10/08

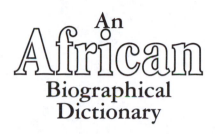

An
African
Biographical
Dictionary

An Africa

Biographical Dictionary

SECOND EDITION

Norbert C. Brockman

Grey House Publishing

PUBLISHER:	Leslie Mackenzie
EDITORIAL DIRECTOR:	Laura Mars-Proietti
PRODUCTION EDITOR:	Toby Raymond
AUTHOR:	Norbert C. Brockman
COPY EDITOR:	Elaine Alibrandi
COMPOSITION:	ATLIS Graphics
MARKETING DIRECTOR:	Jessica Moody

Grey House Publishing, Inc.
185 Millerton Road
Millerton, NY 12546
518.789.8700
FAX 518.789.0545
www.greyhouse.com
e-mail: books @greyhouse.com

Publisher's Cataloging-In-Publication Data
(Prepared by The Donohue Group, Inc.)

Brockman, Norbert C., 1934–
  African Biographical Dictionary / by Norbert C. Brockman — 2nd ed.

    p. : ill., maps, ports. ; cm.

Originally published: Santa Barbara, Calif. : ABC-CLIO, 1994.
Includes bibliographical references and index.
ISBN: 1-59237-112-4

1. Africa–Biography–Dictionaries. I. Title II. Title: Biographical dictionary

DT18 .B76 2006
920.06 B

Cover photography credits, clockwise from right:
  President Marc Ravalomanana of Madagascar—AFP/Jeff Haynes
  Dr. Wangari Muta Maathai, Kenyan environmentalist and activist.
  John Ngugi of Kenya, Olympic medal winning long-distance runner—Getty Images Sport/Gray Mortimore
  Ngugi wa Thiong'o, Kenyan novelist—courtesy of the photographer (Random House).

Table of Contents

x   Table of Contents

xii   Table of Contents

Political map of Africa

European Possessions 1919–1939

Major Natural Resources

Major Religions

Major Slave Trade Routes 1650–1860

Major African States—About 1885

Preface

An African Biographical Dictionary was first published in 1994 by ABC-CLIO of Santa Barbara, California, a publishing house with a long and distinguished record in historical reference work. That first edition book received awards from the American Library Association and other professional groups and was widely praised by reviewers. From the start it was intended to bring together historical personages as well as contemporary ones covering sub-Saharan Africa. For a decade it has served the needs of students, scholars and the general public, but a decade is a long time in the changing world of Africa. It is time for a revision and a new edition.

Since the first edition was published, Africa has been drawn even more tightly into the global economy. The independence movement that began in the 1950s has been completed, but most of the first generation of independence leaders have passed away. Many of the younger notables in Africa were children when independence came, and a substantial minority were not even born. While the first edition listed 10 pages of political figures, there was slightly more than half a page of scientists and a mere four artists. Not only are the arts, sciences and cultures far more represented in this edition, the men and women themselves reflect the increased globalism of our world. In the past, Africans who operated in Europe or America were often in exile, had taken asylum or moved to the West to escape the limitations of apartheid. Today, there are many African writers, performers and intellectuals who are world figures in their own right. They move effortlessly across the international stage, limited only by their talents and opportunities. As a consequence, African artists are far more recognized

than they have ever been; African performers tour the major entertainment venues of Europe, Asia and the Americas; and scientists and entrepreneurs from Africa are found in the laboratories and board rooms of major institutions.

Also striking has been the rise of the number of women leaders in all fields, and the increasing articulation of a distinctively African feminist voice. African women are doing this from a variety of perspectives as world-class writers, political leaders and academics. They are often challenging African patriarchy in the same terms that their parents' generation challenged colonialism.

Just as the independence generation lifted up magisterial figures like Nelson Mandela, Jomo Kenyatta and Léopold Senghor, so the challenges of recent years have generated new leaders. The economic crisis has been a cause of suffering, but it has also created opportunities for African entrepreneurs, a category that barely existed 10 years ago. Health problems are being confronted by research scientists and field workers who deal directly with the immediate needs of Africa.

This second edition presents 713 biographical sketches of historical and contemporary Africans from a wide range of fields of achievement. Of these sketches,170 are new entries, and 349 have been rewritten from the first edition. This represents an increase of 30 percent. Six previous entries have been dropped.

The new entries have greater breadth than that found in the first edition, largely because there are more Africans on the world stage in more and varied fields than ever before. This edition adds more religious leaders, business people, educators, sportsmen/women and scientists. There are also a few in a new category—terrorist.

The revisions range from substantial updates in some cases to smaller factual details in others. The sketches take into account newer interpretations of the importance of certain personalities. Since the first edition, Internet resources have become available, and these have been included in the cross-references.

The format for each entry has not been changed. Each is headed by the name of the person, with the principal name in capitals. Since names have symbolic and even descriptive meaning among Africans, a person may have several names, not to mention a wide variety of spellings when they are rendered into Western languages. In general, the names are alphabetized according to the commonly accepted name, following local customs. Where family names are used—as in Sierra Leone, Liberia and elsewhere—these are given as the principal name. Where custom dictates that the given name is the principal name, that is used.

The name is followed by the present-day country or countries where the person was significant, and the dates of birth and death. It proved too complex and confusing to use contemporary names of states, kingdoms and colonies from various periods, so the current African state was chosen as a means of fixing the location geographically. Dates of birth and death are those most widely accepted, and when the dates can only be approximated, a question mark is used.

The full name is repeated in the first sentence of the entry, with any proper title. Titles have been removed from the heading to avoid confusion with designations in local languages that were sometimes mistaken for proper names. The opening sentence indicates the reason for the person's prominence, and this is followed by a chronological biographical sketch. For cultural personalities, there is also a brief evaluation of their works. When anyone who is profiled in the book is mentioned in another entry, that name appears in capitals on its first use in that entry.

Most sketches close with a brief selection of general references from sources commonly found in universities and public libraries. Any autobiographies and the principal biographies are listed. A few Internet sources are given, including the huge collection of *wikipedia*. Although *wikipedia* articles

are not reviewed or checked, the ones on Africa are of generally acceptable quality and accuracy. Nevertheless, they should never be used without supporting research. It should be noted that articles about prominent Africans from former Portuguese, French and German colonies are often fuller and more complete in those language editions of *wikipedia*. When a person has a Web page, that is given, again with the caveat that these are promotional and not unbiased.

More detailed bibliographies can be found in many of the references or in the excellent UNESCO *General History of Africa*, published in eight volumes between 1981 and 1993 by the University of California Press.

There are several addenda at the end of the volume. One lists present-day states and their capitals, with colonial names. A group of political maps follows. The next appendix gives the political leaders of each state since independence. If more than one name for the country has been used, it is given with the proper years, and this is followed by the year of independence and the last occupying power. A final listing gives all entries by present-day country.

Let me express my gratitude to those who provided assistance and advice. Although he bears no responsibility for this second edition, I wish to acknowledge Henry Rasof, who saw the first edition from an idea to completion when he was editor with ABC-CLIO. Todd Hallman and Susan McCrory served as project editors on the first edition as well. When Grey House Publishing took on the second edition, Ms. Toby Raymond became the amiable and encouraging overseer of this volume.

In the first edition, I thanked librarians and archivists who made the information-gathering possible, especially those from my "home" school, St. Mary's University of San Antonio. I am also in debt to librarians at Rice University, the University of Toronto, Howard University and the Africa Room of the Library of Congress. These days, librarians are known as "information specialists," because new electronic data have transformed their profession. But I am also grateful to the computer sophisticates who took me past several panic attacks—you know who you are!

Norbert Brockman, S.M.

ABACHA, Sani

(Nigeria, 1943–1998)

General Sani Abacha, who engineered coups that first brought Muhammadu BUHARI to power and then removed him, finally took control of the Nigerian government for himself and ruled as a corrupt kleptocrat.

Abacha was born in Kano in northern Nigeria, an area which became his power base. In the early 1960s he attended the Nigerian Military College, and at three different times in his career he was trained at advanced programs in Great Britain. Abacha fought for the federal forces in the 1967–1970 Biafran civil war, rising to colonel. This was followed in rapid succession by training at the Command Staff College and the Institute for Policy and Strategic Studies. In 1982, already a brigadier, Abacha was sent for defense training with the United States Army at Monterrey, California.

On his return, Abacha joined a cabal of senior officers who overthrew Shehu SHAGARI in 1983. He was chosen to announce the coup on Nigerian radio and television, after which he was promoted to major general and appointed to the Supreme Military Council. In 1985, Abacha, by then the most powerful military figure in the country, removed Buhari in favor of General Ibrahim BA-BANGIDA. Abacha was then named Chief of Staff of the army (1985), and five years later became minister of defense, followed by promotion to full general. When Moshood ABIOLA won the 1993 elections, Babangida nullified the results. A transition government was chosen to prepare for new polls, but Abacha sensed his opportunity and seized power.

Abacha moved immediately to suppress all opposition and democratic movements. Political parties were disbanded and elected officers were replaced by army officers loyal to him. Other military officers were purged from the services. Potential competitors for power were imprisoned, including Abiola, Olusegun OBASANJO and Shehu YAR'ADUA. The regime earned international opprobrium for the arrest and execution of Ken SARO-WIWA, the Ogoni activist and writer. The charges against Saro-Wiwa were widely seen as falsified, and his conviction predetermined. After Abacha's fall, his son Mohammed was imprisoned for complicity in the murder of Abiola's wife. Of all these prominent leaders, only Obasanjo survived.

In 1998, Abacha announced a return to military rule, with five newly sanctioned parties—all of which declared him their candidate. This electoral farce was made moot when Abacha died suddenly under mysterious circumstances. Officially, he died of heart failure, but there is evidence that, lured to his palace by prostitutes, he was murdered by military officers.

In five years, Abacha and his family looted the Nigerian oil revenues to a degree almost unprecedented. The later Nigerian government traced some $4 billion hidden overseas in the names of various family members. After Abacha's death, the government reached an agreement with the family for the latter to return $2.1 billion. The Abachas retained approximately $400 million. This deal caused an uproar, with Babangida accused of collaborating in the reward of criminal theft. Even under these most favorable circumstances, however, Abacha's eldest son has always disputed the settlement and claimed that all the money in foreign investments and accounts was legally and properly owned by the family. Their position was bolstered by a statement of Swiss banking authorities that $100 million did "not derive from criminal sources." In exchange for the money settlement, charges against Mohammed Abacha were dropped. Since Great Britain refused to freeze the Abacha accounts in British banks, the deal was perhaps the best that Babangida could hope for, sordid though it appeared to many.

Reference: adb, CB, EB, *wiki.*

ABBOUD, Ibrahim
(Sudan, 1901–1983)

General Ibrahim Abboud was president of the first military government in the Sudan. He began his army career under the Anglo-Egyptian condominium that governed the Sudan until 1956. Commissioned as an engineering officer at age 17, he was educated at Khartoum Military College in the Sudan and then sent to the Royal Military Academy in Sandhurst, England. In World War II he served as an officer in the Sudan Defense Force (SDF), assisting in the liberation of Eritrea and Ethiopia from the Italians and leading troops into action against Field Marshal Erwin Rommel's Afrika Korps in the Libyan campaign. He rose to the rank of SDF deputy commander, in which capacity he served from 1945 to 1956, when the Sudan became independent. Abboud was then named commander and chief of staff, titles he retained until he was toppled from the presidency in 1964.

Abboud masterminded a coup in late 1958, after three civilian governments had brought the Sudan to economic paralysis. His first pronouncements ended all democratic institutions, suspended the constitution, and banned the press, political parties and public assemblies. Parliament was dissolved and replaced by a Supreme Council of the Armed Forces, acting under martial law.

Abboud's economic policies brought temporary economic relief. He sold off a huge cotton surplus to bring in required foreign exchange and negotiated a water treaty with Egypt that met much of the Sudan's needs. As a result, Abboud was able to double the amount of irrigated land and attract foreign investment.

Abboud never grasped the extent of the ethnic gulf between the Islamic north and the animist and Christian south. Economic improvements benefited only the former, and unrest continued to mount in the south until guerrilla warfare broke out. When Abboud suppressed debates at the University of Khartoum on the state of the country, student demonstrations resulted. Government workers and members of the transport unions soon joined the students, and the government was unable to control the situation. Abboud went into exile in England but returned as an elderly man to the Sudan, where he died.

Abboud was a personally austere man, ever the Anglo-Sudanese officer. As president, he lived in a modest brick home with his family and tended his garden. His loyal service to Britain—and his friendliness during his time as head of state—were recognized by several royal honors.

Reference: AO.

ABDALLAH Abderrahman, Ahmed
(Comoros, 1919–1989)

Ahmed Abdallah Abderrahman, the first president of Comoros, maintained a tenuous hold on Comoran politics after independence.

The four islands of the Comoros chain have extremely limited arable land, forcing most sons of peasant families into the class of "the dispossessed." Until 1946, the Comoros Islands were tied to Madagascar, and the young Abdallah went there seeking further economic opportunities. He began working as a trader and returned home to develop a highly successful commodities export business in vanilla and ylang-ylang, a tree extract used for perfume. At the same time, Abdallah never forgot his roots as a member of the landless peasantry. He became a spokesman for the dispossessed on Anjouan, his home island. He was, however, never accepted by the Comoran elite, despite his personal wealth.

Abdallah was elected to the colonial general council for two years after World War II, and when the colonies obtained representation in the French parliament, he was elected to the French Senate, where he served from 1959 to 1972. Abdallah was an ardent nationalist and was well positioned to become the first president of Comoros. In 1972 he became prime minister when his party won elections on three islands, with only Mayotte supporting continued ties to France. In July 1975 independence was declared and Abdallah assumed power. Mayotte has continued to be controlled by France.

Within a month, Abdallah was ousted in a coup led by Ali SOILIH, who used forces commanded by the French mercenary Bob DENARD. Abdallah was exiled to France, but three years later he returned after Denard was hired to lead a second coup to overthrow Soilih. France provided economic assistance, but to gain credibility among nationalists, Abdallah proclaimed Comoros an Islamic republic, drafted a constitution, and held elections. Denard, operating with the covert approval of French military intelligence, remained in Comoros, this time as head of the president's mercenary body-guards.

Abdallah also developed ties to South Africa, and Comoros became a tourist destination for White South Africans. There was considerable South African investment, and vital air links were established with Pretoria, South Africa.

Unsuccessful coups challenged Abdallah's increasingly authoritarian rule in 1983, 1985, and 1987. Each coup attempt was led by mercenaries and each was defeated by Denard's men, whose generous salaries were paid by South Africa. In 1989 a coup resulted in Abdallah's death. He was succeeded by Said DJOHAR.

References: afr, MMA, PLBA.

ABDALLAH Ibn Yasin as-Djazuli
(Mali/Mauritania, ?–1059)

Abdallah Ibn Yasin as-Djazuli was a founder of the Almoravid movement in Islam. Around 1030 he joined the leader of a nomadic clan in a movement of Islamic conversion among the Sanhaja, a Berber people of northwest Africa. Upon his mentor's death, Abdallah faced a mutiny. Deciding to imitate the Prophet Muhammad, he went into seclusion while he gathered together a small band of disciples and instructed them. This period lasted from around 1039 to 1048. The group that emerged from this retreat, the Almoravids, became the basis of a mass conversion movement that created an Almoravid empire stretching from the Mediterranean across the Sahara.

Although Abdallah's history is shrouded in myth and legend, certain facts are clear. Several Berber chieftains, recognizing the superficial nature of Islam among their nomadic peoples, were stirred to ask for a missionary after one of their number had made the *hajj,* or pilgrimage, to Mecca. Abdallah Ibn Yasin, by then a member of a study and meditation center in southern Morocco, was selected and sent into the desert. There he found scores of warring peoples, some nomadic and a few settled. Among the nomads, Islam was worn like a cloak over traditional religious values and social customs.

The settled peoples built mosques but also followed various prophetic movements and Islamic sects.

For the first five years, Abdallah concentrated on his religious mission. He insisted on a true reform of personal morals, stressing strict observance of Islamic law and punishment for those who transgressed. His austere ways and egalitarian values led to a conflict with the Sanhaja chiefs, and in 1053 he was briefly expelled from the desert. Conflict arose over Abdallah's contradiction of social patterns and his disrespect for accepted taboos among the Sanhaja. He caused tension by his harsh insistence that Muslims carry their message by the sword to those of indifferent observance.

One clan, the Lamtuna, became the main agent of Abdallah's drive. He modeled the military tactics of the Lamtuna upon those of the early Arabs who had followed Muhammad. The revivalist movement then became a militant one to carry forth the *jihad,* or holy war. Abdallah shared the leadership of the Lamtuna and even led troops into battle. Numerous clans rallied to the cause (although some accepted its religious reforms and rejected its political unity), and a formidable desert state was created. Where there was active resistance, the Almoravids were pitiless, but most communities submitted peacefully. The Almoravids captured the towns that controlled both the northern and southern ends of the caravan routes, thus guaranteeing economic and military security. Abdallah was killed in a battle with a dissident Islamic sect, but the movement continued to expand, although it divided into two major kingdoms. The Almoravids had great influence on the form and practice of Islam through much of northwestern Africa.

Reference: afr, DAHB.

ABDI ARUSH, Starlin
(Somalia, 1957–2002)

Starlin Abdi Arush, born of a prominent family, was one of the voices of sanity in the collapse of Somalia in the 1990s. Peace activist and humanitarian worker, a leader in many areas, she confronted warlords and United Nations peacekeepers in the same even-handed, blunt manner.

Abdi Arush was born in a small town on the Indian Ocean, and nurtured by a fiercely feminist mother, separated from her husband. Abdi Arush was raised with three sisters and three brothers, all of whom were treated equally. Unmarried, though she was engaged at the time of her death, Abdi Arush never wore the veil. After completing her secondary studies in a convent school run by Italian nuns, she went to Italy for further studies, staying for 13 years studying medicine (her father was a veterinarian) but not completing a degree. She discovered her passion in local government in Turin, where she found success.

Somalia collapsed into fratricidal conflict in 1991, and one of her brothers was killed. Abdi Arush returned to her homeland to share the lot of her people. With her sister, she organized food supplies during the battle of Mogadishu, even as their home was shelled and looted. Somali faction leader Mohamed Farah AIDID had the two arrested and hauled before a tribal court, where they defended themselves of accusations of plotting with foreigners to murder Aidid. "Why would we need foreign help?" Abdi Arush proclaimed to the startled elders. "Why would we not take a knife and do it ourselves?" This bravado showed many times. When Italian aid workers were kidnapped in her home town, she confronted the fundamentalists and vowed to take on the town's desperate needs. She faced down hostile militias more than once, but suffered from rumors and gossip among European aid workers that she was trying to become a warlord herself.

In her home town, where the family and clan had lived for five generations, her achievements were legendary. She reformed the hospital, opened clinics, schools for over 3,000 children, and a camp for demobilized militia. Where several hundred armed thugs had patrolled and looted the hospital, now unarmed men worked.

In 1993, Abdi Arush was the best hope for a ceasefire between Mohamed Farah Aidid and United States peacekeepers. As she was negotiating, the Americans launched an attack on Aidid that ended any hope for an agreement. Abdi Arush never allowed such setbacks, disastrous though they might be, to deter her in her quest for peace and stability in Somalia. She was convinced that the basis for a new social order would have to be the end of tribalism. It was the total rejection of this proposition that caused all attempts to create a Somali nation to founder.

When the United Nations attempted to form a government of national unity in 1999, Abdi Arush was invited to participate. As it became clear that the basis of the new government was to be a tribal quota system, she refused, recognizing immediately that the new government would degenerate into patronage and corruption leading to renewed conflict.

Abdi Arush spent much of her energies in the 1990s working for the Italian NGO Cosv. Her focus was on the creation of small-scale local institutions, especially village governments, from which she believed the Somali state could be reconstituted. One of the signs of her hope was her service, amidst almost total social disorganization, as chair of the Somali Olympic Committee.

Ironically, Abdi Arush, then in exile in Kenya, was on her way to a meeting of Somali warlords when she was murdered in Nairobi, an apparent robbery. In her life she had faced down gunmen, boy soldiers and would-be rapists with dignity and determination.

ABDULLAH, Muhammed Said
(Tanzania, 1918–)

Muhammed Said Abdullah is one of the most prominent Swahili novelists of the modern period, having published seven novels between 1966 and 1984. Because Swahili, although widespread, does not have an extensive reading public, he has spent much of his life as editor of the national agricultural magazine, *Mkulima*. His contribution has been to bring together the traditional Swahili literary tradition with contemporary western styles.

Abdullah has lived his entire life on the island of Zanzibar, a center of Swahili, Muslim and Afro-Arabic cultural blending. In the 1930s, he was educated in Christian missionary schools, where he encountered western literature, which would have been dominant in colonial secondary schools at that time. He took employment with the Colonial Health Department, where he became a writer and editor of *Mkulima* after some years as a field inspector.

In 1953, Abdullah won a short-story contest with a detective story, in which he created a character, Bwana Msa, a reflective and canny investigator. Four detective novels followed, all with Bwana Msa as the chief protagonist. His themes emphasize the cultural mix of Zanzibari society. He is fascinated by Arab, Indian, African and western interaction. Several novels tell the stories of young men and women who fall in love, only to discover that they are long-lost siblings. Abdullah does not hesitate to wrestle with the implications of incest in tiny, closed societies. His stories are set in the pre-revolutionary period, with avaricious Arab landowners as the villains. Abdullah's family endured losses during the revolution, but he has never addressed either those events or post-revolutionary Zanzibar in his writings.

Abdullah's Swahili is widely admired. He uses, in the same work, the traditional classical style of the educated, the common tongue of peasants and fishermen, as well as the broken language of Indians and traders and the street slang (*sheng*) of youth. It is a linguistic tour de force, and Abdullah's books are used as set books (required reading) for national exams in Tanzania.

Reference: adb.

ABDULLAHI Ibn Mohammad
(Sudan, 1846–1899)

Khalifa Abdullahi Ibn Mohammad was the successor to Muhammad Ahmad, the MAHDI, and ruler of a short-lived Mahdist state that he organized along bureaucratic lines. He came from a family of Muslim religious leaders from whom he acquired a passionate belief in the imminent coming of the foretold Mahdi, or final messianic prophet and restorer of the faith. His search led him to Muhammad Ahmad, and Abdullahi became an enthusiastic supporter.

When Muhammad Ahmad began his revolt in 1881, Abdullahi provided essential organizational skills and was soon the Mahdi's chief assistant. Starting from an island in the Nile, the Mahdists defeated the government, drawn from the detested Westernized Egyptian professional class. Abdullahi was named a caliph and was put in charge of much of the Mahdist army. Great Britain intervened, sending General Charles GORDON, but the Mahdists took Khartoum in 1885, killing Gordon. At the height of his triumph, the Mahdi died, and Abdullahi succeeded him, as the Mahdi had desired.

Abdullahi proclaimed himself *Khalifat al-Mahdi*, successor to the Mahdi, and ruled for 13 years. Within three years he had consolidated his power and defeated Ethiopia, his troops killing Emperor YOHANNES IV in battle. Abdullahi's genius was administrative rather than military, however. He created a centralized bureaucratic system under his control at Omdurman. Abdullahi Islamicized the judiciary and dealt in foreign affairs only with "pure Muslim" states. This xenophobic, domineering system worked effectively in the face of agricultural failures, hostile neighbors and famine. Finally, an Anglo-Egyptian force, led by General Horatio KITCHENER, destroyed the Mahdist army at Omdurman, broke its military power, and seized the capital. Abdullahi escaped but was killed a year later in a skirmish with British troops.

References: DAHB, EB, MMA.

ABDULMAJID, Iman
(Somalia, 1955–)

One of the most prominent African women to be accepted as an international fashion supermodel, Iman Abdulmajid has gone on to become a successful entrepreneur and businesswoman.

Iman was born into a prominent Somali family. Her father served as ambassador to Saudi Arabia, a major appointment for Somalia. She was educated in Egypt and later at the University of Nairobi, where she graduated in political science while her parents were in exile in Kenya. Shortly after, she began her modeling career and moved to the United States. A beautiful woman of light color, Iman has the high cheekbones and oval face of a Somali. At 22, she married American Olympic champion and basketball star Spencer Haywood (NBA, 1969–1980), with whom she had a daughter. She took American citizenship. She and Haywood divorced when he left New York and was traded to the New Orleans team. Iman later married British rock star David Bowie, with whom she has also had a daughter.

Iman has dabbled in film roles, playing most notably in *Star Trek VI: The Undiscovered Country*. As she moved from modeling to acting, Iman began a cosmetics firm which has proved successful. She is now a prominent businesswoman.

References: wiki. www.i-iman.com. Iman, *I am Iman* (2001); *Book of Color* (2005).

ABIODUN
(Nigeria, ?–1789)

Alafin Abiodun was the last important *alafin*, or ruler, of the Yoruba state of Oyo. Oyo was located on the frontier between the savannah and the forest areas of West Africa, in what is now Nigeria, and it used its position to control trade between the two regions. From the fifteenth to the eighteenth centuries, it grew into a powerful kingdom. In its later years, the head of the council of state, made up of prominent chiefs, dominated the *alafins,* but Abiodun reversed this trend.

Abiodun took office around 1770 and immediately challenged the unpopular head of the council of state for dominance. In 1774, there was a brief civil war, from which Abiodun emerged victorious. He then had his rival and his rival's entire family executed in a public ceremony and centralized authority in himself, ushering in a brief period of prosperity.

Trade flourished, and according to a Yoruba historian, some 6,600 towns were under Oyo's control during Abiodun's rule. The slave trade was a basis of the country's wealth, and Abiodun used Porto Novo as a major shipping port for slave exports after reducing it to tributary status. The entire Yoruba cultural region, roughly the western half of modern Nigeria and modern Benin, was under Oyo's suzerainty. There were Oyo settler colonies throughout the area, and Oyo traders and agents operated freely. The Oyo cavalry and archers provided armed authority, which some tributary states welcomed as a guarantee of stability. Furthermore, Oyo did not often interfere with local cultures, economic patterns or government.

Under Abiodun, Oyo reached the pinnacle of its greatness. Traditionally, the Oyo army was commanded by slave eunuchs who were totally loyal to the king. In the struggle between the *alafins* and the council, the eunuchs were replaced with Yoruba nobility of divided loyalties. Abiodun gradually became dependent on the army of the subject state Dahomey (in present-day Benin) as a result. It suffered a major defeat in 1783 at the hands of the army of Borgu, a neighboring kingdom, which was followed by successful revolts of subject peoples, including one led by a governor whom Abiodun had appointed. A revolt by the Nupe people cost Oyo the main source of its cavalry horses. By the end of Abiodun's reign, the slave trade, once based so profitably on non-Yoruba captives, had begun to include Yorubas as well. By thus cannibalizing his own people, Abiodun set the stage for the nation's downfall.

Abiodun's successor, Awole, entered into unpopular and disastrous wars that led to his suicide and the rapid downfall of the kingdom. The collapse of Oyo produced a political vacuum that influenced European intervention and imperialism.

Reference: DAHB, *wiki.*

ABIODUN, Adigun Ade
(Nigeria, 1939–)

One of Africa's few space scientists, Adigun Ade Abiodun has served as Chair of the United Nations Committee on Peaceful Uses of Outer Space since 2004. Before that, he was senior special assistant in space science and technology, and for 18 years (1981–1999) chief of Space Applications for U.N. Political and Security Council Affairs.

Abiodun was born in Ogun State, Nigeria, and took his first degree in surveying at the Nigerian College of Arts, Science and Technology. After moving to the United States, he studied at the University of Washington-Seattle, receiving bachelor's and master's degrees in civil engineering and hydraulics. Degrees in hand, in 1966 Abiodun began working for the United States Army Corps of Engineers in 1966. Two years later he began work with the Boeing Company while continuing to study. He also completed requirements to become a professional engineer, licensed by the State of Washington.

After completing a Ph.D. in hydraulic engineering at the University Washington-Seattle, Abiodun took a position on the faculty of the University of Ife, where he stayed from 1971 to 1977, with a year's break as a research fellow of the Research Council of Canada, where he worked at the Canadian Centre for Remote Sensing.

In 1977, Abiodun began a long career with the United Nations, first joining the Outer Space Affairs Office (OSAO) as a remote sensing specialist. Soon after, he was named officer-in-charge of the Space Applications Programme, and by 1981 he was chief of the space section of OSAO. His abilities and public presence were recognized when he was appointed to coordinate U.N. participation in the 1982 International Space Year. He has authored five books and numerous technical articles in hydraulics, remote sensing, satellite meteorology, and various aspects of the economics of space utilization.

ABIODUN, Philip Olayele
(Nigeria, 1943–)

Dr. Philip Olayele Abiodun is a pediatrician who has done pioneering work in oral rehydration therapy, a life-saving method for controlling cholera and diarrhea, major causes of childhood mortality in Africa. Abiodun completed all of his medical studies in West Germany, receiving an M.D. in 1973 and his specialization in children's health in 1978. He continued as a lecturer at a university child clinic in West Germany until 1982. Abiodun then returned to Nigeria, where he took up a post at the University of Benin College of Medical Sciences; he has been associate professor there since 1986. He is a fellow of the West African College of Physicians, the German Pediatric Association, and the German Cystic Fibrosis Group.

Diarrhea and dysentery are major killers of children throughout Africa, causing toxic shock when a child loses so much water that critical minerals are flushed from the system. Because this crisis can occur rapidly, and access to clinics remains difficult for many families, methods of rehydration are needed that can be easily administered by parents. Abiodun has been instrumental in developing different types of rehydration solutions that can be given orally to a child as part of the Child Survival Strategy Program of the Federal Ministry of Health.

Abiodun's concerns for the development of African children encompass a broad range of projects; he has combined his oral rehydration therapy with an expanded program for immunization from childhood diseases, treatments for vitamin A deficiency, and methods for combating malnutrition. He is widely respected in his field, and served on the board of the Commonwealth Association of Pediatric Gastroenterology in the late 1990s.

Reference: PAS.

ABIOLA, Moshood
(Nigeria, 1937–1998)

Chief Moshood Abiola, multimillionaire businessman and a major publisher in Nigeria, was elected president of the country in 1993, only to have the military government nullify the vote. A man of dramatic flair and ostentatious generosity, he had long had political ambitions.

Abiola, a Muslim Yoruba from the south, was educated in a Baptist school before studying accounting at the University of Glasgow from 1962 to 1963. He was progressively deputy chief accountant at the University of Lagos Hospital, controller of Pfizer Pharmaceuticals, and controller of International Telephone and Telegraph (ITT) Nigeria. He built his fortune with ITT as chairman and chief executive from 1971 to 1988. In 1978, when General Olusegun OBASANJO lifted the ban against politics, Abiola became active as a member of the National Party of Nigeria (NPN). At the same time, he founded the Concord Group, which published a daily paper and a weekly news magazine. Despite having his own publications and lavishing the NPN with close to US$1 million, he failed to win the party nomination over Shehu SHAGARI in 1982, and he resigned from the NPN in disgust.

During the 1980s, Abiola turned toward philanthropy, was honored with four traditional chiefly titles, married (four wives), and raised a family. His commercial empire expanded into ownership of an airline, a football team, the Abiola bookshop chain, a bakery, a radio station, and one of the largest mechanized agricultural projects in the country, Abiola Farms. In 1993, when General Ibrahim BABANGIDA announced his system for returning to civilian rule, Abiola returned to national politics as the candidate of the center-left Social Democratic Party. The electoral evidence suggests that Abiola won, but Babangida rejected the results and annulled the election, appointing an "interim" government. The Concord publications were closed, and Abiola went into exile for several months. By the end of 1993 a new military strongman, General Sani ABACHA, had taken over Nigeria, but in June 1994, Abiola announced that he intended to take the presidency that he considered rightfully his. He was arrested and charged with treason, which set off a series of major strikes and a national crisis. By October 1994, total military government had been established by General Abacha. Already in poor health, Abiola died in prison shortly before his scheduled release.

References: afr, PLBA, RWWA, wiki.

ABRAHAMS, Peter Henri
(South Africa, 1919–)

Peter Henri Abrahams, a novelist and one of the most important South African exile writers, has done all his writing in England and Jamaica since 1939. Abrahams, a Pan-Africanist and radical, has set his novels in Africa. Questions of race and politics dominate his works. Born of an Ethiopian father and a Cape Coloured mother, Abrahams was legally and socially Coloured, that is, belonging to a mixed-race, Afrikaans-speaking people who traditionally were aloof from Blacks. Abrahams startled some people when he identified with the Black struggle for freedom.

Abrahams' father died when he was small, and he lived a harsh childhood, which he describes in *Tell Freedom* (1954). He received a limited formal education. At age 10, already working, he learned to read and within a year was writing brief short stories. Failing to find anyone in South Africa who would hire him as a writer, he was forced to leave South Africa in order to write and be free. He signed on as a ship's stoker and after two years at sea settled in England, where he became a journalist for *The Observer* and the Communist *Daily Worker*. In 1941 he published his first novel, *Song of the City*, but it was his second, *Mine Boy* (1946), that attracted critical attention. The story follows Xuma, a young Black miner living in the hostels of South Africa, who is exploited and has no future. *Mine Boy* was one of the first books to realistically describe the plight of South African Blacks. It is regularly used as a set book (required reading) for the national school-leaving exams in Africa.

Abrahams was part of a circle of African intellectuals in England that included Kwame NKRUMAH and Jomo KENYATTA (who was his roommate at a trade union house). Together they were among the organizers of the Pan-African Conference in Manchester in 1946. In 1952 Abrahams returned to South Africa for a visit, which only deepened his disgust at the situation there. He wrote: "It seemed to me that one did not have to die to go to hell. This was hell." In 1957 he and his

family moved to Jamaica, where they have remained and taken citizenship. Abrahams has edited a newspaper and reported on Jamaican radio and television. For two years he served as chairman of Radio Jamaica, during which time he reorganized the public corporation.

Abrahams continued writing, producing eight novels and several other books which have been well received and translated into more than 30 languages. *A Wreath for Udomo* (1965), his second most important work after *Mine Boy*, shows his willingness to criticize Africans who have betrayed freedom and provides a gloomy prophecy of African corruption. His most recent novel, *The View from Coyaba* (1985), looks at the Black quest for freedom from the viewpoint of a family with branches in the United States, Africa, and the Caribbean. For all their depressing settings, Abrahams' novels are optimistic. His answer to racism is found in the hearts of people, where goodwill can triumph over evil. In *Mine Boy*, Xuma refuses to be brutalized by his suffering and oppression. There is an enduring hope for the future. Abrahams says of himself that he "has purged himself of hatred...art and beauty come of love, not hate."

References: AA, adb, afr, CANR, CB, DAHB, DLB, MBW, NRG, wiki, WLTC. Abrahams, *Tell Freedom: Memories of Africa* (1954); Kolawole Ogungbesan, *The Writing of Peter Abrahams* (1979); Michael Wade, *Peter Abrahams* (1972).

ABUBAKAR III, Siddiq
(Nigeria, 1903–1988)

Sultan Sir Siddiq Abubakar III, who served as sultan of Sokoto from 1938 to his death, was the leading Islamic figure in sub-Saharan Africa for half a century. Sokoto, in northern Nigeria, is a major Islamic center in West Africa, and the position of sultan is a politically influential one.

Sultan Abubakar was a calm, steady person. More than once he was a pacifying influence during times of civil strife. A direct descendant of UTHMAN Dan Fodio, founder of the Fulani Empire and first sultan of Sokoto, he was a proud adherent of traditional ways. Always dressed in robes and turban, he lived a simple and unpretentious life. As a follower of Islamic custom, Abubakar was polygamous and fathered more than 50 children. In spite of his deference to the past, he was a cautious modernizer, encouraging the use of modern medicine and hospitals and establishing a representative assembly.

His position as sultan gave him considerable political influence, which he used wisely. Even before World War II, he was concerned about the economic recovery of northern Nigeria. Without hesitation, however, he sacrificed manpower and mobilized Muslims for the British Imperial Army in World War II; many troops saw action in the Burma Campaign against Japan. In 1954, Queen Elizabeth knighted him. When the political crisis and civil war of the late 1960s began, Abubakar remained a strong supporter of the Nigerian national government. In 1966 he calmed the north after the assassination of his popular cousin, Sir Ahmadu BELLO, the northern premier, despite the fact that Bello had criticized him sharply in print. Abubakar also helped mobilize northern troops during the war with Biafra between 1967 and 1970.

Abubakar was revered as the *Sarkin Musulimi*, the spiritual head of Nigeria's Muslims. It was this spiritual authority that gave him political influence, even though formal political power of the Sokoto Empire ended on the day of his birth when his predecessor was defeated decisively by the British. Until his death, Abubakar was president-general of the Nigerian Supreme Council for Islamic Affairs.

Reference: AO.

ABUNGU, George Henry Okello

(Kenya, 1959–)

Dr. George Abungu is a specialist in the archaeology of the Swahili coastal area of the Indian Ocean. Besides serving in various positions in Kenya's museums, he has been president of the International Standing Committee on the Illicit Traffic of Cultural Property since 1999.

Dr. Abungu was raised in northwest Kenya along the coast of Lake Victoria, the world's largest freshwater lake. He studied archaeology at the University of Nairobi, and afterward did graduate work at Cambridge in England. He worked as a research scientist for the National Museums of Kenya while finishing his dissertation. He was posted to the coast as senior researcher and head of the Coastal Archaeology Department. The Indian

Ocean coastal areas of Kenya are among the first in Africa to come in contact with the wider world, receiving Arab and even Chinese trade ships centuries before the arrival of Europeans. Abandoned settlements from that era are readily accessible along the coast. From 1989 to 1995, Dr. Abungu surveyed the coastal areas, supervised digs and developed conservation plans. The Indian Ocean coast is important in East African history as the region where the Swahili people developed their unique culture and language.

Dr. Abungu's work was recognized in his progressive promotions within the Coastal Archaeology Programme. At the same time, he was becoming increasingly visible on the international scene. Abungu recognized the losses that the coastal area had suffered from both cultural looters and casual tourists looking for souvenirs in the ruins of Kilwa and other ancient coastal settlements. He has been a strong supporter of international cooperation in the retrieval of cultural artifacts that have been taken from their natural settings. He also sits on the boards of several international professional associations, including the Global Heritage Fund, the World Archaeological Congress and the International Council of Museums.

From 1999 to 2002, Dr. Abungu was director-general of the National Museums of Kenya (NMK). In 2004, he founded Okello Abungu Heritage Consultants to further these aims. He is married to Lorna Abungu, executive director of the International Council of African Museums and a prominent coastal archaeologist. She has developed the NMK Internet Media Working Group as a training and educational tool.

Reference: adb, I Hear Voices, a Portrait of George Abungu (video, 2002).

ACHEAMPONG, Ignatius Kutu

(Ghana, 1931–1979)

General Ignatius Kutu Acheampong, Ghanaian military ruler from 1972 to 1978, was removed from office and later executed for corruption.

Acheampong worked as a tutor and principal in business schools until entering the army in 1951. His ability was recognized, and he was sent to England for officers' training, after which he spent a year serving in a British battalion before attending the U.S. Army Command and General Staff College at Fort Leavenworth, Kansas. He rose quickly through the ranks and was commander of the Ghanaian troops assigned to the U.N. peacekeeping force in the Belgian Congo in 1962 and 1963. In 1966, Acheampong was made commander of the Sixth Battalion but did not take part in the military coup that toppled Kwame NKRUMAH that year. As a sympathetic officer, however, he was appointed governor of the Western Region.

Acheampong headed an infantry brigade in Accra, the capital, and in 1972 his forces removed the civilian government of Kofi BUSIA, which had come to power in a democratic election. The coup was popular in Ghana because of Busia's failure to improve the depressed Ghanaian economy, and Busia's devaluation of the Ghanaian currency by 44 percent. Acheampong established a military council and banned political parties. He then repudiated some of Ghana's foreign debt and embarked on an ambitious economic program based on self-sufficiency in agricultural production. Several practical changes were also put in place: the introduction of the metric system, worker training schemes, right-hand driving and many infrastructure improvements. He sought trade relations with both Western capitalists and Communist states, and the Ghanaian economy improved for several years. By 1975, however, it had faltered, and two poor harvests deepened the crisis in both 1976 and 1977. Internal security deteriorated and there were riots in Accra. Hoping to bolster his waning popularity, Acheampong held a national referendum on a joint civilian-military government, but he won only because a majority of the people boycotted the voting.

Inflation, shortages of basic goods, smuggling and charges of corruption against the government finally cost Acheampong his last support, and the army forced his resignation in 1978. He was placed under house arrest and was succeeded by Frederick AKUFFO. After the coup by Flight Lieutenant Jerry RAWLINGS in 1979, Acheampong was tried, convicted of corruption, and executed by firing squad, along with Akuffo and five generals.

References: DAHB, DRWW, EB, MMA, PLBA, PLCA, *wiki.*

ACHEBE, (Albert) Chinua(lumogu)
(Nigeria, 1930–)

Chinua Achebe is Africa's most widely read novelist and among the greatest fiction writers in the world today. His work has sold over 20 million copies and has been translated into scores of languages.

An Igbo who returns to his traditions for much of his inspiration, Achebe stands at the crossroads of two cultures, where Western technology, religions, and economic and social systems encounter traditional societies. This encounter, with its built-in tragedy and drama, is the centerpiece of both his writing and his life. The son of a religious teacher who spent his career with an Anglican missionary society, Achebe received an education in colonial schools, which introduced him to the best of British literature. Much as he was impressed by Shakespeare and English fiction and poetry, he felt ill at ease because he could not identify with the characters. When he read Joseph Conrad's *Heart of Darkness,* Achebe realized that he was being seduced into identifying with the European masters. "I realized

(Albert) Chinua(lumogu) Achebe

that these writers had pulled a fast one on me! I was not on Marlowe's boat steaming up the Congo in *Heart of Darkness.* I was one of those strange beings jumping up and down on the river bank, making horrid faces." In a 1975 critical article, Achebe brutally attacked Conrad as a "thoroughgoing racist." At this realization, Achebe began telling his own stories—African stories.

Achebe began working for the Nigerian Broadcasting Corporation in 1954 and started publishing short stories. His first novel, *Things Fall Apart,* was published in 1958. It presents one of the great tragic personalities in twentieth-century fiction, Okonkwo, who lives by the traditions of Igbo society. He achieves success and prosperity, has many wives and is widely respected. When the British arrive, however, he can neither submit to them nor benefit from the valuable aspects of Western culture. Indeed, for Okonkwo, "things fall apart" when the White man arrives. In a state of internal conflict, he hangs himself. The novel was immediately successful; it has been reprinted many times (eight million copies have been sold) and translated into 50 languages.

Achebe followed this success with *No Longer at Ease* (1960), *Arrow of God* (1964), *Man of the People* (1966), and *Anthills of the Savannah* (1987). There have also been collections of short stories, essays, and poetry, including *Beware, Soul Brother* (1971), which won the Commonwealth Prize. All of his books, in one way or another, continue Achebe's quest to make sense of the encounter between African and European civilizations.

Independence came to Nigeria in 1960 and accelerated the breakdown of Nigerian society. In 1967 the Igbo of the eastern region seceded to form the Republic of Biafra, and Achebe, a passionate supporter, became Minister of Information. He was overwhelmed by the death in battle of his close friend, the poet Christopher OKIGBO. The Igbos were crushed, and although Achebe wrote of the war in poetry and short stories, he could not produce another novel for 20 years.

Achebe was able to remain in Nigeria under the general amnesty, and he became a research fellow at the University of Nigeria in Nsukka. He also focused his energy on promoting publishing opportunities for African writers. He helped establish and edit Heinemann's African Writers Series, which has made African writing a major presence in world literary circles. From 1972 to 1976, Achebe taught in the United States before returning to Nsukka and

eventually serving for two years as pro-chancellor of another Nigerian university. He has subsequently lectured during recent years in U.S. universities and received numerous honors, including more than 20 honorary doctorates. Achebe was awarded the Commonwealth Poetry Prize in 1972 and 1979.

In 1990, after attending an international symposium on his work in Nigeria, he was injured in a serious auto accident. He was airlifted to England and spent six months in a hospital. He has since been confined to a wheelchair. In 1991, Bard College in Annandale-on-Hudson, New York, invited him to join its faculty. There he has begun to write again. He published his *Collected Poems* in 2004 and a memoir, *Home and Exile,* in 2000.

Achebe straddles two cultures and is able to draw benefits from both. He never creates plastic characters or mere symbols. Okonkwo, for example, resists imperialism but supports the murder of his adopted son. Achebe's later work is as scathing in its attacks on African corruption as anything written about the evils of colonialism. He finds Christianity both deculturizing and humanizing. Achebe's dual cultural allegiance is perhaps best seen in his ongoing literary argument with NGUGI wa Thion'go, the Kenyan novelist, over the use of Western languages in African writing. For a number of years, Ngugi has refused to write fiction in English, arguing that if his work is good enough, it will be translated from his mother tongue. He has argued powerfully that the last stage of independence is "decolonizing the mind," refusing to submit to the thought processes or the mentality of the West. In contrast, Achebe argues that only Western languages provide access and carry the message to those who most need to hear it. By using European languages, Africans prove that their stories can stand beside Western literature with honor. He pointedly comments that while Ngugi has abandoned English, he continues to use Western fictional forms that are foreign to African traditions. Achebe himself brings together the rhythms of Africa and Western literary forms. For Achebe, the African experience is paramount. An elder in *Anthills of the Savannah* says: "It is the story...that saves our progeny from blundering like blind beggars into the spikes of the cactus fence. The story is our escort; without it, we are blind."

References: AA, AB, *adb, afr,* AWT, CANR, DAHB, DLB, EB, EWB, MBW, NRG, PLBA, *wiki,* WLTC. Catherine Innes, *Chinua Achebe* (1990);

Romanus Muoneke, *Art and Redemption: A Reading of the Novels of Chinua Achebe* (1993).

ACKERMAN, Raymond
(South Africa, 1931–)

Raymond Ackerman is a foremost retailer in South Africa, who popularized the supermarket in that country. He has gone on to be a major philanthropist.

After taking a degree in commerce at the University of Cape Town in 1951, Ackerman joined his family's clothing firm. Shortly after, the family was bought out by a diversified company, and the young manager joined the new firm. Sensing the importance of supermarkets, he persuaded the company to let him develop this form of retailing, and at 24 was put in charge of their food division, Checkers Supermarkets. He took a six-month leave to explore the food retailing world of the United States, returning with new ideas and methods. In 10 years, he managed 85 Checkers, but then was abruptly fired. Ackerman always attributed this to jealousy caused by the fact that Checkers was earning more than all the other company divisions combined.

With two weeks' pay and a wife pregnant with their fourth child, Ackerman invested all he owned and borrowed heavily to buy three Cape Town stores known as Pick and Pay, where he proceeded to reproduce his previous success. Stung by his experience with Checkers, he retained 55 percent control of the new company. Today, Pick and Pay employs 30,000 workers in 470 supermarkets and 14 hypermarkets. It is the largest food retailer in Africa. He continues as chairman of the corporation. Because of his conviction that defending customers will create loyalty, he clashed with the government over price controls. In one notorious tiff, an enraged P. W. BOTHA shook him by the scruff of the neck in a tirade about bread prices.

Ackerman has been a quiet but generous supporter of charities, especially those dealing with hunger relief and small business development. He led South Africa's attempt at an Olympic bid after the country's sports were readmitted following the end of apartheid. In a nasty conflict with the head of the South African Olympic Committee, Ackerman was forced out in 1995, one of his great regrets.

Reference: wiki. Ackerman, *Hearing Grasshoppers Jump, the Story of Raymond Ackerman* (2001) and *Four Legs of the Table* (2005).

ACQUAH, Kobena Eyi
(Ghana, 1952–)

Kobena Acquah is a prominent Ghanaian poet and writer. He has published four volumes of poetry, along with short stories and articles. He is one of a generation of Ghanaian writers who have moved from a Pan-African perspective toward the creation of a true national literature.

Acquah was born and raised in Winneba in central Ghana, an area known for its cultural roots. He studied at the University of Ghana and completed law school. He works as an investment counsel and has been active in civil affairs, serving on the Copyright Board and other commissions. Acquah has also been active with the W. E. B. Dubois Centre for Pan-African Culture, and is president of the Ghana Association of Writers.

Perhaps the most accepted of Acquah's works has been his first, *The Man Who Died* (1984), which has been anthologized and broadcast widely. One finds patterns of the oral tradition in Acquah's verse, which makes it particularly suitable for broadcasting, and radio—which reaches even into the hinterlands in Africa—has brought his work to people throughout the region. He interlaces English with the local language, but does not write in pidgin, as some other West African writers have begun to do. *The Man Who Died* received a Mention for the Noma Prize in 1985.

Acquah's use of the local idiom is wide-ranging, and one can find the rhythm of drumming in his work, something that also makes it perfect for public reading and broadcasting. He incorporates folk tales, riddles that are used to teach moral lessons in the villages, and popular proverbs. His themes, perhaps typical of the newer generation of post-colonial writers, dwell on the collapse of civil order in Africa at the hands of brutal dictators who oppress their own peoples and enrich themselves in the face of grinding poverty. Throughout, his writing does not descend into diatribe, however, as it is suffused with his Christian religious sensibility and faith. Acquah counsels forgiveness in the pursuit of justice, while still calling on the masses to take command of their own future. He confronts the plight of contemporary Africa with hope.

Reference: adb.

ADÉ, Sunny Adeniyi
(Nigeria, 1946–)

King Sunny (Sunday) Adeniyi Adé, who emerged as the leading figure in the juju music craze of the 1980s, remains a major influence on world music as well as a prominent presence in the club scene in Lagos. After experiencing the volatility of the international market for African music, he survived the downturn of the late 1980s and remained a major star.

Juju was born of the encounter between Yoruba traditional music and the palm wine guitar sound. This latter element emerged from the West African coast, where cheap acoustic guitars in the 1930s and 1940s spawned a style that was played in little clubs serving palm wine. The music reveals the nostalgia and sadness of rural people in the city and creates a kind of African blues, with such improbable sources as American country singer Jim Reeves. When it is joined to Yoruba traditional music, the palm wine guitar sound is transformed into juju, retaining some of the softness and sweetness of the guitar sound but with complex underlying rhythms. Juju rose to dominance with the 1967 Biafran civil war. Juju, with its ethnic base, prospered while highlife music went into sharp decline.

Adé is the son of a Methodist minister who disapproved of his music career, so Adé left home at 17 in order to follow his dream. He first joined The Rhythm Dandies, and in 1966 formed his own group, The Green Spots (after 1974, called The Africa Beats). His first hit, "Challenge Cup," in honor of a champion soccer team, sold 500,000 copies, establishing Adé as a musical force to be reckoned with. He went on to become juju's greatest innovator, turning its street sound into a modern big band sound in which Yoruba tradition meets electronics. In his music, guitar and keyboards take a back seat to intricate percussion, created by as many as 10 instruments that make one undulating sound. With interlocking rhythms from guitars, talking drums, and Adé's sweet tenor, there is constant use of call-and-response between star and band. The lyrics typically incorporate Yoruba prov-erbs, snatches of praise songs, or social commentary. The total effect is seamless and airy.

The Green Spots recorded with Africa Song until a total falling out led to an acrimonious court battle and a parting of the ways. As juju came to international attention and Adé's sales rose (averaging 200,000 per album in the 1980s), he was picked up by Island Records, which created the world demand for reggae and internationalized the popularity of Jamaican singer Bob Marley. After three albums, Adé and Island Records also parted company, complaining of creative differences. On Island's side, disappointing international sales were a factor. Adé returned to Lagos, where he has produced all his own records since 1986. His career suffered briefly after the revelation that a 1990 album had been secretly funded by the United States Office of Population as a family-planning project. Adé remains prolific in his production since then, however, with four albums in the 1990s and five in 2000–2003. In addition, he has released a six-disk Classics series on Masterdisc and a recent *Best of the Classic Years* (2003). He tours regularly in the United States and Europe. Adé serves as chair of the Musical Copyright Society of Nigeria.

Juju remains the commanding music of the Yoruba. Adé's *Odu* (1998), a compilation of traditional Yoruba songs, was nominated for a Grammy Award.

Reference: adb, afr, CB, DMM, GEPM, WAM, *wiki.* Christopher Waterman, *Juju: A Social History and Ethnography of an African Popular Music* (1990).

ADEDEJI, Clement Raphael Adebayo
(Nigeria, 1930–)

Dr. Clement Raphael Adebayo Adedeji is one of Africa's leading economists. For 16 years he served as head of the United Nations (U.N.) Economic Commission for Africa (ECA), and he has been a sharp critic of the economic reform programs of the World Bank and the International Monetary Fund (IMF), known as structural adjustment programs.

Adedeji has established himself in both the academic and professional worlds. After graduating from Leicester University in England, he became an assistant secretary for economic planning in Nigeria's Western Region from 1958 to 1960. He obtained a master's degree from Harvard University (1961), then spent two years in the Ministry of Finance before joining the Institute of Administration at the University of Ife. Following the successful defense of his Ph.D. at the University of London in 1967, he was promoted to full professor at Ife. During this period he published several books on African public administration, an area in which he is considered an expert. He also served as chair of Western Nigeria Radio and Television and was a director on the National Manpower Board. In 1971, General Yakubu GOWON appointed Adedeji federal commissioner for economic development. His four-year tenure in that office coincided with the oil boom in Nigeria that produced vastly increased revenue for the national government and ushered in a period of prosperity and economic expansion. Within Nigeria, Adedeji created a National Youth Service Corps.

Perhaps his greatest contribution in that period was the creation of the Economic Community of West African States (ECOWAS). Adedeji conducted delicate negotiations among 16 nations in which post-colonial economies were patterned on English, French and Portuguese models. ECOWAS has been designed as a cooperative venture leading eventually to a free-trade zone, but it has evolved beyond that by taking up regional peacekeeping tasks.

By 1975, Adedeji was seeking a greater challenge, and just before the coup that removed Gowon, he took the post of assistant secretary-general of the United Nations and executive secretary of the ECA. This position provided him with the opportunity to criticize the state of African economic structures. His incisive annual reports and careful addresses won him a respectful audience through the years. He has received a number of awards and honorary doctorates and served on a host of international commissions.

With the passage of time, it became clear to Adedeji that the structural adjustment programs (SAPs) of the IMF and World Bank were not relieving African countries of their economic malaise; they were actually the cause of considerable suffering for ordinary people. The SAPs require severe cutbacks in public-sector services and employment, devaluation of currency, and an end to subsidies on food and services. In 1989, Adedeji published his alternative program, "African Alternative Framework to Structural Adjustment Programmes." Based on international research by over a hundred economists, it argued that SAP demands

exerted pressures for too-rapid change on weak economies. In fact, the evidence showed that SAPs had failed in Africa, ignoring long-term development and failing to offer alternatives. His alternative program promoted multiple exchange rates, differential interest rates, and selective control and price policies to ensure self-sufficiency in food. The report, which was greeted with enthusiasm by the Organization of African Unity (now the African Union), provided a blueprint for economic transformation without great burdens upon the poor.

In 1991, Adedeji stepped down from his post with the ECA but has continued his economic reform campaign. His argument is that the major structural problem for African economies is the crushing burden of external debt, which requires relief. He has also called for a Marshall Plan for Africa, using the model of the Eastern European Development Bank. Adedeji has not laid the blame for the African economic crisis only at the door of Western financial institutions; he has also taken African governments to task, accusing them of "contagious lethargy, monumental opportunism ... and above all, our dependency syndrome."

After leaving the ECA, Adedeji returned to Nigeria to run for the presidency. His attempt to take the nomination of the Social Democratic Party collapsed, however, before the strong position of Moshood ABIOLA.

References: PAS, RWWA, *wik*i.

ADU, Amishadai Larson
(Ghana, 1914–1977)

Amishadai Larson Adu was a civil servant whose service bridged the transition from colonial administration to independence and whose career progressed from national to regional and international levels. A man of great personal and professional integrity, he is credited with establishing high standards for international civil service.

After early education in Ghana, Adu graduated with honors from Cambridge University in 1939. He returned to Ghana and, after several years of teaching at Achimota College, entered public service as a district commissioner. In 1949 he was named joint secretary of the Coussey Constitutional Committee, which was responsible for preparing the constitutional foundation for Ghana's self-government.

As the first African country to achieve independence, Ghana was closely watched and its experience copied by other British colonies in their own moves toward sovereignty. As Adu progressed through the administration, he was often the first African in the posts that he held. In 1950 he was commissioner for Africanization; in 1952, director of recruitment; and in 1955, secretary for external affairs. When Ghana became independent in 1957, he became the first permanent secretary in the Ministry of Foreign Affairs. In the parliamentary system, permanent secretaries direct the daily operations of each ministry and hold the highest civil service positions in the bureaucracy. Many emerging African countries were forced to rely on European permanent secretaries for some years. In 1959, Adu became secretary to the cabinet and head of the civil service.

In 1961 he moved to East Africa as independence was just being achieved, to establish commonwealth and regional organizations. He developed the precursor of the East African Community and served in several United Nations (U.N.) agencies. From 1966 to 1970 he was deputy secretary-general of the Commonwealth of Nations in London and from 1970 to 1975 was the head of Ghana Consolidated Diamonds. He then returned to the U.N. as deputy chair of the International Civil Service Commission. In all of these positions, he was uncompromising in his integrity, even when placed under great political pressure to favor various ethnic groups or political factions.

References: DAHB, MMA. Adu, *The Civil Service in New African States* (1969).

AFONSO I

(Angola/Democratic Republic of the Congo, 1456?–1545)

Manikongo Afonso I, the greatest king of the Kongo, reigned from 1506 to 1545. He worked with the Portuguese to bring Christianity to the kingdom—which was located in the area of present-day Angola, Congo, and the Democratic Republic of the Congo—and was the first African king to be recognized in Europe. In the end, however, he was unable to contain the Portuguese, who wished to develop the slave trade.

Afonso was born Mvemba Nzinga, son of the *manikongo* or king of the Kongo, who in 1482 made the first contact with the Portuguese. Nzinga

converted to Catholicism, taking the name Afonso. When his father, Nzingu Kuwu (João I), adopted the new faith and then reverted to the traditional Kongo religion, Afonso welcomed the expelled missionaries to the province he governed. The Kongo political system provided for the open election of a successor from among the descendants of the first king. Upon his father's death, Afonso's non-Christian brother attempted to deny him the election, but Afonso defeated him in battle and took the throne. He attributed his victory to divine intervention, inspired by a vision of Santiago Matamoros (St. James the Apostle), who was also the symbol of Christian victory over the Muslims during the crusades in Spain and Portugal.

Afonso entered into relations with King Manuel of Portugal to the profit of both countries. Manuel supplied missionaries and craftsmen to the Kongo; Afonso granted trade privileges to the Portuguese. In his domestic policy Afonso pursued a progressive course, building schools and roads and encouraging development.

However, the Portuguese became an increasing problem within the kingdom. Many of the architects, doctors, and pharmacists turned to commerce rather than practicing their professions. They ignored the laws of the Kongo, and in 1510 Afonso had to ask Portugal for a special representative with authority over his countrymen. Manuel responded with an ambitious plan for Westernizing Kongo society in exchange for ivory, copper, and slaves. Afonso rejected most of the plan, but the expanding slave trade presented serious challenges to the

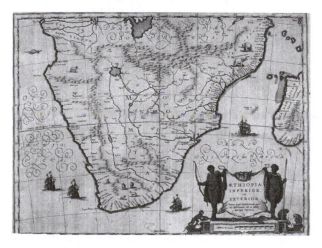

This map of 1635 by Willem Jansz. Blaeu from Aethiopia inferioris shows the Congo Regnum, of Kingdom of Congo that Afonso I would rule.

Kongo's stability. Afonso did not repudiate slavery on principle, but in 1526 he issued decrees to regulate and moderate it.

Initially, slavery was limited to war captives, who were numerous enough because of various local battles and continual border disputes. A commission was set up to see that no one was kidnapped into slavery, but soon almost every Portuguese, including the missionaries, was raiding far into the interior, and the Portuguese craftsmen expected to be paid in slaves. By the 1530s the slave traders had contacts on São Tomé Island, an off-shore colony with a royal trade monopoly from Manuel. Because São Tomé stood to lose by strong bonds between Kongo and Portugal, it made every attempt to sabotage those relations.

The Portuguese were wrongly convinced that the Kongo had vast mineral riches that the king was keeping from them. In 1540 they attempted to assassinate Afonso on Easter Sunday as he attended religious services, and he barely escaped.

Afonso promoted Christianity diligently, destroying traditional religious symbols and building churches and schools, but the few missionaries he was sent proved to be lazy, corrupt, and venal; they took concubines and lived as nobility. The other Portuguese were also poor examples of the new faith, engaging in drunken orgies and theft. In 1529 and again in 1539, Afonso appealed to the pope for intervention against Portuguese abuses, but to no avail. He sent talented young men to Portugal to be educated. Among them was his son Dom Henrique, who was consecrated a bishop in 1518. This attempt at developing an indigenous clergy failed, even though Dom Henrique returned to the kingdom. In spite of difficulties and the scandalous behavior of the Portuguese, Christianity slowly expanded across the kingdom.

When Afonso died, there was a dynastic struggle, and his immediate successor, Pedro I, was overthrown and replaced by a grandson, DIOGO I. The Kongo remained at least nominally Christian for over a century, but the hopeful signs of African-European partnership in international relations were shattered by the Portuguese, who began a ruthless expansion of the slave trade.

In the post-colonial era, Afonso was presented as a great resistance figure who opposed European domination and slavery. He was, of course, a far more complex person. On the one hand a devout Christian who presented himself as monogamous, he somehow left 300 grandchildren at his death. He

destroyed the fetishes of his enemies, but then promoted Christian relics as signs of his personal cult. The churches he built over the graves of the ancestors were dubbed "tombs," and the traditional priests of the water cult were enlisted to care for them and protect the baptismal water. In the end, his kingdom was eroded by the grasping lust for slaves by the Europeans.

References: AB, *afr,* AH, DAB, *dacb,* DAHB, DT, EWB, *wiki.* Elikia M'Bokolo, *Affonso Ier, le roi chretien de l'ancien Congo* (Affonso I, Christian king of ancient Kongo, 1975).

AFRIKANER, Jan Jonker
(Namibia, 1823?–1889)

Chief Jan Jonker Afrikaner was a prominent chief of the Khoikhoi peoples, inaccurately called "Hottentots" in the West. The Afrikaner family governed the Oorlam clan, and around the time of Jan Jonker's birth, his father, Jonker Afrikaner, led them in nomadic wandering throughout Botswana for several years. They spoke Dutch, were Christian, followed European ways, and were on reasonably good terms with British authorities in the Cape.

During Jan Jonker's childhood, the clan settled in what is now Namibia at Windhoek, the current capital. There they established themselves as the dominant group in the region, which had a number of small independent clans. During a territorial skirmish with the Herero in 1863, Jan Jonker's brother, Christiaan, who had succeeded his father in 1861, was killed in battle, and Jan Jonker Afrikaner took his place as chief.

Jan Jonker Afrikaner had hoped to maintain peace, but neighboring groups resented Oorlam dominance. Afrikaner became friendly with MAHERERO, future chief of the Herero, but when Maherero became chief he asserted Herero land claims and the two groups began an intense conflict that lasted from 1863 to 1870. The next decade saw peace, but the Oorlam were exhausted and lost much of their political power in the region. In 1880 hostilities once again broke out and the Khoikhoi, now with the Oorlam clans of Jan Jonker and Moses Witbooi united, suffered further reverses. By 1885, Afrikaner was willing to negotiate with the Germans, who had designs on Namibia, and the next year he granted them a protectorate. Moses Witbooi was killed, and Afrikaner could not get along with his son and heir, Henrik WITBOOI. The Oorlam-Herero alliance collapsed, and the two Khoikhoi clans began fighting each other. Witbooi, however, became a great leader who assumed the mantle of regional dominance. While his power was waning, Afrikaner was assassinated in 1889 by one of his sons, and his branch of the Oorlam clan disintegrated.

Reference: DAHB.

AGGREY, James Emman Kwegyir
(Ghana, 1875–1927)

Dr. James Emman Kwegyir Aggrey, one of the colonial period's most respected African scholars, educators and intellectuals, was a leading advocate of racial equality.

Educated in the Gold Coast (today's Ghana) Methodist mission schools, where he also taught, Aggrey showed early intellectual promise. He assisted in the translation of the Bible into Fante and worked as a deputy editor of the *Gold Coast Methodist Times.* In his position at the *Times* he successfully campaigned against the Lands Bill in 1897, which would have allowed the government to seize all land not in visible use.

In 1898, Aggrey went to the United States to study at Livingstone College in Salisbury, North Carolina, where he was sponsored by the African Methodist Episcopal Zion Church (AMEZ), an African-American denomination. He later worked at Livingstone as registrar and teacher, remaining in the United States until 1924. His stay in the U.S. was a particularly productive period in Aggrey's life. He served as pastor for a number of North Carolina AMEZ churches and furthered his studies at Columbia University and Hood Theological School, where he received a doctorate in theology in 1912. Livingstone considered him for president, but he was first excluded because of his nationality, and later he declined the offer. The Phelps-Stokes Fund, a foundation devoted to furthering the educational opportunities of Africans, African-Americans, and Amerindians, invited Aggrey to be the only African member of its commission on education, which provided him the opportunity to travel in Africa in 1921 and 1924. He visited 11 colonies as well as the independent states of Liberia and Ethiopia in a wide-ranging inquiry into the educational needs of Africans.

Aggrey was a tireless mentor, seeking out promising youth and promoting advanced education (especially African-American education) for them in the United States rather than in Great Britain. Among those touched by him during his endless travels across the continent were Nnamdi AZIKIWE of Nigeria, Hastings BANDA of Malawi, and Kwame NKRUMAH of Ghana. Although he was without a theory of Pan-Africanism, Aggrey championed its practice. He was often greeted enthusiastically as the "herald of an invading band of Negroes" who would resettle in Africa and defeat colonialism. Aggrey did nothing to dispel these fond hopes, although his concerns were more practical. The Phelps-Stokes Commission final report resulted in considerable educational progress within British colonies. Aggrey's frequent public speeches in Britain and the United States earned him international recognition. During this period, he obtained a master's degree from Columbia University and began work on a Ph.D. there.

Aggrey returned to the Gold Coast in 1924 to establish the new university college, Achimota. He worked tirelessly, overcoming both the opposition of colonials and the suspicions of nationalists, who distrusted the government's initiative. He even designed Achimota College's emblem: a piano keyboard symbolizing collaboration of the Black and White races, a cause he supported and promoted constantly. His public successes were not, however, matched by personal ones, and the move to the Gold Coast placed great strain on his marriage. His African-American wife could not adjust to life in the African colony and returned to the United States after a short period. In 1927, Aggrey saw the college opened and functioning. He then took leave to visit his wife and four children and to defend his Ph.D. thesis. He died suddenly in New York of meningitis.

Aggrey had a cheerful, optimistic and open personality. His beliefs in racial harmony stemmed from his strong Christian faith, which he saw as the means of uniting the races. He bore racial slights without animosity, even when he was demoted at Achimota from deputy principal because the British would not allow an African to be acting head during the principal's absence. He was denied lodging with other members of the Phelps-Stokes Commission when he traveled, suffering the usual indignities shown to Africans during the colonial period.

Influenced by the thought of African-American leader Booker T. Washington, he advocated practical education, focusing on agriculture, social service and African culture. His progressive work for African education has made him a national hero in Ghana.

References: DAB, *dabc*, DAHB, MMA. Edwin Smith, *Aggrey of Africa: A Study in Black and White* (1929).

AGGREY, John
(Ghana, 1809–1869)

Chief John Aggrey was ruler of the Cape Coast Fante community. He was the first traditional ruler to organize planned protest against the colonial administration in the Gold Coast. The son of the previous chief, he had no formal education, but he taught himself to read and write in English. He observed carefully as the British expanded their influence and power in Cape Coast. They had made a pact with the Fante, the Bond of 1844, which permitted them to advise the chiefs in judicial matters. Gradually, they extended this prerogative until they had set up their own courts with jurisdiction far beyond Cape Coast Castle—technically their only possession, although they had a protectorate over the Gold Coast in general.

In 1865, Aggrey became the ruler and immediately began asserting his authority. When the British levied a tax and then sought to use most of the revenue to support their own colonial government, Aggrey and the Fante chiefs protested so vehemently that the British revenue policy had to be dropped. Aggrey established his own court and denied the right of appeal to the British court system, arguing that the British were limited to their own possessions. He claimed all land up to the walls of the castle. In 1865 he sent delegates to London to testify before a parliamentary commission, which ultimately advocated British withdrawal from the Gold Coast. Aggrey shrewdly used the talents of Western-educated Africans to argue his cause. He was often in conflict with the local British authorities and on several occasions had the governor's agents arrested. Matters reached a crisis in 1866 when Aggrey demanded total self-government and the governor had him arrested and tried in Sierra Leone. Failing to find grounds for a trial, the British tried to bully Aggrey into submission, but

he held firmly to his claims. He was returned home in 1869 and died shortly thereafter. He is revered in Ghana as the forerunner of nationalism.

References: DAB, DAHB.

AGONGLO
(Benin, 1766?–1797)

Agonglo was the king of Dahomey (in present-day Benin) from 1789 to 1797 during the period in which Dahomey remained under the dominance of the Yoruba kingdom of Oyo. In the face of an economic depression, he fostered and nurtured the European slave trade.

The African system of captivity was sharply different from Western chattel slavery. The slave, usually a male prisoner taken in war, was not normally transferable, he could marry freely, and most West African states had a captive elite that belonged to the royal service. These men were often wealthy and prominent persons. A captive could own property, which in Dahomey could include slaves.

Two forces—one from the north and the other from the sea—transformed this relatively benign slave system into one in which slaves became part of an economic structure in which they provided a necessary labor force and were treated as property. The first force was the expansion of Islam in the hinterland states of West Africa, which introduced Arab slave practices and opened up the desert trade routes to Morocco. The Barbary states of the Mediterranean coast had just had their sea lanes cut off due to the French Revolution, and they sought new sources of slaves. The second force was the role of European traders, who were establishing themselves along the Atlantic coast, seeking a slave labor force for colonies in the Americas.

Agonglo came to his throne as the African and capitalist systems overlapped and the African captive system gave way to the new, more exploitive one. Agonglo was not a popular choice for king, and amid internal disunity he did not have a strong political position. This situation made it difficult for him to take advantage of the weakened status of Oyo, the regional power, and he never was able to free Dahomey from Oyo's domination. He also faced a long, nagging economic depression. The slave trade seemed a possible solution, so he increased raids into the interior to bring back captives to the

Dahomean port of Ouidah and liberalized trade regulations to favor European commerce, but competition was strong along the coast. In his desire to cement relations with Europe, he married a Creole French woman, the first African king to choose a western wife.

Shortly after Agonglo came to power, the slave trade suffered a decline, largely as a result of the French Revolution, which abolished slavery in France and limited it in French colonies. Agonglo turned to Queen Maria of Portugal, because Portugal had a long history as a major slave-trading country. Queen Maria sent two missionaries, and Agonglo converted to Christianity, probably for political reasons. This departure from tradition angered the people, however, and he was assassinated. He left a seriously deteriorated state, marked not only by the brutality of human sacrifice at festivals but also by an attitude of materialism that stemmed from slavery and cheapened human life to the price of alcohol and cowrie shells.

Reference: DAHB, *wiki.*

AHIDJO, Ahmadou

(Cameroon, 1925–1989)

Ahmadou Ahidjo was the first president of Cameroon and the political leader most associated with the unification of the nation. He was elected to the consultative territorial assembly in his early twenties. By 1956 he was president of the assembly, which by then had legislative power, and was poised to move into power at independence. In 1958 he became prime minister after his predecessor was removed for using excessive force against an armed rural rebellion. Ahidjo then initiated negotiations with France and the U.N., and French Cameroon gained independence in 1960. A referendum in the British Cameroons sanctioned the division of that colony; the north joined Nigeria and the south united with Cameroon, the former French trust territory.

Ahidjo continued his efforts after unification. There was considerable economic progress under his regime, and he was able to suppress a Communist-backed insurgency with a combination of amnesty policies and aggressive military actions. After decreeing both French and English as official languages, he created a centralized administration and a single-party state.

Ahidjo was a retiring man who projected an image of quiet competence. A Pan-Africanist, he developed good relations with other states and served as president of the Organization of African Unity (OAU), now the African Union.

In 1982 Ahidjo surprised his nation by announcing his resignation. He left a strong economy based on oil production and trade, but also self-sufficient in food. He had groomed his successor, Paul BIYA, evidently assuming that the younger man would defer to him. Ahidjo kept control of the ruling party but soon clashed with Biya, who emerged as undisputed head of both the ruling party and the state. Ahidjo went into exile in France and Sénégal, clearly regretting his resignation. There were accusations of secret plots against Biya. In Dakar, Ahidjo died a bitter and abandoned leader with few followers.

References: afr, AO, DAHB, EWB, MMA, PLBA, PLCA, *wiki.*

AHMAD Ibn Ibrahim al-Ghazi

(Ethiopia, 1506?–1543)

Imam Ahmad Ibn Ibrahim al-Ghazi, known in the Ethiopian chronicles by his nickname, Grañ ("the left-handed"), was the Muslim leader who came closest to conquering Christian Ethiopia. The early sixteenth century was a period of disintegration in the Ethiopian empire, both politically and culturally, and Ahmad, influenced by the spirit of *jihad* (holy war) carried Islam forward, bringing whole provinces under Muslim control.

Ahmad came from Adel, one of a number of petty Islamic states on the fringes of Ethiopia. During the 1520s he took control of Adel but renounced the title of sultan and declared himself an *imam,* or religious leader. He raised the banner of *jihad* against Orthodox Christian Ethiopia, refusing to pay the traditional tribute. His army, a motley group of nomadic Somalis, was fired up with religious fervor and the desire for conquest. The Ethiopians, under the weak emperor LEBNA Dengel, met Ahmad at Sembera Kure in 1529 and were badly defeated. The Ethiopian army was destroyed and many of the ruling elite killed.

Ahmad then embarked on a war of invasions, and in five years the Muslims had conquered four provinces of Ethiopia and were taking a fifth. The sacred city of Aksum, noted for its monasteries, fell. Most Ethiopians were compelled to accept Islam, countless churches were destroyed, and at Lebna Dengel's death in 1540, all seemed lost for the Christian kingdom.

The new emperor, GALADÉWOS, sought help from the Portuguese, who sent a fleet and troops with firearms. In 1542, Ahmad was routed, but he returned a year later with Turkish support and defeated the Portuguese. He captured and executed their leader, the son of Vasco da GAMA, when he refused to adopt Islam. In a battle shortly thereafter, Galadéwos defeated Ahmad, who died in the battle. With Ahmad's death, his movement collapsed. The Ethiopian church developed a reinstatement ceremony for apostates, and most returned to Christianity. Galadéwos began to reunite the empire, and for several centuries the power of Islam in the region was broken.

References: DAB, DAHB, DT, EB, *wiki.*

AHOMADÉGBÉ-TOMETIN, Justin
(Benin, 1917–2002)

Dr. Justin Ahomadégbé-Tometin, former prime minister of Dahomey (since 1975 known as Benin) and briefly president, served during a period of great instability during which Dahomey had 11 heads of state in 12 years.

Born into Dahomey's royal clan, Ahomadégbé-Tometin was educated at the elite William Ponty School in Dakar, Sénégal, and then studied dentistry at the University of Dakar medical school. After a brief stint as a sergeant in the French army in World War II, he spent 1944–1947 in private dental practice. He entered party politics during this period and in 1947 was elected to the local general council. He was subsequently elected to the Grand Council of West Africa in 1952. In 1947 he left the leading party of Sourou Migan APITHY to found a new party, which in 1956 he formed into a local affiliate of the Rassemblement Démocratique Africain (RDA), the interterritorial party led by Félix HOUPHOUËT-BOIGNY, the dominant regional figure. Ahomadégbé-Tometin and Apithy remained rivals for the rest of their careers.

Ahomadégbé-Tometin continued to assume numerous political positions, which in the French system can be held simultaneously. He became mayor of Abomey in 1956, senator to the French Community, and deputy to the French West African Council. His party fared well in the 1957 and 1960 elections, but not well enough to provide him with a majority. Hubert MAGA, a sometime ally, made an alliance with Apithy, banned Ahomadégbé-Tometin's party, and imprisoned him from 1960 to 1962. In 1964, Maga was removed by a military coup, and Apithy and Ahomadégbé-Tometin divided the powers of the executive branch at the behest of General Christophe SOGLO. The two rivals accomplished little more than a disastrous 20 percent tax increase, and in 1965 Ahomadégbé-Tometin tried to oust Apithy in a dispute over who had the right to appoint supreme court justices. Ahomadégbé-Tometin contacted army elements for support, angering Soglo, who removed both of them.

Following this confusing and self-serving tenure, Ahomadégbé-Tometin, during his exile in Togo and France, plotted several coups to restore his authority, all of which failed. In 1970 the triumvirate of Maga, Apithy, and Ahomadégbé-Tometin was invited back by the military, and after a corrupt and strife-torn election, a Presidential Council was established with a rotating chairmanship. In 1972 Ahomadégbé-Tometin assumed the chair, but he lasted only four months before an exasperated military under General Mathieu KÉRÉKOU removed the council and imprisoned all three until 1981. Ahomadégbé-Tometin went into exile in France until he returned to Benin in 1990 after political liberalization.

References: DAHB, PLBA.

AIDID, Mohammed Farah
(Somalia, 1934–1996)

General Mohammed Farah Aidid emerged from the 1991 campaign to overthrow military dictator General Mohammed SIYAD BARRE as the strongest clan leader in Somalia. His opposition to the invasion and occupation of his country by the United Nations (U.N.) made him an international figure.

Born in Italian Somaliland in 1934, Aidid was trained in the Italian military school near Rome and then returned home to become chief of police in Mogadishu, the capital. In the early 1960s he spent three years in the Soviet Union attending an officers' course, during a period in which Somalia favored the USSR in the Cold War contest for dominance in the Horn of Africa. In 1969, Siyad Barre chose Aidid as chief of staff, but when they clashed, Aidid was imprisoned for six years, largely in solitary confinement. Within a year after his release, Aidid was appointed a colonel and was sent to the Ethiopian front (1978–1979), where Siyad Barre had begun an invasion after the Soviet Union dropped him as a client. The Somali troops were at first successful, but Soviet and Cuban assistance turned the tide against them. Apparently rehabilitated after his field command, Aidid went on to become Siyad Barre's military advisor and then Somali ambassador to India in 1984.

In 1989, Aidid left his post in Delhi to join the political opposition. Within two years his forces had successfully driven Siyad Barre from Mogadishu and across the Kenyan border into exile. A Somali National Movement (SNM) unity government was formed from the guerrilla groups that had opposed Siyad Barre, but there was considerable jockeying for power. Aidid emerged as chairman, while his main rival, Ali Mahdi Mohammed, was named interim president of the country. The sub-clans, pitted against one another under Siyad Barre, soon clashed and divided the country. A drought magnified problems; food supplies ran low and parts of the country experienced starvation conditions.

When large numbers began to die, international aid agencies appealed for help. Stirred by graphic television accounts of the starvation, the United States intervened in late 1992 to bring humanitarian aid. At first Aidid welcomed American intervention, expecting support for his position against Ali Mahdi. When U.N. forces entered and expanded the intervention, they began disarming Aidid's forces. Aidid—whose last name means "he who will not be humiliated"—went into hiding and began harassing the occupying forces. A master of urban guerrilla action, Aidid and his troops staged several ambushes that resulted in serious losses for the U.N. troops. The United States offered a bounty of $25,000 for him, but failed to capture him. Attempts to bomb Aidid's headquarters failed, adding to his aura of invincibility.

Finally deciding that no peace was possible without Aidid, the United States arranged talks among all Somali factions, and Aidid spent much of early 1994 in Nairobi, Kenya, at the negotiations. His notable achievement was to convince the separatists who had established Somaliland, a breakaway republic in the north, that their future lay in a united Somalia. Aidid's Somali National Alliance, formed when he was expelled from the SNM in 1992, became a dominant force in the country, although by no means the controlling one. When American forces abandoned Somalia in 1995, Aidid declared himself president, but the title was a hollow one. The following year, he died of battle wounds after a skirmish with rival factions. Somalia was left with no functional central government.

References: afr, wiki. Mark Bowden, *Blackhawk Down* (1999).

AIDOO, Ama Ata
(Ghana, 1942–)

Ama Ata Aidoo is one of Africa's most forceful feminist writers. She writes in several genres and has published plays, short stories, novels, and poetry. Into all of these literary forms, but especially her plays and short stories, she weaves oral literature: Her writing has the sound and sense of West Africa. Aidoo has commented: "Everybody needs a backbone. If we do not refer to the old traditions, it is almost like operating with amnesia."

Her early plays *Dilemma of a Ghost* (1964) and *Anowa* (1970) both deal with the effect of slavery on Africans. Aidoo has a continuing fascination with the relationship between Africa and the Black diaspora, and it is fair to say that if there is one recurring theme in all her work, it is liberation—personal, social and political. Under this rubric she brings together concerns about the preservation of African culture, the role of women, the fate of the diaspora, and the impact of Western ideas (especially capitalism) on the Third World. Aidoo is an ardent defender of African values, which prompts her to criticize male dominance. Her novels have dealt with issues including marital rape (*Changes*, 1991) and global oppression (*Our Sister Killjoy*, 1977).

Aidoo received her B.A. degree at the University of Ghana and in its drama and writers' workshops completed her first play. Aidoo's sensitive awareness of African traditions comes from her early experiences as a chief's daughter and her upbringing in a royal compound. The rhythms of storytelling, ritual recitations, and the passing on of secret lore became part of her consciousness, influencing her subsequent intellectual development. Her interweaving of African oral techniques and Western literary conventions is most evident in her short fiction. "My stories are written to be heard," she has stated. *No Sweetness Here* (short stories, 1970) focuses on African sexism and *Someone Talking to Sometime* (poetry, 1985) on the collapse of the promise of independence.

Aidoo has pursued a career in teaching and lecturing and served as professor of English at the University of Cape Coast from 1970 to 1982. She was secretary for foreign affairs in the Provisional National Defense Council after Jerry RAWLINGS's second coup, and for the following two years she acted as minister of education. Her ideas on reforming education to meet girls' needs, however, proved too threatening to the government, and she resigned her position. For some years, she lived in Zimbabwe. She now teaches in the United States.

References: adb, afr, AWT, CA, DLB, LKW, MBW, NRG, *wiki,* WLTC.

AJUOGA, Abednego Matthew

(Kenya, 1925–)

Archbishop Abednego Matthew Ajuoga founded the Church of Christ in Africa, known popularly as the Johera, a prominent African Christian denomination in Kenya. He was educated in schools of the Church Missionary Society (CMS), the leading Anglican missionary society in East Africa and one with strong evangelical leanings. Ajuoga was baptized in 1943 and, after working for the railways, he entered the seminary and was ordained in 1954.

Ajuoga was posted to Luoland in western Kenya, an area that had experienced a number of church schisms in response to the *bakalole* ("the saved ones"), a charismatic and evangelical church revival movement. It originated in Rwanda in 1927 and in the late 1930s spread to Kenya, where many Christians began leaving mission churches and joining new African independent churches. Many who remained in the mission churches attempted to transform them from European to African institutions. Ajuoga's first doubts were sewn when he helped translate the Bible into Duluo. It struck him forcibly that the Greek word *philadelphia,* "brotherly love," bore no resemblance to the way the colonial missionaries treated their African disciples. He began to contemplate the need for a completely African denomination, but this would not be triggered until he experienced rejection within Anglicanism.

In western Kenya, the largest renewal group among the Anglicans was known as the Johera ("people of love"). Ajuoga preached unity and opposed separatist tendencies, and was at first a force for keeping the Johera within the Anglican communion. Matters seemed to stabilize when the first five African bishops—all members of the *bakalole*—were consecrated. When relations between the separatists and those within the church became strained, the bishops suppressed the Johera and suspended the clergy, calling in the colonial police for enforcement. Ajuoga led an exodus of seven priests, 130 congregations and 16,000 members.

The schism was wrenching: There were violent outbreaks, 25 churches were destroyed, and the dreaded police Special Branch was deployed. The Johera movement had a political aspect that was not lost on the government; it considered the settler-controlled Anglican state church a pillar of colonial society. Fearing a nationalist movement, the authorities warned the Johera not to identify themselves as a Luo church; thus, they registered under the name "Church of Christ in Africa." It was the first in a wave of independent foundations, now numbering over 500 denominations in Kenya, making that country a center of the independent church movement. By the time of Kenyan independence in 1963, Johera had 50,000 members.

Johera spread throughout Kenya and into neighboring countries and has built a group of religious schools. Unlike many other independent churches, Johera remains traditionally Christian in its teachings.

Ajuoga spent a year of advanced study at Union Theological Seminary in New York in 1964–1965. He remains archbishop and head of the Johera. Widely honored, Ajuoga was president of the African Instituted Churches from 1982–1997. Curiously, his name in Duluo translates as "diviner" or "healer."

References: dabc, DAHB. George Pickens, *African Christian God Talk: Matthew Ajuoga's Johera*

Narratives (1993); F.B. Welbourne and Bethuel Ogot, *A Place to Feel at Home: A Study of Two Independent Churches in Kenya* (1967).

AKINOLA, Peter Jasper
(Nigeria, 1944–)

Archbishop Peter Akinola is primate of the Anglican Church in Nigeria and the leader of a movement in the Anglican Communion to force separation of those Anglican dioceses that support the ordination of active gays or the blessing of gay unions.

Akinola heads the largest and—many would say—most vibrant branch of the Anglican Communion. The Anglican Communion, under the headship of the Archbishop of Canterbury in England, is made up of many national autonomous Churches united by a common faith and history. The Episcopal Church is its American branch.

Akinola was born and educated in Nigeria before becoming a priest and bishop. He is from the evangelical, "low church" wing of Anglicanism, which is the basis of his traditionalist views. His campaign over the recognition of homosexuality in the Church, which he considers an abomination, began when the Canadian Diocese of New Westminister began to bless gay unions in 2002. Akinola announced that in effect, New Westminister had abandoned the historic faith and separated itself from Anglicanism. The issue heated up with the election of a gay bishop in England the following year. Akinola denounced the election as "a Satanic attack on God's Church." When he mobilized African and Asian bishops in opposition, the candidate withdrew his name. Then, when American Episcopalians elected an openly gay bishop who was living with a partner, the matter came to a head. Threatening schism, Akinola gathered opposition from around the world to his cause. Except for those in the Province of South Africa, the African bishops supported him. Opponents—often equally polemical in their denunciations—have suggested that he is positioning himself to head a new Anglican Church, separated from Canterbury.

Events moved quickly. In 2004, Akinola toured Nigerian communities in the United States, making no secret of his intention of cutting them away from the Episcopal Church. He has openly called for a "realignment" of the Church and welcomes secession from those dioceses he considers to be in heresy. In

Peter Jasper Akinola

2005, he redefined the relationship of the Province of Nigeria by removing the clause "communion with the See of Canterbury" with a statement of communion with all faithful churches. He has entered into agreements with breakaway Anglican groups in the United States and Canada.

Akinola has been president of the Christian Association of Nigeria, which represents Protestants, Anglicans and Catholics. From this position, he has spoken out on Muslim-Christian conflicts. When riots took place in the Muslim north of Nigeria in response to blasphemous cartoons of Mohammed, Akinola sarcastically reminded "our Muslim brothers that they do not have the monopoly on violence." In the clashes that followed on this, 80 Muslims were killed.

Akinola is close to President Olusegun OBASANJO and has widespread support from conservative movements outside the Church. He has been funded by several conservative foundations in the United States, and this is a source of criticism. Archbishop Akinola was named one of TIME magazine's 2006 list of "100 People Who Shape Our World."

Reference: wiki.

AKLILU Lemma
(Ethiopia, 1936–1997)

Dr. Aklilu Lemma, Africa's foremost microbiologist, developed the means of eradicating bilharzia, or snail fever, a deadly and common affliction in tropical Africa. The saga of his first discovery is a case study in the use of a traditional medicine, its chemical analysis and replication, and finally, application to the needs of patients.

One day, the young doctor observed an everyday scene: women washing clothes in a stream. They were using a common shrub, *endod* or soapberry, which African women have used for laundry for centuries. What struck Aklilu, however, was evidence of dead snails—the species that carries bilharzia. He realized immediately that *endod* contained some sort of molluscicide that offered a way to destroy the carriers before they infected humans.

Snail fever takes its popular name from the tiny snails that carry the disease, which afflicts some 300 million people in 74 countries in Africa (where it has been epidemic), Latin America and Asia. Most African lakes and rivers may not be used for bathing without serious risk. Only malaria is more deadly in the Third World. Parasitic worms enter the human body with little effort after the snails deposit them. In the body, the worms are paired male/female in constant copulation. They settle into small veins and cause anemia and kidney and liver damage. It is often fatal and always debilitating.

In 1966, Dr. Aklilu established the Institute of Pathobiology at Addis Ababa University and began systematic research. His efforts were met with indifference among pharmaceutical companies, since any likely *endod* product would not be highly profitable. Perhaps more tragic, the medical research community also showed indifference for many years. Only when it was shown that *endod* was also effective in the control of zebra mussels, which infect the Great Lakes of the United States, was his work accepted and followed. Aklilu commented that "the root problems of scientific research in Africa are not only the lack of facilities and funds but also the biases of individuals and organizations in industrialized countries."

After initial studies in Ethiopia, Aklilu graduated from the University of Wisconsin in 1960, and then earned an ScD from Johns Hopkins University. As a doctoral student, he was already interested in bilharzia, and he studied the defense mechanisms of starfish and sea urchins. In the process, he visited Brazil, Egypt and Sudan to see the effects of the disease firsthand.

Back in Ethiopia, Dr. Aklilu started a parasitology program from scratch at the medical college, which he then took a lead in forming into a true medical school, and served as assistant and then dean. A grant from the U.S. Office of Naval Research enabled Aklilu to spend two years at Stanford University, where he worked on the chemical properties of *endod* and its potential applications to snail fever and other parasitic diseases. When the analysis finally isolated the chemical component, it was named Lemmatoxin in his honor. Lemmatoxin has a controlling effect on several other vectors besides snails—mosquitos (malaria), copepods (Guinea worm) and Black flies (river blindness). Commercial applications include contraception, detergents and even strengthening materials for construction materials.

With his research recognized, Dr. Aklilu's team conducted extensive field work using Lemmatoxin. The results were dramatic; among 3,500 children aged one to six, incidence of the disease fell from 50 percent to 7 percent.

In 1989, Dr. Aklilu received the Swedish Right Livelihood Award, sometimes called "the alternative Nobel Prize," for his work on snail fever. Many other awards and honors, including an honorary doctorate, recognized the importance of his work. The income from the patents developed with *endod* go into a foundation to further Dr. Aklilu's work, but not until he had overcome attempts by British scientists to patent Lemmatoxin for themselves and steal his work. Even the World Health Organization attempted to stymie his work, allying themselves with a pharmaceutical corporation whose parallel drug cost 27 times that of Lemmatoxin, and which had to be purchased in hard currency, an impossible burden for poor Third World countries. The hostility extended to convincing the Italian government not to fund field trials. The *endod* story is one of amazing creative research paired with the sordid self-interest of international science. And yet, as Aklilu has argued, "We have found a poor man's medicine for a poor man's disease."

Reference: www.aklilulemma.com.

AKITOYE, Ologun
(Nigeria, 1780s–1853)

Ologun Akitoye, a leading Yoruba chief, was king (*ologun*) of Lagos, a major port city on the coast of the Gulf of Guinea, from 1841 to 1853. Faced with British desires for expanded influence and control, he made concessions but also learned to manipulate the Europeans to his own benefit.

Akitoye was a cousin of the previous *ologun,* who had died without leaving heirs. Both Akitoye and his nephew Kosoko claimed the throne, but Akitoye enlisted the support of the king of Benin, a powerful local figure, and was crowned in 1841. Four years later Kosoko drove him out with backing from Brazilian slavers who coveted the rich slave trade in the region. Akitoye decided to approach the newly arrived British, who were committed to suppressing the slave trade. He received support from missionaries, but lacking firm backing from colonial officials, he tried to negotiate with a Brazilian slaver.

Only in 1851 were the British, under John Beecroft, willing to move against Kosoko. He was expelled from Lagos and Akitoye was reinstated as *ologun*. In exchange, he agreed to prohibit human sacrifice and end the sale of slaves in his territory. His motives were probably self-serving, because his bargaining while in exile showed less concern for human rights than for his return to power. Akitoye died in 1853, and the British, now well established in Lagos, used their power to determine that his son, Docemo (Dosumu), would succeed him. The city of Lagos was ceded to the British in 1861.

Reference: DAHB.

AKUFFO, Frederick

(Ghana, 1937–1979)

Lieutenant-General Frederick Akuffo was the military head of state who overthrew the military government of Ignatius ACHEAMPONG in 1978. He held the office for only one year before being removed by Flight Lieutenant Jerry RAWLINGS, who then had Akuffo executed.

Akuffo joined the army in 1957 as a cadet. He belonged to the first generation of soldiers who had not served in the colonial forces. He was sent for officers' training to the Royal Military Academy in Sandhurst, England, and then qualified as a paratrooper. Like most promising young Ghanaian officers, Akuffo served in the Congo (present-day Democratic Republic of the Congo) in 1960 and 1961 as part of the detachment to the U.N. peacekeeping force. He spent 1967 at the British Staff College.

When Acheampong came to power in 1972, Akuffo was named to the six-man Supreme Military Council (SMC) and rapidly advanced. He was sent to the National Defense College in India in 1973 and then was named army commander the following year. He was next given the difficult job of masterminding the national traffic changeover from driving on the left to driving on the right, which brought him to public attention. By 1976 he was chief of staff and in 1977 headed Ghana's delegation to the Commonwealth Heads of State meeting in London.

In 1978, Akuffo led a bloodless coup that removed Acheampong, accusing him of his inability to work with colleagues on the SMC. Akuffo initiated several popular moves, which included releasing prisoners jailed by Acheampong for opposing his attempts to form a nonparty government, declaring a general amnesty for Ghanaian political exiles, and promising a return to civilian rule within a year. In preparation for this reform, the ban on political parties was lifted, a new constitution was drafted, and elections were set. The economy, however, did not respond to Akuffo's attempted reforms. He reduced the substantial corruption of the Acheampong regime but could not control inflation. There were a series of strikes, and in May 1979 Rawlings attempted a coup. He failed but was freed from jail by fellow junior officers and a month later seized power. Akuffo, along with Acheampong and five senior military chiefs, was swiftly executed.

References: MMA, PLBA.

ALALI

(Nigeria, 1800s–1861)

Alali, head of one of the great trading houses in the kingdom of Bonny in the Niger Delta, amassed power rivaling that of Bonny's king. Bonny was one of a number of city-states in the vast delta of the Niger River, all with economies based on trade.

Alali was of slave origins, which prevented him from becoming king but not from rising to a position of power and influence. In the Niger Delta male slaves were integrated into the community after a ritual in which their heads were shaved like a newborn as a symbol of rebirth. The slave was then assigned as a child to a member of the community, where he assumed full rights and duties. According to his talents, he could achieve authority in his household, marry well, and attain prominence. The "houses" were clan-based trading societies that controlled inland and overseas trade. The expansion of the palm oil trade caused many houses to recruit large numbers of such slaves, and several of the most powerful houses were headed by them. Alali's father,

Modu, made the Opobo House (also called the Anna Pepple House) the wealthiest of the trading houses and even became regent for the underaged king of Bonny. In 1833, Alali succeeded his father as head of the Opobo House and regent.

Alali promoted the slave trade, not only because slaves provided manpower for the palm oil plantations but also because they could be resold to foreign investors. This position earned him the opposition of the British. When young King William Dappa Pepple came of age, Alali refused to cede his regency and the two became rivals. The British exploited this conflict; they became allies of Pepple and deposed Alali in 1837. Pepple, however, was a weak king, and Alali built up his position by absorbing other trading houses until his was dominant. Pepple prohibited the slave trade in exchange for a payment from Britain, but the English soon tired of him, and by intriguing with British merchants, Alali had him removed and deported to England in 1854. Two years later, Alali again became regent, serving in that position until his death (possibly by poisoning). Pepple was then reinstated as king, and JAJA took over Alali's House. By the 1860s, however, the British were the effective rulers of Bonny.

Reference: DAHB.

'ALI Gaji ibn Dunama
(Niger/Nigeria, ?–1497?)

Khalif 'Ali Gaji was one of the greatest Sefawa rulers of Kanem-Bornu, an Islamic state that dominated the Chad region of Central Africa. The Sefawa dynasty ruled for over 1,000 years, the longest reign in African history. The rules governing succession were complex, leading to dynastic wars between two related clans. By the fourteenth century the balance of power had shifted to the chief of the army, who chose the new *mai,* or king, from among the princes of royal blood, often shifting from one line to the other.

'Ali killed the champion of the opposing royal house in battle in 1459, eliminating the rival clan. Even then, however, 'Ali became sultan only after two of his own cousins had ascended the throne. There had been nine *mai* in one generation, and the conflict was not resolved until 'Ali oversaw a change of rules that made succession hereditary by creating

the office of heir-apparent. After a century of bitter division, political stability was achieved.

Upon taking the throne, 'Ali turned his attention to the external threat posed by the nomadic Bulala people, who had taken advantage of strife within Kanem-Bornu to harass people along the borders and destabilize parts of the kingdom. A century earlier the Bulala had been strong enough to force the Sefawa to migrate from Kanem, a desert area, to Bornu, which was easier to defend. In 1471, 'Ali defeated the Bulala in battle. 'Ali's praise song called him "he of the tall towns and long spears" for his military achievements and because he followed his victory by building several fortified towns, including Birni Gazargamu, which was the Bornu capital for the next three centuries.

'Ali brought in a number of Islamic scholars as advisors, thus providing a balance to the military leaders, who had their power reduced. 'Ali seems to have been a sincere Muslim, and he worked at the revival of Islam, which had taken on a number of non-Islamic customs. In 1484 he made his *hajj* (pilgrimage to Mecca) and was invested with the title of *khalif,* which gave him religious as well as secular authority. He was succeeded by his son.

Reference: DAHB.

'ALI, Sunni
(Mali/Niger, ?–1492)

Sunni 'Ali founded and expanded the Songhay Empire, which at its height stretched from the Atlantic Ocean across Central Africa. 'Ali was schooled in the arts of magic and warfare as a boy, in preparation for becoming the fifteenth *sunni,* or ruler, of the little kingdom of Gao in 1464. Gao was tributary to Mali, a large but crumbling empire, and 'Ali exploited its weakness to expand his kingdom at Mali's expense.

In 1468 the Muslim leaders of Timbuktu asked his help in defending themselves. 'Ali seized the opportunity to conquer both Timbuktu's enemies and the city itself. In his conquest he revealed the brutality that (according to contemporary chroniclers) characterized his personality. He sacked the city and murdered its population, singling out Muslim clerics and scholars. In later years his capricious temper would flare up, and even court favorites were executed without reason.

Much of 'Ali's career was spent on the march. He captured small kingdoms shortly after they had wrested independence from Mali, picking them off one at a time. He built a substantial river navy and used it effectively, taking the important port of Djenne in 1473 after a seven-month naval blockade. This conquest gave him control over the lucrative Niger river trade. He was equally adept with cavalry, which gave him mastery over the nomadic groups of the desert. The only people whom he could not conquer were the Mossi, but he managed to keep them at bay.

'Ali saw the rising power of Islam, but he fluctuated between mockingly following its religious practices and openly harassing Muslims. He blended the magic practices of his youth with the new religion, keeping it under strict state control. In his court, he was known to conduct the five daily prayers in one sitting—an obvious insult to Muslim practice. On one occasion, he even executed all the clerics and Islamic scholars at a prominent study center, accusing them of plots against him. 'Ali's behavior led to highly critical accounts of his reign, all written by later Muslim historians, who referred to him as "The Celebrated Infidel" or "The Great Oppressor."

'Ali died as he was returning from an expedition. He may have been murdered by MUHAMMAD Ture, who later seized the throne from 'Ali's son.

References: afr, CWAH, DAHB, EB, EWB, WGMC.

ALIBHAI-BROWN, Yasmin Damji
(Uganda, 1949–)

Yasmin Alibhai-Brown is a prominent and honored journalist in Great Britain, widely recognized for her expertise in multiculturalism. Born into a South Asian-Ugandan family, Alibhai-Brown was educated in Kampala, and graduated from Makerere University in 1972. Shortly after, she went to Oxford University in England for graduate studies in literature (MPhil, 1975).

During her studies abroad, Idi AMIN ordered the expulsion of Asian Africans, and Alibhai-Brown's plans to return to Uganda were crushed. In addition, she married her childhood love and had a

son soon after. Forced to reassess her life, she chose to stay in England, and became a foremost interpreter of the rising multicultural society being created there with the arrival of many Commonwealth immigrants from around the world.

She began writing and found immediate acceptance from prestigious magazines and journals—*The New Statesman*, *The New York Times*, *The Independent* (where she continues to be a regular columnist), and *Newsweek* all published her work over many years. She produced television documentaries for the BBC and became a much-sought-after lecturer. Her reflections of race, gender and identity have helped focus the national debate in Great Britain over multiculturalism. Eight books and an autobiography have all treated the issue, touching on such volatile questions as race hatred, social integration and mixed-race marriage. She and her first husband divorced, and she took her present hyphenated name after remarriage in 1990. After they had a daughter, she explored the dilemmas of mixed-race children in Britain in *Mixed Feelings* (2001).

Alibhai-Brown has been a fellow of the Institute for Public Policy Research, allied with Prime Minister Tony Blair's New Labour Movement. She rejected his support of the Iraq War, and after she was named a Member of the British Empire (MBE) in 2001, she returned the honor in 2003 in protest. She has received many other recognitions, including an honorary doctorate and the George Orwell Prize for Political Journalism (2000).

She has also served on the Home Office Race Forum, where she has been an outspoken critic of racist police tactics. She has not only criticized the racism of White Britons, but also the isolation and nationalism of ethnic minorities. She has challenged the honesty of feminists and liberals in the interracial debate.

References: adb, *wiki*. Alibhai-Brown, *Mixed Feelings* (2001); *Some of My Best Friends Are ...* (2004)

ALLOTEY, Francis Kofi Ampenyin
(Ghana, 1936–)

Dr. Francis Kofi Ampenyin Allotey is a noted West African physicist who also has been prominent in science policy. After graduating from the Imperial

College of Science and Technology, Allotey went to Princeton University, where he received his Ph.D. in 1966. His entire career since then has been at the University of Science and Technology in Kumasi, Ghana, where he has been a professor since 1973. Allotey also served as dean of science at Kumasi from 1974 to 1986, founded the Computer Centre in 1972, and served as its first director until 1987.

Allotey's major research has been on x-ray spectroscopy, a subject on which he has published books and several journal articles. In 1973 he received the Prince Philip Gold Medal (U.K.) and a certificate from the American Nuclear Society for this work. He is a fellow of the African Academy of Sciences, the Royal Astronomical Society, and the International Centre for Theoretical Physics (Trieste). He also has been president or vice president of several mathematics and physics societies. Allotey was chair of the Ghana Atomic Energy Commission from 1972 to 1983 and alternate governor of the International Atomic Energy Agency in 1974. In 1985 he was vice president of the Review Conference on Non-Proliferation of Nuclear Weapons (Geneva), and today he serves on the advisory group of experts on nuclear weapons for the United Nations.

Reference: PAS.

ALO, Babajide
(Nigeria, 1951–)

Dr. Babajide Alo, an organic chemist, has trained, formed, and directs an internationally recognized research team in heterocyclic chemistry, a branch of chemistry that studies heterocyclic compounds. Heterocyclic compounds occur naturally in the human body but also can cause cancer. Consequently, there are important applications of this research.

Alo pursued both undergraduate and graduate studies at the University of Ibadan in Nigeria, completing his Ph.D. in 1979 and then receiving a World Health Organization postdoctoral fellowship. Alo has been a professor at the University of Lagos throughout his career, serving also as associate dean of graduate studies from 1989 to 1991. In addition, he has twice been a visiting scientist at the Natural Products Research Institute at the University of Waterloo in Canada and has contributed to studies of plant extracts that can be developed for medicinal purposes. (African scientists have tended to concen-

trate on studies of materials from the African natural environment, in part because Western science has largely ignored such materials.)

Alo's work has resulted in more than 40 scholarly articles and papers. One of his nonresearch goals is to impress upon students, colleagues and others the importance of receiving an African education. He has been a member of the International Development Research Council (IDRC) Network on Technology Policy Studies and a consultant to several countries on the environment and technology policy questions. He regularly conducts environmental impact analyses.

Reference: PAS.

ALVERE I
(Angola/Congo/Zaïre, 1540s–1586)

Manikongo Alvere I, king of the Kongo from 1567 to 1586, became dependent upon Portuguese military power to stem the tide of foreign invasion during a period of great instability in the Kongo.

Alvere, the stepson of his predecessor, took the throne six years after the death of DIOGO I. During those six years, three other rulers were assassinated or killed in battle. Alvere inherited a kingdom under attack from marauding neighbors and plagued with regional revolts. In particular, he faced the 1568 assault by the Jaga, a fierce group of warriors who had been welded into a nomadic army. They descended upon the kingdom, looted the capital, slaughtered numbers of people, and sold those they captured to slavers. Alvere fled to an island in the Congo River.

Before this time, slavery had been limited to prisoners of war, who had significant civil and human rights. The traders made enormous profits by kidnapping people and shipping them overseas, where they were treated as property without human rights.

Alvere had no choice but to plead for Portuguese intervention. A small force was sent in 1571 and spent two years clearing the country of the Jaga. Alvere returned to his throne under extreme conditions. The Afro-Portuguese slavers of São Tomé Island in the Atlantic ignored any direction from Lisbon and resisted Alvere's attempts to assert his authority. In one desperate move, Alvere offered to become a vassal of Portugal's king, an offer that went unheeded. The São Tomé traders established a rival colony in Angola, depriving the Kongo of much of the legitimate trade from which it had prospered. In spite of these difficulties, stability and royal authority were restored in the interior. Alvere was able to free many people who had been taken illegally into slavery and impose restrictions on the trade. Alvere began a policy of cultivating the Pope as a counterbalance to Portuguese power, but his appeals for support seldom reached Rome, and the new foreign policy had only limited success. At the time of his death, the kingdom was in a state of political crisis and facing disintegration.

Reference: DAHB.

AMADOU Ibn 'Umar Tall
(Senegal/Mali, 1833?–1898)

Sultan Amadou Ibn 'Umar Tall, son and successor of 'UMAR Ibn Said Tall, continually resisted French colonial expansion and died shortly after his empire was overcome. 'Umar had founded the Tukulor Empire in the 1850s.

Amadou took over when his father died in battle in 1864, but only after a complex family struggle that lasted for two years. He spent the first 10 years of his reign recapturing and pacifying kingdoms that had left the Tukulor Empire at the time of 'Umar's death. At the same time, Amadou had to face the advances of the French, who were expanding their colonial holdings throughout West Africa. Amadou pursued a policy of alliance, hoping to compromise with the French rather than to confront them. Taking advantage of internal conflicts within the region, however, the French advanced around the Tukulor Empire, seizing major towns and establishing themselves in critical areas. Amadou, in a poor position with his fractious empire and weak army, was unable to stop them.

Amadou was a competent administrator and set up an efficient government system, but lacking his father's religious stature and charismatic appeal, he did not stir the emotional support of his people as his father had done. As a result, an important element of Tukulor national unity disappeared. In 1887, as part of his campaign to unite the contentious sections of his empire, Amadou allied with the French against Mamadu LAMINE, but the two powers soon began to clash. Colonel Louis ARCHINARD, acting without authorization from Paris, attacked Amadou's strongholds and drew

France into war in 1889. Several kings of small states that were dependent upon the Tukulor Empire and in the advancing path of the French troops, withdrew into Amadou's territory as a final line of defense, but the French made a steady advance on the Tukulor Empire. Capturing major towns and kingdoms and forcing Amadou into a long retreat with his followers, Archinard finally took his last stronghold in bitter hand-to-hand fighting. He installed one of Amadou's sons as a puppet ruler. Amadou fled into exile in Nigeria, where he settled with his remaining followers.

Reference: DAHB.

AMIN Dada, Idi
(Uganda, 1925–2003)

Field Marshal Idi Amin Dada, one of the most notorious contemporary dictators in modern African history, was in exile since his overthrow. Both charming and ruthless, he had a mercurial temper that alternated between extreme generosity and sadistic cruelty. A comic opera figure who brought tragedy to his country, he created a climate of violence and destruction that remained beyond his rule.

Amin was born in West Nile, a turbulent frontier province, and was a member of a small Islamic tribe, the Kakwa. He was raised by his mother, an army camp follower, diviner and herbalist, and received no formal education. He joined the King's African Rifles in 1946. A strapping, powerful man, six feet three inches tall, he excelled in swimming, rugby and boxing, and from 1951 to 1960 was the heavyweight champion of Uganda. In World War II Amin saw action in Burma, and he served in Kenya during the Mau Mau uprising. In Kenya, Amin's proclivity toward cruelty became apparent, and his brutal interrogation sessions almost ended his military career on several occasions. Nevertheless, he rose through the ranks to sergeant-major and in 1960 was made an *effendi,* the highest rank available for an African, and which entitled him to carry a sword.

Preparing for independence, Uganda desperately sought available officers. Amin was appointed as the army's first lieutenant and was sent to suppress cattle raids in the north, where his atrocities caused the British to ask Milton OBOTE, then prime minister, to prosecute him. Amin was, however, merely reprimanded. After receiving further training in England, Amin became a major and returned home in 1964 to find the army in mutiny. When Amin settled the crisis, Obote promoted him to colonel and gave him a battalion command. In 1965, Obote and Amin conspired to assist the followers of the murdered prime minister of the Congo, Patrice LUMUMBA, which Amin did by transporting Zaïrean gold, ivory and coffee from the Congo into Uganda to raise money to establish military camps. When a parliamentary inquiry, sparked by "King Freddie" MUTESA II, the Ugandan president, implicated the two, Obote had Amin promoted to chief of staff and general. In 1969, the royal palace was stormed and Mutesa II was forced into exile. Obote was then in total control of the government.

Subsequently, Obote and Amin had a falling out after it became apparent that educated officers were being groomed to replace the unpredictable general. In a countermove, Amin further extended his control over the army, lavishly dispensing the money looted from the Congo adventure. He supported rebels in Sudan, which led Obote to attempt a new strategy by promoting Amin to a powerless position. In 1971, while Obote was in Singapore for a Commonwealth meeting, Amin staged a coup and assumed authority. It was probably a preemptive strike, because Obote had arranged for Amin to be arrested while he was gone.

At first, Amin proved extremely popular. Mutesa II had died in London, and Amin secured his body's safe return for burial in Uganda. He followed this by freeing political prisoners and disbanding the secret police. At the same time, however, Amin's "killer squads" hunted down Obote's supporters, and parliamentary government was abolished.

Amin's policies were as capricious as his personality. Obote had taken refuge in Tanzania, which, in addition to the border problems with Kenya, prompted Amin to scuttle the East African Community, a trade pact that provided for joint public transport, banking and other facilities. He expelled Israeli technicians and military advisors and solicited military aid from Colonel Muammar al-Qaddafi of Libya. An economic crisis was precipitated when Amin ordered all Asian traders and businessmen to leave the country within 90 days. Their businesses were turned over to Amin's friends. The army was also allowed to run amok and troops were seen drunkenly driving stolen cars throughout the coun-

A caricature of Idi Amin, President of Uganda from 1971 to 1979, as a bloated, powerful figure in military dress and covered in medals and insignias.

tryside until they ran out of fuel or crashed and were abandoned. Approximately 50,000 Asians, the backbone of the business community, were forced to leave the country. In 1972 disaffected officers, mostly from the northern Langi and Acholi tribes, mounted an attempted coup that failed. Retribution was swift and draconian. All Langi and Acholi soldiers were suspect, and many were hunted down in a bloodbath. The Nile Mansions Hotel in downtown Kampala was turned into a brutal interrogation and torture center as people were starved to death, hacked to pieces, or smashed with sledgehammers. Amin became increasingly paranoid and superstitious, moving his residence regularly and changing his bodyguards. Any criticism, no matter how mild, was cause for capital punishment, and he personally ordered the execution of several of his ministers and the Anglican archbishop, Janani LUWUM. No one was safe from his persecution, including the chief justice of Uganda, who was abducted from his chambers and murdered in 1972. Amin is reputed to have murdered one of his wives, over whose body he conducted Islamic prayers. Believing in spirit mediums, he reputedly panicked when he heard that a talking turtle had predicted his demise.

To some extent Amin lost control of his military government, and until his death he protested his innocence and contended that he did not know what was happening. Uganda came under military warlords who owed allegiance to Amin but who ruled their areas with impunity—looting, raping and killing. To maintain some vestige of control, Amin promoted illiterate soldiers and recruited so many foreigners that in his last two years in power, 75 percent of his troops were from Sudan or Zaïre (now the Democratic Republic of the Congo). Uganda became an occupied and terrorized country. Nevertheless, in 1975, the Organization of African Unity elected him president, and the African heads of state blocked United Nations condemnation of the Ugandan political crisis. Any international support for Amin eroded, however, in the general revulsion that followed accounts of his atrocities. Arab countries ended subsidies when they realized the extent of his persecutions, and the United States shifted purchases of Ugandan coffee to other countries in 1978. In Uganda, the rate of inflation rose to 1,000 percent.

In 1978, Amin invaded northern Tanzania, never expecting a counterattack from the Tanzanian army and Ugandan exiles. Despite assistance from Libyan troops, the Ugandan army crumbled, and within six months Amin's regime had fallen. Amin sought exile in Saudi Arabia, where he lived in a villa with his latest wife, who in 1993 bore his forty-third child. After a quixotic trip to Nigeria and Zaïre in 1989 (he remained close to MOBUTU Sese Seko, longtime dictator of Zaïre), he was confined to his compound, where he died of kidney failure.

References: AB, *afr*, CB, DAHB, DRWW, DT, EWB, PLBA, PLCA, RWWA, *wiki*. Samuel Decalo, *Psychoses of Power* (1989); Thomas and Margaret Melady, *Hitler in Africa* (1977). *Id Amin Dada* (video, 1974).

AMIN, Mohamed "Mo"
(Kenya, 1943–1996)

Al-Hadj Mohamed "Mo" Amin was the first and best-known African of the new generation of photojournalists that emerged since the 1970s. Amin was born into a Muslim family in Kenya. At age 17 he joined Camerapix, a news photography agency, and worked for a newspaper in Dar es Salaam, Tanzania. His newspaper reporting led to his arrest and confinement by Tanzanian authorities in 1964 and his return to Kenya. He then entered television and became production manager for BBC-TIME-LIFE's *Search for the Nile* series in his mid-twenties. He produced and shot a number of documentaries. Amin became internationally known, however, for the first films of the 1984 Ethiopian famine, which generated an unprecedented wave of public response. Bob GELDOF, the Irish recording artist who created the famine charity Band-Aid, described him as "the visual interpreter of man's stinking conscience." In 1991, while covering the Ethiopian civil war, he lost an arm in an ammunition blast that killed more than a hundred people, including his cameraman. Undaunted, Amin began working again within a year, using a prosthetic limb.

Amin's photographic books, including a series of travel albums, have met with commercial success, but his most significant photography is found in the account of his own *hajj*, or Islamic pilgrimage, *Pilgrimage to Mecca* (1979). It includes some of the best photos ever taken of each stage of the pilgrimage rites. In the late 1980s, he became head of the Nairobi Bureau of Viznews, a television reporting group owned by Reuters and NBC. He was awarded the 1985 prize of the Royal Television Society and was made a Member of the Order of the British Empire (OBE) in 1992. In 1993, Amin began a weekly news program with Viznews, *African Journal.*

In 1996, while on assignment, Amin was in an Ethiopian Airlines plane that was highjacked over the Indian Ocean, and he died when it crashed.

AMO Afer, Anton-Wilhelm
(Ghana, 1703–1759?)

Anton-Wilhelm Amo was the first modern African philosopher and the first African to receive a doctorate in Europe.

As a small boy, Amo was taken by slavers and shipped to the Dutch West Indies (some say to Amsterdam), where somehow he became a gift to the Duke of Braunschweig-Wolfenbüttel, who gave him to his son. He was baptized at age eight and given a classical education, mastering German, Dutch, Greek, Latin and Hebrew. It is believed that he met the German philosopher Gottfried Leibnitz, and was a sometime guest at his master's palace. Amo then took a law degree from the University of Halle with a dissertation on the rights of Blacks in Europe. The following year (1730), he went to Wittenberg, was awarded a doctorate and became professor of philosophy there in 1733. In the process he studied medicine, which was to influence his thought considerably. He undertook explorations of psychology, bringing his medical training to bear in liberating it from philosophy. His dissertation at Wittenberg was *On the Absence of Sensation in the Human Mind and Its Presence in our Organic and Living Body*. A rising academic star, Amo returned to Halle in 1736 for two years, which saw the publication of his *Treatise on the Art of Philosophizing Soberly and Accurately*. He taught Immanuel Kant, one of the greatest of German thinkers.

In 1740 he moved on to Jena, but here his life began to unravel. The duke's two sons had died shortly before, and his academic patron, the chancellor of Halle, also passed away in 1742. Amidst a growing moralism in the universities, his materialistic worldview fell from favor. The rise in theories of racial inferiority of Blacks brought attacks by enemies and Amo was ridiculed in public entertainments. Without patronage, Amo returned to Ghana in 1753, where he died while living in a Dutch fort.

Since 1994 there has been an annual Anton-Wilhelm Amo Prize awarded to prominent European scientific thinkers.

Reference: wiki. Monika Firla, *Anton William Amo* (2002).

AMPADU, Kwame
(Ghana, 1946?–)

Nana Kwame Ampadu, with his band, African Brothers International (ABI), was at the center of Ghanaian popular music between 1963 and 1975, when highlife was the dominant African popular music and Ghana was one of its focal points.

Highlife, which developed in the colonies of British West Africa, was influenced indirectly by World War II, when Accra was a staging area for troop shipments and supported a lively music club scene. The emerging African middle class went to expensive night clubs wearing full evening dress—hence the term "highlife."

Highlife took two forms. The first incorporated American jazz styles into African dance-hall rhythms, often using traditional melodies and leaning heavily on the use of saxophones and trombones. It was intense, spirited, and danceable; both colonial expatriates and the African elite embraced it. The second strain, which Ampadu dominates, is known as guitar-band highlife. Directly African in its sources, it uses the guitar to reinterpret music traditionally played on the thumb piano (a small handheld plucked instrument) and lute.

While he was still in his teens, Ampadu formed ABI. He honed his guitar skills and won a national competition in which earned him the title *nana*, or "king." In 1966, ABI cut its first record, for Phillips West Africa, which was followed through the years by dozens of others and some 50 albums. Today the band has 20 members.

ABI's lyrics are widely varied, touching on love and death, telling stories, and evoking village scenes familiar to Ghanaian listeners. There has been little political commentary in the group's music, although the title of ABI's first hit (in Twi) translates as "some are living well and others very poorly." The song "African Brothers" became a national and regional favorite. It uses tight vocal harmonies (for which Ampadu is known) that merge with the rhythms of guitars and percussion. Music is the headline act on the group's American and British tours, but in Ghana it shares space with elaborate skits and morality plays.

In the mid-1970s the Ghanaian economy collapsed, which severely affected the music business, including most of the clubs and recording studios. Talented artists left for Europe, but highlife never made the crossover and for the most part has faded both in Africa and abroad. After his 1991 British tour and a similar series of shows to largely African-American audiences in the United States, however, Ampadu saw highlife reach a new concert-hall market overseas. ABI is the only Ghanaian band to have performed for 30 years. In 1994, however, the group almost disbanded, and up to 2003 it only issued compilations of earlier work.

Ampadu underwent a personal transformation in the 1990s, becoming a Christian evangelist. He left his third wife and married a Christian. Ampadu released his first gospel album in 2000, and is working on a debut film. He is a staunch supporter of President Jerry John RAWLINGS, whom he calls his "spiritual friend." He has also been involved in civic affairs as head of the Musicians' Union of Ghana. He has been a district assembly member for Kwahu South for seven years.

References: BPAR,   DMM,   WAM. www.nanakwameampadu.com; Kwadwo Adum-Attah, *Nana Ampadu: Master of Highlife* (1997).

ANDERSON, Benjamin Joseph Knight
(Liberia, 1834–1880)

Benjamin Joseph Knight Anderson was the first notable African explorer in the modern era. Born and educated in Liberia (although a few sources say he was African-American), he became a government official, rising to the post of secretary of the treasury, a position that he held from 1864 to 1866. He had always hoped to explore the interior of Liberia, which was almost unknown to the Americo-Liberians who controlled the colony. In addition, Liberia's ill-defined borders were an invitation to European powers, and more than once, the French had seized territories by right of first exploration. Along with his friend, the Liberian intellectual Edward BLYDEN, Anderson sailed for the United States, where they convinced two benefactors to finance an expedition into the interior. From 1868 to 1869 Anderson led an expedition beyond the forest lands into the interior plateau in French Guinea into the lands of the Western Mandingo. Here he found an advanced and prosperous community involved with trade as far as Timbuktu. There was evidence of gold, and the people had herds of horses. Along with their Muslim faith, this was a sure sign of regular contact with the north.

The Mandingo seemed eager to enter into trade relations with the Liberian coast. Anderson negotiated agreements with Musardo, the main town (and perhaps also the name of the chief) on behalf of the Liberian government, but Liberian officials hesitated to assert control over any parts of the interior. Anderson wrote an account of his explorations, *Narrative of a Journey to Musardu* (1870), which is a valuable description of the West African interior in the nineteenth century.

In 1874, Anderson made a second trip to the interior, again negotiating treaties, and a few years later he conducted a survey of the St. Paul River. He argued for the establishment of a Liberian presence in the interior by trade posts and forts, but there was little official response.

Reference: DAHB.

ANEKE, Nwagu
(Nigeria, 1916?–1990)

Ogbuefi Nwagu Aneke was born into a family of traditional healers and was early on acknowledged to be a diviner and prophet. He was accorded the title of *ogbuefi*, "killer of cows," the most prestigious title in his clan. He soon distinguished himself from other healers, however, by a special revelation. In a dramatic encounter with ancestral spirits in the forests of his native area, he was shown a script for his mother tongue, a dialect of Igbo. The marks appeared on tree bark and leaves, and the system was later named the Nwagu Aneke script. Aneke himself was illiterate in any other system or alphabet.

The 256 characters of the script cover all Igbo syllables. These are put together to form words, and the words to form sentences. But after the alleged discovery, Aneke suffered rejection and ridicule. Previously wealthy and prominent, he lost his friends and all of his property, and was widely seen as insane. Recognition only came after the Biafran civil war (1967–1970), when Aneke used his writing to document meetings and conferences held during the war. He was then named a writer-in-residence at the University of Nigeria-Nsukka, where he composed materials for learning his system. Some scholars suggest that the system was known, if not in wide use, before Aneke presented it.

Reference: adb. Aneke. *The Scriptures of an African Visionary* (1992).

ANKRAH, Joseph Arthur
(Ghana, 1915–1992)

General Joseph Arthur Ankrah was the military head of state from 1966 to 1969 after the coup that toppled Kwame NKRUMAH.

Ankrah entered military service after a brief teaching career. He served in World War II and in 1947 received an officer's commission, only the second given by the British to an African. In 1960 and 1961 he was brigadier of the Ghanaian contingent in the Congo (later Zaïre, now the Democratic Republic of the Congo) as part of the United Nations peacekeeping force. He was awarded the Ghana Military Cross for saving the life of the Congolese premier, Patrice LUMUMBA, and on his return was made deputy chief of staff of the Ghanaian army. In 1966, Nkrumah, fearing a coup, forced Ankrah into retirement; Ankrah thus had no part in the coup that took place later that year. After the coup, because he was well respected in military circles, Ankrah was reinstated by the National Liberation Council (NLC) as army commander and made chairman of the NLC and head of state.

The NLC's goals included a return to civilian government and the scheduled repayment of the country's massive foreign debt. Ankrah, however, proved unequal to the task. The NLC was rife with personal friction and discord, and there were conflicts between the army and the national police. This lack of leadership was exacerbated by a collapsing economy. Ghana, once prosperous, faced hyperinflation as the price of goods became exorbitant for ordinary citizens. Ankrah was accused of petty corruption involving political finances and was forced to resign in 1969. He then went into private business. His nonpartisan position made it possible for him to continue in Ghana without difficulties from later governments, but he did not take part in politics for the rest of his life.

References: DAHB, PLBA.

ANQUANDAH, James Robert
(Ghana, 1938–)

James Robert Anquandah is an archaeologist who has discovered and studied a previously unknown African civilization called Koma in northern Ghana.

Anquandah graduated with an honors degree and diploma in archaeology from the University of Ghana and has spent his career there, beginning as a teaching assistant in 1965. He has been department chair since 1981 and was briefly dean of the Faculty of Social Sciences. In 1980 he received an advanced degree in archaeology from Oxford University. He has received awards for his field work, including a development council award for his book *Rediscovering Ghana's Past* (1982). He has been a member of the Ghana National Commission on Culture since 1989 and served as a consultant on the UNESCO General History of Africa project. He has also been active in such international scholarly groups as the World Archeological Congress and the International Commission on Sites. He is also a member of the Ghana Museums and Monuments Board.

Anquandah's research has focused on West Africa and Ghana, although not exclusively. He has worked on Iron Age archaeology in West Africa and has attempted to trace the origins of agriculture among ancient peoples. In recent years, he has focused on the archaeology of the slave trade. There are 60 slave forts and castles, stretching 300 miles along the coast, some in ruins, others well preserved. Anquandah has been exploring what he terms the "castle culture" surrounding these structures, revealing evidence of schools, metalworking and jewelry-making. The oldest of the forts is Elmina Castle (1482), the oldest European structure in Africa, and the excavation of the area surrounding it has been particularly productive.

Privately, Anquandah is active in ecumenical Christian affairs, serving as a member of the executive of the Christian Council of Ghana and as a consultant to the World Council of Churches in Geneva. His religious interests led to involvement in the study of the archaeology of the Christian Meroitic and Nubian civilizations of the Nile Valley, which were first uncovered by UNESCO at the time of the construction of the Aswan High Dam.

Reference: PAS. Anquandah, *Rediscovering Ghana's Past* (1982).

ANNAN, Kofi Atta
(Ghana, 1938–)

Kofi Annan, perhaps the best-known African in the world, is a Ghanaian diplomat and longtime international civil servant. Since 1997, he has been the seventh secretary-general (SG) of the United Nations, the first to rise through the ranks of the international civil service. He was reappointed to a second term in 2002, which ended in 2006.

Kofi Annan had a privileged education in Ghana at an elite school, graduating in 1957, as Ghana became the first British colony to achieve independence. The country, under Kwame NKRU-MAH, became a symbol of independence across Black Africa, and it was a heady time to be young, talented and African. Annan studied economics in Ghana, then in the United States, where he graduated from Macalester College in Minnesota. He went on to graduate studies in international affairs in Switzerland, and then began his international career with the World Health Organization as a budget officer in 1962. After a few years, he took leave to complete a graduate management degree at the Massachusetts Institute of Technology (1972). Ghana then called him home, where he served as director of Tourism for two years (1974–1976). Returning to the U.N., Annan served tours of duty with the U.N. Economic Commission for Africa in Ethiopia, the U.N. Emergency Force in Ismailia and the U.N. High Commission for Refugees in Geneva.

Annan became assistant secretary-general (ASG) for Human Resources Management and Security in 1987, and worked his way up through increasing responsibilities until he had covered most of the major areas of policy and management. He was progressively ASG for Programme Planning, Budget and Comptroller (1990–1992); ASG for Peace-keeping Operations (1993–1994); and undersecretary (1994–1996). During his tenure as undersecretary, Annan was sent to the former Yugoslavia as Special Representative of the Secretary-General, where he oversaw the implementation of the 1995 Dayton Accords. Similarly, in 1990, he had been sent to Iraq during the First Gulf War to repatriate diplomatic families and begin the delicate negotiations that set up the Oil-for-Food Programme.

During his years as ASG, Annan's style tended to be reactive rather than aggressive. He is naturally a listener, a consensus-builder always looking for a workable compromise. This may have contributed to his cautious approach when he was criticized for inaction during the Rwandan genocide, which took place during his tenure as ASG for Peacekeeping Operations. Canadian General Roméo Dallaire, the U.N. commander in Rwanda, accused Annan of holding back U.N. troops and insisting on rules of engagement that forbade them to intervene in the slaughter. The Rwandan government of Paul KA-GAME boycotted his official visit to Rwanda in 1998, and he was heckled throughout his tour of the country.

On taking charge of the United Nations Secretariat, Annan pledged a renewal and overhaul of its operations. This was largely in response to American criticism, which had caused the United States government to withhold $1.3 billion in back dues. Annan immediately went to Washington right after his inauguration and met with some of the harshest critics, disarming them with his candor and determination to reform the U.N.

In the latter part of his first term, Annan began setting stronger goals for the U.N. He announced a "Call to Action" on HIV/AIDS and fostered the establishment of the Global AIDS Fund. When the United States invaded Iraq in 2001, he called upon President George Bush to work through the U.N. and seek its support and endorsement before beginning hostilities. When this was ignored, he denounced the invasion and declared it illegal.

During his second term, Annan's position was weakened by a series of personnel problems that left the impression that he had covered up corruption in the United Nations. One involved a sexual harassment case against Ruud Lubbers, former prime minister of The Netherlands and U.N. high commissioner for Refugees. Annan ignored the investigation into the charges, which found Lubbers guilty, and exonerated him. Only after the British press leaked the report was Lubbers forced from office in 2005. At the same time, it came out that Annan's son had received payments from a Swiss company that had a lucrative contract under the U.N. Oil-for-Food Programme, which provided basic medical and food supplies to Iraq from its oil revenues, while it was under U.N. trade sanctions. Annan defended his son. An investigative team exonerated both Annans, but criticized U.N. fiscal structures, recommending that some oversight functions be taken out of the secretary-general's office. The report was widely seen as a slap at Annan.

The role of the United Nations under Annan's leadership was recognized with a Nobel Peace Prize in 2001. He has personally received a number of honorary doctorates and, while still criticized in the United States Congress, he is popular and respected elsewhere, especially in the Third World. Annan himself has accepted that part of his job is to serve as a lightning rod for attacks on the U.N. itself.

References: AB, *adb*, *afr*, CB, EB, *wiki*.

ANYAOKU, Eleazar Chukwuemeka (Emeka)
(Nigeria, 1933–)

Chief Eleazar Chukwuemeka Anyaoku, a consummate diplomat, spent most of his career with the Commonwealth Secretariat and held its highest position, that of secretary-general. The Commonwealth, a loosely patterned association of former British colonial possessions, has no legal power but can have considerable moral authority in the hands of influential administrators.

Chief Anyaoku was educated at the University of Ibadan in Classics and at public management institutes in Britain and France. He also spent three years with the Commonwealth Development Corporation before joining Nigeria's foreign service in 1962. His tenure with the Commonwealth Development Corporation was short but useful for his later work, when he was posted to the Nigerian mission to the United Nations.

In 1966, Anyaoku joined the newly founded Commonwealth Secretariat as assistant director of its international affairs division, becoming director in 1971 and assistant secretary-general in 1975. During this period, Nigeria suffered through the Biafran war, and Anyaoku resisted all pressures to involve the Commonwealth Secretariat in the conflict. His official restraint made him a model for other Third World international civil servants. He published *The Racial Factor in International Politics* in 1977, the same year he was elected deputy secretary-general. Anyaoku's professionalism made it possible for the secretary-general to use him on a series of delicate missions. He represented the Commonwealth during the Bangladesh secession, in the imposition of sanctions against Rhodesia (now Zimbabwe) in 1975, and at the lengthy and complex negotiations that brought about the independence of Zimbabwe.

In 1983, already in charge of both administrative and international affairs at the Commonwealth Secretariat, Anyaoku resigned to enter Nigerian politics. Dedicated to civilian government in Africa, he accepted an appointment as foreign minister under Shehu SHAGARI, who had just been elected after civilian government was restored following the military rule of General Olusegun OBASANJO. Within a month the military intervened again and Anyaoku returned to the Commonwealth Secretariat, where the member nations unanimously reelected him to his former post. He came to worldwide public notice when he led the Secretariat team accompanying the Commonwealth Eminent Persons Group to South Africa investigating apartheid in 1986.

Chief Anyaoku used his office to mediate further international conflicts: the Commonwealth Games boycotts of the 1980s and especially the transitions to independence in Zimbabwe, Namibia and South Africa. Sensitive to the financial pressures on smaller Commonwealth countries, he fostered the creation of a central office in New York, from which they could be represented at the United Nations.

Throughout his time as deputy, the secretary-general was Sridath "Sonny" Ramphal, who became both his friend and mentor. Anyaoku was elected to replace Ramphal when he retired in 1990, despite the candidacy of Australia's prime minister. Anyaoku dedicated himself to continuing the campaign against apartheid in South Africa and was committed to South Africa's eventual readmission to the Commonwealth as a democratic state. This was finally achieved in 1994 after the election of Nelson MANDELA as South Africa's president. From 1995–2000, Anyaoku served a second term as secretary-general. After leaving the Commonwealth Secretariat, he became the president of the World Wide Fund for Nature. He has also gone into business in Nigeria, where he is board chair of Orien Petroleum Resources, Ltd. a refinery company.

Reference: RWWA. Anyaoku, *Inside Story of the Modern Commonwealth* (2004); Phyllis Johnson, *Eye of Fire* (2000) [biography].

ANYIWO, Clement
(Nigeria, 1944–)

Dr. Clement Anyiwo, a microbiologist, is a leading expert on AIDS (acquired immunodeficiency syndrome) in tropical countries. After receiving his medical degree in the Soviet Union at the Odessa Medical School, he worked at the Lagos State Hospital in Nigeria for several years and then completed a research degree at the University of London.

Since 1975, Anyiwo has been affiliated with the University of Lagos College of Medicine and in 1981 joined the medical microbiology faculty at Usmanu Danfodio University in Sokoto, Nigeria. In the 1990s, he was periodically dean of the College of Medicine at Nnamdi Azikiwe University, where he founded the Medical Research Society. He was president of the Federation of African Immunological Societies from 1994–1997. That year, he moved to the University of Malawi. Currently, he is senior virologist at the medical faculty of the University of Papua-New Guinea.

Anyiwo's research has centered on AIDS testing. In developing nations, including all African countries, the facilities and resources needed for widespread testing for diseases are often poor or unavailable. AIDS—although its prevalence in Africa has received a great deal of publicity in the Western media—is not a major cause of death in most African countries, and resources must often be channeled to fighting malaria and other more prevalent illnesses. AIDS tests often require expensive equipment and chemicals which are not easily available, especially in rural areas. Anyiwo has addressed this problem by evaluating the existing tests that detect antibodies for HIV (human immunodeficiency virus, the virus that causes AIDS) in terms of Third World countries' needs.

Anyiwo's recommendations have influenced healthcare policy in a number of countries. He serves on several national and international commissions. He has been Commonwealth consultant on AIDS for the West African Health Community and is a member of the National Committee for the Control of STDs, an organization that seeks to limit the spread of sexually transmitted diseases (STDs). His book *AIDS and HIV Testing in Tropical Developing Countries* is used internationally.

Reference: PAS.

APITHY, Sourou Migan
(Benin, 1913–1989)

Sourou Migan Apithy, independence leader and second president of Dahomey (now Benin), participated in a period of confusion and political breakdown that followed independence and lasted for 12 years.

After an education in mission schools that provided him with a lifelong sympathy for Catholicism, Apithy studied in Bordeaux and Paris, where he received a degree in political science and an accounting certificate. He remained in France from 1933 to 1945 both studying and working as an accountant. On his return home, he was thrust into national prominence by his association with a popular French Catholic priest, Francis Aupiais, who was an advocate of African rights. The two were elected to the French Constituent Assembly. Apithy was later elected deputy to the French national assembly (1946–1958), granted membership in the West African Grand Council (1947–1957), elected as mayor of Porto Novo, and appointed to the French United Nations delegation in 1953. Also in 1946 he became vice president of the Dahomean branch of the Rassemblement Démocratique Africain (RDA), the regional party headed by Côte d'Ivoire's Félix Houphouët-Boigny. In 1948 he left the RDA over its Communist affiliations and joined a Catholic party, of which he became president. His party allegiances were elastic, however, and during the 1950s he moved among seven party groupings.

In the 1957 legislative elections he emerged as prime minister in a three-way contest among Apithy, Hubert MAGA, and Justin AHOMADÉGBÉ-TOMETIN. Apithy's party won amid massive electoral corruption; the resulting furor forced him to concede seats and leadership to Maga. Maga and Ahomadégbé-Tometin forced Apithy out of the coalition later that year. After independence, Maga became president and Apithy vice president, but the situation was so uncomfortable that Apithy spent part of his term as ambassador in Europe. The government was removed by General Christophe SOGLO in 1963 and, after reorganization, Apithy emerged as president in a coalition government. Little was accomplished, and strikes and civil strife continued. In 1965, Apithy was overthrown and fled the country.

In 1970, Apithy returned to compete in elections, again opposing Maga and Ahomadégbé-Tometin. He came in a poor third, but civil war threatened and the army imposed a Presidential Council with a chairmanship rotating among the three. They came to be known as the "three-headed monster," and earned little respect. Maga served for two years and Ahomadégbé-Tometin for four months before General Mathieu KEREKOU abolished the council in 1972. Apithy was placed under house arrest until 1981. He was in poor health, and lived quietly in exile in Paris until his death.

References: DAHB, EWB, MMA, PLBA, *wiki.*

APPIAH, Kwame Anthony
(Ghana, 1954–)

Dr. Anthony Kwame Appiah is one of the leading African intellectuals and scholars, with a worldwide following. His academic roots are in philosophy and African studies, but his passion has been the deconstruction of racism.

Born in London of a British mother and a Ghanaian father, Appiah came from a line of distinguished lawyers on both sides. His father was descended from a line of Akan kings, and his mother was the daughter of Sir Stafford Cripps, a leading British political figure. He was raised in Ghana and split his early education between schools there and in England. Finally, he graduated from Cambridge University and took a Ph.D. there. His first position was at the University of Ghana–Legon, where he pursued his interests in the philosophy of language, publishing *For Truth in Semantics* in 1986. At this point, Appiah began to turn toward Black-themed studies. He edited the works of several prominent African-American thinkers and wrote a seminal book, *In My Father's House: Africa in the Philosophy of Culture* (1992). In it he explores the question of African identity, the cornerstone of such movements as *Négritude*, Pan-Africanism and Black Power. He asserts that race is a false European construct. Africa, he insists, is the intellectual invention of Europeans founded on no cultural commonality at all, an extension of the colonial mentality and a means of oppression. By defining Africa and Africans in universal terms, the realities of Africa were ignored. In later chapters of the book, Appiah applies his thought to African politics, religion and literature.

Dr. Appiah has followed his original work with an amazing amount of writing that has looked into every crevice of race theory. He often works with his colleague and close friend, Henry Louis Gates, Jr., whom he first met at Cambridge, and who has forged an intellectual partnership with Appiah. Coming to the United States, Appiah taught at Yale, Duke and Cornell before settling into a position at Harvard in 1991. In 2002, Appiah abruptly announced his departure from Harvard for a position at Princeton. While it was rumored that this resulted from disagreements with the new president of Harvard and his perceived criticism of the quality of scholarship in the Afro-American Studies Department, Appiah insisted that the reasons were personal.

With Gates, Appiah edited a collection of 20 essays on race, class, gender, postcolonialism and globalism, *Identities* (1995). By this point, Appiah and Gates were established as the leading intellectual force dealing with race theory. The following year, in *Color Consciousness: The Political Morality of Race* (with Amy Gutman), Appiah wrote an extended essay challenging the notion of biological differences among races. He debunked the theory that any particular race has heritable characteristics that distinguish their ethical or intellectual abilities. Appiah and Gates followed their scholarly work with two major reference books, intended to demonstrate their theories to a wide public. The first of these, *The Dictionary of Global Culture* (1996), has a massive collection of essays that focus on personalities and movements from the Third World. The denigration of major western figures was so obvious that it was widely criticized for its imbalance. Had they written an encyclopedia of the Third World, without the unpleasant comparisons to western figures, the book would have been more accepted.

With a focus on Africa and its diaspora, Appiah and Gates achieved this in 1999 with *Africana: The Encyclopedia of African and African-American Experience.* A massive work of thousands of entries, it covers movements, personalities and historical events from across Africa (almost half the entries), the United States and the Caribbean. Bowing to the popular use of modern media, it was issued on CD-ROM as *Encarta Africana.* More recently, Appiah has brought his thinking on identity and race together in *The Ethics of Identity* (2005). He has also published four novels, none of which has received either critical or commercial success.

References: adb, BW, CA, CB, EB, *wiki.* www.appiah.net/pages/1.

D'ARBOUSSIER, Gabriel
(Sénégal, 1908–1976)

Gabriel d'Arboussier, a nationalist leader and anti-colonialist, was first known for his radicalism but later became a mainstream minister, politician and diplomat in Sénégal. D'Arboussier was active in West Africa during the period of transition from French colonial authority to independence within the French community.

Born in Mali and son of a French colonial official and his African wife, d'Arboussier was educated as a lawyer and colonial administrator in France. He returned home a Communist and strong anticolonialist and was elected to the French parliament in 1945 from Equatorial Africa. The following year he was instrumental in organizing the Rassemblement Démocratique Africain (RDA), an interterritorial party that chose Félix HOUPHOUËT-BOIGNY as president. At that point, the RDA was a proponent of a West African federation that would be broad-based and inclusive, incorporating all classes and religious, linguistic and ethnic groups.

In 1947, when the Ivory Coast elected d'Arboussier councillor of the French Union, he became active in that country's politics. In the West African rail strike, one of the major events in the move toward independence, only d'Arboussier and Houphouët-Boigny openly supported the strikers, while other African political leaders dithered. When Houphouët-Boigny became secretary-general of the RDA, he decided to cut its ties with the Communists. In the resulting confrontation, d'Arboussier was expelled from the RDA in 1952. With this, the RDA turned away from federalism toward the nationalist pattern favored by Houphouët-Boigny.

D'Arboussier established himself in Sénégal, and five years later he and Houphouët-Boigny were reconciled. Niger then elected d'Arboussier president of the Grand Council of French West Africa. He was an ardent supporter of a federation of the former French colonies, arguing in 1958 that the pre-colonial African states had all incorporated a range of peoples, cultures and kingdoms: "What the organizers of those states did by conquest, we in our day will do by federalism and free consent." D'Arboussier rejected the race-based theory of *Négritude*, then popular among African writers and thinkers, calling it "a dangerous mystification."

The RDA opposed federation, however, and in 1959 d'Arboussier was again forced out of the party. He returned to Sénégal after the breakup of the Mali Federation in 1960, which had included the Sudanese Republic (Mali) and Sénégal. He was Sénégal's first minister of justice until 1960, when he was named ambassador to France. He later served as ambassador to West Germany after a short stint as director of the U.N. Institute for Training.

References: DAHB, MMA.

ARCHINARD, Louis
(Guinea/Mali/Côte d'Ivoire, 1850–1932)

General Louis Archinard was the French military commander responsible for the conquest of French West Africa, and to a great extent he was the creator of this part of the French colonial empire. After completing military school at age 20, the young second lieutenant of artillery was sent to the defense of Paris in the Franco-Prussian War. After France's defeat, Archinard was sent to Indo-China, where he stayed from 1876 to 1878. After this, he was inspector of studies at the École Polytechnique. In 1880, he arrived in what was then known as the Western Sudan to supervise construction of a string of forts to maintain French claims in the interior.

Archinard was appointed to succeed General Joseph GALLIENI as commandant for the Western Sudan in 1888. He initiated a campaign against the Tukulor Empire under AMADOU Ibn Umar Tall and won. Then he occupied much of modern Mali and installed a puppet king. Until that time, French policy had been one of peaceful expansion designed largely to protect trade interests, but Archinard's military offensive—conducted without the French government's approval—committed France to conquest and colonization. Archinard was a career military officer who realized that his personal ambition could best be served by feeding French national pride in the wake of its 1870 defeat in the Franco-Prussian War; therefore, he hoped to create a hero's role for himself by becoming the architect of French imperialism in West Africa. In the political tussle between the officer class and civilian politicians over control of the military, Archinard's adventures played well with the militarists. Well connected politically in Paris, Archinard used his contacts to further his career shamelessly. He ignored the policies of the Colonial Office and ran up large budget overruns. When the Colonial Office attempted to restrain him, Archinard hinted at British imperial designs and brought prominent parliamentarians to his cause. On more than one occasion, he provoked the British with border disputes. By 1890, he had alienated Gallieni by his insubordination.

In 1891, Archinard embarked on a dangerous adventure that was not only unauthorized but also against orders. He moved against SAMORI Touré, who had united the peoples of eastern Mali and Guinea. Archinard struggled against Samori for seven years, harrying Samori's troops through the rainy seasons until many deserted. Finally, he captured Samori in a brilliant surprise attack in 1898. By this time, a hero at home, he had advanced to general.

Archinard was a better military commander than a governor. His attempts to apply "indirect rule" through local chiefs failed, largely due to his constant interference and repression by which he undermined their authority. His policies and military gambles turned the interior chiefs toward the British and Sierra Leone, thus preventing the expansion of trade with France. Economic development stagnated and the slave trade continued. By 1895 the French government had united the various conquered territories under a governor-general, and Archinard was dismissed from his command and posted to the Ministry of Colonies in Paris.

Reference: DAHB, fr.wikipedia.org. A.S. Kanya-Forstner, *The Conquest of the Western Sudan* (1969).

AREOGUN of Osi-Ilorin

(Nigeria, 1880?–1954)

Areogun, a wood carver of the Yoruba people, is among the most recognized traditional African sculptors. His pieces are highly prized and sought after by major museums and collectors. He worked for kings and took public government commissions. Following in his footsteps, his son George BANDELE also became prominent in the transition of Yoruba sculpture to applications to Christian religious settings.

African art was always cultic, used for ceremonies and religious celebrations. The western notion of "art for art's sake" is foreign to traditional African culture, and works are admired not primarily for their elegance or technical brilliance, but for their suitability for use. The African carving tradition began (and largely remained) in religion. Even carving done for kings and to adorn palaces is not purely secular or civic.

It is often thought that African traditional artists—sculptors, weavers, mask-makers—were anonymous. While that is true of many, the best among them were always known by name. Even before there were written records, the carving schools preserved the names of their famous sculptors, the best of whom would have gone on to work for kings.

Like most carvers, Areogun was born to the craft. He came from Osi, along the border between (then) Ekiti and Ilorin Provinces, and continued to work there all his life. He was apprenticed to a prominent local carver, Bamgboshe. Traditional woodcarving degenerated among the Yoruba as tourist art promised better profits with less work. Only among the Ekiti Yorubu in northeastern Nigeria did the old ways and the original quality continue.

Areogun's style used smooth forms and shallow relief. It is compact, and his human figures are rounded and have been described as somewhat bulbous. A statue of the *Three Kings*, done for Father Kevin CARROLL in 1953, shows a Virgin Mary with protruding eyes, holding a young Jesus before her, astride a horse as a sign of his kingship. To one side is a small worshipping woman with pendulous breasts. One of the Magi is presented in the style of a Yoruba ritual mask.

His bowls, house posts and staffs are among the finest examples of Ekiti work. He was prolific, and carved a large number of pieces, which were found throughout the region. His house posts are decorative rather than load-bearing parts of a structure. Commonly, he carved the image of the owner prominently. The most striking of these posts, now in the museum of the University of Ibadan, shows the *oba* or ruler astride a horse, with several attendants. The size of the figures is determined by their rank and importance, so that the *oba* appears dominant and his courtiers far smaller.

"Areogun" was his praise name, but he was known by no other. Literally, it means "he who makes money in the service of Ogun," the god of ironwork of whom Areogun was a devotee. He was recognized by the composition of a praise poem in his honor: "He carves hard wood as though he were carving a calabash; one who knows how to carve for kings; son of those who worship Oyegbe and do not worship falsely, ... he has nothing to hide," it sings, and then more slyly, "being fat does not suit a man." Areogun had a thin, spindly frame.

ARINZE, Francis
(Nigeria, 1932–)

Francis, Cardinal Arinze is the highest-ranking African in the Catholic Church. Since 2002 he has been prefect of Divine Worship and Discipline of the Sacraments in the Vatican. He is widely experienced in ecumenical affairs, and headed the Vatican's Council for Interreligious Dialogue for eight years before receiving his present appointment.

Arinze was born into an animist family, and became Catholic at age nine. At 15, he entered a high-school seminary, and spent three years teaching there after graduation. He then studied philosophy in Nigeria and was sent to Rome to study theology. Arinze was ordained a priest in 1958 and then completed a doctorate with a thesis on sacrifice in Ibo religion. He was in Rome as a graduate student throughout the Ibo civil war which ravaged the country.

Clearly recognized as a leader, Arinze rose quickly in Church circles. He returned to Nigeria to teach liturgy for a year at the seminary where he had studied philosophy, and was named head of Catholic education from the eastern region of Nigeria. He was then sent to London for graduate work in education, but he had hardly used his new studies for a year when he was named coadjutor bishop of Onitsha, a position that entitled him to succeed to the diocese when the incumbent bishop retired. At 32, Arinze was the youngest bishop in the Catholic Church.

Within two years, Arinze was archbishop of Onitsha, a major diocese where over half the population is Catholic. From 1979 to 1984, he was elected chairman of the Catholic Bishops' Conference, but in that year, Pope John Paul II appointed him to the post in charge of interreligious dialogue in the Vatican. Within a year of arriving in Rome, he was named a cardinal. At the consistory of 2005 that elected Benedict XVI, Arinze was widely touted as the "Third World candidate" for pope. After the election, Benedict named him to the

honorary title he had held as a cardinal before hiselection.

Theologically and liturgically conservative, Arinze has been particularly strong in his statements supporting pro-life positions. Yet he is not a negative individual. He is known for his winning, even charming, personality. Those who meet him are impressed by his candor, wit and open spirit. He is a popular speaker at universities and Church events worldwide. Due to his tireless efforts for interfaith dialogue, he was given a gold medal from the International Council of Christians and Jews in 1999.

Reference: adb, wiki. Arinze, *Religions for Peace* (2002).

ASHMUN, Jehudi
(Liberia, 1794–1828)

Jehudi Ashmun was the White American governor of Liberia whose leadership enabled the early colony to survive African resistance and become a viable settlement. Liberia was, like its neighbor Sierra Leone, an artificial nation created for former slaves—in Liberia's case, slaves from the United States. They came as strangers to the continent of their origins, and Liberia was as much a colonial enterprise as any later European settlement.

Ashmun was well educated. He graduated from the University of Vermont and headed a Congregational theological college for two years before being forced to resign due to a misunderstanding over his marriage in 1818. He transferred to the Episcopal Church and edited several Episcopalian publications until he founded the *African Intelligencer,* which promoted the project of the American Colonization Society (ACS) to send free Blacks to Africa to establish a colony.

In 1822, Ashmun, accompanied by his wife, sailed to Liberia at the head of 37 freed slaves. He planned only a brief stay, hoping to obtain a trade monopoly. He found 120 settlers—disorganized, leaderless, and demoralized—under constant threat of attack by local Africans. Ashmun took charge, persuaded the settlers to move off the island where they had taken refuge, and directed the building of fortifications for defense. Five months later, 800 African warriors attacked the settlers, and Ashmun rallied his 35 men and boys to repel them. The following week, they repeated their victory.

The settlement was weakened by malaria, and soon Ashmun and his wife became ill. Although he recovered, his wife died; her death convinced Ashmun to remain in Liberia. He fortified the colony, placing the government in the hands of the White agents of the ACS, with the aid of his assistant, Lott CAREY, a former slave from Virginia. Although he was enlightened and progressive for his time, Ashmun did not accept racial equality. His demanding and authoritarian manner caused dissention among the settlers. In 1824 a coup, led by Carey, forced Ashmun to leave the colony for a time. He returned to assume only limited powers, which he was required to share with a council. From 1824 to 1828 he governed jointly with Carey, who was made vice agent in 1826. When he finally left Liberia, the colony had 1,200 members and some measure of stability.

Ashmun won a truce with the hostile local tribes and expanded the territory under the colony's control, providing Liberia with a period of prosperity. He also suppressed the slave trade, promoted agriculture, and helped to establish a number of new farming settlements. Trade, however, was still the most profitable activity and became the monopoly of Monrovia, the capital.

In 1828 he recommended Carey as his replacement while he returned to the United States, where he hoped to regain his health. He died of malaria shortly after his arrival in Boston.

References: DAHB, EWB. Ralph Gurley, *Life of Jehudi Ashmun* (1835, reprinted 1969).

ASOKHIA, Michael Babatunde
(Nigeria, 1943–)

Dr. Michael Babatunde Asokhia has been at the center of the investigation of toxic dumping in Africa. A geophysicist by training, but equally at home in physics and engineering, Asokhia has been acting head of the physics department at Bendel State University in Ekpoma, Nigeria, since 1989. Earlier, he was head of physics at the University of Agriculture at Abeokuta, and for seven years he was professor and head of geology at the University of Lagos. He received an M.Sc. from Moscow State University in 1971 and then obtained a Mobil Oil Scholarship to study for a diploma in petroleum engineering in Nigeria. Subsequently, he acquired a diploma in computer science in Sweden, and in 1979 he earned a Ph.D. in geophysics at the University of Lagos.

In 1988 it was discovered that an Italian firm had dumped a large amount of toxic waste from Europe in Koto Town, Nigeria. After the Italians bribed local officials, the poisonous chemicals were off-loaded in leaking barrels and abandoned. Extensive investigations, in which Asokhia participated, revealed the danger involved to people in the area as well as to the water table and also uncovered an international conspiracy to dump toxic wastes in vulnerable parts of the Third World.

Asokhia has discovered a number of oil deposits and has applied the knowledge gained through his investigations to analyzing the effect of toxic waste on groundwater and underwater life.

Reference: PAS.

ATTAHIRU Amadu
(Nigeria, ?–1903?)

Sultan Attahiru Amadu was ruler of the Sokoto Caliphate, the most powerful Islamic state in West Africa, at the time of the British conquest. His reign lasted little more than a year. He is best known for leading the resistance against the British.

Little is known of Attahiru's early life, but doubtless it included Islamic education and life at the service of his uncle, Sultan Abdurrahman, an implacable Muslim and a bigoted tyrant. Along with the other rulers of what became northern Nigeria, Abdurrahman totally rejected the expansion of British power by Frederick LUGARD and called for "war as Allah the almighty has enjoined on us." Lugard began his advance on the north just as Abdurrahman died and Attahiru succeeded him. Attahiru was a devout Muslim but, unlike his uncle, he was a decent and open-minded man, not opposed to compromise. Unfortunately, Lugard had no understanding of this essential difference. He proceeded as if there were no possibility of negotiation.

The emir of Kano, a neighboring Islamic state, rushed to Sokoto with half his army, attempting to form a common front against the British. In his absence, Lugard seized Kano. The emir believed that rather than accept defeat, the northern rulers should flee to Arabia—an absurd and fanciful *hejira* in imitation of the Prophet Muhammad's retreat from

Mecca to Medina. As a result, he departed for Arabia in disguise, only to be quickly captured and sold to the British. His army collapsed in confusion. Attahiru was left in a delicate position. He called in his advisors, mostly religious scholars, who promoted a policy of armed confrontation. In the battle that followed, the Sokoto army was decimated before its own walls by British machine guns and artillery, and Attahiru had to be led from the field.

Attahiru absolved his council of its allegiance, and most submitted to the British. Attahiru felt that although as sultan of Sokoto he had been defeated, in his other role as commander of the faithful he still had obligations regarding the safety of his people. Escaping Sokoto, Attahiru moved east with several thousand followers, harassed constantly by the British but picking up other dissidents along the way. Beating off British forces six times, he led his people to a valley where legend said that the Fulani peoples would one day assemble before going to Mecca. Increasingly, Attahiru came under the influence of religious fanatics who had chosen martyrdom over exodus. When the final battle began at Burmi, Attahiru went to the mosque to pray, then walked toward his attackers unarmed; he was shot through the forehead. Large numbers of Fulani continued the exodus, however, and settled in the valley of the Blue Nile in the Sudan.

Reference: DAHB.

AWOLOWO, Obafemi
(Nigeria, 1909–1987)

Chief Obafemi Awolowo was a nationalist and independence leader, one of the great political personalities in Nigeria until his death. For over 40 years he contributed his many talents as a leader, writer and businessman, rising from poverty to prominence as the preeminent representative of the Yoruba people in national politics.

Chief Awolowo was born into a Christian family that was rendered destitute by his father's early death. Initially, he was employed in various positions—teaching, journalism and several clerical jobs—while studying for a business degree by correspondence. In 1944 he traveled to London, where he earned a law degree. In 1946 he returned to Lagos and established a prosperous practice. Even before leaving for England, however, the ambitious young man had entered politics as organizer of a

produce trade association and secretary of a motor transport union. In 1940 he became general secretary of the Nigerian Youth Movement, an early nationalist group, and in London he founded a Yoruba cultural society, which later became the foundation for an ethnic political party, the Action Group (1950). With political activity as his base, Awolowo won election to the Western Region assembly and was a chief minister of that region from 1951 to 1954, the year he became prime minister of the Western Region. He worked hard at building alliances with other ethnic parties, hoping to create a national coalition, but this effort broke down in the 1959 national elections, and Awolowo became leader of the opposition in the federal parliament while losing his regional premiership. A power struggle in the Action Group followed the lost election, and Awolowo won a victory which was so bitter that the federal government suspended the regional constitution.

When Nigeria gained independence in 1960, Awolowo turned to the left, expressing his position in *Forward with Democratic Socialism* (1963) and *Thoughts on the Nigerian Constitution* (1966), both of which he wrote in prison. Accused of plotting a coup, he was jailed between 1963 and 1966 and was released by General Yakubu GOWON's military government, which he joined as minister of finance. After some deliberation, he threw his support behind the national government during the Biafran war. In 1968 he published *The People's Republic,* which outlined his ideas about democratic socialism and federalism, which he felt should be based on ethnicity. This would have provided for separate states, each belonging to a dominant ethnic or religious group. His force of character and personal prestige—he held numerous chieftaincies—sustained him even when political power failed him. Throughout his career, his major issue was free public education at all levels, which his party introduced in the five Yoruba states where it held a majority. Chief Awolowo also opened the first television station in Africa and built West Africa's first sports stadium.

When his political activities were banned, Awolowo practiced law. He returned to politics in 1978 as founder and head of the Unity Party. In 1979 and 1983 he ran for president, losing both times to Shehu SHAGARI and claiming that the elections were fraudulent. An uncompromising man who demanded total loyalty, he was never able to reassure the Muslim north that a practicing Christian could be trusted; as a result, the national presidency eluded him. An old adversary, the Biafran leader Emeka OJUKWU, called him the greatest president Nigeria never had. His death marked the end of an era in Nigerian politics, one in which three powerful regional rivals—Awolowo, Sir Ahmadu BELLO, and Chief Nnamdi AZIKIWE—failed in nation-building. Despite this shortcoming, Awolowo was widely respected, and shortly after his death a Nigerian university was named after him.

References: AA, *afr*, CANR, CB, DRWW, EB, EWB, MMA, PLBA, PLCA, *wiki*. Awolowo, *Awo* (1960).

AWOONOR, Kofi Nyidevu George
(Ghana, 1935–)

Dr. Kofi Awoonor, a leading West African writer in English, uses a wide range of literary forms. He is known primarily as a poet but has also written plays, novels, short stories, essays, biographical pieces, and scholarly studies. Much of this work was accomplished while he was an academic.

After graduating from the University College in Ghana, Awoonor held a research fellowship there in African literature from 1960 to 1964. For the next three years he served as director of films for the Ghana Ministry of Information. During this time he founded the Ghana Playhouse, for which he produced stage and television dramas. He spent a year at the University of London as a Longmans Fellow, receiving an M.A. (1970) for work on African English. Awoonor went to the United States in 1968 for a seven-year stay at the State University of New York, Stony Brook. He was professor and chair of the comparative literature department and also completed his Ph.D. there in 1972. Awoonor developed one of the first American Black studies programs at Stony Brook. In 2001, he became Ford Foundation Writer-in-Residence at Columbia University in New York.

Awoonor's time in the United States was a period of his greatest creativity and one of deepening political consciousness. He was repelled by the violence of Harlem, where he lived with his wife and children, but he also felt at home there. In one poetry reading, he sang Ewe songs from his homeland, accompanied by American Beat poet Allen Ginsberg chanting Native American poems.

Upon returning to Ghana in 1975, Awoonor was arrested by the military government for harboring an opponent of the regime and spent a year in prison. His book *The Ghana Revolution* (1984) is a personal account of that experience. Upon his pardon, he became professor of English, and later dean of arts, at the University of the Cape Coast from 1976 to 1983. In 1985 he served on the National Commission for Democracy.

From 1983 to 1989, Awoonor served as ambassador to Brazil, with accreditation to five other Latin American countries. He traveled widely in South America and in 1989 became ambassador to Cuba. The following year Awoonor was named Ghana's ambassador to the United Nations. He was also Ghana's representative to the "Group of 77," an association of developing countries, and served as its chair. In his diplomatic role, Awoonor proved to be a powerful advocate for Third World concerns. He has been an articulate defender of the sovereignty of poorer countries regarding desertification and the sustainable development of forestry resources. Observing his combination of literary and political careers in the service of human freedom, the *Seattle Times* (1992) called him a "writer and leader of diverse talents who invites comparisons to Czechoslovakia's Vaclav Havel." Awoonor describes his politics as anticolonial, nationalist, and critical of the bipolar politics of the Cold War. Yet, despite his devotion to human rights, Awoonor has been willing to work under Flight Lieutenant Jerry RAWLINGS's authoritarian populist regime.

Awoonor's writing is informed by the richness of his African heritage. These African sources are reflected well in *Until the Morning After: Selected Poems 1963–1985* (1987), which brings together his best poetry and which was awarded the African Regional Commonwealth Poetry Prize in 1989. In the novel *Comes the Voyager at Last* (1992), he recounts the tale of a slave's journey to the United States and his later return to Africa. Thus, two themes alternate and merge in Awoonor's writing: the African cultural tradition (especially from his own Ewe society) and the struggle for personal and political freedom.

Much of Awoonor's poetry can be read autobiographically. Some work explores his feelings of loss at being separated from Ghana, his home, and others explore the experience of being in America. Awoonor's first book of poetry was *Rediscovery*

(1964), which was followed by *Messages* (1970), *Night of My Blood* (1971), and *House by the Sea* (1978), a poetic account of his 1975 imprisonment. His first novel, *This Earth, My Brother* (1971), was followed in 1974 by *Alien Corn* and *Breast of the Earth*, a history of African literature. In 1980 his study of Ewe traditional tales, *Fire in the Valley,* was published. *Ghana: A Political History* (1990) shows his fiercely anticolonial stance. He has been awarded two leading British literary prizes, the Gurrey Prize for Poetry (for his translation of Ewe funeral songs) and the National Book Council Award for Poetry (1979).

As a student, Awoonor rejected his childhood Christianity and dropped his baptismal name, William. As a supporter of ancestral traditions, he discovered his spiritual roots in the Santeria god Ogun, but since returning to Africa, his religion has centered around the veneration of ancestral spirits. He refers to Wheta, his birthplace, as his "spiritual hometown,... ancestral as its shrines and holy groves." Awoonor acknowledges the influence of the spoken traditional poetry of his people and sees his poetry as an umbilical cord from that oral tradition to the new, Pan-African culture that is emerging. His homage to the Ewe oral literary tradition was given form in his poetic work *Guardians of the Sacred Word* (1974).

References: AA, *adb*, *afr*, AWT, BW, CA, CAAS, CANR, DLB, MBW, NRG, *wiki*, WLTC. Romanus Egudu, *Four Modern West African Poets* (1977).

AYENSU, Edward
(Ghana, 1935–)

Dr. Edward Ayensu is a noted international plant physiologist who, in recent years, has assumed significance as a policymaker on international environmental issues.

Ayensu was educated at Achimota College and then took bachelor's and master's degrees in the United States. After his doctoral studies at the University of London, he returned to the United States, where he served as associate curator of botany at the Smithsonian Institution from 1966 to 1969. He was promoted to chair and curator in 1970, a position that he held until 1989. He also served concurrently as director of the Smithsonian's Endangered Species Project from 1976 to 1980. Ayensu is

now based in Ghana, where he directed his own consulting firm on biodiversity issues. For two years, he was chair of the Inspection Panel of the World Bank. In this role, he handled the delicate visit of World Bank officials to China, which was accused of forcing 58,000 Tibetan and Mongolian peasants into arid plains so their land could be distributed to ethnic Han Chinese. He is a chief advisor to the World Bank on biodiversity, directing planning for its US$1.3 billion Global Environment Facility.

In 2005, Ayensu became chair of Haber Mining, Ltd., where he directs their Mercury Abatement Programme. He is involved in the development of an environmentally friendly method of gold extraction which will eliminate the use of mercury.

Ayensu has written widely in his specialty, publishing more than 20 books and 100 professional papers. Chief among these are *Tropical Forest Ecosystems in Africa and South America* (1973) and *Medicinal Plants of West Africa* (1978). He has gone on to do "medicinal plants" books on the West Indies (1981) and China (1984). He has also worked on a simple test for HIV/AIDS, and in 2002 marketed the "Three-Second AIDS Test," which was first used in South Africa. In 2004, Ayensu was awarded the World Medal for Biological Science of the Third World Academy of Science.

It is in his activities outside the Smithsonian Institution that the importance of Ayensu's work emerges. He was executive director of the Association for Tropical Biology between 1969 and 1971 and secretary-general of the International Union of Biological Sciences from 1976 to 1986. In 1988 he became senior advisor on strategic policy planning to the president of the African Development Bank, assuming the position of Central Projects director in 1989. He sits on U.S. State Department panels on science policy in developing nations, acts as a science advisor to UNESCO, represents the United States on the World Council for the Biosphere, and has served many Third World countries on scientific issues.

Ayensu balances his international environmental policy work with his own research. He is a specialist on orchids and enjoys raising and sharing them with the orchid enthusiasts he finds everywhere. He is also an expert on bats and can be found at night, infrared scope in hand, spying on his favorite animal, which he credits with valuable pollination activity and insect pest control.

Reference: PAS. Ayensu, *Ashanti Gold* (1997).

AZIKIWE, Benjamin Nnamdi

(Nigeria, 1904–1996)

Chief Benjamin Nnamdi "Zik" Azikiwe, independence leader and first president of Nigeria, Igbo nationalist, sportsman and journalist, was a powerful presence in almost every facet of Nigerian life from the late colonial era to the present. His impact extended throughout West Africa, where he became a model of anticolonial nationalism in the years before independence.

Inspired by the thinking of Marcus Garvey and the Ghanaian James AGGREY, Azikiwe went to the United States for education. Supporting himself by manual labor, he graduated from Howard University in Washington, D.C., and received M.A.s from Lincoln University in Pennsylvania in politics and the University of Pennsylvania in anthropology, as well as a certificate in journalism from Columbia University.

He returned to Africa to edit a nationalist newspaper in the Gold Coast (now Ghana) from 1934 to 1937, which led to charges of sedition for his outspoken attacks on the government. In 1937 he founded the influential newspaper the *West African Pilot* in Lagos, where "Zik's" columns (as his editorials were known) were soon followed by the African middle class. He argued constantly for independence, traveling to London during World War II to press his case. In 1944 he and Herbert MACAULAY founded the National Council of Nigeria and the Cameroons (NCNC), which brought together more than 40 cultural, political and labor groups. Azikiwe led the NCNC in opposition to the new colonial constitution, calling a general strike that paralyzed the country. He and Macaulay then went on a tour of Nigeria, raising funds for another trip to London so that they could urge Britain to begin the process of decolonization. When Macaulay died on the trip (1946), Azikiwe became president of the NCNC.

Azikiwe was identified with Igbo nationalism, and despite the NCNC's claim to national status, it reluctantly ran him for premier of Eastern Nigeria, an Igbo stronghold. The questions of ethnicity and regionalism established a rivalry that would persist until the late 1960s with Sir Ahmadu BELLO of the Northern Region and Chief Obafemi AWOLOWO of the Western Region. Azikiwe's tenure was dominated by investigations into his government's investments through a holding company, the Zik Group, which managed his extensive range of companies. Azikiwe resigned in 1959 but was returned to office in an overwhelming victory in the following election. In the 1959 national elections, the three regional opponents divided the vote, and a northerner, Abubakar Tafawa BALEWA, was chosen prime minister. With Nigerian independence in 1960, Azikiwe was named governor-general by Queen Elizabeth, and when Nigeria declared itself a republic in 1963, he became president, at that time a largely symbolic position.

Constitutional government collapsed in 1966, despite Azikiwe's desperate attempts to salvage a compromise. When ethnic violence began against the Igbo, the Eastern Region seceded as the Republic of Biafra in 1967. Azikiwe served Biafra as a diplomat, working to gain diplomatic recognition by several African nations before he went into exile in Britain, where he remained until 1972. He returned as chancellor of Lagos University from 1972 to 1976. After democratic politics were again permitted in Nigeria, he ran for president in 1979 and 1983 but was badly beaten both times by Shehu SHAGARI and carried only the Igbo heartland.

Azikiwe, who once wrote that God had created the Igbo to lead the children of Africa from the bondage of the ages, never transcended his essential ethnic nationalism. His other passion was sports; he served as president of the Amateur Football Association and the Nigerian Table Tennis Association and was vice chair of the Boxing Board of Control. Despite his increasing age, he played sports regularly until the death of his wife in 1983, when he went into seclusion. He died in Nsukka.

References: AA, AB, *adb, afr,* CB, DAHB, DRWW, EB, EWB, PLBA, PLCA, *wiki.* Azikiwe, *My Odyssey* (1970); Michael Olisa Michael and Odinchezo Ikejiani-Clark, *Azikiwe and the African Revolution* (1989).

BÂ, Mariama
(Sénégal, 1929–1981)

Mariama Bâ was a prominent feminist and author in West Africa, a progressive voice for women in a predominantly Muslim society. Her grandparents raised her after her mother's death. They opposed schooling for girls, but her father, a minister in Sénégal's first independent government, intervened to give his daughter an elite education, contrary to custom among Muslim families at that time. She finished teachers' college with the highest marks in French-speaking Africa that year.

Already as a student, Bâ began writing on politics and culture for local papers and magazines. While employed as a teacher and schools inspector, she continued to write, but did not publish her first novel until she was 51 and ill. An early essay, often anthologized, reveals her later themes. She sharply criticized the French policy of assimilation: "My mind has been whitened but my head remains Black." She began her lifelong task of exploring the fault-lines in her society: colonial domination, gender, race and culture.

Bâ's first novel, *Une si longue lettre* (*So Long a Letter*, 1979), attacked the custom of polygamy in Muslim society and its effect upon the freedom of women. It was written as a letter to a friend by a recently widowed woman; both the writer and the recipient of the letter suffer from the inequality of their marriages. She poignantly describes the hurt and rejection as her husband took younger, more attractive wives and her distress at having to share her grief with the second wife. It was the first novel to focus upon the situation of Muslim women, and it won the Noma Prize in 1980. It received instant acclaim, and was translated into 12 languages within a few years.

Bâ's second novel, *Le chant écarlate* (*Scarlet Song*, 1981), explores the conflicts in an intercultural relationship, as a marriage between a European woman and a Sénégalese man slowly collapses under the burdens of frustrated assumptions, cultural clashes and family hostility. Both novels have a subtext: how women often undermine one another's happiness and cause marital breakup.

Bâ herself suffered in a failed marriage to a prominent Sénégalese, after she had borne nine children.

References: adb, afr, BW, CA, DLB, wiki.

BABA AHMED, Nafiu
(Nigeria, 1940s–)

Nafiu Baba Ahmed is secretary-general for the Supreme Council for Sharia in Nigeria, making him one of the leading Muslim figures in that country. He has been in the forefront of moves to make *sharia*, the legal code of Islam, part of the legal system of those Nigerian states with a Muslim majority. Baba Ahmed was born in northern Nigeria and educated in Islamic schools.

Human Rights Watch has accused the Supreme Council and the *sharia* courts of ignoring basic human rights, specifically regarding torture, degrading treatment of prisoners and the right to life. They have argued that the Nigerian interpretation of the law is in violation of the *sharia* itself. Baba Ahmed has spoken out in criticism of what he regards as the imposition of western values on Muslims, and defended the right of *sharia* to be practiced in the manner the Supreme Council determines. His style is fiercely polemical and unbending. He has denounced President Olusegun OBASANJO for favoring western dress and customs. He is known as an opponent of Obasanjo, a Christian, and to favor a Muslim president.

In 2002, Baba Ahmed was arrested and charged with treason and arson in connection with religious riots in which over 200 people died. The incident that sparked the violence was the holding of the Miss World contest in Nigeria, which sparked outrage from Muslims when a Lagos newspaper said that even Mohammed would have approved the contest, and perhaps might have chosen one of the contestants as a bride. This insulting reference appalled Muslims, and a *fatwa*, a *sharia*-based legal condemnation, was handed down by the Supreme

Council. This triggered riots in the Muslim areas, including the burning of some Christian churches, and then retaliatory strikes by Christians against Muslims in nasty street fighting. Baba Ahmed pleaded innocent of conspiracy, and ascribed his arrest to political harassment by Obasanjo.

The following year, Baba Ahmed opposed a Ford Foundation sex education program because "it will bring in bad, western ways." It was then banned from the public schools in Kano State.

In 2004, Baba Ahmed led a boycott of polio vaccination in the north, despite the fact that the Muslim region of Kano is the epicenter for polio in the world. A vigorous campaign had reduced polio from 350,000 cases to 1,000 in 15 years, and the 2004 campaign was to eliminate it entirely and end its spread. Baba Ahmed and other conservative clerics condemned the vaccine as an American plot to spread AIDS and sterilize African girls. Although 80 percent successful in the Christian south, the campaign failed in the north.

BABALOLA, Joseph Ayodele
(Nigeria, 1904–1959)

Apostle Joseph Ayodele Babalola, a pioneer in the African independent church movement, was the founder of the Christ Apostolic Church, a major branch of the Aladura movement. The praying or prophetic healing (*aladura*) churches spread across the continent in the 1920s, and among the Yoruba people in Nigeria, they took strong root.

In the 1930s, Babalola, who had previously been a highway department road-grader operator, undertook an amazing preaching ministry. A 1928 vision of Jesus told him to preach the Gospel, clad in palm fronds and decorated with charcoal. This caused him to be judged mad and he was briefly imprisoned, but when smallpox broke out, Babalola returned in a few days, curing the afflicted. Expelled from the Anglican Church, he went to Lagos to join the Faith Tabernacle, a Yoruba independent church that had broken with Anglicanism. Babalola then generated the dramatic Oke-Oye Revival, where he allegedly raised a child from the dead and caused the patients at the Methodist hospital to leave their beds to be cured. Now re-baptized by immersion, Babalola began traveling across Nigeria and into

Ghana, attracting crowds and performing healing ceremonies. Unlike the Zionist churches, which appealed to the poor and marginalized of colonial society, the Aladura movement appealed to urban workers. Thousands flocked to him, and both Anglican and Methodist churches suffered staggering losses in membership.

Babalola preached a Christian healing revival, attacking indigenous religious practices, burning fetishes, idols, and witchcraft paraphernalia in grand bonfires and forbidding polygamy. The Christ Apostolic Church, which he founded in 1955, took its name from a British denomination that helped in its formation. It was neither antimissionary nor anticolonial. Indeed, it has no social or political doctrine at all but instead emphasized spirituality in the tradition of the holiness movement. For these reasons the government did not attempt to attack it, as had happened in the cases of William Wadé HARRIS in Ghana and Simon KIMBANGU in the Belgian Congo. Babalola was jailed for six months on suspicion of participation in a witch eradication campaign, but that was the extent of his conflict with colonial authorities. Babalola headed the church as general evangelist, while its president, Sir I. B. Akinyele, Oba of Ibadan (who was knighted by Queen Elizabeth II), represented its social prestige and public acceptance.

After the death of Babalola, the church continued to grow and in the 2000s had about a million members, with an annual growth of about 15,000. It has several seminaries, a number of secondary schools and a teachers' college. There are missions in West Africa, especially Ghana, and overseas among expatriate Nigerians as far away as Houston, Texas.

References: dacb, DAHB, MMA.

BABANGIDA, Ibrahim Gbadamosi
(Nigeria, 1941–)

General Ibrahim Gbadamosi Babangida, military strongman and president of Nigeria, designed a complex system for a return to civilian rule, only to be the cause of its failure.

A northern Muslim from Niger State, Babangida entered the Nigerian Military College in 1962, then was commissioned and sent to India for training in armor. He served from 1964 to 1966 and then went to England to study at the Royal Armour School. He returned in 1967 in time to lead an infantry battalion during the Biafran civil war. He was wounded in battle, decorated for valor, and posted to the Nigerian Defense Academy as a major. By 1975 he was a colonel and commander of the armored corps. In 1976, General Murtala MUHAMMED was killed in a coup attempt that was foiled by Babangida's decisive deployment of his tanks. He became a hero to the troops and gradually entered military politics. In 1983 he was promoted to major general and continued to build personal support, avoiding ethnic and religious alliances. When oil prices slumped, taking Nigeria from boom to bust, Babangida led a coup against the corrupt government of Shehu SHAGARI in 1983. He hand-picked General Muhammadu BUHARI as head of state; Babangida became army chief of staff. Buhari continued the failures of the previous regime, however, and in 1985, Babangida took over as head of state.

Babangida introduced the austerity measures demanded by the World Bank and International Monetary Fund (IMF) to restore the Nigerian economy, and they met with moderate success. Exports rose and trade improved, but the wages of workers were eroded by inflation, and public services were drastically cut. Babangida was tough in crushing religious riots in the north, after which he defeated two coup attempts with ferocity, executing the perpetrators. He attempted to placate northern sentiment by making Nigeria a member of the Islamic Conference, but this backfired when Christians and traditional religionists saw it as a hostile act.

However, Babangida was still unable to stem the rise of urban crime, which rendered Lagos, then the capital, a center of lawlessness. In foreign affairs, he concentrated on the West African region. In 1990 he took the lead in forming a six-nation task force from the members of the Economic Community of West African States (ECOWAS) to intervene in Liberia's anarchic civil war, and he backed the interim government of Dr. Amos SAWYER.

Babangida's great emphasis, however, was on creating a system of civilian rule that would provide honesty and stability. He announced the creation of a two-party system, founding both parties himself, with one center-right and the other center-left in policies. Elections were postponed until this system was put into effect, which began in 1987 with local nonpartisan elections. He then banned all those who

previously had held high office, including himself, from contesting the presidency. The elections were finally held in 1993, and they were apparently won by businessman Moshood ABIOLA, a former supporter of Babangida. The general, however, nullified the vote and appointed a civilian interim successor, resulting in strikes and civil strife across the country. This decision was disastrous and polarizing. Within three months the government was removed by a new military strongman, General Sani ABACHA, and Babangida found himself on the sidelines.

References: *afr*, CB, PLBA, RWWA, *wiki*.

BADEN-POWELL, Robert
(South Africa/Kenya, 1857–1941)

Lord Robert Baden-Powell, founder of the Boy Scouts, was also a British hero of the Boer War. In recent years, his inflated reputation has been challenged by historians, who have questioned both his character and his achievements. Although he came from respectable but modest origins, his life's work earned him a peerage.

Baden-Powell entered the Indian army as a sublieutenant of cavalry at age 19, but much of his military career involved campaigns to suppress African resistance to colonialism. In treating captives, he had a reputation for harshness. He was also given to bloody entertainments and wrote the standard book on pigsticking (the hunting of wild boars), regarded as a sport among colonial forces.

After the Bechuanaland and Sudanese campaigns of 1884 and 1885, he took part in the Zulu war of 1888, trained African troops for the Asante expedition (1895 to 1896) in the Gold Coast (now Ghana), and developed the night scouting that outflanked the Ndebele rebels in southern Africa (1896). For his military exploits, he earned the nickname *Impeesa,* "the wolf that never sleeps." Baden-Powell used this experience when he assumed his first independent command as colonel of the Fifth Dragoons in India. During this period (1897–1899) he refined his ideas of scouting for soldiers. The civilian version of scouting would adopt features developed at this time, such as the use of merit badges, small unit organization, and tracking. In 1899 he described his program in *Aids to Scouting.*

Robert Baden-Powell

In that same year, Baden-Powell was sent to South Africa in preparation for the impending Boer War. At the outbreak of hostilities, he was surrounded by General Piet Cronje and a vastly superior force at Mafeking. Baden-Powell held out for 217 days, and the relief of Mafeking prompted wild celebrations in the streets of London. He was the hero of the day, was promoted to major general, and was lionized when he returned to England, where he became inspector-general of Cavalry. As a result of his popularity, *Aids to Scouting* became a bestseller, and teachers began to use it as a text on the manly virtues it claimed to inculcate.

In 1908, Baden-Powell formed the Boy Scouts and rewrote his book as *Scouting for Boys*. The response was tremendous, and in 1909 the Boy Scouts held their first jamboree, with 11,000 attending. Baden-Powell retired from the army in 1910 (as a lieutenant-general) to devote his life to the Boy Scouts. In that same year the Sea Scouts were formed, and his sister Agnes began a parallel group, the Girl Guides.

The movement expanded rapidly, especially in the United States. Baden-Powell traveled extensively to promote scouting and from the start intended it to be international. He also created other groups—Wolf Cubs in 1916 for boys below age 12 and Rovers in 1922 for young men above age 18. Because of his military and colonial background, there were early criticisms that scouting was a paramilitary form of imperialism. Baden-Powell always countered these comments by asserting that scouting emphasized character formation and patriotism in both peace and war. In World War I, his scouts provided home service as air raid wardens and as replacements for conscripted agricultural workers. More than 20,000 Sea Scouts replaced coast guardsmen.

As a military commander, however, he was innovative. In maneuvers in the Sudan and Bechuanaland (now Botswana), he pioneered the use of observation balloons, and he taught his troops the woodcraft skills he learned as a schoolboy in the English countryside. These activities resulted in two books, *Reconnaissance and Scouting* (1884) and *Cavalry Instruction* (1885).

Baden-Powell's character was marked by contradictions. For him, character and scouting were inseparable: scouting insisted on the Victorian virtues of propriety, order and discipline. He disdained much of the mindless adulation he was accorded but embellished his own legend as it suited him. He was stuffy, manipulative and uncomfortable with women (he only married in his fifties), yet as a young officer he was an enthusiastic and somewhat gifted actor, and his artistic abilities were noted by shows of his watercolors and sculpture. In India he fell passionately in love with a fellow officer, Boy McLaren, the closest friend of his life. Unsurprisingly, recent historians have debated whether or not he was a homosexual. Although he was certainly an imperialist and an advocate of the superiority of Western culture, his racism and anti-Semitism owed more to contemporary Social Darwinism than to incipient fascist ideas.

In 1939, Baden-Powell settled in the White Highlands of Kenya for his health, and it is there that he is buried. On his gravestone is the tracker's sign for "I have gone home."

References: DAHB, DNB, EB, *wiki*. Baden-Powell, *Lessons of a Lifetime* (1933); Julia Courtney, *Robert Baden-Powell* (1990) [young adult]; Tim Jeal, *The Boy-Man* (1990).

BAGAAYA, Elizabeth
(Uganda, 1936–)

Princess Elizabeth Bagaaya of Toro, co-regent of the child king, was ambassador to the United Nations, foreign minister of Uganda under Idi AMIN, and later ambassador to the United States under President Yoweri MUSEVENI. She is currently ambassador to Germany. Besides these accomplishments, she is a beautiful woman who has been a fashion model and movie actress.

She was born of the royal family of Toro, one of four traditional kingdoms in Uganda. After being educated in England and graduating from Cambridge University, in 1964 she became the first Black African woman to practice law in Britain. After three years of practicing law in Uganda, she returned to London when Milton OBOTE brutally destroyed the Ugandan kingdoms. One evening, her flair and beauty caught the eye of photographers at a charity fashion show, and she was flown off to New York, where her willowy and graceful figure appeared in *Vogue, Vanity Fair, Ebony,* and *Harper's Bazaar.*

Bagaaya came back to Uganda after Obote fell. Idi Amin appointed her roving ambassador and then minister of foreign affairs. In 1974 she chaired the Ugandan delegation to the U.N. and drew attention with a fiercely anti-Western toast at a luncheon hosted by U.S. Secretary of State Henry Kissinger. On her return to Uganda, Amin asked her to become one of his wives. When she declined, thinking that the request was a joke, she was placed under house arrest. Amin then began a crude and outrageous international campaign to discredit her, accusing her of having public sex with a White man in the restroom of the Paris airport. Bagaaya escaped to England and defended her reputation by suing the British tabloids that had printed Amin's lurid accounts. She won 15 settlements. Following this notoriety, she briefly withdrew from political life and became a film actress, winning parts in several films, including *Cotton Comes to Harlem.*

When Obote returned to power in 1980, Bagaaya became a European spokesperson for Yoweri MUSEVENI, the main guerrilla leader challenging the Obote regime. Through her political work she met and married Wilbur Nyabongo in 1981, to whom she was intensely devoted. Museveni appointed Bagaaya ambassador to the United States after winning the civil war in Uganda, but she had just

arrived when her husband died in a plane crash. She spent three months back in Uganda observing traditional rites, which included shaving her head and visiting all the sites of her husband's youth. She then reorganized her embassy and set up a highly successful Washington visit for Museveni. In 1989, Bagaaya was abruptly transferred to Paris as a result of conflicts within the Ugandan Foreign Ministry, but she refused the post. She returned briefly to fashion modeling and then settled on ancestral land in Toro, at the base of the Mountains of the Moon. There she began mixed farming and the creation of a model peasant community. In 1993 her brother Patrick was restored to the throne of Toro, and she took on the traditional social and community roles as *batebe,* or princess royal. After his death, she became co-regent with Queen Mother Best, for the child-king Oyo, enthroned at age three. By 1999 the two were locked in a palace power conflict, when Museveni nominated her for another diplomatic post as ambassador to Germany.

Reference: adb. Bagaaya, *Elizabeth of Toro* (1989).

BAGAZA, Jean-Baptiste
(Burundi, 1946–)

Colonel Jean-Baptiste Bagaza was the military ruler of Burundi for over 10 years. He began as a reformer but became increasingly oppressive until he was overthrown.

Bagaza, who is from the south and a member of the privileged Tutsi ethnic group, was a relative of President Michel MICOMBERO. After education at Catholic mission schools in Bujumbura, the capital, Bagaza joined the army and attended cadet school in Brussels from 1966 to 1970, which was followed by a further year of specialized military training in Belgium. His clan relationship to Micombero led to his appointment to the general staff, and in 1972 he was promoted to lieutenant-colonel and became chief of staff. In 1974 he became first staff chief of the armed forces, making him second in command to the president. In 1976 he led a bloodless coup that removed Micombero on the grounds of centralized power and economic incompetence.

After establishing a revolutionary council, Bagaza promised a return to civilian rule. The deep-seated problem was the bitter discontent among the majority Hutu people, who had for centuries been kept subservient to their Tutsi overlords. Bagaza appointed a few Hutu to his cabinet and abolished the feudal land system, forcing some Tutsi landowners to hand over land to their Hutu peasants. Bagaza was unwilling, however, to concede Tutsi political power. In 1982 a parliamentary election was held, but Bagaza and the army retained firm control. In 1984 he confirmed his hold with an obviously fraudulent presidential election in which he received 99 percent of the vote.

During his regime, Bagaza came in conflict with the Catholic Church, long the champion of Hutu rights. As Bagaza became more authoritarian, he increased his pressures on the Church, deporting missionaries, imprisoning Burundi church leaders, and finally forbidding daily Masses. This policy eventually led to an erosion of Bagaza's support among many Tutsi, and in 1987, while attending a meeting of francophone heads of state in Canada, he was overthrown by Pierre BUYOYA. Bagaza went into exile in Libya, where he continued to plot a return to power.

Buyoya arranged the return to civilian rule and was replaced by a Hutu president in 1993. The army, however, remained Tutsi dominated, with factions still loyal to Bagaza. These soldiers evidently engineered the failed coup that killed the president three months after the return to civilian government. Another failed coup was mounted in 1994. The violent civil war with numerous massacres in neighboring Rwanda leave the political situation in Burundi precarious and open to turmoil.

References: afr, DAHB, PLBA, RWWA.

BAI BUREH
(Sierra Leone, 1840s–1908)

Bai Bureh, the foremost resistance leader against British imperialism in Sierra Leone, was leader of the Temne Hut Tax Rebellion of 1898. His birth name is not known, but he came from the northern area of Sierra Leone, which retained its independence until the 1890s. His father sent him to a training camp for warriors, where he received the name Kebelai, "whose basket is not full," meaning that he had not killed his fill of enemies. After being made a battle commander, Kebelai acquired a fearsome reputation as a powerful military leader from the 1860s to the 1880s.

In 1887, the elders of Kasseh, a minor Temne chieftaincy, elected him chief when they could not find a suitable heir. He then took the title Bai Bureh, which he used as his name, and forged his people into a warrior community. He was not interested in extending Kasseh's control of land, but he often allied his troops with neighboring rulers in regional conflicts. When the British sought treaties with the interior chiefs, he accepted an alliance with them. As a result, he fought for the British several times, even saving them in one campaign in 1892 after they suffered reverses. In 1895, Bai Bureh made an excursion into neighboring French territory, which disturbed the British governor of Freetown, who levied a fine on Bai Bureh and attempted to bring his troops under British control. Bai Bureh refused to travel to Freetown for discussions and cut off contact, although he later met the governor and surrendered 50 guns as a penalty.

In 1896 the British declared a protectorate over all of Sierra Leone and imposed a house, or hut, tax in 1898. Because most people did not possess European currency, the tax, which had to be paid in British shillings, would have forced them to become wage laborers for settlers or the government. The result was the Hut Tax Rebellion, which was precipitated among the Temne when messengers were sent with an order to Bai Bureh to collect the tax. The British dispatched three expeditions to arrest Bai Bureh; when they fired on the people, the Temne retaliated. For 10 months, Bai Bureh fought a well-organized guerrilla war that kept the British at bay, and when the governor offered £100 for his capture, he countered with an offer of £500 for the governor. Other communities that joined the rebellion engaged in murders and atrocities, but Bai Bureh's warriors were well disciplined and avoided such offenses. Bai Bureh was captured, and although he was never accused of a crime, he was exiled to the Gold Coast from 1899 to 1905. He was permitted to return home and was reinstated as chief of Kasseh until his death.

References: DAB, DAHB, MMA.

BAIKIE, William Balfour
(Nigeria, 1825–1864)

Dr. William Balfour Baikie, a Scottish surgeon and explorer, was responsible for breaking the hold of malaria upon Westerners in Africa, which opened

Africa's interior to European exploration. After completing medical school in Edinburgh, Baikie served with the British Mediterranean fleet. In 1854 he was named surgeon and naturalist for an exploration of the Niger and Benue Rivers. When the captain died off the African coast, Baikie assumed command and led one of the most successful inland expeditions to date. He was accompanied by Bishop Samuel Ajayi CROWTHER, who was investigating possibilities for a Niger mission. Not only did they venture 250 miles (about 400 kilometers) farther than any European explorers had previously traveled, but remarkably, they lost no European lives in four months because Baikie had insisted that they use quinine to prevent malaria. This drug was a major breakthrough; for the first time European colonization of the African interior became possible because Westerners did not face almost certain death as they once had.

Baikie's *Narrative of an Exploring Voyage* (1856) brought him fame, and in 1857 he led another expedition, again with Bishop Crowther. The ship was wrecked, but Baikie decided to continue on when his companions returned to England. He took a small boat and two African companions, and moved upriver. He established a settlement at the confluence of the Niger and Benue Rivers and styled himself as the British consul, even though he was more like a local chief. He established relations with neighboring chiefs, who seemed to acknowledge his position, and began a development program. He opened up the navigation of the Niger, created roads, and developed commodities and markets for them among the local people. Baikie also studied the local languages and created written alphabets and dictionaries for 50 of them. He translated the Bible and sections of the *Book of Common Prayer* into Hausa, the dominant local language, used as a trading language through much of West Africa. In 1864, at the age of 39, he died in Sierra Leone while on his way back to England.

References: DAHB, DNB, EWB, *wiki.*

BAKARY, Djibo
(Niger, 1922–1998)

Djibo Bakary remained an important personality in Niger's politics after independence, despite the fact that he had not held a position since he was a leader of the government in the immediate preindependence period.

In 1941, Bakary graduated from the elite William Ponty School in Dakar, Sénégal, and then received a teacher's certificate. While teaching in Niger, he became active in the labor movement, and by the end of World War II he had become a noted unionist, journalist and politician. He founded the Sawaba (Freedom) Party, a Marxist-oriented party affiliated with the Rassemblement Démocratique Africain (RDA), an interterritorial party headed by Côte d'Ivoire's Félix HOUPHOUËT-BOIGNY. Bakary joined the RDA's leadership and was a leading militant in the RDA struggle with the French in Côte d'Ivoire in 1949–1950. He subsequently began to concentrate on building his political base in Niger. He was expelled from the RDA when he refused to accept Houphouët-Boigny's break with the Communists.

In 1956, Bakary ran for the French national assembly against Hamani DIORI, a cousin and political rival. Diori won with heavy assistance from the French, but Bakary was elected mayor of the capital, Niamey. After territorial elections in 1957 placed the Sawaba Party second in the polls, Bakary was made vice president of the executive council. In 1958 a major referendum was held throughout French-speaking Africa regarding the future status of the French colonies. Only Bakary and Guinea's Sékou TOURÉ campaigned for independence and against a French federation, earning them both the enmity of the French government. Sawaba was badly defeated in elections during the following year, the party was banned, and Bakary was exiled. He went to Mali, where he conspired to overthrow Diori, who had become Niger's first president.

In 1974, Bakary was allowed to return to Niger after Seyni KOUNTCHÉ overthrew Diori, on the condition that he not return to politics. Because he violated his pledge, he was arrested and imprisoned until 1980. When Ali SAIBOU came to power in 1987, Bakary joined him in a call for reconciliation and the return of all political exiles. In 1992 a new constitution liberalized politics, and the Sawaba Party was reconstituted. It joined the governing coalition in 1993. Bakary remained a radical critic of French neocolonialism but was no longer a significant figure in politics in Niger.

References: DAHB, PLBA.

BAKER, Samuel White
(Sudan, 1821–1893)

Sir Samuel White Baker was a British adventurer who explored much of the upper Nile and served as an administrator in Sudan under the Egyptian government, which ruled the territory with the British until 1956. His father was a merchant, and Samuel spent two years (1843–1845) in Mauritius, managing his family's interests. He then persuaded two of his brothers to join him in starting a colony in the Ceylon (now Sri Lanka) highlands. It soon prospered, and Baker discovered his chief passion, big-game hunting, while exploring the island.

After his first wife died of typhus in 1855, Baker traveled through the Balkans and Turkey. In 1860, while directing construction of the Danube-Black Sea railway, he met and married a Hungarian woman who was to become his enthusiastic companion in exploration. Financially secure and inspired by the experiences of John Hanning SPEKE, whom Samuel knew, the Bakers joined one of the great adventures of the Victorian age—the search for the source of the Nile.

From 1861 to 1865 the Bakers worked their way up the Nile. The main expedition cast off with a retinue of 96. Most of the armed guards soon deserted, and the Bakers were forced to travel with hostile slave traders. During their journey they were under constant threat of attack by locals and were besieged by clouds of malaria-transmitting mosquitoes. Baker made alliances with chiefs along the way, but most of his new allies proved untrustworthy. In part, his paternalism and racism alienated him from the African societies he encountered. Finally, in 1864, with his wife in a temporary coma from sunstroke and carried on a litter, Baker came to a vast lake, which he named Albert Nyanza (Lake Albert).

Although they made an important contribution to the geography of Africa, the discoverers of Lake Albert failed to resolve the question of the Nile's sources and, in fact, confused the issue further. After they explored Lake Albert, the Bakers sailed for two weeks, discovering and naming the Murchison Falls (after Roderick Murchison, president of the Royal Geographical Society) and mapping the region as well as they could. When they returned to England, the Bakers received public praise and official honors, including a knighthood in 1886. Baker's major book, *The Albert Nyanza,* went through many editions.

In 1869, Baker accepted a charge from Ismail Pasha, the *khedive* (ruler) of Egypt to extend Egyptian authority to Lake Victoria and to end the Sudan slave trade. Baker was appointed governor of Equatoria province of southern Sudan and given the title of *pasha.* His expedition, with 1,200 soldiers, had to cut canals through the floating vegetation, called the *Sudd,* for passage, but Baker was able to set up several stations. In spite of being harassed by slavers, he pressed forward to claim Bunyoro, on Lake Victoria, in 1872. Here he met his match in Mukama KABAREGA, who drove Baker's forces out of his kingdom. Baker had support from MUTESA I, the *kabaka* or ruler of Buganda, but Baker's harsh measures and tactless manner, engendered by his racism and ethnocentrism, prevented working alliances.

Baker was a large and imposing man, fully bearded in the style of the day. He possessed a great store of energy that, combined with determination and courage, made him a notable if eccentric explorer. In 1873 he retired to a life of travel and big-game hunting; the latter won him additional renown.

References: DAHB, DNB, EB, EWB, *wiki.* Richard Hall, *Lovers on the Nile: The Incredible African Journeys of Sam and Florence Baker* (1980).

BAKHITA, Josephine
(Sudan, 1869–1947)

Saint Josephine Bakhita was born into a prosperous Darfur family, but that did not prevent her from being kidnapped into slavery at age nine. She was passed through five slave holders who regularly beat her, once leaving her almost dead. She was then sold to a Turkish general, who had her horribly tattooed with a razor, with six patterns on her breasts and 60 across her body. Around 1882, she was sold to the Italian consul and taken to Italy when the MAHDI captured Khartoum in 1884. As a nanny, she accompanied the family's small girl to school, and alongside her, learned to write and gained knowledge about the Christian faith. When her mistress attempted to take her back to Africa, she refused to go. The Canossian Sisters, who ran the school, enlisted the Cardinal in Venice on her behalf, and the royal Procurator freed Bakhita and pronounced

Josephine Bakhita, FdCC

slavery illegal in Italy. It was a landmark decision that ended legal slavery in all Italian territories.

Bakhita was baptized in 1890 and took the name Josephine. She spent four years studying her new-found faith and felt a call to consecrate herself as a nun. In 1896, she made vows in the Canossian community. She served as porter, seamstress and cook, and nursed the wounded during World War I. Soon she acquired a reputation for holiness and wise counsel, and after her autobiography was published in 1930, she became a celebrity in Italy. Bakhita went on speaking tours, raised money for the schools of her community and counseled an endless stream of suppliants. She never was reputed to perform miracles, but on the contrary lived a simple life.

In old age, her health failed her. As she weakened, in her pain she relived her experience of slavery, begging her nurse to loosen her chains. After her death, Bakhita lay in state for three days with thousands of mourners coming to see "our Black mother."

Bakhita was canonized by Pope John Paul II in 2000. Her feast day is celebrated February 8, especially by Christians in the Sudan, where she is regarded as the patron saint. "Bakhita" means "fortunate one," the name given her by her first captor. She was so traumatized by the abduction that she never remembered her true name.

References: dacb, wiki.

BALEWA, Abubakar Tafawa
(Nigeria, 1912–1966)

Alhaji Sir Abubakar Tafawa Balewa, the first prime minister of independent Nigeria, had a remarkable rise to prominence because of his extremely low social origins.

Balewa was born in northeast Nigeria, the son of a slave who had become a butcher. In a Muslim society suspicious of Western education, he was unusual in finishing secondary school and qualifying as a teacher. He taught and was a headmaster from 1933 to 1945, when he received a scholarship to study at the Institute of Education at the University of London. He was appointed a provincial education officer on his return to Nigeria.

At about the same time a new constitution created a national assembly, and Balewa was elected to the northern house of assembly and then to the Legislative Council (Legco) in 1947. In 1951, Balewa joined Sir Ahmadu BELLO in forming the Northern People's Congress (NPC) into a political party with Balewa as deputy leader. That year another new constitution further advanced self-government, and Balewa became minister of works in the first group of central government ministers. Three years later he was appointed minister for transport. The 1951 constitution also established a federal parliament, and Balewa was majority leader when the NPC took control of the House of Representatives. In 1957, Balewa became Nigeria's first prime minister and formed an all-party national unity government. The NPC won the 1959 elections as well, and a year later Balewa became independent Nigeria's first prime minister and was knighted by Queen Elizabeth II.

From the beginning, the task facing Balewa was daunting. Nigeria was a fragmented society, with sharp divisions between Christians and Muslims, among its three major regions, and among parties. To this problem, he brought great personal integrity and diligent effort. He was a conciliator and unifier, but in the end he was no match for the divisive nature of Nigerian society. His chief ally, Bello, preferred to remain premier of the Northern Region, from where he manipulated national politics. Each year produced a major crisis. In 1962 the federal government took sides in a controversy involving the Action Group (AG), a Western Region party. Balewa was forced to impose martial law, which was followed by a crisis led by the leader of the opposition in the federal assembly, the AG's Chief Obafemi AWOLOWO. Awolowo was convicted of treason and sentenced to prison. In 1963, Nigeria became a republic and Governor-General Dr. Nnamdi AZIKIWE became president. The NPC soon broke with Azikiwe's party, its coalition partner, over the census, which Azikiwe feared favored the north. In the 1964 election Balewa came into open conflict with Azikiwe, who attempted to dismiss Balewa as prime minister on the grounds of election fraud.

Finally, the Western Region elections of 1965 were followed by a collapse of local law and order after flagrant ballot rigging in the area. Three months of riots and murders followed until the army intervened. A faction of the army then attempted a coup against Balewa, and in the confusion he was killed. Within a year, Nigeria was plunged into the disastrous Biafran civil war.

References: AB, *afr*, CB, DAHB, MMA, PLBA, *wiki*. Trevor Clark, *A Right Honourable Gentleman* (1991).

BALLINGER, Margaret Hodgson

(South Africa, 1894–1980)

Margaret Hodgson Ballinger, a teacher and parliamentarian, was a strong advocate of African rights and a prominent liberal spokesperson. She emigrated from Scotland with her parents at age 10 and was educated at Rhodes and Oxford universities. From 1920 to 1935 she was senior lecturer in history at the University of the Witwatersrand in South Africa, where she did pioneering research on the South African protectorates with William Ballinger, a labor organizer, whom she married in 1934. She

was forced to resign in 1935, because married women were not allowed to hold university posts. Together the Ballingers turned to the advocacy of African rights.

The 1935 Representation of Natives Act removed African voters from the common voting rolls in Cape Province and established a separate voting registration for Black Africans, who were allowed to elect four White members of parliament to represent them. Margaret Ballinger was asked by the African National Congress (ANC) to stand for one of these seats. She held a seat, representing two million constituents, until it was abolished in 1960. For some years, her husband also served in parliament as a senator from the Orange Free State.

During her tenure in office, Ballinger was an outspoken opponent of apartheid. In 1953, despairing of any political or economic reforms on the part of the government, she and Alan PATON formed the Liberal Party, and she became its first president. As it moved to the left in the late 1950s, however, she turned away from the party, retiring from public life in 1960. She favored gradual suffrage for Blacks and opposed the Liberal position of "one man, one vote." She also opposed sanctions against South Africa and always put economic and civil rights for Africans ahead of political ones.

After 1960, Ballinger devoted herself to African women's issues through the National Council on Women, the Association of European and African Women, and the Nursing Council. She founded and managed a home for African children with disabilities until the Group Areas Act forced its closure. Along with Paton, she represented the limited extent to which White leadership could support the civil and human rights of Black Africans.

References: AO, CANR, DAHB. Ballinger, *From Union to Apartheid: A Trek to Isolation* (1961).

BAMBA, Amadou

(Sénégal, 1850?–1927)

Cheikh Amadou Bamba founded the Mouride brotherhood, one of several Islamic sects that has grown into a politically potent movement of several million members in Sénégal.

Bamba's father was a *marabout*, or strictly observant Muslim, who taught in the courts of prominent Islamic anti-imperialist resistance leaders, including MABA Diakhou Ba, master of the

Tijani brotherhood. Bamba was initiated into the Qadiriyya brotherhood and spent several years in Mauritania studying Islamic law and theology before returning home to become a renowned preacher. After the end of armed resistance to French colonial expansion in 1886, Bamba had several prophetic visions and became the focus of Islamic hopes of resisting French colonialism. Bamba was a deeply spiritual man who did not encourage rebellion, but the disciples flocking to his village worried the French colonial officials, who finally had him arrested and deported to Gabon in 1895.

During his exile, Bamba developed his religious thought and wrote religious verses. He was permitted to return in 1902, but his followers regarded this as a miracle, so the French used the excuse of a possible holy war to exile him once again, this time to Mauritania, where he resided until 1907.

During this exile, Bamba founded his Mouride brotherhood. Besides traditional Islamic observance, it taught that salvation was attained through hard work and total submission to *marabouts,* or Islamic teachers. "The people produce religion through their work" was one of Bamba's favorite sayings. In 1912, after sending an open letter to his followers that counseled submission to colonial authority, Bamba was allowed to return to his home village. From there the Mouride brotherhood grew into the most powerful rural force in Sénégal. Bamba used this strength to command his followers to cultivate peanuts and to encourage them to enlist in the French army in World War I. He also supported and financed Blaise DIAGNE's campaign for the French parliament.

Bamba's political influence was secondary to his religious concerns, but his political views always had a communitarian aspect. His emphasis on the production of peanuts, for example, led to the colonial government's provision of land grants for the Mourides. Bamba's efforts laid the groundwork for future economic development. Peanuts are now Sénégal's leading cash crop, and the brotherhood controls 40 percent of these exports. The Mourides also dominate public transport and some illegal commerce, such as the drug trade and smuggling. After Bamba's death, four of his sons succeeded him in turn with the title of caliph general. More than a million people make annual pilgrimages to Bamba's tomb in the belief that this site is second only to Mecca as a Muslim shrine.

References: afr, DAHB, MMA. Mouhamed Ane, *La Vie de Cheikh Ahmadou Bamba* (*The Life of Cheikh Amadou Bamba*, 1974).

BAMBATHA
(South Africa, 1865?–1906)

Bambatha was leader of the 1906 Zulu rebellion, a major anticolonial uprising in Natal. The aftermath of the Zulu rebellion was increased pressure for South African unification as a counterbalance to threats of African uprisings.

After the breakup of the Zulu kingdom, Bambatha became chief of a subclan in Natal. His clan numbered 5,500, living in about 1,100 households. Bambatha clashed with the government over his refusal to pay taxes. To the onerous "hut tax" on every dwelling was added a head tax on all males. When Bambatha resisted, the Natal administration deposed him and he fled north into the heart of Zululand (in northeast Natal). Here he met DINUZULU, who had returned from exile in St. Helena. This meeting led to speculation that Dinuzulu gave covert support to Bambatha. Whatever the case, Bambatha seized upon several natural phenomena as signs of impending deliverance from the British and launched a series of guerrilla attacks. Claiming possession of a charm that would deflect bullets, Bambatha inspired his warriors to fight with their traditional *assagais,* or short stabbing spears.

Initially, Bambatha was successful, surprising and ambushing several small forces and infiltrating the African troops under British command. In a pitched battle in the Mome Gorge, however, the rebellion was crushed. Bambatha was killed and beheaded, but many still believed him alive. In order to maintain this myth, his wife refused to go into mourning. About 4,000 Africans died in the rebellion. Dinuzulu was tried for complicity in the insurrection but later was acquitted after a spirited defense by William SCHREINER.

References: DAHB, WGMC.

BANANA, Canaan Sodindo
(Zimbabwe, 1936–2003)

Reverend Canaan Sodindo Banana was an early nationalist and the first president of Zimbabwe. Although the presidency was a largely ceremonial position, Banana distinguished himself as a harmonizing force in the bitter factional conflicts within Zimbabwe after independence, a role that he later extended to international conflicts in Africa.

After local education, including theological school, Banana became a Methodist schools manager. He was ordained in 1966 and became involved in urban industrial missions. He spent a year on a grant traveling throughout Asia and then moved to Bulawayo. With his bishop, Abel MUZOREWA, he founded the African National Council in 1971 to protest negotiations to phase out White rule only after a period of decades. The Council mobilized massive opposition that killed the plan. Banana's relationship with the Methodists was rocky during this period, because his increased political activity brought him into open conflict with his church's opposition to the World Council of Churches' activist stance. He resigned from the Methodist Church for a time but soon returned. By then, however, his life was primarily in politics, although he continued to be chair of the Southern African Urban Industrial Mission until 1973. His passport was withdrawn by the Rhodesian government in 1972, but he slipped out of the country and spent from 1972 to 1975 at American University in Washington, D.C., studying theology and serving as a student chaplain.

When Banana returned to Rhodesia, he was first imprisoned and then detained at various times until 1979. During this period he switched his allegiance to Robert MUGABE's Zimbabwe African National Union (ZANU). In the power struggle after independence in 1980, Joshua NKOMO rejected the offer of the presidency and Banana assumed the position. Although it was a ceremonial office, he proved invaluable to Mugabe, helping to bring together the contending forces that threatened the country's stability. His tenure ended with the new Zimbabwean constitution in 1987, when Mugabe named himself to the new executive presidency. Banana continued his public activities in the economic sanctions movement against South Africa

and became chancellor at the University of Zimbabwe. He led the Eminent Persons Group sent to South Africa in 1989 by the Commonwealth. His conciliation skills were tapped when he was brought in to help mediate a truce that led to a coalition government in strife-torn Liberia in 1994.

All this came crashing down in 1996 when he was accused of homosexual rape by a former bodyguard, on trial for murder. The latter testified that he had killed the man because he was taunted as "Banana's wife." The first reaction was that the accusation was caused by Mugabe, who somehow wanted to disgrace his former colleague. Soon, however, others raised the same accusations, including students from the University. The trial, with salacious details, riveted the country. Banana was convicted on 11 charges of sodomy, and fled to South Africa. He returned and served one year in prison. Later it was revealed that Mugabe had known of the sexual abuse, but had done nothing. Banana died in Great Britain, where his wife had taken asylum after his trial.

References: DRWW, PLBA, *wiki*.

BANDA, Hastings Kamuzu
(Malawi, 1890s–1997)

Dr. Hastings Kamuzu Banda belonged to the first generation of independence leaders. He continued to govern his country until 1994. As an autocrat in a tiny nation, he was able to force development and bring a measure of progress to his country. For Malawians such modernization was paid for at the cost of political repression and the loss of human rights.

Despite his diminutive size, the dapper Banda was, in many ways, larger than life; he rose from peasant status to the presidency by dint of hard work. At age 17 he made a legendary journey to South Africa on foot, stopping in Southern Rhodesia for two years to work as a sweeper in a hospital. It was at this time that he became determined to be a doctor and, with help from missionaries, he began his education in 1925. The poor lad who had barely completed elementary school was allowed to enter Wilberforce College in Ohio because of his age and finished a B.A. degree in three years. He spent a total of 12 years in the United States, receiving an

M.D. at Meharry Medical College in Nashville, Tennessee, in 1937. To complete requirements for British practice, he spent from 1938 to 1941 at the University of Edinburgh. With this background, he established a prosperous practice in London during World War II.

Formal, morally puritanical, and convinced of the value of self-help, Banda had many White friends and moved comfortably in White society. Nevertheless, he was acutely aware of institutional racism and became the patron and a sort of father figure for young African students in London. His home became a kind of salon where such nationalists as Kwame NKRUMAH, Harry NKUMBULA, Peter ABRAHAMS, and Jomo KENYATTA met. This laid the groundwork of personal contacts that would prove invaluable during the anticolonial drive for independence.

The issue that politicized him, however, was the proposed federation of Nyasaland (now Malawi) with the settler colonies of North and South Rhodesia (now Zambia and Zimbabwe). The project infuriated Banda, who had experienced far more racism during his brief stay in Southern Rhodesia than in Britain. When the British Labour government supported the federation in 1953, he left Britain and established himself in the Gold Coast (now Ghana). From there he intensified his campaign against the federation, becoming the acknowledged Malawian leader in exile. When Henry CHIPEMBERE urged him to return to lead the struggle against federation, Banda flew home in 1958. He was 60 years old and had been away so long that he could no longer speak his native language.

Within six months, Banda's fiery oratory (delivered through an interpreter) frightened the authorities into declaring a state of emergency. After spending over a year in prison, Banda led the Malawi Congress Party (MCP) delegation to a London conference but came away with a few concessions. He returned to London in 1960 with Kenneth KAUNDA and Joshua NKOMO, and by then the end of federation was a matter of time. It died in 1963, the same year that Banda became prime minister of Malawi and a year before independence. In 1966 he was chosen president when Malawi became a republic, and in 1971 his title was changed to President-for-Life.

Banda almost immediately put his own stamp on the country. He quickly suppressed any opposition, forcing out democratic voices in the cabinet.

He instituted one-party rule and drove opponents out of the country, but even in exile opponents were not safe from his hit squads. Potential leaders spent long years in prison and several met untimely "accidental" deaths. Banda often favored someone, then dashed his hopes, keeping MCP stalwarts always off center. For example, Banda removed his heir-apparent, John TEMBO, as governor of the central bank, and then as suddenly reinstated him.

Foreign policy was conservative and capitalist under Banda. For years, Malawi was the only African state to exchange ambassadors with South Africa, which provided extensive foreign aid to the country. South Africa funded a new capital at Lilongwe, with an international airport, and subsidized infrastructure. Similarly, Malawi recognized Taiwan rather than the People's Republic of China, and received considerable agricultural development assistance as a result. Banda was pro-Western and anti-Communist and for a time gave covert support to RENAMO, the Mozambican resistance movement that fronted for South Africa.

Domestic policy was equally cautious and marked by Banda's Victorian social attitudes. Bell-bottom trousers and short skirts were forbidden. Arriving male visitors with long hair were spirited into a back room at the international airport and promptly shorn of their "hippie" locks. Malawi never allowed television, and all magazines were censored. It was not unusual to have magazine photos of women in short-sleeved dresses appear with long sleeves drawn in with marking pens. Nevertheless, Banda emphasized modernization and promoted agricultural development, introducing new crops such as rice, which generally improved the lot of the peasantry. With few attractions in its towns, Malawi avoided urbanization. To strengthen national identity, male initiation ceremonies were restored, along with traditional dances. On his frequent trips around the country, Banda was accompanied by a women's dance troupe, and he expected to be greeted by dancers wherever he went. Well into his nineties he would even join them for several hours of vigorous dancing.

Banda also attempted to enforce a national language, Chichewa, but the Tumbuka-speaking north—where he was unpopular—resisted. The only other resistance to his rule came from the Catholic Church. In 1991 the local bishops had a letter read from every pulpit, condemning his human rights abuses. Although one diocesan head, an Irish missionary, was exiled, Banda failed to break the resolve of the African bishops, who were soon joined by their Anglican and Presbyterian counterparts. Internal and international pressures forced Banda to allow a referendum on multiparty government, and the people voted to end one-party rule.

Age, however, was the greatest factor limiting Banda's power. In 1990 he suffered a stroke, and in 1993 he had brain surgery. A presidential council governed during Banda's convalescence, but the MCP nominated him for the 1994 elections. Nonetheless, various forces positioned themselves for the post-Banda era. In late 1993 the army disarmed the Young Pioneers, the MCP-armed youth wing. In the process, the Youth Ministry was sacked and one of Banda's state residences was burned down. In the 1994 elections, Banda was defeated and accepted the decision as inevitable.

References: AB, *afr*, CB, DAHB, EWB, PLBA, PLCA, RWWA, *wiki*. Philip Short, *Banda* (1974).

BANDELE, "George"
(Nigeria, 1910?-?)

Bandele, the son of AREOGUN of Osi-Ilorin, is among the small group of twentieth-century Ekiti Yoruba woodcarvers whose work is recognized internationally.

He did not study under Areogun, but seems to have been influenced by his style. Father Kevin CARROLL commented that "he did not have the same artistic sense as his father." He did, however, have amazing technical skill. Bandele was able to carve with both hands simultaneously, enabling him to work extremely quickly. Bandele worked in several stages: first, shaping the wood with an axe, then producing the form of the work, and finally using a knife for detail work. He chose the subject of the carving according to the natural patterns in the wood, and never worked from sketches.

Bandele joined Carroll's woodcarving workshop at Oyo-Ekiti in 1947, working there until 1954, the year his father died. During this period he undertook a number of Yoruba-style religious commissions for Catholic churches after traditional commissions became scarce. Since the Yoruba woodcarving tradition created pieces either for royal palaces or religious settings—ceremonies and shrines—it was a natural move to carve for Christian churches.

Just as important was Bandele's mentorship of younger carvers who carried on the Ekiti tradition

Among them was Lamidi FAKEYE, who also became renowned for his work. After a period away from the workshop, during which he could find few commissions, Bandele was forced to work as a woodcutter, and so he returned to the Carroll workshop. In 1964, Carroll commissioned him to do two doors for the American headquarters of Carroll's Society of Missionaries of Africa (SMA) in New Jersey, where they now flank the entrance to the African Art Museum. The doors show biblical themes in a Yoruba motif, and are excellent examples of Bandele's work. In 1965, he executed one of his finest pieces, the doors for the chapel at the University of Ibadan. One has scenes from the Hebrew scriptures, the other from the Christian scriptures. The doors complete and parallel the work of Fakeye, who carved a set of doors there in 1954. Bandele's carvings are stylized and incised deeply into the wood. The motifs are Yoruba; when Gabriel comes to Mary at the Annunciation, he finds her pounding yams. There are 10 panels to each door; every one is a complete scene, yet they are balanced harmoniously without a sense of crowding. In the Hebrew biblical set, the scene of Moses at the burning bush is especially strong.

"Bandele" is a name meaning "born away from home," and is a birth-name. He used George as a western name without really adopting it officially.

Reference: Kevin Carroll, SMA, *Yoruba Religious Carving* (1967).

BANNY, Charles Konan
(Côte d'Ivoire, 1942–)

Konan Banny is an international economist and banker who was named head of an interim government in Côte d'Ivoire, in hopes of carrying it through its extended political crisis.

Banny, a native of Côte d'Ivoire, took a graduate degree in economics in Paris in 1968. His banking career began as deputy, then secretary-general of the Inter-African Coffee Organization in 1970, but in 1976 he moved to the West African Central Bank, which manages the common currency of eight francophone countries. He progressed through various positions until becoming governor in 1994. He took leave for several years in the 1980s to serve as head of the International Monetary Fund (IMF) program in Côte d'Ivoire.

Banny was a progressive and competent reform manager at the Bank, reorganizing, introducing technological improvements and developing a regional stock market. There was considerable regional economic integration during his tenure.

Once the most prosperous nation in West Africa, Côte d'Ivoire was split in two when northern rebels seized half the country in 2002, hoping to oust President Lawrence Gbagbo. Six thousand French troops and 4,000 United Nations soldiers monitor a buffer zone between the contending forces.

As the crisis deepened and the country became paralyzed, Presidents Thabo MBEKI of South Africa and Olusegun OBASANJO of Nigeria mediated the dispute. The 2005 elections were cancelled, and President Gbagbo's term was extended for one year. Banny was then called from his position as governor of the Central Bank of West Africa to act as prime minister. He governs until the end of 2006, and is not eligible to run for president. In the process, Banny emerged as a consensus figure in consultations with all factions in the country.

Banny has a reputation as a strong-willed and determined individual, but he faces a huge task of disarming both rebel and government militias. His first months in office brought positive results, with students in the north sitting for exams for the first time in two years, an election scheduled for 2006, the return of exiled leader Allasane OUATTARA, and meetings of all factions in the civil conflict.

Reference: adb.

BARENDS, Barend
(South Africa, 1770s–1839)

Barend Barends was a chief of the Griqua or Gonaqua, a people of mixed Khoikhoi and European ancestry who inhabited the South African frontier. He became the leader of his people just as the frontier was closing, bringing an end to their way of life.

At the turn of the nineteenth century, new societies were evolving along the frontier north of the Orange River. Unable to own land in areas reserved for Whites, the original peoples—the Khoikhoi and San—were forced onto arid pastureland. In this region, the indigenous population combined with Whites and Coloured emigrants from Cape Town to create the Griqua community.

Such frontier societies were often violent because space could be obtained only at the expense of another group, and Whites pressed north constantly, seeking better land. The economy was built on raiding, breeding, and trading cattle, and the Griqua became excellent horsemen. They were a nomadic people, but when cornered, they could rebel, as they had in 1799. Barends came north from the Cape around 1800, probably with a government expedition sent to look into the causes of the uprising.

Barends was a natural leader for the Griqua, because he was able to speak English and understand White ways and customs. He soon gathered a small following. He spent a dozen years as the leader of a wandering band until settling along the Vaal River in 1813 in an area where several Griqua clan leaders had their headquarters. He became their ally in a loose arrangement among the clans and jointly governed the main village, Griqua Town, from 1813 to 1820. In 1823 he joined the chiefs in defending the territory against the large Nguni warrior army fleeing SHAKA's first wave of conquest. When missionaries tried to get the Griqua clans to merge into a unified nation, Barends resisted, left the town, and turned to cattle raiding. In 1831 he attacked the Ndebele, a larger and more powerful people led by MZILIKAZI. Barends' force was decimated, and he spent his last years again as a petty chieftain.

Reference: DAHB.

BARGHASH Ibn Said
(Tanzania, 1837?–1888)

Seyyid Barghash Ibn Said was a younger son of Seyyid SAID, sultan of Zanzibar, the island nation off the coast of what is now Tanzania. He plotted to take the throne on his father's death in 1856, but the rightful heir, Majid, forestalled him. In the 1850s Barghash made two unsuccessful attempts to seize power that led to a two-year exile to India. He then returned home in 1861 to await his brother's death, and in 1870 he succeeded legitimately. He then promptly imprisoned his younger brother, perhaps fearing that he might plot against Barghash as the latter had plotted against Majid. The younger brother was only released when their sister set out on a pilgrimage to Mecca, and Barghash trembled at the thought of a curse put upon him in the Holy City.

A lifelong opponent of British attempts to suppress the slave trade, Barghash came under immediate pressure to end the trade. The Zanzibari clove plantations were dependent upon slave labor, but when a devastating cyclone in 1871 destroyed the island's valuable crops and sank much of the Zanzibari fleet, Barghash was no longer in a position to resist. In 1873 the British exploited Zanzibar's weakness and required Barghash to prohibit the export of slaves and to close the major Zanzibar slave market on the East African coast. Three years later inland slaving caravans were forbidden and African troops were trained to suppress the inland trade. Ultimately, Barghash was forced to submit because of his fear of German encroachment in East Africa.

Barghash turned to the expansion of legitimate commerce as a way out of his dilemma, and, for a time, the ivory and rubber trades flourished. In theory, the mainland owed allegiance to Zanzibar, but it was a fragile relationship. Barghash formed ties with powerful Swahili and Arab traders, such as TIPPU TIP, but by 1885 the Germans had concluded treaties with most of the coastal chiefs and sultans. Barghash's protests that these were chiefs under his jurisdiction drew an ultimatum brought by five German warships, and the British refused to support him. Barghash capitulated, and a French, British, and German commission gave Germany a protectorate over Tanganyika. Barghash then concentrated his attention on Zanzibar, which he developed and modernized. He arranged the import of cheap grain, provided the island with pure water, and restored the clove plantations. He built hospitals and parks and paved the roads. British advisors enabled him to create an efficient army and to modernize the government.

References: afr, DAHB, EB, wiki.

BARKLY, Henry
(Mauritius/South Africa, 1815–1898)

Sir Henry Barkly, the first British governor of Cape Colony without a military background, was a professional colonial administrator who furthered British interests against the Afrikaners.

Barkly was a successful merchant who in 1845 won a seat in the British Parliament as a supporter of strong pro-business policies. In 1848 he was appointed governor of British Guiana (now Guyana) on the northern coast of Latin America, where he owned commercial estates. He was knighted in 1853 and transferred to Jamaica. In 1856 he assumed a governorship in Victoria, Australia.

Barkly thus went to Africa with wide colonial experience and the reputation of a conciliator who highly valued representative government and who showed fairness. From 1863 to 1870 he was governor of Mauritius before being appointed to Cape Town. At the Cape Colony he had to deal with problems of coolie labor from China—a labor practice that he favored and had introduced into Guiana. He handled the question with delicacy and achieved a good labor-business relationship.

Almost immediately after arriving in Cape Town, Barkly was named a high commissioner to settle a jurisdictional dispute over Griqualand West on the frontier, where rich diamond deposits had recently been discovered. The Afrikaner states of the Transvaal and Orange Free State disputed the territory with the Griqua chief, and Barkly decided in favor of the Griqua, who promptly requested British protection. Barkly annexed all of Griqualand West but was later accused of favoring the diamond monopoly by not establishing a strong administrative presence and of allowing the mine interests to control the area.

One of Barkly's concerns was representative government, and in 1872 he was able to introduce a parliament for British subjects in the Cape Colony. He had to overcome a great deal of settler resistance, which he did patiently until he had wide support for White self-government. The legislature showed its independence by opposing Barkly on several major issues. It refused to take responsibility for the governance of Griqualand West, and when the colonial secretary in London pressed for a South African federation, it balked. Barkly argued for a gradualist approach to federation, but the colonial secretary rejected his arguments. When Barkly's term ended in 1877, he was removed and went into retirement in England. His assessment of the tensions in the colony proved accurate, however, as his successor failed utterly and was recalled within three years.

References: DAHB, DNB, EB.

BARNARD, Christiaan Neethling
(South Africa, 1923–2001)

Dr. Christiaan Neethling Barnard performed the first successful human heart transplant in 1967 and was the first African to perform open-heart surgery; he also developed the Barnard valve for use in that procedure. Barnard was emeritus professor of surgery at University of Cape Town Medical School until his death, and was director of surgical research for many years at its Groote Schuur Hospital.

Barnard, one of four sons of a Dutch Reformed clergyman, was raised in poverty. After receiving an M.D. at Cape Town, he did family practice for three years before returning to Groote Schuur as a research fellow. Conditions were so rudimentary that he had to collect dogs from a local pound for surgical experiments. In 1955 he went to the University of Minnesota in Minneapolis to complete his Ph.D. Minnesota was pioneering in heart surgery, and Barnard was attracted to the field; he performed his first heart surgery under the university's auspices.

Barnard returned to Cape Town and spent 10 years doing major heart surgery and continuing his experimental work. In late 1967 he and his team performed the first heart transplant, using the heart of a 24-year-old accident victim. The recipient lived 18 days, and Barnard became an instant international celebrity. He appeared on U.S. television and dined with President Lyndon Johnson. In Europe he drew crowds but also criticism that he was self-serving and a publicity seeker. Barnard, who continued to perform transplants, only noted, "It is the duty of the doctor to … let the people know what is going on." His last patient lived for 24 years after heart replacement. He later performed double transplants and worked with artificial valves.

In Barnard's next operations, White patients received hearts from non-White donors, which was a sensitive issue in South Africa. Barnard, who had never been political, was surprised by the public reaction and grew increasingly uncomfortable with apartheid. Ironically, Barnard suffered from rheumatoid arthritis, which finally ended his surgical career.

References: CB, HH, *wiki*. Barnard, *Christiaan Barnard: One Life* (1970).

BARNATO, Barnett Isaacs
(South Africa, 1852–1897)

Barnett Isaacs Barnato—financier, speculator and diamond merchant—was prominent among the White entrepreneurs who became wealthy in South Africa before the Boer War.

Born Barney Issacs in London, he worked briefly at his father's shop, amusing himself on the side with a vaudeville act that he and his brother Henry had developed. In 1873 he followed Henry to South Africa in search of adventure and fortune. They assumed the name Barnato and established a diamond brokerage. Shrewd and bold, Barney took calculated risks that paid off handsomely. Correctly guessing (after studying the physics of volcanic action) that surface diamonds were only a sign of deeper deposits, he bought up "exhausted" claims that were rich in subsoil deposits. By the 1880s he had formed the Barnato Diamond Mining Company and challenged the industry giant, De Beers Consolidated, led by Alfred BEIT and Cecil RHODES. He controlled almost half the industry when the two companies merged (1888) to avoid economic suicide after a bitter contest.

Barnato was active in local civic affairs and politics in Kimberley, the diamond area, and in 1888 he successfully ran for parliament with Rhodes's support. Although he was reelected in 1894, he proved an indifferent legislator, seldom speaking in or even attending sessions. His passion remained business speculation, and after 1888 he moved to Johannesburg, where he speculated in mining claims and real estate. In one venture he lost £3 million, an astronomical sum at that period (about US$350 million currently). During this time he dabbled in politics, denouncing the 1895 raid of Leander Starr JAMESON into the Transvaal. Afterward, however, he threatened to close his mines (which were staffed by 20,000 White and 100,000 Black African workers) if those accused of involvement in the raid were not freed.

In 1897, Barnato's health began to fail, and during a bout of depression he committed suicide by jumping off a ship. He was a man of generosity, gifted but without pretension. In South Africa he was spared much of the anti-Semitism that would have restricted him in England. Although he belonged to an upper-class club, he had no taste for literature or culture, preferring to amuse himself with boxing and horse racing.

References: DAHB, DNB, EB. Robert Fish, *Rough Diamond* (1981).

BASHIR, Omar Hassan
(Sudan, 1944–)

Lieutenant-General Omar Hassan Ahmad al-Bashir, military head of state since 1989 and president since 1993, has made the Sudan into a center for the Islamic revival through the power of the Islamic brotherhoods.

Bashir went to high school in Khartoum before attending the military college, from which he graduated with a commission in 1966. He received paratrooper training and went to staff college in Malaysia. During the Suez War in 1973, Bashir saw action against Israel, and was decorated for bravery. As a brigadier, he commanded troops in the south against John GARANG's Sudanese People's Liberation Army (SPLA). He had no particular political prominence and avoided most of the intense wrangling of the 1970s and 1980s in Sudan.

Bashir is a devout Muslim, faithfully observing the five daily periods of prayer. Moreover, he is reputed to be a member of the fundamentalist Muslim Brotherhood of Dr. Hassan al-TURABI. Bashir has denied this allegation, but evidence exists of his one-time close connections with al-Turabi. This connection may also have been the motivation that led him to take over the coup movement that toppled Sadiq al-MAHDI in 1989. Immediately, he banned political parties, dissolved parliament and censored the press. Bashir immediately took a hardline stance on public policy. He pursued the war in the south and imposed the *sharia,* the Islamic legal code. Within a year the Islamic fundamentalist nature of the regime became more apparent. The majority of the officers on the ruling Revolutionary Command Council were members of the Muslim Brotherhood. Turabi emerged as the real power in the country, despite the fact that he had no official position other than that of "spiritual advisor." In 1990 there were two attempted coups, which were crushed brutally, but Bashir remains firmly in control. In 1992 persecution of Christians—especially southern refugees forced into the north—intensified. Many were driven into desert areas and then denied food and water unless they embraced Islam. In 1993 the government was reshuffled, with a noted increase in members of the National Islamic Front, Turabi's party.

In 1999, Bashir turned against Turabi and removed him from the post of speaker of the National Assembly (created only in 1996). The government was purged of Turabi loyalists as systematically as the brotherhoods had been included earlier. Turabi himself was imprisoned in 2001.

Peace talks with the SPLA rebels went on through the good offices of several African states, with a settlement finally reached in 2004. The south was promised autonomy for six years, a share in oil revenues, and the option of voting for independence after the autonomy period. John Garang was named vice president, but hopes were soon shaken badly when Garang was killed a few weeks later in a plane crash.

As the conflict in the south ebbed, however, a new crisis developed in the east, in the Province of Darfur. Islamic militias, called *Janjaweed*, have been involved in ethnic cleansing, forcing Black Sudanese from their homes and into slavery. Thousands have been killed, women raped and villages burned. International outrage and the presence of peacekeepers from the African Union have failed to prevent further atrocities. Both the United States and the United Nations have called it genocide and accused Bashir of arming and fostering the *Janjaweed*. Most humanitarian groups have been forced to withdraw due to the violence. Conditions in the south remain chaotic, and the U.S. government has accused the Bashir regime of sponsoring international terrorism.

References: PLBA, RWWA,*wiki.*

BASILIOS
(Ethiopia, 1891–1970)

Patriarch Basilios, the first native-born bishop in the Ethiopian Orthodox Church, later became the first patriarch independent of Egypt.

Basilios was born Gebre Giyorgis and became a monk of Debra Libanos, the dominant monastery and cultural center in Ethiopia. In 1933 he was sent to Jerusalem to take charge of Ethiopian churches and monasteries there. He returned to Ethiopia at the time of the 1935 Italian invasion, where he served in the Battle of Maichew as a chaplain. Basilios returned to Jerusalem during the subsequent Italian occupation, but maintained contact with the resistance movement.

From the time of FRUMENTIUS in the fourth century, all bishops of the Ethiopian church had been sent from Egypt by the patriarch of Alexandria. Because it takes 12 bishops to elect a patriarch, the number of dioceses in Ethiopia was deliberately kept below that number, to the increasing detriment of the Ethiopian Orthodox Church. Negotiations were held between authorities in Addis Ababa and Cairo starting in the 1930s, with the intention of correcting this inequity. The break with Alexandria during the Italian occupation hastened Ethiopia's religious independence, and strong support from Emperor HAILE SELASSIE brought the matter to a head.

In Jerusalem, Gebre Giyorgis was ordained a bishop (1948) in preparation for the transition and became the 111th archbishop in 1950, taking the name Basilios. He was placed in charge of church administration, including management of the extensive church properties. Following church-state traditions in Ethiopia, he was appointed to the senate in 1957. In 1959 he was chosen patriarch, removing him from temporal matters, but vesting all spiritual and religious authority in him. An enlightened man, Basilios was still very much the servant of the emperor and did little to innovate or modernize the church.

Reference: dacb.

BATHOEN I
(Botswana, 1845–1910)

Kgosi Bathoen I was *kgosi,* or chief, of the Ngwaketse—one of the indigenous peoples of Botswana—at a time when several forces were struggling for control of southern Africa. He played an important role as a mediator among the chiefs during the transition to colonial rule and was thus able to influence the direction and extent of colonial control.

Bathoen became the leading figure among the Ngwaketse around 1879 and formally succeeded his father as chief a decade later. The area of modern Botswana was caught among three contending forces during this period: the Transvaal Afrikaners, who coveted its land; the Cape Colony settlers, who wanted to dominate the area; and the major African communities—the Ngwato, Tswana, Ngwaketse,

and Kwena—who hoped for British protection against the other two forces.

Bathoen, who became literate in English during his twenties, fostered education and Christianity and formed an alliance with the London Missionary Society (LMS), which shared his goal of British protection. The LMS assumed the position of national church among the Ngwaketse and helped Bathoen establish a school tax and an education committee in 1902.

Bathoen was instrumental in uniting the chiefs of the smaller ethnic groups to support a common policy. They feared that Afrikaner control would lead to forced labor and that the settler colonialism of Cecil RHODES's Cape Colony would be equally exploitive. They won a British protectorate for Bechuanaland in 1885, but when plans were discussed to turn its administration over to Rhodes's British South Africa Company, Bathoen and other African chiefs formed a strong coalition with the LMS to oppose it. They also shrewdly sought protection from Queen Victoria, which resulted in a trip by Bathoen, KHAMA III, and Sebele to London in 1895, where Rhodes's move was effectively blocked. The policy of resistance through diplomacy left the smaller kingdoms with considerable freedom, while larger, more powerful nations were invaded and subjugated.

In 1908, Bathoen led protests against the incorporation of Botswana into South Africa. He also was part of the 1912 discussions that led to the formation of the South African Native National Congress, which later became the African National Congress (ANC).

Reference: DAHB.

BATTUTA, Ibn
(Kenya/Mali/Niger, 1304–1369?)

Ibn Battuta was a Moorish travel writer and chronicler who left some of the best accounts of life in fourteenth-century Africa along the Red Sea and in West Africa.

Ibn Battuta traveled only within Muslim societies and sometimes stayed for months or even years in one place. His travel writings are a revision of the traditional Maghrebian *rihla,* a kind of travel journal of the *hajj,* or pilgrimage to Mecca. He departed from the style of edifying religious writing to establish a new form of travel journal, recounting what he saw, describing the people and cultures he encountered, and providing insights into popular customs. Thus, we have significant accounts of Islamic religious devotions, miracle stories, and marriage and funeral practices. He describes plants and animals as well as clothing and foods. Some of Ibn Battuta's chronology and details are suspect, but none of these involve his travels in Africa. He married a number of times and fathered many children while supporting himself from gifts given by rulers he encountered and by his service as an Islamic judge.

He left Tangier in 1325 to make the traditional *hajj*. Upon returning in 1354, he dictated his accounts to a scribe. Ibn Battuta's voyage had eight sections. The first, lasting a year, went from Tangier to Syria and then to Mecca. This journey was the *hajj* proper, and his account followed the traditional style of the *rihla*. The second journey went through Syria and Persia, with a three-year stay in Arabia. In each of those years, Ibn Battuta made a pilgrimage to Mecca.

The third journey, from 1330 to 1332, took him around the Red Sea and along the East African coast. He visited the city-states along the way and returned to Mecca for the 1332 *hajj*. The accounts of this trip provide the best existing descriptions of medieval Arab and Swahili trade in East Africa. The fourth and longest journey ventured through Asia Minor, ending in 1333 in India, where Ibn Battuta stayed until 1342. On the fifth journey, he visited the Indian Ocean islands and traveled on to Sumatra and China. On the sixth journey, he returned to Mecca in 1347 by way of Malabar, the Persian Gulf, Iraq and Egypt. In 1349, the seventh trip took him to North Africa and Islamic Spain and then back to Morocco.

On the last journey, lasting 18 months, Ibn Battuta crossed the Sahara by caravan along the desert trade routes and explored the kingdom of Mali at great length. He was the only medieval writer to describe this area. His description of the slave-worked salt mines of Teghaza is vivid, and his judgments of the local chiefs were often scathing when he did not receive the tribute he thought he deserved.

References: DAHB, EB, *wiki*. Thomas Abercrombie, "Ibn Battuta, Prince of Travelers." *National Geographic* (December 1991); Battuta, *Textes et Documents Relatifs à l'Histoire des Voyages d'Ibn Battuta* (*Documents Relating to the Story of the Voyages of Ibn Battuta*, 1966).

BEHANZIN
(Benin, 1845–1906)

Behanzin, the last king of Dahomey (now Benin), was on the throne only five years before he was forced to surrender to the French, who incorporated the kingdom into their colonial empire.

Behanzin was born in Algeria and succeeded his father, GLELE, in 1889. He was immediately faced with French intrigues and attempts by subject peoples to exploit his weakness. Several of the neighboring petty kingdoms sought French protectorate status, which brought Behanzin into constant conflict with France. Behanzin took the name Hossu Bowelle ("Great Shark") in order to assert his determination to resist European encroachment. In a vivid demonstration of his strength and authority, he sacrificed a group of captured slaves at his father's funeral. In 1890, Behanzin attacked Cotonou, a Dahomean port his father had lost to the French. Although he was unsuccessful in his attempt to recapture it, he agreed to a treaty paying him 20,000 francs a year to abandon his claims. The agreement was soon abrogated, and after the French lieutenant-governor's ship was attacked along the coast, the French recalled their premier African officer, General Alfred DODDS, to subdue Dahomey. In passing the order in parliament, the French government justified their actions by referring to human sacrifice and Behanzin's involvement in the slave trade.

Behanzin's forces fought well, including his women's battalion, the Amazons. They could only slow the French advance, however, as Dodd moved on Behanzin's capital. In 1893, Behanzin was defeated in a series of five sharp battles. When he refused Dodds's request to fly the French flag over Abomey, his capital, the city was leveled, and Behanzin fled to the interior. He surrendered later that year by coolly walking into the French camp, puffing on his yard-long pipe. Behanzin was deported to Martinique and later to Algeria, where he died of pneumonia. In 1928 his ashes were returned to Dahomey and buried in the royal cemetery with military honors.

References: DAHB, MMA, WGMC, *wiki*. Joseph Amegboh, *Behanzin: Roi d'Abomey* (*Behanzin: King of Abomey*, 1975).

BEIT, Alfred
(South Africa, 1853–1906)

Alfred Beit, financier and philanthropist, was a German entrepreneur who became a leading figure in South African gold and diamond mining.

After secondary school, the young Beit began working for the Hamburg office of a South African trading firm. The firm next sent him to Amsterdam for a year to learn the diamond trade, and in 1875 he went to Kimberley, where he spent three years as a diamond trading representative. His Dutch experience showed him that Kimberley diamonds were worth far more than they were selling for in Africa. He borrowed £2,000 from his father and set himself up in business. He shrewdly bought land rather than diamonds and later sold it for £260,000—a huge profit in the nineteenth century.

While he was in Kimberley, Beit came to know Cecil RHODES and Barnett BARNATO and joined them to form the De Beers Consolidated Mines in 1888. They were such trusting friends that Beit lent Rhodes £250,000 (about $40 million today) without collateral to aid his scheme of consolidating control of the diamond mines. Beit, who never married, regarded Rhodes as a brother and his most intimate friend. The two complemented one another. Beit was thorough and paid strict attention to detail, while Rhodes was far more dramatic and intuitive.

In 1890, Beit settled in London, having become a loyal supporter of British imperialism. He returned regularly to South Africa, however, and frequently demonstrated his ability to seize economic opportunities. Beit, who owned a number of outcrop gold mines, engineered a method to drive slant shafts in order to mine deeply. He was the first to achieve this technological advance and was able to make another fortune in the process. Always interested in the possibilities of economic development, Beit traveled into what is now Zambia and helped found the British South Africa Company (BSAC) with Rhodes. He supported its expansionist policies and shared Rhodes's impatience with the Afrikaner government in the Transvaal under "Oom Paul" KRUGER. He was involved in the ill-fated Leander Starr JAMESON raid, which attempted to overthrow the Transvaal government. He was forced to resign from the BSAC board and lost some £200,000 in the process. He spent similar sums on military equipment for the troops in the Boer War of 1899–1902.

Beit believed in using his fortune generously. He built a mansion in London and developed a superior collection of Renaissance paintings. He also founded an endowed chair of colonial history at Oxford University and generously donated to Oxford's Bodleian Library. In 1902 he had a stroke but continued his philanthropic work until his death. He left £2 million to charities, most in Africa: £200,000 for education in Rhodesia, a similar sum for fellowships for medical research in South Africa, £1.2 million for the Cape-to-Cairo railway, and various small grants. A shy and quiet man with no social pretensions, Beit had always given privately to causes that touched him, especially those involving relief for the suffering and destitute, and his generosity was revealed by his will.

References: DAHB, DNB, *wiki*. Alfred Beit II, *The Will and the Way* (1958).

BEKELE, Kenenisa
(Ethiopia, 1982–)

Gold medalist Kenenisa Bekele has been a consistent winner in 10,000-meter cross-country competitions, as well as a champion in shorter races. In 2005, he emerged the gold medalist in the 10,000 at the IAAF World Championships after a dazzling 200-meter kick finish. His regular competition has been with his compatriot Haile GEBRSELASSIE, whom he has bested two out of three times.

Bekele was born near Bekoji in the Arsi highlands south of Addis Ababa, an area where boys begin running as youngsters in the high altitude atmosphere. He played soccer football as a boy, when his coaches encouraged him to take up running. He began training with Gebrselassie, who became both a mentor and coach for him.

Bekele took gold in the Athens Olympics in 2004 in the 10,000-meter run and silver in the 5,000. In 2004, he broke the world records in indoor and outdoor 5,000-meter and outdoor 10,000, where he bested Gebrselassie's 1998 record by two minutes, 44 seconds. He took both World Championships in 2005 as well.

In 2002, beginning at age 19, Bekele began a string of four IAAF World Cross Country championships in both the short and long races. No one else has even done both in a single year, much less multiple times. In 2006, he began exploring the mile length, but at first found the conditions strange. The tight curves, which call for different muscle reactions, and the short track made demands on Bekele for which his training had not prepared him. Bekele is short and light at 5'3" and 54 kilos (119 pounds), ideal height and weight for the mile. He placed well in his first mile races, and seems set to dominate that length as well as in cross country.

References: adb, EB, *wiki*.

BELL, Rudolf Douala Manga
(Cameroon, 1873–1914)

Prince Rudolf Douala Manga Bell was educated in Germany as one of a tiny elite group of Africans who were groomed by the German colonial administration. He was the son of the chief who governed Douala, an important town, and he succeeded his father in 1908. Bell had been a loyal servant of the German occupation, but the increased demands of forced labor and the brutal way that the Germans suppressed Cameroonian resistance between 1904 and 1907 seems to have caused Bell to question their policies. Within two years he came into conflict with the colonial authorities over land seizures that were in violation of an 1884 treaty. The incident seemed to turn Bell against the Germans. Relations deteriorated, and the German colonial authorities removed him from his chieftaincy in 1913.

It is difficult to determine his state of mind at the time. He apparently continued to hope for progress under colonialism but considered the Germans too repressive, because when World War I began, he turned toward the French. Finding a kindred spirit in the equally disillusioned resistance leader Martin-Paul SAMBA, Bell supposedly began to lay plans for resistance, but there is no evidence of the conspiracy. The German authorities believed that he contacted the French to coordinate an uprising with a joint British-French invasion of German Cameroon. Arrested and accused of fomenting rebellion, Bell was hanged on 8 August 1914, the same day that Samba was executed by firing squad.

References: afr, DAHB, MMA.

BELLO, Ahmadu
(Nigeria, 1910–1966)

Alhaji Sir Ahmadu Bello was one of the three rival independence leaders, along with Dr. Nnamdi AZIKIWE and Chief Obafemi AWOLOWO, who dominated Nigerian politics during the country's transition to independence. His natural base was northern Nigeria, which held a commanding position in the Nigerian federation thanks in part to Bello. He also achieved international status among Muslims by tirelessly working to restore what he saw as the rightful respect that West Africa had once held in the Islamic world.

Bello was a direct descendant of UTHMAN Dan Fodio, the illustrious leader of the Islamic revival a century earlier. When he finished school, Bello became a teacher. In 1938, however, following the death of the sultan of Sokoto, who then played the most powerful political and religious role in northern Nigeria, Bello aspired to the office. He lost to Siddiq ABUBAKAR, who appointed him *sardauna* (war leader), a largely honorary position. During World War II, Bello began to engage in broader politics, and in 1948 a youth group he had formed merged with the Northern People's Congress (NPC), which was destined to become the leading political party of the north. By 1949 he was a member of the northern assembly, becoming minister for community development and local government. In 1954 he was elected the first premier of Northern Nigeria, a position that he held until his death.

As head of the NPC and premier, Bello was the most powerful individual in Nigeria during the years immediately following independence in 1960. He preferred to stay in the north, but his NPC deputy, Abubakar Tafawa BALEWA, was made federal prime minister. Nigerian public opinion presumed that Bello was the de facto ruler and power behind the throne, and in fact he did expect Balewa to check all major policy issues with him. His open use of northern power to dominate the country made Bello unpopular in the south. He also had opponents in the north, but these he suppressed or kept in check. Bello's monopoly power threatened progressives who resented his conservatism, Islamic orthodoxy, and undisguised political maneuvering. In a failed coup, he and Balewa were assassinated in 1966, ending the First Republic and ushering in a period of military government in Nigeria.

Bello always maintained his interest in Islamic affairs. He made the pilgrimage to Mecca annually, built mosques, and sponsored theological conferences. It was no secret that he hoped to succeed to the sultanate, saying in 1965, "I would rather be sultan of Sokoto than president of Nigeria." Bello engaged in "conversion campaigns" in the north and became vice president of the World Islamic League. He was uncomfortable with Nigeria's recognition of Israel (and disapproved of its use of Israeli technical aid) but avoided entanglement in Arab politics.

Bello's greatest achievement was to move his region from a backward and weak one to a position of prominence and dominance in Nigeria. He was always the aristocrat, never concealing his disgust at the rabble of Lagos, the capital. Nonetheless, Bello remained approachable to working people and peasants and was on good terms with most political leaders, although he always carried the stigma of authoritarianism.

References: afr, DAHB, EWB, MMA, PLBA, PLCA. John Paden, *Ahmadu Bello, Sardauna of Sokoto* (1986).

BELLO, Muhammad
(Nigeria, 1781–1837)

Sultan Muhammad Bello, the son of UTHMAN Dan Fodio, completed the Islamic revolution that created the Sokoto caliphate.

Until the nineteenth century, Islam had spread mostly peacefully and spasmodically in West Africa, but after 1800 there was a series of *jihads* (religious wars) led by clerics who hoped to purify Islam of traditional African beliefs. The clerics also hoped to move beyond Islam's focus on personal faith by creating a state based on Islamic law and practice. Thus, Islam provided a major bond of national unity.

Uthman Dan Fodio began a series of campaigns in 1804 to conquer a number of Hausa-speaking states in what is now northern Nigeria to form a united Islamic state. Bello, at 23, was made a field commander and proved himself especially skilled in cavalry tactics. In 1812, after a series of victories, the conquered Hausa states were divided between Muhammad and his uncle. Muhammad became governor of the eastern half of present-day northern

Nigeria. He established a capital at Sokoto, where he governed until his father's death in 1817. Upon taking the throne, he assumed the title of sultan of Sokoto and began to work at unifying the empire and extending it into the rural areas. He welded the Hausa states together into one empire but constantly had to subdue attempted revolts and external threats. He led his troops into battle more than 40 times. Bello was impartial in the administration of justice in the conquered nations and generous in providing educational opportunities, which gradually won over the Hausa.

Bello was an accomplished historian and poet as well as a distinguished Muslim scholar. He facilitated the political transition from a system of hereditary kings who wielded ritual religious power (often based on magic) to a system in which Allah was the accepted source of authority. Muslim authority is accountable to the community, and therefore, the emirs (the regional governors), chosen for their Islamic fidelity, ruled within a shared system. The principal administration of the caliphate was small and loyal, and was also the center of Islamic courts and scholarship. Many scholars and teachers had died during Bello's *jihad*, but education was nevertheless expanded under his regime. Women teachers were educated—a rarity in Islam—textbooks were printed, the educational system grew to over 50,000 students after Bello's death, and Sokoto became a center for Islamic scholarship. UMAR Ibn Said, for example, studied and resided in the city from 1830 to 1838 and used his learning to lead his own *jihad* and establish the Tukulor empire.

Reference: afr, DAHB.

BEMBA, Jean-Pierre
(Democratic Republic of the Congo, 1962–)

Jean-Pierre Bemba, longtime activist in the Democratic Republic of the Congo (DRC), formerly Zaïre, is presently vice president of the country in its transition government as a result of the 2002 peace settlement. Bemba was the founder and remains the strongman and leader of the Congolese Rally for Democracy-Movement of Liberation of the Congo (RCD-MLC), which he began in the 1990s. Under the agreement, Bemba has the power of appointment of the DRC foreign minister, control of two of the country's 10 military districts, and the appointment of two major national military commanders.

Bemba was born in Equator Province, the son of a wealthy family that was always well connected politically. Bemba is related by marriage to the former dictator MOBUTU Sese Seko, one of whose sons married Bemba's sister. Bemba was educated in Belgium, finishing with a graduate degree in business. Through the 1990s, he prospered in Zaïre as an entrepreneur, especially in aviation and telecommunications. When in 1997 the forces of Laurent-Désirée KABILA took power in Zaïre, Bemba allied himself with them. The following year, he created an armed force to parallel the MLC, the Army for the Liberation of the Congo (ALC).

During the Second Congo War, the ALC was backed by Uganda, acting as a proxy for Yoweri MUSEVENI's interests in the eastern provinces of the DRC. The ALC was known for its brutality (although that was common among all forces in Ituri Province in eastern Congo). The United Nations brought charges of murder, rape and cannibalism against 20 ALC troops, but Bemba managed the trial, which the central government denounced as a sham. Admitting the killings, Bemba defended his men against the charges of cannibalism and rape. Over 350 witnesses to various barbarities were interviewed in the investigation, however.

Reference: fr.wikipedia.org, *wiki*.

BESTER, Willie
(South Africa, 1956–)

The artist Willie Bester has shot from relative obscurity on the international art scene to considerable prominence in a few years. Collectors have been buying his work at prices double their original estimates, and he is sought for in major exhibitions. Several museums have added his work to their collections. In 2004–2006, he exhibited at the Africa Remix, which traveled from Düsseldorf to London, on to the Georges Pompidou Centre in Paris, then closing in Tokyo. It solidified Bester's reputation and gave him important exposure.

Bester was born in the Western Cape. As a child, he learned to be a dental assistant. At 19 he studied art for a year at the Community Art Project in Cape Town, and two years later held his first exhibition. In 1991 he became a full-time profes-

sional artist, the same year he won a major national award, the Merit Prize, at the Cape Town Triennial.

Bester works in mixed media, using rough canvas or sackcloth, found objects, and crushed metal. The metal pieces are welded into large constructions, but his paintings are more modest in size. The themes vary, but many are overtly political and confront issues in South Africa's recent past. His 1999 collage, *Truth and Reconciliation*, swarms with patterns, from which emerge the faces of the oppressed. His 1997 installation, "Die Bybel," was a reference to the use of sacred scripture to justify racism by the Afrikaner community. As a mixed-race, mixed-ethnicity South African, Bester struggles with the meaning of apartheid. As a teen, he was conscripted for forced labor because he had not worked for a White person for three months. He constantly returns to one of three aspects of apartheid: the violence of South African society; the corruption of the Dutch Reformed Church in supporting racism; and the effects of the Group Areas Act, which segregated South Africans by color.

At first, Bester concentrated on mixed media, using photos and found objets in paintings of life in the Black shanty towns. Recent years saw him move into large metal sculptures using welded pieces, forceful in their presentation.

Bester lives and has a studio outside Cape Town. He designed the compound as a living and work space, but also as an architectural statement.

References: adb. www.williebester.co.za.

BETI, Mongo
(Cameroon, 1932–2001)

Mongo Beti, writer and political thinker, is one of the preeminent African novelists writing in French. After attending secondary school in Cameroon, Alexandre Biyidi Awala, as Beti was born, went to France in 1951 for higher education, which culminated in a doctorate in literature from the Sorbonne. After publication of his first novel, *Ville Cruelle* (1954), which he wrote under the name Eza Boto, he adopted his current name for subsequent writing. He has taught Latin, Greek and French literature through the years but has been active primarily as a writer. All of his novels center around the encroachment of Western values and religion on African cultures. Beti uses satire and mockery to describe

Western hypocrisy, but he does not spare his compatriots. African gullibility and naiveté are presented with equal scorn.

Beti published four novels from 1954 to 1958, all concerned with the inner decay of colonialism. After his first work, with which he was dissatisfied, he published his best-known novel, the powerful *Poor Christ of Bomba* (1965), which has been reprinted in several languages. It is a scathing satire of a missionary who attempts to convert the people of a small village in order to protect them from materialism. He discovers to his chagrin that they have become Christians only in order to learn the White man's secrets of wealth. When the missionary discovers that the house where young girls were to learn to be Christian mothers has instead become a den of vice, he returns to Europe, disheartened and defeated. Beti lays bare the soul of well-meaning Europeans who refuse to accept that their "help" is, in fact, a hindrance because they cannot grasp the values—or even the existence—of a vital African culture. The book caused a scandal in France.

Beti's style employs derision and contempt to unmask the colonial enterprise. *Mission Accomplished* (1957) and *King Lazarus* (1958) are farces edged with bitterness. The former presents a debate between a missionary bent on eliminating polygamy, a chief who has just divested himself of 22 wives, and a colonial administrator frightened by the social instability that might result from this change. The latter explores the way that French education has alienated the young African elite from their roots.

Beti sees no alternative to the political novel, calling Western fiction "sophisticated uselessness of gratuitous vulgarity." Political fiction, however, "can ruin tyrants, ... tear a whole people away from endless slavery, in a word, serve ... writing can serve a purpose, and therefore must serve a purpose." Beti is highly critical of African writers who do not accept this premise, attacking Ferdinand OYONO for accepting African despotism and accusing CAMARA Laye of a "folkloric" vision of Africa that lacks political responsibility.

For more than 10 years Beti lived in Normandy, France, with his French wife and taught literature. He did not write again until publishing a polemic in 1972, *The Plundering of Cameroon,* which denounced the neocolonialism following independence. It was banned in France for five years until Beti won a hard-fought court battle. The hollow corruption of postcolonial Africa became the theme of his next group of novels: *Remember Ruben* (1973), *Perpetua and the Habit of Unhappiness* (1974), and *Lament for an African Pol* (1979). All criticize the despotism of independent Cameroon, and all were banned there.

Beti was strongly opposed to the regime of Ahmadou AHIDJO, and he later returned to Cameroon to campaign against the government of Paul BIYA when political parties were legalized in 1991. This resulted in a memoire and polemic, *France contre l'Afrique: retour de Cameroun* (France against Africa: the return to Cameroon,1993). He opened a bookstore in Yaoundé in 1994, but in 1996 the police harassed and physically manhandled him. In 1999 and 2000 he published two of three projected volumes of a trilogy, but died of kidney failure before finishing the third. Despite his long exile, he remains a popular figure in Cameroon.

References: afr, AA, CA, DAHB, MBW, NRG, *wiki,* WLTC.

BEYALA, Calixthe
(Cameroon, 1961–)

Novelist Calixthe Beyala is a leading West African writer in French. She has published 12 novels, six in the 1990s. Besides being prolific, she is also a controversial, strongly feminist writer with a radical bent.

Beyala was born into a large and poor family in the slums of Douala. Despite her disadvantages, she was educated and went to France at 17 to be married. She continues to live in Paris, and has never returned to Cameroon. At 26 she published her first novel, setting on a path of exploring taboo topics—the violence of men upon women, prostitution, and female genital mutilation. Beyala does not shy away from depicting sexual pleasure in women, sometimes in graphic forms. A recent work, *Femme nue, femme noire* (Nude woman, Black woman, 2003) is an frankly erotic novel, proudly feminist.

Beyala argues for a community of women across cultures in essays and her novels. One long essay is addressed to Western women from an African woman, calling for a united front against patriarchal oppression. Her later novels have been set in the French African diaspora as well as in Africa itself. The uniting motif is always the common experience of women, their suffering and the need for liberation.

Beyala's novels have won such prizes as the Grand Prix Littéraire del'Afrique Noire (1993), the 1994 Prix François Mauriac of the prestigious French Academy, the Prix Tropique (1994), and finally, the most esteemed of all, the French Academy's Grand Prize for Fiction (1996).

Reference: adb, WLTC.

BHIMJI, Zarina
(Uganda, 1963–)

Among African artists, Zarina Bhimji is one of the few notable art photographers. For 20 years she has taken part in exhibitions throughout Europe at some of the major museums, beginning in 1985 with the Artists Against Apartheid exhibition in London and three other exhibits.

Bhimji was born in Uganda. As an African of Indian ethnicity, she and her family followed the exodus to England of so many Indo-Africans expelled by Idi AMIN in 1972. At first, the family went into hiding in Uganda, hoping for a reprieve from the 90-day order to leave, but after two years the family fled to Great Britain. Bhimji lives and works in London, where she teaches at the London College of Printing.

Bhimji took up art as a teenager when she studied traditional weaving. In England she graduated from Goldsmith's in 1986, and then spent a year at the Slade School of Fine Art. From the start, she has been associated with the Black Artists Movement. Despite the persecution of East Asians by Amin, her sentiments went with oppressed Black Africans, and her work reflects her interests in gender and race issues, identity and power. When she became fascinated with the race theories of Francis Galton (1822–1911), the founder of modern eugenics, she produced an installation of over a hundred portraits crossing (and crisscrossing) ethnic and racial boundaries. She has famously used preserved body parts as subjects for a 1996 photographic exhibit exploring the boundaries between life and death and beauty in what is thrown away.

Bhimji's work is not limited to photography. She explores the use of mixed media, including found objects. These are usually personal effects of her own, sometimes assembled in small boxes as the ephemera of a life. She has also been experimenting with film as a new media for her. Her first, *Out of the*

Blue (2002), avoids plot, characters and linear forms so that viewers' responses remain their own.

In 2001, Bhimji produced a photo exhibit based on her only return visit to Uganda. She wanted to document her sense of loss and Uganda's deprivation in expelling the East Asian community, very few of whom have gone back from their exile. None of the photos show persons, only emptiness as a metaphor for absence and silence.

Reference: adb.

BHUNU
(Swaziland, 1873?–1899)

Bhunu was paramount chief of the Swazi when British control was imposed on Swaziland. He succeeded to the throne as a minor in 1889 and was placed under the guidance of his mother, who acted as queen regent. He took his full position in 1895.

Bhunu's father, Mbandzeni, had been assisted in gaining the throne by the Afrikaners of the neighboring Transvaal, who wanted a pliable king and found one in the alcoholic Mbandzeni. Mbandzeni sold off major concessions to European traders, including land, minerals, and trading monopolies, and then foolishly allowed an all-White council the right of self-government.

After Mbandzeni's death, this council established joint British-Afrikaner rule (1890) and made Bhunu their puppet. The council confirmed 352 of the 364 concessions, and during his regency, the Transvaal Republic bought up the concessions to lay a legal basis for annexing the kingdom.

The Afrikaners, who governed the Transvaal, were land-hungry expansionists. They were especially interested in annexing Swaziland to gain access to the ocean, where they needed a seaport to protect their trade from being strangled. In all this international intrigue, Swaziland was a weak pawn. In 1894 the British accepted the Transvaal's control of Swaziland on the single proviso that the Afrikaners would not annex it outright. The queen regent and her council protested and sent a delegation to London, but the agreement had been made, and Bhunu was forced to submit. The following year, the Transvaal sent a resident commissioner, who effectively took authority away from the royal family.

Three years later, Bhunu was accused of murdering a Swazi official and had to flee the country.

After paying a fine, he was reinstated as king, but he had no real power. He died suddenly while performing the *Nkwala*, the most sacred Swazi religious ceremony, symbolic of the fertility of the sea, the people and the land. In its final stage, warriors dance around the king's *kraal*, imploring him to emerge from seclusion. When Bhunu's death was announced, many saw it as a sign of the collapse of the power of the chieftaincy. His infant son, SOBHUZA II, succeeded him.

References: DAHB, *wiki.*

BIKILA, Abebe
(Ethiopia, 1932–1973)

Abebe Bikila, a famous long-distance runner whose Olympic marathon records still stand, was also a leader in sports for the handicapped. At the 1960 Rome Olympics, Bikila competed as a virtually unknown athlete and surprised the world by setting a world marathon record of 2:15:15, despite having had an appendix operation six weeks before the race and being allowed only limited training. The thrilling race (the first to be widely seen on television) was decided in the last thousand yards, and Bikila ran barefoot, which made the victory all the more astounding and endeared him to the public. Bikila's only previous organized sports experience had been in amateur soccer, which he had played as a member of Emperor HAILE SELASSIE's palace guard.

At the 1964 Tokyo Olympics, Bikila repeated his feat by breaking his own record with a 2:12:11 win. Four years later, an ankle injury kept him from completing the marathon at Mexico City, where his high-altitude training would have put him at an advantage. The following year, Bikila was paralyzed as a result of an auto accident. He became active in paraplegic track and field events and founded the Ethiopian Paraplegic Sports Association. As a paraplegic athlete, he competed in archery and javelin events. The Germans made him an honored guest at the 1972 Munich Olympics. Upon his death, he was given a national hero's funeral.

Reference: afr, DAHB, *wiki.*

BIKO, Steve
(South Africa, 1947–1977)

Steve Biko was the inspiration and intellectual leader of the Black Consciousness Movement (BCM) and became its martyr. Biko interrupted his medical studies after founding the South African Students Organisation (SASO) in 1969. He articulated a theory of Black consciousness, borrowing radical rhetoric from the American Black power movement but using operative principles from nonviolent liberation programs. SASO began legal aid and medical clinics as well as cottage industries, especially for youth, and Biko became a hero among them. SASO drew support from educated Blacks, churches, and the intelligentsia. The movement attacked the slave mentality of the oppressed and promoted a liberation based on self-reliance and Black identity. Organizationally, in addition to SASO, there were support systems for the families of political prisoners and a wide variety of associations, including sports leagues. In 1972 these banded together in the Black People's Convention, with Biko as president. He was immediately expelled from medical school.

In 1973 Biko was banned by the South African government, which meant that he was prohibited from being quoted or from speaking to more than one person at a time. He was detained and interrogated four times. During the last interrogation (in 1977) he died in police custody.

The minister of justice said that Biko's death resulted from the effects of a hunger strike, attempting to cover up the murder and treating it with coldness. Biko's close friend, journalist and editor Donald WOODS, got into the autopsy room and photographed the bludgeoned body. When the picture appeared in his paper the next day, it caused a sensation. There was autopsy evidence of brain damage and extensive abrasions. Biko had been taken, naked and chained, in a Land Rover for a 12-hour trip to the hospital and died en route. The family sued the government (eventually settling out of court for R65,000 (then about $25,000), and the subsequent court hearing exposed the corruption of the South African police and security systems. The effect of Biko's death was widespread, and a wave of popular revulsion against the apartheid policies of South Africa grew across the West.

Woods, who was himself banned, fled to England in the aftermath of the murder after

Steve Biko

numerous death threats and an attempt at poisoning his daughter. In 1978 he wrote an account of his friendship with Biko and his own escape. In 1987 it was made into a film, *Cry Freedom,* by Sir Richard Attenborough, which brought Biko's case to the attention of a wider public.

References: AB, *afr*, EB, HH, MMA, *wiki*. Donald Woods, *Biko* (1978); *Cry Freedom* (film, 1987); Mamphela Ramphele, *Bounds of Possibility: The Legacy of Steve Biko* (1991).

BINAISA, Godfrey Lukongwa
(Uganda, 1920–)

Godfrey Lukongwa Binaisa, a leading personality during Uganda's first republic, became president after the overthrow of Idi AMIN Dada. Thoroughly Westernized and highly educated, Binaisa is a member of the dominant Baganda people. After completing his undergraduate education at Makerere University, he studied law in London and became the first (and only) Ugandan to be made Queen's Counsel, a prestigious honor.

During the 1960s, Binaisa practiced law in Kampala and was active in the Uganda People's Congress (UPC), one of the country's two major parties. At independence in 1962 he was appointed attorney general by Milton OBOTE. Following Obote's exile of King Freddie MUTESA II and Obote's subsequent self-proclaimed presidency, Binaisa resigned. He had strongly protested Obote's use of his powers of detention without trial. Always a democrat, he opposed Obote's authoritarian style and his suspension of the constitution. During the remaining years of Obote's first period as president, Binaisa substituted juridical activities for political ones. He served as president of the Law Society and as a member of the Judicial Service Committee, and helped organize the Commonwealth Lawyers' Conference. The law firm he established was pointedly interracial, with African, White, and Asian partners. After Amin seized power, Binaisa—who was Israel's lawyer in Uganda—was accused of Zionism and threatened personally by Amin. He went into exile (1972–1979) in the United States, where he practiced law in New York and became involved with exile anti-Amin forces.

When Amin was overthrown, Binaisa returned home and was made president of Uganda (1979–1980) by a coalition of exile groups. He never overcame his earlier association with Obote among the Ugandan people, however, and there were widespread demonstrations against his taking the presidency. The country's economic crisis was beyond his ability to resolve, and he could not contain the political conflicts within the country. His presidency survived only one year and was overthrown by a political cabal working at the behest of President Julius NYERERE of Tanzania, a close friend of Obote, who was restored to office. After a year under house arrest, Binaisa escaped to Kenya, but when Obote sent an assassination squad after him, he again fled to the United States. He had meanwhile allied himself with Yoweri MUSEVENI and his United Patriotic Movement (UPM). Binaisa practiced as a trial lawyer representing the City of New York until retirement.

The retirement years did not last long. In 2002 Binaisa returned to Uganda, where he is the only living ex-president to be pensioned by the government. He plunged immediately back into politics, but his attempts to challenge the Museveni government drew little response. In 2005, he wed Tomoko Yamamoto in a lavish ceremony that was followed throughout the country.

Reference: PLBA, *wiki*.

BINGER, Louis Gustave
(Sénégal/Côte d'Ivoire, 1856–1936)

Louis Gustave Binger was a French explorer and administrator who helped to extend French colonial designs during the critical period when European powers were scrambling for control of Africa.

He first came to the continent in 1880 as a young officer in a military mapping expedition of Sénégal. He returned in 1887 as part of an exploratory team sent into the interior to negotiate treaties with the local chiefs. For two years they traveled through what is now Sénégal, Côte d'Ivoire, Guinea, and Burkina Faso for over 2,500 miles (4,000 kilometers). Binger reached as far as Ouagadougou, the capital of the Mossi Empire (and of modern Burkina Faso) but was unable to obtain a treaty from the Mossi. The French imperial agenda became clear when, treaties failing, military force was used to conquer the Mossi in 1896. Binger wrote a two-volume account of the voyage, *Du Niger au Golfe de Guinée* (From the Niger to the Gulf of Guinea, 1890–1892), a major historical source of information on the region during that period.

In 1893, Binger was named governor of Côte d'Ivoire, which was only nominally under French control. The importance of Binger's explorations is indicated by the fact that the major French colonial thrust into Côte d'Ivoire came from the interior territories, which he had secured, and not from the coast. Binger's administration was dominated by continued military campaigns of consolidation, although he does not seem to have taken part in them personally. The period from 1895 to 1898 was a peaceful one, and Binger was transferred to Paris in 1897 and named director of African Affairs in the Ministry of the Colonies. From 1909 to 1934 the capital of Côte d'Ivoire was in a town on the coast named Bingerville in his honor. The name went unchanged after the end of the colonial period.

Reference: afr, DAHB, wiki.

BIYA, Paul
(Cameroon, 1933–)

Paul Biya, president of Cameroon since 1982, when Ahmadou AHIDJO resigned suddenly, has engaged in a long struggle to maintain his authority.

President Paul Biya of Cameroon with U.S. Secretary of State Colin Powell. Circa 2002.

A Catholic from the south, Biya completed his secondary education in Paris at the Lycée Louis le Grand and then received a law degree at the University of Paris in 1960. He stayed in France to study public law at the Institute of Overseas Studies. Returning to newly independent Cameroon in 1962, he was named head of the foreign aid office directly under President Ahmadou Ahidjo, who became his political mentor. The two became personally close, although their backgrounds and temperaments were quite different. The urbane Biya, who reads Latin and Greek and has a taste for classical music, was a loyal disciple of the Muslim Ahidjo, a former telephone operator with only an elementary education. Until 1975, Biya held a succession of staff positions under Ahidjo, including chief of cabinet, secretary general to the president, and minister of state. In 1975, Ahidjo chose him for prime minister.

In 1982, worried by health problems, Ahidjo resigned and Biya succeeded to the presidency. Although Biya appointed a prime minister from the north of the nation, he replaced many Ahidjo loyalists with southerners who were more loyal to him. Cameroon is the result of a 1961 merger of two trust territories, one British and one French. There has been ongoing tension and rivalry between the two language areas, as well as between north and south. Biya soon found that the northerners entrenched in the bureaucracy would not yield to his direction, and after two bloody coup attempts in 1983, he began to tighten his control. In 1984 elections Biya was returned to office with a comfortable margin. He then challenged Ahidjo, who had remained as head of the ruling party, and at the

1985 party congress, Biya took control of the party. Ahidjo, in exile in France, was tried *in absentia* and convicted for conspiracy in the failed coups.

Biya reacted to challenges to his authority by backing away from political liberalization. While candidates were allowed to contest elections by law, complex and extensive regulations ensured that electoral challenges never took place. Finally, in 1987, bowing to pressures, Biya allowed contests in municipal elections, but only with independent candidates in a non-partisan system, and a qualification procedure so cumbersome as to defeat the purpose. Opposition parties were finally legalized in 1991. Critics called for a national constituent assembly, and backed up their demands with nationwide general strikes. Biya announced parliamentary elections for 1992, which his party narrowly won, and then went on to defeat the leader of the English-speaking region and four other candidates for the presidency in an election that was probably fraudulent. Cameroon has disputed claims of Nigeria to the oil-rich Bakassi Peninsula, and armed clashes broke out between the two countries in 1994 and 1996. An international court has awarded the territory to Cameroon, but Nigeria refuses to remove its troops.

Brutality and extortion are widespread in Cameroon under Biya, and the economy has shrunk by half since he took power. For several years, Cameroon had the dubious distinction of ranking number one on the corruption index. Oil revenues have not been reported as part of the national budget, and Biya has profited from that. Extra-judicial executions, ethnic cleansing and mass graves all point to a vicious, repressive regime.

References: afr, DAHB, PLBA, RWWA, *wiki.*

BLAIZE, Richard Beale
(Nigeria, 1845–1904)

Richard Beale Blaize was the wealthiest African businessman in West Africa in the era before Europeans drove Africans out of commercial competition.

Born in Sierra Leone to recaptive Yoruba parents, who were freed from slave traders by the British navy, Blaize went to Nigeria at age 17. Speaking Yoruba and with the advantages of missionary education, he immediately was accepted in his parents' homeland. Blaize entered the print-

ing business and was head printer for the government for 12 years. In 1875 he established himself as a merchant trader. Recognizing that there was a market for quality cloth, he created designs with African patterns that he had printed in England. His business prospered, and by 1888 he was a member of the Chamber of Commerce and the wealthiest African in the colony.

With his large fortune, Blaize dabbled in a number of ventures and became an active churchman. He founded several newspapers, most of which lost money but which served as voices for his nationalist views. He was critical of the colonial government and used his papers to promote Pan-Africanism. His death marked the close of a period in which African businessmen successfully competed in the newly developing towns and cities. With missionary education, both men and women showed initiative and competence. By 1900, however, European merchants were systematically forcing them out of business by making favorable deals in Europe, where Africans could not compete. Blaize's daughter continued his business, but without the same success.

References: DAHB, MMA.

BLIXEN, Karen
(Kenya, 1885–1962)

Baroness Karen Blixen was a member of Kenyan settler society from 1914 to 1931, and her writings about that era have influenced popular Western impressions of African colonialism.

Born into a prosperous Danish family, Karen Blixen married her cousin, Baron Bror Blixen-Fineke, after a failed love affair with his twin brother. Together they bought a coffee plantation just outside Nairobi. She sailed to Kenya in 1913, becoming a shipboard friend of General Paul VON LETTOW-VORBECK, who was on his way to take command of German forces in their Tanganyika colony. This friendship would make Blixen's loyalties suspect to the British during World War I.

The aristocratic Bror Blixen-Fineke, a big-game hunter, was a notorious philanderer who infected his wife with syphilis, from which she suffered for the rest of her life. For her part, the baroness had various love affairs and engaged in a torrid romance with a dashing, daredevil British settler, Denys Finch-Hatton. She lived with him from 1925 to 1931 and was twice pregnant by him but miscarried. The Blixens divorced in 1921.

The plantation suffered consistent losses because of its poor land and poorer management. When the coffee market collapsed in 1931, Blixen was forced to sell everything and return to Denmark. At the same time, Finch-Hatton was killed when his plane crashed.

During her lover's absences, Blixen had taken to composing tales to share with him on his return. As the farm's financial crisis deepened, she began writing both stories and lengthy letters home. On her return to Europe, these writings formed the basis of *Seven Gothic Tales* (1934), which was an immediate success. In a sharp break from contemporary Danish realistic fiction, *Seven Gothic Tales* was written in English and was a book of extraordinary fantasy, reflecting an atmosphere of indulgence and decadence. Blixen wrote under the pen name Isak Dinesen, which added to the book's mysterious style. She did not reveal her identity until 50,000 copies of the book had been sold. She went on to write five books that were selected by the Book-of-the-Month Club in the United States, where she achieved a large following.

Blixen's second book, *Out of Africa* (1937), drew upon the personalities and characters she had known in Kenya. Presented as an autobiography, it was a hauntingly poetic romance that suppressed the unpleasant and too-personal aspects of her story. It evoked British Kenyan settler society, which she generally disliked, as trivial and boring. As a Dane, she seemed always to feel the outsider among White colonials. A review in the *Saturday Review of Literature* described the book's style as "cadenced, constrained, and [as] graceful as we have today." The Africans in Blixen's work are described with affection and sensitivity but are unfailingly simple, loyal and without insight. Her patronizing attitude was considered progressive in her day. Although the book was popular in the West, she never garnered much respect among Africans.

Writing under her pen name, Blixen became an international literary figure and was nominated for the Nobel Prize in literature several times. Ernest Hemingway, upon receiving that award in 1954, remarked, "This really belongs to Bror's wife." In 1960, shortly before her death, she published *Shadows on the Grass*, another romantic reverie of colonial Africa, which focused on her African servants. There was a tremendous revival of her work after the film *Out of Africa* was made in 1985.

The movie starred Meryl Streep as Blixen and Robert Redford as her lover. It received seven Oscars and was a commercial success. As a result, the book *Out of Africa* sold more than 700,000 additional copies, introducing Blixen's work to a whole new generation. Posthumously, Blixen's collected *Letters from Africa* (1981), written during the most difficult days of her time on the farm, illuminate the shadows so carefully preserved in *Out of Africa*. They reveal the private and often painful truths behind the imaginative romance presented in the latter work.

Despite her literary and commercial success, Blixen was constantly obsessed with not having enough money. She became addicted to amphetamines and ate almost nothing in her later years, until she finally died of malnutrition.

References: CANR, DAHB, EWB, WLTC, *wiki.* Olga Pelensky, *Isak Dinesen: The Life and Imagination of a Seducer* (1991); Judith Thurman, *Isak Dinesen: The Life of a Storyteller* (1982).

BLYDEN, Edward Wilmot
(Liberia/Sierra Leone, 1832–1912)

Edward Wilmot Blyden, born in the Virgin Islands, was one of the most important nineteenth-century Afro-Caribbean intellectuals and the originator of the theory of Pan-Africanism. He also became a prominent educator and political leader in Liberia.

Blyden traveled to the United States to become a clergyman, but when no American theological school would admit him because of his race, Blyden left for Liberia in 1851. He studied at the Alexander High School in Monrovia, where he received a scholarship because of his character and ability. He acquired a broad knowledge of literature, languages, theology and history. In 1856 he wrote an influential pamphlet, *A Voice from Bleeding Africa on Behalf of Her Exiled Children Everywhere,* which had considerable impact on Black nationalists. From 1862 to 1871 he was professor of classics at Liberia College, the first secular English college in tropical Africa, and during this time he entered Liberian politics. He served as secretary of state from 1864 to 1866 and became a close associate of Edward ROYE, Liberia's first Black president. When bitter divisions broke out over color, false moral accusations were made against Blyden by the light-skinned faction, and he was dragged through the streets and almost lynched. He fled to Sierra Leone a few months before Roye himself was murdered. Blyden stayed in Sierra Leone for two years and founded a newspaper—the first to advocate Pan-Africanism.

In 1874 Blyden returned to Liberia, for which he served as ambassador to Britain and president of Liberia College. In 1885 he ran for president of Liberia but lost. After that he divided his time between Liberia and Sierra Leone, where he was director of Muslim education from 1901 to 1906. As an Arabic scholar, he promoted Islam even though he himself was a Christian minister.

Although Blyden's public service was significant, his intellectual contributions were far more lasting. He sought to prove that Africans had a noble history and culture, and he opposed theories of White superiority. Although he was a Christian, he was critical of the racial discrimination practiced within Christian churches and challenged the suitability of Christianity for Africa, especially in his *Christianity, Islam and the Negro Race* (1887). This work also defended such African customs as polygamy.

There were two central points in Blyden's thought: the emergence of an "African personality" and the unity of all African peoples. To foster the first, he favored the use of African names and opposed colonialism, which he was convinced would have a devastating psychological effect on Africans. Blyden sought a modern Africa based on African rather than European culture, with higher education and cultural institutions reflecting the needs of the continent. This emphasis would involve reclaiming the African personality from the degradation of slavery, restoring racial pride, and rediscovering Black history. Blyden argued that miscegenation was contrary to nature, and he asked American sponsors to send only "pure" Blacks to Liberia.

To achieve the unity of Black peoples, Blyden hoped for a single leading African state that would champion the cause of Blacks everywhere and be a focus for their advancement. His original hope was that this nation would arise from the union of Liberia and Sierra Leone, and he spent some years promoting repatriation of former slaves and of Afro-Caribbeans. He subsequently adopted the curious position that Western imperialism and colonialism would be transitional and would promote African unity. Hence, he foolishly took part in several schemes to promote European intervention, including a 1909 attempted coup in Liberia. Although he

was unpopular among many Liberians because of these adventures, in his later years Blyden won widespread respect abroad that brought him honorary doctorates and decorations from Turkey, France, Britain and Tunisia.

References: afr, DAHB, EWB, MMA, WGMC. Hollis Lynch, *Edward Wilmot Blyden: Pan-Negro Patriot* (1967).

BOESAK, Allan Aubrey
(South Africa, 1945–)

Reverend Allan Aubrey Boesak was president of the World Alliance of Reformed Churches (WARC) and a founder of the antiapartheid United Democratic Front (UDF) in the 1980s.

Boesak was born into a family active in the Dutch Reformed Mission Church (NGS), a Reformed denomination established for the Coloured population. The mixed-race Coloureds are an Afrikaans-speaking people who have not been very politically active, in part due to their relatively favorable social and economic position between the dominant White minority and the previously repressed Black majority. Boesak attended the University of the Western Cape and then Bellville Theological Seminary, from which he graduated in 1967. During his college and seminary years he began to react against racial segregation and what he called "ecclesiastical colonialism," the paternalistic and racist attitudes of the Reformed churches. In 1964 he met the Reverend Beyers NAUDÉ, a White minister who had just been forced out of his position as moderator of the White Dutch Reformed Church for his antiapartheid stand. Naudé persuaded Boesak that he could best serve within the NGS, and he was ordained in 1968. Boesak subsequently traveled to the Netherlands and received a doctorate in theology.

Returning to South Africa in 1976, Boesak plunged into politics. He was a key member of the Broederkring, the "Brothers' Circle" of Reformed clergy, which was dedicated to shaping the Reformed churches into an antiapartheid force. In 1981 he was elected as the first president of the Alliance of Black Reformed Christians, which rejected racism, asserted the right and duty of Christians to be involved in politics, and denied the divine institution of the state. The following year, at a Canadian meeting of the WARC, he proposed a condemnation of apartheid as heretical to the Gospel and a betrayal of Reformed tradition. After its passage and his election as president of the WARC, the two White Reformed bodies in South Africa (which supported apartheid) were expelled from membership. The actions of the WARC struck at the heart of apartheid ideology, which was based on a Christian biblical justification of racial separatism.

In 1983, Boesak called for the unity of all antiapartheid groups in South Africa to oppose the new constitution of President P. W. BOTHA, which established Indian and Coloured houses of parliament but excluded Blacks. This led to the formulation of the United Democratic Front, an umbrella group of more than 700 organizations that became the legal opposition during the period when African political organizations were banned. In 1984, Boesak was elected president of the South African Council of Churches (SACC).

Boesak became a tireless campaigner overseas against apartheid. A 1984 trip was instrumental in stiffening opposition to apartheid by the Australian government. He went to Zambia in 1985 to meet with Oliver TAMBO, exiled head of the African National Congress (ANC), and Kenneth KAUNDA, Zambia's president and leader of the Frontline States. In 1985 and 1986 he visited the United States, Switzerland, Thailand and Sweden. He was arrested in 1986 for demonstrating for the release of jailed ANC leader Nelson MANDELA, but charges were later dropped.

In 1986, Boesak, Naudé and Bishop Desmond TUTU formed a religious delegation to discuss with President Botha the violent protests in the African townships outside the urban centers. Botha ignored their suggestions and in 1988 the UDF was banned. The UDF then led a mass defiance campaign against the emergency regulations of 1989, but the election of F. W. DE KLERK as state president that year opened doors to reform. The ANC and other groups were no longer banned, and Mandela and the ANC leadership were freed from prison.

Just as these events took place, Boesak went into political eclipse after it was revealed that he was having an extramarital affair with a prominent White television producer, Elena Botha, the niece of a hard-line apartheid cabinet minister. Boesak was forced to resign from his church and as president of the WARC. He and his wife subsequently divorced, and he married Elena Botha. He led the ANC in the 1994 elections in the Western Cape Province and emerged as leader of the opposition in the provincial

legislature. All that ended in 1999, when he was convicted of fraud and theft of donor funds from a nonprofit development organization that he had established. Much of the money had been given to the organization by the American singer Paul Simon. Another $226,000 was a Swedish government grant, which Boesak used to build a radio studio for Elena. He served two years in prison and four on probation, but was pardoned (with the record expunged) by President Thabo MBEKI in 2005.

References: afr, CB, *dabc*, EWB, GSAP, PLBA, RWWA. David Scholtz, *The Story of Allan Boesak* (1989).

BOGANDA, Barthélemy
(Central African Republic, 1910–1959)

Abbé Barthélemy Boganda was the founding father of his country and a proponent of uniting the French West African states into a federation. He was sent to Catholic mission seminaries for his education after his mother was murdered by French company guards. In 1938 he was ordained as the first African priest in the colony, which was then called Oubangui-Shari. After serving in several missions, he then entered politics in 1946 to defend the rights of Africans. Supported by his bishop, he was elected to the French national assembly on the Catholic party ticket.

Boganda abandoned his church sponsorship and his priesthood in 1950, and in 1951 formed his own party, which quickly dominated politics in Oubangui-Shari. At first he was opposed by the French colonial authorities, but by 1953 they had accepted his unchallenged position. Boganda was able to work with a variety of interests, including French businessmen, who came to support him. In 1956 he tested his popularity by running for deputy mayor of the capital city in a White district against a White opponent and was elected easily. Immensely popular and a charismatic speaker, he had no effective opposition.

Boganda soon turned his energies to regional affairs, where he promoted a "United States of Latin Africa," a federation of former French, Belgian and Portuguese colonies into a powerful state, which he hoped to call the Central African Republic. He worked hard to keep the other French colonies together, but by 1958 independence movements and nationalism had shattered his dream, and he turned again to local affairs. That year, independence for Oubangui-Shari, which became the Central African Republic, was announced with elections scheduled for 1959. During the campaign, Boganda was killed in a plane crash that has never been fully explained.

He was the uncle of Jean-Bédel BOKASSA, who seized control of Boganda's party, a democratic movement, and perverted it for his own ends.

References: afr, DAHB, EB, MMA, *wiki.*

BOGHOSSIAN, Skunder
(Ethiopia, 1937–2003)

Skunder Boghossian was one of the most talented artists working in Africa, and the dean of modern Ethiopian artists. Ethiopians usually go by their first names, as Boghossian did for some years, but after settling in the United States, he followed the Western convention of using the last name. Both usages can be found.

Boghossian showed his talent early, although he had only sketchy art training until he went to England on a government scholarship in 1955. He attended several London art schools with little success but began to achieve his potential when he settled in Paris, where he stayed until 1966. In the meanwhile he had held two one-man shows in New York and displayed works in a number of other exhibitions in Europe and the United States. On his return to Ethiopia, he accepted a teaching position at the Fine Arts School in Addis Ababa (1966–1969) and then moved to Atlanta University in Georgia for five years. Finally, he settled at Howard University in Washington, D.C., where he taught from 1974 to 2000.

Despite his academic connections, he was primarily a working painter. In 1955, Boghossian was the first contemporary African artist to have his work purchased by the Museum of Modern Art (MOMA) in New York. In 1963, he was also the first African artist whose work was purchased by the Musée d'Art Moderne in Paris.

Boghossian's work reflected his interests in the cultures of his homeland, West Africa and Europe. Yet, his surrealist and abstract painting was a bold departure for Ethiopian art. Echoes of traditional Coptic art can be found in his work, often as simple reflections of form or in choice of colors. Coptic style is flat and naive and uses bright primary colors. In one of his best pieces, *Yin and Yang* (1967), the frame of the picture is that of a diptych, a two-paneled religious painting. Boghossian also used the flat, one-dimensional style of religious icons and the traditional reds and browns of Coptic church art. He often startled his viewers with phallic and oval forms that suggest restrained sensuality, but never included anything explicitly sexual. His work was unique in its obvious Ethiopian inspiration, expressed within a surrealistic style. Unlike other modern African artists, he had a long cultural tradition of painting to draw upon, and he was also influenced by Coptic architecture, especially the powerful rock-hewn temples of Lalibela. After one visit to Lalibela, he was so awed that he was "unable to paint for weeks."

Other influences, especially from his Parisian period, are obvious in his abstract, almost surrealist paintings, such as *Explosion of the World Egg* (1963) and *Cosmological Explosion* (1964?). In both paintings, a brightly colored oval sits at the center, but from it dark lines thrust out into a primordial, amorphous space.

Boghossian allowed African-American themes to influence his work, and he often painted with jazz music in the background. He called it "a combination of geniuses, the constant modulation of concepts, the one thing we have, as Black folks, as artists." Boghossian was attuned to the liberation struggles of Africa during his lifetime as well. He spoke of Chiekh Anta DIOP, whom he knew during his Paris years, as an intellectual influence.

BOILAT, Pierre
(Sénégal, 1800s–1853)

Abbé Pierre Boilat was one of the earliest *assimilés,* Africans educated in the French language and acculturated to French ways. A strong adherent of assimilation, he was the first African intellectual to study African culture from a Western point of view.

When the French reclaimed Sénégal from the British in 1817, Catholic missions were established but proved to be a failure. Boilat, a member of the dominant Wolof peoples, was among the first group of Sénégalese selected in 1825 by Anne Marie JAVOUHEY to study in France in her program to revitalize the Catholic missions by Africanizing them. Ordained in France in 1841, Boilat returned to Sénégal to open a secondary school in St. Louis. After four years of difficulties with teachers and the program, Boilat was removed on a morals charge. He moved to Gorée Island, off Dakar, an enclave for *assimilés,* to study the history and cultures of the societies of the interior of the country, which had not come in contact with Europeans. In 1853 he published *Esquisses Sénégalaises* (Sénégalese Sketches) in two volumes, complete with his own illustrations. Besides describing African culture, Boilat argued the case for assimilation.

Accommodation with European culture promised considerable advantages, but at a price. The *assimilés* entered deeply into both African and European cultures but belonged completely to neither. They had to judge in what ways European civilization would benefit Africa without destroying African identity. Boilat belonged to the most extreme school of thought, which argued for the superiority of French civilization and saw African progress in terms of its ability to absorb Western enlightenment. The tools of this achievement were to be religion (to reshape values and the family) and education. In Boilat's attempt to establish a secondary school, he insisted on using the French classical model and resisted every attempt to teach practical trades to Africans. On Gorée Island he became an opponent of polygamy and liaisons between Frenchmen and African women, and credited himself with establishing respect for Christian marriage. Throughout his book, Boilat gave approval to every example of Westernization, from the abolition of slavery to the adoption of French fashion and dances.

References: DAHB. Robert July, *The Origins of Modern African Thought* (1968).

BOKASSA, Jean Bedel
(Central African Republic, 1921–1996)

Jean Bedel Bokassa, one of the most erratic and vicious dictators in modern times, ruled the Central African Republic (CAR) from 1965 to 1979. Often seen as both a comic and a menacing figure, he was capable of harsh and savage reprisals against real or perceived opponents.

Bokassa came from a political family and was one of 12 children. His uncle, Barthélemy BOGANDA, a sometime priest, was the founding father of CAR nationalism, and his cousin, David DACKO, was president both before and after Bokassa.

Jean Bedel Bokassa

When Bokassa was six years old, his father was murdered, and his mother subsequently committed suicide. Raised in mission schools, he was a devout Catholic and considered entering the priesthood. Instead, he joined the French army in 1939 and began a lifelong love-hate relationship with France. He received the Croix de Guerre and the Legion of Honor for combat in the Congo and France during World War II and served the French army with distinction in Vietnam, becoming an officer in 1949. He resigned in 1961 to organize the CAR military for President Dacko and was named commander-in-chief in 1963. When Dacko asked for army support in a government crisis, Bokassa overthrew him and became president.

In 1969, he nullified the constitution, and announced that he was president-for-life in 1972. Then, after a visit to Libyan President Muammar al-Qaddafi, he promptly proclaimed himself a Muslim. In a most bizarre turn of events, he named himself emperor in 1976, simultaneously announcing his return to Catholicism. The coronation followed the ritual used by Napoleon Bonaparte, including exact copies of jeweled crowns and ermine-trimmed robes, and Bokassa—as Napoleon had—crowned himself and his empress. The CAR could hardly afford the $20 million price tag, but France quietly footed the bill.

His behavior then became even more erratic and included a lengthy search for the illegitimate children of his Vietnam days, which resulted in adoptions and forced marriages to Africans for two bewildered Vietnamese. He broke relations with China, restored them, and then recognized South Africa. At French President Charles DeGaulle's funeral, he had to be led away, wailing, "Papa, papa!"

France continued its patronage. Bokassa was especially close to President Valéry Giscard d'Estaing, who ensured a ready flow of money in exchange for uranium. This was found later to have gone well beyond the promotion of French interests—Giscard was treated to lavish hunting *safaris* and gifts of diamonds.

Domestically, Bokassa's rule was harsh. In one grisly incident, he led his troops in beating to death 46 convicted thieves. In 1979 he directed the massacre of 150 children who had refused to buy school uniforms from his wife's company. Body parts were found stored in the freezer of his palace when Bokassa was overthrown. French troops ended Bokassa's reign in 1979 and exiled him to France, where he enjoyed four chateaux, a villa, and a private jet. Quixotic to the end, Bokassa returned to the CAR in 1986 to stand trial. He was convicted of murder, cannibalism and grand theft. He received a life sentence. In 1993, General André KOLINGBA opened all the prisons of the CAR, and Bokassa walked out a free man to 3,000 cheering supporters. Claiming a religious conversion, Bokassa settled into retirement. He had 17 wives and numerous children.

References: afr, DAHB, DRWW, DT, PLBA, RWWA, *wiki*. Alex Shoumatoff, *African Madness* (1990).

BONGO, Omar Ondimba (Albert-Bernard Bongo)
(Gabon, 1935–)

El-Hadj Omar Bongo has one of Africa's longest tenures as a head of state, which he has maintained by conservative economic policies and authoritarian control.

Bongo was educated in Brazzaville, French Congo, where he received a diploma in commerce at the technical high school in 1958. He was a conscript into the French air force from 1958 to 1960. When Gabon achieved its independence in 1960, he joined the Ministry of Foreign Affairs, and two years later he was picked by President Léon M'BA to be on the staff of the presidential cabinet. In 1964 he became minister of national defense while remaining M'Ba's personal aide. In 1966, M'Ba created the new position of vice president so that Bongo could be elected to the position. When M'Ba died eight months later, Bongo became president at age 32.

Bongo is a strong advocate of free trade and private enterprise, often saying "Give me a sound economy and I will give you stable politics." Foreign investment has been encouraged, and Gabon's offshore oil reserves have been leased to the French conglomerate Elf-Aquitaine. He promoted three major development projects: the Kinguele Dam, a port at Owendo, and the Trans-Gabon Railway to open the interior. They have been completed, despite opposition from the International Monetary Fund when it became clear that all the projects were riddled with graft. Few ministers have failed to enrich themselves, nor has Bongo been immune to the same charges. He lives an opulent lifestyle in a lavish presidential palace.

Bongo forged close links with France and with Côte d'Ivoire's Félix HOUPHOUËT-BOIGNY, who is sometimes considered his political mentor. During the Nigerian civil war (1967–1970) he sided with secessionist Biafra and allowed Gabon to be used as a staging area for military supplies for Biafra. In the early 1970s he strengthened ties with North African states, especially Libya, which offered considerable foreign aid. In 1973, Bongo adopted Islam, taking the name Omar, and shortly after made the *hajj*, the Muslim pilgrimage to Mecca. In 1988 he divorced in order to marry the daughter of President Denis SASSOU-NGUESSO of the Congo Republic. He added the name Ondimba in 2003.

The combination of massive development costs, declining oil revenues, and graft produced an economic crisis in the late 1970s. Bongo was able to stabilize Gabon's finances and reduce the debt, but the economic downturn created political opposition. In 1989 a coup plot was discovered among the presidential guard, and Bongo agreed to open the

President Omar Bongo Ondimba of Gabon with U.S. President George W. Bush. Circa 2004.

political system. He was reelected in voting that was marked by serious fraud. Shortly thereafter, the Central African franc was devalued by 50 percent, producing a massive shock of inflation. Riots broke out in the capital, where streets were closed by barricades, and Bongo had to call in paratroops to reassert control. He was inaugurated again in1994 and 2005, the last time with 79 percent of the vote. In 2003, Bongo had the constitution changed to allow unlimited terms for a president, effectively making him president for life. He is extremely wealthy from oil revenues, and was reported to have offered $9 million to Washington lobbyist Jack Abramoff to meet President George Bush. Whether the bribe was paid is unknown, but Bongo did meet Bush within the year.

References: afr, CBB, DAHB, DRWW, PLBA, RWWA, *wiki*.

BONO (Paul Hewson)
(1960–)

A pop music idol, Bono has become one of the leading campaigners for lifting poverty in Africa. Born in Ireland and an indifferent student, Bono drifted into music as a teenager. A friend gave him his stage name from a storefront ad. Before finishing school, he joined with several others to form U2, a rock band in which he was songwriter and sometime vocalist. U2 became a legendary force in rock, and Bono's physical dynamism made its concerts raucous and exciting events.

Bono was always politically aware, if not always very well informed. In 1985, he performed for Bob GELDOF's Band Aid concert for Ethiopian famine relief. (He repeated that role in the 2005 Band Aid 20 concert.) By the 1990s his overweening earnestness and on-stage exhortations brought the band to a crisis. U2 returned with a new format, but Bono's non-stop smoking and recurring nasal infections damaged his voice and sometimes rendered him mute. He was finally forced to have surgery.

Bono found a focus among political issues when he became the spokesman for the Millennium Jubilee 2000 movement to cancel Third World debt. His ability to rally (and some would say, dragoon) celebrities to the cause and to gain access to world figures made him invaluable to the cause of debt forgiveness. He had his picture taken with Pope John Paul II and the Dalai Lama, and met with George Bush and Bill Clinton, not to mention a cast of thousands from the entertainment world. What has made Bono different from most celebrities who champion causes is his persistence and his growing competence in what he talks about.

In 2002, Bono took the U.S. treasury secretary on a four-nation tour of Africa, leaving the politician humbled and impressed, and garnering immense amounts of publicity. Bono followed by founding DATA (Debt, AIDS, Trade in Africa) to confront the major ills of Africa. Bono was a speaker at the inauguration of Paul Martin as prime minister of Canada and has a good relationship with U.S. President George Bush, despite their many differences on issues other than Africa. TIME magazine named Bono a "Person of the Year" for

2005, and he was nominated for the Nobel Peace Prize in 2006, along with Geldof. TIME magazine named him one of "100 People Who Shape Our World" for 2006.

Bono has his critics from both the left and the right. Conservatives find his message of trade equalization threatening and liberals bemoan his socializing with Western world leaders. One British journalist sarcastically called Bono and Geldof, "Bards of the powerful." Political activism has not dimmed public enthusiasm for U2's music, however. The band's last two albums sold 11 million and 10 million copies, respectively, and in 2006, *How to Dismantle an Atomic Bomb* won a Grammy as album of the year. Both albums reflect a return to U2's social roots and away from their lackluster music of the late 1990s.

Reference: EB, *wiki*. www.atu2.com/band/bono.

BOTHA, Louis
(South Africa, 1862–1919)

Louis Botha, soldier and Afrikaner political leader, was instrumental in founding the Union of South Africa. He served as its first prime minister from 1910 to 1919 and was an advocate of reconciliation between Afrikaners and British South Africans.

Born into a Voortrekker family in Natal—one that had made the Great Trek away from British domination in search of Afrikaner independence—Botha was taken at an early age to the Orange Free State (OFS). He was raised on a 5,000-acre farm and had limited education, but he learned both Sotho and Zulu from the African herdsboys.

In 1884 he joined the expedition to restore DINUZULU to the chieftaincy of his father, CETSHWAYO. After their victory, Dinuzulu assigned several million acres to the Afrikaner commandos, and Botha helped establish a short-lived state, the Vryheid Republic, which joined the Transvaal Republic in 1888. Botha held several minor offices but was opposed to President Paul KRUGER's hostile policy toward the *uitlanders,* or foreign White residents. In 1895, Leander Starr JAMESON invaded the Transvaal, expecting a British uprising; Botha was called upon to mobilize forces against him. As a result of Jameson's total defeat, Botha was elected to the parliament, the Volksraad, in 1897. There he espoused a liberal policy toward the *uitlanders,* but the onset of the Boer War in 1899 caused him to throw his full support behind the Afrikaner cause.

Botha proved himself a master of guerrilla warfare and distinguished himself in battle. In one skirmish, he captured Winston Churchill. Botha was put in command of the southern army, which was poised to attack Ladysmith in Natal. In 1900 he was made commander of all Transvaal forces and was able to resist the British advances. His greatest difficulty was in obtaining cooperation from the Afrikaner commanders, who were independent and fractious. After the fall of Pretoria, Botha withdrew from frontal conflict with the British and engaged them exclusively in guerrilla warfare. Nonetheless, the overwhelming British forces made the outcome only a matter of time. At this point, Botha advocated accommodation with the British commander, Lord Horatio KITCHENER, and entered negotiations. He signed the 1902 Peace of Vereeniging and helped to secure concessions that allowed Afrikaners to remain in the region.

In 1905, Botha and Jan Christiaan SMUTS founded Het Volk, an Afrikaner association that they intended to use as a vehicle for reconciliation between the British and Afrikaners. It was the first attempt to bring together the two Afrikaner factions: the "hands up," who accepted British authority, and the "bitter enders," who fought until the end. When his efforts were rewarded with responsible government for the Transvaal, he became prime minister with the intention of leading the province into full union with South Africa. The union became a fact in 1910, and Botha became its first prime minister.

The first problems facing the new administration involved labor issues, especially foreign labor. Botha negotiated with Mohandas GANDHI, the leader of the Indians, who demanded the right to settle permanently in South Africa after completing their indentured labor contracts. In 1913 and 1914, Botha dealt with serious strikes by European goldminers in the Rand and showed that he would use force when necessary to maintain order. When a strike paralyzed the railways, he declared martial law and deported the labor leaders. Tolerant in racial matters, Botha soon alienated the hard-line Afrikaners, who were led by James HERTZOG. Attempts to work with Hertzog failed, and Botha dropped him from the cabinet in 1912.

Botha's next challenge came with the onset of World War I, in which he and Smuts supported the Allied cause. A faction of intransigent Afrikaners supported neutrality and showed some sympathy for the Germans. Botha offered to replace the British garrisons in South Africa so they could be used in Europe and accepted the assignment to invade South-West Africa. Before he could act, however, three Afrikaner commandants took up arms against intervention. Botha was deeply hurt by the prospect of fighting his former comrades in arms, but his sense of duty superseded personal considerations. To avoid any show of ethnic conflict, he called out only Afrikaner commandos and led the troops personally until he had defeated his opponents. Botha then turned to South-West Africa, leading a column against the capital while Smuts led three columns on his flanks. As a result of his careful strategy, the Germans surrendered in 1915 after little combat. Botha and Smuts were delegates to the 1919 Versailles Peace Conference, where they characteristically urged conciliation with Germany. Botha's health was failing, however, and he died soon after signing the treaty.

References: DAHB, DNB, EB, EWB, HWL, wiki. Johannes Meintjes, *General Louis Botha: A Biography* (1970).

BOTHA, Pieter Willem "P. W."

(South Africa, 1916–)

P. W. Botha was prime minister and, in 1984, the first executive president of South Africa. His tenure in office covered the period of South Africa's greatest crisis with apartheid and the beginning of its collapse.

The son of Afrikaner farmers, Botha became active in National Party politics, dropping out of law school to enter party work full-time. Botha also helped found a pro-Nazi movement in 1939 and was threatened with internment. In his first bid for parliament, he lost, but in 1948 he carried a Cape Province district in the National Party sweep of that year. At first Botha attracted little attention in parliament, holding minor ministerial posts concerning Coloured (mixed-race) affairs. In 1966 he was selected as minister of defense and emerged as a powerful political figure. He established the South African Arms Corporation (ARMSCOR) as a government arms production corporation, which was so successful that South Africa became substantially

self-sufficient in military equipment and an arms exporter, despite a British-led embargo. Under Botha's direction, South Africa got its first missile site in 1968. He established a close relationship with the armed forces and joined the State Security Council. In 1975 he was responsible for an invasion of Angola that reached almost to the capital of Luanda and provoked a firestorm of criticism back home.

In 1978, Botha defeated several candidates to become prime minister, keeping his defense portfolio and adding intelligence to it. Immediately, he initiated constitutional reform, eliminating the senate in 1980, reorganizing government bureaus, and increasing the authority of the State Security Council. Botha moved toward representation for Coloureds and Indians, which was an anathema to the Afrikaner right. In 1982, Dr. Andries TREURNICHT and his followers split from the Nationalists to form the Conservative Party over the issue. In a referendum in 1983, however, Botha's proposal was resoundingly endorsed by the White electorate. He became the first state president under the scheme, which abolished the prime minister's office and created three chambers, one for each racial group. In cases of disagreement, the all-White President's Council had the final say. Black leaders denounced the system as a sham, although Botha considered various means of eventually including Blacks. He repealed some aspects of "petty apartheid," such as the prohibition of mixed marriages, and desegregated many public facilities. Nevertheless, to the end he remained a White supremacist.

Botha's foreign policy was confrontational. He refused to withdraw from Namibia, which South Africa held under U.N. mandate. His troops often raided neighboring states, which he accused of harboring rebel African National Congress (ANC) forces. A zealous anti-Communist, Botha regarded all African nationalist movements as dangerously radical and used military force to keep neighboring African states destabilized and weak.

Botha was an uncompromising politician, given to fits of temper. Known by the nickname "the old crocodile," he was wily and tough. His reform tendencies were never deep, and it took little to bring him back to his old racist positions during his last years in office. Botha expected gratitude from Blacks for his reforms, and so the increasing protests and political violence after 1985 angered him. A state of emergency provided him with the authority to crush resistance, and over 4,000 people died, while 45,000 were detained. The international community turned against South Africa, sanctions began to take effect, and the value of the currency eroded, causing economic stagnation. After a 1989 stroke, Botha resigned as party head and was soon forced from office by F. W. DE KLERK.

When Nelson MANDELA and the ANC took political power in South Africa, Botha was summoned before the Truth and Reconciliation Commission headed by Archbishop Desmond TUTU. Botha refused to appear and therefore stood convicted for his part in the repression of Black South Africans. Because of his age, he was fined and given a suspended sentence.

References: afr, CB, DAHB, EB, EWB, GSAP, PLBA, PLCA, RWWA, *wiki.* Brian Pottinger, *The Imperial Presidency: P. W. Botha: The First Ten Years* (1988); Eschel Rhoodie, *P. W. Botha: The Last Betrayal* (1989).

BOTHA, Roelof Frederick "Pik"
(South Africa, 1932–)

Roelof Frederick "Pik" Botha was foreign minister of South Africa for 17 years and one of the more moderate members of the National Party (NP) governments of P. W. BOTHA and Frederik DE KLERK. He became minister of energy and mineral affairs in the government of national unity led by Nelson MANDELA from 1994 to 1996.

Pik Botha attended the University of Pretoria, where he received B.A. and LLB degrees in 1953 before joining the department of foreign affairs. From 1956 to 1959 he served in Sweden, and from 1960 to 1963 in West Germany. In 1963 he joined the legal team defending South Africa's position on South-West Africa (Namibia) before the International Court of Justice in The Hague. In *Ethiopia and Liberia v. South Africa,* Botha ably argued that South Africa had provided for the social progress of Namibia's Black population, and the case was dismissed on technical grounds. Although they had won a narrow victory, the legal team was received back in Pretoria as national heroes by the White population. In 1966, Botha was named legal advisor to the foreign affairs office, and in that capacity he was made a member of seven South African delegations to the United Nations between 1966

and 1974. From 1968 to 1970 he was also undersecretary of state, and in 1974 he was named ambassador to the U.N., but was immediately withdrawn when South Africa was denied further participation in that organization.

In 1970 Pik Botha was elected a member of parliament. He was identified with the *verligte,* or progressive, wing of the National Party, partly due to a U.N. speech in which he declared that the NP would "move away from discrimination based on race or Colour." In 1977 he was named minister of foreign affairs by Prime Minister B. J. VORSTER. When a government scandal forced Vorster out the following year, Botha threw his support to P. W. BOTHA (no relation) and continued in the foreign affairs office. In 1986, Pik Botha commented to reporters that he could foresee a Black president in South Africa if minority rights were guaranteed. The remark caused an uproar in parliament and a public rebuke from the prime minister. Pik Botha replied with a letter acknowledging that a Black president was not government policy, but he made no personal apology.

Through the 1980s, Pik Botha dealt effectively with international relations, even as South Africa was coming under increasing international pressure. He played a key role in negotiations encouraging the mutual withdrawal of South African troops from Namibia and of Cuban troops from Angola, which led to independence for Namibia in 1990. After Mandela's release from prison, Botha was part of the government team in transition talks. A reformer who chose to work within the existing apartheid system, he feels vindicated by the progress made in the first generation of inclusive government. He was elected to the new parliament for the NP and entered Mandela's cabinet as minister of mineral and energy affairs, a key position in a country where mining is the backbone of the economy. It was a signal of continuity for the business community and was warmly received by the mining industry, whose journal commented "the industry seems likely to be well served by the new administration."

After resigning from his ministry in 1996, Pik joined the ANC, calling for national unity. His move was seen as a betrayal by many former NP stalwarts, who had their longtime suspicions of Botha reaffirmed. He had always been the subject of speculation about his loyalties. During the apartheid period, South African Military Intelligence considered him untrustworthy, and perhaps even in the pay of the American CIA. His nickname among his enemies was "Rasputin." In 2004, Pik was diagnosed with colon cancer, but surgery the following year was successful.

References: CB, GSAP, PLBA, RWWA, *wiki.*

BRAIDE, Garrick Sokari Marian
(Nigeria, 1882?–1918)

Prophet Garrick Sokari Marian Braide, a prominent healer and prophet, was a founder of the African independent church movement. Braide became an Anglican catechist (missionary) in the turbulent years following Bishop Samwel CROWTHER's removal as leader of the Niger Delta Pastorate. Semiautonomous status was granted to the Anglican church in Nigeria in 1892, with Bishop James JOHNSON in authority. Although Johnson operated independently, he never cut ties with the sponsoring Church Missionary Society (CMS).

Braide had a gift for healing, and beginning in 1908, people came to him for cures and prophecies. He was said to be able to predict personal difficulties and to bestow good fortune. He retained the support of Johnson because his healing, although unusual, was not far removed from the experience of the evangelical CMS. This toleration also stemmed in part from Braide's success in getting converts to cast out their fetishes and idols. He challenged the priests of traditional cults in a rainmaking contest and then bested them by invoking the Christian God. He spent night vigils in prayer, enforced Sunday observance, and preached peace and reconciliation. He also denounced the use of alcohol so completely that consumption fell dramatically. The loss in excise taxes from the sale of alcohol was so great that when the British moved against him in fear of his growing influence, they listed the decline in revenue as one of their charges.

By 1915, Braide had attracted a following more attached to him than to the Delta ministry or the CMS. His followers were estimated to number more than a million. He was honored as a prophet and began using that title, calling himself Elijah II. Braide had become the focus of a cult. Over two-thirds of the Delta congregation abandoned Bishop Johnson for Braide, and Johnson turned against his protégé. After proscribing the movement for heresy, Johnson asked the British colonial authorities to investigate. They needed little prompting. When Braide was quoted as saying that power was passing from Whites to Blacks during World War I, the British imprisoned him for sedition. Without him, the last tenuous links to the CMS were severed and a new denomination, the Christ Army Church, was founded by his disciples. It was one of the first independent churches founded in African reaction to foreign domination. Braide died in an accident in 1918, and his movement splintered into a number of factions, some continuing his rigorous Christian morality and others adapting Christianity to African customs.

Reference: dabc, MMA.

BRAND, Johannes Henricus
(South Africa, 1823–1888)

Sir Johannes Henricus Brand was president of the Orange Free State (OFS) from 1864 to 1888. An able and aggressive leader, he protected the OFS from British expansion but maintained good relations with Britain. The OFS had been established, along with the Transvaal, in the 1830s as a result of the Great Trek, in which 6,000 Afrikaners and their Coloured servants had gone north, seeking open land and freedom from British domination. In 1854, Britain recognized the OFS as an independent republic.

Brand was born a British subject in Cape Town, the son of the speaker of the House of Assembly. After education in South Africa and the Netherlands, he began a successful law practice in Cape Town in 1849 and was elected to the Cape parliament. In 1864 he was elected to the presidency of the Orange Free State, an office he would occupy until his death. He headed an unstable and often threatened little republic, which had selected him because of its inability to choose among the possibilities of merger with the Transvaal, autonomy, or annexation to Cape Colony.

Brand almost immediately found himself involved in a protracted war with the Sotho king, MOSHWESHWE I, although Moshweshwe was elderly and losing his authority to his sons. OFS commando units were able to inflict decisive defeats on the Sotho. Brand seized large sections of Sotho territory and was poised to take more when the

British intervened (after Moshweshwe's entreaty) and annexed Basutoland in 1868. In the previous year, diamonds had been discovered in Kimberley, and from 1870 to 1871 Brand attempted to assert OFS authority over the diamond fields. Again, the British annexed the area, but this time the OFS received £90,000 of compensation in 1876.

The OFS became known as the "model republic" because of Brand's competent administration. Despite that fact, he had to contend throughout his three terms of office with factions in the republic that favored merger with the Transvaal or annexation to the Cape Colony. Brand continued along the path of autonomy and was skillful enough in his relations with the British to maintain autonomy throughout his life. After the Transvaal War broke out in 1880, Brand served as a mediator between the Transvaal and the British, which left the Transvaal independent and ended British hopes for federation of the republics with Cape Colony. Queen Victoria knighted him for his services in 1882.

References: DAHB, EB. Trafford Barlow, *President Brand and His Times* (1972).

BRAZZA, Pierre Savorgnan de
(Gabon/Congo, 1852–1905)

Pierre Savorgnan de Brazza was a French explorer and imperialist who influenced the establishment of the French Congo and founded the capital city that bears his name, Brazzaville. Although he was born into an Italian noble family, Brazza became a French naval officer and citizen as a young man. His only assignments were in Africa, where he established a French presence in several areas.

From 1875 to 1878, Brazza explored the Ogooué River in Gabon to its source. He returned in 1880, racing Henry Morton STANLEY to the upper Congo River, where he signed treaties with the local chiefs that provided a basis for French claims to the north bank of the river. After the treaties were ratified, Brazza established Brazzaville on the river near Stanley Pool and governed the colonial settlement from 1886 to 1897. In 1891 a French protectorate was declared over the territory. Brazza was recalled to France in 1897, and considerable commercial expansion developed in the following years. He returned only once, in 1905, to

investigate charges of mistreatment of Africans in the colony by the commercial interests that had been granted concessions in the Moyen-Congo. He died in Dakar, Sénégal, on the return trip.

An immensely popular figure in France, Brazza affected the style of the dashing explorer, dressing in robes and Arab desert headdress. His explorations were claim-staking rather than scientific expeditions, and the excitement of his race with Stanley added to the popular clamor in France for the colonization of Africa.

References: afr, DAHB, EB. Pierre Croidys, *Brazza, Conquérant du Congo* (Brazza, conqueror of the Congo, 1947).

BREW, James Hutton
(Ghana, 1844–1915)

James Hutton Brew was a pioneer of West African journalism and an early nationalist. The descendant of an eighteenth-century Irish trader who married into the Fante aristocracy, Brew founded a merchant dynasty that was prominent in Gold Coast (Ghana) politics for two centuries, and he became a strong and articulate advocate of African rights.

Brew's father, a merchant and a member of the Legislative Council (Legco) in the 1860s, sent James to England for schooling from 1852 to 1864. James returned as one of the first African attorneys in the Gold Coast. At the time, the Fante Confederation was being established in an attempt to bring together all the chiefs and kings for common purposes, including defense, the building of roads and schools, and the development of agriculture and mineral resources. The intention was to create an effective central government within the traditional order, and Brew was invited to write the constitution. It was a far-sighted and bold attempt at harmonious cooperation between the educated elite and the traditional rulers. Within three years, the confederation was operative, raising an army of 15,000 and creating courts, a tax system, and a functioning bureaucracy. It collapsed in 1873 under pressure from the British, who viewed it as an anticolonial movement and sought to drive a wedge between the elites and the chiefs. Subsequently, the British subdued the neighboring Asante kingdom by military power and imposed colonial rule. In the interim, Brew served as undersecretary of the confederation and as its spokesman with the British.

When the final constitution was presented to the governor, however, Brew was arrested along with the entire confederation executive.

After British sovereignty was established in 1874, Brew campaigned for the rights of Africans and eventual self-government. He proposed an elected Legco with full powers to govern. His vehicles in these campaigns were the newspapers he founded: the *Gold Coast Times* (1874), the *Western Echo* (1885), and the *Gold Coast Echo* (1888). They became the voice against British encroachment on African rights, defending the distinctiveness of African culture and openly criticizing the colonial administration. One result, perhaps to avoid questions being raised in the British Parliament, was that the governor began appointing Africans to the Legco in 1886.

In 1888 Brew moved to London, where he represented British businesses with interests in the Gold Coast. He also used every opportunity to lobby Parliament and the Colonial Office on behalf of the Asante, then threatened by British expansion into the interior. In 1898 he forced the withdrawal of a bill that would have alienated large tracts of land in the Gold Coast and placed them in British hands. Brew was never trusted by British colonial officials, who thought that, because he was of mixed ancestry, he was a penniless adventurer of poor character. None of this was true, but it was typical of the racism of the day.

References: DAB, DAHB.

BREYTENBACH, Breyten
(South Africa, 1939–)

An Afrikaner poet, writer and artist—and longtime antiapartheid activist—Breyten Breytenbach spent years in exile and in prison for his activities.

Breytenbach studied art at the University of Cape Town, but after a year he went to Paris to expand his career. When he married an Asian woman there, he was banned from returning to South Africa. Even as his first books of poetry in the 1960s won prize after prize for Afrikaans writing, he was forbidden to return home to receive them. While in Paris, he became known to South African intelligence as the founder and leader of an exile antiapartheid resistance group. Regardless, he made an illegal visit home in 1975, where he was betrayed, arrested, and sentenced to nine years

imprisonment for terrorism, serving seven. The first two years were spent in solitary confinement.

An international campaign forced his early release in 1982, and he again went into exile. He took French citizenship in 1983, dividing his time between Paris and Dakar, Sénégal, where he started up an artists' workshop for Africans. After the fall of apartheid, Breytenbach returned to South Africa to the University of Natal, where he taught creative writing. He has been pessimistic about South Africa's future, expressing his misgivings in *Dog Heart* (1999). He has seen the color of leadership change, but not the arrival of justice for the poor.

His work encompasses poetry, essays and fiction, written in Afrikaans and/or English. Without being autobiographical, he writes from his experience as a man in exile much of his life, caught in the cross-currents of politics, art and cultural displacement. He is a prolific writer (30 books of poetry alone), and wrote a four-volume memoir of his prison time. His imprisonment also marks his paintings, which depict people in captivity. Despite the indelible impression that apartheid made on his art, his latest book, *Lady One* (2002), is a collection of love poetry.

References: adb, CANR, DLB, EB, *wiki*, WLTC. Breytenbach, *True Confessions of an Albino Terrorist* (1985).

BRINK, André Philippus
(South Africa, 1935–)

André Philippus Brink, a novelist and playwright, writes in Afrikaans, a national South African language which developed from the Dutch language. Brink, who is White, is the most popular Afrikaans novelist and playwright active today, but because his first novel was the first Afrikaans book to be banned, he also wrote English versions "in order not to be silenced in my own language." Brink's work is widely admired in critical circles, and he has been a nominee for the Nobel Prize in literature. Two of his novels have been shortlisted for the Booker Prize. He continued writing after the end of apartheid, and published four novels between 2000 and 2005.

Like many writers, Brink has another career as a professor of literature. After taking master's degrees in both Afrikaans and English, he spent 1959 to 1961 at the Sorbonne in Paris, then began teaching

Afrikaans and Dutch literature at Rhodes University, where he completed his studies with a D.Litt. in 1975. In 1968 he returned to Paris briefly as a protest against apartheid, expecting to remain in exile. The French student uprisings that year radicalized Brink's thinking, however, and sealed his resolve to return home to confront racist policy. In 1991 he took a position at the University of Cape Town, where he is now emeritus.

Brink is part of the Sestiger group, a loose network of Afrikaans writers who began their careers in the 1960s. The Sestigers brought two elements into Afrikaans literature—the influence of European literary movements and an antiapartheid political consciousness. They opposed the rising authoritarianism in South Africa, which paralleled their own rise to prominence, and they provided a voice against racism in the very language of the dominant National Party, the architect of apartheid. Among the Sestigers, Brink's writing is the most politically committed, which led to many of his works being banned in his homeland until the end of the apartheid era in the early 1990s. Brink has been a supporter of the ANC and its first unity government.

Brink deals with the legacy of slavery (*A Chain of Voices*, 1982), interracial relationships (*Looking on Darkness*, 1973), abuses of police power (*A Dry White Season*, 1979), and materialism (*Rumors of Rain*, 1978). In *A Chain of Voices*, each character speaks his own language, so that they literally cannot comprehend one another. Brink usually writes in Afrikaans and then translates his own work, although he has done some more recent works in English.

In a book of critical essays, *Writing in a State of Siege* (1983), he explored the meanings of political fiction. Brink's recent writing shows the ambiguity of his country's social transition. In *Cape of Storms* (1992) he turned to allegory and myth, which he described as "African magical realism." Some critics, however, considered the book a confused search for a new identity. In 1993 he published his latest work, *On the Contrary,* in which he seems to have found a new voice in historical fiction. The story of Cape Colony's founding as experienced by a French soldier helps restore a history that has been silenced. "It is more imperative than before to revisit that past," Brink has said. Brink defended the African National Congress (ANC) while it was banned, sympathetically representing armed resistance in *An Act of Terror* (1991). Nevertheless, he later broke with the ANC for what he regarded as its own authoritarianism.

References: adb, afr, CANR, DLB, *wiki*, WLTC. Brink, *Before I Forget* (2005).

BRUTUS, Dennis
(South Africa, 1924–)

Dennis Brutus has been a radical opponent of racism, both in the antiapartheid movement in South Africa, and as an exile in other countries. His writing has raised him to the ranks of the major poets in Africa, and he is internationally recognized.

Although born in what is now Zimbabwe, Brutus was raised in South Africa and educated there. He graduated from the University of Fort Hare and then taught English and Afrikaans from 1948 to 1962 in a Catholic secondary school. He left teaching to take a law degree.

Brutus was always active in sports, and was a founder of the South African Sports Association in 1958. Four years later, he was president of the South African Non-Racial Olympic Committee, whose activities got South Africa suspended from the 1964 Olympics in Tokyo because of its race policies. Placed under house arrest in 1963, Brutus attempted to flee but was arrested at the Mozambican border by the Portuguese, turned over to the South African police and then shot when he tried to escape. He was sentenced to 18 months at the notorious Robben Island prison. The brutal conditions forged his first books of poetry, *Sirens, Knuckles, Boots* (1963), and verse letters from prison to his wife, *Letters to Martha* (1968). In both, his political outrage galvanized the poetry, but his work also revealed the tightly crafted and polished style that has been his hallmark. His work occasionally descends to propaganda, but the anger and call for justice is usually restrained by a lyric sensibility. His books were banned in South Africa until 1990.

In 1966, Brutus and his family went into exile in England on an exit permit that forbade return to South Africa. In Britain, Brutus was arrested for interrupting a match at Wimbledon when a White South African was playing, but he won his case after appealing it all the way to the House of Lords. The family moved on to the United States, where Brutus has held a number of posts teaching African literature at various universities, most notably Northwestern, where he spent 10 years in their distinguished African Studies program. In 1986, he joined the Africana Program at the University of Pittsburgh, and is now emeritus. In the United States, Brutus continued his activism; he has joined the anti-globalization movement, has been arrested for demonstrations against the death penalty, and promoted the World Bank bond boycott.

Brutus's earlier works were followed by a series of books, 12 in all. In some, like *Remembering Soweto 1976* (2004), he continues to reflect the experience of apartheid. Brutus's work has never received the recognition in South Africa that it has internationally. Eager to move on, many South Africans have shown less interest in writing about the horrors of apartheid.

References: *adb*, *afr*, CA, CAAS, CANR, BW, DLB, EB, WLTC.

BRYANT, Gyude
(Liberia, 1949–)

Gyude Bryant served as interim president of Liberia from 2003 to 2006, guiding the transition from civil chaos to a new, if unstable, democracy.

Bryant is from the Grebo, an ethnic group not deeply involved in Liberia's disastrous civil conflict. He received a good education and graduated in economics from a Liberian university.

Bryant had a distinguished career in business, politics and civic life. He founded and is president of a heavy machinery import company that deals in mining and shipping equipment. More in the public eye, he has been a stalwart of the Liberia Action Party (LAP), which he helped found in 1984. He has been chairman since 1992. Many believe that the LAP won the election of 1985, when Samuel DOE proclaimed himself elected. Since 1996, Bryant has also been chair of the Episcopal Church, the Liberian branch of the Anglican Communion. Deeply involved in Episcopal affairs for many years and in many capacities, he took leadership especially in their program for rehabilitating boy soldiers.

The choice of the transitional president was part of the peace process brokered by West African peacekeepers and agreed to by the three contending forces at a conference in Accra, Ghana. They chose Bryant because of his record as a consensus-builder and his perceived neutrality. Bryant took on the appointment as interim president as one who had

remained in Liberia throughout the conflict that tore the country apart, forced more than half the population into internal exile and left even the capital city in ruins. Untold thousands had been maimed and killed in brutal fashion, and bands of lawless boy soldiers roamed and looted at will. Bryant was seen as one who braved the worst of the crisis and shared the lot of those who did not have the means or the opportunity to become refugees. At the same time, the Liberia Action Party, which he heads, was always a sharp critic of Charles TAYLOR and the rebel forces. Bryant was frank about his gifts and promoted himself as a healer of the nation, but at the same time, he was never a power in Liberian politics.

Even the interim government was compromised, with the two rebel groups and Taylor loyalists holding half of the ministerial posts. Bryant was not able to be as forceful a leader as conditions demanded, and his administration was riddled with corruption. He turned over authority to the newly elected president, Ellen SHIRLEAF-JOHNSON, in 2006. She inherited an unstable but at least peaceful country.

Reference: *wiki*.

BUCKNOR, Jude Kofi
(Ghana, 1950s–)

Jude Bucknor is an investment banker with wide international experience, and one of those who has strengthened and developed the Ghanaian economy, a success story of recent years.

He was raised in Ghana and graduated from the University of Ghana at Legon before going to Columbia University in New York for an MBA in finance.

Bucknor began his career with Chemical Bank in New York in 1979, and was vice president for three years in the early 1980s. He was then posted to Côte d'Ivoire as regional head of Chemical Bank for West and Central Africa. He stayed in Abidjan to take a position as deputy, then treasurer, of the African Development Bank from 1986 to 1994. He followed with a three-year stint with Lehman Brothers in London, where he was in charge of corporate finance for Africa. In 1994, he also became a director on the board of Ashanti Goldfields back in Ghana. Ashanti has always been a bulwark of the Ghanaian economy. From 1997 to 2000, Bucknor was managing director (president) of the CAL Merchant Bank, and then took on the task of chair of the Ghana Stock Exchange.

Bucknor is widely respected for his expertise. He sits on the boards of a number of corporations from Togo to Australia, including the world's largest gold company. At the time of the1998 currency collapse in Southeast Asia, he served as a member of the Commonwealth's investigative panel on the Asian Financial Crisis. His private consulting firm, J. Kofi Bucknor & Associates, handles major African and foreign clients, both corporate and private.

Reference: adb.

BUDD, Zola (Zola Pieterse)
(South Africa, 1966–)

Known best by her maiden name, under which she became a controversial international sports celebrity in the 1980s, Zola Budd has retired from competitive running and married, now using her husband's name, Pieterse.

Budd shot to prominence when she won the women's 5,000-meter world record at age 17, running barefoot. The image of the diminutive South African girl seemed such an innocent contrast to the ban on South African sports that had been put in place in response to South Africa's race policies. The world record, however, could not be recognized.

South Africa had been banned from the Olympics for 20 years when a right-wing British newspaper convinced Budd's father to have her apply for British citizenship, on the grounds that she had a British grandfather. Her citizenship was rushed through in a privileged manner that caused controversy, but she became eligible for the 1984 Los Angeles Olympic Games. The way in which it was all handled almost ensured that the antiapartheid movement, which was centered in Britain, would protest. When she moved to Britain she was greeted with demonstrations. In all this, Budd was a confused pawn of political interests beyond her understanding. She only knew that her great opportunity to run in the Olympics depended upon this compromise. But from the start, she was the butt of vilification in the British trash press and harassment from the political left, as well irrational

praise and adulation from the right. She had become a symbol.

She was immediately chosen to run the 3,000-meter race for Britain at Los Angeles. It was a disaster. She was pitted against the favorite, American Mary Slaney, and twice the two jostled on the track. After the second time, Slaney fell and never finished the race. Budd took the lead, but amidst a chorus of boos and catcalls from the crowd, she lost heart and ended seventh. In the investigation of the collisions, the Olympic authorities held that Budd was not at fault, but in the popular mind she was guilty. Slaney never forgave her. In the following controversy, the American media took the part of Slaney and the British supported Budd.

Budd went on to set a new world's record in the 5,000-meter in 1985, now able to be recognized officially. She then won the World Cross Country Championships in 1985 and 1986, and the European Championship in the 3,000 in 1986. In each case, she continued to run barefoot. Despite her victories and records, she never escaped the incident that defined her running career at Los Angeles. In 1986, the Commonwealth Games rejected her. In 1988, she returned to South Africa and the following year married and took the name Pieterse. She trains one to five miles a day, but rarely competes at the senior level. In 1992, she went to the Barcelona Olympics to run the 5,000-meter for South Africa, which returned to its first Olympics in a quarter century. She failed to qualify for the finals, but some of her records still stand.

References: adb, wiki. Pieterse, *Budd* (1989).

BUHARI, Muhammadu
(Nigeria, 1942–)

Major-General Muhammadu Buhari was Nigerian military head of state from 1983 to 1985, when he was removed by a military coup.

A career soldier, Buhari entered the Nigerian Military Training College at Kaduna in 1962, and after completing his training he was sent to officer cadet school in England. Commissioned a second lieutenant, he served with the Nigerian contingent in the United Nations peacekeeping operation in the Democratic Republic of the Congo. As he moved up through the ranks, he had an infantry field command during the Nigerian civil war against secessionist Biafra and became head of army supply and transport. In 1975 he played a minor part in the coup that ousted General Yakubu GOWON, and for two years he was a military governor in the north, his home region, gaining valuable administrative experience. He was then made federal commissioner of petroleum by General Olusegun OBASANJO, but he returned to barracks when the military turned over power to civilians in 1980. He had by this time established a reputation for honesty. One oil executive called him "a pillar of rectitude in a jungle of venality."

The civilian government of Shehu SHAGARI proved corrupt and incompetent, and Buhari led a coup in 1983, emerging as president. A retiring and quiet man, although frank and open as well as competent, Buhari was not charismatic and never a popular figure. He was not able to control Nigeria's economy, which was expanding while oil prices plummeted. His solution was an austerity program that turned much of the population against him, especially after the escape of a notoriously venal cabinet minister revealed the depths of corruption that Buhari had failed to root out. Buhari attempted repression and control of the press and the professions, but opposition mounted. It was without much regret that he was removed by General Ibrahim BABANGIDA in 1985. Buhari was detained until 1988 and then retired.

Buharu emerged from retirement in 2003 to contest for the presidency of Nigeria against OBASANJO. As a Fulani, a Muslim and a northerner he hoped to provide a contrast to the Christian Obasanjo, but he failed in his bid and was decisively defeated.

References: PLBA, RWWA, *wiki.*

BUNDU, Abbas(s)
(Sierra Leone, 1944–)

Dr. Abbas Bundu, a longtime international public servant and diplomat, spent five years as secretary-general of the Economic Community of West African States (ECOWAS), transforming it by introducing a political and regional stabilization role when it undertook peacekeeping in Liberia. In 1993, Bundu became foreign minister of Sierra Leone under the military government of Captain Valentine Strasser.

After his early education in Sierra Leone, Bundu took an unusual step in going to Australia rather than to Britain for university studies. He graduated from the Australian National University and was admitted to the bar in New South Wales. He worked briefly as a legal officer in the Australian attorney general's office before attending Cambridge University, where he obtained a doctorate in constitutional law after completing a thesis on coups and rebellions in Africa. He remained in England on the staff of the Commonwealth Secretariat as chief projects officer from 1975 to 1982. During this fruitful period he gained significant international experience in conflict resolution. He served as legal advisor for the Organization of Eastern Caribbean States, for the republics of Belize (in its dispute with Guatemala) and St. Kitts, and for the Pacific nations of Nauru and the Cook Islands. From 1978 to 1979 he served as legal advisor for the Patriotic Front of Zimbabwe (PFZ), the liberation movement that was then supported by the Commonwealth, which had expelled Rhodesia and was preparing the PFZ to become the new government. Bundu also served as secretary to the observer group monitoring the 1980 Ugandan elections. In 1982, President Siaka STEVENS asked Bundu to return to Sierra Leone as minister of agriculture, later shifting him to tourism. When President Joseph MOMOH assumed power in 1985, Bundu remained in parliament and was reelected the next year.

In 1989, Bundu was selected as secretary-general of the Economic Community of West African States (ECOWAS). Although it had been moderately active in the past, ECOWAS was expanded and took on new roles during Bundu's tenure. In 1991 a draft committee began work on proposed revisions of the basic agreement, and in 1992, by the Treaty of Cotonou, an expanded program was set up. A development fund was established as well as a more efficient system for implementing decisions, which are now binding on all members without having to be ratified by individual member nations.

Bundu fostered trade liberalization among the 16 member states, but the greatest change came with the organization's involvement in the Liberian civil war. ECOWAS had always provided for peacekeeping interventions, but the 1990 action in Liberia was unprecedented. Five states supplied troops in a new entity, ECOMOG, under Nigerian command, despite the opposition of three ECOWAS member states. Bundu carefully included these countries in sponsoring peace negotiations, and although there have been serious problems, the peacekeeping effort immensely strengthened

ECOWAS. When Bundu left his position in 1993, ECOWAS was a far more united group.

In late 1993, Strasser named Bundu foreign minister and appointed an electoral commission to prepare for elections and a return to civilian power in 1995. Bundu lasted a year before circumstances overtook both the government and Sierra Leone with the collapse of civil order and the invasion of the country by the forces of Charles TAYLOR of Liberia. When a semblance of order was restored the following year, Bundu put himself forward for the presidency of the Peoples Progressive Party (PPP). He was unsuccessful, and the PPP has drifted into insignificance. In 2006, he was indicted on corruption charges for selling Leonean passports during his tenure as minister of Foreign Affairs. The matter was settled out of court and he received a presidential pardon.

Reference: RWWA. Bundu, *Democracy by Force: A Study of International Military Intervention in the Conflict in Sierra Leone from 1991–2000* (2001),

BUNTING, Sidney Percival
(South Africa, 1873–1936)

Sidney Percival Bunting was the founder of the Communist Party of South Africa (CPSA), but he ran into party resistance because of his determination to make the CPSA multiracial and because of his independence from Soviet control.

Bunting was British and came to South Africa as a lieutenant in the Boer War of 1899–1902. After leaving the service, he became a lawyer in Johannesburg and entered radical politics. He worked in the labor movement and promoted the rights of Africans. In 1915 he helped found the International Socialists' League (ISL) and was convicted of provoking a general strike and the bloody miners' strike of 1918. Bunting believed that only solidarity among Black, White, and Indian laborers would win in the struggle against capitalism. He was an ardent opponent of racism and tribalism and became a pamphleteer. His leaflets—in Sotho, English and Zulu—were widely circulated in workers' hostels, at mining sites, and during rallies.

After World War I, Bunting visited the Soviet Union and joined the Communist Party. In 1921 he brought the ISL and several other groups together to found the CPSA. It was the only political movement that was multiracial and that had a mixed leadership, but like all Communist parties, it was subject to direction from Moscow. In 1928 the Communist International ordered the CPSA to move away from the class struggle and to espouse an independent Black republic. This move threatened the CPSA's one power base, its influence in the Industrial and Commercial Workers Union (ICU). At the same time, Clements KADALIE, the ICU leader, moved to drive out the CPSA members. All of this caused internal dissension and schisms within the party, and in 1931, Bunting was expelled, probably on Moscow's orders. At that time the CPSA had no more than 3,000 members.

Reference: DAHB.

BURTON, Richard Francis
(Equatorial Guinea/Tanzania, 1821–1890)

Sir Richard Francis Burton was a dashing, brave, colorful and eccentric British adventurer and author. An intrepid explorer, he roamed India, Africa, the Americas and the Middle East—where he penetrated forbidden Mecca. He wrote voluminously of these travels in 35 works, 17 in multivolume editions. His enduring fame rests today on his translations of the *Arabian Nights* (1885), the *Kama Sutra*, and a number of volumes of pornography. Called "Dirty Dick" by his enemies but knighted in 1886 by Queen Victoria for his diplomatic service, he was the embodiment of the Victorian era's contradictions.

A man of considerable intellect and ability, Burton mastered some 40 languages and was a competent botanist and gifted explorer. What distinguished his life, however, was his astounding sense of adventure. He spent his early years wandering about Europe with his rootless parents, who provided him with little formal education, despite the tutor who accompanied them. He learned to fence, plunged himself into debauchery, and became a sexual libertine and a heavy user of opium. Amazingly, his father sent him to Oxford to study for an academic career or the clergy. He lasted a year before being dismissed.

At loose ends, he joined the Indian Army, where his quick mastery of languages brought him promotion. He furthered his studies of Arabic by living with Muslim teachers and steeping himself in their customs. He entered into Islamic religious practices, but along with his mysticism he possessed a prurient streak. When he dispatched a vivid report about Indian homosexual brothels used by British soldiers, his career advancement stopped. In addition, Burton's memorandum on Anglo-Indian misrule did nothing to enhance his reputation among officials.

He took leave from the Indian Army to publish four books in India and then plunged into his greatest adventure—the *hajj* to Mecca. Burton set out for the forbidden city disguised as an Afghan physician. He stained his skin brown and had himself circumcised. Facing a constant risk of death if he were revealed, he carefully took part in all the religious observances. The experience brought him closer to Islam, which he would later adopt as a Sufi mystic and a dervish.

In 1854, Burton turned his restless gaze on Africa. He first made a solo trip to Harar, the capital of Ethiopia, never before visited by a European. He then joined three companions to survey the northern Somali coast, but they were ambushed, and Burton and John Hanning SPEKE were badly wounded. Burton had a spear thrust through his face from cheek to cheek. Nonetheless, by 1856, the two were ready to undertake a major inland trek to find the sources of the Nile. They became the first explorers to reach Lake Tanganyika, but when Speke ventured on and sighted Lake Victoria, the true source of the Nile, the two became estranged. After they returned, Burton learned that he was to be left out of further exploration by the Royal Geographical Society. He subsequently undertook the writing of a classic travel book, *Lake Regions of Central Africa* (1860), an important work for understanding early Tanzania.

Burton next made a journey across the United States (which resulted in another book) and married a prim, devout Catholic woman.

In 1861 he accepted a position as British consul in Fernando Po, an island off the West African coast, but his responsibilities extended well inland as well. He thrived in the new atmosphere, easily making friends but also taking time for his own trips. He explored the Cameroon Mountains, went up the Congo River, and twice visited King GLELE of Dahomey. In 1864 he was sent to Brazil for four years as consul, and then to Damascus.

He seems to have remained faithful to his wife despite his previous promiscuity, but he turned his later attentions to translating and editing Eastern erotica. When he died in Trieste, 100,000 people came to the memorial service. His wife then burned his papers, including 40 years of diaries, because of their sexual content. In the process, an immense trove of material that would have been invaluable to researchers was lost.

Besides his explorations, which further opened Central Africa to Europeans, Burton established the popular notion of Africa as an exotic place of curious customs populated by inferior, primitive people. The 1911 *Encyclopedia Britannica* calls his African books and reports "the true parents of the multitudinous literature of 'darkest Africa.'" Even his fascination with erotica, presented as pseudoscientific anthropology, was a titillating version of the sex lives of "savages" used as a proof of their low estate. In *First Footsteps in East Africa* (1856), Burton advocated ruthless imperialism as a solution to African "barbarisms."

References: afr, DAHB, DLB, DNB, EB, EWB, *wiki*. Edward Rice, *Captain Sir Richard Burton* (1990); *Mountains of the Moon* (film, 1990).

BUSIA, Kofi Abrefa
(Ghana, 1914–1978)

Dr. Kofi Abrefa Busia was a nationalist leader and prime minister of Ghana (1969–1972) who helped to restore civilian government to the country following military control. A scholar as well as a politician, Busia alternated between these two professions.

After a brief teaching career, Busia won a scholarship to Oxford University, where he received a Ph.D. His thesis, on the role of chiefs in the modern Ghanaian political system, was an early and significant study of African institutions by an African. He served as a researcher for the Ghanaian government for two years before being appointed the first professor in African studies at the University of Ghana in 1949. He entered politics in 1951 with his election to the Legislative Council and became head of the main opposition party the following year. By 1956, Busia's political activities were so demanding that he resigned his university post, but his party, despite forming coalitions with several others, never matched the popularity of Kwame NKRUMAH's Convention People's Party.

As Nkrumah became more repressive, especially after passage of the Preventive Detention Act, which allowed him to detain opponents without trial, Busia returned to Europe, where he taught first in the Netherlands and then at Oxford. Busia's most productive period as a scholar was between 1959 and 1966, and he was acknowledged as an outstanding African intellectual of international standing. He wrote *The Sociology and Culture of Africa* (1960), *The Challenge of Africa* (1962), and *Purposeful Education for Africa* (1964). He followed these works with a statement of his political philosophy in *Africa in Search of Democracy* (1967). As a research fellow for the World Council of Churches, he completed *Urban Churches in Britain* (1966). During his lifetime, Busia published nine other books as well as several articles.

In 1966, Nkrumah was overthrown and Busia returned to Ghana to serve on the National Liberation Council of General Joseph ANKRAH, the military head of state. He helped to draft a new constitution in preparation for a return to civilian rule. He was elected to parliament in 1969 and was selected as prime minister. Ironically, Busia resorted to the same repressive measures that he had criticized in Nkrumah's regime. He abolished the powerful trade unions—the vehicle of Ghana's independence movement—clashed with the military, and dismissed large numbers of civil servants who had worked for the previous government. His inadequate measures against a failing economy caused popular dissent, especially after he devalued the currency by 44 percent, causing price increases on basic goods. He was overthrown by General Ignatius ACHEAMPONG in 1972 while on a visit to England, and he remained there to take up his old post at Oxford. Despite a £20,000 reward for his capture, he lived peacefully in Britain until his death.

References: afr, CA, DAHB, EWB, MMA, PLBA.

BUTHELEZI, Mangosuthu Gatsha

(South Africa, 1928–)

Chief Mangosuthu Gatsha Buthelezi, former chief minister of the KwaZulu homeland and president of the Inkatha Freedom Party, is one of the most powerful men in South Africa and a leading African opponent of the African National Congress (ANC).

Heir to the chieftaincy of the Buthelezi clan, a grandson of DINUZULU, and a direct descendant of CETSHWAYO, he is steeped in the nationalism and warrior traditions of the Zulu people. He was raised in a traditional household, serving as a herdsboy until being sent off to school. The family also had a legacy of resistance; Buthelezi's uncle was Pixley SEME, founder of the ANC. As a result, when Buthelezi was admitted to Fort Hare University, he joined the ANC Youth League, where he came to know Robert SOBUKWE and Robert MUGABE. He was expelled from Fort Hare for a boycott and demonstration and had to finish his education in absentia. For two years Buthelezi worked in Durban before inheriting his father's chieftaincy and the rule over some 30,000 Buthelezi in 1953.

In 1970 the South African government established a territorial homeland for KwaZulu as part of its racist homeland policy. Buthelezi was elected chief executive by the council of hereditary chiefs, and in 1976, when new powers were attained by the homeland administration, he became chief minister. Buthelezi, who had opposed the homeland policy, now decided to work within its structure. He was already president of a Zulu cultural organization, Inkatha, which had roots in a liberation movement founded by an uncle, King Solomon. Buthelezi transformed the group into the Inkatha Freedom Party, grafting a political base onto its cultural one. Inkatha stood for political, economic and cultural liberation; nonviolent activism; land distribution; foreign investment; and education for equal citizenship. Through the 1970s, Buthelezi used his homeland base to bring together Black leaders as well as to create an alliance of Black, Indian, and Coloured groups. When P. W. BOTHA drafted a plan for a White-controlled, power-sharing parliament, the group split over participation, with Buthelezi campaigning against the proposal.

Buthelezi is a somewhat bombastic and wily leader. He is in the *Guiness Book of World Records* for the longest parliamentary speech ever given—five days and 400 pages—to the KwaZulu legislature. He also clandestinely cooperated with the apartheid government. This was revealed in 1991, and Buthelezi was seriously compromised when it was discovered that Inkatha had received considerable financial support from the government. A follow-up1994 inquiry revealed that the South African security services had supplied Inkatha with arms and missiles for township warfare against the ANC.

Inkatha had grown to over a million members by the early 1980s, although it had difficulty recruiting outside the Zulu homeland. While other antiapartheid groups were banned, it continued to operate. Buthelezi consistently supported capitalism and promoted investment in South Africa as a means of undermining apartheid. Consequently, he came into conflict with the ANC over its large number of Communist leaders and opposed the ANC's call for sanctions during the 1980s. Many left-wing leaders of the ANC regarded him as an anathema and suspected him of too-close collaboration with Whites. Buthelezi's significance as a Black spokesman eroded, especially after Mandela's release from prison in 1990. By then, open violence between Inkatha members and ANC youth had become common, and a "peace agreement" between the two leaders did nothing to end the strife.

To a great extent, Buthelezi represents the desires of Africans with traditional ethnic values, as opposed to the cosmopolitan, Westernized leadership of the ANC. On the one hand, he successfully resisted attempts to cede part of his territory to Swaziland, but on the other he refused to accept recognition of KwaZulu as a nation, insisting on his rights to participate in a central government. Buthelezi's compromises with his own stated values have clearly hurt him politically. He has criticized the ANC for undertaking an armed struggle, but Inkatha has fomented violence itself.

Buthelezi's initial decision to boycott the 1994 elections was a way to avoid sure defeat, but it also reinforced Inkatha's cornered status. He changed his policy only at the last moment, and stickers had to be attached to the ballots for Inkatha. The fall of Lucas MANGOPE's homeland government in Bophuthatswana at the same time left Buthelezi without allies, however. Inkatha won 21 seats in the 1994 elections, and Buthelezi joined the Mandela cabinet as minister for Home Affairs. In September 1994 the king of the Zulu nation, Goodwill ZWELITHINI, broke all ties with Buthelezi. His future as a leader of the Zulus in some question, Buthelezi stayed in the cabinet after the 1999 elections, but broke with the ANC in 2004 and was ousted from his office.

Buthelezi has four daughters and three sons, of whom two died of AIDS in 2004.

References: afr, CA, CB, DRWW, EWB, GSAP, PLBA, PLCA, RWWA, *wiki*. Gerhard Mare, *An Appetite for Power* (1987); Jack Smith, *Buthelezi* (1988).

BUYOYA, Pierre
(Burundi, 1949–)

Major Pierre Buyoya, president of Burundi from 1987 to 1993, and again from 1996 to 2003, attempted reconciliation between the two major ethnic groups in the country and worked at fostering democracy, which led to his own defeat when he allowed free elections.

Buyoya is a member of the dominant Tutsi minority, 14 percent of the population, which has long ruled the Hutu majority of 85 percent. This division has been the source of most of Burundi's political and social problems. Buyoya benefited from his elite status, and was sent to Belgium for secondary and university studies and then to military school. He returned to Burundi in 1975 as a tank commander but later undertook further military training in France and West Germany.

From the start of his military career, Buyoya was politically active. He was promoted to chief training officer of the armed forces the same year that he was elected to the Central Committee of the National Party, the Union for National Progress (UPRONA). At first he was close to his colleague Jean-Baptiste BAGAZA, who had taken power in a 1976 coup. However, as Bagaza began to persecute the Catholic Church, the traditional defender of the Hutu, unrest spread in the country. In 1987, Buyoya led a coup that removed Bagaza.

Buyoya moved quickly both to consolidate his power and to deal with political tensions. He suspended the constitution and UPRONA, freed all political prisoners, and lifted restrictions on the Church. He then made a lengthy tour of the country in an effort to unite the people. He failed, however, to address ethnic tensions quickly enough, and in 1988 the Tutsi-led army engaged in a series of massacres of Hutus that left tens of thousands dead. Buyoya responded by attempting to balance injustice with political involvement. He included Hutus in the cabinet for the first time, even appointing a Hutu prime minister. By 1990, Hutus formed a majority on UPRONA's Central Committee. A Unity Charter was adopted by referendum in 1991, and plans were made for the return to democratic, civilian rule. In the 1993 elections, the first Hutu president, Melchior Ndadaye, was elected over Buyoya by a two-to-one margin.

Buyoya's "quiet revolution" produced a calm and fair election and—after the military was placed under control in the first months of the new government—a peaceful passage to civilian rule. Containing the ethnic strife proved impossible, however. Ndadaye was assassinated, and 150,000 died in the genocidal civil war that followed. In 1994, the prime minister was killed in a plane crash that also took the life of Rwanda's President Juvénal HABYARIMANA and ignited a massive slaughter of Tutsi in Rwanda. Burundi was able to accept large numbers of refugees and remained relatively stable.

Buyoya returned to power in another coup in 1993, and after a deal was brokered for a return to civilian rule, he stayed in office until 2003.

References: afr, PLBA, RWWA, *wiki.* Buyoya, *Mission Possible* (1998).

CABRAL, Amílcar Lopes
(Guinea-Bissau, 1924–1973)

Amílcar Lopes Cabral, the leader of the main liberation movement in Guinea-Bissau, was also the primary ideologist to adapt Marxist theory to the African anticolonial movements. His impact went far beyond his tiny country.

Cabral was raised in the Cape Verde Islands off Guinea, where he was an outstanding student. As a youth he experienced the terrible famines of the early 1940s, when between a quarter and a third of the population died. Cabral was determined to address their two causes: poor agricultural development and Portuguese exploitation. He went to Lisbon to study agronomy and became involved with other African students as well as with Communist cells. Cabral, Agostinho NETO, and others formed a cultural society to affirm African life, going through what they termed "the re-Africanization of the mind," a process that they linked to the French intellectual movement known as *Négritude.* Cabral also became a Marxist, although he never was a Communist party member.

In 1952, Cabral returned to Portuguese Guinea as an agricultural engineer and was assigned to conduct its first agricultural census. This appointment gave him an intimate familiarity with the land, its people and its problems. It also convinced him that the future of decolonization was with the peasantry. From 1955 to 1959 he worked from Portugal as a consultant, which enabled him to visit other African colonies and to make contacts. In 1956 he founded the African Party for the Independence of Guinea and Cape Verde (PAIGC), a liberation movement, with his brother Luís CABRAL, as well as Aristides PEREIRA and others. It was organized into cells and was at first nonviolent. A 1959 dock strike that ended with the massacre of 50 workers demanded a change in tactics, and the decision was made to begin armed resistance. The strike's failure convinced Cabral that orthodox Communist notions of proletarian leadership were not appropriate in Africa, and he determined to base his revolution on the rural peasantry. The president of neighboring Guinea, Sékou TOURÉ, allowed the PAIGC to set up guerrilla camps in his country.

Cabral and his comrades affiliated themselves with broad Lusophone revolutionary groups that worked together toward the liberation of all Portuguese colonies in Africa—Angola, Mozambique, Cape Verde and Guinea-Bissau. This was an extension of Cabral's fellowship with the student revolutionaries during his days in Lisbon.

The armed struggle began in 1963 after extensive training and indoctrination. The PAIGC's cadres infiltrated Guinea-Bissau, slowly converting the rural population to resistance, and by 1969 they controlled two-thirds of the country. They built clinics, schools and trading posts to support Cabral's theory that "people are not fighting for ideas, [but] to live better and in peace, to see their lives go forward." In 1972, after a visit by a United Nations commission, the PAIGC held elections in its areas, and in 1973 the PAIGC-liberated regions declared independence from Portugal. Guinea-Bissau was promptly recognized by a majority of the world's nations, even though Portugal rejected it. In 1974, when a socialist coup in Lisbon ended the right-wing Portuguese dictatorship, the Portuguese withdrew from both Cape Verde and Guinea-Bissau. Cabral did not live to see independence, because in 1973 he was assassinated by a PAIGC activist who was believed to be working for the Portuguese secret police. Luís Cabral became Guinea-Bissau's first president.

References: adb, afr, CA, DAHB, EB, EWB, MMA, PLBA, PLCA, *wiki*, WLTC. Ronald Chilcote, *Amílcar Cabral's Revolutionary Theory and Practice* (1991).

CABRAL, Luís de Almeida
(Guinea-Bissau, 1931–)

Luís de Almeida Cabral, the younger brother of Amílcar CABRAL and also a leading nationalist, became his country's first president. A tough pragmatist, he was always in the shadow of his revolutionary philosopher brother.

Cabral was educated locally, trained as an accountant, and worked for a Portuguese multinational corporation. In 1956 he was one of the six founders of the African Party for the Independence of Guinea and Cape Verde (PAIGC). While his brother was in exile, Luís went into labor organizing. In 1959 he helped organize a dock strike that was brutally suppressed by the Portuguese colonial authorities and resulted in the loss of more than 50 lives. This event, which caused the PAIGC to abandon nonviolence, came as a shock to Cabral. Aware that he was now a hunted man, he slipped over the border to neighboring Guinea, whose radical government under Sékou TOURÉ supported the PAIGC.

In exile, Cabral remained on the party's central committee and served in various capacities. The PAIGC mlitants began taking over areas of rural Guinea-Bissau until they controlled large sections of the country. Returning to the liberated zone, in 1963 Luís Cabral took charge of the strategic Quitafine frontier, and two years later he was appointed to the war council. In 1967 he assumed responsibility for party administration and several times represented the PAIGC overseas, seeking support. From 1970 to 1972 he directed reconstruction in the liberated areas of Guinea-Bissau.

Amílcar Cabral was assassinated in 1973, just as independence was imminent. Luís Cabral thus became Guinea-Bissau's first president. He had good relations with Portugal, where a socialist government had replaced the longstanding fascist dictatorship. Cabral initiated a socialist economy, hoping to overcome the massive dislocation caused by the long guerrilla war, but the economy went from one crisis to another. The government was highly inefficient, due largely to the lack of educated people as well as political corruption. Cabral became politically repressive until he was overthrown by his prime minister, João Bernardo VIEIRA in 1981. Subsequent investigations revealed a mass grave containing 500 of Cabral's political opponents. He was released from house arrest and went into exile in Cuba before moving to Lisbon in 1983. In 1999 he was able to visit Guinea-Bissau again, after Vieira's overthrow.

References: adb, afr, DAHB, PLBA, RWWA, wiki.

CAMARA Laye
(Guinea, 1928–1980)

Camara Laye was one of the most important novelists who pioneered prose writing in the African literary school called *Négritude*. He was born into a nominally Muslim family, and his goldsmith father was knowledgeable in the magic arts associated with that craft as practiced in various traditional societies. His vision of village life, which was fast fading in those days, never left the young writer's imagination.

Camara acquired technical training in Conakry, the capital, and then went to Paris to study engineering. He became an auto mechanic for a Paris vehicle factory, studying at night and writing down the memories of his childhood as a means of overcoming homesickness. A publisher recognized Camara's talent and published his first novel, *The Dark Child* (1953), which was an instant success. It was based on his early years and the loss of his culture as Western education gradually made him a stranger to his own experience. It won the prize for that year's outstanding French novel and was followed by a second work, *The Radiance of the King* (1954). This fantasy recounts the humiliation of a Frenchman—a symbol of colonial France—stripped of all dignity and reduced to being a sex slave, only to be redeemed by the love of a young African king.

These works established Camara's position as a leading presence in the African literary movement called *Négritude*. *Négritude* was rooted in African consciousness, used African themes, and yet was expressed in French, seeking to use the power of that language to express what traditional culture had known but not communicated. Camara was hailed as the leading prose writer of the movement by its father figure and most distinguished member, Léopold Sédar SENGHOR, the premier poet of the period. Camara's use of spirit images and the evocation of a romantic past delighted some and alienated others. His devotion to the nationalist cause was questioned, scorned by Mongo BETI as not anticolonial enough and by Wole SOYINKA as being too reliant upon French literary styles.

For a year Camara served as an attaché at the French Ministry of Youth, but in 1956 he returned to Guinea, where he worked for the colonial government as a technician. With independence in 1958, he became a roving ambassador and then was named director of the Information Ministry's study center. During this period, Camara underwent a personal crisis that affected his ability to write. He had hoped that independence would bring new freedom, but the web of plots and counterplots that surrounded President Ahmed Sékou TOURÉ produced only repression and paranoia. Many intellectuals were executed, and Camara spent 1960 to 1965 under house arrest.

In 1965 he escaped with his family to Sénégal, and in 1966 he published *Dramouss*, a bitter tale of the betrayal of independence by a savage political clique led by a character known only as Big Brute. He supported himself while in exile by editing folktales. Tragically, his wife was imprisoned in 1970 when she returned to Guinea to visit her ill mother. Camara never wrote political fiction again, hoping to protect her, and his last work, *Guardian of the Word* (1978), a historical novel set in thirteenth-century Mali, was based on the oral recitation of a Guinean griot, or storyteller. His last years were scarred by mental problems brought about by his family situation. He took a second wife while his first was in prison, and added three children to the seven he was already trying to support. His first wife divorced him when she finally was released. Camara died impoverished, in exile in Dakar.

His family name is Camara and his given name Laye, but he often reversed them.

References: adb, AA, AO, CANR, DAHB, EB, EWB, MMA, NRG, WLTC. Adele King, *The Novels of Camara Laye* (1980).

CAMERON, Donald Charles
(Mauritius/Nigeria/Tanzania, 1872–1948)

Sir Donald Charles Cameron was a prominent British colonial governor who further developed and applied Baron Frederick LUGARD's theory of indirect rule. Cameron was typical of the best and the brightest British colonial administrators who operated at the height of colonial power—paternalistic yet apparently caring and concerned for his African subjects. Because of a distant and officious manner, he was respected but little loved. His mastery of detail and powers of expression were sometimes overwhelming, but to his intimates he was warm and sympathetic.

Cameron was born in British Guiana and joined the colonial service there. In 1904 he went to Mauritius as assistant colonial secretary. In this position he deeply offended the elected members of the Legislative Council (Legco) in a speech and was saved from censure only by the nominated (government-appointed) members. After threats of violence, Cameron was dispatched to southern Nigeria in 1908 as secretary to the liquor inquiry board. Although he never believed that Lugard appreciated or properly used his abilities, Cameron was greatly influenced by the theory of indirect rule by which Lugard had achieved a measure of respect by using indigenous authorities in the administration of northern Nigeria. When Cameron became chief secretary of all Nigeria in 1921 under Sir Hugh Clifford, he performed well. He was knighted in 1923 and appointed governor of Tanganyika in 1924.

Tanganyika was an undeveloped territory, a former German colony, and a League of Nations mandate that had been under military rule. Cameron adapted indirect rule to the local scene, governing through local institutions in order to create and use an African elite in the colonial government. He organized an African civil service and established a Legco that promoted education and economic development. He successfully opposed an East African Union of Tanganyika, Uganda and Kenya, suggesting that it was not in the interests of Africans. In 1931, Cameron was appointed governor of Nigeria but was unable to turn back the effects of the worldwide depression. He began development in the neglected north, however, and instituted several administrative reforms, including a separate judiciary. His book *Principles of Native Administration and Their Application* (1934) became an influential work for colonial officials. In 1935, Cameron went to London, where he served as an advisor to the Colonial Office.

References: DAHB, DNB. Harry Gailey, *Sir Donald Cameron: Colonial Governor* (1974).

CAREY, Lott
(Liberia, 1780?–1829)

Lott Carey was a co-founder and the first Black governor of Liberia, the colony for freed American slaves that was established by the American Colonization Society in 1822.

In 1813, Carey, a Virginia slave, was able to buy his freedom and that of his two children for US$850, a huge sum at that time. He was ordained a Baptist preacher and joined the original group sailing for Liberia. A few months after its founding, the Colonization Society sent as its agent Jehudi ASHMUN, a White man who intended to become a trader. Ashmun, however, soon found himself in the position of unofficial governor. The two became good friends and Carey served as Ashmun's assistant.

Their first challenge was the unhealthy conditions that bred disease of every sort. Carey nursed the sick and became a self-instructed physician. The two then turned to the pressing need for defense against attacks by the local tribal chief, who claimed the land taken by the settlers. Carey organized the militia and helped build fortifications after moving the fearful settlers from an offshore island to the mainland. Through all their challenges, Carey never lost sight of his original goal. He encouraged the settlers to develop a Christian commonwealth, a vision he shared with their sponsor. He preached to the local people and founded a school for indigenous children, although his efforts had modest results.

Carey later fell out with Ashmun over the latter's policies and perhaps over the paternalism exercised by the project's White overseers. After a settler revolt, Ashmun was forced to leave in 1824 but returned a few months later with greatly reduced authority. After 1825, more immigrants expanded the colony by organizing several new settlements. Once again, Carey's medical experience was invaluable to the newcomers. He was named vice agent in 1826. Ashmun died in 1828 after naming Carey as his successor, but Carey died the following year in a gunpowder explosion.

References: dacb, DAHB. Leroy Fitts, *Lott Carey: The First Black Missionary to Africa* (1978).

CARROLL, Kevin, SMA
(Nigeria, 1920–1993)

Father Kevin Carroll was a British member of the Society of the African Missions (SMA), a Catholic missionary community originally founded in France. He spent most of his professional life in Nigeria, where he established a woodcarving school at Oye-Ekiti in northeastern Nigeria, from which flowed a constant stream of Yoruba art for use in Catholic churches and institutions.

Father Carroll became fascinated by African art as a youth, exploring the African collection of the local museum in Liverpool. He joined the SMA Fathers, was ordained a Catholic priest in 1942, and then posted to the Gold Coast (now Ghana). He spent the next 50 years in Ghana and Nigeria. In Ghana, Carroll mastered the Fante language and put himself under local craftsmen to learn the characteristic pattern weaving, known most prominently for the production of *kente* cloth. He learned the meaning of the patterns and how to weave on the long and extremely narrow looms. Carroll also took on woodcarving and organized his first workshop for teaching youth how to carve everyday items like spoons, bowls and stools. As time went on, he took up bead work, leather, traditional music and metalwork.

When he was transferred to Nigeria, Carroll began to put all these skills to work. With a missionary colleague, he established a workshop to train young carvers in the traditional methods of Yoruba woodcarving. He identified the best of the older carvers and employed them as master carvers, got them commissions from churches and missionary institutions, and had them mentor and train a new generation of Yoruba carvers. In the process, a dying art form took on new life and direction. Among those who worked at the Oye-Okiti center were AREOGUN of Osi-Ilorin, his son BANDELE, and Lamidi FAKEYE. All are recognized as major artistic figures in African sculpture in the twentieth century.

Carroll's workshop is sometimes criticized for influencing traditional art in the direction of Christianity and Western ideas. Certainly the themes of the work were Christian and biblical, but the style remained Yoruba. In between missionary commissions, several of the artists continued to create decorative doors and posts for the palaces of kings, and none of these show any Western influence.

Carroll's work was inspired by a vision of inculturation—creating an indigenous Christianity without copying a Western one. He learned at least four Nigerian languages, and was the first missionary to use African composers for sacred music and African weavers to create church vestments. A few of the artists were Christian, but others were Muslim or followers of traditional cults; the workshop was not used to seek conversions.

Besides his work as an art educator, Carroll was an anthropologist, a linguist who mastered a number of languages, and a photographer. His personal archives contain over 4,000 photos covering all aspects of West African culture, religion and arts. His photos of ritual objects, masks, door posts and textiles are all accompanied by valuable and voluminous notes and documentation. Carroll died in 1993 in Lagos, Nigeria.

References: Carroll, *Yoruba Religious Carving* (1967); Josef Theil and Heinz Helf, *Christliche Kunst in Africa* (Christian art in Africa, 1984).

CASELY-HAYFORD, Adelaide Smith
(Sierra Leone, 1868–1960)

Adelaide Smith Casely-Hayford, pioneering feminist and educator, was a mixed-race child of Fanti and British parents, and always struggled with being both European and African, Black and White, a woman leader in a men's society.

Sierra Leone was established as a settlement for recaptives, African slaves who were liberated by the British navy's Anti-Slavery Squadron from the clutches of slaving ships. Because slavers mixed their captives from different tribes (so that they did not share a common language and could not conspire to escape), Sierra Leone was an African colony without a common African culture. Besides the recaptives, Sierra Leone became a depository for former slaves from Nova Scotia who were expelled from Canada after slavery was declared illegal.

Casely-Hayford's father was English and Fanti; her mother was the daughter of a recaptive and a Nova Scotian. The family were prosperous members of the Creole elite in the capital, Freetown. As a small girl, Casely-Hayford went with the family to England, where she was educated to age 17. She then spent three years studying music in Germany. In both countries, she felt out of place due to her dark color. Although she returned to Freetown as a teacher, she no longer felt at home and experienced prejudice from both White and Creole society. She would later say she was a "White Black woman." She and her sister started a girls' school which had some modest success. Family obligations took her and her two sisters back to England after a few years, and there she met and married Joseph

CASELY-HAYFORD, a Ghanaian widower, lawyer and advocate of African independence. She moved yet again, this time to Ghana, where the couple lived for three years and had a child. Their daughter had medical problems, which took Adelaide and the baby again to England for three years. The marriage suffered by her absence, and the couple separated, though they never divorced.

Except for her school years, Casely-Hayford had not belonged anywhere. This caused her to reflect on the status of women and people of color. She had experienced prejudice on both counts. She returned then to Sierra Leone where she set roots that would last the rest of her life. She taught school and became active, especially in the Universal Negro Improvement Association, which stressed the unity of all Black peoples of Africa and the diaspora. It was the creation of Marcus Garvey, the Jamaican and American Black nationalist.

Determined to start a girls' school in earnest, Casely-Hayford and her niece traveled to the United States on a speaking and fundraising tour, using her husband's many contacts among leading Blacks in the U.S. She appeared everywhere in African dress, and the tour was a grand success. In 1923, she founded the Girls' Vocational School in Freetown, and served as principal until 1940. She hoped to provide an education for African girls but also to foster a pride in being African and being women. In 1935, the king of England awarded her the Silver Jubilee Medal, and in 1950 she was named an MBE (Member of the British Empire).

References: AB, *adb*, DAB. Casely-Hayford, *Reminiscences* (1953); Adelaide Cromwell, *An African Victorian Feminist* (1992).

CASELY-HAYFORD, Joseph Ephraim
(Ghana, 1866–1930)

Joseph Ephraim Casely-Hayford was founder of the National Congress of British West Africa (NCBWA), a group that defended the rights of the African educated class in the British colonies. In the immediate post-World War I period he was the most important nationalist leader in the colonies and was called the "Moses of West Africa."

Casely-Hayford studied at Fourah Bay College in Sierra Leone, briefly served as a teacher, and then for five years (1885–1890) was a journalist. He studied law in London and completed his legal studies in 1896. When he returned to the Gold Coast (now Ghana), he immediately entered local politics. He became the lawyer for the Aborigines' Rights Protection Society (ARPS), helping it defeat a restrictive land act in 1897 and a bill that threatened traditional African forest land tenure systems.

During this period British policy was deemphasizing the role of the educated elite, of which Casely-Hayford was the most prominent leader, and was directing its efforts toward negotiations with traditional rulers. Tensions developed between the two groups, but eased in the 1920s with the appointment of educated chiefs. They cooperated on the Legislative Council (Legco) on issues of justice and reform, and in 1924, Casely-Hayford and the chiefs negotiated the return of the exiled Asantehene PREMPEH I.

Casely-Hayford believed that Western education and African cultural values could be combined. His proposals for a Gold Coast university were instrumental in the 1927 foundation of Achimota College.

Casely-Hayford's thought was influenced by the nonviolent nationalism of Mahatma Gandhi, the Black consciousness of Marcus Garvey, and the attitudes of African intellectual equality taught by the Liberian Edward W. BLYDEN. In 1903 he published *Gold Coast Native Institutions* and in 1911 a novel, *Ethiopia Unbound,* both of which were polemical works. In 1915 he wrote a biography of William Wadé HARRIS, the West African religious reformer. Casely-Hayford's writing, which gave him regional and national recognition, appeared regularly in the *Gold Coast Leader,* a newspaper that championed African political rights and in which his views dominated from 1902 to 1934. He was briefly married to Adelaide CASELY-HAYFORD and they had a child. They lived separate lives but never divorced. Joseph's political views influenced Adelaide, however, and became part of her focus on African racial pride.

From 1916 to 1925, Casely-Hayford served as an appointed member of the Legislative Council (Legco), and from 1927 to his death he was an elected member. His most important political contribution, however, was founding the NCBWA to bring together nationalists from Gambia, Nigeria, Ghana and Sierra Leone. The organization agitated unsuccessfully for self-government, but it did establish the groundwork for future political development. In addition, Casely-Hayford helped found the Gold Coast Youth Conference, which evolved into the first national political party.

References: AA, CA, DAB, DAHB, MMA.

CASSIEM, Achmad
(South Africa, ?–)

Imam Achmad Cassiem is a South African Shia leader, militant and terrorist. Muslims account for only about two percent of South Africa's population, and fewer still are Shia. Although the number of militants is minuscule, they present a danger to South African society. Cassiem has been their organizer and chief ideologue. His name is sometimes given as "Ahmed Cassim."

Little is known of Cassiem's early days, other than the fact that he was educated in Koranic schools. He came to notice with the founding of Qibla in 1979, a group inspired by the Iranian Revolution that year, and created with the intention of establishing an Islamic state in South Africa. Qibla is an Arabic word for the direction toward Mecca that Muslims face during prayer. From the beginning, Cassiem intended Qibla to participate in armed struggle, and militants were sent to Libya for training in guerilla warfare. Cassiem took a small part in the antiapartheid struggle, and the armed wing of Qibla had connections with the Pan-Africanist Congress (PAC). Cassiem was imprisoned on Robben Island, where antiapartheid political prisoners were kept.

Qibla has ties to Lebanese Hezbollah (there is evidence that Qibla members fought in South Lebanon with Hezbollah) and has been named a terrorist group by the United States Department of State. It advocates the use of violence and has been able to mount a number of small but well-placed terrorist actions. None has ever been identified with Cassiem in such a way as to implicate him, but his connections and direction of the group are obvious to intelligence agencies. In the late 1990s, over a hundred members of Qibla were arrested for violence, including murder.

Cassiem appeared on television in the wake of the strike against the World Trade Center on September 11, 2001. He declared that the attacks had been plotted by Jews, and he has made similar anti-Semitic charges in public, such as his widely quoted comment, "In plain English, the Zionist state must be dismantled." After the events of 9/11, Cassiem and Qibla recruited fighters in South Africa to join the Taliban in Afghanistan.

In the 1990s, Qibla began to infiltrate a township (slum) vigilante group in Cape Town called PAGAD (People Against Gangsterism and Drugs). PAGAD targeted drug dealers and gang leaders who operated beyond the reach of the police, often meting out rough justice. As Qibla took over, PAGAD began intimidating and attacking moderate Muslim scholars and leaders. Violence escalated from beatings and warnings to the use of pipe bombs. In 1998, Cassiem ordered a purge of the non-Muslim members of PAGAD, and it became essentially a tool of Qibla. Sham groups have also been set up, mere paper entities, to claim responsibility for terrorist acts and to give the impression of a network of organizations. When Planet Hollywood was bombed, for instance, one of Qibla's shadow groups, "Muslims Against Global Oppression," claimed responsibility. Muslim, Jewish and Christian leaders have united to protest and organize against Qibla.

Cassiem has used other groups as fronts. Since 1995 he has been chair of the Islamic Unity Conference, an umbrella group of 250 Muslim organizations. It has set up an anti-Semitic radio station in Cape Town. In 2005, he engineered his election as head of the Western Cape's branch of the Pan-Africanist Congress (PAC), now a mainstream radical political party. His election was seen as a "nightmare" by many PAC leaders.

Cassiem's reach has extended beyond South Africa's borders. By the early 1990s, Qibla militants were training in Pakistan with the Taliban. In 2005, two of his followers were arrested in Pakistan while plotting to attack the South African parliament and the stock exchange. A year earlier, British authorities had discovered a cache of hundreds of stolen South African passports during a raid in London.

Reference: Cassiem, *Quest for Unity* (1992).

CAVALLY, Jeanne de (Jeanne Goba)
(Côte d'Ivoire, 1926–1990s)

Jeanne de Cavally, a longtime teacher and headmistress, was a leading writer of African French-language children's books.

Jeanne Goba (de Cavally was a pen name, after a river near her childhood home) was born in a large family of 17 children. She was educated in Côte d'Ivoire until after secondary school, when she went to Rufisque in Sénégal to attend a teacher training college. In 1949 she returned to Côte d'Ivoire and began teaching until becoming headmistress a few years into her career. She remained in primary education until retiring in 1983.

Those are the simple outlines of Jeanne Goba's career. She married and had a large family, and lived to see many grandchildren. In every aspect of her life she was surrounded with children.

A few years before her retirement, de Cavally published her first children's book, *Papi* (1978). Three years later came two other books, another in 1985 and her final work in 1987. All were published in Abidjan.

De Cavally's audience was the child between seven and 11 who has begun to master basic French. But her purpose in writing was to provide children's literature suitable for Africans. In this she was a pioneer. "Most of the time," she has said, "we put into the hands of children books that are said to be of great value, but which hardly interest them." Seeing that the available books were about European children, de Cavally determined to write about African subjects for African children. She did not back away from difficulties; her characters experience loss and confusion. In *Boubacar's Christmas Eve* (1981), the young orphan boy "has no one or nothing in the world" after his sister dies from a beating. Wandering the streets, consumed by anger, he comes to a house lit up for Christmas Eve. The story is a contrast between those who rejoice and those who are desolate, and it is not without meaning that the main character has a Muslim name. "Christmas is for me the feast for children. A feast where one can hurt them." Far from writing cheery little books, de Cavally's work confronted suffering in terms children would understand.

CETSHWAYO kaMpande
(South Africa, 1826?–1884)

Cetshwayo, a nephew of SHAKA, replaced his father, Mpande, to become the last independent king of the Zulu. After defeating the British army in the worst rout ever suffered at the hands of an African army, Cetshwayo was overcome by the British and sent into exile. Restored as a nominal king, he ruled only a short time before his death.

As a youth, Cetshwayo faced his half-brother in a struggle for the royal succession. Both organized their supporters, and a civil war erupted in 1856. Cetshwayo killed his rival and took control of the Zulu kingdom, although Mpande, his father, continued to hold the title of king. In 1872, Mpande died and Cetshwayo received the title, but by this time he had already consolidated the administration of the kingdom and strengthened the army. He reinstituted many of Shaka's field strategies, but also armed the *impis* with firearms. He then expelled foreign missionaries from Zulu territory.

In foreign policy Cetshwayo attempted to play the British against the Afrikaners, whom he feared. After the British annexation of the Transvaal in 1877, Great Britain turned against him and supported Afrikaner land claims against the Zulu, suppressing a boundary commission report that favored the Zulu. Cetshwayo, infuriated at what he regarded as betrayal, mobilized his forces. In turn, the British decided to eliminate once and for all the threat of Zulu power in South Africa by destroying Cetshwayo's army in a preemptive attack. Using a pretext, Britain demanded that Cetshwayo dissolve the army. When he refused, they moved against him.

In early 1879, Cetshwayo attacked the British at Isandhlwana and wiped out an entire regiment. The British forces, comprising 1,800 men, were encamped when one of their scouts ventured to the edge of a ravine. He stopped short when he saw 20,000 Zulu warriors sitting in total silence, waiting for the signal to attack. The British deployed themselves in the classic square, with one line kneeling and another standing, to allow rapid volleys of fire. The Zulu alternately threw themselves to the ground and leaped forward until they were inside the square, where their superiority at hand-to-hand combat made British defeat inevitable. Only 50 British soldiers escaped as the Zulu slit open the bodies "to wash their spears" and release the evil spirits.

The British recovered and defeated the Zulus at Cetshwayo's capital, Ulundi, in 1879, using Gatling guns and cannons alongside their riflemen. Cetshwayo was captured and Zululand was divided among 13 independent chiefs. The political situation, however, soon deteriorated into factional rivalries. Cetshwayo appealed to Queen Victoria and was allowed to plead his case in London, where he was an instant favorite among the public and was entertained by the Queen. Largely due to this good impression and the declining situation in Zululand, the British restored Cetshwayo to his throne. Under this arrangement Cetshwayo had no army to enforce his authority and was finally forced to flee as civil war erupted. He died shortly thereafter, officially of a heart attack, but possibly by poisoning.

References: AB, *afr*, CWAH, DAHB, DT, EB, EWB, MMA, WGMC, *wiki*. C.T. Binns, *The Last Zulu King* (1963); Donald Morris, *The Washing of the Spears* (1965).

CHAKA CHAKA, Yvonne
(South Africa, 1965–)

Pop singer, diva, entrepreneur—Yvonne Chaka Chaka is the sort of superstar the media loves. Famous and glamorous, she has successfully made the transition from pop star to businesswoman.

Chaka Chaka lost her father as a child, and was raised by her mother, a gospel singer. In 1981, she was the first Black child to appear on South African television. She sang from childhood, but she burst onto the pop scene with her 1984 hit, "I'm in Love with a DJ," which became an instant sensation all over Africa. It established her distinct form of disco, called bubblegum, as a pop craze. Bubblegum took off from township jive, using vocals that were overlapping call-and-response, a traditional form of singing in Africa. To this, Chaka Chaka added contemporary electronic sound—an electronic drum box and multiple synthesizers. Her powerful alto voice cuts through and dominates the music.

After 1984, Chaka Chaka toured Africa extensively, playing in major stadiums. Bubblegum proved a short-lived style, and she reinvented herself as the "Princess of Africa," adopted African dress and transitioned bubblegum into a meld with soft rock.

As Chaka Chaka's singing career grew, she established her own production company to give herself both artistic and commercial control of her product. In 2002, finished with touring, she became a radio and television personality, a step in her move from performer to businesswoman. She formed Chaka Chaka Enterprises as a Black empowerment project, and in 2005 struck a deal with Gestetner, the multinational office automation giant. Chaka Chaka Enterprises owns 75 percent of Gestetner's South African branch, and Chaka Chaka is CEO. This has not marked the end of her recording career, however. In 2005, she released her first gospel album, a return to her roots.

Chaka Chaka somehow manages a family life with her physician husband and four sons. She received a diploma in Adult Education and a certificate in Local Government Administration in South Africa during her most active singing years, and in 1997, she finished a certificate in Speech and Drama at Trinity College, London.

References: adb, wiki. Minky Schlesinger, *Yvonne Chaka Chaka, Princess of Africa* (1993); *Yvonne Chaka Chaka* (video, 1990); www.princessofafrica.co.za.

CHANDRIA, Manilal Premchand (Manu)
(Kenya, 1929–)

Shri Manilal Chandria is a leading businessman in Kenya, president of the Kenya Association of Manufacturers, and a prominent philanthropist.

Chandria was born of immigrant Indian parents who came to Kenya from Gujurat. Typical of energetic entrepreneurs, his father established a small food shop in Nairobi that later expanded to Mombasa on the Indian Ocean coast. He believed strongly in education as the path to success, and sent his sons overseas for higher education, at great sacrifice. Manu studied engineering in India and the United States. When he completed his master's degree in 1950, the family was already involved in food distribution and tanning, and were testing the waters in metal manufacturing.

Despite business reverses in the 1950s due to speculative investments, Manu and several members of his extended family took over the lagging Kaluworks, with 45 employees, and aggressively

went into the manufacture of steel and aluminum products. By 1958, they had 800 workers making enamelware, kitchen utensils and similar products. They realized that the future of the region involved both national independence from Great Britain and regional cooperation. Kaluworks began to diversify its manufacturing into Tanzania, but fortunately they did not go into Uganda, where Idi AMIN's later expulsion of Indian businesses would have cost them dearly. Instead, they began to market widely to India and throughout Africa as far as Nigeria.

In the 1970s, the family expanded farther overseas to Australia and even Latin America. By the first decade of the twenty-first century, the family holdings were in 40 countries across the globe and diversification had gone from kitchen supplies to a line of steel products, plastics and computer parts. They have been influenced by their Indian business experience to see that the future of manufacturing needed to be connected to the information technology (IT) revolution taking place there. They were also proving that an African company could compete on an equal level with other Third World conglomerates doing business in the developed economies.

Shri Manu brought advanced management styles to the company as well, avoiding family appointments and nepotism. All the companies under the family's control are managed by professionals, regardless of ethnicity and based on competence alone. There is a defined system for identifying potential needs, strategizing around them, and then determining if the family interests should invest, do start-up, or enter into collaborative business relationships.

He is active in several foundations, including a family one, which have sponsored activities as diverse as graduate engineering programs at the University of Nairobi and market opportunities for vegetable sellers.

Shri Manu has received a number of awards for his leadership from the governments of India, Korea and Great Britain. Queen Elizabeth II awarded him the Order of the British Empire (OBE) in 2003, and he has an honorary doctorate. His title of Shri is an honorary one from the Jain community of which he is an active member.

CHASKALSON, Arthur
(South Africa, 1931–)

The Honourable Arthur Chaskalson, former Chief Justice of South Africa and a distinguished jurist, has served on several international tribunals under the United Nations.

Chaskalson had a distinguished career as a barrister before coming to the bench. After taking degrees in business and law from the University of the Witwatersrand in the early 1950s, he entered legal practice in Johannesburg in 1956. In his most celebrated case, he and three colleagues defended Nelson MANDELA at the 1962 Rivonia Trial. Mandela was sentenced to life imprisonment on Robben Island, the vicious maximum security prison for political opponents of the apartheid regime in South Africa.

Chaskalson's career from then on focused on civil rights cases. From 1978 to 1993 he directed the Legal Resources Centre, and he was leading counsel in many cases that challenged apartheid legislation.

After the fall of apartheid, Chaskalson took part in the multiparty negotiations for an interim constitution for South Africa. With the passage of a new South African constitution, Chaskalson was appointed president of the Constitutional Court (1994–2001), which had power to interpret the constitution and laws. From this vantage point, he also undertook a reform of the national judiciary. When the Court was renamed the Supreme Court in 2001, Chaskalson became its first chief justice, serving until retirement in 2005.

While he was fulfilling his duties in South Africa during a time of transition, Justice Chaskalson was tapped to be a member of the International Commission of Jurists (1995) and then appointed to the United Nations Permanent Court of Arbitration (1999). Two years later he was also appointed to the International Criminal Court for the Former Yugoslavia, hearing cases involving genocide and war crimes.

References: adb, wiki.

CHAVUNDUKA, Mark Gova
(Zimbabwe, 1965–2002)

A heroic Zimbabwean journalist, tortured for defending an independent press under the repressive regime of Robert MUGABE, Mark Chavunduka was honored internationally for his principled stand against press censorship.

Chavunduka was born into an educated middle-class family. His father was the first Black African veterinarian in southern Africa and later a nominated member of parliament; his mother was the first Black to be named chief nursing officer in Zimbabwe. After taking a university diploma in journalism, he reported for the *Financial Gazette*, and in two years was the news editor. In 1994 he became editor of *Parade* magazine, at the age of 29. At *Parade* he raised the circulation to two million, a huge number in a region with high illiteracy. In 1997 and until his death, Chavunduka was editor-in-chief of *The Standard*, a new and soon the leading Sunday newspaper in Zimbabwe. Circulation tripled in response to *The Standard'*s nonpartisan and balanced reporting. His lead stories were copied and quoted in the foreign media.

Chavunduka ran afoul of the government in 1999 when *The Standard* reported on an attempted coup against Mugabe, led by 23 army officers. The story hit the international media and infuriated Mugabe. Chavunduka was arrested and tortured with beatings, electric shock and water torture. When an international outcry brought his release, the government denied that torture had taken place, then changed their story to say that—he had tortured himself. The Medical Foundation for the Treatment of Torture Victims in London disproved the government claims, and treated Chavunduka for post-traumatic syndrome. He then returned to *The Standard* and continued its investigative reporting.

His bravery in the face of harassment and threats brought both support and recognition from Harvard University (which awarded a Nieman Fellowship enabling him the take a further degree in journalism), Amnesty International, and the International Press Freedom Award. Friends urged him to stay in the United States, but Chavunduka insisted on returning to Zimbabwe to continue to confront oppression.

When he died at age 36, Chavunduka was managing director (CEO) of *The Standard* and part owner, and had investments in other media outlets.

Reference: adb.

CHEIKH, Said Mohammed
(The Comoros, ?–1970)

Dr. Said Mohammed Cheikh, a leading liberation advocate in his country, became the Comoros' first head of state before they achieved full independence.

Of the island states in the Indian Ocean off East Africa, the Comoros have the strongest ties to the continent. The Comorese speak Swahili, an Afro-Arabic language, and have cultural affinities to the East African coast. During the colonial period, France developed a small class of *assimilés,* people who had absorbed French culture and whom France considered loyal. One of these, Cheikh, descended from two prominent noble families on Grand Comore, the main island, and received an advanced education, becoming the first Comoran-born physician.

As he attracted a popular following in the islands, Cheikh was a natural choice for leadership. His political organization developed into the *Parti Vert,* the Green Party, opposed by the *Parti Blanc* or White Party, which formed around a prince who was the son of the last sultan of Grand Comore. In 1946, when France permitted election of a deputy and senator to the French national assembly, Cheikh was elected to the House of Deputies. He was a supporter of General Charles de Gaulle, the war hero who dominated postwar French politics, and he shared de Gaulle's characteristic charismatic and authoritarian style. In Paris, Cheikh was an effective voice for the tiny colony. A five-year development plan was instituted in 1948, Comoran land reform was approved in 1949, and substantial disaster aid was granted after the cyclone of 1950. Cheikh retained his seat as a member of the Green Party until 1960, when the Comoros received two deputies. Cheikh then shared the honors with his chief rival, and the ruling elite put up a common front.

In 1958 the Comoros Islands voted on independence, which Cheikh strongly opposed, fearing that the islands could not succeed politically or economically. The election was a personal triumph for Cheikh, as 97 percent voted for status as a French protectorate with full internal autonomy. In 1961, Cheikh was elected the first head of state, and in 1965 he carried the islands by 99 percent for de Gaulle in the French national elections. Dissatisfied with the division of authority, Cheikh pressed Paris for greater authority but achieved little success.

In 1968 a student demonstration was suppressed brutally by French paratroops, and the incident fanned the flames of anticolonialism in the Comoros. This incident coincided with the breakdown of the Gaullist government in France, and Cheikh resigned. He made a successful return to political office, but the fragile coalition between the Greens and Whites had been shattered. The grand old man of Comoran politics failed to attract the younger generation. When he died in 1970, the old politics died with him. Total independence came in 1975.

Reference: afr.

CHEPCHUMBA, Joyce
(Kenya, 1970–)

Joyce Chepchumba is a leading Kenyan long-distance runner, a medalist at the 2000 Olympics in Sydney and the winner of the Chicago (twice) and New York marathons. She is regarded as one of the outstanding athletes in the history of her sport.

Chepchumba was raised in Kericho in the Kenyan highlands, a region of the country that has produced a generation of outstanding runners of international caliber. She is a member of the Kalinjin ethnic group, a gathering of several small tribes with common cultural roots.

Chepchumba's record is impressive. She ran for Kenya at the 1996 Atlanta Olympics, but did not place. Beginning with the 1997 London Marathon, however, she posted first-place finishes in Chicago twice (1998, 1999), repeating in London in 1999 (where she set a world record), and taking Tokyo in 2000. That same year, she was the bronze medalist in the marathon at the Sydney Olympics. In 2002 she won the New York Marathon and the Zurich Half Marathon, and two years later the half marathons in Berlin and Lisbon. From 2000 through 2002, she took first at three consecutive Great Scottish Half Marathons.

Few races are as heart-stopping as Chepchumba's finish in the 1999 Chicago Marathon. She stumbled and fell, only to recover her balance and stride and take a photo finish victory by one second.

Inexplicably, the Kenyan national federation passed her over for a spot on the 2004 Athens Olympics team in favor of a less known and less experienced runner (who ended up placing eleventh). In 2005, she had to withdraw from the Berlin Half Marathon due to tax conflicts with German authorities.

Chepchumba trains and lives half the year in Detmold, Germany, with the Volker Wagner Club. Her husband, a former long-jumper who is strongly supportive of her career, lives in Kenya and cares for their son and daughter. As late as 2004, in her mid-thirties, she remained among the top 20 women runners on the list of annual earnings. Her personal best in the marathon was set at London in 1999 (2:23:22), and in the half marathon, 1:08:11 at Lisbon in 2004. She dismisses ideas of retirement: "I will run as long as my legs will be able to carry me."

Reference: wiki.

CHERONO, Stephen (Saïf Saeed Shaheen)
(Kenya, 1982–)

Stephen Cherono, also known as Saïf Saeed Shaheen, is the world record-holding steeplechase runner, a winner of two world championships in his sport, and a gold medalist at the Commonwealth Games in 2002.

Shaheen, as he now prefers to be called, was a talented runner as a youth. At 17 he won the 2,000-meter steeplechase at the World Youth Games. Since then he has gone from strength to strength, posting outstanding results for Kenya, and after his defection, for his new country, Qatar.

Shaheen made headlines and attracted sharp criticism when he defected from Kenya in 2003 and took citizenship in Qatar, an oil sheikdom on the Persian Gulf. In the process he became a Muslim and took an Arabic name. It was reported that he received a million dollars to make the move, along with a guaranteed $1,000 monthly for life. Shaheen openly acknowledged, "Yes, I have moved for the money." He was denounced by President Mwai KIBAKI and his move was regretted by the president of the International Olympic Committee. Some Kenyan runners sympathize with Shaheen's

decision, however, citing the straitened conditions under which many Kenyan athletes are forced to live and the lack of a pension system for athletes in Kenya. Shaheen paid an immediate price, being banned from the 2004 Athens Olympics under a rule that athletes who change their nationality may not compete in international events for three years after their new citizenship takes effect. Only the consent of the Kenyan athletic federation would allow a waiver, and with Kibaki's disapproval, they refused at first. A change of heart came within a year, rumored to be in exchange for a new all-weather track and renovation of a stadium in Eldoret, Kenya.

Shaheen returned immediately to the track, winning the International Athletic Association Foundation (IAAF) Games at Helsinki and the World Championships at Paris in 2003. He holds the world record of 7:53:62 for the 3,000-meter steeplechase, set in Brussels in 2004, his second world record. He has recently begun running flat races at 1,500 meters, 3,000 meters and 5,000 meters, to strengthen his legs to achieve his final goal: a steeplechase record that will stand for many years into his retirement.

Shaheen is a pace setter, with a smooth style that seems effortless as he moves between the barriers without breaking stride. His scrawny body seems frail, but he floats effortlessly over the hurdles.

Reference: wiki.

CHIDZERO, Bernard Thomas Gibson
(Zimbabwe, 1927–2002)

Dr. Bernard Thomas Gibson Chidzero, the minister of finance since independence, presided over the delicate transition of the Zimbabwean economy after the civil war ended in 1980.

Chidzero received his first degree from Pius XII University College in Lesotho (then Basutoland) in 1952. He then studied in Canada, obtaining an M.A. at Ottawa University and a Ph.D. at McGill University, both in political science. He finished his formal education with two years (1958–1960) of postdoctoral research at Oxford University before joining the staff of the United Nations (U.N.) Economic Commission for Africa as a social affairs officer. This position was followed by three years (1960–1963) as representative of the U.N. Technical Assistance Board and three years (1963–1966) as director of the Special Fund Program. He assumed other short assignments, ending his U.N. experience as deputy secretary-general of the U.N. Conference of Trade and Development (UNCTAD) from 1977 to 1980.

All of Chidzero's U.N. experience was in Africa, and by 1980 he was one of the most knowledgeable and able political economists on the continent. He had spent the years of the Zimbabwe guerrilla war outside the mainstream of Zimbabwean life, and his work hardly touched the problems of the Rhodesian regime, which ran a White-controlled state from 1965 to 1980. This separation from his homeland not only allowed Chidzero to gain an international education and experience and to become the most competent Zimbabwean economic specialist, but it also made him one of the few potential leaders uncommitted to any of the factions in the liberation struggle. President Robert MUGABE selected him for his first cabinet as minister of economic planning and development, making him an appointed member of the senate at the same time. In 1985, Chidzero was elected a member of parliament from Harare, the capital.

Zimbabwe's economy has long rested largely in the hands of Whites, and the government's first task was to reassure this minority of their continued role. Chidzero directed the nation's remarkable economic growth during the early 1980s and, when the drop in commodity prices brought on a recession in the mid-1980s, he managed the difficulties in such a way as to avoid a crisis. He restrained the economy, maintained the foreign-exchange balance, and helped the country survive the economic slump with minimal damage. When Mugabe reorganized his government in 1988, Chidzero was made a senior minister in charge of all the economics ministries.

In 1990, Chidzero was a candidate for secretary-general of the United Nations but lost in a close vote to Boutros Boutros-Ghali of Egypt. By 1992 recession had returned to Zimbabwe, and Chidzero had to introduce stringent measures, including tax increases and budget cuts. The pressures of the worldwide recession took a personal toll, however, and in May 1994, Chidzero collapsed and was admitted to a hospital in Harare. He returned to work on a limited basis but gradually withdrew from day-to-day management of the ministry, even as Zimbabwe slid into political and economic chaos.

He was buried with national honors in Heroes' Acre in Harare.

References: CA, DRWW, PLBA, RWWA.

CHIEPE, Gaositwe Keagakwa Tibe
(Botswana, 1926–)

Gaositwe Keagakwa Tibe Chiepe, a diplomat and civil servant, has been a cabinet minister for over 20 years, perhaps the longest leadership record of any female politician in Africa. Her leadership in the widely diverse areas of education, foreign affairs, and mineral resources has been instrumental in Botswana's stability and progress.

After receiving her secondary education in South Africa, Chiepe earned a degree and an education diploma at Fort Hare College in 1947. She was then appointed the first female education officer in the Bechuanaland Protectorate (now Botswana), which was then under British administration. With two years off to complete a master's degree at the University of Bristol in England, she worked her way up through the ranks until she became director of education from 1968 to 1970. She was largely responsible for the framework of the Botswanan education system after independence. At that point, Sir Seretse KHAMA appointed her high commissioner (ambassador) to Great Britain; at the same time she was accredited to five other countries and the European Economic Community (EEC). She took part in the negotiations that led up to the Lomé I Convention that established development and trade policy between the EEC and 70 Third World countries. She also participated in later revisions of the Lomé Convention.

In 1974, Chiepe was the first woman elected to the national assembly and the first brought into the cabinet when she was named minister of commerce and industry. From 1977 to 1984 she served as minister of mineral resources and water affairs. Botswana was going through a major expansion of its mining industry at that time, and she carefully developed key areas that could best contribute to economic growth, laying the groundwork for the country's later economic miracle.

In 1980, President Quett MASIRE chose Chiepe for the sensitive post of minister of External (Foreign) Affairs, in which she had to deal with

South Africa's threat of sanctions as part of its strategy of destabilizing the states on its borders. She dealt patiently with the South Africans over several raids into Botswana, and after 1990 the raids ceased. She served until 1994, when she was named Minister of Education (1994–1999).

Chiepe has remained active after her retirement from government service. In 2000, she chaired the Commonwealth observer team for the Zanzibari elections, which she did not hesitate to denounce as fraudulent, calling for a new poll. In 2004, she was honored by the United States Embassy as one of five outstanding women for Women's Day.

References: EWB, PLBA, RWWA.

CHIKANE, Frank
(South Africa, 1951–)

Reverend Frank Chikane, former general secretary of the South African Council of Churches (SACC), was one of the church leaders involved in the 1980s antiapartheid struggle. It was his leadership that carried the SACC through the transition from apartheid to a multiracial South African society.

Chikane's father was a pastor in the Apostolic Faith Mission (AFM), a Pentecostal denomination, and as a schoolboy Chikane became involved with the Student Christian Movement (SCM). After secondary school he went to the University of the North to study science and became active in SCM activities with Cyril RAMAPHOSA. Both of them became convinced of the evil of apartheid and that the churches cooperating with this racist system had abandoned Christian morality. The SCM took up the student legal aid fund for African political detainees and fostered the beginnings of the Black Consciousness Movement (BCM). Chikane led a weeklong sit-in just before his final examinations and, as a result, collapsed from exhaustion and mental stress. Due to his political activities, he was denied permission to retake the exams and left the university without a degree in 1975.

Chikane began working for the AFM and studying theology by correspondence. He was an assistant pastor for several years before he was ordained in 1979 when he finished his courses. The AFM was a politically conservative group, believing that the church's role should be limited to the spiritual life. When Chikane began a range of projects—including a soup kitchen, adult educa-

tion, and community organizing—he raised concerns among the church hierarchy. He also worked with the Azanian People's Organization (AZAPO), which took up the cause of the BCM when it was banned after Steve BIKO's death. AZAPO's radical challenge to apartheid, based on Black racial solidarity, was opposed by both conservative groups and the African National Congress (ANC).

In early 1977, Chikane was detained for six weeks under the Terrorism Act. Following his release, he was unable to walk because of his torture, which had been conducted by a deacon from his own church. Over the next several years he was detained several times and was beaten, abused and had his hair torn out. On one occasion, his appearance in court so shocked his church that in reaction, a number of youth members slipped over the border to Mozambique to join the ANC guerrilla forces. In 1981, Chikane was defrocked and suspended from the AFM for political involvement. He remained a church member but was not reinstated in his ministry until 1990. In a bizarre event, Chikane collapsed while on a U.S. visit in 1989, and it was determined that his clothing had been impregnated with poison. Those who tried to murder him were refused amnesty by the Truth and Reconciliation Commission, and in 2006 they were indicted and put on trial.

In 1981 Chikane joined the Institute for Contextual Theology, a theological think tank highly receptive to liberation theology, and became its general secretary in 1983. In 1985 a group of 151 clergy released the Kairos Document, a Christian indictment of apartheid that Chikane played a key role in drafting. The document helped to mobilize significant support from churches overseas and formed the basis for a united church front against apartheid. He also helped launch the United Democratic Front (UDF), an antiapartheid umbrella group that provided a legal presence during the banning of African political action organizations. Chikane was a member of its executive, and in 1985 he, Albertina SISULU, and other UDF leaders were detained.

In 1987, Chikane replaced Dr. Beyers NAUDÉ as general secretary of the SACC. The South African government's campaign against the churches intensified until the SACC headquarters were bombed and those of the South African Catholic Bishops' Conference were burned down.

Chikane's task in the SACC, having succeeded Naudé and Desmond TUTU before him, was to bring the conservative churches back into the SACC. He slowly moved the organization from one of political confrontation toward a stance of mediation as the transition to majority-Black government took place. The SACC had a key role in the formation of the Truth and Reconciliation Commission, which allowed those who had tortured and killed in the name of apartheid to confess their guilt and be either granted amnesty or sent to trial.

In 1995, Chikane became the head administrator and chief of staff for the office of the deputy vice president, Thabo MBEKI. When Mbeki became president in 1999, Chikane followed him to the president's office.

References: dacb, GSAP, RWWA. Chikane, *No Life of My Own* (1989).

CHILEMBWE, John
(Malawi, 1870–1915)

Reverend John Chilembwe, the great hero and martyr of Malawi (formerly Nyasaland), is a person of mythic proportions in his homeland because he was the first African with a sense of Malawian nationalism. After founding one of the earliest independent Christian denominations in Africa, he led a dramatic and violent uprising against colonialism.

Around 1890, Chilembwe became a pupil at the Church of Scotland mission in Blantyre, but he was converted by Joseph Booth, a British Baptist missionary, and became his assistant from 1892 until 1895. Booth worked for a number of churches and had no denominational loyalty. He taught a radical equality that resonated with Chilembwe's own sense of Black pride. In 1897, Booth took Chilembwe to the United States, where a Baptist church sponsored him through Virginia Theological College. Here he seems to have come into contact with contemporary African-American thinking, especially the self-help ethic of Booker T. Washington. He returned to Nyasaland in 1900 as an ordained Baptist and founded the Providence Industrial Mission, which developed into seven schools.

Chilembwe preached an orthodox Baptist faith along with a morality that opposed alcohol and emphasized the values of hard work, personal hygiene and personal responsibility. Chilembwe seemed to believe that European-style propriety and etiquette would bring respect and success from Whites. His schools emphasized modern methods of agriculture and by 1912 had 1,000 pupils, plus 800 in the adult section.

Events after 1912 disillusioned Chilembwe. A famine in 1913 brought great hardship and starvation to many peasant farmers. Mozambican refugees flooded into Nyasaland, and Chilembwe deeply resented the way they were exploited by White plantation owners. When World War I broke out the following year, Africans were conscripted into the British army, and Chilembwe protested both from the pulpit and in the local press. The White landowners were infuriated by his nationalist appeal, and several of his schools were burned down. Added to personal problems of declining health, financial difficulties, and the death of a beloved daughter, Chilembwe's sense of betrayal deepened into fury.

In careful detail, Chilembwe planned an attack on the worst of the area plantations, which was known for cruelty to its African workers. Whether Chilembwe thought that his rebellion would spark a general uprising is difficult to determine, because he had no clear long-term goal. With 200 followers, he

John Chilembwe

struck swiftly, and three plantation managers were
killed. One of these, a cousin of David LIVING-
STONE, was notorious for burning down tenants'
chapels, whipping workers, and denying them their
wages. His head was cut off and displayed on a pole
in Chilembwe's church. The rebels, however, scru-
pulously observed Chilembwe's orders not to harm
any women or children. The colonial response was
immediate and ruthless, resulting in the death of
many Africans. Chilembwe was captured and shot
immediately.

Chilembwe must have been aware that the
uprising was suicidal when he called on his men "to
strike a blow and die." It was, nevertheless, the first
resistance to colonialism that went beyond attempts
merely to restore earlier traditional African authority; his rebellion looked toward a future nation. In
this sense, Chilembwe and his followers—mostly
educated, Christian, small businessmen—demanded
for themselves the same place in the modern world
that they saw Europeans enjoying.

References: AB, *afr*, *dacb*, DAHB, EB, MMA,
wiki. Desmond Phiri, *John Chilembwe* (1976).

CHILUBA, Frederick

(Zambia, 1943–)

Frederick Chiluba won the Zambian presidency in
1991 elections, replacing Kenneth KAUNDA and
his tarnished United National Independence Party
(UNIP). The promise of a new order based on
democracy, a liberalized economy, and an end to
corruption has run into hard realities as conditions
have worsened for the country.

Born the son of a Bemba miner in the northern
copper belt, Chiluba lacked the funds to finish
school. As a youth he went to Tanganyika to work
on a sisal plantation and there imbibed the spirit of
nationalism and anticolonialism. He flirted with
communism and spent a few months studying in
East Germany and the Soviet Union. In 1966 he
returned to the copper belt and entered the labor
movement the next year. He became president of
the Building and General Workers' Union in 1971,
which three years later was followed by his election
as president of the Zambian Congress of Trade
Unions, a federation of 18 affiliates. By this time he
had abandoned his socialist views and scorned
Kaunda's failed economic policies. When Kaunda
declared the UNIP the sole legal party in 1972, the

labor movement—one of the few groups able to
muster resistance to the government—became the
unofficial opposition.

In 1973, Chiluba was appointed to Zambia's
United Nations (U.N.) delegation, and he was
profoundly affected by his experience in the United
States. He watched the Watergate investigations of
President Richard Nixon with fascination, convinced that a free press and government accountability were the only paths to freedom. In 1980 he
confronted Kaunda's increasing authoritarianism
with the threat of a national strike, for which
Kaunda expelled the union leadership from the
UNIP. Since the national constitution required all
union heads to belong to the national party, they
were effectively barred from their offices. A series of
crippling strikes followed, and Chiluba, accused of
masterminding a plot, was arrested. After his release
by the courts, Chiluba began an open defiance
campaign, spending much of the 1980s building
support outside the copper belt and his core Bemba
constituencies until he had a multiethnic, national
following.

The collapse of communism in Eastern Europe
and the growing democratization movement across
Africa in 1990 gave the Zambian political opposition the opportunity to demand a free political
system. Disparate antigovernment groups coalesced
into the Movement for Multiparty Democracy
(MMD), and the worsening economy forced Kaunda
to permit open elections. Campaigning on human
rights and economic reform, Chiluba was elected
president in 1991. He lost no time in attacking
Zambia's economic crisis, reducing government
budgets, and cutting food subsidies. The austerity
program caused considerable disenchantment with
the Chiluba government, however, due to evidence
that corruption is still common in higher circles. In
1993 a conspiracy against the government was
discovered, the "Zero Option Plot," causing Chiluba
to declare a state of emergency and to arrest three of
Kaunda's sons. After much international criticism,
Chiluba suspended the state of emergency two
months later.

Chiluba was re-elected in 1996 despite a
challenge that he was born in the Democratic
Republic of the Congo. He turned the tables on
Kaunda's supporters, threatening to deport Kaunda
as Malawi-born. He then attempted to amend the
constitution to allow himself a third term, but that
effort failed. After leaving office in 2002, he was

charged with corruption, but that has not been proved.

References: afr, CB, RWWA, *wiki*.

CHIPEMBERE, Henry Masauko Blasius
(Malawi, 1930–1975)

Henry Masauko Blasius Chipembere, distinguished Malawian nationalist and independence leader, was a member of Malawi's first parliament. At first a supporter of Dr. Hastings Kamuzu BANDA, Malawi's first president, Chipembere later became a center of cabinet opposition to Banda's growing authoritarianism and finally a resistance leader.

Chipembere graduated from Fort Hare University College in South Africa and entered colonial service in Nyasaland (now Malawi). He became active in the Nyasaland African Congress and later the Malawi Congress Party (MCP) and was elected to the Legislative Council (Legco) in 1956, a position from which he attacked the Federation of Rhodesia and Nyasaland for attempting regional dominance by White settlers in Southern Rhodesia (now Zimbabwe). At this time Banda was living in Ghana and was a leading opponent of the federation. Chipembere led a drive to bring him home to lead the nationalist movement.

Accepting Banda's condition that he alone lead the MCP, the two united in a militant campaign for separation from the federation and complete independence. Chipembere, treasurer of the MCP, organized several demonstrations and was imprisoned with Banda in Southern Rhodesia for 20 months during 1959 and 1960. Five months after his release, Chipembere was sentenced for sedition, and he served two years, until self-government was granted to Malawi in 1963. He held several cabinet ministries, and in the cabinet crisis of 1964 he emerged as the leader of those arguing for corporate leadership and shared decision making. He became critical of Banda's friendship with South Africa and the retention of colonial administrators after independence. Although he defended Banda in parliament, Chipembere sided with the liberals and resigned from the cabinet.

Placed under house arrest by Banda, Chipembere fled into Mozambique to organize armed resistance. In 1965 he and his followers invaded Malawi, meeting with initial success, but when his field commander was captured and executed publicly, the movement collapsed. Chipembere went into exile, first to the United States, where he received a master's degree, and then to Tanzania to teach ideology for the Tanzania African National Union (TANU), the national party. In 1969 he returned to the United States to work toward a Ph.D. in history at the University of California at Los Angeles. He also taught at California State University, Los Angeles. In 1975 he died of diabetes in Los Angeles.

References: DAHB, MMA, PLBA.

CHIRWA, Orton Ching'oli
(Malawi, 1919–1992)

Orton Chirwa was a lawyer admitted to the British bar, as was his wife, Vera. He was a founder of the Malawi Congress Party (MCP), headed by Hastings Kamuzu BANDA. At independence in 1964, Chirwa was named minister of Justice and attorney general. It was not long before he fell out with Banda. Chirwa founded the Malawi Freedom Movement (MFM) to challenge Banda's rule. When threats on his life became obvious, he went into exile to Zambia, Great Britain and finally Tanzania. Vera soon joined him.

Both Chirwas were kidnapped in 1981 and spirited to Malawi, where, after a farce of a trial, they were sentenced to death for treason. They were turned over to a so-called "traditional court" and refused either legal assistance or the right to call witnesses. Ironically, Orton had written the law establishing those courts when he was attorney general.

After an international outcry, the sentence was commuted to life imprisonment. During his 11 years in prison, he was tortured regularly. He was forced to squat in shackles for two days at a time, with an iron rod behind his knees. The International Commission of Jurists (ICJ) protested the trial and expressed growing concern for Orton's health as he aged. When he died in prison, the ICJ demanded an independent postmortem, but it was refused. Orton's death came in the midst of the final challenge that would bring down Banda, the open opposition of the Roman Catholic, Anglican and Presbyterian Churches.

CHIRWA, Vera
(Malawi, 1932–)

A fearless human rights activist, Vera Chirwa has suffered for her commitment, spent over a decade in prison and risen above it to continue her crusade for liberation.

Vera married Orton CHIRWA while still a teenager and they had several children. While Orton studied law in London, Vera worked as a clerk for the colonial government.

During the years leading up to Malawi's independence in 1964, Vera was studying in Great Britain. She was admitted to the English bar in 1967 and returned home. After a short time, she returned to England for further studies. Meanwhile, Orton went into exile on Zambia because his opposition to Hastings Kamuzu BANDA's dictatorial tendencies caused him to fear retribution. Vera joined him there. She practiced some law and was a professor at the University of Zambia. They then went on to Tanzania.

With her husband and youngest son, she was seized by Malawian agents on Christmas Eve, 1981, and taken to Malawi for trial. She and her husband were convicted of treason and sentenced to death, which was later commuted to life imprisonment. When Orton died, Vera was refused permission to attend his funeral. She had seen him only once, for a few minutes, after the first eight years of their imprisonment. By the time Orton died, the opposition to Banda had reached a tipping point. Banda pardoned Vera shortly after Orton's death.

After release from prison, Vera plunged into human rights advocacy. Her first activity was on behalf of prisoners, who live in crowded and often disgusting conditions in Malawi. She set up the Malawi Centre for Advice, Research and Education on Rights (Malawi-CARER)

More and more, Vera has devoted her energies to gender issues. She is president of a women's rights group, Women's Voice. Part of her agenda is to change traditional law, which deprives widows of all their property on the death of their husbands. In 2005, she was appointed Human Rights Commissioner of the African Union, the summit organization to which all African states belong.

In 2006 she ran for the presidency of Malawi as an independent, but without a political base in the country, it was a symbolic race. She argued that Africa was ready for its first female president, but before the Malawi elections, that prophecy was fulfilled by Ellen JOHNSON-SHIRLEAF of Liberia.

CHISSANO, Joaquim
(Mozambique, 1939–)

Joaquim Chissano, the urbane foreign representative of the Front for the Liberation of Mozambique (FRELIMO) resistance movement during the last years of colonialism, became president after the sudden death of Samora MACHEL in a plane crash. He has steered Mozambique away from Marxist ideology and has made peace with the Mozambique National Resistance (RENAMO) rebels.

In secondary school Chissano joined a nationalist youth movement begun by Eduardo MONDLANE, the father of Mozambican nationalism. In 1960 he went to Portugal on a scholarship to study medicine, but he soon abandoned his studies to join the exile nationalist movement. Under surveillance by the Portuguese secret police, he left for Paris and then for Tanganyika (now Tanzania) in 1962, where he became a founding member of FRELIMO. Realizing that Portugal would resist all moves toward independence, FRELIMO organized itself as a guerrilla force and established training camps in Tanzania. By 1973, FRELIMO occupied the northern provinces of Mozambique, but instead independence was won by events in Portugal. When the fascist government collapsed there in 1974, the Socialist leaders opened freedom negotiations with all their colonies. Chissano was named prime minister of the transition government that year after taking a leading part in the negotiations. Machel named him foreign minister at independence in 1975.

Mozambique adopted the policy of hosting insurgent anticolonial groups, and it became the base for Robert MUGABE's Zimbabwean African National Liberation Army (ZANLA). In response, Rhodesia (now Zimbabwe) organized RENAMO from disaffected elements and began a systematic terrorist campaign that laid waste to the Mozambican economy. South Africa took over RENAMO's sponsorship in 1980, when Zimbabwe became independent. Chissano during this period represented Mozambique abroad, helping to maintain its links with the Soviet bloc. In 1984, Mozambique and South Africa signed the Nkomati Accord, by which they agreed not to support resistance movements within their own states. Chissano refused to take part in the negotiations but accepted the accord in a spirit of party discipline.

In 1986, after Machel was killed in a plane crash, FRELIMO chose Chissano as president. He began a process of moving Mozambique from doctrinaire Marxism to a more nonaligned position. In 1987, Chissano visited a number of Western states to confirm this shift and to seek support for ending the RENAMO threat. (RENAMO had continued to resist the government, despite the withdrawal of South African support.) He was particularly successful in Washington, where President Ronald Reagan denounced RENAMO and promised assistance in the peace process. Mozambique also received more U.S. foreign aid than any other sub-Saharan country. In 1989, Chissano renounced Marxism and agreed to multiparty elections. These led to direct negotiations with RENAMO, which was legalized in exchange for a ceasefire. Chissano contested in the 1994 elections with Afonso DHLAKAMA, RENAMO's leader, and won. He repeated this in 1999 with 53 percent of the vote. He completed his last term of office in 2005. During his second term he was chair of the African Union (2003–2004).

References: AB, *afr*, CB, EWB, PLBA, RWWA, *wiki*.

CINQUE, Joseph (Sengbe Pieh)
(Sierra Leone, 1813?–1879)

Joseph Cinque (pronounced *sin'gway*) led an 1839 slave mutiny on the Cuban slave ship *Amistad*, which led to a celebrated trial in U.S. courts. The trial held that slaves who had escaped from illegal servitude were free men.

Cinque$,$ a Mende (southern Sierra Leone) farmer, was captured and sold to a Spanish slaver when he was in his twenties. By 1839 the slave trade was prohibited by international law and had been illegal in Spanish domains for 20 years. Nevertheless, Cinque was shipped to Havana, where, along with about 50 other slaves, he was resold and placed on the *Amistad,* a small coastal schooner bound for Cuban sugar plantations. False passports had been obtained for the slaves. After the

schooner was blown out to sea in a storm, Cinque and some of the other slaves seized machetes and killed the captain and the cook. They ordered the remaining two crew members to sail for Africa. The helmsman, however, headed north and landed on Long Island, New York, where the U.S. Coast Guard arrested the men and took them to New Haven, Connecticut, to stand trial for murder.

The U.S. press and President Martin Van Buren favored Spanish demands that the men be sent to Cuba. The trial galvanized the abolitionist movement, which united in support of Cinque and the other Blacks. A portrait of Cinque was engraved and circulated throughout New England to raise money for their defense. At the same time, President Van Buren sent a naval ship to seize the slaves if they lost the case, to prevent any appeal. The lower court ruled that the government had no right to try the captives, because they had been illegally kidnapped into slavery and were therefore free. The prosecution appealed to the Supreme Court, where former President John Quincy Adams took their case and argued for 13 hours on behalf of the *Amistad* defendants, denouncing Van Buren for "utter injustice." In March 1841, the abolitionists won the case.

The Africans were hosted by families who taught them to read and write while money was raised for their return to Africa. They spoke in churches and schools, both collecting funds and inflaming abolitionist sentiments. In 1841 the freed persons were taken to Sierra Leone with several missionaries, who intended to establish a mission settlement, but the Africans soon deserted and returned to their home areas. Cinque visited and stayed at the mission from time to time through the years. Ironically, Cinque reportedly became a slave trader himself, and although he had abandoned Christianity, he returned to the mission to die.

References: afr, DAB, DAHB, EWB, *wiki*.

CLARK, John Pepper-Bekederemo
(Nigeria, 1935–)

John Pepper-Bekederemo Clark, poet and dramatist, has combined a career as a professor and literary critic with that of a playwright and poet. He bases his plays on traditional African tales but often gives them a modern, even melodramatic, treatment.

Clark's poetry is popular, avoiding anything complex or experimental, and has been criticized as suffering from a certain banality. Clark's work and life have been marred by a sarcastic and extremely critical streak that has made his best work marvelous satire but that also has alienated him from others and made his lesser work appear carping.

After undergraduate studies at the University of Ibadan, Clark wrote and produced his first play, *Song of a Goat* (1960), a story of marital impotence and infidelity, which was followed in 1961 by his first volume of poetry. He spent from 1962 to 1963 in graduate study at Princeton (from which he was dismissed), and in 1964 published a scathing travel memoir of his stay, *America, Their America,* in which he describes the United States as obsessed with sex and materialism. After his return to Nigeria, Clark wrote *Masquerade* (1964), a lurid love and murder sequel to *Song of a Goat. Reed in the Tide* (1965) was the first book of poetry by a single Black African to be published in Europe.

In 1966, Clark published *Ozidi,* the first of a series of plays based on a native tradition of the Ijaw people. Clark, by then employed as a research fellow at the University of Lagos, spent 15 years exploring the story cycle, which in its entirety takes over a week to perform. The completed work, *The Ozidi Saga,* was published in 1976 and represents a major scholarly presentation of African epic literature. It is also his masterwork. To make it more accessible, Clark also produced a film based on the chronicle, *Tides of the Delta.* In the meantime, he was promoted to professor and department chair in English in 1972, a position he held until his retirement in 1980.

Clark occasionally falls back on his classical formation in literature. His poems, "New Year" and "Ibadan Dawn," for example, are modeled consciously after Gerard Manley Hopkins, the nineteenth-century Anglo-Irish poet. Clark uses Hopkins's sprung rhythm in both pieces.

Clark could not escape the turmoil of Nigeria, which he often expressed in his bitter political verse. He wrote sarcastic poems about Dr. Benjamin Nnamdi AZIKIWE, Nigeria's president, and a lament for his hero, Chief Obafemi AWOLOWO. His personal circle was divided in loyalties during the Nigerian civil war (1967–1970), where some sided with the federal authorities and others with secessionist Biafra. Clark supported the federal government. Several close friends were killed or executed, and it was years before Clark reconciled with his old friend Chinua ACHEBE, who had supported Biafra.

Since leaving the university—which he called "a cesspool"—Clark has returned to the theater, producing a three-play cycle based on Niger Delta history. With his characteristic satire and dramatic flair, the plays represent a new burst of creativity on Clark's part. He has published critical articles in leading journals, the best of which have been collected and published in *The Examples of Shakespeare* (1970). This compendium contains Clark's essay on the bicultural and bilingual problem of the African writer, "The Legacy of Caliban." Three other volumes of poetry were published in 1965, 1970, and 1981. Popular in style, they also have been critically well received.

Clark long published as "John Pepper Clark" or "J.P. Clark," but later began adding his Ijaw name, which is sometimes used as his surname.

References: adb, afr, AA, AWT, CANR, DLB, EB, MBW, NRG, WLTC, *wiki.*

COETZEE, John M.
(South Africa, 1940–)

Dr. John M. Coetzee, an Afrikaner who writes in English, is a prominent member of the younger generation of South African novelists who explore the dark side of that country's recent history.

Coetzee was raised in Cape Town and the Western Cape, and took degrees in mathematics and English at the University of Cape Town. After the Sharpeville massacre in 1961, Coetzee went abroad as a student and teacher in the United States and as an employee of IBM in Britain. He obtained a doctorate in linguistics at the University of Texas in 1969, using computerized literary analysis, and taught briefly in New York. Coetzee applied for permanent residence in the United States, but was denied due to his activist opposition to the Vietnam war.

In 1972, Coetzee returned to an academic position at Cape Town, where he stayed until retiring in 2002. In the insular world of South Africa, his global perspective and experience set him apart, as did his attraction to postmodernist writing, which is outside the mainstream of South African literary currents.

His first novel, *Dusklands* (1974), places two imperialist characters in counterpoint with one another: an American agent in charge of a social program in Vietnam and an eighteenth-century Afrikaner (pointedly named Jacobus Coetzee) trekking inland from the Cape. The novel examines the common development of the imperialist mentality, a theme that marks all of Coetzee's work. He is interested in exploring the meaning of imperialism as a mental state, examining its hidden recesses, and exposing them to scrutiny. To do so, Coetzee writes from the perspective of his characters.

His 1976 novel, *In the Heart of the Country,* established Coetzee's international reputation. It is a searing tale of a White settler's loneliness and descent into cultural madness as she endures rape and incest, the murder of her father, and gradual mental deterioration that leads her to worship gods springing from her imagination. Coetzee again used an allegorical approach in *Waiting for the Barbarians* (1980), set in a mythical empire about to collapse from the pressure of savages on its borders. *The Life and Times of Michael K* (1983) is set in apartheid South Africa as law and order disintegrates. This novel won the Booker Prize, Britain's most prestigious literary award, but Coetzee—as reclusive and private as any of his main characters—did not go to London to receive it in person. *Age of Iron* (1990) enters most deeply into the mindset of decay, bitterness and evil. Coetzee's narrator, an old White woman who is dying of cancer, writes to her daughter, who has fled to the United States. The old woman is English-speaking, and her anti-Afrikaner venom provides a fine counterpoint for the scenes of apartheid she describes, never understanding how racist and self-indulgent her works of charity are in that context.

In 1999, Coetzee became the first person to win the Booker Prize twice, for *Disgrace*. That incendiary novel, centered about the gang rape of a White woman by three Black men and the use of that horror to strip her of her property, caused a storm of protest in South Africa.

Coetzee writes with great economy, a lesson that he says he learned from his early education in mathematics and years as a computer systems designer. None of his novels exceeds 200 pages. In 2003, Coetzee became the fourth African to receive the Nobel Prize for Literature, although by 2002 he had emigrated to Australia.

References: adb, afr, CA, CB, DLB, EWB, *wiki,* WLTC. Coetzee, *Boyhood* (1998); *Youth* (2002); David Attwell, *J. M. Coetzee: South Africa and the Politics of Writing* (1993).

COGHLAN, Charles Patrick John
(Zimbabwe, 1863–1927)

Sir Charles Patrick John Coghlan, the settler leader who became the first prime minister of Southern Rhodesia (now Zimbabwe), was born in Cape Colony, where he practiced law until moving to Southern Rhodesia in 1900. Elected to the Legislative Council (Legco) in 1908, he quickly became a leader among the elected members. Within the year, Coghlan was chosen to represent Southern Rhodesia at the national convention to form the South African Union. He was knighted in 1910 for his services at the conference but soon found that his enthusiasm for having Southern Rhodesia enter the union was not shared at home, and he decided not to pursue the issue. In 1917, when a proposal was put forth to unite Northern and Southern Rhodesia, Coghlan opposed the move effectively, fearing that the small White population in Southern Rhodesia would face difficulties if faced with the administration and political domination of the large Black population to the north.

Coghlan turned his energies toward securing self-government for Southern Rhodesia. In a 1922 referendum, the White electorate voted for internal self-government rather than union with South Africa, and the following year Coghlan organized the first government. Self-government did not mean separation from Britain, however, and Coghlan favored strong ties to London.

Coghlan's attitude toward Africans was a form of benevolent paternalism. He was convinced, for example, that segregation was in their best interests. His policies were cautious and concerned largely with the economy. White settlers prospered under his administration while Africans achieved some modest educational, social and legal gains. Coghlan died suddenly in office, leaving a legacy of firm control by White settlers.

References: DAHB, DNB.

COILLARD, François
(Lesotho/Zambia, 1834–1904)

Reverend François Coillard, one of the leading Protestant missionaries in southern Africa, was a supporter of British imperialism. Born of a French

Huguenot family, he came under evangelical influence early in life and volunteered for missionary work at age 20. He was trained at the University of Strasbourg and in Paris until 1857, when he was ordained and sent to Basutoland (now Lesotho) by the Paris Evangelical Mission Society.

After being held up for two years in Cape Town by regional warfare, Coillard was finally able to reach Basutoland, where he worked until 1877. He struggled against polygamy and witchcraft, at first without much success due to the king's hostility. He did, however, become an important intermediary and peacemaker between the Sotho and the English, whom he invariably favored over the Afrikaners. In 1866 he was forced out by the Afrikaners but was able to return after a British protectorate was established. He had become influential in the area, especially after the conversion of MOSHWESHWE I in 1870.

In 1877 he and his family crossed the Limpopo River to start a mission among the Shona. The Coillards were arrested by Chief LOBENGULA and expelled. Taking the advice of KHAMA III, Coillard entered what is now Zambia and was again turned back. Finally, Chief LEWANIKA of the Lozi people of western Zambia (Barotseland) invited him to stay, and he established a flourishing mission.

Coillard found himself in an ambiguous position. He negotiated between Lewanika and Cecil RHODES's British South Africa Company, which was then encroaching on various communities in the area. He complained to Rhodes that while he "could not serve two masters," he was willing to bring the two together. He helped to establish a treaty in 1890, which he honestly believed was in the best interests of the Lozi. He later discovered, however, that Rhodes expected him to be responsible for Lewanika's observance of the agreement.

In 1889, Coillard published his memoirs, *Sur le Haut Zambèze*, which was translated into English in 1897. In 1895 he became ill and spent several years recuperating in Europe. He returned in 1899 to what had become Northern Rhodesia and to continual struggles within his mission. A quarter of his assistants had died, and half had quit under the difficult conditions. In 1903 an African independent church movement won away many of his converts. His achievements were not in numerous converts but in the trust he engendered among the British authorities and the diligent way in which he attempted to bring the useful aspects of Western society to Barotseland. He was sincere in his belief that only British colonial government would end civil strife among the Lozi and protect them from their enemies and the exploitation of White gold-seekers. While he refused to become an official imperial agent, he was a decisive figure in the colonization of Zambia.

References: dacb, DAHB, DNB. Coillard, *On the Threshold of Central Africa* (1971).

COMPAORÉ, Blaise
(Burkina Faso, 1950–)

Captain Blaise Compaoré became president of Burkina Faso (formerly Upper Volta) after the military coup that overthrew and killed Thomas SANKARA. While restoring some measure of order to what had become a chaotic situation, Compaoré lacks the broad popular appeal of his predecessor.

The son of a Mossi chief, Compaoré entered the army and was sent to Cameroon for military training. Commissioned a second lieutenant in 1975, he first met Sankara when they served together during paratroop commando training in Morocco in 1978. They became fast friends, and their military and political careers were intertwined thereafter. Sankara became head of the commando training center at Po and made Compaoré his deputy. When Sankara joined the cabinet of Sayé ZERBO in 1981, Compaoré replaced him as commander at Po. A 1982 coup brought Jean Baptiste Ouédraogo to power, and he invited the two comrades to join the ruling military council. Ouédraogo rejected Sankara's pro-Libyan policies, however, and arrested him a year later. Compaoré then mounted a strike force that dramatically liberated Sankara and provided the latter the opportunity to stage a coup and become head of state.

Compaoré was named minister of state and justice, in effect Sankara's second-in-command. He shared Sankara's revolutionary populism, even arresting Zerbo and former president Maurice YAMÉOGO as security threats. While Sankara's inner circle held together ideologically, his increasingly unpredictable behavior led to personality differences. Sankara was outvoted on several key issues as rivalry set in within the core ruling group. In October 1987, Compaoré, fearing for his own future and charging that Sankara had become "a madman," made a preemptive strike. In the firefight

Blaise Compaoré

that followed, Sankara and 13 comrades were gunned down. Compaoré was appalled and devastated by Sankara's death, and spent three days in bed to get over the shock. Because the two had been such close friends, the nation was equally dismayed and there was international protest.

Compaoré took the reins of power with little change at first, but he soon began putting his own stamp on the government. He dismissed Sankara's revolutionary committees, which operated throughout the country, and replaced them with new groups that were unarmed. In 1989 there was a coup attempt by his first and second deputies, and after a trial, both were executed. He dropped some unpopular taxes, relaxed state controls over the economy, and encouraged foreign investment. His father-in-law, President Félix HOUPHOUÉT-BOIGNY of Côte d'Ivoire, encouraged him when he dropped Marxism as the official doctrine in 1991.

At the same time, Compaoré made a cautious move toward political liberalization, legalizing "political formations in the anti-imperialist struggle" and expanding press freedom. He nonetheless kept tight control of the electoral process. His four opponents boycotted the 1992 election, and he was returned unopposed. Ten parties won seats in the assembly, however. Compaoré was re-elected in 1998 and 2005, although the latter was disputed because of a 2000 constitutional amendment that imposed term limits. He argued that the amendment was not retroactive, and he won with 80 percent of the vote.

References: afr, PLBA, RWWA, *wiki.*

CONTÉ, Lansana
(Guinea, 1934–)

Brigadier-General Lansana Conté, military strongman and head of state, succeeded the legendary Sékou TOURÉ as president of Guinea.

Conté attended military schools in Côte d'Ivoire and Sénégal before joining the French army in 1955. When a Guinean army was organized at the time of independence (1958), he transferred there and rose rapidly in rank.

President Touré was supportive of the liberation movement led by Amílcar CABRAL in neighboring Guinea-Bissau, which had its headquarters in Conakry, the capital of Guinea. Around 1961, using Guinean bases, Cabral's forces began occupying sections of Guinea-Bissau, and Conté was assigned to provide assistance. In 1975 he was promoted to colonel and made chief of the army general staff. In 1984, Touré died during heart surgery and the army seized power, with Conté emerging at the head of the governing military council.

Conté acted to remove the most repressive features of the Touré regime as he announced the "end of a bloody and ruthless dictatorship." He released hundreds of political prisoners and invited exiles to return. Press censorship and travel restrictions were lifted. He liberalized the economy, which brought foreign investors back to the country, looking for opportunities in the mining sector. In foreign policy, Guinea began to turn toward the West, repudiating much of its past Marxist dogma. All this change did not sit well with other members of the military council, and in 1985 several officers mounted a coup against Conté. Loyal soldiers, however, crushed the revolt, and Conté emerged with increased popularity among the people. Now freed of political obligations to the military council, he brought numbers of civilians into the government.

In subsequent years, however, Conté became distrustful of subordinates and moved to a more authoritarian style, ruling by decree and ignoring his cabinet. Despite his campaign against government corruption, he has been unable to root it out of his own government, admitting that "incessant embezzlement, laxity in implementing budget estimates and malfunctioning of our administrative system have created a situation that has finally paralyzed all the recovery programs that have been launched." Despite setbacks, however, the economy has shown improvement, and Conté has moved again toward liberalization. Economic reform followed the norms of the International Monetary Fund (IMF), involving currency devaluation and sharply reduced government budgets. Predictably, inflation followed with deteriorating public services. The army mutinied in 1996 over salary payments, but the government survived after loyalist forces barely saved the presidential palace.

Political liberalization has moved more cautiously. Parties were legalized in 1991, and an open election was held in 1993, in which Conté received a slim majority. In 1996, he increased that to 56 percent. A 2001 referendum to extend his term of office passed overwhelmingly, and he was re-elected with 95 percent of the vote in 2003, as the opposition boycotted what they considered rigged elections.

References: afr, PLBA, RWWA, *wiki*.

CRONJE, Wessek Johannes "Hansi"
(South Africa, 1969–2002)

Hansi Cronje was one of the most gifted cricket players in the history of the game. He played for South Africa from 1992 to 2000, and served as captain from 1994. All that came crashing down when it was revealed that he was involved in a game-fixing scheme for money. It became the greatest scandal in cricket history.

Cronje was born in Bloemfontein to an Afrikaner family. He went directly from schoolboy cricket to the Orange Free State team at age 18. After joining the South African national team, he made his international debut against Australia in the opener of the 1992 World Cup in Sydney, which South Africa took by nine wickets. In the semifinals against England he scored 24 on a rain-soaked ground, but the BBC called his later maiden Test

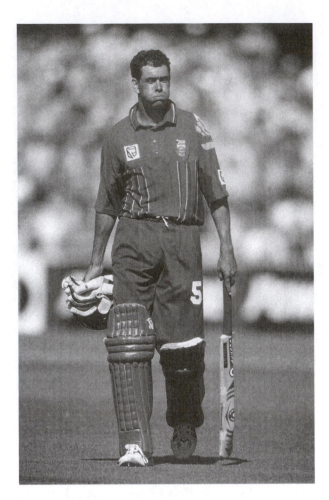

Wessek Johannes "Hansi" Cronje

match against West Indies, "thoroughly forgettable." Cronje hit his stride in late 1992 after this sputtering start, tearing through the Indian team and posting his first Test century, 135 in a first-innings total of 275. His second century came nine months later against a hapless Sri Lanka.

In 1994 Cronje became interim captain and began a string of great games. South Africa bested Australia twice, with Cronje named Man of the Match in the final. By the end of the year Cronje was full captain, leading the team to a series of victories while racking up enviable scores. He went into 2000 carrying the reputation as one of the finest cricketers in the world. Cronje was an intense player, almost to the point of obsession, and his chief obsession was rivalry with Australia, the premier team of that period. He played in South Africa's first Test match after South Africa was readmitted to the world of sport following the 22-year ban under the apartheid government. Cronje, seen as a man of unbending morality and a sincere practicing Christian, became the public face of South African cricket. To much of the world, he represented a renewed South African sport.

With this background, the first rumors of Cronje's involvement in game-fixing were easily dismissed. He had admitted in a newspaper interview that he was offered $250,000 to fix a game against India in 1998, but he had not reported the bribe to authorities. Finally, in April 2000, he confessed to taking gifts and money from bookmakers to influence the results of games. He was convicted by a public commission and banned from cricket for life.

Two years later, Cronje died in a plane crash, when he hitched a ride in a private propjet after missing a scheduled flight. He left a record of 3,714 Test runs in 68 matches, with an average of 38.64, with six Test centuries.

Reference: EB, *wiki.*

CROWTHER, Samwel Ajayi

(Nigeria, 1806?–1891)

Bishop Samwel Ajayi Crowther was the first African bishop in the Anglican church. His appointment was part of the movement to create an indigenous African mission, but the movement failed in the face of colonial British missionary resistance to African leadership.

Crowther was a Yoruba youth when he was captured by Muslim slavers during the civil wars that devastated Nigeria during the early 1820s. His family was sold to Portuguese traders and then liberated when a British cruiser on antislavery patrol seized the ship and released its human cargo in Freetown, Sierra Leone. Sierra Leone was established as a recaptive colony, a settlement where former slaves, who often did not know their origins, could be safely resettled in Africa. Due to the mix of Africans from many tribes and regions, it had neither a common African language nor a shared tribal culture.

In Freetown, Crowther entered a school run by the Christian Missionary Society (CMS) and was baptized a Christian in 1825, taking the name Samwel (Samuel) Crowther. He was sent to England for a year's further schooling and then became the first African to graduate from the CMS's new college, Fourah Bay Institute. Crowther continued as a tutor there and became an evangelist before returning to England in 1841 to be ordained an Anglican priest. He married a woman he had met on the slave ship, who was baptized Susanna. One of their children later became archdeacon of the Delta Mission, which Crowther had founded.

Crowther was the ideal candidate for the CMS's intended purpose of creating an indigenous African church. Intelligent and reliable, soft-spoken and devoted, he was Victorian in his manners and African in his outlook. The progressive secretary of the CMS, Henry Venn, took him under his tutelage and passed on his vision of an African church "independent of foreign aid or superintendence." In 1843, Crowther was posted to Abeokuta, Nigeria. In a poignant moment, he saw and recognized his mother there. In 1848 he baptized her.

Crowther believed that Christianity and trade were inseparable. In 1854 and 1857 he accompanied William BAIKIE's expeditions up the Niger River and wrote two accounts of the voyages.

He remembered much of his childhood Yoruba and preached in the Yoruba language. He translated the New Testament and *The Book of Common Prayer* into Yoruba and published a small dictionary of the language in 1857. Crowther could put aside his natural reticence in his evangelism. He was known to barge into sacred huts to destroy carvings of Yoruba gods. In 1857 he was made head of the Niger Mission and, as the work developed and plans were laid for the first African-staffed diocese, he was the only choice to head it. In 1864, Crowther was consecrated with the title of "Bishop for West Africa beyond British Jurisdiction" and was awarded an honorary doctorate by Oxford University.

The Niger Mission came with serious problems. Crowther's position was not well defined, and he faced opposition from resident Anglicans as well as from Africans. Perhaps most significantly, his personnel from Sierra Leone were inadequately trained, knew little of the local languages, and adapted poorly to the climate. Despite all of this, the mission prospered, and within a few years there were 600 Christians with 10 priests and 14 catechists.

In the contemporary context of Social Darwinism—a doctrine that argued the existence of a scientific basis for racial differences and posited the superiority of Whites—many Europeans believed in the moral obligation of the so-called advanced races to govern those who were "less developed." This theory provided an intellectual (and even scientific) justification for colonialism. Young liberal elements in the CMS dismantled Venn's Africanization policy, and increasing pressure was brought on Crowther by opponents of an African church. Sir George GOLDIE wanted English missionaries who would advance British colonial designs. The new generation of British missionaries, staunchly committed to the Christian duty of colonialism, refused to work under an African bishop, so Crowther was forced to accept a White associate who was given control of finances. Because the establishment of an endowment for the Niger Mission was the key to its future independence, this was a major blow to his prestige and authority.

Crowther was humiliated in a number of ways. His missionary ship, the *Henry Venn*, was taken from him and turned into a merchant vessel, making Crowther dependent on traders for transport inland. Anonymous and unproven accusations were made to the CMS about the management of the mission, and Anglican church law was flouted in the conduct of the investigation. Crowther neither saw the report nor had any opportunity to reply to it. Finally, the finance committee met and suspended the Nigerian priests Crowther had ordained. The bishop, then over 80, resigned his post in protest. Crowther's humiliation was a turning point that thwarted African control and produced a foreign Church. In another, parallel turn of events, it fostered the growth of new African churches that were free of White monopoly.

Crowther was the victim of the twin thrusts of colonialism and Western missionary zeal, both underpinned by racist theories. At no point, however, were any accusations made against Crowther himself, even though he was the obvious target. Almost all Anglican historians have failed to reveal the exact accusations, and their racist nature was not openly discussed until many years later.

References: AB, *afr*, *dacb*, DAHB, DNB, EB, MMA, WGMC. J.F.A. Ajayi, *Christian Missions in Nigeria: 1841–1891* (1965).

DACKO, David
(Central African Republic, 1930–2003)

David Dacko, twice president of the Central African Republic (CAR) and twice removed by military coups, was never able to establish either a coherent economic policy or a representative form of government.

After receiving a local education, Dacko obtained a certificate from a teachers' training college in neighboring Congo-Brazzaville. As a young teacher in the 1950s he was active in experimental education and was highly regarded by the colonial administration, which promoted him to headmaster in 1955. He also began working in the teachers' union and entered politics with the help of his cousin, Barthélemy BOGANDA, a progressive nationalist. In 1957, Dacko was elected to the territorial legislature, and when Boganda formed the first African-led government in preparation for independence, Dacko became minister of agriculture and, later, of the interior. The latter post, giving him authority over internal security, was particularly powerful.

Boganda was cautious about immediate independence and favored a federation with ties to France. This option was defeated in 1958 and the decision to opt for independence was made. When Boganda was killed in a plane crash during the elections in 1959, his ruling party was thrown into disarray. Dacko, using his family ties to Boganda, was chosen to replace him and was elected the first president of the CAR in 1960. His first tenure in office was lackluster at best. He banned opposition parties, arrested Boganda's former vice president, and kept himself in power with the help of the French. His undoing came when he reorganized the economy, which led him into conflict with the dominant French corporations. He was considering resignation when Colonel Jean Bedel BOKASSA, also a cousin, engineered a military coup in 1966.

Dacko spent 10 years in detention before being released to become an advisor to Bokassa. By this time Bokassa had ordered a number of mass killings and was sliding into erratic behavior, including his elaborate and costly coronation when he proclaimed himself emperor. In 1979, with French paratroops,

Dacko deposed Bokassa and resumed the presidency. He was unable, however, to unite the country, and opposition surfaced from students and trade unions. Dacko tried to suppress the demonstrations, but he failed and was removed in 1981 by General André KOLINGBA in another French-supported coup.

Dacko went on to participate actively in politics as leader of the opposition, but was never returned to office.

References: afr, DAHB, PLBA, *wiki*.

DA COSTA, Manuel Pinto
(São Tomé e Prĭncipe, 1937–)

Dr. Manuel Pinto Da Costa, independence leader and first president of his island nation, was one of the first African presidents to accept democracy and open his country to multiparty elections.

Da Costa, the son of a plantation official, was sent to Lisbon in the mid-1940s for education. In 1960, with his friend Miguel TROVOADA and a few other students, he founded the Movement for the Liberation of São Tomé e Prĭncipe (MLSTP), the tiny island country's first anticolonial group. The repressive atmosphere of São Tomé made it impossible for the MLSTP to establish its presence there, so Trovoada set up offices in the nearby country of Gabon. After graduating from the University of Lisbon, Da Costa lived in France, Cuba and East Germany, where he completed a doctorate in economics. In 1972 the MLSTP was reorganized with Da Costa as secretary-general, and the following year it received recognition from the Organization of African Unity (OAU) as the only representative of the people of São Tomé.

The fall of fascism in Portugal brought a swift end to Portuguese colonialism when the new Socialist administration reversed colonial policy and began immediate independence negotiations with Portuguese colonies. In contrast to the strong liberation movements in Guinea-Bissau, Angola, and Mozambique, the MLSTP had no armed wing or presence in its own territory. Independence fever swept the islands in 1974 when the Portuguese recognized the right of self-determination for São Tomé e Prĩncipe. The MLSTP, still in exile, negotiated a transition, and Da Costa was chosen president after elections in which the MLSTP won every parliamentary seat. Trovoada was elected premier.

The euphoria of independence soon waned. Almost the entire Portuguese population of 2,000 abandoned the country, leaving it with a dire shortage of traders, administrators and professionals. While never accepting Marxism, Da Costa led São Tomé e Prĩncipe along a socialist path. The plantations, hated symbols of Portuguese colonial exploitation and slavery, were nationalized, giving the government control of 90 percent of the arable land. The trading sector was reorganized into "people's shops." Private property and investment were permitted, but only as part of a planned economy. The MLSTP became the sole legal party, and Da Costa created a secret police.

Beginning in the early 1970s, factionalism developed within the MLSTP, leading to plots against Da Costa. In 1979 he brought charges against Trovoada and imprisoned him for two years. A far more serious challenge came in a coup attempt in 1988, which, in addition to a declining economy, caused Da Costa to reconsider his socialist goals. He accepted a severe economic reform package from the International Monetary Fund and announced plans for multiparty elections. Trovoada returned from exile to lead the opposition, and Da Costa withdrew when it became obvious that he would lose the 1991 elections. Instead of leading the opposition, Da Costa went to Angola until 1993, when he returned to São Tomé. In 1996, he contested the presidency in democratic elections, getting 48 percent of the vote, but he lost his next bid to return to power in 2001, when his total fell to 39 percent.

References: PLBA, RWWA, *wiki.*

DADDAH, Moktar Ould
(Mauritania, 1924–2003)

Moktar Ould Daddah, the first president of Mauritania after independence, served until he was removed by a coup.

Daddah was born of a devout Berber family of *marabouts,* or Islamic teachers, and he had a strict religious upbringing. After his initial education at an Islamic school, he went to Sénégal to study at a school for sons of chiefs and then to the interpreters' academy. He worked for the French colonial administration until after World War II, when he traveled to France, where he received degrees in law and Arabic.

In 1957, Daddah was elected to the territorial legislative council. When it received increased political authority, he was chosen its president, in effect becoming prime minister of Mauritania at age 33. A year later, in 1960, he became Mauritania's first president.

Mauritania is situated between Arab North Africa and Black West Africa, and its citizens are divided between an Arab Berber majority and a Black minority. Daddah made Arabic the official language and created a one-party state. He saw his country's destiny linked with Arab North Africa and followed an increasingly anti-Western foreign policy, breaking relations with the United States over the 1967 Arab-Israeli War. In 1973 he withdrew from the French franc system and established a Mauritanian currency, further weakening the nation's economy. During the same year he also obtained membership for Mauritania in the League of Arab States. Daddah, a Pan-Africanist, served as president of the Organization of African Unity in 1971 and 1972.

Daddah, a modest and somewhat colorless man, was firm in his policy of "return to Islamic sources." That idea caused suspicion among the Black minority, whose members chafed under Islamicization, especially Daddah's imposition of Arabic in the schools, which led to riots. Blacks felt excluded from government posts, and Daddah had to suppress advocates of federation with Sénégal.

When Spain withdrew from the Western Sahara in 1974, Mauritania laid claim to the southern part of the territory, starting a prolonged war with the Polisario guerrilla movement. The war was unpopular with the army and drained the national treasury, and the military finally overthrew Daddah in 1978. He went into exile in France (and later Tunis), and organized an opposition in exile. Daddah was pardoned in 1985 and returned to Mauritania in 2001.

References: afr, DAHB, DRWW, PLBA, *wiki.*

DADIÉ, Bernard Binlin
(Côte d'Ivoire, 1916–)

Bernard Binlin Dadié, one of the most prolific of the first generation of French-language African writers, has contributed works in almost every genre—plays, poetry, novels, short stories, essays, and collected folk tales. Besides his literary output, Dadié has been a militant nationalist and minister of culture and information for his country.

Dadié's mother, a one-eyed woman, felt that she was under an evil spell that had killed her first three children, so she sent her fourth away to protect him. Living with an elderly uncle, Dadié was steeped in traditional folk tales that he would later incorporate into his writings. He was sent to Sénégal for studies at the prestigious William Ponty School, which required its students to use the folklore they studied to write plays. His early play, *Assemien Débylé,* was staged in Paris in 1937 for the Colonial Exposition. It was Dadié's introduction to academic theater.

Dadié stayed on at the University of Dakar from 1936 to 1947 as an archivist and librarian, and then returned to Côte d'Ivoire as press officer of the Rassemblement Démocratique Africain (RDA), the regional party founded by Félix HOUPHOUËT-BOIGNY. It was also at this time that the French began a campaign to destroy the RDA and separate it from its left-wing support. In a 1949 series of bloody incidents—the *ratissages* (combing out)—villages were burned and terrorist squads murdered peasants. Dadié was imprisoned for a year, during which his first volume of poetry appeared in Paris, *Afrique debout* (Africa standing on its own feet, 1950). It launched his literary career. In 1953 and 1956 two volumes of folk tales were published, the latter a collection of children's stories.

In 1957 Dadié became cabinet secretary for the ministry of education. When France granted Côte d'Ivoire internal government in 1959, he became the national director of information, and shortly after independence he was appointed director of cultural affairs (1961–1977). In 1977 he became minister of cultural affairs, an office that he held until his retirement in 1986. His cultural contributions garnered appointments on many commissions, and he served as member and vice president of the council of the U.N. Educational, Scientific, and Cultural Organization (UNESCO) from 1964 to 1972.

Few writer-politicians have continued their literary output while in public life. Dadié is an exception. His writing began just as the cultural consciousness school of *Négritude* began to intersect with political awareness, influencing his early poetry, which was vigorously anticolonial. Even his later verse deals with Africa's anger at its secondary status in the world. His poetry ranks with that of Léopold SENGHOR in quality. Dadié's first novel, the autobiographical *Climbié* (1953), is an assertion of Africa's beauty in the face of a colonialism that robbed it of its heritage. His later five novels tend toward satire, especially of Western society and its foibles.

It is as a playwright, however, that Dadié is best known, and working on plays is his first love. For many years, beginning in the 1960s, he directed a theater group to provide a showcase for African works and actors and wrote a number of short plays for competitions for this troupe. His own work alternates between satirical or light comedy and serious historical plays. In *Papassidi* (first produced, 1960; published 1968) he presents a confidence man who claims the miraculous power of multiplying bank notes. *Monsieur Thôgô-gnini* (1970) is a farce about an American slave who has returned to Africa, presenting himself to the local traders as experienced at dealing with Whites. He fawningly accepts everything Western as superior, often appearing a fool, as when he puts on sackcloth and proclaims it to be the latest fashion. Dadié has also satirized African corruption, especially in *Les Voix dans le Vent* (Voices in the Wind, 1970) and other plays. His historical plays have revolved around the destruction of Black cultures: *Béatrice du Congo* (Beatrice of the Congo, 1971), which deals with the conquest of the kingdom of Kongo, and *Îles de Tempête* (Stormy Islands, 1973), a theatrical study of the dilemma of the Haitian revolutionary Toussaint L'Ouverture, torn between French culture and liberation. In his later years, Dadié has turned more toward writing short stories, but he has also continued to write plays.

References: adb, afr, AA, CANR, DAHB, EB, MBW, NRG, WLTC, *wiki.* Nicole Vincileoni, *Comprendre l'Oeuvre de Bernard B. Dadié* (Understanding the world of Bernard B. Dadié, 1986).

DANGAREMBGA, TsiTsi
(Zimbabwe, 1959–)

Tsitsi Dangarembga is a Zimbabwean author and film director. She was born in what was then Rhodesia and was sent to England for elementary school. After taking A-levels in Zimbabwe, she studied medicine at Cambridge, but returned to her homeland just as Black majority rule arrived. She continued her studies, this time in psychology, but she supported herself as an advertising writer and then joined the university theater club. These first exposures to writing set her on a new course, and she began writing plays for the club and later for a local stage group.

In the 1980s, Dangarembga's writing began to attract notice. First, a short story appeared in Sweden in 1985, and two years later she published a play, *She Does Not Weep*, about a woman dealing with pregnancy in the face of her family's rejection. Her first novel, the somewhat autobiographical *Nervous Conditions* (1988), was awarded the African section Commonwealth Writers' Prize in 1989. It is unashamedly feminist as it describes the oppression of African women in the colonial period by both the White rulers and the Shona patriarchy. She makes quite clear that while one has been defeated, the other remains in power. The book is widely used in Zimbabwe as a required reading "set book" in the secondary literature curriculum.

She then branched out by studying film direction in Germany. Several of her films were shown at international festivals, and she produced a documentary for German television.

Dangarembga wrote the largest-grossing film in Zimbabwean entertainment, *Neria*. In it a widow, exploited by her brother-in-law who takes her inheritance and her child, finds support from a woman friend. *Everyone's Child* (1996) follows four siblings who have lost their parents to AIDS. She has since turned almost completely to script writing and film direction. *Elephant People* in 2004 was followed by *Mother's Day* in 2005, which was featured at FESPACO, the major international film festival. It tells the harrowing fable of a woman during a famine with nothing but fried termites to feed her children. Her husband murders her with the intention of eating her body, but when he does, she bursts forth from his stomach to embrace her children. It is based on an ancient Shona folk tale, as much of Dangarembga's recent work has been.

Reference: abd, wiki.

DANQUAH, Joseph Kwame Kyeretwi Boakye
(Ghana, 1895–1965)

Dr. Joseph Kwame Kyeretwi Boakye Danquah, a major nationalist figure and a leader of opposition during the presidency of Kwame NKRUMAH, was also a scholar and intellectual.

Born into a distinguished family, J. B. Danquah spent his early years serving as secretary for his brother, a paramount chief, and as assistant secretary of the conference of paramount chiefs. In 1921 he went to London to complete his education, receiving undergraduate and law degrees from the University of London as well as a Ph.D. in ethics in 1927. Returning home, he established a successful law practice in customary and constitutional law and wrote his first books, *Akan Laws* and *Customs* and *Cases in Akan Law* (both in 1928).

In 1931, Danquah began the *Times of West Africa*, the first daily newspaper in West Africa. Through his editorials he became increasingly involved in public affairs, opposing the colonial government on several issues. In 1934 he went to London to argue against a sedition act. He remained for two years, conducting research on early Gold Coast history. This work later provided the basis for adopting the name *Ghana* for the colony when it became independent. Danquah proposed the name, which came from an early African empire. At the same time, his criticism brought a reaction from the colonial authorities, who began censoring his mail after 1934. Danquah then became even more active.

In 1929 he had joined with Joseph CASELY-HAYFORD in founding the Gold Coast Youth Conference to bridge the gap between the educated elite and the chiefs. Danquah revived it in 1937 and forged a coalition between the chiefs and urban leaders to oppose controlled prices in cocoa. The cocoa boycott aroused nationalist sentiment throughout the colony, and the chiefs appointed Danquah as their representative to a constitution committee. Although this was rejected, Danquah had a notable success in 1946 when he joined the Asante Confederacy Council and the Gold Coast colony into a single Legislative Council (Legco). As an elected member of Legco, Danquah was able to propose that a cocoa marketing board be established and to press for other reforms. In 1947 his frustration with the inadequacies of British colonial government and insufficient African political representation led him to found a nationalist party, the United Gold Coast Convention (UGCC). Nkrumah returned from England to be general secretary.

A crisis developed within a few months, with street riots and demonstrations against inflation. The British suppressed one demonstration by war veterans by firing into the crowd. The UGCC announced to the colonial authorities that it was willing to provide a stable government and called for a public protest. A state of emergency was declared, and the UGCC leadership was detained. In the investigations that followed, it was agreed that a constitution should be written that would lead to independence within 10 years. When Nkrumah was excluded and Danquah appointed to the commission, Nkrumah left the UGCC to form a new party, the Convention People's Party. Danquah accepted gradual constitutional reform while Nkrumah endorsed mass organization and public confrontation, which won the nationalist movement to his side. When Nkrumah formed the first government under internal rule in 1951, Danquah became leader of the opposition.

The rest of Danquah's life was defined by his opposition to Nkrumah. He criticized the bribery and corruption that appeared in Nkrumah's administration and formed a united opposition in 1952 by merging the UGCC with several other parties. In 1954, Danquah lost his seat in the legislature. He failed to win it back again in 1956.

After independence in 1957, Nkrumah began to institute restrictions on civil liberties. Danquah fought against the Preventive Detention Act, and when it was passed, he defended two parliamentarians held under its provisions. He continued his protests against the rising authoritarianism of the Nkrumah regime. In 1960 he stood for president against Nkrumah but was badly defeated. The following year, as Nkrumah drifted more and more toward the Soviet bloc, the economy began to falter. Danquah challenged the legitimacy of the government, and as a result he was imprisoned and held for a year under the Preventive Detention Act. In 1964, after an attempt on Nkrumah's life, Danquah was again detained, this time under extremely harsh conditions. He was chained to a bare floor, refused medication for his asthma, and starved. Danquah's

cause as a prisoner of conscience cost Nkrumah much of his international support, but before Danquah could be released, he died. Despite Nkrumah's animosity, Danquah was given a hero's burial.

Danquah's literary and scholarly work was part of his deepening concern for fostering Akan culture. He wrote several long dramas, two of which were published: *Nyankonsem* (1941, in Twi) and *The Third Woman* (1943). Both concern African religion and tradition and provide a prologue for his masterwork, *The Akan Doctrine of God* (1944). These studies reveal a concern for Christianity and the need to harmonize it with local tradition. His final work was a history, *Revelation of Culture in Ghana* (1961), which explores the prehistoric migration of the first Akan peoples to Ghana.

References: afr, AA, DAB, DAHB, EB, EWB, MMA, PLBA, *wiki*. L.H. Ofosu-Appiah, *The Life and Times of Dr. J. B. Danquah* (1974).

DAWUD
(Mali/Niger, ?–1582)

Askia Dawud was one of the principal rulers of the Songhay Empire in the sixteenth century. He was one of the sons of MUHAMMAD Ture, who established the Askia dynasty, the name which each of his sons took as a title.

Dawud held several high offices (probably including provincial governor) and was experienced in public affairs. In 1528, Muhammad Ture was deposed by one of his sons, Muhammad Bunkan, was exiled to an island, and then was brought back to Gao by another son, Ismail. Dawud peacefully replaced Ismail when he died in 1549, only a year after Muhammad Ture's death. He set to work restoring the empire as it had been under his father, who was still revered, reclaiming parts that had broken away. After reorganizing the army, he systematically subdued a series of small kingdoms of the old Mali Empire and defeated the Tuareg, a powerful nomadic clan. With its borders thus defined and secured, the empire prospered.

Chronicles of the period present him as a pious Muslim, but he was deferential to the traditional tribal religions, practiced magic, and never made the pilgrimage to Mecca. His syncretic brand of Islam was suitable for unifying the empire, however, and Islam was certainly at the center of a flowering of culture over which Dawud presided. He was generous to Muslim scholars and rebuilt the Friday mosque in Tombouctou (Timbuktu). The Islamic scholars in Tombouctou formed an elite group, and Dawud always came to the city as a simple pilgrim, setting aside ceremony and court protocol. While the scholars rebuked his acceptance of pre-Islamic superstitions, Dawud recognized that Islam and traditional African magic provided him with two sources of legitimacy, and he could not forge national unity without both.

Songhay reached the pinnacle of its prosperity under Dawud. The Niger River valley was intensively cultivated, trading towns were active, the trans-Saharan caravans carried goods to North Africa, and taxes and duties made the empire prosperous. Thousands of tons of grain were collected in Dawud's warehouses, and he established a treasury of coins. He was even able to strike an agreement with the powerful sultan of Morocco, who claimed the valuable salt mines of Taghaza. Dawud contributed generously to the sultan's Islamic programs, but Songhay's ownership was respected.

Dawud hoped to end dynastic feuds by limiting succession to his direct line rather than having it passed down among his various sons; this attempt was not, however, successful. On his death in 1582, his first-born son was excluded in a vote of the sons and senior officials of Songhay. A series of nasty intrigues followed among the sons, and imperial decline set in rapidly. Dawud's friendly relations with Morocco deteriorated quickly, and this set the stage for an invasion in 1591 that effectively ended the empire under ISHAQ II.

Reference: DAHB.

DÉBY Itno, Idriss

(Chad, 1954?-)

Colonel Idriss Déby, Chadian military head of state who came to power through the long civil war, has his base in the small Zaghawa ethnic group from the northeast region. Déby joined the army as a young man and completed officer cadet school in 1975. He was then sent to France to qualify as a fighter pilot.

In the confused situation of the late 1970s, when as many as 11 armed factions were alternately involved in military action and negotiating for a united national government, Déby cast his lot with Hissène HABRÉ, who was then prime minister. In 1978 he was named chief of staff of Habré's Armed Forces of the North (FAN), directing the campaign that placed Habré in the presidency. A brave frontline commander, Déby earned the nickname "Cowboy of the Sands." In June 1982 he led his troops into the capital, N'Djamena, driving out President Goukouni OUEDDEI, Habré's old rival. He went on to take southern Chad, was promoted to colonel and made commander-in-chief of the army. When Oueddei counterattacked in the Aozou, a northern border area claimed by Libya, Déby led FAN troops to hold the line against them. In 1985 he was sent to Paris for advanced military training, and he used the time to develop his connections with French military officials. Because French forces fought in the Chadian conflicts and had administered the north until 1975, 15 years after independence, these were to become critical personal contacts.

Déby returned in 1986 to become Habré's military advisor. He found that the atmosphere of paranoia and plotting left him increasingly on the margins of power. Nevertheless, the next several years were marked by notable victories over the Libyans, who in 1987 abandoned their largest base in the Aozou Strip, leaving US$1 billion worth of sophisticated equipment to FAN. In 1989, after Déby was involved in a coup attempt that failed, he and loyal troops fought their way across the country to sanctuary in Sudan. In 1990 he returned and swept across Chad in a little over two weeks, defeating FAN forces in pitched battle. Habré fled the country and Déby took control of the government.

As president, Déby inherited an exhausted country, and sporadic civil strife has continued. Déby took measured steps toward liberalizing the government by inviting exiled dissidents to return and holding a national conference in 1993, which was attended by more than 40 parties and six rebel groups. He finally settled the bitter territorial dispute with Libya over the Aozou Strip, which was turned over to Chad in June 1994. In 2006, the World Bank suspended its loans to Chad over the misuse of oil funds intended for schools and hospitals. Parliament voted to allow their use for the military, and then doubled the funds available to the president without oversight. In 2005, Chad had the unhappy distinction of beating out Bangladesh for the position of most corrupt nation on Earth. Since it began exporting oil in 2003, Chad receives about $100 million a year in revenues.

Idriss Déby with Secretary-General of the United Nations, Kofi Annan

Déby was voted in again in 1996 and 2001 in questionable elections, and repeated this in 2006, after a referendum suspended constitutional term limits. Déby has provided stability to Chad, but difficulties remain. The country must deal with 300,000 Sudanese refugees from the Darfur region, and Chad is one of the poorest in the world.

Chad hit another major crisis when the opposition, organized from camps in the Darfur region of the Sudan, invaded in 2006. Darfur refugees were forced into the guerilla army, which advanced almost to the suburbs of the capital. With the assistance of French troops providing intelligence, and armed with American-supplied equipment, Déby's forces defeated the poorly trained invaders, although some had penetrated into the capital's streets. Déby's position remained fragile, however, and the hostility of the Sudanese government (his earlier patrons) added to the instability of the region.

Reference: afr, RWWA, *wiki*.

DE JONG, Dennis Harold
(Zambia, 1930–2003)

Bishop Dennis De Jong of Ndola in northern Zambia was a prominent churchman best known for his early and vigorous crusade against HIV/AIDS. Due to his unflagging activism, he was made an African Prize Laureate by the Hunger Project.

De Jong was a mixed-blood Zambian, and when he wished to study for the Catholic priesthood during the colonial period, no seminary was permitted to accept him. In 1958, he was finally ordained after studies in Rome on a scholarship. He was one of very few diocesan priests at the time, since most African clergy entered missionary orders instead. After ordination, De Jong was sent to London for a year to study education, and then he returned to

Zambia as teacher and later rector of Francisdale Minor Seminary.

In 1975, De Jong became the first African bishop of Ndola, and from 1978 to 1984 he was president of the Zambian Catholic Bishops' Conference. He was the Church's spokesman, presenting strong advocacy for programs for the poor and challenging the government on its more authoritarian policies.

In 1988, the HIV/AIDS pandemic infected 27 percent of the Ndola population. The diocese began some simple responses, but without funds could not open care centers. In 1993, Bishop De Jong instituted the Integrated AIDS Programme (IAP) in his diocese to bring all the activities together, a model that was later copied by other Catholic dioceses and other churches. It provided for the care of AIDS patients and preventive anti-AIDS education. The care portion was home-based, which required challenging African notions of rejection of those with HIV/AIDS. Community-based schools struggle to provide for the 80,000 AIDS orphans in the Ndola area.

De Jong fostered open dialogue about sexuality and responsible sexual behavior, a forthrightness foreign to African sensibilities. The IAP serves 26 shanty towns in the northern copper belt region of Zambia. Seven hundred fifty volunteers care for 7,000 clients. Core teams have been trained in mining companies and military barracks—two major sources of HIV infection—to do outreach education with families. On his death, De Jong's leadership was recognized as from a great heart that produced the courage to confront a stigma that others ignored.

DE KLERK, Frederik Willem

(South Africa, 1936–)

Frederik Willem De Klerk was the last Afrikaner president of South Africa and was leader of the National Party (NP). He helped to negotiate the transition to African rule and supported political reform that ended his presidency and forced his party out of power.

De Klerk's background gave little indication of his later reform activism. Born into an Afrikaner family of strong NP convictions, he received his

Frederik Willem De Klerk

higher education at Potchefstroom University, a Calvinist Afrikaner institution. His uncle, J. G. Strydom, was prime minister during De Klerk's university years (1954–1958). De Klerk was active in local party affairs while practicing law from 1959 to 1972, when he won a by-election to parliament in 1972. By 1978 he was a cabinet minister, achieving rapid promotion by South African standards. At various times until 1989, De Klerk held portfolios for social welfare, sports, post and telecommunications, mines, environmental planning and energy, budget, internal affairs, and national education in the cabinets of Balthazar VORSTER and P. W. BOTHA. He was thus well versed in a wide range of government policy by the time he became chair of the executive that managed the White chamber of parliament in 1985.

In early 1989, President Botha resigned as NP leader after suffering a stroke, but he retained his position as state president. De Klerk was elected party leader in a caucus. He seemed a natural successor—committed to moderate apartheid policies, including the maintenance of the homelands. De Klerk appeared to be a cautious progressive who was still willing to use coercion to maintain the existing social order. Tensions, however, developed between De Klerk and Botha, and in a confrontational caucus meeting later in 1989, Botha was forced to resign, making De Klerk acting state president. He immediately called a general election, which the NP won with a reduced majority by fending off parties from the right, which attacked the government as too soft on Black activists. The right's fears were well founded, as De Klerk immediately loosened the strict regulations against mass demonstrations. Within a month he released eight political prisoners, including Walter SISULU. At the 1990 opening of parliament, he announced the unbanning of the African National Congress (ANC), the Pan-Africanist Congress (PAC), and the Communist Party. In February, Nelson MANDELA was freed from prison after 25 years of confinement.

De Klerk realized the need to move quickly to avert political chaos, economic crisis, and civil war in South Africa. He held his first negotiating sessions with Mandela in May 1990 and then embarked on an extensive overseas trip to nine European nations. He hoped to undermine economic sanctions and return foreign investments to South Africa. By that fall De Klerk had lifted the state of emergency and opened the NP to multiracial membership. In early 1991 the remaining apartheid legislation, including the Group Areas Act, was repealed as part of a settlement with the ANC by which it would end the armed struggle. In March parliament enacted land reform, enabling a million Blacks to become landowners. These events were shocking for NP stalwarts, but De Klerk was able to bring most of his White constituency with him.

Elections under a new constitution were announced for 1994, under a one-person, one-vote standard. Accepting inevitable defeat, De Klerk nevertheless waged an active campaign. The NP was seriously compromised a month before the elections when it was revealed that paramilitary units of the Zulu-based Inkatha Freedom Party of Mangosuthu BUTHELEZI , armed by and working with the state police, had engaged in political assassinations and terrorist bombings against the ANC. De Klerk was not held responsible, but there was widespread public concern that he was not in control of his government.

Long before ceding the presidency, De Klerk began involving Mandela in decisions. This policy paid off during several crises, especially the collapse of Bophuthatswana in 1994, when that homeland refused to allow election plans to proceed. De Klerk, with Mandela's blessing, neutralized the government of Lucas MANGOPE and sent troops to disarm and arrest White radicals who had invaded the homeland. Mandela also significantly assisted the ailing national economy by adding his prestige to a call for ending international sanctions.

Together, De Klerk and Mandela received the Nobel Peace Prize in 1993, but there have been moments of strain and tension in their relationship. After one confrontation, they hardly spoke for most of 1991. They have suspected each other of not using their respective positions to curb the township violence that has cost several thousand lives each year. Moreover, they also represent the fears of their specific constituencies. De Klerk and Mandela have been chained together by history rather than welded together by common ideals.

De Klerk is above all a politician who believes in negotiation. He is a man of personal courtesy and deep religious convictions and compassion, which was recently demonstrated by his calm reaction when it was revealed that his son was involved in a relationship with a Coloured woman—a potentially explosive situation in South Africa.

In the 1994 elections, De Klerk led the New National Party (NNP) to a strong second position, entitling him to the post of second deputy president and leader of the opposition. He did not work well within a Mandela administration, however. In 1998, his reputation was badly damaged by a contentious divorce from his wife of many years, and a quick remarriage to a much younger woman. Now politically powerless and without much of a following, he resigned from the NNP in 2004.

References: AB, *afr*, CB, EB, EWB, GSAP, PLBA, PLCA, RWWA, *wiki*. De Klerk, *F. W. De Klerk: The Man in His Time* (1989).

DELAMERE, Hugh Cholmondeley
(Kenya, 1870–1931)

Hugh Cholmondeley, Lord Delamere, was the leading champion of settlers' rights and privileges during the colonial period in Kenya, which was then known as the British East African Protectorate. His White supremacist approach shaped the settler mentality for several generations.

Born a British aristocrat, he became the third Baron Delamere of Vale Royal at 17. After a brief period in the military, he made three big-game hunts in Somaliland, the last of which was followed by a trek through the desert to the Aberdare Highlands of Kenya. When he returned home, his restless nature was too confined to be a country gentleman, and in 1903 he returned to Kenya, where he remained for the rest of his life.

The colonial commissioner granted him 100,000 acres of prime Kenyan highland on a 99-year lease. The land legally belonged to no one, because the British ignored the presence of the Kikuyu, many of whom were resettled or compelled to become agricultural workers. Delamere was instrumental in creating the policy that the White Highlands, as the Aberdares came to be known, should be restricted to European settlers. He based his policy on the fiction that the Africans were the only ones adapted to the malarial lowlands. Delamere began an ambitious agricultural program on his own lands, transforming them into a valuable source of exports. He did this by a series of experiments, none of which was well planned. When New Zealand sheep failed, he imported new breeds of cattle. Finally, he settled on wheat and began experimenting with rust-resistant varieties until he was successful.

Delamere rose quickly to settler leadership, becoming president of the Colonists' Association within a year of his arrival in the colony. In 1907 he was one of the first two observers on the Legislative Council (Legco). In World War I he served in British intelligence on the Kenya-Tanganyika border until malaria forced his evacuation. Delamere was elected to the Legco for the Rift Valley in 1920, when Europeans were given the vote, and became the settler spokesman. He believed in the superiority of White civilization and dreamed of an East African dominion in the British Commonwealth along the lines of South African White supremacy. These views led him into conflict with colonial authorities as well as with non-Whites. He resisted the shift of British colonial policy embodied in the 1923 position that "Kenya is an African territory, and ... the interests of the African natives must be paramount." That year he led a settler delegation to London to protest the new policy, but it failed. From 1925 to 1927 he organized and paid for three annual East African intercolonial conferences to champion "the solidification of the White ideal." He also opposed the enfranchisement of Indians and their further immigration.

Lord Delamere was a passionate and authoritarian man, powerful in argumentation. Always something of the adventurer and pioneer, he detested bureaucrats. At times he was fiery and expansive, impulsive and loyal; he was a formidable foe and a generous friend. On his political convictions regarding European primacy in Kenya, he was above all consistent and unbending.

Delamere was financially devastated by the dramatic fall in commodity prices after 1929. In 1930 he made his last trip to London to defend settler interests, but his political activities along with the attempts to save his farms further strained his heart, first weakened by his 1915 bout with malaria. He died on his farm in 1931.

References: DAHB, DNB, EB. Elspeth Huxley, *White Man's Country* (2nd ed., 1953).

DENARD, Bob
(Comoros, 1929–)

Mercenary, soldier, coup leader, perhaps assassin, Bob Denard is one of the dashing yet corrupt figures of postcolonial Africa. Born Gilbert Bourgeaud in Bordeaux, France, he is also known by his Arabic name, Saïd Mustapha Mahdjoub.

Denard served with the French army in Indochina in his late teens and early twenties, leaving in 1952 to join the colonial police in Morocco. He was convicted of joining an assassination attempt on the French prime minister and served a year in prison. Denard re-emerged in the early 1960s as a soldier of fortune, working for the secessionist Congolese leader, Moïse TSHOMBE. He then moved from one adventure to another—Yemen, Congo-Zaïre, and finally the Comoros. Here he would become part of African history.

With 50 mercenaries, Denard seized control of the Comoros in 1978, toppling President Ali SOILIH, who was killed "while attempting to escape." Denard placed the exiled Ahmed ABDALLAH in the presidential palace and became head of the Presidential Guard—effectively his own private army. Abdallah forged ties with South Africa, which funded Denard generously. In return he turned back three coup attempts against the president. The two finally fell out, however, and as Abdallah moved to fire Denard, the former was killed. Denard was present, by his own admission, but insisted that it was Abdallah's bodyguard who had murdered the president. In all, Denard overthrew four Comoros governments.

In the last incident, Denard had lost his undercover patron, the French secret service. In 1989, the French moved against him with a naval task force and 3,000 soldiers. He was arrested and spent 10 months in French jails. He then went into exile in South Africa for five years, then returned to France to face charges stemming from a failed coup in Benin. After prominent French officials spoke up for him and he showed that the coup attempt had been done with the support of the French government, Denard was given a suspended sentence. He was tried again in 1999 on the charge of the murder of Abdallah, but was acquitted.

Denard has been married seven times polygamously, after becoming a Muslim. He has taken Comoros citizenship.

References: EB, *wiki.* Samantha Wienberg, *The Last of the Pirates: The Search for Bob Denard* (1994).

DHLAKAMA, Afonso
(Mozambique, 1953–)

Afonso Dhlakama, a guerrilla leader long in the service of Rhodesia (now Zimbabwe) and South Africa as head of the Mozambique National Resistance (RENAMO), has in recent years agreed to participate in unifying his country.

Dhlakama attended a Catholic seminary before graduating from business school in Beira, Mozambique, in 1969. In 1973 he joined the Front for the Liberation of Mozambique (FRELIMO), the nationalist liberation group led by Samora MACHEL, but Dhlakama proved unreliable and was expelled during a 1974 anticorruption campaign.

In 1976 the White minority government of Rhodesia decided to organize a guerrilla force to destabilize Mozambique, which was then being used as a staging ground for the Zimbabwe African National Liberation Army (ZANLA) of Robert MUGABE. Joining RENAMO shortly after its formation, Dhlakama was put in charge of supplies for forces in the local province. RENAMO at that time was hardly more than an extension of the Rhodesian army, and it was initially led by disaffected Portuguese settlers. Rhodesia wanted RENAMO to appear more African, and so Dhlakama rose quickly in the movement. In 1980, after the death of RENAMO's founder, Dhlakama became president, eliminating some of his rivals by execution.

That same year Zimbabwe became independent, and RENAMO attracted a new sponsor: South Africa.

Through the 1980s, RENAMO operated as a terrorist organization, destroying schools and clinics and dynamiting bridges and railroads in an attempt to render Mozambique ungovernable. By 1986 there were 250 skirmishes a month with national troops, 85 percent initiated by RENAMO. FRELIMO forces made every attempt to capture Dhlakama, once almost cornering him when they surrounded his headquarters and then dropped Zimbabwean paratroopers on the camp. His escapes contributed to a mystique surrounding him, even as RENAMO's atrocities against the population mounted. Support came not only from South Africa (secretly after 1984) but also from right-wing organizations in the United States, which viewed RENAMO as a bulwark against communism. The U.S. government, however, favored the ruling government in Mozambique after Joaquim CHISSANO became president, and the Reagan administration denounced RENAMO in strong terms.

By 1990, FRELIMO and RENAMO were ready to meet and discuss a ceasefire, largely out of mutual exhaustion. Despite several false starts, these negotiations led to a settlement in 1992 which provided for RENAMO's recognition as a political party, elections within a year, merger of the two armies, and political amnesty. Dhlakama suffered a setback in May 1994 when other opposition groups refused to support his candidacy for president, leaving him only the support of RENAMO adherents. He agreed, however, to respect the election results and has promised not to return to guerrilla resistance. Chissano received 53 percent of the votes and Dhlakama only 34 percent. With most minor parties eliminated and his image softened in the public mind, he raised his total to 48 percent in 1999, but still lost. He tried again in 2004, but the FRELIMO candidates defeated him 64 percent to 32 percent. He has been called "the long-distance runner," "the survivor," and less kindly, "the eternal candidate" as his influence wanes.

References: PLBA, *wiki.* Alex Vines, *Terrorism in Mozambique* (1991).

DIAGNE, Blaise
(Sénégal, 1872–1934)

Blaise Diagne created the first African political party in the French colonies and was the first Black African to be elected to the French Chamber of Deputies. His career began in radical politics, but his policy of working through compromise eventually moved him to the right.

Diagne was born on Gorée Island, a former shipping depot for slaves, off Dakar. After notable success in school, he entered the French colonial service in 1892, assured that any talented African could be assimilated into French society as an equal. Experience proved otherwise, and Diagne found himself passed over for promotion because of racial discrimination. Disgruntled by his treatment, he became an outspoken critic of the oppression of colonial subjects, which led to his being labeled a troublemaker and given frequent administrative transfers. He was in turn posted to the customs service in Benin, Gabon, Congo, Réunion, and Madagascar.

In 1908 he took sick leave in France, where he married and made contacts with French politicians and colonial activists. In 1910 he was assigned to French Guiana in South America, where corruption in the service further radicalized him.

In 1913, Diagne returned to France, where he gave public lectures and debated issues related to colonialism. This political exposure influenced him to seek a seat in the parliament. Sénégal had been electing deputies to the Chamber of Deputies since 1848, but none had ever been African. Diagne had no political base in Sénégal, but he soon built one with support from three sources: the major youth group; the African civil servants; and the leader of the largest Islamic sect, Amadou BAMBA. The French, who attempted to limit the civic rights of Sénégalese with full citizenship, provided Diagne with an obvious campaign issue. He was elected in 1914 in a runoff election.

Diagne sat with the Socialists in parliament and operated by offering concessions in exchange for his political goals. Thus, he agreed to conscription of Africans as a trade-off for securing full citizenship rights for them. When the manpower pressures of World War I became severe, Diagne was offered a minor cabinet post if he would go to Sénégal as commissioner of military recruitment. He refused until he obtained a tax exemption for Africans living in France and the construction of hospitals, a medical school, and an agricultural school in Sénégal. He enlisted 60,000 men, and in the elections of 1919 made these veterans the base for the first French African political party, the Republican Socialist Party. Diagne swept back into office, and his party carried all the local elections as well. Diagne had become an international figure and presided over the 1919 Pan-African Congress.

Following this success, Diagne began to focus on domestic issues and won concessions from the French, thus allowing the excluded indigenous peoples of the interior their first representation on an enlarged legislative council. This continuing pressure for Africanization and equality alarmed and mobilized the French settlers and the *métis,* or people of mixed heritage. Fearing permanent exclusion from power, these two groups made an alliance with the Bordeaux businessmen who controlled trade with France in order to block further social reform. Diagne responded by offering to bring his opponents into the party and the legislative council in exchange for their support, but this compromise, called the Bordeaux Pact, angered and factionalized his African followers. Even his most loyal associate, Galandou DIOUF, stood for election against Diagne. By then, however, the colonial government openly supported Diagne, and he won his seat, but it is likely that the 1928 election was rigged to defeat Diouf.

Diagne became closer to the French government in his last years. In 1930 he defended the detested forced labor policy before the League of Nations, which appalled his supporters at home but led to his appointment as undersecretary of state for the colonies. Nonetheless, he was still able to benefit his people, and during the Great Depression he negotiated farm subsidies for Sénégal. Diagne believed in the equality of Franco-Africans in the French community, suggesting that with racial justice, colonialism could benefit all citizens. He did not support independence, which was a major reason why more radical African leaders ignored him and subsequently bypassed his efforts.

References: *afr,* DAHB, EWB, MMA, WGMC. Amady Dieng, *Blaise Diagne, Deputé noir de l'Afrique* (Blaise Diagne, Black deputy from Africa, 1990).

DIANGIENDA, Kuntima Joseph

(Democratic Republic of the Congo, 1918–1992)

His Eminence, Joseph Diangienda was second head of the Kimbanguist Church, officially called the Church of Christ on Earth, the largest and most prominent denomination in the African independent church movement. The denomination was founded by his father, Prophet Simon KIMBANGU in the then Belgian Congo (now the Democratic Republic of the Congo or DRC). The independent churches bring together Christian beliefs and African values and customs. They have a wide variety of practices, but commonly emphasize healing and freedom from witchcraft.

Diangienda is one of three sons, each of whom has been active in the Kimbanguist movement. From the beginning, however, Diangienda was the acknowledged leader.

Considered a threat by Belgian colonial authorities and strongly opposed by Catholic missionaries, Kimbangu was imprisoned in 1921. During the years of his imprisonment and isolation (1921–1951), Kimbanguism suffered from a lack of leadership. Numerous prophetic personalities claimed the fallen mantle, and Kimbanguist sects sprang up that rejected Kimbangu's doctrine of submission to the state. They resisted taxes and reintroduced polygamy. The original Christian biblical inspiration was replaced by animist elements, which were reinforced by visions.

According to Kimbanguist tradition, when he entered prison, Kimbangu predicted that his baby son, Diangienda, would succeed him. Diangienda was raised by a White missionary couple who took him in when his father was imprisoned, and he was brought up in a Baptist atmosphere, but educated at a Catholic school. Faithful to his father's prophecy, however, Diangienda took charge of the movement when he became an adult and forged a united community even though Kimbanguism was proscribed and persecuted by the colonial government. In 1948, Diangienda was allowed to visit Kimbangu in prison and was formally named successor to his father, the prophet.

With Kimbangu's death, Diangienda moved to unite the disparate groups of his disciples. In 1954 they acknowledged Diangienda, then secretary to a provincial governor, as leader. The movement then took steps to obtain recognition and legitimacy in both the DRC and Belgium. In 1956 a Church council was formed to lead the movement, with the formal name Church of Christ on Earth through the Prophet Simon Kimbangu (EJCSK). A confessional statement professing respect for the government and exclusively religious goals finally won acceptance from Belgium. The colonial government granted legal recognition to the church in 1959, but it was again restricted after national independence. To be granted government acceptance and achieve unification, Diangienda also had to pull together those groups that had formally belonged to the Catholic and Protestant missions while secretly adhering to Kimbanguism, thus completing the transition from religious movement to denomination. Many Kimbanguists had gone underground in the mission churches.

The confessional statement affirmed that Kimbangu was "not God . . . but the envoy of Christ." It stated that Kimbangu "died, rose again, and is with us in spirit." Diangienda himself claimed miraculous powers, and his disciples believe that he raised the dead and called down rain during droughts.

Under Diangienda's leadership, the church built a seminary and a network of schools, clinics and social services. It has over five million members in some 5,000 parishes. In 1981, the EJCSK built a massive cathedral seating 37,000. It is part of a complex that includes an amphitheater, several residences, its own hydroelectric plant, a school and a hospital.

Diangienda led the church into membership in the World Council of Churches in 1969. It was the first independent African Church to be granted membership. It was also close to the dictator MOBUTU Sese Seko, who, as part of his "authenticity" campaign, helped to promote the EJCSK as a counterfoil to the Protestant and Catholic Churches.

Diangienda took the title "eminence" rather than "prophet." He was a quiet and simple man in appearance, with a plain, straightforward style of preaching. After his death, he was succeeded by an older brother, and after his death by Diangienda's son.

References: dacb, Diangienda, *Histoire de kimbanguisme* (History of Kimbanguism,1984).

DINGANE
(South Africa, 1795?–1840)

Dingane murdered his half-brother SHAKA and succeeded him as paramount chief of the Zulu from 1828 to 1840. While Dingane maintained Zulu power, his encounters with Europeans were calamitous, involving the slaughter of a large number of Afrikaners, which was followed by the disastrous defeat of the Zulu army.

Dingane had been spared from the general massacre of Shaka's relatives because he had not taken sides against Shaka's right to the throne, but this same indecisiveness plagued him all his life. Lethargic and inconsistent, he could not exert control as Shaka had. Several sub-chiefs defected and, although Dingane reinstituted Shaka's system of terrorism, he was not as effective a leader, nor did he inspire the same loyalty in his troops. Although he had hoped to end much of Shaka's incessant military adventures, he had a huge and restless army on his hands, and he busied them with various campaigns such as defending his territory twice against MZILIKAZI's Ndebele. In 1833 his troops destroyed the Portuguese garrison at Delagoa Bay, Mozambique.

Dingane realized that Shaka had made a major error in tolerating White settlement in Natal and in permitting the establishment of Port Natal (now Durban), which became a refuge for several thousand Zulu refugees. In 1837, Dingane was confronted by a large group of Afrikaners who were part of the Great Trek moving into the interior of South Africa from the Cape Colony to escape British rule and establish an Afrikaner homeland. Dingane treacherously granted them a large land grant but then ambushed and massacred a delegation of Afrikaner leaders under Piet Retief. By night the rest of the Afrikaner camps were attacked and destroyed. A year later, Andries W. J. PRETORIUS returned with a well-armed force and, at the Battle of Blood River, inflicted a total defeat upon the Zulu, massacring the best of their troops. By 1840, Dingane's half-brother had deserted with thousands of followers and entered an alliance with the Afrikaners. He then returned north with modern arms and defeated Dingane, who was murdered a few months later while a refugee.

References: afr, CWAH, DAHB, EB, EWB, *wiki.*

DINGISWAYO
(South Africa, 1770s-1816)

Dingiswayo, paramount chief of the Nguni confederation, paved the way for SHAKA's efforts to centralize chiefdoms. Dingiswayo was powerful just before momentous change in southern Africa that included a complete realignment of ethnic and cultural patterns. He was also the last important leader in the region before significant European penetration. Consequently, some of his history is traditional and perhaps mythic, ascribing achievements to him that may have been accomplished before his time.

Dingiswayo was exiled as a youth after a quarrel with his father, a sub-chief among the hundreds of Nguni clans. He spent some years as a wanderer and took his name, meaning "the wanderer." When he returned home on horseback, he had acquired a legendary aura. In 1805 he killed his brother, who had succeeded his father as chief, because he considered him a usurper. Recognizing that the old system of multiple chieftaincies was no longer workable because of expanding population pressures, Dingiswayo began gathering the related chiefdoms into a confederation. In this strategy, he had two competitors who were moving in the same direction: the Ndwandwe and the Swazi.

Dingiswayo's Mthethwa federation was based on collaboration as well as military force. He organized circumcision classes into military age groups, an idea that Shaka would build upon. Young men spent long periods preparing for circumcision, the life passage that entitled them to be warriors. During the preparation time, spent separate from the tribe, strong bonds of friendship were forged, making them ideal companions for military service. Using his troops where necessary, Dingiswayo created a strong confederacy with himself as paramount chief and a large number of sub-chiefs under his authority. As needed, he intervened in the choice of clan leaders to make sure that loyal chiefs would govern the various groups, but he rarely interfered in internal matters. In this way, he dispatched Shaka, who had become a trusted leader in the Mthethwa army, to take over the Zulu throne after his father's death and supplied troops to enforce Shaka's position. In 1816, the paramount chief of the Ndwandwe lured Dingiswayo into a trap and had him murdered, some say with the connivance of Shaka. The confederation then began to disintegrate, with Shaka seizing the opportunity to take the paramount chieftaincy and forge the confederacy into a unified empire.

References: CWAH, DAHB, *wiki.*

DINUZULU
(South Africa, 1869–1913)

Dinuzulu, king of the Zulu, ruled during the transition from independence to incorporation into South Africa. When he was a boy, his father, CETSHWAYO, was banished and his kingdom divided into 13 jurisdictions, each headed by a chief. Cetshwayo was restored briefly to a truncated kingdom but died soon after. Dinuzulu succeeded him in 1884 with support from the Afrikaners, who demanded land concessions in exchange. Locked into a struggle with the British over domination of Natal, the Afrikaners hoped to carve out what they called the "New Republic."

The British and the Afrikaners negotiated with no further consideration for Zulu concerns. In 1888 the New Republic territory was incorporated into the Transvaal, and the British annexed Zululand, which was divided into judicial districts under British magistrates. In vain, Dinuzulu protested and tried to assert his independence. When a former rival for the throne sent warriors into Zulu territory, Dinuzulu repulsed them but was brought to trial for treason. He was convicted in 1889 and deported to the island of St. Helena. In 1898 he was allowed to return as a minor chief on a government stipend, but he never surrendered his hereditary title.

In 1906, Chief BAMBATHA of the Zondi clan led a revolt against a new head tax. It was the last armed revolt by the Zulu against colonial absorption. Bambatha was deposed by the British for his opposition, and before organizing his warriors into guerrilla bands, he met with Dinuzulu. There is no evidence that Dinuzulu encouraged the rebellion, but he was accused of treason by the Natal government, and the case became a sensational trial. Dinuzulu was defended by William SCHREINER, who had just been reelected to parliament and was the champion of native rights in the new South Africa. Dinuzulu was convicted only of tacitly supporting the revolt; he was deposed and banished to internal exile in the Transvaal, where he died in 1913.

References: CWAH, DAHB, MMA, *wiki.* C.T. Binns, *Dinuzulu: The Death of the House of Shaka* (1968).

DIOGO I
(Democratic Republic of the Congo/Angola, 1510?–1561)

Manikongo Diogo I, the grandson of AFONSO I—the first Christian *manikongo,* or king, of the Kongo—continued his grandfather's policy of attempting to gain control over Portuguese settlers and regain authority over trade.

He came to the throne in 1545 after Dom Pedro I, who was toppled in an insurrection and forced to take sanctuary in a church. Diogo, a popular choice for election, was also favored by those Portuguese who were faithful to the king of Portugal because he had bestowed royal trade prerogatives on the Kongo. A second faction was loyal to the traders at nearby São Tomé Island, who ignored both Kongolese rights, as well as orders from Lisbon, in their greed to control the lucrative slave trade. Diogo immediately set about trying to limit the latter group. Throughout his reign, Diogo had to deal with supporters of Dom Pedro. In 1550 a conspiracy against Diogo was crushed, revealing the various factions opposed to Diogo.

Diogo was able to retain the Kongo's control of trade caravans going into the interior, but the São Tomé faction petitioned Lisbon, claiming that he was creating commercial interference by maintaining high customs duties and limiting opportunities for Portuguese traders. In turn, Diogo complained of São Tomé smuggling, refusing to carry Kongolese cargo, and looting of local fisheries. In 1556 this conflict erupted into a war over rights to deal with the peoples of Ndongo, to the south. Diogo was defeated, and Portugal began to trade directly with Ndongo, which laid the groundwork for the establishment of the colony of Angola. In 1560 the Portuguese changed their policy and withdrew the royal prerogative, allowing São Tomé settlers to trade directly anywhere along the coast.

Diogo's religious policy was similarly unproductive and strife-ridden. The bishop of São Tomé, who had jurisdiction over the Kongo, arrived in 1547 to establish a monastery to train Kongolese Dominicans, but Diogo forced him to leave after their relations soured. The Jesuits, in turn, came to the Kongo in 1548 to establish a school but quickly became supporters of Pedro and the São Tomé faction. In the aftermath of the failed 1550 conspiracy, they were expelled. Diogo himself did not accept those parts of Christianity that challenged Kongolese social customs on marriage. He kept concubines and married close relatives, which were necessary practices for maintaining links with powerful families.

References: DAB, DAHB.

DIOP, Alioune
(Sénégal, 1910–1980)

Alioune Diop was one of the most influential African intellectuals and writers in the years spanning the transition from colonialism to independence. His pioneering Parisian publishing establishment became the foremost resource for bringing French-speaking African writers to the attention of the West. In 1982 the ministers of culture of the sub-Saharan African states established a literary prize in Diop's name to recognize his critical place in African literature.

Diop is associated most often with Pan-Africanism in his thinking, but his concern extended to the entire Black world, including the diaspora in the United States and the Caribbean. His focus was not on traditional Black cultures but on the emerging Black consciousness, which was being expressed in literature and the arts. He was also the major cultural figure in the anticolonial movement.

Born in Saint-Louis, one of the four privileged communes whose residents were citizens of France, Diop received a good education, including university studies in Algeria and Paris. After brief tenures as a teacher and colonial officer, he was elected from Sénégal to the French Senate in 1947, and returned to Paris. There he joined a diverse group of intellectuals and writers who asked him to establish a journal that would foster a debate between Africa and the West.

The journal *Présence Africaine* immediately became a lively arena in which contrasting views were expressed. Although the journal was anticolonial and Afrocentric, it had no doctrinaire position and was open to Communists and liberals, Caribbeans and Africans, Americans and Europeans. It also had no literary limits; the journal published essays, poetry, and fiction. In 1960 an English edition was initiated. *Présence Africaine* became a showcase for the writing of political leaders such as Julius NYERERE and Sékou TOURÉ, poets such as David DIOP and Léopold Sédar SENGHOR, and other literary figures such as Wole SOYINKA, Chinua ACHEBE, and John Pepper CLARK. These prominent African writers were placed alongside leading Black writers of the Caribbean (Aimé Césaire and Eric Williams) and the United States (Amiri Baraka, formerly Leroi Jones). Within two years, Diop established a publishing house, also called Présence Africaine, which began to bring out the books of African writers.

Diop was a close associate of Senghor and a leading figure in his *Négritude* movement, which stressed the African sources of Black culture. Within *Présence Africaine,* the African cultural personality was asserted as a direct challenge to colonial ideology. In the 1960s, a period of intense political consciousness in Africa, *Présence Africaine* became increasingly political in content. Despite this emphasis, the bulk of Diop's own writing consisted of essays on the role of the arts in modern African life and culture.

Diop was raised a Muslim but converted to Catholicism, although he wrote essays that were bitterly critical of Christianity. He regarded many Christian institutions as colonialist in orientation and out of tune with the cry for freedom throughout Africa. He saw the Africanization of Christianity as the most crucial element of *Négritude,* and when the Congress of Black Writers and Artists met in Rome in 1959, Diop helped to assemble a group of African theologians. This session, and the three congresses that followed, typified the large number of international conferences for which Diop was the moving spirit. Through his central association, *Société Africaine de Culture* (Society of African Culture) (1956), he reached out into every area of culture to bring together Black intellectuals, artists and writers. His efforts reached diverse groups and led to his Festivals of Black Arts and various Congresses of Black Writers and Artists. In every case, Diop brought in cultural figures from throughout the Black world. He felt an intense gratitude that Black Americans and Caribbeans had spoken up for Africans before they had the power or the voice to speak for themselves. In tribute to Diop after his death, his journal called him a "sign of double alliance—first, the alliance of Black people among themselves, and second, the alliance of the latter with other people of the world."

Reference: adb.

DIOP, Birago Ismael
(Sénégal, 1906–1989)

Dr. Birago Ismael Diop, folklorist and poet, was a great popularizer of West African traditional stories. An early friend of Léopold SENGHOR, Diop was also a partisan of the *Négritude* movement in literature.

Educated in veterinary science at the University of Toulouse in France, Diop spent a year in Paris before practicing his profession in French West Africa from 1933 to the late 1950s. In Paris he entered the circle of Black intellectuals and writers who were affirming Black cultural values and became enthusiastic about the value of African folk tales as a vehicle for Black consciousness. Senghor, one of this group, published several of Diop's poems in 1948, but he was already known for *Les Contes d'Amadou Koumba* (1947), adaptations of a collection of Wolof folk tales. The book was highly praised, and Diop subsequently published two further volumes of Wolof traditional stories in 1958 and 1963. The folk collections follow a story cycle about Leuk (the hare) and Bouki (the hyena) locked in eternal combat. The stories are often humorous but always revealing of human foibles. Diop adopted the narrative style of the *griot,* a West African storyteller and keeper of family histories. Repetition, plays on words, legends and current matters are combined to reflect his heritage and provide entertainment. Poetry, song and story alternate in such a way as to create a rhythm that, even in French, evokes the experience of the Wolof tale being told aloud.

Diop reinforces several traditional values: living within the bounds of nature, reverence for the sacred, and the primacy of the community. Bound as he was to his tradition, Diop shared the vision of the *Négritude* writers that fused Black culture and humanism: "The *négritude* that claims to be a movement must arrange to go beyond itself and open up to the world of tomorrow."

When Sénégal achieved independence in 1960 and Senghor became its first president, he appointed Diop as ambassador to Tunisia. In that same year *Présence Africaine*, the leading African literary and cultural journal and publishing house, published a volume of Diop's poetry. In 1964, Diop left public service and established a veterinary practice in

Dakar while working on his multivolume autobiography and memoirs, which are a valuable source for the history of the African intellectual movement in Paris in the 1930s.

References: adb, AA, AO, CA, DAHB, EB, MBW, NRG, WLTC, wiki. Diop, *Mémoires* (5 vols., 1978–1989); Mohamadou Kane, *Birago Diop: L'Homme et l'Oeuvre* (Birago Diop: The man and his work, 1971).

DIOP, Cheikh Anta
(Sénégal, 1923–1986)

Dr. Cheikh Anta Diop, opposition politician and well-known historian, was one of the preeminent African intellectuals of the twentieth century. *The African Origin of Civilization* (1955), his seminal work on the origins of Western civilization, has influenced both the current Afrocentric movement in the United States, and later historians, especially through the United Nations' *General History of Africa,* to which he was an important contributor.

Diop's central thesis was that ancient Egyptian civilization was Black, which suggests predominantly African origins for Western and Near Eastern civilization. Diop propounded his theory in his doctoral dissertation at the Sorbonne in Paris, but the dissertation was initially rejected. His book won wide acclaim when published by the French periodical *Présence Africaine* in 1955, and Diop subsequently received his degree. In several later books, Diop advanced and refined his theory. Starting with the work of Louis LEAKEY, Diop argued that "the whole human race had its origin at the foot of the Mountains of the Moon" and was "ethnically homogeneous and negroid."

Diop first studied physics in Paris under Frederick Joliot-Curie and went on to develop Africa's first carbon-14 dating laboratory at the Institut Fondamental d'Afrique Noire. Using scientific data and other information, he reinforced his basic proposition. With microscopic analyses of skin samples from mummies, he demonstrated that the melanin level in both the epidermis and the dermis is consistent only with a negroid population. The same levels cannot be found among either Caucasian or Semitic peoples. He augmented this evidence with analyses of blood types and bone measurements.

Diop's thesis caused great scholarly controversy that continues today. Traditional Egyptology was severely threatened, and some scholars accused Diop of an ill-concealed racism. Much criticism is based on trivialized sensationalism such as *Time* magazine's cover story, "Was Cleopatra Black?" Such headlines distorted Diop's careful research findings. Despite much criticism, his work continues to be strengthened by independent analysis, although his linguistic analysis is not generally accepted.

An active student leader as a young man, Diop was Pan-Africanist and anticolonial. In Sénégal, however, he was never fully accepted as a leader. Opposing another towering African intellectual, the pro-French President Léopold SENGHOR, Diop founded three political parties. The first was founded in 1961 and folded in 1963 when all the other leaders defected to Senghor; the second was banned in 1965; the third (1973) was only recognized in 1981. Diop came in a poor third in the 1983 presidential elections, but he and his parties remained aloof from the needs of the average Sénégalese. His one great political success was to foster the nationalist Wolof language movement against French as a medium of education. A leading Sénégalese university is named for him.

References: adb, afr, CA, EWB, MMA, PLBA, *wiki.* E. Curtis Alexander, ed. *Cheikh Anta Diop: An African Scientist* (1984).

DIOP, David Mandessi
(Sénégal, 1927–1960)

David Mandessi Diop, a leading figure of the *Négritude* movement, died in a plane crash before realizing his full potential as a poet. His influence lies largely in his almost mythic position in African literature as the poetic standard-bearer of Black nationalism.

Diop was born in Bordeaux of African parents and was educated in France. He studied medicine, but ill health dogged him all his life, forcing him to abandon plans for a medical career. The major intellectual influence on Diop was his teacher, Léopold SENGHOR, who was then just beginning to reject the French assimilationist philosophy and assert the importance of Black consciousness. Diop developed a passionate interest in the poetry of Blackness. After World War II he joined the group that founded *Présence Africaine,* which became the

most prominent African cultural journal and champion of the literary Black consciousness movement known as *Négritude.* Diop contributed both articles and poems to the journal. In 1948, in his important anthology of Black poetry, Senghor introduced Diop to a wider public. In 1956, Diop published his only book, *Coups de Pilon* (Hammer Blows), and returned to Dakar to teach, becoming principal of a college in Guinea after a year. He and his wife were killed in a plane crash while returning from a Paris holiday. All his unpublished manuscripts—reputedly including a novel, many poems, and a textbook on African literature—perished with him.

Diop weighed in on the language argument, asserting that those who wrote in colonialist languages had submitted to assimilation, and he called the use of Western literary forms a kind of bastardization. Yet he himself felt compelled to do both.

Diop's poetry positioned him as a leading advocate of African consciousness. Militant and antiassimilationist, the most extreme of the *Négritude* writers in his condemnation of European cultural superiority, he championed a return to Black cultural roots as a basis for the rebirth of Africa within an emerging international community that seemed so fresh and promising in the 1960s. His writing did not represent nostalgia for an African mythic past but a triumphant affirmation of a new Africa. Perhaps because his vision was so compelling, Diop—despite the slim body of his work—remains one of the most widely anthologized poets of his generation.

References: adb, AA, DAHB, EB, MBW, MMA, NRG, WLTC.

DIOP-MAMBÉTY, Djibril
(Sénégal, 1945–1998)

Djibril Diop-Mambéty was one of the leading figures in the first generation of African filmakers. His *Touki Bouki* (The Voyage of the Hyena, 1973) is the story of a young African couple who go to extreme lengths to fulfill their dream of seeing Paris. It is widely accepted as the best African comedy written to date, and one of the finest African films of any type.

Diop-Mambéty began his professional career as an actor on stage and in several African and Italian films. After graduating in drama, he worked with the National Theater, from which he was dismissed for lack of discipline. Diop-Mambéty took his expulsion as a challenge and plunged into film making.

In his first feature film, *Touki Bouki*, Diop-Mambéty was already testing the limits of contemporary African cinema. He used sound and creative camera work to expand beyond the linear storytelling modes of the founders of African cinema, like Ousmane SEMBÈNE. The film was critically acclaimed, and won the International Critics' Award at the Cannes Film Festival and the Special Jury Award at the Moscow Film Festival.

For a long time Diop-Mambéty produced only shorter films, but in 1992 he returned to full-length with *Hyènes* (Hyenas), intended as the second part of a trilogy with *Touki Bouki*. It is a slashing attack on African elites, their greed and corruption and failure to realize the promise of liberation.

From this, he turned toward short films about the lives of ordinary Africans. Again he planned a trilogy. The first, *Le Franc*, won the best short film award at FESPACO (the major African film festival) in 1995. It shows the devastating effect of the 50 percent devaluation of the Central African franc on a man who comes to base his last hope on winning the lottery. By extension, Diop-Mambéty is saying that life has been reduced to a crap-shoot for the poor. The second part of the trilogy, *La Petite Vendeuse du Soleil* (The Little Sun-Seller, 1999) tells the story of a crippled girl who struggles to compete with street boys selling newspapers. Neither trilogy was completed before Diop-Mambéty died of lung cancer.

Reference: adb.

DIORI, Hamani
(Niger, 1916–1989)

El-Hadj Hamani Diori led his country to independence and served as its first president from 1960 to 1974, when he was removed by a military coup.

Diori's father was a public health official in the colonial service, and so the young Hamani received a good education, at first in Niger, then in Dahomey (now Benin), and finally at the prestigious William Ponty School in Sénégal. He returned to Niger as a teacher in 1936, but two years later went to Paris to teach Hausa at the Institute of Overseas Studies. After returning home in 1946 to assume the position of headmaster in a school in Niamey, he

entered nationalist politics for the first time, cofounding the Progressive Party of Niger (PPN) as the local branch of Félix HOUPHOUËT-BOIGNY's regional party, the Rassemblement Démocratique Africain (RDA). Diori was elected that year as an African member of the French National Assembly. Diori and Houphouët-Boigny became close friends as well as political allies. Diori's relations with his cousin, Djibo BAKARY, turned into rivalry at the same time, and Bakary defeated Diori in 1951 after Bakary broke away from the PPN.

Diori returned to teaching until 1958 at a new school named for him, and spent his political energies in reorganizing the PPN. In 1956 he narrowly defeated Bakary for the French assembly, but the following year the PPN lost the majority of the territorial assembly to Bakary's party. In the key referendum of 1958, however, Diori triumphed, having gathered a coalition of chiefs, traditionalists, and the Hausa, Fulani, and Djerba ethnic groups. The referendum was a resounding 78 percent "yes" vote for autonomy within the French community. Diori was named prime minister of the autonomous republic that year and became president of the newly independent state in 1960. He was re-elected in 1965 and 1970.

Diori's first years in office were marked by mediation in various African conflicts and leadership in regional organizations. In 1968 he was spokesman for the Afro-Malagasy Joint Organization at negotiations to associate the French-speaking states with the European Community. His prestige was such that four nonmember states asked him to represent their interests.

French support for Diori gradually cooled, however, when he did not follow the French lead in international affairs. He established diplomatic relations with the Communist bloc and, during the Nigerian civil war (1967–1970) he favored the federal government over secessionist Biafra. Neither position pleased Paris. The French exerted pressure on Niger, but Diori remained loyal to his Hausa neighbors in Nigeria as well as supportive of fellow Muslims. Relations with Nigeria remained cordial, but there were occasional differences with Ghana. The major one occurred when Dr. Kofi BUSIA expelled 200,000 Niger workers in 1969 as part of an economic stabilization program.

Diori's domestic position was far more fragile than his growing international reputation suggested. From his exile, Bakary mounted border skirmishes and plotted attacks. A 1965 mosque bombing almost cost Diori his life. He subsequently established his authority by firm action, but the economy continued to deteriorate. Moreover, Diori's frequent trips abroad led to corruption and mismanagement by those to whom he delegated responsibility. Many felt that by the late 1960s he had lost touch with the needs of the people. Matters came to a head when a pervasive drought hit Niger in the 1970s; massive foreign aid was mismanaged and siphoned off to corrupt officials. Diori was overthrown by a 1974 military coup led by Colonel Seyni KOUNTCHÉ, during which Diori's wife was killed. Diori was imprisoned for six years and then held under house arrest until 1987. He spent his final years in Morocco.

References: afr, DAHB, DRWW, MMA, PLBA, *wiki.*

DIOUF, Abdou
(Sénégal, 1935–)

Abdou Diouf was the hand-picked presidential successor of the legendary Léopold SENGHOR. A wily political operator, he has kept himself in power by a combination of openness and conciliation toward his opponents and strong support from rural Muslim leaders.

Diouf was educated at the elite Lycée Faidherbe in Saint-Louis, and then at the University of Dakar and the Sorbonne, where he received his law degree in 1960. He entered the civil service and proved himself an able administrator in a series of appointments during the 1960s. In 1968 he entered parliament and was named minister of planning and industry. Senghor became his political mentor, and when he decided to retire from the presidency, he arranged for Diouf to be his successor. The position of prime minister was established in 1970, and Diouf held that office for 10 years, with considerable freedom of action regarding the economy. He began to build a political base among the powerful rural Muslim leaders, the *marabouts,* but he also became the respected leader of the middle class and the technocrats in government. In 1980, Senghor announced his retirement, and the following year Diouf succeeded him in office.

Diouf tended to steer a moderate course for his country, devoid of ideology. In 1982 he formed a Senegambian Confederation between Sénégal and the Gambia, but the inequality of the two states led to its breakdown, and it was abandoned in 1989. Far more serious was the racist violence that broke out between Sénégal and Mauritania in 1990, leading to border skirmishes and the mutual expulsion of tens of thousands of expatriates from each country.

Diouf handled internal political crises with tact and avoided divisive situations. Feeling that the ruling party was too strong, he encouraged opposition but has regularly defeated opponents in elections. His major opponent, Abdoulaye WADE, who alleged electoral fraud, was detained by the government. International observers declared the 1993 elections "free and fair," but in the aftermath, the vice chair of the supreme court charged with certifying the results was murdered, and Wade was accused of complicity in the crime.

Diouf took a firm stand against two guerrilla movements, one an urban Muslim fundamentalist group that has been involved in terrorist bombings and the other a secessionist movement in Casamance, in the southern part of the country. Diouf maintained his Islamic credentials by being elected head of the Islamic Conference in 1994.

In the 2000 elections, Diouf again faced off against his longtime opponent, Wade, and led in the first round, 41 percent to 30 percent—not enough to win outright. In the run-off, he lost to Wade, 58 percent to 41 percent, after the opposition united against him. Diouf handed over authority peacefully. In 2003, he became secretary-general of La Francophonie, the association of French-speaking countries.

References: afr, DAHB, DRWW, PLBA, RWWA, *wiki.* Momar Diop, *Le Sénégal sous Abdou Diouf* (Sénégal under Abdou Diouf, 1990).

DIOUF, Galandou
(Sénégal, 1875–1941)

Galandou Diouf was an African pioneer in French politics as the first Black city council member elected in Sénégal, as well as its first Black mayor.

For some years Diouf toiled as a petty bureaucrat. His contact with racial discrimination made him a critic of French colonialism and a defender of African workers' rights. He subsequently became an accountant with a prominent Muslim merchant and won the respect of the Bordeaux business establishment that controlled Sénégalese trade. At the same time, he helped organize the Young Sénégalese, a pressure group advocating equal pay for equal work, greater access to higher education, and fuller civil rights for Africans. He made a coalition of these two groups of supporters and was elected to the General Council in 1909. He began a newspaper to promote his ideas and was later elected mayor of Rufisque, his hometown.

Diouf was an early and faithful supporter of African politician Blaise DIAGNE and swung his support to Diagne in his first electoral campaign for the French Chamber of Deputies. After World War I, however, the two fell out when Diagne began turning to the right. By 1920, anticolonial sentiment had rallied around Diouf, and the more radical elements had deserted Diagne and rejected his position advocating colonialism with equality. In 1928, Diouf ran against Diagne but was unable to unseat him in an election that was marked by widespread voting fraud. With powerful colonial newspaper support, Diagne repeated his success in 1932, but when he died, Diouf was elected to replace him.

Diouf repeated Diagne's pattern of appeasement and conciliation once he was in Paris. He supported French colonial policies, and as a result his support at home evaporated. His trusted lieutenant, Lamine GUÈYE, became his main opponent.

Like Diagne, Diouf relied upon business and settler support, which kept him in the Chamber of Deputies until the fall of France in 1940, when the Nazi occupation and the collaborationist Vichy regime suspended representative politics. Diouf lent his support to the Vichy regime.

References: DAHB, MMA.

DIPEOLU, Olusegun Oladipupo
(Nigeria, 1941–)

Dr. Olusegun Oladipupo Dipeolu is a leading veterinarian specializing in the control of cattle ticks. Dipeolu investigates tick control through genetic rather than chemical methods, thus helping to reduce the extensive use of pesticides in Africa's fragile environment.

Dipeolu received a doctorate in veterinary medicine in West Germany in 1968 and then pursued further studies at the University of Edin-

burgh, where he received a Ph.D. in tropical parasitology in 1972. He joined the University of Ibadan, becoming a full professor of veterinary parasitology in 1977 and serving as dean of the School of Veterinary Medicine from 1981 to 1985. He spent the next three years in the United States as a professor and director of research in the department of veterinary medicine at Tuskegee Institute in Alabama.

Dipeolu is internationally renowned in his field, has served on many councils and committees and has received numerous awards. He was recognized by National Taiwan University in 1983 and received the University of Pennsylvania's centennial award in 1984. Dipeolu has been made a fellow of many scientific groups, including the Royal Society of Entomology, and has written several dozen scholarly articles and conference papers.

The work that has earned this recognition has centered on controlling cattle ticks by natural means. Cattle ticks are one of the natural pests that keep large sections of Africa deficient in beef production. Nomadic peoples are often largely dependent upon cattle for their subsistence; therefore, reducing cattle pests can dramatically decrease malnutrition and improve lives. In 1988, Dipeolu's interests led him to become director of and principal researcher for the tick control program at the International Centre of Insect Physiology and Ecology (ICIPE) in Kenya. He worked there with the international African team led by Dr. Thomas ODHIAMBO and headed up efforts to discover genetic means of tick control.

Currently Dr. Dipeolu is director of the Centre of Tropical Diseases and International Travel Medicine at the American University of Antigua College of Medicine in the Caribbean. He has been doing research in tropical disease and community health.

Reference: PAS.

DJOHAR, Said Mohammed
(Comoros, 1918–)

Said Mohammed Djohar, president of Comoros from1990 to 1996, walked a swaying tightrope in attempting to join the ethnic and political factions in the Comoros Islands. The Comorese are an amalgam of African, Arab, Malagasy, Malay, and

Indian strains. French economic and political dominance, although it is resented, lies just below the surface of Comoran politics, and South Africa was long a major player in local affairs.

Djohar brought to this instability both longevity and political skill at infighting. Born in Madagascar, he joined the French colonial administration of the Comoros Islands and was named a local official by the French in 1947. For 13 years he held various ministerial posts after internal self-government was granted, and he became speaker of the national assembly in 1972. Djohar was well placed when his friend and associate Ahmed ABDALLAH Abderrahman declared independence from the French and named Djohar ambassador to Madagascar, which was probably the most important diplomatic post after Paris. When his half-brother, Ali SOILIH, ousted Abdallah and seized power, Djohar relinquished his position until Soilih's death and Abdallah's return in 1978.

By 1987, Djohar was head of the Supreme Court, and when Abdallah was killed in 1989, he became interim president. Utter confusion followed, during which French paratroops had to dislodge mercenaries under Bob DENARD, who attempted to create a pirate kingdom for themselves. In 1990, Djohar narrowly won highly contested elections amid allegations of fraud. He embarked on a program of moderate democratization that was highly progressive by Comoran standards. While he espoused multiparty government, managing the confusion and deadlocks that resulted was difficult, though a new constitution was drafted. His successor as president of the Supreme Court attempted to remove Djohar in 1991, alleging Djohar's weakness due to age, but he survived that political crisis.

Djohar's administration was rife with corruption, and in the face of interparty confusion and lack of parliamentary leadership, he became more authoritarian. Things came to a head when Denard engineered yet another coup and detained Djohar. Again the French intervened, but Djohar was sent into exile.

Reference: *afr*, RWWA, *wiki*.

DLAMINI, Makhosini
(Swaziland, 1914–1978)

Prince Makhosini Dlamini, the first prime minister of Swaziland after its independence from Great Britain, helped his country take its first steps toward a modern democratic system.

The Dlamini clan is an extensive part of the royal family. Prince Makhosini Dlamini, a nephew of SOBHUZA II, studied locally. He then lived from 1938 to 1940 in South Africa, where he received teacher training, after which he taught for several years and became a headmaster. In 1947 he resigned from teaching to spend more time in politics, serving as a rural development officer and supporting himself by farming. In 1950, after his father's death, he was appointed a senior chief.

Swazi politics were dominated by the king, who also led the nationalist movement. Dlamini, who served as the king's assistant on several occasions, was appointed to every constitutional conference through the early 1960s. He was responsible for the 1961 proposal, rejected by the British, that came to be known as the "50–50 Constitution." It called for a legislative council of 12 Europeans and 12 Swazi, with some of each group elected by both Black and White voters. This plan was typical of Dlamini's moderate and balanced approach to political problems.

In the period just prior to independence, Dlamini was appointed prime minister in the first Swazi parliament in 1964. The king had also founded his own party, the Imbokodvo National Movement (INM), and Dlamini was made its leader in 1964. He led the INM to victory in parliamentary elections in 1964 and 1967, thereby continuing as prime minister when the government became fully autonomous in 1967 and when Swaziland became independent the following year. He always respected the preeminent position of the king but gradually emerged as a respected leader in his own right. He was popular and admired; he used his respect and standing to take a moderately progressive position in African affairs. Already in 1965 he had represented Swaziland at the Organization of African Unity in Accra, where he entered into close relations with other African states. At the same time, Swaziland's dependence upon the South African economy made him cautious in his policies, and this approach was respected by the other African countries.

In the 1972 elections, the INM lost a few parliamentary seats to a small radical group, the Ngwane National Liberation Congress. In response, the king centralized legislative and executive power in himself as monarch. The constitution was annulled, opposition parties were banned, and a detention act was proclaimed. Dlamini remained as prime minister but without a parliament. He was removed by the king in 1976 and died two years later.

References: DAHB, MMA, PLBA.

DODDS, Alfred Amédée
(Sénégal, 1842–1922)

General Alfred Amédée Dodds, a gifted general, was one of the first African citizens of France to rise to a high position both in the colonies and in France.

The son of parents who were both mulattoes, Dodds entered Saint-Cyr, the French military academy, and graduated first in his class. He first saw combat under Marshall François Bazaine in Mexico in 1862–1863. He became a captain during the Franco-Prussian War of 1870–1871, where his heroism at the Battle of Sedan brought him to the attention of his superiors. Wounded and twice captured, he escaped both times to rejoin the army and eventually served in the defense of Paris. He received the Legion of Honor on the battlefield.

Dodds returned to Sénégal, where from 1871 to 1883 he led campaigns against local African chiefs and gradually expanded French control over Sénégal. From 1883 to 1887 he served in Indochina, where he distinguished himself by destroying the Tonkin pirates, who preyed upon shipping in the China Sea. He returned to Sénégal a colonel. (In contrast, it should be noted that at this time no African served above the rank of sergeant in the British army.) Dodds was an outstanding example of the *assimilées,* those Africans who rose in French society and received citizenship. He was a large, strong man with dark features; a contemporary described him as a "keen-eyed, slender man with a long, drooping mustache." He thought of himself as French and did not see the paradox in being both an African and one of the leading French imperialists of his time.

In 1891, Dodds was promoted to regimental command in France, where he trained his men for a major operation in Dahomey (now Benin). Returning the following year with a company of artillery and several companies of marines, he picked up two battalions of Sénégalese riflemen and settled into a protracted campaign against BEHANZIN, the last king of Dahomey. After blockading the coast to prevent the Germans from bringing in relief supplies, Dodds moved inland and, in a series of well-

executed battles, captured Abomey, the Dahomean capital, and within it, the royal flags. Dodds offered terms that included a symbolic role for the king, but Behanzin refused. The king was finally captured and Dahomey was dismembered with its regions absorbed into the French colonial empire.

Dodds was promoted to general, given a major command in France, and in 1900 commanded the Western allied armies in China during the Boxer Rebellion. Here he faced racism from the American and British troops, who refused to serve under a mulatto general. He was inspector general of French colonial troops from 1903 to 1907 and retired from the army in 1912. In 1914, Dodds was reactivated to become military governor of Paris and a member of the Supreme War Council. He was overshadowed by the heroes of World War I, however, and was deeply offended at being excluded from the victory parade in 1919.

References: EB, WGMC.

DOE, Samuel Kanyon
(Liberia, 1950?–1990)

Master Sergeant Samuel Kanyon Doe, a corrupt, incompetent, and often violent president, represented the revolt of the oppressed indigenous peoples of Liberia against the ruling Americo-Liberian elite.

Since statehood in 1847, Liberia had been ruled by an oligarchy of families descended from American ex-slaves who settled in the territory. In 1980 they constituted about two percent of the population, governing through the True Whig Party and the Masonic order. Sporadic attempts were made to improve the lot of the upcountry indigenous peoples, but little progress was made.

Doe was born into the Krahn tribe, one of several neglected groups in the north, and after dropping out of school he entered the army, rising to sergeant in 1975. He excelled in marksmanship and hand-to-hand combat, and in 1979 was chosen for U.S. Green Beret training. Doe was ignorant of politics but took advantage of a current crisis. There was an ongoing economic depression and increasing anti-Americanism, which resulted in violent demonstrations. In part, these events reflected the policies of President William TOLBERT, who had recognized the Soviet Union and Communist China, voted against Israel in the United Nations, and generally strained relations with the United States, even though Liberia continued to be its client state.

In 1980, Doe led 17 soldiers in an attack on the presidential palace. The president was bayoneted and his body mutilated as he lay in bed. Most of his cabinet were executed at dawn on the beach, with the executions played later on national television. Doe installed a "people's redemption council," made up of sergeants and corporals, all of whom were indigenous Africans. Further executions of Americo-Liberian leaders followed, while Doe embarked on a policy of repression and personal enrichment. At first, African nations were appalled (at his death, Tolbert had been head of the Organization of African Unity), but they soon accepted Doe, who was initially popular in Liberia.

The continued failure of the economy eroded Doe's public support, however, especially when his closest followers were seen to live extravagantly. Unemployment exceeded 50 percent. The middle class deserted Doe, as did many army officers. There were nine coup attempts between 1980 and 1990, usually resulting in the summary execution of Doe's opponents. Doe did, however, permit elections, and in 1985 he was elected president (probably fraudulently) with 51 percent of the vote. Doe's regime was cruel and violent, as well as corrupt, and was sustained by an army packed with Krahn supporters. He did, however, improve relations with the United States, reestablish diplomatic relations with Israel, and authorize U.S. experts to draft a plan for the Liberian budget in 1987. As a result, American economic aid flowed into the country, and Doe was received at the White House by President Ronald Reagan. His close ties to the United States fed rumors that the Americans had engineered the original coup against Tolbert.

In 1989 an upcountry rebellion against Krahn domination resulted in numerous atrocities and widespread destabilization of the rural areas. The army responded with its own massacres but was then forced back to Monrovia. The rebel forces divided, enabling Doe to hold out in the presidential mansion while total anarchy engulfed Liberia. Five neighboring countries sent in a peacekeeping force, but during a truce meeting Doe was kidnapped at gunpoint. His captors made a video of his torture and mutilation and then executed him.

References: afr, AO, CB, DAHB, DT, EB, EWB, MMA, PLBA, PLCA, *wiki*.

D'OLIVEIRA, Basil "Dolly"
(South Africa, 1931–)

Dolly D'Oliveira (sometimes spelled D'Oliviera) is one of the premier cricketers of the twentieth century.

D'Oliveira was raised in Cape Town and classified as "Coloured" under South African race laws. In his youth, he played both cricket and soccer for the national non-White teams, but was barred from joining first-ranked teams, which were limited to White players. In 1960 he emigrated to Great Britain, where he played cricket exclusively and became a citizen in 1964. Two years later he was chosen for the English national team as an outstanding all-rounder.

In 1968, D'Oliveira hit 159 in the five-Test Ashes against Australia to tie the series. He was kept off the England side because it was scheduled to play with South Africa, but the hue and cry forced his being chosen when another player dropped out. Infuriated, President Balthazar VORSTER threatened to cancel the tour if D'Oliveira was to play. He thundered that the team was not representing England but the antiapartheid movement. When Dolly was reinstated, Vorster made good on his threat, and the tour was cancelled. The resulting publicity focused international attention on apartheid. It was the death-knell of tours to South Africa. After Australia's 1969 tour, no others were held until the end of apartheid. In the 1970s, D'Oliveira attempted to mediate between the White and non-White leagues in South Africa, but to no effect. He retired from the pitch at 40, far past his prime but still playing solid cricket.

D'Oliveira played in 44 Test matches, with 2,484 runs scored and a batting average of 40.06. He had five centuries and 15 halves. His bowling average was 39.55.

As he has aged, D'Oliveira suffers from debilitating Parkinson's disease. In 2003, South Africa gave him the Order of Ikhamanga (silver) for contributions to culture, and the following year, a trophy was named in his honor, to be awarded to the best player in the England-South Africa Test series. He was also named a Commander of the British Empire (CBE) in 1995 by Queen Elizabeth II.

Reference: wiki. Peter Osbourne, *Basil D'Oliveira: Cricket and Conspiracy* (2005).

DO NASCIMENTO, Alexandre

(Angola, 1925–)

Alexandre Cardinal do Nascimento is the first Angolan to become a cardinal in the Catholic Church, the majority religion in his country.

Dom Alexandre, as he prefers to be called, was ordained a priest in 1952. He studied in Angola and went to Rome, where he took degrees from the Gregorian University in philosophy and theology. He returned to Luanda, the capital, where he was professor of theology at the seminary from 1953 to 1961, along with responsibility for Catholic media. He was also named official preacher at the cathedral.

When the civil war broke out in 1961, he went into exile in Lisbon for 10 years. While there, he worked with refugees and student groups. When he returned in 1971, do Nascimento became professor at the Pius XII Institute for Social Sciences, with a ministry to students and political prisoners.

In 1975, do Nascimento was appointed bishop of Malanje, his home diocese. With the reorganization of the Angolan Catholic Church, he was named archbishop of Lubango two years later. Dramatically, he was kidnapped by rebel forces in 1982 and held for a month. Pope John Paul II launched an international appeal for his release, and when that took place, promoted him to cardinal. He was named Archbishop of Luanda in 1986, and retired in 2001.

While in office, do Nascimento worked tirelessly for unity in Angola. One of his main projects was the establishment of a Catholic University of Angola, and he was the driving force behind its realization. It was opened in 1999 with the unique funding system of a tax of one cent on every barrel of oil exported from Angola, which brings in approximately $3 million a year.

DOS SANTOS, José Eduardo

(Angola, 1942–)

José Eduardo Dos Santos, an early nationalist and president of Angola since 1979, finally succeeded in reaching a peace accord with rebel Jonas SAVIMBI after a dozen years of conflict, only to see it collapse after Savimbi lost in a national election.

Dos Santos joined the Popular Movement for the Liberation of Angola (MPLA) in 1961. He went to both the Democratic Republic of the Congo (then called Zaïre) and the Congo Republic as youth leader and representative of the MPLA, which had offices in both countries. In 1963 he went to Moscow to attend the Patrice Lumumba University, which had been set up by the Soviets for African students. In 1969 he received a degree in petroleum engineering and then stayed another year to study telecommunications in order to be more useful to the guerrilla army. He was assigned to the northern front from 1970 to 1973. The following year he was made a member of the MPLA central committee, just as a revolution in Portugal ended the fascist dictatorship there and caused the colonial power to agree to independence. Dos Santos was named foreign minister. In 1979 he succeeded to the presidency when Agostinho NETO died of cancer.

Dos Santos inherited a shattered country that was deeply involved in a war with Savimbi's National Union for the Total Independence of Angola (UNITA). At independence, the three liberation groups—MPLA, UNITA, and Holden ROBERTO's National Front for the Liberation of Angola (FNLA)—had been accorded equal status, but the MPLA soon squeezed the others out, and the FNLA and UNITA began armed resistance. UNITA received substantial aid, including air and artillery support, from South Africa and the United States. It initiated its operations from South-West Africa (now Namibia) and the Democratic Republic of the Congo. Angola turned to the Communist bloc and received large numbers of Cuban troops. Neither side could achieve a full victory, but in the process the country became a Cold War pawn of the Soviet and Western blocs.

Dos Santos determined to pursue diplomacy as the avenue to peace, assumed the post of foreign minister, in addition to the presidency, and began negotiations. He dropped several hard-line Marxists from his cabinet and in 1988 achieved a major breakthrough. Accepting a U.S. principle of "linkage," he agreed to withdrawal of the Cuban troops in exchange for the withdrawal of South African forces and Namibia's independence. From 1989 to 1991 he and Savimbi negotiated a power-sharing agreement while operating under a series of ceasefire arrangements. In 1991, Dos Santos accepted multiparty elections, which were held in 1993 under

José Eduardo Dos Santos

United Nations supervision. Savimbi received 41 percent of the vote and was entitled to a runoff, but he refused to accept his loss and returned to armed conflict. Within a few months he had captured his former headquarters in a fierce battle that cost more than 12,000 lives. More significantly, UNITA captured the diamond-mining area, which provided ample funding for the continuing civil war.

Savimbi's refusal to participate in open elections led to recognition of Dos Santos's government by the United States and other countries. Finally, UNITA was defeated, but at a loss of over 300,000 Angolan dead. Among them was Savimbi, killed in a fire fight in 2002. His death led to the collapse of UNITA and a final peace accord. Dos Santos has struggled with the Angolan economy, despite its riches in diamonds and oil.

References: afr, CB, DAHB, EWB, PLBA, RWWA, *wiki.*

DUBE, John Langalibalele
(South Africa, 1871–1946)

John Langalibalele Dube was an early political activist and the first president of the African National Congress (ANC). He was also the first Zulu writer and, as such, had an important influence on Zulu literature.

Dube, the son of one of the first African pastors, was educated at Oberlin College in Ohio and ordained a Congregational minister in 1897. In the

United States he met W. E. B. Du Bois and Booker T. Washington, whose ideas influenced him for the rest of his life. He founded the Ohlange Institute in 1901 on Washington's principles of thrift, industry, capital accumulation and education. The institute subsequently gained recognition as an important center for African education. In 1903, Dube founded the first Zulu newspaper, *Ilanga lase Natal* (Natal Sun), to defend the rights of Africans against land seizures by Whites. His consistent position was to appeal to Great Britain's sense of duty in promoting African human rights. He also used his newspaper to encourage young Zulu writers. But when Dube incurred the wrath of the authorities for his vigorous support of Chief BAMBATHA, leader of the 1906 Zulu rebellion, the paper was temporarily closed.

In 1910, Dube and Pixley SEME founded the African National Congress (ANC), and Dube served as its president until 1917. During his term he led the opposition to the 1913 Land Act, which dispossessed Africans of land in territories claimed by Whites. In 1914, Dube went to London to protest against the racist law, but to no avail. Divisiveness in the ANC caused him to break with Seme, and Dube resigned his presidency in 1917, although he remained head of the Natal branch of the ANC until his death.

Dube was never completely comfortable with the ANC's multiethnic national focus. As he became increasingly conservative, he turned toward his Zulu tradition. He served as an advisor to the Zulu royal house and began writing Zulu songs. In 1922 he wrote the first Zulu novel, *Isita esikhulu somuntu omnyama nguye uqobo lwake* (*The Black Man's Greatest Enemy Is Himself*). He completed an English novel in 1926 and another Zulu novel in 1933, which was based on the life of SHAKA, founder and first chief of the Zulu nation. Among his nonfiction works is a biography of the Zulu prophet Isaiah Sembe.

Although weak from age and illness, Dube was elected to the Native Representation Council in 1942, which by then was considered "safe" by the government. He was the senior spokesman of the council, and on his death he was succeeded by Albert LUTHULI.

References: AA, *afr*, *dacb*, DAHB, EB, EWB, MMA, *wiki*. Shula Marks, *The Ambiguities of Dependence in South Africa* (1986).

DU TOIT, Stephanus Jacobus
(South Africa, 1847–1911)

Reverend Stephanus Jacobus Du Toit was an early champion of Afrikaner nationalism and an architect of Dutch Reformed cultural thought. Born and educated in the western part of the Cape Colony, he was ordained a Dutch Reformed minister in 1875. By this time, the church had enforced segregation upon its congregations for almost 20 years.

Du Toit became prominent both within and outside the Church as a writer. He is best known, however, as the founder of a movement to promote recognition of the Afrikaans language, the Society of True Afrikaners. With the young men of his parish, Du Toit attempted to elevate a language scorned by many Afrikaners and forbidden in schools by the British. In 1876 they founded the first Afrikaans newspaper, *Die Afrikaanse Patriot* (*The African Patriot*), which Du Toit edited off and on until 1904. To *Die Patriot*, Du Toit soon added a children's magazine.

In 1876 he produced a grammar of Afrikaans and a year later wrote a landmark history of South Africa that laid the groundwork for later Afrikaner nationalist historiography. It was also the first book in Afrikaans, which made it a symbol of pride. It set forth a national mythology through which Afrikaners could envision themselves as a distinct people with a common destiny, bonded by the Calvinist ideal of a national calling. It was also the basis for resistance to British cultural imperialism.

Du Toit supported resistance to the British occupation of the Transvaal (1877–1881), and after restoration of the Transvaal Republic, he became superintendent of education (1882–1888). In 1879 he was a founder of the Afrikaner Bond, a nationalist party and the first political party in Cape Province. Du Toit intended it to be a Pan-Afrikaner party and established chapters in the Transvaal and Orange Free State, but it soon became exclusively a Cape party after control passed to its parliamentary leaders. Du Toit was the acknowledged intellectual father of Afrikanerdom but never became a major political leader.

Reference: *dacb*, DAHB.

EBOUÉ, Adolphe Félix Sylvestre
(Central African Republic/Mali/Chad, 1884–1944)

Adolphe Félix Sylvestre Eboué, the first Black to hold the rank of governor-general in colonial Africa, was an early supporter of General Charles de Gaulle and the Free French movement in World War II.

Eboué, the grandson of slaves, was born in French Guiana as a French citizen. His talents were recognized early, and he was sent to France for education, first in Bordeaux and then at the colonial school for career administrators. When he completed his education in 1908, he asked to be appointed to Africa and was sent to Oubangi-Shari, now the Central African Republic. There he established his unvarying style. He worked tirelessly against inertia and indifference in administration, promoted progressive development, and resisted the underlying racism in the colonial service. Throughout his career Eboué encouraged the appointment of Africans in the civil service. Although he was not a native African but a descendant of slaves taken to South America, he learned local languages, worked whenever possible through the chiefs and indigenous institutions, and made a point of understanding local cultures.

In 1931 he published *The Peoples of Oubangi-Shari* and in 1935 a linguistic study, *The Musical Key to Drum and Whistle Languages*. At the same time, Eboué supported colonialism as necessary for the progress of "less-advanced peoples" and even endorsed forced labor for economic development. He cultivated liberal contacts in Paris, affiliated with the Masonic Lodge, and while on leave in France in the 1920s, he became friends with Blaise DIAGNE, the Sénégalese deputy and the most influential French African of the period. These contacts both aided and restricted his career, as Eboué had to contend with the rise and fall of ideological tendencies in the French government.

In 1932, Eboué was promoted to senior grade in the colonial service and was sent to Martinique as acting governor. In 1934 he returned to Africa as secretary-general of French Sudan (now Mali), and then was returned to the Caribbean in 1936 as governor of Guadeloupe. Here he introduced a number of progressive reforms, which gained him enemies in France, and he was reassigned to Chad as governor in 1938. His appointment was a sensitive one; just as fascism was on the rise in Europe, Eboué was appointed as the first Black governor by a Jewish cabinet minister. Moreover, he was placed in an area adjoining territory that was coveted by Mussolini's Italy. Eboué increased military preparations and criss-crossed the northern desert with new roads that would later be vital in the attack on Libya in World War II.

Eboué's leadership during World War II was critical to the western Allies and the Free French.

Charles de Gaulle, chief of Free France, is welcomed to Chad by Governor-General Eboue of Free French Africa.

When France fell in 1940, Eboué rejected the authority of the Vichy regime established in collaboration with the Nazis. He was the first governor to rally to General de Gaulle's Free French government-in-exile. Within days other governors had joined Eboué and French West Africa was solidly Free French. By the end of the year, Eboué was appointed governor-general of all of French Equatorial Africa, and the first military action under Free French command was launched against the Italians from bases in Chad. The entire series of events gave much-needed credibility to the Free French.

Eboué used his new position to further develop African talent, although he remained opposed to nationalist and anticolonial movements. He tripled budgets for education and built secondary schools in every district. His expenditures included subsidies for mission schools, despite his own socialist and Masonic leanings. His policies increased the numbers of mid-level civil servants, especially from Gabon, which had been neglected. Eboué then fostered the integration of Gabonese staff into the career service, despite stiff opposition from other parts of French Equatorial Africa. In 1944, de Gaulle honored him by holding the conference for developing postwar colonial policy in Brazzaville, his capital. Eboué died of pneumonia on a trip to Egypt and is the only African buried in the Pantheon of heroes in Paris.

References: afr, DAHB, EB, EWB, WGMC, *wiki*. Brian Weinstein, *Eboué* (1972).

ECKEBIL, Jacques Paul
(Cameroon, 1939–)

Dr. Jacques Paul Eckebil, an agronomist who has specialized in plant breeding, is a recognized international scientific figure in plant research and development. He was sent to France for higher studies and graduated from the University of Toulouse in agronomy just as Cameroon achieved its independence. In 1966 he was awarded the higher diploma and licentiate of the Overseas Office of Scientific Research and Technology in Paris.

Eckebil served as head of the Sorghum and Millet Improvement Program in Cameroon from 1966 to 1971 and then completed a Ph.D. at the University of Nebraska, doing dissertation research on sorghum. Following the introduction of non-native grains to Africa, especially rice and wheat,

consumer tastes have begun to change. Due to the increased competition from new cereals, agricultural scientists have begun studying the means for making traditional grains more productive and attractive to African consumers. Increase in the use of traditional cereals reduces dependence on chemical fertilizers and improves the economy's foreign exchange balance. Both sorghum and millet are basic foods that were eaten for thousands of years in Africa but lately have been ignored, especially by educated Africans.

Eckebil was awarded the Order of Valor for his contribution to Cameroon in 1971 and again in 1984. He served as head of the Center of Food Crops and Fruits from 1975 to 1980 and then moved to the Institute of Agronomic Research, where he worked until 1987, when he became deputy director general of the International Institute for Tropical Agriculture in Nigeria. Because Eckebil helped to establish the Cameroon National Agricultural Research System (NARS) as one of the strongest such organizations in Africa, he has been tapped by the World Bank to draft guidelines for similar programs elsewhere on the continent.

Dr. Eckebil has continued his international service as head of Research and Technical Development for the Food and Agricultural Organization (FAO), a post he filled from 1999 to 2002. He then became assistant director-general for Sustainable Development for the FAO.

Reference: PAS.

EKWENSI, Cyprian Odiatu Duaka
(Nigeria, 1921–)

Cyprian Odiatu Duaka Ekwensi is a Nigerian novelist who has created popular fiction as well as more enduring novels. He is one of Africa's most popular writers, read widely by the general public.

Educated as a pharmacist in England, Ekwensi worked for the Nigerian Medical Service and taught at the School of Pharmacy in Lagos while beginning to write. His *People of the City* in 1954 was the first major Nigerian novel and provided a colorful, spirited account of urban life in Africa. It earned him an appointment with the Nigerian Broadcasting Corporation in 1956.

His first two children's books were published in 1960. He continued to distinguish himself as a writer of children's books (his most recent was in 1992). In 1961 he published *Jagua Nana* (1961), another urban novel, which was far better crafted than *People of the City* and is his best work. It tells the story of a lusty, ostentatious prostitute (her name is a play on the Jaguar sports car), who narrates the story.

Ekwensi then embarked on a prolific period in which he published between 30 and 40 books, plus short stories and children's fiction. Five books appeared in 1966 alone. His work is not stylistically polished, but his writing is lively and colorful. He makes no apologies for being a popular "writer for the masses," gently mocking what he calls "the sacred writers." Nevertheless, some of his later work shows a greater concern for style, and he has matured into a significant, if not great, author. Unlike his contemporaries, especially Chinua ACHEBE, he has little interest in history. His work continues to expose the gritty daily life of contemporary urban Nigeria. His major theme for over 40 years has been the immorality of African city life.

In 1961, Ekwensi was appointed director of the Federal Ministry of Information, but in 1966 he joined the secessionist Biafran cause in the civil war. Two books came from that experience: *Survive the Peace* (1976) and *Divided We Stand* (1980). After the war he returned to pharmacy for a few years and then began writing for a national newspaper while directing the state-owned Star Publishing Company. He continues to own a pharmacy and trading company while writing his autobiography.

References: adb, afr, AA, AWT, CANR, DAHB, DLB, EWB, MBW, NRG, PLBA, *wiki,* WLTC. Ernest Emenyonu, *Cyprian Ekwensi* (1974).

ELESBAAN (Kaleb)
(Ethiopia, ?–550?)

King St. Elesbaan was the last important Axumite king of Ethiopia to maintain Axum's position as a Red Sea power. Axum is the basis for the later Ethiopian Empire, and it reached its height during EZANA's reign in the fourth century. Elesbaan is often also known as Kaleb.

Much of the information available about Elesbaan comes from Greek historians who were contemporaries of his, including the Emperor Justini-

an's official court historian, Procopius. Although educated in Ethiopian Orthodox Church schools, Elesbaan revered Byzantine Greek culture and fostered trade with the Byzantines through the Red Sea ports. Greek inscriptions, some ordered by Elesbaan, have been copied and preserved. Large numbers of coins from his reign indicate that Ge'ez was the common language and that the arts flourished in this period. The general picture of prosperity is reinforced by records that Axum controlled much of the Red Sea trade and dealt with the East as far as India and China. The Byzantines had ceded the silk trade to the Axumites, partly to eliminate rival Persian merchants.

During this time, much of southern Arabia was under an Ethiopian protectorate. A Yemeni chief challenged that domination by converting to Judaism and bringing together the large Jewish communities of the region into a proto-state. When he began persecuting Christians, they appealed to Axum for help. Elesbaan responded and conquered Yemen in 525, annihilating the Yemeni army. The Axumite kingdom was at its political apogee at the time. It was recognized as the third power in the East after Byzantium and Persia, and it exchanged ambassadors with other courts. Some modern historians argue that in the expedition, although Elesbaan received tribute and controlled Yemen, Axum overextended itself and became vulnerable to later attacks.

Little more is known of Elesbaan. Both Greek and Ethiopian sources say that he abdicated in favor of his son and retired to a monastery. He is one of the rare saints in the Ethiopian Coptic Church who is also recognized by both Greek Orthodox and Roman Catholics. His feast day is 28 May.

Reference: DAB, *dacb, wiki.*

EMECHETA, Buchi Florence Onye
(Nigeria, 1944–)

Buchi Florence Onye Emecheta is a leading African writer who explores feminist issues in her fiction. She rejects the word *feminist* and vehemently denies that she is one, yet her writing speaks out constantly for women. An expatriate who has lived most of her life in England, she also refuses to be identified as an

African writer, preferring to be considered an international author.

Orphaned in her teens, Emecheta married because "nobody was going to look after me." Repudiating the dependence that her marriage represented, she left her husband, raised five of her children alone, and completed an honors degree in sociology. She supported her family as a cleaning woman, library clerk and community worker. Throughout this period she wrote, but for years no editor would review her work. Her breakthrough came not in fiction but in a book of columns, *In the Ditch* (1972), an account of her life as a single mother in London. She followed that in 1974 with *Second Class Citizen,* based on her failed marriage and "the cumulative oppression resulting from being alien, Black and female."

Her next three books were set in Nigeria and are among Emecheta's best work. *The Bride Price* (1976) is actually her first book, but it had to be recreated after her husband burned the manuscript. It explores marriage taboos, revealing Emecheta's ambivalence toward them. On one hand she is a traditionalist, but on the other she yearns for freedom from the power of custom. She mourns the heritage that is decaying under the assault of Western culture but also seeks the freedom of modernity. In *The Slave Girl* (1977) Emecheta casts a harsh light on the exploitation of women in traditional society with a searing comparison of marriage and slavery. *The Joys of Motherhood* (1979) mocks the romanticism surrounding motherhood, which defines a woman's value in much of African society. Forced into an unwanted marriage, bearing child after child to ensure enough male children (female babies do not count), Nnu Ego, the central character, dies lonely and embittered. The novel is an open assault on polygamy and male domination.

Emecheta has begun to focus on her current environment and to present the concerns of British Blacks. In *Gwendolen* (1989, published in the United States as *The Family*)$,$ the main character is Afro-Caribbean and the theme is the incest taboo. Emecheta remains an African writer, however, insisting that her "emotive language" is Igbo and that its rhythms influence her English. Widely respected in England, Emecheta has served as a juror for the Booker Prize, Britain's top literary prize, and teaches creative writing at the University of London. She is a regular writer for the *Times Literary Supplement*, *The New Statesman* and other journals.

References: adb, afr, CA, DAB, NRG, *wiki,* WLTC. Emecheta, *Head above Water* (1986).

ENWONWU, Benedict Chukwukadibia
(Nigeria, 1921–1994)

Chief Benedict Chukwukadibia Enwonwu, a leading African sculptor, worked in a variety of media, including bronze and wood. He also did oil painting and murals. He was the first Western-trained African artist with an international reputation. At age 16 he exhibited in London, and at 21 he held his first one-man show in Lagos. Shell Oil Company sponsored his study in England, which he undertook at Goldsmith's College (University of London), Ruskin College (Oxford University), and Slade College of Art. During this period (1944–1948), he was represented in the UNESCO Exhibition in Paris (1946) and had four one-man shows in London (1948–1955) as well as in Washington and New York in 1950. Enwonwu received the Empire Art Prize in 1957, was made a Member of the Order of the British Empire, and held three traditional Nigerian titles.

In 1950, Enwonwu took part in the first exhibit of contemporary African art in the United States, at Howard University in Washington, DC. From the early 1950s until 1966, he was the first African federal art advisor in Nigeria, a position that gave him a platform for his ideas and the freedom to work without economic concerns. Clearly recognized as a leader, he emerged as an advocate for African art. Enwonwu argued consistently that Europeans cannot fully grasp or appreciate African art. Nevertheless, his work, whether inspired by European styles or the more obvious African traditions, is widely appreciated outside Africa, and he remains, both critically and commercially, the most successful African artist.

Enwonwu received a number of significant commissions. In 1957 he finished a life-size bronze of Queen Elizabeth II, which was commissioned by the government of Nigeria along with doors and a speaker's chair for the Parliament building. The statue was removed after independence but was restored to display in 1990. Nigeria also commissioned Enwonwu to do a bronze for the United Nations. The work *Anyanwu (The Awakening)* is a

The 1956 bronze sculpture "Anyanwu" by Ben Enwonwu.

striking statue of a woman in full Benin royal court dress. She is almost seven feet tall, commanding and powerful.

Enwonwu threaded his way comfortably between the demands for Western representational art and his own desires to work in African motifs. In his terra cotta work he brought these together with naturalistic sculptures of Africans, such as his *Head of Kofi* and *Head of Koyi*. The best known of these works is the bas-relief on the front of the Nigerian Museum in Lagos, *The Awakening,* an abstract female figure with realistic face and hands, based on the original at the United Nations, as mentioned above.

Enwonwu was also a master of Yoruba woodcarving. His life-sized *Risen Christ* at the Protestant University Chapel, Ibadan (1961), both contrasts with and complements Osagie Osifo's crucifixion scene there. Enwonwu used the same topic in Western style for the chapel doors of the Vatican embassy (1965). In his last years he moved away from naturalism to explore African styles in paint-

ing as represented by his murals for the Nigerian Corporation Building in Lagos. His *Ibo Dancers*, a stylized painting of nudes, bears resemblance to Ibo mud dancers. He also did the book illustrations for Amos TUTUOLA's novel, *The Brave African Huntress.*

Enwonwu retired from teaching in 1975, but never from art. His last major exhibition, in Germany and the United States, was completed shortly before his death.

Reference: EB, EWB.

EQUIANO, Olaudah
(Nigeria, 1745–1802?)

Olaudah Equiano was taken at age 11 as a slave from what is now Nigeria and spent much of his adult life as an articulate opponent of slavery. His master gave him the name Gustavus Vasa or Vassa, after the Reformation king of Sweden. He disliked his slave name, but he became known by it. He was sold to a British naval officer and traveled widely in the Americas, Europe and Turkey for 30 years. Equiano became an acute observer of slavery, and after deep disappointment at being denied his freedom following service in the Seven Years' War, he found himself in the West Indies in 1763, under a new master. This man, a Quaker, allowed Equiano a small business of his own, with which he was able to purchase his freedom within three years.

Equiano then sailed for Britain, where he worked on ships and in trade. A trip to the Arctic resulted in his conversion to evangelical Christianity. He hoped to become an Anglican missionary to Africa, but his efforts met with Church disapproval. His energy then turned to abolition, which was a growing cause among evangelicals. He had a role in the public outcry over the 1783 *Zong* atrocity, during which 132 slaves were cast overboard and then claimed for cargo insurance loss. He also became active in the repatriation movement that established Freetown in Sierra Leone as a haven for freed slaves, but he was dismissed after intrigues among the sponsors.

To defend himself, Equiano wrote his autobiography, which has been his lasting legacy. It was the first slave narrative and a valuable document on slavery. Beyond that, it includes his valuable recollections of precolonial Africa. The book argues against both the immorality of slavery and its economic backwardness. Equiano's stance helped to provide the basis for the views of later abolitionists. The book went through eight editions during Equiano's life, and he traveled throughout Britain lecturing on it and related topics. He married an Englishwoman in 1792, and they had two daughters.

References: AA, AB, *afr*, *dacb*, DAHB, DLB, *wiki*. Equiano, *The Life of Olaudah Equiano, or Gustavus Vasa, Written by Himself* (1789).

EUSEBIO (Eusebio da Silva Ferreira)
(Mozambique, 1942–)

Eusebio was the first African to gain international soccer stature due to his electrifying effect on the Portuguese team in the 1960s. He was a powerful striker for the Portuguese national team and for Benefica.

Eusebio (professionally he used only one name), "The Black Panther" to his fans, was born in the region of the Mozambican capital, and acquired a reputation as a schoolboy. After being scouted by the coach of Benefica, there was a contract battle between that team and Sporting Lisbon, the sponsoring team of F. C. Lourenço Marques, where Eusebio was playing. Amidst a media frenzy, his contract was transferred to F. C. Benefica for the small sum of £7,500, and he burst upon the European soccer scene in 1961. He went from triumph to triumph, and in 1962 he led Benefica to victory over the powerful Real Madrid side to help Portugal take the European Cup. In 1966, at the World Cup in London, he was top scorer with nine goals, four of them in a single match.

Eusebio's score of 44 goals for Portugal's national team remained a national record until 2005. He played 15 years for Benefica during years when the team dominated Portuguese football. He was top scorer in the Portuguese league seven times and top European scorer twice, with 40 and 42 goals, respectively. The final total before his retirement is equally impressive—727 goals in 715 games. In 1998 he was elected to FIFA's Football Hall of Fame, among many other honors, and was the first recipient of the Golden Boot Award in 1968.

Besides his scoring prowess, Eusebio was a fast runner. As a teen, he was the Portuguese champion in the 100-meter, 200 and 400 races. He retired in 1976, but he continues to assist with the Portuguese national team as a volunteer.

References: adb, wiki.

EVORA, Cesaria
(Cape Verde, 1941–)

Her smoky voice caressing the songs of the *morna* (a genre of Cape Verdean music), Cesaria Evora has emerged from a twilight as a Verdean singer to international prominence as one of the leading figures in world music.

She was born into a family with a long musical tradition (she sometimes sings songs written by an uncle) and by age 16, Cesaria was singing in the bars of her native Mindelo. Four years later she performed on national radio and became a local star, nicknamed the "queen of *morna*." She sang for tour

Cesaria Evora

groups but could never make the breakthrough into the European music scene. In disgust, she retired in the 1970s and entered into three failed marriages that left her cynical about love. In 1985 she emerged from her retirement for a second career when she took up an offer to record and perform in France. She has produced 16 albums since.

Evora sings in an African-Portuguese Creole. *Morna*, her preferred type of music, is a plaintive, sad music related to Portuguese *fado* and African-American soul music. Never bitter, but always mournful, it can deal with love lost or with the historical ravages of the slave trade. *Morna* is a traditional Verdean music in a slow beat with minor-key melodies. It evokes memories, longing and yearning—for a loved one or a happier past time. Evora's throaty voice is the perfect instrument for melancholy. As one critic commented, "If she were a man, I would call it a whiskey tenor."

Stocky, chain smoking and fond of liquor, she often performs in a house dress and bare feet, which has become a signature effect. Her first album, *The Barefoot Diva* (1988), reinforced the image. Several albums later, and with growing critical appreciation and a cult following, Evora produced her first international hit album, *Miss Perfumado* (1992). It was followed by tours in Europe and the United States, where she performs regularly. *Cesaria Evora* (1995) went gold and was nominated for a Grammy as best world music album. She received a second Grammy nomination two years later for *Cabo Verde* (1997) and finally won in 2004 for *Live d'Amour* (2004). Despite the tours and her late success, Evora is unimpressed with the West and remains in Cape Verde.

References: adb, afr, EB, wiki.

EYADÉMA, Gnassingbé Étienne

(Togo, 1937–2005)

Gnassingbé Étienne Eyadéma was the military dictator of Togo for over 35 years, even though a National Conference attempted to strip him of his powers in 1991. He stayed in power through brutal force and intimidation.

Eyadéma was a member of the Kabré ethnic group from the north of Togo. As a poor youth, he excelled at sports, especially wrestling. With no opportunities at home, he and a group of other 16-year-olds slipped over the border into Dahomey and joined the French army. Eyadéma served in Indochina and Algeria until 1960. After independence, he and a number of Kabré were excluded from the Togolese army because President Sylvanus OLYMPIO, a member of the controlling Ewe elite, feared the expansion of a Kabré-dominated military. In 1963, Eyadéma led a group of noncommissioned officers on a raid in which he personally executed Olympio before the gates of the U.S. embassy. Nicolas GRUNITZKY emerged as the new president and expanded the army, making it possible for Eyadéma to be promoted to full general by 1967. He was popular among his troops, and in 1967 he overthrew the government, which was in a state of collapse.

Eyadéma ruled by combining authoritarianism and benevolence. He established a one-party system and governed through a group of loyal assistants while shrewdly developing a personality cult. In 1974 he survived a plane crash in which all others aboard died, which created a miraculous aura of invincibility. Through the 1970s, stability and prosperity brought him widespread support. He nationalized the French phosphate mines, constructed a decent road system, and modernized the capital. Eyadéma courted popularity with his policy of Africanizing culture. As part of this policy, he adopted his father's name (which means"courage" in Kabré), and stopped using his given name, Étienne.

Eyadéma's development campaign was accomplished at a high price. The party maintained neighborhood and village watch committees, and disrespect for the president could result in severe punishment. Torture of prisoners was common. In the early 1980s political corruption increased and the economy stalled. Togo was forced to accept an austerity program from the World Bank and the International Monetary Fund.

Much of the country's stability began to unravel after 1985, when there were a series of bombings in the capital. Pressures began building for democracy, and demonstrations became violent, with high death tolls. In 1991, Eyadéma allowed the creation of a National Conference, which quickly turned against him and seized power. He maneuvered successfully to maintain his position when the army refused to accept civilian control. With the new prime minister under house arrest and many members of the National Conference in hiding, Togo was paralyzed. Elections were announced for mid-1992, but one candidate was murdered and another was wounded. Voting finally took place during 1993. Eyadéma won (with French endorsement) amid evidence that he regained his former authority. Both the United States and France withheld foreign assistance in the wake of mounting evidence of state terrorism and a breakdown in public safety.

Eyadéma was a crude and uneducated leader, halting in his command of the French language and an indifferent administrator. In foreign affairs, he was equally inept, but he longed for international respect. In 1975 he helped found the Economic Community of West African States (ECOWAS), which he chaired three times. From 1975 to 1990, he hosted the Lomé Conferences with the European Community, whose Third World trade compacts are named for the capital.

Eyadéma died suddenly, leaving over 100 children and a political vacuum. His son Faure became president amid a Togolese and international outcry. ECOWAS and the African Union (AU) forced his ouster. Later that year, however, Faure was elected on his own.

References: adb, afr, CB, DAHB, DRWW, PLBA, PLCA, RWWA, *wiki.* Ahmadou Kourouma, *Waiting for the Wild Beasts to Vote* (1998); Comi Toulabor, *Le Togo sous Eyadéma* (Togo under Eyadéma, 1986).

EZANA
(Ethiopia, Fourth Century)

King St. Ezana was king of Axum from around 330 to about 356. His reign marked the final development of the fourth-century Ethiopian highlands culture. During his time, Ge'ez became the national language and Christianity, in its unique Ethiopian Orthodox form, became the national religion. Axum thus became the cradle for later Ethiopian civilization.

As a youth, Ezana was tutored by FRUMENTIUS, the first apostle to Ethiopia, who introduced him to Christianity. When Frumentius returned as first bishop, he converted Ezana, and by the year 345, the king had become protector of the new faith. With Christianization came a long period of internal peace and unity. Ezana extended Axum's boundaries, opening them to territories across the Red Sea. He treated subject peoples well, offering them prime land in order to cement their loyalty,

and discontinued the ancient custom of enslaving conquered populations. Ezana shifted the balance of power in the region with his conquest of Meroë, thus completing the downfall of the northern Sudanic kingdom of Kush.

This political growth and stability was accompanied by prosperity based on international trade. Ezana built up trade with Mediterranean countries, especially Greece, and maintained the Nile trade routes to Egypt. Coins with his inscription have been found as far away as India, indicating trade across the Indian Ocean.

Ezana left extensive stone inscriptions describing his conquests. According to tradition, he died in battle and is buried in a rock-hewn church in Axum. The Ethiopian Coptic Orthodox Church recognizes him as a saint.

References: DAB, *dacb*, DAHB, EWB, WGMC, wiki. S.C. Munro-Hay, *Aksum* (1991).

EZZIDIO, John
(Sierra Leone, 1812?–1872)

John Ezzidio was a recaptive who became a successful entrepreneur and the first African to take part in representative government in Sierra Leone.

Ezzidio was captured by Brazilian slavers in Nigeria when he was about 15 years old, but the ship was intercepted by the British navy's Preventive Squadron and he was set free in Sierra Leone. British anti-slavery policy assigned a naval squadron to the African Coast, where slave ships were seized and their human cargos deposited in Sierra Leone, which thus became a multiethnic, multitribal settlement. While a few liberated slaves were able to return to their home villages, most were not.

Ezzidio was apprenticed to a French trader and later became an agent before establishing his own commercial network. Because colonialism had not yet taken root, opportunities were abundant, especially in trade. Ezzidio bought a home that became a center for trade negotiations, and he visited Britain on business trips in 1842 and 1859. These visits provided him with the contacts to import directly from England a wide variety of goods desired by both Africans and Europeans. His newspaper advertisements list cotton trade goods, European clothing, foodstuffs, medicine, and a collection of wines.

Ezzidio became a major figure in Freetown as a result of his business position. He entered local politics and was mayor of Freetown for a term. During the 1840s and 1850s he became the spokesman for the Creole population's grievances against the governor, defending Creole rights when attempts were made to limit them. In 1863 the government created a Legislative Council (Legco) and Ezzidio was elected by the Creole business community as its representative. In time, however, the British regretted having established the principle of election, and they abolished it, leaving Ezzidio with the distinction of being the first and last elected official in Sierra Leone for over half a century.

Ezzidio was active in the Methodist church, which he helped build and in which he served as a preacher. He was also far-seeing and ecumenical in his thinking, which was rare for the time. He promoted interfaith cooperation, and on the Legco he supported government grants for the Anglican Church, which had begun a program of native pastorates. This effort earned him opposition among the Methodists, whose British superintendent opposed African leadership. For a time, work on Ezzidio's church was stopped and the conflict began to affect his health. Along with some business reverses, it forced him into semiretirement until his death.

References: DAB, DAHB, MMA.

FAKEYE, Lamidi Olonade

(Nigeria, 1928–)

El-Haji Lamidi Fakeye is one of the finest contemporary woodcarvers and sculptors to come from the famous school and craft shop of Father Kevin CARROLL in Oye-Ikiti in northeastern Nigeria. He is the fifth generation of a line of woodcarvers named Fakeye (sometimes "Lamidi" is given as his family name by mistake) and began his craft at an early age. His birth-name, "Olonade," means "the carver has arrived."

In the early twentieth century, Yorubaland returned to peace after years of foreign invasions and devastation. Local chiefs began to commission lavish palaces, all of which featured carved posts, doors and thrones. With the simultaneous building of Christian churches, there was an economic demand for the revival of traditional Yoruba sculptural woodcarving as well as other arts, especially weaving, pottery and *batik*. Into this opportunity stepped Father Carroll with his sculpture workshop.

Fakeye recounts that he and his brothers all began carving at about age nine. He attended school to sixth grade and was literate, but he did not enjoy carving. Having no other options, he produced a mix of "tourist art" and household items such as spoons, bowls and trays for a few years. His eyes were opened when he visited the palace of an oba, or chief, where he saw a set of pillars carved by AREOGUN of Osi-Ilorin with Yoruba figures, one a nursing mother and the other a horse and rider. He realized his own limitations.

For a few months, Fakeye taught carving at an Anglican missionary trade school where he met Father Carroll, who invited him to his craft shop in Oye-Ikiti. When he saw BANDELE's work there, he felt ashamed but also motivated. Bandele became his mentor, and he was apprenticed to him for three years and "suffered much," in his own wry admission. On his own time, he continued working and slowly perfecting his technique. His first commission was a set of doors and pillars for a royal gate house. In 1954, Carroll took him to Lagos, the capital, to carve the doors of the Catholic chapel at the University. Despite his Christian training, he is

a Muslim convert and in 1995 he made his *hajj* to Mecca.

After this, Fakeye worked largely on his own. In 1955, he carved the doors, chairs and thrones for the House of Assembly of Chiefs in Ibadan. As his reputation spread, Fakeye traveled to and exhibited in the United States, France and Great Britain. Later, he did carvings for the office of the premier of the Western Region. In the United States, he carved the magnificent doors of the Kennedy Center in Washington, DC. He also began taking his own apprentices, chosen, as is customary, from his family, including two younger brothers. He has also been artist-in-residence at Obafemi Awolowo University.

Fakeye's work is rooted in Yoruba traditional carving, but as his horizons widened, it has matured. His early work shows symmetrical figures faced front formally. Later work reveals emotion, as in mother-and-child statuettes. The finish on his carvings is all done with steel knives, and produces a satiny effect. Despite his Muslim faith, Fakeye's work today most often uses figures and gods from Yoruba traditional religion.

Reference: Fakeye, *Lamidi Olonade Fakeye: A Retrospective Exhibition and Autobiography* (1996); Kunle Filani, *Patterns of Culture in Contemporary Yoruba Art* (2004).

FAKU

(South Africa, 1777?–1867)

Chief Faku was paramount chief of the Mpondo during the breakdown of southern African society caused by the *mfecane* or *difeqane* ("the crushing"), during which whole peoples were scattered, new nations were formed, and the political and ethnic landscape of southern Africa was reshaped. Faku not only kept the Mpondo people intact but also provided a barrier against expansion of the *mfecane* into or beyond Natal.

Faku became paramount chief sometime before 1820, as SHAKA was coming to power in Zululand. Faku ably defended his territory (much of present-day Natal province in South Africa) against attacks by the Zulu to the north and the Xhosa and Thembu to the south, but he was forced to pay tribute in cattle to Shaka of Zululand. In 1828, Shaka mounted a major campaign against the Mpondo that plundered most of their cattle but left the Zulu warriors exhausted. This campaign led to Shaka's assassination by his brother DINGANE. Dingane, however, could not maintain complete control over Zululand. Faku took advantage of the situation and recovered to maintain his military power, and in 1829 he defeated two breakaway Zulu chiefs who were trying to exploit Dingane's weakness to expand their authority. Faku showed brilliant generalship in routing superior forces. The Mpondo were never again seriously threatened by neighboring communities.

After 1830, Faku's main concern was maintaining balanced relations with White settlers. He invited Methodist missionaries into Pondoland and used them as intermediaries with the Whites. As more and more Afrikaners moved into the area, however, Faku grew alarmed, especially after an 1840 raid on a neighboring community by Andries PRETORIUS. Faku invited British protection, and in 1844 the British occupied Natal. Faku proved a passive ally, however, and refused to join the British in their two campaigns against the Xhosa in 1846 and in 1850–1853. After the Xhosa destroyed their own power in a religious frenzy of cattle-killing led by the prophet MHLAKAZA, Faku was less important to the British, and his prestige declined. As he aged, his two sons began to assume authority and divided the chiefdom between them after his death.
Reference: DAHB.

FALOLA, Toyin
(Nigeria, 1953–)

Dr. Toyin Falola, distinguished historian and author, has been for many years a professor of modern African history. Since 1991, he has held an endowed chair at the University of Texas at Austin. Besides an enviable record as a historical writer, he has received several awards for excellence in teaching, and the Ibn Khaldun Award for research excellence. His colleagues have dedicated two books of essays in

his honor. He built the graduate program in African history in Texas, where he heads its Center for African and African-American Studies.

Falola was educated in his native Nigeria, and took his Ph.D. at the University of Ife (now the Obafemi Awolowo University) in 1981. Before graduate studies, he taught school and worked for the government in Nigeria. His academic career at Ife lasted from 1981–1988. He then spent a research year at Cambridge University in England before going to York University in Canada for a year and then to Texas. He has lectured all over the world and is a fellow of several universities.

His output is prodigious. Between 2000 and 2005 alone, he published or edited 12 books on topics as diverse as African urbanization, teen life, methodology in African studies, slavery and colonialism, culture, the modern African military and Black business and economic power. There are few areas of African history and culture of modern Africa that he has not investigated, and few areas where his intellectual influence is not felt. "My inspiration has been drawn by the challenge ... to keep correcting a barrage of misleading interpretations about the continent."
Reference: CA.

FARAH, Nuruddin
(Somalia, 1945–)

Nuruddin Farah is the leading modern Somali novelist and dramatist. Although his hopes of returning to Somalia after 20 years of exile were dashed by the Somali civil war and United Nations occupation in 1992, he remains the major cultural figure in Somali society. He attempted a return to Somalia in 1996, but since 1998 he has lived in South Africa with his second wife.

Farah received a good colonial education in Somalia and pursued higher education in India. In 1970 he published his first novel, *From a Crooked Rib,* one of several treatments that he has given to women's issues. Its heroine is a nomadic girl who breaks away from traditional society. It is a sensitive account of triumph over social oppression, which so impressed Farah's editor that Farah was asked for a photo of himself in order to prove that he wasn't a woman. Nigerian feminist writer Buchi EMECHETA praised him as being a woman in a man's body.

Farah taught in Mogadishu for four years while continuing to write. An extended trip through the Soviet Union, Greece (under military rule), Egypt and Hungary in 1973 helped to confirm his convictions against authoritarianism. In 1974 he left for Britain after his writing in the national newspaper was censored by the government of Mohammed SIYAD BARRE, who was then increasingly supported by the Soviet Union. Siyad Barre banned all Farah's writings and ordered him assassinated.

In Britain, Farah explored playwriting and worked with the Royal Court Theatre. In this productive period he completed two full plays for the stage and two for the British Broadcasting Company. He also began writing short stories and published several dozen, although few have been collected. In 1976, *A Naked Needle* appeared. A more explicitly political novel than *From a Crooked Rib*, it depicts the psychological decline into hatred and muteness of a man—symbolic of Somalia—who has no convictions or political values and who lives only for survival.

Farah settled in Rome from 1976 to 1979, later moving to England and West Germany before returning to Africa in order to avoid becoming "a European mercenary." Farah regards this peripatetic period as a form of nomadic life in the pattern of his forebears; he inhabits what he calls "a country of the mind." Farah disputes NGUGI wa Thiong'o's claim that Western languages are instruments of cultural oppression. "When I come to define who my people are, not only are Somalis my people, but the whole of Africa," Farah has said.

In Rome, Farah began a trilogy that he calls "variations on the theme of African dictatorship." The first work was *Sweet and Sour Milk* (1979), a mystery thriller about a twin searching for his brother's murderer in an atmosphere of political fear. The second, *Sardines* (1981), is another feminist novel, a bold rejection of female circumcision, which ties women's oppression to wider political issues. "When women are free," Farah has said, "then and only then can we talk about a free Somalia." The last novel of the trilogy is *Closing Sesame* (1983), written through the eyes of an old independence fighter now despairing of the freedom for which he sacrificed.

In 1986, Farah began another trilogy on the theme "blood in the sun," with *Maps,* perhaps his best work. It examines the interaction between two men, both struggling with their social creation of self in a society in which definitions are breaking down around them. It is full of high drama as well

as psychological depth and is both a serious literary work as well as a popular thriller. The second part of the trilogy was a love story entitled *Gifts* (1993). The third work, *Secrets* (1998), explores the deceptions of a family scarred by tribal hatreds. Currently, Farah is exploring film production and screenwriting, out of the conviction that "the cinema is made for Africa," but he continues to write novels—his most recent being *Links* (2002).

References: afr, AA, CA, DLB, NRG, *wiki,* WLTC. Farah, *Yesterday, Tomorrow: Voices from the Somali Diaspora* (2000); Patricia Alden and Louis Tremaide, *Nuruddin Farah* (1999).

al-FARSY, Abdullah Saleh
(Kenya, 1912–1982)

Sheikh Abdullah Saleh al-Farsy was for many years a Chief Kadhi, first in Zanzibar (1960–1967) and then in Kenya (1974–1980). He was a respected Islamic scholar and historian.

Sheikh al-Farsy was born in Zanzibar into a prominent and devout Muslim family who sent him to study under leading Islamic scholars of the time. During the colonial period, Zanzibar excelled as a center of Islamic learning, and prominent scholars vied for the privilege of teaching there. He was mentored by some of the greatest names in Swahili. From an early age al-Farsy showed his zeal for the Holy Qur'an and he became a *hafiz,* one who had memorized the entire Holy Book in Arabic, in which he became completely fluent.

In 1950, al-Farsy embarked on his most ambitious work, a faithful translation of the Qur'an into Kiswahili, which he completed 17 years later. He later wrote a Swahili life of the Prophet Mohammed (1960) and a 1971 book on religious teaching. Since Islamic themes are embedded in Swahili poetry, he also studied that literary form, wrote Swahili verse, and edited a basic work of Swahili poetry. He also wrote Arabic verse. His doctoral dissertation, *Great Muslim Scholars of East Africa,* led to the writing of over 100 biographical sketches of Islamic sages.

Al-Farsy's translation of the Holy Qur'an was intended as a counterweight to two previous translations done by Anglican missionaries, and was meant to provide background for missionary understanding. In response, a Pakistani translation was drafted, but many Sunni Muslims considered it an apologetic translation to justify the tenets of the sect of its scholars. Al-Farsy chose to do as true a translation of the original as possible, free of sectarian bias, and in elegant Swahili. It was a magisterial work. The Sultan of Qatar subsidized the publication.

Al-Farsy spent his earlier career in secular education, first as a school teacher and then inspector-general of schools under the colonial regime. During the 1950s he served as headmaster for the main Muslim secondary schools of Zanzibar.

In 1960, the colonial government appointed al-Farsy as Chief Kadhi, making him the highest authority on Muslim law and the Islamic Supreme Court judge. After independence, the 1967 radical revolution in Zanzibar broke out in a murderous frenzy that forced the Sheikh into exile. The brutal regime that followed was anti-Islamic. Al-Farsy went first to Malawi, where he conducted Islamic classes, and then to Kenya. There President Jomo KENYATTA appointed him Chief Kadhi in 1974 upon the recommendation of the retiring Chief Kadhi. Al-Farsy retired in 1980.

In 1982, Sheikh al-Farsy moved to Oman to be with his family, and died there a few months after his arrival. A gentle, engaging and generous-hearted man with a smiling face, Al-Farsy was remembered with affection as well as respect.

Reference: adb.

FASILADAS
(Ethiopia, ?–1667)

Emperor Fasiladas became emperor of Ethiopia when his father, SUSNEYOS, abdicated in 1632 after the disastrous religious war between Catholics and followers of the Ethiopian Orthodox Church. Fasiladas restored the religious and cultural authority of the traditional Ethiopian church, expelled foreign missionaries, and established a new capital at Gondar.

When Susneyos proclaimed Catholicism in 1622, it was the culmination of a long development during which Jesuit missionaries had tried to unite Ethiopian Coptic Orthodoxy with Rome. This was part of a century-long opening of Ethiopia to the West and to European ideas. When a fanatic Jesuit began reforms that threatened the identity of its Church, an essential part of Ethiopian culture, religious quarrels broke out, dividing even the royal

family. In 1632, after a bitter battle in which more than 8,000 were killed, Susneyos resigned in favor of Fasiladas. Within a year Fasiladas expelled the Jesuits, broke relations with Portugal, and closed the borders to all missionaries. He entered into relations with neighboring Muslim states as a counterbalance to the European Christians. Fasiladas also promoted the return of all Ethiopians to the Ethiopian Church and restored its authority. By taking sides in complex theological debates, however, Fasiladas alienated other factions and came to depend largely on his personal guard made up of Muslims, the Falasha (Ethiopian Jews) and slaves.

The reign of Fasiladas saw a restoration of national identity and tradition, but it was also an isolationist period in foreign policy. The preoccupation with religious concerns and the constant need to suppress rebellions left the kingdom open to the aggressive Galla people in the south, who began to enter the kingdom in large numbers. They destroyed the royal army in 1642, and Fasiladas withdrew to build a new capital at Gondar. This action fostered greater provincial autonomy, further weakening the emperor's central power. The pattern of decentralization characterized Ethiopia until the reign of TEWODROS II in the nineteenth century. In essence, Fasiladas's reign represents the beginning of a long period of decline in Ethiopian history.

References: DAB, DAHB.

FATUNLA, Tayo
(Nigeria, 1961–)

Tayo Fatunla is a popular cartoonist with a worldwide following. For 15 years he was cartoonist for *West Africa* magazine, which is published in London and circulated internationally.

Fatunla was raised in Nigeria and began cartoon drawing as a teenager. By 17 he was published in children's magazines until he went to the United States, where he graduated from the Joe Kubert School of Cartoon and Graphic Art. Even while in school, he continued to sell his work, especially with the leading comic book publisher, DC Comics, known for publishing Batman and Superman comics. He began contributing to Nigerian daily newspapers and magazines, and since then has consistently worked for several.

Fatunla is in demand as a freelance cartoon artist, doing caricatures, political cartoons and educational pieces. Best known among these would be his series on Black history, which was serialized by over 30 American newspapers and later appeared in book form. Tayo (as he signs his work) also teaches cartooning workshops and has been cartoonist-in-residence at Lewisham College, London, where he lives with his family. His work has been distributed by the New York Times Syndicate and the British Broadcasting System (BBC). Tayo has received many awards for his work, most notably the Crayon de Porcelaine in 2001.

Tayo uses whatever style suits his topic. His editorial cartoons can evoke strong emotion or be biting caricatures. A sample appears on his Web page. For the historical series he uses naturalistic portraits.

References: *adb*, www.tayofatunla.com. Fatunla, *Tayo Thro' the Years* (2000); *Our Roots: Black History Sketchbook* (2004).

FONCHA, John Ngu
(Cameroon, 1916–1999)

Honourable John Ngu Foncha was prime minister of (British) Southern Cameroon during the last days of colonialism, bringing it into federation with French Cameroun as the Cameroon Republic. He spent his political career championing federation and the rights of English-speaking Cameroonians. After World War I, Kamerun had been taken from Germany and apportioned between France and Britain, the British sections being administered as part of Nigeria.

Foncha was educated in Catholic mission schools and served as a teacher's aide until completing teachers' training school in 1939. After a year spent teaching agriculture in Nigeria (1941–1942), he served as a principal in Catholic schools until 1954. Alongside his educational career, Foncha founded a youth league and a teachers' union, which gradually drew him into politics. He was elected to the Eastern House of Assembly in Nigeria from 1951 to 1954, but that year he formed the Kamerun National Democratic Party (KNDP) and began a lifelong advocacy of reunification.

In 1959 the KNDP became the official opposition in the Southern Cameroons. It won the elections, making Foncha prime minister. He negotiated an arrangement with President Ahmadou AHIDJO of the Cameroun Republic, which had

won independence from France, and they agreed on a bilingual federal system. In a 1961 referendum, Foncha's proposal won a resounding victory in the Southern Cameroons, while the northern province opted to join Nigeria. Foncha became vice president of the new federation and prime minister of what was called Western Cameroon. In 1965 he was reelected on a ticket with Ahidjo but became increasingly cool toward Ahidjo's plans for a unitary government. In 1970 he was forced from the ticket in favor of a longtime rival, Solomon Muna, and in 1972 the federation was abolished in favor of a unitary state.

Foncha retained considerable influence among English-speaking politicians and was partially rehabilitated in 1979 with an honorary title as Grand Chancellor of National Orders. He was vice president of the national party under President Paul BIYA, who took over upon Ahidjo's resignation in 1982, but in 1990 he and Muna resigned together and endorsed multiparty government after an English-speaking rally of 20,000 was broken up by security forces. The leading Anglophone party still opposed federation, however, and the two old rivals united in fighting for English-speaking rights in Cameroon.

References: DAHB, PLBA, RWWA.

FOSSEY, Dian
(Rwanda, 1932–1985)

Dr. Dian Fossey, an American primatologist and environmental conservationist, spent 20 years studying and defending mountain gorillas. In the process she authored a bestselling book and became an international figure when a film was based on it. Her life became a symbol of the struggle to save endangered species, and for many her murder at her research station made her a martyr of the environmental crusade.

In 1963, Fossey first visited Africa, where she met Louis and Mary LEAKEY, who encouraged her to pursue her study of the mountain gorilla. Louis Leakey took a personal interest in the young scholar, visiting her in the United States and becoming her mentor at critical points in her career. In 1967 she began studying gorillas in the eastern region of the Democratic Republic of the Congo, but barely escaped following arrest and several weeks of imprisonment during that country's civil war. She

Dian Fossey

then moved to Rwanda, where she established the Karisoke Research Centre in a national park in the Virunga Mountains. In 1974 she received a doctorate from Cambridge University, using her gorilla research for her thesis.

Mountain gorillas live in close-knit groups and avoid strangers, so Fossey had to develop methods of approaching them, learning their habits, and communicating with them until her presence was accepted. She followed four families of 51 individuals, recording their social patterns and identifying some 15 sounds that they used to communicate. She discovered strong family ties and evidence of self-sacrifice among the gorilla units. Fossey conducted her studies alone for several years before permitting research assistants in her camp.

She soon encountered opposition from poachers hoping to exploit the gorillas. In 1978 she began a campaign against poachers who killed gorillas for collectors or who kidnapped the young for European zoos. The poaching struggle convinced Fossey that exposure to too many humans would only be confusing to the gorillas and led her to support keeping tourists away as well. In 1981, when a census revealed that the number of gorillas had declined precipitously in recent years, she and student volunteers began poacher patrols.

Fossey also opposed encroachment on the gorillas' territory by human settlements on the edge of the national park. Rwanda is the most densely populated country in Africa, and population pressure had gradually reduced the gorillas' habitat. In her stubborn single-mindedness, Fossey took strong measures, driving grazing cattle from the park, burning African homes, and destroying hunting traps. She was even known to present herself as a sorceress to frighten off the local people. A close friend said that Fossey "didn't care about people except to keep them away from the gorillas." She became increasingly eccentric and a loner with long bouts of moodiness.

In 1980, after another six years in Virunga, she taught briefly at Cornell University and completed *Gorillas in the Mist* (1983). The book, which would make her well known throughout the world, recounts her personal affection for the gorillas, whom she named and with whom she established "personal" relationships. The trust she established with the mountain gorillas allowed her (and later researchers) to receive what another scholar called "the privilege of honorary gorilla group membership." At the same time, her scientific observations

were detached, and nonjudgmental. They represent the most accurate extant record of the lives of gorilla families.

In late 1985, Fossey was murdered at her station, probably by poachers at the instigation of the then-governor of the province, known to be involved in profiting from poaching and smuggling. She was buried in the cemetery where she had interred the gorillas killed by poachers. In 1988, Sigourney Weaver portrayed Fossey in a film biography, *Gorillas in the Mist,* which further popularized her work. After her death, her foundation reversed Fossey's ban on tourists, taking the position that limited access would help guarantee protection for the gorillas by making them a valuable resource. With about 250 remaining mountain gorillas, one group of families was allowed to be observed regularly by tourists, while others were protected and encountered only by researchers. The foundation's approach brought financial support from the Rwandese government, which took over the project in 1990.

By early 1993 the area around the Karisoke Research Centre was home to over half the mountain gorillas in existence. It also lay along the front lines in the civil war between forces of the Rwandan government and the Rwandan Patriotic Front. The facility was abandoned, looted and eventually destroyed by government soldiers.

References: CB, EB, EWB, HH, *wiki.* Fossey, *Gorillas in the Mist* (1983); www.dianfossey.org.

FRANCO (François Luambo Makiadi)
(Democratic Republic of the Congo, 1939–1989)

Franco, a dominant influence in the creation of Afro-Pop, was the leader of TPOK Jazz (*Tout Puissant Orchestre Kinois*, "all powerful Kinshasa orchestra"), the most famous band in Africa. *Le Grand Maître* (the great master), as he was known, recorded some 150 records, the first one in 1953. For over 30 years he was the focal point of the first truly African popular music, variously called "Congo Music," the "Lingala Sound," or *soukous.* It is a distinctive form, emerging out of the clubs and *shabeens,* or speakeasies, that were the favored recreational sites of the urban proletariat. Coming from several ethnic traditions, club music used African languages such as Kiswahili and Lingala, often combining them with French.

Franco's use of African instrumentation made soukous unique. One can detect influences such as American soul in saxophone riffs (Franco liked guitar-saxophone duets). In addition, the disco beat introduced the bass drum over the conga. *Soukous* is a dance music, but always includes a counterpoint of vocal melody and instrumental solos. A piece typically lasts from 15 to 20 minutes, with several distinctive sections; it may include call-and-response, refrains, and electric guitar solos. Despite the percussion and guitars, the music is lyrical in style, and often described as "cool." Guitarists, for example, strike clear tones with no echoes of heavy metal sound. The singing uses African modes, and lyrics tend toward social commentary. Franco sang of infidelity, family problems, land expropriation, and the fortunes of his favorite soccer team. There was a minor scandal when it was revealed that Franco's 1987 recording, *Attention Na SIDA!* ("Watch out for AIDS!"), had been secretly funded by the U.S. government.

Franco supported MOBUTU Sese Seko's *authenticité* campaign, when Mobutu changed the name of the country to Zaïre, required citizens to take African names and stressed local culture. Franco was decorated by Mobutu, but he was also imprisoned at least twice, in part because he was known to attack corrupt politicians in his lyrics. But when Franco went into the hinterlands to popularize Mobutu's program, he rediscovered traditional African music, and this provided another element in his music.

TPOK Jazz has been called "a musical university," and playing in the group was "akin to earning a degree." Hundreds of musicians, each carefully auditioned, passed through the band. Tabu LEY Rochereau, Franco's only real rival for popularity, Sam Mwangwana, and Hugh MASEKELA all played or recorded with OK Jazz at various times. When Sonodisc of Paris released a series of Congolese popular recordings, they included no fewer than 18 second-generation bands that sprang from OK Jazz. Franco's influence was immense and is obvious in the work of such performers as Pepé KALLÉ, Orchestre Virunga in Kenya, Mbaraka Mwinshehe in Tanzania, and Peterson Mutebi in Uganda. The impact of Franco's music can be best seen in the fact that he made Lingala a true national language. In parts of East Africa, it is a common lingua franca among urban youth.

Franco performing in his prime was inspiring. He was a consummate guitarist, winning the praise of a *New York Times* critic who commented, "He played his guitar as if it were an indigenous African instrument, nimbly plucking intricate arpeggios in complex rhythms." At over 300 pounds, playing powerful music while backed by his svelte dancing Francolettes and surrounded by a worshipping crowd, Franco delivered great entertainment. He also lived in grand style in a Kinshasa mansion, shared with several wives and some of his 18 children. In the 1980s, Franco conquered Europe, especially France and Belgium. That year, the government named him Grand Master of Zaïrean Music. He went through a period of patriotic music, some would say pandering to the government of Mobutu. He gained weight alarmingly and reconverted from Islam (which he had accepted and never practiced) back to Catholicism (which he also rarely practiced). In 1987 he brought out a single on AIDS as he began to show signs of the disease himself.

The main OK Jazz had about 40 musicians, and by 1989, there were three touring OK Jazz bands, one permanently based in Belgium. That year, Franco collapsed from kidney failure while on a European tour and died in Namur, Belgium. He had denied persistent rumors of AIDS, even as he

Franco (François Luambo Makiadi)

lost weight due to illness, but it was almost certainly a contributing cause of his death. His last album featured a track entitled "Toujours OK." He was given a national funeral, to which heads of African states came along with tens of thousands of fans.

References: AO, BPAR, CB, DMM, GEPM, MMA, WAM, *wiki.* Al Angeloro, *Franco* (2005).

FREDERICKS, Frankie
(Namibia, 1967–)

Frankie Fredericks was for over a dozen years a leading international sprinter. His career spanned the period in which South African-controlled Namibia was banned from international competition to its readmittance after independence and the end of apartheid.

Fredericks was born and raised in Windhoek in South-West Africa, as Namibia was then called, but went to university in the United States, where he took a degree in computer science on a track scholarship and support from a uranium company. He caught the attention of Brigham Young's sprint coach at the South African Junior Championships while training and working for the mining company. He later took an MBA and continues to work for the uranium corporation.

When Namibian independence came in 1990, Fredericks was able to compete on the world scene. Between 1991 and 2002, Frankie took 16 championships or medals in international competition. His strongest race was the 200 meter, where he took silver in the World Championships in 1991, gold in 1993 and 1995, and silver again in 1997. In 1994, Namibia competed in its first Commonwealth Games. Frankie first took the bronze medal in the 100 meter dash. He topped this with a Games record of 19.97 seconds in the 200 meter, taking gold. He repeated the gold in the 200 meter at the 2002 Commonwealth Games.

At the 1992 Olympics in Barcelona, Namibia's first appearance, Fredericks took silver medals in both the 100 and 200 meter races. He repeated the silvers at the 1996 Olympics in Atlanta, being bested only by two runners who established world records. He skipped the 2000 Olympics due to injuries, and at the Athens 2004 Olympics, he finished a disappointing fourth. After that, he retired from competition. He set his personal bests

in both the 100 and 200 meter races in 1996, the year he also established a world record in the 200 meter indoor run, 19.92 seconds.

Frankie has been well aware of the meaning of an international champion to a country with little sports history and few models. He has always been known in racing circles as a gentleman, and even paid for his and his coach's trips when Namibia could not afford it, saying "my brothers and sisters died for that freedom and if I can afford that cost of going to the Games, so be it."

References: afr, wiki.

FRUMENTIUS
(Ethiopia, Fourth Century)

Saint Frumentius, first bishop of Ethiopia, is widely accepted as the person who introduced Christianity into the ancient kingdom of Axum, from which Ethiopia developed.

Although there are numerous legends about Frumentius, accurate accounts provide a basic outline of his life. Frumentius and his brother Saint Aedisius were taken captive along the Red Sea. They probably were traders, for they were appointed court officials in Axum. Frumentius used his position to favor Christian tradesmen. It seems that the two brothers served under the queen-regent of Axum as tutors for the prince, EZANA. When Ezana took the throne, Aedisius returned to Syria, and Frumentius went to Alexandria to request a missionary bishop from the patriarch Athanasius.

Athanasius appointed Frumentius himself as the first bishop. This appointment began a custom (which lasted until 1960) of appointing an Egyptian chosen by the patriarch of Alexandria to be head of the Ethiopian Coptic Orthodox Church. In about 341, Frumentius returned to Axum, where his preaching won many adherents. The documentary record is blank for the next 15 years until 356, when Byzantine Emperor Constantius II challenged Frumentius's ordination because it was at the hands of an Orthodox rather than Arian patriarch. The Arians, Christians who denied the divinity of Christ, were engaged in a long struggle for power with the traditional, or orthodox, Christians, and Constantius was a patron of their doctrine. Ezana ignored the Byzantine emperor's request to have Frumentius reordained, and following this incident Frumentius disappears from history. He is reputed to have headed the Church for many years, being called Abba Salama, the Father of Peace. That title has been adopted by several of his successors.

References: dacb, DAB, *wiki*.

FUGARD, Athol
(South Africa, 1932–)

Athol Fugard, the leading playwright of South Africa, revealed the evil at the heart of the apartheid system in his home country. Several of his plays, especially *Sizwe Bansi Is Dead* (1974) and *Master Harold . . . and the Boys* (1982), have been widely performed in Europe and the United States. In addition, Fugard often acts in his own works.

After a spotty education in auto mechanics and philosophy, Fugard left home to travel across Africa. He sailed in Asia as a merchant seaman for two years and then in 1956 returned to South Africa, where he began writing for the South African Broadcasting System. His actress wife and he then established an experimental theater group for which he wrote. During the next few years Fugard became acutely aware of the injustice of the apartheid system, a theme that has influenced all of his writing. His style is gritty and personal, and he was content to expose the effects of apartheid on people's lives rather than indulging in polemics. *No-Good Friday* (1959) came from his experience working in an African court, and *Nongogo* (1959) is the tale of a mineworkers' prostitute. These plays gained him enough attention for him to be hired as stage manager for the national theater. *The Blood Knot* (1961) was the first of a trilogy about family conflicts. Two brothers, one light and the other dark, clash over a White girl desired by the dark-skinned brother and scorned by the other.

In 1964, Fugard became a full-time playwright. *Hello and Goodby* and *Boesman and Lena* (both 1969) tell stories of Black families cheated by the South African legal system. The government soon forbade mixed acting companies, and after the British Broadcasting Company televised *The Blood Knot* (in which Fugard acted), the government confiscated his passport for four years. Allowed to travel in 1971, Fugard produced most of his plays overseas, mainly in London. In 1974 he published *Sizwe Bansi Is Dead,* the story of a Black man whose work permit is taken from him and who assumes the identity of a man found dead in a ditch.

Fugard has also appeared in films. He played Boesman in *Boesman and Lena* (1976) and Byleveld in *Marigolds in August* (1984), both written by him. In better-known international films, he played General Jan SMUTS in *Ghandi* (1982) and Dr. Sundeval in *The Killing Fields* (1984).

His work has won a number of awards, most notably a Tony Award for Best Play in 1975 for *Sizwe Banzi is Dead.*

Master Harold . . . and the Boys (1982), his greatest work, is a favorite of university theater groups but was banned in South Africa under apartheid. It is a searing encounter between teen-aged Harold and two older employees of his mother's tea shop who try to console him over his conflicts with his parents. He turns on them, making them scapegoats for his feelings. Fugard, who is White, admits that the play is autobiographical and represents "the most painful writing experience of my life." Harold is Fugard's legal first name, which he never uses.

He has called himself "an old liberal fossil," because he is unsure if writing is a significant form of action. All of his plays remain very personal and can be performed with minimal staging, precisely so that they can be presented by and to ordinary people. His most recent works have been written in workshop form and lack the polish or the punch of his best work, but he remains unsure about his ability to write for the changing South Africa. He admits "you could give me five Nobel Prizes, but . . . I will be as frightened and uncertain of myself as I was with every play I have written."

References: adb, afr, CANR, DLB, EB, EWB, *wiki,* WLTC. Fugard, *My Cousin* [autobiography] (1995); Russell Vandenbroucke, *Truths the Hand Can Touch: The Theatre of Athol Fugard* (1985); Dennis Walder, *Athol Fugard* (1984).

GALADÉWOS
(Ethiopia, 1522?–1559)

Galadéwos was *negus,* or emperor, of Ethiopia from 1540 to 1559, when the kingdom was at one of its lowest points. The son of Emperor LEBNA Dengel, he was raised in a period of unremitting attack from Muslims in the east, nomadic Galla warriors in the south, and Turkish invaders in the north (from what is now Eritrea). Churches and monasteries were plundered and burned, and general slaughter and forced conversions occurred.

Crowned emperor at age 18, Galadéwos rallied his people, and in 1543, using a small force of Portuguese musketeers alongside his troops, he defeated the Muslims and killed their leader, AHMAD Ibn Ibrahim al-Ghazi (Ahmad Grañ). While they regrouped, Galadéwos consolidated his victory by thwarting moves by several provinces to take advantage of the weak monarchy in order to secede. Turning to the Muslims again, he captured their leaders, and by the 1550s, Ethiopia was reasonably secure within its ancient borders.

Galadéwos realized that rebuilding his country involved more than military defense. Although he concluded treaties with the Portuguese, he was wary of their intentions and distrusted the Jesuit missionaries who accompanied them. Galadéwos was a deeply religious man, who wrote a confession of faith to affirm traditional doctrines and involved himself in the spiritual revival of the Coptic Orthodox Church, which he saw as the kingdom's cultural backbone and basis of unity. He also concerned himself with development and built irrigation works and roads.

The Muslims were able to mount later campaigns, but in 1559 Galadéwos took their capital, Harar, and sacked it. In 1559 on Good Friday, a day of fasting that weakened the Ethiopian soldiers, Galadéwos was lured into battle and was killed.

References: DAB, DAHB.

GALLIENI, Joseph Simon
(Guinea/Mali/Sénégal, 1849–1916)

Marshal Joseph Simon Gallieni was the French military commander who successfully overcame several major Islamic empires in West Africa and consolidated French colonial presence there.

Gallieni graduated from the French military academy at St-Cyr before being commissioned in the Marines. Like many other young officers who served in the Franco-Prussian War, Gallieni was sent to Africa in the 1870s, and from 1879 to 1881 he was political director of Sénégal. In the Upper Niger region, he was captured in a skirmish with forces but was able to negotiate his freedom and a preferential position for French interests. He rose quickly in the colonial military ranks, first being posted to Martinique and then returning to West Africa as governor of French Sudan. He expanded the French military presence in the region by taking Bamako, later the capital of Mali. Following a series of failed alliances with Muslim leaders, he became convinced that the Islamic kingdoms would have to be subjugated and that the best method of doing so was to ally himself with various Islamic factions and create dissention while expanding French influence and authority. When Mamadou LAMINE mounted a serious threat to Gallieni in 1887 and forced the French into retreat several times, he struck Lamine a final decisive blow and ended the rebellion. In 1888 he passed his command on to Louis ARCHINARD, who completed Gallieni's designs.

Gallieni spent 1892 to 1896 in Indochina. He was brought back to Africa to lead the French forces that completed the conquest and occupation of Madagascar, where he was known for his brutality. In Madagascar he did not face tribal societies, but an organized state with long traditions and strong leadership. Gallieni suppressed opposition with power and force, and executed many prominent figures. That task completed, he stayed on in Madagascar as governor-general until 1905. His administration was widely regarded as progressive and humane once he had taken full command.

He returned to France in poor health, which caused him to decline an appointment as supreme commander of the French army in 1911. He was recalled from retirement in 1914 and took command of the defense of Paris in World War I. He then served for a year as minister of war. Five years after his death, he was posthumously named a marshal.

References: afr, DAHB, EB, *wiki*. Pierre Lyautey, *Gallieni* (1959).

GAMA, Vasco da
(Mozambique/Kenya, 1460?–1524)

Admiral Vasco da Gama, a Portuguese explorer, was the first European to sail to India around the Cape of Good Hope in South Africa.

In the fifteenth century, Portugal's presence in Africa consisted of only a few trading posts for safe haven and supplies. Africa held little allure for the Portuguese at the time and was in fact an obstacle to finding a direct route to the Far East, where trade in spices could bring immense wealth. But when da Gama rounded the Cape of Good Hope in 1497, Europe outflanked the rival Muslims, who up to then controlled the Indian trade.

During the same year, da Gama was given command of a fleet of four ships, which sailed to the Cape in four months. It had been reached nine years earlier by Bartolomeo Dias, but no European had penetrated beyond this point. Da Gama's ships anchored at several points along the Mozambican coast, where he encountered his first Muslim towns and traders and at first pretended to be a Muslim himself. The fleet then resorted to piracy, raiding Arab ships. They reached Mombasa (Kenya) in April 1498, but the local authorities were hostile, so he moved on quickly to Malindi. There he was received warmly, took on provisions, and was allowed to set up a pillar, which still stands. Most importantly, da Gama obtained the services of Ibn Majid, a pilot who knew the routes to India. The trip was successful from an exploratory point of view, but two of his ships and two-thirds of his crew did not make it back to Portugal.

After an inconclusive visit to Calicut, India, da Gama returned along the African coast in 1499. In Lisbon he was knighted, and in 1502 he sailed again, this time with 20 ships and the title of Admiral of the Ocean Sea. On his return trip da Gama bombarded the port of Kilwa in present-day Kenya and forced the ruler to swear allegiance to Portugal. When the Arabs sent a fleet against him, da Gama dispatched it and again took up plundering in the area. This attack marked the beginning of a period of increasing Portuguese domination of the trading ports and created a legacy of hostility toward the Portuguese along the coast. Da Gama died in India as governor of the state of Goa, which was part of Portuguese India at the time. He was lionized in Portugal. The *Lusiads*, Portugal's greatest epic, is about his voyages, and the Jeronimós Monastery in Belém, the finest jewel of Manueline architecture, was built in his honor. It sits across a broad plaza from the modern Monument of the Discoveries.

Da Gama's voyages were part of the thrust of sea exploration that had begun with Prince Henry the Navigator (1394–1460), and included such illustrious figures as Bartolomeo Dias before him and Ferdinand Magellan after him. Besides the desire for exploration and trade wealth, da Gama's motivations seem to have been partly religious. He was a member of the knightly Order of Christ, a military religious order originally founded to combat Muslim expansion.

References: afr, DAHB, EB, *wiki*.

GANDHI, Mohandas Karamchand
(South Africa, 1869–1948)

Mahatma Gandhi, honored sage and iconic leader of anticolonial liberation in India, spent 20 years in South Africa developing his understanding of nonviolence and beginning his lifelong advocacy of freedom for colonized peoples. He was universally revered as the "Mahatma," or "Great Soul."

Gandhi was born in Gujarat, India, of a prominent Hindu family. He would be guided all his life by the values of tolerance among faiths and castes and the principle of *ahimsa* (never to harm a living being), learned from the large Jain community in Gujarat. He entered an arranged marriage at age 15, and four years later sailed for England and legal studies. He held to his Hindu values in an alien land, becoming a convinced vegetarian. He

M.K. Gandhi circa 1913, during his tenure as a solicitor in South Africa.

also studied Buddhism and Christianity, which he respected but found unconvincing. When once asked his opinion of Christianity, he commented wryly that it was wonderful, and that someone should try it some time!

Ghandi returned to India and experienced total failure as a barrister. In his first and only case, he was so tongue-tied he could not utter a word and fled in disgrace. With relief, he accepted a minor position with an Indian firm in South Africa. An indifferent, morbidly shy man who lacked self-confidence, Ghandi was transformed by Africa.

In South Africa, he was confronted with deep-seated racism for the first time. One incident after another humiliated him and steeled him against injustice. After dealing with the case he had been brought to South Africa to settle, he began to organize the Indian business community against a bill in parliament to deprive all Indians of the vote. Although they failed, a new Gandhi emerged. He became politically astute, hard-driving, yet steeped in nonviolence and a sense of selfless service. The condition of the Indian poor in South Africa was appalling. Mostly indentured servants, illiterate and exploited, they had no idea of their rights. And

indeed, there were none. They were required to travel third class on the trains, and if any White chose, the Indians could be expelled from that to the running boards outside the cars. They could not share a sidewalk with Whites and education was closed to them. Those who finally emerged from indenture found the land tenure that they were promised when they were recruited blocked by impossible fees and taxes.

Gandhi persisted, fundraising in India and campaigning in England, where he got a sympathetic hearing in the press that almost cost him his life when he was attacked by a White mob on his return. In response to rejection, Gandhi organized 1,100 Indians into an ambulance corps for the British Army in the Boer War. What he got from this generous gesture was the 1907 Asian Registration Act and further restrictions on Indians. This caused Gandhi to develop his theory of passive resistance, *satyagraha*, political confrontation that was neither verbally nor physically violent. General Jan SMUTS seemed to favor repealing the Asian Registration Act and the hated tax on former indentured workers, but not only did this not happen, but the Supreme Court invalidated all non-Christian marriages. The reaction was swift and dramatic, and the Indian miners struck. When 2,000 marched with their wives and children to a subsistence farm Gandhi had set up, he was arrested and they were forced back underground. In prison Gandhi was treated miserably, and both London and Delhi denounced South Africa's "blood and iron" policy. In the end, Gandhi and the Indians won the marriage and tax issues and free travel was permitted.

Gandhi returned to India in 1914 a transformed person, his earlier vague conviction honed in service in Africa. His greatest years, of course, lay ahead.

References: CAAS, EB, EWB, *wiki.* www.mkgandhi.org; *Gandhi* (film, 1982); Gandhi, *Gandhi, an Autobiography* (1957).

GANTIN, Bernard
(Benin, 1923–)

Cardinal Bernard Gantin (his name means "tree of iron"), a Roman Catholic cardinal, is the highest-ranking African in the Vatican. Gantin, who was close to Pope John Paul II, was given progressively more important positions until he was sometimes mentioned as a possible successor to the pope.

Gantin was sent to Rome for theological studies after ordination in 1951, where he took advanced degrees in theology and church law. Within five years he was named auxiliary bishop of Cotonou, the capital city of Benin. From 1960 to 1971 he served as its archbishop, where he reorganized the diocese, expanded schools and fostered indigenous clergy and sisterhoods. In 1971, as part of Pope John Paul's program to internationalize the Vatican bureaucracy, Gantin was called to Rome and made deputy head of the Congregation on Evangelization, which oversees all Catholic Third World mission dioceses. Soon, Gantin came into conflict with Mathieu KÉRÉKOU, head of Benin's Marxist government, when Gantin protested from Rome the arrests of priests (including his successor as archbishop) and the suppression of religious education. He was barred from visiting Benin.

By 1977, Gantin was head of the Vatican Commission on Justice and Peace and was made cardinal. Over the years, tensions with the Benin government eased, and in 1982, Gantin accompanied John Paul on a visit to that country, where he received a tumultuous welcome. In 1984 he was appointed head of the powerful Congregation for Bishops, which gave him jurisdiction over the appointment of all Catholic bishops worldwide.

Although he was originally viewed by the Church as a "mild man without much political weight," Gantin proved a firm supporter of John Paul's conservative tendencies and is close to Opus Dei, the archconservative lay movement in the Catholic Church. With his friendly, open, outgoing personality, he has been an effective administrator. In 1993, he was elected dean of the College of Cardinals, a prestigious but largely ceremonial post that involves directing papal elections. The choice shows his wide acceptance by other cardinals throughout the church. In 2002 he retired to Benin. He tuned 80 shortly before the election of Pope Benedict XVI, thus losing his voting rights.

References: dacb, wiki.

GARANG de Mabior, John
(Sudan, 1945–2005)

Colonel Dr. John Garang de Mabior, leader of the rebel Sudanese People's Liberation Army (SPLA), kept the south from northern domination for over 20 years until a settlement allowed him to share power as vice president.

An orphan from a poor Dinka family from the southern Sudan, Garang was educated in Tanzania and then graduated from Grinnell College in Iowa in 1969. At first he joined the Sudanese army, but he soon quit to join the Anyanya (Scorpion) rebel movement in the south, which had been involved in a southern liberation fight since the 1950s. Garang returned to Tanzania to study agricultural economics, and there joined the African Revolutionary Front, where he became friends with a later ally, Yoweri MUSEVENI, future president of Uganda.

In 1972 a truce was agreed upon with General Gaafar NIMEIRY, president of the Sudan. The rebel troops were integrated into the Sudanese army, and Garang rose to become deputy director of military research and an infantry battalion commander. He also received infantry officer training in the United States and received a doctorate in agricultural economics in 1981 from Iowa State University.

In 1983, Garang founded the Sudanese People's Liberation Movement (SPLM) and its military wing, the SPLA, in opposition to the imposition of Islamic law on the south. At various times, the SPLM has advocated the liberation of the Sudan from authoritarianism, regional autonomy for the southern provinces, and radical nationalism. The SPLM received support from Ethiopia under MENGISTU Haile Mariam, but its local support rested upon the dissatisfaction of the southerners (who are Christian or followers of traditional religions) with the government's attempts at cultural genocide. Major issues have been the introduction of Arabic as the only language of instruction in schools, the imposition of Islamic law (*sharia*), and the reintroduction of Black slavery by northern Arabs. Garang and the SPLA have continued a guerrilla war against a series of Sudanese regimes, not always showing willingness to negotiate. In particular, Garang rejected the overtures of Sadiq al-MAHDI when he was prime minister in the late 1980s. Garang's African critics sometimes accused him of narrow Dinka tribalism. The war devastated southern Sudan, destroying its economy and creating large numbers of refugees.

Since 1989, Garang faced an implacable foe in General Omar BASHIR, who was less willing to compromise. After losing its Ethiopian bases in 1991 after the fall of the Mengistu regime, the SPLA split into two groups along ethnic lines. In a campaign begun in 1993, Garang's forces were driven from most major towns, and they lost two headquarters. The SPLA and its factions also engaged in attacks on one another. Still, he refused at first to negotiate, but finally in 2005 a peace compact was brokered. He signed a power-sharing agreement with Bashir and became vice-president. Garang also became chief of the southern administrative district, with a referendum scheduled for 2011 with the option of independence for the south.

All this was thrown into doubt when Garang's helicopter crashed into the southern mountains, killing all aboard. Though all sides agreed there was no foul play involved, riots followed, and the state of the peace settlement remained cloudy.

References: afr, CB, PLBA, RWWA, *wiki*.

GATSI Rusere
(Zimbabwe, 1559?–1623)

Mwene Mutapa Gatsi Rusere is perhaps the best-documented early ruler of the Mutapa Empire, an expansive Shona kingdom that lasted from the early fifteenth century until the beginning of the twentieth century. He initiated contact with the Portuguese and unintentionally allowed them to extend their influence in the kingdom.

Gatsi's father declined the throne on the death of his father on the condition that his son be first in line for succession. When Gatsi became *mwene mutapa* (king) around 1589, his authority was challenged by a rival political faction led by the family of the previous ruler. Gatsi sought military aid from the Portuguese, who were happy to expand their influence by providing assistance to the rebellion. Although the Portuguese at this time paid an annual tribute to the *mwene mutapa,* they sought to secure control of the kingdom. During Gatsi's reign they insinuated themselves into the kingdom's politics and increased their trade. Nevertheless, the Mutapa kingdom was prosperous and powerful. The *mwene mutapa* dressed in silk and

covered his court walls with finely woven cloth. He could raise 100,000 men as needed, although there was no standing army.

In 1592 the state was invaded by two large bands, one of which chose to assimilate while the other was hostile and had to be driven off. Gatsi was dissatisfied with his commanders' military efforts and executed several officers, touching off a protracted civil war. Because the main person executed was his uncle, the war became a dynastic feud, which was made worse by Portuguese intervention. The Portuguese, who operated with several thousand recruited African warriors from the area around Lake Malawi, were brought in to stabilize matters, but strife continued until 1609. The Portuguese price was a treaty that ceded land, including gold mines and other mineral resources. The Portuguese were in no position to exploit these, but they used the prestige of the treaty in future dealings. Despite this concession, Gatsi maintained his power, although civil strife continued throughout his reign. He was only staving off the inevitable, however, for in the generation after his death, the authority of the *mwene mutapa* became seriously compromised.

Reference: DAHB.

GEBREMARIAM DESSU, Gebrelu
(Eritrea, 1965–)

Gebrelu Gebremariam Dessu is a noted Eritrean artist. He uses mixed media to express his spiritual insights, drawn from his Orthodox tradition.

Dessu graduated from the Addis Ababa School of Fine Arts as an accomplished muralist, but spent his early years honing his skills as a graphic artist and photographer. Perhaps his best-known work, however, is a monumental mural done for the Ethiopian Orthodox Church in Nairobi, Kenya. This work, *Angel*, shows his creative skill at bringing together fresco, mosaic and stained glass. He stayed in Nairobi as a studio artist for an art center while exhibiting at the National Museum of Kenya in 2002 and 2004.

Gebrelu (as he signs his work) paints in water colors, acrylics and oils on such materials as animal skins as well as the more traditional canvas or wood. He incorporates string and found objects such as bits of ceramics and small statues into his work.

Each piece, however, reflects the iconic tradition of Ethiopian Orthodox art. Religion has had "an enduring influence" on his art, regardless of whether the specific topic of a work is religious or secular. To Gebrelu, the circle is the ultimate religious symbol, and is integrated into every piece he creates. "It explains life, light, motion and feeling, all of which radiate, rather than emerge, from the circle. Everything is to be either found in the circle or will come from it." He comments that "I crave to bring to life religious art ideas inspired by Byzantine techniques I was exposed to as a child."

In 2004, he settled in San Diego, California, where he exhibits at the Sharp Gallery. He often gives his name as Gebrelu G. Dessu. He has also exhibited in Kenya, Italy and Germany.

Reference: http://gebrelu.com

GEBRSELASSIE, Haile
(Ethiopia, 1973–)

One of the great distance runners to arise out of East Africa in the last quarter of the twentieth century, Haile Gebrselassie follows in the tradition begun by Abebe BIKILA at the 1960 Tokyo Olympics, after which East African runners have totally dominated the distance events. Gebrselassie may well be the greatest of the African distance runners.

Born in a small village 8,000 feet above sea level, Gebrselassie and his nine siblings ran 10 miles each way to school every day. His peculiar running style reflects this—he runs with his left arm pressed against his body as he did when holding his textbooks. He first came to international attention in 1992 when he won both the 5,000 meter and 10,000 meter World Junior Championships. Two years later, he took the world record in the 5,000 meter. Within another year he added the world records in the two mile and the 10,000 meter. For a decade he was a major contender, setting an Olympic record in winning the gold medal in the 10,000 meter at Atlanta in 1996. He repeated that gold in Sydney in 2000. Gebrselassie has held over 15 world records. His overwhelming closing sprint in long races became legendary, running gracefully on the balls of his feet.

After 2000, Gebrselassie's consistent rival has been his younger countryman Kenenisa BEKELE, who has finally moved past him to take several of his world records. Gebrselassie held the World Indoor record for the 5,000 meter from 1998 to 2003, when Bekele bested it by one minute, 59 seconds. Still, as late as the 2004 London Super Grand Prix, Gebrselassie could take first in the 5,000 meter run with a respectable 12:55.51. After the 2004 Athens Olympics, when he ran with a tendon injury and finished fifth (Beleke took gold), Gebrselassie has concentrated on the full marathon. He had already won the World Championship in the half marathon in 2001.

With success came rewards for the boy whose father could afford only one pair of running shoes for him and a brother and sister to share. With appearance fees and bonuses for setting world records, Gebrselassie made over $1 million a year for some time, and took away winning gifts, including several Mercedes-Benz sedans. Gebrselassie never learned to drive any of his cars, and used his wealth to care for his family and build a house for his father. He lives simply and gives generously to the poor and his church. In 1998, he played himself when Walt Disney Productions made a film of his life. In 2003 he was elected a member of the IAAF Athletes Commission.

References: afr, CB, *wiki. Endurance* (film, 1998).

GEINGOB, Hage Gottfried
(Namibia, 1941–)

Dr. Hage Gottfried Geingob, first prime minister of Namibia, has been a lifelong activist in the South-West African People's Organization (SWAPO).

Geingob attended Augustineum Secondary School and teachers' training college in Okahandja after being expelled from primary school for student activism. After teaching for several years, he became a member of SWAPO in 1962 after joining its protests that year against the poor quality of African education. SWAPO sent him to Botswana as its representative there. He was then singled out for advanced education abroad as part of SWAPO's leadership preparation program. After a year at preparatory school, he attended Fordham University in New York City, receiving a BA in 1970. In 1972 he received an MA in political science from New York's New School for Social Research. Along with his studies, Geingob was made SWAPO's representative to the United Nations (U.N.) and its spokesman in the United States from 1964 to 1972. During this period, Geingob wrote and spoke widely and was partly responsible for the general shift from the colonial name South-West Africa to international acceptance of the name Namibia. In 1969 he was appointed to the SWAPO central committee.

In 1972, Geingob joined the U.N. as a political officer in the Secretariat, being replaced as SWAPO representative by Theo Ben GURIRAB, who became SWAPO's foreign affairs spokesman. Geingob became associated with the U.N. Commission on Namibia, which oversaw the trusteeship arrangement under which South Africa governed the country. In 1975 he was made director of the U.N. Institute for Namibia, located in Lusaka, Zambia. The institute was responsible for training future administrators for Namibia. During this period he remained active in SWAPO affairs, and when independence arrangements were completed, he became coordinator of SWAPO's election campaign in 1989. Chosen chair of the constituent assembly to draw up the new Namibian constitution, he drafted the final model that provided for a democratic multiparty system. It was a long and fractious project, and Geingob credits Dirk MUDGE, the leading White politician, with making the final draft possible. Geingob was rewarded for his achievement with the position of prime minister in 1990.

Geingob necessarily worked closely with President Sam NUJOMA but was primarily responsible for government business in parliament, much of which Nujoma delegated to him. He negotiated an amicable accord with the De Beers mining conglomerate and worked out a system for land reform acceptable to both indigenous peasants and foreign owners. A good deal of Namibia's successful political transition and subsequent stability can be attributed to Geingob's achievements. He likes to quip, "An African country that isn't in the news must be doing something right."

At the closure of his long service as prime minister in 2002, he took a sabbatical from politics to finish a Ph.D. in Great Britain. He returned to Namibia in 2004 to take up his position as a SWAPO member of parliament.

References: PLBA, RWWA. Geingob, *State Formation in Namibia* (2004).

GELDOF, (Robert Frederick) Bob
(1951–)

Bob Geldof, rock star and indefatigable champion of the poor of Africa, has become a gadfly of the Western power structure and decision makers on behalf of debt and famine relief.

Geldof worked at various trades until becoming a writer for Melody Maker. In 1975, he formed a rock band that eventually became the Boomtown Rats. It was successful in his native Ireland and in Great Britain, but never achieved much in the American market.

In 1984 Geldof was profoundly moved by the television reports of the famine devastating Ethiopia. He co-founded Band Aid in response to the famine. They released "Do They Know It's Christmas," which became the Christmas season number one single that year and twice in later years. Some of the best-known artists of the time have taken part. In 1984 this included Geldof, Sting, Paul McCartney, David Bowie, Bono, Phil Collins and Criss Cross. Each time it has been re-recorded with a new group of musicians and reissued. The last time was in 1989 in response to the second Ethiopian famine. It has raised £8 million (about US$15 million) for the Band Aid Trust. In total, the funds raised for the Trust have exceeded $100 million. The morning after the initial recording, Geldof promoted the record on British television. When the government refused to cancel the value-added tax, Geldof confronted Prime Minister Margaret Thatcher with well-publicized indignation, and she agreed to donate the tax to the Trust.

The following year the Trust started Live Aid, which has raised 10 times as much as the original single. To dramatize the cause, two live concerts were held, in New York and London, with 1.5 billion people listening on television and radio.

The name Band Aid was chosen to reflect two things: that it was a musical charity and that its efforts were no more than a bandage on a gaping wound. In 2005 Geldof returned to that theme with Live Aid 8, but this time the agenda went beyond famine relief to indebtedness across Africa, AIDS and trade barriers. He assembled another star-studded set of performers for five shows in Paris, London, Rome, Berlin and Philadelphia, For the first time, an African took part, Youssou N'DOUR.

The shows were scheduled shortly before the G8 economic summit (of the eight largest world economies) met in Scotland. It was perhaps the most progressive economic summit in dealing with African issues, especially debt relief.

Geldof has now received entree to the offices of the powerful, and with that has come inevitable criticism. Many liberals accuse him of basking too easily in the reflected light of President George Bush (whom he has praised for his AIDS initiative) and of compromising his values. He and Bono have worked together on African debt relief. While they have raised the profile of African issues, their policy effect is harder to gauge.

In 1985, Geldof was nominated for the Nobel Peace Prize. In 2005, he was named the Nobel Man of Peace, an honor given by the vote of the living Nobel Prize winners, and in 2006, he was again nominated for the Peace Prize, with Bono. He received an honorary knighthood from Queen Elizabeth II. His personal life has not been so happy. His former wife left him and subsequently died of a drug overdose. He is involved in legal wrangles with the Boomtown Rats, but he has brought out several successful solo albums.

Reference: wiki.www.bobgeldof.info; Geldof, *Is That It?* (1986).

GEZO
(Benin, 1797–1858)

Gezo, one of the greatest kings of Dahomey in present-day Benin, was responsible for its expansion and secured its freedom from external domination. After 40 years of depression, in part caused by British curtailment of the slave trade, Gezo's predecessor had lost all popular support and Gezo mounted a successful coup in 1818. He legitimized his rule by creating an oral tradition claiming that he was a grandson of AGONGLO, but this was a fabrication.

Gezo restructured the armed forces and included an elite women's fighting corps, the "Amazons," many of whom were his wives. The Brazilian slavers who had been alienated by his predecessor were the only avenue to reviving the slave trade, and Gezo made peace with them. With renewed economic and military stability, he moved to break the humiliating control exercised by the Yoruba state of Oyo, which extorted tribute from Dahomey each year.

After his army defeated Oyo, Gezo began expanding into the territories of neighboring states until Dahomey became the major regional power.

Gezo restored the slave trade but realized that it had little future in the face of European hostility. He agreed to a gradual end of the trade to give Dahomey time to establish legitimate exports such as cotton and palm oil and to improve agriculture with new food crops. In 1858, Gezo was assassinated and was succeeded by GLELE.

References: AB, DAHB, MMA. Adrien Djivo, *Guezo, la Rénovation du Dahomey* (Gezo, the rebirth of Dahomey, 1977).

GITHUKU, Ndungi
(Kenya, 1974–)

Ndungi Githuku is an activist-playwright who has used his art for both street plays and the revival of small-scale theater in indigenous languages.

Githuku was radicalized as a young secondary student under the regime of President Daniel arap MOI when his government became increasingly corrupt and repressive of dissent. In 1991 an informal movement, the Mothers of Political Prisoners, staged an all-night vigil that was broken up by the police, and Githuku was arrested. It would turn out to be the first among his innumerable arrests for protest action.

Post-independence Kenya kept the repressive laws of the colonial era in order to suppress dissent and maintain a one-party state. Under Moi, torture, exile and police brutality were common. The press was forced into submission. Githuku was arrested many times and tortured. A multiparty system and widespread agitation forced Moi into retirement, but the hoped-for gains have not materialized under President Mwai KIBAKI, whose government has also been riddled with corruption.

Githuku founded the Pamoja Theatre Group in 1998 as a vehicle of protest, which he calls "artivism." The group's name is Swahili for "together." The 18 members go into the streets and public parks to enact short, biting theater pieces exposing corrupt politicians. His poetry rings with the images of persecution from the past as well as the present. Recalling a hero of the Mau Mau rebellion against the British, he sings in one: "They have killed KIMATHI again." Jeans-clad and with a crop of Rasta-style dreadlocks, Githuku is the very image of the angry young man railing against those who oppress the poor. He belongs to what has been called "the Uhuru Generation," the "Freedom Generation" that has come of age as the postcolonial period ends.

Githuku has also been deeply involved in Kikuyu-language theater. As English and Swahili theater have waned in Kenya, small venues are producing short plays in Kikuyu. A lively scene has developed, often in bars, with plays running for months. It has proved so successful that the most popular plays have replaced house bands as the regular entertainment. The characters are often thinly veiled exposés of government ministers and powerful figures. Githuku's *Walking Shadows: Undying Spirits* (2004) is a mocking indictment of Moi's 1985–1987 torture campaign against his opponents. That year Githuku was arrested for defacing the Nyayo ("Footsteps") Monument on Moi Day. Moi was gone, but his legacy remained.

In 2001, Githuku was one of four recipients of the Reebok Human Rights Award, given to people under 30. The $50,000 award must go to a human rights organization, and Githuku gave his to the Mulika Communications Trust, which he founded that year. It has become the sponsoring arm of the Pamoja Theatre Group, but it also uses media to give out information on human rights abuses and strengthen community groups. It describes itself as "an early warning system for impending human rights violations."

in 2006, Githuku was chosen one of the Young Global Leaders, an honor established by the World Economic Forum of international corporate leaders.

GLELE
(Benin, 1814?–1889)

Glele took over the throne of the kingdom of Dahomey, in what is now Benin, after the assassination of GEZO in 1858. He continued Gezo's expansionist policies, defeating several rival states and extending Dahomean power. He maintained Gezo's economic policies as well, seeking to supplement the slave trade with palm oil exports.

Although the slave trade had been largely eliminated along much of the West African coast by the mid-nineteenth century, Dahomey continued to export slaves as long as there was a market, despite pressures from French and British abolitionist

forces. Increasingly, however, palm oil sent to France replaced slaves destined for Brazil as the center of the export trade. The new legitimate trade meant that slaves and captives were used more regularly as workers and porters for the palm oil plantations, and fewer captives were hunted down for export. During Glele's reign, the transition from slave export to legitimate trade was substantially completed, and when Brazil abolished slavery in 1888, Dahomey's economy was no longer dependent upon the slave trade. Glele did continue internal slavery, however, and owned many to work his plantations. They were also used as sacrifices to the gods, so-called "messengers to the ancestors."

Glele was forced to deal with the problem of the encroaching European powers. He was unable to control the coast, where both Britain and France attempted to gain a foothold. They were opposed to Dahomey's continued slave trade with Brazil and contended between themselves for control of legitimate commerce. At first Glele allied himself with the French to place a royal prince in the chieftaincy of the coast, but when Tofa attacked Dahomean troops, the British took advantage of the situation to attack Glele. Finally, Glele contented himself with controlling the frontiers of his kingdom. The French proclaimed a protectorate over Dahomey's port of Cotonou in 1878, although at first they only set up a customs office there. Glele withdrew into the interior and built a new capital.

In 1889 a French official arrived to press French rights under a treaty signed by Gezo in 1851, but he met little acceptance. One of Glele's techniques was to shock visiting French negotiators with gory displays of human sacrifice. This strategy had the opposite effect, however, providing the French authorities with a stronger argument for military action "in the name of humanity." They did not act, however, until after Glele's death, which occurred during the meetings with the French official sent to insist on French treaty rights. There were persistent rumors that the elderly and infirm Glele committed suicide by poison because of the impending French conquest. He was succeeded by his son, BEHANZIN.

References: CWAH, DAHB, *wiki.*

GLOVER, Emmanuel Ablade

(Ghana, 1934–)

Dr. Emmanuel Ablade Glover is one of the prominent artists currently working in Africa. Although his painting, sculpture and textiles have roots in African traditional art, Glover is a modern artist who works in contemporary styles and several media.

Born in Accra during the colonial period, Glover began his art education at the Presbyterian Teacher Training College and the University of Science and Technology (UST) at Kumasi, where the art program, the oldest in West Africa, dates from the 1930s. Glover continued his art studies overseas, first at the Central School of Art and Design in London from 1959 to 1962, then at the University of Newcastle-upon-Tyne, and finally at the Ohio State University, where he took a Ph.D. When Glover returned to Ghana, he tutored at Winneba Teacher Training College, whose art program was then under the distinguished leadership of the sculptor Vincent Kofi. Glover began exhibiting in the 1960s and had his first show in London. He is a Fellow of the Royal Society of Arts. In 1965 he was named lecturer in printed textiles at UST (now Kwame Nkrumah University of Science and Technology) and later was appointed chair of art education and finally dean of the College of Art. Kumasi has become both a center of art education and a gathering place for Ghanaian artists.

Glover combines both African and European styles of art and uses a wide variety of media. In addition to textiles, he has worked in wood sculpture. In printed media he was a poster artist for the Ghana Information Services for several years. In recent years he has painted in oil impasto, using vibrant colors. He uses a palette knife rather than a brush, layering his colors carefully until the painting takes on almost a three-dimensional aspect. His work plays with the theme of order emerging from chaos. Seen close up, his paintings seem totally abstract and random, but upon stepping away, the viewer sees images form and evolve. One of his regular subjects is the female form.

In the mid-1960s he opened the Heritage, a private gallery in London that provides a European showcase for his work. Glover also maintains a gallery called Omanye ("Happiness") in Accra. He was among six African artists chosen for the opening show in a major series of multimedia exhibitions displayed in London and Virginia that began in 1993–1994. This exhibition has showcased West African artists working in modern styles that are inspired by traditional African themes. Glover exhibits widely in Europe, Asia and the United States, and his work is in major collections.

GODDARD, Keith

(Zimbabwe, 1960–)

Keith Goddard is an ethnomusicologist, cinematographer, and since 1992, the leading southern African gay human rights activist. He has been the director of Gays and Lesbians of Zimbabwe (GALZ) since 1997.

In 1991, Goddard founded the Kunzwana Trust to promote Zimbabwean music, and he remains a trustee. Their Tonga.Online Project works to preserve the music of the Tonga people, who were forcibly displaced in the building of a dam. Kunzwana also provides computers for Tonga schools and beads to restore traditional beadwork. He has been a consultant on Zimbabwean traditional music for Afropop International and has also worked as a cinematographer for nine films, including the five *Absolutely Fabulous* short comedies in 2001.

Goddard has acquired fame and notoriety primarily as a gay activist, however. President Robert MUGABE, a rabid homophobe, has called gays and lesbians "worse than pigs" and says they have no rights at all. In a repressive dictatorship that provides justification for persecution and harassment, Goddard has suffered for his stands. In 1998, he was arrested and charged with rape at gunpoint on a trumped-up accusation that may have been a police trap. He has been a prisoner of conscience for Amnesty International, but the case was never brought to trial.

In 1995, Goddard received worldwide media attention in the wake of a campaign against Zimbabwe's international book fair. GALZ applied for a display booth and was rejected, causing some groups, including the influential Publishers' Association of South Africa, to boycott the book fair. When GALZ won in court and set up an anti-AIDS display the following year (with its stall shunted off into a corner), the booth was trashed by a gang of youths. Even so, it has displayed each year since.

The anti-gay campaign widened, with orders to the government-owned newspaper to vilify GALZ and homosexuals in general. Churchmen joined the denunciations ("God commands the death of sexual perverts" was one leading cleric's pronouncement) shortly before the World Council of Churches was to meet in Harare in 1998. To this was added the high-profile persecution and conviction of former President Canaan BANANA on sodomy charges and the arrest of the head of Zimbabwean national television for public lewdness. Mugabe replied to international criticism of Goddard's arrest by announcing "the world can go to hell." Despite the incessant harassment, Goddard has expanded GALZ's activities to support gay groups in South Africa, Namibia and Swaziland. A major achievement was the opening of the GALZ Resource Centre in 2004.

Reference: Goddard, *A Fair Representation* (2004).

GOLDIE, George Dashwood Taubman
(Nigeria, 1846–1925)

Sir George Dashwood Taubman Goldie, an Englishman, revived the chartered company, an institution that had been used extensively in earlier British imperialist expansion, and made it the means of establishing British control over Nigeria.

After several years in the Royal Engineers, Goldie arrived in Nigeria in 1877 and found a disordered state of affairs. Parliament had declared itself opposed to any colonial responsibilities in the interior of Equatorial Africa, and the scene was left to a number of British trading companies that were engaged in ruthless competition for the coastal trade. Although William BAIKIE had explored the Niger, few others were interested in exploiting the riches of the interior. Goldie proposed a royal chartered company for the Niger valley, which was largely free from non-British commercial and missionary competition. He began by uniting the existing traders into the United Africa Company in 1879. Meanwhile, two French companies settled on the river, and Goldie bought them out after a price war.

In 1884, Germany surprised the other European powers by entering the colonial race and helped to launch the "scramble" for Africa by calling an international conference in Berlin. To secure its claims in Nigeria, Britain (with Goldie present) argued that "the whole trade of the Niger basin is exclusively in British hands." Britain won Nigeria, and Goldie won a knighthood for his services to the crown.

Recognition of British claims did not deter Germany and France from competing for further domination in the unmapped interior, so Goldie pleaded with the British government for a charter that would enable him to negotiate treaties with the local chiefs on a par with government agents. His request was finally granted in 1886, and the Royal Niger Company (replacing the United Africa Company) was born. The company was empowered to govern its territories, sign treaties, and even to establish new protectorates. Goldie quickly monopolized trade by excluding both other Europeans and Africans. In 1897 he moved against the Islamic states, which were taking slaves from African communities that were under company protection. With a disciplined African force of 800 men, Goldie defeated 15,000 troops from Nupe in northern Nigeria, deposed the emir, and banned slavery. Soon other Muslim states were forced to follow suit. The Royal Niger Company controlled much of the trade in palm oil, which it sold on the European market for huge profits.

By 1899 it was clear that the chartered company had had its monopolistic limits; direct colonial government was necessary for unity and development. The charter was revoked, and the company was awarded a £865,000 indemnity (US$95 million today). Goldie left Nigeria and spent some years in South Africa and Rhodesia before settling in England, where he died.

References: DAHB, DNB, EB, *wiki.* Dorothy Wellesley, *Sir George Goldie, Founder of Nigeria* (1977).

GOODALL, Jane
(Tanzania, 1934–)

British-born Dr. Jane Goodall has devoted her life to the study of wild chimpanzees, and in the process she has popularized the cause of wildlife preservation and developed new field work techniques for studying primates.

Goodall first went to Africa as a tourist, but an encounter with the paleontologist Louis LEAKEY changed her life. She became his secretary for three years until he helped her establish a field camp at the Gombe Stream Chimpanzee Reserve in Tanzania, where she began observing chimpanzees. Aware of her academic limitations, she returned to England to take a Ph.D. in animal behavior at Cambridge University, admitted on Leakey's recommendation and the basis of her experience, since she had no undergraduate degree.

Goodall adapted the participant-observer methods of field sociology. She won the trust of a troop of chimpanzees and sat among them and played with them. Slowly, she began to uncover the network of relationships among them, their patterns of social standing and their clan and family traits. Goodall discovered hitherto unknown aspects of chimpanzee life, such as their ability to use tools, something that scholars had long held was only done by humans. She observed them fashioning sticks so they could get ants and termites from anthills as part of their diet. To the surprise of many, she also proved that chimpanzees were meat-eaters and engaged in cooperative hunting with monkeys. She charted the differences between chimpanzees and bonobos, and their relationship to gorillas.

In the mid-1960s, Goodall's work came to international attention through articles in the *National Geographic* and a documentary brought out by the National Geographical Society. She used her fame to establish the Jane Goodall Institute for Wildlife Research. She has received numerous awards and honors, including being made a Dame of the British Empire (DBE) in 2004 by Queen Elizabeth II. Goodall received the Hubbard Medal of the National Geographic Society and is the only non-Tanzanian to receive the Tanzanian Kilimanjaro Medal. In 2004, she was named one of *Time Europe*'s Heroes of the Year. She devotes all her time today to wildlife conservation.

References: afr, CA, CANR, EB, EWB, *wiki*. Goodall, *40 Years at Gombe* (2000); *Reason for Hope: A Spiritual Journey* (2002); *Jane Goodall's Wild Chimpanzees* (film, 2002); www.janegoodall.org.

GORDIMER, Nadine
(South Africa, 1923–)

Nadine Gordimer, the preeminent White novelist of South Africa and its first Nobel Prize winner in literature (1991), was a foe of apartheid and one of the leading White voices in support of the African National Congress (ANC). Her writing and her politics went hand in hand as she moved from the White liberal tradition to more outspoken radicalism.

Born into a middle-class immigrant family near Johannesburg, her early environment was so apolitical that her subsequent awareness of it was a personal discovery: "I lived with and among a variety of colours and kinds of people. This discovery was a joyous personal one . . . as time has gone by it has hardened into a sense of political opposition to abusive White power." She has always described her life in terms of "the tension between standing apart and being fully involved." As a child, Gordimer was a Jewish girl in a Catholic convent school, and as an adult she developed into a personal consciousness writer in a literary tradition wedded to realism. Hers was the White voice that could speak when Black voices were stilled, "a stranger among people who were strangers to each other."

Gordimer began writing in her teens while still a student at the University of the Witwatersrand. In 1949 she published her first collection of short stories, *Face to Face*. A number of stories had already appeared in leading U.S. magazines, including *The New Yorker* and *Harper's*, and they showed the finely crafted work of a young professional. The collection included one of her best, "Is There Nowhere Else We Can Meet?" The story tells of a young White woman's encounter with a poor Black man who robs her. It examines her decision not to report the incident as she comes to understand his poverty and desperation.

Gordimer continued writing short stories, publishing 10 more collections by the 1980s, but her novels have been given the greatest recognition. Her early novels explored the bourgeois world of English-speaking South Africa and its mounting isolation and disintegration in the wake of the Afrikaner political triumph and the imposition of apartheid. The first four novels came together in *The Late Bourgeois World* (1966), based on the reflections of a woman whose ex-husband has just committed suicide. She remembers him as a failed revolutionary and a traitor to African nationalism.

A turning point is apparent in *Burger's Daughter* (1979), which brings together the Soweto riots and the Black-power rejection of White liberalism in a story about the daughter of a leading Communist who tries to create a nonpolitical life after her father has died in prison. Middle-class White liberal politics are portrayed as irrelevant, paternalistic and lifeless. In 1974, Gordimer had published *The Conservationist,* in which the central character, Mehring, is a symbol of White South Africa: materialist, racist, privileged and abusive. That year it won the Booker Prize, Britain's leading literary award. In *July's People* (1981) Gordimer explored the dependence that Whites have on Blacks, which the former continue to deny. *My Son's Story* (1990) has a Coloured man as its main character, and through his being "somebody who was in an indefinite state," Gordimer explores the meaning of race. In late 1994 she published *None to Accompany Me*, the account of two couples, one Black and one White, and their struggles to adjust to the new South Africa. Her writing has garnered criticism as being a reflection of White privilege, albeit staunchly antiapartheid. There was speculation whether Gordimer would be able to rise above being a protest writer after the end of apartheid, but in *The House Gun* (1998) she showed that she could explore the tragedies of post-apartheid South Africa.

When Gordimer won the 1991 Nobel Prize, it was after a number of failed nominations. President Frederik DE KLERK, whose predecessors had banned four of her novels, called her prize an "exceptional achievement" and an "honour to South Africa." Others noted that she was also the first woman laureate in a quarter century. Gordimer has remained unwavering in her support of the ANC and has written abundant tributes to Nelson MANDELA. She has been a sharp critic of White liberals, such as Helen SUZMAN and once said of herself, "I am a White South African radical. Please don't call me a liberal."

References: AB, *adb, afr,* CANR, CB, DLB, EB, EWB, *wiki,* WLTC. Stephen Clingman, *The Novels of Nadine Gordimer* (1992); Gordimer, Nadine. *The Essential Gesture: Writing, Politics, and Places* (1988).

GORDON, Charles George "Chinese"
(Sudan, 1833–1885)

General Charles George "Chinese" Gordon was a contradictory figure in British imperialism, alternately a religious eccentric who received his mission in visions, a self-sacrificing servant of the poorest, and a romantic military leader who became a martyr-hero for a generation of British.

Gordon was already an artillery lieutenant at age 19, and his reckless bravery in the Crimean War brought him to the attention of his superiors. In 1860 he joined British forces fighting in China and took part in the occupation of Beijing, in which he directed the burning of the emperor's summer palace.

In 1862 he built bastions around the foreign trading compounds in Shanghai and then took over the ragtag defense force pompously known as the Ever-Victorious Army. Gordon was named a mandarin (a Chinese imperial court official) and lieutenant-colonel and proved his ability by forging a decent fighting force, dismissing incompetent officers, and engaging the enemy. Personally brave, he faced down a mutiny among his men by executing its ringleader in public. He always led his troops unarmed except for a riding crop, which the superstitious peasant soldiers regarded as a magic wand. He halted the Taiping Rebellion but was betrayed by the local governor. Infuriated by this action, Gordon refused the emperor's gifts and withdrew. After several months, during which the rebels regrouped, Gordon returned to command on his own terms and soon crushed the rebellion, returning home to great honor. Thereafter, he was always known by the nickname "Chinese" Gordon, although his detractors also referred to him as "Half-Cracked" Gordon.

From 1865 to 1871, Gordon did routine military engineering near London. He lived austerely, sponsoring schools and clinics for the poorest ragpickers and taking young boys into his home and caring for them. During this period he began having mystical experiences. One night, "with palpable feeling," he had a revelation that God was within him and had plans for him beyond anything the world could understand. He began to see his work in spiritual terms, adding to this vision a moral imperative, that it was God's will that he break the slave trade.

In 1872, Gordon was named governor of Equatoria province in southern Sudan, succeeding Sir Samuel White BAKER. He set up a line of posts along the Nile as far as Uganda, attacked the slave trade, and established a communication link with Cairo. By 1876 he had come into conflict with the governor-general of the Sudan over slavery, and Gordon resigned. Within a few months, the *khedive* (ruler) of Egypt begged for him to return, and he did, but as governor-general with total control. He moved against the slave trade, at one point confronting 6,000 armed defenders of the slave routes.

In a long series of forced marches, Gordon secured much of his territory from the slavers. He negotiated with Emperor YOHANNES IV of Ethiopia on behalf of the *khedive* but was later captured by some of Yohannes's troops. After he escaped, Gordon tendered his resignation because he was in ill health and returned to England in 1880. The next 18 months found him restlessly moving around Switzerland, India, China, Ireland and Mauritius. In 1882, "tired of doing nothing," he applied for a post in South Africa, where he was made commander of British forces in Cape Colony for a year. Again he resigned in a dispute after being betrayed by a colonial official in dealings with the local chiefs. He considered an offer to become a mercenary for the king of Belgium in the Congo Free State and then spent 1883 in Palestine, visiting the holy places.

By this time, matters in Egypt and the Sudan had seriously deteriorated. The Egyptian army revolted and the British invaded, occupying the country. In the Sudan, Muhammad Ahmad, the Mahdi, had begun a *jihad,* or holy war, after announcing that he was the Mahdi$,$ the promised one who would bring Islam to fulfillment at the end of time. Britain decided on a strategic retreat after a catastrophic defeat at the Mahdi's hands, and Gordon was recalled to service to complete the evacuation of the garrisons in the Sudan that he had established. He evacuated 2,500 people and proclaimed an independent Sudan, a pointless statement under the circumstances, since the Mahdi had already occupied most of it.

Within a month, Gordon was under siege at Khartoum, leading a yearlong struggle with his usual bravado and military skill. In Parliament the British government hesitated until it was too late, sending a relief force from Britain after the Nile rains had begun. Eventually, Gordon was the last European in Khartoum, and the city fell in March 1885 with a slaughter of the inhabitants. Gordon was speared by a group of dervishes and his head was presented to the Mahdi. Chinese Gordon became a martyr of imperialism, a symbol of undying devotion; a national monument to him was placed in Trafalgar Square in London. As a result of its mishandling of the affair, the Liberal government fell and the Liberal Party remained out of office for 20 years.

Only after a generation did historians begin to suggest that Gordon's defense of Khartoum was both unnecessary and foolhardy, perhaps even a death wish. He had claimed, "People may say 'You tempt God, in putting yourself in positions like my present one,' yet I do not care. I do not do it to tempt Him; I do it because I wish to trust in His promises." The Mahdi, a fanatic Islamic revivalist, encountered a Christian who was as convinced, inspired and driven by the spirit as was the Muslim leader. When the Mahdi offered Gordon freedom if he would convert to Islam, he could not have selected a better means of confirming the righteousness of Gordon's convictions.

A man of deep contrasts (and perhaps deeper conflicts), Chinese Gordon was a compulsive person who needed constant activity and who was also prone to moody contemplation. He was celibate, in a way that made companions uncomfortable, but evidence exists that he may have been sexually involved with the boys he rescued from poverty—his "little kings," as he called them. In his generosity and his stern sense of duty, as well as in his weaknesses, he was the epitome of the Victorian imperialist.

References: DAHB, DNB, EB, EWB, HWL, *wiki.* Lytton Strachey, *Eminent Victorians* (1918); John Waller, *Gordon of Khartoum* (1988).

GOULED Aptidon, Hassan

(Djibouti, 1916–)

Hassan Gouled Aptidon was the first president of Djibouti, a tiny enclave on the Red Sea. Formerly French Somaliland, it has retained its close ties to France, which maintains a military base there. It is also the site of the only American military base in Africa.

Gouled left his nomadic Issa family in his teens and became a street peddler. He worked his way into contracting and became an Issa leader, championing their cause for greater representation. He represented the colony in the French senate from 1952 to 1958 and later in the national assembly from 1959 to 1967. During this period he was a Gaullist and a proponent of local autonomy for Djibouti as an overseas French territory. In a 1958 referendum he defeated the candidates urging independence. Two factors influenced Gouled's political turnabout: he became impatient with the slow pace of reform toward autonomy, and later he was dismayed at French favoritism toward the minority Afar clan. A second referendum in 1967 also rejected independence, but by then Gouled was on the other side.

Gouled emerged from independence negotiations with France to lead his country to a resounding 99 percent vote for independence, and in 1977 he became president of Djibouti. Ethnic tensions dogged his regime from its beginnings. Gouled attempted to stress a common Arab heritage and appointed several Afar vice presidents, but ethnic rivalry continued to be a problem. Djibouti has been a single-party state since 1982, but limited opposition was permitted in the 1991 presidential election, which Gouled won with 60 percent of the vote.

The Issa are Somali-related, while the Afar are ethnically related to Ethiopia, so conflicts between Somalia and Ethiopia have squeezed Djibouti and threatened to spill over its borders. Gouled worked to bring the two nations together and played a major role in the peace agreement between them in 1988. Nevertheless, Djibouti was involved in the Somali civil war in favor of Issa clansmen. An opposition Afar group, Front for the Restoration of Unity and Democracy, began low-level guerrilla action against the Gouled regime in 1991. Gouled reacted harshly, recruiting Issa from Somalia for his army. In a 1993–1994 campaign, he drove the guerrillas from their strongholds with such ferocity that he was accused of ethnic cleansing. Rape, executions and well poisonings were common. The army, which tripled in size, consumes 35 percent of the national budget, and the war is crippling the Djibouti economy. Unemployment hovers around 60 percent. Gouled Aptidon retired from the presidency in 1999.

References: afr, DAHB, PLBA, RWWA, *wiki*.

GOWON, Yakubu Dan Yumma "Jack"
(Nigeria, 1934–)

General Yakubu Dan Yumma "Jack" Gowon was military leader of Nigeria during the civil war and the architect of the reconciliation policy that followed. His decision to make every effort to maintain Nigerian unity helped to guarantee the country's future.

The son of a Christian evangelist from the Muslim north, Gowon was educated as a soldier at Great Britain's Royal Military Academy at Sandhurst and in several advanced courses in England. He did two tours of duty with the United Nations (U.N.) Peacekeeping Force in the Democratic Republic of the Congo (DRC) during the Congo's post-independence crisis of 1960–1961. None of this, however, prepared him for being thrust into a vortex of coups, assassinations and civil war. While Gowon was out of the country in 1966, Nigeria's first prime minister, the northerner Abubakar Tafawa BALEWA, was assassinated. Gowon was appointed chief of staff by the coup leader, who was himself assassinated in another coup six months later. Mounting clashes between Igbo and northern soldiers made conditions precarious, and Gowon, although he was a Christian, was chosen to head the northern-dominated military government at the age of 32.

Nigeria has been divided economically and culturally between north and south since Frederick LUGARD united the two regions under one colonial administration. There had been previous violence, but now there was mutual slaughter of Igbo and Hausa. In 1967 the Eastern Region declared itself independent as the Republic of Biafra. It was led by a friend of Gowon (who had served with him in the DRC), Chukwuemeka OJUKWU. The two met in Ghana in a final attempt at reconciliation, but when the military council turned down some of the concessions that Gowon was prepared to make to Biafra, the die was cast.

Gowon never ceased attempting to reassemble a unified country while continuing the war vigorously. He restored discipline in the army to make it a more effective force and to end wildcat excursions against the Igbo. He released a number of political prisoners, including Chief Obafemi AWOLOWO, the Yoruba leader. He abolished the Nigerian regions and replaced them with 12 states, allaying fears of northern domination. Throughout the war he invited international observer teams to tour the war zone. Along with improved army discipline, this policy helped to reduce allegations of genocide against the Igbo. Gowon tolerated food relief flights into Biafra, refusing to accept starvation as an instrument of policy. Despite peace initiatives, Biafra refused to surrender until 1970. Relief supplies and medicines were brought in, although Gowon clashed with several international relief agencies, and starvation and disease were reversed in the east within a year. Gowon completed his policy of national reconciliation by integrating the Igbo into the government and rejecting any revenge.

Gowon relied on a network of bureaucrats, and after 1970 corruption began to dominate the administration. In 1974, Gowon announced that his proposed date for return to civilian rule in 1976 was unfeasible, thereby disappointing many and weakening his authority. In 1975, while attending a summit of the Organization of African Unity (he had been president the year before), a coup removed him from office. Gowon immediately pledged his loyalty to the new government, retired on pension, and went into exile in England. He lost his rank and pension when he was accused of plotting a 1976 coup in which General Murtala MUHAMMED was killed. In 1981, however, President Shehu SHAGARI pardoned Gowon and invited him to return to Nigeria. After a visit, Gowon returned to England to finish a Ph.D. in political science at Warwick University (1984). He finally returned to Nigeria and served in the Senate.

References: afr, CB, DAHB, DRWW, DT, PLBA, PLCA, RWWA, wiki. John Clarke, Yakubu Gowon: Faith in a United Nigeria (1987); Isawa Elaigwu, Gowon: The Biography of a Soldier (1985).

GRAZIANI, Rudolfo
(Ethiopia, 1882–1955)

Italian fascist General Rudolfo Graziani spent only a few years in Africa, but they were enough to earn him a reputation as one of the most vicious colonial tyrants in history. He was known as the "butcher of Addis Ababa" and "the hyena" for his atrocities.

Graziani was a career soldier. His first posting was in Eritrea (1908–1912). He was part of the Italian occupation of Libya in 1912 and returned there as commander between 1930 and 1934, attaining a reputation for savagery. After a year as governor of Italian Somaliland, Graziani was made commander of the southern command in the Italian invasion of Ethiopia. Within two months, he was named viceroy of Ethiopia and initiated a ruthless campaign of repression.

In 1937, Graziani was wounded in a grenade attack by the Patriots, the underground Ethiopian resistance movement. The incident occurred at a public gathering when Italian soldiers fired wildly into the crowd of women and children, killing hundreds. Graziani further retaliated with a three-day massacre that cost thousands of lives, including those of Patriot prisoners who had surrendered under amnesty as well as 350 monks of Debra Libanos, the main Ethiopian monastery. Bishop Petrus was publicly executed when he refused to broadcast a pro-Italian message to the Patriots. After thousands of deaths failed to quell the resistance, Graziani was removed, given an aristocratic title, and made honorary governor of East Africa. Despite his gruesome record, he returned to Rome a hero, feted with royal ceremony.

He was transferred back to Libya in 1939 and commanded the invasion of Egypt despite his concerns that his army could not match the British tank forces. After a decisive defeat, he resigned. When Mussolini fell in 1943, Graziani joined the Nazi-led occupation government as Minister of Defense. He was sentenced as a war criminal in 1950, but served only a few months of a 19-year sentence. An unrepentant fascist, he headed the Italian neo-fascist movement until his death.

References: DAB, EB, wiki. www.it.wikipedia. Porg.

GRUNITZKY, Nicolas
(Togo, 1913–1969)

Nicolas Grunitzky served as prime minister of an autonomous Togo in the French Union and later returned (after a coup) to be president for four years before being overthrown himself. Grunitzky was the son of a Polish officer in the German army and a Togolese mother. Within a year of his birth the British and French had driven the Germans out of

Togo during World War I. Grunitzky was educated in France, where he took an engineering degree. In Togo he worked for a time in the civil service before establishing a successful construction business.

Grunitzky entered politics during World War II, siding with the Free French when the colonies were taken over by the fascist Vichy government, which was in league with the German occupation forces. Grunitzky earned Gaullist support after the war for his loyalty, but it was not enough to win him election to the French assembly in 1946. The opposition to his pro-French party was led by the nationalist party of his brother-in-law, Sylvanus OLYMPIO. Between 1951 and 1958, however, Grunitzky held a place in the French national assembly. When Olympio boycotted the 1955 territorial elections, Grunitzky's group took control of the territorial assembly. In 1956 Grunitzky became prime minister, but his close ties to the colonial administration made him highly unpopular.

In 1958 the United Nations' supervised elections swept Grunitzky from power, and Olympio led Togo to independence in 1960. Grunitzky founded a new party, but it lost every seat it contested, and he left the country to pursue business in Côte d'Ivoire. He returned to Togo to become president after the assassination of Olympio. Grunitzky attempted to govern with a multiparty coalition and with northern support, but he failed. Demonstrations against his government dogged his four years in office, the economy slumped, and the government was badly divided. The army finally intervened and removed Grunitzky, who returned to Côte d'Ivoire and his prosperous transport business there. He died in an auto accident while in exile in Paris.

References: DAHB, MMA, PLBA, *wiki*.

GUÈYE, Lamine
(Sénégal, 1891–1968)

Dr. Lamine Guèye, an early nationalist leader, organized French-speaking Africa's first modern political party. A transition figure between colonial resistance and independence, he remained active in politics until his death.

Like most early African leaders in Sénégal, Guèye was a founding member of the Young Sénégalese, an activist group of educated elite. He fought in France in World War I and stayed there to study, receiving a doctorate. In 1921 he became the first Black lawyer in French-speaking Africa. As part of the anticolonial opposition to Blaise DIAGNE, who dominated African politics, Guèye was elected mayor of Saint-Louis and served from 1924 to 1926. The two later reconciled, and Diagne arranged Guèye's appointment as a magistrate in Réunion, 1931–1934. Guèye continued to challenge African politicians who supported government colonial policy, however, and in 1934 and 1936 he ran against Galandou DIOUF, whom he had supported against Diagne and who subsequently had moved away from an anticolonial position.

In 1935, Guèye took over the Sénégalese Socialist Party, reorganized it along modern lines to attract the educated elite, and affiliated it with the international Socialist movement. During World War II all political activity was suspended, but by 1945, Guèye's Socialist Party was the best-prepared party in the country. With his protege, Léopold Sédar SENGHOR, Guèye was elected to the French National Assembly. Until that time, full French citizenship had been enjoyed only by a small group of Sénégalese, but Guèye championed the rights of all colonial subjects in West and North Africa, winning the right of French citizenship for colonial subjects in a stunning victory. Guèye and Senghor rejected Félix HOUPHOUËT-BOIGNY's formation of an interterritorial progressive party, effectively taking Sénégal on a separate political path.

In 1946, Guèye became mayor of Dakar, Sénégal's major city, a position that he held until 1961. He lost his seat in the French Chamber of Deputies in 1951 after Senghor broke with him and began another, mass-based party. The two reconciled, however, over the issue of federation for the former French colonies, which was opposed by Houphouët-Boigny, who feared that Côte d'Ivoire would be held back by less developed states. Guèye and Senghor advocated federation but found their position rejected. Sénégal then formed the Mali Federation in 1959 with Mali, but it soon became embroiled in conflicts over leadership and was dissolved in 1960. Sénégal became an independent republic with Guèye as president of the National Assembly.

References: afr, DAHB, EWB, MMA, PLBA. Guèye, *Itinéraire Africain* (African journal, 1966).

GUNGUNYANE
(Mozambique, 1850?–1906)

Gungunyane was the last independent ruler of Gaza, an empire in southern Mozambique, and was a leader of the resistance to Portuguese colonialism. When his father died in 1884, the royal succession was unclear. With Portuguese support, Gungunyane seized the throne in a coup, but several rivals escaped into neighboring areas, where they continued to harass him throughout his reign. The Gaza empire was multiethnic and based on the assimilation of various Nguni linguistic groups as well as other conquered peoples. Gungunyane therefore faced two challenges: maintaining national unity and confronting Portuguese expansion.

At first, Gungunyane asked the British to establish a protectorate, but the Portuguese blocked this effort by claiming that they ruled the region. An Indo-Portuguese settler and trader had established a foothold and was expanding his private empire into Gazan territory, and added to this, Gungunyane's subject communities in the south were asserting their independence. In 1889, trying to bypass the trader's territory and consolidate his control in the south, Gungunyane moved the bulk of his people to the coast. This migration of 60,000 people caused economic dislocation, and the empire was seriously weakened.

His relations with Portugal experienced the same breakdown. He entered into a nonaggression treaty but at the same time harbored chiefs who were staunchly anti-Portuguese. He constantly intrigued with the British, inviting envoys and discussing mineral concessions with Cecil RHODES's British South Africa Company. Finally, the Portuguese moved against Gungunyane, and after a series of battles he was captured in 1895. The Gaza empire was dismembered, and Gungunyane and his 10 wives were exiled to the Azores, where he died. In 1985 his remains were returned to Mozambique, and he was enshrined as a national hero.

References: DAHB, MMA.

GURIRAB, Theo Ben
(Namibia, 1938–)

Theo Ben Gurirab, foreign minister of Namibia since independence, was the foreign affairs spokes-man for the South-West African People's Organization (SWAPO) and its representative to the United Nations (U.N.).

Gurirab was educated at mission schools and completed teacher training at the Augustineum Training College in Okahandja. Subsequently, he was sent to the United States for higher education in a program that SWAPO had established in the early 1960s to prepare future leaders for Namibia. He received BA and MA degrees in international relations from Temple University in Philadelphia and was named SWAPO representative in the United States. In 1972, Gurirab was appointed chief of the SWAPO mission at the U.N. This position was a key post, because South-West Africa was not a colony of South Africa, but technically a mandated territory administered for the U.N. by that country. There was a U.N. commission for South-West African (later Namibian) affairs, and in 1972, Hage GEINGOB was appointed a political officer on the commission. The goal of the two SWAPO representatives was to prevent any extension of apartheid into South-West Africa and to work for independence. Gurirab urged a complete arms embargo against South Africa, arguing that many of these arms were in fact transferred to Rhodesia, which was under U.N. sanctions.

Gurirab also worked on the 1978 U.N. formula that called for U.N.-directed elections at an early date. In 1981, Gurirab represented Namibia at the U.N. Geneva Conference, and in 1986 he was appointed secretary of foreign affairs for the SWAPO politburo. Because South Africa was using bases in Namibia to launch attacks against Angola, the withdrawal of South African troops from Namibia was linked to a settlement of the Angolan civil war. In 1988 the South Africans suffered serious political and military reverses and became open to implementing the 1978 U.N. formula. In exchange for a Cuban troop withdrawal from Angola, South African troops were withdrawn from Namibia, to be replaced by a U.N. peacekeeping force. Gurirab returned to Namibia to prepare for the elections, which were set for 1990.

Gurirab was appointed foreign minister in the new government and immediately began to negotiate its most difficult international issue: the future of Walvis Bay. This site was a South African enclave in Namibia that was not surrendered when Namibia became independent because it was not part of the U.N. trusteeship. It is Namibia's only deepwater port and housed a major South African military base. By 1994, Gurirab had negotiated a complete cession of sovereignty for Walvis Bay with guarantees for the property and civil rights of South African investors and residents. In 1999–2000 he chaired the United Nations General Assembly. He returned to Namibia to become prime minister, 2000–2005, and then speaker of the National Assembly.

References: RWWA, *wiki*.

HABRÉ, Hissène

(Chad, 1936?-)

Hissène Habrè was a leader of northern dissidents and later was president during a tumultuous period of civil war and invasion in Chad.

The northern territories in the Sahara Desert have always resisted central control and are virtually impossible to govern. During various periods since independence in 1960, the French have had to continue policing the area. Habré was born in the north and worked as a clerk for the French army. Both the French and President François TOMBALBAYE sought out talented northerners, and Habré became a deputy prefect. He was then sent to France for higher studies in overseas administration, which he followed by obtaining a degree in law.

Returning to Chad in 1971, Habré worked in the ministry of foreign affairs. After being sent to Tripoli to negotiate with the head of the National Liberation Front (Frolinat), he defected to the opposition. He allied himself with Goukouni OUEDDEI in a separate faction and at one point captured several prominent Germans, for whom they were paid a large ransom. The two split over the incident, and Habré was reduced for a time to leading a few hundred soldiers. In 1976 he had his first major clash with Libyan troops, who had invaded to take advantage of the situation. By 1978 there were several Frolinat factions and counterfactions. Habré made his peace with the new president, Félix MALLOUM, who appointed him prime minister in a government of national union. Within a year, fighting once again erupted, and Habré took control of the capital, Ndjamena. Civil strife, negotiations by regional powers, and turmoil characterized the next several years in Chad. At one point in 1980, Habré, who was defense minister, and President Oueddei both had forces contesting one another for control of the capital. Libya moved into this political vacuum in 1981, forced Oueddei to sign a treaty of union between the two countries, and helped him defeat Habré. The treaty with Libya angered most Chadians and caused a strong reaction among other African states. Habré regrouped his forces, the Libyans were forced to withdraw, and

Oueddei was defeated. Habré became president in 1982.

Oueddei's forces continued to fight, using Libyan aid, and Habré soon attracted further foreign support, including French troops. The struggle continued until 1987, with Habré steadily advancing. He captured the main Libyan air base that year, closing off Libya's air cover and seizing a billion dollars' worth of equipment. In 1990 the victorious armed forces under General Idriss DÉBY turned against Habré in a sudden coup and within a month had swept him from office. Habré took political asylum in Sénégal, ending a confused and destructive period in north-central Africa. In Sénégal he has proved an embarrassment to President Abdoulaye WADE after Belgium indicted Habré on charges of mass killings and torture during his presidency. A Chadian inquiry accused him of 40,000 political murders and 200,000 cases of torture. Wade placed Habré under house arrest but refused to extradite him to Belgium amidst a storm of protest over handing an African over to a former colonial power. In 2006, the case was referred to the African Union heads of state, who rejected the idea of a trial outside Africa.

References: afr, CB, DAHB, PLBA, RWWA.

HABYARIMANA, Juvénal

(Rwanda, 1937–1994)

General Juvénal Habyarimana, military president of Rwanda for over 20 years, worked at easing ethnic tensions between the majority Hutu population and their traditional overlords, the Tutsi. His assassination came at a crucial juncture in peace negotiations and touched off a wave of violence and slaughter that shocked the world.

Habyarimana was born in the far north of Rwanda and was educated in the Belgian Congo (now the Democratic Republic of the Congo), where he spent a year in medical school before dropping out to become a soldier. His military success was immediate; two years after being commissioned one of the first officers in Rwanda's National Guard in 1961, he became chief of staff, and in 1965 he was made minister of defense under President Grégoire KAYIBANDA.

The adjustment to independence was painful for Rwanda, where the feudal Tutsi rulers had been favored for education and leadership by the Belgian colonial office. The first years of independence were marked by open clashes between the Tutsi and the Hutu, the latter of whom had taken power at the independence elections by virue of their much greater numbers. In 1963 a group of Tutsi exile rebels invaded, and Habyarimana successfully repulsed them, but this action was followed by a bloodbath of revenge in which 10,000 Tutsi died and more than 150,000 were driven into exile. In 1969 even larger numbers were killed and exiled, mostly north to neighboring Uganda.

Deteriorating economic conditions and discontent among junior Hutu officers led Habyarimana to stage a bloodless coup in 1973. He immediately set to work to relieve ethnic tensions, but he gave most of his government appointments to northerners, adding regional resentments to ethnic tensions. He imposed a single-party system but also eliminated ethnic identity cards (which were later reinstated) and attempted to mend relations with Burundi and Uganda, both of which had received large numbers of Tutsi refugees.

Several events influenced Rwanda's political crisis by the early 1990s. One of the most densely populated countries in the world, Rwanda is mountainous and has little arable land. The drop in world coffee prices in 1989 caused the president to introduce an austerity program that was extremely unpopular. Habyarimana began cautious political liberalization and authorized a political opposition, partly in response to pressure from foreign aid donors. In 1990 a large Tutsi rebel force, led and armed by Ugandan army officers from the refugee population there, invaded from the north. They were contained at great cost and only with French military support, but the Rwandese army was unable to expel them, and they settled into semipermanent camps in the Ruwenzori Mountains, the "Mountains of the Moon."

Habyarimana accelerated his reform program and opened peace talks with the rebels. The early 1990s, however, saw growing paranoia in the administration, and Habyarimana retreated from his conciliatory position to one of blaming the Tutsi for all of Rwanda's problems. By 1993 the invaders were close to the capital, and in April 1994, before any political resolution was possible, Habyarimana's jet was brought down by rockets that killed him and the president of Burundi. There is evidence that the plane was destroyed by elements of the hardline Hutu Presidential Guard, which opposed the peace talks. They subsequently unleashed a vindictive slaughter of Tutsi that was unprecedented even in Rwanda's bloody history. At first, all supporters of reconciliation were targeted, including moderate Hutu leaders. Then the carnage spread to mass killings of Tutsi, including the elderly and children. It is perhaps the saddest chapter in Rwanda's tortured history, and the world's worst genocide since World War II.

References: afr, DAHB, DRWW, PLBA, RWWA, *wiki*.

HAGGARD, H(enry) Rider
(South Africa, 1856–1925)

Sir H. Rider Haggard was an English romance novelist and one of the most popular writers of his generation. Although he lived in South Africa only briefly, the impact of his writing was such that it shaped popular Western images of the continent for generations.

At age 19, Haggard went to South Africa as secretary to the governor of Natal. When the Transvaal was annexed to the British Empire in 1877, he was on the special commissioner's staff. He stayed in the Transvaal to become registrar of the high court, but in 1879, after only four years in South Africa, he returned to England. There he married an heiress, and thereafter he returned to South Africa for only one brief visit. He studied law and was admitted to the bar in 1884, but largely devoted himself to writing.

On the basis of his limited experience, Haggard wrote popular adventure literature about Africa. He portrayed the continent as romantic, exotic and full of opportunities for a European to prove his heroic stature through generous bravery. In all his novels, his African characters are cardboard creations with little real personality. It should be noted, however, that Haggard did little to develop character in his writing; adventure was the main feature.

Haggard wrote an astounding 76 books, mostly potboilers ground out at a rate of three or four a year. Of the 58 novels, *King Solomon's Mines* (1885) and *She* (1887) are the best known. Both are still in print and show his writing's limited imagination, drama and narrative. *King Solomon's Mines* is based on legends of fabulous cities and gold mines in the interior of Africa, and the story has been filmed several times. The novel's style creates breathless suspense as the reader is led from one adventure to another. The White adventurers are always handsome and brave, while the Africans are always treacherous or simpleminded (with an occasional loyal retainer who turns out to be a secret prince). These images fixed a generation's notions of Africans as being primitive, in awe of the superior White man, with no enduring cultural values and steeped in superstition.

Haggard remained active in public life and in contact with the colonial establishment. He also had a genuine concern for the plight of the poor. His *Rural England* (1902) was a trenchant description of the breakdown of rural society. In 1905 he was appointed to a commission studying resettlement in South Africa for British slum dwellers, but he did not favor the scheme. He spent five years traveling around the world as a member of the Dominions Royal Commission and made several other overseas trips on behalf of colonial resettlement strategies for war veterans. His various writings on public policy were numerous and are better than his fiction in quality. His enduring legacy is his shaping of popular Western ideas about Africa and Africans.

References: DAHB, DLB, DNB, wiki. Haggard, *The Days of My Life* (1926); Norman Etherington, *Rider Haggard* (1984); D.S. Higgins, *Rider Haggard: The Great Storyteller* (1981).

HAIDALLA, Mohammed Khouna Ould
(Mauritania, 1940–)

Lieutenant-Colonel Mohammed Khouna Ould Haidalla, military prime minister and president of Mauritania for four years, was removed in a coup after the failure of his policy in the disastrous conflict with the Polisario revolutionary movement in the Western Sahara.

After finishing secondary school locally, Haidalla joined the army. He was sent to Saint-Cyr, the French military academy, from 1962 to 1964, and was commissioned a second lieutenant. He held several commands and received further training in France.

In 1976, Mauritania joined with Morocco to divide the former Spanish Sahara (also known as Western Sahara or the Shawari Republic), despite the existence of a nationalist movement, Polisario, which began fighting to establish an independent country. In 1976, Haidalla received a formal commendation for his defense of Nouakchott, the capital, and went on to distinguish himself for his desert campaigns. When Mauritania was unable to extricate itself from the war, the army removed Prime Minister Moktar DADDAH in 1978, and Haidalla was named prime minister and chief of staff by the military council. In 1980 he led a council coup that removed the acting head of state, and Haidalla proclaimed himself president.

At first Haidalla followed a liberal policy. He abolished slavery (Mauritania was the last government to do so) and began to bring civilians into the government. After several coup attempts, however, he retreated and in 1981 named Colonel Maawiya Ould TAYA as prime minister to replace a civilian leader. He then established Islamic law (*sharia*) as part of the penal code, allowing its more severe punishments such as amputation, to be imposed. Moreover, slavery had not been suppressed and soon reappeared in Mauritanian society.

Haidalla's greatest successes were to sign a peace treaty with Polisario, renounce all claims to the Western Sahara, and withdraw Mauritanian troops. The military leadership was split over this issue, and in 1984, Taya led a bloodless coup that removed Haidalla. He was placed in detention, was released on an amnesty in 1988 and retired. He emerged to contest unsuccessfully for the presidency in 2003.

References: DAHB, PLBA.

HAILE MICHAEL, Kidane Mariam
(Ethiopia, 1940–)

Dr. Kidane Mariam Haile Michael is a plant physiologist engaged in field research to increase the yield of potato crops. He has developed at least two varieties of potato and has organized a national program for Ethiopia, where food shortages and famine have been continual problems.

After graduating from the University of Addis Ababa in 1962, Haile Michael studied at the University of California, Davis (MA, 1965), and the University of Wisconsin (Ph.D., 1972). From 1962 to 1981 he was associated with the University of Addis Ababa, becoming director of research for the College of Agriculture and head of its horticulture program. The famine of the late 1970s and the increasing repression of the Marxist government under MENGISTU Haile Mariam finally made conditions intolerable. The 1976–1978 Red Terror period, during which educated Ethiopians were purged, also made life increasingly hazardous for anyone with a foreign education, especially an American one. In addition, by 1981 the government had nationalized 820,000 acres of commercial farmland for state farms, and Ethiopian agriculture was in crisis. Research was almost impossible under these conditions.

Haile Michael left for neighboring Kenya in 1981 to join the staff of the International Potato Centre, which does research on new varieties of potatoes and protects the gene pool so that variants do not become extinct. From 1983 to 1986 he was a visiting scientist at the University of Wisconsin. Then he rejoined the Potato Centre in charge of its eastern and southern Africa programs. At the Potato Centre, his major research interests have been incorporating genetic resistance to late blight and bacterial wilt.

Reference: PAS.

HAILE SELASSIE
(Ethiopia, 1892–1975)

Emperor Haile Selassie was the last emperor of Ethiopia. His death ended a long line of emperors and empresses going back centuries. He brought his country into the mainstream of African politics in the modern period. With Haile Selassie, the Ethiopian Empire reached its high point and then abruptly ended. As the best-known African in the world during the twentieth century because of his heroic stand against Italian fascism, Haile Selassie became a symbol of freedom to Africans across the continent.

He was born into a royal family and named Tafari Makonnen. His father was a cousin and chief advisor of Emperor MENELIK II. Marked for advancement, Tafari became governor of a small province in his teens and then governor of Harar, an important center. He took the title of Ras Tafari, by which he is often known. Provincial governors had considerable independence and often operated as warlords, jockeying for power and contending with one another. The emperor was dependent upon them for troops in times of crisis. Ras Tafari built his base shrewdly and soon emerged as the most powerful provincial leader in the country. He became the leading candidate to be the next emperor, both because of his ability and because he was a member of the line that traced its descent to King Solomon.

Ethiopian palace politics were a network of intricate intrigues, and the succession process was the most complex and potentially dangerous of these. In 1909, MENELIK became incapacitated and real authority passed to his empress, TAITU. She hoped to succeed her husband, but he named a grandson, IYASU V, who took the throne in 1913 but was never officially crowned. Iyasu was a weak and ineffectual ruler, increasingly enamored of Islam. His intentions of converting Ethiopia into an Islamic state upset the Coptic Christian nobility. In 1916, after attempting to remove Ras Tafari as governor and replace him with a Muslim, Iyasu was deposed. In 1916, when Iyasu fled, his father marched on Addis Ababa, the capital, but was killed. Iyasu himself was captured in 1921 and imprisoned for life. At this point Ras Tafari was not yet powerful enough to take the throne on his own, and so Taitu installed her choice, her stepdaughter ZAUDITU, as empress. There were two conditions for her assuming the position: that she divorce her husband and rule alone and that Ras Tafari be regent.

Zauditu was conservative, religious and bent on maintaining traditional society. Ras Tafari was a progressive who wanted to modernize the state. As a power behind the throne, he was able to implement many of his ideas. He obtained membership for Ethiopia in the League of Nations in 1923 and toured Europe and the Middle East the following year, seeking diplomatic recognition. Under Ras Tafari's reforms, schools were built and slavery was abolished. For 10 years he maneuvered and positioned himself, gradually eliminating the threats to his authority. In 1926, Zauditu's chief minister died

Emperor Haile Selassie of Ethiopia rides in parade along with U.S. President John F. Kennedy, October 1963.

and Ras Tafari took command of his army. Zauditu became alarmed at his growing power, so she made moves to curb him in 1928, but she was too late. Her maneuvers provided Ras Tafari with the opening to make her give him the title of *negus,* or king. He then ordered her estranged husband, Gugsa Wolie, to report to the capital, and when he refused he was killed in battle in 1930. Zauditu died of shock upon hearing the news, and Ras Tafari was crowned emperor in a lavish ceremony. He took the name Haile Selassie ("Might of the Trinity").

Haile Selassie immediately used his power to promulgate a new constitution limiting the powers of parliament and extend his authority into the provinces. He strengthened the police and army and phased out feudal taxation in favor of a modern system. Army reform was the most important element in his program. Using his own Harar force and the army he had obtained from Zauditu's chief minister as his base, he began to establish a standing army trained by Belgians and Swiss to replace the feudal armies under the control of provincial governors. His plans, however, were cut short by the Italian invasion of Ethiopia in 1935. The feudal levies were totally inadequate, and Ethiopia went to war with a ragtag collection of peasants bearing spears and single-shot rifles against a modern, well-equipped force that was anxious to prove its mettle and to avenge the Ethiopian defeat of Italy at Adowa in 1895.

The Italian invasion and occupation of Ethiopia became a symbol far greater than its actual international impact. It was seen by many African leaders as the last gasp of imperialism, Europe's final gambit in the scramble for Africa, and a call to resistance. In the West it was often interpreted as a rehearsal for World War II, an opportunity for Italy to test its war machine. In Italy itself it was viewed as a great triumph, making Italy at last a major power and infusing the nation with a sense of national pride. It was Haile Selassie who transformed the Western understanding of the situation as the destruction of a proud and ancient civilization under the jackboot of fascism. Going into exile in 1936, he appeared before the League of Nations in a dramatic appeal for support: "God and history will remember your judgment ... it is international morality that is at stake." As he walked off to an embarrassed scattering of applause, Haile Selassie muttered prophetically, "It is us today. It will be you tomorrow."

After a short, brutal occupation, Haile Selassie formed an exile army in the Sudan, and British and Ethiopian forces successfully retook the country in 1941. After regaining his throne, Haile Selassie began a program of development that altered Ethiopian society irrevocably. In the process, he centered all authority around himself, and his court took on some of the same elements of intrigue and conspiracy that had plagued courts of earlier emperors. He also ignored the claims of various regions and subject peoples, because he was intent on preventing regional rulers from regaining independent authority. He failed to recognize that the new dynamic of regionalism was not dependent upon warlords but upon rising ethnic consciousness, fueled by the spectacle of the African independence movement all across the continent. One major achievement in this period was the creation of an autonomous Ethiopian Coptic Orthodox Church with an Ethiopian patriarch independent of Cairo.

The challenges to Ethiopia were significant: political threats and severe economic limitations. The first concern was to limit the influence of the British, who did not withdraw immediately after the liberation. They administered Eritrea until 1952 under a United Nations (U.N.) mandate and occupied the Ogaden and other areas of Ethiopia until 1955. Haile Selassie was also dependent upon Britain for foreign aid. In addition, he had to redefine province borders and appoint governors loyal to him. Until the end of his reign he faced a series of insurrections, especially in Eritrea. A coup mounted by the palace guard in 1960 was defeated by the army, but not before the guard had executed a number of power brokers in the court.

The economic problems were also long-lasting. Ethiopia had a basic infrastructure of roads, bridges and public buildings, mostly built by the Italians with forced labor. Haile Selassie sought extensive foreign aid and, at various times, received assistance from the United States, Israel, the Soviet Union and the Scandinavian countries. He was able to improve education considerably, building a university and many schools, and he modernized communications, banking and electric power. Italy and Yugoslavia built dams for him. The national airline became competitive and profitable, and the military was trained and professionalized. Nevertheless, land reform, which was often attempted, was never realized, so the lives of peasants improved little. Haile Selassie made only token attempts at democratizing the political system, leaving the growing number of professionals and educated Ethiopians increasingly dissatisfied. University students increasingly became a new source of opposition to the emperor.

Haile Selassie worked at establishing Ethiopia as a leading voice in Africa. As the only other African state besides Liberia that was never colonized, it had an aura in the postwar period that reflected on the emperor himself. The Economic Commission for Africa was established in Addis Ababa in 1958, and in 1960 the second conference of independent states was held there. This meeting was followed in 1963 by the first continental meeting of African heads of state, over which Haile Selassie presided. The headquarters of the Organization of African Unity (OAU) was established in Addis Ababa in 1964. As a major voice in this organization, Haile Selassie was responsible for including in the OAU charter a provision respecting the borders established by the colonial powers. While this provision avoided numbers of clashes (and protected his claims to the Somali-speaking Ogaden), it also ratified often irrational colonial boundaries that divided ethnic groups. In various other ways, Haile Selassie made himself a respected African figure. He offered support to African independence movements, sponsored ceasefire talks between the Biafran rebels and the Nigerian government in their civil war, and helped negotiate the 1972 settlement between General Gaafar NIMEIRY and the southern Sudanese.

After the 1960 coup attempt, Haile Selassie made further efforts to broaden political participation. He allowed the prime minister to appoint the cabinet and arranged for elections. He did little to loosen the reins of power, however, and opposition to the pace of change mounted amid his hints about possible retirement. The "creeping revolution" began in 1973 with a serious drought that killed over 100,000. The government attempted to minimize the importance of the crisis, and angered many peasants. Opposition became widespread in a series of strikes, army mutinies and student demonstrations. By mid-1974, Haile Selassie had been isolated, and a military council had established control. Over the summer his government was dismantled, and in September he was placed under house arrest. He was murdered in his cell in 1975 by order of the Dergue, the Marxist military regime that replaced him. His body was recovered from an unmarked grave in the palace in 1992 and was buried with honors.

Haile Selassie was a short but imposing man with piercing eyes and regal carriage. He operated in modern offices surrounded by flamboyant symbols of power. When he was driven in one of his Rolls-Royces, his subjects prostrated themselves beside the road. He was guarded by cheetahs and lions (his noblest title was Lion of Judah) and trailed by attendants. He was the incarnation of the benevolent patriarch, but he used his power to dismantle the Ethiopian imperial systems and destroy its feudal network of allegiances. He was not able, however, to create a modern state to replace it.

References: AB, *afr*, CB, DAB, DAHB, EB, HWL, MMA, PLBA, PLCA, WGMC, *wiki*. Selassie, *My Life and Ethiopia's Progress, 1892–1937* (1976); Colin Legum, *Ethiopia: The Fall of Haile Selassie's Empire* (1975); Hans Lockot, *The Mission, the Life, Reign, and Character of Haile Sellassie I* (1989).

HAMALLAH Haydara, Amadou

(Mali/Mauritania, 1886–1943)

Sheikh Amadou Hamallah Haydara was the proponent of the doctrine of an Islamic mystical brotherhood that turned from religious reform to insurgency and later evolved into an independence movement.

As a youth, Hamallah was known for his precocious knowledge of the Koran and other Islamic works. He was recognized as a *marabout*, a Muslim teacher and spiritual guide, and joined the Tijaniyya brotherhood. Each brotherhood teaches a unique way (*tariq*) to reach mystical communion with God, and for the Tijaniyya it is a form of prayer beads. During Hamallah's youth a reform movement to purify the sect began among the Tijaniyya. Hamallah seems to have allied himself with this new group, and in 1909 he was chosen as successor to the leader after a nine-year search by a

wandering disciple seeking mystical signs of who might be the "chosen one."

Hamallah's influence grew, and he soon acquired a large following throughout the region. Wearing white, never preaching, and rarely going out in public, Hamallah devoted himself to prayer and mortification. He regularly entered ecstatic states in which he communed directly with Allah or the Prophet Muhammad. He began sending out disciples who converted large numbers of Africans, swearing them to lifetime personal obedience to Hamallah. They recruited heavily among slaves, Blacks, and other socially marginal people. Although he taught radical ideas, such as the freedom of youth from parental authority and the equality of women at worship, Hamallah ignored other social and secular questions.

Because the Tijaniyya supported the French, breakaway groups such as the Hamallists were regarded with suspicion. Hamallah himself attempted to ignore the French and never spoke out against them, but he could not control his most tempestuous followers. While the subsequent violence appeared to be over religious orthodoxy, it actually masked Hamallist resentment with factions that supported colonialism. Conflicts broke out between the Hamallists and other brotherhood sects in 1917 and 1923, and when a bloody clash occurred in 1924, the French deported Hamallah to Mauritania in 1925. In 1930, following an assault on a district office that resulted in considerable loss of life, Hamallah was charged with fomenting dissent and was transferred to Côte d'Ivoire. Instead of isolation, however, Hamallah drew the support of Ivoirian leaders, especially Galandou DIOUF and Lamine GUÈYE. Freed in 1935, he returned to a hero's welcome. Some followers thought he was the Mahdi, the savior who would usher in the final victory of Islam, and began to pray in the direction of his capital rather than toward Mecca.

Violence peaked in 1940 when three of Hamallah's sons led an attack on a rival group, killing over 400, including many women and children. The French executed the leaders, including Hamallah's sons, and deported Hamallah to France, where he began a fast that contributed to his death in 1943. The brotherhood went underground during this period, but Hamallism continued after his death, at first with armed resistance, and then as the core of the Rassemblement Démocratique Africain (RDA), a new anticolonial party, which led the way to independence in French West Africa.

References: DAHB, MMA.

HANI, Chris Martin Thembisile

(South Africa, 1942–1993)

Chris Martin Thembisile Hani was one of the most charismatic leaders of the South African antiapartheid struggle and a chief exponent of armed resistance. Until his assassination, he was a dominant figure in the African National Congress (ANC) and the Communist Party of South Africa (CPSA) as well as the acknowledged leader of the younger generation of Black activists who came to adulthood after apartheid was in place.

As a youngster, Hani aspired to the Catholic priesthood, but his father refused him permission to enter the seminary. He read Latin at Fort Hare and Rhodes Universities. Intense study of the conflict between the Roman nobility and the commoners, combined with the impact of Charles Dickens's fictional portrayals of Victorian England, influenced his class-focused interpretation of politics. His political formation was completed by his family. His father, an ANC activist, was banished and sought asylum in Lesotho the year Hani received his degree. In addition, one of his uncles was a member of the CPSA.

Hani became a member of the ANC Youth Wing at age 15, and two years after its 1960 banning he joined Umkhonto wa Sizwe ("Spear of the Nation"), the ANC's guerilla military branch. At Fort Hare, he joined protests against the takeover of the university by the Department of Bantu Education and in 1961 was expelled for political activism. Within a few months of Hani's involvement with Umkhonto, he was a member of the leadership cadre, the Committee of Seven. A few months later he was arrested under the Suppression of Communism Act, the first of several arrests. By 1963, with his appeals exhausted, Hani went underground and was sent out of the country for military training.

The next years were spent in exile in Zambia, Botswana, Lesotho and Southern Rhodesia (now Zimbabwe), where he served the liberation struggle. In Rhodesia, he took part in three battles as commissar of the Lutuli Brigade in a joint ANC-ZAPU (Zimbabwe African People's Union) campaign against Rhodesian forces. After moving to Botswana in 1967, he was sentenced for weapons possession and served two years in prison. By 1974 he was secretly back in South Africa as a political organizer for the ANC. He was subsequently elected to the National Executive at age 32. In 1978, Hani returned to Lesotho and the guerrilla forces. In 1982 there were several attempts on his life, including a car bombing, and the ANC moved him to Zambia, where its political leadership was centered.

Hani was political commissar (1983–1987) and later chief of staff and deputy commander of Umkhonto wa Sizwe (1987–1992?), assuming responsibility for political discipline among the guerrilla forces. During 1983, in one of the first challenges to his discipline, dissident ANC members (who were confined in detention camps) mutinied against their harsh treatment, and Hani was a key figure in the suppression of the uprising. He always denied that he took part in the torture and murders that followed, however.

In 1990, when the ban on the ANC was lifted, Hani returned to South Africa. By this time he was well known as a member of the CPSA and a close associate of Joe SLOVO, its general secretary and his colleague on the ANC Executive. These two men represented the worst fears of conservative South African leaders and stirred deep feelings of dread and dismay. But with the freeing of Oliver TAMBO and Nelson MANDELA, a new and legal chapter of the ANC's history began. By 1992, Hani had stepped down as head of Umkhonto wa Sizwe in order to devote more time to CPSA organizing. The Communists, although they were a major presence in both the ANC and the Council of South African Trade Unions, were under fire. The collapse of Marxism in Europe had discredited the movement, and with it the old policy of infiltration into other antiapartheid groups instead of independent action. A further crisis faced the first legal meeting of the CPSA in December 1991—the revelation that Joe Slovo had cancer.

Hani was elected secretary-general to replace Slovo, effectively removing him from consideration as a possible successor to the aging Mandela. Radicals were dismayed as they watched the shift in the ANC toward a more moderate leadership. The CPSA began to define itself independently under Hani, making clear that it would take part in constitutional negotiations with the government as a separate entity. Simultaneously, a massive recruitment campaign began in the townships, often pitting the CPSA against the ANC. Overall, the CPSA came out the winner, especially among young people with no memories of pre-apartheid days and with little commitment to the democratic ideals of Mandela and the mainline ANC. Smiling, energetic, passionate and charismatic, Hani began to attract a cultlike following. A number of squatter camps were named in his honor. He was also the only national leader able to rein in the radical township self-defense groups that had shed the ANC's authority.

In April 1993, as Hani was returning home to the racially mixed suburb where he lived with his wife and three daughters, he was assassinated by an anti-Communist Polish refugee with close links to the White nationalist Afrikaner Resistance Movement. Hani's death shocked the nation and in particular staggered members of the ANC and the CPSA. His death also came at a critical moment, just as the CPSA was achieving independent status. Lacking basic organization, and bereft of funds because of European communism's collapse, the party was thrown into disarray by this major setback. There was no one of Hani's stature or charisma to replace him. Despite some minor violence, however, Hani's assassination did not derail the constitutional negotiations, a sure sign of the distance that the antiapartheid movement had traveled toward stabilization.

References: afr, GSAP, PLBA, RWWA, *wiki*.

de la HARPE, Wendy
(South Africa, 1940s-)

Wendy de la Harpe, a founding member of the Zimbabwe National Ballet Company, has been for some years the director of Outreach for the Ballet Idaho in Boise. She is one of the most prominent African choreographers.

De la Harpe was trained at the Arts Educational Trust in London, and is a registered teacher of the Royal Academy of Dance. She has taught ballet and jazz in England, South Africa, Zimbabwe, Canada and the United States. In addition, she has brought her skills to television and the stage. In her early years she was dance director for Sun City, the largest and most developed resort in Africa. She also choreographed musicals for South African national television (SABC).

In the United States during the 1980s, de la Harpe choreographed a number of successful musical productions—*West Side Story*; *Applause, Applause;* and *Little Shop of Horrors* on Broadway, and *Grease* in Los Angeles. In Portland, Oregon she choreographed a ballet in tribute to Nelson MANDELA on his release from prison. Her television work includes two recent productions for SABC for African Renaissance for President Thabo MBEKI and the Africa Telekom Conference. For 10 years, she was artistic director for the Colombia Dance Ensemble in Vancouver, British Columbia.

De la Harpe has also produced her own *African Experience* for the 1999 Edinburgh Festival. She trained youth from the Soweto slums in the style used for informal dance in the worker's hostels in the South African mines. They dance in the only footwear they have, gumboots (rubber galoshes), producing a rhythmic stomping effect. Along with dancers from Mali, they also performed traditional fertility and war dances.

Her credits include many corporate events for clients like Nedbank, JP Morgan, and numerous international automobile corporations. One of her favorite programs is the annual fundraiser for The Sports Trust of South Africa, for which she returns to South Africa each year. Her reputation is such that she draws performers of the caliber of Bill Cosby and global celebrities such as President Nelson Mandela and Senator Hillary Clinton. She arranges, choreographs and directs these extravaganzas with aplomb and professional competence. As one amazed colleague remarked, she "has achieved what no one believed possible."

Similar comments are made about her current work in dance education. She has served as an artist-in-residence in elementary schools under a National Endowment for the Humanities grant. "My philosophy is to get children to love it." Through all her other commitments, de la Harpe returns regularly to work on projects in South Africa.

Reference: adb.

HARRIS, William Wadé
(Ghana/Côte d'Ivoire/Liberia, 1865?–1929)

Prophet William Wadé Harris was one of the earliest figures at the beginnings of the independent church movement, which brings together Christian and traditional African practices. Although his church was suppressed, separatist groups invoking him as their founder flourish today in Côte d'Ivoire and Ghana.

Harris became an Episcopalian lay preacher and school principal in Liberia after spending his youth as a sailor. In 1907 he was appointed as a government interpreter, but due to his advocacy of interior peoples' rights against the Americo-Liberian elite, he was fired the following year. When he protested, he was unfairly accused of complicity in a British coup attempt against President Arthur Barclay and was jailed. In prison he had a vision of the archangel Gabriel, who told him he would become a prophet.

On his release in 1912, Harris began preaching along the coast in Côte d'Ivoire and Ghana. In 1914 his Ivoirian crusade baptized more than 100,000. Wearing a white robe and turban, carrying a staff topped by a cross, and with a full white beard, he fostered the image of himself as a biblical prophet. Harris taught a strict opposition to witchcraft and many traditional religious practices and was popularly accepted as an exorcist and faith healer. Nonetheless, he accepted polygamy, and several of his wives accompanied him on his travels. In his preaching, which was initially accepted by the French colonial administration, he insisted on temperance and hard work. As his converts increased, however, the French felt threatened by the political implications of a mass movement. They forbade preaching in any language other than French, arrested and deported Harris to Liberia, and burned his churches. Meanwhile, Catholic and Methodist missionaries took advantage of the revival to recruit from among those Harris had evangelized. Harris continued to preach in Liberia but was never very successful in his homeland.

It is unclear whether Harris intended to establish a full-fledged independent church, although his chief disciple declared that before his death, Harris had ordained him to carry out such a mission. The Église Harriste, a congregation descended from the 1914 converts, is a significant Christian church in Côte d'Ivoire. In 1998, the Harrists joined the World Council of Churches, and membership has also spread into Europe and the United States with African immigrants. Harris was the first of the major prophetic African leaders, and he had the greatest impact of any itinerant preacher.

References: dacb, DAHB, MMA. Gordon Haliburton, *The Prophet Harris* (1973); Sheila Walker, *The Religious Revolution in the Ivory Coast* (1983).

HAYATU Ibn Said
(Nigeria, 1840?–1898)

Sultan Hayatu Ibn Said was one of the Islamic religious and political leaders in the Mahdist revival movements of the 1880s.

Hayatu was a great-grandson of UTHMAN Dan Fodio, founder of the Sokoto caliphate in northern Nigeria. He hoped for a high position in the caliphate, and when he was unsuccessful, he left Sokoto for the town of Adamawa in the southeast area of the empire. Since the 1820s, the authority of the Sokoto caliphate had been so strong that neighboring areas had adopted social institutions under its influence. One result was the rise of chiefs among peoples who had not previously had such central political figures.

In 1881 in the Sudan, Muhammad Ahmad proclaimed himself the MAHDI, the chosen one of Allah who would rise to purify Islam and bring a reign that would drive out the infidels and create a new society. As the Mahdi began his campaign against the British, Hayatu became his proponent in Sokoto. The memory of the recent Islamic revival was still fresh, and Hayatu attracted numerous followers and established himself as a regional power. He took the title of sultan and preached a messianic doctrine of deliverance through the Mahdi. The Sokoto empire, however, refused to recognize the Mahdi, and its leadership considered him and Hayatu to be heretics.

When the Mahdist movement continued after its founder's death, Hayatu's growing power left the Sokoto empire uncomfortable for both religious and political reasons. In 1892, Zubeiry, the governor of Adamawa, challenged Hayatu in battle. Zubeiry was defeated, which only increased alarm in the other emirs (regional governors). Hayatu next turned toward the kingdom of Bornu, against which he allied with Rabeh Zubair, another Mahdist leader. Bornu fell in 1893, but Hayatu did not become its ruler, and Bornu was taken by Rabeh. Chafing under his secondary position, Hayatu tried to establish his political independence. He was killed in 1898 in a battle for supremacy with Rabeh. Nonetheless, Mahdist religious consciousness continued to grow and soon became a rallying point for resistance to British colonial expansion.

References: DAHB. Said, *Sultan Sa'idu Bin Hayatu Tells the Story of His and His Father's Life* (1978).

HEAD, Bessie Emery
(South Africa/Botswana, 1937–1986)

Bessie Emery Head, unlike many other South African exiles, remained along the borders of her homeland. Rejecting the urban and cultured European settings possible for her as a noted novelist, she lived in an experimental settlement based on rural self-sufficiency.

Born Bessie Amelia Emery in a mental asylum, illegitimate daughter of a wealthy White woman and one of the family stablehands, she spent her early life in foster care or orphanages. Her mixed-race status as the daughter of an illegal liaison always dogged her. After teacher training, she taught for four years and then began writing as a journalist for *Drum* magazine, the leading Black South African periodical. In 1964 she left a broken marriage and traveled to Botswana with her son to begin a new life. Granted refugee status, Head taught and began writing fiction based on her experiences. Finally, in 1979 she was granted Botswanan citizenship. She suffered from mental problems and spent a period in an institution as a result of bizarre behavior.

Her first novel, *When Rainclouds Gather* (1969) resulted from her refugee experience. It explored the tensions between her new freedom from oppression and the "extremely brutal and harsh" treatment that she received from Black Botswanans. Head returned to the question of ethnicity in *Maru* (1971), in which a new teacher, although educated and attractive, becomes a center of bitter conflict because of her heritage. In 1974, Head published *A Question of Power,* which is often regarded as her best work. The novel portrays the disturbing descent into the hell of mental breakdown. It explores an intense and convulsive disintegration that alternatively reflects the advancing madness of the heroine and of the racist society that breaks her spirit. All three of these novels deal with the outcast theme—the experience of one who lives in exile, physical or spiritual. She has often been identified as a feminist writer, but she rejected the label.

By the 1970s, Head had become involved in a rural collective at Serowe that helped to shape her response to the psychological struggles she experienced. Head paid tribute to the experience by saying: "All my life I lived in shattered little bits. All those shattered bits began to grow together here ... I have a peace against which all the turmoil is worked out." *The Collector of Treasures* (1977) is a short story anthology focusing on rural women's lives, in which the stories are told in a folkloric manner. In *Serowe* (1981), Head went further and based her novel on the oral histories of women whom she came to know at Serowe. It sweeps across a century of Botswana's history, closing with a lingering and affectionate view of life in the collective. At the age of 48, Bessie Head died of hepatitis.

References: AA, AB, *afr*, CANR, DLB, MMA, NRG, *wiki*, WLTC. Head, *A Woman Alone* (1990); Gillian Eilerson, *Bessie Head: Thunder Behind Her Ears* (1995).

HERTZOG, James Barry Munnik
(South Africa, 1866–1942)

Dr. James Barry Munnik Hertzog, a general in the Boer War, was prime minister of South Africa from 1924 to 1939. He placed South African interests before those of the British Empire and worked toward separate development for English-speaking South Africans and Afrikaners.

Hertzog was a native of the Orange Free State (OFS). Although he was the grandson of German immigrants, he identified completely with the community's Afrikaner roots, and in 1892, after local education, he received a doctorate in law in Amsterdam. He practiced law in Pretoria until 1895, when he became a judge of the OFS high court.

In 1899, Hertzog resigned his judgeship, and in 1900 he was appointed a general in the Free State forces in the Anglo-Boer War, rising to become deputy commander to General Christiaan De Wet. He proved himself a bold and resourceful guerrilla leader, taking his irregular forces on raids into the Cape Colony. He opposed negotiations with the British but finally accepted the inevitable and took an active and decisive role in the peace settlement.

Hertzog represented the hard-line Afrikaners and obtained important concessions, including Afrikaans language rights for the defeated Afrikaner republics.

After the war Hertzog became a dominant figure in OFS politics. He founded a party, Orangia-Unie, that fought for internal self-government, which the British granted in 1907. Hertzog became attorney general and minister of education in the first cabinet, where he followed his Afrikaner cultural policy firmly, dismissing school officials who did not accept his views on the superiority of Afrikaans over English. He was a delegate to the convention that drafted the South Africa Act by which the Union of South Africa was created, and Louis BOTHA appointed him to the first national cabinet as minister of justice.

In the cabinet Hertzog articulated his vision of separate but equal development for Afrikaners and English-speaking South Africans while segregating and subordinating the Black population. When Hertzog challenged Louis Botha in a 1912 public speech by advocating both his "Two Streams Policy" and "South Africa First," Botha forced him out of the cabinet. In 1914, Hertzog formed the National Party (NP) on a platform of South Africa's complete independence from Britain and opposed Botha's support of the Allies in World War I. Although never openly treasonous, Hertzog made no secret of his sympathy for the 1914 rebellion led by De Wet and defeated by military forces under General Jan Christiaan SMUTS. The NP steadily gained in each election and, after Botha's death in 1919, actually outpolled the South African Party, then under the leadership of Smuts, who was forced to govern with a coalition. Hertzog was the undisputed spokesman of the Afrikaners, who rejected Smuts as having sold out to international and imperial interests.

In 1924, with Labour Party support, Hertzog became prime minister. Although he was forced into a coalition with Smuts in 1933 (and merged their parties a year later into the United Party), he remained prime minister for a quarter century, placing his stamp on the country. Hertzog never wavered from Afrikaner nationalism and South African independence. Afrikaans was made an official language, and a segregationist racial policy was placed in effect. His greatest nationalist triumph was the Statute of Westminster (1931), in which Great Britain accepted South Africa's independent status. Hertzog adopted a new national flag to symbolize the new country. The restrictions on Blacks were the result of Hertzog's conviction that

Africans were inferior. Nonetheless, he had also to contend with their hostility in the Cape, where Black voters joined the English in opposition to anything hinting of Afrikaner nationalism. The political influence of Clements KADALIE's union movement was of particular concern to Hertzog. He sharply limited the franchise of the Cape African population, giving him the parliamentary majority necessary to legislate a coercive labor system. This legislation laid the legal groundwork for the later development of apartheid.

The United Party merger, a marriage of convenience demanded by the Great Depression of the 1930s, unraveled during World War II. Smuts favored strong support for Britain, while Hertzog, a tacit supporter of the German cause, favored neutrality. His government fell over the issue, and Smuts formed a wartime coalition. During Hertzog's last administration, the opposition had been a new hard-line Afrikaner party, the Purified Nationalists, led by Daniel MALAN. Hertzog joined them and briefly became leader of the opposition. He retired from politics in 1940, however, after a rancorous dispute over equal rights for English-speaking South Africans.

References: DAHB, EB, EWB, HWL, MMA. Oswald Pirow, *James Barry Munnik Hertzog* (1958).

HINTSA
(South Africa, 1790?–1836)

Hintsa was a central figure in the 1834–1835 Sixth Frontier War, sometimes called Hintsa's War. As the paramount chief of a major division of the Xhosa people in South Africa, he was a powerful ruler, but British treachery betrayed him and cost him his life.

There had long been tension between European settlers and the Xhosa, who resented the loss of their ancestral lands. Raids and the killing of isolated individuals and families were not uncommon. The foremost problem that Hintsa inherited when he acceded to the chieftaincy, however, was the continual conflicts among Xhosa groups and the effects of the *mfecane* or *difaqane,* the destructive wave of Nguni migrations influenced by the rise of the Zulu under SHAKA. At first, Hintsa allowed Nguni refugees to settle in his territory, but he soon took a defensive posture as larger, armed groups attempted to enter his territory. In 1828 he joined with the

Thembu and the British to turn back a marauding army that threatened his state.

Hintsa then had to turn to the internal problem of his refugees. Traditionally, refugees had been absorbed into the Xhosa community, increasing its population and providing a means of expansion. In 1827, however, Hintsa allowed the Methodists to establish a mission, which immediately attracted refugee adherents. The mission began to champion grievances (mostly imaginary) against the Xhosa and created an unnatural separation between the refugees and their Xhosa hosts. This instability stirred up more conflict, which now involved the Europeans. When tensions erupted into conflict between the Xhosa and the British, the refugees sided with their European patrons. They agreed among themselves not to invade British territory, to protect missionaries, and to provide intelligence to British forces.

Hintsa's branch of the Xhosa was at first isolated from much of the frontier war that erupted in 1834 because of its position north of a major river. His position as paramount chief, however, caused the British to regard him as responsible for the conduct of all Xhosa. This was not the case, however, because Hintsa's position was titular and carried no direct authority. Nevertheless, Hintsa was swept up in the war when 16,000 refugees took 15,000 Xhosa cattle and escaped across British lines. The British ordered Hintsa to stop the war, which was beyond his power, although he did attempt to negotiate a settlement. During a meeting in 1835, the British arrested Hintsa and he was forced to sign a treaty and pay an indemnity of livestock. While helping in the roundup, his horse bolted. The British shot Hintsa and then mutilated his body publicly in the presence of the English commanding officer.

Reference: DAHB.

HOLOMISA, Bantu(bonke)
(South Africa, 1955–)

General Bantu Holomisa, former military leader of the South African homeland of Transkei, was a progressive benevolent dictator there. He was commander of the Transkei Defence Force from 1987 to 1993. He took power in 1987 after engineering two coups against corrupt predecessors. Transkei is the center of Xhosa culture and the birthplace of Nelson MANDELA, Chris HANI, and Desmond TUTU. Holomisa became one of Mandela's firmest allies, as well as a personal friend, although he treats Mandela with the deference due a revered elder.

Holomisa has an unassuming, almost boyish character, and his regime avoided all the trappings of dictatorship. He was never tainted with corruption and lived in a simple home, insisting that the palace remain empty until there was a democratically elected president. Available to people and a master manipulator of the media, he often went on local radio talk shows and fielded questions—including hostile ones—from the public. Freedom of expression existed in Transkei during his regime, and both the African National Congress (ANC) and its more radical rival, the Pan-Africanist Congress (PAC), were active. Indeed, the expansive Transkei bureaucracy provided most of the ANC and PAC leadership with government jobs. At that time, Holomisa was probably one of the most popular Black leaders in South Africa.

The son of a Xhosa chief, Holomisa was educated in a school for traditional elites, primarily the sons of chiefs. His background and education provided him with a strong ethic of duty and honor. Even though he was trained in the South African Army College as part of the government's program to maintain dominance over its homelands, Holomisa proved to be independent of Pretoria. A supporter of reuniting the homelands with South Africa, he was accused of harboring forces of the Azanian People's Liberation Army (APLA)—the armed wing of the PAC—which attempted to destabilize other homeland governments, especially Ciskei. Holomisa denied this, but at one point Pretoria restricted the Transkei borders in retaliation for APLA raids.

Holomisa at first claimed no interest in a political future in the new South Africa, though he was elected to parliament as an ANC delegate and was deputy minister of Environment and Tourism in Mandela's first administration. In 1994, he received the most votes in an ANC poll for National Executive.

Holomisa soon fell out with the ANC due to his uncompromising opposition to corruption and willingness to name names before the Truth and Reconciliation Commission. When he accused Vice President Thabo MBEKI of being in the pay of a corrupt businessman, that was the end. Mandela tried to pull him in, but Holomisa remained stubborn. The party expelled him in 1996 and published a booklet attacking him with strong language and half-truths. It continues to be available on the Internet.

Along with Roelf Meyer, recently expelled from the conservative National Party, Holomisa formed a new party in 1997, the United Democratic Movement (UDM). They surprised everyone when they placed in six provincial parliaments and took 13 seats in the national assembly. Holomisa continued his campaign in parliament, and his accusations against Vice President Jacob ZUMA finally forced the latter's resignation and indictment. The UDM has struggled. In 2005, Homomisa expelled seven parliamentarians who threatened to defect to the ANC. In 2006 it held six seats.

In his twenties, Holomisa was a gymnast, rugby player and manager of a football club, and he has served on several national sports commissions. He still plays rugby.

Reference: adb, GSAP, *wiki*.

HORN, Mike
(South Africa, 1966–)

Mike Horn is one of the new breed of adventure athletes whose exploits pit them against the worst conditions in the world.

Horn was born in Johannesburg and studied human movement at Stellenbosch University. He began his adventure sports career in 1991, paragliding and rafting in the Peruvian Andes. In 1994 he descended Mont Blanc in Switzerland on a body board, which earned him membership in the Sector No Limits Sporting Team. The next year he descended Peru's Colca Canyon, twice the depth of the Grand Canyon in the United States. He went from high in the Andes to the river's exit into the Pacific by hydrospeed. The same year he made the first descent of the Pascuare River in Costa Rica, and set a world record for waterfall descent on a hydrospeed (72 feet). In 1997, he crossed South America from west to east, first on foot from the Peruvian coast to the headwaters of the Amazon and then descended 7,100 kilometers (4,400 miles) on a one-man hydrospeed to the Atlantic Ocean. At one point, he was swimming in a black wet suit when local natives thought he was a devil, and he was barely rescued by Peruvian marines in a helicopter.

The same year he won the Multicoques Grand Prix sailing race.

As if those achievements were not enough, Horn set up Latitude Zero, a solo circle of the globe at the Equator. It took him 17 months in 2000–2001 by a combination of means. He began in Gabon in Central Africa, crossing the Atlantic in 19 days at one of its widest points by trimaran. He went from Brazil to Ecuador on foot, pirogue (dugout canoe) and bicycle. He then went through the Amazon Jungle and climbed the Andes Mountains. This was followed by the Pacific crossing by trimaran again, to the Galapagos Islands and Indonesia. He trekked by foot and sailboat through the jungles of Borneo and Sumatra, then sailed across the Indian Ocean to Somalia. By the time he returned to Gabon, he had walked, sailed, biked and canoed some 29,000 miles (47,000 km). He braved a 137 mph cyclone at sea with 197-foot waves. He was stood before a firing squad and rescued at the last moment, and forced to detour around war zones in Africa. Crossing the Democratic Republic of the Congo at the height of its lawlessness was in itself an act of either extreme bravery or foolhardiness.

In 2002, Horn created the Arktos Expedition, circling the North Pole and following the Arctic Circle. The journey took two and a half years and 12,400 miles, using skis, sled, a bike and a sailboat. In the process he crossed the Norwegian Sea from the North Cape of Norway, across Greenland, Canada, Alaska and Siberia. He almost lost his hands to frostbite.

He leads rafting and adventure trips for clients worldwide. In his extreme sports, he is sponsored by the Swiss Watch Federation. In 2001, he received the Laureus World Sports Award. He presently lives in Switzerland. Of his adventures, he says, "When you are about to reach the end, you think, . . . what am I going to do after this?"

Reference: www.mikehorn.com

HORTON, James Africanus Beale
(Sierra Leone, 1835–1883)

Dr. James Africanus Beale Horton, an early West African intellectual, was a pioneer of African nationalism and an advocate of modernization.

Born into a family of Nigerian recaptives (people liberated from slave ships by the British slave squadron and resettled in Sierra Leone), Horton attended Fourah Bay Institute and then went to Great Britain to study medicine, graduating from the University of Edinburgh in 1859. In Britain he encountered the pseudoscientific racist theories of the day and took the name Africanus in reaction. He joined the army medical service and was posted to the Gold Coast (now Ghana). There he began a career that would take him along the coast for 20 years, allowing him to retire with the rank of lieutenant-general.

Horton made his greatest contribution in his writings, which had considerable influence in the precolonial period. These works ranged from botanical and medical studies to social and political theory. His most important book was the 1868 *West African Countries and Peoples,* which combined perceptive description and analysis of coastal institutions with proposals for political development. Horton argued that Africa, now opened to Western society, should develop along European patterns, utilizing Western education and technology. Some have interpreted this as his accepting the theory of African cultural inferiority, and Horton's reputation has suffered in comparison with that of his friend and fellow intellectual, Edward BLYDEN. Blyden argued the existence of a unique African identity, an idea that is seen as a forerunner of modern African nationalist thought. Horton rejected that notion by arguing for a universal humanity that made theories of racial inferiority unjustifiable. In *An African View of the Negro Place in Nature* (1865) and *The Vindication of the African Race* (1868), he refuted the ideas of racial inferiority then common and ascribed the differences in European and African development to external factors.

Horton was also a Pan-Africanist, a logical position considering his insistence upon universals in culture. He compared the state of Africa to Europe's barbarism in the early medieval period and offered a vision of an Africa governed by modern principles, educated and developed. Horton's ideas influenced the formulation of the Fante Confederation in 1871, which was based on a written constitution, and they provided a means of creating modern government in West Africa. His philosophy was not allowed to develop as a result of the advance of colonialism. Horton died before being able to publish anything that took the new circumstances into account.

References: AA, DAHB, MMA, *wiki.* Abioseh Davidson Nicol, *Africanus Horton and Black Nationalism* (1969); Christopher Fyfe, *Africanus Horton, 1835–1883* (1972).

HOUPHOUËT-BOIGNY, Félix

(Côte d'Ivoire, 1905?–1993)

Félix Houphouët-Boigny, founding father of his country, was a dominant figure in French-speaking West Africa for a generation. His death left a vacuum in leadership just as his country experienced a serious economic crisis.

Houphouët-Boigny, the son of a Baoulé chief, was educated as an African doctor and assigned to the southeast, where he practiced medicine for 15 years and gained a reputation as a healer. He also organized his first African planters association in 1933. After he inherited large tracts of land in his home area, he continued as an organizer and advocate of African landowners. In 1944 his African Agricultural Union (AAU), with 20,000 members, became one of the first anticolonial movements in Côte d'Ivoire. In 1945 he transformed the AAU into the country's first political party, the Democratic Party of the Côte d'Ivoire (PDCI), and was elected to the French general assembly. He increased his following immensely and became a hero by obtaining the repeal of the detested *corvée,* a colonial system that required Africans to "donate" a number of days each year to forced labor on public projects.

The early post-World War II period was significant for Houphouët-Boigny's development. He forged links with General Charles de Gaulle, added the political name Boigny ("irresistible power"), and formed an intercolonial party, the Rassemblement Démocratique Africain (RDA). The party suffered a major drubbing after its allies, the Communists, fomented a series of disastrous strikes in 1950 that resulted in a warrant for Houphouët-Boigny's arrest. Parliamentary immunity saved him from prison, but, having learned his lesson, he completely cut himself off from the Communists. This strategy and the RDA victory in the 1956 elections made him the trustworthy confidant of the French authorities. He was named to the cabinet and helped draft the framework for internal autonomy for the French colonies. At the same time he

Félix Houphouët-Boigny

served as mayor of the capital, Abidjan, and president of both the Côte d'Ivoire assembly and the Grand Council of West Africa, holding offices on local, national, regional and metropolitan French levels.

As Côte d'Ivoire and other French West African colonies prepared for eventual independence, they faced two options: federation into a single West African union or individual national independence with links to France. Houphouët-Boigny was anti-federal, opposing Léopold SENGHOR of Sénégal on that issue. An interterritorial referendum was called. With de Gaulle campaigning for him, Houphouët-Boigny triumphed, carrying the referendum everywhere except in Guinea. He undermined the Mali Federation, and, with individual states assured, became president of Côte d'Ivoire in 1960.

The country was directed through a one-party system that was paternalistic yet effective. His policies were pro-Western and capitalist, and he made it clear that foreign investment was welcome under generous conditions. The result was impressive economic growth, the "Ivoirian miracle," that continued until the 1980s. Houphouët-Boigny's French contacts enabled him to garner preferential commodity deals for Ivoirian cocoa, timber and coffee while other nations languished. As the nation prospered, Abidjan became one of the most modern capitals in West Africa, called "the Paris of Africa." Houphouët-Boigny was thoroughly at home in French circles and retained large numbers of French bureaucrats in his government.

Ivoirian foreign policy, while pro-Western, was always independent. Houphouët-Boigny recognized Biafra in its futile secession attempt from Nigeria in the 1960s and advocated dealing with South Africa. In 1985, Côte d'Ivoire was the first African state to restore diplomatic relations with Israel following the general rupture between Africa and Israel in 1973 over the Lebanon invasion. Houphouët-Boigny balanced this action by exchanging ambassadors with the Soviet Union.

Houphouët-Boigny cautiously opened the domestic political process in the 1970s by establishing national palavers based on the African custom of open dialogues with the chief. One result was the recognition that educated Ivoirians were being slighted in favor of French employees, and Houphouët-Boigny moved to correct the imbalance. Nonetheless, major disparities between the elite and the peasants continued to exist, and the booming economy provided few benefits for the poor. Gradually, political parties were legitimized, but no challenge was allowed to "Le Vieux," the "old man." Despite reforms, there were strikes and student disturbances as the sliding economy began to influence everyday life. Houphouët-Boigny, however, retained the support of the public, and when he permitted a contested election in 1990, he won officially 81 percent (unofficially 65 percent) of the popular vote.

The folly of Houphouët-Boigny's old age was the massive Catholic basilica constructed in his home village, Yamoussoukro. Built of imported materials in a totally European style, it cost about $200 million, which Houphouët-Boigny insisted came from his own resources. It is the largest Christian church in the world, holding 7,000 in air-conditioned comfort. The pope had requested that it be a few feet shorter than St. Peter's, but he reluctantly consecrated it in 1989. At the same time as this massive structure was consecrated, Côte d'Ivoire was forced to suspend its debt payments and introduce austerity measures.

Houphouët-Boigny's death passed peacefully, because his declining health had already provided for considerable jockeying for power within the government. France's best friend in Africa was honored at his funeral with a delegation led by President François Mitterrand and included a past president and seven premiers or former premiers of France.

References: AB, *afr*, CB, DAHB, DRWW, EWB, PLBA, PLCA, RWWA, *wiki*. Jacques Baulin, *La Succession d'Houphouët-Boigny* (1989).

HUDDLESTON, Trevor
(South Africa, 1913–1998)

Archbishop Trevor Huddleston, one of the founders of the antiapartheid movement and its heart for many years, was an Anglican clergyman who served as a missionary in Tanganyika, Mauritius and South Africa. It is with South Africa and its liberation movement, however, that his life is forever connected.

At Oxford University in the 1930s, Huddleston turned pacifist and Christian Socialist under the influence of the student movements of the Depression. This background led him to join the Resurrection Fathers, a tiny Anglican religious order committed to social action and popularly known as the Mirfield Fathers. In this order he found a congenial fellowship of monastic spirit that was devoted to social justice and that he always called "my home." In 1943, Huddleston was sent to South Africa to bolster a small mission effort. He began working in Sophiatown, a squatter township of 60,000 outside of Johannesburg, where he encountered the plight of Africans in a racist society. Within a few years he became regional superior of the order and moved to another township mission in nearby Rossetenville. Mirfield sponsored St. Peter's, a large school that Huddleston used to develop Black leadership. The novelist Peter ABRAHAMS was an alumnus, and African National Congress (ANC) leader Oliver TAMBO and writer Ezekiel MPHALELE were teachers. Hugh MASEKELA, a student, received his first trumpet from Huddleston, who helped him form a jazz band.

When apartheid became codified in South Africa in the early 1950s, Huddleston was among the first to protest. Sophiatown was crushed beneath bulldozers in 1955 and its people were scattered and replaced by a White neighborhood cynically named Triomf ("triumph"). In response, Huddleston wrote *Naught for Your Comfort* (1956), a devastating indictment of racism, bigotry and legalized persecu-

tion. The book received worldwide publicity and sparked controversy, thrusting Huddleston into more political activity. He helped organize the congress that drafted the Freedom Charter, the ANC's statement of principles. At the congress, he received the ANC's highest honor, the Isitwalandwe, for his work. After this accomplishment, he was called back to England to be director of novices for the Mirfield community. He calls the transfer "the toughest bit of obedience I've ever had to face up to, a terrible bereavement." While obedient to his superiors, he experienced periods of depression. The move proved providential, however, because Huddleston brought the antiapartheid campaign to England and internationalized it.

In 1960, Huddleston was elected bishop of Masasi, Tanganyika, a rural diocese that was a totally new environment for him. Within eight years he had trained an African successor and returned again to Britain. He was next chosen to be

Archbishop Trevor Huddleston with Nelson Mandela.

assistant bishop of London in charge of Stepney, a slum in London's East End. He felt the contrast: "Deprivation in an *affluent* society is infinitely worse than poverty in a Third World society, which has marvelous values of community." If Huddleston had hoped to retire to Mirfield after another 10 years, he was surprised by his election as archbishop of the Indian Ocean, which sent him to Mauritius. From this post he saw something new: a multicultural society of many races, religions and ethnic groups, living in partnership. In 1981, he was elected president of the Antiapartheid Movement (AAM).

Huddleston returned to Britain in 1983 to continue the work of the AAM. He criticized White liberalism, arguing that it had "done so much to keep the apartheid structure in place ... by its essential philosophy of evolutionary change." A radical and combative man, Huddleston led the move for economic sanctions against South Africa. In Xhosa, his nickname is "the dauntless one." When the ANC was unbanned in 1990, he flew to Sweden for a moving ceremony in which he introduced the ANC leadership to a cheering crowd of supporters.

Author Alan PATON described Huddleston as "one burning to serve the world," a prophetic critic of social evil, yet with "an absence of all prudery and censoriousness." Tall, spare and frail, with a penetrating gaze, Huddleston came across as intensely personal. His inner serenity and transparent holiness seemed integral to his commitment to justice, yet his personal piety was of the reserved, nondemonstrative Anglican variety. A delightful companion, he enjoyed a good meal with good wine. He was equally at ease with Nelson MANDELA or legions of small children. Above all, people were at ease with him. Paton modeled the priest in *Cry, the Beloved Country* on Huddleston. Although they later went separate ways politically, Paton still called Huddleston "one of the most human of saints." Nadine GORDIMER confessed "I have no religious faith, but ... I see godliness in a way I can understand deeply. I see a man in whom prayer functions."

Huddleston's last years were spent back in the Mirfield Community after several falls in 1994. He tried a nursing home in South Africa, but could not stand being a privileged White served by Black attendants. At Mirfield he was not a docile patient. His mind remained acute as he weakened, and he had little tolerance for his condition. He endured it but raged against it, finally surrendering.

Reference: afr, dacb, EB. Robin Denniston, *Trevor Huddleston, A Life* (1998).

HUGGINS, Godfrey Martin, Lord Malvern
(Zimbabwe, 1883–1971)

Sir Godfrey Huggins was prime minister of Southern Rhodesia and the first prime minister of the Federation of Rhodesia and Nyasaland. Born in England, where he became a surgeon, Huggins came to Southern Rhodesia in 1911 for his health, intending to stay for only a short time. Realizing the opportunities for a physician there, he took up residence.

In 1923, Rhodesia (now Zimbabwe) became self-governing, and Huggins entered politics as an elected member of the legislative assembly in the Rhodesia Party of Charles COGHLAN. He became a champion of settlers' rights, as he saw them, and argued forcefully for racial segregation as the best means of securing benefits for White citizens. When the Rhodesia Party did not move as strongly on the race issue as Huggins felt it should, he left in 1931 to form his own group, the Reform Party. In the 1933 elections the Reform Party took advantage of the worldwide economic depression to defeat the Rhodesia Party, and Huggins became prime minister and secretary of native affairs. He moved to merge his new party and the Rhodesia Party, and in 1934 he called a snap election in which the new United Party won overwhelmingly. Huggins remained prime minister for 21 years, setting a record for Commonwealth countries. He was knighted in 1941 by King George VI.

Throughout his long tenure, Huggins promoted a racial policy of segregation that he called the "two pyramid" theory. It emphasized separate but independent White and Black political development. In practice it came to very little more than opposition to the empowerment of Blacks, but it did provide a convenient theory to consolidate White farmers' support for Huggins's plans for Southern Rhodesia. He supported the amalgamation of Southern and Northern Rhodesia (now Zambia) during much of the 1930s, partly out of fear of being absorbed into South Africa and coming under the domination of the rising Afrikaner political movements. When it became clear that Great Britain would not approve uniting the two Rhodesias, Huggins began to promote the idea of a federation, including Nyasa-land (now Malawi).

The 1940s brought serious challenges to the United Party, and in 1946, Huggins survived with a minority government. He introduced a registra-tion and residence law restricting Black residence in urban areas, which contributed to his convincing plurality among White voters in the 1948 elections. Thus strengthened, Huggins pushed his plans for federation, enlisting the support of Roy WELEN-SKY of Northern Rhodesia. He began federation discussions with the British government by includ-ing Joshua NKOMO in the London negotiations. Huggins dropped his talk of the "two pyramids" in favor of a "partnership" theory that assuaged British concerns about the rights of Blacks. The British government hoped for a counterbalance against the apartheid system being introduced in South Africa and, despite Nkomo's opposition, the federation was approved in 1952.

Huggins resigned his premiership in favor of Garfield TODD and became prime minister of the new Federation of Rhodesia and Nyasaland, called the Central African Federation. The federation made some progress, improving educational opportuni-ties, founding a university, and building Huggins's dream project, the Kariba hydroelectric dam. Few of these benefits aided Blacks, however, and Huggins continued to keep political control out of their hands. In 1955 he was made a viscount, and the following year he retired from politics.

References: DAHB, EB, *wiki.* Lewis Gann, *Huggins of Rhodesia* (1964).

HURLEY, Denis, OMI
(South Africa, 1915–2004)

Archbishop Denis Hurley was the first Catholic archbishop appointed in South Africa, an interna-tional churchman and a foe of apartheid.

Denis Hurley was born in Cape Town and raised on Robben Island, the site of the prison where later, leaders of the African National Congress (ANC) would be kept. He entered the Oblates of Mary Immaculate (OMI), a Catholic missionary order, as a youth, and was sent to Ireland for his first training. He then went to Rome for studies in philosophy and theology, and was ordained a priest in 1939. When Italy entered World War II, he

escaped through Spain and took a freighter home. After several years in Durban as a curate, he was appointed to several positions within the OMI until 1946, when he was named a bishop. At 31, he was then the youngest Catholic bishop in the world.

The Catholic Church in South Africa was considered a missionary region and was not formally organized until 1951, when the various mission districts were structured into dioceses, and Hurley was made archbishop of Durban, again the youngest in such a post in the world. At that point in his life, Hurley saw himself as a loyal churchman charged with developing a missionary territory. He regularly went to Europe and the United States to raise money, and on one of his fundraising trips in Germany, he experienced a revelation on a train ride while meditating. He realized suddenly how much he was part of the oppressor class in South Africa, not a servant Christian but a master. It transformed the rest of his life.

Hurley began advocating against apartheid. He was opposed both within the Catholic community and by the government. There was strong resistance to his attempts to integrate Catholic schools, but he forced the issue. In 1957, he mobilized the South African bishops behind a national pastoral letter in which they condemned apartheid as "intrinsically evil." In the 1970s, he began a daily protest outside a government building in Durban, standing silently with a placard denouncing apartheid. He was placed under house arrest several times and threatened with banning, although by that time he had acquired such an international following that the government feared moving on him. He was close to the Community of Sant'Egidio in Rome, and was a secret collaborator of theirs in the negotiations that settled the civil war in Mozambique.

Finally, in 1985 Hurley was charged with treason for revealing atrocities committed by South African forces in Namibia. When the case came to trial, the courtroom was filled with bishops from all over the world, sitting in silent solidarity. The trial was adjourned and the charges dropped. Hurley settled out of court and received 25,000 Rand. He retired in 1992, after the first free election. He was honored for his leadership with 10 honorary doctor-ates and medals from France, Italy and South Africa. Author Alan PATON paid tribute by calling him "the guardian of the light."

In Church affairs, Hurley was a moderate liberal. He was elected head of the South African Bishops' Conference, and as such served on the

Preparatory Commission for the Second Vatican Council. In 1968 and again at the Synod of Bishops in 1980, he respectfully questioned the papal teaching against birth control, and it is widely believed that this killed any chance of being named a cardinal. From 1975 to 1991 he chaired the International Commission on English in the Liturgy, which made the transition from Latin to English in religious services. In defining the theological issues involved in opposition to apartheid, Hurley worked with the Dominican theologian Albert NOLAN, OP.

Reference: wiki. A. Gambley, *Denis Hurley: A Portrait by Friends* (2001).

IBUKUN, Lawrence Olu

(Nigeria, 1932–)

Dr. Lawrence Ibukun, distinguished engineer and physicist, has been a prominent figure in the United Nations Educational, Scientific and Cultural Organization (UNESCO) African programs for science and technology. After studies at University College, Ibadan, he received doctorates in applied physics (Imperial College, London, 1957) and engineering (University of London, 1963). Ibukun also earned graduate diplomas in economics and linguistics. From 1957 to 1965 he was a lecturer and research fellow at the University of Ibadan, and from 1965 to 1968 he was affiliated with the University of Lagos.

Ibukun's primary contributions have been made outside the university setting. In 1957 he was on the staff of the Nigerian program for the International Geophysical Year, and in 1965 he became deputy director for UNESCO's Regional Centre for Science and Technology for Africa. He moved to Paris in 1967 as program specialist for the UNESCO Africa Section, after which he began a long tenure (1970–1983) in Nairobi, Kenya, as director of the UNESCO Regional Office for eastern Africa. Ibukun also represented UNESCO to the Organization of African Unity (OAU) and the U.N. Economic Commission for Africa. In 1983 he returned to Paris as head of the UNESCO's Technological Education and Training Programme. At UNESCO his interests have been in technology education and the social ethics of engineers and scientists.

Chief Ibukun holds the traditional title of Ajagunna II of Ogbagi-Akoko. He served single terms in the federal (1964–1966) and Western Nigerian (1959–1960) parliaments. A man of wide interests, he has published a novel (*The Return,* 1970) and is a sportsman.

Reference: PAS.

IDRIS Aloma

(Niger/Nigeria, 1542?–1619?)

Mai Idris Aloma, the most famous of the rulers or *mai* of Bornu, took a weakened state and strength-ened it with new administrative and military power. He also encouraged the spread of Islam as a religious and cultural basis for its society.

When Idris was an infant, his father died, and the rule passed to another branch of the Sefawa dynasty. When Idris reached the throne, 20 years after his father's death, Bornu faced serious political and economic problems. Nomadic clans raided the empire at will, a long famine had weakened the economy, and there were continued inter-dynastic conflicts. Idris began by building a powerful army, which used muskets that he first encountered when he made his *hajj,* or pilgrimage, to Mecca in 1571. He also instituted new military strategies, such as a camel cavalry for long-distance campaigns. Following a series of successful campaigns, he made Kanem a tributary state and signed a boundary treaty. Idris then successfully repelled the nomads from his territories.

Having reduced external threats, Idris turned to internal organization. He ended the custom of appointing relatives to administrative posts and replaced them with trusted persons loyal to him, thus reducing the chances of coups based on dynastic feuds. The economy was stabilized around a fair tax system, tribute and the slave trade, but fishing and salt and natron mining were also developed. Idris established a regional trade in these products as well as in slaves, hides, ivory and leather.

To unite the country, Idris fostered Islam by building mosques and establishing the legal system on Islamic principles. He had a progressive foreign policy and established contacts with the sultans of Morocco and the Ottoman Empire. Clerics were used as mediators with warring communities and, in one case, to stop an attack upon the city of Kano. Muslim religious observance became common in the towns, and Islamic traditions regarding burial, naming and other social customs became accepted. Adultery and obscenity were suppressed and education was introduced.

Idris's *hajj* has been called his "finest hour," and it was certainly a defining point for his reign. He set out with thousands of soldiers, retainers and bearers, visiting Islamic communities along the way. The impact of this contact with Islamic learning and devotion (as well as Idris's introduction to firearms) had a lasting influence.

All Idris's achievements—military, religious and administrative—ushered in a golden age in the history of Bornu, and by appointing an official historian, he provided future generations with a wealth of detail about his rule. The dating is confusing, however. The best research places his reign from 1569 to about 1600; estimates of his date of death range from 1596 to 1619.

Reference: DAHB. Eldridge Mohammadou, *Idriss Aloma* (1983).

IHONVBERE, Julius
(Nigeria, 1956–)

Dr. Julius Ihonvbere is a political scientist known primarily for his radical politics and critical commentary on African dependency and underdevelopment. He graduated from Obafemi Awolowo University, where he was active in student groups. In 1979 he received the Award of Honour of the Pan-African Youth Movement and the Merit Award of the Association of Campus Journalists. Ihonvbere received an MA from Carleton College in Minnesota and a Ph.D. from the University of Toronto in 1984. From 1983 to 1986 he was a lecturer in political science at Ogun State University and from 1986 to 1990 was senior lecturer at the University of Port Harcourt. After a year as visiting professor of African Studies at the University of Toronto, he joined the political science department at the University of Texas, Austin, where he has authored dozens of scholarly papers and seven books. While at the University of Toronto, he was active in the local community, taking up an interim board appointment at the Africa Centre in the wake of a corruption scandal. After leaving Texas, he was program officer for Africa for the Ford Foundation, and instrumental in directing grants toward projects to promote democracy.

Influenced by theories of classical Marxism, Ihonvbere has concentrated his research on labor history, state and social class, and the economic aspects of security issues. In this last area, he has been studying the effects that peace and military conflict have on the economy. He was the first to apply Marxist critiques to studies of the Economic Community of West African States (ECOWAS). In 1994 he published *Nigeria: The Politics of Adjustment and Democracy*, in which he analyzes the relationship between economic adjustment and political power, identifying the middle class as a primary cause of national decline.

In recent years, Ihonvbere has been special advisor for Policy to the President of Nigeria. His willingness to speak frankly and even publicly has caused clashes with powerful figures, including President Olusegun OBASANJO himself.

Ihonvbere has been critical of African elites, as well as of the Hunger Project's Africa Prize, which he has denounced for ignoring the efforts of grassroots workers, whom he calls "the real heroes." He said, "The prize is a recognition of those already recognized. It's not about people who are out there keeping the country alive."

References: adb, PAS.

ISHAQ II
(Mali/Niger, ?–1591)

Askiya Ishaq II was the *askiya,* or ruler, who suffered the defeat and dismemberment of the Songhay Empire.

He was a son of DAWUD who succeeded his father after a brutal dynastic conflict in which brothers imprisoned, executed and deposed one another in a series of conspiracies that several times erupted into civil war and weakened the empire. In 1588 one brother had himself proclaimed *askiya* at Timbuktu and marched at the head of the armies of the western provinces to complete his conquest. Ishaq, who was *askiya* of Gao, the empire's administrative center, annihilated the western forces in battle and cruelly ended the rebellion. The empire was sundered, and the division never healed. Half the army had been lost, and Songhay was seriously wounded.

An even greater challenge, however, came from Morocco, and Songhay was too divided to resist it. Sultan Ahmad al-Mansur had just defeated Portugal around 1589 and received huge sums of ransom for the Christian slaves he had seized. As an international Muslim leader, he planned the unification of African Islam and revived the *jihad* or holy war for the spread of Islam. At the same time, Songhay was in the way of Morocco's favored trade routes to the

Sudan and its large slave supply, and it also controlled the valuable desert salt mines. The sultan took two desert oases to position himself and sent spies to Ishaq's court. After gathering intelligence and convincing his reluctant councilors, al-Mansur mounted a campaign in 1590. Ishaq's manner of taking the throne had so alienated the western leaders that many received the Moroccans as liberators and joined them.

Ishaq foolishly waited until the last minute to mobilize, but he assembled a massive force of 40,000 to confront the 5,000 Moroccans. Without firearms or cannon, however, he suffered total defeat at Tondibi in 1591. Gao fell and the empire was ended. Ishaq tried to negotiate with the Moroccan commander, Judar Pasha, but al-Mansur permitted no settlement and Ishaq was driven to his death in the desert. Songhay resistance continued for a few years, but the Moroccans garrisoned the river and finally assumed control.

References: DAHB, *wiki.*

ISSAIAS Afeworki

(Eritrea, 1945–)

Issaias Afeworki is the nationalist leader of the Eritrean People's Liberation Front (EPLF) and the first president of Eritrea.

Eritrea was an Italian colony until the end of World War II, when it was administered by Great Britain as a United Nations (U.N.) mandate until it was federated to Ethiopia in 1952 and annexed 10 years later. The federation was never accepted by the majority of Eritreans, and Ethiopian control was seen as a new form of colonialism. The origins of the liberation war were in the 1961 Eritrean Liberation Front (ELF), a Muslim-dominated group from which the EPLF split off in 1970. The EPLF gradually controlled large areas of the Eritrean countryside, establishing its own social services and schools.

Little is known about Issaias's early life, except that he joined the EPLF as a soldier around 1965, became military commander in 1975, and was elected EPLF secretary-general in 1987. After the defeat of MENGISTU Haile Mariam and his Marxist tyranny in Ethiopia in 1991, the United States supported Issaias's proposal for an Eritrean national referendum on independence. Issaias established a provisional government, and in April 1993 the independence referendum carried by 99.8 percent in an open and fair election. After Ethiopia accepted the results a week later, Issaias automatically became president. Two weeks later, Eritrea was admitted to the U.N., and in July, to the Organization of African Unity (OAU). Issaias startled his hosts at his first OAU meeting by boldly criticizing them for lack of support during the EPLF liberation war and for bearing a share of responsibility for Africa's economic crisis. It was typical of his blunt manner of speaking, taking little notice of diplomatic niceties and suggesting that, as one official aide commented, "He is still fighting a war."

Shortly before the referendum, Issaias contracted cerebral malaria and was airlifted, unconscious, to Israel, where his life was saved. This incident cemented his growing appreciation for Israel, which was an early contributor of technical assistance, especially in agriculture, fisheries and water management. The EPLF was founded as a nonsectarian group, and Issaias's friendship with Israel has offended Muslim states. In 1994, Eritrea applied for membership in the Arab League but was rejected after false rumors circulated that Israel was planning to build a base in Eritrea.

Issaias faced a daunting task in attempting to restructure the country, because it was devastated by 30 years of conflict, and its Red Sea port of Massawa had been rendered inoperable by Ethiopian bombing raids. Reconstruction has proceeding slowly, hampered by a lack of hard currency. Issaias has begun a policy of limited economic liberalization and an investment program tailored to attract expatriate Eritreans living in Europe and North America.

The main barrier to development has been the ongoing conflicts with Ethiopia over the borders between the two countries. He has had a complete falling-out with Meles ZENAWI, Ethiopia's president, and in 1998–2000 the two countries fought a devastating war that cost 100,000 lives. Skirmishes continue to flare along the border, an arid and worthless piece of land, but one that is rumored to have oil. Conflict continues despite a mediator's decision to award the disputed territory to Eritrea.

Issaias has a reputation as a centralizer and an autocrat. In 2001 he closed the private press and maintains strict censorship.

Reference: David Pool, *Guerillas to Government* (2005).

President Issaias Afeworki of Eritrea and U.S. Secretary of Defense Donald Rumsfeld shake hands.

IYASU V

(Ethiopia, 1896–1935)

Emperor Iyasu V governed Ethiopia from 1909 until he was deposed in 1916. Although he assumed the powers of emperor, he was never crowned, and his increasing involvement with Islam during his reign made that impossible.

Raised in the royal court at Addis Ababa, he was the son of Ras Mikael, the Muslim governor of Galla, who wed a daughter of Emperor MENELIK II. At age 13, Iyasu was married and proclaimed heir to the throne, despite the intrigues of Menelik's wife, TAITU, who favored her stepdaughter, ZAU-DITU. After a series of strokes, Menelik had fewer lucid moments, and the court became a center of conspiracy and plotting. Iyasu was under the supervision of a regent who died in 1911 when Iyasu was 15. Iyasu assumed authority at that time—thwarting an attempt by the nobility to set up a regency council—and began appointing officials loyal to him. This included naming his father *negus* or emperor of Zio, Wollo and Tigray.

Iyasu's rule was one of the most eccentric in Ethiopian history. He engaged in many undignified activities, some insulting to traditional religion and others merely irresponsible. He was intemperate and chewed khat, a narcotic plant. He had at least 13 wives and numerous children. He became increasingly enamored of Islam, visited the Muslim provinces often and made furtive contacts with Islamic leaders. He "discovered" a forged genealogy that showed him as descended from the Prophet Muhammad through his father as well as from King

Solomon, the legendary ancestor of Ethiopian emperors, through his mother.

Iyasu increased Islamic influence, to the mounting alarm of the nobility, and he made no secret of his plans to Islamicize Ethiopia. When he attempted to appoint a Muslim to replace the governor of Harar, Ras Tafari Makonnen (later HAILE SELASSIE), a coup became inevitable. He was declared deposed and was replaced by Zauditu, with Ras Tafari as her regent. Both Iyasu and his father raised armies and took the offensive, but after decisive defeats, Iyasu was excommunicated from the Ethiopian Church and went into hiding for four years. In 1921 he was captured when he attempted to escape to Tigre. He spent the rest of his life in prison, but in 1935, the invading Italian army dropped leaflets attempting to rally Ethiopians around Iyasu, whom they hoped to use as a puppet emperor. He died shortly after under unknown circumstances.

References: DAB, DAHB, *wiki.*

JABAVU, John Tengo
(South Africa, 1859–1921)

John Tengo Jabavu founded the first African-language newspaper in South Africa and was active in Cape politics in the period when educated Africans had the vote.

Jabavu was a mission-school teacher before he began his newspaper career in 1881 with *Isigidimi sama Xhosa*, the Xhosa edition of a Methodist paper. He left the paper to manage the African side of a White politician's campaign. In 1884, White liberals founded a Xhosa weekly, *Imvo Zabantsundu* (*Bantu Opinion*), which Jabavu edited. The paper gave him a platform to become the dominant African political figure in the Cape Colony until the end of the nineteenth century. He advocated African support of White Liberal Party candidates, even when the party turned increasingly anti-Black under Cecil RHODES. Rhodes attempted to undermine Jabavu by helping to start a rival Xhosa paper in 1897, and Jabavu switched his allegiance to the Afrikaner Bond, a moderate party. When they failed to live up to expectations as supporters of African rights, Jabavu lost credibility with his African constituency. Late in the Boer War (1901–1902), the government shut down the paper, creating serious financial losses from which *Imvo Zabantsundu* never recovered.

Jabavu remained active in African politics, but he made several blunders that cost him much of his following. In 1909 he went to England as part of a delegation protesting the proposed South African constitution, which made no provision for votes for Africans. In 1913, however, he supported the Native Land Act, despite criticism from Solomon PLAATJE, the other major African journalist of the time, who called him a White puppet. Within a year, *Imvo Zabantsundu* was undermined by a rival paper controlled by the African National Congress (ANC). In 1914, Jabavu destroyed his political career by waging a revenge campaign for Cape Provincial Council against the ANC candidate, the only African incumbent, thereby assuring the victory of a White candidate.

During his last years, Jabavu shifted his energies to African education. He raised funds to establish the South African Native College, which became the University College at Fort Hare (1916) and sat on its council until his death. Fort Hare became a major center for the formation of African leadership, and Jabavu's son became the first African professor there. His second son took over the newspaper at Jabavu's death.

References: AA, *dacb*, DAHB, MMA, *wiki*.

JAJA
(Nigeria, 1821?–1891)

King Jaja, also known as Jubo Jobogha, created and ruled the trade state of Opobo in the Niger River delta from 1869 to 1887. He was one of a new generation of nonroyal rulers who appeared as the West African economy was shifting from slaves to palm oil. He stoutly resisted British trade expansion until the British removed him from office and sent him into exile.

Jaja, an Igbo, was sold into slavery as a child. In African slavery, as distinct from that in the West, the slave became a member of the household and could rise within it. Jaja became the slave of the chief of the Anna Pepple House in Bonny, one of two houses of royal blood (the other was the Manilla House). These houses were the basis of Niger delta society, involving clan members, slaves and persons in various stages of integration into the clan house. Each house owned a number of large trading canoes, and rivalry among the houses was highly competitive, which made it necessary to promote by ability rather than by birth.

Jaja began as a canoe paddler, but made the transition into trading because of an outgoing personality and an agreeable nature, which made him popular with up-country producers of palm oil as well as the crews of American and British cargo ships on the coast. Jaja was the perfect middleman and soon became wealthy, buying himself out of slavery. In 1861 the head of the Anna House, ALALI, died leaving a large debt. After all the eligible chiefs declined the headship, Jaja was elected in 1863 and paid off the debt within two years. He reorganized the house's finances and began to absorb smaller, less prosperous houses.

The expansion threatened the head of the Manilla House, also a former slave, and several incidents aroused mutual antagonism and subsequent conflict. In 1864, Christianity was introduced to the area. It was welcomed by the Manilla House but was rejected by Jaja, causing the missionaries and many European traders to side with Manilla House. Although a former slave could head a house, he could not be king, so when the king of Bonny died in 1865, the two houses contended for control of the throne. At first the conflict was of low intensity, but in 1868 a fire raged through the Anna House properties, destroying most of Jaja's arms. Jaja surprised his opponent by suing for peace and then invited the British consul to preside over the talks. As negotiations stretched out over weeks, Jaja slyly moved his families and goods to a strategic point at the mouth of a river that controlled the trade routes. In 1870 he established a new center called Opobo and proclaimed himself king. Of 18 houses affiliated with Bonny, 14 followed him to Opobo. It prospered at the expense of Bonny, whose trade languished, to the consternation of the British, who had significant investments there.

Jaja ruled for 18 years, welding his kingdom together, creating a well-equipped army and monopolizing the palm oil trade. He was able to block the British traders and even shipped palm oil directly to England, bypassing the British middlemen. In 1873, Great Britain recognized the kingdom, but the relationship did not last. In 1884, Jaja signed a treaty of friendship but deliberately excluded free trade. A depression in the 1880s forced competing traders to bypass Jaja's control of the interior palm oil markets, and in 1885, Britain declared a protectorate over the area. In 1887 Jaja refused to stop taxing British traders, and the English consul, Henry Hamilton JOHNSTON, invited him to discussions. Johnston arrived on a river gunship, and once aboard, Jaja was promptly arrested and exiled to the West Indies, where he lived on a pension. He was permitted to return to Nigeria in 1891, but died on the voyage.

References: DAHB, HH, HWL, MMA, *wiki.* Sylvanus Cookey, *King Jaja of the Niger Delta* (1974).

JAMESON, Leander Starr
(South Africa/Zimbabwe, 1853–1917)

Sir Leander Starr Jameson, friend and confidant of Cecil RHODES, a leading figure in early South African politics, is best remembered as the commander of a disastrous military attack against the Transvaal Republic, for which he was tried and imprisoned.

Born in Scotland, Jameson was educated as a doctor in London and established a successful medical practice until his health broke from overwork. He went to South Africa to recuperate and settled in Kimberley, the center of diamond mining. There he had the Ndebele Chief LOBENGULA and Transvaal President Stephanus KRUGER among his patients, and he and Rhodes became good friends. Lobengula was so pleased with Jameson's work that he gave him an honored title, which made him a useful intermediary in the 1889 negotiations with the chiefs that opened the way to the formation of the British South Africa Company (BSAC). In 1890, Jameson abandoned his medical practice and led an expeditionary force into what is now eastern Zimbabwe, which he occupied in Rhodes's name and christened Rhodesia. His move prevented the Portuguese in neighboring Mozambique from claiming the area, and Jameson was made a director of the BSAC and the administrator of the territory from 1891 to 1894. During this time, he expanded company territory until he had taken over all of Zimbabwe.

Taking advantage of a political crisis in the Cape Colony, which he believed would support further expansion and the eventual union of all southern Africa, Jameson and Rhodes (then prime minister of the Cape Colony) plotted an invasion of the Transvaal Republic, an independent Afrikaner state under "Oom Paul" KRUGER. Convinced that foreign workers, who had no legal rights in the Transvaal, would revolt, Jameson moved on Johannesburg in late 1895, despite orders from the British High Commissioner not to intervene. The rebellion never materialized and Jameson's support collapsed. He drove within 20 miles of Johannesburg before being forced to surrender to Boer forces. Rhodes resigned as prime minister in disgrace, the Company was forced to pay a large indemnity, and Jameson was taken to London for trial. He was received as a popular hero and was sentenced to 15 months in prison (from which he was later pardoned).

His brief time in prison damaged Jameson's health, but he returned to South Africa to embark on a political career. He was elected to the Cape parliament in 1900, took over the Progressive Party after Rhodes's death in 1902, and was prime minister from 1904 to 1908. He played a leading role in writing the constitution of the Union of South Africa and was a member of its first parliament (1910–1912). He retired to England in 1912 after having been made a baronet, and was then elected president of the BSAC. As he had requested, he was buried near Rhodes in Zimbabwe, on a hilltop "with a view of the whole world."

Intensely loyal to Rhodes and their shared vision, Jameson was a man of great personal charm and infectious gaiety, which he combined with daring and strong leadership that inspired loyalty in others.

References: afr, DAHB, DNB, EB, EWB, *wiki*. Elizabeth Longford, *Jameson's Raid* (1960).

JAVOUHEY, Anne Marie, C.S.J.
(Sénégal, 1779–1851)

Blessed Anne Marie Javouhey was responsible for the revival of Roman Catholic missions in Africa. The suppression of the Jesuits from 1773 to 1814, the ravages of the French Revolution, and the Napoleonic Wars that followed left Catholic overseas missions in a state of almost total collapse. These events took place just before an explosive revitalization of religious orders, however, which resulted in a new missionary era that would parallel, and in some ways be part of, Western colonial expansion. Javouhey was the pioneer of this missionary movement at a critical juncture.

Javouhey was the daughter of a devout peasant family that hid priests who had refused to take the anti-clerical oath of allegiance to the French Revolution. One of the priests encouraged her to take up religious life as a sister, and she left for Switzerland to pursue her goal. With three companions, she began a community of sisters, which was formally founded as the Sisters of St. Joseph of Cluny.

From the start, the Cluny sisters focused on Africa. The first St. Joseph mission was on the Indian Ocean island of Réunion (1817), but more important were the missions of Sénégal, where the sisters opened hospitals in 1819. Javouhey arrived at Gorée Island in 1822 to discover a struggling and demoralized Catholic community. She came to the conclusion that the future of the Church in Africa had to be indigenous and set to work to provide African leadership. Her first attempt was to found a Christian village, but this project failed after an epidemic. At the invitation of the British governor, she went to the Gambia in 1824 to reorganize the hospitals there and in Sierra Leone, an achievement that helped her refine her goal of church Africanization. She then returned to France to arrange for Africans to be sent there for education, some as priests and others as teachers. The first went in 1825, and by 1840 three Sénégalese priests had been ordained.

Javouhey proceeded to found a seminary in Sénégal and established an interracial religious order open to both French and African candidates. At first the seminary prospered, and by 1833 there were six priests and nine seminarians, along with a group preparing to be religious brothers. Africanization, however, threatened the missionary authorities, not to mention the direction of a seminary by a woman. The local bishop opposed her plan and after a tuberculosis epidemic, the project collapsed. Her lasting contribution, however, was the direction she gave to a struggling missionary group, the Holy Spirit Fathers. Due to her interventions, they regrouped from a low point and went on to become a major instrument in African Catholic missions.

Javouhey was also involved in the anti-slavery movement, and in 1828 she sailed with 36 sisters to French Guinea, the site of her most remarkable achievement: a self-supporting colony of freed African slaves. She was largely responsible for emancipation in that settlement, which still exists as a model town. In all her efforts, Javouhey faced considerable resistance, both because of her opposition to slavery, which had been abolished in France but not in the colonies, and because she was a woman. One French bishop attempted to take over the colony, and the clergy in Guiana refused her the sacraments for two years, which was a terrible rebuke at that time. She outlasted all her adversaries, and at her death more than 300 sisters worked in foreign missions, most in Africa.

She has been declared blessed by the Church, with a feast day on 15 July. In Sénégal she is especially remembered, and her home on Gorée Island, a short distance from the former slave pens, is maintained as an anti-slavery memorial.

References: dacb, C.C. Martindale, *Life of Mère Marie Javouhey* (1953); Frances J-B. Delaplace, *Blessed Mother Anne Marie Javouhey* (1979).

JAWARA, Dawda Kairaba
(The Gambia, 1924–)

Sir Alhaji Dawda Kairaba Jawara, one of the longest-serving presidents in Africa, governed within a multiparty democratic system and was a constant beacon of constitutionalism in a region plagued by military coups.

The Gambia, with fewer than a million people, is a tiny sliver of a country along the Gambia River. It is 200 miles long and no more than 10 miles wide at any point. A former British colony, it is totally surrounded by Sénégal. Its existence is a result of European colonial politics. Jawara was born in the Upper Gambia River area to a Muslim Mandingo family but received both an Islamic and a Christian missionary education. From 1945 to 1947 he served as a nurse trainee and then spent a year studying science at Achimota College in Ghana before entering the University of Glasgow to study veterinary surgery. He qualified in 1953 and returned to become the first veterinarian in The Gambia, holding the post of principal veterinary officer until 1960.

In 1959, Jawara entered politics by transforming the Protectorate People's Society into a political party, the People's Progressive Party (PPP), which governed The Gambia from independence until 1994. It had its base in the rural areas but also attracted support from the developed coastal area and the capital, Banjul. In the 1960 and 1962 elections the PPP took comfortable majorities, and Jawara became premier. He was subsequently named prime minister at independence in 1965 and president when The Gambia became a republic in 1970.

Jawara's commitment to democracy was unwavering. He resisted ethnic pressures as well as calls for a single party system. The opposition regularly took about 30 to 40 percent of the vote. In 1981 an attempted coup by a Marxist group took place while Jawara was in Britain, and

Lady Jawara and several family members were held hostage. The coup was thwarted by Sénégalese troops under a mutual aid pact. Although strict adherence to due process made the subsequent trials models of justice in Africa, Jawara realized The Gambia's vulnerability. In 1982 the Confederation of Senegambia was formed with Jawara as vice president. Political unification was never fully accepted because of Gambian fears, and the confederation was dissolved in 1989. An economic agreement has been reached with Sénégal to limit smuggling, and the two states continue to recognize their interdependence. The Gambian economy relies on groundnuts, although Jawara adopted a diversification policy. He introduced rice to reduce the hard currency drain to Asia and promoted tourism, now a major source of hard currency earnings and employment.

Jawara became a Christian in 1955, but in 1965 he reverted to Islam. During this period he was known as David, which is the English version of his name. He was knighted in 1966. In 1992, Jawara was re-elected to what he announced would be his last term as president.

A committed Pan-Africanist, Jawara assigned a portion of The Gambia's 800-man army to peacekeeping duties in Liberia when the Economic Community of West African States (ECOWAS) sent a combined force to that country in 1990. When the troops returned to The Gambia, they complained that they had not received their pay, and in 1994 a group of junior officers took over the government in a bloodless coup. Jawara took shelter on a visiting U.S. naval vessel and went into exile in Sénégal until 2002.

References: afr, DAHB, DRWW, EWB, PLBA, PLCA, RWWA.

JOHNSON, James "Holy"
(Sierra Leone/Nigeria, 1836?–1917)

Bishop James "Holy" Johnson, a West African proto-nationalist, became the second African to be ordained an Anglican bishop and was a critical figure in preserving his Church in the face of separatism led by independent churchmen.

Johnson was born in Sierra Leone to Yoruba parents who had been taken into slavery but recaptured and released by a British anti-slavery patrol. He graduated from Forah Bay Institute, was ordained, and became a pastor of the Church Missionary Society (CMS) assigned to the "native pastorate." He advocated the evangelization of Africa by Africans, under African leadership, and thus did not make an easy colleague for British missionaries. In 1874, due to his command of the Yoruba language and his popularity with African nationalists, he transferred to Nigeria to assume the Yoruba mission there.

Because of his views on African leadership, Johnson became a natural leader of the educated African elite in Lagos. He was an open critic of imperialism, encouraged educational opportunities for Africans, and promoted an autonomous, self-supporting church. Johnson began to raise a £10,000 fund to endow the Niger Mission and end dependency on England. This effort so frightened his opponents that he was physically ejected from his parish. Johnson argued that Christianity was the only value that Europeans had to offer, and the sooner Christianity shed Western control, the better: "It is more helpful that a people should be called to take up their responsibilities . . . than be in the position of vessels taken in tow." In 1886 he joined the Legislative Council (Legco) in Nigeria, where he was a spokesman for African interests. Johnson was a colleague of Bishop Samuel CROWTHER, the head of the Niger Mission, but he was more flexible than Crowther in dealing with traditional religions. He felt that Christianity could learn from them by entering into dialogue with diviners. He incorporated Yoruba religious names into Christian baptismal rituals. He drew the line at separatism, however, and opposed every attempt at division within Anglicanism. The solution for Johnson was an Anglican Church with African leadership, African philosophies and African theology. He showed his Anglican loyalties after the deposing of Bishop Crowther when he accepted and supported the CMS decision.

In 1900, Johnson became assistant bishop of the Niger Mission, a position earned by his loyalty to the CMS and because he presented the only real hope for retaining the Nigerian elite, who were being attracted to newly founded African independent churches. Johnson excommunicated his former associate Garrick BRAIDE and ultimately preserved the Anglican Church despite great losses, during a time in which it might have disappeared in Nigeria. Personally rigorous and self-demanding, he became known as "Holy Johnson" for his personal piety and prayerfulness.

References: afr, dacb, DAHB, MMA. Emmanuel Ayandele, *Holy Johnson: Pioneer of African Nationalism* (1970).

JOHNSON-SHIRLEAF, Ellen
(Liberia, 1939–)

Ellen Johnson-Shirleaf became the first woman to be elected president of an African country when she took office in Liberia in 2006. Johnson-Shirleaf has spent her entire life obtaining the experience necessary to face the daunting task of bringing Liberia back from the brink of a failed state. In 2006, *TIME* magazine named her to its annual list of "100 People Who Shape Our World."

Liberia has always been divided between the Americo-Liberians, descended from former slaves from the United States who founded the country, and the indigenous peoples of the interior. Johnson-Shirleaf's father was the first "native" elected to the national legislature. She married shortly after high school and went with her husband to America, where she graduated from college. Later she took a graduate degree in public administration from Harvard. As a professional economist, Johnson-Shirleaf has been a vice president of Citibank and then senior loan officer of the World Bank until becoming president of Kormah Development and Investment Corporation and then of the Liberian Bank for Development and Investment. She was named secretary of state for Finance in Liberia in the William TOLBERT administration for a year in the 1970s, and then minister of Finance in 1980.

She criticized Samuel DOE for his harsh and corrupt regime, and was thrown in prison in 1985. The 15 men who shared her cell were executed the first night, and she narrowly escaped rape. At first she supported Charles TAYLOR's rebellion, but they soon fell out and he accused her of treason. Nevertheless, her early endorsement has haunted her reputation in Liberia.

As Liberia descended into chaos, she moved to Kenya as vice president of Citibank's Africa Regional Office for three years and then to Washington as vice president and executive board member for the Equator Bank from 1986 to 1992. All the while, Liberia went from one disaster to another as towns were looted and people were murdered and maimed. Buildings in the capital are pockmarked by artillery strikes and the country has not had electricity since 1991.

She became director of the United Nations (U.N.) Development Programme's regional bureau for Africa for the next five years, and then re-entered Liberian politics. In 1997, she was the presidential candidate of the Unity Party, losing badly to Taylor, but in a seriously flawed election. As part of a U.N.-brokered peace agreement, she took the reins of the Commission of Good Governance from 2004–2005, but resigned after making charges that the transition administration could not control corruption. She then ran for president.

Her major opponent was the soccer football star, George WEAH. Weah was immensely popular among the young, but Johnson-Shirleaf was a sign of empowerment for women, who ended up voting overwhelmingly for her. In the first round of voting, lesser candidates were eliminated, with Weah in the lead. A bruising runoff left Johnson-Shirleaf the winner. Weah challenged the results, alleging electoral fraud, but lost his case. In the volatile atmosphere of Liberia, it seemed at first as if the country could again slide into open conflict, but Weah finally conceded. The new president's first act, fulfilling a promise to attack corruption, was to go to the Ministry of Finance and dismiss the entire staff personally. By mid-2006 she had requested Taylor's extradition from Nigeria, where he had been given safe haven, and he was flown to Sierra Leone to be tried by a United Nations court for war crimes.

Reference: adb. Liberia: A Fragile Peace (film, 2005).

JOHNSTON, Henry Hamilton "Harry"

(Liberia/
Malawi/Nigeria/Tanzania/Uganda,
1858–1927)

Sir Henry Hamilton "Harry" Johnston was a British explorer and scholar who pioneered in establishing colonial administration. His greatest importance

was the critical role he played for Britain during the European scramble for control of Africa. Johnston was a sickly youth who alternated between school studies and periods of private study of botany, anatomy and painting. At age 21 he traveled to Tunisia, where he learned Arabic and made his first contact with Africa. In 1882 he joined a scientific expedition into Angola and then pushed on alone into the Congo Basin, where he made the acquaintance of Sir Henry Morton STANLEY, who was establishing the administration for the Congo Free State. As a result of this expedition, the Royal Society sent Johnston to explore Kilimanjaro. He also undertook a covert political mission to negotiate treaties with local chiefs, a mission which later became the basis for the British East African Protectorate. In 1885 he was formally appointed to the Foreign Office and made vice consul of the protectorate of the Niger Delta and the Cameroons. He confronted JAJA, the powerful merchant who controlled the palm oil monopoly along the Niger River by using armed river boats, and had him arrested and deported.

In 1889, Johnston was part of the delegation that arbitrated Portuguese and British spheres of influence in southern Africa. He was then posted as consul to Mozambique, where he came to know Cecil RHODES. When the Portuguese attempted to extend their authority to Lake Malawi, Johnston declared it a British protectorate. Rhodes supplied funds for Johnston's campaign against the Arab and Yao slavers who operated along the lake. Within a year he had defeated them, made numerous treaties, and enlarged the protectorate to all of Nyasaland and Northern Rhodesia and parts of Tanganyika. When he was appointed British commissioner, Johnston organized the administration of Nyasaland, stimulated economic development, and suppressed the slave trade. He set up the first tax system, which earned him the opposition of the traders, and then curbed the missions, which were accustomed to acting as local governments.

Johnston spent 1897 to 1899 in Tunis as consul-general after fever sapped his health. Then he went to Uganda, where he faced a difficult and delicate situation. Religious wars had torn the country apart and Sudanese troops had rebelled against their British officers. Johnston spent two years working for a peaceful solution. His immense tact resulted in the Uganda Agreement (1900) with Apolo KAGGWA. It gave the Baganda nation dominance in the protectorate and set the pattern for Ugandan administration throughout the colonial period.

During this time, Johnston kept up his enthusiasm for natural science: he explored the Ruwenzori Mountains, found fauna new to Western science, and wrote *The Uganda Protectorate* (1902) to describe the country. When he left the foreign service in 1902, Johnston had been instrumental in adding 400,000 square miles of Africa to the British Empire. Johnston then spent from 1904 to 1906 reorganizing the government of Liberia. A prolific writer, he published more than 30 volumes of scholarship, natural science, memoirs and fiction. His last major work was the monumental two-volume *Comparative Study of the Bantu and Semi-Bantu Languages* (1919–1922), which initiated linguistic scholarship in that field.

References: DAHB, DNB, EB, EWB, *wiki*. Roland Oliver, *Sir Harry Johnston and the Scramble for Africa* (1958).

JONATHAN, Leabua
(Lesotho, 1914–1987)

Chief Leabua Jonathan was the first prime minister of his country following independence. A conservative nationalist, he dominated Lesotho politics for over a generation.

Jonathan was a great-grandson of MOSH-WESHWE I, founder of the Basotho state. After completing primary school he went to South Africa to work as a clerk in the mining industry, returning to Basutoland (the colonial name of Lesotho) in 1937 to take a position in the local administration of the paramount chief regent. He became president of the Basuto courts the following year and assessor to the judicial commissioner in 1951. In the 1950s, he entered politics and was elected to the district council in 1956; he was subsequently elected to the national council, where he received the title of chief. He was seen as a popular and progressive leader who respected tradition, and he was chosen to represent the national council at the constitutional convention in London in 1958. He was at that time a member of the Basutoland Congress Party (BCP), but in 1959 he broke away and formed the Basutoland National Party (BNP), which emphasized policies of economic stability and good relations with South Africa. In 1960, Jonathan was elected to the Legislative Council (Legco), but the BCP formed the

government. Around that time, he converted to Catholicism and forged a link with Catholic leaders, who became a base of his support. In the Legco, Jonathan championed minority interests, especially those of Indians and women, who had not yet received the right to vote. In 1964 he led the delegation to London that negotiated independence, and in the first elections in 1965, the BNP won by a slim margin, and Jonathan became prime minister.

Within a few months, he clashed with King MOSHWESHWE II, the constitutional monarch, over the king's continuing interference in politics. He forced the king to assume a ceremonial role, but this action, along with his friendly relations with South Africa and economic problems, threatened his re-election in 1970. As the ballots were being counted, Jonathan suspended the constitution and arrested the king, later sending him into exile. Jonathan ruled by decree and became repressive. Meanwhile, the presence of BCP rebels in South Africa began to strain relations with that country. In particular, the economy began to be affected, since Lesotho is completely surrounded by South Africa, its major trading partner. As tensions with South Africa mounted in the 1980s, Jonathan became increasingly critical of apartheid and South African policy. He openly protected members of the African National Congress (ANC), and South Africa retaliated with raids into Lesotho. In 1985, when Jonathan refused to turn over ANC agents who were operating from Lesotho, Pretoria imposed an economic blockade until the Lesotho army intervened and deposed Jonathan in 1986. He was confined to his farm, where he died.

References: DAHB, EWB, MMA, PLBA, *wiki*.

JOSEPH, Helen Beatrice
(South Africa, 1905–1992)

Helen Joseph was a leading White political dissident and one of the most prominent White antiapartheid leaders.

Born in England, she graduated from the University of London and then went to India to teach. She moved to South Africa in 1931, married, and became a social worker. During World War II she served as a welfare officer where she ran community centers and a medical aid society. In response to the passage of the apartheid legislation after World War II, she organized the Congress of

Democrats, the White wing of the African National Congress (ANC). In 1955 she worked on the Freedom Charter, the ANC call for a multiracial South Africa.

In 1956 she and her longtime friend Lillian Ngoyi organized a march of 20,000 African women to protest the 1952 passbook laws, which required all African women to carry racial identification with them at all times. For this and other ANC work, Joseph was placed under house arrest in 1957 and charged with treason. She had the distinction of being the first person banned by the South African government. A bruising four-year trial followed, and after being acquitted, she wrote *If This Be Treason* (1963), a book that was promptly banned. Much of the rest of her life was spent under restriction. *Tomorrow's Sun* (1966), which was also banned, was the account of her visits and interviews with Black leaders under banning orders. She was soon restricted again, this time for 10 years until 1971. The last banning order was lifted when she was 80.

Joseph was threatened many times, had bullets fired into her home, and a bomb attached to her front gate.

Courageous and feisty, strong yet caring, she was a devout Anglican and a friend of Trevor HUDDLESTON, whose religious and political vision she shared. In 1975 she interrupted her activism to take a diploma in theology at the University of London. In 1978 she was jailed for refusing to testify against Winnie MANDELA. When Mandela went to prison, Joseph helped raise Nelson and Winnie Mandela's daughters. In 1983, Joseph became a sponsor of the United Democratic Front, the legal arm of the ANC, which campaigned for international trade sanctions and the freeing of political prisoners. In 1988 the ANC gave her its Isitwalandwe Award, bestowed only on distinguished comrades.

Joseph's funeral was a tribute to her life. The casket was draped in the ANC tricolor, Nelson MANDELA gave a eulogy to "my friend, my sister, my comrade," and Desmond TUTU preached. Joseph is buried alongside Lillian Ngoyi and is the first White allowed into Soweto's Avalon Cemetery.

References: *wiki.* Joseph, *Side by Side* (1986).

JUGNAUTH, Aneerood
(Mauritius, 1930–)

In 1993, Sir Aneerood Jugnauth, the dominant figure in post-independence Mauritian history, achieved his longtime goal of having Mauritius become a republic. He has successfully diversified the country's economy, initiating economic stability and growth.

Mauritius is among the few African countries that has had free multiparty democracy since independence, although divisions along class, caste and racial lines make politics complex. Jugnauth is an East Indian, a group that makes up two-thirds of the population. After local education, he studied law at Lincoln's Inn in London and passed the bar in 1954. Upon returning home he entered politics and was elected to the legislative assembly in 1963, joining an all-party coalition government as minister of labor in 1965. Two years later he quit parliament after a disagreement with the prime minister and joined the public service as a magistrate (1967–1969) and then as crown counsel (1969–1971). In 1971 he joined the more radical Mauritian Militant Movement (MMM), and from 1971 to 1973 he was chairman of the party and reorganized it while most of the MMM leadership was in detention under the state of emergency imposed by Sir Seewoosagur RAMGOOLAM in the aftermath of fighting between Muslims and Creoles.

In the 1976 elections the MMM polled the largest number of votes, but a coalition of its opponents formed the government and Jugnauth became leader of the parliamentary opposition. The MMM scored a clear victory in the 1982 elections,

Prime Minister Aneerood Jugnauth meets with U.S. President George W. Bush in the Oval Office, June of 2003.

making Jugnauth prime minister, a position that he has maintained since that time. The next year the MMM split into factions over a government crisis, and he was expelled from the MMM. He then formed the Militant Socialist Movement (MSM). He has been able to maintain power since then by a series of coalitions.

There have been a number of political scandals involving members of the cabinet, including the 1985 arrest of four ministers in Amsterdam on drug charges. Because they were not members of MSM, Jugnauth did not resign, but many of the cabinet did. In 1987 and 1988 he survived two assassination attempts, which he attributes to his campaigns against drugs.

In 1990 he began to press for his goal of removing Queen Elizabeth II as titular head of state and making Mauritius a republic. In the 1991 elections his coalition received more than the 75 percent necessary to change the constitution, and he was able to move on his plan.

The chief foreign policy issue has been a dispute with Great Britain concerning jurisdiction over Diego Garcia Island, which the United States has leased from Great Britain until 2016 for a major air base. Britain removed the island from Mauritian dependency in 1965, three years before independence. Great Britain was amenable to a transfer of rights until the base proved of major value in the 1991 Gulf War, and it now refuses to discuss the issue.

References: afr, PLBA, RWWA, *wiki. Aneerood Jugnauth: Le Premier Ministre du Changement* (Aneerood Jugnauth: Prime Minister for Change, 1982).

KABILA, Laurent-Désiré

(Democratic Republic of the Congo, 1939–2001)

Laurent Kabila was president of the Democratic Republic of the Congo (DRC) from 1997 to 2001. He came to power through a long guerilla and military campaign and was assassinated in office.

Kabila was born in the southern province of Katanga and was educated in France and Tanzania. There he met and became a lifelong friend of Yoweri MUSEVENI, later president of Uganda. When Kabila returned to the Congo, he became a leader in a youth movement allied to Patrice LUMUMBA, the radical prime minister of the country. In the turmoil that spun the Congo out of control in the aftermath of independence, Lumumba was kidnapped and murdered, Katanga attempted secession, and the Congo collapsed into chaos. Foreign intervention by United Nations (U.N.) forces and covert involvement by both the American CIA and Soviet agents only served to complicate matters and drag the country into the context of the Cold War.

Along with other supporters of the fallen Lumumba, Kabila fled into the eastern jungle as MOBUTU Sese Seko came to power. In 1964, Kabila organized one of the first revolts against the new regime in the Congo, by then renamed Zaïre. Because Mobutu was widely seen as a pawn of the West, especially the United States, Kabila got support from Cuba, and Che Guevara, a stalwart of the Cuban revolution who was in charge of exporting it to the Third World, arrived with a hundred men. The two leaders soon fell out, Guevara withdrew, and Kabila's insurgency was suppressed. In 1967, Kabila created a Marxist state in the east, far from the reach of most of Mobutu's forces. This time his Communist ally was China, and state lasted until it was also suppressed in 1977. Kabila was widely rumored to have been killed.

Far from dead, Kabila spent much of the 1980s in Tanzania with the remnants of his forces, and reappeared in 1996. By this time, the eastern Congo had been convulsed in the events following the slaughter of 800,000 Tutsi in the Rwandan genocide. Militias being pursued by the army of Paul KAGAME fled across the border into the eastern Congo, destabilizing and terrorizing the region. At the same time, Mobutu was losing his grip on power, his army mutinied, and Zaïre, now a failed state, began to fall apart. Again choosing his allies with care, Kabila launched the First Congo War with not-so-secret support from Kagame's Rwanda, Burundi and Uganda. Within a year, Kabila's forces swept across the country. Peace talks failed and Mobutu, now in frail health, fled into exile. Kabila took Kinshasa, the capital, proclaimed himself president, and renamed the country the Democratic Republic of the Congo.

Kabila's hold on the DRC was flimsy, and his former allies deserted him to promote a rebel force that tried to topple him in what came to be known as the Second Congolese War. The ever-wily Kabila forged new alliances with Angola, Namibia and Zimbabwe, which all sent troops and money. In a coup attempt, Kabila was mortally wounded and died in the hospital in Zimbabwe. His son Joseph succeeded him, and has formed a tenuous government of national unity, although there have been several more coup attempts.

References: afr, EB, wiki.

KABAREGA, Mukama

(Uganda, 1850?–1923)

Mukama Kabarega was the last independent *mukama* (king) of Bunyoro, one of the four traditional kingdoms of Uganda. He led a long and forceful resistance to British conquest and is regarded by many Ugandans as a national hero.

Kabarega succeeded his father as *mukama* in 1869 after a conflict with his brother that devastated the country. Kabarega set out to restore Bunyoro's power by reorganizing and professionalizing the administration and building a standing army trained with modern weapons. At the same time, he initiated a strong defense policy, resisting the expansion of the kingdom of Buganda to the west and the Egyptians to the north. In 1872 the Egyptians sent Samuel BAKER with a Sudanese force to occupy the headwaters of the Nile, but Kabarega repulsed him. Throughout the 1870s, Kabarega reconquered provinces and kingdoms that his weaker predecessors had lost, and the Egyptians gradually withdrew before his increased power.

Kabarega now turned to his longtime rival, Buganda, resulting in a long, intermittent war throughout the 1880s. This culminated in a major invasion attempt in 1886 by MWANGA II, whom Kabarega defeated. The British provided the greatest challenge, however, and in 1891, Frederick LUGARD placed a pretender on the throne of Toro, a kingdom that Kabarega had reclaimed only a few years earlier. In 1893 the British withdrew their troops from Toro, and Bunyoro immediately seized it again. The British then joined with Buganda in a protracted war against Bunyoro in which Kabarega waged perhaps the first effective guerrilla conflict in East Africa. The cause was futile, however, even though Mwanga broke with the British and eventually joined Kabarega. Bunyoro was defeated and both kings were seized. Kabarega was banished to the Seychelles in 1899. He returned to Bunyoro in 1923, but died shortly after.

References: DAHB, MMA.

KADALIE, Clements
(South Africa, 1896–1951)

Clements Kadalie, South Africa's first Black trade union leader, was the founder of the Industrial and Commercial Workers' Union (ICU) in 1919 and its dominant figure for its first 10 years. The ICU was the first African mass movement, and it presented the first Black working-class challenge to the ruling White elite.

Born in northern Nyasaland, the son of a paramount chief of the Tonga, Kadalie arrived in Cape Town in 1918. His rise to prominence was swift and dramatic. In the same year as its founding, the ICU held its first industrial action, a strike by unskilled workers on the Port Elizabeth docks. The government arrested Kadalie, and in the following demonstration, 24 supporters, including a European, were killed. This clash catapulted the ICU to prominence, and the strike led to three successive pay raises from the dock management. Other strikes followed.

In 1923, Kadalie established a Black workers' newspaper, the *Workers' Herald*. He became disenchanted with Prime Minister Jan Christiaan SMUTS after his administration suppressed the miners' strike in the industrialized Rand district, and in 1924, Kadalie endorsed the Afrikaner nationalist James HERTZOG, swinging the Black vote in Cape Province, where a limited franchise for Africans existed at that time. By then he had weathered an attempted deportation and had led the ICU to its first national conference, which was attended by 17 branches.

By 1927 the ICU had peaked at 100,000 members and was deeply involved in politics. Kadalie did not choose his allies wisely, however. After the Hertzog government proved more repressive than Smuts's regime, he accepted Communists into the ICU, only to expel them when they tried to take over the union. His rejection of Communists brought White liberal support to the ICU. In 1927, Kadalie traveled to Europe, where he established relations with Socialist labor movements. Nevertheless, an attempt to gain recognition by the International Labor Organization failed.

Kadalie returned home to find dissension within the ICU. The British labor movement sent an advisor, William Ballinger, but the two could not work together. Several major ICU branches seceded, and by 1929, Kadalie had been isolated and was forced to resign. Although he was a brilliant orator, the Native Administrative Act (1927) restricted his public speeches, which were critical of the government.

Kadalie was unable to overcome the forces against him in both South African society and the ICU. He remained politically active as a member of the African National Congress (ANC) but was barred from running for the Native Representative Council because he was Malawian. Kadalie was regarded as a respected community leader in East London, where a small local union continued to be loyal to him, but his sporadic attempts to assume a national role all failed.

References: afr, CWAH, DAHB, EWB, MMA. Kadalie, *My Life and the ICU* (1970).

KAGAME, Alexis
(Rwanda, 1912–1981)

Abbé Alexis Kagame was a Rwandese historian, ethnologist and philosopher who became the intellectual leader of the Tutsi people by articulating their cosmology in contemporary terms.

Kagame was born into a family of court historians and soon became intimately familiar with the oral traditions of the Tutsi. His family converted to Catholicism after World War I, and Kagame attended a missionary school as well as a school for the sons of chiefs. He entered a seminary in 1929 and was ordained in 1941. By 1938, while still a seminarian, he was an editor of a Catholic newspaper. He also taught at the novitiate of the Brothers of St. Joseph (Bayozefiti), one of the first African religious communities, and continued to do so for five years after his ordination. During this time Kagame became a close friend of King MUTARA III and rose to prominence in the country. Kagame's abilities would have been apparent under any conditions, but he had the good fortune of achieving public attention as Catholicism became a pervasive force in the country.

In 1943, Kagame published his first book, an oral history of ancient Rwanda. This book was followed by several volumes of poetry and finally by a multivolume creation epic, published in French as *La Divine Pastorale* (1952–1955). It presents a Rwandese creation myth and history of the world, revealing parallels between Tutsi traditions and Christian teaching, which was a favorite theme of Kagame's. In the 1970s he added several critical studies of Rwandese dynastic poetry.

In 1952, Kagame wrote *Le Code des Institutions Politiques du Rwanda,* a stirring defense and vindication of the Tutsi feudal system. The Belgian authorities found his nationalist work disturbing and conveniently arranged for Kagame to be sent to Rome for higher studies. He became a member of *les prêtres noirs* (the Black priests), a loose association of young African theology students who were undertaking a nationalist reading of Christianity. Kagame's doctoral thesis in Rome became his most noted work, *The Bantu-Rwandese Philosophy of Being* (1956). In it Kagame made African thought available in Western terms, by attempting a synthesis of Bantu thought patterns with Scholastic philosophy. It not only replied effectively to missionary interpretations of African thought but also began a dialogue on the nature of African religion and its relationship with Western Christianity.

After returning home, Kagame began teaching at the Catholic seminary and published a history of Rwanda and a study of the Kinyarwanda language. In 1959, after the death of the king, the Hutu overthrew the feudal system in a vicious bloodbath of revenge. Kagame, despite his identification with the former ruling class, was unaffected due to the general respect for his scholarship and thought. He was appointed to the National University when it was founded in 1963 and subsequently received many international honors, which included serving on the prestigious UNESCO committee for writing a general history of Africa.

During this later period he also championed the Africanization of Christianity, using the documents of the Second Vatican Council to argue against maintaining missionary attitudes. With the importance of Catholicism in Rwandese society, this was a statement that went far beyond religious issues. Kagame's lasting influence is his argument on the indigenization of the Church. In this he was strongly opposed by the Apostolic Delegate, the diplomatic representative of the Vatican, and a group under the Belgian Brothers of Charity, the "Groupe Scolaire." In many ways, the debate went beyond the issues of religion to the wider questions of the integrity of African cultures under the impact of western ideas. Despite his eminence, Kagame was a transitional thinker, mediating African thought in Western terms but making it possible for a newer generation of intellectuals to begin a more integrally African philosophy that at the same time has a place in the contemporary world. To the end he remained a staunch monarchist and defender of the traditional rights and role of the king.

Early on, Kagame collected dynastic poetry and his collections, many translated into French, are the only surviving collections of dynastic verse from the royal court. His collections of oral poetry were massive, but he also wrote his own verse. *La Divine Pastorale* (1952) is a poem in 24 cantos, and is perhaps the greatest work of Afro-Christian poetry.

References: *adb*, AA, *dacb*, DAHB, EB, MMA. Joseph Nsengimana, *Alexis Kagame: L'Homme* (Alexis Kagame: The Man, 1987).

KAGAME, Paul
(Rwanda, 1957–)

President Paul Kagame has been head of the government of Rwanda since he led his forces to victory in the invasion of Rwanda as the general in command of the Rwandan Patriotic Front (RPF).

Rwanda has been wracked by periodic spasms of ethnic conflict between the educated minority Tutsi and the Hutu majority, largely small-holding peasants. During the colonial period, the Tutsi were given privileged status, and the fallout has often been tragic. In 1959, The Hutu overthrew the last Tutsi monarch, killing 20,000 Tutsi and forcing over 100,000 into exile in neighboring Uganda, where the infant Kagame was raised in a refugee camp. As a youth he joined the rebel forces of Yoweri MUSEVENI against the dictator Milton OBOTE. Museveni came to power in 1986 and Kagame became chief of military intelligence. A year later, with Museveni's support, Kagame helped found the RPF as a guerilla force in western Uganda. The RPF trained and prepared itself and launched an invasion of Rwanda in 1990, while Kagame was attending an advanced officers' training program in the United States. Kagame immediately returned home, and when the RPF leader was killed, he assumed command.

The RPF found itself with a base in the Ruwenzori Mountains, but was unable to venture further, held back by a combined force of French, Belgian and Democratic Republic of the Congo (DRC) forces. The RPF made another attempt to push out of their redoubt, and then in 1993 Kagame signed an agreement with President Juvénal HABYARIMANA, calling for a transition to multipar-

Paul Kagame

ty democracy and the repatriation of Rwandan exiles. Habyarimana's concessions did not sit well with his own army and many radical Hutus. In 1994, Habyarimana's plane was shot down over the military base outside the capital. This touched off a genocidal massacre, in which 800,000 Tutsi were hacked, burned and shot to death in an orgy of slaughter. United Nations forces were forbidden to intervene, but the RPF took to the field and moved quickly on the capital. Fearing retaliation, 1.5 million Hutu, including many of the worst militias, the *Interahamwe*, fled the country, mainly to the DRC.

Kagame was now the undisputed leader. He appointed a Hutu RPF-loyalist as president and a second Hutu as a vice president in a gesture of national unity, reserving for himself the second vice presidency and the Ministry of Defense. With parts of the Hutu forces reforming in the DRC and attacking Rwandan border towns, Kagame became a supporter of Laurent-Désiré KABILA's rebellion against MOBUTU Sese Seko. Rwandan forces also crossed over the border to attack their enemies lodged in the DRC.

After a falling-out with his chosen president, Kagame took over the office in 2001. He then won a landslide victory in elections in 2003 against his protégé, who organized a militia as part of his opposition party until he was defeated, arrested and sentenced to 15 years' imprisonment. Kagame's domestic policies have largely focused on national unity and repairing a shattered economy. He has insisted on the importance of bringing the perpetrators of genocide to some sort of justice, but given the extent of involvement among the people, he has fostered local village courts to hear cases and decide the guilt of ordinary citizens in the genocide.

References: adb, afr, EB, *wiki.* Colin Waugh, *Paul Kagame and Rwanda* (2004).

KAGGIA, Bildad
(Kenya, 1921?–2005)

Bildad Kaggia was a radical leader among the Kikuyu, the largest ethnic group in Kenya. He was convinced of the necessity of Africanizing postcolonial society, was active in the liberation movement, founded an African independent church, and became a leading socialist labor leader in Kenya.

Because he was unable to raise school fees, Kaggia became a government clerk until being recruited into the British army in 1940. He was sent to the Middle East, and the experience radicalized him when he realized that the British, whom he had been led to believe were superior, could be defeated. He returned home a revolutionary, seeing no future in the existing African cultural association, which he considered elitist and conservative. Instead, inspired by a visit to Jerusalem that led him to reject missionary Christianity, he founded an African Christian Church to reinterpret Christianity with an African voice. Kaggia was arrested several times for holding unlicensed meetings, but his Friends of the Holy Spirit spread across Kenya as a reaction to the "*mzungu* [White] church of the Pharisees."

Kaggia supported himself as a bank clerk and formed the Clerks and Commercial Workers Union, which he affiliated with the Labour Trade Union of East Africa, an organization that he later headed. During this same period he joined Jomo KENYATTA's political party, using his union following to take control of its Nairobi branch in 1951 and radicalize it. Secretly, he had also joined the central committee of the Mau Mau guerrilla movement. In 1952 he, Kenyatta and others, the "Kapenguria Six," were arrested and imprisoned until 1959 under the emergency proclaimed by the colonial authorities. This was followed by two years of restriction under house arrest. Kaggia always found it amusing that the British considered Kenyatta the head of the Mau Mau, when it was actually Kaggia who told Kenyatta the names of its leaders.

Kaggia was elected to parliament at Kenyan independence in 1963 and made an assistant minister of education, but he clashed with Kenyatta over land policy and was removed. When Kenyatta offered Kaggia a land grant, he refused because the poor had not been resettled. Kaggia defended the rights of squatters and former freedom fighters and called for cooperatives to be established on confiscated White farms. He became a leader of the backbenchers and an open critic of the government. He was finally forced, with Oginga ODINGA, to leave and form an opposition party. Kaggia lost his seat in the next election, and in 1968 he was arrested for holding an unlicensed meeting, which led to a six-month prison term. Following his service on government commodities boards, he retired from politics in the early 1970s. He always

lived simply, and died in poverty, neglected by the nation he has helped found.

References: dacb, Kaggia, *Roots of Freedom, 1921–1963* (1975).

KAGGWA, Apolo
(Uganda, 1860s–1927)

Sir Apolo Kaggwa served as *katikiro,* or prime minister, of Buganda, the largest kingdom in what is now Uganda, during the critical period during which the area came under British control. When factions developed along religious lines, he became the leader of the Protestants and the most powerful African political personality in Uganda during the first 40 years of the colonial era.

Although it was ruled by an absolute monarch, Buganda allowed for talented people to rise in political and social status through ability rather than birth or class. The usual route to advancement was through court service, and around 1877, Kaggwa became a page to MUTESA I. He arrived around the time that Christian missionaries began to achieve success among the pages, and Kaggwa became a candidate for conversation to Anglicanism. Candidates were called "readers," because they were made functionally literate in order to read the Bible. Kaggwa was baptized around 1884, when MWANGA II became king.

The king was a moody and volatile youth who played off various factions, which included the traditional chiefs, influential Islamic traders and their converts, and the growing Anglican and Catholic communities. In 1886, Mwanga instituted an anti-Christian purge that resulted in the deaths of over a hundred, including the bloody executions of 44 Christians. Kaggwa escaped with only a beating as the Christians, supplied with martyrs, began to flourish. Kaggwa, although probably not a devout Christian, immediately saw advantages in Christianity as a path to education and modernization. Mwanga, in a characteristic switch, appointed him commander of the royal guard in 1887.

The kingdom entered a brief period of complex alliances and confusing power struggles that first saw Mwanga overthrown by a Christian-Muslim alliance in 1888. Kaggwa joined many other Christians in exile in the neighboring kingdom of Ankole, but returned within a year at the head of a Christian force that placed Mwanga back on the throne, this time under Kaggwa's influence. Kaggwa was appointed *katikiro* and when the British arrived in 1890, he signed a treaty of alliance with Sir Frederick LUGARD. Tensions between Anglicans and Catholics progressed into open conflict, and Lugard sided with the Protestants, enabling them to defeat the Catholic faction, many of whom migrated west to settle around Masaka. A British protectorate over Uganda was declared in 1894.

Mwanga, chafing under the loss of his powers, attempted an anticolonial coup but was deposed by the British with Kaggwa's assistance. Mwanga was forced into exile, and his infant son inherited the throne. Kaggwa became regent and the most powerful person in the kingdom. In 1900 he negotiated a treaty that was highly favorable to the Baganda, allowing them to keep their *kabaka* (king), parliament and court system. Kaggwa also received a large land grant, and in 1905 he was knighted. Throughout his life, Kaggwa insisted that the treaty was a pact between equals, but the British insistence upon their dominant position caused constant friction between him and the governor. In 1914 the *kabaka* acceded to his throne, ending the regency. Kaggwa continued as *katikiro,* but opposition to him grew among the chiefs, who had never been pleased with the 1900 agreement. In 1926 the *kabaka* used a disagreement over beer permits as an excuse to remove Kaggwa. Kaggwa elevated the dispute to one of the equality of the partners in the 1900 treaty, which removed any further support he had from the British colonial authorities. He left for England to press his rights but died in Kenya on the way.

Kaggwa's main achievement was to bring the Baganda into a favored position in Uganda. They gained preferential treatment in education and development over other neighboring peoples. In addition, he wrote several books in Luganda on the customs and history of the Baganda. These are valuable resources for the last 25 years of the precolonial period.

References: afr, DAHB, MMA.

KAHARI, George Payne
(Zimbabwe, 1930–)

Dr. George Payne Kahari is chair of the Department of African Languages and Literature at the Universi-

ty of Zimbabwe, and the leading literary analyst of Zimbabwean literature.

Kahari was born into a herding family but was sent to school, where he fell in love with writing in Shona, his mother tongue. After teaching and heading a school, he took a degree from the University of South Africa, and then studied in England for a year before receiving a Ph.D. from the University of Zimbabwe. He then commenced his lifelong study of Shona names and writing in indigenous Zimbabwean languages. Among others, he has analyzed and popularized the little-known fiction of the national hero, Bernard CHIDZERO.

Kahari joined the faculty of the University of Zimbabwe in 1965, and has been a prolific writer on African literature. He has published 17 books and innumerable articles in his field. He began his work under the colonial regime when Shona fiction was banned and all writing in local languages was censored. He believes strongly in the close relationship between politics and literature, citing a number of novels with political themes. Independence in 1980 allowed a flood of new writing, and Kahari has been the leading literary critic of the movement. From 1980 to 1989 he served as dean of the Faculty of Arts at the University.

Kahari's position and eminence as a scholar led to diplomatic appointments, and he served as ambassador in Germany, Italy and Czechoslovakia from 1989 to 1993. In 1993 he was awarded both Gold and Silver Liberation Medals by President Robert MUGABE. The following year he became director of the National Gallery of Zimbabwe, a position he held until 2003.

Kahari has been a Fulbright Scholar in the United States and a visiting professor at several universities. He has also been a leading figure in the establishment of a Catholic University of Zimbabwe. In 2005, Kahari was appointed to the controversial Zimbabwe Electoral Commission by President Mugabe.

Reference: adb.

KALLÉ, Pepé
(Democratic Republic of the Congo, 1951–1998)

Pepé Kallé, one of the leading seminal figures in the *soukous* mainstream of Congolese popular dance music, was one of the few recording artists who refused to emigrate to Paris.

Soukous was originally a dance popularized in the 1960s, but the word soon became a generic term for any Congolese dance music. Kallé insisted on retaining *soukous*'s dance roots, not only by performing in dance halls but also by creating new dances to fit his new compositions. Although his recordings reflected rigid studio performances, Kallé in a live concert displayed a fuller range of his band's performance.

Born in the capital, Kinshasa (then called Léopoldville), the center of new African music from the 1950s through the 1980s, Kallé grew up exposed to the best bands on the continent. In his teens he left school to perform, and by 1968 he was part of the leading Congolese popular band, Kallé Kabasele's African Jazz. Despite the name, it played Congo rhumba based on such Latino dance music as merengue, mambo and beguine. Pepé Kallé moved on in 1970 to begin his own group, called African Choc. A year later, MOBUTU Sese Seko, who had stabilized the country under an authoritarian dictatorship, launched his *authenticité* campaign, an Africanization program that changed the national name from Congo to Zaïre and required all Western names to be replaced with African ones. African Choc became Empire Bakuba, the name by which it has since been known. Kallé rose to stardom on the wave of youth music that carried along a number of musicians in the 1970s.

Empire Bakuba plays a rock-influenced *soukous* that does away with horn sections. Older bands (such as Tabu LEY's Afrisa) use a two-part structure, starting with a long, sometimes languid, slow section before breaking into a frenetic explosion of dynamic sound. Empire Bakuba starts with a fast beat that never slows, gradually weaving guitar lines into the music until they provide an intricate network of cross rhythms. The roots of Kallé's *soukous* were in Afro-Cuban rhumba, a dance music that was introduced to the area during World War II, although its essential rhythms originated in Africa. Empire Bakuba has made many recordings, but among the best have been *Kwassa Kwassa* (1989), which showcases the band's unique style, and *Gigant-Afrique* (1990). The last work before his sudden death was *Full Option* (1997), which was well received. The band has continued without Kallé, but it has struggled and produced few recordings. Several posthumous recordings have been issued from work done before Kallé's death.

Kallé, a large man (six feet, six inches and over 330 pounds) with an imposing stage presence, was affectionately known as "Le Bombe Atomique" and "The Elephant of Zaïre." Despite his size, he was agile on stage. He had a strong high tenor voice that fit well into the total sound of his band.

Reference: GEPM, WAM, *wiki*.

KAMWANA, Elliot Kenan
(Malawi, 1872–1956)

Elliot Kenan Kamwana was the founder of the Watch Tower movement and a Christian separatist leader, one of the forerunners of the African independent church movement.

He began as a Scots Presbyterian and between 1899 and 1903 led a highly successful revival movement. On a trip to South Africa he met Joseph Booth, a peripatetic English missionary who founded many sects and had baptized John CHILEMBWE. Kamwana became an Adventist and then a Jehovah's Witness. Returning to Malawi (then the British colony of Nyasaland) in 1906, he established a branch church known as the Watch Tower, taking the name from the newspaper of the Jehovah's Witnesses, and within three years he had baptized 10,000 followers. Kamwana preached that Armageddon would arrive in 1914 and that at his second coming, Christ would abolish hut taxes and expel all Europeans. The British authorities responded by deporting Kamwana to South Africa (1909–1914) and banned the Watch Tower movement.

During Kamwana's exile, his churches continued as an underground movement. Without organization, the Watch Tower movement spread to Northern Rhodesia (now Zambia) and the Belgian Congo (now the Democratic Republic of the Congo, or DRC), continuing to preach the end of colonialism. Whole areas of the western DRC converted to the new religion. Although it was pacifist, colonial authorities suppressed it whenever possible. The Watch Tower movement continued to follow Jehovah's Witness teaching, using its symbolism. It was often known as *Kitawala* or "Kingdom," a central Witness theme, and preached the imminent coming of Christ, although it was non-Christian in its focus.

The failure of the millennium to arrive in 1914 as predicted by Kamwana did not deter the growth of the movement. Kamwana preached briefly in Mozambique but was promptly deported to Malawi. During the Chilembwe revolt (1915) he was placed in preventive detention and then deported to Mauritius in the Indian Ocean because his followers refused to enter the army. In 1937, Kamwana returned to Malawi to take charge of the movement, but it was much reduced by then. He quietly continued to lead it until his death.

References: dacb, DAHB.

KANDA Bongo Man
(Democratic Republic of the Congo, 1955–)

Kanda Bongo Man is the leading African musician based in Paris, which since 1980 has become a center of African popular music. He grew up not far from Kinshasa, the capital of the Democratic Republic of the Congo (DRC), during the era when the new urban pop music of the Congo was taking form and its first big bands—FRANCO's OK Jazz (1956) and Tabu LEY's Afrisa (1965)—were being established. They brought together what was to be the basis of Congo *soukous,* a synthesis of traditional African music, Afro-Latin rhythms and American jazz.

Kanda's father (also called Bongo Man) and grandfather were both local musicians, and there seems to have been family opposition to his going to Kinshasa as a teenager. But by 1972 he had gotten his first permanent job with a group called Bella Bella. At that time, more than 30 bands were working in the capital and competition was fierce. Kanda has a high tenor voice that blended well with Bella Bella's melodic emphasis, and he readily admits that this band was a major influence on his style. He was ready to leave, however, by the end of the decade, when it became clear to him that a successful recording industry would never develop in MOBUTU Sese Seko's Zaïre, as the country was then called. In 1979 he departed for Paris, never returning home. Since that time Kanda has become the most prominent of the large number of Congolese musicians in Paris who both perform and record there.

Iyole, Kanda's first solo album, was released in 1981. It was followed by *Djessy* in 1982. Kanda was invited to the 1983 WOMAD (World of Music, Arts, and Dance) festival, and his career was launched. After several more successful records, Kanda invested financially in his own work. He is one of the few African artists who controls his own production, for both artistic and financial reasons. In 1984 the new Bongo Man recording label released *Amour Fou,* which used a synthesizer for the first time. Kanda admits that technology has shifted his high-energy dance music further away from its African roots, although he has never wavered in his use of the basic rhumba beat. Kanda has even experimented with high-tech Caribbean music. It is the ability to use technological advances such as these plus the community of Congolese talent that has kept Kanda in Paris. Because of the availability of musicians, Kanda puts together a new group for each album, with the exception of his lead guitarist, who has worked with him since 1982.

Kanda has developed a high-speed *soukous* style that he is able to maintain, despite never having formed his own band. He moved away from the earlier styles of *soukous,* which begin slowly and then move into what is called the *sembène,* a fast passage led by the lead guitar. Kanda begins his songs with the *sembène,* producing a high-energy dance sound from start to finish. The effect created the *kwassa kwassa* dance style, with swinging hips and hands moving in rhythm. He sings in Lingala, which has become the *lingua franca* of Congolese pop. He has expressed dissatisfaction at the pace with which *soukous* has been accepted outside Africa, although he tours extensively in Japan and the United States to demonstrate the accessibility of his music on the world scene. In 2005, he performed at BONO's Live 8 concert in Cornwall.

References: BPAR, GEPM, WAM, *wiki.*

KANEMI, Muhammad al-
(Niger/Nigeria, 1779?–1835?)

Sheikh Muhammad al-Kanemi was the religious and political leader of Bornu who saved his nation during the Fulani *jihad,* or holy war.

The son of a sheikh, as a young man he studied to become a Muslim scholar and made the arduous pilgrimage to Mecca, the *hajj.* Shortly after his return, the Fulani people under the mystic and empire-builder UTHMAN Dan Fodio began a *jihad* to extend and purify Islam. When they captured

Bornu around 1808, al-Kanemi organized resistance forces to aid the *mai,* or ruler, of Bornu, who had pleaded that as a fellow Muslim he should not be attacked. Although this plea was ignored, al-Kanemi and the *mai* routed the Fulani, and al-Kanemi was given rule over four communities. He became the most important person in the kingdom but never became *mai.*

In 1813, after the *mai* had been deposed by nobles who were jealous of al-Kanemi's rise to power, al-Kanemi conspired to restore the *mai.* As a result of his success in this counter-coup, al-Kanemi became an even more dominant figure in Bornu. His clansmen moved into the kingdom and assumed positions of power to strengthen his authority. He built a new capital, leaving the *mai* in his palace as a figurehead. By 1820 the *mai* was chafing under this secondary role, so he plotted with a neighboring king to invade the new capital. The plan was to have the *mai* turn upon al-Kanemi in battle, trapping him between the two forces. Al-Kanemi learned of the ruse and maneuvered so that the two attacked one another, and the *mai* was killed. Al-Kanemi now chose a completely compliant person to hold the title. After 1820, al-Kanemi was able to establish the borders of Bornu and develop a strong centralized government. His son removed the last *mai* and established a dynasty that still governs Bornu.

Like Uthman Dan Fodio, al-Kanemi was a religious leader. He believed that he was guided by divine authority and continued his Islamic studies throughout his life. At one point he engaged in a long correspondence with Uthman Dan Fodio and his son Muhammad BELLO, debating the appropriateness of holy war as a means of reform. He constantly professed his desire to return to religious reflection but felt that his governance was a divine commission. He is reputed to have stated that if he could, he "would be out of here like a runaway slave." Al-Kanemi lived in simplicity and was noted for his upright character and religious piety.

References: DAHB, MMA.

KASAVUBU, Joseph
(Democratic Republic of the Congo, 1913?–1969)

Joseph Kasavubu, first president of the Congo (now the Democratic Republic of the Congo, DRC),

presided over a total collapse of order in the nation until he was finally removed from office in a military coup.

Kasavubu was educated at a Catholic mission school before he entered a preparatory seminary. He continued to study for the Catholic priesthood from 1928 to 1937 but was asked to leave before taking orders. At that point, political organizing being forbidden, cultural societies offered the only outlet for nationalist activities. In 1950, when the cultural group Abako was founded to promote Bakongo culture and language, Kasavubu became active and turned it toward political mobilization. He was elected president and used that platform to become a leading spokesman for Congolese rights. In 1955 a national dialogue was begun on the future independence of the Congo. Kasavubu contributed to the discussion with the blunt assertion that a slow-paced preparation would be unjust and insisted on immediate independence with full freedom of the press, speech and association. He rejected colonial patronage and insisted that only Africans could decide their destinies.

When Belgium permitted the election of Africans for urban posts in 1957, Abako won about 65 percent of the vote. A year later, French President Charles de Gaulle visited the French Congo and offered that colony independence. The effect was electrifying across the border in the Belgian Congo. After a riot following an unemployment demonstration in 1959 resulted in 50 to 100 deaths, Kasavubu was arrested and then briefly deported to Belgium. Abako boycotted elections that year, forcing the Belgians to convene negotiations in January 1960. Kasavubu demanded that the discussions be binding and then forced through several major concessions, which ended with an agreement on independence by June.

The first national election was won by Patrice LUMUMBA, but lacking a clear majority, he became prime minister while Kasavubu was named president. Left out of all consideration was Moïse TSHOMBE, the leader of Katanga province. To this point, Kasavubu had advocated a loose confederation, but he now favored a centralized system, much to the dismay of Tshombe, a staunch supporter of semiautonomous provinces. The matter was left unsettled constitutionally. Within two weeks of independence, the army mutinied. Panic spread throughout the country, and Tshombe took advantage of the situation to declare Katanga independent. Kasavubu and Lumumba asked for U.N. help, and a peacekeeping force was sent in to restore order. Relations between Kasavubu and Lumumba completely broke down shortly thereafter and each declared the other deposed from office. In this confused state of affairs, U.N. troops from Ghana supported Lumumba, while others supported Kasavubu. The houses of parliament endorsed Lumumba, and Kasavubu made an alliance with MOBUTU Sese Seko, commander of the Leopold Battalion. In November 1960 the U.N. seated Kasavubu's delegation, refusing to allow Lumumba to fly to New York to present his case. Lumumba was captured while trying to escape to his stronghold in Kisangani (then called Stanleyville) and was turned over to Tshombe's forces. When they killed him shortly afterward, world opinion fixed much of the blame on Kasavubu.

In 1961, a U.N.-brokered conference accepted a new constitution with a confederation of independent states under Kasavubu. When Tshombe rejected the compromise, he was arrested and held for two months, then left the country. During his absence, Tshombe plotted his return while matters deteriorated in the Congo. A popular revolt spread across the country, involving Lumumbists, various bandit groups and regional factions. After a 1964 state of emergency proved useless, Kasavubu invited Tshombe back. He returned with his former troops and foreign mercenaries and brutally suppressed the revolt. The two leaders never trusted one another, however, and Kasavubu removed Tshombe. This action precipitated another constitutional crisis, and finally Mobutu intervened and took over the government in a military coup. Kasavubu cooperated with the coup and retired peacefully. A man of gentle and unassuming ways, he was caught up in events far greater than he could manage. Kasavubu attempted to mediate among powerful forces that eventually brought him down.

References: afr, CB, DAB, DAHB, EB, EWB, MMA, PLBA, *wiki.* www.kasa-vubu.info.

KAUNDA, Kenneth David

(Zambia, 1924–)

Kenneth Kaunda, father of Zambian nationalism and leader of the Frontline States against South African apartheid, was one of Africa's longest-serv-

ing heads of state and one of the few to accept defeat in a fair election and retire to private life.

Kaunda was educated at mission schools in Northern Rhodesia (now Zambia), and after completing teacher training he taught school in Tanganyika (now Tanzania) in 1945. He then returned to Northern Rhodesia's northern Copper Belt region, where he worked as a welfare assistant and organized a farmers' association. He joined this association with Harry NKUMBULA's African National Congress (ANC), becoming its secretary-general in 1953. When Kaunda became increasingly unhappy with Nkumbula's moderate views, his faction split from the ANC in 1958. Kaunda was imprisoned in 1959 after clashes with the colonial government, but upon his release he formed a new party. Following local self-government in 1962, Kaunda joined an all-party cabinet, but in 1964 his United National Independence Party (UNIP) swept the elections and governed alone. That year, Kaunda became president of an independent Zambia.

Kenneth David Kaunda

Kaunda's first domestic crisis came from a separatist religious sect, the Lumpa Church, led by Prophetess Alice LENSHINA. Her disciples had rejected government authority and barricaded themselves in fortified villages. With British help, Kaunda disbanded the Lumpa Church, destroyed the towns, and interned Lenshina. He was widely criticized for the violence of the repression, which cost over 700 lives.

Kaunda's first years in office were prosperous ones for Zambia, which was dependent on copper exports. So long as copper prices were high, the economy soared, and Kaunda provided generous social benefits, including universal free education and health care. After commodity prices fell in later years and substitutes for copper wire closed traditional markets, Kaunda's weak management of the economy became obvious. Intent on a socialist policy that did little to attract foreign investment, he set in place programs that damaged the economy. Parastatal (government-owned) companies became riddled with corruption, although Kaunda himself was never tainted with impropriety. Massive state-run farms produced less than peasants had previously. The economy went into a consistent decline that reduced some areas of the country to subsistence and brought the main cities to the brink of gridlock with constant electrical failures, water shortages, food distribution problems and rampant inflation. Kaunda initially accepted and then rejected an International Monetary Fund reform package that he regarded as demanding too much sacrifice from his people.

Kaunda's entire tenure was dominated by regional political conflicts with White-dominated governments, which increased pressure on the Zambian economy. In 1965, Ian SMITH declared Southern Rhodesia (now Zimbabwe) independent of Great Britain and established a minority White government. Because Zambia shared hydroelectric power grids and transport networks with Rhodesia, it was plunged into crisis. An international boycott of Rhodesia closed the common borders, forcing Kaunda and Julius NYERERE of Tanzania to obtain Chinese support to built the Tazara railroad link to the Tanzanian port of Dar-es-Salaam. Nonetheless, the Zambian economy suffered from inflationary prices due to shipping costs, and internal strains caused a split in the UNIP. In 1972, Kaunda suspended all opposition parties and declared a one-party state, which lasted until 1991.

The liberation wars in Rhodesia and Angola also led Kaunda to declare a state of emergency in 1976.

In solidarity with the liberation movements of South Africa, he allowed the leadership of the South African ANC to establish its headquarters in Lusaka, close to his presidential compound, taking the personal risk of South African air strikes. ANC guerrilla training camps were set up in Zambia as well, and Kaunda took the lead in forming neighboring countries into a Frontline alliance against apartheid. His own relationship with South Africa, however, was ambivalent. Unable to survive without South African goods, Zambia tolerated imports while denying investment and maintained no official diplomatic contacts. Harboring ANC activists resulted in regular cross-border raids and bombings.

With his trademark white handkerchief dabbing at his eyes, Kaunda is an extremely emotional man, exhibiting a flamboyant style and given to fits of public weeping. He proposed a national ideology called "socialist humanism," a romantic and vague concept of human dignity, which reflects his personal gentleness and idealism. Socialist humanism was based on Kaunda's admiration of Gandhi's nonviolence as well as on a sentimental vision aimed at returning Africa to its precolonial state. Kaunda is a deeply religious man with a strong sense of mission. Although he was committed to democracy, this religious attitude produced a personal authoritarianism. Besides outlawing organized opposition, Kaunda extended his control over the media, labor unions and the army. The University of Zambia, a constant source of political opposition, was closed on numerous occasions for a year or more. Still, Kaunda has been a figure of great personal stature, leading a weak and poor country under extreme external pressures. He consistently sacrificed himself and his people for the ideals of African liberation.

The extent to which Zambians shared his extreme devotion to Pan-African liberation is questionable. As shortages and difficulties mounted, food riots became common. There were major disturbances and an attempted coup in 1988. This dissent led eventually to Kaunda's concession of a referendum on multiparty government. In 1991, the UNIP lost the first free election it contested, and Kaunda was replaced by Frederick CHILUBA, the leader of the trade unions. Chiluba later tried to deport Kaunda on the grounds that he was Malawian, and when that failed, he prevented any Zambian with foreign-born parents to stand for the presidency. Chiluba then accused him of plotting a coup against the government, and Kaunda retired from public life. Kaunda lives simply, having amassed no fortune in office, and cares for his ill wife.

References: AB, *afr*, CB, DAHB, DRWW, EB, EWB, HWL, PLBA, PLCA, RWWA, *wiki*. Kaunda, *Zambia Shall Be Free* (1962).

KAYAMBA, Hugh Martin Thackeray
(Tanzania, 1891–1939)

Hugh Martin Thackeray Kayamba was an African civil servant and supporter of colonial authority as a limiting force on White settlers. His advocacy of colonialism has caused some to regard him as antinationalist or a traitor to African interests, even though he saw the colonial government as the only protection for Africans against settler expansion. A member of the tiny African elite of the period, he was an equivocal leader from an ambiguous social class.

Born on Zanzibar, then a British possession, to two Anglican mission teachers, Kayamba was well educated for the time. During World War I he was detained for a year by the Germans because he was a British subject. When the British took over the administration of Tanganyika under a League of Nations mandate after World War I, he entered colonial service and headed the first all-African district office. He organized the country's first trade union, the Tanganyika Territory African Civil Service Association (TTACSA), which also provided classes and sports activities for its members. In 1929, Kayamba's prominence was recognized when he was appointed to an advisory commission on African affairs.

The issue that galvanized the African elite was the possible union of British East Africa into one jurisdiction. Tanganyikans feared the loss of their special mandate status and the imposition of Kenya's settler pattern, with its widespread land alienation and oppressive farm labor conditions. As a representative of the tiny African middle class, Kayamba was unfamiliar with typical peasant village life, but he ably defended the rights of rural Africans. In 1931 he was invited to London with several other prominent African leaders to report to a parliamentary commission. In his 1937 book, *African Problems,* he defined three threats to African

development: interference by missionaries, loss of land, and migrant labor. Strongly opposed to reservations, Kayamba argued for increasing African participation in colonial administration.

Kayamba expressed himself in rather romantic terms. He tended to idealize African village life and similarly praised the progress brought by White colonialism. Kayamba was neither a leader of mass movements nor a radical—some African historians have regarded him as self-serving and elitist in the extreme, characterizing him as a colonial underling. Yet he had a national vision of Tanganyika, and the TTACSA later evolved into Tanganyika's national political party.

Reference: DAHB.

KAYIBANDA, Grégoire
(Rwanda, 1924–1976)

President Grégoire Kayibanda was the first president of independent Rwanda and successfully introduced majority Hutu rule.

For generations, the Tutsi minority had ruled Rwanda, with the Hutu in feudal subordination as peasants and herdsmen. Under German (and later Belgian) colonial authority, the Tutsi were favored for education and advancement. The Catholic missions provided some opportunities for Hutu development, and Kayibanda was educated in mission schools and the major seminary. He left the seminary to become a teacher, and in the 1950s he was employed as inspector of schools. After a short period as a colonial information officer, he assumed the editorship of two Catholic newspapers, one published in French and another in Kinyarwanda. He was invited to Rome (a visit sponsored by Church officials) and spent from 1958 to 1959 in Belgium, studying journalism and serving an internship at a missionary press center.

Throughout the 1950s, Kayibanda also emerged as a Hutu political leader. A cooperative movement that he founded in 1952 developed into a political party, the Muhutu Social Movement, in 1957. It was established to campaign for Hutu rights, with peasants organized into local cells as a form of political education. When he returned from his stay in Belgium, he found Rwanda in turmoil. King MUTARA III died (apparently, he had been murdered), and Tutsi nationalists began rounding up Hutu leaders. Hutu-Tutsi clashes erupted into bloody riots. Kayibanda, who had founded another new political party, Parmehutu, had to be protected by Belgian authorities.

Kayibanda and other Hutu leaders hoped to slow the pace of independence in order to allow the Hutu to develop their political leadership, but the Belgians were determined to hold elections in 1960. After Parmehutu won a clear majority, Kayibanda was made prime minister. The new king went into exile and a republic was proclaimed, which was confirmed in a referendum. As a result, Kayibanda became executive president in 1961, a position that he retained at independence a year later. He attempted to unite the country but faced age-old animosities. In late 1963, an invading Tutsi force attempted to take control, coming within a few miles of the capital. The Hutu turned on the Tutsi in vengeance, killing more than 10,000 and sending 150,000 refugees into neighboring countries.

A modest person, Kayibanda was never tainted by corruption. When Parmehutu took all the parliamentary seats in the 1965 elections, he banned other parties but respected the rule of law and other democratic institutions. He was not able, however, to master the deteriorating economic situation, which reflected the conditions of an overpopulated country with limited resources. When further ethnic clashes broke out in 1973, resulting in several hundred deaths, General Juvénal HABYARIMANA took power in a bloodless coup. Kayibanda died of a heart attack while under house arrest.

References: DAHB, DRWW, MMA, PLBA.

KAYIRA, Legson Didimu
(Malawi, 1942?–)

The novelist Legson Kayira is known as much for his dramatic and touching story of overcoming adversity as he is for his fiction.

Kayira was born to abjectly poor parents in northern Nyasaland near the Tanzanian border. His distraught mother, unable to feed a new baby, threw him into the Didimu River in despair. When he was rescued, its name became his birth name. He showed determination at an early age, and as a teen he decided to be the first to earn an American college degree. He began to walk across Africa, subsisting on bananas and learning three words in each language region through which he passed: "food, water, job."

In Uganda he came across a directory of American colleges and applied to Skagit Valley Community College in Washington State. The college was so astounded at his story that when he applied, he was accepted with a full scholarship. The student body raised the money for his passage. When he arrived in 1960 he had walked over 3,000 miles toward his goal. *TIME* magazine featured his odyssey and his story appeared in *Reader's Digest* and *Guideposts.* After completing studies at Skagit Valley, he enrolled at the University of Washington and graduated in 1965, the same year he wrote his autobiography. This was followed by a string of novels.

Kayira's work is less impressive than his life story, which has been repeated through the years in inspirational accounts and sermons. Nevertheless, he was the first novelist from Malawi. His four novels begin with rather pastoral stories of his native Karonga village, but in his third book, *The Civil Servant* (1971), he expands his vision to begin to address social issues. *The Detainee* (1974), written during the oppressive regime of Kamuzu Hastings BANDA, is a satire upon the plight of Malawi under the old autocrat. Kayira is a gently comic writer who uses irony to explore the relationship between his characters and their world. After graduate studies at Cambridge University in England, Kayira took a position there and married a British wife.

References: adb, CA. Kayira, *I Will Try* (1965); Cynthia Kersey, *Unstoppable* (2004).

KEINO, Kipchoge Hezekiah
(Kenya, 1940–)

Kipchoge Hezekiah Keino, a brilliant and fleet-footed middle-distance runner, set world records in the 3,000 and 5,000 meter races. He also clocked the second-fastest mile in history. He may be the greatest all-round distance runner ever.

Kip Keino, like the vast majority of Kenya's notable runners, is a Nandi, one of several branches of the Kalenjin people. Born within a kilometer of Henry Rono and Mike Boit, two other outstanding medalists, Keino ran track in school but became serious only after joining the national police academy, where he excelled at sports. Keino attracted the attention of officials who were looking for promising officers to replace expatriates in the period just prior to independence, and he was appointed physical training instructor at the police academy. Within a year he held all the Kenyan records in the one, two, and three mile distances and in the relay. He took the East African championship in 1962 and placed well in the Commonwealth Games in Australia that year.

At the 1964 Tokyo Olympics, Keino placed only fifth in the 5,000 meter race, but the following year he set a world record for the 3,000 meter race with a time of 7:39, and ran the 5,000 with a time of 13:24. At the same time, he was winning a long list of other international meets. Keino trained moderately but always at high altitude, and he never depended on a coach. His altitude training made him the favorite at the Mexico City Olympics in 1968, but gall bladder problems limited him to one gold medal. He added a second gold in steeplechase at the Munich Olympics in 1972. Keino became a professional the following year and retired from competition in 1980.

Keino is a shy, easygoing man. For years he and his wife have taken in abandoned or homeless children. Sometimes 50 children are living with them at one time. He has invested wisely and owns a tea estate, a sporting goods store, and a farm, but his generosity has helped determine the modesty of his lifestyle. Keino is a hero for hundreds of youthful Kenyan runners, who try to imitate his form. Four of his children have been educated in the United States, and two of these have been varsity runners. He is president of the Kenyan Olympic Committee, and in 1996 he was inducted into the World Sports Humanitarian Hall of Fame.

References: afr, CB, *wiki*. Wayne Coffey, *Kip Keino* (1992) [young adult]; Francis Noronha, *Kipchoge of Kenya* (1975?).

KEITA, Modibo
(Mali, 1915–1977)

Modibo Keita was the first president of Mali and ruled from that country's independence in 1960 until he was overthrown by a coup in 1968. He spent the rest of his life in detention, dying only a few weeks after his release.

Born in Mali, Keita was educated at the elite William Ponty Teachers' College in Dakar, Sénégal, where he was first in his class. He returned to Mali to teach and was co-founder of the West African teacher's union.

Always a Marxist and anticolonialist, Keita entered politics in the French Sudan (now Mali) at age 30. He was one of the founders of the Rassemblement Démocratique Africain (RDA), an intercolonial party pressing for greater autonomy from France. During this period he was close to Félix HOUPHOUËT-BOIGNY and the French Communist Party. After suppression of the RDA in 1950, Keita was sent into internal exile in the Sahara. He organized schools for nomads near Tombouctou, where he had previously been a teacher. Following an easing of repression he was elected mayor of Bamako, the capital, and went to Paris in 1956 as an elected member of the French Chamber of Deputies from Mali. He became France's secretary of state on two occasions. Keita championed a federation of French West African colonies, which caused a split with Houphouët-Boigny.

In 1959, Keita became president of the Mali Federation, which collapsed after a year under pressure from Houphouët-Boigny, who kept Côte d'Ivoire out and pressured Dahomey (now Benin) and Upper Volta (today's Burkina Faso) to withdraw. At independence, Keita became president of Mali. Always a Pan-Africanist, he attempted several unions with other states, but none ever developed. In 1963, he was an instrumental figure in the drafting of the charter of the Organization of African Unity (OAU).

Under Keita, Mali remained underdeveloped and attracted no Western support. His uncompromising left-wing, anti-Western stance earned him the Lenin Peace Prize in 1963, but he received only small amounts of Soviet aid. He tolerated no opposition parties, and in 1967 he attempted a national purge in the style of the Chinese Cultural Revolution. His creed was stern: "Men have died . . . to make independence possible. If it is necessary to ruin and to kill men in order to stay independent, we shall do so without pity or regret." In 1962, Keita withdrew from membership in the Franc Zone by which France backed the currencies of its former colonies. The Malian economy was crippled by inflation as a result. Keita finally agreed to rejoin but was overthrown in a 1968 military coup led by Moussa TRAORÉ. He was imprisoned and died there, but after Traoré's own fall, his reputation has been rehabilitated.

References: afr, CB, DAHB, DRWW, EWB, MMA, PLBA, PLCA, *wiki*. Oumar Diarrah, *Le Mali de Modibo Keita* (The Mali of Modibo Keito, 1986).

KENYATTA, Jomo
(Kenya, 1891?–1978)

Mzee Jomo Kenyatta was the first president of Kenya and the leading figure in his country's independence movement. Born into the dominant Kikuyu culture, he became the chief interpreter of its traditions to Western society.

Kenyatta entered politics in 1924 with the Kikuyu Central Association (KCA), which opposed the alienation of Kikuyu land by White settlers. He served as editor of its journal from 1924 to 1929, and by 1928 he was its general secretary.

In 1929, Kenyatta went to London to lobby for Kikuyu land rights and to advocate the right to establish African schools. He failed on the first issue but won on the second and began a Kikuyu school when he returned. This move toward creating independent African institutions was opposed by colonial authorities but was to be a pattern of Kenyatta's opposition. In 1931 the KCA sent him back to England, where he stayed for 15 years and married a British woman. He first studied at the Selly Oak Colleges in Birmingham and then spent a year (1932–1933) at the Comintern Institute in Moscow.

Returning to London, Kenyatta studied at the London School of Economics (LSE) under anthropologist Bronislaw Malinowski, for whom he wrote *Facing Mount Kenya* (1938), a brilliant description and defense of Kikuyu traditional society. *Facing Mount Kenya* presents Kikuyu life as Kenyatta experienced it: as a member of the last generation to see it in a form unaffected by Western influences. The book details the customs and practices of Kikuyu society, as well as the spirit behind them, in a way that Europeans could grasp and appreciate. The book, which Kenyatta called "a text in cultural nationalism," was an assertion of the value of African society. Perhaps most controversial was his defense of female circumcision, which was strongly opposed by colonial authorities and Protestant missionaries. Kenyatta argued that the tradition was part of the total Kikuyu culture and could not be eliminated without damage to the whole. He accused Western thinkers of ignoring the ritual

meaning of traditional practices, thus rendering them merely exotic or curious. *Facing Mount Kenya,* which is still in print, had a great impact in Britain and remains a classic study of traditional African life. During the same period, Kenyatta published several other works, including a study of the Kikuyu language (he was for a time an assistant in phonetics at the LSE).

Kenyatta also became active in expatriate African circles, where he came to know anticolonial leaders from other parts of the continent and from the diaspora. The home of Dr. Hastings BANDA—the future president of Malawi, who was stranded in London by World War II—became a gathering place for Kenyatta and Kwame NKRUMAH, as well as the novelist Peter ABRAHAMS, Isaac WALLACE-JOHNSON of Sierra Leone, Harry Mwaanga NKUMBULA of Northern Rhodesia, and the Caribbeans George Padmore and C. L. R.. James. Together they formed the Pan-African Federation, which in 1945 convened the notable Fifth Pan-African Congress in Manchester, England. The conference restated the anticolonial message and laid the intellectual and strategic groundwork for the goal of African unity.

Kenyatta's long stay in England isolated him from the factional rivalries that afflicted the growing Kenyan independence movement. On his return in 1946, he was received as the one leader who could unite the anticolonial forces. He transformed the Kenya African Union (KAU), a Kikuyu cultural association, into a truly national party. Simultaneously, he became principal of a teachers' college to prepare staff for the African independent schools. Nevertheless, the colonial situation between settlers and Africans deteriorated, and Kenyatta was unable to control the Kikuyu extremists, for whom the land issue had become paramount. A guerrilla movement, the Mau Mau, began armed resistance, causing the British to declare a state of emergency. The KAU was accused of complicity in the Mau Mau uprising, and in 1952 the KAU was banned and its leadership arrested. In a sensational trial, using perjured evidence, Kenyatta and five others known as the "Kapenguria Six," were convicted and sentenced to seven years. The confinement was in Lodwar, an isolated desert post that was almost inaccessible. His main support during this period was his daughter, Margaret KENYATTA.

In Jomo Kenyatta's absence, leadership in the nationalist movement passed to Tom MBOYA. The British army crushed the Mau Mau rebellion and

Jomo Kenyatta

the emergency was lifted in 1959. The following year a new party, the Kenya African National Union (KANU), was formed with the jailed Kenyatta as president. It campaigned for his release, which came in 1961, with the proviso that he was ineligible for public office.

The British granted internal autonomy to Kenya in preparation for its full independence, and KANU was victorious in 1962 elections. The party refused to form a government until Kenyatta was able to lead it, and so became the parliamentary opposition. In 1963, KANU repeated its victory, and this time Kenyatta was allowed to become prime minister. In 1964, Kenya became independent with Kenyatta as its president.

Kenyatta was a powerful image of national unity and a widely revered force for moderation. His nickname *Mzee*, Kiswahili for "old man," became a proud and affectionate title. The White settler community, however, which presented the worst image in British Africa of racism, feared retribution and land expropriation. At a packed meeting in the White Highlands, the coffee plantation heartland of the settlers, Kenyatta confronted their fears and outlined a program of conciliation, asking them not to flee the country but to share in its development in the spirit of his slogan *Harambee!* ("let us all pull together").

Kenyatta followed a pro-Western and capitalist development approach, which alienated him from the more socialist leaders in the African nationalist movement, especially his vice president, Jaramogi Oginga ODINGA. As Odinga and others soon discovered, Kenyatta tolerated little opposition, and Kenya gradually became a one-party state. Several critics died under mysterious circumstances, and the large Kenyatta family enriched itself. Nevertheless, corruption was not extensive, nor did Kenya become a repressive state. The press moderated itself and was generally uncensored, and there was widespread prosperity. At his death, Kenyatta was succeeded by his third vice president, Daniel arap MOI.

References: AA, AB, *afr*, CA, CB, DAHB, DRWW, EB, EWB, HWL, MMA, PLBA, PLCA, *wiki*. Kenyatta, *Facing Mount Kenya* (1938) and *Suffering Without Bitterness* (1968); Azhar Chaudry, *Jomo Kenyatta* (1969).

KENYATTA, Margaret Wambui
(Kenya, 1928–)

Margaret Wambui Kenyatta, one of two children of Jomo KENYATTA and his first African wife, was her father's mainstay and support throughout his seven-year imprisonment. She then emerged as a women's leader in her own right and as an able administrator.

For an African woman of her time, Kenyatta received a good education at mission schools and the prestigious Alliance High School. She grew up in England during her father's long absence from Kenya (1931–1946) and idolized him. From 1948 to 1952 she taught in a normal school, preparing primary teachers for the independent Kikuyu schools that were run by her father as part of his nationalist program. During the emergency declared by the colonial authorities, the normal school was closed. It was only natural that when her father was detained in 1952 she would devote her time to him. He was imprisoned in an isolated desert area in the far north of Kenya in a small cottage. Living by various jobs as a telephone operator, bookbinder, and accounts clerk, Margaret Kenyatta regularly made the difficult trek to visit him, serving as a confidante, advisor, and conduit of information from others. Her public image of fidelity became fixed in the Kenyan mind during this period.

Kenyatta entered politics in 1960 with the formation of the Kenya African National Union (KANU) shortly before her father's release. She was elected a county councilor in Kiambu and began a second career of civic activities. She served the Red Cross, Girl Guides, and YWCA and was president of the Council of Kenyan Women for three terms. In 1963, when KANU swept the elections, she was selected as a councilor in Nairobi. By 1969 she was deputy mayor, and from 1970 to 1976 she served as mayor, using her background in social work to concentrate on public health issues. Her tenure was uneventful, but she proved a competent and effective administrator.

In 1976, Kenyatta was named permanent representative to the United Nations (U.N.) Environment Programme, and in 1979 adding an appointment to the U.N.'s Habitat. Because Nairobi was the international headquarters for these U.N. programs, she became a prominent figure. She extended this influence to the U.N. Year of the Woman, for which she became active on behalf of Third World women and a strong presence at the 1986 concluding conference held in Nairobi. She retired from public life shortly after this event as a highly respected woman in her own country and abroad.

References: DRWW. Louise Crane, *Ms. Africa* [young adult, 1973].

KÉRÉKOU, Ahmed Mathieu
(Benin, 1933–)

Brigadier-General Ahmed Mathieu Kérékou, military president of his country for 20 years and a remarkable survivor in an unstable political climate, permitted the introduction of competitive politics in 1990 and was defeated in a free election the following year, only to return to office by election.

Kérékou joined the French army after secondary school in Sénégal and attended the Fréjus Military Academy in France. In 1961, a year after Dahomey became independent, he transferred to its new army. He was named President Hubert MAGA's aide and received his first command in 1963. Dahomey endured 10 changes of head of state in its first 12 years, but Kérékou continued to progress in the armed services until he was named commander of the paratroop commando force and deputy chief of staff in 1970. That year saw the collapse of civilian government, with the only possible arrangement being a presidency rotating among the three major politicians: Maga, Sourou Migan APITHY, and Justin AHOMADÉGBÉ-TOMETIN. Two years later, in 1972, Kérékou distinguished himself by his restrained handling of an army mutiny, rehabilitating a fragmented and demoralized military and emerging as its leading figure.

Political leadership stagnated, and Kérékou took power in 1972, setting up a military government composed entirely of officers under 40. In 1974, he announced that Dahomey had become a Marxist state, and the following year he marked the transformation by changing the name of the country to Benin. The economy was nationalized and the government expanded. Kérékou proclaimed a civilian government in 1980, but with himself as president and with a strong military presence throughout the state. The same year he allied with Libya, converted to Islam and took the name Ahmed. This failed, however, to secure the aid he needed for the devastated economy, and in 1985 he approached the International Monetary Fund (IMF) for support. This link resulted in some liberalization of the economy and painful adjustments that caused internal dissension. Kérékou stepped back from his more radical alliances, abandoned Islam and became a born-again Christian.

By 1989 the government was not able to meet its payroll, and unrest intensified. Kérékou announced that Benin would follow the lead of Eastern European countries in abandoning Marxism. A national conference in 1990 sharply limited his powers—he called it "a civilian coup d'état"—and in 1991 elections Kérékou became the first African dictator to be defeated in free and open elections. He asked for forgiveness for the "deplorable and regrettable incidents" of his years in office. He was granted a full amnesty by the new government of Nicephore Soglo.

In the 1996 elections, Kérékou returned to office after defeating Soglo in a runoff, and was re-elected in 2001. During this second presidency, Kérékou followed a liberal economic path and the economy of Benin has improved. Finishing his term in 2006, Kérékou retired from public life.

References: afr, CBB, DAHB, DRWW, PLBA, RWWA, *wiki*.

Ahmed Mathieu Kérékou

KHAMA III
(Botswana, 1837?–1923)

Khama III, *kgozi* or paramount chief of the Ngwato, a Tswana people, was a leading supporter of Christianity in southern Africa. He became a prominent ally of the British as they expanded their colonial control.

In 1860, already heir to the chieftaincy, he was baptized and became a supporter of the London Missionary Society (LMS), one of the chief Protestant groups working in Africa at that time. In 1863 he repulsed the attacks of the Ndebele chief LOBENGULA and became a popular figure among the Ngwato. These events led to conflict between Khama and his father, Sekgoma I, who feared Khama's popularity and regarded his Christianity as a betrayal of ancestral customs. Sekgoma convened a traditional initiation ceremony that Khama, as a Christian, refused to attend, and he was removed as heir. In 1872, Khama seized the throne but was exiled a year later by his enemies. In 1875 he returned with an army and defeated his father's forces, and from that time he reigned unchallenged.

Khama's Christianity was a major cause of the rift in Ngwato society, especially as he undertook to Christianize his people. He abolished initiation ceremonies, declared Christianity the official religion, and instituted sabbath observance. He abolished witchcraft, circumcision and bride payments and restricted polygamy and alcohol, which gave him considerable control over the itinerant White traders in the region. He expanded his chieftaincy by absorbing numbers of neighboring peoples and integrated them without tolerating slavery. He built schools, initiated scientific cattle breeding, and created a mounted police corps. This stern and paternalistic progressivism earned Khama the respect of the British and the strong support of the LMS, which flourished within the kingdom.

Khama's main challenge was to maintain Ngwato autonomy in the face of colonial intrusions. His territory was pressed from several sides—Afrikaners from the south, Germans from the west and Ndebele expansion from the north. He was especially suspicious of the Afrikaners infiltrating from the Transvaal Republic and sought British support against them. As a result, when Britain established a protectorate over Bechuanaland, Khama supported the move, which protected him from both the Afrikaners and his traditional African enemies. He

was not so successful in his dealings with Cecil RHODES's British South Africa Company (BSAC). Although he personally led his troops in a campaign with the BSAC against Lobengula, when the company attempted to administer Khama's territory, he resisted. Accompanied by two Tswana chiefs, BATHOEN and Sebele, he went to London, where they won major concessions. Khama continued to be an autocratic and a respected and loved ruler until his death. He is known in Botswana as "Khama the Good."

References: afr, AH, CWAH, DAHB, EB, MMA, WGMC, *wiki*. J. Mutero Chirenje, *Chief Kgama and His Times* (1978).

KHAMA, Seretse
(Botswana, 1921–1980)

Sir Seretse Khama, nationalist leader and first president of Botswana, made the transition from traditional rule into the postcolonial period, making his country a model of democracy and stability.

Seretse Khama was the grandson of KHAMA III and heir to the Ngwato chieftaincy after the death of his father, who ruled only two years. Seretse's uncle, Tshekedi KHAMA, held the chieftaincy as regent, and Seretse never became *kgozi,* or paramount chief. He was educated in South Africa and graduated from Fort Hare College in 1944. He deferred taking up his ruling position in order to study law in England. In London he married an English woman without permission, which threw Bechuanaland (the colonial name of Botswana) into a political crisis. In addition, the marriage infuriated South Africa, which had just made interracial marriages illegal. He returned home and received acceptance of his wife as queen from the elders but was summoned back to Britain by the secretary of state. He was offered a pension to renounce his claims to be *kgozi,* and when he refused, he was banned from returning home from 1950 to 1956, when he and Tshekedi Khama both renounced any royal claims.

Seretse Khama retained immense prestige in Botswana during his exile, and his absence from everyday administration made him more of a national than an ethnic leader. In 1962 he founded the Botswana Democratic Party (BDP), which has dominated politics since independence. He helped negotiate the terms of Botswanan independence and became prime minister in 1965 and president the following year. He was knighted in 1966. Khama used his prestige to bring together various ethnic groups and to transfer the powers of the traditional chiefs to the new democratically elected government. This was a major accomplishment considering the loose collection of communal authorities that operated under a listless colonial administration. He established an efficient and honest government rooted in free and fair elections.

Botswana became an African success story under Khama. At independence, it was one of the weakest economies in Africa. Khama initiated a strong economy based on mineral wealth and farming, despite Botswana's arid climate and poverty. Throughout Khama's tenure in office, Botswana had the highest growth rate of any economy in the world, spurred on by major discoveries of diamonds. Dependence on South Africa caused tensions, but Botswana was always a moderate among the Frontline States. Although he refused to allow liberation movements to establish camps in Botswana, he permitted them transit to camps in Zambia. As a result of this policy, Botswana suffered several South African and Rhodesian raids. Khama took a prominent role in negotiating a peaceful transition from the White-led Rhodesian government to independence for Zimbabwe. An opponent of racial politics, he said upon taking the presidency: "We stand virtually alone in our belief that a non-racial society can work now, but there are those . . . who will be only too delighted to see our experiment fail."

References: AB, *afr*, AO, CB, DAHB, DRWW, EB, EWB, MMA, PLBA, PLCA, *wiki*.

KHAMA, Tshekedi
(Botswana, 1905–1959)

Tshekedi Khama was regent (until 1949) and acting chief of the Ngwato people from 1925 to 1952. He was the son of KHAMA III, but his nephew, Seretse KHAMA, was the heir-apparent because he was the son of Khama III's successor.

Tshekedi Khama, although he was a young man when he assumed the regency (his nephew was a child of four), was a strong chief with independent ideas. He took advantage of the delegated authority that had enhanced the power of chiefs under the colonial system and built up considerable political strength. He overrode local administrators where

necessary and learned how to use the British appeal system to his own advantage.

The critical issue for Botswana—then Bechuanaland Protectorate—was to maintain its separation from South Africa, because annexation would mean a loss of freedom, racial discrimination, alienation of land, and a reversal of progress. Bechuanaland was one of three territories that were planned to be incorporated into South Africa under the South Africa Act (1909), which had not been carried out. Tshekedi Khama successfully resisted attempts by the British South Africa Company to extend its mining claims in Bechuanaland, taking the issue to the secretary of state for the colonies. In 1936, South African Prime Minister James HERTZOG attempted to incorporate the British protectorates of Bechuanaland, Lesotho, and Swaziland, and Khama was instrumental in defeating the proposal. He made alliances where useful, helping to keep Jan SMUTS from annexing South-West Africa (Namibia) in 1949 by joining with Chief Hosea KUTAKO to block the move in the United Nations (U.N.). Every issue he faced in foreign policy was colored by the threat of South Africa. During World War II, Khama even enforced a bitterly unpopular conscription program in order to keep his men out of army units that were under South African control.

In addition to external problems, he had to deal with the ongoing issue of Seretse Khama's status. In 1944, Tshekedi Khama asked Seretse to take the chieftaincy, but Seretse deferred this until completing studies in England. In 1948 he married an English woman, which caused a political crisis. Tshekedi Khama feared the result of this action among the Ngwato, but Seretse gained support when he returned home. Tshekedi also realized that a White wife would make Seretse unacceptable to South Africa. Pressures mounted until both Khamas were forced into exile and resigned their claims to the chieftaincy. The position went unfilled from 1950 to 1953, a period of some disorder. Within a few years, however, Botswana was on the road to independence.

References: DAHB, MMA.

KHUMALO ARBS, Michael
(Malawi, 1960–)

Michael Khumalo Arbs has made his mark among the rising group of stone sculptors from Zimbabwe, which has emerged as the center for modern sculpture in Africa.

Khumalo Arbs began carving as a young man by watching local carvers and learning from them. He never studied sculpture formally in school nor apprenticed himself to a single artist. Nevertheless, the influence of his friends and associates gave him ample opportunity to develop his own style.

Khumalo Arbs works in stone, and he began his work in this medium. That is unusual for an African sculptor, who usually begins in wood. In recent years he has also expanded to the use of stoneware, clay that has been fired at such high temperature that it becomes, in essence, stone. Khumalo Arbs's forms do not emerge from the stone itself but from his experience of the environment of Zimbabwe. They are rounded and soft, often suggesting human figures but at other times completely abstract.

His own informal and self-taught experience has inspired Khumalo Arbs to become a teacher through educational workshops rather than affiliate himself with an art school. He hosts demonstrations regularly at venues where his work is exhibited, at art galleries and shows. He has done workshops for professional artists as well as in schools at all levels. He has exhibited around the world, but the bulk of his exhibits are in England, where he enters shows from four to six times a year. Since moving to Great Britain, where he is now based, he has become a member of the Royal British Society of Sculptors and several other professional groups.

Reference: http://khumalo.myexpose.com.

KIBAKI, Mwai
(Kenya, 1931–)

Mwai Kibaki is a longtime public figure in Kenya, a member of parliament for 40 years, a holder of several ministry posts and the vice presidency, and Kenya's third president since 2002. In that post he has struggled as his control over the government has eroded.

Kibaki posted one "first" after another in school, initially at the prestigious Mang'u Secondary, then at Makerere University in Uganda. Sent to England, he took a further degree in finance at the London School of Economics and returned to Makerere to teach. With independence coming, he returned to Kenya as executive for the Kenya African National Union (KANU), the leading national party, and worked on the drafting of the Kenyan constitution. He was elected to parliament in 1963.

From the start, Kibaki was made an assistant minister (Finance), and then minister of Commerce in 1966, and minister of Finance in 1969. In 1974, *TIME* magazine named him among the top 100 potential leaders in the world. When Jomo KENYATTA died, President Daniel arap MOI made Kibaki his vice president. By 1988, the two were at loggerheads, and Kibaki was replaced, but kept in the cabinet as minister of Health.

Kibaki was restless under Moi and increasingly disturbed by the rampant corruption in the government. In 1991, when contested elections were allowed and one-party rule ended, Kibaki quit KANU and founded the Democratic Party (DP). He failed in his first bid for the presidency in 1992, but came in second in 1997. In both instances, the opposition to KANU was badly split among several parties. By 1997, Kibaki was in open and critical opposition with Moi. In 2002, the DP united the opposition into the National Rainbow Coalition (NRC), and Kibaki won an overwhelming victory over Moi's hand-picked candidate, a son of Jomo Kenyatta.

Kibaki had campaigned on a platform of change, transparency, the end of ethnic persecution, and reform of corruption. His victory was hailed in the West, especially among countries with heavy investments in the Kenyan economy. Kibaki proved to be a delegator, in sharp contrast to the centralized micro-managed control practiced by Moi. His hands-off approach has proved to be his undoing, but he has also had to contend with a cabinet spread out among the many factions that make up the NRC, and his own frail health.

In 2005, Kibaki attempted a major revamp of the constitution which would have given him expanded powers. Many citizens considered the proposal a betrayal of his promises to reduce the strongman role of the presidency, and in a plebiscite it was brought down by a 57 percent negative vote.

Seven members of the cabinet campaigned against the proposal and the vote split on ethnic lines.

At the start of his term, Kibaki appointed an investigator to root out corruption. By 2005, it was clear that corruption extended into the highest reaches of government, and Kibaki was doing little to deal with it. As they were exposed, ministers—and even the vice president—resigned. Fearing indictment, bribes and rake-offs began to be refunded secretly to the Central Bank, some $300 million in all. The anti-corruption czar fled to England in fear for his life. From there he revealed more corruption, including a billion-dollar deal for diamonds that never existed. In the aftermath of the revelations, Kibaki's government has gone into continual crisis.

References: adb, EB, *wiki.*

KIDJO, Angelique
(Benin, 1960–)

Angelique Kidjo is a leading African rock artist who writes in a rebellious style, preferring the international rock scene to links to traditional African music. "I won't do my music different to please some people. I am not going to play traditional drums and dress like bush people." Despite that assertion of independence, she often sings in Fon, a tonal language, although she records in France and performs there and in England and the United States. She has not performed in Benin for many years.

Kidjo's early influences were the Beatles, Carlos Santana and Simon and Garfunkel, although she has always admired Miriam MAKEBA. Encouraged by her parents, she studied jazz in Paris in the 1980s. Her first recordings earned respectable sales, but she gained international attention in 1994 with *Ayé,* and the title song became a hit single. *Fifa* (1996) was her first album to include English lyrics. In later years her music has shown Brazilian influences, especially after a visit to Bahia. In *Black Ivory Soul* (2002), she blends Brazilian, Caribbean and African beats into an organic whole.

On stage, Kidjo is a dynamic and dominating presence. Her voice interacts with the musicians, and when she sings in Fon, the tonal aspect of the words weaves into the music in unique ways. Kidjo has been nominated for a Grammy and received the Prix Afrique (1992), the Danish Music Award as Best Female Singer (1995) and the Kora Award as Best African Female Artist (1997).

References: afr, adb, EB, *wiki.* http://ayemusic. free.fr.

KIGERI IV Rwabugiri
(Rwanda, ?–1895)

Mwami Kigeri IV Rwabugiri, last independent king of Rwanda, extended the borders of his kingdom to their furthest limits. The kingdom had been established in the fifteenth century by the Tutsi, whose economy was based on cattle. Gradually, they dominated the majority agricultural Hutu people and became the aristocratic ruling class of Rwanda. Because it was in a mountainous area, the kingdom remained largely isolated from outside contacts until the colonial period.

When Kigeri became *mwami,* or king, around 1865, he was forced to confront the serious problem of a land shortage for an expanding population. He reorganized the kingdom along centralized lines, extending the social system of caste superiority. The army was consolidated and based on conscription, and Hutu men served as warriors under Tutsi officers. He modernized the army and armed them with modern firearms. Kigeri then abolished hereditary posts in the government, appointing officials who were both competent and loyal to him.

Kigeri made Rwanda into a major expansive state in the region and was able to complete Rwandan expansion by subjugating the last Hutu chiefdoms. In general, the Hutu were subordinated to the Tutsi economically and socially. When Tutsi became poor or lost status, they often joined the Hutu. Large numbers of Tutsi also emigrated during this period. Because cattle remained the basis of wealth, trade goods were not desired, and Kigeri was able to check European imperial and commercial penetration, keeping out traders until 1894. The only significant foreign items that were sought were firearms, which were obtained from neighboring communities and were limited to use by the army.

Kigeri died in 1895 as monarch of a powerful centralized kingdom that was ruled by a small aristocracy and supported by a huge population of Hutu serfs. His death touched off a struggle for succession, and the final victor allied himself with the Germans to maintain his authority. Within 10 years, Rwandan independence was ended.

References: DAHB, MMA, *wiki*.

KIMATHI, Dedan Waciuri
(Kenya, 1920–1957)

General Dedan Kimathi was an anticolonial revolutionary leader, a general in the Mau Mau uprising, and a martyr to the cause of Kenyan independence.

Kimathi was raised in the White Highlands of Kenya, where he worked on colonial plantations. In 1941 he entered the colonial forces in World War II, but was expelled for insubordination. Some accounts, probably apocryphal, say that he was sent with African troops to the Burma front, where combat against the Japanese opened his eyes to the realization that people of color could defeat White troops. Kimathi returned home, taught school (until fired for misconduct) and took a string a small jobs. At first he joined a Kenyan political party, but along the way he became radicalized. In 1950 he joined the Mau Mau by taking the illegal blood oath. By 1952 he had forsaken traditional politics for guerilla tactics. The British declared a state of emergency and arrested Jomo KENYATTA. The repression caused hundreds of Kikuyu warriors to flee to the hills. Kimathi was arrested several times, and then formed the Kenya Defense Council to unite all the forest warriors.

Using jungle warfare tactics he supposedly learned in Burma, he led a resistance that paralyzed the Kenyan colonial forces. In 1952 he organized a mass oathing ceremony with thousands of Kikuyus in attendance, and when the local chief appeared, he was beaten to death. Kimathi was betrayed and arrested shortly after, but he bribed sympathetic guards and escaped into the mountains. Finally he was captured, sentenced to death and was executed by the British. He was buried in a mass grave that has never been identified, and to this day, the British government resists all efforts to open its records to reveal the place of his burial. Even the interventions of Nelson MANDELA have failed to get it revealed.

Kimathi has always been something of an enigma to Kenyan authorities, who have done nothing to keep his memory alive. Mandela caused an international flap on his 1990 visit to Kenya when he asked President Daniel arap MOI for permission to meet Kimathi's widow. Despite official indifference, the legend of Dedan Kimathi has been embroidered until he has become a national hero in Kenya and a symbol of resistance to colonialism.

References: MMA, *wiki*. Ngugi wa Thiong'o, *The Trial of Dedan Kimathi* (1977).

KIMBANGU, Simon
(Democratic Republic of the Congo, 1887?–1951)

Prophet Simon Kimbangu was the most important of the prophet founders in the African independent church movement. The Church of Jesus Christ on Earth by the Prophet Simon Kimbangu is one of the largest of such communities and was the first both to establish a theological school and to be admitted to the World Council of Churches. Little of this was foreshadowed by Kimbangu's life, however, most of which was endured in prison.

The outlines of his life are simple. Although his father was a traditional religious leader, Simon Kimbangu was converted by the Baptist Missionary Society in 1915. He worked for several years as a catechist, a religious teacher who prepares candidates for baptism, and then had a vision in which God gave him a divine commission to preach and heal. To escape the divine command, he fled to Léopoldville, the capital of the Belgian Congo, where he did migrant work. In 1921 he cured a sick woman and returned to the Lower Congo region to preach. This mission, which lasted only six months, had astounding effects. He drew crowds, to the extent that workers left the plantations to hear him speak and hospital beds were emptied of those hoping for cures. The word spread that an *ngunza* (prophet) and *mvuluzi* (apostle, messiah) was among the Congo people. Kimbangu cured the sick and was said to raise the dead. His village, Nkamba, was renamed New Jerusalem. The mission became a mass movement and began to take on nationalist overtones, disturbing both the Baptists and the Belgian colonial authorities. His healing ministry had a powerful impact, as followers proclaimed his cures and miracles. In all this were echoes of the messianism of KIMPA Vita two centuries earlier.

Kimbangu employed Christian symbolism, seeing himself as a Christ figure. He appointed 12 apostles to assist him and laid down three moral rules: the abolition of all traditional religious symbols; the eradication of erotic dancing and the destruction of dance drums; and the end of polygamy. He opposed witchcraft and sorcery and forbade the use of alcohol and tobacco. To the shock of the missionaries, who had worked toward these goals for years with little result, Kimbangu's disciples conformed to his rules without a murmur.

Africans often believed that the missionaries held back the secrets of Christianity that were the source of European power and wealth, and therefore Kimbangu's leadership provided a way to unlock these secrets by using a prophet who had talked directly to God. Kimbangu identified God with *nzambi*, the Congo supreme being, and preached God's closeness to his people.

The movement also fed on anti-European feeling and thus aroused the Belgian government's concern. Prodded by missionaries, especially the Catholics, the government panicked. Machine guns were posted in the capital in expectation of an African uprising. The first attempt to take Kimbangu failed when he slipped away from a rally, resulting in stories of his miracle-working. Kimbangu turned himself in to authorities, was charged with sedition, and was sentenced to death. King Albert I commuted the sentence to life imprisonment with 120 lashes, and Kimbangu was sent a thousand miles away, where he died after 30 years in isolation from his followers.

If the Belgians thought that this would silence the movement, they were mistaken. During his trial, Kimbangu assumed the stance of the martyred Christ during his passion, and in detention his figure took on iconic proportions. Even traditional Christians admired his acceptance of his fate, his obvious prayerful piety, and the evidence of his deep personal holiness. Although he could not preach in prison, his demeanor was patient and loving, and he shared his meager food rations with other prisoners. His followers begged him to use his miraculous powers to escape but continued to build his movement without him. The Belgians cracked down on Kimbanguists, but the Church went underground, led by his son, Joseph DIANGIENDA. Several related sects soon appeared, all acknowledging Kimbangu as their spiritual father. Kimbangu also became a symbol of Congolese nationalism, and Kimbanguism fostered group cohesion. By dimin-

ishing the power of magic and witchcraft, it helped to develop mutual trust and community. It also challenged the authority of the local chiefs, who were seen—quite rightly—as the lackeys of the Belgian authorities.

A church council was established in 1956, five years after Kimbangu's death, and his three sons, led by Diangienda, took over. The Belgian authorities finally recognized the Church in 1959. In 1991, President MOBUTU Sese Seko posthumously amnestied Kimbangu and awarded him the National Order of the Leopard. The day of his death (October 12) is observed as a holiday.

References: AB, *afr,* DAB, *dacb,* DAHB, MMA, *wiki.* Marie-Louise Martin, *Kimbangu: An African Prophet and His Church* (1976).

KIMPA Vita
(Democratic Republic of the Congo, 1683?–1706)

Kimpa Vita was a popular prophetess in the kingdom of the Kongo, a precursor of the prophetic figures of the independent Churches, and the creator of a movement that used Christian symbols but revitalized traditional Kongo cultural roots.

The latter half of the seventeenth century was one of cultural disintegration and political disarray in the Kongo (which included parts of present-day Congo, The Democratic Republic of the Congo and Angola). Portuguese forces had defeated the Kongo, the Christianity of AFONSO I had fallen into a syncretic mix of Christian and African traditional religions, and three ruling families contended for power. Into this political and cultural vacuum a number of messianic prophets arose to proclaim their socioreligious visions. The most important of these was Kimpa Vita, a young girl who believed herself possessed by the spirit of St. Anthony of Padua, a popular Catholic saint and miracle worker. She began preaching in the Kongolese city of San Salvador, which she said God wished restored as the capital.

Kimpa Vita was born into a noble family in what is now Angola, and was baptized. From childhood she had visions, and her spiritual gifts were recognized early. She was trained as a *nganga marinda* or spirit medium. She fell ill in 1704 and began receiving visions of St. Anthony, whom she claimed to have taken over her body. Her message was that Christ was angered by civil wars and division in the Kongo, and that the people must unite. Her call to unity drew strong support among the peasants, who flocked to the city, which Kimpa identified as the biblical Bethlehem. She told her followers that Jesus, Mary and other Christian saints were really Kongolese.

Kimpa conspired with the general of Pedro IV, one of the contenders for the throne, but she was captured after Pedro determined to destroy her mounting influence. Both Kimpa and her baby—conceived by her "guardian angel"—were burned at the stake for heresy, at the instigation of Capuchin missionaries.

The Antonian movement, which Kimpa began, outlasted her. Her ideas remained among the peasantry, appearing in various messianic cults until, two centuries later, it took new form in the preaching of Simon KIMBANGU. Some sects believe that Kimbangu is a reincarnation of Kimpa Vita.

References: afr, DAB, dacb, DAHB, wiki. John Thornton, *The Kongolese Saint Anthony: Dona Beatriz Kimpa Vita and the Antonian Movement* (1998).

KING, Charles
(Liberia, 1871–1961)

Charles King was a public figure and for 10 years president of Liberia.

Until recently, Liberia was governed by an Americo-Liberian elite that was descended from the freed American slaves who had colonized the area. King, a member of this elite, achieved early success, becoming a prominent lawyer and head of the National Bar Association. He was a member of the True Whig Party, which governed Liberia from 1878 to 1980. He was appointed attorney general and served as secretary of state throughout World War I. In 1920 he became president.

At that time Liberia was in the midst of an economic crisis, and King mounted an austerity program after attempts to float an American loan failed. He then sought a more permanent solution. At first he negotiated with Marcus Garvey, who promoted a "Back to Africa" movement in the United States and was interested in Liberia. This movement threatened the position of the traditional elite, however, and King turned to the Firestone Rubber Company. In 1926, Liberia signed a 99-year

lease for a million acres under terms very favorable for Firestone. Nonetheless, King obtained considerable concessions for Liberia, including a duty on rubber exports and a US$5 million loan. He embarked on a public works program that provided electricity for the capital, created a paved road network, and built hospitals and schools. This ushered in an era of economic stability that carried Liberia through the depression of the 1930s. King also improved relations between the government and the indigenous African chiefs of the hinterland.

In 1927, King was re-elected by a margin of 234,000 votes—a figure that was 15 times the total electorate. This fraudulent election was followed by charges that senior officials were involved in forced labor and slave trading on their plantations. An international investigation cleared King of any wrongdoing, but when his vice president was implicated, he resigned in 1930. In 1947 King reentered public life as ambassador to the United Nations (U.N.) and to the United States—Liberia's most important diplomatic post. Five years later he retired, having regained the nation's esteem and appreciation.

References: DAHB, MMA, wiki.

KINGSLEY, Mary Henrietta
(Congo/Gabon/Democratic Republic of the Congo, 1862–1900)

Mary Henrietta Kingsley, English explorer and writer, greatly influenced European ideas about Africa and its people. She was a critic of colonialism, believing in the value of indigenous customs and the desirability of a British policy supporting traders and merchants over settlers.

Kingsley was raised in a sheltered atmosphere within her family and was educated at home by her father. After nursing her parents through their final illnesses, she experienced a totally new sense of freedom, and in 1893 she sailed for West Africa to study African religion in order to complete a book begun by her father. She traveled along the bend of the Gulf of Guinea, collecting specimens for the British Museum. She lived among local tribes, who tutored her in the ways of jungle survival. Then she followed the rivers into the area of present-day Congo and Gabon, through dangerous territory where she had several narrow escapes. None of this area had been previously explored by Westerners. Of limited means, she supported herself by trading in rubber and oil as she traveled, which gave her insight into areas of African experience not seen by other observers.

These adventures made her a popular lecturer when she returned to England in 1896. Her first lecture (to a medical school) was entitled "African Therapeutics from a Witch Doctor's Point of View." She also published two popular books showing her strong sympathies for Africans and arguing that, although they were different, African cultures were in no way inferior to those of the West. The first, *Travels in West Africa* (1897), recounts her experiences and presents the case against colonialism, arguing that traders could best develop the interior areas of Africa and maintain law and order. Kingsley had made contacts with the major trade figures in West Africa, some of them powerful regional chiefs. She represented their views in London unofficially but persuasively.

She also rejected theories of cultural and racial inferiority in *West African Studies* (1899), citing attempts to change or replace African social and political institutions as serious mistakes. Her influence was extensive and included direct access to the Colonial Office, where she presented her views. After 1890, British policy clearly showed greater concern for retaining African social institutions, partly as a result of Kingsley's campaigning.

Kingsley was a most unlikely explorer, yet she was a highly successful one. Of the hundred or more species of fauna that she brought back to the British Museum, three fish were previously unknown and were named after her. Kingsley planned another trip to Africa, but when the Boer War broke out, she instead volunteered as a nurse. She went to South Africa in 1899 and died of typhoid fever contracted while nursing the sick. She was buried at sea with full naval and military honors.

References: afr, DAHB, DNB, EB, *wiki*. Katherine Frank, *A Voyager Out: The Life of Mary Kingsley* (1986); Robert Pearce, *Mary Kingsley: Light at the Heart of Darkness* (1990).

KINJIKITILE Ngwale "Bokero"
(Tanzania, ?–1905)

Kinjikitile Ngwale was a prophetic, spirit-possessed cult leader in German East Africa who inspired the last major uprising against German imperialism in that colony.

Kinjikitile was already a wandering prophet when he appeared along the Tanzanian coast in 1902 as a miracle worker. His arrival coincided with a period of particularly strong German repression, in which harsh measures were used to force Africans into commercial farming. The Africans lost their lands and received trivial compensation for their work, under conditions no better than those of serfdom. Consequently, Kinjikitile's apocalyptic message of the Germans' ultimate expulsion fell upon receptive ears. Traditional religious belief held that all human misfortune was explainable and that cures should be sought. The German oppression with its attendant social turmoil and suffering was often attributed to sorcery and witchcraft, which, following a tradition of antisorcery cults, called for powerful medicine and rituals to overcome evil. A serious drought in 1905 crippled cotton production and set off open resistance. The Africans had never dealt with cash crops before, and cotton growing disrupted community life and well-defined gender roles. Thus, when the Germans insisted upon a full quota of cotton despite the crop failure, the people were forced into desperate measures.

Kinjikitile is known to have been middle-aged when he began his crusade. Tall and with imposing presence, an eloquent speaker and obviously schooled in the esoteric arts of a diviner and medicine man, his background gained him wide respect. He was familiar with the traditions of the people among whom he moved and easily synthesized their religious and social values into his prophetic messages. He took local beliefs in spirit possession and the power of traditional medicine and used them to create a religious movement that promised the people a new age of unity and divine protection. He was believed to be possessed by the spirit Hongo, sent by the high god Bokero. Kinjikitile offered a ritual for driving out the Germans—a sacred water (*maji* in Kiswahili) mixed with oil to protect people from bullets and create a bond of unity. A complex of religious themes thus resonated with local belief. Powerful water and river deities were invoked, and *maji* was connected to snake cults. Adherents of various snake cults were among the first to join the Maji Maji Rebellion, as the anticolonial revolt came to be called.

The Maji Maji Rebellion broke out in 1905 on the cotton plantations. The German authorities immediately arrested Kinjikitile and hanged him. The rebellion lasted for two more years and involved over a third of present-day Tanzania, but it was eventually suppressed. The struggle and the following famine cost 75,000 lives and several hundred thousand were displaced from their homes.

Reference: DAHB, *wiki*. Michael Adas, *Prophets of Rebellion* (1977).

KITCHENER, Horatio Herbert
(Sudan/South Africa, 1850–1916)

Lord Horatio Herbert Kitchener, one of the most notable British imperialist military leaders, reconquered the Sudan for Britain and led British forces during the second phase of the Boer War.

Kitchener was commissioned in the Royal Engineers in 1871 and served in the Middle East before being made commander in 1886 at Suakin, the only Sudanese town that the British held after the collapse of Anglo-Egyptian forces under attack by the MAHDI. Kitchener was made commander of the Egyptian army in 1892 and four years later was selected to direct the campaign against the Mahdists in the Sudan, who were led by ABDULLAHI Ibn Muhammad. The Madhist struggle took two years, starting with a river campaign. It was waged methodically but with incredible brutality, fueled by British memories of the humiliating defeat of General Charles "Chinese" GORDON.

With 25,000 troops—8,200 of them British—using gunboats and high explosives, Kitchener faced 70,000 Sudanese troops who were lightly armed but who were led by the fanatical dervishes. They met in the battle of Omdurman, where the Mahdists were utterly crushed by the superior firepower. It was a classic slaughter in which the Mahdists made charge upon charge into the fire of British machine guns. Only 60 British and 160 Egyptians died. After the battle, Kitchener ordered the massacre of 20,000 wounded enemy forces—"all done as humanely as

possible." They then bombed the tomb of the Mahdi and dumped his bones into the Nile, keeping the skull as a souvenir that Kitchener had made into a tobacco canister. British forces pursued Abdullahi and killed him in battle, effectively ending the threat of the Mahdists. People in Britain were both appalled and entranced by Kitchener. He was denounced in Parliament as the "butcher of Omdurman who made war on women and children." Nonetheless, he was also the popular hero of the day, the man who had avenged Gordon and restored British pride.

Kitchener then revealed another side of himself. He faced a potentially explosive situation at Fashoda, on the Nile River, where a small French expedition was trying to extend French sovereignty into parts of the Sudan. Kitchener approached the French, faced them down, and delicately avoided an international incident. Kitchener returned to London in triumph to receive his first peerage as Baron Kitchener of Khartoum and Aspall. In the Sudan, Kitchener moved swiftly to provide a basis for lasting peace. He rebuilt the mosques, made Friday a day of rest and guaranteed freedom of religion, while preventing evangelical missionaries from attempting to convert Muslims. He also established the first free schools.

In 1899, now one of the most trusted military figures in Britain, Kitchener was posted as chief of staff to South Africa, where the British were locked in the Second Boer War with the Afrikaners. Within a year Kitchener was made commander in chief and began occupying Afrikaner territory. The Afrikaners resorted to guerrilla warfare, and Kitchener again used his most oppressive tactics. The countryside was closed off with barbed wire and blockhouses, and farms were destroyed to prevent the guerrillas from receiving supplies. Afrikaner women and children were herded into concentration camps with minimal sanitation facilities. The death rate was considerable, and the inhumane British actions created a longstanding bitterness that has contaminated British-Afrikaner relations ever since, and which contributed to the growth of both anti-British feelings and Afrikaner nationalism.

Kitchener directed that Boers disguised in British uniforms be executed summarily, and then denied having issued the order. In a notorious case, several Australian officers, including the renowned "Breaker" Morant, were tried and shot by a firing squad for having executed disguised Boers. Australians have always interpreted this as a cover-up on

Kitchener's part. He was again widely criticized in Britain, but the title of viscount was added to his other honors.

From 1902 to 1909, Kitchener was commander-in-chief in India, where he reorganized the army. After achieving the rank of field marshal, he became proconsul of Egypt and the Sudan from 1911 to 1914. In 1914 he was made an earl, received two other titles, and was appointed secretary of state for war. He drowned during World War I when his ship struck a mine and was sunk near the Orkney Islands.

Kitchener, a dashing and brave soldier as a young officer, disguised himself and reconnoitered the Nile Valley during an Egyptian army revolt. During the siege of Khartoum, he undertook intelligence forays into the Sudanese desert at great risk. Even as governor-general he led raids and was seriously wounded in one. He inspired his junior officers and was a gifted strategist. At the same time, he was an autocrat who had difficulty in delegating authority. His bursts of vicious bloodletting often came after disgust with his predecessors. When he took command in the Boer War, he scornfully called it "a game of polo with intervals for afternoon tea." Serving in the cabinet during World War I, where his fellow ministers did not share the popular adulation for his leadership, Kitchener was unable to cooperate with his colleagues.

References: DAHB, DNB, EB, EWB, HWL, *wiki.* Philip Warner, *Kitchener: The Man Behind the Legend* (1986).

KIVULI, David Zakayo
(Kenya, 1896?–1974)

David Zakayo Kivuli was the founder of the African Israel Church Nineveh (AICN), which has grown into one of the largest independent African Churches in East Africa. He became a preacher and school supervisor for the mission of the Pentecostal Assemblies of Canada in 1925, but it was only in 1932 that he began speaking in tongues and claiming the gifts of the Holy Spirit. To this Kivuli added the gift of faith healing, and he began to develop a considerable personal following, especially among the Luo and Luyia peoples of western Kenya. In 1942 he separated from the Pentecostal Assemblies and founded the AICN. His movement spread into Uganda and Tanzania.

Kivuli's movement appeared in a period that was ripe for the foundation of independent Churches in East Africa. A religious revival, the *Balokole* or "Saved Ones," swept through the Christian churches beginning in the 1930s. It was based on lay communities of prayer and fellowship, which created fertile ground for separatism from the missionary Churches. Revival communities also became homes for anticolonial sentiment, and new Church bodies free from missionary control appeared throughout East Africa. Kenya became a center for the independent Church movement, which was also flourishing—as the result of other factors—in southern Africa.

Kivuli drew members from the Pentecostals as well as from the Quakers (Society of Friends). The AICN is a curious mixture of traditions. Their services on Fridays (their day of worship) include dancing, spirit possession, and the wearing of white clothing. The church's members revere a religious center (called Nineveh) where vast numbers of the faithful gather to celebrate Christmas. They also have an elaborate doctrine of sin, including confession and physical taboos about touching certain places on the body where sins are located. The Church discourages polygamy among the laity and forbids it among the clergy. Unlike other independent Churches, however, the AICN is not divorced from modern life. It is active in development projects and promotes modern medicine.

The AICN has been eager to develop ecumenical contacts. When the evangelical agency World Vision held the first all-pastors' conference in Nairobi in 1968, the AICN had the largest delegation. Kivuli attempted to join Kenya's National Christian Council in 1957 and was rejected, but by 1970 the AICN had become a probationary member. In 1975, one year after Kivuli's death, it became affiliated with the World Council of Churches.

References: dacb, DAHB.

KIWANUKA, Joseph, WF
(Uganda, 1899–1966)

Archbishop Joseph Kiwanuka, WF, was the first African to be named a bishop in the Catholic Church in 400 years, and used his position to work toward an African-directed Church.

Kiwanuka was born in Buganda and was singled out to be sent to a mission school, where he excelled. He entered seminary and was ordained in 1929, and then joined the Missionaries of Africa, popularly called the White Fathers. He was sent to Rome, where he became the first African to take a doctorate in canon law in 1932. He became a professor at Katigondo Seminary. His patron was Bishop Henry Streicher, a forward-thinking missionary who groomed him for leadership. In 1939, Pope Pius XII named him a bishop along with several others from colonial areas, and he was appointed vicar of Masaka. This vicariate was limited to African clergy, to prove their ability to succeed without European supervision. Soon Kiwanuka was in charge of the entire diocese.

He began by appointing 56 African priests in charge of parishes, and Masaka became the first Catholic diocese to be completely directed by Africans. He developed elected lay councils in the diocese as well. He worked toward a democratic Uganda as independence arrived and served on the constitutional commission in 1955, warning against charismatic but authoritarian figures such as Milton OBOTE.

In 1961, Kiwanuka was promoted to the archdiocese of Rubaga (Kampala), the capital, in time to join the celebrations around independence. He again warned against authoritarianism and issued a stirring pastoral letter on democracy. He died suddenly, and the day following, Obote took power and abolished the constitution.

Kiwanuka was also an influence in the White Fathers community. In 1947 he argued forcefully for the internationalization of the missionary effort and the rejection of the British policy of allowing only Commonwealth citizens to operate as missionaries in Africa. He was well aware that his own episcopal ordination had been delayed for several years by the opposition of colonial authorities. He took part in the Second Vatican Council, and joined—openly weeping—in the canonization of the Uganda martyrs, Karoli LWANGA and his companions, in 1964. These were the first recognized African saints in the Church in centuries, and their cause had been promoted actively by Kiwanuka.

References: afr, dacb. John Mary Waliggo, *A History of African Priests* (1988).

KOENA, Moeketsi
(South Africa, 1971–)

Moeketsi Koena is a South African dancer and choreographer who is executive and artistic director of the Inzalo Dance and Theatre Company, which he co-founded in 1999.

Koena studied dance at the Soweto Dance Theatre from 1990 to 1993. He received a certificate as a community dance teacher and two diplomas. In 1995–1996 he studied in the Netherlands, followed by two years at the Research Training Studios in Belgium. He continues to study and apprentice with such groups as the Bates College Dance Festival and the Alvin Ailey American Dance Center in New York.

Koena fuses South African *kwaito*, a form of hip-hop, with traditional African dance and western contemporary styles. He describes himself on stage as "dynamite exploding" to reflect his dynamic style and innovative choreography.

Koena dances and choreographs with a number of companies in South Africa, Belgium and the Netherlands. He has been four times nominated Most Promising Male Dancer (1992 to 1995). In 1996 he received the Vita Award for Most Outstanding Performance. He performed with Moving Into Dance, one of the companies he regularly dances with, at the inauguration of President Nelson MANDELA in 1994. With the Soweto Dance Theatre he toured Europe and Australia (1992–1999), and since the beginning of the Inzalo Dance and Theatre Company he has danced in Europe and throughout Africa. Inzalo's repertoire focuses on intercultural dance expression. Several dances mix European youth dance with South African hip-hop and African modern youth dances. Inzalo is also involved in dance teaching and encouraging youth by offering performance workshops.

Reference: adb.

KOLINGBA, André Dieudonné
(Central African Republic, 1936–)

General André Kolingba was head of state in the Central African Republic (CAR) from 1981 to 1993, after overthrowing President David DACKO in a peaceful coup. Kolingba maintained a firm but humane administration, moving slowly toward political liberalization.

Kolingba attended the Leclerc Preparatory Military Academy in Brazzaville, French Congo, before entering the French army at 18. He was sent to the military academy at Fréjus, France, and then received training as a signals officer. He was serving in this position with a French armored squadron when the CAR became independent in 1960, and he transferred to the new CAR army. He rose quickly to the rank of general by 1973 under the presidency of Jean-Bédel BOKASSA. During the years of Bokassa's dictatorial excesses, Kolingba was overseas as ambassador to Canada and, later, to West Germany. After Dacko reconstituted the government, Kolingba was made chief of staff in 1981, but it was apparent that the Dacko government was weak and indecisive, unable to control public dissatisfaction. In elections that year, Dacko was returned with less than 51 percent of the vote.

In September 1981, Kolingba demanded Dacko's resignation in order to end mounting violence and strikes. He announced that the military council would work toward restoring civilian government, but he forced the leader of the main opposition, the former prime minister Ange-Félix Patassé, into exile. He did, however, begin to introduce civilians into government ministries. In 1985, after Kolingba was given the title of president, he permitted parliamentary elections. This move led to pressures for a multiparty system, to which he agreed reluctantly, in 1991. Patassé was elected president in 1993 elections, and Kolingba accepted the verdict, although in a fit of pique he released all political prisoners, including Bokassa.

Kolingba's tenure in office was marked by increasing pressure from outside. France was his patron for some years, and there are persistent rumors that the French garrison in the CAR supported Kolingba's coup. By 1990, France had joined a chorus of countries and Non-Governmental Organizations (NGOs) in calling for democratization. At the same time, the World Bank, donor nations and the International Monetary Fund (IMF) demanded decision-making authority over aspects of the CAR economy.

In 2001, there was a coup attempt against Patassé, and Kolingba was implicated. He fled to Uganda, and only returned to the CAR after Patassé himself was overthrown two years later. Failing health has kept Kolingba on the sidelines since.

References: afr, PLBA, RWWA, *wiki*.

KONARÉ, Alpha Oumar
(Mali, 1946–)

Dr. Alpha Oumar Konaré, archeologist and scholar, was president of Mali for 10 years and is now the chair of the Commission of the African Union (AU).

Konaré was born the fifth of 14 children to a schoolteacher. He was educated in Mali and Sénégal, and took a degree in history in Bamako, the capital of Mali. He then went to the University of Warsaw to study archeology for his Ph.D. He taught archeology and history, and then was named head of historic patrimony in the Ministry of Sports and Culture. He has been involved with several professional associations and for 10 years he was a consultant for the United Nations Educational, Scientific and Cultural Organization (UNESCO).

Konaré was an early opponent of the military regime of Moussa TRAORÉ, but from1978 to 1980, he accepted an appointment as minister of Sports and Culture. He resigned and for a time, he worked with the underground democracy movement. In 1989, he stepped forward as a spokesman for democracy against the military. Konaré began an opposition newspaper and a radio station shortly before Traoré was swept away by a military transition group that immediately laid plans for multiparty elections. In a three-way race, Konaré was elected in a run-off in the most transparent and free election Mali had known. He was re-elected in 1997.

Konaré served as president of Mali for two terms, 1992–2002, and stepped aside at the end of his term with no attempt to extend it beyond the constitutional limit. In office, he developed the Malian economy, despite its weak base, and fostered democratic reforms. True to his academic background, he took special interest in preserving the cultural heritage of the country, but he also went a long way toward developing information technology in Mali. His economic policies implemented reforms requested by donor countries, but without harsh results for the peasants and herdsmen. The Malian economy showed growth throughout his presidency.

One of his first crises was the Tuareg rebellion in the north. Feeling culturally oppressed and suffering from persistent drought, the nomadic Tuareg harassed the army and destabilized the region. Konaré reached a settlement in 1995 and curbed the spread of small arms. In celebration, the Tuareg held a bonfire of 3,000 guns, the "flame of peace," and the insurrection faded. The Tuareg have now been largely incorporated into the Malian economy.

Konaré struggled with corruption in his administration and disturbances that caused him to cancel legislative elections, which brought international criticism. Though there were some violations of human rights, he encouraged complete media freedom, and there is a lively debate in the country on every issue. He also instituted an annual *palaver*, a meeting where any citizen may speak openly and critically to the president and his ministers. It is based on an ancient tradition of dialogue with chiefs.

Konaré stood for election to the chairmanship of the AU in 2003, and was chosen by a two-thirds vote. The major African powers, most notably Nigeria and South Africa, openly supported him. His reputation as a Pan-Africanist was a deciding factor with many countries. Konaré also served as head of the Economic Community of West African States (ECOWAS) in 1999. He has received several honorary doctorates and awards from international groups, especially for his development of sport in Mali.

References: CB, *wiki.*

KONY, Joseph
(Uganda, 1961?–)

Joseph Kony is a terrorist, spirit medium and rebel leader who has maintained a devastating insurrection in northern Uganda for almost 20 years.

Kony was raised Catholic in the north and gave no signs of his future depravity as a youth.

In the wake of the Holy Spirit Movement of Alice LAKWENA, a number of millenarian groups sprang up in northern Uganda, fed by the discontent of the Acholi people at what they felt was the neglect and disrespect shown by the government of Yoweri MUSEVENI. Kony has been the most important of these dissidents, and is believed to be a cousin or nephew of Lakwena's. He began his Lord's Resistance Army (LRA) around 1988, after Lakwena was defeated and fled to Kenya.

Kony claims to be a spirit medium, at various times channeling the spirits of a former government minister under the dictator Idi AMIN and a Chinese

general, along with seven other "angels," including three Americans. His hold on his followers is sustained by a mix of prophetic vision and sheer terror. Using a mix of ritual and strict rules, he insures complete obedience. As they go to flight, the soldiers must make a sign of the Cross on their chests, foreheads, shoulders and their rifle, lest they be killed in battle. The oil used is a sign of the Holy Spirit. Kony says he will restore rule by the Ten Commandments, to which he has added an eleventh: "Thou shalt not ride a bicycle"! He teaches a melange of witchcraft, Christian customs and terrorism. Islamic elements have been incorporated ever since the Sudan began supplying arms to the LRA. Prayers are now offered facing Mecca, and Friday as well as Sunday are days of observance.

The LRA kidnaps children, especially from the displaced persons' camps, and presses them into his fighting force. The LRA has taken some 20,000 children as soldiers or sex slaves. Boys are made to kill their parents, so they have no homes to return to. Ugandan forces have been unable to break Kony's grip on the north, since it would involve going to war against Sudan, where Kony keeps his main base.

In 2005, the International Criminal Court (ICC), urged on by Museveni, issued arrest warrants for Kony and four of his lieutenants for criminal actions. There were 21 counts of war crimes, including murder, attacking civilians, pillaging, rape and forcing children into the ranks of the LRA. There were also 12 counts of crimes against humanity–enslavement, rape, murder and sexual enslavement. The ICC chief prosecutor charged Kony with "abducting girls to offer them as rewards to his commanders." He himself is reputed to have 60 "wives" at his service.

Reference: wiki. Invisible Children (film, 2006).

KOUNTCHÉ, Seyni
(Niger, 1931–1987)

Major-General Seyni Kountché, first military president of Niger, was known for his personal integrity and austere life. He dealt effectively with his country's economic crisis and maintained a balanced foreign policy.

Kountché's Djerba clan completely dominated the officer class in Niger; therefore, it was natural for him to enter the French army school. He

completed his education at a secondary school in
Sénégal and joined the French army in 1949. By
1959 he was commissioned and saw combat in
Indochina and Algeria before transferring to Niger's
new army in 1961, a year after independence. He
moved through the ranks and received further
training in France before being made chief of staff in
1973. A year later he led the coup that removed
Hamani DIORI and replaced him with a military
council with Kountché as president. The coup came
amid widespread corruption in the government and
a scandal involving the sale of food aid that had been
intended for drought victims.

Kountché moved immediately and effectively
against the worst of the drought conditions, seeing
that food was distributed and punishing those who
had profited illegally. Benefiting from the end of
the drought, he began an aggressive agricultural
program and expanded Niger's uranium mining
exports. The resulting improvement in the economy
gained him considerable popularity, which he
enhanced by pardoning political prisoners and
inviting exiles such as Djibo BAKARY to return,
under the condition that they not participate in
politics. This latter policy did not last, and Bakary
was imprisoned in 1975. Kountché made cautious
progress toward including civilians in the government but did nothing to restore democratic politics.

In foreign policy he was similarly conservative.
He based his views on a frank assessment of Niger's
minor status alongside its powerful neighbors. He
backed away from Diori's significant involvement in
international affairs to focus on good relations with
regional states, and in 1975 he was instrumental in
establishing the Economic Community of West
African States (ECOWAS). He maintained good
relations with France, where he was respected, and
established ties with conservative Arab states as a
counterbalance to Libya, whose erratic foreign policy
disturbed him. Between 1981 and 1984 he broke
relations with Chad but then supported Chad when
it was invaded by Libya. He kept on good terms
with the United States, the major source of food aid
during the drought years.

Kountché's personal austerity and work habits
made him personal enemies, while his brusque and
abrasive manner made him few friends. Moralistic
and demanding, he arose before dawn to work an
18-hour day, lecturing those in the bureaucracy who
were less devoted. Associates close to him were
mainly army comrades and relatives, and when he
developed a brain tumor, his cousin, Colonel Ali

SAIBOU, took over his responsibilities and then
replaced Kountché after his death.

References: afr, AO, DAHB, MMA, PLBA,
wiki.

KOUYATÉ, Kandia
(Mali, 1960s–)

Kandia Kouyaté is a *griotte* or *jalimusolo*, a traditional
praise singer, honored with the title of *ngara*, one
who is strong, loyal and never lies. She sings in
Mandinka and Bambara and is a superstar in West
Africa.

Kouyaté received a good education, where she
shone especially in French and mathematics. In love
with music and born to the griot life as her destiny,
however, she learned the traditional forms from her
mother and grandmother, despite strong opposition
from her father. She has a strong and penetrating
voice with a broad range, well suited to praise songs
and genealogies. She is the only Malian woman to
sing shouting songs, because of the respect shown to
her voice.

Mandingo music is based on a number of
traditional songs recognized by everyone. Their
melodies may be used in newer compositions, and
while most songs are in praise of great heroes of the
past, a few praise more recent people of events. The
songs usually include a long improvisation on the
descendants of the one praised, thus providing an
oral history of the genealogy of his family. On her
debut album *Kita Kan* (1999), she presented an
eight-minute shouting song in honor of SUNDIA-
TA Keita, a thirteenth-century king who established the Malian Empire. Some songs honor
patrons for their generosity ("The Hundred Giver"),
and will include the names of his wives and family.

While she has produced successful records,
Kouyaté has followed the common path of taking
support from rich patrons, who vie to provide for
her. One even gave her a plane and built an airstrip
for her village. In the pre-colonial era, kings and
Muslim *marabouts* were patrons; today they are more
likely presidents or wealthy businessmen. The
relationship is not sexual or even social, but one of
mutual friendship. A great *jalimusolo* will have a
number of patrons.

Kouyaté broke away from reliance on traditional
praise songs by expanding her repertoire to include
love songs, which are now regarded as her staple.

She also does not shy away from controversial topics—she has sung against arranged marriages and female circumcision, to which she was subjected. Yet while rejecting certain customs, she continues to steep herself in the tradition. Despite her fame, she brings kola nuts as an act of respect and asks questions of the elders. A practicing Muslim, she has made the *hajj* to Mecca three times.

Reference: wiki.

KRAPF, Johann Ludwig
(Ethiopia/Kenya/Tanzania, 1810–1887)

Reverend Johann Ludwig Krapf, missionary pioneer of East Africa, played a leading role in evangelizing and exploring the region. His linguistic work on Swahili, Amharic, and Ge'ez provided some of the earliest scientific investigations of those languages.

Krapf was born in Germany and educated at the Basle Mission School in Switzerland and at Tübingen University, where he completed theological studies in 1834 and was ordained a Lutheran clergyman. After several unhappy years as a pastor, he joined the Anglican Church Missionary Society (CMS) in order to take part in their new missionary campaign in Ethiopia and was sent there in 1837. In 1843 all Protestant missionaries were expelled from Shoa Province, and Krapf decided to work among the Galla people of southwest Ethiopia. His account of his travels, which were supposed to start from the Indian Ocean coast through present-day Kenya, is a valuable source of Swahili coast history in this period, particularly trade patterns and political developments. In Zanzibar, where he began, Krapf met Sultan Seyyid SAID and received a permit to stay, making him the first Protestant missionary on those shores "sole and single to attack the old bulwarks of darkness." Disgusted by the Zanzibari population, who were three-quarters slaves and morally "scarcely superior to Sodom," he settled further north in the Kenyan town of Mombasa. Conditions were appalling. Krapf's wife and newborn infant died of fever, and he was too delirious even to name the baby. Associates betrayed him or died of tropical illnesses. Malaria, the climate, and close living conditions made daily life a misery. Nonetheless, while he was in Mombasa, Krapf translated the Bible into Swahili and determined to travel inland.

Between 1847 and 1849, Krapf made six inland journeys of exploration, and on one of these he became the first European to see Mount Kenya. On another, he was the only survivor of an ambush and was almost trampled by a rhinoceros. He staggered back to his mission in tatters after two weeks of hiding in the bush. Krapf competed with the Muslims, who reviled Christianity at every turn, and on his journeys his pitifully small escort carefully avoided the Muslim slave caravans, which often traveled with a thousand armed men. The Muslims accused him of foreign intrigues and spread the rumor among Africans that he was a cannibal. When his plan to establish a chain of mission stations failed to materialize, he returned to Germany in 1853 to write his memoirs.

Even when he was back in Germany, Krapf sought to return to Africa, and in 1862 the Free Methodists sponsored him. In 1867–1868 he accompanied an expedition into Ethiopia as an interpreter, but his health failed and he returned to Germany for the last time. His missionary work was little developed—it is said that in his first 10 years he made two converts—but he gave inspiration for later projects in both Kenya and Tanzania that were successful in employing his plans. His linguistic studies resulted in the first Swahili grammar book (1850) and dictionary (1882), as well as a comparative vocabulary of six Bantu languages (1850). He published 25 books before his death and mastered at least a dozen languages from Bantu to Hebrew, modern and ancient.

References: afr, dacb, DAHB, *wiki.* Jeremy Murray-Brown, *Faith and the Flag* (1977).

KRUGER, Stephanus Johannes Paulus "Oom Paul"
(South Africa, 1825–1904)

Stephanus Johannes Paulus "Oom Paul" Kruger, was a Voortrekker, one of the Afrikaners who traveled inland from the Cape Colony to escape British control. The builder of the Afrikaner nation, he was a four-time president of the Transvaal but died in exile after the disastrous Boer War.

Kruger was raised in the interior and had almost no formal education. In 1836 his father joined 40 families emigrating to the Orange Free

Stephanus Johannes Paulus "Oom Paul" Kruger

State (OFS). At the battle of Vechtkop they defeated 6,000 Ndebele warriors whom they encountered, interpreting the victory as a sign from God of his protection.

Young Kruger handled himself well and became a frontiersman, married at 17, and established a cattle ranch. His exploits became legendary; he was known as a cool and competent fighter. In one commando raid in 1854 he rescued his superior officer's body under withering fire. He also had various narrow escapes from attacks by wild animals. As a youth he had been chosen a field cornet, a local post with military and civil responsibilities, and he was present for the signing of the Sand River Convention in 1856 when the British acknowledged the Transvaal's independence. The Afrikaner republics were characterized by their fierce independence and lack of a sense of a greater national identity. The burghers so resented authority that they undermined even their own governments. Kruger was instrumental in conciliation and prevented the outbreak of civil war in 1857. He pressed for a written constitution, which was adopted two years later. Conflict continued, however, and Kruger took the lead in unifying and pacifying the dissident

factions in the Transvaal. He was elected commandant-general in 1863 and continued to pursue wars against the local African communities.

By 1877, Kruger was vice president of the republic, and when the British annexed the Transvaal, he made a trip to London to protest. Treated with contempt and lampooned by the British press, he returned to the Transvaal determined to organize resistance. In the 1870s, Afrikaner national consciousness was developing under the influence of Stephanus DU TOIT. In 1879, Kruger convened a meeting of "bitter enders" who swore an oath to regain their freedom. The next year they declared their independence under the triumvirate that included Kruger and Andries PRETORIUS. Two sharp defeats forced Britain to recognize the Transvaal in 1881.

In 1883, Kruger was elected president of the republic, a position that he held until 1902, when the British regained the Transvaal. During the 1880s, Kruger was embroiled in conflict over the western border, where Cecil RHODES sought a land corridor to the region north of the Limpopo River. Kruger was forced to back down and accept a British protectorate over Bechuanaland (now Botswana), which Kruger had hoped to keep out of British hands. The greatest challenge came with the flood of European (*uitlander*) miners who entered the republics after the discovery of diamonds (1869) and gold (1886). Kruger faced the challenge of his old enemy Rhodes, who dominated both diamond and gold mining and had been elected prime minister of the Cape Colony in 1890. Kruger enacted discriminatory legislation against the *uitlanders,* taxed them heavily, and virtually denied them all political rights.

Rhodes correctly saw Kruger and the Afrikaner republics of the Transvaal and OFS as the main barriers to his dream of a united British South Africa. He had the support of the *uitlanders,* the Rand capitalists, and even of many Cape Afrikaners, who had made accommodation with their situation in the colony and did not support the Afrikaner republics. Rhodes miscalculated badly, however, when he assumed that the Transvaal would crumble at the first attack, and when he sponsored the ill-fated raid under Leander Starr JAMESON, it resulted in a major setback. Kruger handled the matter well and emerged with heightened support at home and respect abroad. Rhodes was forced into the background, but the British colonial office now intervened and demanded concessions in favor of the *uitlanders.* When no compromise could be reached, both sides prepared for war. After some initial Afrikaner successes, the British captured both republics. Kruger went into exile in Europe in 1900, pleading the Afrikaner cause. The new British commander, Lord Horatio KITCHENER, took up a scorched-earth policy, burning crops and farms and placing families in concentration camps, where more than 28,000 died under wretched conditions.

Kruger was a narrow-minded, bigoted and often ill-informed man who held to Afrikaner nationalism with a dogged determination. He was a Dopper, a member of the Dutch Calvinist sect that was convinced that God's special favor rested on the Afrikaners. Kruger liked to compare the Voortrekkers with the Children of Israel during the exodus, seeking and occupying their chosen land as the elect of God. He saw his own leadership as divinely ordained. The Doppers were biblical literalists, and Kruger once retorted to an American who claimed to be on a trip around the world: "You don't mean *round* the world ... it is impossible!" Doppers accepted White supremacy as a fact of nature and had few scruples in their dispossession of Africans from their lands or in the practice of slavery.

References: AB, DAHB, EB, EWB, HWL. John Fisher, *Paul Kruger: His Life and Times* (1974).

KUTAKO, Hosea
(Namibia, 1870–1970)

Chief Hosea Kutako was paramount chief of the Herero people, replacing the exiled Samuel MAHERERO. Kutako continued the Herero tradition of resistance to foreign domination, in this case South African rule, and became a leading figure in the Namibian independence movement.

Wounded and captured in the Herero revolt of 1904 against the Germans, he was released after the decimation of his people, three-fourths of whom either died or were driven out of the country in the slaughter that ended the rebellion. Kutako served quietly as a teacher until the German defeat in World War I led to a South African mandate over South-West Africa (now Namibia) under the League of Nations. In 1917 the government appointed him chief of the Herero, which was confirmed in 1920 by Samuel Maherero, who had been driven into exile in Bechuanaland (now Botswana) by the Germans.

South-West African interests were subordinated to those of South Africa under the mandate, and White land possession doubled by 1937. All African males over age 14 were required to carry racial identification cards, and controlled labor systems were put in place that forbade Africans to find their own jobs. "Native reserves" were set up, despite Kutako's opposition. Quietly but forcefully, he also opposed the absorption of South-West Africa into the Union of South Africa and petitioned the United Nations (U.N.) for independence after World War II, despite the fact that South Africa refused to accept the transfer of the League mandates to U.N. jurisdiction. When Jan SMUTS, the South African prime minister who wrote the preamble to the U.N. Charter, asked to have South-West Africa annexed to South Africa, Kutako and others mounted a campaign against the proposal. Refused permission to travel, he sent a missionary as his delegate to plead his cause. South Africa lost its case both in the U.N. and before the International Court of Justice. Kutako became the most prominent independence leader until his death and helped include the question of Namibian independence as part of the mounting international opposition to apartheid.

Reference: DAHB.

KUTI, Fela Anikulapo-
(Nigeria, 1938–1997)

Fela Anikulapo-Kuti, a musician who achieved international status, was also a controversial figure in Nigerian politics. His musical talents enabled him to create a unique style, Afrobeat, and his dramatic public persona revealed him to be a confrontative, anti-establishment political activist, which earned him several stays in prison.

Born into a distinguished family of Christian clergy and civil servants, the Ransome-Kutis, Kuti—or Fela, as he is popularly known—abandoned the English name Ransome in favor of Anikulapo, meaning "having control over death" in Yoruba. Kuti considered himself an *abiku,* or twice-born, one who has been reincarnated, the last time as his own brother. He is a follower of the Yoruba deities, the *orishas,* and in 1981 he claimed that he was possessed by one, who became the source of his inspiration. His father was a noted composer and teacher, and his mother, Funmilayo RANSOME-

KUTI, Nigeria's leading women's rights campaigner, was known for her left-wing political views. A friend of Kwame NKRUMAH, she traveled to China, where she met Mao Zedong, and she received the Soviet Union's Lenin Prize. Most of Kuti's family has been involved in radical or human rights activism.

Kuti was a flamboyant performer, given to extended (and even all-night) concerts. Because his group, Egypt 80, included some 30 musicians and dancers, his tours were limited, and most performances were given at his nightclub, The Shrine, in Lagos. In Nigeria, he was a major musical force, but Egypt 80's first U.S. tour took place only in 1986; he returned in 1991. Both tours received positive reviews, and Kuti achieved a small but growing American following.

Afrobeat, his signature sound, brings together African rhythms with elements of American blues and jazz. His lyrics were usually political, sometimes little more than slogans or statements repeated over and over until they become woven into the fabric of the total sound. His discography is so extensive that it is difficult to trace, but it includes more than 50 albums.

Kuti studied classical music at Trinity College, London, from 1958 to 1962 but was attracted to jazz. He formed a jazz group for a year and then returned to Nigeria, where he was influenced by the soul music of Otis Redding and James Brown. His breakthrough came on his first visit to the United States in 1969, when he encountered Sandra Smith, who became his lover and then his wife and collaborator. She introduced him to the writings of Malcolm X and challenged him to get in touch with Africa, Black power, and revolutionary Pan-Africanism. He introduced African instruments, and his new amalgam of African pop and scathing social commentary proved explosive. He attacked Nigeria's government, mocked women who aped Western styles, and ridiculed the incompetence and corruption of the African elite. *Beasts of No Nation* (1988) criticized Ronald Reagan and Margaret Thatcher. His appeal was to the urban masses, especially the poor and the unemployed.

Kuti was jailed on a variety of offenses during the 1970s, but in 1977 he infuriated General Olusegun OBASANJO by declaring his compound an independent republic and by issuing *Zombie,* an antimilitary album. In a police raid the compound was burned down, and Kuti was beaten. His arm was so badly hurt that he was never again able to play saxophone. During the attack, a number of his wives (in 1978 he married 27 women as a protest against Western culture) were abused and raped, and his mother, Fumilayo RANSOME-KUTI, was thrown from a window. When she died of her injuries sometime later, Kuti left her coffin at the gates of Obasanjo's palace and released an album entitled *Coffin for Head of State.* Kuti spent two years in prison, from 1984 to 1986, until international pressure (Fela was an Amnesty International case of conscience) achieved his release. He then formed a political party, the Movement of the People, but it was refused permission to compete in elections. After opposing military dictator General Ibrahim BABANGIDA, he was falsely accused of murder and was again imprisoned in 1993.

His views on women were sexist in the extreme. He criticized feminism and argued that women are naturally submissive and exist for men's service. He practiced polygamy without any sense of fidelity, saying that "sex should be worshipped every day!" His lifestyle and politics made him an outrageous figure, but he was also a consummate musician with a dedicated international following. He died from complications due to AIDS.

References: AB, *abd, afr,* BPAR, CBB, CM, DMM, EB, GEPM, WAM, *wiki.* Miael Veal, *Fela: The Life of an African Musical Icon* (1997); Tejumola Olaniyan, *Arrest the Music! Fela and His Rebel Art and Politics* (2004); *Fela Live!* (video, 1981).

LA GUMA, (Justin) Alex
(South Africa, 1925–1985)

Comrade Alex La Guma, a lifelong Communist activist, was a South African fiction writer, perhaps the finest short-story writer from that country, who used his work to expose the sufferings of ordinary South Africans under apartheid.

La Guma was educated in Cape Town and through correspondence courses. He did factory work and through union activity, he joined the Communist Party, where his father had been active from before Alex's birth. He was listed as a "known Communist" under the Suppression of Communism Act, and was always under suspicion. He worked as a journalist in the 1950s, but he was imprisoned following the 1960 Sharpeville Massacre, where 69 peaceful demonstrators, including children, were shot down. Following his release, he was detained twice more until he was exiled to London, where he was named the official representative of the African National Congress (ANC).

Though he was a prominent short-story writer, his novels were better received. They portray the grim and unyielding conditions of grinding poverty and hopelessness forced upon Blacks at the time. They are unflinchingly brutal is descriptions of prison conditions, and prostitution and violence in everyday life. La Guma himself was legally of a Coloured (mixed-race) family, of French, Malagache and African stock. His first novel, *A Walk in the Night* (1962), describes the social and political situation in District Six, the main Coloured area. *The Stone Country* (1967) presents prison as a metaphor for Black existence under apartheid. His fiction develops strong characters and shows their disintegration under the pressures of legalized racism.

In 1978, the ANC posted him to Cuba and the Caribbean as their representative there, and he died in Havana.

References: abd, afr, EB, MMA, *wiki*, WLTC. La Guma, *In the Fog of the Season's End* (1972); Kathleen Balutansky, *The Novels of Alex La Guma* (1990).

LAKWENA, Alice
(Uganda, 1956–)

Alice Lakwena, born Alice Auma, was a spirit medium, rebel leader and terrorist. She founded the Holy Spirit Movement, the predecessor of the Lord's Resistance Army (LRA) headed by her reputed nephew, Joseph KONY.

Colonial policy in Uganda favored the Bantu south, which was organized into kingdoms, while the Nilotic peoples of the north were considered fit only for the military. Education and development was concentrated in the south and west, while the Acholi and other northern peoples supplied farm labor and security guards. This built up generations of resentment. After Yoweri MUSEVENI defeated the Acholi General Tito Okello, who toppled Idi AMIN, many Acholi soldiers fled into the bush. A peace accord was signed with the Museveni government, but some Acholi refused to accept it and followed Alice Lakwena into the Holy Spirit Movement.

Alice Lakwena is a priestess and spirit medium who claims to channel an Italian military officer. She converted from Anglicanism to Catholicism at some point, but in 1985 she became spirit-possessed after spending 40 days in a forest. At first she served as a healer and oracle until her spirit told her to go to war to eliminate evil.

The Holy Spirit Movement melded traditional Acholi religious elements with Christian ones. Soldiers were anointed with holy oil, which was said to deflect their enemies' bullets from their bodies. They went into battle singing the Catholic refrain, "Christ has died, Christ is risen, Christ will come again!" in Acholi. They marched south, winning a series of skirmishes, until they were ready to storm the capital, Kampala, in 1986–1987. In the resulting battle, the Holy Spirit warriors were cut down by Ugandan artillery, with horrific loss of life.

Lakwena's spirit deserted her after her defeat and she fled across the border to Kenya by bicycle, where she has been interned in a United Nations

Refugee Camp. She has become a caricature of her former self, now extremely obese and ranting about a return to Uganda as she sits on a wooden throne in her mud hut. She was invited back to Uganda by Museveni in 2003 under an amnesty act, but he withdrew the offer after she claimed to be able to cure AIDS. It was feared she would begin another cult, or perhaps link up with her nephew's LRA.

References: wiki. Heike Behrend, *Alice and the Holy Spirits* (1999).

LALIBELA
(Ethiopia, 1150s–1225?)

St. Lalibela was an Ethiopian monarch and church builder. The penultimate king of the Zagwe dynasty, he was the most renowned, especially for the 11 rock-hewn churches built in his capital. These edifices are among the major medieval monuments of Africa. Lalibela provides a striking example of the union of church and state in Ethiopia and is revered as a saint in the Ethiopian Coptic Orthodox Church, where his feast is observed on June 6.

Lalibela, meaning "bees obey him," was a birth-name noting that at his birth a swarm of bees alighted on him without harming him. As a youth, Lalibela claimed to have visions and spent some time as a hermit. In 1180 he made a pilgrimage to Jerusalem. Upon his return, Lalibela only reluctantly took the throne from his half-brother Harba with support from the clergy, who opposed Harba's contacts with the papacy. He took the name Gabra Masqal, Servant of the Cross, and began his reign with a long fast. He was *negus* of Ethiopia from about 1187 to his death.

Lalibela attempted a Christian policy of charity and peace, which was largely successful. He began by reconciling with Harba. He secured his borders with new monasteries and developed good relations with the Sultan Saladin, thus easing pressures on the Christians of Egypt and protecting the Ethiopians in Jerusalem. His greatest feat, however, was creating the amazing network of churches, courtyards and water systems in his capital. Legend—and Lalibela's life is surrounded by legend—has it that he carved it by night, assisted only by angels. Since the entire complex is carved from natural rock below ground level, it has survived intact. Lalibela's tomb is also located there.

References: AB, *afr*, DAB, *dacb*, DAHB, *wiki*. Taddesse Tamrat, *Church and State in Ethiopia* (1972).

LAMINE, Mamadu
(Sénégal/Gambia, 1835?–1887)

Mamadu Lamine, an Islamic ruler in the Senegambia (the Gambia River basin), led the Soninke resistance movement against French imperialism in the late nineteenth century.

Born the son of a Muslim cleric and provided with an Islamic education, Lamine spent much of his youth in the service of UMAR Ibn Said Tall—known popularly as al-Hajj Umar—who was establishing the Tukulor Empire, the dominant Islamic expansionist state of the region. In the 1860s, Mamadu made his own *hajj,* or pilgrimage to Mecca, which, under the transportation limitations of the time, often took several years and involved a considerable security guard. When he returned, Umar had died and been succeeded by his son, AMADOU Ibn Umar Tall, who promptly placed Lamine under detention, probably over religious differences within the Tijaniyya brotherhood, although he was certainly aware that Lamine might be a potential leader for the restive Soninke.

In 1885, Lamine began a brief but dramatic career as a national leader. Returning to the Senegambia, he encountered French expansionism, aimed largely at the Tukulor Empire, its main competitor in the region. The Soninke had long chafed under Tukulor dominance and had a history of rebellion. Their experience of European imperialism was more recent—forced contract labor to build a railway to Niger. The high death rate under perilous conditions and daily humiliations stiffened Soninke resistance. A charismatic leader who knew how to use religious symbols, Lamine fanned the embers of Soninke nationalism against both the French and the Tukulor and attracted a substantial following. He preached the orthodox doctrine that Muslims should not allow themselves to be governed by infidels. He declared a *jihad* or holy war in 1886 and quickly seized control of most of the Senegambia, placing more than 10,000 men in the field. With spies in the camps of collaborators, Lamine defeated the French several times and forced General Joseph GALLIENI to make peace with Amadou and SAMORI Touré so that he could consolidate his forces on the Gambia River basin. Able to concentrate his troops, Gallieni defeated Lamine in a decisive battle at Toubakouta in 1887. Lamine died either during or shortly after the battle.

Reference: DAHB.

LAMIZANA, Aboubakar Sangoulé
(Burkina Faso, 1916–2005)

Aboubakar Sangoulé Lamizana was three times head of state in Upper Volta (since 1984 called Burkina Faso). Once he was elected, and twice he gained the position through coups. Although he joined the French army in 1936 and spent much of his career in the military, he nevertheless made several attempts to maintain civilian government in Upper Volta until 1980, when the government was overthrown.

Lamizana joined the French army at age 20 and served in Morocco, Algeria and Vietnam, where he was awarded the Legion of Honor. In addition to his field experience, he twice served as adjutant to military commanders in Mauritania and Côte d'Ivoire and was an instructor at the Center for African and Asian Studies in Paris. When Upper Volta gained independence in 1960, his wide experience made him a logical choice for the national army's chief of staff.

By 1966 it was clear that President Maurice YAMÉOGO had lost control of the deteriorating situation in Upper Volta. The powerful labor unions, joined by the Church and the civil service, called for his overthrow, and Lamizana seized power. In office, he proved tough and purposeful. He worked for a return of elected government and announced that the military would govern only for the duration of the four-year development plan. He tamed the unions, balanced the budget, and drafted a new constitution that provided for civilian rule with a strong military presence. In 1970, true to his word, elections were held, and Lamizana turned over authority to Gérard Ouédraogo. By 1973 the oil crisis and inflation had once again undermined the economy, but Ouédraogo refused to resign after losing a vote of no confidence. Lamizana deposed him but announced elections for 1977. Again he initiated a fiscal policy that improved economic conditions and, while retaining his army position, was elected president with 56 percent of the vote. It was one of the most democratic and fair elections held in West Africa up to that time.

Lamizana supported a multiparty system while suppressing corruption, and American President Jimmy Carter called Upper Volta one of the most progressive African states in the field of human rights. The economy, however, could be maintained only under strict austerity measures. Foreign aid exceeded the national budget, and expatriate Burkinabè workers sent home much of the money coming into the country. The food deficit was 65,000 tons a year, and the local economy produced little. Once again the trade unions challenged the government, generating a bitter confrontation that included conflict with armed union militants. At the threat of civil war, Colonel Sayé ZERBO seized control and imposed public order.

Lamizana was placed under house arrest, and in 1984, when Captain Thomas SANKARA took power, he was accused of corruption and plotting a coup. He was acquitted and went into semi-retirement. In 1987 he was elected chairman of the National Union of Burkinabè Elders.

References: DAHB, DRWW, PLBA, *wiki.*

LANGALIBALELE
(South Africa, 1818?–1889)

Langalibalele was the chief and traditional leader of the Hlubi, a small clan in Natal. His arrest and mistreatment made him a symbol of the exploitation of Africans.

Langalibalele's people, the Hlubi, had been scattered by the *difaqane,* the enforced migration of various southern Africans that resulted from the formation and expansion of the Zulu nation. Around 1845 he gathered the remnants of the Hlubi together and settled them in the Drakensberg Mountains, where his following grew to about 10,000. He became renowned as a medicine man and rainmaker. The Hlubi peasants prospered, causing concern among nearby White farmers. Many Hlubi were, however, forced to work in the diamond mines in Kimberley, where they were able to buy guns with their earnings. This factor aroused concern among Whites, and wild rumors of an impending uprising spread through Natal. In 1873 the Natal secretary of native affairs ordered that the guns be registered, but Langalibalele refused and also ignored several summonses to explain his decision. An armed force was sent against him and three Whites were killed in a skirmish. Enraged White farmers demanded suppression of the "rebellion," and Langalibalele fled into Lesotho, where Molapo, a Sotho chief, arrested him in exchange for the right to loot Hlubi villages. The Hlubi lost their lands, more than 200 men were killed, and the women and children were distributed to area farmers as indentured laborers.

Langalibalele's trial for murder, treason and rebellion was a sham. He was sentenced to life imprisonment and sent to Robben Island. At first Langalibalele's only support came from John William Colenso, the Anglican bishop of Natal, but soon London intervened and removed the lieutenant-governor. Langalibalele remained in prison or exile until 1887, when mounting outrage brought about his release, and he returned to the Natal region.

References: DAHB. Bill Guest, *Langalibalele: The Crisis in Natal* (1976).

LATTIER, Christian
(Côte d'Ivoire, 1925–1978)

Christian Lattier was one of the foremost sculptors of the mid-twentieth century. He came from a prominent Ivoirean family and was sent to France for education in 1935. He spent the World War II years there and then attended the Académie des Beaux Arts in Paris from 1947 to 1956, where he apprenticed under several leading masters of sculpture, wood carving and architecture. He emerged with a strong commitment to modern sculpture, using new forms and experimenting with unusual materials. Lattier exhibited in Paris, Munich, Rome and Abidjan before sending pieces to the Festival of Black Arts in Dakar, Sénégal, in 1966. Competing with art works from all across sub-Saharan Africa, he won the Grand Prize with one of his rope-on-iron sculptures, *Panther*.

In his lifetime, Lattier would create over 3,000 designs, destroy most of them and keep the best. His first impact was made with his rope sculptures, and his 10-foot *Leopard* caused a furor in artistic circles, but it won the Chevenard Prize in 1954. In 1955 he received the French Cathedral Grand Prize of the Fine Arts Academy, which had not been given for 10 years because no one was considered worthy

of it. It brought him a contract to work on the restoration of Chartres Cathedral, one of the finest Gothic structures in Europe. In 1957, he executed his first work in Côte d'Ivoire, the decoration of the Abidjan City Hall. He then spent several years exhibiting before returning to Côte d'Ivoire permanently.

In 1962, Lattier was appointed professor of sculpture at the National Institute of Arts in Abidjan. Four years later he took part in the World Festival of African Arts in Dakar, where he was awarded the World Prize for the body of his work, in addition to the prize for *Panther*. Until his death, Lattier worked in Côte d'Ivoire, where he ornamented a number of public buildings, both civic and religious. He did much of this work in laterite, a clay-like substance that hardens into a form of stone. Throughout, however, Lattier continued his string sculptures where the string, usually plastered, demonstrated traditional African motifs with American minimalist style. One such was *Mask* (1975), a modernized interpretation of a traditional African ritual mask.

References: MMA. Yacouba Konaté, *Christian Lattier: le sculpteur aux mains nues* (Christian Lattier: the bare-handed sculptor,1993).

LEAKEY, Louis S. B.
(Kenya, 1903–1972)

Dr. Louis S. B. Leakey was the paleontologist who first proved that Africa was the cradle of humanity. Leakey, born in Kenya to missionary parents, spoke Kikuyu before English and was initiated as a Kikuyu warrior at age 13 with the name Wakariugi, "Son of the Sparrow." He even became a Kikuyu elder with his age-set. Although he regarded himself as a Kenyan nationalist, he was still respected by the British, whom he served during World War II and as an interpreter at the trial of Jomo KENYATTA.

Leakey began his archeological career as a paleontologist at age 20, when he left Cambridge University to do field work in Tanganyika. After completing his Ph.D. back at Cambridge, he continued explorations in the Great Rift Valley and was rewarded in 1929 with his first major find, a 200,000-year-old settlement. In 1948, he found the skull of *Proconsul africanus*, a common ancestor of both humans and apes. With his wife Mary

LEAKEY and sons, he concentrated his research on the Olduvai Gorge in northern Tanganyika, finding over a hundred forms of extinct prehistoric animals and further evidence of early humanoids, most notably *Homo habilis*. Leakey was able to challenge the theory that humans originated in Asia, showing that the hand-axe culture diffused out from Africa. He also disproved the accepted theory that human evolution was linear, demonstrating that there were parallel humanoid developments. Much of his work was supported by the National Geographic Society, and he, along with Mary, received its Hubbard Medal in 1962, among many other awards. Leakey also supported field research on primates, convinced that by observing them in their natural settings, one could begin to grasp the patterns of evolution.

Leakey was flamboyant and given to dramatic announcements of his archaeological discoveries. His personal life was a checkered one, and at various times he was estranged from his sons. He also engaged in various romantic affairs and, after separating from Mary, he took up openly with young women. He was also able, however, to mentor young women. Jane GOODALL and Dian FOSSEY, both of whom did important work on primates, began under his direction.

References: AB, *afr*, CA, CB, EB, HH, MMA, *wiki*. Leakey, *By the Evidence* (1974); Anne Malatesta, *The White Kikuyu* (1978).

LEAKEY, Mary Douglas
(Kenya/Tanzania, 1913–1996)

Mary Douglas Leakey was born in England but spent most of her life in Kenya as an associate of her husband, Louis LEAKEY. Their amazing discoveries of the evidence of early humans altered scholarly debate on evolution. She first worked with the discoverer of the prehistoric rock paintings in southern France, and then spent four years on neolithic sites in southern England. She was only 20 years old when she met Louis Leakey, a married man 10 years her senior. Their romance became a source of gossip. Louis was fired from his position at Cambridge University over the affair, and Mary joined him at the Tanganyikan site of Olduvai Gorge, living with him until his divorce made their marriage possible in 1936. Their three sons, Jonathan, Richard LEAKEY, and Philip, have all been involved in "the family business," as paleontology

came to be regarded by them. "I had no intention of allowing motherhood to disrupt my work," she commented.

Mary Leakey was instrumental in the discovery of the skull of *Proconsul africanus* in 1947 on Rusinga Island in Lake Victoria. It was the first of its kind to be found. In 1959 she made her most important find, 400 fragments of a hominid that she called *Zinjanthropus*. Spying a jawbone with teeth, she rushed back to Louis at camp, crying out, "I've found our man!" *Zinj* (called "Dear Boy" by the Leakeys) proved to be 1.75 million years old. In the same stratum were the remains of other hominids, which led to the novel idea that two species of hominids had coexisted. Besides her discoveries, in 1951 she used her considerable artistic talents to record 1,600 Stone Age rock paintings in Tanganyika. Her 1983 book, *Africa's Vanishing Art*, describes them.

Mary increasingly worked alone while Louis lectured and traveled, and she grew more independent. In the 1960s they grew apart and rarely saw one another in his last years. After Louis's death in 1972, Mary became a more public person, speaking and writing. In 1978 she discovered a trail of hominid footprints, two adults and a child, in volcanic ash dated 3.6 million years. With no tools to be found in the stratum, it became clear to her that walking upright was what preceded all technology. "This freed the hands for myriad possibilities.... The brain expanded to meet it. And mankind was formed."

Mary Leakey retired from fieldwork after losing sight in her left eye in 1982, and she lived in Nairobi until her death.

References: AB, *afr*, CANR, CB, EB, EWB, HH, *wiki*. Leakey, *Disclosing the Past* (1984).

LEAKEY, Richard Erskine
(Kenya, 1944–)

Richard Erskine Leakey, one of the sons of Mary LEAKEY and Louis LEAKEY, has been a safari leader, museum director, paleoanthropologist and environmentalist—all with a high-school education. Always a rebel, he resisted working with his famous parents. Finally, his father hired him to handle camp arrangements. He snuck out of camp to make his own finds, and at a later meeting with National Geographic officials, left his father speechless as he obtained a grant that Louis thought surely was his.

Richard Leakey's most important discovery was made in 1984 at Lake Turkana in Kenya, where he found the bones of *Homo erectus*, a 1.6-million-year-old youth. While his parents concentrated on the hominid ancestors of humans, Richard looked for the evolution of specifically human qualities—consciousness, morality, language, creativity. Leakey argues that human evolution was possible only because of cooperation and rejects the contention that violence is innate is humans. He has had a long and acrimonious rivalry with Donald Johansen, the discoverer of "Lucy," the 3.5-million-year-old skeleton from Ethiopia, which is accepted by most anthropologists as a common ancestor of humans. They have been known to engage in shouting matches at professional meetings.

In 1968, Leakey was named director of the Kenya National Museums, giving him a base for continuing his field research. In 1989 he surprised everyone by accepting an appointment as director of the corrupt Department of Parks and Wildlife. With an aggressive style and direct access to President Daniel arap MOI, Leakey reformed the organization. He fired 1,700 employees and began a revitalization of the department. He armed, trained and paid his rangers well, outfitting them with the latest equipment with money raised abroad. When he announced a "shoot to kill" policy against poachers, elephant poaching dropped drastically. Leakey then convinced the World Bank to provide $300 million for Kenyan wildlife conservation, at the same time that it was cutting funds to the government in Nairobi over human rights issues.

Brazen at self-promotion, Leakey uses the media dramatically. His ability to dominate media attention is best exemplified by the single-handed way he brought about the international ivory ban in 1989, mobilizing forces from all sides, who were treated to a huge bonfire of 60 tons of elephant tusks confiscated from poachers.

In 1993 Leakey crashed while piloting a small plane. He lost both legs but returned to his position, stoically continuing to work even after nine operations left him in excruciating pain.

His success has not endeared Leakey to politicians, and in 1994, smelling the money attracted to his department, calls went out for his removal. Environmentalist Wangari MAATHAI accused critics of hoping to loot the game parks and use their

vast lands for ethnic cleansing in the bloody tribal conflicts engineered by Moi's faction. Leakey submitted his resignation, but in a dramatic show of support, Moi reinstated him a few months later. Leakey's policies always placed conservation above population pressures, and many were angered by being excluded from lands they felt were rightfully theirs. After a few weeks, Leakey realized that his opponents had prevailed, and he resigned again.

In 1995, Leakey and several Kenyan leaders formed a new anti-corruption political party opposed to Moi. He was again admitted to the government as cabinet secretary in 1999, at the insistence of international donors appalled at the level of financial mismanagement in the government. He was finally forced out in 2001.

References: AB, *afr*, CANR, CB, EB, EWB, HH, *wiki*. Leakey, *One Life* (1984) and *Wildlife Wars* (2001).

LEBNA DENGEL
(Ethiopia, 1496–1540)

Emperor Lebna Dengel ruled Ethiopia from 1508 to 1540, a period that was marked by a major expansion of Islam, which he initially contained before it ravaged the country by the 1530s. He was also known as Dawit (David) II.

He succeeded to the throne at age 12, and the country was ruled by a regency, during which the Muslim sultanates to the south were kept in vassalage. In 1516 there was a rebellion by Adalite Muslims, but Lebna Dengel defeated them at the Red Sea port of Zeila. Fearing the expansion of Islamic power, however, the queen regent invited the Portuguese to assist Ethiopia, and Lebna Dengel entertained (or possibly detained) a Portuguese diplomatic mission for six years. The emperor had a keen interest in modernization and wrote both the king of Portugal and the pope, requesting economic, military and technical assistance. He sent an ambassador to Lisbon and promoted the cooperation of all Christian nations against the Muslims. These policies gave rise to false hopes in Rome that Lebna Dengel wished to unite the Ethiopian church to Catholicism.

Lebna Dengel governed in a rather arbitrary way, alienating many of the nobility. In 1527, Adal again rebelled, and a combination of its determination and the lackluster response of the nobility led to a disastrous defeat for Lebna Dengel in 1529. The Ethiopian army was no match for that of AHMAD Ibn Ibrahim, known as Grañ, "the left-handed." Grañ had taken over Adal around 1520, named himself an imam and proclaimed a *jihad* (holy war) against Ethiopia. Grañ swept across Ethiopia with almost no resistance in his path, destroying monasteries and forcing the conversion of over 90 percent of Ethiopian's Christians. Lebna Dengel fled to the isolated monastery of Debra Damo, on top of a mountain, where he died, perhaps in battle. He was succeeded by his son GALAWDÉWOS, who defeated Grañ three years later with Portuguese military assistance.

References: DAB, DAHB, *wiki*.

LEGUM, Colin
(South Africa, 1919–2003)

Colin Legum was a distinguished South African journalist, known internationally as an interpreter of African affairs.

Legum was born in the Orange Free State and worked his way up from office clerk to chief parliamentary correspondent for the Johannesburg *Sunday Express* from 1936 to 1939. After this stint, he became editor of two left-wing papers, *The Mineworker* and *The Forward*. He became affiliated with the socialist wing of the Labour Party and in 1942 he was elected to the Johannesburg City Council. In 1948, after the apartheid system came into force, he left for Great Britain. For 30 years he was a correspondent and associate editor for *The Observer*, a leading London paper. He developed close relations with many South African leaders in exile, especially Oliver TAMBO and Donald WOODS. In 1991 he returned to South Africa.

Legum's contribution to journalism was his astute commentary on world affairs and his ability to bring the issues of Africa to world attention at a time when the continent was largely ignored in the media. His concerns included apartheid, but was by no means limited to it. With press censorship in place in South Africa, and a controlled media in most other countries, Legum's writing was a valuable and trustworthy source of information. He also did research and writing on Middle Eastern and Indian Ocean security questions. From 1982 to 1995 he published a newsletter on world affairs, *Third World Reports*, with analysis of international

affairs from the perspective of the Third World. His press clips alone comprise 17 volumes. All of his research materials and writings have been made available for use on University Microfilms. His papers are held by the University of Edinburgh.

References: CANR, EB. Legum, *Africa Since Independence* (1999).

LEKHANYA, Justin Matsing
(Lesotho,1938–)

Major-General Justin Matsing Lekhanya replaced the unpopular administration of Chief Leabua JONATHAN and governed Lesotho for five years, during which time he forced King MOSHWESHWE II to abdicate and made the Lesotho monarchy a constitutional one.

Lekhanya was educated in mission schools, spent a year working in the South African mines, and then in 1960 joined the Basutoland police, the colonial force. In 1965 he was appointed the only African officer in the police mobile unit. When Basutoland became independent as Lesotho in 1966, Lekhanya rose quickly in the army ranks. When Jonathan engineered the 1970 coup to keep himself in power, Lekhanya supported him and enforced the state of emergency by arresting Jonathan's opponents. From 1972 to 1973, Lekhanya went overseas for further military training in Scotland and the United States. Shortly after his return he became police commander and began the process of developing the police force into a national defense force, which was completed with an independent force in 1977. Lekhanya was noted for his attention to his men's welfare. He improved their living conditions, set up a night school at the police barracks, and eventually established a clinic and a bus service for them. All these programs were operated by police as after-hours employment and also served the public.

During this period, Lekhanya served the Jonathan regime effectively, but by 1985 conditions had deteriorated. Jonathan canceled elections and appointed the parliament, the economy was in a shambles, and South Africa had begun a blockade because of Jonathan's friendship with the Communist nations of Eastern Europe. In 1986, Lekhanya stepped in and turned executive authority over to the king. Lekhanya settled conflicts with South

Africa by agreeing to a pact of mutual nonsupport of armed opposition forces. He was strengthened by South Africa's withdrawal of support for a guerrilla group that had been harassing Jonathan, and Lesotho expelled militants of South Africa's African National Congress in return. Most of the Communist embassies were also closed.

Internally, Lekhanya's primary issue was a power struggle with the king, who used two scandals involving Lekhanya to weaken his position. Lekhanya responded in 1990 by removing several of the king's supporters from the military council, which had been investigating Lekhanya's personal actions. The crisis deepened, and Lekhanya forced the king into exile and then stripped him of his authority and replaced him with his son, King Letsie III. In 1991, Lekhanya was removed by Colonel Elias RAMAEMA and went into exile in South Africa. Later he returned to Lesotho to head the Basotho National Party, which has been a small minority in parliament.

References: PLBA, RWWA, *wiki.*

LENSHINA Mulenga Mubisha, Alice
(Zambia, 1924?–1978)

Prophetess Alice Lenshina Mulenga Mubisha was the founder of a powerful African independent Church movement at the time of Zambian independence. Beginning as an anti-witchcraft movement, it clashed with the new government when it rejected secular authority.

Lenshina was a baptismal candidate with a Presbyterian mission when she received a series of visions in which she believed that she was taken to heaven and given divine messages instructing her to destroy witchcraft and sorcery. She claimed to have died and been resurrected four times. In 1953 she began a movement called *Lumpa* (meaning "better than all others" in Bemba) in a town that she renamed Zion. She took the name Lenshina, meaning queen. Despite her claims, a Presbyterian pastor baptized her, an event that seems to have had a profound impact on intensifying her visions. She and her husband were expelled from the Presbyterians in 1955, however, and began their preaching mission. Crowds of adherents soon joined them, and by 1959 there was an organized Church with

ministers and between 50,000 and 100,000 members, most of whom had left either Presbyterian or Catholic missions.

Lenshina preached a basically Christian doctrine but with baptism as the only observance. Baptism was a special ceremony administered by Lenshina herself. She attacked witchcraft and sorcery, which placed her in the long tradition of witch eradication movements in Central Africa, but to these she added the condemnation of alcohol and polygamy. The Lumpa composed spirited Bemba hymns, far superior to the wooden translations in use among Protestants and Catholics. The religion gathered its members into villages, where the hymns and rejection of traditional religious practices created what she promoted as a new, cleansed society worthy to receive the Saviour when He came again. The grand cathedral built at Zion in 1958 has a pillar upon which Jesus Christ was to descend for His second coming.

The problematic teaching of the Lumpa Church was its opposition to earthly authority, a doctrine it seems to have accepted from the Watch Tower Society, itself a splinter sect of the Jehovah's Witnesses.

By 1958, Lenshina had rejected government registration of her Church as an approved organization. The Lumpa also rejected taxes and formed their own villages, which threatened the traditional authority of the chiefs. Lenshina challenged the dominant United National Independence Party (UNIP) of Kenneth KAUNDA, which witnessed a decline in membership when her followers withdrew from political groups. UNIP regarded the Lumpa Church as a rival, and there were an increasing number of violent clashes between the two. At Zambia's independence in 1964, the Lumpa Church constituted an open challenge to the new government's supremacy. Lumpa followers fortified their villages, and the subsequent conflict resulted in the death of 1,500 church members during police and army attacks. The skirmishes lasted for three months, ending with the banning of the Church and Lenshina's arrest. The Church remained banned but an amnesty was declared in 1968, whereupon 20,000 Lumpa went into exile in the Democratic Republic of the Congo. Lenshina was only released in 1975 and was arrested again two years later for holding a church service. By that time, however, the movement was effectively dead. Lay movements, such as the Catholic Legion of Mary, reclaimed many of the members for their churches, often by incorporating the very hymns that had resonated with Bemba national feelings.

References: AB, *dacb*, DAHB, MMA, PLBA, *wiki*. Andrew Roberts, *The Lumpa Church of Alice Lenshina* (1972).

LETTOW-VORBECK, Paul Emil von
(Namibia/Tanzania, 1870–1964)

Major-General Paul Emil von Lettow-Vorbeck, commander of German East African forces in World War I, became an accomplished guerrilla leader who pinned down vastly superior numbers of Allied troops.

After serving in Cameroon, von Lettow-Vorbeck was assigned to the colonial forces in South-West Africa (now Namibia), which were then being strengthened in order to suppress the Herero rebellion led by Samuel MAHERERO from 1904 to 1907. German forces in the colony pursued a genocidal extermination policy that caused the loss of over 70 percent of the local population and devastated the economy. Von Lettow-Vorbeck gained valuable experience in bush warfare, especially on open plains. He received an eye wound and recuperated in South Africa, where he became a friend of General Jan SMUTS, whom he would later fight. He was then posted to Cameroon as commander of colonial forces there.

Von Lettow-Vorbeck was appointed commander of German forces in East Africa when World War I broke out in 1914. The British were able to maintain a naval blockade throughout the war, preventing any reinforcements from reaching his undermanned detachment. The governor favored having German East Africa (now Tanzania) declared a neutral territory, with German forces interned. Ignoring this counsel of defeat, von Lettow-Vorbeck realized that he could affect the outcome of the war by tying up large numbers of Allied troops in East Africa. He proceeded—with never more than 3,000 German soldiers—to keep 150,000 to 300,000 British, Belgian and Portuguese soldiers engaged in protecting their colonies and attempting to defeat him. He armed and trained 11,000 African *askaris* (native militia), who fought effectively and made use of their familiarity with the countryside. This military strategy particularly frightened British settlers in Kenya, who were adamantly opposed to arming any Africans.

In 1917, General Smuts commanded a massive offensive with 45,000 troops against von Lettow-Vorbeck but was unable either to capture him or destroy his forces. Under von Lettow-Vorbeck's command, the Germans invaded Mozambique, German East Africa and finally Northern Rhodesia, where he surrendered after the armistice in Europe. He returned to a hero's welcome in Germany, and a promotion from colonel to major-general. A staunch conservative, he led an attempted putsch against the radicals in 1920 and later briefly served in the Reichstag. In later years he was an anti-Nazi and was involved in the conservative opposition to Hitler.

References: DAHB, EB, *wiki*. Edwin Hoyt, *Guerilla: Colonel von Lettow-Vorbeck and Germany's East African Empire* (1981).

LEUTWIN, Theodor
(Namibia, 1849–1921)

Theodor Leutwin ruled German South-West Africa from 1894 to 1904, consolidating German authority over the colony, but was finally removed after a disastrous rebellion that he had not anticipated and for which he had not prepared.

Leutwin arrived in South-West Africa as a young administrator with a clear mandate: to make as much land available for German settlers as possible and to govern with a minimum of personnel. He therefore moved quickly against the Khoikhoi chief Henrik WITBOOI, defeating him and making him an ally. Witbooi, who had opposed German domination, became a supporter, providing supplies and even troops on occasion. Leutwin followed a policy of governing through the local chiefs as much as possible and maintaining divisions among them.

In 1904 this policy collapsed in the final surge of anticolonial resistance. As Leutwin was subduing the Nama (with support from Witbooi, who personally led his warriors), the Herero under Samuel MAHERERO moved to seize lands previously taken from them. They killed more than a hundred German farmers, which resulted in settler protests and aroused opposition to Leutwin in the German government. Leutwin was forced to reach a disadvantageous settlement with the Nama in order to meet the Herero threat. When the Herero were subdued, Leutwin was replaced by a harsh commander, Lothar Von Trotha. At that point, Witbooi—who had supported Leutwin because of a personal bond rather than out of general support for German rule—launched his own land reclamation war. He was killed in battle, the Herero were decimated, and Leutwin's indirect rule policy was abandoned.

Reference: DAHB.

LEWANIKA Lubosi
(Zambia, 1845?–1916)

Lewanika Lubosi, king of the Lozi (or Barotse) from 1878, built his kingdom into the most powerful in what is now western Zambia. Recognizing that European expansion spelled the end of independence, he decided to ally himself with the British rather than the neighboring Portuguese, and he brought his kingdom under British protection.

Lewanika came to power after a coup and during troubled times. The kingdom was politically factionalized and had to deal with the recently arrived traders and missionaries, who were introducing new and uncontrollable influences. He survived an attempted coup, eliminated his rivals, and undertook a successful military campaign against the Ila people. In 1884 he was forced into exile, but after a year he returned, determined to consolidate his authority. He took the praise-name *Lewanika,* "the uniter," and began to eradicate every possible rival faction.

Fearing both internal crises and external pressures, Lewanika made contact with KHAMA III, a progressive chief who had obtained a British protectorate in Bechuanaland. He began petitioning for the same status. At the same time, he formed a close friendship with a French Protestant missionary, François COILLARD. Lewanika was indifferent to Christianity but did look to Western education as a means of modernizing the kingdom. In addition, he abolished slavery and slave trading in Barotseland. In 1890 he signed a mining concession with Cecil RHODES's British South Africa Company (BSAC), the first of a number of BSAC treaties that whittled away his authority and reduced him to a figurehead paramount chief. He was able, however, to obtain a school system that produced an educated elite, who brought about a Lozi revival after his death.

References: DAHB, EB.

LEY Rochereau, Tabu
(Democratic Republic of the Congo, 1940–)

Tabu Ley Rochereau, a superstar performer of African popular music, ranked just behind the inimitable FRANCO. He has numerous recordings and maintains high professional standards.

Ley was a precocious musical talent, playing with a number of bands, and was sought after for his eloquent voice and styling. In 1961 he joined Africa Jazz, a seminal group that had great influence on Ley and Docteur NICO, with whom Ley performed. Financial conflicts led Ley, Nico, and others to form African Fiesta in 1963. It became an immediate hit, but recording contracts generated dissension. In 1965, Ley launched his own band, Afrisa, and it began performing in Kinshasa and making its own recordings locally. Papa WEMBA was part of the group, which became one of the most successful in African music, selling over a million albums. Ley reflected on those days with nostalgia, saying: "What we'll never be able to recapture is the spontaneity, the concentration of the musicians of that era."

Ley is credited with creating a style known as *soukous,* which has become a generic term for all Congolese dance music. *Soukous* blends Cuban rhythms into extended jazz-style pieces that move from slow and sensual introductions to hard-pounding dance beats. Singing in French and Lingala, Ley has a warm, sweet high tenor, and on stage he is a riveting personality. For 30 years Ley and Franco dueled for the title of greatest pioneer of African music, each producing several thousand songs and attracting devoted followings. In 1992, Senachie Records culled thousands of Ley's singles to produce an album of older music, *Man from Kinshasa,* which he used on a U.S. tour.

Ley's album, *Exil-Ley* (1993) was a sardonic comment on his estrangement from his homeland. For many years, Ley opened every concert with "Djalelo," a praise song in honor of MOBUTU Sese Seko, the tyrant of the Democratic Republic of the Congo (DRC), which Mobutu renamed Zaïre. but as the country descended into chaos, most of the prominent musicians, including Ley, left for Paris. With the death of Franco in 1989, Ley became the grand old man of *soukous*. Even in exile, he remained perhaps the most popular person in the DRC. In the 1990s, Ley lived and recorded in California, where he began integrating Samba rhythms and English lyrics. There are at least four albums from this period. After Mobutu's death, Ley returned to the DRC. He was born Pascal Tabu, and sometimes goes by Rochereau.

Reference: DMM, GEPM, WAM, *wiki*.

LIVINGSTONE, David

(South Africa/Botswana/Zambia/Tanzania, 1813–1873)

Dr. David Livingstone, the famous Scottish explorer who revealed Africa to nineteenth century Europe, was a missionary forerunner of modern Christianity in Africa.

Livingstone was raised in poverty; the family of nine lived in a single room in a Lanarkshire cotton mill tenement. Working 14 hours a day while studying at night school, he prepared himself and saved what little he could until, in 1836, he was able to study medicine and theology at the University of Glasgow while still working part-time as a cotton spinner. In 1838 he went to London to offer his services as a medical missionary to the London Missionary Society (LMS), which he chose because of its nonsectarian character. Livingstone was a devout evangelical Christian whose conversion came when he realized that faith and science were compatible.

In London, Livingstone completed his internship and, through the LMS, met the South African missionary Robert MOFFAT, who attracted him to Africa. In 1840 he received his medical license, was ordained, and set sail for Cape Town. His first assignment was in Bechuanaland (now Botswana), where he was to found a mission station north of Moffat's. Here he began what was to become his standard practice. He traveled into the interior and stayed with the local people until he learned their language, preaching and studying the botany and natural history of the area. These expeditions were not without risk. In 1844 he was badly mauled by a lion, so thereafter he was forced to fire his rifle from his left shoulder.

Between trips he ran his mission, building a chapel, setting up a printing press, preaching and healing. In 1845 he married Mary Moffat, Robert's eldest daughter, and began a family while moving about setting up new mission stations. The Royal Geographical Society (RGS) awarded him a prize and a gold medal for his discovery of Lake Ngami in the Kalahari Desert in 1849. In 1851 he reached the Zambezi River. When he returned to the mission, however, he found that the Afrikaners, smarting from his constant rebukes of them for practicing slavery, had burned down the mission and destroyed his home. In 1852, Mary and their four children were sent to Great Britain for their protection.

With the family's departure, Livingstone embarked on a series of long explorations that were unprecedented at the time and that would take up the rest of his life. His determination was clear: "I shall open up a path into the interior or perish," he said. Livingstone was convinced that Christianity, commerce and civilization would deliver Africa from slavery and barbarism. He hoped to find a route to the Atlantic Ocean that would open legitimate commerce and undercut the slave trade while providing opportunities for missionary work. In 1852 he went north to the Zambezi and east to Luanda in Angola. On his return, he followed the Zambezi to the Indian Ocean, encountering along the way the spectacular falls called by the Africans *Mosi-oa-Tunya* ("the smoke that thunders"), which Livingstone renamed Victoria Falls in honor of the queen. In 1856 he returned to England a national hero and undertook a six-month speaking tour while preparing *Missionary Travels and Researches in South Africa* (1857), which made him financially independent and allowed him to provide for his family and resign from the LMS. England was deeply affected by a Christian religious revival at the time, and a series of Livingstone's addresses at Cambridge University so fired young students that the Universities' Mission to Central Africa (UMCA) was founded in 1860.

David Livingstone returned to Mozambique as British consul at Quelimane, charged with exploration "for the promotion of Commerce and Civilization with a view to the extinction of the slave trade." The 1858 to 1863 expedition was equipped with a paddle-wheel steamer, six Europeans, and 10 Africans. Nothing worked as expected, however. The ships (he went through three) could not navigate the Zambezi, Livingstone's moody character caused dissension, and Mary died of fever in 1862, three months after joining David. The British recalled the expedition, and Livingstone sailed the last steamer, which was unsuitable for travel on the high seas, all the way to Bombay, India, to be put

David Livingstone

up for sale. Despite the sense of failure, the second expedition later proved among Livingstone's most useful. He was the first European to discover both the Shire River and Lake Nyasa, and he exposed the atrocities of the Arab slave trade along the lake, especially at Nkhota Kota.

In 1865, back in England, Livingstone published *Narratives of an Expedition to the Zambezi,* and the RGS underwrote the costs of his next expedition, which was to search for the sources of the Nile River. He pushed further inland, discovering Lakes Mweru and Bagweulu in present-day Zambia. He reached Ujiji on Lake Tanganyika after great hardship, including Ngoni raids and desertions among his retainers. To avoid punishment on their return, the deserters spread the false rumor that Livingstone had been killed by the Ngoni. Nonetheless, the intrepid Livingstone pressed on until he reached the Congo River, the westernmost point reached by any European explorer. At this juncture, after five years, the world considered him lost, and the *London Telegraph* and *New York Herald Tribune,* sensing a popular cause, sent the flamboyant journalist Henry Morton STANLEY to search for him. According to the legend, he met him in a dramatic encounter, doffing his hat and addressing the only White man within a thousand kilometers with the words: "Dr. Livingstone, I presume?"

Stanley reprovisioned Livingstone's expedition and traveled with him around Lake Tanganyika, but the weak and ailing Livingstone refused to leave Africa with him. In 1873 his servants found him dead. They embalmed the body and carried it overland to the Indian Ocean, a journey of nine months. He was buried in Westminster Abbey in a solemn national funeral. Livingstone's achievements were notable. His discoveries—geographical, botanical, medical and social—were far-reaching. Most significantly, however, his explorations made him a forerunner of Western imperialism.

References: *afr, dacb,* DAHB, DNB, EB, EWB, *wiki.* Jeremy Murray-Brown, *Faith and the Flag* (1977); Andrew Ross, *David Livingstone: Mission and Empire* (2002).

LOBENGULA Kumalo
(Zimbabwe, 1836?–1894)

Lobengula was the last independent chief of the Ndebele, an Nguni nation founded in the 1830s by his father, MZILIKAZI. His kingdom was the last in southern Africa to be destroyed by the colonial powers.

The Ndebele kingdom was at the crossroads of European colonial ambition, separating Portuguese colonies in Mozambique and Angola, German ones in present-day Tanzania and Namibia, and British territories in South Africa and Kenya. It was formed from Zulus who fled during the *mfecane,* "the great killing," the sweep of the Zulus across southern Africa that cost over a million lives. Mzilikazi had been a Zulu commander who fell out with SHAKA. By the time Lobengula inherited this chieftaincy, the original band of about 1,000 had, through conquest and absorption, grown to a nation of five million.

On the death of Mzilikazi in 1868, Lobengula was proclaimed chief in place of his brother, Nkulumane, who had disappeared years earlier. Royal pretenders would claim the throne throughout Lobengula's reign and would be manipulated by the British. Further complicating the political setting was the new aggressiveness of the British in the aftermath of the Berlin Conference (1885), which allotted spheres of influence to the colonial powers.

Lobengula accepted traders and missionaries and thus welcomed Reverend John Moffat, son of the famous Robert MOFFAT and brother-in-law of David LIVINGSTONE. Moffat won Lobengula's confidence and, acting as a British agent, persuaded him to sign an agreement that he would not enter into treaties with any other nation without ratification by the British High Commission in South Africa. Having thus fended off other European powers, Moffat helped to negotiate the Rudd Concession (1888), by which Lobengula granted Cecil RHODES prospecting rights in exchange for rifles and ammunition. Rhodes somewhat duplicitously interpreted this treaty as a land grant and began encouraging European settlement, and in 1889 he was awarded a royal charter allowing him to take over administration of the area. The great prize was the unexploited gold fields around Bulawayo, Lobengula's capital.

Rhodes used his trusted associate, Dr. Leander Starr JAMESON, to take over the territory, and he began to wean away Lobengula's tributary chiefs. By 1893, 1,500 White settlers had been given large land grants. In that same year, Lobengula raided the Shona, a neighboring people, to reassert his diminishing authority. Jameson used this as an excuse to declare war. He defeated the Ndebele easily, and Lobengula fled to the north but died of smallpox along the way.

References: AB, AH, CWAH, DAHB, EB, EWB, HWL, MMA, *wiki.* Ngwabe Bhebe, *Lobengula of Zimbabwe* (1977).

LOTSHE
(Zimbabwe, ?–1889)

Lotshe, an Ndebele military commander and member of its royal council, became an advocate of accommodation with the British when he realized that armed resistance was impossible.

Lotshe served under King MZILIKAZI and was prominent enough to head the delegation that searched for his missing heir. Satisfied that the heir had died, Lotshe threw his support behind LOBENGULA for the kingship and remained loyal to him throughout the various challenges to his rule by pretenders. Lotshe became a military commander and the primary supporter of Lobengula during the brief civil war in 1870. He led the increasing number of cattle raids and campaigns against neighboring peoples and, although he was personally brave in battle, he did not develop new military tactics, even though other nearby groups were using horses and new weapons. In 1885 he commanded a disastrous assault against the Tswana at Lake Ngami in Botswana with great losses. With his forces weakened, Lotshe's influence waned.

Nonetheless, Lotshe remained an *induna,* or royal councilor. In the council, he increasingly became the voice of accommodation with the British, who were pressing for land and mineral concessions. Perhaps fearing the consequences of armed confrontation, Lotshe advocated signing the Rudd Concession (1888), which was to allow limited mining by Cecil RHODES's group in exchange for modern arms, including 1,000 rifles and an armed riverboat. When the concessions were published in the British newspapers, Lobengula was furious, because all of his stipulations had been removed. He attempted to repudiate the agreement and strengthen his position, but to no avail. To symbolize his rejection, Lobengula ordered the execution of Lotshe along with his wives, children and cattle.

Reference: DAHB.

LUBWA p'CHONG, Cliff
(Uganda, 1946–)

Cliff Lubwa p'Chong is a Ugandan playwright and poet from the troubled and undeveloped north of the country. His work incorporates Acholi folklore.

Lubwa p'Chong was born and raised in Gulu in West Nile Province, the heartland of Idi AMIN. The region has known little peace throughout its history, and the Acholi have suffered from prejudice and social bias. They are largely a pastoral people. Lubwa p'Chong moved to the capital, Kampala, to attend Makerere University, where he studied literature. He was the editor of the literary magazine at the university and then founded and edited the magazine of the National Teachers' College. He began publishing his poetry there and in other East African journals, especially in Kenya. At the time, there was a burst of interest in African writing, which gave Lubwa p'Chong the opportunity to have his work included in anthologies. His poetry deals with tradition, and reflects the same concerns as another Acholi writer, OKOT p'Bitek.

Lubwa p'Chong's best-known work, however, is contained in his plays. He was particularly prolific in the 1980s, when he was writing almost a play each year. His best work is his 1976 play, *Words of My Groanning* (sic), a satiric and searing exposé of the failure of the promise of independent Africa.

References: adb.

LUGARD, Frederick John Dealtry
(Nigeria/Uganda, 1858–1945)

Lord Frederick John Dealtry Lugard was a British imperialist and colonial administrator who drafted the most comprehensive theory of colonialism, which became the basis of much British colonial management.

Born in India of British missionaries, he was educated at the Royal Military College in Sandhurst, England, after which he saw combat in the Afghan War (1880), the Suakin Campaign in the Sudan (1885), and in Burma. Restless after being placed on medical leave and depressed after a broken love affair, he went to Africa to seek adventure. After he was refused entry to the Italian army, which was then attacking Ethiopia, his services were sought by the British consul in Mozambique, who sent him with a small relief column to northern Malawi to the village of Karonga, which was besieged by slave traders. He secured the stockade but was badly wounded in an attack on the slavers. His bravery attracted attention, and he was asked by the Imperial East Africa Company to open a trade route to Uganda. In forced marches through Maasai territory, he reached the capital of Buganda in 1890.

Buganda was in political chaos. Protestant, Catholic and Muslim groups had developed sizable followings among the palace elite and had formed religious factions. The ruler, MWANGA II, was decadent and effete, and a religious civil war had left him politically unstable. Lugard persuaded Mwanga to accept a British protectorate over Buganda and then pacified the surrounding kingdoms of Bunyoro, Toro and Nyankole. Following this success, he promptly marched over the Mountains of the Moon to bring back 600 Sudanese soldiers who had been abandoned there and used these forces to bolster his position in Buganda. After returning from this mission, Lugard found that war had again erupted in Buganda, and he chose to enter the conflict on the Anglican faction's side. Once the Catholics were defeated and isolated toward the west, he persuaded Sir Apolo KAGGWA, the *katikiro,* or prime minister, to assume leadership.

After these events, Lugard was stunned to receive orders to abandon Uganda, and he returned to England to argue his cause and raise funds from missionary groups. Cleverly using the anti-slavery argument and defending himself from charges of atrocities, he wrote *The Rise of Our East African Empire* (1893) and won government support for his position.

His work in Uganda completed, Lugard went to Nigeria to forestall French territorial ambitions by obtaining a treaty with a major chief in the interior. He next worked for a year in Bechuanaland (now Botswana), expanding trade there. Finally, in 1897, the British secretary of state recalled him to Nigeria to organize the West African Frontier Force.

For two years Lugard served as commissioner for Northern Nigeria in order to defend the title of the Royal Niger Company from competing French and German claims. By diplomacy and authority, he avoided a potential war with the French, and when Great Britain ended the company's monopoly and declared a protectorate, he was named high commissioner of Northern Nigeria.

Lugard's years in the region (1900–1906) shaped his thought on colonial administration. With a tiny staff and inadequate forces attempting to extend British authority over powerful Hausa states, he realized that he could govern only through existing traditional structures. Not understanding local customs, lacking financial resources, and with few British officials, he accepted the governance and judicial jurisdiction of the emirs. He treated them as autonomous but dependent rulers and demanded only an end to the slave trade and the collection of modest taxes. This approach, which allowed for minimal personnel and investment in the colonial enterprise, came to be known as "indirect rule." This system did not go unchallenged, and from 1901 to 1903 he had to proceed against the most powerful Hausa states, Sokoto and Kano. After their conquest, the others posed little threat and accepted British dominance.

From 1907 to 1912, Lugard languished as governor of Hong Kong, and he readily accepted the offer to return to Nigeria to complete his work there by uniting the northern and southern protectorates of the region. Completing this task in two years, he was named governor-general of what became the largest British colony and held that office until his retirement in 1919.

Lugard was as active in retirement as he had been in the colonial service. In 1922 he published his influential book, *The Dual Mandate in British Tropical Africa,* which shaped colonial administration until its demise. He provided a justification and process for colonialism that attempted to blunt the criticisms of imperialism that arose after World War I. He argued that colonialism, which benefited the industrial expansion of the great powers, could be judged by the way in which it helped indigenous peoples to progress to a higher plane of civilization. African peoples should be brought forward morally and economically and be prepared for self-government, he argued. Although his position assumed the superiority of Western culture, Lugard himself lacked the blatant racism found among many other imperialists.

From 1922 to 1936, Lugard was a member of the League of Nations Mandates Commission. He opposed any international intervention in colonial affairs but still served on the International Slavery Committee and several groups promoting African education.

References: *afr,* DAHB, DNB, EWB, *wiki.* Arthur Thomson, *Lugard in Africa* (1959).

LUMUMBA, Patrice Emery

(Democratic Republic of the Congo, 1925–1961)

Patrice Emery Lumumba, independence leader and first prime minister of the Congo (later named Zaïre and today the Democratic Republic of the Congo), led the struggle for his country's independence. His political execution made him a martyr of Pan-Africanism and a symbol of anticolonial resistance.

During his missionary education, Lumumba encountered the writings of Karl Marx and Jean-Paul Sartre, which shaped his political ideas. Hoping to take advantage of the privileges allowed the educated elite, he worked 11 years for the Belgian colonial service in the Congo, primarily in the postal system. He campaigned for independence through newspaper articles and cultural associations, which the Belgian authorities tolerated. In the meantime, he broadened his contacts within the colonial administration, establishing relations with the minister for colonial affairs, and was granted two interviews with King Baudouin when he visited the Congo. Eventually, he began to move away from the cause of the elite toward advocacy of the masses. Lumumba was sent on a goodwill study tour of Belgium by the government in 1957.

On his return from Brussels, Lumumba was imprisoned for embezzling 126,000 Belgian francs (about US$2,500) from the post office, and when he admitted his guilt (but never revealed his reasons), he was sent to prison. On his release a year later, he moved to Kinshasa and took a position with a brewery. When political activity was allowed by the Belgians in 1958, Lumumba became head of a small Catholic party, the Congolese National Movement (MNC), and was invited to the All-African People's Conference in Accra, Ghana. This event was a turning point in his life. He was profoundly impressed with Kwame NKRUMAH and embraced Pan-Africanism enthusiastically. On his return he made a major speech before a large crowd, demanding independence. The Belgians, who had banned the ethnic party headed by Joseph KASAVUBU, attempted to make concessions, but they could not restrain the anticolonial fervor, and riots followed. The disturbances were crushed with considerable loss of life. The Belgians, now shaken, announced a program for independence. Lumumba worked at recruiting smaller nationalist groups into the MNC, which changed its character and led to a major split in party unity. The result was two contending programs: Lumumba's faction of the MNC favored a strong centralized government, and the Kasavubu party favored federalism, which would have allowed regional interests to control their own provinces.

Lumumba began a series of demonstrations that resulted in deaths, and he was again imprisoned, this time for inciting violence. The Belgian program for self-government collapsed at this point, when it became clear that they could not control the rural areas, and they agreed to immediate discussion of independence. As other Congolese leaders demanded Lumumba's freedom, he was brought to Brussels to join them. Belgian resolve totally collapsed, and the colonial government agreed to unconditional independence within a few months. Lumumba won the elections at the end of June 1960 and became prime minister with Kasavubu as president. When King Baudouin of the Belgians gave a terribly impolitic and even insulting speech at the independence celebrations, Lumumba seized the microphone and spoke with energizing eloquence to the frenzied crowd.

Without a normal decolonization transition, the results were disastrous. On 5 July the army

Patrice Emery Lumumba

mutinied against its Belgian officers, creating total confusion. Within days, Belgians had fled in such numbers that administrative posts were abandoned and offices were inoperable. Belgian colonial policy, one of the most backward in Africa, had educated not a single doctor, military officer or lawyer and had produced only one engineer. Belgian soldiers were sent to the Congo to protect their nationals, but Lumumba demanded their withdrawal and appealed for United Nations (U.N.) forces. With Belgian paratroop protection, the copper-rich Katanga Province in the south broke away under Moïse TSHOMBE. Other secessionist movements contributed to the continuing political crisis. Within six weeks of independence, Lumumba broke diplomatic relations with Belgium and U.N. troops began to arrive, but they failed to dislodge the Belgians. Lumumba, who was now having difficulties with the U.N., appealed to the Soviet Union. Such a declaration, made out of desperation, lost almost all Western support for Lumumba, and Kasavubu broke with him and attempted to replace him. Lumumba retaliated by dismissing Kasavubu as president. The country was now in chaos, army bandit groups engaged in terrorism in the countryside, and there was widespread looting.

The U.N. forces closed all Congolese airfields, supposedly to prevent the arrival of Soviet troops, and took over the national radio station. The parliament returned both Lumumba and Kasavubu to their offices, and the U.N. troops were ordered to leave. At this point, all resolutions and orders were moot. In an army coup, Joseph MOBUTU (later MOBUTU Sese Seko) took over the country, promoting himself to commander. After being assaulted, Lumumba asked for protection and was placed under house arrest in the capital, Léopoldville (now Kinshasa), with a ring of Ghanaian U.N. troops protecting him from arrest and another ring of Mobutu's soldiers preventing his escape. Meanwhile, an international debate raged over the Congo's future. The USSR and Ghana led an Afro-Asian bloc supporting Lumumba, while the West, hardening its attitudes in light of the Cold War, supported Kasavubu and Mobutu.

Learning of a plot between the American Central Intelligence Agency and Kasavubu to arrest him for treason, Lumumba escaped with his wife, baby and two colleagues and attempted to drive to Stanleyville (now Kisangani), which remained loyal to him. On this quixotic trip he spoke to crowds along the way, rallying support. He was arrested at a river crossing, returned to Léopoldville, and severely beaten in the presence of foreign correspondents. He was then flown to Elizabethville (now Lubumbashi), Tshombe's headquarters, and was killed on arrival. Three firing squads, commanded by Belgian officers, executed Lumumba and several associates. Tshombe stood by in attendance. The body was first buried and then exhumed and dissolved in acid. In 2002, Belgium issued a formal diplomatic apology.

Lumumba's death provoked demonstrations at the U.N. and in a number of European capitals. The Soviet Union established a university in his name in Moscow for students from Africa and other Third World countries. Lumumba is revered as an anti-imperialist martyr through much of the postcolonial world. A passionate, impetuous and often imprudent nationalist, Lumumba was a victim of the Cold War. He was actually without Communist or Western sympathies, but he became a symbol and a caricature in the West.

References: AB, *adb*, *afr*, CB, DAB, DAHB, EWB, HWL, MMA, PLBA, PLCA, *wiki*. Nikolai Reshetnyak, *Patrice Lumumba* (1990); L. De Witte, *The Assassination of Lumumba* (2002).

LUTHULI, Albert John Mvumbi
(South Africa, 1898–1967)

Chief Albert John Mvumbi Luthuli, president of the African National Congress (ANC) until his death, was the first African winner of the Nobel Prize for Peace. His tenure as ANC president covered the years 1952–1967, during which apartheid legislation was implemented, the Sharpeville massacre occurred, the ANC was banned, and its leaders either were imprisoned or forced into exile.

Luthuli was born in Southern Rhodesia, the son of a Congregationalist Church worker. He spent 17 years as a teacher in a mission school and then in 1935 was elected chief of the mission reserve Zulus, the Abasmakholweni. Previously insulated from racism by his mission environment, Luthuli was plunged into the realities of life for the Zulu, who were deprived of most of their land and constantly demeaned by the police. In 1945 he joined the ANC and became president of the Natal chapter in 1951. In 1946 he was elected to the Natives Representative Council, a toothless consulting group, which he entered in order to block a government collaborator. When Luthuli mounted a peaceful protest in 1952 called the Defiance Campaign, he was called in by the government and told to resign either his chieftaincy or his ANC post. He refused, saying: "I have joined my people in the new spirit that moves them today, the spirit that revolts openly and boldly against injustice." He was removed from chiefly office by the government but was immediately swept into the national presidency of the ANC on a wave of nationalist enthusiasm. Nelson MANDELA from the ANC youth wing was elected deputy. Within days Luthuli, Mandela and more than a hundred others were put under banning orders, which forbade their attendance at any gathering of more than three people, except for church services. Luthuli was restricted to his farm.

The first ban was renewed at its expiration in 1954, and in 1956 Luthuli was arrested for treason, then released after a year. In 1959, he undertook a speaking tour through the Cape Province, and his nonviolent moderation began to attract Whites. The moderate position, calling for justice and interracial reconciliation, was not, however, universally well received, and a radical wing moved against the Luthuli-Mandela leadership in 1959. Failing to assume leadership, the radicals left the ANC. Under the direction of Robert SOBUKWE, they established the Pan-Africanist Congress (PAC). Luthuli was again banned, and when he was summoned to Johannesburg in 1960 for a hearing, a demonstration supporting him turned violent. Seventy-two Africans were shot, and more than 200 were wounded. Infuriated, Luthuli publicly burned his pass book, the hated government identification required of every African. Numbers of Africans assembled at police stations without their pass books, courting arrest in order to clog the machinery of justice. In Sharpeville, the police opened fire, wounding 187 and killing 67; most were shot in the back. The government declared a state of emergency and banned all African political groups.

The Sharpeville massacre was a watershed. Nonviolence was the main casualty. The PAC launched several hundred bomb attacks against police stations and post offices. Umkhonto we Sizwe (Spear of the Nation), the ANC militant wing, went underground and began training for guerrilla warfare. Plans laid earlier saved some of the ANC leaders. Oliver TAMBO, who succeeded Luthuli, went into exile in Northern Rhodesia (now Zambia). Mandela and Walter SISULU were sent to prison on Robben Island, where they languished until 1990. Luthuli alone remained, although under internal exile. In 1971 he was allowed to accept the Nobel Prize for Peace, and in his address he restated his beliefs in nonviolence and racial harmony. The United States offered him political asylum, but he returned to South Africa, where he died in 1967 after being hit by a train at a crossing near his home.

Luthuli was a man of dignified bearing and great civility, courtly and kind. He was intensely religious and exerted strong moral leadership, although his constant banning severely limited his actual leadership of the ANC. He was deeply offended by the treason charges that he had plotted the violent overthrow of the government and that he was a Communist. He remained true to his nonviolent ideology, which was Christian rather than Gandhian. He was a reformer and a liberal social democrat but never a radical.

References: AA, AB, *afr*, CB, DAHB, EWB, MMA, PLBA. PLCA, *wiki*. Luthuli, *Let My People Go* (1962); Mary Benson, *Chief Albert Lutuli of South Africa* (1963).

LUWUM, Janani
(Uganda, 1924–1977)

Archbishop Janani Luwum, an Anglican archbishop and martyr, was an implacable foe of Idi AMIN, who had him murdered.

From 1956 Luwum worked as a parish priest. He was elected bishop of Northern Uganda in 1969, and in 1974 he was chosen archbishop of Uganda, Rwanda, Burundi and Boga-Zaïre. He confronted the injustices and atrocities of the Amin regime almost immediately, at first with private remonstrances and finally in a radio address at Christmas in 1976. The sermon was censored before he completed it. Luwum threatened a public demonstration, and for a time he united Catholics and Protestants behind him, a major feat in religiously divided Uganda.

Amin reacted swiftly and without mercy, sacking Luwum's home. The Anglican bishops responded with a stinging denunciation of Amin's abuses. Luwum was detained and questioned by Amin personally. Two days later Luwum was publicly accused of sedition and arms smuggling while participating in a large public rally in Kampala. This event provided an excuse for a second arrest, and by the end of the day, Luwum was dead. The cause of death was listed as a car crash, but it was later revealed that Luwum, along with two government ministers, had been shot on orders from Amin. Some witnesses later claimed that Amin himself fired the fatal shot.

Luwum was recognized immediately as a hero of resistance to tyranny, and he has been recognized as a martyr in the Anglican Church. His feast is celebrated on February 17. Luwum's statue is among the twentieth-century martyrs recently placed on the front of Westminister Abbey in London.

References: dacb, MMA, *wiki*. Margaret Ford, *Janani: The Making of a Martyr* (1978).

LWANGA, Karoli (Charles)
(Uganda, 1860?–1886)

St. Karoli Lwanga was the head page at the court of the Kabaka MWANGA in the kingdom of Baganda. He was of the first generation of Christians and the leader of the group that formed the "martyrs of Uganda," executed for their faith in 1889 on orders of Mwanga.

Lwanga was a member of the Bush-Buck clan in the service of a local chief. On a visit to Rubaga, the royal capital, he encountered several young Ganda attached to the court, who were studying Christianity. They were a mix of Catholics and Anglicans, both of which had rival missionaries there. Rubaga was a town of some 40,000, and Baganda had an efficient army and a navy on what later became known as Lake Victoria. Under Mwanga's father, MUTESA, the Christians had competed freely with Arab Muslim traders, but Mwanga was a paranoid, volatile and somewhat dissolute youth who suspected the foreigners of plotting against him.

The process of becoming Christian was long. The Anglicans first taught their candidates to read ("the readers" would become their derisive nickname) so they could understand the Gospels. The Catholics insisted on a lengthy catechumenate of several years' instruction. Lwanga followed the instructions of the French White Fathers and lived in a community of young Christians. In 1884, he entered the service of the kabaka as a page. Talented and with an engaging personality, he was soon in charge of the pages. He was admired for his athletic ability as a wrestler and won the hearts of his young charges, many of whom were barely in their teens. Lwanga saw his obligation to protect them from the temptations of the court, and in the process, he began to recruit many to Christianity.

Kabakas commanded total obedience, and Mwanga suspected that the pages were being won over to a rival authority. He was infuriated when the Christian candidates refused his homosexual advances, since refusing the kabaka anything was unheard of in the kingdom. He rightfully suspected Lwanga of shielding them from him.

Mwanga began a campaign against Christianity, and hundreds died or were castrated in the purge that followed. It began when Mwanga was rebuked for his pederasty and, in a fury, he struck down his chief steward. Lwanga then gathered the pages by night to seek baptism. He took the Christian name Karoli or "Charles." Mwanga demanded that the pages renounce their faith, which they refused to do, and Lwanga himself baptized the five youngest. Twenty-four youths—11 Anglican and 13 Catholic—were taken on a forced march and then confined for a week, which they spent in prayer. As the leader, Lwanga was burned first, wrapped in reeds and with a slave yoke around his neck. The fire began at his feet and slowly consumed him alive, but he never complained or cried out. After his death, the others were also burned alive. Twenty-two Catholics were canonized in 1964, and an equal number of Anglicans have been recognized as martyrs in the Anglican Communion.

Reference: dacb, wiki. J.F. Faupel, *African Holocaust* (1965).

MAATHAI, Wangari Muta

(Kenya, 1940–)

Dr. Wangari Muta Maathai, environmentalist and activist, is one of the most dramatic figures on the African political scene. By turns an environmental scholar, feminist, international celebrity and political gadfly, she was named "The Forest Queen" by *New African* magazine. U.S. Vice President Albert Gore, Jr., praised her work in his book *Earth in the Balance.*

Dr. Maathai was a surprise choice for the Nobel Peace Prize in 2001, but she argues that saving the environment is an issue of world peace. The Nobel Committee lauded her for standing up against the oppressive regime of Daniel arap MOI, which imprisoned her several times and harassed her. She has also received many other international awards, including the shared $100,000 Africa Leadership Prize of the Hunger Project in 1991. She was a featured speaker at the 1992 Rio Earth Summit. Maathai has also been beaten and teargassed by police, criticized in the tabloids, and denounced by President Moi, who accused her of circulating false coup rumors and restricted her travel. She won the right to attend the Rio meeting only after a court battle. In response to her defeating the government in court, 150 troops surrounded her home, and she was arrested.

After graduating from St. Scholastica College in the United States, Maathai was the first Kenyan woman to earn a doctorate (biology), to be appointed to a professorship, or to become a university department chair and dean. In 1977 she began the Greenbelt Movement, the most successful environmental program in Africa. This program is a grassroots effort involving rural women, whom she has helped to empower. At any one time it employs 50,000 women in the part-time planting of indigenous trees, such as fig, baobab, blue gum, and acacia, that were destroyed during the colonial period. Greenbelt's goal is reforestation and the restoration of Kenya's natural habitat. Its accomplishments are impressive: 12 million trees planted, 1,000 nurseries, 90,000 members and a multimillion-dollar annual budget. As a result of this program, Kenya is one of the few African countries dealing effectively with its deforestation threat.

Mass movements cause tremors of fear among some politicians. Maathai embodied their worst fears when she opposed the 1989 attempt by the national party, the Kenya National African Union, to build a massive 60-story office tower in the main greenspace of central Nairobi. The building would have cast a shadow over the central business district for several hours each day. Using her international connections to persuade the World Bank and other granting agencies that the project was environmentally unsound, she successfully prevented construction. Even the American ambassador publicly criticized the project.

Maathai has paid a high personal price for her convictions. Her husband, a businessman and member of the Kenyan parliament, was ridiculed for having such a powerful and highly educated wife

Wangari Muta Maathai

287

"beyond his control." He buckled under social pressure and attacks on his masculinity and divorced her. The bitterness of the divorce filled the newspapers, and their breakup became the subject of common gossip. It was this public attempt to degrade her that influenced Maathai to unite women's issues with environmental ones. Most dramatic was her defense of eight mothers of political prisoners, who staged a sit-in that drew thousands of participants. Finally, she resigned her position at the University of Nairobi to run for parliament but was disqualified on a technicality. The university refused to take her back.

Maathai's views can be startling. She rejects having African women move into the mainstream of society because that mainstream denies full participation even to men. Women in Africa lead miserable lives, she concedes, but "we forget that these miserable women are married to miserable men. They are oppressed together." She advocates the development of Kiswahili over both English and other African languages as a common language. She has sharply criticized the African educated class to which she belongs as "an elite club to exploit Africans, no better than the world which colonized us."

Despite her fierce convictions and tireless activism, Wangari Maathai is a soft-spoken, simple woman. Only when questions of the environment, justice and women's issues are raised does her voice get steely, her words more measured and biting. She caused considerable controversy when she claimed that AIDS was the result of failed bio-engineering, a conspiracy theory that was originally disseminated by the Soviets during the Cold War. She blurted out that AIDS was created by Western scientists "to punish Blacks." Her comments stirred denunciations in the scientific community and she later modified them somewhat.

Maathai was elected to parliament when Mwai KIBAKI defeated Moi, and in 2003 she was appointed assistant minister of Environment, Natural Resources and Wildlife. She has been a visiting fellow at Yale University since 2002.

Reference: AB, *afr*, CB, EB, *wiki*. Maathai, *The Greenbelt Movement: Sharing the Approach and the Experience* (2003).

MABA Diakhou Ba
(Sénégal/Gambia, 1809–1867)

Maba Diakhou Ba was the religious and military leader responsible for the revival of Islam in much of the Senegambia. A Koranic scholar, he came under the influence of UMAR Ibn Said Tall, the leader of the major Islamic revolutionary movement of the mid-nineteenth century and a member of the same clerical class. Umar designated Maba representative of the Tijani brotherhood within the *marabout* faction of Islam. The *marabouts* were a devoutly observant sect and responded immediately to the Tijani emphasis on strict Koranic observance and *jihad* (holy war) to spread Islam. The Tijani also had mass appeal, and Maba soon gathered a considerable following.

When he was attacked by an anti-revivalist group in 1861, Maba defeated them, which brought large numbers of Muslims to his side. Soon his movement had become a *jihad* on behalf of Islamic minorities within the Senegambian tribal states. Maba's forces conquered a number of smaller states and then turned toward the larger kingdoms that had no Muslim presence. Maba's authority was extended until it encountered expanding French military power. In an 1867 battle against combined French and African forces, his troops were defeated. Maba died in battle, and his nascent empire dissolved. His lasting influence came from his followers, who proceeded to seize power throughout the region. They eventually dominated Senegambia and were responsible for the Islamization of the region.

Reference: DAHB.

MABOGUNJE, Akinlawon Ladipo
(Nigeria, 1931–)

Dr. Akinlawon Ladipo Mabogunje is the leading African geographer and is widely recognized for his contributions to city planning. While his early work, including his groundbreaking *Yoruba Towns* (1962), dealt with the description of postcolonial urbanization, Mabogunje's concerns have shifted to the impact of urban planning on achieving development goals. Comparing industrialized nations, he has demonstrated the importance of a society's spatial reorganization at the time of its transformation from a preindustrial culture and economy to an industrialized culture. Mabogunje has published 13 books and numerous articles, but *The Development Process* (1980) best embodies his later thought.

After undergraduate work at the University of Ibadan, Mabogunje received his Ph.D. at the University of London in 1961. From 1958 to 1981 he was professor of geography at Ibadan. Since then, he has been vice president of PAI Associates (Nigeria) as an urban planner and consultant. Dr. Mabogunje has been rewarded with visiting professorships at universities on three continents and has held a Commonwealth professorship in England. He has honorary doctorates from Michigan State University and the Stockholm School of Economics and has received the David Livingstone Medal from the American Geographical Society, the Nigerian National Merit Award, and the Murchison Award of the Royal Geographical Society.

Mabogunje has worked on many public service commissions and has served on the U.N. secretary-general's Committee on Regional Development (1972–1976) and as a consultant to the U.N. Educational, Scientific, and Cultural Organization (UNESCO). He was a member of the Population Council's board (1977–1985) and since 1982 has been a board member of the Settlement Study Centre in Rehovot, Israel. During his tenure as president of the International Geographical Union (1980–1984), Mabogunje was able to bring the People's Republic of China back into the organization.

References: CANR, PAS.

MACAULAY, Herbert Samuel Heelas
(Nigeria, 1864–1946)

Herbert Samuel Heelas Macaulay was the founder of Nigeria's first political party and a major figure early Nigerian nationalism.

Macaulay was a member of a pioneering family. His grandfather was Samuel CROWTHER, the first African Anglican bishop, and his father founded the first grammar school in Nigeria. Macaulay himself was the first government-sponsored Nigerian sent for higher education to England, where he studied civil engineering. A zealous empire loyalist, he

began working as a surveyor for the colonial service in 1893.

As a surveyor, Macaulay was confronted with the massive injustices of the colonial system. In 1899 he resigned in disgust to establish a private practice. He began to defend Africans who had been defrauded of land, and in 1912 he opposed the policy to place Nigerian lands in trust under colonial governors. Failing in his efforts in Nigeria, Macauley planned to appeal to the Colonial Office, but he was arrested and imprisoned on a trumped-up charge to prevent his departure for London. In 1921 he had his greatest victory when he took the case of a chief to London, where the Privy Council rejected a paltry colonial land payment of £500 and ordered one of £22,500 (approximately $18,000 and $1.2 million, respectively, in current value).

The colonial government retaliated by deposing another chief who had supported Macaulay. Realizing that individual efforts would not bring justice, Macaulay began the organizing efforts that would lead to the foundation of the Nigerian National Democratic Party (NNDP) in 1922. It was the first political party in Nigeria. The NNDP won the restoration of the deposed chief in 1931.

After the Legislative Council (Legco) in Lagos was opened to African electors in 1923, the NNDP dominated all Legco elections until 1948. In 1944, Macaulay and Dr. Nnamdi AZIKIWE formed a union of 40 associations into the National Council of Nigeria and the Cameroons (NCNC) to press for independence, and Macaulay was chosen president. He died on a national speaking tour for the NCNC.

References: DAHB, EWB, MMA, *wiki*. Tekena Tamuno, *Herbert Macaulay: Nigerian Patriot* (1975).

MACHEL, Graça
(Mozambique/South Africa, 1945–)

Madame Graça Machel is the current wife of Nelson MANDELA, former president of South Africa, and the widow of Samora MACHEL, founding president of Mozambique. She is, in her own right, however, a leading revolutionary and cultural figure.

After early education in Mozambique, Graça Machel went to Portugal for higher education, where she met bright youth from the colonies who were ardent supporters of independence. She began to form the networks that would be part of the anticolonial struggle in the years to come. She returned home in 1973 to become a school teacher and joined the Mozambican Liberation Front (FRELIMO). The following year, Mozambique received sudden and unprepared independence when the Socialists won the election in Portugal that overturned decades of fascism. The new government immediately began a hasty decolonization process, neither planned nor well administered. Despite Portugal's official withdrawal, however, behind the scenes the Portuguese secret service conspired against the new postcolonial countries. Graça Machel was named minister for Education and Culture in 1975, the same year she married the president, Samora Machel. She served in her ministry until 1989, when she resigned to chair the United Nations (U.N.) Study of the Impact of Armed Conflict on Children, published in 1994. It was a major exposé of a problem that bedeviled a number of African insurgencies.

After President Machel's death in a plane crash in 1986, she continued her work. She had known Nelson Mandela for some years, and after the collapse of his marriage to Winnie MADIKIZELA-MANDELA they became confidants and then lovers. After Archbishop Desmond TUTU gently chided them for giving a bad example to the youth, they married in 1998. She proved herself a gracious and popular first lady during the last year of Mandela's term. Since 1999, she has held the honorary post of chancellor of the University of Cape Town.

Machel has been recognized for her work by receiving the Nansen Medal of the U.N. High Commission on Refugees (1995), and in 1992 she was named a laureate of the Africa Prize of the Hunger Project.

Reference: wiki.

MACHEL, Samora Moïses

(Mozambique, 1933–1986)

Samora Moïses Machel, the leader of the independence struggle in Mozambique and its first president, was one of the foremost Marxist revolutionaries in Africa. A gifted guerrilla commander, he also proved himself to be a worthy and resourceful national president.

Samora Moïses Machel

Machel came from a peasant family that was dispossessed by Portuguese settlers and forced to work in the South African mines, where one of his brothers was killed. After nurse's training, Machel worked briefly until the founding of the Front for the Liberation of Mozambique (FRELIMO) in 1962. A year later he was sent to Algeria for military training. After his return, he led the first armed strike against a Portuguese border post. Machel rose rapidly through FRELIMO, gaining progressively greater military responsibilities until taking overall command of the guerrilla forces in 1966. He expanded the number of troops and extended their operations.

Machel became secretary of defense after the 1969 assassination of Eduardo MONDLANE, FRELIMO's founder. A year later he assumed the presidency. In this role he negotiated independence after the collapse of the dictatorship in Portugal in 1974. Independent Mozambique inherited an economy in shambles in 1975. Portuguese authorities decamped hastily with 250,000 settlers, who took everything portable. The new civil servants did not find typewriters, furniture or even paper in their offices.

Under these circumstances, Machel emphasized order and the continuation of services as his highest priorities. FRELIMO transformed the government into a one-party system that functioned through local councils called *grupos dinamizadores,* (animating committees), which operated in villages and neighborhoods as well as workplaces. The legal profession and customary law were abolished, and banking, insurance, refining and hospitals were nationalized. The twin thrusts were expanding education and health care, which had both been severely restricted under Portuguese colonialism. To this end, a basic literacy program was established and mission schools were nationalized, and by 1979 the population of elementary schools had doubled. Clinics were established throughout the country, and large numbers of healthcare workers were trained.

The coup in neighboring Rhodesia, which brought the White settler government of Ian SMITH to power from 1965 to 1980, greatly hampered Mozambican development. Machel provided sanctuary for Zimbabwean guerrillas and closed the borders in 1976, despite significant losses in trade. Smith supported a subversive movement, the Mozambican National Resistance (RENAMO), which soon also received covert South African support as well as funds from right-wing Portuguese interests. After the fall of the Smith regime, Machel drafted an ambitious 10-year plan for the 1980s and took part in forming the Southern African Development Coordination Conference (SADCC) to reduce economic dependence on South Africa. Machel began moving away from doctrinaire Marxism toward a more mixed economy. He sought Western aid and investment and reduced military aid from the Eastern bloc. (After his death this process was accelerated and Marxism was officially abandoned.)

Machel also provided safe sanctuary to the African National Congress' (ANC) guerrilla forces. South Africa's support of RENAMO increased in response, and Mozambique found itself in the midst of a major civil war. Whole provinces were laid waste, transport and communications were interrupted, and the economy teetered on the edge of collapse. Machel finally negotiated the Nkomati Accord with South Africa, by which both nations agreed to mutual expulsion of ANC and RENAMO fighters in their territories. South Africa, however, merely returned to a more covert strategy.

Returning from a Front-Line States summit in Zambia in 1986, Machel was killed in a plane crash just inside the South African border. African opinion immediately accused South Africa of radar manipulation, although later investigation laid blame on the Soviet flight crew, which may have been intoxicated. Machel was succeeded by the foreign minister, Joaquim CHISSANO. Throughout his presidency, Machel was supported by a fellow revolutionary, Graça MACHEL, who became his wife and a minister in his government.

References: afr, CB, DAHB, DRWW, EB, EWB, MMA, PLBA, PLCA, *wiki.* Iain Christie, *Samora Machel* (1989).

MACHUNGO, Mario Fernandes da Graça
(Mozambique, 1940–)

Dr. Mario Fernandes da Graça Machungo, prime minister of Mozambique from 1986 to 1994, is a professional economist who had responsibility for rebuilding Mozambique after the long civil war that followed independence in 1975.

Machungo comes from a family of *assimilados,* a tiny elite group of Westernized and educated Africans who possessed expanded civil and legal rights under the Portuguese colonial system. As favorites of the colonial power, they were often regarded with suspicion by other Mozambicans. Although Machungo did not participate in the armed struggle for independence, he was a Front for the Liberation of Mozambique (FRELIMO) militant from his youth and was expelled from his studies in Lisbon for anticolonial organizing. His social status and lack of experience in the guerrilla war kept him for many years on the fringes of power in Samora MACHEL's government.

After finishing a master's degree in economics in 1969 in Lisbon, Machungo returned to Mozambique and worked as an economist for the National Development Bank during the last years of colonialism. Following the Portuguese coup and the end of formal colonial rule in 1974, he was minister of economic coordination in the transitional government. He assumed a succession of ministries after independence in 1975: energy and industry, agriculture, and planning. In 1977 he was elected to the Central Committee of the ruling politburo. From 1983 to 1986 he had the sensitive position of governor of Zambezia Province, the center of the RENAMO guerrilla movement that was waging a devastating war, with South African assistance, in order to destabilize Mozambique.

In 1986, Machel named Machungo prime minister, a primarily administrative post. Within three months, Machel died in a plane crash and Machungo's position took on new importance. He was instrumental in the rejection of Marxism and led the move toward a free market economy and a democratic system of government. He served until 1994, and then became chair of the Banco Internacional de Moçambique. Later he was also named chair of the Commercial Bank of Mozambique, where he has had to fend off accusations of favoring a banking monopoly in the country.

References: PLBA, RWWA.

MACÍAS NGUEMA Biyogo Negue Ndong, Francisco
(Equatorial Guinea, 1924–1979)

Francisco Macías Nguema Biyogo Negue Ndong was the first president of his country, a despot and a psychotic tyrant.

Macías Nguema worked for the Spanish colonial administration before completing the process that provided him with the status of an "emancipated" African. This gave him a standing above that of an African subject and entitled him to better education. Even as a young man he possessed an unstable personality, deferring to foreigners and demeaning people he considered to be of lower status. Macías Nguema adopted Spanish manners and took a Spanish name. He was rewarded with the position of senior administrator and made mayor of the city of Mongomo. By 1964 he was a provincial deputy and held the ministry for public works. He attended the Madrid conferences that led up to independence and won the first election for president in 1968. Shortly thereafter, he had his opponent assassinated. It was the first of many political murders.

Macías Nguema held office until 1979 in a reign of terror that was steeped in paranoia, which earned the country the nickname "the Auschwitz of Africa." Early in his regime the Spanish residents left, leaving the economy paralyzed. Twenty thousand Nigerian workers were repatriated, which crippled cocoa production, and Macías Nguema resorted to forced labor. One-third of the population fled the country, even though Macías Nguema sold the fishing fleet and all fishing rights to the Soviet Union so that there would be no boats for escape.

His inferiority complex caused him to fear educated people, and most of the elite were killed during his rule, including the parliamentary president and secretary, his United Nations (U.N.) ambassador, several cabinet ministers and the heads of the major parties. The last colonial prime minister was starved to death in prison and Macías Nguema's vice president was murdered in jail. After negotiations over conflicts with neighboring Gabon regarding territorial claims, he seems to have exchanged several islands for a bribe, and this money may have paid for his $12 million fortified palace. He banned the Catholic Church, whose members included almost 80 percent of the population, and ordered all to change their Christian names to African ones. He then stopped using his own Christian name. On National Day in 1978 he ordered 32 executions. The psychosis of power seemed to have completely consumed him. During this same period he awarded himself the titles "The Unique Miracle" and "Grand Master of Science, Education, and Culture."

Finally in 1979, he was overthrown by his nephew, Lieutenant-Colonel Teodoro OBIANG NGUEMA Mbasogo. Macías Nguema was tried for terrorism and executed.

References: afr, DAHB, MMA, PLBA, *wiki*. Randall Fegley, *Equatorial Guinea: An African Tragedy* (1989).

MADAMOMBE, Colleen
(Zimbabwe, 1964–)

A leading stone sculptor who uses her work to express the joys and tragedies of womanhood, Colleen Madamombe is both an artist and a feminist.

Madamombe is a prominent figure among Zimbabwean stone sculptors, who have risen to international acclaim by using African motifs in modern styles. She is considered among the most gifted artists of the "second generation" of Zimbabwean sculpture, and the only woman.

The theme of womanhood at all stages of life dominates her work. She presents the African woman of the villages and fields as indomitable, self-assured and inspiring. Every emotion is portrayed—pride, humor, sadness and suffering—but above all, endurance. This reflects her own life. Madamombe is divorced (from a sculptor) and raised seven children herself. She has struggled to prove herself as an artist in a world where women are taught not to believe in their abilities. She stoutly argues that "women can work as sculptors as well as men." She respects the less strenuous crafts often practiced by women in weaving and making pots, but defends the right of any woman to undertake the heavy "masculine" effort involved in large stone work.

In the past, Madamombe did carvings of insects, especially ants, which fascinate her. But in recent years, her work has been of proud African women, based on the traditional roles of Shona women. The bodies are left in rough finish with smooth, glossy polished faces and hands that provide a sharp contrast. She achieves this by working in hard black sandstone, which allows her to vary her textures.

Reference: Joceline Mawdsley, *Chapungu: The Stone Sculptures of Zimbabwe* (1997).

MADIKIZELA-MANDELA, Winnie Nomzamo
(South Africa, 1934?–)

Winnie Nomzamo Madikizela-Mandela, women's leader in the African National Congress (ANC) and former wife of Nelson MANDELA, created a political following during the years that her husband was imprisoned. She has since gone on to attempt to create a personal political base separate from him.

She was a Xhosa born in the Transkei. Her father represented their district in the territorial council and was later minister of Agriculture in the Transkei homeland government. She was given the prophetic birth name Nomzamo, "she struggles through trials." Her parents, both teachers, insisted on a demanding education for their daughter. After finishing secondary school, she entered the Jan Hofmeyer School of Social Work in Johannesburg, and in 1957 she became South Africa's first African medical social worker, working in a Soweto hospital. She was already politically active in the Federation of South African Women, founded and led by Helen JOSEPH and allied with the ANC. The federation was an active partner among the groups that convened the Congress of the People in 1955, which adopted the Freedom Charter that called for democracy and racial equality. The government responded with further repression, and a year later 156 leaders, including Nelson Mandela and Oliver TAMBO, were indicted for treason.

Tambo's fiancée introduced Winnie Madikizela to Nelson Mandela. His first marriage was already strained by political demands and his constant absences, and Mandela was immediately attracted to the vivacious, dedicated young woman. Their affair was controversial among the ANC leadership, but in 1958, Nelson divorced his first wife and married Winnie. She was perhaps the perfect partner for him—totally dedicated to her husband while sharing his life's work.

Also in 1958, Winnie Mandela joined the Federation's mass protests against the pass laws and, despite being pregnant, she was imprisoned. She was dismissed from her job but found employment as a field worker for the child welfare office in Soweto. Following the 1960 Sharpeville massacre, Nelson went underground for 15 months. Winnie and her two small children saw him only by using elaborate routes and up to 10 changes of vehicles. She once feigned labor pains to get through a police roadblock. In 1962, Nelson was captured and sentenced to hard labor after a sensational trial. For Winnie it was "the end of any kind of family life."

Within two months she was placed under banning orders because of her membership on the national executive of the Federation. The order, which lasted until 1974, banned her from attending meetings, gatherings and communications with other banned persons; from preparing, compiling, publishing, printing or transmitting documents, books, pamphlets, records, posters, photos or drawings; and from entering schools, universities or publishing houses. Police harassment was constant: on one occasion she was arrested for violating the banning order by handing a grocery list to her brother-in-law; on another she was arrested for chatting with two neighbors about the price of a chicken (she was permitted to speak to only one person at a time). The order was made more stringent in 1965, and she again lost her job. She took a number of temporary jobs in shoe repair, dry cleaning and furniture repair, only to be fired when the police frightened her employers. She was charged with violating her banning several times without being convicted, but this allowed the police to keep her in solitary confinement for 17 months in 1969–1970. Her daughters, expelled from several schools, were finally sent to Swaziland for their education. The 1962 banning order was followed by another set, restricting her to Soweto from 1974 to 1977. Finally, she was banished to Brandfort in the Orange Free State until 1986.

At first her separation from Nelson, the police harassment, and her own "loneliness worse than fear" were paralyzing, but with help from friends, she began to emerge into the spotlight that events had turned on her. "I rediscovered the value of my soul . . . I had ideas and views of my own. I had my own commitment and I wasn't just a political ornament," she said. As Nelson became the icon and hero of the resistance movement with the passing years, Winnie became his alter ego and the visible presence of his authority. Despite the handicap of her bans, she formed a parents' action group, set up soup kitchens and child clinics, and established self-help groups. When her Brandfort home and clinic were firebombed in 1985, she defied her orders and returned to Soweto. During the state of emergency in 1986, all restrictions against Winnie were suddenly lifted, apparently in a public relations gesture by the South African government. She immediately entered the campaign for economic sanctions against South Africa.

After 1985, Winnie Mandela began to develop her own public persona and her own following. Immensely popular among radical township youth who had no memory of her husband, she began to adopt an absolutist style that brooked no opposition. Her new home in Soweto was a mansion set amid small houses, and she was protected by a bodyguard of young thugs who enforced "people's courts" in a form of rough local justice. After members of the Mandela United Football Club, as it called itself, raped a girl at a neighboring school in 1988, Winnie's home was burned down by an enraged group of schoolmates. In 1989, Winnie was arrested for her involvement in the murder of a youth who was being held in her home. The ANC began to distance itself from her, placing responsibility for the team's acts on her. Nelson Mandela and Oliver Tambo even asked that the youth group be disbanded. The alleged "coach" of the team was convicted of the murder, and Winnie was implicated but not sentenced, even after the judge angrily called her "an unblushing liar."

Under this cloud, Winnie's political career was regarded as finished, especially after Nelson Mandela and the ANC leadership were released from prison in 1990. Winnie and Nelson became further estranged after the publication of an impassioned love letter from Winnie to her defense lawyer. She had also entered into a bitter rivalry with Albertina SISULU, who wrested the presidency of the ANC Women's League from her and then had Winnie suspended from membership in 1993 after she criticized the ANC leadership, including Nelson. By then, far more politically radical than her husband and chafing under an ANC leadership that was too conciliatory for her taste, Winnie began to cultivate her own following. She assumed the mantle of the martyred Chris HANI, the one ANC leader who commanded respect among the township youth, and by the 1994 election she was such an independent political activist that she could no longer be kept on the ANC sidelines. Her political return was as dramatic as her fall. By late 1993 she had regained her position in the Women's League, defeating Albertina Sisulu, and was elected to parliament in the first national elections.

The personal toll of separation caused the Mandelas to grow apart, and in 1992 they separated. This was followed by a 1996 divorce that was excruciating and humiliating for the president when he was forced to testify in court about their lack of intimate relations. The break was complete. Winnie was not invited to the inaugural party, and it was Albertina Sisulu who nominated Nelson for president. In the first round of cabinet appointments, Winnie was not included, but within a few days she was appointed deputy minister of arts, culture, science, and technology, a position that did not entitle her to attend cabinet sessions on a regular basis. After allegations of corruption, she was dismissed in less than a year.

Despite her reverse, Winnie remained the standard-bearer of the radicals, and she was elected president of the ANC Women's League in 1993 and 1997, and even toyed with the idea of running for president of the ANC. In 2003, she was convicted on 43 counts of fraud and 25 of theft, based on a sham insurance scheme from which she and her broker stole. She was sentenced to five years' imprisonment, with one year suspended, but in 2006, the entire sentence was suspended on appeal.

References: AB, *adb*, *afr*, CA, CB, EB, EWB, GSAP, HH, PLBA, *wiki*. Madizikela-Mandela, *Part of My Soul Went with Him* (1985); Anne Marie du Preez Bezdrob, *Winnie Mandela* (2003).

MAGA, Hubert Coutoucou

(Benin, 1916–2000)

Hubert Coutoucou Maga was the moderate in the triumvirate that dominated Benin politics for a brief period, along with Sourou APITHY and Justin AHOMADÉGBÉ-TOMETIN, Apithy and Ahomadégbé-Tometin became his bitter rivals and joined forces against him, and this mutual animosity was a major divisive force in Benin. Maga twice served as president of Dahomey, as Benin was known until 1973. On both occasions he was removed from office.

During a brief period in which he worked as a teacher and principal, Maga represented the northern region in Dahomey's General Council. He was then elected a deputy to the French parliament, where he served from 1951 to 1958, becoming undersecretary of state during his last year. Simultaneously, he was also a deputy in the territorial assembly.

In the period immediately preceding independence in 1959, Apithy and Ahomadégbé-Tometin's political rivalry resulted in a standoff, and Maga took the coveted position of prime minister. Within a year he was the first president of the new republic. He promptly jailed Ahomadégbé-Tometin and embarked upon a spree of extravagance that included the building of a lavish presidential palace. In 1963 he was removed by the army. After two years of house arrest, he and his two rivals took advantage of another coup to flee into exile.

Maga retained his popular support in the northern region, however, and Dahomey became ungovernable without its cooperation. As a result, in 1970 he returned to share a rotating presidency with his two adversaries. Maga held office from 1970 to 1972 and was again lavish with the public purse. He turned the presidency over to Ahomadégbé-Tometin, but within a few months all three old foes were placed under house arrest by General Ahmed KÉRÉKOU, where they remained until 1981. Maga was never again a figure of major influence, as the three aging rivals were replaced by a new professional class of leaders.

References: DABH, DRWW, PLBA, *wiki*.

MAGANDE, Ng'andu Peter

(Zambia, 1947–)

Peter Ng'andu Magande—businessman, banker, administrator—has been a central figure in recent Zambian affairs. He is currently minister of Finance.

Magande was educated in his home country and graduated from the University of Zambia in 1970. He took a leave from the civil service a few years later to take an MA in economics at Makerere University in Uganda. Much of Magande's career was spent in the Zambian civil service, where he rose from an entry position to permanent secretary over a period of 23 years. He was permanent secretary, the highest civil service position in the country, for nine years. In this post, he had responsibility for the personnel of all ministries. During this time, he was seconded to be managing director (CEO) of Lima Bank and of the Zambia National Commercial Bank, and executive director of the Industrial Development Corporation of Zambia. These are parastatal banks, government-owned corporations. He reorganized the banking system and restructured the entire agricultural credit system, and also began the process of liberalization and privatizing of agriculture. In his last year in office, he reorganized 21 parastatal companies and began a process of privatizing them.

Before moving into the Ministry of Finance in 1981, Magande was in the Ministry of Agriculture as Planning Coordinator. He initiated contacts with international development agencies and began forming partnership arrangements.

By far the most important part of his career, however, was the four years from 1996 to 2000 that he spent as secretary general of the African, Caribbean and Pacific Group of States (APC). The APC handles combined foreign aid grants from the European Union (EU) to the member countries and fosters trade between them and the EU. It is sometimes referred to as the Lomé Group because it was established and refined by a series of treaties signed in Lomé, Togo. The work of the secretary general involved extensive negotiations among member states, the EU, the parliaments of EU countries and numerous Non-Governmental Organizations (NGOs) with aid and development interests in the Third World. Magande's main achievement was to shepherd a new 20-year Partnership

Agreement through the maze of governments until there was a new treaty between the APC and the EU. The package was worth £13.5 billion (about US$16.2 billion) in direct aid. In addition, he organized the first and second summits of APC heads of state and created networks with many other international bodies.

In 2003, Magande became minister of Finance for Zambia, which has been struggling with an underperforming economy and high unemployment. He is also a tobacco farmer. In 1989, the Tobacco Association named him "Best Tobacco Farmer," the first indigenous African to receive that award.

Reference: adb.

MAHDI, The (Muhammad Ahmad)
(Sudan, 1844–1885)

The Mahdi was a charismatic Islamic religious figure, the founder of a dervish religious brotherhood, who declared himself the Mahdi (meaning "messiah"). This is to be the divinely guided Muslim leader foretold by Islamic tradition (although the concept does not appear in the Koran). In a holy war, he restored Islamic rule in the Sudan, defeating and killing General Charles "Chinese" GORDON and inflicting a serious blow to British imperial designs.

Muhammad Ahmad was raised in a religious atmosphere and attended Koranic school in Omdurman. He joined a Sufi brotherhood but switched to another that he considered less worldly. The brotherhoods, which are similar to both religious orders and secret societies, teach that one can attain a mystical experience of God through some religious practice, or *tariq*, which varies from group to group. Muhammad Ahmad's brotherhood—called *Ansar* or "Helpers"—followed the *tariq* of mystical dancing until they collapsed into ecstasy. They were part of the larger movement known as dervishes. In the 1860s, Muhammad Ahmad gathered his disciples around him on an island in the White Nile south of Khartoum, where he soon acquired a reputation for holiness and mystical power. Muhammad, who was a protonationalist, began to preach against the oppression of the Egyptian occupation. The *khedive,* the Ottoman viceroy of Egypt, had gone into bankruptcy and European banks managed much of

the economy and government. In 1882 this economic crisis resulted in a British takeover of Egypt. Muhammad Ahmad touched a chord of resistance among the Sudanese, who resented Anglo-Egyptian control and European ways and who also responded to the call to religious unity and purity.

In 1881 Muhammad Ahmad proclaimed himself to be the Mahdi, the awaited redeemer who, in the eyes of some Muslims, was to come at the end of time to inaugurate a kingdom of justice. Many believed that this would happen in 1300 on the Islamic calendar, which was 1881. The Mahdi believed himself sent by Allah to purify Islam, to drive out the infidels (the Europeans and their allies), and to preside over a new age of Islamic glory. To this end, he declared a holy war and easily defeated the forces sent against him by the Egyptians. The Mahdist movement spread like wildfire, and in 1883 he laid siege to el-Obeid, captured it as well as Darfur, and then routed a British-led Egyptian army. These victories were seen as miracles, and the Mahdi's armies were said to be led by angels. His followers, angered by years of brutality and injustice and gripped by religious fanaticism, showed no mercy to those they defeated. They slaughtered the wounded and captives. For all his brutality, the Mahdi was a hero all over the Islamic world.

The British, concerned about saving their investments in Egypt, ordered Egyptian forces out of the Sudan, and sent General Charles "Chinese" Gordon, who had been governor-general of the Sudan from 1877 to 1880, to direct the evacuation. By the time of Gordon's arrival in 1884, the Mahdi controlled most of the Sudan. Gordon attempted, in vain, to defend Khartoum. Hoping for a relief column that never came, he both valiantly and foolishly tried to defend the city, but his forces were overwhelmed in early 1885 after a siege of almost a year. Gordon was slain by a group of dervishes who cut off his head and displayed it on a spear. The Mahdi, victorious, established himself across the river in Omdurman and began to organize the Sudan into an Islamic religious state. Suddenly, after only six months, he died of typhus, and the leadership passed to his chosen successor, ABDALLAHI Ibn Mohammad, who maintained the Mahdist state for 13 years. The *Ansar* continues to exist as an influential conservative Islamic brotherhood in the Sudan. The Mahdi is regarded as a great hero, especially by fundamentalist movements in contemporary Islam.

References: AB, CWAH, DAHB, DT, EWB, MIW, MMA, WGMC, *wiki.* Byron Farwell, *Prisoners of the Mahdi* (1967).

MAHDI, Sadiq al-
(Sudan, 1936–)

Imam Sadiq al-Mahdi, twice prime minister of Sudan and great-grandson of the MAHDI, had both religious and political prestige but was unable to deal effectively with the civil war in the south or with the rise of Islamic revivalism.

Born into one of the Sudan's oldest and most revered religious families, he was raised in a breeding ground of political and religious activism. His father revived the Ansar sect, a Sufi Mahdist movement that combined nationalism with Islamic revivalism. Sadiq al-Mahdi was provided with a Western education at Comboni College, Khartoum, and Oxford University. In 1958, upon his father's death, he became the imam (leader) of the Ansar, and in 1961 he succeeded as leader of the Umma Party. Although he was elected to parliament, he was too young to be accepted as a government leader. Finally, in 1966, he became prime minister. He attempted to deal with the intractable problems in the south, where civil war had been going on since 1955. Factionalism in the Umma Party brought down the government in the 1968 elections, and General Gaafar NIMEIRY took power in a military coup d'état. The Ansar sect openly confronted Nimiery's regime, losing after a pitched battle in which more than a thousand were killed. All Ansar property was confiscated and Sadiq al-Mahdi was arrested for treason but was allowed to go into exile in London, where he plotted several coups that failed.

After lengthy negotiations, Mahdi returned home but soon fell out with Nimeiry over the imposition of Islamic law, *sharia.* When Nimeiry fell in 1985 and elective government was revived, the Umma emerged as the largest party in the 1986 elections. Mahdi was chosen prime minister, and he immediately reached out to the south, promising to abolish the *sharia.* His overtures were rejected by Colonel John GARANG, leader of the Sudanese People's Liberation Army (SPLA). This provoked a crisis in which Mahdi's coalition fell, forcing him to seek support from the Muslim brotherhoods and their fundamentalist leader, Dr. Hassan al-TURA-

BI. Al-Turabi demanded full application of the *sharia,* while the army and the SPLA demanded its abolition. In 1989, Mahdi was overthrown by General Omar BASHIR, who was secretly a member of the brotherhood. Mahdi was placed under house arrest but continued from time to time to speak out against the government until he was arrested again in 1993. He made a daring escape from house arrest in 1999 and settled in Cairo. He leads the Sudanese opposition in exile. One of his continuing interests has been the water shortage in the region, and in 2004 he was appointed to the Arab Water Council.

Although raised in a refined and cultural atmosphere, al-Mahdi lives an austere life. Even in office, he refused the use of an official car and residence. He returned his salary to the government. He is a democrat who believes he can return to power through the ballot box, and he detests the militant Islamic movement that has ripped the Sudan apart. He is at odds with his brother-in-law, Hassan al-TURABI on the role of Islam in the Sudan.

References: MIW, PLBA, RWWA, *wiki.*

MAHERERO
(Namibia, 1820?–1890)

Maherero was the paramount chief who united the Herero chiefdoms into one kingdom and liberated them from Khoikhoi domination. He accomplished this unification despite a long period of war in which his opponents had the advantage of firearms.

The Herero were nomadic herders, and when drought forced them into the central plains of Namibia, they encountered resistance from neighboring Khoikhoi, who were Afrikaans-speaking people with European settler connections. The Khoikhoi proved superior and took over the central plains, even capturing the Herero capital, Windhoek. In the 1840s the young Maherero went to live among them to learn about firearms and the use of horses. He also became a friend of Jan Jonker AFRIKANER, their future chief.

Upon his father's death around 1861, Maherero became a clan chief and renewed resistance to the Khoikhoi. After making an alliance with a White trader who supplied guns and strategic advice, Maherero defeated Afrikaner in 1868. A truce was signed in 1870, leasing the town of Windhoek to Afrikaner and leaving Maherero, now the paramount chief, supreme in the region between the Orange and Kunene Rivers. Later there were further skirmishes with the Khoikhoi, and Maherero destroyed an entire settlement. The British played one side against the other until Maherero allied with the Germans in 1885. Subsequently, the British retreated to the post town of Walvis Bay. The Germans proved unreliable, but their increasing military power in Namibia convinced Maherero to remain their collaborator. His son, Samuel MAHERERO, succeeded him as paramount chief.

References: DAHB, MMA.

MAHERERO, Samuel
(Namibia, 1854?–1923)

Samuel Maherero, paramount chief of the Herero people, fought one of the major anticolonial wars of resistance against the Germans in South-West Africa (today's Namibia) in the early part of the twentieth century. He is regarded as a national hero and celebrated on Herero Day each year.

Samuel Maherero succeeded his father in 1890, although others also attempted to claim the chieftaincy. He sought German support and recognition as paramount chief, and this alliance with the Germans caused a rift between him and several of the chiefs.

At first, the German presence was light and had little impact, largely because German imperial policy called for the containment of British expansion rather than colonization. In 1892, Maherero made an alliance with Henrik WITBOOI, leader of the Witbooi clan, against Afrikaner expansion from the Transvaal. This move alarmed the Germans, who precipitated war by attacking Witbooi. Governor Theodor LEUTWIN moved his troops against them and was temporarily successful. Then the Germans began expropriating land which the Africans believed could only be owned collectively. The Herero at first protested but then settled peacefully.

Maherero sought greater German protection even though he realized that his pro-German policy was costing him support among his own people. He agreed to back the Germans in any future conflicts and gave up cattle and land in exchange for food allotments. The Germans were thus able to end resistance.

With few cattle left, the Herero were increasingly forced into contract labor, and colonial settlers took over the cattle market. A crisis was reached in 1903, and when the Germans sent their forces south against a Nama uprising, Maherero called for solidarity with them, reversing his earlier policy of cooperation with the Germans. Several African communities joined the Herero, including the Ovambo kingdoms in the north, and in 1904 the rebels, under Henrick Witbooi, entered the fray. At first, Maherero's troops forced the abandonment of the frontier settlements, and Leutwin was forced to resign. Issuing an "extermination order," the new German field commander, Lothar von Trotha, defeated the Herero, drove them into the desert, and set up a defense line beyond the waterholes. German policy sought nothing short of genocide. The Herero were reduced from about 80,000 to fewer than 15,000. Witbooi also attempted to attack the Germans, but it was too late for coordinated resistance. By the end of the war in 1907, Maherero fled into Botswana with 1,500 followers and eventually lost his chieftaincy. The Herero who survived in Namibia were reduced to serfdom by German farmers.

References: AB, *afr*, CWAH, DAHB, HWL, MMA, *wiki*. Horst Drechsler, *Let Us Die Fighting* (1966).

MAKEBA, Miriam Zensi
(South Africa/Guinea, 1932–)

Miriam Zensi Makeba, the preeminent African female singer, was significant in popularizing African music in the West and became a popular figure in the antiapartheid campaign.

Makeba began singing at home and in church choirs and eventually was invited to join a local touring band. She became a regional musical figure, and Coca-Cola even used her picture on billboard advertising aimed at African customers. In 1957, Makeba had a cameo singing part in a semidocumentary antiapartheid film, *Come Back, Africa*. She attended the Venice Film Festival and then went to London, where she met Harry Belafonte, the leading Black American entertainer at the time, who became her mentor and sponsor.

When she went to the United States with Belafonte, Makeba became an immediate star performer. The reviews were effusive after Belafonte introduced her as "the most revolutionary new talent to appear in any medium in the past decade." Her concerts sold out, and her albums achieved

Miriam Zensi Makeba

immense sales. She made her nightclub debut at the Village Vanguard, a popular club in New York's Greenwich Village. Her visits to Africa were triumphs—she sang at the liberation ceremonies for Côte d'Ivoire, Tanzania and Kenya, and at the inauguration of the Organization of African Unity (OAU).

Makeba's professional career was accompanied by, and for a long time suffered as a result of, upheavals in her personal life. She was forced to become an exile from South Africa when, after attempting to go home to visit her dying mother in 1960, the government canceled her passport and banned her music. In 1962 she had her first bout with cervical cancer, and her marriage to musician Hugh MASEKELA ended. In 1968 she married the radical African-American activist Stokely Carmichael (later named Kwame Touré), which had disastrous effects on her professional career. Her recording contract and concerts were canceled, and for 17 years she suspended touring. The FBI followed the couple constantly until they fled to Guinea, where

they became honorary citizens. The marriage dissolved in 1978. In 1985 she lost her only child, Bongi, who died in childbirth.

In 1987 her career was revitalized when she took part in Paul Simon's Graceland tour, which showcased African musical talent. In 1990 she finally was able to return to South Africa. One of the positive things that happened to her during this period was becoming the protégé of President Sékou TOURÉ, who appointed her to represent Guinea at the United Nations.

Makeba's repertoire is eclectic. She has sung Hebrew dance songs, Portuguese *fado*, and various ballads and love songs. Her best-known single recordings have been popularized versions of African music, the most dramatic being her trademark "Click Song." Sung in Xhosa, which uses a series of clicking sounds, it plays on words in a style more commercially clever than musically memorable. It is, however, her renditions of traditional African songs that are most enduring. With these songs she retains some of the township *kwela* sound, a South African type of jazz marked by the use of instruments such as penny whistles and sticks. She returned to this music in her album *Sangoma* (1988), dedicated to her mother, who was a *sangoma,* or traditional spirit medium. In recent years she has reissued recordings from her earlier years.

Makeba has received a number of awards, including a Grammy (1965), the Polar Music Prize (2002) and a Kora Life-Time Achievement Award. In 2005–2006, she began a farewell tour, with concerts booked in every country where she had performed.

References: AB, *afr*, CA, CB, DMM, GEPM, LKW, *wiki*. Makeba, *Makeba: My Story* (film, 1987) and *The Miriam Makeba Story* (2004).

MAKHUBU, Lydia Phindile
(Swaziland, 1937–)

Dr. Lydia Makhubu is a leading chemist in southern Africa who has become prominent in the study of the chemical qualities of traditional medicine.

After graduating from Pius XII College (now the University of Lesotho), she went to Canada and took advanced degrees in medicinal chemistry at the University of Alberta and the University of Toronto.

She was the first Swazi woman to earn a Ph.D. Her entire career has been at the University of Botswana and Swaziland, where, in addition to her professorship, she was appointed dean of science and then vice chancellor in 1988. (The head of state always holds the title of chancellor, so the vice chancellor is in fact president of the university.) Makhubu has been one of the first women to head an African university. She retired from that position in 2003.

Makhubu has become a leader in studying the applications of science to economic development and is a notable researcher in the field of traditional medicine. Long dismissed as folklore or witchcraft, traditional medicine has begun to be taken seriously as a means of discovering effective indigenous remedies that are unknown to Western science. Makhubu's research has focused on the chemistry of medicinal plants and the control of snail fever by using natural plant poisons. She has been involved in the research on the use of endod in snail fever. She has served on the Royal Swazi Commission on Traditional Medicine, the OAU Committee on Traditional Medicine and Medicinal Plants, and the World Health Organization Medical Research Council. She has also been a member of the allocation group for the U.N. Financing System for Science and Technology. In 2003, she was president of the Third World Organization of Women in Science.

Reference: PAS.

MALAKI, Musajjakawa
(Uganda, 1875?–1929)

Musajjakawa Malaki was a Christian leader who formed a separatist Church, the Society of the One Almighty God, popularly known as the Malakites.

Malaki, a Baganda, was twice refused baptism by Anglican missionaries, and in 1914 he founded the Malakite movement, which soon developed into a formal denomination that claimed more than 90,000 adherents within seven years. The Malakites were also the first independent Church in Uganda.

Although the Malakites were a religious group, they also carried the seeds of anticolonial dissent. The movement was confined almost entirely to the Baganda, Uganda's dominant ethnic group, which by 1914 was almost entirely Christian. Malaki taught that Western medicine was to be rejected, a tenet that created conflict with both the missionar-

ies and the government. Perhaps more serious was his advocacy of land redistribution. The Malakites proposed that ancestral lands be the property of clans rather than of individuals. This proposal was a threat to the local chiefs. The incident that brought about the suppression of the Malakites by the colonial government, however, was their refusal to cooperate in a vaccination program. Malaki himself died as the result of a hunger strike.

The movement declined swiftly from its peak in 1921 until it disappeared around 1930. The Malakites' Church was among the very few large independent Churches in Africa that have collapsed. Its appearance, however, caused the missionary Churches to reconsider their attitudes toward African religious aspirations, and it helped prepare them for the wave of African separatist religious movements in the next generation.

References: dacb, DAHB.

MALAN, Daniel François
(South Africa, 1874–1959)

Dr. Daniel François Malan, prime minister and champion of Afrikaner nationalism, formed the first Afrikaner government in South Africa and began apartheid.

Raised in the western Cape Colony, Malan studied at the predecessor of Stellenbosch University and took a doctorate in divinity at the University of Utrecht in the Netherlands. In 1905 he was ordained a minister of the Dutch Reformed Church and spent several years as an itinerant preacher in South Africa, the Belgian Congo (now the Democratic Republic of the Congo), and Southern Rhodesia (now Zimbabwe). He entered politics in 1915 over the issue of neutrality in World War I. Malan joined the National Party (NP) and became editor of its newspaper, *Die Burger,* which defended Afrikaner nationalism and opposed support of Britain during the war. He entered parliament in 1918 while he was leader of the Cape NP. He was later selected to join James HERTZOG's first cabinet in 1924 as minister of the interior, education, and public health.

In 1926 a bitter controversy erupted over the national flag, and Malan emerged as the exponent of Afrikaner intransigence, arguing against any appearance of the hated British ensign in the flag design. He also obtained recognition of Afrikaans as an official language, replacing modern Dutch. When the worldwide depression of the 1930s forced a coalition government on Hertzog, Malan remained in the cabinet but was increasingly at odds with the NP leadership. Thus, it was no surprise that when the NP merged with Jan Christiaan SMUTS's South African Party in 1933, Malan bolted, taking 19 other parliamentarians with him to form a new group, the Purified National Party, which became the official opposition.

Malan's sympathy for Nazi Germany in World War II narrowed his popular support, but with considerable skill he built his following among nationalistic Afrikaners. He emerged in the 1943 elections with 43 members of parliament. In 1948, help from the Afrikaner Party enabled his reconstituted NP to take control of the government, ushering in almost half a century of Afrikaner dominance. Malan had campaigned on a platform of apartheid, which was defined as White supremacy, racial separation, and the return of Black Africans to communal reserves. As prime minister, he played on the fears of Whites over the influx of African workers to the cities, and the NP began to put its proposals into legislation.

The architect of apartheid was Malan's minister for native affairs, Hendrik VERWOERD, the leader of the NP in the Senate. His legislation removed the last vestiges of the non-White franchise and imposed segregation in all areas, including land ownership, residence, marriage and employment. All adults were now defined by race, and passes were required to be carried at all times. There was stiff resistance to apartheid, but the Suppression of Communism Act (1950) gave the government special powers to suppress all opposition. During the Defiance Campaign of 1952, Malan imprisoned Chief Albert LUTHULI, and in 1953, under the Bantu Education Act, he removed African education from mission school control and placed it under the government. By 1954, when the 80-year-old Malan retired and handed the reins of power to Johannes Strydom, the entire apartheid structure was in place.

References: dacb, DAHB, EB, EWB, MMA, *wiki.*

MALAN, Magnus André de Merindol
(South Africa, 1930–)

General Magnus André de Merindol Malan, former chief of the South African Defense Forces (SADF) and minister of defense through the 1980s, was a chief enforcer of apartheid and one of the most powerful figures in the government.

Although Malan was the son of a chemistry professor and parliamentarian, he sought a military career. After graduating in commerce from Stellenbosch University, he received a second degree in military science at the University of Pretoria and was commissioned in 1953. He rose rapidly through the ranks, taking a number of military courses and holding a variety of posts. In 1962–1963 he attended the U.S. Army Command and General Staff College at Ft. Leavenworth, Kansas, and then became commander of the South-West Africa (Namibia) Command, where he was responsible for fighting the guerrilla war against the South-West African People's Organization (SWAPO) liberation forces. From 1968 to 1972, Malan headed the South African military academy before taking another field command for a year. He was army chief from 1973 to 1976 and chief of the SADF from 1976 to 1980.

During his tenure as SADF chief, Malan never wavered from his belief that the African National Congress (ANC) and other antiapartheid groups were essentially Communist. He cooperated closely with P.W. BOTHA when he was minister of defense and later prime minister, and was instrumental in helping to create a national armaments industry that was sufficient to supply most domestic military needs and to compete on the world market. Botha and Malan saw eye to eye on national security policy and together developed the "total onslaught" strategy against armed opponents. The SADF entered the Angolan war on the side of Jonas SAVIMBI, fighting directly against Cuban troops. It also launched cross-border raids against ANC camps and staging areas.

In 1980, Malan retired from the SADF to enter parliament and take the post of minister of defense, because he was convinced that a political role was far more important than a military one in combating unrest. He was appointed to the National Security Council, which under Botha functioned almost as an executive cabinet. By 1983 Malan had integrated army units into police patrols in the most restive African townships, and, when the 1986 state of emergency was imposed, he commented that political rights were not a relevant concern for Blacks.

Reluctantly, after several major defeats for the SADF in the field, he took part in peace talks with Angola and oversaw the South African withdrawal in 1988, the same year that Namibia achieved its independence. The South African negotiating party was booked on Pan Am flight 103 to New York, but they cancelled their reservations at the last minute. The plane was destroyed by a bomb planted on board.

At home, the SADF created covert paramilitary units to engage in political kidnapping and assassinations and funneled money and logistical support to the armed wing of Mangosuthu BUTHELEZI's Inkatha Freedom Party (IFP), the scourge of the ANC in the townships. When this support for Inkatha was revealed in 1991, it became a national scandal (dubbed "Inkathagate") and Malan was demoted to the ministry of forestry and water affairs. In 1993, when the government of F. W. DE KLERK had made a multiracial, Black-led government inevitable, Malan resigned and left politics. He did not participate in the 1994 elections.

In 1995, Malan was charged and tried for the murder of six adults and seven children in 1987, as part of a scheme to foment open conflict between the ANC and the IFP. After a seven-month trial that inflamed passions in South Africa over its revelations, Malan was acquitted.

References: GSAP, PLBA, RWWA, *wiki.*

MALLOUM, N'gakoutou Bey'ndi Félix

(Chad, 1932–)

General N'gakoutou Bey'ndi Félix Malloum, president of Chad in the late 1970s, was one of the few national leaders without a regional base or a personal army.

Félix Malloum is from the south, the more heavily populated and Westernized section of the country. He attended military school in the French Congo and then was sent to Fréjus military academy in France. As a sergeant in the French army, he served in Indochina from 1953 to 1955 and was rewarded by being sent to officer candidate school in

France. He saw further action in Algeria before returning to Chad in 1961. He rose quickly in Chad's new national army, although President Ngartha François TOMBALBAYE distrusted him. He was suspended for three months in 1966 but was reinstated. He led Chadian troops against several rebellions and served in the cabinet as minister of defense. His position as the real military strongman was recognized when he was named chief of staff in 1971, and a year later he became overall commander. In a bizarre turn of events, Tombalbaye arrested Malloum in 1973 for sorcery, accusing him of using animal sacrifices to bring down the government through witchcraft. Following the 1975 coup, Malloum was released and was chosen head of state by the military council.

Malloum set out to bring together the factions and regional warlords into a national government. He had success at first, although the opposition group controlling the north, Front de Libération Nationale du Tchad (FROLINAT), would not cooperate and continued the civil war. In 1977, Malloum brought Hissène HABRÉ into his government as prime minister. Habré was commander of FROLINAT's northern army, which continued its attacks on government forces. In 1978, Habré attempted a coup, which ended in a month of inconclusive, bloody fighting in the capital, N'Djamena. Goukhouni OUEDDEI took advantage of the stalemate to advance on the capital and take it. A four-party truce was achieved, but as a symbol of the defeated south, Malloum was sent into exile in France, then moved to Nigeria. He returned to Chad in 2002.

References: DAHB, PLBA.

MALULA, Joseph Albert

(Democratic Republic of the Congo, 1917–1989)

Cardinal Joseph Malula, the leading modern champion of the Africanization of Christianity, had the unenviable task of leading the Catholic Church in the Congo through the crisis of decolonization.

After being educated at the Grand Séminaire in Kabwe, Malula was the first African priest assigned to the capital, Léopoldville (now Kinshasa), where he confronted firsthand the paternalism of Belgian missionaries. In 1952 he founded study circles for consciousness-raising to compensate for the almost total neglect of African higher education by the Belgians. From this movement came a number of postcolonial politicians and several government ministers. In 1958, Malula became the acknowledged leader of the Black clergy following a speech at the Léopoldville exhibition on the place of the Church in Congolese society. He was made auxiliary bishop the following year, just in time to attend the Vatican Council, where he quickly became the spokesman for francophone Africa. In 1964 he was named archbishop of Kinshasa, and in 1969 he became a cardinal.

A consistent progressive, Malula clashed with both his government and the Church. He condemned ethnic conflict as the "scourge of Africa" and defended the rights of women in a famous speech denouncing those who reduced them to "slaves or instruments of lust." After the crisis of persecution and destruction that followed independence, he began his great work, the Africanization of Catholicism, a program he called "authenticity." He began to replace Western forms of worship and European ideas and approaches with African ones.

By 1970 the mercurial dictator MOBUTU Sese Seko had imposed order on Congo's chaos and began a program of national unity. The country changed its name to Zaïre, and Mobutu dropped his Christian name and demanded that all citizens do the same and be rebaptized. He called his program *authenticité*, a term he adopted from Malula. When Mobutu began to place cells of his party's youth wing in Catholic schools and seminaries, Malula led the opposition. The issue of Christian names became symbolic, but for Malula the real issue was Mobutu's dictatorship. In the presence of King Baudouin of Belgium, Malula preached against Mobutu, then he issued a pastoral letter denouncing government policy. Mobutu's response was swift and severe: all religious schools were seized and religious instruction was forbidden. Religious festivals were banned and holidays were abolished. Malula's life was threatened and his home was pillaged. Malula went into exile at Belgium's Louvain University in 1972, leaving negotiations to diplomats. He returned after compromises were reached and turned his energies toward the Africanization of the Church.

When he returned, two projects absorbed him: creating a truly African liturgy and holding an African Council to set directions for Catholicism on the continent. He achieved the first goal brilliantly. Carefully following the guidelines of the Vatican Council and using the best scholarly consultants,

Malula produced a rite that went beyond the mere introduction of local styles of music or customs and radically reshaped the style and impact of the Catholic Mass. Resistance from Rome was overcome with the minor concession that leopard skins would not be used as vestments. The incorporation of dance, talking drums, and African literary forms was most striking. While visiting Kinshasa in 1980 and 1985, Pope John Paul II participated in services using the new rites. It is the first (and only) indigenous rite for the Catholic Mass.

Malula hoped for a married clergy, but when Rome forbade even the discussion of that option, he strengthened the existing role of lay catechists into *bakambi* ("guardians") or village religious elders. Vatican officials regarded him with suspicion, but the pope appointed him co-chair of the 1985 Synod of Bishops as a sign of his personal support. Malula wanted, with a continental council, to confront and resolve the issue of Christianity and African identity. His influence among African bishops waned, however, with the massive increase of indigenous bishops chosen by John Paul II. The pope approved only a synod of African bishops, using an agenda drawn up by the Vatican. Malula believed firmly, as he often said, that "yesterday the foreign missionaries christianized Africa, but today Black Africans will Africanize Christianity."

References: dacb, DRWW, MMA.

MAMDANI, Mahmood
(Uganda, ?–)

Dr. Mahmood Mamdani, Herbert Lehman Professor of Government at Columbia University, is a leading political scientist studying Africa, and the director of the Institute of African Studies at Columbia.

Dr. Mamdani graduated from the University of Pittsburgh and did graduate studies at the Tufts University's Fletcher School of Diplomacy and Harvard, where he took his Ph.D. in 1974. He has taught at Makerere University in Uganda, the University of Dar es Salaam (Tanzania) and the University of Cape Town (South Africa). He has been president of the Council for the Development of Social Research in Africa (CODESRIA), based in Sénégal. *Citizen and Subject* (1996), his study of the effects of late colonialism on Africa, won the Herskovits Award of the African Studies Association in 1998, and has been touted as one of the best books ever written on Africa. Dr. Mamdani has also written on the Rwandan genocide (*When Victims Become Killers: Colonialism, Nativism and the Genocide in Rwanda*, 2002). His research has wider limits, however, and he has authored books on the Iraq War (2004) and the roots of terror, *Good Muslim, Bad Muslim* (2004). Currently, he is studying civil wars in Africa.

MANCHAM, James
(Seychelles, 1939–)

Sir James Mancham was his country's first president but was overthrown in a 1977 coup.

Educated in the Seychelles, a tiny island chain in the Indian Ocean, Mancham studied law in Paris and London before being admitted to the bar in 1961. Two years later he was a founder of the Seychelles Democratic Party (SDP). Initially, the SDP opposed independence, favoring some sort of continued association with Great Britain. A partially elected council was set up in 1967, followed by a legislative assembly in 1970. In every pre-independence election, the SDP emerged victorious, and Mancham served as chief minister from 1970 until the Seychelles achieved full independence in 1976. The opposition was led by France-Albert RENÉ. The two have formed twin poles of Sechellois politics since that time.

Mancham reversed his colonial position in the 1974 elections and won easily, forming a government of national unity with René. With independence in 1976, Mancham became president and René became prime minister. Mancham had always been a politician with flair and flamboyance, but his tenure in office only underscored his playboy image. The British newspaper *The Guardian* described Mancham's government as "a kaleidoscope of Arab princes, pop stars, film stars, and land deals at sky-rocketing prices." After a year, René's party staged an armed uprising while Mancham was in London for a Commonwealth conference, and placed René in the president's chair.

Mancham is widely believed to have been behind several coup attempts engineered against René from overseas. At least two of these coup attempts have been mounted with the involvement of South African mercenaries. Mancham is well connected to foreign capitalist interests that would like the opportunity to develop the islands' tourist

potential. At present, tourism is deliberately kept minimal and under the control of citizens.

Recently, René has felt more secure and has extended democratic reforms. Mancham even emerged to contend the 1993 elections. In a bizarre oddity, Mancham held the winning $20,000 ticket in a national lottery to raise funds for René's campaign. It was all Mancham won, however, because he received only 34 percent of the vote in what was regarded as a fair election. Mancham had promised foreign investment, but the economic boom enjoyed by the Seychelles made this campaign promise moot. He flew into the Seychelles before the election to reconcile with René, who agreed to consult him on major matters and to move toward parliamentary democracy. Mancham attempted a return to office in 1998, but garnered only 14 percent of the vote as a candidate of the Democratic Party.

Reference: PLBA. Mancham, *Paradise Raped: Life, Love, and Power in the Seychelles* (1983); Christopher Lee, *Seychelles: Political Castaways* (1976).

MANCOBA, Ernest
(South Africa, 1904–2002)

Ernest Mancoba was a pioneering Black painter in South Africa who worked in oils and watercolors.

Mancoba never received any formal training in art, although he took teachers' training and taught from 1925 to 1929. Throughout, he had an insatiable interest in both European and African art, and studied them as much as he could. In 1934 he exhibited as part of the South African Academy Exhibit. In South Africa, Mancoba established himself as a sculptor, with commissions from churches and civic venues. Already he was attempting to Africanize the dominant norms of Western sculpture. His *Bantu Madonna* (1929, and now in the Johannesburg Art Gallery) was the earliest African interpretation of the Virgin. He used local yellow wood and presented the Virgin barefoot and with marked Negroid features. The work shocked Christians by its unconventionality. Mancoba felt that his religious carving should keep to a traditional African community role. He was pleased that the statue was carried to the Anglican Cathedral in Johannesburg in 1936 in a food drive for drought victims.

He returned to school to take a degree in 1937, and then left South Africa for the greater opportunities of Paris. During World War II he was interned by the Germans as a citizen of an enemy nation. In the internment camp he met and married his wife, a Danish sculptor. After the war, he could not return to South Africa because apartheid had taken hold. With friends, he formed COBRA (for Copenhagen/Brussels/Amsterdam), an artists' group that influenced painting for several decades. Their intention was to express the unconscious without intellectual design. He later took French citizenship.

Mancoba's style was abstract and spontaneous, allowing bright color to speak for itself. From the start he worked with watercolors, and only did his first oil painting two years after going to Paris. That work, *Composition* (1940), is a slash of color in patterned designs, as if for a fabric. It was a style to which he would return again and again. In 1960 he set up a small gallery in Paris and worked from there. He returned often to the theme of mother and child, however, that he had begun in his statuary.

In 1994, Mancoba returned to South Africa for the first time for a Retrospective Exhibit of his lifetime work in Joahnnesburg. The next year he also had a retrospective at the National Gallery in Cape Town.

References: adb. Elza Miles, *Lifeline Out of Africa: The Art of Ernest Mancoba* (1994); *Ernest Mancoba at Home* (video, 1994).

MANDELA, Nelson Rolihlahla

(South Africa, 1918–)

Nelson Rolihlahla Mandela, the first Black president of South Africa, is perhaps the best-known and most widely respected African leader of modern times.

Mandela's father was head counselor for the paramount chief of the Thembu, the largest ethnic group in the Transkei in South Africa's Eastern Cape Province. As a boy, Mandela was groomed to be a chief, but after his father's death in 1930 he was sent to a Methodist boarding school, from which he emerged a strong Christian with a sense of service. Throughout his education, Mandela maintained contact with traditional society, returning in 1934 for the three-month circumcision ceremonies that

marked his adulthood and allowed him to retain his hereditary right to a chiefdom (which he later renounced when he went into legal practice).

In 1938 he entered Fort Hare College, South Africa's first university college for Blacks. There he befriended Oliver TAMBO, with whom he led a student strike that resulted in their expulsion in 1940. When Mandela returned to the Transkei, the response to his expulsion was an arranged marriage, which he avoided by moving to Johannesburg, where he worked as a gold mine policeman. Experiencing the life of the mine workers shocked him and further deepened his determination to work for social justice. He soon moved into Alexandra, a Black suburb, where he was introduced to Walter SISULU and his fiancée Albertina, and they moved into a large house together. At night, Mandela studied for his BA, which he received by correspondence from the University of South Africa in 1941, and then began legal studies at the University of the Witwatersrand. His study partner was Seretse KHAMA, future prime minister of Botswana.

In 1944, Mandela married a cousin of the Sisulus, and the four, with Tambo and four others, formed the Youth League (YL) of the African National Congress (ANC), hoping to revive the

Nelson Rolihlahla Mandela

moribund organization, which they described as "a dying order of pseudo-liberalism and conservatism, of appeasement and compromise." They advocated an action program based on Black nationalism, gaining the approval of Dr. Alfred XUMA, the ANC president. Mandela endorsed African autonomy, keeping a distance not only from White liberals but also Communists and Indian nationalists. In 1948 he was elected secretary, and in 1950 he became the YL president. In 1949, Mandela joined the ANC national executive. The 1948 elections had put the National Party (NP) in power under Daniel MALAN, who began a relentless enactment of apartheid legislation. Despite his separatist views, Mandela advocated a common front with Indians and supportive Whites against the new racist laws.

In 1952, Mandela and Tambo formed the first Black legal practice in South Africa. Shortly thereafter, the ANC began the Defiance Campaign, a program of civil disobedience and passive resistance directed by Mandela. As a result, 8,500 people, including Mandela and Sisulu, were arrested and charged under the Suppression of Communism Act. Mandela was banned from attending any meetings for two years and was restricted to Johannesburg. The banning orders were renewed regularly for the next nine years. Mandela began the "M-plan" to reorganize the ANC into small cells in case it was forced to go underground. In 1953 his banning order required him to resign from the ANC. From then on, his leadership was clandestine, except during his treason trial.

In 1956, Mandela and 155 other ANC leaders were arrested and charged with treason. The trial dragged on for five years until they were found not guilty. A defining moment came in 1960, when Robert SOBUKWE of the Pan-Africanist Congress (PAC), in connection with the ANC, called for a nonviolent national program of civil disobedience against the pass laws. When between 10,000 and 20,000 demonstrators assembled in the township of Sharpeville, refusing to carry their racial identification cards, the police fired into the crowd, leaving 72 dead and 186 wounded. The incident internationized the antiapartheid cause and brought about the first U.N. condemnation of apartheid.

After the Sharpeville massacre in 1960, the ANC was declared illegal and was forced to consider a future without legal political activity. Fearing a new banning order, Mandela went underground for 17 months. He realized that nonviolent protests, strikes and demonstrations would now be met with police violence, and he made a basic shift in his philosophy from advocating nonviolent action to accepting the necessity of forming a guerrilla force for armed resistance. In early 1962 he was smuggled across the border and made a dramatic appearance in Addis Ababa, Ethiopia, at a meeting of the Pan-African Freedom Movement. At this conference he articulated the ANC's new justification of political violence. He next went to Algeria to undertake guerrilla training, then to London to meet with Tambo, and was in exile there. He returned to South Africa in July and was captured a few weeks later. He was sentenced to five years' imprisonment. In December the new armed wing, *Umkhonto wa Sizwe* (Spear of the Nation) took its first action: a series of bombings of electrical installations.

While Mandela was in prison, the secret farm housing the ANC's underground headquarters was raided, and in 1962 the ANC high command was put on trial for sabotage, conspiracy to overthrow the government, and assisting armed invasion. Called the Rivonia trial, after the location of the farm, it provided an unprecedented opportunity for the ANC to make its case to the world, revealing apartheid in all its ugliness. Mandela gave a memorable four-hour address, parts of which were later released as a recording. He ended by saying, "I cherish the ideal of a democratic and free society in which all persons live together in harmony and with equal opportunities. It is an ideal I hope to live for and to achieve. But if needs be, it is an ideal for which I am prepared to die." The Rivonia Eight were sentenced to life imprisonment on Robben Island, South Africa's high-security political prison.

Mandela remained in prison for 28 years while his prestige increased throughout South Africa and the world. He became a symbol of dignity under oppression and a rallying point for resistance to racism and political repression. His second wife, Winnie MADIKIZELA-MANDELA, became his alter ego within South Africa, and despite her continuous banning, she attempted to provide a focus for opposition to the government. After 1978, when P. W. BOTHA became president of South Africa, Mandela's prison conditions improved. He was no longer forced to do hard labor and could mix with the general prison population. He formed ANC discussion groups and reached out to more radical groups. In 1982 a "Free Mandela" campaign was begun internationally, and he and Sisulu were transferred to a Cape Town prison. Botha offered Mandela a conditional release several times, the condition being his renunciation of violent action, but Mandela steadfastly refused. Foreign governments began to demand his release, and in 1988 there were worldwide celebrations of his seventieth birthday, including a television concert that was broadcast to more than 50 countries. That same year, he was moved to a prison hospital and then to a cottage on prison grounds. He was surreptitiously prepared for release by being taken secretly on tours of Cape Town so that he could understand the changes in society since his imprisonment.

In 1989, President Frederik DE KLERK released Sisulu and several other political prisoners. A year later Mandela gained his release and emerged to a tumult of adulation, drawing hundreds of thousands of people at his first appearances. He was restored to his position as deputy chairman of the ANC, but everyone recognized him as the true leader, because Tambo, who was chairman, had suffered a stroke and was hospitalized.

In 1990, Mandela led the ANC delegation in talks with the government before undertaking a tour of Europe and North America. He was greeted everywhere by massive crowds. Returning to South Africa, he began to deal with the extreme expectations that his release had brought. He forged a close working relationship with De Klerk, which was always civil, if not cordial. De Klerk, on his part, began to consult with Mandela on major decisions. Mandela's biggest challenge was to rein in the young militants in the African townships who were engaged in bloody confrontations with Chief Mangosuthu BUTHELEZI's Inkatha Freedom Party.

In 1991, Winnie, who had built her own political base in the townships during her husband's absence, was convicted of kidnapping and being an accessory to the death of a youth murdered by her bodyguard. Nelson distanced himself from her, and the two became estranged and later divorced. Nelson remarried, to Graça MACHEL, the widow of Samora MACHEL of Mozambique.

Made president of the ANC in 1991 when Tambo retired, Mandela began to organize for the elections that would mark the beginning of a new South Africa. In 1993, after he and De Klerk received the Nobel Peace Prize, Mandela proclaimed, "Let a new age be born!" The 1994 elections confirmed what was widely expected—a convincing ANC victory. Extremists on both the right and left were politically marginalized, and Mandela took the presidency of a five-year transitional government with two deputies, De Klerk and

Thabo MBEKI. He intended to step down in 1996, but continued to serve until 1999.

Mandela provided a transition of peace for a new South Africa. He encouraged the formation of the Truth and Reconciliation Commission and appointed Archbishop Desmond TUTU to head it. Together, those two magisterial figures defused the tensions of decades of apartheid. He mediated between Libya and Great Britain to bring the terrorist bombers of Pan Am 103 to trial. He also served as president of the Non-Aligned Movement during his last year in office.

Mandela has remained active even as he has slowed down due to age. After his eldest son died of AIDS in 2005, he admitted his own neglect of the issue as president and became active in the campaign against the disease.

References: AB, *adb*, *afr*, CA, CB, CBB, DAHB, EB, EWB, GSAP, HH, PLBA, PLCA, RWWA, *wiki*. Mandela, *Long Walk to Freedom* (1995); Fatima Meer, *Higher than Hope: The Biography of Nelson Mandela* (1990).

MANGOPE, Lucas Manyane
(South Africa, 1923–)

Kgosi Lucas Manyane Mangope, raised in a traditional family of Tswana chiefs, was president of Bophuthatswana, the most important of the ethnic homelands created by the South African government as part of the apartheid system.

Mangope received teacher training and taught until 1959, when he became chief of a mixed ethnic group and joined the local regional authority. In 1961 the Tswana Territorial Authority was established, and Mangope became vice chairman. In 1972 he became chief minister of Bophuthatswana as the territory was being prepared for internal autonomy under the bantustan scheme, a part of the apartheid policy of South Africa. Bantustans were segregated reservations that were to be nominally independent states, while in reality being under South African domination. At this point Mangope was convinced of the need for separate development of the races, but following a trip to the United States in 1973, he began to support equality within South Africa on a one-man, one-vote basis as an eventual goal. In 1974 he founded the Bophuthatswana Democratic

Party (BDP), which swept the polls when "Bop" (as it was popularly called) became nominally independent in 1977 with a population of 2.5 million.

At the independence ceremonies, Mangope attacked the Pretoria regime for the fragmented condition of the new mini-state, which was broken into seven parts. Nevertheless, he managed the new country even when no other nation outside South Africa recognized it. Using its putative independence as a shield against sanctions, he established a lucrative tourism industry with casinos to lure both South Africans and Europeans. Moreover, the development of platinum deposits made Bophuthatswana economically viable. Mangope's gradualist approach won him few friends and generated considerable opposition, however, and his tenure was marked by constant disturbances. When South African President P. W. BOTHA made a state visit in 1985, student riots caused the closing of the university and were followed by bus and school strikes. The following year, 11 died in clashes with police, and in 1988 there was an attempted coup in which Mangope was seized and freed only by South African troops. Despite those political events, however, Mangope did achieve a situation in which the daily political violence so common in South Africa itself was unknown. In addition, 70 percent of secondary school students graduated—twice the average for Black South Africans. Interracial couples lived together freely, and other aspects of petty apartheid did not exist.

Mangope was a continual opponent of the African National Congress (ANC). He naively offered to serve as a negotiator between the ANC and the South African government in 1986 but was rebuffed. Nelson MANDELA called him a "puppet leader" after Mangope accused the ANC of being behind 1990 demonstrations in favor of integration with South Africa. In 1994, in advance of the South African elections, Mangope refused to cooperate in allowing the electoral commission to operate in Bophuthatswana. Mounting discontent produced a strange turn of events, as armed reactionary White separatists swarmed into Bophuthatswana to defend it from integration with South Africa. The Bophuthatswana forces reacted and killed a number of the invaders, and the South African army then entered the homeland and effectively ended its short history. Mangope fled the homeland to South Africa amid widespread rejoicing and celebration.

Mangope was found guilty of corruption in 1998. He is now head of the small South African Christian Democratic Party.

References: GSAP, PLBA, RWWA, wiki.

MAPANJE, Jack
(Malawi, 1944–)

Jack Mapanje is a leading African poet and linguistic scholar who was persecuted for his forthright defense of freedom under the authoritarian Dr. Hastings Kamuzu BANDA.

Mapanje was educated in local Catholic schools and took teacher training before graduating from the University of Malawi. He then took a Ph.D. in linguistics at University College, London. There he compiled his first collection of poetry, *Of Chameleons and Gods* (1981). In it Mapanje wrote a veiled, subtle attack on tyranny, using imagery from Malawian mythology, and it was promptly banned by Dr. Banda, why had grandly styled himself president-for-life. In *Chameleons*, Mapanje uses the traditional praise-poem form to mock a fictitious "chief," whom he styles "his Royal Blindness." He returned to Malawi to take a post in linguistics at Chancellor College, by then Malawi's only university. He became chair of Languages and Linguistics and then founded the Linguistics Association for southern Africa.

When *Of Chameleons and Gods* was reprinted in 1987, Banda had Mapanje arrested, and he spent four years in prison, unable to communicate with his family. Amnesty International began a campaign on his behalf as a Prisoner of Conscience, and he was released in 1991. It was widely believed that the campaign was the only thing that kept him from being murdered in prison. Mapanje took his family to Great Britain and published his prison writings, *The Chattering Wagtails of Mikuyu Prison*, in 1993. In one searing poem, he wrote of scrubbing the walls of the blood stains of previous prisoners.

Mapanje was well received in Great Britain and taught at York University and lectured throughout the country. He visited Malawi in 1995 after Banda's removal from office and returns now on a regular basis. In 1998 he published *Skipping Without Ropes*, which continues the themes of detention and release. His latest collection is *The Last of the Sweet Bananas* (2004).

Mapanje's verse reflects the various stages of his life. What is consistent is his use of Malawian traditions, first as a young man excited about the fusion of African ways with Western thought, and then bringing to bear his linguistic scholarship. Though he has written in Chichewa, the bulk of his work is in English. With the end of the worst oppression in Malawi, Mapanje has continued to explore social themes from a wider Africa, writing of the genocide in Rwanda and developments in South Africa.

References: adb, afr, DLB.

MARGAI, Albert Michael
(Sierra Leone, 1910–1980)

Sir Albert Michael Margai was the brother of Sir Milton MARGAI and his successor as prime minister of Sierra Leone. Like his brother, he first followed a medical career, working as a nurse and pharmacist for 12 years. In 1944 he went to England to study law and in 1947 was admitted as a barrister. He was the first Sierra Leonean lawyer.

Until 1951, Sierra Leone, which had been founded as a haven for liberated slaves, had only a single center of education and development, the capital, Freetown. Because the freed people came from many places in Africa, the Creole elite in Freetown had little sense of ethnic identity. In the interior, "the protectorate," the opposite was true, and the Margai brothers became leaders among the indigenous peoples when the protectorate obtained the right to vote. Under the banner of the Sierra Leone People's Party (SLPP), they swept to power in spite of some political differences between them. At independence, Albert served in Milton's government after 1962 in three ministries. Upon Milton's death in 1964, Albert succeeded him but never enjoyed his popularity.

Albert Margai never favored multiparty democracy because he feared that parties would become tribally based. He openly opposed the involvement of traditional rulers in national politics. Mounting criticism over government corruption, favoritism towards Margai's Mende tribe, and centralization of power rallied public support for Siaka STEVENS, who won the 1967 elections. Margai mounted a coup, which was followed by two others. In the end, disgraced, he went into exile in England.

References: AO, DAHB, MMA, PLBA, *wiki.* John Cartwright, *Political Leadership in Sierra Leone* (1978).

MARGAI, Milton Augustus Striery
(Sierra Leone, 1895–1964)

Sir Milton Augustus Striery Margai was the first prime minister of Sierra Leone and created the national coalition that led his country through the independence period.

Born of a paramount chief in the undeveloped interior of Sierra Leone, he was the first "protectorate native" to graduate from Fourah Bay College, despite prejudice from the dominant Creoles, the descendents of liberated slaves whom the British had settled on the coast. Subsequently, he studied medicine in England, becoming the first physician from the protectorate. For a quarter of a century he practiced in the colonial medical service, professionalizing midwifery in the rural areas by working through the women's secret society and publishing two books on the subject. Through his work he gained the trust of the local chiefs and a popular following.

Margai formed the Sierra Leone People's Party (SLPP) with Siaka STEVENS in 1951, winning the elections to the Legislative Council (Legco) that year. The acknowledged leader of the up-country indigenous African population, insultingly called "foreigners" by the Creoles, he was able to defuse the potentially polarizing ethnic tensions and include Creoles in his party and, later, his administrations. His brother, Sir Albert MARGAI, challenged Milton's cautious leadership of the SLPP and won by one vote, becoming prime minister in 1958. Milton was knighted and appointed parliamentary leader and minister. In 1960 he led an all-party delegation to London for independence negotiations. He became prime minister in 1961, when independence was granted.

An essentially conservative pro-British leader, Sir Milton was firmly committed to democracy and defended the rights of the opposition. Avoiding ethnic rivalries, he worked toward national unity. He encouraged foreign investment and regional cooperation and created a stable and productive economy. When he died in office, he was succeeded by his brother Albert.

References: CB, DAB, DAHB, MMA, PLBA, wiki. John Cartwright, *Political Leadership in Sierra Leone* (1978).

MARKER, Laurie
(Namibia, 1950s–)

Dr. Laurie Marker is co-founder and executive director of the Cheetah Conservation Fund (CCF) and a prominent animal scientist and environmentalist.

The cheetah, the world's fastest mammal, clocked at 60 mph in hunting bursts, is also the world's most endangered cat. clocked at 60 mph in hunting bursts, is also the world's most endangered cat. It is now limited to Africa, with fewer than 200 left in Iran, and it is extinct in South Asia. The 15,000 left in Africa is half the number of a generation ago. While the cheetah may live for 12 years in the wild, it lives longer in captivity, and the CCF has an active captive breeding program to reintroduce greater numbers to Africa.

Marker began her work at the Wildlife Safari in Oregon from 1974 to 1988, creating the most successful cheetah breeding program in the world there. In 1977, she took a captive-raised cheetah to Namibia to see if hunting was innate or needed to be taught. She founded the CCF in 1990 to develop the expansion of the cheetah population in its native habitat. A foundation helped the CCF purchase an 18,000-acre farm in Namibia, and with support from Chevron, United States AID and the De Beers Corporation, a field research center for animal biology was established with a visitors' educational center. Marker moved to Namibia to manage the program, choosing it because Namibia is one of the last strongholds of the cheetah.

She had to face the opposition of some local farmers, who lost farm animals to cheetah attacks, so she developed a guard dog training program that supplies dogs to the farmers to protect their flocks. The basic research program focuses on the cheetah's lack of genetic variation, and since 1988 she has published and updated a comprehensive cheetah stud book. The CCF does biomedical research on diseases and ecosystem research.

In 2000, Marker was named one of *TIME* magazine's "Heroes of the Planet" for her conserva-

tion work. Since 1988, she has also been executive director of the Center for New Opportunities in Animal Health Sciences at the Smithsonian's National Zoo in Washington, DC. She has received numerous environmental and conservation awards.

Reference: adb. www.cheetah.org.

MARKHAM, Beryl Clutterbuck
(Kenya, 1902–1986)

Beryl Clutterbuck Markham—aviator, horse trainer, writer—was one of the generation of White settlers whose lives spanned colonialism and independence and who were prominent in both eras.

Her father brought her to Kenya at age four after his wife abandoned them. Markham grew up with Kipsigis children, learning to hunt barefoot and speaking the local languages. She was reckless in the face of danger and once barely survived a lion attack. Her mother's abandonment scarred her emotionally, and this was exacerbated when her father went to South America when she was 17.

She became a race trainer, and her horses won eight Kenya Derbies and numerous other races. After a brief marriage to a rugby player, she married British coal heir Mansfield Markham. She abandoned him in 1927 for Raoul Schumacher, a screenwriter with whom she lived in California from 1936 to 1947. She then deserted Schumacher as he lay dying and returned to Kenya.

Manipulative and jealous, she had a compulsive need to prove her allure by male conquests. She had notorious affairs with the Prince of Wales and the Duke of Gloucester, resulting in her receipt of a small annuity as hush money. Writer Karen BLIXEN (Isak Dinesen) described her as "pantherine," and with good reason, because the passion of Markham's life was Dinesen's lover, Denys Finch-Hatton. When he died in a plane crash in 1931, Markham was bereft.

Markham learned to fly in 1930 in order to entice Finch-Hatton, who was an amateur pilot. She became a bush pilot and flew often from Nairobi to London. In 1936 she made the "impossible" east-west solo flight from England to North America and was awarded a ticker-tape parade in New York. She wrote beautifully of the flight in her memoir *West with the Night* (1942). The book was forgotten in the distractions of World War II but was rediscovered after a reference to it as "bloody marvelous" was found in a letter written by Ernest Hemingway. *West with the Night* was reissued in 1983 and stayed over 40 weeks on *The New York Times* bestseller list, selling over a million copies. It has been the subject of much literary controversy and is considered by some to have been ghostwritten by Raoul Schumacher, whose style is evident in it.

Markham, who was never wealthy, supported herself by training and racing horses until the royalties from the reissue of her book gave her a comfortable old age.

References: CA, CB, LKW, *wiki*. Mary Lovell, *Straight on Til Morning* (1987); Errol Trzebinski, *The Lives of Beryl Markham* (1993).

MASEKELA, Hugh Ramopolo
(South Africa, 1939–)

Hugh Ramopolo Masekela, the leading South African jazz artist and an outspoken critic of apartheid, lived in self-imposed exile from his homeland from 1960 until 1994.

Born in a mining town 100 miles from Johannesburg, Masekela came as a child to Sophiatown, a Black suburb of Johannesburg, where he was enrolled at St. Peter's School. He came under the influence of Father Trevor HUDDLESTON, the Anglican pastor and antiapartheid campaigner who gave him his first trumpet and launched him with the Huddleston Jazz Band. When Huddleston was expelled from South Africa in 1955, St. Peter's was closed.

Sophiatown was leveled in the government's attempt to destroy any urban African cultural identity. It was then replaced by the housing blocks of Soweto. During these years Masekela performed widely, inspired by the music of Dizzy Gillespie, Miles Davis, and other African-American artists. Shortly after the Sharpeville massacre in 1960, Masekela left South Africa with the help of American performer Harry Belafonte. Masekela enrolled in the Manhattan School of Music, where he completed the album *Trumpet Africa* in 1962.

Masekela began to gain popular attention in the 1960s, when he did musical arrangements for and performed with Belafonte and singer Miriam MAKEBA, to whom he was married for several years. He began mixing traditional American jazz with African elements, such as enhanced percussion and a repetitive vocal quality that infused the music. In 1968 his single recording "Grazing in the Grass" was number one on the musical charts for several weeks. Masekela, however, was increasingly restless with jazz, and in 1973 he left the United States to return to Africa and visit the popular musical community there. He traveled extensively in West Africa, and in Nigeria he met Fela KUTI, the master of Afrobeat. Kuti in turn introduced Masekela to the Ghanaian musical group Hedzoleh Soundz, whose music had a powerful effect on both Kuti and Masekela. Their compositions used a base of African folk music with jazz overtones and the insistent rhythms and contrapuntal trumpet solos of Afro-Cuban music. Masekela recorded five albums with Hedzoleh Soundz and took them on a U.S. tour, but the group, although well received, broke up.

In 1983, Masekela settled in Gaborone, the capital of Botswana, to be nearer the African musical scene. Here, in a mobile studio, he began recording with bands that crossed the South African border. During this period he toured with Paul Simon and Ladysmith Black Mambazo as part of the controversial *Graceland* tour. In 1984, at the suggestion of Winnie MADIKIZELA-MANDELA, he collaborated on the antiapartheid musical *Sarafina!*, the story of the Soweto student uprising, which had a two-year run on Broadway and later became a movie.

Masekela's hit single, "Bring Him Back Home," became the anthem for the campaign to free Nelson MANDELA in the 1980s. At Mandela's request, Masekela ended his self-imposed exile and made a tour of South Africa in 1991. After Mandela's election as president of South Africa, Masekela returned to live there. In 1994 he and Makeba made their first tour together in 20 years. In recent years, Masekela has returned to the *mbaqanda* sound of his first youth group, a fusion of rural *marabi* (keyboarding reminiscent of ragtime) and *kwela* (the township street music based on the sprightly sounds of the tin pennywhistle).

References: adb, afr, CBB, CM, DMM, GEPM, EB, WAM, *wiki*. Masekela, *Grazin' in the Grass: The Musical Journey of Hugh Masekela* (2004); *Amandla!* (Film, 2003).

MASIRE, Quett Ketumile Joni

(Botswana, 1925–)

Sir Quett Ketumile Joni Masire, independence leader and Botswana's second president, was responsible for maintaining its record of unbroken democratic government.

Masire came from a peasant family and was a herdsboy until he began school at age 13. In 1949 he finished high school and began teaching, at the same time becoming the leader of a band of young educated Ngwaketse, his ethnic group. He was often in conflict with the tribal authorities, but he began his political career with election to the Ngwaketse Tribal Council in 1958. When the Botswana Democratic Party (BDP) was founded in 1962, Masire became a full-time organizer and the editor of its newsletter. He was close to the BDP's founder, Sir Seretse KHAMA, but he also had his own following. Masire was the organizational genius behind the BDP, which has never lost a Botswanan election. Masire garnered widespread support, including the backing of chiefs and most of the White population.

Independence was achieved in 1966, and Masire became vice president and minister of finance. When Khama died in 1980, Masire was the obvious choice to succeed him. Masire has been the architect of the strong Botswanan economy, which has grown at an average of 13 percent a year since independence. As minister of finance and development, he avoided central planning and encouraged foreign investments. As president, he has diversified the economic base to include tourism and diamond processing and has improved agriculture to complement copper-nickel and diamond mining. About a third of the nation's income has been used for social benefits, especially public education. By 1994, Botswana had foreign reserves of about $4 billion and was the only African nation lending money to the World Bank and International Monetary Fund. At the same time, the country is perhaps as open and free politically as anywhere in Africa There is a free press, and harassment of the opposition is rare. Masire stepped down in 1998.

Masire's foreign policy was cautious, because Botswana shares a long border with South Africa. While maintaining cool but correct relations with the White apartheid regime in Pretoria, Masire quietly allowed the African National Congress (ANC) to transit Botswanan territory. He did not, however, permit camps or any ANC military presence. Despite this policy, South African forces mounted a number of raids into Botswana in the 1980s, and in 1986, Masire expelled ANC representatives from the country. Tensions eased when F. W. DE KLERK became president of South Africa and improved markedly after the election of Nelson MANDELA in 1994.

After several forays into international diplomacy after leaving office, Masire took the non-managing position of chairman of Global Afrika Resource and Energy Corporation (Garek), a South African company with a dicey record for lack of transparency and questionable practices. Garek is a major company with a value in billions of rand. Its shares are sold illegally in South Africa, and it remains unlisted. It also is vague about its activities and the nature of its business. There has never been a satisfactory explanation of why Masire would serve as a front man for such a group, risking his reputation for integrity.

References: afr, DRWW, PLBA, PLCA, RWWA, *wiki.*

MASIYIWA, Strive

(Zimbabwe, 1961–)

Strive Masiyiwa is a telecommunications entrepreneur who has risen from being principal engineer for Zimbabwe Posts and Telecommunications Corporation (ZPT) to CEO of Econet Wireless Holdings and a board member of the Southern African Enterprise Development Fund.

Masiyiwa was educated in Great Britain, but after high school he returned to Zimbabwe to join the anticolonial resistance. The leaders sent him back to England because they needed future business leaders more than they needed another 17-year-old freedom fighter. He returned to newly independent Zimbabwe in 1984 with an engineering degree and went to work with the telephone company, a state-owned parastatal. He quickly rose to become principal engineer.

In 1993, Masiyiwa attempted to set up the first cellular network in Zimbabwe, and offered to share the project with ZPT. Protecting their monopoly over land lines, ZPT refused to grant him a license, and Masiyiwa sued the government and won in the Supreme Court. Econet began expanding to other countries and won a coveted license for Nigeria to deliver GSM cellular services. In the space of five years, Africa's mobile connections jumped from two million to over 35 million, and Econet has become one of Africa's five largest telecom companies, riding this crest.

At every turn as he was starting, Masiyiwa was hampered by the corruption and cronyism of the Zimbabwean bureaucracy. His success has made him something of a national hero. Even after he began setting up base stations with Swedish help, President Robert MUGABE forbade mobile phones, and decreed a two-year prison sentence for violators. ZPT suddenly showed interest in mobile technology, with a sweetheart deal being given to a member of Mugabe's family. Masiyiwa was offered bribes and threatened, but in the end the high court vindicated him. A week after he set up his first operation, he had 100,000 customers.

Econet Wireless has revenues of over $300 million a year and has operations in eight countries, including Great Britain and New Zealand as well as six across Africa. For his outstanding achievements despite a weak Zimbabwean economy, Masiyiwa has earned the inevitable comparison: he is regularly called "the Bill Gates of Africa."

In 2002, *TIME* magazine named Masiyiwa one of its Global Business Influentials of the year. He has also been named Entrepreneur of the Year in Zimbabwe (1998) and Businessman of the Year (1990).

Reference: adb.

MASSEMBA-DÉBAT, Alphonse
(Congo, 1921–1977)

Alphonse Massemba-Débat, president of the Congo Republic from 1963 to 1968, was caught between the army and the forces of the ideological revolution that he initiated. The conflict, which has plunged the country into long periods of confusion and violence, was his undoing.

Massemba-Débat became a teacher in 1940 and served in Chad, where he was active in the local society of educated Africans and the Chadian Progressive Party, the local affiliate of the Rassemblement Démocratique Africain (RDA), the interterritorial party formed by Félix HOUPHOUËT-

BOIGNY of Côte d'Ivoire. Massemba-Débat returned to Congo in 1947 and joined the RDA's Congolese branch under Abbé Fulbert YOULOU. In 1958, Youlou, then prime minister, appointed Massemba-Débat to a government post, and in 1959 he was elected to the national assembly. He was chosen president of the assembly and in 1961 became minister of state but disagreed with Youlou's pro-French policies, which led to his resignation in 1963. This departure proved to be a clever move, because Youlou survived only three more months until popular demonstrations brought down his government.

Massemba-Débat returned to take over the new government, which was facing serious internal problems. Most notably, the economy was in shambles. His support rested with the student and labor union movements, which had unrealistic expectations for immediate change. Massemba-Débat moved the country sharply left, nationalizing mission schools and establishing an armed youth movement to counter the army. He kept Congo in the French franc zone, the hard currency region supported by France, despite criticism of this policy as representing a form of neocolonialism. Mounting opposition from both the left, which demanded a more Marxist economic policy, and from the army gradually placed Massemba-Débat in an untenable position. In 1966 he tried to incorporate the army into his new armed militia, prompting the junior army officers to mutiny. Massemba-Débat attempted to conciliate the army by giving in to most of its demands, making the leader of the officers, Major Marien NGOUABI, his chief of staff. After an unsettled two years, a power struggle followed for several months in 1968 with Major Ngouabi emerging as the new head of state. Massemba-Débat was placed under house arrest for a year and then went into retirement. When Ngouabi was assassinated in 1977, Massemba-Débat was accused of complicity in the murder and was executed without trial. His involvement has never been proven.

References: afr, DAHB, DRWW, MMA, PLBA, *wiki.*

MASUPHA
(Lesotho, 1820?–1899)

Masupha was a military commander and governor in Lesotho. A junior son of MOSHWESHWE I, he seemed always to have resented his brother Letsie, who became king in 1870, and he often defied Letsie's authority. Masupha established himself as a capable commander in campaigns that eliminated one of his father's rivals and by defeating the Afrikaners from the Orange Free State.

In 1871 the administration of Lesotho was taken over by the Cape Colony, and Masupha was made governor of Thaba Bosiu, Moshweshwe's capital and legendary fortress, from which he had maintained the independence of the Sotho people. Masupha's position was important both because of his rank (he was one of four governors) and because of Thaba Bosiu's symbolic significance. Cape rule, however, was not onerous at first. The Sotho kept their troops, who were increasingly equipped with firearms. This led to attempts to disarm the Sotho and to the hostilities that followed, the so-called "Gun War" of 1880–1881. Leadership in the kingdom split, with King Letsie supporting the colonial government. Masupha resisted attempts to disarm him but did not engage in battle.

Masupha retained his position even after Lesotho was returned to British protectorate status in 1884. Distanced from political conflicts within the kingdom, Masupha contributed to factionalism by his autonomy. After Letsie died in 1891, his son, Lerotholi, gradually asserted control over the regional governors, saving Masupha for last. Thaba Bosiu was stormed and taken in 1898, and Masupha was arrested and removed from office. The fortifications were then torn down.

Reference: DAHB.

MATAKA Nyambi
(Tanzania, 1805?–1878?)

Mataka Nyambi forged a trading enterprise among his Yao people into a strong regional chieftaincy. He capitalized on the growth of the slave trade into the interior around Lake Malawi, causing the disruption of society on the one hand and creating new chiefdoms on the other.

The Yao traders had long been successful in the interior, and Mataka began by organizing a small village as a base and by gathering followers. They wove baskets that he traded for iron hoes, which in turn he traded for slaves. At first the slaves were outcasts and criminals, but as the export of ivory began to demand large numbers of porters, the Yao

acquired firearms and began taking slaves by raiding. This upset a delicate balance in which slavery had been a means of social control of criminals and deviants in societies that had no prisons. For the Yao, slavery now became an extension of a new economic structure to meet external demands.

Mataka was one of the most successful in exploiting this shift. By the 1860s he controlled much of what is now interior Tanzania. He raided with gangs of *ruga-ruga,* youth of mixed parentage who were often the offspring of enslaved women. These outcasts had no social position and were thus loyal only to Mataka. Their marauding expeditions terrorized everyone in their area because their raids were marked by brutality. One Arab trader in 1861 reported traveling for over two weeks through burned villages without seeing a living soul. Mataka's mini-state was one of half a dozen that controlled the region, and the slave and ivory trades expanded dramatically during this period.

Mataka's capital was an administrative center with Arab scribes and was visited by the British explorer David LIVINGSTONE. Mataka was impressed with Swahili and Arab cultures, which he attempted to copy in his capital. He even introduced mango trees and the wearing of the *kanzu,* the long white Swahili gown. Mataka, however, never adopted Islam. Mataka's successor, Mataka II Che Nyenje, began the custom of using his name as his title.

Reference: DAHB.

MATEMERA, Bernard
(Zimbabwe, 1946–2002)

In the explosion of modern sculpture in Zimbabwe in the last part of the twentieth century, Bernard Matemera stood out as one of the masters. His smooth, almost glass-like works, grotesque to some eyes, reflected a strongly emotive sense. He is regarded as one of the finest stone sculptors of the period.

As a young man, Matemera worked in clay and wood carving. He joined the Tengenenge Workshop, where he was introduced to stone carving. Tengenenge is a major center for Zimbabwean stone sculpture and Matemera soon began to absorb the craft from the other sculptors there. His first recognition came with *Great Spirit Woman* (1982), which won first prize at an exhibit at Zimbabwe's National Gallery. This massive piece is in Matemera's characteristic presentation, half human with animal features. It is a tribute, he said, for "throughout our history there have been individual women possessed of great spiritual powers."

Matemera's work is deeply African. Its themes are drawn from the dream and spirit world: *Great Spirit Woman*, *The Man Who Ate His Totem* (1998) and *Bird Boy*. Of *The Man Who Ate His Totem*, he said: "My totem is 'Nguruve' the wild pig. I have disobeyed the law by eating its delicious flesh. Now both my son and I change into our totem animal." It is a tortured sculpture of human-and-pig, the father and son clinging together in desperation.

Matemera's work is smooth and rounded, like great boulders. Even his human figures have animal qualities, and his monumental works bear comparison to the polished stone of Inuit (Eskimo) stone carvers in Arctic Canada. The figures often have three toes and three fingers, an anomaly also found in excavations of the prehistoric figures of northern Zimbabwe.

Matemera's last year before his untimely death was very productive, and there has been a frenzy among collectors to acquire his last pieces.

Reference: adb.

MAWA
(South Africa, 1770s–1848)

Princess Mawa, a Zulu princess, was the aunt of SHAKA, DINGANE, and two other Zulu kings. She was the youngest sister of Senzangakhona, the king who disgraced himself by his incestuous relationship with NANDI, mother of the future king Shaka. Because this took place shortly before he came of age to take the throne, Mawa was quite young and escaped the bitterness that came out of that scandal. She seems to have remained on good terms with her nephews. After Shaka came to power, he appointed her royal representative of a military town, which she continued to govern throughout his reign (1815–1828) and also under the kingship of Dingane (1828–1840).

In 1840 the Zulu kingdom began to break into factions, each led by large sections of the army that broke away. Dingane attempted to shift his Zulu troops to Swaziland, but half the army rebelled and challenged him. Upon Dingane's death in battle, a

dynastic struggle began among Mawa's three remaining half-brothers. Mpande, the winner, who had toppled Dingane and received the support of Afrikaners in Natal, began to eliminate his rivals. Mawa had sided with one rival, but picked a loser. Because as royal princess she had no power of her own, but only that reflected upon her by a king and patron, Mawa was forced to flee.

Mawa witnessed the contests for power in the region, which included not only the Zulu claimants but also Afrikaners and British. In 1843 the British established Natal as a colony, and at the same time the nephew backed by Mawa lost the struggle for kingship and was executed. This certainly would have been her own fate, but Mawa was a shrewd leader and apparently used her long tenure as royal representative to good effect. When several thousand warriors panicked in fear of the new king, Mawa took command and led these troops (with their families and cattle) into Natal, where she gathered in other remnants of the Zulu nation. Her stabilizing influence on these wandering groups earned her the accommodation of the British, who allowed her to settle in Natal and form a permanent settlement.

Reference: DAHB.

MAZRUI, Ali Al'Amin
(Kenya, 1933–)

Dr. Ali Al'amin Mazrui, political scientist and scholar, is a leading Africanist who has affected both scholarship and popular ideas of Africa. He is the scion of the ancient Mazrui dynasty from coastal Kenya. After receiving his doctorate at Oxford University, Mazrui was professor, chair and dean at Makerere University in Uganda, until he openly criticized dictator Idi AMIN Dada. Advised to "shut up or leave the country," Mazrui took a position at the University of Michigan in 1973. A number of distinguished visiting professorships at various universities punctuated his 17-year tenure there until 1990, when New York Governor Mario Cuomo personally offered him the Albert Schweitzer Chair at the State University of New York at Binghamton.

Mazrui has written some 25 books, but by far the best known is *The Africans: A Triple Heritage* (1986) issued simultaneously with a six-part television series of the same name. Unreservedly anticolo-

M'BA, Léon

316 M'BA, Léon

nialist and somewhat anti-Western, it makes accessible the central thesis of much of Mazrui's work: African society can be understood as the interplay of traditional, Islamic and Christian cultural elements. The series was attacked as "a pretentious fraud" by *The New York Times* and called "biased and preachy" by *The Washington Post*. The National Endowment for the Humanities, a partial funder, even asked to have its name removed from the credits. Mazrui responded that he was merely restoring balance to the previous colonialist interpretations of Africa and saying what Westerners did not want to hear. "The United States is a great communicator, but a poor listener," he commented.

Furthering his argument for reading Africa from an African perspective, Mazrui edited the volume in the UNESCO General History of Africa dealing with Africa since 1935. In the 1990s he coauthored two books on the political culture of language, and in 2005 he applied his triple heritage theory to the contemporary issues of globalism and counterterrorism. All of his work reflects on African identity as reflected in the intertwining of religion, culture and politics.

Another enduring theme in Mazrui's ideology has been his proposal for a *Pax Africana* (African peace) based on a Pan-African peacekeeping force. He denounces U.N. peacekeeping efforts as "disguised recolonization." He has further antagonized some Westerners by suggesting that a Black South Africa will become a nuclear power. He has stated, "Maybe the West can be persuaded to give up nuclear arms when people like us have them."

Despite his strong positions, Mazrui is soft-spoken. The son of Kenya's chief Islamic law judge, he is proud of his Islamic heritage. He has served on the board of the American Muslim Council. He sees his role as that of an intellectual ambassador from Africa, bringing its insights to an ignorant West.

References: adb, afr, CANR, DLB, PAS, *wiki*. Sulayman Nyang, *Ali Mazrui* (1981); Seifudein Adem, *Paradigm Lost, Paradigm Regained: The Worldview of Ali A. Mazrui* (2002).

M'BA, Léon
(Gabon, 1902–1967)

Léon M'Ba, independence leader and first president of his country, was a lifelong supporter of close ties with France.

M'Ba was a Fang, a member of a large immigrant ethnic group that was looked down upon by other African communities and distrusted by the French colonial administration. M'Ba's brother was the first Fang priest, but despite a mission education, Léon turned to politics as a means of preserving African society from European influence. He studied African customary law and began working for the colonial government in various clerical positions. He was active in the nationalist movement and led a revival movement of traditional ceremonies as part of a cultural renewal. In 1933 these activities led to charges of witchcraft, for which M'Ba was imprisoned by French authorities for three years and exiled to Oubangi-Shari (now the Central African Republic) until 1946.

On his return to Gabon, M'Ba plunged into local politics, forming a new party that became the Gabon affiliate of the interterritorial Rassemblement Démocratique Africain (RDA) of Félix HOUPHOUËT-BOIGNY of Côte d'Ivoire. When he assumed leadership in reducing tensions concerning Fang ethnic problems, M'Ba earned credibility with the French authorities. He was elected to the territorial legislature in 1952, and in 1956 he became mayor of Libreville, the capital of Gabon. A year later M'Ba was named vice chair of Gabon's executive council. In 1958 he became president after a decisive win in national elections.

His great strength derived from his ability to bring together diverse interests and ethnic groups, a talent which made him the accepted choice for president when Gabon achieved independence in 1960. He had opposition from radical groups, however, which considered him too pro-French and conservative, but after a brief period of instability, he was confirmed in office by a landslide majority in 1961 elections. In 1963 he absorbed the opposition into a single party but was unsuccessful in integrating the various factions. The army attempted a coup in 1964, but it was defeated by French paratroops. M'Ba responded by becoming increasingly authoritarian and ultimately ending democracy in Gabon. He remained unchallenged as president, and was reelected shortly before his death. His hand-picked successor, Albert-Bernard (Omar) BONGO, became president.

References: afr, DAHB, MMA, PLBA, *wiki*.

MBARUK bin Rashid al-Mazrui
(Kenya, 1820s–1910)

Mbaruk bin Rashid al-Mazrui was the son of the last independent ruler of the Mazrui dynasty in Mombasa, on the Indian Ocean coast of Kenya. He was an implacable enemy of the Busaidi dynasty, which overthrew his father in 1837, and became the leader of an important rebellion against the British.

Mbaruk's father was defeated by Seyyid SAID of Zanzibar and barely escaped with his life to the south. Around 1865 he succeeded to leadership of the southern remnant of his people, and the Zanzibaris recognized his leadership and awarded him an annual allowance. He remained hostile to the Busaidi, however, and under the regime of Sultan BARGHASH bin Said there were constant clashes. From 1870 to 1888, Mbaruk lived essentially as a fugitive bandit leader, regularly harassing the Busaidi with his force of several thousand, made up mostly of slaves. He attempted to involve the Germans, who had imperial designs on Zanzibar, but to little effect. Finally, the chartered Imperial British East Africa Company (IBEAC) established itself along the coast, and Mbaruk returned to settle there. His relations with the IBEAC were cordial, and he gave the company support in various ventures. In turn, Mbaruk became a prosperous trader, controlling the sale of food crops along the coast by becoming the middleman for the Mijikenda and Giriama peoples.

This arrangement was disturbed by the proclamation of a British protectorate in 1895. In the unsettled months between the end of IBEAC authority and the arrival of a British commissioner, open conflict broke out over the succession to leadership in one of the Mazrui clans. The IBEAC chose the new governor in defiance of Islamic law, and when the news reached the Mazrui that the British would soon take over, they took up arms. The Mazrui revolt soon united all the clans and swept along the coast. The Giriama and several smaller communities joined the alliance, and several coastal towns were attacked. The British were forced to bring in troops from India to quell the rebellion, but they were unable to capture Mbaruk, who escaped to Tanganyika (now Tanzania). He surrendered to the German authorities and received political asylum from them. Mbaruk retired to Dar es Salaam on a German pension, and the authority of the Mazrui dynasty effectively ended. Mbaruk was pardoned by the British in 1907 and was invited back to Kenya, but he chose to remain in Tanganyika, where he died.
Reference: DAHB.

MBEKI, Thabo Mvuyelwa
(South Africa, 1942–)

Thabo Mvuyelwa Mbeki, longtime African National Congress (ANC) activist and its international expert, was first deputy president under President Nelson MANDELA and succeeded him.

The son of Govan Mbeki, an ANC companion of Mandela's who spent 25 years in prison with him, Thabo Mbeki joined the ANC Youth League (YL) at age 14. After a school strike led by the YL, the student body was expelled, and Mbeki completed his exams independently. In 1960 the ANC was banned, and Mbeki's father was consistently harassed, arrested, detained and finally forced to go underground. Thabo Mbeki also went underground from 1960 to 1962, organizing among the youth, but in 1962 the ANC asked him to leave South Africa. He was arrested in Southern Rhodesia (now Zimbabwe) and was about to be deported to South Africa when the British government intervened. He was granted asylum in Tanzania and then went to Great Britain for studies, receiving an MA in economics at Sussex University in 1966. At the university he became active in antiapartheid student organizing both in Britain and internationally.

Until 1970, Mbeki worked for the ANC's London office, then moved to Lusaka, Zambia, where ANC exile headquarters had been established. He became the ANC's representative to the Frontline States, those which bordered South Africa and joined together to oppose apartheid. He served in Botswana, Swaziland, Tanzania and Nigeria during this period. In 1975 he joined the ANC Executive and in 1985 was appointed director of information. In this capacity he met the increasing number of delegations of White business and community leaders who visited Lusaka during in that period to make unofficial contact with the ANC. In 1989 he was transferred to head the ANC department of international affairs.

Thabo Mvuyelwa Mbeki

Following legalization of the ANC, Mbeki joined the ANC team that negotiated transition arrangements with F. W. DE KLERK's South African government. Considered flexible and sophisticated, he was appointed deputy president in Mandela's government, beating out his rival, Cyril RAMAPHOSA, head of the Congress of South African Trade Unions (COSATU). The selection made him the leading contender for the presidency when Mandela retired and, therefore, the center of a power struggle within the ANC. Mbeki did not have the local base of support that Ramaphosa had, but his lengthy ANC credentials made him a party insider. He forged an alliance with Winnie MADIKIZELA-MANDELA, the president's former wife and the leader of a powerful grassroots following. In 1997, he became president of the ANC.

In 1999, Mbeki succeeded Mandela as president. He lacks Mandela's charisma, and he does not have the same public authority in Africa. Nevertheless, he has used his position to mediate and bring together contending forces in the Sudan, Kenya, the Democratic Republic of the Congo (DRC) and Côte d'Ivoire. Twice, in Equatorial Guinea and in São

Tomé e Principe, he foiled attempted coups, and in 2003 he helped arrange the exile of Charles TAYLOR from Liberia. He has placed South African peacekeepers in the DRC and Burundi, and observers in the Sudan and Ethiopia. He not only sees the role of South Africa as the "economic engine of Africa" but also as a guarantor of continental peace. His only signal failure has been attempting to mediate between the dictatorial regime of Robert MUGABE and the democratic opposition in Zimbabwe. Many felt that Mbeki was manipulated by Mugabe into tacit support for his repressive thuggery.

If his international efforts have achieved some results, at home his policies have seen less success. The program to provide desperately needed housing in South Africa has moved slowly, corruption has begun to appear in high places, unemployment stands at a minimum of 40 percent and economic recovery has been sluggish.

By far his worst attitude has been his position that AIDS is not caused by HIV. He has accused scientists of being "stooges of foreign drug companies." Mbeki evidently relied on Internet blogs and unreliable sources in forming his opinions, and in the end, he was held up to ridicule. Although he dropped this view without repudiating it, South Africa has one of the worst HIV/AIDS policies in the Third World. Little money and less effort goes into antiviral drug therapies, and the national treatment program is in shambles. Infection rates continue to soar, and South Africa has one of the largest groups of infected citizens in the world.

Mbeki projects a rather imperious style, brooking little dissent in the ANC and ramming home his policies. He tends to rely on a small coterie of trusted allies rather than consulting the wider party leadership. He handles criticism poorly, using the media to lash out at anyone he differs with. Even his brother has called him "stubborn and self-righteous." When retired Archbishop Desmond TUTU criticized Mbeki for dependence on his small circle of advisors and indifference to the plight of the poor, Mbeki denounced him as "an icon of the White people."

References: afr, EB, GSAP, PLBA, RWWA, *wiki*.

M'BOW, Amadou Mokhtar

(Sénégal, 1921–)

Amadou Mokhtar M'Bow was a top civil servant and international diplomat as head of the United Nations Educational, Scientific, and Cultural Organization (UNESCO) from 1970 to 1987. His controversial direction caused several member states to withdraw from membership.

M'Bow came from humble origins and entered the French army during World War II. He was 26 before he completed university entrance requirements, but he went on to receive a degree from the Sorbonne in 1951. He taught for two years in Mauritania and then spent four years on the UNESCO staff in its basic education program. He was called back to Sénégal in 1957 to become minister of education in the preindependence government. He left after a year over a dispute with the national leader, Léopold SENGHOR, and returned to teaching. In 1966 he reconciled with Senghor and was reappointed minister of education from 1966 to 1968. After student strikes in 1968, he was transferred to the ministry of culture. During this time he served on UNESCO's board and was twice head delegate to UNESCO from Sénégal.

In 1970, M'Bow was elected UNESCO's assistant director general for education, and in 1974 he took over the top post of director general. M'Bow was the first Black African to head a U.N. agency, and he proved a highly controversial director. He moved political issues such as disarmament, Third World concerns, and South African apartheid to the forefront. The focus of UNESCO before his administration had been on scientific collaboration and cultural exchange. M'Bow's support came from developing nations and the Soviet bloc, and his opposition derived from Western nations and developed Asian states such as Singapore and Japan. His programs placed M'Bow in the center of Cold War controversy, which dogged his time in office. There was sharp disagreement with the way he was politicizing social and cultural programs.

UNESCO met in Belgrade in 1981 after M'Bow had been unanimously re-elected director general. There he unveiled his New World Information Order (NWIO) to meet the criticisms of developing countries that the Western media misrepresented them to the world. The NWIO called for the licensing of journalists and mandatory publication of governmental replies to disputed statements. The NWIO became a rallying issue for M'Bow's Western opponents, who accused UNESCO of censorship, and cost him his last support among Western intellectuals and liberals. In 1982 the Western bloc rejected budget increases, and the United States (which contributed 25 percent of the budget) threatened to withdraw from UNESCO. A year later the Americans made good on their threat and were followed by Great Britain and Singapore.

M'Bow weakened his position by centralizing decision-making power in himself. The governing bodies deferred to him, and he controlled policy. Under his leadership, 80 percent of UNESCO's budget went to its central office in Paris, where the bureaucracy grew while the field staff declined. There was also evidence of cronyism and nepotism in his appointments as well as a strong national bias, which were contrary to U.N. personnel policies. Accountability and auditing procedures were lax, leading a number of member nations to call for reform, with the implicit threat of further departures. By 1986, UNESCO was experiencing a serious budget shortfall and was unable to fund its programs or maintain its staff. M'Bow appeared ready to stand for a third term in 1987, but when the Soviet Union withdrew its support for his candidacy, he dropped out. He returned to Sénégal in retirement.

References: EWB, PLBA. Thassinda Uba Thassinda, *Amadou Mahtar M'Bow: Un Sahélien à l'UNESCO* (Amadou Mahtar M'Bow: A Sahelian at UNESCO, 1989).

MBOYA, Tom (Thomas Joseph Odhiambo)

(Kenya, 1930–1969)

Tom Mboya, Kenyan nationalist and labor leader, was a man of intellectual ability who had a democratic vision for his country. His potential for being one of the great African leaders of the postcolonial period was cut short by his assassination.

Mboya was educated at Catholic mission schools and completed secondary school at the prestigious Mangu High School. His parents were poor Luo agricultural workers, and Mboya supported himself with odd jobs but could not raise enough money to pay for the final course to prepare for the national examinations. From 1948 to 1950 he studied at the sanitary inspectors' school, which he chose because it paid a small stipend during training. He was assigned as an inspector in Nairobi and shortly thereafter was asked to take a vacancy as secretary of the African employees' union. In 1952, Mboya founded the Kenya Local Government Workers' Union (KLGWU).

In 1951 the Mau Mau rebellion against British colonialism led to the declaration of a state of emergency the following year. The leading African political organizations of the time were identified with the largest Kenyan ethnic group, the Kikuyu, which also made up almost all the membership of the Mau Mau. The Kikuyu political leaders, including Jomo KENYATTA, were arrested. Mboya became treasurer of the Kenya African Union (KAU), Kenyatta's party, and assumed tacit leadership of the nationalist movement. He continued to expand his base in the labor movement, establishing more than 1,300 branches of KLGWU. The British Labour Party provided Mboya with support and advice, and in 1953 he united five unions into the Kenya Federation of Labour (KFL). Shortly thereafter, the KAU was banned, and the KFL became the largest African organization in the country. Mboya led protests against the detention camps, mass removals of people, and the secret trials of African leaders. As a result, he made several trips to Great Britain and the United States to gather support for Kenyan independence. In 1955 he settled an acrimonious dockers' strike, winning a 33 percent wage increase for the workers. It was one of the first times an African labor leader had represented African workers in a strike settlement.

The British Labour Party arranged a scholarship for Mboya (1955–1956) to study industrial management at Ruskin College, Oxford University. He used the time to meet other nationalists and to explore British socialism. When he returned, the Mau Mau insurgency was over and Africans were allowed to form political parties. Mboya founded the People's Convention Party, and in the 1957 elections he joined the first elected Africans to sit on the White-dominated Legislative Council (Legco). The other elected Africans immediately formed a bloc behind Mboya and demanded equal representation, which led to 14 Africans (representing six million) being seated along with 14 settlers (representing 60,000 Whites). Mboya called for "undilut-

ed democracy" with every adult having a vote. In 1958, when African nationalists from across the continent gathered in Accra, Ghana, for the All-African People's Conference, Mboya was elected the chairman and called it "the proudest day of my life." In the same year he was elected to the executive board of the International Confederation of Free Trade Unions, and in 1959 he received his first honorary doctorate. He had became a national and international symbol of the independence movement.

In 1960 the Kenya African National Union (KANU) was founded with Mboya as secretary-general. All African leaders in Kenya deferred to Kenyatta, who was then still in detention, but party factions were threatened by ethnic divisions. Mboya's Luo background gave a sense of national unity to the predominantly Kikuyu party, and he proved a brilliant tactician and organizer. Among his projects was the famous "air lift," which organized scholarships for talented Kenyans regardless of tribe and sent more than 1,000 students to the United States for higher education. When independence was achieved in 1963, Mboya was elected to the national assembly and was named minister of labor, a post that he had held in the transitional government. In 1965 he was promoted to the Ministry of Economic Planning, where he led Kenya to a position of prosperity. He opposed nationalization and adopted a capitalist, mixed economy.

Politically, Mboya stood for non-ethnic, open politics. A brilliant debater and charismatic speaker, he enjoyed open disputation. The critical issue for him was that all politics be conducted in public rather than through secret negotiations that were immune from challenges. As a consequence, Mboya was a highly visible person, both at home and on the international scene. His main opposition came from a fellow Luo, Vice President Oginga ODINGA, whose leftist policies were in opposition to Mboya's unabashed Western leanings. They clashed primarily over White-owned land, which Odinga wanted expropriated and distributed to landless peasants, while Mboya favored purchasing land at market prices. Odinga left KANU in 1968, by which time Mboya was widely seen as Kenyatta's heir.

Mboya's power and position presented a threat to many in the Kikuyu elite, who were further angered when Mboya raised charges that they were enriching themselves at the expense of the country. When his charges touched upon members of Kenyatta's family, the situation became volatile. In

1969, Mboya was shot and killed in public by a Kikuyu attacker with connections to prominent officials. When Kenyatta attended the funeral, a violent demonstration broke out against him on the common belief that he was behind Mboya's murder.

References: AB, *adb*, *afr*, CB, DAHB, EB, EWB, HWL, MMA, PLBA, PLCA, *wiki*. Mboya, *Freedom and After* (1963); E. Gimode, *Thomas Joseph Mboya: A Biography* (1996); P. Mwanji Kagwanja, *The Legacy of Tom Mboya* (1999).

McKENZIE, Precious
(South Africa, 1936–)

Precious McKenzie, a diminutive sportsman known as "the Pocket Rocket," overcame personal, political and professional adversity to become a world champion weightlifter.

McKenzie was born in a rural area of South Africa, and shortly after his birth, his father was killed by a crocodile. A weakling who had nearly died as a baby, he was named "Precious" by his mother in gratitude for his survival. His mother was unable to cope with five children, and Precious was placed in a foster home, where he was abused. The abuse was so severe that it stunted his growth, and Precious stands only 4 feet 10 inches tall. Nevertheless, he began gymnastics in school.

As a small youth, he trained as a circus acrobat, which was his path to discovering weightlifting. He soon began winning competitions, but was turned down for the South African teams for the Empire Games in 1958 and for the Olympics in 1960 because of his race. When he could not compete due to the international boycott of South African sports, he went to England, where the minister of sport put him on a fast track to citizenship, waiving the five-year residence rule. Now in a position to train professionally, he graduated from Bisham Abbey Academy in kinetics and began competitive weightlifting in earnest. He won his first gold at the Commonwealth Games in Jamaica in 1968. He would repeat at bantamweight or flyweight classes the next three Games. Now retired from that level of competition, McKenzie still sets records in the over-sixties class, the most recent in 2004.

The story is told that Queen Elizabeth II was so determined to see McKenzie win his third Commonwealth gold medal that she quietly rearranged her official engagements. Whatever the reality of that account, McKenzie went on to produce what became listed as one of the Ten Greatest Commonwealth Games Moments with his third Commonwealth record and gold medal.

McKenzie was nine times British weightlifting champion, 10 times power lifting champ and five times world power lifting champ. He went to three Olympics on the British team. McKenzie is still the World Masters Power Lifting Champion. He held eight world masters power lifting records between 1999 and 2002 and accumulated four consecutive gold medals at the Commonwealth Games. The Queen recognized his abilities by naming him a Member of the British Empire (MBE) in 1974. McKenzie now lives in New Zealand, where he serves on the New Zealand Safety Council and works in the area of back injury prevention and workplace safety.

References: wiki. www.preciousmckenzie.co.nz. Marion Connock, *The Precious McKenzie Story* (1975).

MDA, Zakes (Zanemvula Kizito Gatyeni)
(South Africa/Lesotho, 1948–)

Novelist and playwright Zakes Mda is a polymath, gifted not only as a literary writer, but as a journalist, poet, scholar, painter and film producer.

Mda was raised in Soweto, the Black reservation surrounding Johannesburg, before going to Lesotho, where his father had been exiled for activity in the Pan-African Congress (PAC). Zakes Mda began writing poetry as a youth, but his first mark was made with his play *We Shall Sing for the Fatherland* (1973), which won the first Amstel Playwright Award in 1978. He won again the following year for *The Hill* (1978). His plays were collected in a volume in 1980, which caught the attention of Ohio University in Athens, Ohio, a center for African Studies. Mda was given a scholarship for a master's degree in theater. He returned to Lesotho as a lecturer at the university and in 1989 received a Ph.D. from the University of Cape Town. Since then, he has been prolific in his writing. In 1994, Mda returned to South Africa as a professor at the University of the Witwatersrand.

Mda's plays focus on social issues, but in his novels the social realism gives way to a mystical overtone, a blend of mystical fantasy and realism known as magical realism. Like his compatriot, the Afrikaner J. M. COETZEE, Mda injects magical realism into a South African world. His first novels, both published in 1995, were *Ways of Dying* and *She Plays with the Darkness*. Three more have followed in rapid succession, the latest, *The Whale Caller*, in 2005. This last work illustrates his approach. Its anti-hero is a whale caller, a man who communicates with whales. He is unlike the official whale crier who tries to bring the animals near shore for tourist sightings. Like Mda himself, the whale caller has returned to his home village after years away. No one knows him anymore, but one whale becomes his soul-mate. Only in a mysterious and hidden relationship is communication possible.

Mda credits the end of apartheid with triggering his latent ability to write novels. He freely admits that under apartheid, poetry and short stories were written not for art's sake, but for politics. The end of apartheid meant the lifting of that burden and a freedom to explore themes at length on their own terms.

Mda is a "staunch republican," a defender of the need for reconciliation both between races in South Africa, but also among Blacks themselves. He has seen the temptations of power and warns that "we must make sure that the liberators do not become the oppressors." His work is suffused with compassion and forgiveness, the only path to the reconciliation that can provide the basis for a new South Africa. Yet, he is unblinking in facing the evils of the past. In *The Heart of Redness* (2000) he describes the sexual exploitation of Black girls by Afrikaner farmers in explicit language, and then turns to scenes of Black shame and violence.

Several times, Mda has been made writer-in-residence at major universities, enabling him to complete plays and fiction. In 2001, Mda won the Commonwealth Writers' Prize for *The Heart of Redness*.

References: adb, DLB, *wiki*.

MENELIK II
(Ethiopia, 1844–1913)

Menelik II, the third of three great sovereigns who ruled Ethiopia in the nineteenth century, expanded the empire, repelled an Italian attempt to make Ethiopia a colony, and promoted modernization and progressive policies.

Menelik II

Menelik was crown prince of the Shoa kingdom in central Ethiopia when TEWODROS II seized it in 1855, killing the king and taking Menelik prisoner for 10 years. Menelik escaped in 1865 and proclaimed himself *negus* or emperor. After Tewodros's suicide in 1868, YOHANNES IV took power, but Menelik maintained his autonomy. By 1887 he had the best-equipped army in the region and had established diplomatic relations with European powers. He conquered Harar, the chief Muslim province, acquiring vast stores of ivory, gold and tax revenues from the Islamic slave trade. When Yohannes went to war with the Italians, who had occupied the coast (today's Eritrea), Menelik remained neutral, but after Yohannes's death in battle with the Mahdists in 1889, Menelik easily seized the throne of all Ethiopia.

Menelik signed a peace treaty with the Italians (known as the Treaty of Ucciali), but the Italian and Amharic language versions differed on the crucial point of whether Ethiopia had consented to an Italian protectorate. The Empress TAITU boldly confronted the Italian ambassador and accused Italy of dishonesty. The Italians, confident of an easy victory, responded by invading Ethiopia. Menelik mobilized his people and defeated the Italians in a series of battles. He inflicted a crushing defeat on them at Adowa in 1896, assuring Ethiopia's independence. Soon, other European powers accepted the empire's complete sovereignty, and for a number of years Menelik worked to guarantee the security of his borders against colonial encroachment. He negotiated borders with the British over the Sudan and Somalia, and got their support in suppressing arms smuggling to the Mahdists in the Sudan.

Menelik was now in a position to achieve what he had denied his predecessors: the unity of all Ethiopia. He was a brilliant administrator and immediately began organizing the empire along new lines. A standing army was established, a national tax system was put in place, and a centralized administration was created. Under the influence of Taitu he established a new capital at Addis Ababa, with paved streets, hospitals and schools. Menelik instituted a national currency, a printing press, and a postal system and began a rail link to the coast. Beginning in 1906 he suffered a series of strokes, and Taitu gradually assumed the powers of regent. As Menelik's health declined, court factions conspired to gain the throne. His grandson, Lij IYASU V, succeeded him. He and Taitu (who was married five times) had no children, but Menelik fathered ZAUDITU, who later became empress in her own right (1916–1930).

Menelik was a man of astonishing energy, and despite the royal mythology that he was a descendant of Solomon and the Queen of Sheba (which made Ethiopian emperors almost superior beings), he was accessible to his people. In the famine of 1890 he worked in the fields alongside the peasants. He had a child's delight in new inventions but an administrator's keen appreciation of their uses. In his old age, he learned to drive the first automobile in Addis Ababa, abandoning his horse and racing along, laughing and gasping for breath.

References: AB, DAB, DAHB, EB, EWB, HWL, MMA, WGMC, *wiki*. Ray Prather, *The King of Kings of Ethiopia, Menelik II* (1981).

MENETEWAB
(Ethiopia, 1706?–1773)

Menetewab, empress and regent of Ethiopia, was the de facto ruler of Ethiopia for almost 40 years. She stands in a long line of powerful women in Ethiopian political history.

Menetewab (Beautiful Queen) became the consort of Emperor Bakaffa around 1722, shortly after he was enthroned. She was one of his secondary wives and gave birth the following year to a son, the future IYASU II. She spent much of her marriage in internal exile separated from her son but in 1728 was granted the title *etege,* or empress, which she kept after the emperor's death in 1730. After

Bakaffa's death, she took up with a young lover and had three daughters.

Iyasu became emperor, with Menetewab as regent. She gained political support among her family and clan, but in 1732 a major revolt against her broke out among the nobility. Menetewab and Iyasu were besieged in their palace for several weeks, but after the suppression of this revolt there was never another serious challenge to her leadership. Even when Iyasu came of age and was crowned, Menetewab retained her title as co-ruler.

Her policy was one of conciliation, and Ethiopia enjoyed a period of peace and tranquility under her rule. She did not challenge the independence of the provincial governors, and in the few instances when neighboring peoples invaded the empire, they were easily repulsed. She avoided religious controversies, maintaining peace between the two major monastic centers. Her reign was noted for an artistic flowering, as she encouraged and supported manuscript illuminators and painters as well as the decorative arts, which she displayed in the impressive churches and palaces that she built.

Iyasu died in 1755, and Menetewab set up a new regency in the name of an infant grandson, Iyoas. The lord of the major region of Tigre, Mikael Sehul, threatened this arrangement, but Menetewab was able to come to terms with him by marrying one of her daughters to him and another to his son. This did not stop Mikael Sehul, however, and in 1769, Iyoas was assassinated and Menetewab was removed when a coup she mounted against Mikael Sehul failed. She then retired to the palace complex she had built for herself in Gojjam. Eventually, she was guaranteed safety by Mikael Sehul and the new emperor, and she returned to Gondar to lend her prestige to their rule.

References: DAB, DAHB, WWR, *wiki*.

MENGI, Reginald Abraham
(Tanzania, 1940s–)

Reginald Mengi is a media baron in Tanzania, the owner and executive chair (CEO) of IPP Limited, and an industrialist. He has twice been voted among the most respected businessmen in East Africa.

Mengi began his career as a chartered accountant, and rose to become managing partner of

Coopers & Lybrand in Tanzania. In the mid-1980s he took over the IPP Group, which manufactured ballpoint pens in a small assembly plant. Mengi turned IPP into a major conglomerate with interests in soap, toothpaste and cosmetics, some of the easiest start-up manufacturing products for a Third World country with few natural resources. It then expanded into bottling in a joint venture with Coca-Cola. Beyond consumer goods, IPP has a financial consulting firm and an extensive media empire. It publishes eleven newspapers, five in English and six in Kiswahili. Outside of print media, IPP runs three radio stations and tri-state (Tanzania, Kenya, Uganda) television programming. It controls the Tanzanian prints of major British newspapers and the ITV network from Great Britain.

Mengi has a long and distinguished record of civic service, something not very common among African entrepreneurs. He has funded the Kilimanjaro Afforestation Campaign to restore the woodlands on the flanks of Africa's highest mountain and has been a patron of the Global Environmental Network. He has also served as chair of the National Environment Management Council and the Poverty Alleviation and Environment Committee. For his sustained work on behalf of environmental causes, Mengi has been recognized and honored. He was named Environmentalist of the Century (the Kilimanjaro 2000 Award) and given the East African Environmental Leadership Award. Tanzania has presented him with two national decorations. Besides his environmental interests, Mengi has set up programs for youth employment and persons with disabilities.

Professionally, Mengi has been chair of the National Board of Accountants and Auditors and the Tanzanian Chapter of the International Chamber of Commerce. He serves on the board of the Commonwealth Business Council.

Reference: adb. www.ippmedia.net.

MENGISTU Haile Mariam

(Ethiopia, 1939?–)

Lieutenant-Colonel Mengistu Haile Mariam was the military ruler who brought an end to the ancient Ethiopian monarchy and forcibly transformed Ethiopian society into a doctrinaire Marxist state.

Mengistu's origins are shadowy. Supposedly the orphan of a southern soldier, he was raised among the extended family of an army commander and former governor. He entered military service as a boy, transferring to the regular army at age 18 after finishing grade nine. Mengistu entered Holeta Military School and was commissioned in 1962. Assigned to the Third Division as an ordnance officer, he rose to major by 1974 and was popular with other junior officers. The corruption and favoritism of the imperial government deepened his resentment toward the Amhara, the ethnic elite who ruled the country, and he supported the army's "creeping bloodless coup" in 1974, when 200 officials were arrested for corruption. By the end of the year, the aging and senile Emperor HAILE SELASSIE was deposed.

Mengistu was elected the Third Army's delegate to the Provisional Armed Forces Committee, popularly known as the Dergue (Shadow). It had 120 members of all ranks, and Mengistu became one of its deputy executives. He was soon running the Dergue behind the scenes, and by the end of the year, the Ethiopian press acknowledged him as the "true moving force" behind the revolution. Mengistu was ruthless in removing those who stood in his way. He executed 60 of the leading nobility and may have taken part in the fierce gun battle that ended with the death of the Dergue chairman, General Aman Mikael Andom. Mengistu manipulated Andom's successor and finally executed him and the other deputy in 1977. The Dergue was purged until only 60 loyalists who shared Mengistu's views were left. He suppressed student dissent, abolished civil liberties, and at the same time vigorously pursued the war against secessionist forces in Eritrea.

The Dergue began its transformation of Ethiopia into a Marxist nation by nationalizing industry and land in order to form state farms and cooperatives. The patriarch of the Ethiopian Church was executed, and Church lands and monasteries were seized. Mengistu moved against competing Marxist groups in early 1977, and the Ethiopian People's Revolutionary Party (EPRP) began a terrorism campaign, the "White Terror," against the Dergue. Mengistu responded with the "Red Terror" of 1977–1978, in which students, intellectuals and educated people were indiscriminately killed. In several incidents, in a convulsive reaction against anyone influenced by Western ideas, youths were shot for wearing school uniforms. To drive the lesson home, the bodies of the tortured were displayed on national television. Relations with the United States became increasingly strained, and Mengistu forged new links with the Soviet Union and Cuba.

Mengistu's military control of the country was in danger of being lost in 1978 as monarchist forces reached the edge of Gondar, the ancient capital, while the Somali army was poised to take two major southern cities and control the rail line to the Red Sea. Cuba and the Soviet Union poured arms into Ethiopia, turning against their former ally, Somalia, and Mengistu was able to prevail. The Cubans quietly sent troops as well.

Although Mengistu's land reforms led to increased food production, the country was drained by military demands. The Dergue was harassed by the EPRP internally and by the Eritrean People's Liberation Front (EPLF), which was attempting to wrest that province away from Ethiopia. Despite Mengistu's initial successes, the EPLF forces could not be decisively defeated. The Tigrean People's Liberation Front (TPLF) expanded in the Tigre, and it appeared that Ethiopia might be balkanized. Almost 50 percent of the national budget went for defense, and the war debt to the Soviets mounted to almost US$4 billion.

In 1983 and 1984, the country was hit by unprecedented drought and famine. Despite massive food aid, tens of thousands died, and even larger numbers became refugees. International food relief was often off-loaded from European ships to Soviet ones while they were in port, to pay the arms debt. This happened to the aid purchased from the receipts of Bob GELDOF's famous Band Aid Concerts. The situation deteriorated further until 1988, when the EPLF and TPLF launched major campaigns, inflicting huge losses on the Ethiopian army. A generals' coup in 1989 failed, but only after most of the top officer corps were either killed in the coup or executed. By 1990, facing defeat, Mengistu renounced Marxism and initiated peace talks with the rebels. Despite this final effort, rebel forces continued to advance. As they entered the capital in 1991, Mengistu fled into exile in Zimbabwe as a guest of Robert MUGABE. Mengistu has always blamed the Soviet Union for abandoning him after the fall of Communism.

References: afr, CB, DAHB, EWB, PLBA, PLCA, RWWA, *wiki.*

MHKLAKAZA
(South Africa, 1800?–1857)

Mhklakaza was a Xhosa religious leader whose prophecies destroyed Xhosa society and caused the Xhosa people to lose their independence to British colonialism.

The British were aggressive in what they called their "civilizing policy," which introduced White settlers among the Xhosa, reduced the power of their chiefs, and forced them into contract labor. Whites were settled in Xhosa lands in a checkerboard pattern, and the chiefs' authority was severely limited, with White magistrates assuming much of their jurisdiction. Chiefs were compensated with stipends and were expected to collect a hut tax from the people as well as to enforce labor on public works such as roads. The loss of land and economic dislocation caused enormous population pressures as groups were shifted off their lands and refugees were forced to migrate from neighboring expropriated areas.

In this crisis, the Xhosa turned to a religious prophet, Mhklakaza, who was already a prophetic priestly figure in the court of a major chief. In 1856 his niece told him of a dream in which she had been given messages from the ancestors. Using her as a spirit medium, Mhklakaza called the Xhosa to a ritual purification in which they had to destroy all their worldly goods. Then the ancestors would send a whirlwind to cast the English into the sea, and ancient warrior heroes would rise from the dead, returning with vast stores of grain and cattle and even White man's trade goods. A new age of Xhosa wealth and power would be ushered in. The king and people were swept up into this vision, and in 1856–1857 no crops were planted, grain stores were burned, and over 150,000 cattle were slaughtered.

The promised day, 18 February 1857, came without the millennium, but Mhklakaza announced a new date, 28 May 1857, which also passed uneventfully. By then some 20,000 people had starved to death. An even larger number fled to Cape Colony, seeking employment to survive. The British governor seized the opportunity to expropriate land and establish a Ciskei district government. Mhklakaza died during the crisis, and Xhosa independence was utterly destroyed.

Reference: DAHB.

MICOMBERO, Michel
(Burundi, 1940–1983)

General Michel Micombero, the prime minister who made Burundi a republic and was its first president, is best known for unleashing a campaign of genocide against the Hutu people that resulted in the slaughter of more than 100,000 people.

A Tutsi from the south of the country, Micombero attended Catholic mission schools and then the local preparatory seminary, where he excelled in Greek and Latin. He joined the army in 1960 and was sent for officer's training in Belgium but was called home in 1962 as part of the army's indigenization program in preparation for independence. Within a few months, Burundi became independent and Micombero was promoted to captain. He joined the ruling party, which was closely allied with the cause of the king, Mwami MWAMBUTSA IV. So tiny was the educated class of Tutsi that Micombero was given the defense portfolio in the government at the age of 23. An uprising by the Hutu was suppressed with thousands of deaths, and Micombero was promoted to chief secretary of state. Mwambutsa, who had gone to Europe during the insurrection, continued to govern from overseas.

In 1966, Micombero conspired with Mwambutsa's son, Crown Prince Charles, to depose the monarch; Charles was proclaimed Mwami Ntare V. In turn, Micombero was named prime minister, but he and Ntare were soon at odds. Ntare failed in an attempt to dismiss Micombero, and Micombero took advantage of the *mwami*'s absence on a state visit to depose him, proclaim a republic, and assume the presidency. Micombero announced a policy of national reconciliation, freeing a number of Hutu political prisoners and denouncing tribalism. Unfortunately, his actions belied his words. The Hutu constituted 85 percent of the population and the Tutsi only 14 percent, but Tutsi domination at all levels continued. By 1969, however, there was serious dissension among both groups, with the Tutsi rallying around the monarchist cause and the Hutu fearing that they would be the objects of government pogroms.

Ntare returned to Burundi in 1972 at a particularly tense time during a trial of alleged Tutsi conspirators. Micombero had the *mwami* arrested and executed and then dismissed his cabinet, ruling by decree. Returning Hutu exiles rose against him, and in a bloody reprisal, Micombero had them massacred. Almost all the educated Hutu were killed, and the final estimates of deaths range from 100,000 to 200,000. More than 100,000 again fled into exile. Micombero descended into alcoholism and became erratic. Burundi sank into confusion, harried by Hutu guerrillas and with an economy in the midst of collapse. In 1976 the military under Jean Baptiste BAGAZA deposed Micombero and he went into exile in Somalia, which was ruled by his close friend General Mohammed SIYAD BARRE. He earned a degree in economics at the University of Somalia a year before he died of a heart attack.

References: afr, DAHB, DRWW, MMA, PLBA, *wiki*.

MILINGO, Emmanuel
(Zambia, 1930–)

Archbishop Emmanuel Milingo, deposed Catholic archbishop of Lusaka, Zambia, has been at the center of a bitter controversy affecting Christianity in Africa. In attempting to silence his views by removing him to Rome, the Vatican has in fact internationalized the controversy and created partisans for Milingo's beliefs.

Milingo is an Nguni who was raised in the warrior tradition. At age 12, after four years as a cattle herder, he ran away to enter a mission school. It was an astounding break with his childhood. Milingo was illiterate, spoke only Nguni, and had never been outside his village. But he also possessed the qualities of tenacity, strength and single-mindedness. Within two years he spoke and read English and Chewa and was ready for further education. Until 1958 he attended seminaries in Nyasaland (now Malawi). Then he served as a parish priest from 1958 to 1965, with a two-year hiatus in which he obtained diplomas in sociology in Rome and education in Dublin.

In 1965, Milingo went to Lusaka as an assistant for communications to the Zambian Bishops' Conference, and his radio ministry made him a popular national figure. He also started the Zambia Helpers' Society, a volunteer group, to bring health care to the shantytowns. He participated in their work on a daily basis following his other responsibilities. In 1969 he was named the first African archbishop of Lusaka.

Milingo's tenure as archbishop fostered a religious and spiritual revolution. Recognizing how deeply his Western education had separated him from his African background, he began Africanizing institutions, practices and attitudes, making many foreign missionaries uncomfortable. He set up women's councils at all levels and fostered grassroots Basic Christian Communities (BCCs). He also founded a community of sisters, the Daughters of the Redeemer, which has become the center of his thought and work in Africa. Milingo did not operate in Western style, and some Christian followers and colleagues found him paternalistic and overbearing.

Milingo believes in the existence and everyday significance of a spirit world, including the power of the devil. Increasingly, people came to him for healing, until there were complaints that he had time for nothing else. The sick besieged his home, lining the stairs, and his healing services at the cathedral were crowded. He drove out evil spirits, cured the sick, and mobilized the people. In 1976, at a training session in Ann Arbor, Michigan, Milingo found a spiritual bridge between his African heritage and his firm (and rather conservative) religious faith. He joined the Catholic charismatic renewal movement that was then growing throughout the Catholic and Episcopal Churches and found allies in that movement for his later conflicts. He continued his social reforms as well and began to denounce the wealthy African elite for commercialism and exploiting the poor.

The issue that Milingo brought to a crisis was inculturation—the development of an authentic African Christianity growing out of African values, including spiritual ones. Inculturation challenged Western control of African Christianity and its Western cultural roots. It was not enough for Milingo to use local languages or include traditional dancing in services; the African Christian's mentality had to be liberated from colonialism. Africans had to overcome a sense of cultural inferiority and validate their religious experience. Although the arguments over inculturation often concerned the spirit world, the heart of the controversy was the assumption that peoples of color are not inferior but that they have wisdom that the West neither possesses nor acknowledges.

Opposition was swift in making itself felt. The Jesuits, who had founded the Zambian Catholic missions and named the previous bishops, were strong opponents of the new approaches. In addi-tion, Milingo's fellow Zambian bishops were equally troubled. Accusations focused on his healing ministry and exorcisms, which attracted over a thousand people to each cathedral service. Milingo was accused of heresy, witchcraft and misuse of money. Outrageous stories were fabricated about him, and although they were disproved, they left a legacy of mistrust. Among the worst tales his pastoral coordinator reported secretly to the Vatican was that Milingo had made the superior of the Daughters pregnant and then arranged an abortion. The result of the controversies was a discreet diplomatic request to the Vatican by President Kenneth KAUNDA, followed by an investigation led by a conservative African cardinal known for his hostility to recognizing the spirit world. In 1979, Milingo was forced to cease healing services, and in 1982 he was ordered to Rome for a rest and psychiatric examinations.

The doctors cleared Milingo, but by that time he was too divisive a figure to return home. He resigned from his diocese and accepted a minor post on the Vatican Commission for Migration and Tourism. He continued his healing work, both with individuals and before large crowds at a monthly service in Rome. Then came Milingo's most bizarre behavior. He became a supporter to Reverend Sun Myung Moon's Unification Church and in 2001, he married a Korean woman chosen for him by Reverend Moon. After Pope John Paul II reprimanded him, Milingo annulled the marriage and reconciled with the Church. He then spent a year in prayer and penance in Argentina.

Milingo's influence, especially through the charismatic renewal movement, was felt throughout the Catholic Church. He has retired and keeps a low profile today.

References: *dacb, wiki.* Gerrie Ter Haar, *Spirit of Africa* (1992); www.archbishopmilingo.org.

MKHATSHWA, Smangaliso Patrick
(South Africa, 1939–)

Reverend Smangaliso Patrick Mkhatshwa is one of the generation of religious activists, along with Beyers NAUDÉ, Desmond TUTU and Frank CHIKANE, who brought the Churches into the anti-apartheid movement in South Africa.

After studies at St. Peter's Seminary during its period of integration, Mkhatshwa was ordained a Catholic priest and spent five years in parish work. In 1970 he began working for the South African Catholic Bishops' Conference, but after a year he was sent to Belgium, where he took philosophy and theology degrees at Louvain University.

Returning to the Bishops' Conference in 1973, Mkhatshwa headed a number of offices, including Justice and Peace, Ecumenism, and finally, in 1981, he became general secretary. His appointment was a major statement on the part of the Catholic bishops, because by 1981 Mkhatshwa was a leading exponent of South African liberation theology. By 1974 he had already organized the Black Renaissance Convention, a dialogue of Black African, Coloured, and Indian leaders.

After the Soweto riots, he was imprisoned for four months. Upon his release he was placed under a five-year banning order, which forbade him to receive guests or to enter any Black township or educational institution. Beginning in 1977, he was imprisoned for another five months during the government crackdown on African community organizations. Then, after attending a prayer meeting at the University of Fort Hare, he served five months more in the Ciskei Homeland in 1983 and 1984. The Ciskei court denied him visits, mail and exercise during his confinement.

His keynote address to the National Education Crisis Conference at the University of the Witwatersrand in 1985 was a major influence on the freedom movement's acceptance of student participation. The following year, he was a member of the delegation of South African Church leaders that met with the exiled leadership of the African National Congress (ANC) in Lusaka, Zambia.

In 1986, Mkhatshwa was arrested under emergency regulations, along with Zwelakhe SISULU, Sister Bernard NCUBE, and other religious figures. During this imprisonment he was tortured for 30 hours by members of the South African military, and upon release he sued and won R25,000 ($10,000). It was the first time the government had been forced to pay compensation to a South African political prisoner. Shortly thereafter, he was received by Pope John Paul II in Rome in a demonstration of solidarity by the Vatican. He has been awarded honorary doctorates by Georgetown University in Washington, DC, and by Tübingen University in Germany.

Mkhatshwa left the Catholic Secretariat in 1988 and became general secretary of the Institute for Contextual Theology, a leading research center. In the 1994 elections he was elected to the South African parliament as an ANC member. In 1999 he became deputy minister of education, and the following year he was elected to the ANC National Executive.

Mkhatshwa was elected mayor of Tshwane (Pretoria) in 2000. This city is now a merger of 11 municipalities, and it has major challenges supplying water, sanitation, electricity and housing. He has attacked these problems with characteristic organization and verve, producing, for example, some 10,000 housing units a year during his term. In 2006, his term was not renewed, evidently due to infighting in the ANC and a new quota system requiring that half of all ANC election lists comprise women.

References: dacb, GSAP.

MKANDAWIRE, Thandika

(Malawi, 1940–)

Since 1998, Thandika Mkandawire has been executive secretary of the United Nations Research Institute for Social Development (UNRISD). For 16 years (1980–1996) he was deputy, then executive secretary of the Council for the Development of Social Science Research in Africa (CODESRIA).

As a young man, Mkandawire was an editor at the *Malawi News*. He then began studies overseas, with degrees in economics from the Ohio State University and the University of Stockholm. During this time he spent a year in Ecuador and a period as a research and teaching fellow at the International Institute of Labour Studies in Geneva. After finishing studies, Mkandawire taught at the University of Zimbabwe before joining CODESRIA in 1980.

CODESRIA is the premier social-science coordinating group on the continent, with links to scholarly associations in the United States, Canada and Europe. It facilitates Pan-African collaboration in the social sciences across disciplines, language groupings and geographic regions. Mkandawire's multidisciplinary competence served CODESRIA well as it expanded into considerations of gender politics.

Mkandawire's writing (eight books and a number of articles and reports) covers a range of African issues with depth of analysis. He has published two works on the effects of structural adjustment programs on agriculture and several on democratization on the continent. His most recent work departs from those economic issues to take up the question of intellectual leadership in Africa. In *African Intellectuals* (2005), Mkandawire discusses the interconnections among gender, politics, language and development. His current research and writing concerns crisis management in African states.

He serves on the editorial boards of four scholarly development journals and a number of international councils and federations, mostly dealing with labor issues.

Reference: www.codesria.org.

MKWATI
(Zimbabwe, ?–1897)

Mkwati was a prophetic cult leader in the service of Mwari, the high god in Shona traditional religion. He was involved in a revolt against the British. Because he was a religious figure endowed with magical powers, accounts of his life are often embroidered with legendary details, but the main outlines of his life are clear.

Mkwati was born in what is now western Zambia, where he was captured by Ndebele raiders and taken as a slave. He was working in a military town when he became a "messenger" of the high god, Mwari. He continued his religious duties throughout the British occupation of 1893–1894, establishing a prophetic shrine, a place where the gods would send messages to the people. The collapse of the Ndebele kingdom with the establishment of British rule in Southern Rhodesia (now Zimbabwe) only increased Mkwati's popular following. He achieved considerable status among the Ndebele and was able to marry the daughter of a Shona chief. The Ndebele, like several other ethnic groups in southern Africa, included a majority of members who had been adopted, absorbed after conquest, or joined the community voluntarily after their own clans had broken up. Mkwati attracted these immigrant fragments.

Around 1896, Mkwati led an anti-British revolt at the same time that the Ndebele leadership also mounted an insurrection. The extent of the collaboration between these two movements is disputed, as is the degree to which the two simultaneous rebellions were religiously or politically motivated. Robert BADEN-POWELL, chief staff officer in the British forces, wrote that Mkwati was a *mlimo,* a god-like personality, and certainly warriors in both rebel groups regarded him as a man of magical powers. By late in the year, however, the Ndebele chiefs were willing to negotiate with Cecil RHODES, and Mkwati angrily left for Shona territory to join a separate uprising that had begun there. He allied himself with Shona religious cult leaders to attempt to persuade the chiefs to resist the British, but the savagery of the British response caused many to come to terms with them. As Mkwati moved further north, he was assassinated by a Shona group who had lost faith in his magic and his policy.

Reference: DAHB.

MKWAWA
(Tanzania, ?–1898)

Mkwawa, paramount chief of the Hehe peoples, offered the stiffest military resistance to the Germans during the period of their imperialist drive on Tanganyika. His formal name was Mkwavunyika Munyigumba Mwamuyinga, and the shortened form means "Conqueror of Many Lands."

Mkwawa was the son of a chief who first unified the Hehe by adopting the technique of military organization by age-sets and absorption of captured foreigners into society as quickly and completely as possible. The Hehe ably defended themselves and created a small kingdom in what is now southern Tanzania. Mkwawa succeeded his father in 1879 after a brief struggle with a rival. At first, he continued his father's policy of expansion eastward, subduing neighboring peoples and supporting his campaigns by cattle and ivory raids. The Germans, however, were pressing inland against resistance. Coastal Arabs rebelled against them, and several African groups actively stood firm. The Germans tried to court Mkwawa with a treaty, but he was suspicious and unwilling to travel to meet them; he even cut the trade routes from the coast. The Germans sent a military force, while Mkwawa dispatched a delegation bearing gifts, to seek a peace agreement. Thinking them warriors, the Germans killed them all. Mkwawa mounted an ambush with

3,000 warriors in which he killed the German commissioner and 290 troops, at that time one-tenth of the entire German force in East Africa.

The Germans now concentrated their forces against the Hehe. For three years the war went on, with Mkwawa attacking trade caravans and German patrols. Finally in 1894, a large German force took Kalenga, Mkwawa's fortified capital. Mkwawa retreated into the bush to continue with guerrilla warfare for four more years, but his followers gradually dropped away until he was left with only two young pages. In 1898 a German patrol found him, and Mkwawa shot himself to avoid capture. With his death, the resistance to the Germans ended.

Reference: DAHB, *wiki.*

MMANTHATISI
(Lesotho/South Africa, 1781?–1835?)

Queen Mmanthatisi was regent and leader of the Tlokwa peoples, a clan of the Sotho, during the *difaqane* or *mfecane,* the period of general Nguni migrations and political changes that resulted from the destructive expansion of the Zulu empire under SHAKA. The Zulu and the Ngoni, under ZWAN-GENDABA, expanded outward in a series of migrations, destroying the existing clan system, absorbing the remnants, and creating new national societies. All the smaller and weaker groups either had to copy their methods or retreat into secure mountain areas.

Mmanthatisi was the principal wife of the Tlokwa chief, and her son, the heir, was only 13 years old when the chief died. To avoid having the chieftaincy taken by her husband's brother, Mmanthatisi ruled as regent while she sent the boy away for the traditional circumcision ceremony, which involved lengthy coming-of-age rites. Female regents were not unknown among the Sotho, who also had battalions of female warriors led by the daughters of chiefs. Almost immediately she had to contend with attacks from the Nguni, and she chose to lead her people in a migratory pattern. The Tlokwa raided and absorbed smaller groups as they wandered over the next several years.

Mmanthatisi received numbers of refugees from shattered communities, and the Tlokwa became a powerful force as their numbers swelled. Because she was a woman, fearsome stories were told of her prowess as a warrior, and the Tlokwa were credited with a number of raids that were actually conducted by others. This general fear and respect served as a useful protective shield, but Mmanthatisi also suffered her share of defeats. When she invaded Lesotho, MOSHWESHWE I drove her back. In one major battle, she had sent her troops out to forage for food when the enemy attacked. Lining up the women and children, she charged the surprised foes, who fled in terror when they saw an endless line of what they thought were warriors. Her military genius and audacity saved the day.

By 1824, exhausted by wandering, Mmanthatisi settled the Tlokwa in what is now northern Lesotho, and her son, Sekonyela, assumed the chieftaincy. She continued to exercise authority as queen mother and chief advisor to her son until her death. Deprived of her wise counsel, Sekonyela challenged Moshweshwe for dominance and was badly defeated, and the Tlokwa were absorbed into the Sotho kingdom.

Reference: DAHB. David Sweetman, *Woman Leaders in African History* (1984).

MMUSI, Peter Simako
(Botswana, 1929–)

Peter Simako Mmusi was vice president of Botswana from 1983 to 1992 and also has held a number of ministerial posts. Raised in South Africa, where his father worked in the mines, he completed teacher's college there and taught in Botswana for 10 years before entering government service. As part of the transition to independence in 1965, Mmusi was appointed commissioner of labor, a secure civil service position from which he resigned in 1974 in order to enter politics.

Mmusi was a favorite of President Sir Seretse KHAMA, who appointed him to several ministries, including the major one of Home Affairs, where he was in charge of all internal security. In the 1979 elections Mmusi defeated the leader of the opposition, Dr. Kenneth Koma, further ingratiating himself with Khama. Mmusi was elected Botswana Democratic Party (BDP) chairman in 1981. He continued to serve in the cabinet after Khama's death, and President Quett MASIRE appointed him vice president in 1983. The following year Mmusi retained his seat against Koma, but ballot tampering was discovered, and in the subsequent election Mmusi was defeated. Masire then made him a "nominated" (appointed, rather than elected) member of parliament. Although Mmusi lost considerable influence during this time, he reestablished himself in the 1989 elections by winning handily in his home district. However, he lacked a strong popular base and is politically dependent on the BDP.

Mmusi is a technocrat of great competence and has represented Botswana well in international economic matters. He has been chair of the Southern African Development Coordination Conference since its foundation and is the acknowledged leader of African delegations to the International Monetary Fund and the World Bank. His influence was again damaged, however, when he was implicated in a land transaction scandal, and he was forced to resign as vice president in 1992. He remains on the leadership team of the BDP in a very reduced role.

References: PLBA, RWWA.

MNTHALI, Felix
(Malawi/Botswana, 1933–)

Dr. Felix Mnthali is a leading Malawian poet and a longtime critic of repressive government in his country.

Mnthali was educated at the University of Lesotho. He later took advanced degrees at the University of Alberta in Canada. He returned to teach at the University of Malawi, where he was a founder of the Writers' Group in the 1970s, with Jack MAPANJE and a few others, mostly poets. Not only did the Writers' Group foster the development of a robust poetry scene, it also provided a covert space for dissidents under the autocratic government of Dr. Hastings Kamuzu BANDA. They were soon exposed, and on the day he was to receive his full professorship, Mnthali was arrested and spent a year in the notorious Zomba Prison. When he was released, he could not find work and went into exile in Botswana. He has been a professor of English at the University of Botswana ever since.

Many of the themes of Mnthali's poetry come from current issues about which he feels passionately. During the regime of Dr. Banda, he often wrote of oppression and censorship, and the mindless suppression of intellectuals. He has continued his political poetry since Banda's fall, indicting not only the successor government but also that of other countries. His denunciation of Malawi's government

after Banda shows his dashed hopes: "The fear we thought we had banished from our political consciousness . . is now back."

His elegy for Ken SARO-WIWA is a powerful voice for the voiceless peasants of the Niger Delta. His range can be broader, however, as in "Letter to a Feminist Friend," in which he attacks the influence of Western ideas of women's liberation on African women. He shows his disappointment in the failed dreams that independence promised and never delivered.

Perhaps the most noted of his poems has been the biting "The Stranglehold of English Literature," in which he laments the effects of classical British literature on the educated African mind. That he chose not to frame his lament in an essay makes it all the more pungent, and the piece is widely anthologized in collections of postcolonial literature. Mnthali's work weaves Malawian and African symbols with his vision of African Christianity.

Reference: adb.

MOBUTU Sese Seko
(Democratic Republic of the Congo, 1930–1997)

Mobutu Sese Seko, a tyrant and ruthless opportunist who has ruled his country for 30 years, took over a nation that was in chaos and violence, and imposed order on it through state terrorism. In the 1990s, the Democratic Republic of the Congo (DRC) again slid into anarchy as his power came to an end.

Born Joseph-Désiré Mobutu in the Équateur Province of what was then the Belgian Congo, Mobutu was unruly as a child, moving from one school to another until he assaulted a schoolmaster in 1950, for which he was expelled and conscripted into the colonial army for seven years. When he was mustered out, having reached the rank of sergeant-major, Mobutu attracted the attention of a Belgian publisher, who employed him as an editorial writer in Léopoldville (now Kinshasa). His new prominence earned him a trip to the 1958 Brussels World's Fair, and he used the opportunity to obtain an internship with the Congolese propaganda bureau and to develop useful contacts with the U.S. Central Intelligence Agency (CIA). At the same time, he joined with Patrice LUMUMBA, the leading radical Congolese nationalist. Mobutu directed Lumumba's Brussels office and represented

Sese Seko Mobutu

his movement at pre-independence talks with the government in early 1960.

The Belgian Congo became independent on 1 July 1960 with little preparation. Lumumba was named prime minister and Joseph KASAVUBU, a moderate, was made president of the new Congo Republic. There were fewer than 20 university graduates, and among these there was not a single physician, lawyer, engineer, military officer, economist or public administrator. Any sort of training or ability was in demand, and Mobutu was named army chief of staff. Within a few weeks, the army mutinied and the country tottered on the brink of civil war. Mobutu traveled tirelessly around the country, rallying the troops during July and August 1960. In effect, he was building a power base for himself, sending unreliable units to remote districts and breaking up those with tribal allegiances. By controlling payrolls and promotions, he bound officers to his personal service and directed foreign military aid to units loyal to himself. He received support from the U.S. government through the CIA, which deeply distrusted Lumumba's ties to the Communist bloc. By September, Kasavubu and Lumumba were locked in a struggle for power.

Katanga (now Shaba), the mineral-rich southern province with its own army, declared independence under Moïse TSHOMBE. Mobutu intervened, capturing Lumumba and turning him over in February 1961 to Tshombe (who had him murdered). Kasavubu was retained in office, but over the next four years Mobutu was the real power. When Kasavubu attempted to act independently in 1965, Mobutu removed him and named himself president.

Until 1972, Mobutu followed the common path of African despots, creating a one-party state built upon a security apparatus. He eliminated competing military detachments, including the Katanga forces, regional paramilitary units, and the European mercenaries he had used to maintain power during several rebellions. Besides his own troops, Mobutu created a state security agency that suppressed all opposition. The vast Belgian multinational holdings were reduced, but new linkages were forged with Western banks and multinationals without colonial experience in the country. State income came from selling mineral rights to foreign corporations, extensive foreign aid grants, and higher taxes on foreign investors. Much of this money disappeared into the pockets of Mobutu and his closest associates, as affairs came to be run by extortion and bribery.

Mobutu positioned himself well in the Cold War as a staunch anti-Communist with U.S. ties. When critics of his human rights abuses questioned U.S. support for his regime, he would threaten to switch to Soviet patronage. In 1973 he made an ostentatious visit to China and North Korea as a demonstration of his "independence" from the West. Mobutu continued this cynical approach to foreign policy, taking aid from both sides. Under U.S. President Jimmy Carter, who was very critical of his human rights record, Mobutu still received one-half of all U.S. aid going to sub-Saharan Africa. When Ronald Reagan became U.S. president, Mobutu allowed the CIA to establish secret bases in the DRC from which to pursue covert operations on behalf of Jonas SAVIMBI and Holden ROBERTO, who were then conducting guerrilla warfare against the Marxist government of Angola.

At home, Mobutu developed an elaborate personality cult that presented him as the "guide of the revolution," or, finally, "the messiah." The television news opened always with a picture of Mobutu descending from the heavens on a cloud. In 1972 he began his campaign for "African authenticity" (*authenticité*), identifying the national destiny with himself. He dropped his Christian names and became Mobutu Sese Seko—in full, Mobutu Sese Seko Nkuku Ngbendu wa za Banga, "the all-conquering warrior, going from strength to strength, leaving fire in his wake." He renamed the country Zaïre and ordered all Christians to take new African names. Until this time Mobutu's only internal critic had been the Catholic Church, and this new policy brought the conflict to a crisis. The Church's head, Cardinal Joseph MALULA, was forced into exile, Catholic youth movements were closed down, and in 1974 religious schools were nationalized. Mobutu's great mistake in this campaign of "authenticity" was what he called "the Zaïrianization of the economy." He nationalized foreign holdings and then looted them, passing some of the stolen funds to his cronies. When the businesses were returned a few years later, few could be rebuilt, and the economy began a slide into total collapse.

Mobutu's leadership was not without opposition. Besides early Lumumbist revolts, there were invasions from Shaba Province in 1977 and 1978 and numerous coup attempts. In 1980, 13 members of parliament, led by Étienne wa Malumba TSHISIKEDI, challenged the regime and advocated a multiparty system. Mobutu responded by imprisoning Tshisikedi in a psychiatric hospital. In 1981 his prime minister fled to Belgium and began criticizing the government from exile. By 1989, Mobutu's reputation cost him much of his support, and U.S. disengagement from the Angolan crisis left him a relic of the Cold War. That same year, after Mobutu scorned a Belgian offer of debt forgiveness, the Belgian media (using obvious leaks from the government) exposed the estimated US$5 billion that he had in overseas bank accounts and his extensive property holdings in Europe, including 11 palaces.

In 1990, Mobutu came under intense pressure to introduce reforms. After 100 students were killed in a confrontation with police, Mobutu announced political reforms but was unprepared for the suppressed antagonism that was unleashed. A 1991 National Conference was attended by 200 new political groupings who chose Tshisikedi as prime minister. Mobutu fired him after a few months, but Tshisikedi refused to leave, and Zaïre now had two competing governments. In the meanwhile, Mobutu's term of office expired, and the National Conference elected Archbishop Laurent Monsengwo, Mobutu's leading Church critic, as its president pending elections. This event led to two competing congresses as Mobutu rejected the National Conference and convened his own under the protective guns of the presidential guard.

After 1991 there was an unceasing round of strikes, riots, urban lawlessness, and at least two regional ethnic conflicts. The government introduced three new currencies in attempts to curb inflation, but the money became worthless almost immediately. The latest currency had lost 93 percent of its value in three months, and by December 1993 it was being exchanged at 110 million zaïres to the dollar. Inflation varied from 1,000 to 6,000 percent a year. In 1993, the army mutinied when it was paid in worthless five-million zaïre notes, which no stores would accept. Exports fell by 90 percent between 1990 and 1994. Whole regions of the country were without any governmental authority, and much of the infrastructure had broken down. Amid all this chaos, Mobutu rarely left his pink marble palace in Équateur Province. When forced to go to Kinshasa, he stayed on his yacht in the Congo River, perhaps in fear for his life. In May 1994, *The New York Times* described Zaïre as "the stateless country."

In 1996, Motubu went to Europe for cancer treatment, and in his absence, the Rwandese genocide spilled over into Zaïre. Laurent KABILA marched on Kinshasa, gathering strength as he moved across the country. Mobutu finally fled to Morocco, where he died, unmourned.

References: AB, *afr*, CB, CBB, DAHB, DRWW, DT, EB, EWB, HWL, PLBA, PLCA, RWWA, *wiki*. Michael Schatzberg, *Mobutu or Chaos?* (1991).

MODISE, Johannes "Joe"
(South Africa, 1929–2001)

Johannes "Joe" Modise, former commander of Umkhonto we Sizwe (Spear of the Nation), the armed guerilla wing of the African National Congress (ANC), was minister of defense in the first government of Nelson MANDELA.

After dropping out of secondary school, Modise worked as a truck driver and joined the ANC Youth League at age 18. He began working as a youth organizer in the early 1950s and led resistance to the Bantu Education Act (1953), which mandated inferior education for Blacks. He was arrested in 1954 during resistance to the Sophiatown removals, when Blacks were deported to rural areas so that Sophiatown could be made into a White suburb of Johannesburg. In 1956 he was accused of treason, although the charges were later dismissed. His open activities ended when the ANC was banned in 1960 and Umkhonto was formed, with Modise in its military high command. For three years he recruited and sent young militants out of the country. When his role was revealed to the South African police by captured recruits who had been tortured, he left the country.

To that point, the cadres had engaged in bombings and other acts of destabilization but had had little formal training. Modise went to Czechoslovakia and the Soviet Union for a year, and after Mandela's arrest and trial (1962–1964), Modise was named commander of Umkhonto in 1965. He arranged arms shipments and established training camps in Tanzania, dividing his time between Tanzania and Zambia, where he had Umkhonto join operations against Rhodesia, in concert with Joshua NKOMO's Zimbabwe African People's Union (ZAPU). During the early 1970s, Modise concentrated on building up underground guerrilla groups within South Africa, and in 1976 they began military action. That year the Soweto student riots brought a flood of new recruits, many of them street youths with little discipline or ideological commitment to the ANC. Some were secret agents of the South African police. There were camp mutinies and serious discipline problems, which were dealt with harshly, often by torture and beatings. In 1993 an ANC investigation commission criticized Modise for his improper arrests and involvement in human rights abuses in the camps in the early 1980s. Modise could act with vengeance when he thought it necessary. At one point, he plotted the assassination of Chris HANI, whom he suspected of planning a coup against the ANC leadership. Only Oliver TAMBO stopped it

As a longtime member of the ANC executive, Modise took part in negotiations with the government after the ANC was legalized. In Mandela's new government he was named minister of defense, a post he held from 1994 to 1999. Here he faced a difficult task, not only to reduce the forces to free up a budget heavily committed to the armed forces, but also to find employment within the army for 30,000 former Umkhonto fighters and soldiers from homeland forces who had been promised that they could continue their careers. This problem was only slightly relieved by the end of conscription. Modise reappointed the White generals he had fought against, and agreed with them that South Africa's short-term solution to financing the military lay in entering the international trade in arms. He was criticized for giving contracts for arms to friends and was suspected of corruption.

After leaving government, Modise became chair of Labat Africa, a brewery. He was a late convert to capitalism, but entered business with the same enthusiasm he had brought to everything he did.
References: *adb*, GSAP, RWWA, *wiki*.

MOFFAT, Howard Unwin
(Zimbabwe, 1869–1951)

Howard Unwin Moffat, prime minister of Southern Rhodesia from 1927 to 1933, was born in South Africa, the grandson of pioneer missionary Robert MOFFAT.

Moffat served in the Bechuanaland Border Patrol, and in 1893 he joined the stream of White migrants to Southern Rhodesia, where he prospered as a settler. He saw military service against the Matabele and in the Boer War.

The British South Africa Company administered the colony and, during the last years of this arrangement, Moffat was elected to the Legislative Council (Legco), serving from 1920 to 1923. In 1922 the settlers voted for self-government, which Britain granted. Moffat entered the new Legislative Assembly and immediately became a member of Charles COGHLAN's cabinet as minister of mines and public works. This role put Moffat in a prominent position, and after Coghlan died in 1927, he succeeded him as premier.

From 1900 to 1935, Southern Rhodesia had one of the largest White populations in sub-Saharan Africa, reaching over 35,000. About a third were born in the Rhodesias, one-third were immigrants from Britain, and one-third were immigrants from South Africa. The alienation of land was the most serious issue facing Moffat's administration, especially because Whites had created huge commercial farms that placed the greatest amount of arable land in the hands of a tiny minority. Africans could not compete for desirable land. Under Moffat's administration Africans controlled 45,000 acres compared to 31 million acres owned by Whites. Much of the White land was not farmed but was held for speculation. The Land Apportionment Act (1931) resolved the question in favor of the White settlers, and by allotting sections of the country by racial groups, it became the basis for later segregation. Refused permission to grow the most valuable cash crops, African peasants were forced into farm labor for Whites at starvation wages. The extent of this forced labor was greater in Southern Rhodesia than elsewhere in British Africa.

The challenge of worldwide depression that began during his term caused Moffat's downfall, as commodity prices plunged for all of Rhodesia's exports. In 1931 a new group, the Reform Party, formed around Godfrey HUGGINS, and by 1933, Moffat had resigned, alleging poor health. Within a year Huggins was prime minister and Moffat retired to private life.

Reference: DAHB, *wiki.*

MOFFAT, Robert
(South Africa, 1795–1883)

Robert Moffat, a pioneering Scottish Protestant missionary and Bible translator, was the father and founder of missionary work in South Africa.

Moffat came from a simple Scottish family and was apprenticed as a gardener. After a conversion experience, he applied for missionary work and was accepted by the London Missionary Society (LMS) in 1816. His first years in South Africa were spent in Namaqualand, where he converted a chief who was sought by the local colonial authorities. Moffat earned government support when officials realized that he had solved a problem through his religious efforts. Moffat also explored the Kalahari Desert and, as a result, was named to head a mission station. On his way he encountered a flood of refugees fleeing the advance of the Ndebele under MZILIKAZI. These people soon took over a number of villages, and Moffat rushed to warn the neighboring communities. In a fierce struggle, the refugees were driven off. Moffat's reputation among the people he saved was immensely enhanced.

In 1824 he went on to Kuruman, the northernmost outpost in South Africa. Here, despite raids by bandits and other difficulties, he stayed for half a century. Moffat was an indefatigable linguist. Within a year he had completed a grammar of SeTswana and had begun translating the Gospel of Luke. In 1829 his missionary work finally bore fruit, and his services were crowded. Within a few years there were well-instructed converts, a flourishing school, and a permanent church.

Moffat made contacts with Mzilikazi and accepted an invitation to visit him in his kraal; as a result, a warm relationship developed between the two. In 1837 the Afrikaners began to penetrate the area and came into conflict with the Ndebele, causing the destruction of an American mission and the loss of many cattle. The Ndebele emigrated, and for a time Moffat lost contact with them. He used the time to take a sabbatical in England (1839–1843), where he completed his translation of the New Testament and Psalms and wrote a series of scripture lessons. He also met David LIVINGSTONE and recruited him for the mission. Livingstone was one of a group of young men who extended Moffat's work into the hinterland. On a recuperation visit to Kuruman, Livingstone met and married Moffat's daughter, Mary, in 1844.

This period was one of organizing and systematic evangelizing in southern Africa. Mission stations spread across the north of the country, and Moffat maintained supplies and communication. At the same time he completed his SeTswana Bible (1857), a translation of *The Pilgrim's Progress,* and a hymn book. He traveled extensively, even though he was by this time more than 60 years old. In 1854 he set out across the Kalahari Desert, covering over 700 miles (approximately 1,120 kilometers), a good deal of it by compass over uncharted country. He finally found his old friend Mzilikazi, and after reestablishing their friendship, he made arrangements for a permanent mission among the Ndebele. He returned in 1857 and again in 1859, personally manning the forge and taking part in constructing the necessary buildings. Moffat assumed a mythical and prophetic character among the Ndebele. A persistent—but false—legend has it that Moffat had foretold the coming of the Afrikaners before the Great Trek began and told the Ndebele to travel north.

By 1870 two of his children were dead, another was widowed, and his wife's health was precarious. The Moffats then returned to England, where his wife died. Covered with honors, Moffat spent his last years lecturing and promoting missionary work. He wrote several volumes of memoirs, which are valuable sources for the history of the region.

References: dacb, DAHB, DNB, EB, *wiki.* Jeremy Murray-Brown, *Faith and the Flag* (1977); W.C. Northcott, *Robert Moffat: Pioneer in Africa* (1961).

MOFOLO, Thomas Mokopu
(Lesotho, 1875?–1948)

Thomas Mokopu Mofolo, the first African novelist, was also an important influence on the development of writing in African languages.

Born into a devout Protestant family, he was educated in mission schools and received a teaching certificate. While he was teaching in South Africa and Lesotho, his inclination for storytelling caused friends to encourage him to begin writing. In 1906 he published *Moeti oa Bochabela* (translated from the Sesotho as *Traveller of the East* in 1934), which is considered the first novel by an African and the first in an African language. In 1910, Mofolo wrote *Pitseng,* and in 1912 completed his major work, *Chaka,* a historical romance about the Zulu king SHAKA. A later manuscript, a romantic novel about the Sotho ruler MOSHWESHWE I, was destroyed in a fire.

Mofolo's first two novels are more important for their historic than for their literary value. *Moeti* is a moral allegory about a young chief's conversion to Christianity that makes clever use of praise poems and traditional stories. *Pitseng* is an attempt at writing a European romance, but neither its style nor its themes are successful. Nevertheless, it went through nine printings, a sign of the hunger for vernacular writing among Sotho readers. In *Chaka,* however, Mofolo creates a heroic tragic character whose success breeds his downfall into cruelty, tyranny and insanity. It is a major work and has been translated into English, German, French, Igbo and Italian. Moving away from the Christian idealism of his earlier works, *Chaka* presents African religion in all its vigor, as Shaka sells his soul into sorcery in exchange for power. The mission press, Mofolo's only outlet, rejected the novel, and it was not published until 1925. It became a bestseller, but by then a disappointed Mofolo had given up writing.

In addition to writing, Mofolo held a variety of jobs, which included recruiting contract labor for the South African gold mines, shopkeeping, and farming. Evicted from his land in South Africa by the Bantu Land Act (because his plot adjoined that of a White owner), he returned to Lesotho destitute. He subsequently became active in the nationalist movement through the Basutoland Progressive Association.

References: AA, CA, DAHB, DLB, EB, EWB, MBW, MMA, WLTC. Daniel Kunene, *Thomas Mofolo and the Emergence of Written Sesotho Prose* (1989).

MOI, Daniel Torotich arap
(Kenya, 1924–)

Daniel Torotich arap Moi weathered numerous challenges to maintain himself in power since becoming president in 1978. In a country where powerful tribes coexist uneasily, he is a member of a minority group, the Kalenjin, a collection of even smaller ethnic groups that is best known for providing many of Kenya's outstanding long-distance runners.

Moi was educated in schools of the African Inland Mission, and the Government African School from 1943 to 1945, and then completed a teaching certificate at the Kapsabet Teachers' Training College in 1947. He taught and was a headmaster until 1955, when he was appointed to one of the African seats in the Legislative Council (Legco). In 1957, when the first elections were held, Moi was returned to the Legco with seven other Africans, including Oginga ODINGA and Tom MBOYA. Moi was sympathetic to the independence movement and visited Jomo KENYATTA during his long detention in the northwestern desert. Later official histories made much of Moi's hiding five Mau Mau guerrilla warriors who were being pursued by the British, but if it were true, the event was an exception to his usually cautious approach to independence politics. Odinga described him as "influenced by the missions, overawed by settler power and making a slow adjustment to political trends." He also called him "a giraffe with a long neck that saw from afar."

By 1960 he was head of the moderate Kenya African Democratic Union (KADU) and was named a delegate to the Lancaster House Conference in London that negotiated the terms of Kenya's independence. KADU brought the minority groups together and sought a regional constitution with significant authority given to local authorities. It also joined the common call for Kenyatta's freedom

Daniel Torotich arap Moi

and joined a coalition government with its main rival, the Kenya African National Union (KANU), Kenyatta's party. Moi became minister of education and then minister of local government.

After independence, Moi became head of the opposition in parliament, but Kenyatta brought him into KANU as a counterweight to more radical elements of his own party, including Odinga and Bildad KAGGIA. Moi became minister of home affairs, a powerful post that controlled police, internal security and immigration. When Odinga, the most important leader of the Luo people, was forced out as vice president in 1967, Moi was chosen as vice president and leader of government business in parliament. The selection avoided conflict among the powerful factions of the predominant Kikuyu ethnic group's elite and isolated the Luo entirely. Moi proved loyal to Kenyatta, shielding him from several crises, including the controversy following Mboya's assassination. In 1976, Moi was openly challenged by the main Kikuyu faction, wealthy business interests, and members of Kenyatta's family. Rallying minority politicians and a smaller Kikuyu faction, he outmaneuvered the opposition, which then conspired to assassinate him. When

Kenyatta died suddenly, Moi dramatically evaded police roadblocks set up to capture him. Officials loyal to the constitution came to his aid, and Moi was proclaimed president in 1978.

Moi swiftly consolidated his power. Convinced that tribalism was the root of political instability, he outlawed tribal political organizations. At the same time he placed his own Kalenjin people in high positions and allowed the Kikuyu leaders in his entourage to struggle for power among themselves. To counter continued Kikuyu dominance, he reached into the business community and helped to place minorities in posts where they would neutralize Kikuyu control of the economy. When several banks did not cooperate, he removed government deposits to destabilize their financial security. The end result was a stable but increasingly authoritarian government directed by a small group of cronies close to the president. This strategy enabled him to survive an attempted coup in 1982 that was led by the air force.

Moi announced a program called *Nyayo* (Footsteps) to show his continuation in the tradition of Kenyatta, the country's revered father. Moi remained popular for many years because Kenya enjoyed economic expansion and remained close to Great Britain. The country benefited from substantial Western foreign aid. Moi balanced a populist appeal to Africanization of the economy with protection for Indian business interests and foreign investments. Moreover, corruption was at first kept moderate. After Moi became more repressive and his confidants began to make excessive bribery demands, the populace turned against him as they experienced the effects of inflation and the growing world recession. In the early 1990s, political repression became more obvious and open. The press was placed under censorship, several magazines were banned and confiscated and their editors imprisoned. Student movements were savagely suppressed and the universities closed on several occasions. The Churches became his most severe critics, and an Anglican bishop was killed in a suspicious auto accident. Although Moi was usually able to manage his opposition with his considerable political skills, in 1990 his minister of foreign affairs was murdered and several members of the cabinet were implicated.

During the early 1990s, government policies encouraged violence between the Kalenjin and the Kikuyu, producing more than 50,000 internal refugees. The U.S. ambassador began a series of public criticisms of the government, forcing Moi to release political prisoners and allow greater judicial independence. In 1992, when his international aid donors made political reform a condition of assistance, Moi authorized multiparty elections. Again showing his political shrewdness, he encouraged divisions among his three rivals for the presidency and emerged with a plurality in the 1993 elections, receiving 36 percent of the vote to his nearest rival's 26 percent. He continued to maintain his balance as head of a fractious country, remaining in office by a combination of astute politics and manipulation. He again won in 1997, but by 2000, he had lost much popular appeal. Corrupt deals, one costing the Kenyan economy 10 percent of its GDP, were exposed and Moi and his sons were implicated. He was swept from office in 2002 by Mwai KIBAKI, his former vice president. His only foray into politics since retirement has been to oppose Kibaki's proposed constitution, which was defeated in a national referendum.

References: AB, *afr*, CB, CBB, DAHB, DRWW, EB, PLBA, PLCA, RWWA, *wiki*.

MOMOH, Joseph Saidu
(Sierra Leone, 1937–2003)

Major-General Joseph Saidu Momoh was the chosen successor of his mentor, President Siaka STEVENS, who governed Sierra Leone from 1968 to 1985. Momoh, however, lacked Stevens's political skills or popular following to maintain stability, and under him Sierra Leone began to face political and economic collapse.

Momoh completed secondary school in Freetown, the capital, before entering the army in 1955. After several years as an enlisted man, he was sent to Ghana and Nigeria for officers' training and was commissioned in 1963. During his training, Sierra Leone achieved its independence (1961). Momoh advanced rapidly as nationalization of the army occurred. He was a major and commander of the army training center by 1967, quartermaster-general the following year, and battalion commander in 1969. He was made armed forces commander in 1971 and was promoted to brigadier in 1973. In 1983 Momoh was the first Sierra Leonean to be appointed to major general.

In 1974, Stevens appointed Momoh to parliament as one of the members chosen by the president, and he was also appointed to the cabinet as minister of state for defense. Stevens and Momoh worked closely together, the general providing security for the elderly leader and Stevens becoming Momoh's political mentor, grooming him for the presidency. Stevens seems to have been disappointed in the caliber of civilians available and looked for a firm hand to continue his policies. In 1985, Momoh was elected president with broad public support.

Stevens evidently intended to govern from behind the scenes, and he soon began complaining that Momoh was not following his advice. The challenges Momoh faced, however, were massive. The government was thoroughly corrupt, the economy had seriously declined, and there were new political pressures for greater democratization. Momoh struggled unsuccessfully with the economic crisis. Inflation followed the imposition of strict economic controls mandated by the International Monetary Fund, and the government had to contend with the public disturbances that followed. Momoh fired a number of cabinet members for corruption and tried to stop smuggling and hoarding, but the level of venality was beyond his control.

The final crisis came from outside the country: a spillover from the civil war in neighboring Liberia. Momoh had favored a West African peacekeeping force to intervene and govern Liberia. Angry rebel forces from Liberia invaded Sierra Leone in retaliation. The Sierra Leonean army was hard-pressed to expel the invaders and only succeeded with support from Nigeria and Guinea. To garner broader domestic support in his exhausted country, Momoh agreed to multiparty elections for 1992. Before these elections could be held, Momoh was deposed by a coup led by junior officers, and he fled to Guinea. From there he sponsored a guerrilla force that controlled part of the country and hoped to reinstate him. Events overtook Momoh, however, and he was sidelined by the crisis and civil war that racked Sierra Leone. He died in exile.

References: PLBA, RWWA, *wiki*.

MONDLANE, Eduardo Chivambo
(Mozambique, 1920–1969)

Dr. Eduardo Chivambo Mondlane was the founder of FRELIMO, the Mozambican liberation movement, and Mozambique's greatest national hero.

Mondlane was educated in mission schools before going to South Africa for secondary education in 1944 because Portuguese policy allowed post-elementary education only for the elite. At the University of the Witwatersrand he was popular and was elected to the student council by the White student body. In 1948 new apartheid regulations led to his deportation. The Portuguese secret police (PIDE) accused him of having "been infected with the Communist virus" and recommended that he be sent to Portugal to keep him from infecting others. The result was exactly the opposite of what the Portuguese had sought. Mondlane forged bonds with nationalist leaders from other colonies, including Agostinho NETO of Angola and Amílcar CABRAL of Guinea-Bissau.

After a year of police harassment and raids, Mondlane accepted a scholarship to study in the United States, where he finally graduated from Ohio's Oberlin College in 1953. He went on to Northwestern University in Illinois, obtaining an MA and Ph.D. in anthropology. In 1957 he joined the staff of the United Nations (U.N.) Trusteeship Council. In 1961 he served on the plebiscite commission overseeing the elections in Cameroon, and then, protected by his U.N. passport, he visited Mozambique. He was warmly greeted by crowds everywhere and made contacts with underground liberation groups. He began teaching at Syracuse University in New York in 1961, but at the end of the school year he went to Tanzania to meet with the three main Mozambican resistance groups. In 1963 he moved his American wife and children to Tanzania.

After fashioning the resistance movements into the Front for the Liberation of Mozambique (FRELIMO), Mondlane's first task was to bring unity out of differing ethnic and ideological values. He himself preferred a socialist alternative to colonialism, but he operated within FRELIMO by democratic methods. FRELIMO's central committee was representative of various views and even included a few hardline Marxists, such as Samora MACHEL. The leftists accused Mondlane of pro-Western sympathies, and some to his right wanted a military end to Portuguese domination without a basic social transformation. Mondlane worked tirelessly to keep the two wings of the party together and also carried the burden of overseas diplomacy and fundraising. American Protestant churches were a financial mainstay for FRELIMO, as was the World Council of Churches.

In 1964, Mondlane announced the launch of the armed struggle against Portuguese colonialism. Networks within Mozambique were used to form internal resistance units and for recruitment of youths. Algeria provided military training. Between 1964 and 1968 about one-third of Mozambique was liberated through the guerrilla struggle, making it possible to hold FRELIMO's second congress within the country.

While the armed struggle went on, Mondlane founded the Mozambican Institute in Dar es Salaam, Tanzania, to educate refugee youths but also to provide a place for experimenting with the new Mozambican curricula. In 1968 a power struggle broke out within FRELIMO that resulted in several deaths. The Portuguese teachers at the institute were expelled, and the institute itself was closed in a conflict over race that targeted Mondlane's wife, Janet. In 1969 Mondlane was assassinated in Dar es Salaam by a parcel bomb. Only in the 1990s was it revealed that a secret "stay-behind" army of Portuguese soldiers working underground had killed him. Machel succeeded him. Mondlane is still revered as a national hero in Mozambique.

References: AB, DAHB, EWB, MMA, PLBA, PLCA, *wiki.* Mondlane, *The Struggle for Mozambique* (1983).

MONTEIRO, António Mascarenhas
(Cape Verde, 1944–)

Dr. António Mascarenhas Monteiro, longtime president of the supreme court and the most widely respected opposition figure for many years, became president of Cape Verde in 1991. He is one of the new democratic leaders to have emerged from public service rather than from the military or party politics.

After secondary school in Praia, the capital, Monteiro went to Portugal and studied law at the University of Lisbon and then received a master's degree at the University of Coimbra. Cape Verde was regarded in the colonial period as an integral part of Portugal, and when Monteiro became subject to military conscription, he left Portugal for Belgium, where he obtained his doctorate in law at the Catholic University of Louvain and began teaching. He joined the African Party of Independence for

Guinea and Cape Verde (PAIGC) in 1969 but two years later left in a dispute over its Marxist ideology. In 1977, Monteiro returned to Cape Verde, which had become independent in 1975. He became secretary-general of the national assembly, a senior staff post. He helped guide the country's first constitution through the assembly, and when it was adopted in 1980, Monteiro was named president of the supreme court. He was an activist jurist, leading Cape Verdean delegations abroad and working on legal questions for the Organization of African Unity (OAU), for which he helped draft a new charter of human rights.

In 1990 the ruling party, following democratic currents elsewhere in Africa, permitted popular election of the president and the registration of other political parties. A Lisbon-based opposition group, the Movement for Democracy, established itself first and negotiated a timetable for elections. In 1991 it won the parliamentary elections, and Monteiro, its presidential candidate, easily defeated Aristides PEREIRA, who had been president since 1975. He was re-elected in 1996 with 80 percent of the vote, but chose not to stand for re-election in 2001. Monteiro agreed to move toward a new constitutional arrangement that reduced his powers from those of executive president to those more typical in a parliamentary system. Cape Verde also began an economic reform policy based on International Monetary Fund conditions.

Reference: afr, RWWA.

MOSHWESHWE I
(Lesotho, 1786–1870)

Moshweshwe I, a gifted diplomat and ruler, was the founder and first king of Lesotho. Out of the disintegration of southern African traditional society caused by the *difaqane* or *mfecane* (the crushing), the Sotho people emerged as one of the few intact nations due to his foresight and ability. The name is often rendered Moshoeshoe.

Born the son of a petty chief of the crocodile clan of the Basuto, Moshweshwe established a small village as a base for cattle raiding, but by the 1820s it had become untenable. The impact of the *difaqane* began to reach into the central plateau, producing constant raids and warfare. The destabilization, in part caused by the rise of the Zulu empire under SHAKA, had a ripple effect as fleeing African communities, often devastated by earlier attacks, marauded over the plains in military bands. Roaming Nguni refugee groups touched off a series of regional wars lasting 20 years. Moshweshwe joined his father in the Drakensberg Mountains, moving until they found a small plateau on a steep-sided peak that provided natural defenses. This impregnable fortress was named Thaba Bosiu, "the mountain climbed at night." Thaba Bosiu came under attack several times, but as its reputation for security spread, refugee bands and whole clans began to seek its safety. Moshweshwe began to assimilate these disparate groups into a new nation, which called itself Sotho. One group introduced horses, which gave the Sotho mobility and control of the mountain valleys. By 1834, Moshweshwe ruled some 25,000 people, a number that would increase to 150,000 at the time of his death.

Moshweshwe formed a series of alliances against incursions, granting land to groups that formed buffers between Lesotho and potential enemies. He made close friends among the missionaries from the Paris Evangelical Mission, and although he never became a Christian, these contacts proved invaluable.

As the threat from the *difaqane* subsided, a new one appeared. Afrikaners, during the Great Trek northward from the Cape Colony to escape British rule (1835–1843), began to encroach on Sotho territory. Moshweshwe appealed to the British at Cape Colony for help, but while they defined the borders, they did nothing to dislodge the Afrikaners. A sequence of boundary limitations whittled away at Lesotho's borders, and Moshweshwe also had to contend with raids and continuing military conflict with the Afrikaners. In 1850 the British also attacked Thaba Bosiu but were repelled. Moshweshwe subsequently used diplomacy, employing missionary contacts in London to put pressure on the Colonial Office to forbid further military actions against the Sotho and to return some occupied lands. Despite this effort, the Cape governor determined to break Moshweshwe's power and marched a well-armed force to Lesotho, where he demanded 10,000 cattle as an indemnity, knowing that this would mean war. The governor now realized that he faced a confrontation that would surely be disastrous for both sides. Moshweshwe allowed the battle to last one day and then proclaimed himself a British subject. Accepting a "gift" of 3,000 cattle, the governor withdrew with his dignity intact.

Moshweshwe I

When the Orange Free State (OFS) was established as the first Boer republic in 1854, Moshweshwe was at first able to establish friendly relations with it. Within a year, however, a hostile president was elected, and armed skirmishes against the Sotho became common. Moshweshwe never abandoned diplomacy and negotiated procedures for settling disputes. Despite this, in 1858 the OFS attacked Thaba Bosiu, but Moshweshwe outflanked the Boer commandos and forced them to retreat. The two sides then signed the Treaty of Aliwal North to confirm their respective borders. Border conflicts continued to break out, and as Moshweshwe aged, his sons began to act independently. After a Sotho-Boer war that lasted from 1865 to 1866, Moshweshwe signed the Treaty of Thaba Bosiu, in which he lost the best of his farm lands. In 1867 another war broke out, but this time Moshweshwe was determined to accept British intervention.

By 1868 it was clear that power in southern Africa was moving into the hands of settlers as opposed to the British Colonial Office. The British, therefore, became a balance against local domination, which rarely considered any African personal or property rights. Moshweshwe had previously petitioned for a British protectorate without success, but in 1868, Lesotho gained that status, which allowed for internal self-rule and ended any Afrikaner attempts to encroach on its territory. Moshweshwe achieved autonomy for his people in a southern Africa that was otherwise mastered by Whites.

References: AB, DAHB, EWB, HH, MMA, WGMC, *wiki*. Peter Sanders, *Moshoeshoe, Chief of the Sotho* (1975).

MOSHWESHWE II
(Lesotho, 1938–1996)

Motlotlehi Moshweshwe II, paramount chief of the Sotho and former constitutional monarch (*motlotlehi*) of Lesotho, was long at the center of conflict in Lesotho politics, often exceeding his limited constitutional role and spending periods in exile or under house arrest. His name is often given as Moshoeshoe.

Moshweshwe was a direct descendant of MOSHWESHWE I, founder of Lesotho. He inherited the throne at age two when his father, Chief Seeiso Griffith, died. His stepmother acted as regent until 1960, when he returned home from Oxford University and was installed as paramount chief. He was an observer at the 1958 and 1964 constitutional conferences in London, but as independence approached, he urged caution and delay, expressing the traditional Sotho fear of South African dominance without British protection. When the new constitution denied him authority over defense and foreign affairs, he refused to sign the conference reports. Moshweshwe clashed with the prime minister, Chief Leabua JONATHAN, who demanded his abdication, and their dispute boiled over into violence during the summer of 1966. At independence in October, Moshweshwe was proclaimed king, but Jonathan placed him under house arrest before the end of the year and forced him to sign a document accepting the constitutional limitations on his office.

In 1970, Jonathan staged a coup after it became clear that he was losing the election. As a result, the king was deported to the Netherlands for seven months. He returned, but with severe restrictions on his political activities, and spent the next 15 years as a ceremonial head of state. Reserved and conservative in his personal life, Moshweshwe was politically left of center. He spent much of this time working at various social programs. He established scholarship trusts, brought several international service agencies into Lesotho, and lent his prestige to a number of social programs. His enforced retirement ended in 1986 when the military, under General Justin LEKHANYA, toppled Jonathan and restored the king to full powers. In practice, however, the military council kept Moshweshwe on a short leash, and the king and council had sharp disagreements over South African policy. Moshweshwe continued his traditional stance of wariness and opposition, opposing Lekhanya's state visit to Pretoria and conciliatory moves made to please South Africa.

The conflict came to a head in 1990 when the king refused to swear in three council members who were appointed to replace those who had been loyal to him. He was dethroned, sent into exile in England, and replaced by his son, Crown Prince Letsie. In 1992 a compromise was worked out whereby Moshweshwe returned to Lesotho as head of the royal family, with Letsie retaining the title of king. The constitutional crisis over the role of the monarchy was not successfully resolved even after democratic elections in 1993. Letsie several times suggested returning the throne to his father, and this finally took place in 1995. It was a short-lived resolution, however, because Moshweshwe was killed in an auto accident a year later and Letsie was reinstated.

References: DAHB, PLBA, RWWA, *wiki.*

MOTHOPENG, Zephania Lekoane
(South Africa, 1913–1990)

Zephania Lekoane Mothopeng, an uncompromising militant who rejected negotiation with the apartheid regime, was a founder of the Pan-Africanist Congress (PAC).

He was born in the Orange Free State and taught science and mathematics in Soweto. When the Bantu Education Act of 1953 was passed, reinforcing the subordinate role of Blacks in South Africa, Mothopeng was president of the Transvaal African Teachers' Association. He led the opposition to the law and was fired from his teaching job in 1952. After two years of teaching in Lesotho, he returned to South Africa and became active in politics, supporting himself as a law clerk.

Mothopeng was a member of the African National Congress (ANC), briefly serving on the executive council of its youth league. After 1955, with Robert SOBUKWE, he joined the "Africanist" wing, which was critical of the ANC leadership for its moderation and its willingness to collaborate with White and Indian Communists. They called for Black-led liberation of the land that they called Azania, urging guerrilla warfare and rejecting any form of negotiation. "Our liberation will be brought about by Africans themselves by having to struggle for it," he argued. "They will not achieve it at the negotiating tables." In 1959 the Africanists broke from the ANC and founded the Pan-Africanist Congress (PAC).

For his opposition to apartheid, Mothopeng spent three periods in prison. He was first jailed for two years in 1960 for taking part in the Defiance Campaign against the hated pass laws, which were used to restrict the movement of Blacks. The PAC was also banned as a result of the campaign. Mothopeng was detained in 1963 and imprisoned again from 1964 to 1967, serving time on Robben Island with Nelson MANDELA, Walter SISULU, and other ANC leaders. He was placed under a banning order upon his release, which severely limited his movements until 1971. He then became director of the Urban Resources Centre, a community service organization in Soweto. The Soweto student uprising of 1976 led to Mothopeng's arrest again. He refused to plead at his trial, saying that he did not accept the jurisdiction of the court, and he was sentenced to 15 years under the Terrorism Act. In prison he was elected president of the PAC (1986), but shortly afterward he was diagnosed with throat cancer and finally was released in 1988.

Despite his age and poor health, he returned to politics and lived to see the PAC unbanned and restored to legal status. Mothopeng remained steadfast in his refusal to participate in negotiations with the government of F. W. DE KLERK. His death in 1990 left the PAC in disarray, with no clear leadership. Although it finally decided to contest the 1994 elections, it received less than five percent of the vote as the ANC swept to total victory.

References: GSAP, MMA, PLBA.

MPHALELE, Es'kia (Ezekiel)
(South Africa, 1919–)

Dr. Es'kia (Ezekiel) Mphalele is a writer of the apartheid generation in South Africa and an important literary critic who spent two decades in exile from his homeland. An academic writer of polished skills and Western tastes, he writes works that reflect the struggle of his life to rise from urban poverty to a position where his abilities can be recognized and accepted.

After completing teacher's college, Mphalele obtained an honors AB (1949) and an MA (1956) at the University of South Africa. Until 1957 he taught school and was fiction editor of *Drum Magazine,* where he began publishing his short stories. At first he taught at institutes for the blind until he was banned from teaching in South Africa for protesting the Bantu Education Act, which lowered standards of education for Blacks. In 1954, Reverend Trevor HUDDLESTON provided him with a teaching position at St. Peter's Secondary School in Sophiatown, where one of his students was Hugh MASEKELA.

After working briefly at *Drum* when St. Peter's was forced to close, he left the country in 1957. He lectured at the University of Ibadan in Nigeria (1957–1961), was director of African Programmes for the Congress for Cultural Freedom in Paris (1961–1963), and was director of the Chemchemi Creative Centre in Nairobi, Kenya (1963–1965). He was a witness to independence movements throughout Africa, with the exception of South Africa, where repression was increasing. He left for the United States and obtained a Ph.D. in literature at the University of Denver, where he stayed to teach, with the exception of brief appointments at the University of Zambia and the University of Pennsylvania. In 1977 he returned to South Africa, but the government withdrew the university appointment that had been offered. He subsequently did become professor of African literature at the University of Witwatersrand, where he stayed until his retirement from teaching in 1987.

By the time Mphalele had gone into exile, he was an established short story writer. In 1961 his work was banned in South Africa, and the last restrictions were lifted only in the 1990s. His first novel, *The Wanderers* (1971), based on his own inner experience, is a cry of pain for rootless exiles who search in vain for a true homeland. Mphalele agreed with some of his critics who felt that his work in exile lacked contact with his homeland and even lacked a sense of place throughout that period. To nourish his intellectual life, Mphalele relied upon close friendships with other African authors, especially Kofi AWOONOR. When he returned to South Africa in 1977 he said: "I want to be part of the renaissance that is happening in the thinking of my people." At the same time, he described himself as "the personification of the African paradox, detribalized, Westernized, and still an African."

In 1980 he published a second novel, *Chirundu,* the story of an African torn between tradition and modernism, community and individualism. It reflects Mphalele's own life tension, one that he neither rejects nor avoids. It is also a richly satisfying novel of ideas, which puts it outside the canon of most post-independence fiction in Africa. It is in his short stories that Mphalele enters into the daily experience of South Africa. His urban slums are alive with reality; his portrayals are unyielding and unsparing. It is striking that Mphalele can also write as trenchantly of the life of wealthy White families (in what he calls the "White ghetto") as he does of Black poverty. His short stories have been published in several collections: *Man Must Live* (1947), *The Living and the Dead* (1961), and *In Corner B* (1967).

In addition, his critical essays have had considerable influence on the study of African fiction. In *The African Image* (1962) he explored Kwame NKRUMAH's concept of "the African personality" in literature and society. *Voices in the Whirlwind* (1972) continued the themes of African identity. In his essays Mphalele never limits himself to commentary but engages in an intellectual dialog with the writer he is contemplating. As in his fiction, Mphalele returns constantly to what might be seen as his major theme—the "tyranny of place," the magnetic draw of the homeland, the place of one's formation, and the community that is the cradle of a person's life and dreams. He has endorsed Wole SOYINKA's opposition to the theory of *Négritude,* arguing that it lacks revolutionary potential. He also has joined in the views of NGUGI wa Thiong'o that writing in colonial languages lessens the ability of fiction to reach the masses or raise their consciousness. Despite that, he has always written in English himself.

References: adb, afr, AA, AWT, CANR, DLB, MBW, NRG, WLTC. Mphalele, *Afrika My Music* (1984); Ursula Barnett, *Ezekiel Mphalele* (1976); www.eskiaonline.com.

MPINA, Edison
(Malawi, 1942–)

Edison Mpina is one of the generation of Malawian poets who arose in the 1970s. Unlike his contemporaries Jack MAPANJE and Felix MNTHALI, he was not part of the Writers' Workshop that developed so much of Malawi's poetic explosion.

Mpina graduated from secondary school in Zomba, but entered banking rather than attend university. His poetry reflects his differences with the Writer's Workshop School in being less academic and not as overtly political. Part of this latter element stems from the fact that he began writing only in the late 1970s. He did share one important experience with the Writers' Workshop poets—he was imprisoned without cause under the regime of Dr. Hastings Kamuzu BANDA.

He first broke into public awareness when his poem, "Summer Fires of Mulanje Mountain," won the British Broadcasting Company's prestigious Arts and Africa Award in 1981. Mpina has published only one book of his poetry, *Raw Pieces* (1986), but his work has been extensively anthologized in volumes of contemporary African poetry. His writing deals with the struggles of everyday living. Partly to distance himself from the Writers' Workshop School, he founded his own group, the Lingadzi Writers' Workshop in the capital, Lilongwe. It is an apt center for something that breaks with tradition, a raw and new city (some would say "sterile") with little tradition behind it.

In more recent years, Mpina has been writing novels. The first, *The Low Road to Death* (1990), explores the effects of consumerism on Malawians. He followed this with *Freedom Avenue* (1991), an anticolonial work on forced labor.

Reference: *adb*.

MROIVILI, Ali "Napalo"
(Comoros, 1961–)

Ali Mroivili is a Comorean artist whose neoconceptual sculptures have attracted international attention. He also writes poetry in Shikomoro, a creole fusing Kiswahili and Arabic.

Mroivili, who prefers his pseudonym "Napalo," was educated in France from 1987 to 1992, and then spent a year at the Rijksacademie in Amsterdam, a country he now makes his home.

Beginning in 1988, he began exhibiting in museums and public settings. He has been in scores of major shows, averaging three to five a year. Most of his installations have been in Western Europe, including such venues as La Défense in Paris, the Rijksmusem in Amsterdam and Palais de Beaux-

Arts in Brussels. His work has also appeared in the Indian Ocean countries—the Seychelles, Réunion and the Comoros.

His art consists of installations of cultural objects found in everyday life, but transformed. Typical was his chair and piece of luggage placed together and covered by wallpaper. Another, *The Strongest Democracy* (2000), is a painting of a form draped with a *faux* military shirt with bogus decorations. Beside it is another painting of a pair of jackboots with flowers springing up from them, and a backless, seatless empty chair. *Decolonizing Images* (1997) is a tropical hat as often worn by colonial officials, hanging from a wall rack. Half the crown is cut away to expose an empty globe. Like all Mroivili's work, it stimulates questions: is it on the rack because colonialism is now gone? Or does it imply that neocolonialism still covers half the world? A piece of public art, low stone walls in a field, is entitled *Wherever You Are Is the Centre of the World*, with the subtitle *The North Is Not the Centre of the World*. That little bit of whimsy, satire touched with humor, is another characteristic of Mroivili's art. His work is provocative without being overwhelming. Mroivili calls it "fruitful confrontation."

Reference: *adb*. www.napalo.com.

MSWATI II
(Swaziland, 1820s–1868)

King Mswati II was the second and greatest king of the Swazi, who took their name from him. He was the son of the founder of the Swazi kingdom and became heir on his father's death in 1840. During his long rule he extended the kingdom north into what is now Zimbabwe, lands that were later lost by the kingdom.

Mswati was a great warrior king. Swaziland had been created as a result of the expansion of the Zulu under SHAKA and DINGANE, whom Mswati's father either appeased or avoided by taking to the easily defended mountains. Mswati armed the Swazi and trained them along the lines of the Zulu regimental system, stationing regiments at each of the royal residences. At first he was challenged by several revolts, but the royal regiments remained loyal. Mswati consolidated his position by centralizing the regimental command and creating military villages headed by members of his clan who were personally dependable. In 1846, shortly after he had completed his circumcision rite, a half-brother who had been acting as regent attempted a coup that involved White missionaries and Zulu imperialists. Mswati signed a treaty with the Afrikaners in the Transvaal, who protected him from the Zulu. He continued this protective foreign policy, becoming close to the British after they helped him expel a Zulu invasion in the 1850s and creating a legacy of friendly relations between Swaziland and Great Britain.

Mswati received his only setback from the Pedi, a branch of the Sotho, in the 1850s. In 1859 he aided a pretender to the kingship of Gaza, a small empire in what is now southern Mozambique. When the Portuguese entered the conflict on the other side, Mswati withdrew and gave the pretender asylum in Swaziland.

Domestically, Mswati dealt successfully with the reality of Swazi society, which was a cobbled-together collective of refugee clans with a distinct Swazi minority. He reinforced his father's policy of integrating other groups on an equal basis and married into as many clans as possible. The general populace followed his lead until intermarriage produced a common society.

References: DAHB, EB, MMA.

MSWATI III Makhosetive
(Swaziland, 1968–)

King Mswati III Makhosetive, who inherited his throne from his illustrious father, SOBHUZA II, has been a steady but determined modernizer for his small kingdom. He has struck a delicate balance, trying to maintain tradition without being conservative and to be progressive without alienating supporters of the Swazi nation's heritage.

Prince Mswati was the second-last of Sobhuza's 70 sons. He qualified as heir by being the left-handed son of a mother with no brother and no later children. He was named heir by Sobhuza before the latter's death and was sent to England for secondary education. Meanwhile, in Swaziland an intense factional rivalry between traditionalists and reformers developed around the queen mother and regent. The regent was deposed and replaced by Queen Ntombi, Mswati's mother. Mswati was then brought home from England to be introduced to his people as their future king. Shortly after his nineteenth birthday in 1986, he was enthroned amid lengthy ceremonies in the royal cattle kraal. The Western media, taken up with the theatrical aspects of the event, highlighted his fondness for reggae music and American fast food, leaving the impression of an immature and easily manipulated young king. Quite the opposite turned out to be true.

From the beginning of his reign, Mswati III has taken full authority, determining how and when power should be shared. He disbanded the powerful Liqoqo, or Supreme Council, dismissed the prime minister in a dramatic move, and had a number of Swazi officials arrested and convicted for treason and conspiracy. By the time he received full powers at age 21 in 1989, Mswati had established himself as the nation's ruler. He recognized that many people were impatient for real political reform and that delaying or rejecting it would lead eventually to unrest. Political changes in South Africa, which completely surrounds Swaziland, were beginning to affect the Swazi. In the aftermath of any turmoil there, Swaziland could simply be swallowed up. South Africa has posed the main policy question for every Swazi king. Mswati began an electoral process to move the kingdom toward democracy. A new parliament was chosen in 1993 as Mswati began the process of becoming a constitutional monarch limited to traditional and ceremonial powers.

Two-thirds of Swazis are younger than the young king, and the urban educated reformers argue that Swaziland has no future as a traditional kingdom governed by elders. They advocate that the complex and secretive nobility who retain powers in the court and who plot palace intrigues be swept away in favor of a modern civil service. Yet, Mswati understands the powerful pull of traditional symbols. He has 11 wives chosen carefully from a wide spectrum of young women who represent clan alliances. Each year at the Reed Dance, some 50,000 girls dance before him, carrying reeds to be used to rebuild the royal *kraal*. He may pick a bride from among them. He uses ceremonial dress and accepts his ancient titles: The Lion, Sire of the Herd, The Sun, and The Milky Way. Mswati remains the visible sign of his people's unity.

References: afr, PLBA, RWWA. Zodwa Ginindza, *Umntfwana! A Pictorial Biography of the New King of Swaziland* (1986).

Mswati III

MUDGE, Dirk Francis
(Namibia, 1928–)

Dirk Francis Mudge was the first White politician in power in Namibia to advocate majority government, while it was still under the South African apartheid system. After the independence of South-West Africa (SWA) as Namibia, he emerged as the leader of the opposition in parliament.

Mudge was born in South-West Africa and educated in South Africa, where he received a BComm in 1947 at Stellenbosch University, a center of Afrikaner ideology and culture. He returned home to run the family farm, joined the National Party (NP), and was elected to the SWA territorial legislature in 1961. He became NP party leader in the legislature in 1969 and a member of the South African prime minister's advisory council in 1973. In 1977, after failing to take the NP leadership in SWA due to his liberal proposals for racial equality, he quit the NP and formed the Republican Party.

In 1975, South Africa attempted to forge an internal alliance of forces to create an independent Namibia that would be friendly to apartheid South Africa and hostile to the South-West African People's Organization (SWAPO). Mudge convened a national conference at the Turnhalle (gymnasts' hall) in Windhoek, the capital. The groups present represented rather narrow ethnic factions, but in 1977, Mudge was able to bring them together in a multiracial coalition, the Democratic Turnhalle Alliance (DTA). Its core was Mudge's White-based Republicans and the party of the Herero people, with smaller groups representing the Tswana, Ovamba, Nama and mixed-race Coloureds. The DTA advocated equal parliamentary representation for Europeans, Coloureds and Africans, and dominated the elections for the Constituent Assembly and the National Assembly that it created in 1979.

Mudge was selected to head the multiracial internal government.

The Ministers' Council, which Mudge headed from 1980 to 1983, took part in the United Nations (U.N.) Geneva (1979–1980) and Lusaka (1983) conferences, which met with SWAPO. In 1983, however, he resigned in disgust, calling the South African arrangement "a futile exercise." Pretoria disbanded the government and reassumed direct rule. South Africa established a transitional government from 1985 to 1989, which Mudge joined as minister of finance. In the 1989 elections for the first independent Namibian parliament, the DTA emerged second to SWAPO, with 28.6 percent of the vote and 21 seats. The DTA's goals of proportional representation and a two-chamber parliament were achieved, and Mudge became leader of the opposition. After the election it was revealed that the DTA had received R65 million (about US$26 million) in election support from South Africa. In 1993, Mudge was pressed to resign his chairmanship of the party on the grounds that the South African subsidies had compromised the DTA among the electorate. Instead, he resigned from parliament and retained his party chairmanship.

Reference: RWWA. At van Wyk, *Dirk Mudge* (in Afrikaans, 1999).

MUDIMBE, V(alentin) Y(ves)

(Democratic Republic of the Congo, 1941–)

Dr. V. Y. Mudimbe, a philosopher, linguistic scholar and novelist, has long lived and worked in the United States. Although his interests and scholarship have ranged over many topics, he is best known for his thinking and work on cultural identity.

Mudimbe became a Benedictine monk for two years, immersing himself in Latin, Greek and Western philosophy. After withdrawing from the monastery, he took a degree at the Louvanium University in the Democratic Republic of the Congo (DRC) and then a doctorate in French linguistics at Louvain in Belgium in 1970. He taught at several universities in the DRC, then known as Zaïre, until emigrating to the United States in 1981. He had refused an offer to join the central committee of the

national party under MOBUTU Sese Seko and went into exile. After several other teaching posts, he became a professor at Duke University in 1988.

Mudimbe's early work in the 1970s focused on French language, both in technical studies and teaching texts. He also published several novels and volumes of poetry. His first novel, *Entre les Eaux* (*Between the Waters*, 1973), was awarded the Grand Prize for International Catholic Literature in 1975. In it an African priest (with the same name as Mudimbe's as a monk), struggles with his dual spirit—African and Western at the same time. His second novel, *Le Bel Immonde*, followed in 1976 (published in English as *Before the Birth of the Moon*), and confronts the corruption of postcolonial Africa. Two others in 1979 and 1989 explore the question of the duality of the African intellectual caught between his culture and his education.

By far Mudimbe's greatest contribution, however, has been his philosophical writings on the nature of African identity. *The Invention of Africa* (1988) won the Herskovits Prize from the African Studies Association the following year. *The Idea of Africa* (1994) capped this, along with many articles in philosophical and cultural journals. Mudimbe explores the question, "Why did colonialism happen?" by looking at the various explanations that historians have proposed. He then dismisses this as the wrong question, since regardless of the theory of origins, it ignores the final question, "What *is* colonialism?" He argues that colonialism starts with "organization and arrangement." There are three elements to this: domination of space, primarily land; the colonization of the indigenous mentality through education in Western thought patterns and religion; and the integration of local economies into service of European wealth. The consequence of this pattern is the marginalization of local societies and cultures. It produces a "Eurocentric" society in the colonized communities.

Eurocentrism is based on a mode of thinking that makes sense of the universe in terms of dualities—good versus evil, urban versus rural, traditional versus modern, subsistence versus cash economies, and in literature, the basis of learning, oral versus written. The "word" becomes, in the European mindset, the final arbiter of truth, be it by treaties, legal structures or literature. He then points out the folly of redesigning development programs for the Third World as if the marginalization created by colonialization were merely a failure of an otherwise efficient process. He even criticizes the conception of African studies as a Western construct, the need to refashion reality into an academic discipline. He explores the meaning of African art in the West, where collectors and museums think in terms of fine art, while African art was always made with an application in mind, be it religious ritual or to honor royalty.

Mudimbe points out that colonialism was intertwined with the emergence in Western thought of the superiority of the White race and its obligation to "civilize" the barbarian or "savage" societies of the world. The proponents of this Social Darwinism not only felt justified in subjugating peoples, but also saw it as a sacred duty to bring them the benefits of advanced cultures.

Mudimbe is widely recognized for his contributions to philosophical thought. He has received several honorary doctorates and has been awarded government honors from the former Zaïre, Japan and the French-speaking community.

References: BW, CA, *wiki*, WLTC.

MUGABE, Robert Gabriel

(Zimbabwe, 1924–)

Robert Gabriel Mugabe, nationalist leader and guerrilla fighter, won the battle against the White secessionist government of Rhodesia (now called Zimbabwe) and has served as prime minister (1980–1987) and as president (1987–) of Zimbabwe. In his last years he has become a despotic ruler who has destroyed his country's prosperity.

Mugabe graduated from Fort Hare College in South Africa and embarked on a teaching career. At Fort Hare he met members of the African National Congress and studied the philosophy of GANDHI but was not politically active. From 1957 to 1960 he taught in Ghana, which was then newly independent, and completed his political education by studying and adopting some Marxist ideas on popular struggle. He returned home and entered the liberation movement as a youth organizer. He joined the Zimbabwe African Political Union (ZAPU), the party of Joshua NKOMO, but broke with him by 1962 to join Ndabaningi SITHOLE's Zimbabwe African National Union (ZANU) Party. Nkomo and Mugabe became wary rivals, which they remained up to Nkomo's death. Mugabe was

arrested at least three times in the next two years. The last time he was held in detention camps for 10 years. He spent his time studying, completing several degrees by correspondence. Although he was not a major figure, Mugabe successfully challenged Sithole for the leadership of ZANU while he was in prison, although it took several years before he was accepted. He opposed the settlement then being discussed between Ian SMITH, head of Rhodesia's White separatist government, and Bishop Abel MUZOREWA and was determined to win liberation through guerrilla war. In 1974 he was one of the resistance leaders amnestied by Smith.

While his leadership of ZANU was still tenuous, Mugabe faced a bloody rebellion among his recruits, followed by the assassination of a major guerrilla leader in Zambia. Mugabe and a companion made a dramatic escape over the highlands to Mozambique, led through the passes by an elderly chief. Subsequently, young men from Zimbabwe poured over the border, and Mugabe spent the late 1970s organizing armed struggle. He worked at attracting international support while training his men and securing arms. In the meantime he shuttled back and forth to international reconciliation conferences, where various settlements were debated. By 1976 the Patriotic Front (PF) brought ZANU and ZAPU together to coordinate armed struggle and negotiations. In 1979 a compromise constitution was agreed upon, providing majority control to African citizens. In the 1980 elections, Mugabe defeated the opposition party of Bishop

Robert Gabriel Mugabe

Muzorewa and immediately began a policy of binding old wounds.

Mugabe's first success was to merge the two guerrilla forces with the former Rhodesian army. It was less easy to merge the victorious parties, and resistance from ZAPU-dominated regions continued. In 1985, Mugabe crushed the resistance in Matabeleland. Nkomo fled to London, and Muzorewa was detained. Nkomo and Mugabe then negotiated themselves out of a potential crisis in 1987. Mugabe became executive president and Nkomo vice president. Despite Mugabe's Marxist leanings, there was no nationalization policy during this period, and in only a few key areas did the government even invest substantially. In 1991, ZAPU formally rejected its Marxist dogma. Mugabe developed an aggressive agricultural policy, increasing peasant production from 8 percent to 64 percent of marketed food. He convinced most White farmers to remain, which was critical, because Zimbabwe's foreign currency reserves were based on farm exports.

In 1993, however, Mugabe sent tremors of fear through the White commercial farming industry when he announced the expropriation of 70 large farms, which were divided into small holdings for peasants. The issue shook the confidence of foreign investors and left the Zimbabwean economy unsteady during the worldwide recession. Mugabe was forced to accept an economic adjustment plan, slashing subsidies, reducing government employment, and revaluing the currency. All these factors increased unemployment. Platinum and gold discoveries eased the situation somewhat, but a 1992 drought turned Zimbabwe into an importer rather than an exporter of grain. He then held back for seven years the implementation of his plans for land expropriation.

In office, one of Mugabe's most successful efforts was the improvement of basic education. Zimbabwe now has Africa's highest literacy rate, 85 percent, a tribute to aggressive policies in education. In foreign policy Mugabe returned the support that Mozambicans had given him and aided them in their fight against the RENAMO guerrillas. Apartheid South Africa proved a continuing problem, as its security forces regularly sent commandos across the border and clandestinely supplied arms to the ZAPU resistance fighters. Tensions eased considerably after former President Frederik DE KLERK prepared South Africa for a transition to majority rule.

In the late 1990s, Mugabe turned on the White farmers who controlled 70 percent of the country's land and earned most of its foreign exchange. Promised land reform had not been pursued, despite offers of financial support from Britain. In 1999, Mugabe began a policy of forced evacuations, which plunged Zimbabwe into a financial crisis. It became dependent on foreign food supplies as farm production plummeted after commercial farms were cut into small holdings and modern agriculture was abandoned. It soon became clear that the land was being distributed to Mugabe's supporters, although he called them former "freedom fighters." The opposition was harassed, its candidates beaten, and some murdered. Food aid was stolen for members of Mugabe's party as malnutrition spread throughout the country. Opposition members of parliament were arrested and tortured, and the press came under strict censorship. Foreign journalists were expelled. In all, a reign of terror broke out in Zimbabwe.

Mugabe's power base is in rural Mashonaland, and he has struck at the urban masses who support the opposition. Under a program called "Drive Out Trash," slums and housing quarters in the capital, Harare, were bulldozed in 2005–2006. The people were scattered into rural areas under the government's control.

Mugabe and many of his ministers are banned from travel in the European Union, and the United States has issued harsh economic sanctions against Zimbabwe, which was suspended from the Commonwealth of Nations and then formally withdrew. In Africa he has drawn as many critics: Archbishop Desmond TUTU called him a "caricature of an African dictator," and Wole SOYINKA dismissed him as a "disgrace to the continent." Among his chief opponents in Zimbabwe, besides the political opposition, has been Bishop Pius NCUBE, who has received death threats for praying for Mugabe's early death. In many ways, this is the sad story of a great liberator turned tyrant.

References: AB, *afr*, CB, DAHB, EB, EWB, PLBA, PLCA, RWWA, *wiki*. Stephen Chan, *Robert Mugabe: A Life of Power and Violence* (2003); Martin Meredith, *Our Votes, Our Guns: Robert Mugabe and the Tragedy of Zimbabwe* (2002).

MUGABE, Sally
(Ghana/Zimbabwe, 1932–1992)

Sally Mugabe was the popular first wife of Robert MUGABE, president of Zimbabwe. Her memory is revered by ordinary Zimbabweans, often in contrast to their dislike of her husband.

She was born Sally Haytron in Ghana, where she met Mugabe in 1959 while he was teaching at a teacher-training school in Accra, the capital. They married in 1961 and had one child, who died in infancy. She went to London as a student in 1957 and stayed there when Robert was imprisoned in what was then apartheid Southern Rhodesia in 1964. For a number of years the couple remained separated as Robert remained imprisoned for 10 years and then directed the Zimbabwean liberation struggle from Mozambique.

Meanwhile, Sally supported herself in London and applied for residence. She was rejected on the grounds that she should have gone to Ghana to apply. In 1969 and 1970, Robert pleaded for her from prison, but she was rejected. Fearing the implications for a future state leader in Southern Rhodesia (Britain was harshly critical of the minority White government of Ian SMITH), the matter went to Cabinet and was finally resolved. Sally worked during that time for the Africa Centre, the main cultural venue for Africans in London.

When she was finally allowed to go to Zimbabwe, Sally joined the resistance, organizing women's groups. She was imprisoned for her activities.

As First Lady, Sally Mugabe campaigned, without much success, against bride price, the custom that a suitor had to provide his fiancée's family with money and gifts before he could marry her. She argued that it encouraged illicit relationships and in-law problems, and burdened the poor. She was also active in various charities such as the Leper Society and the Child Survival Movement, which she founded.

She was a champion of women's rights, and became secretary of the Women's League of the national party. Sally was personally aware of the dichotomy of women's sacrifice for liberation and their continued oppression in a male-dominated society. For years, she lived with Robert's infidelity with his secretary, who bore him three children. Finally, Robert married his secretary in a traditional ceremony as a second wife, even as Sally was dying of kidney disease. He later married his second wife

in a church wedding, but many have never forgiven him for wronging Sally, a beloved figure.

Reference: adb. Zimbabwe Department of Information, *Sally Mugabe: A Woman with a Mission.*

MUGO, Micere Githae
(Kenya, 1942–)

Dr. Micere Mugo is a poet and playwright, perhaps best known for coauthoring the historical play, *The Trial of Dedan Kimathi*, with NGUGI wa Thiong'o. She is also a leading African scholar and feminist.

Mugo was born and raised in Kenya, but she has had Zimbabwean citizenship since 1984. The first African to integrate a prestigious girls' school, she graduated with high honors. Mugo then turned down a scholarship to Oxford to attend Makerere University in Uganda. She graduated in 1966 and took a teaching diploma the next year at the University of Nairobi. She went on the University of New Brunswick in Canada for a Ph.D. in literature. Returning to Kenya, she taught at the University and became the first woman dean there (and perhaps in all of Africa). After she criticized the government of Daniel arap MOI for its human rights abuses, she was harassed and remanded several times. Finally, her passport was seized and she and her two daughters went into exile in the United States (she calls herself an "exmatriate"). She joined the faculty of the African-American Studies Department at the University of Syracuse, where she still teaches.

Mugo has published a number of books on women's issues, which concern her deeply. She has written two books on Muthoni wa Kirima, a field general in the Mau Mau rebellion against colonialism, and has written on other Third World women heroes, the "matriots." She also lectures widely. Her reputation was most enhanced, however, when she and Ngugi wrote *The Trial of Dedan Kimathi*, which was first produced in London in 1977 to strong reviews. When it was finally performed in Nairobi, the audience spilled into the streets in celebration.

Her two collections of poetry both express the concerns and joys of womanhood. *Daughter of My People, Sing!* (1976) was her first, and *My Mother's Poem and Other Songs* (1994) her most recent. In the latter she celebrates the wisdom of elder women. The poetry is a tribute to the oral tradition and way of speaking.

Reference: adb.

MUHAMMAD Abdullah Hassan

(Somalia, 1864–1920)

Hajj Muhammad Abdullah Hassan was a powerful Islamic religious reformer and the leading poet in Somali literature, who for 20 years led a resistance movement that paralyzed British and Italian imperialism in the Horn of Africa.

A gifted Islamic scholar, Muhammad began preaching as a youth. He visited the Sudan, then the center of Islamic defiance, where the MAHDI had defeated the British and established an Islamic nation. In 1894 he made his *hajj,* or pilgrimage to Mecca, and there joined the Salihiya sect, a puritanical reform movement of the Ahmadiya brotherhood. When he returned to Somaliland, he was profoundly shocked and offended by the aggressive work of Christian missionaries who had been introduced during his absence.

In the 1890s the British, French and Italians divided Somalia. The British got the impoverished northern region, which had scant value and poor trade possibilities. They governed it as a dependency of India and regarded the region as having little importance. To win the favor of Ethiopian Emperor MENELIK II and to contain the threat of the Mahdi in neighboring Sudan, the British made trade and land concessions to Ethiopia. This policy led to plundering Ethiopian military expeditions, customs duties, and humiliating harassment in northern Somalia. Local protest was easily suppressed, but the spectacle of two Christian nations dividing up Somali territory and the introduction of missionaries inflamed the sensibilities of the Muslim Somalis.

Precolonial Islam took the form of brotherhoods, or traditional Sufi religious orders. These now were replaced by radical and messianic sects, one of which was the Salihiya. In 1896, Muhammad led a group of followers inland to found a pure Islamic community away from contamination by European ways. Three years later he declared that he was the Mahdi, the chosen one of Allah who would appear to bring together Muslims in a final victory over infidels. It was the same claim and the same title that had been assumed by Muhammad Ahmad in the Sudan.

A small incident involving the Ethiopians sparked rebellion among Muhammad's followers, and in 1900, having quietly assembled a substantial force, they declared a holy war and struck against the hated Ethiopians. In one victory after another, Muhammad took Ethiopian border forts, pushed back their detachments, and reclaimed Somali territory. It was the start of a 20-year period in which the "Mad Mullah," as he was soon called, tied up the combined efforts of the Ethiopian, British and Italian forces and challenged foreign domination of Somalia. The alien powers assembled large forces, including a joint naval flotilla, and finally inflicted a devastating defeat on Muhammad at Jidbale in 1904. The mullah himself remained at large, however, and was able to regenerate his army with new recruits. By this time he was attracting many Somalis who shared his nationalism but not his religious intensity. Regarded as a religious fanatic by the colonial powers, the mullah became a rallying point for Somali resistance, a symbol of Somali nationalism, and ultimately a hero to his people.

Realizing that the threat would not disappear, the Italians signed a peace treaty in 1905 with Muhammad that gave him control of a central coastal province. Peace lasted three years, when border disputes triggered the revolt again. Muhammad then moved out of Italian Somalia and conquered most of British Somaliland, confining the English to their coastal settlements for over 10 years. He fortified a number of towns, established a capital and, during World War I, even negotiated for Ottoman protection. Gradually, however, many followers from other regions left Muhammad to return home, and more moderate religious orders disowned him. In 1920 the British mounted a campaign against Muhammad that dislodged him from his stronghold. He died, possibly of influenza, while on retreat with his last devoted disciples, and his movement died with him.

While known in the West as an Islamic revivalist and resistance leader, in Somalia Muhammad is revered as a great poet. His work is based on the style of impromptu Somali verse, which is easily memorized and thus quickly taken up in a culture with a strong oral tradition. The origins of his poetry were in feelings of despair. In 1904 the mullah's movement seemed crushed after the Battle of Jidbale, where he was betrayed by an ally and abandoned by his own clansmen. The path of retreat was littered with bodies of men, women, children and cattle. A terrible drought had brought his disciples to the brink of starvation. He then composed *Jiinley,* a powerful invocation of his authority (based on *karamah* or divine grace), the justice of his holy war, and the shame of abandoning the cause. It was written in 33 three-line verses, reminding its hearers of the 99 names of Allah—a sacred invocation. This poem includes the claim: "It is I who said to the infidel: this land is not yours . . . Now I can only look to Allah for my just reward." The poem electrified the Somalis. The deserters returned, and the movement came to life again. The mullah regarded his poetic expression as divine in origin. Muhammad often composed aloud—he had an official memorizer who recorded his compositions—and declaimed his verse in sermons to celebrate victories or to trumpet his cause. He left 120 known poems having sentiments which range from brutish attacks on the British to paeans of praise to Allah, and even the occasional bantering humorous piece. Muhammad's range was impressive, and his impact on Somali literature was profound.

References: DAHB. Abdi Sheik-Abdi, *Divine Madness* (1993).

MUHAMMAD Ture
(Mali/Niger, 1440s–1538)

Askia Muhammad Ture, the leading general and favorite of Sunni ALI, founder of the Songhay Empire, deposed Ali's son to found the Askia dynasty that ruled the empire for a century. Although Muhammad may have been Ali's nephew and was certainly his devoted servant, he also was apparently a ruthless actor in the destruction of the Sunni dynasty. Perhaps it was Ali's unpredictable temper, which several times threatened Muhammad's life, or Ali's undisguised contempt for Islam, but Muhammad felt no compunction in seizing his patron's throne in 1493 and exterminating all members of the Sunni dynasty. When one of Ali's daughters called him *askia* ("usurper"), he took it as his title and established his own dynasty.

Muhammad stabilized the military by strengthening the cavalry and infantry while maintaining the powerful river navy. He continued Ali's expansion until Songhay extended a thousand miles (about 1,600 kilometers) along the Niger River. He was an able administrator as well and established 10 provinces, plus a kind of cabinet for national affairs. He standardized weights and measures, provided security to caravans (and taxed them), and traded as

far east as Baghdad and as far north as Portugal. The great cities of Songhay, especially Tombouctou (Timbuktu), became centers of culture and learning.

Muhammad championed the Muslim cause and made it a basis of his empire. He saw himself as an Islamic reformer and sponsored young men at the leading Muslim schools. From 1496 to 1498 he made the *hajj*, the pilgrimage to Mecca, with such pomp that the chroniclers hardly needed to use exaggeration. Preceded by a musical troupe of tambours (royal dummers) and trumpeters, and surrounded by a vast armed guard, he marched in regal splendor. As a sign of his wealth and power, as well as gratitude, he donated a great amount of gold to the holy cities.

By 1538, Muhammad was old and blind, facts that he concealed because everything he said was given out through a trusted secretary. He was deposed and exiled to an island in the Niger as his sons fought over the empire. Finally freed, he died a natural death.

References: DAHB, DT, WGMC.

MUHAMMED, Murtala Ramat
(Nigeria, 1938–1976)

General Murtala Ramat Muhammed was only briefly president of Nigeria, but his administration had a significant effect on his country's future.

A northerner, Muhammed joined the Nigerian army in 1957 after completing secondary school and was sent to the Royal Military Academy at Sandhurst in Great Britain for officer training. After further military training, he spent a year with United Nations (U.N.) peacekeeping forces in the Democratic Republic of the Congo, then known as Congo-Kinshasa. Muhammed moved ahead as his talents were recognized and in 1962 was made aide-de-camp to the military administrator of the western region of Nigeria, where he witnessed political crisis and public disorder. In 1964 he was promoted to major and was made commander of a signal squadron in Lagos, the national capital. He took no part in the military coup of January 1966, which was led largely by Igbo officers. In the aftermath, with rising ethnic tensions and mounting numbers of deaths, Muhammed joined a group of young officers who led the coup and established General Yakubu GOWON as head of state.

During the Biafran war, Muhammed led an infantry battalion that pushed the Biafrans out of Bendel State and took Onitsha after a difficult campaign. Muhammed was promoted to brigadier and made federal commissioner for communications in 1974. A year later he deposed Gowon in a bloodless coup and became head of state. Muhammed became tremendously popular by taking bold steps to attack Nigeria's most serious problems. He resolved the issue of land ownership of properties abandoned during the civil war, cleared the ports of congestion, improved the supply of fuel oil, reduced inflation, and dramatically cut 10,000 positions from the army and civil service. Muhammed used the restored sense of national confidence to prepare a new constitution with a reorganized group of states. His diplomatic initiatives were similarly active and earned him widespread respect across Africa.

A devout Muslim, Muhammed lived a simple life without the elaborate trappings of office. This austerity was his downfall, because the absence of an armed escort made him easy prey for a group of officers who ambushed and assassinated him during a failed coup. He has become a martyred symbol of national unity in Nigeria, and the international airport is named for him. He was succeeded by General Olusegun OBASANJO, who completed Muhammed's project for returning governance to civilian rule.

References: DAHB, DRWW, MMA, PLBA, *wiki.*

MULUZI, (Elson) Bakili

(Malawi, 1943–)

A longtime politician in Malawi, Bakili Muluzi became president in the country's first free elections after the ouster of Dr. Hastings Kamuzu BANDA.

He began his career with a prison term for fraud after he stole funds from a charity for divorced women. Somehow, he rose from that and at age 33, he was named Banda's minister of education. After a year, he remained in Cabinet as a minister without portfolio, in essence an advisor to Banda. In 1981 he became minister of transport and communications in one of Banda's regular cabinet shuffles. He founded the United Democratic Front in the wake of Banda's concession allowing multiparty elections.

Muluzi was in the right place at the right time, and although he had served Banda for years, he benefited from name recognition to win election. He had formed a new party, the United Democratic Front (UDF) which easily defeated Banda's discredited Malawi Congress Party (MCP). During the campaign he presented himself as the champion of democracy. He carried the thickly settled south of the country, which had always been a Banda stronghold.

Muluzi took office in 1994 and served two terms. In 2002 he attempted a constitutional amendment to allow himself a third term, but there was such a public outcry that he backed down. The people of Malawi had too many bad memories of a president-for-life to abandon term limits so soon. Muluzi continued as head of the UDF.

In the aftermath of 30 years of Banda's authoritarian rule, Muluzi had a mandate for reform and a fund of general goodwill. He began well, setting up an Ombudsman's Office, a Law Commission and an Anti-Corruption Bureau. Soon, however, corruption began to return. By Muluzi's second term, it had become so blatant that the major foreign donors—the United States, the European Union, the World Bank and the International Monetary Fund—banded together to withhold $100 million in grants and loans. Denmark closed its embassy after its criticism was rejected out of hand. Muluzi's business interests expanded during his presidency, and he became a wealthy man.

Controversy followed Muluzi in office. In one disastrous move, he sold the country's grain reserves just before a drought that left many farmers without crops. The famine that followed caused great suffering with many deaths among children and the elderly. The money from the food reserve sale, which might have been used to buy food on the international market, has never been traced. It is widely assumed to have been looted by Muluzi and his cohorts. Despite his failures, Muluzi remained popular. His open, gregarious style endeared him to many who had resented the dour, self-centered Banda.

Since leaving the presidency in 2004, Muluzi has been dogged by health problems. In 2006 he went to Great Britain at Malawian government expense, to have spinal surgery.

Reference: wiki.

MUMIA wa Shiundu
(Kenya, 1849?–1949)

Nabongo Mumia wa Shiundu was the last independent *nabongo,* or king, of the Wanga, the leading subclan of the Luyia in western Kenya. His father, Shiundu, had begun a policy of favoring Arab traders in order to obtain firearms, which were necessary in maintaining independence. Mumia became *nabongo* in the early 1880s and continued his father's policies, although he increasingly sought accommodation with the British. His central town, simply referred to as "Mumia's," became an important way station between the coast and Uganda, and several important British explorers and officials had reason to be grateful to Mumia for either hospitality or refuge.

In 1888 the Luyia were included in the British East African Protectorate, a fact imparted to Mumia only when a British agent arrived in 1894. Rather than resist—Mumia was well aware of the fates of MWANGA and KABAREGA in neighboring Uganda—he became one of the most enthusiastic proponents of British colonialism. Mumia's capital became the base for expeditions against neighboring African peoples, and thousands of Luyia warriors were made available for these campaigns. The rewards of loyalty were significant for both Mumia and his people. Because the Luyia were the only centralized state within the protectorate, the British delegated Mumia's kinsmen as headmen in non-Wanga areas in 1907. Two years later, Mumia was declared paramount chief, effectively putting him in charge of a small subcolonial regime. For 10 years Luyia power was at its height, but it did not go unchallenged by the subject peoples who resisted. Mumia's chieftancy and his servitude toward British interests have made him a figure of some scorn in Kenyan history for being a colonial collaborator.

In 1920 the colonial administration was moved to Kakamega, which was on the rail line, and Mumia's influence declined. In 1926 the British withdrew his title as paramount chief, for which he regarded the colonial government as ungrateful. One of his sons was named headman of the Wanga in his stead, and Mumia was reduced to a symbolic figure. As such, however, he was not without sway over the Luyia, and during his last days he lent support to the nationalists under Jomo KENYATTA.

References: DAHB. John Osogo, *Nabongo Mumia of the Baluyia* (1966).

MUSA, Mansa
(Mali/Sénégal, ?–1337)

Mansa Musa, king of the Mali empire during a united and prosperous period, is known primarily (and perhaps unfairly) for his lavish and ostentatious pilgrimage to Mecca.

Musa was the grandson of SUNDIATA Keita, founder of the Malian Empire. Little is known of his life before 1307, when he succeeded to the throne as *mansa* or king. From then on, the chronicles of the period give extensive accounts of his reign. Musa's predecessor had been weak, and the empire he inherited was disunited. Musa set about the task of centralization, which involved obtaining the loyalty and obedience of provincial governors as well as the submission of nomadic peoples, who were often little more than bandit clans. When the empire and his routes were secure, Musa made preparations for his *hajj,* or pilgrimage to Mecca, in 1324.

Contributions were demanded of every province and trading town. The entourage was huge, even when one allows for the overstatement of the chroniclers. Some 500 personal servants and 60,000 porters are reported to have accompanied him, along with 10,000 soldiers. Exaggerated or not, a large retinue was an absolute necessity, if only for safety. Musa's predecessor had been killed by nomads while on the *hajj.*

Musa is reported to have been a young man at the time of his *hajj,* although he was probably about 50 years old. He was described as handsome, with a brown complexion. His arrival in Cairo was a stunning event that was discussed and remembered for generations. He cut a magnificent figure on horseback, surrounded by troops and attendants. He carried a huge amount of gold to be given out in alms along the way. One account says that he had over 20 tons of gold, another reports "80 packages of gold dust, each weighing three *kintars* or 3.8 kgs . . . and 500 slaves, each carrying a golden staff weighing over 500 *mithkal,* about 3 kgs." Although the account may be embellished, it was reported that Musa's visit caused a period of inflation in Cairo and depressed the price of gold by 12 percent. Mali held at that time almost half the world's known gold supply.

The impression of a great ruler of a powerful empire was just the one Musa wished to leave, and he used his pilgrimage to establish cultural and trade relations with those he visited. He also extended diplomatic contacts with the Moroccan sultanates and protected the security of the trans-Saharan trade routes. The result was a period of prosperity and unity within the empire that brought it to its highest point. Musa also was inspired to erect great buildings along the lines of the palaces and mosques that he had seen in Cairo and Arabia, and he brought architects back with him for this purpose. Although most of these works, made of beaten earth, have disappeared, the Friday Mosque at Djenné remains as an example of the Sudanese style introduced by Musa.

Musa attempted to revive and extend Islam in the empire but had less success in his religious policy. He had learned a good deal about Islamic orthodoxy from the pilgrimage, and he built Koranic schools and encouraged Arabic poetry. His diplomatic contacts with Morocco introduced scholars into his empire, but Islam remained primarily the religion of the towns, while traditional religion was followed in the rural areas. One of the subject peoples, the Bambara, even formed a secret society during Musa's reign to resist Islamization and preserve their traditional religion.

References: AB, *afr*, CWAH, DAHB, EWB, HH, *wiki*.

MUSEVENI, Yoweri Kaguta
(Uganda, 1944–)

Yoweri Kaguta Museveni, the revolutionary leader who overthrew the unpopular regime of Apollo Milton OBOTE, has been president of Uganda since 1986.

He studied in Tanzania at the University of Dar es Salaam, where he worked for FRELIMO, the exiled Mozambican liberation movement. He received his first guerrilla training with FRELIMO and subsequently undertook training in counterintelligence from the Israelis. After a year working in Obote's first administration, he returned to Tanzania when Idi AMIN Dada seized power. Museveni soon formed the Front for National Salvation for Uganda (FRONISA) and in 1979 led 9,000 Ugan-

President Yoweri Museveni of Uganda meets with U.S. President Ronald Reagan, October 1987.

dan exile troops when Tanzania invaded Uganda. In the rigged elections of 1980, his Uganda Patriotic Movement (UPM) was soundly defeated, and Museveni returned to his rural strongholds to form the National Resistance Movement (NRM).

Museveni campaigned against Ugandan ethnic, religious and regional tensions. His NRM proved disciplined and formidable, and when Obote fell in an army coup, it was largely because the NRM had fatally weakened him. The army proved as weak as the dictator it had toppled, and in a lightning campaign, the NRM occupied Kampala and most of the country in less than a month.

Once in power, Museveni found the transition from guerrilla leader to political leader to be a difficult one. The economy was in shambles. Warring ethnic groups and bandit bands of irregulars terrorized the north, and the old religious and political divisions reappeared. Museveni, never comfortable with multiparty democracy, consolidated the power base with National Resistance Councils organized at every level. Security was established in the south, and the north was somewhat pacified by 1991.

Born of a Nyankole father and a Rwandese mother, Museveni has always received strong support from the substantial Rwandese refugee population in Uganda. In downsizing the army in 1990, he dropped many Rwandese, and he disappointed them further by not making good on promises of citizenship for Rwandese refugees. They transferred their loyalties to the Rwandese Patriotic Front and launched an invasion of their homeland from Uganda. All the senior officers were from the Ugandan army, as were supplies and arms, yet Museveni denied any knowledge of the plot. This event, plus a blunt and abrasive style, has alienated

Museveni from many African leaders, although he was elected president of the Organization for African Unity (OAU) in 1990. He is a poor speaker, enigmatic and contradictory in his statements. Moves intended to be popular have often been misinterpreted, such as the establishment of Kiswahili as a national language and the 1993 restoration of the four traditional monarchies in Uganda.

In the West, however, Museveni was held up as an African success story, and Uganda was favored by donors such as the European Union and the United States. Outside of African issues, his foreign policy favored the West. Within the region, however, he has embroiled Uganda deeper into conflicts. Museveni became involved in the civil war in the Democratic Republic of the Congo, and supported those who overthrew MOBUTU Sese Seko. He has taken sides in the civil war in the Sudan, in part because of the spillover into Uganda's northern provinces.

Worst of all has been the lackluster response to the lingering and deadly civil strife in the north, where the Lord's Resistance Army of Joseph KONY has continued to ravage the countryside. Museveni's army has been either unable or unwilling to protect the refugee camps from attack, and Kony continues to kidnap youth and press them into his service through terror.

On the domestic front, Museveni was more successful. He declared a moratorium on political parties and elections, declaring that national unity was foremost in a crisis and that parties would foment ethnic division. At the local level Resistance Councils were established, elected by the people to manage local affairs, including the distribution of subsidized basic commodities. When multiparty elections were finally permitted in 1996, Museveni won easily. He then changed the constitution to abolish term limits. He handily won the 2006 vote, but only after his opponent was harassed and jailed in elections that were tainted by fraud. It was a sign of Museveni's increasing intolerance of opposition or criticism.

Museveni improved the failed economy, restarted some industries and invited back the Indian investors who had been expelled by Idi Amin a generation earlier. While only a few took up his offer, the economy grew under new free-market policies. Museveni abandoned his earlier Marxism and became an enthusiastic supporter of the World Bank's economic policies.

Another marked success has been Museveni's anti-AIDS campaign, which has taken Uganda from among the highest rates of infection to among the lowest in the Third World.

References: AB, *afr*, CB, PLBA, PLCA, RWWA, *wiki*. Museveni, *What Is Africa's Problem?* (2000).

MUTARA III Rutahigwa
(Rwanda, 1913–1959)

Mwami Mutara III Rutahigwa ruled as *mwami* or traditional king of Rwanda from 1931 to 1959. Unlike most traditional rulers during the colonial period, he was not a mere figurehead but exercised real authority. The maintenance of this authority, in the face of attempts by Belgium and the United Nations (U.N.) to reduce it, was the overriding policy issue during Mutara's reign.

Mutara was a Tutsi, the son of Mwami Yuhi IV Musinga. The small Tutsi minority in Rwanda formed a feudal elite over a large Hutu majority. Social, economic and political inequality were a constant source of friction, and Mutara was the last *mwami* to maintain Hutu subordination. In this policy he was consistently opposed by Belgian colonial authorities, who sought both to encourage democratic forms in preparation for independence and to forge alliances with the majority as a political counterbalance to the *mwami*.

The Belgians deposed Yuhi IV in response to his constant conflicts with subordinate chiefs. The *mwami's* power was considerable when Mutara took the throne, and he enhanced it as the symbol of Tutsi domination in Rwanda, with the entire feudal edifice resting on his office. In theory and practice, the *mwami* owned all of the land, which was especially significant in a land-poor country. He controlled the subordinate chiefs and managed the population through them.

After World War II, the U.N. changed the Belgian mandate to a trusteeship, with the Belgian commissioner accountable to the U.N. The U.N. policy favored reforms leading to decolonization and democracy, including the opening of opportunities for Hutu advancement and education. In this the Catholic Church, which controlled the school system, was an active supporter. Mutara resisted these changes but was unable to contain the rise of Hutu political organizations.

When Mutara died under suspicious circumstances, chaos followed. Tutsi monarchists installed his brother as Mwami Kigeri V, but he was soon driven into exile, and the Hutu rose against the Tutsi, resulting in massacres. Order was restored only with a Hutu government, led by Grégoire KAYIBANDA, who ended the monarchy.

References: DAHB, MMA.

MUTESA I
(Uganda, 1838?–1884)

Kabaka Mutesa I, one of the most powerful rulers of Buganda (the main kingdom in Uganda), made the first contacts with Europeans and ushered in a period of change that ended only with the establishment of British colonial rule.

Mutesa was in his teens when his father died of smallpox in 1856. The Buganda kingdom was highly centralized, with the *katikiro* (prime minister) wielding great authority with respect to political succession. He chose Mutesa from about 80 possible contenders, hoping for a pliable and inexperienced youth. The losing candidates for *kabaka* (king) were exiled to an island, from which they attempted a coup that Mutesa defeated. He then asserted his independence and surprised his courtiers by his authority and control. A fine network of roads and a system of informers kept him in contact at all times with developments anywhere in Buganda. He also imported firearms from Arab traders, although initially all foreigners were forbidden entry into the kingdom.

In 1861 reports reached Mutesa that two White men had been seen at Lake Victoria. One, John Hanning SPEKE, arrived within a few months and was astonished and impressed with the *kabaka's* compound, which housed hundreds of family members and retainers. The two developed a mutual respect for one another. At this point, Mutesa was concerned about attempts by Egypt to expand its authority to the headwaters of the Nile, and he was prepared to negotiate with possible allies. He also invited Zanzibari traders, from whom he learned some Swahili and Arabic, and began to read the Koran and follow traditional Islamic rituals, but his refusal to undergo circumcision prevented his formal conversion.

By 1875, Henry Morton STANLEY had arrived at Mutesa's court, and the *kabaka* asked for Christian missionaries, not for religious purposes but with the hope that they would help stem the Egyptian advance. Basically, Mutesa, who ruled a secular state, was not religious, although he realized religion's importance for diplomatic contacts, and he did not forbid his people to convert to new faiths. He enjoyed religious debates, however, which he held regularly in his court between Muslims and Christians.

The Anglican evangelical organization, the Church Missionary Society (CMS), arrived in 1877, followed two years later by the French White Fathers. The missionaries, wary of one another but thrown together, were forced to stay at the *kabaka's* court, where they found numerous converts among the pages and courtiers. As a result of their efforts, Buganda underwent a profound change with the introduction of new ideas about allegiance and loyalty among the future elite of the kingdom. While not obstructing them (or the Muslims), Mutesa continually attempted to manipulate these religious factions for his own purposes of state. When General "Chinese" GORDON, in the employ of the *khedive,* or ruler, of Egypt, attempted to conquer Buganda, Mutesa, calling himself "His Most Christian Majesty," contemptuously arrested the troops. When the CMS missionaries arrived, Mutesa was disappointed that they did not bring him arms but was pleased when Britain opposed any attempts by Egypt to annex Buganda.

The missionaries were detested by the Muslims in court, partly because they were opposed to the slave trade. They also garnered the animosity of the chiefs, most of whom adhered to traditional beliefs and were far more conservative than the *kabaka.* Only Mutesa's political skills maintained a shaky balance, as they did in external relations. In his last years, Mutesa's health deteriorated and more authority passed to court administrators, but he left a strong, centralized, and independent state when he was succeeded by his son MWANGA.

References: AB, *afr,* DAHB, EWB, MMA. M.S.M. Kiwanuka, *Muteesa of Uganda* (1967).

MUTESA II, Edward Frederick
(Uganda, 1924–1969)

Kabaka Edward Frederick Mutesa II was the first president of independent Uganda and *kabaka,* or king, of the Baganda kingdom. He was deposed in a coup by Milton OBOTE and sent into exile. He was popularly and affectionately known as "King Freddie."

Born a Baganda royal prince, Edward succeeded his father as *kabaka* in 1939 but deferred his coronation until 1942 because of his age. He completed his education in England and received military training there. Baganda was the largest of four Ugandan kingdoms, all operating with limited delegated power under a British protectorate. Although the king was initially unpopular among his people, when the British attempted in 1953 to impose a unitary state on Uganda, Mutesa led the Baganda opposition to the move. He refused to submit the British proposals to his parliament, the *Lukiko,* demanding instead separation from the rest of Uganda and independence for Baganda. He was deported and replaced by a regent, but his support grew and his return was arranged in 1955 after he and the British agreed to a compromise.

Mutesa returned as a national hero and played a prominent part in the constitutional discussions leading up to Ugandan independence. He boycotted the 1960 elections for internal government to protest the lack of autonomy for Baganda. Mutesa then formed a royalist party, the Kabaka Yekka, that allied itself with Obote's Uganda People's Congress (UPC). The coalition won the first national elections in 1962, and Obote became prime minister with Mutesa as president. Mutesa also remained constitutional monarch of Baganda, although he had no executive powers. In 1966 a government crisis occurred when the opposition accused the UPC of complicity in smuggling gold from neighboring Congo-Kinshasa. Obote suspended the constitution and began to consolidate his power.

As a result, Obote and Mutesa clashed. In 1966, Mutesa rejected a new constitution that allowed Obote to become executive head of state. When Mutesa ordered all Ugandan troops out of Baganda (which included the capital), Obote ordered his arrest and had the *kabaka's* palace stormed by Colonel Idi AMIN. Mutesa escaped and again went into exile in England, while Obote abolished all the Ugandan kingdoms the following year. Mutesa died in London of alcohol poisoning. While British authorities declared it suicide, there is reasonable suspicion that he was murdered.

References: DAHB, EB, EWB, MMA, PLBA, *wiki.*

MUTINGA, John Mutuku
(Kenya, 1939–)

Dr. John Mutuku Mutinga made his career as an entomologist at the International Centre of Insect Physiology and Ecology (ICIPE), the unique scientific research center founded in Kenya by Dr. Thomas ODHIAMBO to combine both theoretical biological investigation and applied experimentation to attack problems of African health, food supply and development.

Dr. Mutinga graduated from Union College in Nebraska and received an MA from the University of Missouri in 1968. Returning home, he received his Ph.D. in entomology from the University of Nairobi while working for the Kenya Ministry of Health. He joined the ICIPE in 1979 as a research scientist and head of the Program in Medical Vector Research, which studies disease-bearing insects that transmit disease to humans. Mutinga kept this post until 1985, when he was promoted to ICIPE deputy director, a position that he held for a year. Since 1986 he has been the ICIPE's principal research scientist.

His major research has dealt with leishmaniasis, or Black-water fever, which causes liver and spleen damage in humans and can be fatal. Mutinga was the first to demonstrate that the disease exists in goats and can be transmitted to humans by animal parasites. In addition, he has studied malaria, also a vector-borne disease. He developed the ICIPE Sticky Trap, a device for controlling sandflies; it is simple enough to be used effectively by nomads and illiterate peasants.

Mutinga supplements his research with a wide variety of natural science activities that benefit the public, including membership in the East African Natural History Society and on the Kenya Museums board. He is vice chancellor of the University of Eastern Africa (UEA) at Eldoret. Since the national president is ex officio the chancellor of every university, Mutinga is in effect the president of the UEA.

Reference: PAS.

MUTOLA, Maria de Lourdes

(Mozambique, 1972–)

Maria de Lourdes Mutola is Mozambique's best-known athlete and runner. She has amassed 12 gold medals in indoor and outdoor races, including one at the 2000 Olympics.

Beginning in 1993, Mutola began a streak of wins that lasted for over 10 years, taking gold in nine World Championships, another at the 2000 Sydney Olympics and at the 2002 Commonwealth Games. In the 1996 Atlanta Olympics she took bronze and has twice taken silver at World Championships. Throughout this period, Mutola has seemed to own the 800 meter race, with almost no real competition.

Mutola loved sports as a girl, and without any facilities for women in Mozambique, she played soccer with boys' teams. Her talent was recognized early, but training opportunities were haphazard. Her first real competition was at the African Games in 1987, where she won a silver medal with almost no preparation. The following year, at age 15, she made the Mozambican Olympic team, but did not place at Seoul. She won gold at the African Games in 1990 and the next year received a grant to train in the United States. It was her first consistent training with a professional—a high-school coach who has remained with her.

Mutola established a junior world record that year. After a poor showing at the 1992 Barcelona Olympics, she began the streak of wins that established her as the leading 800 meter woman runner in the world. Along the way, in 1995 she broke the 1,000 meter world records for both indoor and outdoor races.

In 2003 Mutola was undefeated in every race, which brought her the million dollar prize for any athlete who won every race in the IAAF Golden League. In 2004, she suffered from hamstring injuries and finished fourth in the Athens Olympics. Her injuries have continued to keep her from her past form.

Reference: wiki. www.flmutola.org.mz.

MUTWA, Vusamazulu Credo

(South Africa, 1921–)

Credo Mutwa is a traditional healer and high witch doctor with a large following in South Africa. He has popularized his teachings in bestselling books.

Mutwa descends from a line of witch doctors. His father was the keeper of his clan's history and a Catholic catechist. His mother was the descendant of generations of Zulu medicine men, and the marriage broke up when she refused to convert to Christianity. Mutwa, however, continues to use his Christian name. His maternal grandfather, a medicine man and healer, taught him the secret lore. He lived with his father for many years, worked in a notions shop and did not revisit his mother and grandfather until 1954. On a visit to them, he was commanded to renounced Christianity and accept his calling. He underwent a purification ceremony and began learning the tribal secrets.

In 1963, Mutwa was named a high witch doctor or *sangoma*, based on his esoteric knowledge and healing powers. The following year he shocked traditionalists when he broke his oath of secrecy and revealed the inner arcana of his craft. The book, *Indaba, My Children*, sold a quarter million copies in South Africa, an amazing number in such a small market. He has followed this up with an autobiography and a further exposé of shamanism, *Song of Stars: Lore of a Zulu Shaman* (1995). Both of his books on shamanism take the form of stories or parables, rather than analytical presentation. Mutwa had a collection of fetishes, or sacred ritual objects used for magic, which he claims were destroyed by Zulu terrorists during political strife in 1985. They consisted of talismans, a leather phallus and several engraved tablets. From these he divined that extraterrestrial reptiles were infesting the world. He has spoken of visitors from the stars, and his UFO-tinged ideas have attracted the interest of New Age mystical devotees in America. He has also weighed in on the AIDS controversy, arguing that certain natural remedies will cure the disease, while pharmaceutical medicines are false forms of exploitation of the sick. In a country with a huge AIDS-infected populace, this is explosive teaching.

Mutwa lives in the Eastern Cape, where he directs a healing center that he founded.

Reference: Mutwa, *Indaba, My Children* (1964) and *Zulu Shaman* (2003).

MUZOREWA, Abel Tendekayi
(Zimbabwe, 1925–)

Bishop Abel Tendekayi Muzorewa, Methodist bishop and nationalist leader, was prime minister of the coalition government called Zimbabwe-Rhodesia, which failed in its attempt to create a biracial government to end the civil war.

In 1947, Muzorewa was appointed a lay preacher for five tiny congregations while he studied theology. He was ordained in 1953 and was appointed a circuit preacher for five years before spending 1958 to 1963 at Methodist colleges in the United States, where he completed a master's degree. By the 1950s he supported his people's rising nationalist feelings and, after his return, he took up a conference post as youth director, where he could channel his ministry into political activity. He led protests against the deportation of Bishop Ralph Dodge, who opposed the increasing political repression of the Ian SMITH government, which unilaterally proclaimed the independent White-ruled nation of Rhodesia in 1965. In 1968, Muzorewa was elected bishop to succeed Dodge, becoming the first African head of a major Church in Rhodesia. He came into conflict with the Smith regime, which banned him from tribal trust lands, where most of the Black Methodists lived. He continued to criticize the racist policies of the government and became a national symbol of resistance.

In 1971 the British struck a deal with Smith that provided for a transition to majority rule over decades in exchange for an end to sanctions against the government. Muzorewa joined with an inexperienced cleric, Reverend Canaan BANANA, to form the African National Congress (ANC) to oppose the settlement. (This is not to be confused with the South African ANC.) It was so successful that the proposed referendum was withdrawn. Muzorewa found himself a national leader and an international personality. The liberation movements—the Zimbabwe African National Union (ZANU) of Reverend Ndabaningi SITHOLE and the Zimbabwe African Political Union (ZAPU) of Joshua NKO-MO—both placed themselves under the ANC umbrella even though they had some doubts when Muzorewa founded a national party. The ANC was the only legal Black party once ZANU and ZAPU undertook guerrilla warfare, which it rejected. Muzorewa is a man without cunning or political guile, which was both his appeal during the 1970s and the reason for his failure. He was the acknowledged African leader, but he lacked ambition and avoided the factional politics that fueled the independence movements, but which also led to ethnic violence and bloodshed in internecine battles. Muzorewa saw himself as a Moses leading his people out of bondage; ZAPU and ZANU saw him as a figurehead maintaining a legal front while they fought the real battle for liberation.

In 1975 Sithole and Nkomo were released from the restriction that had confined them to their home villages since 1964. They promptly moved to seize control of the ANC from Muzorewa. Talks with the government collapsed, Nkomo and Sithole abandoned the ANC to begin their own splinter movements, and Muzorewa temporarily left the country. After 14 months he returned to a tumultuous welcome. Nkomo tried to outflank the bishop by joining with guerrilla leader Robert MUGABE to form the Patriotic Front (PF). After the collapse of U.S.-brokered conciliation talks in 1977, Muzorewa found himself increasingly isolated politically. The neighboring African states endorsed the PF's civil war, and Muzorewa turned to direct negotiations. In 1978, Muzorewa and Sithole (who had lost control of ZANU to Mugabe), signed an agreement with Smith for installing a majority government within a year. All citizens over 18 had the vote, but seats were reserved for Whites and they were allocated a quarter of the cabinet positions.

From the start, the transitional government was doomed to failure. Muzorewa became prime minister when his ANC carried the elections, and the country's name was changed to Zimbabwe-Rhodesia. The PF denounced the arrangement, however; the war continued, and no international recognition was forthcoming. When Muzorewa attempted to address the United Nations Security Council the day after Nkomo and Mugabe, he was not permitted to do so. The security situation deteriorated until government supporters were unsafe beyond the region around the capital. Large numbers of Whites emigrated, leaving the economy in shambles. Finally, an international all-party arrangement led to the arrival of a British administrator along with Commonwealth troops to oversee a ceasefire. In 1980 independence was achieved, and Mugabe's ZANU swept to power. Muzorewa was elected to parliament, but the ANC won only two other seats. Banana became president of Zimbabwe, with Mugabe as prime minister. Muzorewa remained in parliament but was detained from 1983 to 1984. In 1985 he returned to the United States. In 1995, Muzorewa stood for president against Mugabe, but lost badly. He divides his time between Memphis and his farm in Zimbabwe.

References: dacb, CB, DAHB, DRWW, PLBA, RWWA, *wiki*. Muzorewa, *Rise Up and Walk* (1978).

MVENG, Engelbert, S.J.
(Cameroon, 1930–1995)

Reverend Engelbert Mveng, S.J., a leading West African intellectual, combined interests in history with work in religion and the arts. He was a historian, poet, artist, theologian and a potent advocate for liberation.

After completing secondary school, Mveng joined the Jesuits and studied at the universities of Dakar, Sénégal, and Lyons, France (at the international Jesuit faculty of Fourvières) before obtaining a doctorate from the Sorbonne. In 1965, after three years of teaching at a Jesuit college, he joined the history department at the University of Yaoundé, which he chaired at various times.

Mveng's interests were wide ranging, crossing cultures, disciplines and narrowly defined fields of scholarship. This made him a Pan-Africanist politically and an interdisciplinary scholar intellectually. Mveng was deeply involved in the critique of African inculturation in Western institutions, chiefly in the arts and religion. He has written three books on the arts, the most recent being *L'Art et l'Artisanat Africain* (*African Art and Craftmanship*,1981). In 1985 he published the standard history of the Cameroon, in two volumes. The following year, his studies of African Christianity were capped with *Spiritualité et Libération en Afrique*. He has written other works on the history of African art, the Greek sources of African history, and African Christianity.

In the past decade Mveng's painting has received increased notice, and his murals in the chapel of the African Jesuit school of theology in Nairobi were featured in *TIME* magazine in 1989.

In 1983 he completed a massive (16- by 24-foot) mural for Holy Angels Parish in Chicago, the largest African-American Catholic church in the United States.

Mveng served as a consultant to the United Nations Educational, Scientific, and Cultural Organization (UNESCO) (1963–1966) and as head of cultural affairs for the Cameroonian Ministry of Education and Culture (1966–1974). As a Pan-Africanist, he has taken leadership in a number of professional associations, all groups with an activist tinge. Since 1980 he was secretary-general of the Ecumenical Association of African Theologians, and from 1981 to 1986 he was secretary-general of the Ecumenical Association of Third World Theologians. He was co-president of the World Conference on Religion and Peace and executive director of the Pan-African Movement of Christian Intellectuals. Mveng was also a member of the Academy of Overseas Sciences of the Académie Française.

He stirred up a furor when, in his historical studies, he denounced Africans who had taken part in the slave trade for being as culpable as the slavers from foreign countries. He argued that African chiefs and slavers had profited hugely from the trade and ignored the humanity of their own people.

In his later years, Mveng's thought became more politically current. He argued that poverty, not inculturation, had become the dominant theological issue in Africa. He defined this as "anthropological poverty," one that degrades one's humanity and goes beyond merely living simply. Mveng became increasingly critical of President Paul BIYA's authoritarianism, the collapse of the economy, corruption and widespread lawlessness. Protesting clergy and sisters were assassinated and their deaths not reported or investigated. Mveng suffered the same fate, murdered in his apartment at night, with the culprits never identified.

Reference: Jean-Paul Messina, *Engelbert Mveng* (in French, 2003).

MWAANGA, Vernon Johnston
(Zambia, 1939–)

Vernon Johnston Mwaanga, politician and businessman, has alternated between diplomatic posts for his government and management of several successful business enterprises. After a long absence from public life due to conflict with President Kenneth KAUNDA, he emerged in the early 1990s as a leader of the multiparty democracy movement.

Mwaanga's talent was recognized early, and he was sent to the Institute of Commonwealth Studies at Oxford University and later spent a year at Stanford University in California. Groomed for leadership when Zambia became independent, he received training at the British embassy in Rome in 1963, and the following year he served as an administrator in the prime minister's office. He was appointed Zambia's first deputy high commissioner in London in 1964, and the following year he became one of the youngest ambassadors in the world when he was named ambassador to Moscow. After a tour as permanent secretary in Kaunda's office (1966–1968), Mwaanga was named permanent representative to the United Nations, with ambassadorial appointments to four Caribbean nations from 1968 to 1972. A one-year tenure as editor of the government newspaper, the *Times of Zambia,* was followed by two years as minister of foreign affairs. It was a meteoric rise, since at this point, Mwaanga was slightly over 30.

In 1977, Mwaanga left public service to take up a variety of business interests. He became a consultant for Lonrho, the huge Anglo-African conglomerate, and chairman of the Bank of Credit and Commerce and three other corporations. All these activities were brought to an abrupt halt when Kaunda had Mwaanga detained during 1985 and 1986 on charges of foreign currency dealing and drug smuggling. At the same time, a tour company he headed was closed down by the government without explanation. During his detention, Mwaanga defended his reputation by writing an account of the events in a book titled *The Other Society: A Detainee's Diary.* He was released without formal charges being laid and resumed his business career.

An advocate of free markets and democracy, Mwaanga emerged as one of the challengers to the Kaunda regime in 1990, when he became the spokesman for the Movement for Multiparty Democracy (MMD). After the MMD victory, President Frederick CHILUBA appointed Mwaanga to his previous post as foreign minister in 1991. He began by restoring diplomatic relations with Israel and establishing them with South Africa, one of Zambia's major trading partners. He next moved to break relations with both Iraq and Iran on the grounds that their diplomats had assisted a coup

attempt involving one of Kaunda's sons. By far the most difficult issue for Mwaanga came in 1993, however, when Zambia's national soccer team was killed in a plane crash off Gabon shortly before a major international match. Mwaanga accused Gabon's security forces of complicity in the crash, especially after Gabonese authorities refused to allow outside participation in the investigations.

In 1994, Chiluba initiated moves against corruption in his government, and the old drug trafficking charge against Mwaanga appeared again. This time, foreign donor nations pressured Chiluba, and Mwaanga was forced out. Although he was not implicated in the financial irregularities that brought down several other cabinet ministers, Mwaanga resigned in anger, accusing the cabinet of being "infested with dishonest men."

He retained his influence in the governing party, however, and returned to office as minister for Information and Broadcasting in 2001. He has been an exponent of removing the American monopoly on governance of the Internet so that national governments might have greater control of it.

Reference: RWWA. Mwaanga, *An Extraordinary Life* (1982).

MWAMBUTSA IV
(Burundi, 1912–1977)

Mwami Mwambutsa IV was *mwami* (king) of Burundi from 1915 to 1966, throughout the colonial period. He came to the throne after the unexpected death of his father, who had held royal authority during much of the German colonial occupation. Within a year of his becoming *mwami,* the Germans were defeated in World War I and were replaced by the Belgians, who administered the protectorate jointly with Rwanda, its northern neighbor. Mwambutsa, unfortunately, proved to be a weak ruler. The *mwami* had retained some autonomous authority, but this was largely lost under Belgian pressure and clan and factional conflicts within the kingdom. The Belgians tolerated his indolence and sexual escapades, because they kept him from initiating resistance.

Mwambutsa himself had little influence, but his family led the nationalist movement; one of his sons, Louis Rwagasore, became the first prime minister just prior to independence. Rwagasore, however, was assassinated soon after achieving leadership, and a series of bloody conflicts followed between the dominant Hutu people and the minority Tutsi, many of whom were killed. The coups and ethnic clashes made for an unstable independence in 1962, when Burundi became a constitutional monarchy. These unsettled political conditions provided Mwambutsa with the opportunity to try to take power, and he conspired with a group of Hutu military officers to engineer a coup in 1965. It failed, and he was forced to flee the country and settle in Switzerland. A young son, Charles Ndizeye, usurped the throne and was installed as *mwami* the following year, but he was deposed by his own prime minister, Michel MICOMBERO, who declared Burundi a republic and executed the young king in 1972. Mwambutsa himself died in exile in 1977 in Geneva.

Reference: afr, DAHB, *wiki.*

MWANGA II
(Uganda, 1866?–1903)

Kabaka Mwanga II, the last independent *kabaka,* or king, of the Baganda, presided over a social and religious breakdown that transformed the kingdom and brought on British colonial rule.

When he succeeded his father, MUTESA I, Mwanga inherited a centralized kingdom already poised for profound change. Before Mutesa's time, the power base of the *kabaka* had been the hereditary chiefs, but a strong court bureaucracy had begun to centralize power. This process accelerated during Mutesa's reign and, with the introduction of Islam and Christianity, this powerful group was divided among Protestant, Catholic and Muslim courtiers. Unfortunately, the stable and sophisticated hand necessary to control this power struggle was not Mwanga's. The youth was weak and capricious, given to explosive fits of anger that he later regretted. Alongside the questioning of authority that the new religions introduced was the spectacle of a *kabaka* who did not deserve respect.

Mwanga responded to the complex politics of the kingdom by attempting to remove threats to his rule, but he did so neither decisively nor well. He removed the older chiefs who had served his father and began a sporadic persecution of the religious factions, despite his various superstitions. In 1885 he rashly approved the ambush and killing of an Anglican missionary bishop being sent to Bugan-

da[NOTE: Should this be "Baganda"?] because the bishop's route took him through an area from which ancient tradition maintained the fall of the kingdom would come. In 1886, Mwanga began a purge of Christian courtiers after several refused his sexual demands. Flying into a fury at being disobeyed and shamed, he executed a number of Christians, who were immediately considered martyrs by their brethren. Others—such as Apolo KAGGWA, who became *katikiro,* or prime minister—were restored to positions of authority after being flogged.

Finally, in 1888, Mwanga moved against all three religious factions at once, completely misjudging the erosion of his authority. The three groups united against him and swept him from power, driving him out of the country. The factions now fell upon one another, with the Muslims temporarily taking control. Ironically, the Christians then rallied around Mwanga and restored him in 1890. At this point, the European powers intervened. After Germany and Great Britain agreed that the area was in the British sphere of influence, Frederick LUGARD established a protectorate over Uganda. The British favored the Protestant cause, and the Catholics were defeated in battle in 1892 and were forced to retreat to the west of the capital. Mwanga again fled and again returned, chafing under sharply reduced authority under Kaggwa. In 1897 he led a rebellion, supported this time by the traditionalist chiefs, and maintained a guerrilla struggle for two years, joining in the resistance of Mukama KABAREGA of the neighboring kingdom of Bunyoro. They were captured and exiled to the Seychelles, where Mwanga died.

References: DAHB, EWB, *wiki.*

MWANGI, Meja
(Kenya, 1948–)

Meja Mwangi is a popular novelist whose writing exposes the gritty underbelly of urban slum life in contemporary Africa.

By far the most read of Mwangi's dozen novels is his first, *Kill Me Quick* (1973), the story of two friends in slow descent into despair as they try to grapple with poverty and lost opportunities in Nairobi, Kenya's capital. The title comes from a nickname for the cheap rot-gut liquor that they use to cloud reality. Mwangi followed with *Going Down River Road* (1976), an equally bleak account. River

Road is the heart of the city center, where it attracts drifters, thieves and a mixed collection of losers. Mwangi has twice won the Kenyatta Prize for Literature.

The Last Plague (2000) moves from the city to a village called Crossroads, and explores the ravages of AIDS. He also wrote two earlier novels that were set in the Kikuyu Highlands during the Mau Mau rebellion. In all of his work, naturalistic realism is tempered with a sardonic humor, as if looking over his shoulder at tragedy that would crush him if he did not find some of the bizarre in life.

Mwangi has also written books for young readers, and he does not soften his description of things as they are. His most recent book, *Mzungu Boy* (2005), is the account of the blossoming friendship between an African boy and the White grandson of the farm owner, as the two grapple with the impending violence of the Mau Mau in the 1950s. It is both a thriller and something deeper in its depiction of relationships and the ways in which social and political drama are played out in people's lives.

Before turning to writing, Mwangi worked as a sound technician with French television and as a film librarian for the British Council. He was assistant director of the film of Karen BLIXEN's *Out of Africa* (1986), and worked on *White Mischief* in 1988. His only formal education in writing was the Iowa Writers' Workshop, in which he participated in 1975–1976.

References: adb, CA, DLB, wiki.

MWINYI, Ali Hassan
(Tanzania, 1925–)

Ali Hassan Mwinyi, a quiet career civil servant, began the process of transition from a one-party system to a multiparty democratic one in Tanzania.

Mwinyi received a teaching certificate in 1944 and spent 20 years teaching, with a two-year sabbatical to obtain a degree at the University of Durham in 1956. Independence and the union of Zanzibar and Tanganyika placed great demands on the few educated Tanzanians, and Mwinyi was pressed into service on a number of boards and commissions, including the Film Censorship Board, the East African Currency Board, and the Zanzibar State Trading Corporation. He showed himself to be a valuable committee member who was hard-work-

ing, pragmatic, and not attached to any ideology. In 1964 he was named principal secretary to the Zanzibar Ministry of Education.

President Julius NYERERE appointed Mwinyi to the national cabinet in 1970 and made him minister of Health in 1972. In 1975 he was moved to Home Affairs but resigned as a matter of honor in 1977 after misconduct was discovered at lower levels in the ministry. Mwinyi returned to the cabinet as minister of natural resources in 1982 and then became a minister of state in the office of Vice President Aboud Jumbe. Up to this point, Mwinyi had proved himself a loyal, competent man of integrity but had not shown great political leadership. In 1984, however, when Jumbe, who was also president of Zanzibar, was forced to resign over secessionist activity there, Mwinyi became acting president of Zanzibar and was confirmed in office a few months later. He liberalized trade, improving the economy noticeably and bringing calm to the island. In 1985, when Nyerere announced his retirement, Mwinyi was chosen by the ruling party, Chama cha Mapinduzi (CCM), to succeed him as president of Tanzania.

Mwinyi faced an immediate economic crisis, the consequences of years of Nyerere's socialist experimentation. Despite opposition from the left wing of the CCM, which was still headed by Nyerere, Mwinyi accepted an economic reform package from the International Monetary Fund. He opened up the economy, cut subsidies, and reduced government employment by firing large numbers of corrupt and inefficient bureaucrats. Gradually replacing Nyerere's appointees with his own, by 1990 he had ousted the last hard-line socialists from the cabinet and forced Nyerere to turn over the leadership of the CCM to him.

Firmly in control, Mwinyi legalized opposition groups in 1992. Zanzibar continued to be disturbed, however, both by secessionist sentiment and by a small but vocal Islamic revivalist movement. A national crisis developed when Zanzibar joined the Islamic Conference (IC) in 1993. Under the union constitution, Zanzibar has no authority in international affairs, and when Mwinyi attempted to keep peace by accepting Zanzibar's act, parliament rebelled. Nyerere came out of retirement to convince Zanzibar to withdraw from the IC, but the constitutional union of Tanzania is likely to remain an issue for years to come.

Mwinyi's free-market economic policies produced some progress in an economy that was overwhelmingly dependent on foreign aid. Inflation was a serious problem throughout his term of office, however, due to a lax monetary policy that oversupplied cash into the economy. After leaving office, Mwinyi lives in retirement in Zanzibar.

References: afr, CB, CBB, DRWW, PLBA, RWWA, *wiki.*

MZILIKAZI
(Zimbabwe/South Africa, 1795?–1868)

Mzilikazi, founder of the Ndebele kingdom, was one of the great warrior-kings during the *mfecane,* a time of destructive upheaval in southern Africa. He became chief of Kumalo, a territory in South Africa's Zululand, when his grandfather murdered his father in the power struggle surrounding the ascendancy of SHAKA Zulu.

Mzilikazi allied himself with Shaka from 1818 to 1823, but after a clash he fled with several hundred warriors. Beginning as a roving outlaw band, they progressively integrated captured peoples until they had a formidable army. Mzilikazi, a former regimental commander for Shaka, taught his men Zulu tactics, including the use of the stabbing spear and shield. He formed a firm friendship with the missionary Robert MOFFAT, although he never embraced Christianity.

The Ndebele, numbering some 20,000, expanded and settled near present-day Pretoria. Their right to live there, however, was constantly challenged. In 1831, Barend BARENDS, the Griqua chief, attacked with a thousand men but was decisively defeated. A year later Zulu attacks under DINGANE forced a westward move. By 1835 to 1837, Boer encroachment provided a constant challenge. In a series of skirmishes, the Ndebele lost half their army and thousands of cattle.

Mzilikazi then began an epic trek north, splitting his people into two bands. Once they reached their destination, he confirmed his total power by executing the leaders of the second band and establishing his kingdom in Matebeleland beyond the Limpopo River, where he conquered and absorbed many Shona people. He founded a royal house and a government of regional chiefs that reported directly to him. The capital was established at Bulawayo, and the Ndebele grew to number over 100,000. In 1854, Moffat visited him, and Mzilikazi thereafter opened relations with the Afrikaners. Missionaries and traders were admitted, and a peace treaty was negotiated with the Transvaal Republic. When he died, Mzilikazi was succeeded by his son, LOBENGULA.

References: AH, DAHB, EB, EWB, MMA, *wiki.* R. Kent Rasmussen, *Mzilikazi of the Ndebele* (1977).

NANDI

(South Africa, 1760?–1827)

Queen Mother Nandi was the mother of SHAKA and the queen mother of the Zulu nation. She protected her son during his childhood, promoted his succession to the chieftaincy of the Zulu, and remained one of his chief advisors throughout her life. Much of her life is known either through oral traditions or the accounts of Shaka's enemies.

As an adolescent, Nandi had an affair with Senzangakhona, the chief of a small Zulu kingdom, and bore him a son. Some historians suggest that she and Senzangakhona married, but even if this did occur, Nandi was disgraced. After several years of persecution, she took Shaka to her own clan. They were not well received there either, so they finally settled with the Mthethwa, where Shaka entered the service of DINGISWAYO, rising to the rank of regimental commander. Upon his birth father's death, Shaka seized the chieftaincy from his legitimate brothers with Dingiswayo's support.

Nandi, after years of constant humiliations, used her new position to settle old scores. Those who had abused the mother and son were impaled on long spikes and left to die as warnings of Shaka's total power. Shaka never married and took no official concubines, so Nandi assumed an even greater role than that usually accorded the queen mother. In many African societies the mother of the king (rather than his wife, who might be only one among many) was an important counselor. Nandi maintained a small court of her own and had retainers to do her bidding.

In 1827, Nandi died and Shaka decreed a period of mourning that triggered a bloodbath. Thousands were slain and symbols of motherhood were attacked so that everyone would realize what it was to lose a mother and to mourn as Shaka mourned. Pregnant women and their husbands were killed, cows with calves were slaughtered and crops were forbidden to be planted. Even milk, an essential of the Zulu diet, was forbidden. There were rumors that Shaka had had Nandi killed, and his psychotic behavior seriously weakened his control. Within a year of Nandi's death, Shaka was assassinated.

References: afr, DAHB, *wiki*.

NASCIMENTO, Lopo Fortunato

(Angola, 1942–)

Lopo Fortunato Nascimento, veteran activist with the Popular Movement for the Liberation of Angola (MPLA), has become the government's leading pragmatist as it moves away from Marxist ideology.

Nascimento is a native of Luanda, the capital, where he was educated at a commercial school. At age 14 he became a resistance activist with the MPLA, and he was arrested by the secret police for the first time at age 17. He was imprisoned from 1963 to 1968, after which he went into labor organizing, and in 1974 he joined the MPLA central committee. Although he had not participated in the armed struggle, when the Portuguese granted Angola independence in 1975, he was the MPLA representative on the three-party transitional government. At independence there was already conflict among the MPLA, Holden ROBERTO's National Front for the Liberation of Angola (FNLA), and Jonas SAVIMBI's National Union for the Total Independence of Angola (UNITA). In 1975 the FNLA attempted to assassinate Nascimento.

When the MPLA established the first independent government, Nascimento was appointed prime minister by President Agostinho NETO, although the post held little power. (It was abolished in 1978 and then restored in 1991.) Nascimento's appointment was widely interpreted as a move against the pragmatists on the part of Marxist hard-liners, who felt that they were not ideologically strong enough. In the meantime, the MPLA government was locked in a bitter civil war with UNITA, which was increasingly dependent on Soviet aid and Cuban troops, while Savimbi received supplies from the West and military assistance from South Africa. Nascimento became executive secretary for the United Nations Economic Commission on Africa until José DOS SANTOS succeeded Neto. Nascimento then headed the ministry of trade until 1982 and the ministry of planning until 1986, at which point he became provincial commissioner in the southwest region. In this last post he created a model for the rehabilitation of war-torn areas that was later adopted on a national level.

After the MPLA rejected Marxism in 1990, Nascimento was recalled to act for the MPLA in the peace settlement with UNITA and then was made territorial administrative officer. In 1994, marking the MPLA's further shift from Marxism, he was elected secretary-general of the party.

Reference: RWWA.

NAUDÉ, Christiaan Frederick Beyers
(South Africa, 1915–2004)

Reverend Christiaan Frederick Beyers Naudé was a leading Afrikaner critic of apartheid and an important witness of conscience.

Naudé's father, a Dutch Reformed minister, was a central figure in the Afrikaner cultural revival as a pioneer in promoting the Afrikaans language and as one of the founders of the Broederbond, the Afrikaner secret society. He named his son for a general with whom he had fought in the Boer War (1899–1902). Naudé followed the family tradition, studying at Stellenbosch University, the center of Afrikaner thought, where he received an MA in languages and a degree in theology in 1939. During that year he became the youngest member of the Broederbond and was ordained in the Dutch Reformed Church (DRC). For 20 years he was a pastor at various places throughout the country; among Afrikaners he served as a respected clergyman who was convinced of apartheid's biblical basis. His last position was in a wealthy Pretoria church attended by several cabinet members.

In 1960, Naudé was profoundly shaken by the Sharpeville massacre, in which 69 Africans were killed while peacefully demonstrating against the pass laws, which restricted movement and work for Africans. Deeply disillusioned, he began an intense study of the Bible and concluded that apartheid was unjust and unsupported by the scriptures. In Sharpeville's aftermath, the World Council of Churches (WCC) convened a meeting of the leadership of the world's eight major Reformed bodies to discuss apartheid. Naudé had became acting moderator of his church district and then moderator, the

highest local office. He directed the DRC to accepting the final statement that rejected apartheid. In opposition, the South African prime minister, Dr. Hendrik VERWOERD, led a conservative backlash that reaffirmed the argument that there was a biblical basis for apartheid, and this position led to the withdrawal of the DRC from the WCC. Naudé refused to alter his position in the face of the Church synod's fury. In 1963 he resigned as moderator and founded the Christian Institute (CI), an ecumenical organization to pursue reconciliation through interfaith dialog. For this action he was defrocked, and he subsequently left the Broederbond. He commented to his wife, "We must prepare for 10 years in the wilderness."

Both Naudé and the CI were harassed from the start. When invited to address a DRC youth meeting, he was dragged from the building by DRC officials. The security police raided his home and the CI offices. Naudé spoke out against the rising tide of Black violence as well as against apartheid, but as CI became more radical, it allied itself with the liberation theology of Steve BIKO's Black Consciousness Movement (BCM), which rejected both White racism and liberal paternalism. Many CI staff were banned or had their passports withdrawn.

Naudé and the CI began a campaign of consciousness-raising among Christian Churches. Deflecting accusations of left-wing WCC interference, he stated that "if blood runs in the streets of South Africa it will not be because the World Council of Churches has done something but because the Churches of South Africa have done nothing." This bold statement prompted a parliamentary inquiry into CI and several other Christian groups in 1973, but Naudé refused to testify. In 1977 he was banned for five years. In 1980 he resigned from the DRC and was received by the African Reformed Church, which accepted his orders and gave him a pulpit. He succeeded Desmond TUTU as secretary-general of the South African Council of Churches in 1984 and held that post until his retirement in 1987. Although he was never connected to the African National Congress (ANC), Naudé was named to its negotiating team for the 1992 constitutional talks with the government of F. W. DE KLERK. Ill health dogged him in his later years and he withdrew from active politics.

References: afr, dacb, GSAP, wiki. G. McLeod Bryan, *Naudé: Prophet to South Africa* (1978); Peter Randall, *Not Without Honor* (1983).

NCUBE, Bernard Nekie Zellie

(South Africa, 1935–)

Sister Bernard Nekie Zellie Ncube is a women's activist and longtime opponent of South African apartheid. She served in ANC governments after the end of apartheid.

A member of the Companions of Angela, a Black Catholic religious order founded by the Ursulines when apartheid laws prevented White religious communities from accepting African members, she received teacher training and a diploma in theology at Roma College in Lesotho. She taught in Catholic schools in Johannesburg until 1980, when she turned to adult education. There she became involved primarily with consciousness-raising among African women. She also spent seven years on the staff of the South African Bishops' Conference (SABC), coordinating training programs for Catholic nuns in rural areas. During this period Sister Bernard became closely allied with Father Smangaliso MKHATSHWA, the general secretary of the SABC. She began working with mothers and in 1984 formed the Federation of Transvaal Women (FEDTRAW), which she has led since then. Using community organizing techniques, FEDTRAW—which focuses on the social, legal, economic and political status of women—has become an action group affiliated with the United Democratic Front (UDF), the multiracial political organization that represented the African National Congress (ANC) during its banning.

FEDTRAW was concerned that the liberation movement would bypass women, and its position (stated in its Women's Charter) was that the freedom of women had to parallel that of the general population. Ncube was detained six times under apartheid, including once when she spent three months in solitary confinement under the emergency regulations of 1986. Her cause came to international attention, along with that of detainees MKHATSHWA and Zwelakhe SISULU. She was subsequently freed but then was rearrested with a number of others and charged with sedition and subversion. Finally, however, the state withdrew the charges when they could not be substantiated.

In 1989, Ncube was part of the UDF delegation that met with President George Bush, and since 1991 she has been a member of the National Executive Committee of the ANC. In 1994 she was elected to the South African parliament on the ANC ticket. She served eight years, at various times chairing the parliamentary committees of ethics and arts, culture, science and technology. Her positions have followed the ANC line, but on free bills she has shown a streak of independence. She defended abortion in the debates on the Abortion Bill. Her sometimes strident feminism and unorthodox positions have earned her opponents in her Church, although her sisterhood has stood by her.

Ncube became mayor of the West Rand region, where she supervised four municipalities, mostly under women deputy mayors. All of them received high marks for integrity, transparency and fiscal responsibility, and Ncube has acquired a reputation as a good administrator. In 2006, she announced her intention to retire from politics.

Reference: dacb, GSAP.

NCUBE, Pius Alick Mvundla

(Zimbabwe, 1946–)

Archbishop Pius Ncube has been the leading public figure to oppose the growing autocracy of President Robert MUGABE of Zimbabwe. He has mobilized a wide spectrum of Church leaders of various Christian denominations, even though he has also run into opposition within his own Catholic Church.

Raised in a rural peasant family, Ncube became Catholic at age 14, walking alone for 10 kilometers to his baptism because his family disapproved. He was already determined to enter the seminary. Ordained in 1973, he took graduate studies in theology in Rome and was then assigned to Matabeleland. After working in city parishes, he was named the first Black archbishop of Bulawayo, the capital, in 1997.

Ncube was radicalized in the early 1980s when Mugabe's North Korean-trained special forces ravaged the Matabele heartland, murdering and raping in atrocities that cost 20,000 lives. People had to watch as their loved ones were herded into huts and burned alive while they were forced to dance and sing songs of praise to Mugabe. Catholic authorities painstakingly documented the barbarities, but only some of the Zimbabwean bishops endorsed the final report. Ncube is one, and he has been a staunch defender of those who have suffered under Mugabe. He organized other Christian leaders into a faith coalition against injustice and poverty. Together they have provided a voice as the only community organizations able to reach a majority of the people and speak independently.

In 2005, Ncube spoke out against the government's food distribution system, arguing that malnutrition would add to the death toll from AIDS, already at 700 persons per day. His criticisms of Mugabe have been directed at him personally. Ncube has accused the government of treason and called on the populace to rise up in a peaceful revolution to remove Mugabe from power. He compared Mugabe to Pol Pot, the murderous tyrant of Cambodia. In one of his regular radio broadcasts, Ncube asked for prayers for Mugabe's death, "since the man will not go on his own." In a press interview he commented that "death cannot come too soon for evil Mugabe." He even suggested that the international community remove him from Zimbabwe.

For his stands against the oppressive regime in Zimbabwe, Ncube was awarded the 2005 Humanitarian Award of Robert Burns International, and the Human Rights Award of Human Rights First in 2003. United States Secretary of State Colin Powell praised him for his forthright positions. For every award of praise, Ncube has received criticism at home. Mugabe called him a "liar," and the national government paper has called him "demented" and suggested that he be excommunicated. He has received death threats. In 2003 Ncube suffered a stroke, but he continues his activism.

Reference: wiki.

NDABANEZE, Pontien
(Burundi, 1952–)

Dr. Pontien Ndabaneze, a botanist, has done his main work on grasses and grasslands. Among his major publications is a pharmacopoeia of Burundi that lists the medicinal plants found in the country.

Ndabaneze studied science at the University of Burundi before traveling to Belgium for graduate studies. He received his MA in ecology from Louvain University and, in 1983, a Ph.D. in botany from the University of Liège. Beginning in 1977 he was a lecturer in sciences at the University of

Burundi and was promoted to professor in 1983. Ndabaneze headed the biology department there from 1984 to 1986 and became dean of the faculty of agronomy the following year.

Ndabaneze is one of a growing group of African biologists who study traditional uses of healing plants, including herbal medicine. Some Western scientists have dismissed this research as being without value, arguing that the practice of traditional healing has being based on witchcraft and superstition rather than on sound scientific principles. But in recent years strictly controlled experiments have demonstrated the curative effects of some herbs and traditional practices on specific diseases. Western medicines can be inappropriate for treating illnesses found largely in Africa, and the study of traditional medicine opens up new approaches that Western research would not consider. The study of traditional medicines also has an economic benefit for African countries, because it produces medicines less costly for African health systems. One of the main avenues of this research is to identify the beneficial chemicals in medicinal plants. Ndabaneze, who has done research on plants containing essential oils, is working on this problem.

Dr. Ndabaneze served as the African representative on the Plant Committee of the Council on International Trade in Endangered Species (CITES), which identifies plants to be protected from exploitation under the CITES treaty, to which most nations are signatories.

Reference: PAS.

N'DOUR, Youssou
(Sénégal, 1959–)

Youssou N'Dour, a leading figure to emerge from the world music movement of the 1980s, influenced the direction of Sénégalese popular music and became well known in Europe, although only since the 1990s has he been recognized in the United States.

As a teenager, N'Dour found the local music scene dominated by Cuban *pachangas* and American soul music. Within a few years he had transformed that scene by the introduction of African rhythms and other traditional elements, creating the *mbalax* sound. Multiple percussionists, guitarists and saxophonists provide a pulsating rhythm through which

Youssou N'Dour

N'Dour's high tenor bobs and weaves. He sings in his native Wolof and in French with remarkable control and power. *Mbalax* is a griot word for the sound of talking drums. Even in its fused form, it is a direct descendant of Congolese rhumba, which derived from Cuba, which in turn was born from West African music.

N'Dour was born into a clan of griots, whose historic task is to preserve family histories by composing genealogies, reciting and singing them at traditional rituals. He joined his first professional group at age 15. N'Dour achieved immediate popularity in Sénégal and then went to Paris, where he formed the band Super Étoile—Superstar.

N'Dour's music reflects his heritage with its echoes of the Islamic call to prayer and lyrics inspired by family, local proverbs and daily life. For his first American tour (1987) he released an album, *Nelson Mandela,* to highlight the political crisis of South Africa. He also sang on Paul Simon's *Graceland* album and toured with Bruce Springsteen, Sting and other artists on the Amnesty International Human Rights Tour in 1988. In 1992 he made a second U.S. tour, featuring songs from *Eyes Open,* an album released by filmmaker Spike Lee. N'Dour produced the album in his own studio in Dakar. He continues to be prolific, and his discography includes over 20 albums and 30 cassettes. Eleven original albums and three compilations have come out since 2000. He was a finalist for the Kora Awards in 2001 after being named best artist in 1996. The year before he had won Song of the Year at the World Music Awards.

According to N'Dour, African musicians need to be in touch with their traditional sources but should not limit themselves stylistically. As a result, he has experimented with rock, hip hop and jazz influences. His most recent album, *Egypt*, is a celebration of Islamic Sufi mysticism, where the griot elements—traditional drumming and praise-singing styles—have come to the fore over the Afro-Cuban sound. He bristles at criticism by such fellow African stars as Remmy ONGALA that his adaptations have compromised African music: "Isn't it time to leave behind such tired ways of listening? I am no longer afraid of interacting with other music," he has said.

The music journal *Rolling Stone* extolled his achievements and his promise: "If any Third World performer has a real shot at the sort of universal popularity enjoyed by Bob Marley, it's Youssou, a singer with a voice so extraordinary that the history of Africa seems locked in it."

References: adb, *afr*, CB, CBB, CM, DMM, GEPM, WAM, *wiki*. www.youssou.com.

NELSON, (Barima) Azumah

(Ghana, 1958–)

Azumah Nelson was a three-time world champion boxer who continued to contend for titles until his retirement at age 39.

Nelson was a fine amateur boxer with 50 wins in 52 bouts before turning professional at age 21. Within a year he was Ghanaian and African champion in his weight class. He made his mark in 1982 when a mixed-up schedule caused him to be substituted in a bout with the featherweight World Boxing Commission (WBC) titleholder, and fought him for 15 rounds before taking a loss on points. The previous unknown was now in demand, and two years later he captured the WBC title. He defended the title six times before moving up to the super featherweight class in 1988 and taking that title as well. Although he failed in an attempt to take the lightweight title, Nelson defended super featherweight six times, including one draw.

In 1993 in Mexico City, Nelson defended his title before 120,000 fans, the largest boxing crowd in history. That same year he began a legendary series of four fights with Jesse James Leija. Two of his losses were against Leija. In his final fight in 1998, he lost to Leija in a bout for the International Boxing Association (IBA) lightweight title. Nelson broke his left hand in the fifth round but went the full 12-round bout. In 2004, he was elected to the International Boxing Hall of Fame.

In retirement from boxing, Nelson has been active in civic affairs. He began a campaign to get wealthy business people to support special education, starting off with a contribution of 10 million cedis (about US$1,100). He is active in promoting eco-tourism and was named Environmental Ambassador in 2004.

References: adb, wiki.

NETO, Antônio Agostinho
(Angola, 1922–1979)

Dr. Antônio Agostinho Neto, the founder and first president of independent Angola, was deeply involved in the liberation movement in his country to oust the colonial Portuguese from power.

From his youth, Neto was politically active. He worked in the colonial health services until 1947, when the people of his village banded together to gather funds to send him to Portugal to study medicine. In Lisbon, he joined youth groups and became openly anticolonial. He cooperated with Amílcar CABRAL and other anticolonial leaders. Neto was imprisoned three times for his activities and writing. In 1958 he received his medical degree and returned to Angola to establish a private practice in gynecology. He was already involved in the Popular Movement for the Liberation of Angola (MPLA), founded in 1956.

In 1961, Neto was arrested, and when a popular demonstration resulted, the police killed 30 people. The Portuguese deported Neto to Cape Verde and later to Lisbon, where he was placed under house arrest. He escaped to Congo-Kinshasa (now the Democratic Republic of the Congo), where he became president of the MPLA and directed the armed struggle that had begun in Angola. The movement went through a period of crisis with rival factions led by Holden ROBERTO—who was recognized by Congo-Kinshasa and the Organization of African Unity (OAU)—and the National Union for the Total Independence of Angola (UNITA), led by Jonas SAVIMBI and assisted by South Africa. Neto concentrated on organization within Angola, where MPLA policies, based on socialism and nonracial equality, soon attracted a mass following. In 1965 the OAU recognized the MPLA as an accredited liberation movement, and in 1968 it withdrew its recognition of Roberto's faction. The 1974 revolution in Portugal altered the situation dramatically, when the new socialist government decreed the immediate independence for Portuguese colonies. Angola achieved its independence the following year, with Neto as president.

His time in office was marked by armed conflict. MOBUTU Sese Seko, the dictator of what was then named Zaïre, actively opposed him and supported Roberto, his son-in-law, while UNITA guerrillas operated with South African and American support. Neto turned to the Soviet Union for military aid and to Cuba for troops, but he was never able to resolve the unity crisis among the three nationalist forces. Neto's economic policy was less dependent on socialist states, and he encouraged Western investment, especially in oil production and trade. He died of cancer in Moscow and was succeeded by José Eduardo DOS SANTOS.

Neto was a quiet person—reserved, cautious and moderate—preferring the intellectual life to a public one. He remains the most prominent Angolan poet, and his work has been published in many editions in a dozen languages. Much of it deals with the theme of freedom, and some poems became popular liberation songs. Chinua ACHEBE memorialized him in a poem at his passing: "I will celebrate/The man who rode a trinity/Of awesome fates to the cause/Of our trampled race!/Thou Healer, Soldier and Poet!"

References: afr, AA, CA, DAHB, DRWW, DT, EWB, MMA, NRG, PLBA, PLCA, wiki. Agostino Neto (film in Portuguese, 2000)

NGOUABI, Marien
(Congo, 1939–1977)

Major Marien Ngouabi, a military ruler who came to power through a coup, attempted to develop the Congo into a Marxist state, altering traditional social and political patterns and creating a climate of repression and instability. The Congo Republic should not be confused with the Democratic Republic of the Congo, which borders it. At independence, it was commonly known as Congo-Brazzaville to distinguish it from Congo-Kinshasa.

After secondary school, Ngouabi joined the army in 1960, the year of Congolese independence from France. He was subsequently sent to France for officer's training. He returned to spend a year in charge of a small garrison before being promoted to captain and being assigned to establish a paratroop battalion in the capital, Brazzaville. From 1963 to 1966, Ngouabi was part of a circle of junior officers who became his political base. They shared a common interest in Marxism, which was also the professed ideology of President Alphonse MASSEMBA-DÉBAT. In 1966, Ngouabi was reassigned, and this event, along with a plan to incorporate the army into the national militia, touched off an officers' revolt. Ngouabi, as a leader in the mutiny, was demoted, but the merger plans were dropped and the head of the army was removed.

Over the next several years, political conditions in the Congo were turbulent. Ngouabi was assigned to the general staff, but amid rumors of an impending coup in 1968, he was arrested. His loyal paratroops freed him from prison, but after several days of confusion, Massemba-Débat reestablished himself in the presidency, with Ngouabi as army chief of staff and chair of the National Revolutionary Council (NRC). After a few months Massemba-Débat was forced out of office and Ngouabi became president in 1969, following a brief struggle for power within the NRC.

Ngouabi began to inaugurate his version of communism, changing the national party into a workers' party, introducing a red national flag with hammer and sickle, and establishing the Communist hymn, the *Internationale*, as the national anthem. He nationalized the critical oil industry, causing the United States to impose tariff restrictions on the Congo. He also abolished bride price, which customarily bound together the families of a prospective bride and groom through a traditional exchange of cattle, gifts and money. Ngouabi's real power lay in the army, which he made into one of the most politicized in Africa. When he was challenged by a series of plots, attempted coups and public opposition, he purged the army and civil service several times and merged all military and paramilitary forces under one command.

In 1973, Ngouabi attempted to broaden his political base and permitted a national assembly to function. This effort did little, however, to dampen opposition. In 1976 the unions called a general strike, which the government suppressed harshly by jailing the labor leadership. The following March, during a failed coup attempt, Ngouabi was assassinated. Massemba-Débat was executed for complicity in the coup, and in the following week a number of national leaders were also murdered, including the cardinal-archbishop of Brazzaville. The army, under Colonel Joachim YHOMBI-OPANGO, confirmed its authority and declared a month of national mourning for Ngouabi.

References: afr, DAHB, DRWW, MMA, PLBA, *wiki*. Théophile Obenga, *La Vie de Marien Ngouabi* (*The Life of Marien Ngouabi*, 1977).

NGUGI wa Thiong'o
(Kenya, 1938–)

Ngugi wa Thiong'o is a leading Kenyan novelist, social and political critic, writer, and prominent dissident. Not only are his novels and critical works among the most significant to appear by an African author, but his theories of African writing have had a profound effect across the continent.

Ngugi studied at Makerere University in Uganda and at the University of Leeds in Britain before joining the English Department at the University of Nairobi in 1967. By this time he had already published *Weep Not, Child* (1964), *The River Between* (1965), and *A Grain of Wheat* (1967). All three emphasize Kenyan historical themes: the Mau Mau rebellion, life among the Kikuyu during the period in which colonial rule destroyed local traditions, and the struggle against British rule. In 1970, in sympathy with a student strike over the banning of a campus appearance by Oginga ODINGA, Ngugi resigned and spent a year teaching at Northwestern University in Evanston, Illinois. He then returned to Nairobi to reform the curriculum, replacing the English Department with one of African languages and literature. In 1973 he published *Homecoming*, his critical essays on African and Caribbean literature and culture. All this early work established the theme for his later writing: the need to free African societies of the remnants of neocolonial thinking. At this time he gave up his Christian name, James, to return to ancestral religion.

Ngugi's fiction creates memorable characters sketched with economy yet with psychological depth. Sometimes the characters present a serious political message, but Ngugi's sense of irony and outrage fuel a passion for justice that engages both the fictional personalities and the reader. His 1986 novel, *Matigari,* for example, is an allegory concerning a freedom fighter who emerges from the bush seeking truth and justice. He discovers that both have been betrayed by the new masters. At the end, Matigari digs up his buried weapons and takes off his belt of peace.

Ngugi has always considered the corruption and venality of African leaders to be a product of colonialism. In 1977 he began an adult literacy program that involved political education. As a result, he was imprisoned for a year by the government of President Jomo KENYATTA. His Gikuyu play, *Ngaahika Ndeenda (I Will Marry When I Want)* was suppressed as "too provocative." A new novel that year, *Petals of Blood,* was a slashing indictment of the Kenyan elite. In 1982, Ngugi went to London for the publication of his prison journals. While he was in England, an attempted coup against Kenyan President Daniel arap MOI took place, and several of Ngugi's friends were implicated in the conspiracy. Fearful of returning, Ngugi remained in exile.

Since his self-imposed exile, Ngugi's focus has shifted from colonialism to neocolonialism, the dependency and exploitation created by Western economic forces in collaboration with corrupt African leadership. Since 1977 he has culturally underlined this view by writing fiction only in Gikuyu or Kiswahili, although all of his later work has been translated. He has said: "Language is a carrier of a people's culture, culture is a carrier of a people's values; values are the basis of a people's self-definition. When you destroy a people's language, you are destroying that which helps them to define themselves . . . that which embodies their collective memory as a people." He has stated his views most forcefully in *Decolonizing the Mind: The Politics of Language in African Literature* (1986), *Moving the Center: The Struggles for Cultural Freedom* (1993), and

Penpoints, Gunpoints and Dreams (1998). In the second he argues for the empowerment of cultural centers in Asia, Africa and Latin America to end the dominance of Eurocentrism. Ngugi's work since 1977 has been influenced by Marxist analysis.

After a lecture tour of the United States, Ngugi joined the Yale University faculty from 1989 to 1993, moved to New York University, and has been at the University of California at Irvine since 2002, where he is head of the International Center for Writing and Translation.

In 2004, he returned to Kenya for his first visit since going into exile. While there, thugs broke into his hotel room, raped his wife and brutally beat him.

References: *adb, afr,* AA, AWT, CANR, DLB, EB, EWB, MBW, NRG, *wiki,* WLTC. Carol Sicherman, *Ngugi wa Thiong'o: The Making of a Rebel* (1990).

NGUGI, John
(Kenya, 1962–)

John Ngugi is an outstanding member of the new generation of Kenyan long-distance runners who burst upon the scene in the late 1980s and have subsequently dominated many international events. Before 1964, Black Africans had won only 20 Olympic gold medals, but since that year, the first in which independent nations from Africa competed, there have been over 80 gold medals, a third of which have been awarded to Kenyans in track and field. Ngugi won five cross-country titles in his short career.

Ngugi followed the pattern of this legion of great runners and has been at the head of the pack. He was raised in the hills along the Rift Valley and ran to school every day, as other Kikuyu boys ran in the thin air at 5,000 feet, or about 1,500 meters, to visit other families and to herd cattle. The Kikuyu diet of milk, corn meal, and vegetables is high in carbohydrates, which contributed to his athletic development. Ngugi joined the Kenyan army as a young man, and in regular training he averaged about 19 miles (30 kilometers) of running daily, including the famous long Agony Hill, on which many Kenyan running greats have trained.

Ngugi had an unorthodox style but ran a conservative race with little flash. He started slowly but steadily, building a lead that requires little kick at the end. He used a long, loping stride, with his left arm hanging at his side. In 1986, Ngugi entered and won the world cross-country championships—the first time he had run the 12-mile distance (about 20 kilometers). He then repeated his success for each of the next three years. Showing versatility, Ngugi then took the 5,000 meter gold medal at the 1988 Seoul Olympics. He ran a blistering race, leading from the start and never faltering. After 1989, however, he went into a slump and for several years did not win a major race.

Ngugi returned to the headlines dramatically in 1992, winning his fifth world championship in cross-country, running in Boston's snow and bitter winds. He ran perhaps his best race, taking the lead before the half and never relinquishing it. However, he failed to qualify for the Kenyan Olympic team later that year.

In early 1993 he refused a routine drug test by International Amateur Athletics Association (IAAA) doctors who came to his village. He claimed that he was duped, but a four-year suspension was slapped on him and then lifted amid intense negotiation between the IAAA and the Kenyan association. An independent tribunal exonerated Ngugi. At that point he retired from competition. His later business investments failed and in 2005 he was dismissed from the army without a pension. He has alleged that all his misfortunes are the result of personal enemies, but many are critical of Kenya's national policy of denying support to retired athletes who have represented the country internationally.

Reference: wiki.

NICO, "Docteur"
(Democratic Republic of the Congo, 1939–1985)

Docteur Nico was an influential guitarist and orchestra leader whose work strongly influenced younger musicians throughout Africa. In the 1960s and 1970s his crisp guitar style was dominant at the height of the popularity of Congo music, which fused jazz and Latin rhythms. Nico launched his career supported by the best musicians of the time.

Nico's parents were themselves performers, but he encountered his major cultural influences when the family migrated to the capital of Kinshasa (then Léopoldville) in the late 1940s. The clubs and first

recording studios (which supplied instruments and became informal centers for jam sessions) generated scores of opportunities for contacts, performing, and sharing ideas and techniques. Musicians took the availability of the Hawaiian guitar, the popularity of Cuban rumba, and their familiarity with African music and fused those elements into a new sound.

In 1953, Nico and some friends formed a group called African Jazz. Nico was too young to perform in public, but he could record, and he would slip out after school until he was eligible for a work permit. African Jazz was chosen to make a Belgian tour during the Belgian Congo's independence negotiations in 1960, which provided Nico's first European exposure. After independence, the band incorporated Tabu LEY Rochereau and other well-known performers and became Orchestre African Fiesta. Ley formed his own group after a few years, but Nico and Ley remained friends. That was not the case with Nico and FRANCO, another major musician, with whom Nico built an intense rivalry. Fans were divided between loyalty to Nico's progressive sound and Franco's more traditional sound, and the two took to writing songs that mocked each other. For 10 years Nico was a major presence in west and central Africa, attracting large crowds. He made very little money, however, because recording companies paid no royalties and often demanded taping sessions for up to a hundred songs for a small flat fee. His discography is almost impossible to trace.

One of Nico's nicknames was "God of the Guitar" for his virtuosity. Perhaps the greatest African guitarist, he is credited with creating several dance styles, and some consider him as the one who began *soukous*, the dominant dance idiom of Congolese pop.

By the late 1970s his own recording company collapsed, and Nico stopped performing. In 1983 he began recording again, but his health soon declined and he died in 1985. Two of his posthumous albums from this period are *Adieu* (1989) and *Dernière Mémoire* (1990).

References: BPAR, DMM, GEPM, MMA, WAM, *wiki*. www.muzikfan.com/africaframe.html. Gary Stewart, *Rumba on the River* (2000).

NICOL, Davidson Sylvester Abioseh

(Sierra Leone, 1924–1994)

Dr. Abioseh Nicol was a Leonean scholar, diplomat and writer with a varied career, in each part of which he made significant contributions.

Nicol was always enamored of science and worked as a lab technician before going to Great Britain to study medicine. After graduating from Cambridge University, he was rejected by a leading London medical school because of his race, but persisted until he found a placement where he finished medical studies for the MD. He practiced medicine in England and then took a Ph.D. in sciences in 1956. The following year he was named a fellow of Christ's College, Cambridge, the first Black African so honored. He then returned to Africa to teach at the University of Ibadan in Nigeria. Later he was named the first Leonean principal at Forah Bay College, then was made vice chancellor, 1966–1969. Since the position of chancellor is an honorary one usually given to the national president, he was in effect the president of the university. At the same time, he continued his research, which led to the discovery of human insulin, which has a profound effect on the treatment of diabetes.

In 1969, Nicol entered the Leonean diplomatic service as permanent representative (ambassador) to the United Nations (U.N.), and from 1971 to 1972 high commissioner (ambassador) to the United Kingdom. He was then tapped to be undersecretary-general of the U.N. for 10 years as executive director of the U.N. Institute for Training and Research (UNITAR). He finished his academic career with brief stints at two American universities as a Distinguished Professor of International Studies. Throughout both his academic and diplomatic careers, he wrote on international and African affairs. To this he added a number of short stories, some of which were published in collections, and others anthologized. He was influenced by the African-American writer Langston Hughes, who encouraged him to write fiction. His stories drew on the Creole culture of Sierra Leone, and explored the relations between Africans and colonial authorities. He wrote fiction under the name Abioseh Davidson.

Reference: adb.

NIMEIRY, Gaafar Mohammed

(Sudan, 1930–)

Major-General Gaafar Mohammed Nimeiry was Sudan's military dictator for 15 years. At first he insisted on national unity and negotiated with the separatist movement in the southern provinces, but in the last years of his regime he began to introduce Islamic revivalist policies that alienated them.

Nimeiry attended the elite Hantoub School, which educated many of Sudan's leaders, but he was at first known more for his soccer abilities than his studies. He grew into an ardent nationalist at Hantoub, joining a seven-month student strike in 1946 against the Anglo-Egyptian administration of the Sudan. In 1949 he entered the Sudanese Military College, graduating with a commission in 1952. He served in several battalions and was twice sent to Egypt for advanced training in armor. There he was impressed with Gamal Abdel Nasser and his anticolonial military regime, and Nasser became his role model and hero. In 1953, Nimeiry formed the Free Officers' Association (FOA), a secret society with the same name and goals as one set up by Nasser when he was plotting his coup in Egypt. The FOA was nationalist but not ideological, and it lasted until 1957, when the Sudan declared its independence and the new government moved against all suspicious groups. Nimeiry was arrested along with a number of other junior officers and cadets and was dismissed from the army.

After the 1958 coup of General Ibrahim ABBOUD, Nimeiry was reinstated and quietly began to reestablish the FOA. He was assigned to the Juba command in the south, where he saw the results of the government's program to Arabize the southerners. He became convinced that a military solution to conflict between the Arab Islamic north and the Black Christian and animist south was impossible. In 1963 he was sent away by the authorities to take military courses in Cyprus, Libya and West Germany to cool his revolutionary ardor. He returned in time to join the coup that replaced Abboud in 1964. Nimeiry was arrested on counter-coup charges but was cleared and sent to the United States, where he did graduate studies at the U.S. Army Command and General Staff College at Fort Leavenworth, Kansas.

During the period of ineffectual government in Sudan from 1964 to 1969, Nimeiry was alternately rewarded, then shunted aside to desert posts. In 1969 he was serving as the head of the infantry school in Khartoum when he initiated another coup and seized power. He formed a government of Communists and Nasser-style nationalists, with the most serious opposition coming from Islamic revivalists, especially the Ansar sect led by Sadiq al-MAHDI. In 1970 there was an open clash in which about 1,000 Ansar followers died and the movement retreated. Nimeiry then turned against the left, causing radical officers to arrest him in 1971. Freed in a dramatic rescue, Nimeiry purged the army and had his coup confirmed in a fraudulent election in which he received 98.6 percent of the vote.

In 1972 he negotiated a settlement in the south, allowing regional autonomy in exchange for the southerners' abandonment of their secessionist demands. Pressed by expanding Islamic fundamentalism, he reneged on parts of the agreement, and in 1983 he introduced elements of the Islamic law, *sharia,* including the banning of all alcohol and the use of severe physical punishment. This only served to reignite the civil war between the Islamic north and the Christian and animist south.

Nimeiry fostered the exploration and development of oil and gas deposits throughout his term, and negotiated contracts with the American firm, Chevron. In later years this would become Sudan's main source of foreign exchange, but when a drought and economic decline led to a famine in 1984, Sudan faced a crisis. Nimeiry became increasingly authoritarian, even turning on the Muslim Brotherhood, which he had been trying to placate. In 1985, while he was in the United States seeking famine aid, he was deposed and went into exile in Egypt. He returned to the Sudan in 1999.

References: afr, CB, DRWW, PLBA, RWWA, *wiki.*

NKETIA, J(oseph) H(anson) Kwabena

(Ghana, 1921–)

Professor Kwabena Nketia is Africa's leading musicologist. He has had a profound effect on the study of ethnomusicology throughout the world. He is recognized as the leading figure in the study of African musical theory.

Nketia was first trained as a teacher in Ghana, and then received a scholarship to study linguistics at the School of Oriental and African Studies at the University of London. He took the opportunity to plunge himself into a personal study of Western music. He began to bring his studies of linguistics and social anthropology together with his increasing competence in music. He then studied for a period at Trinity College of Music in London and New York's Juilliard School of Music.

As he began to publish his research on African music after his return to Ghana, recognition came for his pioneering work. He began to divide his time between the University of Ghana, where he was director of the Institute of African Studies from 1966 to 1981, and various universities in the United States. During this period he taught at UCLA and then settled into the University of Pittsburgh from 1983 to 1991. Besides these appointments, he has twice been a visiting professor in Australia, once as a Commonwealth Fellow.

Professor Nketia's articles and research broke new ground in African music studies. He published several works on Ghanaian music as well as broader analyses of music across Africa. His *Music in Africa* (1974) became the defining text on the subject. Viewing the music theory approach that divided music into art music, popular music and traditional music, Nketia chose to dwell on the last. He has argued persuasively that the essence of African music could be found in its traditional forms, where one finds the roots of modern popular music. His later *African Art Music* (2004) is the leading work on that subject.

Besides his scholarly work, Nketia is a composer of note. He composes for piano and has published both classical works and piano pieces for teaching. He has also published several choral pieces and song cycles in Twi, his mother tongue. He has received the UNESCO Award for Distinguished Service to Music and the Prince Claus Award from the Dutch government in 1997.

Reference: adb, CA, DMM.

NKOMO, Joshua Mqabuko Nyangolo

(Zimbabwe, 1917–1999)

Joshua Mqabuko Nyangolo Nkomo, was the father of Zimbabwean independence, guerrilla leader and vice president of his country. He was a national figure throughout the history of modern Zimbabwe.

After higher education in South Africa, Nkomo returned home to work for the Rhodesian Railways, where he became a labor organizer. By 1951 his African Employees' Association was one of the strongest unions in central Africa. In 1952 he accompanied the Rhodesian premier, Sir Godfrey HUGGINS, to London for consultations on the possibility of a federation of the Rhodesias and Nyasaland. Correctly perceiving the federation as an attempt at settler domination, Nkomo opposed it. He became president of the Rhodesian African National Congress (ANC) and in 1957 became its national head. (This ANC was not connected with the better-known South African ANC.) He was abroad when the ANC was banned by the government of premier Edgar WHITEHEAD in 1959, and he went into exile in Britain. From there he continued his international advocacy, building the liberation movement, gathering funds, and pleading the cause before one forum after another. Together with Dr. Hastings BANDA of Nyasaland (now Malawi) and Kenneth KAUNDA of Northern Rhodesia (now Zambia), Nkomo opposed the federation. He successfully brought the Rhodesian question to the United Nations, obtaining its recognition as an international issue in 1962. By this time he was president of a successor organization to the ANC, the Zimbabwe African People's Union (ZAPU). When he returned to Rhodesia from his self-imposed exile in Tanzania, ZAPU was restricted for three months. Nkomo was the most popular African leader in the country at the time.

Upon his release, Nkomo attacked the Rhodesian Front, the right-wing White party that he called "the suicide squad" for leading Rhodesia to "unilateral independence" in 1965 as a segregationist state. Nkomo petitioned for British military intervention, and he was once again arrested. By this time there was serious unrest in the townships, riots in the capital, and repressive police action resulting in a number of deaths. Nkomo spent the next 12 years facing a series of detentions, jailings and restrictions that severely limited his organizational abilities. In one incident, when courts voided a detention order, another was dropped by parachute into the detention camp, and he stayed where he was. During this period he could receive mail, but his only outside contacts were a few meetings with British cabinet officials consulting on constitutional arrangements for Rhodesia. Respect for Nkomo never declined, but his inability to organize, especially among the youth, compromised his later position. In 1963, Robert MUGABE left ZAPU to form a more militant group, the Zimbabwe African National Union (ZANU).

When Nkomo was finally released in 1974, contention among the resistance leaders almost matched their animosity toward the government. Under pressure from supportive African countries, the two factions fashioned a unity movement called the Patriotic Front (PF), which formed a common effort against the compromise transitional government of Bishop Abel MUZOREWA. In the meantime, both movements had well-established and armed guerrilla wings harassing government forces. ZAPU was operating out of Zambia with Soviet support, and ZANU was working out of Mozambique with Chinese backing. When the Zambian borders were closed in 1973, Nkomo's forces were placed at a disadvantage, and ZANU was situated in the forefront of armed struggle. It began receiving the bulk of the young men pouring across the borders to join the guerrillas.

ZANU and ZAPU competed in the first elections in 1980, and ZAPU was soundly defeated, garnering 12 seats to ZANU's 57 (20 were reserved for Whites and three were taken by Muzorewa's party). Nkomo was offered the largely ceremonial presidency but rejected it in favor of the ministry of home affairs, which controlled internal security. Nkomo wanted to ensure that his armed followers would not upset the constitutional election, but in 1982 a ZAPU arms depot was discovered and Nkomo was accused of complicity in a plot, a charge almost certainly without foundation. Nevertheless, ZAPU adherents deserted the army, and armed resistance to the ruling ZANU government sprang up in Matabeleland, Nkomo's stronghold. Mugabe sent his crack troops into the area and crushed the rebellion with loss of life totaling about 10,000, while Nkomo again fled to London.

He returned to Zimbabwe, although all of his property had been confiscated, and contested the 1985 elections with no better results than in 1980.

Mugabe threatened to form a single-party system with or without Nkomo. In 1987, Nkomo accepted the best of a bad arrangement and joined a new national unity regime as senior minister. He surprised many by being a loyal and competent minister, and in 1990 he was named vice president, where he served until 1999. Many of his followers thought he had sold out, and his influence waned.

A hefty, lumbering man given to caution, Nkomo became the leading advocate of African nationalist aspirations before international bodies and a hero at home for his continual imprisonment and detention. Nevertheless, he never achieved the political base in Zimbabwe that might have given him real power. His vision of a united Zimbabwe where Whites and Blacks could work in harmony to build the nation failed utterly in the face of Mugabe's racism and authoritarianism.

References: AB, *adb*, *afr*, CB, DAHB, DRWW, EB, EWB, HWL, PLBA, PLCA, *wiki*. Nkomo, *Nkomo: The Story of My Life* (1984).

NKRUMAH, Kwame Francis Nwia Kofi
(Ghana, 1909–1972)

Kwame Nkrumah, Ghana's first president and for a decade the spokesman for the aspirations of independent Africa, was in part defeated by his economic policies and authoritarianism. In the end, he became a rejected prophet. Despite a tragic downfall, he was the first president in independent Africa and a source of immense pride for Africans and Black people everywhere.

Nkrumah began his career in a pattern rather typical of African leaders: education at mission schools, the government teacher training institute in the Gold Coast (as Ghana was called in the colonial period), successful teaching (1930–1935), and an opportunity for study abroad. In 1939 he graduated from Lincoln University, Pennsylvania, in sociology, receiving a degree in theology in 1942 and two MA degrees in education and political philosophy from the University of Pennsylvania. He read voraciously, especially Marx, Lenin, and GANDHI, as well as the Black American thinkers W. E. B. DuBois and Marcus Garvey, who inspired his thinking about Pan-Africanism. The Caribbean radicals C. L. R. James and George Padmore spent time with him

Kwame Francis Nwia Kofi Nkrumah

and taught him political organization. From 1943 to 1945 he taught at Lincoln while also serving as president of the African Students Association of the United States and Canada.

Abandoning Ph.D. studies before beginning his thesis, Nkrumah went to London to read law at Gray's Inn and study at the London School of Economics. The next two years were ones of intense activity. He edited a radical magazine, *New African,* for the West African Students' Union. He cast aside his studies when he was appointed secretary-general of the working committee directing the Fifth Pan-African Congress in Manchester. Nkrumah came to know the leading figures of Africa, forming relationships that would affect his life and work: Jomo KENYATTA of Kenya, Félix HOUPHOUËT-BOIGNY of Côte d'Ivoire, Léopold SENGHOR of Sénégal, and Obafemi AWOLOWO and Nnamdi AZIKIWE of Nigeria.

Nkrumah's abilities also attracted attention at home, and in 1947 he was invited back to the Gold Coast to be general secretary of the United Gold Coast Convention (UGCC). Immediately, he began implementing his own approach, the creation of a mass party to agitate for independence. In 1948 he organized war veterans' and workers' demonstrations against postwar inflation, and he organized a boycott of non-African shops. In the subsequent riots, 30 were killed and several hundred were wounded, leading to Nkrumah's arrest. The leadership of the UGCC was dismayed at his radical actions. As a result, Nkrumah was forced to resign, and in 1949 he formed his own political organization, the Convention People's Party (CPP), a vehicle for his ideas of immediate independence and an eventual union of African socialist republics. The CPP formed a powerful coalition with youth movements, trade unions, peasants and ex-servicemen. It promoted "positive action," by which it meant nonviolent confrontation and civil disobedience. "We prefer self-government in danger to servitude in tranquility," Nkrumah stated.

The wave of strikes and demonstrations in 1948 had convinced the British colonial authorities to consider constitutional reform. When the study committee's final report did not include independence, Nkrumah launched the Positive Action campaign in January 1950. The country came to a standstill with a general strike that closed down factories and the railroads, and protests became violent. Within a week, the army was brought in and a state of emergency was declared. The CPP was suspended and Nkrumah was arrested and sentenced to three years' imprisonment as a subversive. He served a year of the sentence, during which he ran the affairs of the CPP from prison. In February 1951, the CPP won a stunning victory in national and local elections, with Nkrumah receiving 98 percent of the vote in his own Accra Central constituency. The British governor invited his prisoner to become "His Majesty's Leader of Government Business" in the legislature. Within a year he was prime minister, and in 1953 he passed his "Motion of Destiny," calling for independence "at the earliest possible time."

Nkrumah won two further elections in 1954 and 1956, despite a hard core of opposition from cocoa growers and traditional chiefs. In 1957 the Gold Coast gained its freedom, taking the name Ghana and becoming the first Black African colony to achieve independence. Nkrumah's goals for his new state were ambitious, and he entered office with resources of US$400 million in foreign reserves, strong popular support, an educated leadership, and an international reputation. In 1959 the second Five Year Plan was put into effect. The first, which had controlled cocoa prices at an artificially low level, had been the impetus for forming the main

opposition party. The second called for a massive Volta River Project and the building of more than 600 new factories. Only the Volta River Dam was completed The rest of the plan was scuttled in 1961 with a $150 million loss. Nkrumah made a further disastrous move in the early 1960s when he began shifting trade from Ghana's established markets in the West to the Soviet bloc, where exports were not paid for in hard currency. He began funding his projects from reserves, and it became apparent that a fair percentage of the national wealth was being siphoned off by corruption, while the rest was simply mismanaged. Nkrumah dropped a few minor officials from the party after a scandal revealed that one official possessed a gold-plated bed. Nevertheless, the more avaricious politicians merely scaled back their thefts for a time. By the end of Nkrumah's tenure, over a billion dollars had been spent, leaving an enormous national debt.

His vision of unity made Nkrumah the leading exponent of Pan-Africanism. On the world stage he was an inspiration and the most prominent African of his generation. In the wake of the independence movement of early 1960s, he convened the All-Africa People's Congress in 1958, the precursor of the Organization of African Unity (OAU), but the OAU's lack of any provision for real political integration disappointed him. His enthusiasm for unity took him beyond the continent, and he became a leader in the Nonaligned Movement, hoping to avoid both the perils of neocolonialism and the pitfalls of becoming enmeshed in the Cold War. Once in power, however, he became more and more a tool of the USSR.

Nkrumah's transition from democratic advocate of mass participation to president was made rather poorly. His paranoia was fueled by reports of assassination plots and, later, by three actual attempts to kill him. Very quickly, Nkrumah accelerated his repressive measures. He dismissed the Supreme Court and took over its appeal functions. In 1958 he passed the Preventive Detention Act, using it liberally against his foes. More than a thousand people were detained, the most noted being the prisoner of conscience J. B. DANQUAH, who died in prison when he was deprived of sufficient food and medical care. The media were made totally submissive, and in 1964 opposition parties were banned and Nkrumah proclaimed himself president-for-life. He became dependent on Soviet and Chinese advisors, whom he introduced in large numbers, and the Soviet ambassador became his chief consultant on foreign affairs. More ominously, the Soviet Committee of State Security (KGB) was given management of the security forces and all police communications. At this point, President Julius NYERERE of Tanzania publicly denounced Nkrumah for his excesses.

Nkrumah fostered a personality cult that was excessive even by the standards of most dictators. He liked to be called *Osagyefo,* the Redeemer, and had his name put up in lights all over Accra. His fortress palace with its private zoo kept him isolated and the prey of petty informers and flatterers. The praise-songs in his honor were lavish. Postage stamps carried Nkrumah's likeness, and coins proclaimed him Conditor Ghanaensis (Founder of Ghana). He soon attempted to formulate a political theory to accompany his anticolonial nationalism. Rejecting European thought, even Marxism, he produced an abstruse and meandering theory that he expressed in a 1964 book, *Consciencism.* The Kwame Nkrumah Ideological Institute was established to promulgate the theory, and all government employees were obliged to follow it.

In 1966, soon after the inauguration of the Volta Dam, Nkrumah traveled to Beijing on a diplomatic mission, and the army deposed him during his absence. There was a general sense of relief in Ghana that was followed by public celebrations. Nkrumah went to Guinea, where his longtime friend and fellow radical, Sékou TOURÉ, provided him asylum and named him "co-president." While alive, he was treated as a threat to later Ghanaian governments, but after his death from cancer he was buried in Ghana with traditional honors.

References: AB, *adb, afr,* AA, CA, CB, DAB, DAHB, EWB, HLW, MMA, PLBA, PLCA, *wiki.* Basil Davidson, *Black Star* (1973); Nkrumah, *Ghana: The Autobiography of Kwame Nkrumah* (1957); David Rooney, *Kwame Nkrumah: The Political Kingdom in the Third World* (1988).

NKUMBULA, Harry Mwaanga
(Zambia, 1916–1983)

Harry Mwaanga Nkumbula, a militant who was one of the fathers of Zambian nationalism, went on to be a major opposition leader after independence.

Nkumbula graduated from teachers' training college in 1934 and established the Kitwe African Society during his early years of teaching. The society became increasingly political and anticolonial, causing the authorities to offer him a scholarship abroad to dampen his political agitation. In 1946 he left Northern Rhodesia for Makerere College in Uganda. He then went to London, where he spent two years studying education before embarking on an economics degree at the London School of Economics. Rather than discourage Nkumbula's anticolonialism, London only provided further opportunities for its development. He spoke at rallies, criticizing colonial policy and actively attacking plans for the proposed federation of the two Rhodesias and Nyasaland (the present-day countries of Zimbabwe, Zambia and Malawi). In London he also met and came to know other African nationalists such as Hastings BANDA of Malawi and Kwame NKRUMAH of Ghana.

Nkumbula returned to Northern Rhodesia in 1950 and, by a stroke of luck, discovered a cache of cowrie shells on Snake Island. Cowries were used as money in some parts of Africa, and Nkumbula traded his supply for cattle, giving him financial independence which he used to enter politics. He became president of the Zambian African National Congress (ANC). the first national anticolonial organization in Northern Rhodesia. (This organization was not connected with the South African ANC.) The immediate issue for the ANC was opposition to the federation, which would give ascendancy to White settlers. He was joined by Kenneth KAUNDA, who became the ANC's secretary-general. When the effort failed and the federation was established in 1953, Nkumbula's credibility as a nationalist figure was damaged, and the younger, more militant ANC members began to drift away from him.

Opposition within the ANC simmered until 1958, when Kaunda led a group of former ANC members to form the Zambia National Congress, which later became the United National Independence Party (UNIP). In the critical period from 1961 to 1962, Nkumbula was imprisoned for reckless driving after he killed a man in an auto accident. In the 1962 elections for the Legislative Council (Legco), the ANC fared badly against UNIP, but they joined in a coalition against the White United Federal Party. When Zambian independence was achieved in 1964, UNIP scored a convincing victory, and Nkumbula became the opposition leader. He challenged the creation of a single-party system, but when it was imposed by Kaunda in 1972, Nkumbula joined UNIP. He attempted to stand for president against Kaunda in 1978 but was disqualified and retired from politics.

References: afr, AO, DAHB, MMA, PLBA. Goodwin Mwangilwa, *Harry Mwaanga Nkumbula: A Biography of the Old Lion of Zambia* (1982).

NOLAN, Albert, OP
(South Africa, 1934–)

Father Albert Nolan is the most prominent liberation theologian in Africa and a coauthor of the Kairos Document, with which Christian leaders created a theological rationale for opposition to apartheid.

Nolan began as a conventional South African White cleric. He joined the Dominican Order in 1954, studied in South Africa and was sent to Rome for graduate work in theology. After several routine posts, he was named a university chaplain in the 1970s, where the students, both Black and White, began to raise his consciousness about the evils of apartheid.

Nolan first came to notice for a simple book that became a bestseller, *Jesus Before Christianity* (1976), which was later translated into nine languages. He found that the university students had little interest in traditional theology, so he built his course around the person of Jesus. As he commented, "very often we wear ourselves out giving answers to questions that people are not asking." He discovered that people responded to a theology that dealt with a person and not a theory, and to those understandings that arose from their experience. Nolan began to grasp what would become contextual theology. He began working at the Christian Institute, an ecumenical center, and later he became a full-time activist at the Institute of Contextual Theology (ICT). In 1983, the antiapartheid parties and movements, including church groups, banded together to form the United Democratic Front.

Nolan and a few other South African thinkers, especially Frank CHIKANE and Beyers NAUDÉ, began to explore the implications of apartheid for theology. Nolan had visited South America and studied the liberation theology developing there, but felt that the South African situation called for a different response. South Africa, through the domi-

nant Dutch Reformed Church, had a state theology that justified apartheid on biblical grounds. Other Christians lived with a "Church theology" which disapproved of racist policies but sought reconciliation and avoided confrontation. The third option that the ICT developed was uniquely South African, "clearly and unambiguously taking a stand." In 1985, the ICT issued the Kairos Document, with 150 churchmen signing it. The name comes from the biblical notion of *kairos*, a time of grace when God calls to prophetic action. It called for participation in the liberation struggle, and did not shy away from the fact that this would involve armed resistance to evil.

Nolan began speaking out about the evils of apartheid and attracted the suspicion and opposition of the government. In 1988 he had to go underground to avoid the security police, and during that time he wrote *God in South Africa* (1988).

The Dominican Order in South Africa is quite small, an amalgamation of former Dutch and English missions. In 1968 it was organized into a vicariate, the lowest level of Dominican structure. Nolan was elected to be the superior twice, 1974–1984 and 2000–2002. In 1980 he was also elected to head the worldwide Order, one of the most influential and distinguished in the Catholic Church. To everyone's surprise he refused, the first time in the 800-year history of the Order that anyone had ever done so. He had a simple argument: I am more needed in South Africa. He campaigns today against the poverty and injustice that still plague South Africa, and in 2003 he was awarded the Order of Luthuli for his contributions to nation-building.

NUJOMA, Sam Daniel Shafishuna
(Namibia, 1929–)

Sam Nujoma, nationalist and leader of the South-West African People's Organization (SWAPO), spent 30 years in exile before becoming the first president of Namibia.

Nujoma was born into a farm worker's family in the poorest clan of the Ovambo people, Namibia's largest ethnic group. He lived with relatives at several places in the country and received a few years of spotty education. At age 20, he learned English

Sam Daniel Shafishuna Nujoma

and began to work for South African Railways as a sweeper. He was fired for union activities in 1957. Two years later he was suddenly thrust into national and world attention by his role in a campaign against the introduction of apartheid regulations into Namibia. There were demonstrations against the removal of Namibians who were Black or of mixed race from neighborhoods being turned over to Whites. Public transportation and facilities were boycotted, and in one street demonstration, 11 Blacks were killed and buildings were burned. The only nationalist group, the Ovambo People's Organization (OPO), had sponsored the demonstrations, and its leader, Animba TOIVO ja Toivo, was jailed. From that point on, Nujoma was a marked man. He was followed, jailed on several occasions, and harassed in many ways. He managed to escape through Tanzania and Ghana and went to the United Nations (U.N.) to plead the OPO case. In 1959, SWAPO, a pan-ethnic nationalist group, was founded.

SWAPO headquarters were set up in Tanzania (and later Lusaka, Zambia), and guerrilla war was begun in 1966 with attacks on South African targets within Namibia. The raids led to the 1968 arrest of a number of SWAPO activists, including Toivo. At the same time, Nujoma achieved several major victories on the diplomatic front. In 1968 the Organization of African Unity recognized SWAPO as the sole legitimate authority in Namibia, and the U.N. followed in 1973 by providing its support. U.N. recognition was important because South-West Africa was technically a U.N. mandate under South African administration. After 1975, South Africa attempted to negotiate an internal settlement with existing parties and groups in Namibia, but in 1978 the U.N. established a formula calling for the "independence of Namibia through free and fair elections under the control and supervision of the U.N."

From 1985, the U.N., South Africa, and Angola were involved in complex negotiations regarding both Namibian independence and the end of the civil war in Angola. South Africa forces, supporting Jonas SAVIMBI, mounted attacks from bases in Namibia, claiming that the presence of 50,000 Cuban troops in Angola justified their intervention.

In 1988, South African forces were defeated at Cuito Canavale in Angola. It then became possible to link the withdrawal of South African troops from both Angola and South-West Africa to the withdrawal of Cuban forces from Angola. Namibia came under U.N. transitional management, and Nujoma returned in triumph to direct an election campaign. He won with 57 percent of the vote and began a multiracial administration, appointing two White members to his cabinet. As he said, "memories of bitter and long years of conflict, racial hatred, and deep distrust among us Namibians must be buried forever." Nujoma also toned down his socialist rhetoric and pledged his government to a mixed economy and respect for property rights.

Nujoma became president of Namibia in 1990 as the world economy entered a recession. With unemployment standing at 50 percent, economic development became his first priority. Heavily dependent on South Africa, its major trading partner, Namibia steered a careful course. The Namibian dollar, first issued in 1993, is pegged to the South African rand. A possible area of conflict between the two states was the jurisdiction over Walvis Bay, a South African enclave within Namibia with a military base. Negotiations by Theo Ben

GURIRAB, the foreign minister, resulted in South African acceptance of Namibian sovereignty over Walvis Bay, with a guarantee of South African property rights there. This settlement, along with the success of multiparty democracy, has led to a smooth and peaceful political transition. Nujoma instituted a land reform scheme to address the inequities in land holdings left over from the apartheid era. Although this has gone gradually and fairly smoothly because compensation has been given to White farmers, Nujoma defended the seizures of White-owned land in Zimbabwe under Robert MUGABE.

Nujoma retired from the presidency in 2005.

References: AB, *afr,* CB, DAHB, EWB, PLBA, PLCA, RWWA, *wiki.*

NWANKWO, Clement Okechukwu

(Nigeria, 1962–)

Clement Nwankwo is a civil rights activist in Nigeria and was the founder and longtime executive director of the Constitutional Rights Project. Before that, he began Nigeria's first human rights group, the Civil Liberties Organization, in 1987.

Nwankwo has consistently taken the position that Nigeria's law must conform to international standards for human rights. To push this agenda he founded the Constitutional Rights Project in 1990 and was executive director until 2002. Since Nigeria is Africa's largest (and one of its most powerful) states, bringing its legal system into harmony with international standards would have a profound effect throughout the continent. The project has made its case, not in the parliament, but in the courts. Nwankwo has teams of lawyers defend the accused *pro bono,* especially those held in detention without being charged, a common device for removing dissidents from activism as well as a means for local officials to remove opponents.

A major effort of the Constitutional Rights Project has been providing training programs for judges, lawyers and police to provide an understanding of their role in defending human rights and avoiding abuses.

Nwankwo has written four books on human rights in Nigeria, including one on the sensitive issue of rights in the Niger Delta. There has been a low-level struggle in the Delta over the effects of oil drilling on the local people, who have found their environment spoiled, water contaminated, and the air polluted. Armed guerillas have begun harassing oil workers, and the government's only response has been harsh repression. The issue rose to international prominence with the execution of Ken SARO-WIWA in 1995. Nwankwo has always argued that negotiation and arbitration can avoid most such regional conflicts.

Nwankwo's work has been recognized by governments and international human rights groups. The United States' National Endowment for Democracy gave him its highest award in 1999, and he has been honored by Human Rights Watch and Amnesty International. He has also been named a member of the International NGO Advisory Committee of the Harvard Institute for International Development.

Reference: adb.

NYANHEHWE

(Zimbabwe, ?–1480s)

Mwene Matope Nyanhehwe was *mwene mutapa* or ruler of the southern African kingdom often called Munhumutapa. The title means either "master pillager" or "lord of the metals," a reference to the fact that the *mwene mutapa* held a monopoly on all gold mined in the kingdom.

The kingdom was founded by Nyanhehwe's father Mutota in the early fifteenth century by gathering together Shona-speaking peoples from the plateau who were escaping the authority of Great Zimbabwe, the dominant regional empire. Evidently, the original foundation of Munhumutapa was based on the existence of salt deposits along the Zambezi River.

Nyanhehwe succeeded his father around 1450 and promptly began a period of expansion. He captured large herds of cattle, which he then lent to chiefs in exchange for their becoming his vassals. The political system seems to have been developed along the lines of the Zimbabwe empire, which had collapsed suddenly a short time earlier, probably due to agricultural failure and general exhaustion of the land. This economic history would also explain the power wielded by the main cattle-holder in the region, because cattle would have become the new basis of the economy. Because the Shona probably had been influenced by earlier Zimbabwean political structures, they were familiar with its organization. Most of present-day Zimbabwe and central Mozambique were part of Mutapa state, and members of Nyanhehwe's family were appointed governors of more distant provinces. After Nyanhehwe's death, the empire did not survive beyond his successor, but the central kingdom lasted long after the arrival of the Portuguese in the sixteenth century.

Reference: DAHB.

NYERERE, Julius Kambarage
(Tanzania, 1922–1999)

Mwalimu Julius Nyerere, father of Tanzania, one of Africa's outstanding independence heroes, and the leading political intellectual in Africa, was the architect of a massive experiment based on an African theory of community known as *ujamaa.*

Nyerere was born to the fifth wife (of 22) of a chief of the Zanaki people in northern Tanganyika, a trust territory administered by the British since World War I. After local primary school, he was sent to a mission secondary school in 1937, the only one in the country open to Africans, and was baptized a Catholic around 1945. He attended Makerere University in Kampala, Uganda, from 1943 to 1945 to obtain a teaching certificate. It was there that he formed the first nationalist Tanganyikan student group. He returned to teach at a Catholic mission school, and then in 1949, went to the University of Edinburgh, where he received an MA in economics and history in 1952, making him the first African in Tanganyika with a university degree. In Edinburgh he came in contact with the anticolonial movement, especially Fabianism, an anticolonial socialist movement. He taught for three years at another Catholic school near Dar es Salaam and became active in the Tanganyika African Association (TAA), which was essentially a study group on social questions.

In 1954, Nyerere transformed the TAA into Tanganyika's first political party, the Tanganyikan African National Union (TANU). It espoused independence, nonviolence, ethnic equality and harmony, and multiethnic politics. He was appointed to the Legislative Council (Legco) in 1954, and the following year he gave up teaching for a political

career. He proved a talented recruiter and organizer, bringing 250,000 new members into TANU the first year and establishing branches across the country. He took advantage of Tanganyika's position as a trust territory to testify before the United Nations (U.N.) Trusteeship Council in 1955 and 1956, presenting the case for a timetable for Tanganyikan independence. With this effort he was established as the leading Tanganyikan nationalist. Insisting on nonviolence, he allowed TANU to contest the 1958 elections, even though he strongly disapproved of its division of elected seats in the Legco into White, Black African, and Indian. TANU carried 28 of 30 elected positions (34 were still appointed), and Nyerere quipped: "Independence will follow as surely as the tickbirds follow the rhino."

Nyerere's prediction was accurate; in 1960 limited self-government was granted by Britain, with an African majority in the Legco. Nyerere was sworn in as first minister after another TANU sweep, and in 1961 he became prime minister of independent Tanganyika. He established a one-party state, outlawed strikes, and created a centralized administration. He also developed a theory of the one-party state, arguing that within it could be both collaboration and unity without the suppression of a variety of views. He rejected European and American systems as reflecting class and power distinctions that were foreign to Africa. Nyerere expressed the fear that multiple parties in Africa would lead only to ethnic conflict. He attempted to adapt African modes of decision making, especially the *palaver,* a consensus-building discussion that proceeds until all are satisfied.

To build national unity, Nyerere also fostered Kiswahili as the national language, making it the medium of instruction in schools at all levels. Tanzanian Kiswahili, as a consequence, is considered elegant in its expression, and Nyerere contributed to the language by translating Shakespeare's *Julius Caesar* (1963) and *The Merchant of Venice* (1969). But in this, as in other ways, Nyerere became doctrinaire. Kiswahili's limitations in technical and medical fields meant that Tanzania lagged behind other African countries in technology.

In early 1962, Nyerere abruptly resigned the premiership to spend a year turning TANU from a liberation movement into a governing party and sharing his plans for the country. By December, Tanganyika was a republic, and he returned to office as president. Shortly thereafter, tensions built in the island nation of Zanzibar, off the Tanganyikan coast, erupting in 1963 into a bloody coup that set Black Africans against Arabs. Coup fever spread to the mainland, and the Tanganyikan army mutinied in 1964. Nyerere went into hiding and was forced to call in British troops. With order restored, he announced the merger of Zanzibar and Tanganyika into a new nation, the United Republic of Tanzania. Later, in 1977, he merged TANU and Zanzibar's Afro-Shirazi Party into a national party, Chama Cha Mapinduzi (CCM, literally "Association of the Revolution").

With the major issues of national unity settled, Nyerere moved to promote his system of African socialism. In 1967 he proclaimed the Arusha Declaration, which became the basis for the Tanzanian system. Its centerpiece was *ujamaa,* community or familyhood, a program for independent self-help that would keep Tanzania from becoming dependent on foreign aid. In 1970 he followed with a villagization program that organized rural life into village collectives. At first these were voluntary, but resistance was met with coercion, and after 1975, with forced villagization. Almost 80 percent of the population was organized into 7,700 villages that, despite planning, led to a sharp drop in agricultural production. Tanzania went from being Africa's leading exporter of food to being its greatest importer. This result was only one of several contradictory elements in Nyerere's program, which was often a triumph of theory over reality. Tanzania became almost entirely dependent on foreign aid grants for hard currency as its small export base shrank to negligible proportions, and by the 1980s, it was the largest per-capita recipient of foreign aid in Africa. In 1971, Nyerere nationalized property after introducing state ownership of banking and plantation agriculture.

In other areas there were unchallenged social and economic achievements: infant mortality was reduced by 50 percent and adult literacy increased to 90 percent. In the late 1960s, China built the Tazara railroad to link Dar es Salaam with Zambia and increase commercial transport.

Nyerere's foreign policy was dominated by two decisions: to support neighboring liberation movements and to take military action against the Ugandan despot Idi AMIN. Tanzania became a favorite venue for training camps and offices, which often cost support and trade opportunities with important states, such as South Africa. In 1970, in response to an incursion into northern Tanzania by

Amin's forces, Nyerere mobilized his army and invaded Uganda with 20,000 troops. He gave support to the Ugandan forces that defeated Amin, and then engineered the election of his friend Milton OBOTE to the presidency. The military campaign, however, had a destructive effect on the Tanzanian economy.

Uganda was not Nyerere's only intervention. In 1977 he was behind the coup that brought France Albert RENÉ to power in the Seychelles. In that case, he was worried over increasing South African influence in the Indian Ocean states.

In 1984, Nyerere stepped down from the presidency in favor of Ali Hassan MWINYI, although he remained head of the CCM. When Mwinyi began to dismantle some of the *ujamaa* program and begin privatizing the economy, Nyerere interceded from behind the scenes. He did not step down from the CCM chair until 1990, by which time he had agreed that some of his policies had failed and that a multiparty system should be considered.

In retirement, Nyerere worked at finding a resolution to the Great Lakes Crisis, and he encouraged Tanzania to accept large flows of refugees fleeing Rwanda and Burundi. He received the Nansen Medal for his work for refugees.

Nyerere remained deeply respected in Tanzania and was always referred to by his honorific title, *mwalimu* (teacher). A man of simple tastes and an austere lifestyle, he retired from public life with little fortune, accepting a farm from the government. As he traveled the country to say farewell, villages vied to present him with cattle. Nyerere spoke out bitterly about corrupt officials who had grown rich from their positions, and he seemed delighted to be endowed by his people. His political philosophy has been published in several collections: *Uhuru na Umoja* (Freedom and Unity, 1967), *Uhuru na Ujamaa* (Freedom and Community,1968), and *Uhuru na Maendeleo* (Freedom and Development, 1973).

References: AA, AB, *adb, afr,* CA, CB, DAHB, EWB, HWL, PLBA, PLCA, RWWA, *wiki.* Robert Jackson and Carl Rosberg. *Personal Rule in Black Africa: Prince, Autocrat, Prophet, Tyrant* (1982); William Smith, *We Must Run While They Walk* (1971).

NYUNGU ya Mawe

(Tanzania, 1840s-1884)

Nyungu ya Mawe was a member of the Nyamwezi chiefly family who rallied his people after they had been badly shattered by Arab raiders. He was to become the most powerful of the nineteenth-century warlords in Tanzania. His name is a praise title meaning "pot of stone."

As a youth, Nyungu served the chief of the Nyamwezi, in whose court he was part of a faction opposing Arab control of the ivory and slave trade. When the Arabs deposed and killed the chief in 1865, Nyungu (who was only part Nyamwezi) was excluded from succeeding to the chieftaincy, so he assembled a personal army of *ruga-ruga*, who were unattached warriors, usually abandoned children, mixed-race sons of slave rapes or other social outcasts. Nyungu gave them social status and a purpose, and in return he received their intense loyalty. Nyungu commanded them with complete authority but rewarded them well with spoils from raiding expeditions.

At first Nyungu was unable to seize the trading routes, but after 1870 he systematically absorbed the Kimbu clans, who lived in more than 30 petty chiefdoms. He replaced their chiefs with seven personally loyal governors who had no local ties. By 1880 his empire covered 20,000 square miles of present-day western Tanzania, and he was no longer dependent upon the *ruga-ruga* for his military power. He received all ivory in his empire as tribute. Due to his empire's political stability, it passed without incident to his daughter Mgalula after his death in 1884. She ruled it well and proved to be an able field general. Unfortunately, 1884 was also the year of the Berlin Conference to partition Africa among European powers, and it marked the arrival of the first colonists. Chief Mgalula entered into an alliance with the Germans in 1895 and was thus able to maintain autonomy, which was finally lost under her successor.

Reference: DAHB. Aylward Shorter, *Nyungu-ya-Mawe* (1969).

NZAMUJO, Godfrey Ubeti, OP

(Nigeria/Benin, 1940s–)

Father Godfrey Nzamujo, founder of the Songhai Centre in Benin, is a proponent for creating African forms of development.

Nzamujo, a Nigerian, was one of the early members of the Dominican Order in Africa, and he studied and later taught electronics for five years in the United States. His studies abroad convinced him that development from the West ignored the African people and fostered dependence.

Nzamujo has long argued that Africans need to set their own agenda for development, not rejecting support and aid but not accepting direction from outside. He rejects the idea that African-led development needs to be basic. He endorses and uses advanced technology, including the Internet, powering it in rural areas with solar panels. On the farms, all waste materials are recycled for fertilizer and as biogas for fuel. He sees the new technology as a chance to leap-frog over the older infrastructures that were never developed in Africa. Nzamujo calls the new approach "antenna-receiver." Africans, even those from peasant cultures, need to be able to access information from anywhere in the world and then discern what is relevant to their situation. He criticizes the "pitfall of passive information consumerism." From this conviction was born the Information and Communications Network for Sustainable Agriculture to optimize access and the quality of information available. Direct satellite communications link all the centers to the Songhai hub.

Nzamujo began his plans in Nigeria in the early 1980s, hoping to create model farms that would revitalize the agriculture of the region. He found rejection in state after state, and left in disgust for Benin, where his ideas were welcomed. In 1985 the Songhai Centre began. He understood that food production—Songhai's only focus—required more than farm training. He sought human empowerment through social, cultural, spiritual and technical human development, the creation of a community on the land. There are three facilities—livestock, crop production and aquaculture. Yield has increased 10 percent a year over traditional farming.

It is ironic that the first Songhai program outside Benin is in Nigeria. The Nigerian project, with government help and support from Shell Oil, is located in the sensitive Niger Delta, where large numbers of unemployed youth have generated violence. The project there is intended to provide employment with dignity and to return numbers of young men to farming, which many had rejected. The regimen is strict and operated with military-like discipline. Nzamujo has also been in dialogue with local people in Southeast Asia about adapting these approaches there. In 1993, he received the Africa Prize of the Hunger Project.

NZINGA Mbande, Anna
(Angola, 1582?–1663)

Nzinga Mbande, daughter and sister of kings of the Angolan kingdoms of Ndongo and Matamba, was about 36 years old when the Portuguese conquered parts of the region. She became a Christian in hopes of gaining Portuguese support, but they favored her brother over her. Nevertheless, she negotiated Portuguese recognition of her authority in northern Angola, rejecting payment of tribute but permitting the release of Portuguese captives. When the colonial governor attempted to humble her by forcing her to stand in his presence by removing the chairs, Nzinga ordered a slave to kneel and used him for a throne. Then she haughtily had the slave slaughtered in front of the governor. In 1624, after four years' rule, her brother died and Nzinga had her nephew strangled, thus succeeding to the Mbundu kingdom of Ndongo's throne.

From the first, Nzinga asserted her power against the Portuguese, and in 1626 they chose her sister as a puppet ruler. The people remained loyal to Nzinga throughout five years of retreat into the mountains, after which she returned from the bush with a remarkable guerilla strategy. Nzinga's effective use of women warriors (her palace bodyguards were trusted women) was perhaps the origin of the legend of the Amazons.

Forming alliances with neighboring kingdoms and with the Dutch, she effectively took the Portuguese slave trade for herself. Thus enriched, she conquered the kingdom of Matamba and made herself "king." In the 1640s she mounted three successful military campaigns against the Portuguese and by 1656 forced them to negotiate a peace settlement that included sharing the slave trade. Nzinga was an imperious and brutal woman, given to gory atrocities to demonstrate her power. She

kept some 30 male slaves as concubines, executing them when they no longer pleased her. She never married, presumably to avoid rivalries for her throne. She forbade the use of the title "Queen," insisting that she be addressed as "King."

After reaching a peace agreement with the Portuguese, Nzinga turned herself to the reconstruction of the country. After renouncing Christianity during her period of resistance, Nzinga embraced it again before her death, evidently with some sincerity. She abolished polygamy and the sacrifice of captives and encouraged missionary activity. She began to develop an alternative economy less dependent on slaving.

References: AB, *afr*, DAHB, LKW, WGMC, WWR, *wiki*. Ibrahima Kake, *Anne Zingha, Reine d'Angola* (1975).

NZO, Alfred Bephethuxolo
(South Africa, 1925–2000)

Comrade Alfred Bephethuxolo Nzo, one of the older-generation stalwarts of the African National Congress (ANC), was ANC general secretary for over 20 years and served as foreign minister in the first ANC government.

After attending a Catholic mission school, Nzo spent a year at the Healdtown Missionary Institute and then entered Fort Hare University College. At the university he joined the ANC's Youth League, becoming so politically active that he had to drop out of school in 1946. Despite Nelson MANDELA's opposition to forming a coalition with the Communists, Nzo followed the lead of Walter SISULU and joined in the bloody May Day strike in 1950 and the follow-up national strike protesting the Suppression of Communism Act. He was also an organizer for the 1952 Defiance Campaign, the program of civil disobedience against the apartheid laws. At the same time, Nzo pursued further studies at a technical school and qualified as a health inspector in 1951. He worked in Alexandra township outside of Johannesburg, where the appalling conditions under which African workers were forced to live further radicalized him. In 1957 he organized a three-month bus boycott in Alexandra, and the following year Nzo was elected to the ANC's Transvaal and national executive committees. When

NZO, Alfred Bephethuxolo   389

he lost his job as a result of his activism, he began working full-time for the ANC.

The government began harassing Nzo almost immediately. Without his previous job, he no longer was entitled to a residence permit in Alexandra. Until 1964 he endured a number of banning orders, arrests and jail sentences. At that point, the underground leadership (the ANC itself had been banned in 1960) decided to use Nzo as part of its international effort, under the direction of Oliver TAMBO. Nzo was deputy of the ANC's Cairo office from 1964 to 1967 and then head of its delegation in India. In 1969 he was elected secretary-general of the ANC and transferred to Morogoro, Tanzania, the ANC headquarters. His next years were spent in administrative activities, until Tambo had a stroke in 1989. Nzo assumed many of Tambo's duties and provided continuity at an important time for the ANC struggle. As the South African government indicated a willingness to negotiate an end to apartheid, Nzo drafted a detailed program. When Mandela and Sisulu were released from prison in 1990, Nzo was made part of the ANC delegation in constitutional talks with the government. In 1991 he was replaced as secretary-general by Cyril RAMAPHOSA, a younger, more militant activist. Nzo's appointment as South African foreign minister in 1994 was something of a surprise to foreign observers. As expected, foreign policy was to be set by the deputy president, Thabo MBEKI, longtime ANC spokesman abroad, with Nzo providing administrative and internal leadership. Nzo suffered a stroke in 1999 and withdrew from office.

References: EB, GSAP, RWWA.

OBASANJO, Olusegun
(Nigeria, 1937–)

General Olusegun Obasanjo, military head of state of Nigeria in the late 1970s, became a widely respected international senior statesman, and then twice took on the challenging job of president of Nigeria, Africa's largest and most populous country.

Obasanjo never intended to enter politics, and his military career reflects the background of a professional soldier. After high school he entered the Nigerian army and was sent to Mons Officer Cadet School in Ghana, then to England and India for further training, receiving his commission in 1959. After service in the United Nations (U.N.) peace-keeping mission in the Congo (now the Democratic Republic of the Congo), he joined the Army Engineers and was promoted to captain and commander of the engineering unit. He received military engineering training in England and India from 1965 to 1967, and, when the Nigerian civil war broke out that year, he returned in charge of the Ibadan Garrison, which he headed for two years. As commander of the Third Marine Commando Division in 1970, he accepted the surrender of the Biafran forces.

When the war was over, Obasanjo returned to command the Army Engineers and was promoted to brigadier in 1972. He spent a year in command training in London before being appointed commissioner of works by General Jack GOWON, who was then head of state. He joined in the officers' coup that removed Gowon in 1975 and was appointed chief of staff by General Murtala MUHAMMED. Muhammed's plans to return the country to civilian rule were abruptly halted by his assassination. Fearing a return to confusion, the military council looked for stability, and Obasanjo reluctantly found himself the head of state from 1976 to 1979.

With a southern Christian replacing a northern Muslim, unrest was expected, but Obasanjo proved even-handed and fair in dealing with all regions and groups. At the same time, he did not hesitate to reject Muslim attempts to extend *sharia,* Islamic law, under the proposed new constitution. He attempted to control Nigeria's overheated economy, which had been swollen by money from the oil boom. Despite increased government revenue, he reduced the size of the military and reorganized the trade unions, rebuffing attempts at unnecessary expansion.

Obasanjo clashed with students from his Yoruba ethnic group, and many of his compatriots turned against him. Then, in a terrible mistake, he ordered a raid on the compound of the music star, Fela KUTI, a national personality and fellow Yoruba. Kuti's mother, the distinguished Funmilayo RANSOME-KUTI, died from injuries sustained during the raid. Fela Kuti became a scathing critic. Yet, Obasanjo took on few of the trappings of power, and he adhered strictly to Muhammed's timetable for restoring civilian rule, transferring power to Shehu SHAGARI in 1979.

Obasanjo retired from the army and turned to farming, at least partly to challenge the stereotype of the ignorant peasant and to provide an example for others. From time to time, he emerged to criticize succeeding governments for corruption as the benefits of the 1970s oil boom were squandered. As his stature grew, Obasanjo began to receive appointments to international commissions: the Palme Disarmament Commission, the Inter-Action Council of past heads of state, and the chairmanship of the 1986 Commonwealth Eminent Persons' Group, which had the task of attempting to open a dialog with South Africa that would lead to a multiracial future. Although this group had no immediate success, the negotiating concept that Obasanjo proposed became the basis for the constitutional formula used four years later when President F. W. DE KLERK began the democratic transition. Obasanjo was also one of the six candidates endorsed by the Organization of African Unity (OAU) for secretary-general of the U.N. in 1991. He lost to another OAU endorsee, Boutros Boutros-Ghali of Egypt. His mediation during this period reads like a litany of the contemporary political crises in Africa: Angola, Burundi, Mozambique, South Africa, Sudan.

Corrupt politics continued the path of failure in Nigeria, however. There were coups and counter-

Olusegun Obasanjo

coups until Moshood ABIOLA apparently won the 1993 election, only to be denied it. General Sani ABACHA took power the following year and imprisoned Abiola. Obasanjo became a critic of the Abacha regime, which was both kleptocratic and brutal. Obasanjo was charged with treason in a trial where one witness spoke against him, a colonel who had been tortured to force his false testimony. Obasanjo spent three years in prison, in solitary confinement and under constant threat of poisoning. When Abacha died under questionable circumstances, Obasanjo was freed and immediately announced his intention to stand for the presidency.

Obasanjo became Nigeria's first elected president in 16 years in 1999. He inherited a Nigeria rife with extreme corruption, divided into bitter north-south sectionalism and constantly in danger of violent religious conflict. He was re-elected in 2003 over General Muhammadu BUHARI, who had been Obasanjo's minister of petroleum in the interim presidency. The vote was a strict north-south divide and candidates Buhari and Chukwuemeka OJUKWU charged fraud.

References: *afr*, CB, DAHB, PLBA, PLCA, RWWA, *wiki*. Obasanjo, *Not My Will* (1990); Onukaba Ojo, *Olusegun Obasanjo* (1997).

OBIANG Nguema Mbasogo, Teodoro

(Equatorial Guinea, 1942–)

Brigadier-General Teodoro Obiang Nguema Mbasogo overthrew his uncle, Francisco MACÍAS NGUEMA, to become president of his country.

Educated locally, Obiang then joined the Spanish army and was sent to the Saragossa Military Academy in Spain for training in 1963. He was commissioned a second lieutenant in the territorial guards in 1965, and when Macías became the first president in 1968, Obiang was made military governor of Fernando Po.

Fernando Po, an important island off the coast, enjoyed considerable autonomy at first, but when Macías decided to limit its privileges, it was Obiang's unpleasant task to enforce the order. Obiang was promoted to command of the national guard in 1975 and became even more deeply involved in Macías's systematic program of state terrorism and repression. When a hundred senior officials requested modifications in government economic policies, Obiang arrested them, leading to the murders of the head of the national party, the vice president, and a number of other people. Obiang was one of Macías's tiny inner circle of confidants, and the army remained loyal to him. He seems to have begun to plot his coup against Macías after one of his brothers was executed on Macías's orders.

In 1979, Macías was overthrown, tried for murder and abuse of power, and executed by firing squad. Obiang released more than 5,000 political prisoners and invited Equatorian exiles (who were over a quarter of the population) to return home. Obiang secured foreign aid from Spain and France, which admitted Equatorial Guinea to the franc zone in 1985. This provided a stable currency tied to the French monetary system. Any hopes for liberalized politics or an end to political repression, however, were illusory. Obiang continued his uncle's policies of absolute personal control and extensive corruption. He took over companies he coveted, executed opponents, and ruled through a one-party state. A series of coup attempts were harshly subdued. Although the oil industry has been developed for several years, no trace of its revenues has ever appeared in any public budget.

In 1991, Obiang promised to introduce democracy, and he legalized political parties and ran sham elections in 1992 and 2002. The result has been the election of only two members who are not from Obiang's party. Harassment has continued, including the imprisonment of prominent opposition leaders. He also fosters the growth of a cult of personality, regularly claiming to be God and giving himself extravagant titles.

In an outlandish turn of events in 2004, Obiang accused Spain, the United States and Great Britain of plotting his overthrow. He cited as evidence a planeload of armed mercenaries who were detained in Zimbabwe en route to Equatorial Guinea to mount a coup. A group was also arrested in Malabo, the capital. The leader, a notorious South African arms dealer and mercenary, was sentenced to 34 years in prison. Equatorial Guinea now faces further destabilization, since Obiang is in declining health due to cancer and is losing control of his power.

References: afr, PLBA, RWWA, *wiki*.

OBOTE, Apollo Milton

(Uganda, 1925?–2005)

Apollo Milton Obote ruled his country twice, from 1962 to 1971 and from 1980 to 1985. An autocratic leader, he never attracted the worldwide opprobrium of the more flamboyant and violent General Idi AMIN, who controlled Uganda between Obote's two tenures in office.

Obote, a member of the Lango ethnic group and a northerner, was educated in the north and then at Busoga College, a breeding ground for nationalism. He studied at Makerere University in Kampala, the capital, for two years, dropping out in 1949. He was determined to enter politics through the trade union movement and went to Kenya, where he worked in a sugar mill and at construction. He became active in labor and political circles, working with Tom MBOYA until political parties were banned in Kenya.

Returning to Uganda in 1957, Obote was elected to the Legislative Council (Legco). Known for his forthright dealings with colonial authorities, he acquired the ability to negotiate the complexities of Ugandan ethnic, regional and religious divisions. In 1960 he founded the Uganda People's Congress (UPC), one of several factional parties that would represent these divisions in modern Uganda. While

Apollo Milton Obote

it had some national support, the UPC was largely a northern and Protestant party. The parties hardened the conflict between the nationalists and the four traditional kingdoms, whose kings were dissatisfied with their proposed role after independence. The largest and most powerful kingdom, Buganda, boycotted the first direct elections in 1961, allowing the Democratic Party (DP), largely southern and Catholic, to form the transitional government. Obote became the leader of the opposition.

Realizing his mistake, Sir Edward MUTESA II, kabaka (king) of Buganda, formed a royalist party, Kabaka Yekka (KY), whose name ("The King Alone") was also its slogan. It formed a coalition with the UPC in exchange for exempting Buganda from direct elections, permitting the kabaka and his royal parliament, the Lukiko, to choose their delegates for the proposed national assembly. The coalition won the 1962 national elections handily, and Obote led Uganda to independence as prime minister, with the kabaka, "King Freddie," as president. Buganda's privileged status and Baganda sentiments of ethnic superiority were unpopular elsewhere in Uganda, however, and in 1962 Obote had to use force to quell separatism in the west. The uneasy alliance with the KY foundered, while the UPC itself became riven by religious, ethnic and ideological divisions.

In 1966, a scandal erupted over a cache of gold and ivory captured by Ugandan forces during a revolt in neighboring Congo (now the Democratic Republic of the Congo). Obote and his army commander, General Idi AMIN, were implicated.

Just as the inquiry was to proceed, Obote arrested five of his cabinet ministers, abrogated the constitution, and assumed the presidency. The kabaka protested and ordered the national government out of Buganda. Amin's troops stormed the kabaka's palace and King Freddie fled into exile during the battle, in which large numbers were killed. Obote abolished the four traditional monarchies but could not unite the country. Opponents were imprisoned, and all political parties except the UPC, were banned in 1969. The opposition was forced underground.

In 1971, Idi Amin took over the government while Obote was out of the country. Amin launched a reign of terror and left the economy in a shambles. Obote bided his time in exile in Tanzania until Amin invaded northern Tanzania in 1978. President Julius NYERERE mobilized his army and counterattacked, driving out Amin in two months. After a short period of confusion, Obote returned to campaign for the presidency. With open support from the occupying Tanzanians and the ruling military commission, who supplied vehicles and security, Obote won the election. Electoral irregularities abounded, from the creation of extra districts in the UPC's northern strongholds to the disqualification of 17 DP candidates. When it seemed that the DP's Paul SSEMOGERERE still might win, the chair of the military commission took over the counting of ballots. The Election Commission chairman fled into asylum in Great Britain and another commissioner disappeared. "Obote II" had begun.

Several factions began to wage guerrilla war against the regime, the most prominent being led by Yoweri MUSEVENI, the third-place candidate in the election. Whole sections of the country became ungovernable, and Kampala, the capital, became a shuttered city every evening as roaming bandit gangs raided with impunity. Obote was never able to assert control over his army, who used the excuse of counterinsurgency to pillage, rape and engage in ethnic cleansing. Obote revived Amin's dreaded State Research Bureau, which returned to its system of arrest, torture and execution. In 1985, the army overthrew Obote, who fled into exile in Zambia, leaving a legacy of bitter ethnic conflict and a shattered economic and political structure.

References: *afr*, CB, DAHB, DRWW, PLBA, PLCA, *wiki*. Francis Bwengye, *The Agony of Uganda: From Idi Amin to Obote* (1985).

OCLOO, Ester Afra
(Ghana, 1919–2002)

Ester Ocloo, "mother of microbanking for the poor," was a pioneer in business for women in Africa.

Ester Ocloo was born to a poor peasant family but received a secondary education on a scholarship from the Cadbury Corporation. In 1941 she began Ghana's first food processing plant with less than an American dollar in her pocket. Her first product was 12 jars of marmalade, on which she turned a profit. In six years that profit turned into Nkuleni Industries, and by 1949 she had made enough to fund two years to study food technology in Great Britain. After she returned, she built Nkuleni into a major food processing company with a wide variety of products, all from local produce. From the start, Ocloo paralleled this with training in agriculture and crafts for young women. In 1958 she founded the Ghana Manufacturers' Association.

At the first United Nations (U.N.) Conference on Women in Mexico City in 1975, she stated her position thus: "Why are we talking about women as victims or passive beneficiaries of social services? Poor women are the world's farmers, traders, informal sector industrialists. Women need access to financial services—nor charity, not subsidies." And she practiced that credo, founding Women's World Banking (WWB) as a network of women in banking serving women across the Third World. She created WWB Ghana as a microlending institution that gave access to finance to the poorest.

Microbanking is the system of lending very small sums of money to entrepreneurs who are capable of small trading, services or manufacturing. It makes loans available to the woman who opens a vegetable kiosk in a market, or who sews school uniforms for children or makes simple products. Microbanking is the banking of the poor because it makes loans to those that banking institutions cannot afford to serve. Ester Ocloo herself began by selling jars of marmalade in the market; she knew the hardships and the frustration. She also knew that small loans were not enough, and WWB affiliates trained women in small-scale business, record keeping and marketing. They taught skills to girls: how to sew, dry fish or buy products for sale.

By the time of the U.N. Women's Conference in Beijing in 1995, WWB was operating in 40 countries with tens of thousands of clients. It had developed enough credibility to be able to work

Ester Afra Ocloo

with ministries of finance to build financial programs that served the poor. By the time Ocloo died in 2002, WWB had expanded to a program serving 10 million women.

Ocloo served on a number of boards and commissions besides her work with WWB. In 1991, she also founded the Sustainable End of Hunger Foundation. In all, she began eight non-profit development organizations. In 1990 she was named the Africa Prize Laureate from the Hunger Project. The Cambridge Biographical Society named her one of the Foremost Women Leaders of the twentieth century. Recognitions, including an honorary doctorate (of which she was very proud), came from the United Nations, Ghana, and groups in Switzerland and the United States.

Reference: adb.

ODHIAMBO, Thomas Risley
(Kenya, 1931–2003)

Dr. Thomas Risley Odhiambo, founder and head of the International Centre of Insect Physiology and Ecology (ICIPE) from 1970, was a world-renowned expert on insect life. His work on the hormonal control of insect reproduction not only broke new ground in theory but had an immediate impact on the lives of millions of people.

Odhiambo obtained his Ph.D. from Cambridge University after working for several years as an agricultural officer in Kenya and Uganda. During his earliest research, he concentrated on the life

Thomas Risley Odhiambo

cycles of dangerous insects. By studying the chemistry of the tsetse fly, which transmits diseases to both humans (sleeping sickness) and cattle, he was able to devise natural means of destroying that insect. The tsetse, which means "cattle killer," makes huge fertile areas of Central Africa uninhabitable. It infects more than 25,000 persons a year—many fatally—and reduces the beef yield by over 1.5 billion tons annually.

Odhiambo was also appalled by the hazardous effect of highly toxic pesticides and was determined to create a means of control that did not damage the land or endanger people. Using sophisticated chemistry, he developed traps based on pheromones, natural chemical substances that lure over 99 percent of tsetse flies to their deaths. Best of all, the traps can be set and maintained by uneducated nomadic herders. Cattle urine is put in traps that attract the flies to their deaths in large numbers.

Odhiambo applied his methods to the control of locusts, which devastate Africa as well as other parts of the world, often triggering famine. A swarm of billions of locusts weighing thousands of tons can strip an area of all crops, trees and grass. Odhiambo's research focused on finding the pheromones that signal the time for the locusts to swarm and to break that cycle.

Odhiambo's enduring work was the ICIPE, with its staff of 50 scientists and teams of field workers. The institute directs a graduate research Ph.D. program with about 70 students, and Odhiambo was proud that none of its graduates have left Africa. It operates in collaboration with 25 African universities. The ICIPE's core program includes control of crop pests, livestock ticks and medical vectors, besides the work on tsetse flies and locusts. In the 1990s work began on mosquito control. This personal commitment to applied research earned Odhiambo international recognition, including the first prestigious Hunger Award (1987) and the Albert Einstein Medal (1979). He held membership in numerous scientific societies. In 1985 he founded the African Academy of Sciences.

Odhiambo was a visionary, scornful of what he calls "the fire brigade" approach to crop loss and famine. He was convinced that without science, Africa could not have a stable economy and believed that developing countries can teach one another. His system, based on the approach that made Mexico a world leader in steroid chemistry in a decade, was to start with a cadre of research fellows, recruit professors from the ranks of the world's best scientists, and focus on problems that have "ultimate economic payoff."

Reference: PAS. www.icipe.org.

ODINGA, Jaramogi Oginga
(Kenya, 1911?–1994)

Jaramogi Oginga Odinga, independence leader and longtime political figure in Kenya, spent much of his career in the political opposition, promoting his ideals of democratic socialism in the face of increasing authoritarianism in his homeland. Odinga was the acknowledged political boss of the Luo people, the second-largest ethnic group in Kenya. He was also revered as their *ker* or spiritual leader.

After taking a diploma in education, Odinga taught from 1940 to 1946 before going into business as managing director of a local trading company. Simultaneously, he entered African politics, taking over and restructuring the Luo Union. In 1957 he became one of the first Africans elected to the Legislative Council (Legco) and headed the African members' caucus. When internal government was delegated to Kenyans by the British in 1963, Odinga was elected to the House of Representatives and was made minister of home affairs by Prime Minister Jomo KENYATTA.

Kenyatta chose Odinga as his vice president when independence came the following year. It was a marriage of convenience, and Odinga soon began separating himself from Kenyatta. Odinga challenged Kenyatta's alliance with foreign capital and Western powers in the Cold War. He founded the Lumumba Institute with money from socialist countries and moved to the left. The two strong personalities clashed, and in 1966, Odinga resigned from the vice presidency and also from the Kenya African National Union (KANU), Kenyatta's party. He and Bildad KAGGIA formed a new party, the Kenya People's Union (KPU). In 1969 the KPU was banned and Odinga was detained after a public shouting match between Odinga and Kenyatta led to riots and 11 deaths. In 1971 Odinga was released from prison and rejoined KANU. He bided his time while he directed the Luoland branch of KANU.

President Daniel arap MOI appointed Odinga to a marketing board within a year after Kenyatta's death, but Odinga also ran afoul of the Moi regime, which he accused of corruption by calling for a "second liberation." In 1982, Odinga's son was accused of complicity in an attempted coup, and Odinga himself was again expelled from KANU and restricted to his home city. He continued to criticize the government, and only his personal prestige gave him immunity from arrest. Always direct and blunt, Odinga made few friends but became a voice for democratic pluralism. When international pressure forced Moi to agree to multiparty elections in 1992, Odinga joined the opposition, later deciding to form a personal party. In the elections, he exposed serious government corruption involving losses of almost seven percent of the Kenyan money supply. Odinga, however, was embarrassed when it was revealed that he had accepted a US$57,000 "gift" from a central figure in the scandal. Odinga easily won a parliamentary seat but came in last in the presidential polls, with 12 percent of the vote. His age, his image as a critic, and the taint of corruption combined to defeat his presidential aspirations.

References: afr, AA, DRWW, EB, EWB, PLBA, *wiki.* Odinga, *Not Yet Uhuru* (1967).

OGOT, Grace Emily Akinyi
(Kenya, 1930–)

Grace Emily Akinyi Ogot is a novelist and writer, and in her own country she is known as a political figure. Originally trained in England as a midwife, Ogot has worked in a variety of fields. For several years she was a writer with the British Broadcasting Corporation (BBC) and had a popular weekly program for the BBC in the Dhuluo language. Subsequently, she served as an executive with Air India, and presently she owns and manages two successful clothing boutiques in Nairobi. Her marriage to Bethwell A. Ogot, a distinguished historian, supported her interest in Luo history.

Ogot was among a small group of women who were groomed for leadership by President Daniel arap MOI. In 1975 she was a Kenyan delegate to the United Nations (U.N.) General Assembly, and the following year to the U.N. Educational, Scientific, and Cultural Organization (UNESCO). In 1983 she was appointed to parliament by Moi, but she resigned in 1985 to contest an elected seat in her own right. Her risk proved worthwhile, and she won the parliamentary seat for Gem district. She became assistant minister for culture until 1992, when she was defeated along with almost all cabinet ministers in a major rebuke to Moi and KANU, the ruling party.

She remained a KANU loyalist, however, and was appointed to head the Kenyan delegation to the 1995 U.N. Women's Conference in Beijing. When the Moi government was swept from power by the coalition of Mwai KIBAKI's National Rainbow Coalition in 2002, she retired from politics.

Ogot's primary literary contribution has been as a short-story writer, although she also has published three novels, *The Promised Land* (1966), *The Graduate* (1980), and *Miaha* (1983). Ogot uses the traditions and folklore of the Luo people and in the process creates historical fiction. She interprets this background widely to include the clash of traditional values with those of the new urban Africa. Returning often to women's issues, Ogot stands strongly by tradition, presenting women who sacrifice individuality for the sake of family and clan. She reconciles the dissonance between these female characters and her activist life by pointing out that the communal standard is one that she imposes on men as well. In one of her best short stories, "The Professor," she explores the conflicts surrounding the first Kenyan heart transplant. While the story's protagonist, a surgeon, makes history, the taking of the heart from a dead man and giving it to another man is portrayed as a forbidden act of witchcraft. The struggle between modernity and deep-rooted tradition destroys the protagonist, who is unable to submit to tradition.

Three volumes of Ogot's short stories have been published: *Land without Thunder* (1968), *The Other Woman* (1976), and *Island of Tears* (1980). She writes in Dhuluo, Kiswahili and English.

References: adb, afr, AA, DLB, EWB, LKW, NRG, *wiki.*

OGUNYEMI, Wale
(Nigeria, 1939?–2001)

The playwright Wale Ogunyemi published six plays in his lifetime and also adapted Shakespeare's *Macbeth* (1969) for the Nigerian stage under the title *Aare Okogun*. He was also known as a popular and gifted actor.

Ogunyemi entered the theater as an actor and remained one all his life. Without any formal training, he began performing with Nigerian television in the 1960s, then joined a touring theater group, honing his skills as he performed across the country. Wole SOYINKA brought him into his Orisun Theatre Group, which gave Ogunyemi a higher profile. This began a lifetime association in which Ogunyemi took major parts in Soyinka's plays for many years. His balance between comedy and drama made him an ideal actor for Soyinka's work.

In 1967 he joined the staff of the Institute of African Studies at the University of Ibadan and began writing. At the same time, he embarked on a one-year intensive course in theater and stagecraft. Most of his plays were written in English between 1968 and 1991. Besides his six published plays, nine others have been performed, and Ogunyemi wrote numerous radio and television scripts.

Several of Ogunyemi's plays are historical, tales of pre-colonial Yoruba wars. In general, his work comes from Yoruba myth and history. He shows the effects of civil conflicts in such a way as to draw parallels with the contemporary Nigerian collapse of order. Others were more typical dramas, the best of

which was *The Vow* (1971), which won numerous awards. *The Divorce* (1977), his most performed play, is a domestic comedy, and along with the overwrought *Partners in Business* (1991), hardly rises above soap opera.

It is in his other works that Ogunyemi's contributions lie. He weaves Yoruba myths of the interaction of the gods and the people, using dialogue and musical backgrounds.

Even after his writing days were over, Ogunyemi continued to perform, appearing in Soyinka's *The Beatification of Area Boy* in 1995 in England and in television and film. He never limited himself to African theater, however, performing in plays by Shakespeare, Chekhov and Bertolt Brecht, among others.

Reference: adb, CA.

OJUKWU, Chukwuemeka Odumegwu
(Nigeria, 1933–)

Chief Chukwuemeka Odumegwu Ojukwu was leader of the Biafran secession from 1967 to 1970 and remains a significant political figure in Nigeria.

Emeka, as his followers call him, came from a wealthy Igbo family in eastern Nigeria. He was educated in Lagos before studies in England, where he earned a degree in history from Oxford University in 1955. Upon returning home, he spent two years in the colonial service, directing community development in rural areas. In 1957 he entered the army, "the only truly federal organization that was likely to remain intact." After officer's training in England, he was commissioned in 1958 and was posted as an instructor at the Frontier Forces Training School in Ghana. Shortly after Nigerian independence (1960), he became quartermaster general at the Kaduna Barracks before being sent to the Congo (now the Democratic Republic of the Congo) with the United Nations (U.N.) peacekeeping force. There he administered Kasai Province, adjacent to the troubled Katanga (now Shaba) Province.

From 1964 to 1966, Ojukwu commanded the Fifth Battalion, which was stationed in northern Nigeria. He took no part in the 1966 coup that ended with the assassination of Sir Abubakar Tafawa BALEWA, but he was appointed military governor of the Eastern Region. It was a time of turmoil, and within a few months, more than 200 Igbo officers were murdered in a counter-coup that brought to power General Jack GOWON, a classmate of Ojukwu. Things continued to deteriorate until September, when northern soldiers joined civilian mobs in slaughtering tens of thousands of Igbos living in the north. More than two million Igbo refugees poured into the Eastern Region. Ojukwu favored a loose federation of regions, each with its own dominant ethnic group, but Gowon opposed weakening the central government.

In March 1967, Ojukwu kept back federal revenues in order to care for refugees. Because the Eastern Region was blessed with oil, industry and palm oil, it was the wealthiest, and Ojukwu's policies sparked mounting reactions until he proclaimed the independence of the region as the Republic of Biafra in May. A naval blockade was set up along the coast, and federal troops invaded in July. The Biafrans at first held their own, but initial success was followed by the encirclement of Biafra and its gradual strangulation. Military supplies were given generously to the federal government by the Soviet Union, Great Britain and Egypt, which had a squadron of jets fighting for Nigeria. With the disruption of farming and an effective blockade, starvation began to spread among the civilian population until deaths reached more than 8,000 per day. Biafra collapsed in early 1970, and Ojukwu went into exile in Côte d'Ivoire.

In 1982, Ojukwu was pardoned by Shehu SHAGARI and returned home to an ecstatic welcome. He became active in the National Party of Nigeria (NPN) but was unsuccessful in a bid to be elected to the national senate. When General Muhammadu BUHARI overthrew Shagari, Ojukwu was detained for a year, and after his release he went into private business. In 1993 he threw his support to the center-right Republican Party because he thought it would be the best guarantor of eastern interests in national politics. He contested the presidency in 2003 as one of many against Olusegun OBASANJO, but got a pitiful three percent of the vote.

References: CB, DAHB, DRWW, PLBA, RWWA, wiki. Frederick Forsyth, *Emeka* (fiction, 1982); Valentine Obienyen, *Ojukwu: The Last Patriot* (2206).

OKIGBO, Christopher Ifekandu
(Nigeria, 1932–1967)

Christopher Okigbo, perhaps the best Nigerian poet of his generation, died a patriot for his region in the Biafran War.

Okigbo graduated in Greek and Latin classics from the University of Ibadan and worked as a teacher, literary editor and librarian while he began writing. In 1961, he was invited to be one of the founders of the Mbari Club, an association of writers and artists that would have a profound effect on African arts. Here he collaborated with Wole SOYINKA (for whom he played jazz accompaniment when Soyinka sang in local clubs), Chinua ACHEBE, Es'kia MPHALELE, John Pepper CLARK, Amos TUTUOLA and various artists.

After 1963, he became West African representative for the Cambridge University Press, which allowed him to travel around the region and to Great Britain. His poetry was collected in four books: *Heavensgate* (1962), *Limits* (1964), *Silences* (1965) and the posthumous *Labyrinths with Paths of Thunder* (1971). His verse shows the influences of his classical education and his familiarity with American writers, but it is steeped in Igbo mythology. His images come from his background, and his poetry is complex and sophisticated. It reflects the oral tradition, using repetition and chanting styles, and is best read aloud, even declaimed. He saw himself as one who cries out to people, but he called to them through ancient myths, poetry in the rhythms of drums and melodic chants. Okigbo's self-image as a poet was that of the seer, prophet and high priest, speaking a truth that others may not see. His grandfather had been a priest of the water goddess Idoto, and he often evokes the image of water. *Heavensgate* opens with the oft-quoted lines: "Before you, Mother Idoto, naked I stand/Before your watery presence a prodigal." It marked a conscious return to Yoruba religious myth.

Okigbo rejected the theory of *Négritude* that was popularized by Léopold Sédar SENGHOR, the reigning African poet of the post-World War II era. When shortly before his death he was offered the Langston Hughes poetry prize at the 1966 Festival of Black Arts in Dakar, Sénégal, he turned it down with the comment, "There is no such thing as Negro art."

Okigbo's writing was cut short by the Biafran War. He entered the Biafran army as a major and was killed in battle. Prophetically, he had written a year earlier: "The elephant has fallen/The mortars have won the day."

Reference: adb, *afr*, EB, MMA, *wiki*, WLTC. Dubem Okafor, *The Dance of Death* (1998). http://echeruo.syr.edu/okigbo.

OKOSUNS, Sonny
(Nigeria, 1947–)

Sonny Okosuns (or Sunny Okosun), although not a seminal figure in West African popular music, has been a popular performer and lyricist in the Afropop movement and originated a reggae sound that he calls *ozzidi*.

Okosuns was born in Enugu in Nigeria's eastern region, to parents who were traditional musicians. He grew up admiring the music of Elvis Presley and the Beatles. His first band, the Postmen, was formed in 1965 as a Beatles clone and imitated their songs, their dress and even their hair styles. When the eastern region attempted to secede from Nigeria, precipitating the Biafran civil war of 1967, Okosuns fled to Lagos with his family. There he worked for Nigerian television as a stagehand, but with the flight of most Igbo entertainers to Biafra, Okosuns was able to pick up playing jobs and in 1969 joined a group that toured Europe and Japan. At the end of the war, he struck out on his own.

After struggling while he played American rock, in 1974 Okosuns formed a new group named Ozzidi. The name came from two sources: the novel *Ozidi* (1966) by John Pepper CLARK, featuring an Ijaw god of that name, and the Igbo words *ozi di*, "there is a message." Ozzidi's first songs, all set to a slow, rolling reggae beat, were popular successes. Bob Marley praised his work, and Okosuns soon began receiving offers to tour.

Okosuns writes all his own material, and almost all of it has political and social commentary. "I didn't want to go into love singing at all. I wanted to sing something meaningful, protest songs," he says. His songs have been appropriated by political leaders for their own purposes, particularly in Nigeria, where the fortunes of several of Okosuns's songs have risen or fallen with the fates of various governments.

In the 1970s and early 1980s, *ozzidi* enjoyed considerable success. The best albums of that period are from 1978, *Holy Wars* and *Fire in Soweto*. His liberation songs became anthems of the struggle in South Africa and Namibia. Both feature protest songs of the same names that were bestselling singles. *Togetherness* (1983) was an appeal for national unity at the time of Shehu SHAGARI's re-election and subsequent overthrow by the military. After this album, Okosuns entered a withdrawn period, with fewer club dates and little recording activity. In 1991 he issued *African Soldiers,* his first American release featuring all new material. It was uneven and not up to his earlier work.

After the 1990s, Okosuns had a pentecostal conversion experience, and now calls himself an evangelist. Since 2000 he has released several albums of gospel and religious music: *A Great Change* and *Celebrate and Worship in Caribbean Rhythms* (2000), and the most recent, *The Glory of God* (2005?).

Okosuns has refused to live and work outside Nigeria, which has kept his work fresh and noncommercial but which also limits his opportunities for regular contact with international music. Fifteen of his albums have gone platinum.

References: BPAR, GEPM, MMA, WAM.

OKOT p'Bitek
(Uganda, 1931–1982)

Okot p'Bitek appeared dramatically on the African literary scene with an epic poem, *Song of Lawino,* in 1966. Unlike most previous African poets, who owed much to the literary influences of the European languages in which they wrote, Okot used the form of African oral literature. The work was an astonishing tour de force.

Okot, an Acholi born in Gulu in northern Uganda, went to England as a member of the national soccer team and decided to stay. He successively completed a diploma in education and degrees in law (Wales) and social anthropology (Oxford), for which he wrote a thesis on Acholi traditional songs. After his return home, he joined Makerere University, studied traditional oral literature, and organized the Gulu Festival of the Arts. The recognition that came to him after the publication of *Song of Lawino* gained him an appointment as director of the National Theatre and Cultural

Centre. Okot's prestige was not enough, however, to protect him when he criticized the government of President Milton OBOTE. In 1967 he left Uganda for Kenya. After a year (1970–1971) with the Writers' Project at the University of Iowa (Idi AMIN's coup prevented his return to Uganda), Okot took a post at the University of Nairobi, where he stayed from 1971 to 1978. He joined forces there with NGUGI wa Thiong'o to replace the English Department with one emphasizing African literature. After Amin's fall, Okot returned to Makerere but died suddenly after only four years there. *Song of Lawino* was written in Acholi and transposed into English—recreated rather than translated. In the poem, Lawino defiantly celebrates the life and culture of her people in order to win back Ocol, her husband, who has alienated himself and taken on Western ways. Composed of 13 song-poems of irregular length, the poem captures the cadence of the original Acholi. Each song takes up a different aspect of life, and each describes Western customs as unconnected, in contrast with the rootedness of African village life. It does not denounce the West but pleads with Ocol for tolerance: "I do not understand/The ways of foreigners/But I do not despise their customs./Why should you despise yours?"

Okot's subsequent work is prefigured in this first epic poem. *Song of Ocol* (1970), an attempt to respond to Lawino's challenge in her husband's voice, never lives up to its predecessor, perhaps because Okot cannot really put himself in Ocol's place. Ocol remains inarticulate in defense of his adopted ways and ends a confused and pathetic figure. Unlike *Song of Lawino,* however, *Song of Ocol* has a broad geographical and chronological scope, ranging across Africa and through its history, conjuring up noble kingdoms and a heroic history. In *Song of a Prisoner* (1971), Okot exposes the dilemmas of failed hopes in newly independent Africa.

Okot's Nairobi years were also a time of great scholarly creativity. In 1971 he published two studies, *Religion of the Central Luo* and *African Religions in Western Scholarship*. He collected his trenchant critical essays in *Africa's Cultural Revolution* (1973). These works shared the same dynamic emphasis as the poems, "dedicated to the total demolition of foreign cultural domination and the restoration and promotion of Africa's proud culture to its rightful place." To this end Okot also translated and edited two volumes of Acholi folk tales and songs.

References: AA, AWT, DLB, MBW, MMA, NRG, *wiki*, WLTC. Monica Wanambisi, *Thought and Technique in the Poetry of Okot p'Bitek* (1984).

OKRI, Ben
(Nigeria, 1959–)

Sir Ben Okri burst upon the international literature scene in 1991 with a stunning novel, *Famished Road*, but the years leading up to his "discovery" had been ones of growing recognition.

Okri was raised as a small child in London, but his family returned to Nigeria in 1968. He went back to Great Britain for university and published his first novel, *Flowers and Shadows* (1980), at 21. It tells the story of a young man's disillusionment at discovering his father's corruption. The parallel with the growing cynicism in Nigeria was not lost on its readers. The following year he published *The Landscapes Within*, which marked a transition from traditional plotted fiction to a mix of realism and mysticism. It set the trend for all his later writing.

Okri spent the next six years as a writer for BBC Television while writing short stories. In 1986, his collected stories, *Incidents at the Shrine*, won both the Aga Khan Prize and the Commonwealth Prize for Africa. *Famished Road* won the Booker Prize. It is a brilliant example of magic realism. Azaro, the protagonist, is a spirit-child who has entered the land of the living and chosen to remain, despite the constant temptations of his spirit companions, who try to trick him back. He takes part in the travails of his human family, but always feels the tug of the other side. It is a tour de force of exploration of the landscape of the imagination, the term he prefers over "magic realism." He continued the story of Azaro in *Songs of Enchantment* (1993), which takes the boy even deeper into the spirit world. As he once commented: "The dead are not really dead, the ancestors are still part of the living community and there are innumerable gradations of reality."

Awards and recognition followed immediately. Besides the Booker, *Famished Road* won several other international literary prizes. Okri has received several honorary doctorates and was knighted by Queen Elizabeth II.

Okri's later work includes half a dozen novels, two books of poetry and a volume of essays. He continues to live and write in London.

References: AB, *adb*, *afr*, CA, DLB, EB, *wiki*, WLTC. Robert Fraser, *Ben Okri: Towards the Invisible City* (2002).

OLAJUWON, Hakeem
(Nigeria, 1963–)

Hakeem Olajuwon was the most outstanding basketball player to come out of Africa and the only player in National Basketball Association (NBA) history to rank among the top 10 in scoring, rebounding, blocked shots and steals for three seasons.

Olajuwon studied at the Muslim Teachers' College in Lagos and began playing basketball when his school team needed a player at a sports festival in Sokoto. In 1980 he played for Nigeria in the All-Africa Games before arriving at the University of Houston. In Houston he established an exceptional record, playing in the National Collegiate Athletic Association (NCAA) Final Four Tournament on three occasions. Olajuwon was drafted by the Houston Rockets in the first round of draft picks in 1984.

Once he joined the NBA, Olajuwon scored in double figures in 98 percent of the games in which he played and averaged 20.6 points per game. From 1987 to 1989 he was elected to the first-team all-NBA, after missing by one vote in 1986. He suffered an eye injury on the court in 1991 and missed 25 games as a result. In 1996, for the NBA's golden jubilee, he was named one of the NBA's 50 best players of all time. He was elected to the all-NBA First Team six times.

For several years with the inconsistent Rockets, Olajuwon distrusted his teammates and played a highly individualistic game. He became known as a malcontent and even made it clear at one point that he would welcome playing for another team. In 1993, however, his viewpoint changed, and the *Houston Chronicle* recognized his development into "the consummate team player." Settling his differences with the Rockets' owner during an all-night flight to Japan, Olajuwon signed a US$25.4 million contract binding him to the Houston team until 1999.

Olajuwon ascribed his new self-confidence and cooperation to "Islamic willpower." An observant Muslim, he renewed his faith since moving to the United States, where he became a dual citizen in 1993. In 1994 he purchased an unused bank building in Houston and converted it to a mosque. He observed the daily Islamic times of prayer, which the Rockets accommodated in team practice scheduling. He also kept the annual Islamic fast, abstaining from all food and drink during daylight during the month of Ramadan. In 1996 he married an 18-year-old Nigerian woman in a traditional Muslim marriage. His name was originally "Akeem," but he added an "H" in 1991 after persistent misspellings in the press. "Olajuwon" in Yoruba means "always on top."

He was chosen the NBA most valuable player (MVP) in the 1994 season, with *The New York Times* calling him "the dominant player of his era." He finished the season by being named MVP of the

Hakim Olajuwon

championship series when the Rockets beat the New York Knicks in seven games.

In 2001 Olajuwon was traded to the Toronto Raptors, where he played his final NBA season. In his career he played in 1,236 NBA games and scored 26,946 points for a 21.8 points-per-game average. He had over 12,000 rebounds and holds the NBA record for blocked shots at 3,830. He also won a gold medal with Dream Team III at the Atlanta Olympics, and received the NBA's Sportsmanship Award in 2000. He is a man of culture who speaks three Nigerian languages plus English, French and Arabic, and has an interest in fine art.

Reference: afr, wiki. George Rekela, *Hakeem Olajuwon* (young adult, 1993).

OLATUNJI, Babatunde
(Nigeria, 1927?–2003)

Babatunde Olatunji, a legendary drummer and drum teacher, was the major force in popularizing African drumming in the United States, where he lived from 1950 to his death. Olatunji's early (and probably best) album, *Drums of Passion* (1959), was reissued in 1989.

Following his schooling, Olatunji worked for the colonial civil service in Nigeria before attending Atlanta's Morehouse College, where he was sponsored by the Rotary Club. He supported himself and his American wife with cultural performances while completing most of the work on a Ph.D. in public administration at New York University. The allure of performing became too great, however, and in 1958 he abandoned plans for an academic career and signed with Columbia Records to begin his pioneering introduction of Worldbeat, the use of African percussion in American popular music.

At first, he performed with little public notice, although he appeared alongside musicians such as Bob Marley, John Coltrane, and Carlos Santana. In one memorable performance, he played at the Village Gate in New York City with Jack Kerouac. By 1966, after six albums, Columbia had lost interest. Olatunji then spent almost 20 years touring with his Center of African Culture, a peripatetic lecture, music and dance troupe. He completed two books and also did consulting for educational television.

When Mickey Hart, the drummer for the legendary Grateful Dead, asked Olatunji to open for the group on New Year's Eve, 1986, a new era began for him. With Hart and Santana, Olatunji recorded two albums and began exploring forms of music such as traditional Yoruba prayer songs to the gods, using complex layered rhythms and choral call-and-response forms. He was always interested in music education and developed a method for teaching drumming.

By the 1990s, Olatunji had assumed the prominence of an old master. He was called upon for special events, master classes and concerts. His teaching was legendary, and Hart is among his many students. He also helped Bob Dylan at a critical point in his career, assisting him in getting his first record contract. Without straying from his natural home in Worldbeat, Olatunji introduced the African drum into many popular venues that had never heard it before. He became a staple at national conferences of the men's movement, with its emphasis on drumming as a form of therapeutic play. With his flowing Yoruba robes and dark glasses (the legacy of a year's blindness due to cataracts), Olatunji was a striking stage presence. Alternately formal and passionate in his attacks on the drums, he moved his audiences and always ended with his fans dancing on stage and in the aisles.

References: BPAR, DMM, GEPM, MMA, WAM, wiki. www.olatunjimusic.com; http://babaolatunji.com.

OLONISAKIN, 'Funmi
(Nigeria, 1965–)

Dr. 'Funmi Olonisakin is one of the leading security specialists in the world.

Olonisakin graduated from the University of Ife and then took an MA in war studies at King's College, London. Later she was the first African woman to receive the Ph.D. in war studies. She stayed there as a research associate, directing a project on United Nations (U.N.) peacekeeping operations and regional organizations. Much of this focused on the efforts of the Economic Community of West African States (ECOWAS), through its joint military task force, to stabilize Sierra Leone. In 1998 she went to the Institute of Strategic Studies at the University of Pretoria to study women in combat and the issue of child soldiers. She returned to King's College to found the celebrated Africa Security Unit.

In 2000, Olonisakin was appointed Special Representative for Children in Armed Conflict in the U.N. Secretary General's Office, then moved to the Centre for Defence Studies at King's College, London, where she was later named MacArthur Foundation Research Associate. Her work has always combined policy formulation with the effect of armed conflict upon vulnerable groups, especially women and children. She has assisted in policy concerning the reintegration of child soldiers into society after demobilization. She has also been active in many groups as an advocate for African women's leadership. She represents the Pan-African Movement on JusticeAfrica.

Reference: adb. Olonisakin, *Reinventing Peacekeeping in Africa* (2000).

OLOWE of Ise
(Nigeria, 1875–1938)

Olowe of Ise is the greatest of the Yoruba traditional sculptors, and the most famous. His Ikere door is known internationally. When it was sought for the Nigerian Pavilion of the British Empire Exhibition in London in 1924, the Ogaga of Ikere at first refused to release it. The British bargained with the Ogaga for a British royal throne, the door was given to the Exhibition in exchange, and Olowe carved a new door for the Ogaga's palace. One of the two original doors depicts the 1897 visit of a British official to the palace.

Olowe of Ise

Olowe's other famous work is a bowl carved from a single piece of wood. That in itself would not be remarkable, but this *olumeye*, a ritual bowl in honor of a female messenger to the spirits, is unique. It features four female dancers on the lid, while the bowl itself is supported by kneeling male nudes. Both these features are unknown in other Yoruba carving and they reverse the gender presentations in traditional Yoruba carving. Inside the frame formed by the kneeling figures holding up the bowl is a carving of a human head. The head moves about inside its "cage" but it cannot be taken out, a demonstration of Olowe's superior carving skill.

Nothing is known of Olowe's apprenticeship or who his carving mentors might have been. That this was the path by which traditional artists were trained is without dispute, however. What is known is that he apprenticed and later practiced in Ise, hence his name. He attracted many patrons, petty chiefs and kings of the region, who had him carve posts and doors for their palaces as a means of exalting their grandeur.

Olowe's carving has distinctive characteristics. His reliefs are deeply incised, to the extent that the raised parts cast shadows. While most Yoruba carvers seldom raised their figures more than a centimeter, Olowe's figures seem to rise up out of the background, sometimes as much as 12 centimeters. A master of composition, Olowe's work shows dynamism, with active and moving figures. His reliefs are packed with images of men in many poses and everyday activities. His style features elongated forms and textured surfaces in bold geometric patterns combined with vivid colors. As an indication of the high regard in which he was held by other Yoruba sculptors, praise-song poems were written in his honor. Toward the last decades of his life, Olowe began signing his work, using a triangle.

Reference: Roslyn Walker, *Olowe of Ise* (1998).

OLYMPIO, Sylvanus Epiphanio
(Togo, 1902–1963)

Sylvanus Epiphanio Olympio was the father of Togolese independence and the country's first president.

Olympio was born to a wealthy family when Togo was under German colonial authority. He was sent to Austria for secondary education and attended the University of Vienna before taking a degree at the London School of Economics in 1926. He worked for the United Africa Company until 1938 in Nigeria, Gold Coast (now Ghana) and Togo, where he became the highest-ranking African in a multinational corporation. During this period he was also active in the All-Ewe Conference, an association promoting the unity of the Ewe people, who were divided among the Gold Coast, French Togo and British Togoland. In 1941 he founded the Committee for Togolese Unity (CUT) to work for Ewe unification. Being open in his criticism of both French and British colonial powers, Olympio was arrested by the French in 1942 and was deported to Dahomey (now Benin). When General Charles de Gaulle came to power at the end of World War II, Olympio was freed and returned to French Togo.

In 1946, Olympio led the CUT to victory in the territorial elections and became president of the assembly. When he spoke out against the division of the Ewe in a strong speech to the United Nations (U.N.), the French government had the United Africa Company transfer him to Paris. He refused the false promotion and was arrested on trumped-up currency violations charges. Banned from office for five years by the French, Olympio was superseded by Nicholas GRUNITZKY, who was elected prime minister in 1958. When the U.N. held elections for the trust territory, Olympio won the office with an overwhelming victory. The ban was lifted so that he might become prime minister of an autonomous Togo. He pressed for full independence, and when it was achieved, he was elected president in 1960.

Olympio was a popular leader, but his economic policies produced opposition. He encouraged foreign investment and developed the phosphate industry, which became a cornerstone of export earnings. His budgets, however, were strict and failed to respond to the plight of the unemployed. When Kwame NKRUMAH closed the border after failing to absorb Togo as a province of Ghana, Olympio instituted economic austerity. Specifically, he reduced the army to 250 men and refused to accept demobilized veterans of the French army. The veterans attacked Olympio's palace in 1963, joining with disgruntled noncommissioned officers who wanted a larger army with greater opportunities for promotion. The coup was unplanned, but as Olympio attempted to escape, he was killed at the gates of the United States embassy by Gnassingbé EYADÉMA, a junior officer who later became

president. Olympio's longtime rival Grunitzky succeeded him as president.

References: DAHB, EWB, MMA, PLBA, *wiki*.

OMBÉDÉ, Phillipe Louis (René Philombe)
(Cameroon, 1930–2001)

Phillipe Ombédé, who wrote under the pen name Réné Philombe, was the author of a score of books. He was also a leading cultural and political activist for much of his life. He belongs to the first generation of Cameroonian writers, with Ferdinand OYONO and Mongo BETI, to whom he is often compared as a writer.

In his late teens, Ombédé joined the national police, where he immediately began union organizing. By his mid-twenties, however, he was progressively rendered infirm by spinal disease, and he turned to writing. After 1958 he was confined to a wheelchair. He began several newspapers as a start on his writing career. His first works were short stories; *Tales from My Hut* was written in 1957 but published in collected form 20 years later. It recounted his everyday life as his handicap overtook him and won a literary prize from the prestigious French Academy. This was followed by several novels: *Sola, My Darling* (1966), about the inequity of marriage customs; *The White Sorcerer of Zangali* (1970), the tale of missionary and colonial bureaucracies; and two works published in 1978 as cautionary tales against dictatorship. He also published five volumes of poetry and five plays.

In 1960 he helped found the Cameroonian writers' association, and served as an officer in 1981. Ombédé was active in a banned left-wing, Marxist party, both during the colonial period and after independence. Despite his infirmities, Ombédé's activities resulted in arrests and several prison terms under President Ahmadou AHIDJO, whom he lampooned in political pamphlets. On his last release from prison in 1981, he was kept under house arrest. Despite the continued persecution, Ombédé never went into exile. After he was cheated by his publishers, he went into an almost hermit life in his village after 1983 and published no more work. In 1992, he received the Fonlon Nichols Award of the African Literature Association for the body of his work.

Reference: Richard Bjornson, *The African Quest for Freedom and Identity: Cameroonian Writing and the National Experience* (1991).

ONGALA, Remmy
(Tanzania, 1947–)

Remmy Ongala, the most popular musician in Tanzania, has only recently become an international figure. His original name was Ramathan Ntoro Ongala.

Born in eastern Belgian Congo to a father who was a singer and entertainer, he was introduced to music from childhood, but he was orphaned at nine and raised by his extended family, who disapproved of a musical career. Despite their disapproval, he was performing by age 17 and in 1969 had two hit singles sung in Swahili. His early influences were the Congo recordings he heard on the radio from Kinshasa, especially those of FRANCO, whose guitar-picking style is still echoed in Ongala's performances.

Ongala played for various bands in Uganda and Kenya in the 1970s, and then moved to Tanzania in 1978 to join an uncle's band. In 1980, settled in Dar es Salaam, Tanzania, he helped form Orchestre Matamila and soon became its leader. Tanzania is a much poorer country than its neighbors but has experienced almost none of their civil strife. The result has been a benign government attitude that neither promotes nor censors music. The economic status of the country cannot support recording or production because of the shortage of hard currency. The few recordings that are made are produced in small numbers, usually in Kenya, and cassette piracy is widespread. Because little income results from recording, Super Matimila is primarily a live band, playing almost nightly in clubs in Dar es Salaam and occasionally on Tanzanian radio.

Lacking local opportunities to reach a wider audience, Ongala sent a tape to England. In response, he received an invitation to join the 1988 WOMAD Tour (World of Music, Art and Dance). WOMAD simultaneously issued an album of Matimila's earlier work, *Nalilia Mwana,* which some regard as its finest work. Ongala was invited back for the 1989 WOMAD Tour, from which came his album, *Songs for the Poor Man* (1990). It was recorded in England in a professional studio and was co-released by Real World and Virgin Records.

Georges Collinet, the dean of Afropop music criticism, listed it in his 1992 *Afropop Worldwide* with his highest recommendation and played it in the United States on Public Radio International.

Ongala is lead guitar and singer in a lineup of three guitars, bass, sax, trumpet, and drums in a characteristic *soukous* mode. He has been careful to maintain his African roots and has been sharply critical of such performers as Youssou N'DOUR, whom he considers a compromiser of African music. Ongala is also a musician with a message, writing lyrics that attack poverty and racism, two themes that he returns to constantly. One of his most poignant lines is, "Love has no color, love has no race," but he speaks out on every social issue. In 2001, his "Mambo Kwa Socks," urging the use of condoms, was included in *Spirit of Africa*, the AIDS awareness album. In recent years he has had to curtail his touring because of diabetes.

References: BPAR, DMM, GEPM, WAM.

OPPENHEIMER, Harry Frederick
(South Africa, 1908–2000)

Harry Frederick Oppenheimer, head of the De Beers industrial empire, was for years the most powerful businessman in Africa. When Nelson MANDELA, who became South Africa's president, was released from prison, Oppenheimer was one of the first people he asked to see. His support proved critical to the future of South Africa.

Oppenheimer was born in Kimberley, the diamond center of South Africa, and educated at Oxford University. In 1945 he became managing director of the Anglo-American Corporation, and from 1948 to 1958 he was a member of parliament. His was one of the rare voices in parliament against apartheid, and he left parliament only upon his father's death in order to devote himself to family business interests full-time. However, he continued as the main support for the Progressive Party even when it was reduced to only one member in parliament, Helen SUZMAN. In part, his distaste for apartheid was related to its anti-Semitism. A cultivated, modest man, he has been caricatured and vilified as "Hoggenheimer" in the right-wing press, even though he is a lifelong Anglican of Jewish ancestry. Oppenheimer was, however, a longtime supporter of Jewish charities and of Israel. He personally approved raw diamond sales to Israel so that it could develop a diamond-cutting and polishing industry.

Oppenheimer was chairman of the Anglo-American Corporation until 1983 and of its subsidiary, De Beers Consolidated, until 1984. He headed the family holding company and came to his office daily until shortly before his death. The two firms reach into every continent and a multitude of industries, including basic manufacturing, mining, automobiles, wine, diamonds, food production, tourism and hotels. De Beers controls approximately 80 percent of world gem diamond production, and Oppenheimer's personal assets were estimated at US$15 billion.

Oppenheimer was an early business opponent of apartheid, deeming it both morally wrong and economically disastrous. De Beers and Anglo-American lobbied successfully to eliminate the job reservation system, which eliminated job opportunities for Black South Africans. He also championed trade union rights for Blacks in 1974 and, when the government allowed them five years later, his companies were the first mining enterprises to recognize Black unions and to enable them to form more easily. Anglo-American has set up a cadet plan to train Black corporate managers. Yet even Oppenheimer admitted it was not enough: "We went on saying how wonderful we were ... and then didn't go on pressing."

Reference: CB, *wiki.*

OSEI Bonsu
(Ghana, 1779–1823)

Osei Bonsu, was *asantehene* (king) of Asante from 1800 to 1823, when the state was at the pinnacle of its power. He centralized the imperial bureaucracy and spent much of his rule maintaining his authority over subject peoples and keeping trade routes open.

On Osei Bonsu's accession to the Golden Stool, the Asante throne, he was faced immediately with an insurrection in favor of Osei Kwame, a previous king who championed Islam. Osei Kwame sided with the local chiefs, who feared that Islam would undermine the traditional religion. The rebels were defeated, and Kwame was executed in 1803, thereby initiating a long period of peace in the north. Osei

Bonsu reinforced the peace with a tolerant religious policy, and Muslims were respected and appointed to positions of influence in later years. After subduing the north, Asante controlled all of present-day Ghana except the coast, which he proceeded to occupy. Using the excuse that they were harboring two fugitives, Osei Bonsu mounted a campaign against the Fante kingdom, which ruled the coast, in 1807. By 1816, he had added the coastal provinces to his kingdom. It was at this point that he took the name *Bonsu,* meaning "whale" or "master of the seas."

Osei Bonsu favored education and developed Kumasi, his capital, into a city of substance. He founded the first African museum, the Palace of Culture, to showcase his collection of Asante arts and crafts. Asante's economy depended upon open trade routes, and Osei Bonsu went into competition with the private trading families, even to the extent of subsidizing those individuals who traded with Europeans rather than with the traditional trading houses. He centralized and streamlined the bureaucracy, making it accountable to him directly. Although he replaced the hereditary council of elders with one of his appointees, he allowed regional chiefs of the other ethnically related Akan states a measure of autonomy.

The British attempted to extend their influence after 1816, especially in order to replace slavery with legitimate trade and to replace the Dutch traders, whom Osei Bonsu favored over the British. The British conspired to organize a number of coastal chiefs against Asante, and Governor Charles Macarthy led a combined force of anti-Asante rebels against Osei Bonsu. In 1824, Osei Bonsu defeated them at Nsamankow, and Macarthy was killed. Shortly after, Osei Bonsu died, leaving Asante at its imperial zenith.

References: DAB, DAHB, *wiki.* Kwami Segbawu, *Osei Bonsu: Warrior King of the Asante* (1977) [young adult].

OSEI Kofi Tutu
(Ghana, 1636?–1712?)

Osei Tutu, *asantehene* (king) of Asante from 1680, established the traditions of the Asante nation and founded the Asante Union.

In the seventeenth century the Akan peoples settled in the north of what is now Ghana and founded a number of small states. They were tributary to a powerful state, Denkyira, which maintained their allegiance by keeping hostages from each subordinate petty kingdom. Sent as a hostage to Denkyira, Osei Tutu escaped to Akwamu, another clan's territory, where he received warrior training and learned about firearms. Returning home with Akwamu advisors and soldiers, he began to consolidate his power, the basis of which was a reorganized Asante army, which was modeled, according to tradition, upon the movement of fire ants on the march. In reality, the military structure was based on an earlier model, which subordinated smaller units under the *asantehene*.

Osei created a sense of national destiny by establishing powerful cultural institutions. He made use of the magical authority of a close friend, a shrine guardian from Akwamu, who became chief priest. After establishing the capital at Kumasi, Osei sought to forge national unity through various institutions, such as Odwira, a religious festival in which the bones of defeated enemies were displayed for ritual insults. Another unifying institution was the king's throne, the Golden Stool, which was said to embody the soul of the Asante people and which was displayed on ceremonial occasions. The Golden Stool became a commanding symbol of national unity, as it was not allowed to touch the ground and only the king was allowed to sit on it. The Asante Empire existed until the British seized the Golden Stool in 1900, even though the last ruling king, PREMPEH I, had been exiled four years earlier. Osei created a number of other stools, which he awarded to important officials such as the treasurer, the head of the metalsmiths, and the chief trader.

His first expansive move was to pacify the neighboring clans. He then began to unify the smaller Akan states into a coalition that was dependent upon Kumasi. The Asante Union was primarily military, but Osei did not rule as an autocrat. He respected the rights of the paramount chiefs, governing as first among equals in a quasi-feudal system of mutual rights and obligations. In 1699 the Asante army moved against Denkyira to the south and defeated it in 1701 at Feyiase. Here the Asante seized a major prize, their agreement governing Elmina Castle, the Dutch coastal trading post, especially for the slave trade. This accord opened the trade routes to the coast, and the Dutch acknowledged his hegemony.

Osei Tutu developed the slave trade and expanded commerce in gold and. In a later campaign, he was killed in an ambush when he stopped to pay reverence at the graves of his ancestors and allowed his army to go ahead of him. The date is disputed as being either 1712 or 1717. In commemoration, an oath taken on the anniversary of the king's death was considered most solemnly binding. Osei Tutu, the first *asantehene*, is considered the founder of the Asante Empire.

References: afr, CWAH, DAB, DAHB, WGMC, *wiki*. Basil Freestone, *Osei Tutu: The Leopard Owns the Land* (1968); K.Y. Daaku, *Osei Tutu of Asante* (1976) [young adult].

OSHITELU, Josiah Olunowo
(Nigeria, 1902–1962)

Prophet Josiah Olunowo Oshitelu was founder of the Church of the Lord (Aladura) in 1930, one of the major branches of the Aladura religious movement. Oshitelu, an Anglican catechist and teacher, was dismissed in 1926 because he claimed to have visions, which were brought on by extensive fasting and devotions.

Aladura, "owners of prayer," began in 1918 as a prophetic healing movement and received its greatest impetus under Joseph BABALOLA. During three years spent in seclusion and spiritual discipline, Oshitelu received in a vision a revealed script with holy words and names that had miraculous power. He was assisted in interpreting his dreams and visions by a spiritual master who later became his apostle to West Africa. Oshitelu emerged in 1929 to begin an independent preaching and healing ministry in the Aladura tradition. He attacked idolatry, traditional medicine and fetishes, and healed by using prayer, fasting and holy water. He condoned polygamy, and he himself had seven wives. In 1930 he founded his church. It soon spread into all regions of Nigeria, including the Islamic north, where its use of Islamic dietary rules and prayer forms made it a breakthrough Christian presence. The Church of the Lord also incorporated a series of dramatic spiritual acts—rolling on the floor and jumping and clapping, all accompanied with characteristic cries and shouts.

Oshitelu taught that continuing revelation comes to the Church through the prophets, but he considered his movement to be Christian. He brought it into the World Council of Churches.

The Church of the Lord began its successful expansion beyond its base in Nigeria throughout West Africa after 1947. It found support among prominent persons, including a daughter of PREMPEH I in the Gold Coast (now Ghana). Aladura later spread abroad to England and the United States. Aladura includes some 500 separate sects, so it is no surprise that the Church of the Lord has spawned more than 25 breakaway groups since its foundation. The original Church, however, has about three million members. It is well organized under a primate, with local captains and ministers, but the position of prophets remains one of high honor.

Reference: dacb.

OSMAN, Aden Abdullah
(Somalia, 1908–)

Aden Abdullah Osman was the first president of Somalia and became the conscience of the nation. Born into the Hawiye clan in the south, he enrolled in elementary school at age 14 and in 1928 entered colonial service as a medical assistant at a Mogadishu hospital. In 1941, Osman started a small business and in 1944 joined the Somali Youth League (SYL), which became his vehicle to political power.

Osman was active in trusteeship politics during the period of United Nations-sponsored Italian administration. He entered the Territorial Council in 1951 and later became vice president. In 1956 he was elected to the Territorial Assembly as an SYL delegate, and was its president until 1960. That year Somalia was united and Osman became the first president of the new nation. He was a partisan of a "Greater Somalia" that would unite all Somalis, regardless of clan or jurisdiction. He supported the integration of the former British Somaliland and took a confrontational stance toward the Somali provinces of Kenya and Ethiopia.

In 1967, as a result of a clan conflict in the government, Osman resigned the presidency a few days before his term expired. He did, however, remain a member of the assembly. When the democratic government was overthrown in 1969 in a coup engineered by General Mohammed SIYAD Barre, Osman was arrested and detained until 1973. In retirement Osman continued as a spokesman for

Somali national unity as competing clans divided the country. In 1990 he was again imprisoned after he signed the Mogadishu Manifesto, which protested Siyad Barre's human rights abuses.

When Siyad Barre was toppled, Osman survived the breakdown of Somali society. Today, Osman tends a banana and grapefruit farm, refusing the protection of guards. Despite the lack of security, his farm and home have remained untouched throughout the continuing civil strife since the early 1990s. It is a tribute to the deep esteem in which he is held by the Somali people.

References: DRWW, PLBA, *wiki.*

OUATTARA, Allasane Dramane
(Côte d'Ivoire, 1943–)

Dr. Allasane Dramane Ouattara, distinguished international economist and administrator, was appointed the first prime minister of Côte d'Ivoire in 1990. He represents the new wave of professionals coming to power in the aftermath of the democracy movements sweeping Africa in the early 1990s. These new leaders are untouched by corruption and unbound to ethnic loyalties.

Ouattara was a teenager at independence and does not fit the mold of the older elites, who were French-educated, culturally assimilated and anticolonialist. In contrast, Ouattara went to the United States for his education, graduating from Drexel Institute of Technology in Philadelphia and remaining to obtain a doctorate in economics at the University of Pennsylvania. From 1968 to 1973 he served as an economist for the International Monetary Fund (IMF). Ouattara next worked with the Central Bank of West African States (BCEAO), becoming the deputy governor by 1983. He returned to the IMF in 1984 as director of the African department and advisor to the director-general. During this period Ouattara oversaw the difficult and controversial imposition of IMF Structural Adjustment Programs (SAP) on faltering African economies. The SAP conditions for aid and loans required the reduction of bloated bureaucracies, the end of food subsidies, privatization of state-owned businesses, and the adoption of free market economics. These programs caused hardship and generated political turmoil in some cases, but Ouattara has remained a strong supporter of the SAP. His integrity and professionalism earned him respect internationally as well as throughout Africa.

In 1988, Ouattara returned to the BCEAO as governor, but soon President Félix HOUPHOUËT-BOIGNY selected him to head a cabinet-level commission on the Ivoirian economy. Long the economic miracle of west Africa, Côte d'Ivoire's economy began to falter in the recession of the late 1980s. Ouattara announced a program of 100 days to stabilize the economy and of 1,000 days to establish its growth. Privatization was begun, government workers were either laid off or lost privileges, and international debt was rescheduled (a point where Ouattara's contacts proved indispensable).

At the same time, because of HouphouËt-Boigny's advanced age, Côte d'Ivoire was experiencing political upheaval. Opposition parties were permitted for the first time in the 1990 elections in the wake of mass demonstrations, and the position of prime minister was created, which Ouattara obtained along with the portfolios for finance and the economy. He clashed with student groups and others angered by his strict economic program, and in the power struggle after HouphouËt-Boigny's death in 1993 he was ousted, apparently with the support of the United States and France.

Ouattara is a northern Muslim, and because his name is one found on both sides of the border, he has been accused of being of immigrant background. This excuse was used to disqualify him from running for president in 2000, but in fact, it was part of the longstanding tension between Muslim north and Christian south. A constitutional clause was drafted specifically to block Ouattara's candidacy, but his exclusion from the voting was a major incident generating the resulting civil war. He returned from exile in France in 2006, and has been permitted to contest the elections under United Nations supervision.
Reference: RWWA, *wiki.*

OUATTARA, Bakari
(Côte d'Ivoire, 1957–)

Bakari Ouattara is an Ivoirian painter who brings together African and Western themes, and uses symbols and materials from both cultures.

Ouattara was raised in Côte d'Ivoire, where his father practiced both traditional medicine and was a Western-trained surgeon. He received an education in French-language schools, but was also initiated into a secret society in his traditional religion. After high school, he moved to Paris to study art and began exhibiting in 1986. He became a close friend of the influential Haitian artist Jean-Michel Basquiat, who introduced him to the New York art world. At the same time, Ouattara brought Basquiat to his home village. Today Ouattara divides his time among Paris, New York and Abidjan, but he exhibits around the globe.

Ouattara's work brings together materials from his culture. A common background is large concentric circles, a symbol of the summoning of spirits, but the painting may have a number of found objects attached to it, such as small stones, children's toys and coffee beans. The paintings are often monumental, and he paints at night "because it is more mystical; the evil spirits are sleeping." His mysticism pervades his works and dictates the choice of the objects he attaches to his paintings. He incorporates Egyptian designs and Amharic script from Ethiopia. For the Last Century Exhibit (Germany 1994, New York 2001), with the theme of independence and liberation movements, he showed a piece (mixed media on wood), *Hip Hop Jazz Makoussa,* which celebrated the cross-fertilization of African, African-American and Afro-Caribbean cultures. His work has appeared in over 20 major exhibits.

Nevertheless, Ouattara is capable of sly ironies. *Dark Star*(1996), for example, shows a skeleton placed against footprints and handprints, but with the distinct impress of Nike sneakers, a play on Western consumerism. All of his work toys with the interaction of cultures.
Reference: adb.

OUEDDEI, Goukouni
(Chad, 1944–)

Goukouni Oueddei, past president of Chad, is one of several figures at the center of the country's unstable politics.

A northerner who lost four brothers in the guerrilla wars against the southern dominance of President Ngartha TOMBALBAYE, he has always functioned as a regional warlord. The northern

Saharan areas have long resisted central control, and for 15 years after independence (1960–1975) they remained under French military administration.

In 1972, Oueddei joined the guerrilla wing of the Chad National Liberation Front (FROLINAT) under Hissène HABRÉ, serving as his deputy commander. FROLINAT's goal was to force the central government to accept autonomy for the Muslim north. After a 1974 raid in which Habré captured two Europeans whom he held for ransom, Oueddei broke with Habré. He took command of the northern armed forces in 1977 and the chairmanship of FROLINAT's central committee in 1978. The two leaders became deadly rivals, each making alliances to topple the other. French intervention brought Habré into the government in 1978, while Oueddei allied with Libya, which had designs on the Aouzou Strip, a northern borderland reputed to be rich in mineral deposits.

By 1979 there were four main armies contending for control of Chad, and a consortium of African states, led by Nigeria, brought the leaders together to form a transitional Government of National Unity (GUNT). Oueddei was chosen president, but conflict continued, especially among smaller warlord armies. The French began their withdrawal, but the Libyans took advantage of the situation to increase their troop presence. By the fourth peace conference, 11 armed factions were represented. Habré, serving as minister of defense in GUNT, kept his own forces, and by 1981 his and Oueddei's armies were fighting in the streets of N'Djamena.

Turning to his old ally, Oueddei signed an accord with Libya for the future merger of the two countries, but this only united all the other factions against him. Libya was driven from the north and Habré emerged victorious. Oueddei fled to Algeria, from which he regrouped and counterattacked in 1983 with Libyan support. Anti-Libyan French and American help stopped him, and Habré again triumphed. Oueddei retreated to Libya, where he and GUNT remained as an exile opposition. After Habré was overthrown in 1990, Oueddei made a highly publicized visit to Chad to meet with President Idriss DÉBY. He remains respected by many in Chad as a potential mediator and took part in the Sovereign National Conference in 1993 to chart future directions for the country. Nevertheless, he remains an opposition figure and has used the unsettled conditions along the Sudan border to maintain a guerilla force.

Reference: RWWA, *wiki.*

OUÉDRAOGO, Bernard Lédéa
(Burkina Faso, 1930–)

Bernard Ouédraogo is founder of one of the largest and most successful grassroots development programs in Africa. It has been especially effective in the desert-prone Sahel region among small-scale farmers.

Ouédraogo graduated with an education degree and taught for 13 years before becoming a rural extension worker. He soon realized that his programs were having little effect and began to study Mossi tribal society to see what social structures would prove most useful to development. In 1977 he received a Ph.D. in development studies from the Sorbonne.

Ouédraogo is president of the Naam movement. He realized early on that government-sponsored self-help schemes got little cooperation from peasants, who experienced these approaches as unconnected with their everyday reality. He began Naam in 1967 to pattern a self-help agricultural development program on traditional ways that people would recognize and accept. Naam is a traditional custom that brings together young men and women for a mix of farming, social and cultural activities. All were equal in the group and leadership was chosen by ability, not family or political connections. It became the perfect forum for adapting new approaches from traditional ones and introducing farmers to cash crops and marketing. Storehouses were built for grain purchased during the harvest and kept until the annual droughts, when it could be sold to avoid the seasonal fluctuation in prices that had taken place in the past. In another instance, a traditional three-stone stove was adapted in such a way as to reduce wood consumption by half. Old approaches to water conservation were re-established. Today there are over 7,000 groups in Burkina Faso with over 350,000 members, half women.

The Naam groups not only foster agricultural development, but they also extend into small-scale production. They build dams and wells, produce storage facilities and run credit banks. All this has caused changes in Mossi society, which had been rigidly hierarchical. Now women may own livestock, participate in decision-making and take their place in a productive economy.

He also co-founded Association Six-S in 1976 and has been the executive director since 1978. Six-S are initials for "serving the dry season in the savannah and the Sahel" in French. It is a federation of peasant groups scattered across nine West African countries, and the membership runs into the hundreds of thousands. Small grants are made to individual groups, which determine their own priorities in using the funds, but according to strict accountability standards. Naam itself is a member group.

Ouédraogo has been honored many times: the United Nations (U.N.) World Prize for Peace and the UNESCO Peace Prize (both 1987), the Right Livelihood Award (1990) and several national awards. He was the 1989 Africa Prize Laureate of the Hunger Project. One of the highest tributes came from the Red Cross: "No other African in recent years has had such an influence on the lives of African farmers."

OUÉDRAOGO, Idrissa
(Burkina Faso, 1954–)

Idrissa Ouédraogo is, next to Ousmane SEMBÉNE, the leading filmmaker in Africa. Cultural and financial ties between francophone west Africa and Paris mean that many Africans have received French training and work only in France. There has been little development of film in Africa itself. An exception is Burkina Faso (formerly Upper Volta), where the Pan-African Cinema of Ouagadougou has taken place since 1969.

In 1977 the African Institute for Film Education opened in Ouagadougou, and Idrissa Ouédraogo joined its first class. Expelled from university for leading student demonstrations, he left Burkina Faso to study filmmaking in Moscow and Paris, where he graduated from the Institute for Higher Film Studies in 1985.

Ouédraogo's first works were shorts. *Poko* (1981) is a tragedy about a pregnant woman who dies due to Burkina Faso's inadequate medical care. *Les Ecuelles* (*Wooden Bowls*, 1983) is a study of traditional ritual in making crafts, and *Issa le Tisserand*(*The Weaver*, 1985) depicts the deplorable decline of crafts in the face of Westernization. These films all won international awards, two of them at FESPACO, the leading African film festival. Ouédraogo directed two other shorts, both con-

cerned with the seduction and cheapening of African culture by powerful Western images and materialism.

Ouédraogo's feature films are less didactic and more in touch with universal human feelings. *Yam Daabo* (*The Choice*, 1986) tells of a peasant who leaves his land during a drought to find his own solution in a new area. In *Yaaba* (*Grandmother*,1989), Ouédraogo confronts intolerance and fear by showing the emerging relationship between a young boy and a scorned old woman who is accused of being a witch. It won the top award at FESPACO and the Critics' Award at the Cannes Film Festival, and it was shown at international festivals in New York, Tokyo and Chicago. *Yaaba* was commercially successful in the United States and established Ouédraogo's reputation. *Tilai* (*Code of Honor*, 1990) shows two people caught in unchanging customs. It is the tragedy of a man who must be killed by his brother for breaking a marriage taboo. It won the Special Jury Prize at Cannes in 1990 and the Grand Prize at FESPACO. The acceptance of these films has given Ouédraogo the financial support to use more sophisticated film techniques.

In *Samba Traoré* (1993), which won the Silver Bear Award at the Berlin Film Festival, Ouédraogo took the step toward making popular films, which, in an African setting, will speak to an international audience. It is the story of Samba, a criminal who hides out in his village by posing as a rich benefactor. In this story of the "innocent guilty man," Ouédraogo attempts to move African film out of its particular cultural niche into a universal form of entertainment. Ouédraogo uses many nonprofessional actors and no constructed sets, so his work appears unaffected and simple. Nothing comes between the viewer and the universal life experiences that the film explores. In this context, Africa is not exotic but simply the natural place where the story unfolds.

Some of Ouédraogo's work is topical. In *11/09/01-September 11* (2002), a group of boys plot to capture a man who looks like Osama bin Laden, and claim the reward. After the man eludes them and they lose their dreams of wealth, they decide to pool their meager resources to pay the school fees of the poorest of the group.

Reference: afr, CB, *wiki*.

OUÉDRAOGO, Rasmané

(Burkina Faso, 1950s–)

Rasmané "Raso" Ouédraogo is an actor and president of the African Actors and Actresses Association. His film and television credits have made him a recognized figure in French-speaking Africa. Ouédraogo has acted in films made in Burkina Faso, a center for French African film, and in Belgian, French and Tunisian movies.

Among Ouédraogo's best-known roles was in *Tilai* (1990), made in Burkina Faso by the notable Burkinabé director, Idrissa OUÉDRAOGO (no relation; the name is common in Burkina Faso). Raso played the lead, Saga, a man who returns to his village after a long absence to find that his intended bride has been married off to his father. His acting received praise from critics in Europe and the United States, as well as in Africa. Ouédraogo also played the African slaver king in the 2001 Ivoirean film *Adanggaman*, about the complicity of Africans in the slave trade. In 2002, he starred in a 12-part television series, *Sita*, about forced marriage. It played in Burkina Faso, Gabon and Mali.

In 2003, Ouédraogo also played in another of Idrissa Ouédraogo's films, *Anger of the Gods*, and in 2004 he played Tomoto, the village idiot, in *The Night of Truth*. Tomoto ruins all attempts at peace between factions in a long civil war, and Ouédraogo's acting was a tour de force. The film won the Grand Prize of the Fribourg Film Festival in 2005, and was a finalist at the Paris Film Festival.

In his leadership of the African Actors and Actresses Association, Ouédraogo has organized acting workshops where older, experienced actors and actresses train younger ones. He sees this as an alternative to the financially prohibitive acting schools. He is also organizing national acting unions in several countries.

OUMAROU, Ide

(Niger, 1937–2002)

Ide Oumarou, a man of many talents, was primarily an international civil servant but has been prime minister of his country and also a successful popular novelist.

In the waning years of colonialism, he was educated at the William Ponty School in Dakar, Sénégal, and at the Institute for Advanced Overseas Studies in Paris. He began his career with the Ministry of Information in Niger in 1960, the year of the country's independence. For two years he edited the newspaper *Le Niger* and then served as director of information (1963–1970) and commissioner (1970–1972). Oumarou subsequently spent two years as director of posts and communication.

When General Seyni KOUNTCHÉ took power in 1974, he chose Oumarou as a trusted aide, appointing him chief of cabinet from 1974 to 1979. With his intimate knowledge of government policy, Oumarou was well suited to represent Niger abroad, and he began his international career as Niger's delegate to the United Nations (U.N.) from 1979 to 1983. Oumarou was well respected by his colleagues and was often chosen to chair the African group of delegates. In 1980 and 1981 he presided over the Security Council. Kountché recalled him to be minister of foreign affairs in 1983.

In 1985 the position of secretary-general of the Organization of African States (OAU) had been open for two years, because it was tied up in an intense controversy involving the seating of a delegation from the Polisario movement of the Western Sahara and a Libyan boycott. Oumarou became a candidate for the position. Naturally reserved and professional, Oumarou lacked the political power base of some candidates but appealed to countries that wanted a nonpolitical secretary. It took seven rounds of voting before he won the position, but he immediately moved to stabilize OAU operations. His strategy involved cost-cutting measures, including closing several regional offices. Oumarou placed emphasis upon economic issues and saw to it that they were debated at OAU meetings. He also took part in consultations with the Frontline States who were leading the resistance to apartheid South Africa. Oumarou successfully defended his administration against charges of mismanagement and generally emerged from his tenure as a successful secretary-general. In 1989 he was defeated in his bid for a second term by Salim SALIM of Tanzania.

Oumarou was first and foremost a civil servant and diplomat. A Muslim who neither drank nor smoked, he was a devoted family man whose one indulgence was writing fiction. He has published several bestselling novels, including *Gros Plan* (1978), which won the Grand Prix Littéraire de l'Afrique Noire.

Reference: RWWA.

OYONO, Ferdinand Léopold

(Cameroon, 1929–)

Ferdinand Léopold Oyono, a novelist writing in French, has also served his country as a diplomat. He is one of several authors who, during the 1950s, wrote satirical novels attacking colonial rule. Other writers included Mongo BETI, Bernard DADIÉ and Ousmane SEMBèNE.

Oyono's mother, a devout Catholic, left her husband when he continued to keep several wives. The young Oyono helped support the family as a houseboy for the local mission and used these experiences in his later writing. His father finally provided Oyono with an education, which culminated with a law degree in Paris. While in Paris he published his first two novels in 1956, *Une Vie de Boy* (*Houseboy*) and *Le Vieux Nègre et la Médaille* (*The Old Man and the Medal*). *Houseboy* takes the form of a diary kept by a Cameroonian houseboy named Toundi, who is captivated and astonished by the White world. Passed from master to master, he becomes disillusioned and radicalized, as when he discovers to his shock that his master is not circumcised. To an African, this meant that the master, never having gone through the rituals to become an adult, was immature, unreliable and unclean. "It killed something inside me. I knew I would never be frightened of the Commandant again." *Houseboy* has also been rewritten as a play. *The Old Man and the Medal* is a bitter satire on a peasant's reward for great devotion to France, which consists of losing two sons in French wars and having his land confiscated. *Chemin d'Europe* (*The European Way*, 1960) describes the confusion of a young man who is more educated than his friends but not enough to ensure him a career. Oyono has been working on a large novel about Western society as seen from within, but it has never satisfied him and has been in continual revision for 20 years.

Oyono's diplomatic career has been distinguished although undramatic. Unlike Beti, who went into exile, Oyono has never turned his satire against postcolonial corruption and has faithfully served his country. He was twice minister to the European Community and has been ambassador to France, Liberia and the United States as well as delegate to the United Nations (U.N.). He was later made minister of Foreign Affairs in the government of Paul BIYA from 1992 to 1997, and is currently minister of Culture.

References: adb, *afr*, AA, NRG, *wiki*, WLTC.

PANKHURST, Richard
(Ethiopia, 1927–)

Dr. Richard Pankhurst is the foremost historian of Ethiopia, the author of some 23 books and the editor of another 17, along with numerous articles.

Pankhurst was the illegitimate son of suffragist Sylvia Pankhurst and Silvio Corio, an Italian socialist. His mother, a radical feminist, refused to marry or to take a man's name. She had lived in Italy and saw the rise of fascism, which she detested, and was among the first to realize that Ethiopia was slated to be the first victim of fascist expansion. Becoming a campaigner for Ethiopia, she started a newspaper to further the cause. She first exposed the atrocities of General Rudolfo GRAZIANI, and as she became more anticolonial, she befriended such Pan-Africans as Jomo KENYATTA. Through her, Richard became familiar with Ethiopia and absorbed her fascination with the country. He graduated from the London School of Economics and later took a doctorate there.

In 1956, Richard Pankhurst moved to Addis Ababa to teach at the new university being founded. Soon after, he founded the Institute of Ethiopian Studies, which became his life's work. He went back to London in 1976 following the Ethiopian revolution, but returned to Ethiopia permanently in 1986.

Pankhurst has long campaigned for the return of Ethiopian artistic treasures looted by foreign invaders. His special interest has been the Aksum Obelisk, an ancient stele of great historical and cultural value. Following the 1947 peace treaty with Italy, it was to have been returned, but Italy has refused to honor its pledge. He is also active for the repatriation of artifacts looted by the British and the return of part of the Ethiopian archives still held by Italy.

Reference: Pankhurst, *The Ethiopians* (2001).

PARK, Mungo
(Gambia/Nigeria, 1771–1806)

Mungo Park, a Scottish surgeon and explorer, was one of those adventurers who influenced the minds of Europeans about Africa in the years immediately preceding the colonial period. A restless and utterly fearless character, Park was admirably suited to the peripatetic life he set for himself. He was sponsored by the president of the Royal Society, who recommended him as medical officer on a voyage to Sumatra. Impressed by Park's achievements, the society appointed him to explore the course of the Niger River, and he embarked in 1795.

Park learned to speak rudimentary Mandingo and set out with only an African servant. Imprisoned for four months by an Arab chieftain, Park escaped and proceeded toward Gambia on foot. Slowed by fever, harassed by bandits, and physically exhausted, he reached the coast after a two-year trek. When he returned to England, Park wrote an account of his adventures, *Travels in the Interior Districts of Africa* (1799). The book went through three editions, and Park became an instant celebrity who was lionized everywhere.

For several years Park lived in Scotland, practicing some surgery and marrying the oldest daughter of his former employer, the Duke of Buccleuch. Sir Walter Scott became a close friend, and the Duchess of Devonshire wrote a popular song about one of his exploits. Surgeons at this time had little professional respect, because they were not physicians, so his notoriety created a breathless ascent for a 30-year-old of humble origins.

Nevertheless, Park was restless and jumped at an offer from the Colonial Office to return to Africa. It took two years to make arrangements, during which Park learned Arabic, but he finally departed in the company of his brother-in-law in 1805. Joined by a company of soldiers, they marched for 14 weeks to Bamako in present-day Mali, but only 11 of the 40 Europeans survived. In another 12 weeks, only Park and three soldiers had survived the terrible effects of climate, fever and malaria. Park built a double-hulled canoe, hoisted the British flag, and started out again. His last letter, sent back by an African guide, ended: "If I could not succeed in the object of my journey, I would at least die on the Niger." Park's tiny party disappeared, and four years later it was discovered that all had drowned in the Niger while under attack from the shore.

References: afr, DAHB, DNB, EB, *wiki*. Kenneth Lupton, *Mungo Park: The African Traveler* (1979).

PATON, Alan Stewart
(South Africa, 1903–1988)

Alan Stewart Paton was one of the great twentieth-century novelists of South Africa and a leader of White liberal politics in his country. As such, he was more often appreciated outside South Africa than within it. His writing was considered patronizing by Blacks and radical by many Whites. Nevertheless, Paton's novels were the vehicles by which many in the United States and Britain were awakened to the realities of apartheid.

Raised by staunchly religious Methodist parents who inculcated a sense of moral duty, Paton converted to Anglicanism in 1930 and was thereafter increasingly influenced by his religious faith. The connection between spirituality and social conscience was nurtured by his long friendship with Archbishop Trevor HUDDLESTON, although the two often disagreed on political strategies against apartheid. Paton wrote several warm and affectionate sketches of Huddleston, and in his first novel, *Cry, the Beloved Country*, Huddleston appears as a priest in a poor Black community.

After graduation from the University of Natal, Paton spent 20 years as a teacher, the most formative ones as headmaster of a reformatory for African boys. He was repelled by the destructive nature of the prison system and began a lifelong crusade for prison reform. On a postwar worldwide trip to observe modern prisons, he found himself seated in Norway's Trondheim Cathedral before its luminous rose window. Overcome with emotion, he returned to his hotel and began a novel. He finished it on the trip in less than 90 days. The instant popularity of *Cry, the Beloved Country* (1948) made Paton an international celebrity and financially independent. He then resigned from government service to devote himself to writing.

The novel appeared in South Africa just as the Afrikaner-led Nationalist Party took power on a platform of apartheid. It is the story of Stephen Kumalo, a Zulu clergyman, in search of his son Absalom, who has murdered a White man. Stephen loses his faith on the journey, only to rediscover it. This novel is about racial tension but also describes forgiveness and reconciliation. The theologian Reinhold Niebuhr called it "the only recent religious novel that succeeds," and reviewers uniformly praised it. It was translated into 20 languages and sold more than 15 million copies. It still sells over 50,000 a year in English alone. In 1949, Kurt Weill and Maxwell Anderson created a musical version that ran for nine months, and in 1952, it was made into a film. In the English-speaking world, it fixed the image of South Africa as a racist, oppressive and backward nation. In South Africa, the reception was much less enthusiastic. Afrikaners dismissed it as sentimental, although it did have an impact upon English-speaking Whites. Many Africans rejected its simplistic stereotypes of Blacks as victims with little personality or depth.

In 1953, Paton completed a second novel, *Too Late the Phalarope*. By then, apartheid legislation was in place, and this book examined the impact of the Immorality Act, which prohibited sexual relations between different races. It recounts the story of an alienated young White man who becomes involved with a Black woman, only to be arrested and see his world destroyed. Paton was dissatisfied with the novel, and he took a break from writing to work in a tuberculosis settlement with his wife. His social conscience would not allow him to take refuge in simple charity, however, and in 1953 he helped found the Liberal Association, replacing Margaret BALLINGER as president two years later. He developed it into the South African Liberal Party (SALP) and served as its only president. The SALP advocated the universal vote and held four seats in parliament as part of the franchise for non-Whites. The government moved against the SALP in the 1960s, banning several leaders and eliminating its base by ending the non-White franchise. In 1968, multiracial parties were made illegal, and the SALP was disbanded. Despite his political activity and open criticism of the government, Paton was never personally banned, although from 1960 to 1970 he was denied a passport and confined to South Africa. In 1953, *Too Late the Phalarope* was banned. The death of his first wife and that of the party, both in 1968, marked the end of Paton's political activity other than writing.

After his two novels, Paton published two volumes of short stories, a play, and about 20 volumes of nonfiction, including religious and political writings. The best of these are his two volumes of autobiography and his sensitive and loving memorial to his first wife, *Kontakion for You Departed* (1969). His later political views remained liberal, but he was increasingly passed up by more radical Whites. He opposed economic sanctions, causing Huddleston to comment sarcastically, "I just hope I don't get hardening of the arteries which might make me reactionary!" Paton was despised by Afrikaner leaders and rejected as ineffectual by Blacks. He took cautious, moderate positions, such as acceptance of the limited but segregated franchise for Asians and Coloureds in 1984 and support for Chief Mangosuthu BUTHELEZI. Throughout the decline of South Africa into increasing political violence, Paton remained a figure of optimism, saying shortly before his death, "I still believe there is hope."

References: AB, *adb*, *afr*, AO, CANR, CB, *dacb*, DAHB, DLB, EWB, MMA, *wiki*, WLTC. Paton, *Towards the Mountain* (1980) and *Journey Continued* (1988).

PATTEN, Anna

(Mauritius, 1960s–)

Anna Patten is a leading dancer from Mauritius who has revived Indian traditional dance and blended it with contemporary styles.

Patten was born of South Indian parents in Mauritius, an Indian Ocean country with a broad mix of races and cultures. With her partner, Bhimjee Sanedhip, she has carried the revival of traditional Indian *kathak* dance to India itself and around the Indian Ocean coast. Sanedhip was her first disciple, and together they founded the Indigo Ocean troupe, with some 150 dancers. Through the 1990s she choreographed a series of *kathak* pieces for her dance group and performed them widely. *Kathak*, or story telling, is the major classical dance of northern India. It originated in the temples and palaces there, and at various times it was used as a form of religious ritual and at others as simple entertainment. In time, the story-telling aspect faded and kathak became more abstract. It is precisely this aspect which has made it possible for Patten to use *kathak* as a form of modern dance, incorporating newer styles. In the tradition, it was the profession of female dancers, something that the colonial British frowned upon. Patten has been one of the postcolonial dance theorists to work at its revival.

The dance is accompanied by various traditional musical instruments, of which the sarod (a lute), sitar (a long-necked stringed instrument) and tabla drums would be most familiar to Westerners. At least another 10 instruments are also used. *Kathak* has always emphasized the role of the solo dancer, even in later forms where groups performed. Here Patten takes the stage as the narrator of the tale embodied in the dance. Patten's dances invoke the spiritual tradition of *kathak*, opening with an invocatory dance, almost a kind of meditation. The next movement takes up classical Indian dance and then moves into the modern aspects, blending them harmoniously. The dancers harmonize their facial expressions with bodily movements in such a way that the story line becomes clear even without lyrics or spoken lines. Patten uses a line of dancers moving in perfect synchronicity, their quick footwork following the sound of their ankle bells. The effect is both energizing and hypnotic.

Patten brings *kathak* to life in a new way, returning the experience of the Indian diaspora to India itself, where her work has been warmly received, both in theater settings and on national television.

PAULOS

(Ethiopia, 1935–)

Abune Paulos, fifth patriarch of the Ethiopian Orthodox (Tawahedo) Church, has held that office since 1992. He suffered imprisonment, exile and persecution and governed the Church during a time of great tension in Ethiopia and within the Church.

Abune Paulos is Tigrean. He entered a monastery as a youth and was taken to Addis Ababa for seminary studies, sponsored by his mentor, the patriarch Abune TEWOFLOS. He was clearly chosen as a promising student, and Tewoflos sent him to New York to finish seminary and begin graduate work at Princeton Theological Seminary. When the Communist Dergue under MENGISTU Haile Mariam overthrew Emperor HAILE SELLASIE in 1974, it immediately moved to control the Church, the leading social unifier in Ethiopia. In 1975 Paulos was called home and ordained a bishop by Tewoflos without government approval. Paulos was promptly thrown in prison for seven years. In

1982, he was released and sent into exile. He went to the United States for 10 years, during which he returned to studies at Princeton Theological Seminary, taking master's and doctor's degrees.

While Paulos was in exile, Tewoflos was deposed and executed in prison, and replaced with a puppet patriarch. The Dergue fell in 1991 and the second government-managed patriarch was pressured into resigning. He tried to retract his resignation, but the Church Synod declared the office vacant and authorized a new election. In 1992, Paulos was elected to replace him. The ex-patriarch, in exile in Kenya, has refused to recognize Paulos's election, generating a small group of splinter congregations abroad, especially in the United States. Abune Paulos has been accused of being too close to the ruling party, and while Paulos was leading religious processions in 2006, demonstrations broke out that resulted in several deaths. A monk was killed when he attempted to assassinate the patriarch in 1997. This is a confused situation, because Paulos has supported the All-Party Conference of Democratic Forces, which is opposed to President Meles ZENAWI.

Despite controversy and tensions, Paulos has presided over a time of regrouping and expansion for the Orthodox Church. He obtained the return of much of the Church's confiscated properties, re-opened the seminary and restructured the patriarchate. He has improved relations with other faiths, including cooperative programs with the Muslim Society of Ethiopia. In Ethiopia alone, there are 30 million Orthodox with 400,000 clergy of various ranks. Muslims almost equal that number. There are also about six million Ethiopian Orthodox in the diaspora. After Eritrea became independent, its Orthodox faithful petitioned and obtained their own patriarch, and Paulos, though loath to grant it, finally accepted the decision.

Paulos has been active in the peace negotiations between Ethiopia and Eritrea, which have had a series of border wars. He intervened three times between 1998 and 2000. He has also made the Orthodox Church into the main relief organization in the country, serving war refugees and those suffering from drought. His refugee work was recognized by the United Nations High Commission for Refugees, which awarded him the Nansen Medal in 2000.

Reference: wiki.

PEREIRA, Aristides Maria

(Cape Verde, 1924–)

Aristides Maria Pereira was an early independence leader and comrade of Amílcar CABRAL and Luis CABRAL and a founder of the African Party for the Independence of Guinea and Cape Verde (PAIGC). He was president of his island country for 16 years.

After secondary school, Pereira trained as a telegraph technician in Bissau, Portuguese Guinea (now Guinea-Bissau). In 1952, Amílcar Cabral returned from Portugal, and he and Pereira began working together to organize resistance cells on the Communist model. In 1956 the PAIGC was founded as a liberation group for both Cabo Verde and Guinea-Bissau, with the hope of bringing the two colonies to freedom as one nation. In 1958, Amílcar Cabral left for newly independent Guinea, where Sékou TOURÉ offered a safe haven for the PAIGC infiltration of neighboring Guinea-Bissau. Pereira remained in Cabo Verde, and in 1959 a dock strike that he organized was crushed by the Portuguese with considerable loss of life. It was the spark that set off the armed struggle.

Pereira, who had risen to head of telecommunications in Guinea- Bissau, slipped out of the country in 1960 and joined Amílcar Cabral in exile in Guinea. There Pereira set up the PAIGC exile headquarters and established an information program to broadcast radio reports to friendly nations. Placed in charge of international affairs, he was successful in securing aid from the Soviet Union, Scandinavian countries, and the Organization of African Unity (OAU). The guerrilla struggle, limited entirely to Guinea-Bissau, began in 1963. Although Pereira took part, especially in organizing underground sabotage groups in Bissau, it was not his major focus. When Amílcar Cabral was assassinated in 1973, Pereira was kidnapped in Conakry and was put on a boat for Bissau. At the last moment he was rescued by the Guinean naval patrol before he could be handed over to the Portuguese. He immediately took charge of the armed struggle and brought it to a successful conclusion. With independence, Luis Cabral became president of Guinea-Bissau (1974), and Pereira returned to Cape Verde. He was elected overwhelmingly as president in 1975.

Initial plans called for the merger of the two countries, but in 1980, Luis Cabral was overthrown by João VIEIRA. Pereira led Cabo Verde jointly with his associate, Pedro PIRES, who was prime minister throughout Pereira's tenure in office. While it was friendly with the West, Cape Verde maintained ties to the Communist states. The major challenge, however, was economic survival. Cape Verde's limited land area cannot support its burgeoning population, and large numbers of people are forced to emigrate. In 1990, responding to changes in both Africa and Eastern Europe, Pereira introduced a multiparty system. He was then soundly defeated by Antonio MONTEIRO in 1991, which led to his retirement from politics.

References: afr, DAHB, DRWW, PLBA, RWWA, *wiki*.

PHILIP, John
(South Africa, 1775–1851)

Reverend John Philip was a highly controversial Scottish missionary who championed the rights of Africans and was a strong advocate of direct British rule.

A self-assured man who started working at the age of 11, Philip had a stern moral sense. In 1794 he quit a good job in protest against child labor and eventually became a Congregational minister in Aberdeen. Philip took an active interest in the London Missionary Society (LMS), which invited him to visit South Africa in 1818 for an investigation of mission conditions. He found the mission stations neglected and the local peoples oppressed by the settlers. His report to the LMS condemned the Society in the harshest terms. The LMS responded by establishing a central mission house in Cape Town and appointing Philip superintendent for South Africa.

Philip returned to his new post in 1822 and built a chapel in Cape Town, from which he traveled throughout the colony. Because the LMS missionaries were often the only Europeans in outlying areas, Philip's access to information on current conditions made him influential in Cape Town. His earlier criticisms did not abate; if anything, they became stronger. His censures resulted in considerable improvement in the legal status of the Khoikhoi, the original indigenous people, after he published *Researches in South Africa*

(1828) to plead their cause. He used this tract to lobby the British Parliament into passing an act supporting his recommendations. When he returned to Cape Town, he encountered a hostile reception. A prominent settler whom he criticized sued him for libel, and Philip lost. Friends paid his fine, but even they found him to be too shrill in his criticisms. He clashed with Robert MOFFAT, who thought Philip vain and too sure of the benefits of mission stations for British trade.

Philip was more resourceful and effective on behalf of African rights in Parliament than in Cape Town, where he was resented and disliked. His frequent trips to England, lecture tours, and lobbying efforts produced the policies he sought but also alienated the settler community. He had close contacts with the Clapham Sect, an evangelical band of reformist parliamentarians who were instrumental in ending the slave trade. Philip shared their moralistic zeal and sense of righteousness. In 1836 his campaigning brought about the removal of Cape Town's governor, and for some years after, Philip became the arbiter of Cape policy regarding African affairs. His pet project was the establishment of a series of small African states along the frontier of South Africa to prevent Afrikaner expansion. He negotiated with several African chiefs, but in 1846 the Xhosa War brought an end to his dreams and his influence. In 1848 a further frontier war dashed any remaining hopes of a peaceful belt of African states in the borderlands. Philip resigned the following year and retired.

To those who admired him, Philip was a noble defender of the oppressed, a humanitarian and a progressive. His opponents regarded him as a master of intrigue and manipulation, not above dishonesty in his self-willed drive for control. He was the most powerful political figure in the Cape Colony for over 30 years.

References: dacb, DAHB, DNB, EB.

PIRES, Pedro Verona Rodrigues
(Cape Verde, 1934–)

Pedro Verona Rodrigues Pires was a guerrilla commander during the liberation struggle against Portugal in the 1970s and became prime minister at independence in 1975. He held that position until

420 PLAATJE, Sol(omon) Tshekisho

1991, making it one of the longest tenures in modern Africa. He became president of Cape Verde in 2001.

Pires studied science at the University of Lisbon but returned home in 1961 to join the African Party for the Independence of Guinea and Cape Verde (PAIGC), which had been founded in 1956 by Amílcar and Luis CABRAL to work at the liberation of Portuguese Guinea (now Guinea-Bissau) and Cape Verde. That year, Pires was sent as a delegate to the conference of nationalist organizations in Portuguese colonies, which met in Morocco. In 1965, Pires became a member of the PAIGC central committee and in 1967 was named commander of the south front in the Guinea-Bissau guerrilla war. The PAIGC favored the union of the two colonies and worked as a common front. Pires negotiated the independence of both territories in late 1974, and the following year, Cape Verde formed a government with Aristides PEREIRA as president and Pires as prime minister. The two would hold those positions until leaving office together in 1991.

The unity issue remained unresolved, with both countries promising referenda. When the PAIGC government of Luis Cabral was overthrown in 1980, however, Cape Verde removed all references to unity from its constitution, although good relations between the two countries were maintained. Besides close relations with the other Portuguese-speaking countries, Cape Verde pursued a nonaligned position in world affairs, refusing a Soviet offer to build a naval base on the islands. Cape Verde was governed in tandem by Pires and Pereira in a moderate fashion, without harsh repression. In 1990, responding to the democracy movement across the continent, Pereira stepped down from party leadership and was replaced by Pires. Open elections were set for 1991, and the ruling party was defeated by António Monteiro. Pires became the leader of the opposition as head of his party.

In 2001, Pires was elected president. He has pursued a moderate socialist agenda. In 2006, he narrowly won re-election with 51 percent of the vote.

Reference: afr, RWWA, *wiki.*

PLAATJE, Sol(omon) Tshekisho
(South Africa, 1876–1932)

Sol(omon) Tshekisho Plaatje was a journalist and author who helped found the African National Congress (ANC). His writing became a vehicle of protest against the growing oppression of Blacks in South Africa.

Plaatje, the fourteenth child in his family, took his father's Afrikaans nickname (meaning "short and stocky") as a family name. After serving as a postal clerk in Kimberley, he became a court interpreter for the British in the Cape Colony. With the outbreak of the Boer War in 1899, he was made an interpreter and signal man for the British army. At the siege of Mafeking, which lasted for seven months, he had his first opportunity to write. Plaatje learned typing, an unusual skill at the time, and did some war correspondence.

On the basis of this slim experience, Plaatje launched the first SeTswana newspaper in 1901, *Koranta ea Bechuana* (*Newspaper of the Tswana*). He became one of the leading African newspaper editors of the period and a strong advocate of indigenous rights. He argued for African representation and ably presented the case for protection of African rights in the constitutional discussions that followed the end of the war. In 1909 he moved on to Kimberley to become editor of *Tsala ea Bechuana* (*Friend of the Tswana*) and then *Tsala ea Batho* (*Friend of the People*). His move coincided with the creation of the Union of South Africa.

Plaatje brought great language skills to his writing. He spoke seven languages and translated Shakespeare into SeTswana. At one time, he held majority interest in three newspapers. He would also be the first African to write a novel in English, *Mhudi* (1913).

Plaatje became increasingly involved in politics after 1910. In 1912 he was one of the founders of the African National Congress (ANC) and was elected the first general secretary. The galvanizing issue was the Native Land Act of 1913, which severely restricted African rights to ownership and was an important step toward segregation. In 1914, Plaatje went to London with a delegation opposing the bill, but they were ignored by the Colonial Office. He remained in Britain during World War I to write. His first book, *Native Life in South Africa*

(1916), was a powerful attack on the Land Act and a defense of the rights of Africans. In moving and emotional tones, he described the act's effects on the peasant farmers as they were driven from their farms in the dead of winter, carrying a few possessions and begging for shelter, "as if these people are so many fugitives escaping from a war." The book received the attention that the delegation had not and was widely and favorably reviewed. At home, the South African parliament debated the issues the book had raised.

The other two books that resulted from Plaatje's stay in England were studies of SeTswana, reflecting his desire to preserve the language and save it from linguistic corruption in the face of social change. The first was a collection of 732 proverbs, with translations and comparable European sayings, where these existed. The second book was a linguistic study, applying the phonetic alphabet to the SeTswana language and was the first time that such an analysis had been attempted for any African vernacular.

Plaatje returned to South Africa in 1917. In 1919 he went to Europe to present African grievances at the Versailles peace discussions, with no success. Again he remained behind, this time to attend the first Pan-African Congress in Paris. Making useful contacts, he traveled in France, Canada and the United States, lecturing and trying to win support for the Black cause in South Africa. He returned home, however, in 1923, convinced that outside intervention would not be forthcoming from any quarter. For the rest of his life, Plaatje continued to write for various publications and to work on his SeTswana studies. He translated six of Shakespeare's plays, two of which were published and sold well to Tswana schools. He also polished and published a novel, *Mhudi: An Epic of Native Life 100 Years Ago* (1930), which he had written earlier. It is the first novel in English by an African writer, and it remains in print. It is a historical novel of the nineteenth century, mixing traditional storytelling techniques with Western plot and character development. The central character is a woman, and on several levels it sympathetically explores the contributions of women to society, possibilities for racial harmony, and the necessity of justice.

Plaatje remained active in political affairs. He joined the temperance movement and founded an interracial society to improve relations. He traveled to the Belgian Congo, and his report comparing conditions there and in South Africa resulted in the increase of African employment on the South African railways. Although he wasn't radical, in 1930 he joined the Communist protests against the pass laws after the ANC refused to support them. He died of pneumonia while on a trip.

References: afr, AA, CWAH, DAHB, DLB, EB, EWB, MBW, MMA, *wiki*. G.E. De Villiers, *Servant of Africa: The Life and Tomes of Sol Plaatje* (2000).

PLAYER, Gary Jim
(South Africa, 1935–)

Gary Jim Player, one of the outstanding golfers of the twentieth century, was only the third person in history to win all the major world golf titles: the British Open (three times), the U.S. Masters (twice), the U.S. Open, and the Professional Golfers' Association (PGA) championship (twice).

As a teenager in the 1950s, Player was coached by Bobby Locke and Ben Hogan but primarily by Jock Verwey, whose daughter he married. He turned professional in 1953 and won his first three tournaments two years later. At age 24, he was the youngest competitor to win the British Open. In 1961 he competed in all 12 PGA tournaments, was the top money winner, and won the Masters. In his banner year, 1963, he won nine tournaments. He ranks first in professional wins (167) and is fourth in major championship victories (nine). In 1974, he posted the lowest round ever in professional golf, a 59 at the Brazilian Open.

Player is a fitness fanatic and a devotee of health food. He neither smokes nor drinks. A devout Christian who reads the Bible daily, Player is a political conservative. Although he was a critic of apartheid, he disagreed with Black voting equality in South Africa and spoke out against it. At the PGA Championship in 1969 he was harassed by an antiapartheid crowd and had to finish the round under heavy police escort.

Player designs golf courses (he has done over 200), especially in Asia and the Middle East. He has had a running argument with environmentalists about the value of courses, which he defends as "natural green belts." He divides his time between a home in Orlando, Florida, and a 1,000-acre farm near Johannesburg, where he breeds thoroughbred horses. The farm supports an elementary school for 400 Black children from poor families. He was in the first class inducted into the World Golf Hall of Fame in 1974. In 2003 he was awarded the Order of Ikhamanga by the South African government for excellence in sport, and he has three honorary doctorates. He still plays on the Champions Tour. At age 55 he took his third Senior PGA Championship title.

References: afr, CB, *wiki*. www.garyplayer.com.

POLLOCK, Graeme
(South Africa, 1944–)

Graeme Pollock was one of the greatest left-handed batsmen in international cricket. His first test match was against Australia in 1963, and he finished with a last test against the same team in 1970. In each of those series he had a double century.

His debut test in Australia was brilliant. He opened with 25 runs in the first match, slowed to 19 the second, and then posted an astounding 122 in the first innings of the third. The legendary Sir Donald Bradman wired: "The next time you decide to play like that, send me a telegram." He finished the series with 399 runs. Pollock was a mere 19 years old.

His last test was one of his greatest, but also one of the saddest. Pollock set a South African record of 274 runs in the first innings as the Springboks triumphed against a strong Australian team. But it was to be Pollock's last test because the international ban on South African sport went into effect, not to be restored until over 20 years later.

Pollock was 26 when sports sanctions fell on South Africa, but he continued to play until he was 43. He retired with a record of 71 centuries and 110 fifties; seven and 11 of these, respectively, were in test matches. In tests he scored 2,256 runs, and 20,940 in first-class matches. His batting style was smooth and seemingly effortless. One prominent cricketer called it "A poetic quality mixed with the spirit of the eternal schoolboy." His leg-side strokes were the stuff of sports stories.

Pollock's test average was 60.97, the second-highest in cricket history. His first-class career spanned almost three decades, 1960–1987. In 2000, South Africans voted him Cricketer of the Century.

Reference: wiki.

PREMPEH I
(Ghana, 1871?–1931)

Asantehene Prempeh I, king of Asante from 1888, was the last great ruler of the Asante kingdom. He inherited a crumbling empire after the death of his brother and spent six years repressing rebellions and attempted secessions from the Asante Union. He resisted British attempts to extend a protectorate over the Asante and in 1894 was ceremoniously installed on the Golden Stool, the throne of the kingdom, which served also as its national symbol.

The British, however, considered restoration of Asante authority, threatening and continuing to conspire against Prempeh. They spread stories of harshness and human sacrifice, which Prempeh countered by sending a delegation to England to defend his reputation. The colonial authorities supported the coastal states against him, and in 1896 they sent troops to Kumasi to demand submission and payment of an indemnity. Prempeh decided that resistance was futile, promised the payment, and attempted to negotiate. The British deposed him and arrested him along with several members of the royal family and other Asante leaders. They were exiled to the Seychelles Islands. After a rebellion during which the British attempted to seize the Golden Stool, Asante was annexed to the Gold Coast colony in 1901.

In 1924, Prempeh was allowed to return to the Gold Coast as a private citizen, although the people always revered him as king. The British compromised by appointing him ruler of the Kumasi region under their system of indirect rule. He had, in fact, considerable authority, although the title of *asantehene* would only be restored to his nephew and successor, PREMPEH II.

References: AB, DAB, DAHB, WGMC. Thomas Lewin, *Asante before the British* (1978).

PREMPEH II
(Ghana, 1892–1970)

Asantehene Prempeh II was king of Asante during the colonial and early independence years in Ghana. Asante custom provides for succession in the female line, and Prempeh II was the maternal nephew of PREMPEH I, whom he succeeded in 1931. Given a Western education, he worked for a European firm until his election to the Golden Stool, the Asante throne. In 1935 the British colonial government decided to create the Asante Confederacy Council, and Prempeh II was recognized officially in a spectacular ceremonial coronation.

As head of the Asante Confederacy Council, Prempeh wielded considerable power, and his position as chairman resulted in his knighthood in 1937. He retained the traditional mode of consensus government and benefited from the immense reverence attached to the Golden Stool, Asante's greatest symbol of unity. During the 1930s Prempeh resisted some British policies, using a boycott of European products in one case. He was more often than not successful in asserting Asante rights, but in the 1940s he could not accept the more radical politics of the nationalists, who were led by Kwame NKRUMAH. In 1954, Prempeh backed an opposition group, but he later switched his allegiance to Nkrumah. His authority continued to diminish with the decline of traditional rule generally, although Nkrumah hastened the process by abolishing chiefs' councils following Ghana's independence in 1957. After 1958, Prempeh retreated from politics, although from 1969 to 1970 he was a member of the Council of State, which helped to govern Ghana during a period of instability.

References: DAB, DAHB, MMA.

PRETORIUS, Andries Wilhelmus Jacobus
(South Africa, 1798–1853)

Andries Wilhelmus Jacobus Pretorius, a founder of the Transvaal Republic, was one of the leaders of the Great Trek, during which much of the Afrikaner population moved away from British dominance to establish their own independent states.

Pretorius was born in the Cape Colony and was educated on the family farm by itinerant teachers. He participated in several frontier wars against the Xhosa and became a prosperous settler with several large farms. By the mid-1830s, there was serious dissatisfaction with British rule among the Afrikaners. British opposition to forced labor interfered with the Afrikaner economy; moreover, English speakers displayed little sensitivity toward Afrikaner attitudes and culture. Large organized groups began moving north with their cattle, servants and goods

until about 6,000 Afrikaner settlers—representing about 20 percent of the Afrikaner population of the Eastern Cape—had moved across the Orange River and beyond British colonial frontiers.

At first this migration was loosely organized and Pretorius was not involved. Subsequently, his interest grew, and in 1837 he made an exploratory trip into the interior. He was a leader in the battle of Mosega, in which MZILIKAZI was defeated, and shortly thereafter he was invited to lead a punitive military strike against DINGANE, who had lured the main Afrikaner leader into his camp, had slaughtered more than 300 Whites and 200 Coloured servants, and had taken 35,000 livestock.

Pretorius's task was daunting; the Afrikaner settlers were fiercely independent and unused to military discipline. When Pretorius reached Natal, he formed a commando of 464 men and insisted on proper discipline. On 9 December 1838 he bound them together by a sacred vow that they would mark any victory by a day of Holy Sabbath in thanks to God. The anniversary of this event became a sacred national observance among Afrikaners. Before 1994 it was called the Day of the Vow, but it remains a national holiday under the new name, Day of Reconciliation.

A week after, the group formed a laager, a tightly knit circle of more than 50 wagons, providing an instant defensive position. When some 10,000 Zulu warriors attacked, the commandos' withering fire decimated them, leaving 3,000 dead in what is known as the Battle of Blood River. Pretorius followed up this blow by giving support to a revolt against Dingane, joining his forces to the usurper's, and defeating Dingane decisively in 1840. An Afrikaner republic was proclaimed in Natal, with Pretorius as commandant-general. It was an enclosed society limited to Afrikaners, who dominated larger groups of Coloureds and Blacks, termed *skepsels* (creatures) to indicate that the Afrikaners considered them subhuman.

This settlement, which reproduced the seventeenth-century life and values of the Afrikaners, was short-lived. FAKU, chief of the Mponde, protested through his missionaries about the treatment of the Africans, and the British intervened. Although the Afrikaners were at first able to repel the British, by 1842 the Natal Republic was taken over. The Afrikaner response was to move further out, and a series of tiny "republics," some hardly larger than a single clan, sprang up on the high veldt. Pretorius and his followers settled across the Vaal River far to the northwest. Here they encountered expanding chiefdoms and strong kingdoms, such as those of the Griqua and MOSHWESHWE's Sotho.

The British, in a series of mistakes, attempted to annex the area between the Orange and Vaal Rivers but were unable to maintain their authority. In 1854, Pretorius signed the Sand River Convention, by which the British ceded the territory to the Afrikaners, abandoning both their claims and their defense of the Africans. Independence was recognized; Andries's son Martinus PRETORIUS became the first president of the republic that followed. He named the South African capital Pretoria after his father.

References: afr, DAHB, EB, EWB, *wiki*.

PRETORIUS, Martinus Wessel

(South Africa, 1819–1901)

Martinus Wessel Pretorius, one of the chief personalities in the Afrikaner independence movement, served as president of both the Transvaal Republic and the Orange Free State. The eldest son of Andries PRETORIUS, he joined him in the Great Trek to Natal and followed him to the Transvaal in 1848. There he was named one of four commandants-general after his father's death in 1853. He drafted the first constitution for the nascent Transvaal Republic that Andries had made possible.

Martinus's goal was the union of the various small clan-based Afrikaner "republics" that had proclaimed themselves along the Vaal River. He worked to bring them together until the South African Republic, an amalgamation of most of the Afrikaner settlements, was proclaimed in 1857, with Martinus Pretorius as president. The fierce spirit of independence among the Afrikaners made this a considerable achievement, but Pretorius's determination and high-handed style overcame most opposition. He seemed to be capable of uniting the Transvaal states with the Orange Free State (OFS) when he was elected president of the OFS in 1860. This effort plunged the Transvaal into confusion, and he was asked to choose between the two presidencies. Opting for the OFS, his efforts to bring about a union of the two Afrikaner states failed, and he returned to the Transvaal in 1863 when civil war broke out there. He was again elected president of the South African Republic, brought the contending forces together, and stabilized the frontiers.

Pretorius was able to obtain diplomatic recognition from the United States and several European powers, and he was re-elected in 1868. Shortly after these achievements, diamonds were discovered along the Vaal River, but Pretorius mishandled the republic's claims on the territory, and he resigned in 1871 over the matter. At first he retired from public life, but after the British annexed the Transvaal in 1877, Pretorius became the leader of the passive resistance. The Afrikaners rebelled in 1881, and Pretorius was chosen as a member of the ruling triumvirate and helped negotiate the Pretoria Convention by which independence was restored. It was Pretorius's last public activity.

References: DAHB, EB, *wiki*.

QUAISON-SACKEY, Alexander
(Ghana, 1924–1992)

Alexander Quaison-Sackey was born into a prominent family in Gold Coast (now part of Ghana) and became politically active while a student at Achimota College. After graduating from Oxford and receiving his MA from the London School of Economics, he studied law and was admitted to the bar in London. When Ghana became independent in 1957, Quaison-Sackey began a lifelong career in diplomacy. He was first posted to London as high commissioner (ambassador) from 1957 to 1959. Then, until 1965 he was ambassador to the United Nations (U.N.) and simultaneously accredited to Cuba and Mexico. In the U.N. he served in 1961 on the conciliation group to the Democratic Republic of the Congo and as chair of the peacekeeping committee. The high point of his career was his election as the first African president of the U.N. General Assembly for the 1964–1965 session.

Quaison-Sackey was a close associate of Kwame NKRUMAH, who appointed him minister of foreign affairs in 1965. A year later, he was with Nkrumah on a peace mission to Vietnam when the Ghanaian government was toppled by a coup. After a few months of house arrest, Quaison-Sackey quietly resumed his law practice in Ghana until a new government appointed him ambassador to the United States and Mexico, a position that he held from 1978 to 1980. He then returned to Ghana and private practice, which he pursued until his death.

Reference: wiki. Quaison-Sackey, *Africa Unbound* (1963).

QUAQUE, Philip
(Ghana, 1741–1816)

Philip Quaque, a pioneering educator in Gold Coast (now part of Ghana), was not only the first African to be ordained an Anglican priest, but was also the first African missionary. Quaque, son of a chief, was taken under the wing of the Reverend Thomas Thompson, the first missionary of the Society for the Propagation of the Gospel (SPG). Quaque was one of three Fante youths sent to England to be educated and was the only one who survived. In 1765 he returned home accompanied by a British wife. For the next 50 years he served as chaplain for Cape Coast Castle, the headquarters of the British business community in the Gold Coast.

Quaque attempted to use his position to evangelize his compatriots, but he had little success. He was thoroughly assimilated and had lost his ability to speak Fante after his sojourn in England, so he had to use an interpreter. On the one hand, he was isolated from his family and people; on the other, he was rejected by the British. Hence, his ministry proved largely ineffective. The SPG gave him little support and often failed to pay his meager salary. As a result, Quaque had accumulated considerable debt by the time he died in 1816.

Over time, Quaque turned toward education, opening a school for Anglo-African children, primarily to train clerks for the colonial administration. In fact, most of the school's students, including members of the BREW family, went into local businesses and later formed the core of African leadership in Ghana. After his British wife's early death, he married an African woman, but he only began to rebuild his contacts with African society in his later years.

References: DAB, *dacb,* DAHB.

RABÉARIVELO, Jean-Joseph
(Madagascar, 1901?–1937)

Jean-Joseph Rabéarivelo was the leading poet in Madagascar and the founder of modern Malagache literature. His life was short, simple and tragic.

Born the only child of a high-caste mother, he lived in poverty. He attended mission schools that were free for promising young men who planned to enter the seminary, but when he refused to be a seminarian, he was expelled at age 13, thus ending his formal education. Determined to perfect his ability to speak French, Rabéarivelo plunged into reading the French writers Baudelaire and Mallarmé. By his early twenties he was writing in French, Spanish and Hova, his mother tongue.

Rabéarivelo was unable to find financial support even after his work had been published, so in 1924 he took a proofreading job, which he considered demeaning. Moreover, he suffered from the colonial authorities' refusal to recognize or support his writing. Depressed and ill, Rabéarivelo increasingly took refuge in drugs, alcohol and gambling. His last years were marked by a downward spiral of self-destruction. He felt inadequate in his attempts to provide for his wife and five children, and the death of his baby daughter in 1933 was a crushing blow. Rabéarivelo seems to have believed in assimilation as a Frenchman, and he was deeply disappointed when the colonial authorities refused to allow him to emigrate to Paris to live and write. In 1937 he committed suicide.

Rabéarivelo's early poetry was derivative, much of it influenced by French models. Gradually, he allowed it to be inspired by the traditional Malagache verse style known as *hainteny,* a ballad form in free verse that gave his poetry a songlike character. Rabéarivelo used Malagache verse rhythms to shape his choice of French expressions, and some poems contain rhythmic plays on words. Exceptionally imaginative and surrealistic, the poetry reflects the nature of the Madagascan countryside. Rabéarivelo published hundreds of individual poems. Between 1924 and 1936 he published eight books of verse, many brought out by the publisher he worked for. His impact on later Malagache poets remains notable, and a Friends of Rabéarivelo group has been editing his collected works.

References: AA, *wiki*. Robert Boudry, *Jean-Joseph Rabéarivelo et la Mort* (*Jean-Joseph Rabéarivelo and His Death*, 1958).

RADEBE, Lucas
(South Africa, 1969–)

Lucas Radebe went from the depths of apartheid South Africa, where his opportunities in soccer were denied because of his race, to become one of the star players in the English Premier League. He was South Africa's first soccer superstar.

Radebe's youth was spent in the Soweto townships during the era of rising crime and violence. Radebe, one of 11 children, joined the antiapartheid student movement and took part in "direct action," a euphemism for organized vandalism against government property. He was also a member of a "disciplinary committee," another euphemism for gangs that dispensed rough justice on lawbreakers with warnings, beatings and worse. His parents hoped to keep him from trouble by sending him off to Bophuthatswana, a client Black homeland created by the South African government, nominally independent though actually a Black reservation. Here Radebe, bored and casting around for some activity, began playing soccer.

Radebe's natural talent blossomed, bringing him both praise and envy. In one incident, opponents wounded him in a drive-by shooting, and he spent some time recovering. When he returned to soccer, Radebe found himself in demand because South Africa, suspended from international football in 1964, had just been readmitted to play after the end of apartheid. He played in South Africa's first games in 1992. He was the best player with the Kaizer Chiefs from 1989 to 1994, when the opportunity came to go to Great Britain.

Leeds United of the English Premier League paid £250,000 ($590,000 in current US dollars) for Radebe's contract. It was a rocky start; he was sidelined with an injury and played too few games to maintain his residency permit. He slowly returned to form and in 1996 he was seconded to his country team, Bafana Bafana, to play for South Africa in the African Nations Cup. The South African team was the most racially integrated in South African history, and the final victory was sweet revenge for years of exclusion.

Returning to Leeds, Radebe found a new coach who inspired him, and after 1996, he became one of their finest players and perhaps one of the best defensive players in soccer. Leeds began a climb up the ranks in the English Premier League. In 1998 Radebe was made Leeds captain, the first African in English Premier history. He stayed with Leeds throughout his career in England.

Radebe became captain of Bafana Bafana, and in 1998 he took the team to the finals in the World Cup, losing only to the final winner. In all, Radebe played in 70 games for Bafana Bafana. In 2002, controversy broke out over the division of his time and energies between his club (Leeds) and his country team (Bafana Bafana). At 33, it was getting increasingly difficult for him to maintain both, especially after he spent the 2001–2002 season sidelined with a knee injury. He left Bafana Bafana and international play in 2002, and retired from Leeds in 2005. He is working with Leeds United as a coach.

Radebe has always been a credit to sport. The international football federation (FIFA) gave him its Fair Play Award in 2000 for his work to eliminate racism in sport, and he has long been an active supporter of SOS Children's Villages.

References: adb, wiki.

RAMAEMA, Elias Phisoana

(Lesotho, 1933–)

Colonel Elias Phisoana Ramaema, a professional police officer, took power in Lesotho in 1991 after a military coup but later transferred authority to civilian government.

He was educated locally, taking a degree in 1956 at Roma College (now the University of Lesotho). As with many Lesotho men, limited employment opportunities forced him to spend two years in the South African mines. In 1959, Ramaema returned home to join the Lesotho police. He received police training overseas in 1978 and 1984 and transferred to the mobile police unit, which later became the Paramilitary Force (PMF), finally becoming a colonel in 1986. After the military coup that removed Chief Leabua JONATHAN in 1986, Ramaema became a member of the military council that governed the country and soon was deputy to General Metsing LEKHANYA, its leader and de facto head of state. He headed five ministries: planning, economic affairs, information, public service, and social welfare. In 1991, dissent over low pay in the civil service and the army began to come to the surface. In a bloodless coup, Lekhanya was removed and Ramaema replaced him.

Ramaema's chairmanship of the military council represented no changes in policy, and many regarded the coup as merely cosmetic. He faced the same economic problems as his predecessor, which were compounded by a 10 percent drop in the number of Sotho employed in South African mines. Absorbing the unemployed and adjusting to the drop in their repatriated income remain major challenges. The ban on political parties was repealed and a new constitution drafted with the approval of King Letsie III. The previous king, MOSHWESHWE II, in exile after being deposed in 1990, was allowed to return in a face-saving move, making him head of the royal family but not ruling monarch. When the 1993 elections were held, the Basotho Congress Party (BCP) won all parliamentary seats and Ramaema retired from politics.

Ramaema's retirement was interrupted by a bizarre incident, when an Irish aid worker was abducted, robbed and murdered in 1999. His vehicle and its keys were found at Ramaema's home, along with other incriminating evidence. Ramaema was imprisoned along with other members of his family.

Reference: RWWA.

RAMANANTSOA, Gabriel

(Madagascar, 1906–1979)

General Gabriel Ramanantsoa was a reforming military head of state for three years.

Born into a wealthy family, Ramanantsoa was educated in Marseilles, France. He was the first Malagache to study at the French military academy at Saint-Cyr, from which he graduated in 1931 with a commission in the French colonial army. In the 1930s he served in North Africa, but when Germany invaded France in 1939 he went to the front, where he was promoted to captain for bravery in the field. After the French surrender, he returned to Madagascar. In 1940 he established a school of physical education, where he stayed until 1946, when he was posted to the Paris headquarters of the colonial army in the Ministry of Defense. He returned to the Ministry of Defense from 1950 to 1953 and again from 1955 to 1959. In between these assignments he was responsible for military veterans in Madagascar and was a field commander in Indochina during France's ill-fated attempt to hold on to Vietnam.

Ramanantsoa was involved in independence negotiations in 1960, being appointed the first commander-in-chief of Madagascar's new armed forces that year. During the 1960s he organized the military into a unified land-sea-air command, and his long loyalty to France made him a congenial colleague of President Philibert TSIRANANA, who was pro-French. Tsiranana's ties to South Africa, however, made him increasingly unpopular. A general strike and workers' riot shook the country, and matters reached a crisis in 1972 when the police killed 400 at a protest demonstration. Tsiranana resigned and turned the government over to Ramanantsoa.

After releasing all political prisoners, Ramanantsoa undertook a series of reforms that were generally popular: he lowered taxes, reduced the civil service and introduced a merit system, and replaced French government employees with Malagache citizens. His foreign policy, designed by Admiral Didier RATSIRAKA, focused on Africa and turned away from the West. In 1972, Madagascar broke diplomatic relations with South Africa and became a contributor to the Organization of African Unity (OAU)'s liberation fund. Madagascar also distanced itself from France, closing French military bases on the island and withdrawing from the franc zone in order to create an independent Malagache currency.

Despite these successes, Ramanantsoa was never comfortable in a political role, nor could he work with the opposition. When there was an attempted coup, he dissolved his government in 1975 and handed it over to the military. There was a short period of violent confusion before Admiral Ratsiraka succeeded him. Ramanantsoa died in Paris four years later.

References: MMA, PLBA.

RAMAPHOSA, Matamela Cyril
(South Africa, 1952–)

Matamela Cyril Ramaphosa, secretary-general of the African National Congress (ANC) since 1991 and chair of the committee writing the new South African constitution, came to prominence in South African politics through the trade union movement.

After secondary school, Ramaphosa entered the University of the North, where he became active in the Student Christian Movement (SCM), a religious group with a long tradition of social action. He met and was influenced by Steve BIKO and his Black Consciousness Movement (BCM). He was arrested in 1974 and imprisoned for 11 months for being involved in a student demonstration. On his release he began a round of activities with various organizations, punctuated by periods in prison. He completed his university studies by correspondence and began studying law. Disgusted at the mercenary attitude of many lawyers, he became legal counsel to the Council of Unions of South Africa (CUSA) instead of going into private practice. When in 1982, CUSA decided to form a mineworkers' union, Ramaphosa became its first secretary-general. Within four years under his leadership, the National Union of Mineworkers (NUM) went from 6,000 to 340,000 members and became the first Black union to be recognized by the South African government. In 1985 and 1986 he led the NUM in the first legal strikes by a Black union in South African history.

Ramaphosa gave the keynote address at the 1985 formation of the Congress of South African Trade Unions (COSATU), a national federation of labor groups, and a year later he led a COSATU delegation that met with the ANC leadership in exile in Lusaka, Zambia. He was forced into hiding after that meeting, eventually going to Great Britain for several months. In 1987 the NUM mounted a massive strike that involved 40 mines and more than 300,000 workers. It failed to win salary increases but showed the NUM's ability to sustain a long, difficult strike. Future differences were negotiated with mining management and resulted in improved conditions.

COSATU took an active part in the antiapartheid movement and was a key player in the United Democratic Front, which brought together the antiapartheid movement during the period of greatest government repression. Ramaphosa's growing affiliation with the ANC and its leader, Nelson MANDELA, paralleled his withdrawal from the Black consciousness movement and racial exclusivism and represented his acceptance of a future multiracial society in South Africa. In 1987 he led the NUM to endorse the multiracial principles of the ANC's Freedom Charter.

With the end of apartheid, Ramaphosa was regarded as a contender for a major post in the new government, but he rejected any other appointment but deputy presidency. Lacking extensive ANC credentials, and seen as too abrasive and radical, he was defeated by his longtime rival and ANC insider, Thabo MBEKI. Mandela instead made Ramaphosa chair of the commission drafting the new South African constitution, and he was also elected to the new parliament.

In 1997, Ramaphosa made a bid to succeed Mandela as president, and when that went to Mbeki, he turned to business and left politics. His contacts made him invaluable to corporations trying to integrate their boards, and he took directorships with eight companies. He is also executive chair of Millennium Consolidated Holdings, and on the advisory councils of Coca-Cola and Unilever. Internationally, he was appointed an inspector for the disarmament of the Irish Republican Army (IRA) in Northern Ireland and to several other commissions.

References: CB, EWB, GSAP, PLBA, *wiki.*

RAMGOOLAM, Seewoosagur

(Mauritius, 1900–1985)

Sir Seewoosagur Ramgoolam was the father of his country and its central political figure for 40 years. He was also the first African leader to be voted out of office in a free election.

Born into a Hindu family, Ramgoolam was the first East Indian from Mauritius to receive higher education in England, where he qualified as a physician and cardiologist. For 12 years he remained in Great Britain, where he met Mahatma GANDHI and was inspired by his vision of the rights of Indians. When he returned home, he became active in Indian affairs but did not enter politics until 1940, when he was elected to the city council of Port Louis, the capital, after which he became deputy mayor and then mayor. Although Indians were the majority ethnic group, they had been virtually excluded from public affairs. Ramgoolam was appointed to the Legislative Council (Legco) as the Indian representative. When the Legco became elective in 1948, Ramgoolam won a seat in a district that he continued to represent, both under colonialism and after independence, for 34 years.

Ramgoolam joined the dominant Mauritius Labour Party (MLP) in 1953 and began a campaign to end British colonial rule. With independence in 1968 he became prime minister. He undertook the delicate task of bringing together the diverse ethnic and racial groups in Mauritian society, reassuring the non-Indian minorities and avoiding a mass exodus from the country. Ramgoolam became a binding force among the different groups and was fondly known to all as *"chacha"* (uncle). Although he was committed to democratic government, he had to deal with tensions between Muslims and Creoles, which broke into open conflict. A state of emergency was declared from 1972 to 1978, but Ramgoolam never used it to suppress opposition or limit civil rights. He was awarded the United Nations Prize for the defense of human rights in 1973.

In foreign policy, Ramgoolam remained close to the West, which was concerned about Mauritius's strategic position in the Indian Ocean. He served as president of the Organization of African Unity (OAU) from 1976 to 1977 and was active in the Commonwealth. His only conflict with the West was over the status of Diego Garcia, a nearby island in the Chagos Archipelago, which was transferred from Mauritian authority in 1965 and then leased to the United States for 50 years. Diego Garcia became the site of the chief American air and naval bases in the Indian Ocean. Diego Garcia's status was protested by Ramgoolam, but he was only able to obtain £4 million of compensation for the resettlement of families, all of whom were expelled from the island. This is valued at approximately $94 million in 2005.

Ramgoolam instituted an extensive program of free education, social benefits and pensions, and free health care. This social policy proved difficult for the Mauritian economy to sustain, and when sugar prices dropped, the currency had to be devalued. In 1982 elections, a left-wing alliance swept Ramgoolam from power, but a grateful British government appointed him to the ceremonial post of governor-general, which he held until his death.

References: afr, AO, MMA, PLBA. Ramgoolam, *Our Struggle: 20th Century Mauritius* (1982).

RAMPHELE, Mamphela Aletta
(South Africa, 1947–)

Dr. Mamphela Ramphele has had a distinguished career as a physician, academic and international businesswoman.

Dr. Ramphele took an M.D. at the University of Natal in 1972, where she also became a founding member of the Black Consciousness Movement (BCM) with Steve BIKO. She remained a member of the BCM inner circle until it was banned by the government. She and Biko also became lovers and she bore two children with him. One died in infancy, and the other was born just as Biko was murdered; she named the baby Hlumelo, "shoot of the dead tree."

Her medical work was an extension of her activism, but that was always joined to a feminist agenda. She has said that "it was not the desire to serve which influenced my career choice, but the passion for freedom to be my own mistress in a society where being Black and woman defined the boundaries within which one could legitimately

Mamphela Aletta Ramphele

operate." She began village development programs with the BCM, which resulted in government banishment to internal exile from 1977 to 1984.

She went on to further studies and took a Ph.D. in social anthropology from the University of Cape Town, a degree in business, and diplomas in public health and tropical medicine. She went to the University of Cape Town in 1986 as a research fellow, and after the fall of apartheid, she was promoted to deputy chancellor (vice president) in 1991. She was named vice chancellor (effectively the president, since the head of state automatically holds the honorary title of chancellor). She also joined the corporate board of Anglo-American Mining.

Four years later, Ramphele became one of the four managing directors of the World Bank, in charge of human development, health, nutrition and population issues. She has received many awards, including 18 honorary doctorates.

An unabashed radical and feminist, Ramphele does not shrink from criticizing Black leaders and activists who think that liberation was completed when they came to power.

References: adb, CB, *wiki*. Ramphele, *Across Boundaries* (1995); Judith Harlan, *Mamphela Ramphele: Challenging Apartheid in South Africa* (1999).

RAMSAMY, Prega
(Mauritius, 1950–)

Dr. Prega Ramsamy, a development economist, is executive secretary of the Southern African Development Community (SADC). He has held that position since 2001.

Dr. Ramsamy is of East Asian (Indian) ethnicity, an important part of the population of the Indian Ocean republic of Mauritius. Like many Indian ethnics, he studied at the University of Delhi, but he then went on to take a post-graduate diploma in population and development from the United Nations Centre for Population Studies in 1977. From 1975 to 1982 he worked for the Mauritian government in the Ministry of Economic Planning and Development.

In 1982 he also received a certificate from the International Development Centre of Japan, and then went to the United States to complete his graduate studies for an MA (1985) and Ph.D. in development studies (1986).

Throughout 1983 to 1997, Ramsamy worked as an economist with the Common Market for Eastern and Southern Africa (COMESA), where he had a series of increasing responsibilties: senior trade expert, chief of technical cooperation, and finally director of development finance in 1997. That year he joined the SADC Secretariat as chief economist. Within a year he was named deputy chief secretary.

The SADC is a regional coordinating organization that works toward the development and integration of the economies of the southern African states, with a view to the eventual establishment of a regional development community. Its current emphasis since 2005 has been on food supplies and the plight of the Indian Ocean states in the face of global warming. The small Indian Ocean states—Mauritius, the Seychelles, the Comoros and Réunion—are particularly vulnerable to rising ocean levels caused by the melt of the polar ice caps.

RANAVALONA I
(Madagascar, 1788–1861)

Queen Ranavalona I was the wife of Radama I, who first united Madagascar into a single kingdom. Radama ended the slave trade to please the British and introduced Anglican missionaries, who included craftsmen. On Radama's death in 1828, Ranavalona took the throne, beginning a remarkable succession of women rulers.

Ranavalona promptly had all rivals put to death and reversed Radama's pro-European policies. She was described by a leading Malagasy historian as a monarch "absolute in authority, firm in decisions, rigorous in principles." Her reputation for cruelty has perhaps been exaggerated, but without doubt she was ruthless in pursuit of her aims. In eliminating rivals, she assassinated most of her extended family.

Key to her policy was modernization without Western domination. Although she sought self-reliance, she also promoted trade. She expelled missionary tradesmen and worked to restore ancestral religion. Ranavalona came into conflict with the Anglicans and in 1835 attempted to execute adherents to Christianity. Perhaps 200 were slain, providing Christianity with martyrs. Many others fled into the mountainous forests. Protestants were largely wiped out, but a remnant of Catholics survived, led by Victoria, one of the royal princesses.

Stylized portrait of Queen Ranavalona I of Madagascar.

It was from the vicious torture deaths of Christians that her reputation as a sadistic monster came. Anyone found with a Bible was killed, and the deaths were particularly barbarous: dressed in the bloody skins of animals with hunting dogs turned on them; starved to death in the jungles; boiled alive in great pits. She ended up detested and feared by her own people.

The British and French, with island bases in the Indian Ocean, attempted to resist Ranavalona's policies and finally sent a joint expeditionary force to Madagascar. Ranavalona defeated them at Tamatave in 1845 and closed the port to trade. Trade—and, gradually, friendly relations with Britain—resumed only after 1853, but Madagascar lived in a closed economy, importing only firearms, alcohol and Western clothing.

In 1857, Ranavalona's son Rakoto attempted a coup, causing her to become increasingly paranoid and oppressive. Restless, energetic and domineering, she remained an absolute monarch and was battling a French invasion when she died.

References: AB, *afr*, MMA, WWR, *wiki*.

RANAVALONA III
(Madagascar, 1861–1917)

Queen Ranavalona III was the last monarch of Madagascar, with much of her reign spent as a mere titular ruler. She succeeded her cousin Ranavalona II, who made Christianity the official religion and reopened Madagascar to Western influence. In 1883 she ascended the throne and married the prime minister, Rainilaiarivony, who had been the consort of both preceding queens and the dominant figure in Malagasy politics since 1864.

Despite the apparent dominance of her husband and prime minister, Ranavalona and Rainilaiarivony shared both power and common convictions. A long and exhausting war against French forces ended in 1885, with Rainilaiarivony negotiating a peace treaty giving France control over foreign policy and permission to maintain a small group of soldiers in the country. The queen and her consort hoped to preserve as much Malagache independence as possible in the face of encroaching colonial power. She played off European powers against each other. Great Britain, however, recognized French hegemony in exchange for French recognition of British claims in Zanzibar. France again invaded Madagascar in 1895, and Ranavalona was forced to agree to a protectorate that left her as titular queen. Her husband was deported to Algiers. Ranavalona met a similar fate the following year after a Malagache insurrection, and she spent most of the rest of her life in Algiers.

References: MMA, WWR, *wiki.*

RANSOME-KUTI, Funmilayo
(Nigeria, 1900–1978)

Chief Funmilayo Ransome-Kuti, one of the first modern feminists in Africa, was an international figure as a fighter for women's rights and as a political personality.

Her husband, an Anglican priest and educator, founded the Nigerian Union of Teachers, the first multiethnic and nationalist association in the country. Initially, Ransome-Kuti engaged in traditional women's civic activities, establishing in 1942 the Abeokuta Ladies' Club (ALC) for educated women involved in charitable work. Under the colonial system of indirect rule, which removed the checks and limits of chiefs and priests, authority was concentrated through the Sole Native Authority (SNA) system. Women were effectively stripped of traditional authority. A literacy project brought her into close contact with the market women, uneducated but shrewd and intelligent traders who controlled food distribution. Ransome-Kuti's women's groups protested poll taxes, exorbitant water rates, abuses of dowry, food price controls and oppression of market women.

When it became clear how exploited they were by the *alake,* the traditional ruler who governed in the name of the British, she combined the ALC and her working women's group into the Nigerian Women's Union (NWU). They challenged the authority of the *alake,* who was profiteering from his control of provisions for soldiers in World War II. He also extorted excessive taxes without providing public services. The NWU progressively confronted the *alake* by petition, legal processes, and audits of his records. When all else failed, 10,000 women camped around his palace, singing derisive anticolonial songs with words such as "White man, you will not get to your country safely." The tax on women was abolished, the *alake* was forced to abdicate in 1949, and Ransome-Kuti became a national figure. Four women were appointed to the Egba Central Council, which replaced the disgraced SNA. It was a limited success but a stunning victory over colonial domination.

This activity naturally moved Ransome-Kuti into a wider political arena, and in 1947 she was a member of a delegation to London on Nigerian independence led by Dr. Nnamdi AZIKIWE. Critical of Azikiwe's imperious style, she broke with him and used her time to form international networks with women's associations. Her closest contacts were with the Fabian Colonial Bureau and the Women's International Democratic Federation (WIDF), a socialist group with definite Marxist leanings. In 1956 the WIDF funded a trip to China for her, and she returned full of praise for socialist progress there. The following year, alleging Communist influence in the NWU, she was refused a passport renewal. After independence in 1960, when she could travel on a Nigerian passport, Ransome-Kuti visited many of the Eastern bloc countries, including the Soviet Union. She was never a Communist and never allowed the NWU to affiliate with the WIDF, but she did have marked socialist leanings. The Eastern bloc was the only place she saw evidence of commitment to women's social and political equality.

Ransome-Kuti always exhibited her ideals of gender equality. Her boys, who included the famous entertainer and political gadfly, Fela KUTI, learned to cook. Her daughter, a hospital head nurse, received the same educational opportunities as her sons. A friend called her marriage "an egalitarian relationship out of its time."

Ransome-Kuti crossed Nigeria organizing women without regard to class or ethnic lines. NWU chapters operated mother-and-child clinics, built cooperatives and ran literacy programs. She also assisted women's groups across Africa, and in 1960 presided over the inauguration of the Ghana women's movement at the invitation of President Kwame NKRUMAH. Her activism often went beyond her party loyalties. Eventually, the increasing conflict with Azikiwe ended with her expulsion from his party in 1959. Her work for women and the poor won her honors and awards, however, including the Lenin Peace Prize in 1970.

In 1977 she was staying with her son Fela when government troops raided the compound to punish him for his criticism of the military junta. The house was burned, several of Fela's wives were raped and brutalized, and Ransome-Kuti was thrown from a second-story window. She died of injuries and shock a year later. She faced death as defiantly as she had lived. To protest her death, the motorcade that brought her body to Abeokuta for burial left the casket at the gate of Dodan Barracks, the residence of General Olusegun OBASANJO. Fela named his next album *Coffin for the Head of State*.

References: AB, MMA. Cheryl Johnson-Odim, *On Behalf of Women and the Nation* (1995).

RAPONDA-WALKER, André
(Gabon, 1871–1969)

Monsignor André Raponda-Walker, the first Gabonese priest and a prominent clergyman, is the country's most noted scholar.

Raponda-Walker was the child of a Gabonese woman from a royal family, and a British business agent who was also an explorer of inner Gabon. Around 1867 he set up the first factory in Gabon. Raponda-Walker was educated in Gabon and in 1899 became the first African priest in the country. Seven months after a mission was established at Notre-Dame de Trois-Épines, Raponda-Walker became the first African pastor in the country after traveling there for three days by pirogue. Over a 50-year period, he was posted throughout the country as a pastor and teacher, and in every place, he gathered data about the local area. From 1905 to 1933 he worked in Sindara and studied the Pygmies, the first anthropologist to do so. In time, he emerged as the leading scholar of the peoples, cultures, languages and especially the botany of Gabon. In 1959 he published the first of several volumes of his studies, *Plantes Utiles des Gabon* (*Useful Plants of Gabon*), a major contribution to botany and the only source for the medicinal use of many plants used by Africans in the interior of the country.

His cultural studies followed: *Notes d'Histoire du Gabon* (*Notes on the History of Gabon*, 1960) and *Rites et Croyances des Peuples du Gabon* (*Rites and Beliefs of the Peoples of Gabon*, 1962). The latter is one of the few sources for the religious practices and beliefs of traditional peoples before the impact of modern society and Christianity. His autobiography is also an important reference for Gabonese history, since his life spanned much of the modern period. Raponda-Walker is respected as the "premier writer and expert" of Gabon, in the words of the director-general of the National Archives. In 1981, he was honored with a postage stamp bearing his picture. A number of volumes of his extensive unpublished work have been brought into print since his death by the Raponda-Walker Foundation, including collections of proverbs, grammars and dictionaries, an etymology of Gabonese names, and further botanical studies.

After the attempted coup against the government of President Léon MBA in 1964, the regime became increasingly intolerant and repressive. Raponda-Walker wrote an essay in a Paris newspaper criticizing the use of violence by Mba's supporters, and the rising tide of tribalism which Mba fostered. On orders from the president, a gang broke into Raponda-Walker's apartment, destroyed his valuable library and expelled him from the church residence. The 93-year-old was beaten unconscious.

Because the title "Monsignor" is often used in French for bishops, some sources incorrectly say that he was a bishop in the Church. As a churchman, he was keen to apply his cultural studies to Christian liturgy and worship, and he regretted deeply that

Gabon had the lowest percentage of Africans in the priesthood on the continent.

Reference: MMA. Raponda-Walker, *Souvenirs d'un Nonagénaire* (*Recollections of a 90-Year-Old*, 1993).

RATSIMAMANGA, Albert Rakoto

(Madagascar, 1907–2001)

Dr. Albert Rakoto Ratsimamanga, a distinguished biochemist and physiologist, played a role in Madagascar's transition to independence and served in his country's diplomatic service for 13 years, holding one of the most important ambassadorial posts.

Ratsimamanga, who was a member of the Malagache royal family, was the grandson of the last premier of Queen RANAVALONA III, who was executed by General Joseph GALLIENI. Refused education in colonial schools because he was Malagache, Ratsimamanga went to Anglican mission schools, then received his medical degree from the University of Paris. He stayed in Paris, rising to become research director of the Centre National de la Recherche Scientifique and director of the École Pratique des Hautes Études. Ratsimamanga's interests lay in pharmacology, and among other work, he discovered a potential liver antitoxic factor and a new antidiabetic drug. He was a consultant to the Food and Agricultural Organization (FAO) and served as vice chair and member of the executive council of the United Nations Educational, Scientific, and Cultural Organization (UNESCO).

Because of his education and wide contacts in Paris, he took part in the independence negotiations between France and Madagascar in 1960. In that same year, the new government named him ambassador to France, where he remained until 1973. This period coincided with the regime of President Philibert TSIRANANA, whose strongly pro-French views Ratsimamanga shared. While holding the Paris post, he was also ambassador to West Germany (1961–1968), Sierra Leone (1963–1973), and (for brief periods) the Soviet Union and China. After the collapse of the Tsiranana government in 1972, Ratsimamanga retired from public life.

After leaving his diplomatic career, he founded the National Center for Applied Research in Mada-

gascar, where he did extensive research on medicinal plants used in traditional medicine. He was the major researcher on a native weed, *Centella asiatica,* which he refined into a wound-healing drug known as Madecassol.

Ratsimamanga also worked with a native plum, *Eugenia jamolana*, for over 20 years. He experimented with its seeds until he extracted a substance that returned the glycemic levels of type 2 diabetics to normal in 75 percent of cases. The discovery came from his profound respect for traditional healers and willingness to do field work among them. He observed that they diagnosed diabetics by having them urinate on an ant hill. Ants flee from human urine, but that of diabetics is high in sugar, and they did not reject it. Thus secure in their diagnosis, they used the special plum as a curative.

References: PAS. Raymond Rabemananjara, *Prince Albert Rakoto Ratsimamanga* (2 volumes, 2003).

RATSIRAKA, Admiral Didier

(Madagascar, 1936–)

Admiral Didier Ratsiraka, military strongman in Madagascar for almost 20 years, was defeated in free elections in 1993 but remains a power within the country.

Ratsiraka completed his secondary education at the elite Lycée Henri IV in Paris and then joined the French navy. After completing studies at the French naval academy, he served as a signals officer on corvettes. In 1963 Ratsiraka transferred to the Malagache navy, and he was promoted to captain after attending the advanced naval officer's institute in Paris, earning diplomas in engineering and mathematics. From 1972 to 1975 he was military attaché at the Malagache embassy in Paris.

When General Gabriel RAMANANTSOA took over the government in 1972 from Philibert TSI-RANANA, Ratsiraka was brought in as foreign minister. He rejected Tsiranana's policy of dialog with South Africa and cut diplomatic ties with that state. He also broke relations with Taiwan and established them with China and North Korea. His fiery radicalism did not gain the approval of many in the military cabinet, but Ramanantsoa only asked him to temper his rhetoric. Ratsiraka's major foreign policy achievement was in relations with France, where he renegotiated all military agreements and forced France to withdraw its troops from Madagascar and close its bases and its Indian Ocean headquarters.

After Ramanantsoa's resignation there was a period of confusion until the military council chose Ratsiraka as head of state in 1975. His foreign policies as president, generally anti-Western, followed previous ones. In domestic policy, a new area for Ratsiraka, he took a socialist path, nationalizing the oil industry and mineral resources, banking and insurance, and the major shipping company. As a result, the economy collapsed and he was forced to reverse many of his initial programs in order to maintain credit privileges with the International Monetary Fund.

Ratsiraka harassed the opposition but never suppressed it, and he was popularly elected to the presidency in 1982 and re-elected in 1989. Opposition parties always kept some seats in parliament, but economic conditions also brought unorganized opposition in the form of urban unrest. There were several coup attempts, each followed by widespread disturbances. By 1991 there were irresistible demands for reform, and when Ratsiraka refused, he was forced to use the army to maintain order. A state of emergency was declared, and when demonstrators defied it, hundreds were killed in clashes with the military. After an opposition rally of over 300,000, Ratsiraka formed a unity government and established a national forum to draft a new constitution. In 1992–1993, he stood for president and was defeated in two rounds of balloting. He remained a powerful figure, however, and was re-elected in 1997 after his successor was impeached.

By 2001, Ratsiraka had lost most public support. A close election with Marc RAVALOMANANA, the popular mayor of the capital, was to have led to a run-off, but both sides claimed they had won. Ratsiraka controlled much of the upcountry, while Ravalomanana commanded the capital. With much foreign pressure, Ratsiraka's base eroded and he went into exile.

References: DRWW, PLBA, RWWA, *wiki.* Ferdinand Deleris, *Ratsiraka, Socialisme et Misère à Madagascar* (*Ratsiraka, Socialism and Misery,* 1986).

RAVALOMANANA, Marc
(Madagascar, 1949–)

Marc Ravalomanana has been president of Madagascar since 2002, after a bruising election and armed conflict between himself and his predecessor, Admiral Didier RATSIRAKA. He is a member of the dominant Merino ethnic group.

Ravalomanana became mayor of Antananarivo, the capital, in 1999. He threw himself immediately into urban renewal, building parks, theaters, schools and health centers. Much of the money came from the European Community and the French national development fund. His policies and achievements made him a national figure.

Ravalomanana built a new party around himself under the name Tiako Madagasikara ("I love Madagascar"). He contested the 2001 elections, coming out ahead of his rival, the military strongman Ratsiraka, 44.4 percent to 40.6 percent. Both claimed victory, but a projected run-off was never held. Instead, Ratsiraka attempted to occupy the country with his military forces. He controlled much of the rural area while Ravalomanana held on to the capital. They established rival governments. Gradually, Ratsiraka's support waned and he finally fled the country after the national constitutional court declared Ravalomanana the winner. He quickly moved to legitimize his government, receiving international recognition and re-entering the Organization of African Unity (OAU), which had suspended Madagascar under Ratsiraka.

Announcing a "struggle against poverty," Ravalomanana focused his first term in office on rural development. He proclaimed a universal right to health care and promised a progressive attack on plague, malaria and cholera—the triple scourge of the country. Madagascar has one of the world's lowest rates of HIV/AIDS, but Ravalomanana has designed programs to prevent its spread. In 2005 Madagascar was the first country to receive a grant under the United States Millennium Challenge Fund ($110 million). It is being used for rural credit and reform of the feudal land system. In the southeast of the country, its poorest region, Ravalomanana secured a $500 million investment from the mining conglomerate Rio Rinto in 2005.

Ravalomanana has also begun an aggressive environmental protection program. Madagascar, as a large but isolated island, has a large number of unique flora and fauna. In 2003, Ravalomanana

Marc Ravalomanana

commented: "It is important to stress the positive impact biodiversity conservation has on economic development." Protected areas are to be expanded by 28,000 square miles by 2008. The present area that has been withdrawn from development is the size of Cyprus.

Ravalomanana has long been a leader of the Protestant Churches in Madagascar, and he is known for his strong personal faith. He has been vice president of the national council of the Reformed Church (FJKM), and is a pillar of the national ecumenical Christian council. About 45 percent of Malagache are members of FJKM, and Ravalomanana has used his religious ties to bolster his political aims.

There have been criticisms that Ravalomanana, after promising to respect the media, has continued Ratsiraka's harassment. He owns several media outlets, including a newspaper and a television station. His business interests have made him independently wealthy. He is the principal of TIKO Corporation, with over 5,000 employees. It has diversified into a number of areas, including an airline, and it holds monopolies on oil and dairy products.

Reference: wiki. fr.wikipedia.org.

RAWLINGS, Jerry John
(Ghana, 1947–)

Flight Lieutenant Jerry John Rawlings was a charismatic populist reformer, initially popular but later turning to authoritarianism. Despite this criticism, Rawlings has been an exemplar for a new style of African leadership: a responsible radicalism that detests corruption and privilege and espouses reforming the economy for the benefit of the masses.

Born to a Scottish father and an Ewe mother (the Ewe are a people of southeastern Ghana), Rawlings attended Achimota College near Accra, the capital, and then entered the military academy in 1968, becoming a pilot officer in 1969 and being promoted to flight lieutenant in 1978.

The great promise of Ghana's early years of independence under Kwame NKRUMAH (1957–1966) ended with the economy weakened and civil liberties damaged. Succeeding military and civilian governments were marked by rapacious corruption, and Rawlings was appalled by the way in which senior officers enriched themselves and the economy was looted by Lebanese businessmen. In 1979 he led 13 junior officers in a coup to overthrow General Frederick AKUFFO. It failed, but at his trial, Rawlings so ably defended himself with his speeches on the corruption of the regime that he was applauded in court. A group of fellow officers freed Rawlings, and the second coup succeeded. He celebrated by flying his jet across the country, buzzing remote villages.

To the surprise of Ghanaians, Rawlings kept his promises to proceed with scheduled elections and to return the country to civilian rule. In the meantime, he undertook what he called "housekeeping," including the trial and execution of Generals Ignatius ACHEAMPONG, Akuffo, another former president, and several generals and ministers—all for "economic sabotage." Price controls were put in place, with public flogging for those caught exceeding them, and half the Lebanese business community left the country. The purge took 90 days and made Rawlings a national hero.

The new president, Hilla Limann, faced an impossible task, however. Inflation was at 80 percent, with industry running at 25 percent of capacity. Moreover, cocoa, the main export, was at a 20-year low in price. Rawlings hovered in the background, but his supporters were gradually sent to overseas posts, and finally Rawlings himself was forced into retirement from the military. He responded by becoming the de facto leader of the opposition, criticizing Limann at every turn and threatening to remove him.

In 1981, Rawlings made good on that last promise and took over the government. He suspended the constitution, dissolved parliament, and banned political parties. A number of opponents were executed, and the Lebanese were forbidden to trade in coffee, cocoa and peanuts. Rawlings had no clear economic program but was inspired by the Marxist revolution in Ethiopia and Colonel Muammar Gadhafi's program in Libya, which Rawlings called "a revolutionary dream." Rawlings experimented with various extremist Marxist ideas, such as closing the national university and sending its students and staff into the countryside to work on farms. "People's committees" ran neighborhoods and villages and "people's tribunals" handled local legal disputes. His attempts to transform the institutions of government and the military were never completely successful, however, and he turned to older, failed means—staffing important posts with loyal friends and members of his own Ewe ethnic group. Civil liberties were abused, culminating in the murder of four high court justices in 1982. By 1983 the radical phase of the Rawlings revolution was exhausted.

Rawlings abandoned his attempts to collectivize the economy, which had caused most of the skilled labor force and professionals to flee the country. Facing a serious drought that crippled food production, and forced to absorb a million Ghanaian workers expelled from Nigeria in 1983 and 1985, he instituted an austerity program to prevent total economic collapse. The national currency was devalued, subsidies were cut, and the government budget was slashed. This economic policy earned Ghana renewed credit with the International Monetary Fund but lost Rawlings support from his base among workers, urban youth and radicals. The economy, however, did improve somewhat, and Rawlings began to court the rural chiefs and urban commercial interests.

The 1987 assassination of Burkina Faso's Thomas SANKARA was a devastating personal blow to Rawlings, who had been a close friend and political ally. At one point, they had even considered merging the two countries' economies. Rawlings began political liberalization in 1988 in response to both local dissent and Ghana's increasing isolation. In 1991 he announced a return to multiparty elections in the face of rising dissent. Political exiles were allowed to return to Ghana, and a new constitution was prepared. Although many expected Rawlings to be rejected, his demoralized opponents collapsed, and he triumphed in the 1992 elections by a larger margin than even he had anticipated. The Commonwealth Observer Group certified the election as "free and fair" and "free from fear." He was re-elected in 1996 and stepped down at the end of his term in 2001.

Rawlings, despite his authoritarian tactics, continued to project an image of honesty and commitment to national reform, but he struggled to mobilize Ghana around a coherent solution to its social and economic problems. During his administration, food production increased dramatically, and in 1993 he received the World Hunger Prize. In foreign policy, his primary goal—somewhat successful—was to bring stability to the region and end conflicts in Sierra Leone, Côte d'Ivoire and Liberia.

References: AB, *afr,* CB, DAHB, PLBA, PLCA, RWWA, *wiki.* Kevin Shillington, *Ghana and the Rawlings Factor* (1992).

RENÉ, France-Albert
(Seychelles, 1935–)

France-Albert René, president of the Seychelles from 1977 to 2004, moved his Indian Ocean island country from one-party autocratic rule to a cautious restoration of democratic freedoms.

René trained for the priesthood before changing his mind and deciding to study law in London. At the London School of Economics (1962–1963) he imbibed a socialist approach to policy and became active in the British Labour Party. On his return to the Seychelles he founded the forerunner of the Seychelles People's Progressive Front (SPPF). He also formed the country's first trade union in 1964. The following year he was elected to the legislative assembly. René was a consistent voice against continued British colonialism, opposing his rival, James MANCHAM. The two contended throughout the closing years of colonial administration, but when Mancham won the 1974 elections (after switching to an independence position), he shared power with René.

With independence (1976), René became prime minister while Mancham took the presidency. Mancham's administration emphasized land deals, overseas investment under dubious conditions, and flashy but insubstantial politics. In 1977, after only a year, an armed group of SPPF activists overthrew Mancham's government while the president was out of the country at a Commonwealth conference. René denied involvement in the plot, but there is evidence that Tanzania backed the plot out of concern for growing South African involvement in the Seychelles. René suspended the constitution and dissolved the national assembly.

René took a moderate leftist position, nonaligned but not Marxist. He liked to call himself "an Indian Ocean socialist." He introduced a one-party system and ruled by decree, an autocratic approach reinforced by five failed coup attempts in which Mancham was involved. In two of these, foreign mercenaries were landed but arrested. In one instance, a submachine gun fell out of a piece of luggage when mercenaries arrived at the national airport. Racing through airport security to take hostages, they highjacked an Air India jet and flew to South Africa, where they got off lightly. South Africa paid the Seychelles $3 million ransom for the terrorists who had been captured.

Mounting discontent with the lack of political pluralism showed itself in large-scale abstention in the 1991 presidential election, and René moved to permit a multiparty system. In the 1992 elections he was returned handily, but Mancham still received 34 percent of the vote. The two old rivals reached a power-sharing agreement under which Mancham was consulted on major policies and free elections were assured. What emerged was a de facto two-party system. The independent power of the SPPF has also been curbed.

René's tenure was marked by a steady and strong growth in the economy, and when he left office the Seychelles had one of the most developed economies in the African region. Unemployment is virtually nonexistent and per-capita income has gone from US$1,000 to $5,500. The boom has been based on tourism, deliberately kept small and in the hands of the local people. Foreign investment in the tourist trade has been severely limited and no large developments have been allowed. Copra continues to be the main export, but there is now a thriving re-export business (mainly airline and shipping fuel) and a free-trade manufacturing zone. The middle class of the tiny nation (population about 75,000) is probably the largest in Africa. This economic growth is the base for René's political stability. Education, health care and environmental protection have been well handled, and infant mortality and literacy are among the best in Africa.

René possesses personal wealth, some of it from properties expropriated by the state. In retirement he has moved to Australia where he owns a ranch.

References: afr, PLBA, RWWA, *wiki.*

RHODES, Cecil John
(South Africa, 1853–1902)

Cecil John Rhodes, financier and entrepreneur, was the most notable of the nineteenth-century British imperialists. The founder of the international diamond industry and one of the greatest philanthropists of modern times, he shaped the modern history of southern Africa, leaving two of its largest colonies, Northern and Southern Rhodesia (now Zambia and Zimbabwe), originally named after himself.

Rhodes's father was an Anglican priest from a family of prosperous farmers, but as a curate with 11 children, he did not share in that prosperity. At 16, Cecil went to Natal, South Africa, to assist his brother in starting a cotton farm, hoping to make enough to be able to afford university studies. Cotton proved inadequate at making a fortune, and Rhodes yielded to "diamond fever" the next year when the rush to the Kimberley diamond fields began. He began working an open-pit mine, personally supervising his African workers, sorting diamonds, and earning a modest fortune. In 1873 he returned to England to enter Oxford University, and he spent the next eight years alternating between the university and Kimberley until by sheer determination he received BA and MA degrees in 1881. Tall and fair, a loner with sharp features, a high voice and eccentric manners, he was considered something of an oddity at Oxford.

More than his personality set Rhodes apart, however, as the Oxford years were a time in which he formulated his philosophy of life. In 1875 he spent six months alone on foot in an oxcart, wandering the plains of the Transvaal, South Africa, formulating his vision of an unconquered Africa open for development. In 1877 at Oxford, he composed a "Confession of Faith," which became the basis of his "dream" of a new world order led by a secret brotherhood of elite Anglo-Saxons. The confession spoke of "the occupation by British settlers of the entire continent of Africa, the Holy Land, the Valley of the Euphrates ... the ultimate recovery of the United States of America as an integral part of the British Empire ... and finally the foundation of so great a power as hereafter to render wars impossible." This grandiose scheme, based on notions of Anglo-Saxon racial superiority, provided the basis for Rhodes's later political activities, imperialist designs, and ultimately the foundation of the Rhodes Scholarships.

While at Oxford, Rhodes was making rapid progress in his South African career. His original diamond claim (on land owned by a farmer named Nikolaas De Beers) expanded to a number of holdings. One of the most capable speculators, Rhodes was also shrewd in allying himself with others. Alfred BEIT became his financier, and together they formed the De Beers Mining Company in 1880, the same year Rhodes was elected to the Cape parliament from an Afrikaner district. His major rival at the time was Barnett BARNATO, and the two entered a furious competition until Rhodes bought out Barnato in 1888 for £5 million (over US$25 million then, approximately $700 million today). De Beers Consolidated Mines was created in 1887 and by 1891 controlled 90 percent of world diamond production. Rhodes also acquired a large stake in the Transvaal gold mines, although he never considered that investment as important as diamonds.

In Cape politics, Rhodes incessantly pursued his vision of a British Africa. He saw the danger of the expansion of Afrikaner republics to the north, and his efforts were instrumental in causing Great Britain in 1884 to annex Bechuanaland (now Botswana), of which Rhodes was made deputy commissioner. He successfully negotiated a settlement of Afrikaner claims with Transvaal's President Paul KRUGER, giving the British the corridor necessary for expansion into central Africa. When it became clear that the British would not undertake a protectorate over the northern territories, Rhodes extracted concessions in 1888 from LOBENGULA, the successor of MZILIKAZI as chief of the Ndebele. The colonial office then provided a royal charter to the British South Africa Company (BSAC), granting commercial, political and administrative rights in the name of the British crown in a vaguely defined area north of the Limpopo River. Company agents immediately began to move into Lobengula's kingdom until they had effectively taken it over. The new territory was named Rhodesia. It was not separated into Northern and Southern Rhodesia until 1924.

In 1890, Rhodes was elected prime minister of the Cape Colony with support from both British residents and the Afrikaners. He supported a generous agricultural policy, which benefited the Afrikaners but moved to limit the freedoms of Black Africans. The Cape had included Africans in the

Cecil John Rhodes

electoral system, but by the Franchise and Ballot Act (1892), Rhodes placed financial and educational limitations on Blacks, sharply reducing the number of eligible voters. Sensitive to the prejudices of the Afrikaners, whom he saw as essential for the creation of a South African federation, Rhodes enacted the Glen Grey Act in 1894, setting aside residential areas for Black development. Residents of these areas were denied the right to vote and were taxed unless they worked outside the district. This provided both a source of cheap labor and a prototype for the apartheid system of bantustans 60 years later.

His northern expansion stalled, however, as Belgium occupied the mineral-rich Katanga region of the Belgian Congo (now the Democratic Republic of the Congo), closing off the Northern Rhodesian border. Then Lobengula tried to reclaim his authority, but a military expedition subdued the Ndebele and killed Lobengula. One major obstacle to Rhodes's designs for expansion remained: the Afrikaner republics. With the Cape Dutch behind him because of old resentments against Kruger, Rhodes determined to face Kruger down. In 1895, Rhodes's administrator in Bechuanaland, Leander Starr JAMESON, launched a raid into the Transvaal, fully expecting the British residents (*uitlanders*) to rise up and join him. The colonial secretary in London was aware of the plan, which Rhodes had approved, and he even funded the movement within the Transvaal.

The Jameson Raid was a complete disaster. The raiding party of some 500 was captured, Jameson was sent to prison in Great Britain, and Kruger emerged stronger than ever. Rhodes was forced to resign as prime minister and from his directorship of the BSAC. The British House of Commons appointed a select committee to look into the matter, and in the final report, Rhodes was pronounced guilty of "grave breaches of duty" both as prime minister and as director of the BSAC.

Rhodes devoted the remainder of his life to developing Rhodesia, building a railroad that was part of his scheme for a Cape-to-Cairo line to link all British colonies south to north. In 1899, Oxford honored him with an honorary doctorate, and at that time he signed his will, leaving his fortune for the establishment of a scholarship program to benefit talented potential leaders from the colonies and the United States—the elite he had always envisioned. When the Boer War broke out that year, he went to Kimberley and stayed there throughout the six-month siege. His already frail health was further damaged by this experience, and he died two years later.

References: *afr*, DAHB, DNB, EB, EWB, HWL, *wiki*. Brian Roberts, *Cecil Rhodes: Flawed Colossus* (1987); Robert Rotberg, *The Founder: Cecil Rhodes and the Pursuit of Power* (1988).

ROBERT, Shaaban
(Tanzania, 1909–1962)

Sir Shaaban Robert was the writer responsible for forming the modern Kiswahili language. Denied an education because he was a Muslim who refused to convert to Christianity, he worked throughout his life as a clerk for the colonial civil service in customs, the game department, and the survey office. As a devout Muslim and Pan-African patriot, he was influenced by both Islamic moralism and anticolonialism. In the independence struggle, he was an ally of Julius NYERERE.

Robert is an important literary figure, not only because of his prolific output of high-quality writing, but also because of his impact on Kiswahili. Kiswahili is primarily a trading and conversational tongue, but Robert gave it a place in modern literature. Robert crafted the transition from classical Kiswahili to a modern language. Among his innovations was replacing Arabic script with the Roman alphabet for the written language. It became the national language of Tanzania, and his influence contributed to the reputation of Tanzanian Kiswahili as the most advanced and elegant form of the language. It is also the official language of Kenya, Uganda, and the Democratic Republic of the Congo, and is widely spoken in eastern and central Africa.

It is Robert's Kiswahili poetry that anchors his reputation. He wrote *utenzi*, four-line verses with internal rhyme in the first three lines and a final rhyme that continues in the fourth line of each verse. The complexity of this form may be appreciated when one realizes that a single poem may run several thousand lines. He also wrote in *tendi*, a verse form in which the final lines do not rhyme. His greatest work, published posthumously, is an epic of 3,000 stanzas on World War II, *Utenzi wa Vita na Uhuru* (*Epic of the War of Freedom*, 1967).

He also published four novels, four volumes of essays (a genre that he introduced to the language), an autobiography and a Kiswahili translation of the

Rubaiyat of Omar Khayyam. Robert's biography of the popular Zanzibari singer Sinti Binti Saad emphasizes the struggle of Islamic women for acceptance in Muslim society.

Robert's achievements were recognized in his lifetime. He served on the East African Swahili Committee and in the East African Literature Bureau, among other organizations, and was knighted by Queen Elizabeth II. Unfortunately, despite his importance, little of his work has been translated into Western languages, and Robert is virtually unrecognized outside of Africa.

References: adb, AA, DAHB, EWB, MMA, WLTC. Robert, *Maisha Yangu* (*My Life*, 1949) and *Baada ya Miaka Hamsini* (*After 50 Years*, 1960).

ROBERTO, Holden Alvaro

(Angola, 1923–)

Holden Alvaro Roberto, a nationalist and guerrilla leader, has spent most of his life outside his country, turning his National Front for the Liberation of Angola (FNLA) from the liberation war against Portugal to harassment of the elected Angolan government after independence.

Born into a branch of the Kongo royal family, Roberto was educated at mission schools in the Belgian Congo (now the Democratic Republic of the Congo, DRC). In 1941 he began working for the Belgian colonial administration and then joined a business firm in 1949. He entered Angolan exile politics in the 1950s and in 1958 was sent, under a pseudonym, to the All-African People's Congress in Accra, Ghana, where he made a number of contacts with liberation figures from across the continent. The following year he traveled to Guinea, where he was issued a passport and attached to Guinea's United Nations (U.N.) delegation in order to be able to plead the cause of Angola before the U.N. He returned by way of Tunisia, where he attended the second All-Africa Congress and received support from President Habib Bourguiba. Once back in the DRC, Roberto began weekly radio broadcasts in Portuguese from Kinshasa.

Roberto spent much of 1961 training guerrilla forces, and by spring the first anticolonial military actions began within Angola. In 1962 he merged the main independence groups into the FNLA and

proclaimed an Angolan government in exile, which in 1963 received the recognition of the Organization of African Unity (OAU). His patron and brother-in-law, President MOBUTU Sese Seko of the DRC (then named Zaïre), prodded him until he entered into an agreement with Agostinho NETO, the other major Angolan liberation leader, head of the Popular Movement for the Liberation of Angola (MPLA). In the liberation struggle within Angola, however, Neto emerged as the recognized leader, and the OAU's recognition was transferred to the MPLA in 1968.

With the overthrow of Portugal's fascist dictatorship in 1974, Portugal rushed to rid itself of its colonial empire, and Roberto reentered Angola for the first time since childhood. He discovered that the MPLA had a far more popular base than the FNLA and, in 1975, Neto was installed as Angola's first president. Both Roberto and Jonas SAVIMBI of the National Union for the Total Independence of Angola (UNITA) refused to accept the results of the election and began guerilla attacks against the MPLA government. Roberto, despite bearing responsibility for several atrocities, was a major recipient of U.S. military aid. Nonetheless, the combined antigovernment forces were badly beaten and forced to withdraw to their bases in Zaïre. In 1979, Mobutu asked Roberto to leave Zaïre, and he settled in Paris, attempting to keep his movement alive from Europe. In 1986 he appeared before a U.S. congressional panel seeking funding for further guerrilla action but was rebuffed. In 1992, Roberto returned to Angola to contest the presidential elections, but by that time he was little more than a historical footnote to the Angolan people, who gave him only 2 percent of the vote.

References: DRWW, PLBA.

ROBERTS, Joseph Jenkins

(Liberia, 1809–1876)

Joseph Jenkins Roberts, an American freedman, was the first president of Liberia. He achieved international recognition for his new country but also reinforced the Liberian pattern in which free Blacks colonized other Africans.

Born in Virginia, Roberts and his family emigrated to Liberia in 1829 under the sponsorship

Joseph Jenkins Roberts

of the American Colonization Society (ACS), which had been formed to create an African homeland for freed American slaves. Roberts became a trader on the coast, making contacts and learning the ways of the local peoples. The Liberian government engaged him to collect debts from the chiefs, which they were forced to pay in land, thus increasing the territory held by the ACS. In 1839 he performed well in skirmishes against the indigenous population and was elected lieutenant-governor of the colony, in charge of native affairs. Two years later, the White American governor died and Roberts succeeded him.

Roberts's term as governor was marked by two issues: expansion at the expense of the local chiefs and conflict with Britain and France. He called a chiefs' council, which accepted Liberian domination, and used his position to extend sovereignty over increasing amounts of territory. The British and French, however, regarded Liberia as a private religious and commercial venture, not a government, and refused to respect its borders or customs regulations. In 1846 the ACS withdrew its control in favor of independence, and the American government, uncomfortable with sponsoring a Black colony, encouraged the move. The following year, independence was proclaimed, and Roberts was elected president.

His first move was a visit to Queen Victoria, who recognized Liberia and presented him with a patrol boat for curbing the slave trade, at which he was extremely effective. By 1853 he had pacified the coastal chiefs who depended upon the trade and freed some 80,000 captives. He sought international recognition and was successful everywhere in Europe. The United States granted Liberia diplomatic recognition in 1862.

Roberts was re-elected until 1856, when he peacefully turned over authority to his successor. Afterward, he spent his time fundraising and establishing Liberia College, which he served as its first president. Roberts also continued to be involved in politics and was a general in the militia. A color-conscious man, he favored lighter citizens and was probably behind the coup that deposed the unpopular and dark-skinned Edward ROYE in 1872. Roberts replaced Roye and served until 1876, although he was in failing health.

References: DAHB, MMA, *wiki.* Calvert Tazewell, *Virginia's Ninth President: Joseph Jenkins Roberts* (1992).

ROCKSTONE, Reggie (Reggie Osei)
(Ghana, 1960s–)

Reggie Rockstone is the premier hip-hop artist in Africa, responsible for its acceptance and integration into African pop music. He is the pioneer of rap music in Ghana, and sings in Twi.

Rockstone was born Reggie Osei of Ghanaian parents in London. He went to the United States for college but fell in love with American rap. He returned to London and began his career there with a group called PLZ (Parables, Linguistics and Zlang). In 1994 they were invited to Panafest in Ghana, and when their turntable broke down, they began to freestyle in Twi, and the crowd went wild. The experience convinced Rockstone that Afropop elements and local languages could be integrated into hip-hop. He performs and works in Ghana.

Rockstone calls his music "hip-life," after hip-hop and the high-life street sounds of the 1950s. His first number-one single, "Maaka Maaka" ("I Said It Because I Said It," 1997), later became a bestselling album. His most successful album, however, was *Me Na Me Kae* (*I Was the One Who Said It*, 1999), which sold over two million copies. By this point, Rockstone was touring widely, eventually performing in 44 countries. Altogether, he has issued five albums. *Ah*, which was Rockstone's entry for the Kora Awards, is a bitter account of the breakdown of his marriage due to his wife's infidelity with his best friend. He has touched on a variety of social issues in typical rap fashion—opposing abortion, criticizing government denial of visas, and the struggles of everyday life.

Rockstone has built his own independent label, Kassa Records, in Accra. In 2003 he announced his retirement, but nevertheless continues to tour.

ROSE, Tracey
(South Africa, 1974–)

Tracey Rose is an installation and video artist with a powerful way of making statements about race and politics, both about formerly apartheid South Africa, but also in the social and cultural transition to a new society. As a Coloured woman, she experienced both the oppression of not being White, and the privilege of not being Black. Duality and identity are themes to which she returns again and again.

Rose was born in Durban and graduated in Fine Arts from the University of the Witwatersrand in 1996.

Some of Rose's work is shocking, and meant to be. In her video *Cross/ing* (1997), she appears naked and proceeds to shave her body hair, a symbol of vulnerability, removal of protection, and a satire on the Western notion of beauty that demands shaved legs on women. She recorded the video using surveillance cameras. Rose intends the message to be about "demasculinising and defeminising the body, ... This kind of desexualization carries with it a certain kind of violence." She uses this confrontational approach to the crossover of South Africa as it sheds pretense after the end of apartheid. She has appeared nude in romantic video scenes with Black males, an unsettling image of intimacy across racial boundaries. In *TKO* (2000), she plays off images of a nude boxer working with a punching bag and shots from inside the bag, to lure the viewer into an aggression/oppression experience. She considers it her masterpiece, an expression of passionate art. It began when she took boxing lessons in South Africa, but came to fruition during a year as resident at ArtPace in San Antonio, Texas.

Her most recent exhibition, at a group show called Africa Remix, has been in Germany in 2004, then moved to London and Paris the following year and Tokyo in 2006.

Reference: adb.

ROWLAND, Roland Walter "Tiny"
(Zimbabwe, 1917–1998)

"Tiny" Rowland—international businessman and entrepreneur, friend of presidents and guerrilla leaders, and developer of the greatest multinational corporation in Africa (with some 900 subsidiary companies)—rose from obscurity to international power and immense wealth.

Rowland was born in India in a World War I detention camp, the son of a German merchant who placed him in a British school in 1934. He changed his name, Roland Fuhrhop, at the start of World War II, when his parents were interned in Britain as enemy aliens (his mother died in the camp). He served in the British army during the war. An embittered Rowland left for Southern Rhodesia (now Zimbabwe) in 1947 to try his hand at farming and later worked for the Rio Tinto mining company. Lonrho Corporation, which began as a sleepy mining company founded in London in 1909, hired Rowland in the 1950s to stimulate its growth. By 1961, Rowland had bought out its holding company and established the mixed investment pattern he would follow: a range of companies in mining, a pipeline and several auto franchises. Rowland began an expansionist entrepreneurial policy that drained cash reserves but acquired platinum and copper mines. He also developed the administrative pattern that he never abandoned—Rowland and Rowland alone made the decisions. When he could, he excluded outside board directors, accepted no limits on his authority, and took little advice from associates.

Events at Lonrho reached a crisis in 1973 when it seemed that Rowland would be ousted by the directors, but at a dramatic stockholders' meeting, his opponents were jeered, shouted down and voted off the board. Rowland reigned supreme, and Lonrho began a long climb to the top tier of multinationals. Between 1961 and 1991, Lonrho's group sales multiplied 767-fold and pretax profits rose by 1,365 percent. Besides mining and oil pipelines, he entered publishing (London *Observer*, *Glasgow Herald*, Scottish and Universal Publishers); agricultural machinery; auto and motorcycle distributorships; beer, tea, sugar and food processing; textiles; cold rolled steel; pharmaceuticals; casinos, hotels, tourism and resorts; and insurance. There are companies in five North and South American countries, in 17 African states, and in various other nations around the world.

One acquisition battle made headlines for its drama and ferocity. In the late 1970s and 1980s, Rowland fought for control of Harrods, the prestigious London luxury department store, but failed. It was one of the few times that the secretive giant emerged from the shadows. A loner, he joined no clubs and lived quietly with his wife. The failed move on Harrods signaled Lonrho's entry into service industries, however, which are now a cornerstone of its profits.

Rowland's political activities were always at the service of his corporations. At various times, he has been close to Kenneth KAUNDA of Zambia, Milton OBOTE of Uganda, and MOBUTU Sese Seko of Zaïre. In Kenya, he was connected to Daniel arap MOI through Mark arap Too, party head and rumored illegitimate son of Moi, whom Rowland made head of his Kenyan interests. In 1992 he called Libya's Colonel Muammar Gadhafi "a super friend." One London newspaper labeled this choice of despot friends as "unblemished by signs of good judgment." In 1973, British Prime Minister Edward Heath called him "the unacceptable face of capitalism," a gibe that stung Rowland. He once retorted, "You can never have enough enemies," and he did not lack them, either in business or politics.

His connections with conservative rebel leaders made him a negotiator since 1985 between the central government of the Sudan and John GARANG, although his shuttle diplomacy yielded few results. He had more success in Mozambique, where he helped broker the 1992 agreement that brought Afonso DHLAKAMA to the peace table with President Joachim CHISSANO.

Rowland's shareholders turned from him as profits sagged and his high-handed methods wore thin. In 1993 he brought in a German investor who began selling off less profitable companies and then installed outside directors who placed curbs on Rowland's free-wheeling ways. He effectively lost control of Lonrho in 1994. Nelson MANDELA

awarded him the Order of Good Hope in 1996. When he died, the media estimated his personal wealth at between £150 million and £650 million ($262 million and $1.13 billion).

References: wiki. Tom Bower, *Tiny Rowland: A Rebel Tycoon* (1993).

ROYE, Edward James
(Liberia, 1815–1871)

Edward James Roye was a businessman and political leader who defended the rights of Black citizens in racially polarized Liberia and served briefly as president. Roye was born in Ohio of wealthy Black parents and became a prosperous businessman. Unhappy over racial prejudice toward Black freedmen, he emigrated to Liberia in 1846. There he studied law and founded a shipping line, the first to fly the Liberian flag, and was soon a leading merchant.

In Liberia, Roye joined the True Whig Party and was elected to the legislature, becoming speaker of the House in 1849 and then a senator. By the 1850s he was leader of his party, which championed the cause of dark-skinned Liberians in opposition to the aristocracy of light-skinned Republicans. Roye ran for president unsuccessfully in 1855, but in 1864 he was appointed chief justice of the supreme court. He ran for president again in 1867 and lost, but finally achieved his goal two years later.

Roye drew up an ambitious economic development plan and funded it with a huge loan from British bankers, which was made at disadvantageous rates. This loan, along with his progressive policies promoting Blacks, alienated him from the race-conscious legislature. Then, in confusion over the results of a referendum on the subject, Roye declared that his term had been extended two years. Impeachment proceedings began, but as street violence escalated, Roye was arrested and removed from office. Although he reportedly died during a prison escape before he was sentenced, Roye was probably murdered. He was succeeded by Joseph ROBERTS, Liberia's first president and a bitter opponent of Roye's.

References: DAHB, MMA, *wiki.*

SACRANIE, Iqbal
(Malawi, 1952–)

Sir Iqbal Sacranie, a native of Malawi, is secretary general and spokesman for the Muslim Council of Britain (MCB), where he has worked tirelessly at improving relations between Muslims and others in Britain. There are about 1.2 million Muslims in Great Britain, and the MCB represents some 350 British Muslim organizations. Sir Iqbal Sacranie was knighted by Queen Elizabeth II in 2005.

Sacranie comes from an East Indian (Asian) family that was prominent in Malawi. His father was a supporter of the independence movement. Sacranie was raised in Malawi and went to England for higher studies in 1969. He maintains close ties with political figures in his home country and is well respected there. In Great Britain he is active as an accountant and is a fellow of the Institute of Financial Accountants. He is managing director (CEO) of his family's business interests in Britain.

For 30 years, however, Sacranie has been best known for his volunteer work, especially among Indians and Pakistanis. He raised £1.2 million ($2.1 million) from the East Asian community for a London sports complex and community center to be used by all ethnic groups. He serves on the Interfaith Foundation, the Prince's Trust and many other charitable groups.

He is chairman of Muslim Aid in Britain, and has been secretary general of MCB since its founding in 1997. As the head of Muslim Aid, Sacranie has supported education and food projects in Malawi. His primary work has been in Great Britain, however, where he has served on the advisory council of a series of home secretaries under both Labour and Conservative governments. While his particular interest has been the defense of the rights of British Muslims, he has devoted himself to relations among ethnic and faith communities.

Sacranie has also been the source of controversy, which has sometimes overshadowed his ecumenical efforts. He has been a strong opponent of the Iraqi War and the occupation of Palestine. In 2005, he publically boycotted a Holocaust memorial observance on the grounds that it did not also commemorate the Muslim victims of the Palestinian intifada.

Sacranie argued that other European ceremonies for the sixtieth anniversary of the liberation of Auschwitz included remembrances of the victims of all genocides, including those of Rwanda, Palestine and Bosnia. He was also highly critical of Salman Rushdie, the Muslim British author, for what Sacranie regarded as his blasphemous novel, *Satanic Verses*, when he suggested that "death is perhaps too easy" for Rushdie. Sacranie has led the MCB through the difficult period after the 9/11 attacks on the United States and the tube bombings in London that resulted in over 50 deaths.

Sacranie has been opposed by radicals within the Muslim community who disrupted the MCB's election in 2005. He has been seen as too close to the government, and an MCB letter to British mosques asking them to condemn terrorism brought accusations of fostering Islamophobia.

References: adb, *wiki*. www.mcb.org.uk.

SAIBOU, Ali
(Niger, 1940–)

General Ali Saibou, a benevolent military autocrat, ruled Niger from 1987 to 1993. While maintaining close control of his country, he began a process of limited liberalization.

Saibou was educated in West African military schools in Mali and Sénégal, and entered the French army in 1960. He saw action in Cameroon and was wounded. After independence in 1960, he transferred to the new Niger army and was commissioned an officer after training in France in 1964. As he moved through the ranks he undertook further training in France as an infantry officer and later at the staff school. In 1973 he became head of the Malian military academy for a year. In 1974 his cousin, Seyni KOUNTCHÉ, staged a coup against the longtime government of Hamani DIORI. Saibou was a willing and enthusiastic participant, bringing his mechanized troops to the capital in a 24–hour drive across 600 miles of open territory. He served in the cabinet until later in the year, when he was appointed armed forces chief of staff, a position from which he crushed several coup attempts, including one in which he was briefly held prisoner. By the time Kountché died in 1987 of a brain tumor, Saibou seemed his inevitable successor, having been acting head of state several times while Kountché was in Paris for lengthy medical treatment.

Saibou, a man with a cheerful and outgoing personality, attempted to heal the wounds of past conflicts. He freed political prisoners, including Diori and Djibo BAKARY, the main opposition leader. He formed a new ruling party but also lifted the ban on other political organizations, announcing that this decision was "the final step in [the] normalization" of politics in Niger. Actually, the final step seems to have been the convening of a national conference of 24 political parties and 69 mass organizations. When it met in 1991, the conference assumed sovereignty, and Saibou reluctantly accepted a largely ceremonial role. Under the new constitution, Saibou was forbidden to contend for office, and in the 1993 elections he was replaced by the former prime minister. He retired to his farm thereafter.

References: PLBA, RWWA, *wiki*.

SAID, Seyyid
(Tanzania, 1791–1856)

Sultan Seyyid Said was the founder of the Busaidi dynasty in Zanzibar (now part of Tanzania) and a prominent Arab trader. At age 16, he became sultan of Oman, and when a serious depression followed the end of the Napoleonic Wars, Said turned toward Britain. He offered to end slaving with Christian nations in exchange for his protection for commercial interests on the East African coast.

In the 1820s, Said began a series of expeditions to subdue the East African coastal towns, using the powerful Omani fleet to end the domination of the Mazrui family. In 1840 he moved his capital to Zanzibar and became, in effect, an African ruler with an Omani outpost. Within a year Said had established his suzerainty from Mogadishu in Somalia to northern Mozambique. It was essentially a trading empire based on shipping, slaving and cloves. Said then took the honorific title *Seyyid*

("learned one"), which would become the dynastic title.

Said introduced cloves, a spice valued in Europe for meat preservation, to Zanzibar. Using the plantation system, he created the major African slave system that paralleled the North American form in atrocity and exploitation. Slaves not used in farming were sold to Arab countries from what became the largest slave market in Africa. Prosperity came also from trade in ivory, grain and coconuts, as well as a highly profitable banking business based on Indian investment capital. A significant cultural result of this commercial activity was the spread of Kiswahili as the common language along the coast. On Said's death, his empire was broken into Omani and Zanzibari sections, which were separately inherited by his two sons.

References: DAHB, EWB, HWL.

SALIM, Salim Ahmed
(Tanzania, 1942–)

Salim Ahmed Salim, longtime diplomat and former prime minister, was secretary-general of the Organization of African Unity (OAU) from 1989 to 2001, an unprecedented three terms.

Salim was a wunderkind—a Zanzibari student activist as a teen, and at 19 he was named deputy chief of the Zanzibari Office in Havana, just as Fidel Castro was coming to power. He returned to Zanzibar after a year and was named editor of a daily newspaper on the island and head of the All-Zanzibar Journalists' Association.

Salim graduated from the University of Delhi in India in 1967 and received an MA in international affairs from Columbia University in New York in 1974. His studies were pursued while he was on diplomatic missions for his government. As a supporter of the antisultanate revolution that led to Zanzibar's merger into Tanzania, he was sought after by the new government, which badly needed talented and loyal Zanzibaris for its civil service. At age 22 he was ambassador to Egypt and a year later became high commissioner in Delhi. After six months in China (1969), he was posted to New York from 1970 to 1980 as permanent representative to the United Nations (U.N.) and simultaneously was ambassador to six Caribbean nations. For most of this time he chaired the committee on decolonization and was well respected. He was nominated to replace Kurt Waldheim as secretary-general of the U.N. in 1981 but was opposed by the Western powers.

In 1980, President Julius NYERERE called Salim back to Tanzania to become foreign minister, and he was promoted to prime minister in 1984 when the incumbent died in an accident. He was a leading candidate to succeed Nyerere as president but was defeated by Ali Hassan MWINYI. He spent four years as deputy prime minister until running for OAU secretary-general against the incumbent, Ide OUMAROU of Niger.

Following the end of White domination in Africa (after the 1994 election of Nelson MANDELA as president of South Africa), Salim helped the OAU face its two main issues: the increasing marginalization of Africa in the world economy and the need to serve as a peacemaker in African conflicts. He supported the African Economic Community treaty, which was modeled on the European Economic Community, and sees economic integration as one solution to Africa's problems. Responding to negative African reactions to the American invasion of Somalia, Salim made an African peacekeeping force his top priority.

Salim is a member of the National Executive of the Tanzanian governing party and remains a prominent figure in the country. He serves as president of the Julius Nyerere Foundation and on several international boards and commissions.

References: adb, PLBA, RWWA, *wiki*.

SAMBA, Martin-Paul
(Cameroon, 1870?–1914)

Martin-Paul Samba, an anticolonialist resistance leader, led an abortive uprising against the Germans in 1914 that led to his execution. He is revered as a martyr and national patriot in Cameroon.

German colonial repression in Cameroon was especially harsh, and resistance continued during most of the colonial occupation. Samba was of the Bulu people from the southern forests, a dense bush area that was occupied by the Germans in the 1890s as they moved inland. Sometime in his late teens, Samba came into the service of Curt von Morgen, a German ethnographer who was attached to the colonial forces. Von Morgen became Samba's mentor and took him along to Germany, where he spent three years in a German academy and then enrolled

in an officers' training school for another three years. Samba was appointed to the German imperial army as an officer, which was a relative rarity for colonial subjects.

Samba returned to Cameroon in 1895 as a colonial supporter. He became chief of the Bulu, helped extend German authority over his people, and joined in the pacification program. There was a major uprising among the Bulu from 1898 to 1901, which Samba helped to suppress. It is not known what turned Samba against the Germans, but by 1914 he was disillusioned enough to have plotted against them. Because of his heroic status in Cameroon, many legends surround him, including one that the Germans had chosen him to be governor, but he was later rejected. Another says that he had a magic handkerchief whose powers failed him or that, in another version, kept him in thrall to the Germans until it lost its powers.

Whatever the causes, by 1914 Samba was planning a revolt against the Germans. He left the army—where he held the rank of Hauptmann, or major—and trained some Bulu troops. As part of Samba's planning, he made contact with Rudolf BELL in an attempt to link anti-German forces. When he attempted to contact the French, who were then invading Cameroon as part of the World War I African campaigns, the message was intercepted, and Samba and Bell were arrested. Both were executed on the same day.

References: afr, DAHB, MMA. Madeleine Mbono, *Martin Samba: Face à la Pénétration Allemande au Cameroun (Martin Samba: Confronting the German Penetration of Cameroun*, 1976).

SAMORI Touré
(Guinea/Mali/Sierra Leone, 1830?–1900)

Almany Samori Touré, a Muslim trader and empire builder, created a powerful kingdom in west Africa in the late nineteenth century.

At age 17, Samori became a *dyula*, one of a class of professional Muslim traders, and within three years had built up a major commercial network that extended from Guinea to Sierra Leone. When his mother was taken in a raid, Samori joined her captors to free her, rose to become a war chief, and learned the use of firearms. Returning home to Konyan in present-day Guinea, he soon amassed a following and began a brutal campaign of expansion by defeating and slaying a number of chiefs and enslaving the men who did not join his forces. In 1864, El Hadj UMAR Said Tall died, and his empire began to splinter as warlords seized parts of its territory. Samori took advantage of the situation to try to become the dominant power in the region.

By 1874, Samori had established his own state, and within five years it covered several hundred thousand square miles. In 1884 he declared it officially Muslim, opening schools and mosques and imposing Islam on all his subjects. He then took the title *Almany*, "the commander of believers."

Besides religion, Samori's policy of advancement within the army based on merit rather than ethnicity provided a powerful force for national unity. The state's economic foundation was trade in slaves, gold and ivory, which were exchanged for modern firearms. Samori had great organizational ability, dividing the empire into 10 administrative districts, each with an army unit of 5,000, which spent half the year in farming and half in military training.

Beginning in 1882, Samori clashed with the French, whose colonial designs conflicted with his own imperial expansion. Samori made contact with the British in Sierra Leone and from them secured a supply of breech-loading rifles. The French countered with artillery, which made the defense of Samori's fortified towns impossible. Sporadic warfare with the French continued, alternating with increasingly restrictive treaties, until 1894, when, in desperation, Samori moved his kingdom eastward, pursuing a scorched-earth policy. Everywhere he was harassed and often defeated by General Louis ARCHINARD, but now he also met resistance from local chiefs. Finally, he lost half his troops in a terrible retreat over the mountains to Guinea. Samori was captured in 1898 and died of pneumonia in exile in Gabon.

References: afr, DAHB, MMA, WGMC, *wiki*.

SANÉ, Pierre T.
(Sénégal, 1948–)

Dr. Pierre T. Sané was secretary-general of Amnesty International from 1992 to 2001. Before that he had a long career as an international civil servant, especially in development. He studied in France, taking degrees in marketing, administration and finance. He completed his education with an MS in public administration from the London School of Economics and a Ph.D. in politics from Carleton University in Ottawa, Canada.

Sané worked briefly for the Sénégalese Pharmaceutical Association before joining the Ottawa-based International Development Research Centre (IDRC) in 1978. After working as regional comptroller for research institutes and universities in Dakar and Nairobi, Sané became associate director for policy and budget in 1985 and regional director in Africa for the following three years. He took responsibility for project development, strategies and implementation throughout the continent. He was also a founding member of PANAF, an African Non-Governmental Organization (NGO) with the goal of Pan-African unity, and served as president of PANAF's Sénégal chapter.

In 1992, Amnesty International (AI) recruited him as secretary-general at a critical juncture in its history. With over a million members and 47 national branches, AI is a major worldwide force for human rights. One of Sané's first projects was the 1993 international Human Rights Conference in Vienna, launched under AI sponsorship, with the responsibility of drafting a successor document to the United Nations Declaration on Human Rights. Working under the most intense political pressures, he maintained a balance among competing interests and emerged as a respected leader in the field. Sané was able to harness his IDRC experience in economic rights to gain legitimacy among Asian Third World spokespersons who hoped to assert economic rights over political/legal rights. He also used his AI credibility with Western proponents of civil rights. His ability to negotiate conflicting positions was one of his strongest assets.

His strategy for AI was to further implant it in Third World countries so that it could not be considered a colonialist association with foreign values. He worked through local NGOs in Third World regions and fostered joint action with parallel groups.

Sané faced several internal and external problems, such as AI's weak financial position, lack of younger members, and changing needs following the end of the Cold War. Sané began an ambitious program to bring AI to the forefront of international civil rights activism. He described himself as "a militant of optimism" in this task. After leaving Amnesty, Sané was named assistant director-general for Social and Human Sciences at the United

Nations Educational, Scientific and Cultural Organization (UNESCO).

Reference: wiki.

SANKARA, Thomas
(Burkina Faso, 1949–1987)

Captain Thomas Sankara was a charismatic revolutionary who attempted to revitalize the spirit of nationalism in his country while modernizing it. He became one of the leading African opponents of neocolonialism.

Sankara was born into a low-status, former slave family and was a Catholic in a country where the vast majority of people adhere to traditional religions or Islam. He attended a military secondary school, where he passed the baccalaureate examinations and went on to a military academy in Madagascar. In 1974 he returned to Upper Volta, as Burkina Faso was then called, after completing paratroop training in France and Morocco. He became involved in trade union activities and with left-wing political groups, forming a loose association of like-minded junior officers who shared his nationalist views. Among them was his close friend Blaise COMPAORÉ. Later in 1974, Sankara distinguished himself in the war between Upper Volta and Mali and was promoted to commander of the paratroop battalion.

In 1981, Colonel Sayé ZERBO came to power through a coup, and Sankara was appointed minister of state in the new president's office. He soon, however, grew disgusted with the corruption of the regime and resigned after denouncing the government. He was stripped of his rank and spent several months in prison. During the following several years, Upper Volta went through a period of instability, with coups attempted by several groups. In 1983, Zerbo was overthrown and Sankara joined the 120–man governing council. At first he refused any position, but in January 1983 he accepted the post of prime minister.

Jean Baptiste Ouédraogo, the president, was too conservative for his radical premier, and he arrested Sankara in May and had him interned. An internal struggle followed, and Sankara was released and placed under house arrest. Sankara's following was too powerful to be restrained, and in August, Compaoré set him free in a daring raid. Ouédraogo was deposed, and Sankara emerged as chairman of the National Revolutionary Council (NRC) and national leader. He set forth a policy "to take power out of the hands of our national bourgeoisie and their imperialist allies and put it in the hands of the people." In a move to popularize the revolution, local committees for the defense of the revolution (CDRs) were established in every village and workplace to promote collective dialog and to mobilize those who had been on the margins of Upper Volta's society. These committees were also to be Sankara's link with the masses.

Sankara displayed a passionate commitment to independence and self-reliance. The CDRs took charge of local development and mounted a massive vaccination campaign that inoculated more than three million children. They built several hundred water storage tanks, began a program that doubled the literacy rate, and attacked the advance of the Sahara Desert with a tree-planting program. All arable land was nationalized and agriculture was based on collectives. The national budget was opened for discussion by the CDRs, resulting in a surplus by 1985. Sankara's tax system, based on the ability to pay, raised opposition and, when the teachers went on strike, he fired them and then rehired them on his own terms. Sankara was also criticized by the labor unions, which disputed the military dominance of the CDRs as well as the priority given to rural progress over the development of urban workers. In addition, he alienated the traditional chiefs, whose powers he sharply reduced by ending their right to forced labor.

Sankara remained generally popular, however, partly because of his personal austerity. He never owned property. As minister of state he had gone to work in the presidential palace on a bicycle, and as head of state he rejected chauffeured limousines in favor of driving his own cheap Renault 5. He was an ardent champion of women's progress, appointing many women to government posts and forming a national women's organization, despite the fact that this policy ran counter to conservative national traditions. His personal guard was made up of a women's motorcycle troupe.

In 1984, Sankara changed the name of the new nation to Burkina Faso, "land of the upright people." His zealotry and disrespect for tradition, along with a blunt and abrasive style, strained his relations both within the country and abroad, but outside of official circles he retained a large popular following.

Internationally, Sankara's alliances gave Burkina Faso an unaccustomed prominence. He forged links with what he regarded as other "people's republics," such as Cuba, Angola, North Korea and Libya. Within Africa he became known as a critic and opponent of countries allied with the West. He was openly contemptuous of Félix HOUPHOUËT-BOIGNY, president of Côte d'Ivoire and the senior statesman of the region (and Compaoré's father-in-law). An attempt on Sankara's life while he was visiting Côte d'Ivoire in 1985 only deepened his isolation from his neighbors, and he was passed over for chairman of the Economic Community of West African States (ECOWAS) when it was Burkina Faso's turn.

In 1987 internal dissension within the NRC came to a head over the trial of a number of Marxist labor union leaders who were accused of subversion. Sankara supported drastic sentences, but Compaoré, as minister of justice, ordered some of the accused set free. Sankara may have been moving against his opponents in the NRC when Compaoré countered this gambit and counterattacked. In a shootout between his bodyguard and Compaoré's soldiers, Sankara was killed. Although he was formally accused of dictatorship after his death, the new government had difficulty controlling the popular demonstrations that followed. Despite an economic revival under Compaoré, nostalgia for Sankara persists in Burkina Faso. There is a significant Sankarist Youth Movement dedicated to his ideals as well as several political parties bearing his name. The revolution that he preached and practiced may, in fact, have destroyed him. As he said in 1985: "You cannot carry out fundamental change without a certain amount of madness.... We must dare to invent the future."

References: afr, MMA, PLBA, PLCA, wiki. Bruno Jaffre, Burkina Faso: Les Années Sankara (Burkina Faso: The Sankara Years, 1989).

SANKOH, Foday
(Sierra Leone, 1937–2003)

Foday Sankoh was one of the most brutal terrorists in modern African history. In a 10–year civil war he started in 1991 in Sierra Leone, upwards of 200,000 died, many in grisly and disgusting ways.

Sankoh began as a soldier in the Leonean army, and spent a tour of duty as a United Nations (U.N.) peacekeeper in the Democratic Republic of the Congo. He took part in the protests against a new Leonean constitution which brought Siaka STEVENS back to power in 1971, and was imprisoned for seven years as a result. On his release, now a hardened criminal, he began to organize rural resistance groups. He then went to Libya for guerilla training, and there met Charles TAYLOR, a like-minded ally. Taylor helped him form the Revolutionary United Front (RUF). The RUF infiltrated rural Sierra Leone, and promised the poor peasants schools and clinics, to be paid for with the revenues from Sierra Leone's diamonds. He took the diamond fields and used the money to fund arms and bribes, but he never paid his soldiers. They were expected to forage for themselves and to live by looting. Pay came in the form of bonuses to boy soldiers who turned in the most amputated hands, limbs or ears.

Sankoh's terrorism began with his own troops. Young boys would be seized and forced to kill their own parents on pain of their own deaths. Now unable ever to return to his village, the boy would be further brutalized until he became a ruthless, amoral killing machine who would murder for sport. One game was to guess the sex of a fetus, then cut it out of its pregnant mother with a bayonet. Looting, rape and sex slavery were common among the troops.

In 1997, Sankoh went into exile in Nigeria, which imprisoned him. He returned to the RUF in 1999, by which time Sierra Leone was reduced to being the poorest country on earth, devastated and demoralized. Ceasefires were established, then broken. At one point, Sankoh captured 500 U.N. peacekeepers and only released them when a crack British army force moved against him with orders to kill. He was captured by a mob in 2000 and turned over to the international court for crimes against humanity in Sierra Leone. He died, apparently having gone insane, in captivity.

Reference: wiki.

SARO-WIWA, Ken(ule) Beeson
(Nigeria, 1941–1995)

Ken Saro-Wiwa, a promising Nigerian writer, is far better known as the martyred leader of protests on behalf of the Ogoni people against the central government and international oil corporations. His resistance and death became an international cause.

In the 1950s, oil began to be exploited in the Niger Delta, in the homelands of the Ogoni people. They found themselves displaced and their land fouled by leaks and dumping. Two European oil giants, Royal Dutch Shell and British Petroleum, worked together to extract as much profit as possible from the deposits.

Saro-Wiwa advocated autonomy for Ogoniland, for which he was dismissed from a post as minister of education in Rivers State. He continued his activism on a small scale during the 1980s while he built up his business interests in real estate and a grocery chain to support his writing and television work. In 1990, he founded a nonviolent resistance group, the Movement for the Survival of the Ogoni People (MOSOP) to demonstrate, petition and bring the issue to the attention of the international community. Alongside MOSOP, however, gangs began tapping into the pipelines to steal and resell the oil. The corporations and the government seldom distinguished between MOSOP and the criminals. At one point, Shell was discovered smuggling small arms into the Delta and building up its own forces. In 1992 Saro-Wiwa was jailed by the military government of Ibrahim BABANGIDA.

In 1993, half the Ogoni populace went on marches around their homelands. Shell withdrew from the Delta, even though the marches had been peaceful. On its own side, Shell had colluded with the government of Sani ABACHA to suppress opposition. The Nigerian army destroyed Ogoni villages and massacred thousands.

In 1994, Saro-Wiwa and eight MOSOP colleagues were arrested and accused of inciting the murders of several Ogoni chiefs. They were held for a year, tried outside the regular court system, and hanged in 1995. There was a worldwide protest and revulsion at the sentence, led by Nelson MANDELA, and the Commonwealth of Nations suspended Nigeria's membership. It is widely regarded as judicial murder. They were buried in unmarked graves, but in 2000, American forensic experts exhumed the bodies and Saro-Wiwa was buried in 2004 in his home village. *Sozaboy, A Novel in Rotten English* (1985) was a 1987 mention for the Noma Prize for African Writing. In it, Saro-Wiwa recounts the story of a village youth who enters the secessionist Biafran army during the Nigerian civil war and experiences disillusionment and loss of innocence. The novel was written in a mix of

standard, broken and pidgin English, a clever play on language. He described it as "having no rules and no syntax. It thrives on lawlessness and is part of the dislocated and discordant society in which Sozaboy must live."

Saro-Wiwa returned to the Biafran War for his memoir, *On a Darkling Plain* (1989), based on his war diaries. He was also a television producer and developed a soap opera series that was highly popular. In all he wrote five novels, a book of poetry, eight plays, 12 children's books and three books of non-fiction. *A Forest of Flowers* (1986), a collection of his short stories, received the 1987 Commonwealth Writers' Prize. For his environmental work, he received many awards, including the Right Livelihood Award in 1994.

References: adb, afr, CA, CANR, EB, *wiki.* Ken Wiwa, *In the Shadow of a Saint* (2001).

SASSOU-NGUESSO, Denis
(Congo, 1943–)

General Denis Sassou-Nguesso has governed a divided country as a military dictator. As political liberalization has spread across Africa, he has been reluctant to accept it but has finally been forced to surrender most of his powers.

After graduating from teachers' college, Sassou-Nguesso joined the army, was sent to Algeria for training, and then went to France for infantry training. He became an officer and later commander of the airborne infantry. From the start of his career he was politically involved as a supporter of President Marien NGOUABI and joined the dominant Congolese Labour Party (PCT), which elected him to the central committee in 1968, the same year he became minister of defense. When Ngouabi was assassinated in 1977, Sassou-Nguesso became deputy chair of the military committee ruling the country after Joachim YHOMBI-OPANGO was made head of state. The two strongmen became rivals, and Sassou-Nguesso assumed power in 1979 when Yhombi-Opango could no longer manage the economy or the resulting social discontent.

Sassou-Nguesso pledged to continue Ngouabi's Marxist path, but while he kept up a radical rhetoric to please the extreme left, in practice he took a pragmatic approach, even including economic liberalism. He negotiated for Western companies to manage the vital oil and mineral deposits. Though he signed a friendship treaty with the Soviet Union, he still maintained good relations with France.

Denis Sassou-Nguesso

From 1986 to 1987 he chaired the Organization of African Unity (OAU) and from that point took a greater interest in international affairs. Sassou-Nguesso played an important role in settling the 1987 war between Chad and Libya, and the following year he mediated negotiations leading to Namibian independence.

Challenges to Sassou-Nguesso's authority did not come from either end of the political spectrum, however, but from ethnic divisions within the country. Several coups were mounted in the 1980s, and in 1987 an armed uprising involving the main opposition leader ended in a bloody shootout. After being confirmed in office by the PCT in 1989, he announced cautious moves toward political liberalization. In 1991 opposition parties were legalized. The PCT lost the 1992 elections but rejected the verdict. Unprepared for democracy, the country erupted into conflict between Sassou-Nguesso's Mbochi ethnic group from the north and two groups from the south. During Sassou-Nguesso's tenure in office, the Mbochi dominated both government and the army, and conflict was suppressed. In 1993 clashes degenerated into ethnic battles that forced 40,000 people to flee Brazzaville, the capital. Kidnapping and hostage exchanges became a bargaining tool. Sassou-Nguesso spent 1994–1997 in Paris, but the dapper former paratrooper spent his years out of office as a spokesman for Africa. He resurfaced in time for the 1997 elections and took the presidency again in a short but bloody civil war after his villa was attacked. He again allowed reasonably free elections and was elected overwhelmingly in 2002, due to a boycott from his main rival. The 2002 Constitution allowed him a seven-year term.

In 2006, Sassou-Nguesso edged out Omar Hassan BASHIR of the Sudan to become head of the African Union (AU), the successor group to the Organization of African Unity (OAU), which he had previously chaired. It is hoped that Sassou-Nguesso's mediating skills will help settle the Darfur crisis.

References: afr, DAHB, PLBA, RWWA, *wiki.*

SAVIMBI, Jonas Malheiro
(Angola, 1934–2002)

Dr. Jonas Malheiro Savimbi, head of the National Union for the Total Independence of Angola (UNITA), maintained a guerrilla war against the national government from 1975 to his death in battle.

Although Savimbi's father worked for the railroad, he was also a part-time Protestant church worker, whose efforts were so successful that he was in regular conflict with the dominant Catholic missions. Savimbi attended mission schools and then received a scholarship from the United Church of Christ to study in Lisbon. Already imbued with his father's spirit of independence and resistance, he was soon active in anticolonial student groups. After he was detained three times by the Portuguese secret police, he left for Switzerland, where he studied at the Universities of Fribourg and Lausanne, from which he graduated in 1965 with an honors degree in political science. For years, Savimbi called himself "doctor," until it became a common honorific title for him, but there is no evidence that he ever pursued a doctorate.

At a student conference in Uganda in 1961, Savimbi met with Kenya's Tom MBOYA, who suggested that he join Holden ROBERTO in forming an Angolan resistance group. Savimbi became a leading figure and in 1962 negotiated the formation of the National Front for the Liberation of Angola (FNLA) by the merger of several splinter groups. He represented the FNLA to the United Nations (U.N.) that year, but he split with Roberto in 1964 and formed UNITA two years later. In the interim he received a year's guerrilla training in China, after being rebuffed by the Soviets. Savimbi wanted a movement with both social and military programs and not one based upon ethnicity, which was his major criticism of the FNLA. Divisions within Angolan society were such, however, that each of the liberation movements—UNITA, the FNLA, and Agostinho NETO's Popular Movement for the Liberation of Angola (MPLA)—had major ethnic and regional bases. UNITA became dominated by the Ovimbundu people of the south, the largest ethnic group in Angola.

UNITA built up a following in the east and south of Angola and soon dominated there, with

Savimbi leading his forces. As well as resisting the Portuguese, however, UNITA and the MPLA fought one another. When Portuguese opposition to independence collapsed with the end of fascism there in 1974, UNITA was the weakest of the three liberation movements joining in negotiations for a transition. In the election campaign that followed, Savimbi's status as the major anticolonial leader to have remained in Angola throughout much of the resistance war, his oratorical gifts in six languages, and his appeals for national unity made him a popular figure. He promised a place for the Portuguese settlers, no nationalization of property, and nonalignment in the Cold War. The electoral process broke down despite three attempts by Savimbi to bring the three groups together, and the MPLA suddenly went on the offensive against UNITA. By the end of 1975 there was full-scale civil war.

From the start, the conflict was entangled in the Cold War. The United States shipped arms to UNITA, while the MPLA government received aid from the Soviet Union. Cuban soldiers were airlifted into Luanda, and the West countered with an armored column from South Africa. The foreign involvement accelerated until there were some 60,000 Cuban troops on one hand and South African air cover and artillery along with U.S. Central Intelligence Agency (CIA) covert support on the other. UNITA received financial aid from France, China and several Arab states. Control of large sections of the country frequently changed, and it became clear that the stalemate would be broken only through negotiations. In José DOS SANTOS, the MPLA had a more flexible leader, and between 1985 and 1988 talks led to a U.S.-brokered agreement on mutual withdrawal of Cuban and South African troops, independence for Namibia, and open elections. With their foreign patrons withdrawn, the two competing political factions signed a peace treaty and agreed to merge their armed forces. Savimbi carefully undercounted his troops and used the transition period to move his forces from guerrilla status to that of a fully organized army. When he lost the 1993 elections, which were supervised by the U.N., he rejected the results and returned to armed struggle. UNITA captured over two-thirds of the country, including the vital diamond mines, which yielded Savimbi about US$1 million per week.

In 1994, a new accord was signed and Savimbi was offered the vice presidency of Angola. He rejected the offer and after several years, returned to the bush. He died in a firefight. A ceasefire was signed shortly after.

References: afr, CB, EWB, PLBA, PLCA, RWWA, *wiki*. Fred Bridgland, *Jonas Savimbi: Key to Africa* (1987); Windrich, Elaine. *The Cold War Guerilla* (1992).

SAWYER, Amos
(Liberia, 1945–)

Dr. Amos Sawyer became interim president of Liberia after the government's complete collapse during the chaos of civil war in the 1990s. Under the protection of peacekeeping forces from the Economic Community of West African States (ECOWAS), he worked to bring the factions together and lead Liberia toward some sort of political stability.

After completing his undergraduate studies at the University of Liberia, Sawyer received a Ph.D. (1973) in political science from Northwestern University in Evanston, Illinois. He began teaching at the University of Liberia while being active in social and political programs. He taught at the Marcus Garvey Night School at the time when Sergeant Samuel DOE was a student. During the 1970s, Sawyer was involved with MOJA (Number One), the radical opposition to the True Whig Party, which had dominated Liberian politics since the country's foundation. Although he was harassed by the government, Sawyer stood for mayor of Monrovia in 1979 and was so popular that the election was postponed by officials who feared that he would win.

Following Doe's 1980 coup, Sawyer chaired the constitutional commission but was soon sidelined by Doe and in 1984 was detained. By this time Sawyer was Doe's leading rival for the presidency and head of the Liberian People's Party (LPP), which he helped found. The LPP was banned from presidential elections after he refused to campaign as Doe's running mate. In 1984, Sawyer went to the United States to teach at the Indiana University African Studies Center. From this base he formed an opposition group, the Association for Constitutional Democracy in Liberia.

In early 1990 a regional uprising turned into a major challenge to the Doe regime, spreading swiftly until Monrovia, the capital, fell to several rebel factions and atrocities became common. In August, after the United States and the United Nations (U.N.) refused to take action, ECOWAS sent a multinational African peacekeeping force into Liberia. Sawyer flew to Gambia, where he announced a government-in-exile. Doe was murdered in September, and, after four faction leaders proclaimed themselves president, ECOWAS recognized Sawyer and installed him as interim president. For the next four years ceasefire negotiations alternated with outbreaks of war that involved neighboring states. Liberia lay in shambles, with massive numbers of refugees, little economic activity, and terrorism ruling the rural areas. Water, sanitation and electricity were almost nonexistent. Sawyer's authority largely rested on the ECOWAS troops, but stability was finally asserted. In 1994 an all-party transitional government was established to prepare for national elections. Sawyer handed over his authority to a four-person council and announced that he would withdraw from politics and enter business. Soon, however, strife erupted again and Charles TAYLOR took power.

Sawyer returned to the University of Indiana where he has settled into an academic life. In the 2005 elections he supported Ellen JOHNSON-SHIRLEAF.

References: PLBA, RWWA, *wiki.* Sawyer, *Beyond Plunder: Toward Democratic Governance in Liberia* (2005).

SCHNITZER, Eduard Carl Oscar
(Sudan, 1840–1892)

Dr. Eduard Carl Oscar Schnitzer, best known as Emin Pasha, was a German adventurer who helped both British and German authorities extend their influence in Africa. A talented linguist who taught himself Arabic, Turkish and Persian, he was also an acute observer who wrote a large number of articles for German journals on African natural history, geography and culture.

After becoming a physician in Germany, he went to Albania in the medical service of the Ottoman empire. There he took his Turkish name of Mehemet Emin. In 1875 he came to the Sudan, which was then under Egyptian administration, and General "Chinese" GORDON, acting as an agent of the *khedive* of Egypt, appointed him as his medical officer in Equatoria Province in the far south. When Gordon left for his new post as governor-general in 1878, Schnitzer succeeded him as governor of Equatoria, receiving the title of *bey.* Schnitzer completed Gordon's project to eradicate slavery and generally governed wisely and well. He traveled throughout the region, always making surveys and noting cultural and natural features of the territory. He penetrated as far as Uganda, negotiating with King KABAREGA of Bunyoro and exploring neighboring regions.

In 1885, when Khartoum fell to the MAHDI's forces, the Egyptians abandoned the Sudan, and Schnitzer—now promoted to the rank of *pasha*—was abandoned and isolated. He held out for three years until his Sudanese troops mutinied and he was left in an impossible position. A massive expedition was mounted and sent for his relief from the East African coast under the leadership of the explorer Henry Morton STANLEY. Schnitzer was still reluctant to leave his post, but Stanley prevailed, and their force of 1,500 made their way to Bagamoyo in 1889. Schnitzer was then invited by the Germans to make an exploratory expedition inland, but this venture was canceled after the signing of a new treaty between Britain and Germany. Schnitzer set out instead to cross the continent, and in the Belgian Congo (present-day Democratic Republic of the Congo) he was ambushed and murdered by Arab slave traders, who had always considered him their enemy.

References: DAHB, EB, *wiki.* Alphonse Symons, *Emin: Governor of Equatoria* (1950).

SCHREINER, Olive Emilie Albertina
(South Africa, 1855–1920)

Olive Schreiner, a South African of British descent, was a leading feminist and the first important South African novelist.

Born into poverty, Schreiner was largely self-educated and an omnivorous reader. She was forced to support herself as a governess for wealthy Afrikaner farmers, which gave her time to immerse herself in the writings of Herbert Spencer, John Stuart Mill, and Charles Darwin. Unlike many of their English counterparts, Afrikaner women worked alongside Afrikaner men and owned property. Schreiner's friendship with such women influenced the development of her feminist sensibility, which led her to reject stereotyped gender roles and to embrace an image of shared labor.

Schreiner was a woman of powerful intellect and great energy. Her views were not only progressive, but they were also held tenaciously and passionately. Perhaps due to the deep contrasts between these convictions and the beliefs that she had been brought up with, she was subject to depressions that paralleled her enthusiasms in their intensity. In addition, she was affected throughout her life by severe bouts of chronic asthma.

The atmosphere of her evangelical Victorian upbringing was so vivid that she had nightmares of hellfire. Her reading and her rebelliousness combined to lead her on a painful pilgrimage away from her parents' religion and values. At age 15, while in the Griqualand gold fields, she met a Swiss businessman and had a love affair. Following the end of the relationship, Schreiner began to write and quickly completed two novels. Taking her savings, she sailed for England to seek a publisher and to fulfill a lifelong dream of studying medicine.

Schreiner's health was not strong enough for medical studies, but in 1883 her autobiographical novel, *The Story of an African Farm,* was published to general acclaim under the pseudonym Ralph Iron. She began studying the social conditions of women and formed friendships with young socialists. She had a brief affair with Havelock Ellis, the distinguished sexologist, and then an emotionally draining relationship that caused her to despair of heterosexuality. She subsequently had a romance with the poet Amy Levy, who killed herself over it in 1889. Schreiner was ready to return to South Africa in 1891.

Schreiner's brother, William SCHREINER, was at the time attorney general in Cecil RHODES's government, and the author was romantically attracted to the charismatic Rhodes. However, her feelings soon turned to utter disdain and opposition. In 1897 she published *Trooper Peter Halket of Mashonaland,* a bitter attack on Rhodes's militaristic expansion policy and subordination of Africans. In the novel, Christ appears to Peter in a dream and leads him into confessing the atrocities of the English—rape, murder and looting. Schreiner's outraged English friends immediately cut her off. By this time, however, she had found support,

stability and comfort in marriage to a man who shared her views and encouraged her work.

The Boer War devastated Schreiner. Her home was looted, her papers were destroyed, and she was interned for a year for her support of the Afrikaner cause. When she was freed, she reconstructed her lost notes and began in earnest to write her feminist credo, *Women and Labour* (1911). She presented the goal of a time when "new men" and "new women" would create a society of equality in which women would be free to pursue any career. She spent the World War I years in England in declining health. Always controversial, she championed the rights of conscientious objectors. In 1920 she returned to South Africa but died within months.

Her husband wrote her biography and edited her letters, but did a poor job with both. More importantly, he published *Man to Man* (1926), with which she had struggled over for a number of years. It recounts the story of two sisters and their search for self-fulfillment. It is her most ardent fictional statement on justice for women.

References: afr, DAHB, DLB, DNB, EB, LKW, *wiki,* WLTC. Ruth First and Ann Scott. *Olive Schreiner: A Biography* (1990); Gerald Monsman, *Olive Schreiner's Fiction: Landscape and Power* (1991).

SCHREINER, William Philip
(South Africa, 1857–1919)

William Philip Schreiner, a liberal prime minister of Cape Colony, was an early and strong advocate of the voting rights of Africans in South Africa. Born of missionary parents sent to South Africa by the London Missionary Society, he was a brother of novelist and activist Olive SCHREINER. After a brilliant record in law studies in London, he was admitted to the English and Cape bars and made Queen's Counsel in 1892, an honor awarded to the most respected lawyers. He married the sister of the chief justice (and later president) of the Orange Free State.

Schreiner entered the Cape parliament in 1893 and was twice attorney general in Cecil RHODES's government. He broke with Rhodes over the JAMESON Raid scandal (1895) and formed the South Africa Party. Schreiner won the party's first election and was prime minister from 1898 to 1900.

His party fell after factional conflict over the Boer War. Schreiner pursued every effort for peace, serving as a conciliator between the forces and even attempting to make the Cape a neutral area.

Schreiner was a man of peace, a gentleman who believed in and supported the civic virtues. He opposed radicalism, racist appeals and polarization, always speaking out for political moderation. He set the highest standard of probity in the legal profession. His sense of fairness and justice made him a natural ally of racial reform forces.

In 1908, Schreiner was embroiled in the defense of DINUZULU, who was charged with treason after the BAMBATHA rebellion. After a long trial, Dinuzulu was exonerated but was fined and banished for not having opposed the rebels. Schreiner returned to parliament that same year as an independent. There he forcefully supported the non-White franchise for Blacks, Coloureds and Indians. When he was unsuccessful, he led a delegation to London, but to no avail. At the formation of the Union of South Africa in 1910, Louis BOTHA appointed him to a senate seat representing non-Whites where he continued to oppose discriminatory legislation.

In 1914, Schreiner was appointed high commissioner to Great Britain, where he died, partly as a result of exhaustion from overwork during World War I.

References: DAHB, DNB. Eric Walker, *W.P. Schreiner: A South African* (1937).

SCHWEITZER, Albert
(Gabon, 1875–1965)

Dr. Albert Schweitzer was the preeminent Christian medical missionary in Africa, a towering figure in twentieth-century Protestant thought and philosophy, and a renowned musician. Although his reputation has been somewhat eclipsed since the end of the colonial period, during his lifetime Schweitzer was one of the most respected and honored personalities in the world. In 1952 he received the Nobel Peace Prize for being an exemplar of the "Brotherhood of Nations."

Schweitzer, born in Alsace under German governance, was the son of a Reformed pastor. After studies at the University of Strasbourg, where he received doctorates in both philosophy and theology, he became pastor of Strasbourg's St. Nicholas

Church. He had interspersed his academic work with study of the organ and was simultaneously appointed organist of the Bach Society of Paris.

In 1905 he published *J.S. Bach: The Musician-Poet,* in which he presented Bach as a religious mystic whose music was an entry point to understanding nature's cosmic forces. Schweitzer's reputation as a foremost interpreter of Bach was strengthened, and the book was an immediate success. The following year he published *The Quest of the Historical Jesus,* which established Schweitzer as a world figure in theology and which has been a benchmark in modern biblical theology ever since. In addition, Schweitzer was a popular, witty and charismatic preacher with a devoted following.

During this period, Schweitzer was evolving what was to become the dominant theme of his life and thought—"reverence for life"—an ethical norm that he extended to all life and all social forms, including civilization itself. In 1905 his thinking culminated in a religious conversion that turned him away from worldly success toward a life of Christian service. Along with his teaching and preaching, he began studying to become a medical missionary and to live out what had become his dominant philosophy. Subsequently, he met Hélène Bresslau, an artist and musician who gave up her career to become a nurse and join him. They married in 1911, a year before Schweitzer took his MD. In 1913 they departed for Gabon, in what was then French Equatorial Africa, sponsored by the Paris Evangelical Mission Society.

The Schweitzers built a hospital at Lambaréné, working alongside African laborers. In 1917 and 1918 they were interned in France because of their German background, and they remained there until 1924. Schweitzer used the period for reflection, publishing the first volume of his *Philosophy of Civilization* in 1923. In this work, he offered a complete statement of his ethic on reverence for life. It argued that all forms of life contain a force that impels them toward their completeness or perfection—the glory of creation. This ethic of life imposes a duty on humanity, whose striving is conscious, to enter into the lives of other, lower forms. Schweitzer sums up: "To him all life as such is sacred. He shatters no ice crystal that sparkles in the sun, tears no leaf from its tree, breaks no flower, and is careful not to crush any insect as he walks."

In 1924, by then fully grounded in his approach to his mission, Schweitzer returned to Lambaréné, to find that his hospital had decayed and had been partially reclaimed by the jungle. He rebuilt several miles upstream on the Ogowe River. The hospital's hallmark was simplicity, and Schweitzer became an early advocate of what would later be called appropriate technology. The hospital operated in what Schweitzer perceived as a style suitable for an African setting. He avoided a Western atmosphere, which he felt only separated Africans from medical care and reinforced the power of local priests and traditional healers. Families were encouraged to live with the patients, who were housed in a number of small structures built around the hospital. Relatives prepared the meals, often keeping goats and other small animals to provide milk or meat.

At its height, there were 350 patients (plus relatives), as well as 150 patients in a leper colony built a few years after the hospital. There were 30 to 40 White doctors as well as nurses and African workers. Schweitzer supported this staff from his own income, which he supplemented by highly successful Bach recordings and organ recitals in Europe. Benefactors, including the Mellon family and the Unitarian-Universalist Church, also supported the hospital. Amidst all the activity at Lambaréné, Schweitzer continued editing Bach's organ works and wrote several books on theology.

Schweitzer's approach was autocratic and paternalistic, and he had a low expectation of Africans' intellectual capability. Nevertheless, he always showed respect for both workers and patients and was beloved by many. He held that "ethics are pity," and he seemed to have no illusions about the equality of traditional and Western civilizations. His biblical model came from the parable of Lazarus and the rich man (Luke 19:16–31). Schweitzer saw himself as the rich man at the table, obligated to share with the poor beggar what he had. He criticized the exploitation of Africans but primarily because he saw it as a sign of the civilized West's moral failure rather than because of an inherent sense of injustice.

Schweitzer has become a symbol of altruism and self-sacrificing dedication to the poorest and the suffering. He was awarded the Nobel Peace Prize in 1952. Yet, Africans rarely share this awe. The writer and diplomat Conor Cruise O'Brien argued that he stood for "the most irritating, if not the most noxious, aspects of the White man in Africa: paternalism, condescension, resistance to change." The African intellectual Davidson NICOL accused him of equating Africans "with insects as two

inferior forms of life which must nonetheless be 'respected,' since *all* life is sacred."

Schweitzer's reverence for life was not absolute and did not include the concept of "rights." He was convinced of the Darwinist principle of natural selection and conceded that people kill that which threatens them. One can kill either mercifully or ruthlessly, but mercy must always be chosen, he believed. This was an ethic for the superior, benevolent protector of the inferior. When, in the 1950s, Schweitzer opposed nuclear testing, it was because of its effects on plant and animal life, not in opposition to the use of nuclear weapons, if that should be necessary. His viewpoint was a colonial perspective, which was both refined and paternalistic. Schweitzer died in Lambaréné while still active and is buried there. He left instructions that the hospital be modernized, and his daughter has continued his work.

References: dacb, DAHB, EB, EWB, *wiki*. Norman Cousins, *Albert Schweitzer's Mission: Healing and Peace* (1985); *Le Grand Blanc de Lambaréné* (*The Great White Man of Lambarene*, film, 1995); James Brabazon, *Albert Schweitzer: a Biography* (1976).

SEMBÈNE, Ousmane
(Sénégal, 1923–)

Ousmane Sembène is best known as the foremost African film director, but he is also a significant novelist and writer. He balances the role of revered elder of African cinema with that of youthful innovator. Combining experience and creativity into increasingly complex works has brought Sembène to the forefront of international filmmakers, one of the few Africans to be accorded that level of recognition.

Sembène was born and raised in the fractious and secessionist province of Casamance, and his early life reflected the tensions, separatism and antiauthoritarianism of that district. Raised by a devout Muslim uncle who lost his teaching post in a dispute with a colonial administrator, Sembène went to Dakar upon his uncle's death. As a teenager in the capital, he joined the fringes of the urban cultural scene. In one form or another his marginality would be a major element in his creative evolution, linking him to the Sénégalese adaptation of African tradition and modernity. He absorbed much of this cultural mélange from griots and musicians, but also by returning to his religious roots. Islam in Sénégal has always revolved about the Muslim brotherhoods that emphasize mystical union with Allah, and at age 17, Sembène returned to the practice of Islam after a profound mystical experience.

In Dakar, Sembène also studied for the French colonial service, but his rebellious nature brought swift expulsion. By rights a French citizen, the young Sembène soon learned the limitations of that status for an African. This understanding expanded his political consciousness, which would influence all his literary and cinematic work. An enthusiastic admirer of General Charles de Gaulle, who organized his Free French Resistance in French West Africa, Sembène volunteered for the army and served in Italy, France and Germany, primarily as a dockworker. When he was discharged with a bad conduct record, he returned to Dakar to enter trade union activities, which at that time formed the nucleus of African political life. He was much affected by the bitter 1947–1948 railroad strike, which was a turning point in anticolonial African resistance in French West Africa. From 1950 to 1960 Sembène was a member of the Communist Party.

From his dock experience came an autobiographical novel, *The Black Docker* (1956). Soon after publication, a spinal injury forced Sembène to give up manual labor, and his initial success as an author led him to follow a career in writing. In 1957 he followed with *O My Country, My Beautiful People!*, the story of the rejection of a young African who returns home from France with a White wife and ideas of change. It was well received in Europe, and Sembène traveled widely there and also in Vietnam and China.

In 1960, Sembène published *God's Bits of Wood*, a sweeping epic of the railroad strike. It established his reputation, was translated into a number of languages, and intensified Sembène's literary output. In 1962 he followed this novel with a collection of short fiction, *Voltaïque*, a trilogy, *Harmattan*, and two novellas (1965), which won the literature prize of the Dakar Festival of Black Arts.

Sembène was recognized as the leading writer of the post-*Négritude* generation. He consciously stood aside from that movement, regarding it as romantic. Nevertheless, he was still struggling with his own cultural identity. He wrote in French, saying, "I could have written in Wolof, but who would have read it?" Sembène wrestled with a situation in which the interpretation of the Black experience was dominated by African-American and Caribbean writers. He was conscious that his main audience was not African but European.

The dichotomy between writing and life brought Sembène to seek another medium that would give him immediacy in speaking to the ordinary African. He spent 1962 in the Soviet Union at the Moscow Film School and as an intern with Gorki Studios. In 1963, Sembène produced his first picture, a 19–minute short film on the life of a Dakar cart driver. *Borom Sarret* established Sembène's cinematic approach—the use of amateur actors only, a *cinéma verité* style, and the integration of personal and political themes. *Borom Sarret* has been described as "one of the most accomplished shorts in African cinema."

In 1966, Sembène released his first full-length film, *Black Girl*, acknowledged as the first major African film. It is the account of an African woman degraded by her work as a house servant in France and driven to suicide. Its biting social criticism was not lost on the African postcolonial elites, whose treatment of servants was often as demeaning. Sembène's criticism of the colonial French officials and settlers parallels that of the neocolonial elites who succeeded them at independence. *Black Girl* established a pattern he would follow in almost all of his later work: developing a screenplay from one of his works of fiction (or sometimes vice versa). *Black Girl* originated in a short story Sembène wrote for *Présence Africaine*.

These first films established Sembène's reputation as a filmmaker, and in 1967 he was named a juror at the Cannes and Moscow film festivals. The French Ministry of Culture supported his next film, enabling him to do a feature in color. *Mandabi*, the resulting work, was Sembène's first comedy and helped cement his reputation. There were both French and Wolof versions, and the film was a commercial success. *Emitai* (1971), an anticolonial film that alienated the French government, resulted in censorship by the Sénégalese authorities and a limited audience. Sembène then returned to comedy in *Xala* (1974), which was simultaneously released as a novel.

In *Xala* (Wolof for "impotence") the lampoons a pompous bureaucrat who has prospered by catering to the corrupt ruling elite. Alternately hilarious and devastating in its portrayal of those whom Sembène scorns as "the deformed children of imperialism, the cultural bastards," the film reduces its protagonist to the humiliation of sexual impotence. He bears the ironic title "El Hadji" as one who has made the pilgrimage to Mecca, but he nonetheless is forced to turn to witch doctors in his desperation. After the president's personal *marabout* (Islamic teacher) fails, El Hadji goes from one healer to another until, desperate and penniless, he is cornered by a mob that includes the man who placed the *xala* curse upon him. The film closes as El Hadji submits himself to final debasement at the hands of beggars and cripples. *Xala* is a parable of the powerlessness of post-independence Africa, degraded and shamed.

Cultural dissonance is a theme to which Sembène returns regularly. He has been honest enough to face this in himself, and in *Ceddo* (1977), Sembène explores the depersonalization of Africans by Islam and the complicity of Islamic slavers in the slave trade. Sembène played a bit part as a reluctant convert and even shaved his head for the role. In Muslim Sénégal, the film was banned and has rarely been seen anywhere in Africa. Sembène's exposé of colonialism, *The Camp at Thiaroye* (1990), highlights the contradictions between French values and practice as well as the depravity of colonialism. In *Guelwaar* (1993) the plot explores village tensions that are revealed when it is discovered that a Catholic man has accidentally been buried in a Muslim cemetery. After 2000, Sembène has done several films for television. *Moolaadé* (2004), which deals with the sensitive topic of female genital mutilation, won an award at both the Cannes Film Festival and FESPACO, the main African film festival.

Sembène is a tall, imposing man, usually puffing his trademark pipe. In 1974 he married an American student of his work, and they live in Dakar with their son. He has no illusions about his own place in African culture; he has said, "There used to be griots, now there are filmmakers."

References: adb, afr, AA, CA, CB, DAHB, MBW, NRG, *wiki*, WLTC. Françoise Pfaff, *The Cinema of Ousmane Sembène* (1984); Samba Gadjigo, *Ousmane Sembène: The Life of a Revolutionary Artist* (2005).

SEME, Pixley ka Izaka
(South Africa, 1880?–1951)

Pixley ka Izaka Seme, one of the first Black South Africans admitted to the legal profession, was the moving spirit behind the African National Congress (ANC) and served as its president from 1930 to 1936. For 25 years he was also the leading African journalist, editing the first national newspaper for Blacks, *Abantu-Batho*.

Seme studied in the United States, where he graduated from Columbia University and came in contact with the ideas of Black leader and educator Booker T. Washington, whom he admired. After law studies at Oxford University, he returned to Johannesburg. The formation of the Union of South Africa in 1910 jolted him into a broader political consciousness. Racial separation was enshrined in the law, and Seme, a Zulu nationalist, began to think in wider, national terms.

In 1910, he established *Abantu-Batho,* a newspaper published in English, Zulu, Xhosa and Sotho. He also helped start up a national farmers' association that owed much to the ideas of Washington; it fostered agricultural training of peasants while serving as a forum for presenting their needs to the government. In 1912, Seme was one of the founders of the South African Native National Congress, which was later renamed the African National Congress (ANC) in 1923. John DUBE was its first president, and Seme was elected treasurer. In 1928, Columbia University awarded Seme an honorary doctorate that provided him with prestige which he used to be elected president of the ANC.

Cautious and conservative, he did little to develop the ANC, and it declined during his presidency. He did not have a collegial style of leadership and opposed more radical African groups, such as Clements KADALIE's Industrial and Commercial Union (ICU). When he was voted out of office in 1936, *Abantu-Batho* also folded, and Seme returned to legal practice. However, he remained active in the ANC until his death.

References: DAHB, MMA. Richard Rive, *Seme: The Founder of the ANC* (1992).

SENGHOR, Léopold Sédar
(Sénégal, 1906–2001)

Léopold Sédar Senghor, father of Sénégalese independence and the country's first president, is also one of the leading French poets of the twentieth century and the founder and guiding spirit of the

Léopold Sédar Senghor

literary movement called *Négritude.* His lyricism, nourished by sources in the oral tradition of Africa, owes something as well to European verse, especially that of Paul Claudel and Saint-John Perse. Senghor's life was dedicated to promoting a synthesis between African culture and European humanism toward a "universal civilization." Because the first forms of nationalism are often literary, Senghor moved successfully from the poetry to the politics of independence. Also a unifying agent politically, he fought for the federation of French West Africa.

Senghor was an unlikely leader for Sénégal. He was a Catholic from the Serer ethnic group of the interior, while the country was dominated by the Muslim Wolof and the educated *assimilés* of the coastal towns. The four coastal communes were legally part of metropolitan France, and their residents were citizens with representation in Paris. Senghor's family were mere subjects. His father was a prosperous trader, however, and at eight, Senghor was sent to a mission school, where he learned French and Latin.

The acculturation was thorough. Senghor would later say that he only realized he was African when he went to France, and that he would resolve the personal conflict between African culture and modern life by what he called a "conciliatory agreement." For his French teachers, however, the goal was assimilation, and they fostered the young Senghor's gifts. At age 16 he entered a seminary in Dakar, where he was steeped in scholastic philosophy. Attracted by Thomas Aquinas's synthesis of Arab, Greek and Christian thought, he flourished intellectually, but his strong temperament ran afoul

of the rector, who thought all Africans "savage." After a confrontation, Senghor was dismissed—to his profound shock—and entered the local *lycée* (high school) as the only African student. Here he won all the prizes, excelling in Greek, and gained a coveted scholarship to Paris. With this achievement, Senghor began his second uprooting.

Senghor spent 1928–1929 at the Lycée Louis-le-Grand to prepare for the university entrance exams. His closest friends were Georges Pompidou, later president of France, and Thierry Maulnier, later a member of the Académie Français. In that secular republican atmosphere, Senghor was a devout Catholic and a fervent monarchist. He was an equally passionate student, taking his licentiate in 1931 and becoming the first Black to receive the French postdoctoral degree, the *aggregé,* in 1935. He completed his assimilation by taking French citizenship and being conscripted into the army. He then taught in several *lycées* until World War II, when he spent two years in German prison camps before returning to France to teach and work in the resistance movement.

The postwar period saw the fruition of Senghor's intellectual development. As complete as his assimilation might have appeared on the surface, it was tempered and then challenged by a rising awareness of his African roots. Besides Pompidou and Thierry Maulnier, he had become friends with the radical Afro-Caribbean intellectual Aimé Césaire. The Depression caused Senghor to lose many of his illusions about France. During this period of despair, Senghor experienced—as if for the first time—the squalor of Paris, the oppression of its proletariat, and the arrogance of its individualism. Incapable of bitterness or rejection, he looked for a reconciling element and found it in a rediscovery of his Blackness. He later called it "discovering Africa in France," reclaiming his "childhood kingdom," feeling his "pagan sap which prances and dances." This heady mix of Black consciousness and French culture began to take shape in verse, in philosophical reflection, and in long conversations with expatriate friends.

There was a close circle of Blacks, including Senghor's pupil, the gifted poet David DIOP; Alioune DIOP, with whom Senghor founded *Présence Africaine* in 1947; and the West Indians Paulette Nadal and Césaire. The circle also included diaspora Blacks, such as the American writers Langston Hughes and Countee Cullen, and the Guyanan intellectual Léon Damas. What arose from their collaboration, thought and writing was the literary movement known as *Négritude*. *Négritude*, Senghor has said, "is the sum total of the values of the civilization of the African world. It is not racialism; it is culture." Senghor always saw his theory as a contribution to a universal civilization. The contribution is in Africa's uniqueness—the rhythms and song styles of its oral literature and the auditory sense of its poetry, but also its social values of communalism, traditionalism, earthiness and religious faith. Senghor sought out newer writers and thinkers and became their mentor and support. He emerged as a major influence in the development of African intellectual life. Perhaps the greatest single work to this end was the 1948 publication of his *Anthologie de la Nouvelle Poésie Nègre et Malgache de Langue Française* (*Anthology of New Black and Malagache Poetry in French*). In it he introduced David Diop and other unknown African poets to the literary world. His efforts were not, however, without opposition. Gabriel d'ARBOUSSIER, the Sénégalese intellectual and diplomat, called *Négritude* "mystification" that ignored the class struggle. Others called it elitist and out of touch with the African masses. And of course, Senghor was reproached for writing in French, the language of colonial oppression.

Senghor's own writing was at the heart of the movement, fusing surrealist and mystical influences from such diverse sources as Paul Claudel and Walt Whitman with African motifs and song styles. Essentially a lyric poet, he often used *woman* as a symbol for Mother Africa. He could be bitter in approaching Africa's history or gentle in his love poetry. His first book, *Chants d'Ombre* (*Shadow-Songs*, 1945) was followed by a number of others. Perhaps the most acclaimed was *Éthiopiques* (1956), in which he struggled with his dual African and French allegiances. It includes "Chaka," a poetic version of Thomas MOFOLO's novel, in which Senghor tested his theories of the unity of poetry, dance and music—which he saw as the core of African art. In 1983, Senghor was elected to the Académie Française, but the Nobel Prize for Literature eluded him.

During his presidency, Senghor not only continued his own writing, but became a patron of the arts in general. Painters, choreographers, muralists and sculptors flourished with government support, extending the spirit of Pan-Africanism and *Négritude* far beyond literature. The 1966 World Festival of Black Arts made Dakar the premier center for post-independence art for a generation.

Another aspect of Senghor's formation in Paris also came to fruition in the postwar years. His Parisian guardian as a youth was Blaise DIAGNE, the first African deputy in the national assembly. Gatherings at his sponsor's home were Senghor's first introduction to politics, both French and African. As a result, Senghor and his colleagues gradually evolved a theory of African socialism, neither capitalist nor Marxist, that was the political and economic expression of *Négritude*.

In 1946, the same year that his first book of poetry appeared, Senghor was offered a place on Lamine GUÈYE's ticket to represent upcountry Sénégal, and he was elected to the French national assembly, where he remained for 10 years. He also sat in on the constituent assemblies that established the Fourth Republic, France's new constitutional government after World War II. He embraced the politics of the peasantry, strongly affirming the values of village life. For him, this was the Africa of *Négritude*. Soon Senghor parted company with Guèye, rejecting his dependence on the urban elites, and built a powerful following in the rural areas. His new political party swept the Sénégalese elections of 1951 and 1952. International acclaim followed his national recognition; Senghor served in the French cabinet (1955–1956), was involved in the Council of Europe, and took part in the formation of the French Community.

The major contest of the 1950s concerned the future of French West Africa, and it became Senghor's greatest political defeat. He was strongly committed to regional unity and campaigned against de Gaulle's 1957 proposal to allow for immediate and complete independence from France. Senghor committed a tactical error by boycotting a conference to form a regional party, fearing that it would be dominated by Communists, and he was outflanked by Félix HOUPHOUËT-BOIGNY of Côte d'Ivoire, who opposed regional union. From that point, Senghor fought a losing battle against dismemberment of the West African Federation. He supported (and was president of) the ill-fated Mali Federation, from which Mali soon disengaged. With the collapse of his federalist dream, Senghor became Sénégal's first president in 1960, which he remained until retiring from politics in 1980. He continued his efforts for Pan-Africanism as a founder of the Organization of African Unity (OAU) and the Economic Community of West African States

(ECOWAS) and with strong support of the French Community and various regional development compacts.

Until 1974, Senghor ruled through a one-party system, but after that time he gradually began to permit multiparty democracy. He survived several attempted coups, usually absorbing the organized opposition afterward. The most difficult standoff came in 1962 after his removal of Mamadou DIA, his prime minister. Dia's army and Senghor's paratroops faced off, but Senghor won the day and took total control of the country. The national assembly and a referendum confirmed his authority. In 1970 he cautiously reestablished the prime minister's position, filling it with Abdou DIOUF, and in 1978 he permitted Abdoulaye WADE to challenge him in the presidential elections. When he retired he became the first African president to do so freely. He was succeeded by Diouf, whom he had groomed for the job.

Senghor's impact has been considerable, and it continues. His political philosophy is matched in Africa only by that of Julius NYERERE in its intellectual depth. Younger African critics have attacked *Négritude* as a compromise with neocolonialism, a refusal to complete the decolonization of the African mind. The philosopher V. Y. MUDIMBE calls him the "myth that is endlessly discussed."

References: AA, AB, *afr*, CA, CB, DAHB, DRWW, EB, EWB, HWL, MBW, NRG, PLBA, PLCA, *wiki*, WLTC. Senghor, *Ce Que Je crois* (*What I Believe*, 1988); Janet Vaillant, *Black, French, and African* (1990); Elisabeth Harney, *In Senghor's Shadow* (2004).

SEXWALE, Mosima Gabriel "Tokyo"
(South Africa, 1953–)

Tokyo Sexwale is a prominent businessman in South Africa and a former antiapartheid campaigner who was imprisoned for his activism.

Sexwale was raised in the Black slums of Soweto, and joined the Black Consciousness Movement (BCM) as a teenager. After graduating from high school, he joined the African National Congress' (ANC) guerilla wing and was sent to Swaziland. He took up further studies there and then went to the Soviet Union for military officer's training. On his return in 1976, he was captured during an engagement with South African forces. In 1977 he was sentenced to Robben Island for treason and spent 13 years there before he was released.

By 1990, when Sexwale returned to Johannesburg, the ANC had been legalized, and he took up a post at the ANC central office. In the elections of 1994, Nelson MANDELA (a companion on Robben Island) named Sexwale premier of Gauteng Province, which included Pretoria, the capital. He served until 1998, having settled conflicts in the townships and bringing a measure of security to the city and province. He braved the men's hostels in the East Rand's violent no-go areas, and brought the miners over to his side. The daily death toll of 20 dwindled into single digits. After 1998, he did not re-enter elective politics, although many consider him the leading rival of Cyril RAMAPHOSA to succeed Thabo MBEKI when Mbeki steps down in 2009. Sexwale has upstaged the president in public appearances, and once commented, "The president's shoes are huge and Thabo has small feet."

Sexwale is a charismatic campaigner with a populist message. He helped secure South Africa's bid to host the World Cup in 2010 and launched the country's Grand Prix auto racing team. He argues for an inclusive South Africa: "If Blacks get hurt, I get hurt. If Whites get hurt, that's my wife, and if you harm Coloured people, you're looking for my children. Your unity embodies who I am."

Sexwale's later activity has been as a successful businessman in mining, diamonds and oil. His holding company is one of the largest Black-owned companies in the country. He has been particularly successful in the diamond trade. Even Harry OPPENHEIMER praised his competence in diamonds, where he has forged strong ties to Russian conglomerates. His company is the third-largest in South Africa. He also chairs the boards of a bank, an electronics company and a gold mining corporation. He is estimated to be worth £130 million ($227 million). Sexwale knows how to use the government's Black empowerment policy, but has never accepted any grants. Needless to say, his meteoric rise to wealth in seven years has earned him enemies and critics. He argues in reply that his trusts benefit many poor people—1,000 former political prisoners and 60,000 former ANC fighters are stakeholders.

Reference: wiki.

SHABALALA, Joseph
(South Africa, 1940?–)

Joseph Shabalala is inseparable from the group he created and crafted into a major South African musical presence, Ladysmith Black Mambazo. The bestselling recording group in South Africa, they have also become popular figures in the United States.

Ladysmith's 10 members (seven basses and three tenors) sing *a capella* in a Zulu harmonic style known as *iscathamiya,* or tiptoeing. It was born in the all-male hostels that house migrant workers in industrial centers and is a fusion of stomp dancing (the Zulu *ingoma),* traditional music and gospel. Dramatic effect is created through contrasts and swelling volume, with highly controlled tone modulation. Zulu is a tonal language in which changes of pitch change meaning, and it uses "click" sounds found only in a few African languages. These and other elements have shaped Ladysmith's sound. *Iscathamiya* is a variant of the *mbaqanga* sound ("township jive") that has emerged from the Black townships around Johannesburg. The albums *Inala* (1986) and *Shaka Zulu* (1987) showcase Ladysmith's best work.

In 1986, Ladysmith Black Mambazo took part in Paul Simon's Graceland Concert, the first major South African performance by Black and White artists in many years. Two of their songs appeared on the album, and after touring with Simon, Ladysmith shared the Grammy Award in 1987 for the album. Since then, Ladysmith has appeared on American television and in 1993 made its debut on Broadway in *The Song of Jacob Zulu*. Ladysmith now tours regularly in the United States.

Joseph Shabalala is the autocratic master of Ladysmith, and its soul. Convinced that angels have revealed Ladysmith's style to him in dreams, he is the perfectionist master of every tone, every movement. When Ladysmith was barred from hostel competitions in 1972 (because they always won), Shabalala decided to take the risky move of turning professional. Within a year Ladysmith was singing full-time. In 1981 Shabalala became a priest in his sect, the Church of God of the Prophets. He feels that the spirit of God communicates directly to him.

Primarily a gospel group, Ladysmith Black Mambazo avoided overt political statements when apartheid was still in force, causing some to regard the members as collaborators with apartheid. Many of its lyrics, however, concerning daily life in the homelands among migrant laborers and in the mines, convey social criticism. Shabalala's political reticence was breached when he was approached to do a musical about his cousin, a young Black activist who was murdered by a South African security guard. Shabalala describes *Jacob Zulu* as a musical about how "a kid who wanted to stay away from politics has been brought step by step, inevitably, to become a terrorist." Shabalala was further influenced by the murder of his brother (and Ladysmith bass), Headman Shabalala, in 1991. Further violent tragedy struck when his wife was shot dead outside their home in 2002. Joseph was wounded in the attack. His next album, *Raise Your Spirit Higher*, was a tribute to his wife.

Ladysmith Black Mambazo has avoided ethnic partisanship and remains aloof from the Zulu political movement that is influential in the hostels. Ladysmith sings in Xhosa, Sotho and English, as well as in their native Zulu.

References: CM, DMM, GEPM, WAM, *wiki.* *On Tip Toe: Gentle Steps to Freedom* (film, 2000); *Ladysmith Black Mambazo* (video, 1990)

SHAGARI, Shehu Usman Aliyu
(Nigeria, 1924–)

Alhaji Shehu Usman Aliyu Shagari was an important government figure in the first Nigerian republic and executive president during the second. A man of intelligence and integrity, he was unable to control the economic and political forces gripping his country.

Shagari was one of the first Nigerian leaders to come from the Muslim north. He was educated to be a teacher and taught science from 1945 to 1950 before serving as a headmaster from 1951 to 1954. He organized a cultural society in 1949, which in 1951 became the Northern People's Congress, one of three major parties in the period before independence. He was elected to the House of Representatives in 1954 and in 1958 was appointed parliamentary secretary to Sir Abubakar Tafawa BALEWA, who became his political mentor. After independence (1960), Shagari was named to the cabinet, and until the Balewa government was toppled by a military coup in 1966, he held a series of ministerial posts. He was a tireless and competent administrator and was responsible for upgrading the civil service, instituting prison reform, and planning for Niger River hydroelectric development. After the coup he retired to his farm but shifted his interests to community service. He established an educational development fund that built more than a hundred schools.

The government of General Yakubu GOWON called on Shagari to represent it abroad during the Biafran civil war, which he did in Switzerland, France and Italy. In 1970 he was invited to Lagos to take charge of the postwar national relief and rebuilding program. The following year he replaced Chief Obafemi AWOLOWO as federal commissioner of finance. He stayed in that position until being forced out after the 1976 coup led by General Murtala MUHAMMED. The new government, however, appointed him chairman of Peugeot Automobile, where he tripled the output of its Kaduna factory and instituted new training programs for technical workers. Shagari's reputation for honesty, diligence and loyalty to the country made him an unthreatening and competent choice for administrative positions regardless of the group in power. When General Olusegun OBASANJO announced his intent to return Nigeria to civilian control, Shagari was appointed to the constitutional committee.

Shagari was one of five candidates to run for the presidency, and his National Party of Nigeria had the support of much of the educated elite, businessmen and military. In the 1979 elections he received a plurality of votes over Awolowo and formed a coalition with Dr. Benjamin Nnamdi AZIKIWE. He had hoped for a union government, but Awolowo resisted.

Shagari had to contend with serious problems, beginning with a major scandal in the oil industry, which showed a US$4.76 billion shortfall in assets. Shagari suspended the board of the National Petroleum Company but could not combat the underlying corruption that permeated the government and its many parastatal (government-owned) corporations. Shagari embarked on an ambitious agricultural development program and followed a liberal economic policy favoring business growth. The collapse of the world oil market in 1982, however, made his programs unworkable and led to a national crisis. Nevertheless, Shagari was re-elected in 1983,

despite accusations of ballot tampering. Religious and political violence escalated to intolerable levels.

Later that year, the military, led by Major-General Muhammadu BUHARI, ousted Shagari in a bloodless coup. He was held in detention until 1986 and then released by General Ibrahim BABANGIDA when no evidence of personal wrongdoing could be found. He was banned for life from ever holding public office but remains a respected figure throughout the country.

References: CB, DAHB, DRWW, PLBA, RWWA, *wiki.* David Williams, *President and Power in Nigeria* (1982).

SHAKA
(South Africa, 1787?–1828)

Chief Shaka forged a new nation out of an assortment of Nguni clans and made this Zulu people one of the greatest powers of Africa in his time. The social upheavals he generated have marked southern Africa since. Both a famous conqueror and a hard and unfeeling despot, Shaka was a brilliant military tactician and an organizational genius. This dramatic combination has made him one of the most romantic and heroic figures in African history.

Shaka, the son of a minor chief, was raised among his mother's people, the Langeni, because his parents, belonging to closely related subclans, had violated customary law with their relationship. His mother, NANDI, was despised and finally driven away, and so they settled among the Mtetwa. When he was 23, Shaka's age group was called up for military service by DINGISWAYO, a great Mtetwa war chief. After Shaka had served with distinction for six years, his father died, and with Dingiswayo's help, Shaka seized the vacant position of Zulu chief. When Shaka took them over in 1816, the Zulu were the smallest of the numerous Nguni communities, with fewer than 1,500 members. He immediately murdered most of his relatives to avoid dynastic feuds of the chieftaincy, and took absolute command.

Shaka began by reorganizing the weak Zulu warriors into a formidable fighting force. He trained his warriors to run barefoot over thorns to toughen their feet, and those who hesitated were killed on the spot. His troops could cover 50 miles (about 80 kilometers) in a day and still be able to fight. Shaka ordered the men to discard their light throwing

Shaka

spears and substituted the *assagai,* a short stabbing spear that forced the warriors to fight at close quarters. Each received a toughened, full-length cowhide shield that was capable of turning aside the light spears used by other peoples. The army was organized into *impi* (regiments) based on age groups that lived together in separate stockaded villages, segregated from the rest of society. Only members of the bravest regiments were allowed to marry. Shaka thus built a powerful bond and death-defying loyalty among his troops.

Shaka developed standardized tactics that he used to devastating effect. The army attacked in a formation called the buffalo, with the most seasoned warriors in the frontal assault ("the chest") and two "horns" of younger, faster men encircling the enemy. The reserve ("the loins") could be thrown into the battle at any point. Because the shields

could catch thrown spears, the army formation often closed upon almost defenseless enemies, who were slaughtered. Shaka killed as many of his enemies as possible to prevent any regrouping and to destabilize their communities. The remnants of the defeated were integrated into the Zulu nation, with the result that within a few years, Shaka had a fighting force of 60,000 men and 10,000 women.

He first conquered the neighboring clans and then sought out the Langeni for revenge. He chose those who had humiliated him as a youth and impaled them on long stakes so that they would die in slow agony. This torture became his favored form of execution for sexual infractions, especially adultery. Shaka's methods instilled fear into his opponents, and when Dingiswayo was murdered around 1818, he was able to make himself paramount chief. He defeated his major rivals and in a series of campaigns destroyed the network of clans throughout the region. By 1823 present-day Natal was depopulated by the constant strife. Extended families and clan structures were obliterated, and the people had no choice but to turn their loyalties toward the new Zulu nation, which helped to establish a powerful sense of unity. Kings and chiefs, including such prominent figures as MOSHWESHWE of Lesotho and SOBHUZA of the Swazi, paid tribute to Shaka.

Shaka's ruthless expansion had a widespread ripple effect. Clans fled at his advance, and community fragments became marauding bands, until much of southern Africa was destabilized by the outward thrust of migration and conflict. Some able tributary chiefs, such as MZILIKAZI, took whole tribes on nomadic treks into central Africa, where Shaka's military techniques were used to disrupt the region. The intricate clan structures of the interior were broken up in a movement known as the *difaqane* or *mfecane,* "the crushing," which caused some two million deaths. One side effect of Shaka's emptying of Natal was that it remained open for White settlement, which he did not discourage.

Shaka came under the influence of sorcerers soon after taking over his father's throne, and his paranoia and cruelty increased with the years. Executions became more common and were often meted out less for failures than to instill terror. He refused to marry and wanted no heir, and when one of his concubines presented him with a son, he smashed the baby's head. When his mother died in 1827, he killed thousands "in sympathy," including pregnant women and their husbands. He forbade milk—a Zulu staple—and even killed milk cows so that their calves would know what it was to lose a mother. After an exhausting campaign in 1828, Shaka refused the *impi* any rest due to some minor transgression and sent them on another campaign to Mozambique. Weakened by disease, they were defeated. In the aftermath, Shaka's half-brother DINGANE—one of a few relatives he had not killed—stabbed him to death. At his death, Shaka's empire included about 250,000 people. The Zulu nation remained a powerful element in southern Africa until its defeat by the British in 1879. The Zulu have remained a united people and an important factor in modern South African politics.

References: AB, *afr*, AH, CWAH, DAHB, EB, EWB, MMA, WGMC, *wiki*. Donald Morris, *The Washing of the Spears* (1966); Diane Stanley, *Shaka, King of the Zulus* (1988) [young adult].

SHONIBARE, Yinka
(Nigeria, 1962–)

Yinka Shonibare, born in London of Nigerian parents and raised in Nigeria from the age of three, is a prominent African artist with an international following.

After a comfortable but strict education in Nigeria, Shonibare returned to London to study at the Byam Shaw School of Art from 1984 to 1989. He later studied at Goldsmith's College. When a teacher suggested he work from traditional African art, he had to go to the British Museum to see what he meant. "None of my English friends were being asked to make traditional English art and I resented the implications. It taught me to question stereotypes."

In 1997, he burst into public consciousness at the Young British Artists' Show, "Sensation." The theme of the show was the role of art in redefining the nature of British identity. Shonibare used antique Victorian dresses made from African fabrics to confront and reverse the colonizer/colonized experience of the English and their former subjects. He also teased British society about its own gradual absorption of colonized cultures into its emerging multicultural scene. He played with the ambivalence of interactions between the "mother country" and its many "children," with wit and irony, yet not without empathy. His pieces show humor and clever juxtapositions of upper-class society and immigrant

sensibilities. In a video performance, *Diary of a Victorian Dandy* (1998), Shonibare plays on the themes of Oscar Wilde's "The Picture of Dorian Gray," with its Victorian (im)morality. He can also poke fun at Black consciousness, as in his *Afro-Alien Disfunctional Family* (1999). "Art is better than life; you can construct your own history, your own fantasy within a range of artifices." One of Shonibare's interests is the use of the Dutch wax method of batik on cotton cloth. Created by Dutch colonizers in Indonesia and taken up by British cloth manufacturers, it became popular in west Africa. Today it has become a signifier of African cultural identity, and Shonibare comments, "It's the fallacy of that signification that I like. It's the way I view culture—it's an artificial construct."

Shonibare was shortlisted for the Turner Prize in 2003 for "Double Dutch," an exhibition in Rotterdam with works begun in 1994, and his work from the "Africa Remix" exhibit in London.

References: adb, wiki.

SHUTTLEWORTH, Mark
(South Africa, 1973–)

Mark Shuttleworth is an Internet entrepreneur who has parlayed his business success into personal adventure. He was the second space tourist and the first African citizen in space in 2002.

Shuttleworth heads a venture-capital company that invests in technology, particularly uses of the Internet. He had a fascination for all things electronic from a young age in Cape Town, but in business school at the University of Cape Town (UCT), where he graduated in 1995, he took an interest in the Internet and its applications to business. He founded a consulting firm in his last year at UCT to develop Internet security systems for businesses, and it became the leading certifying authority outside the United States. He sold that business to an American company, then founded HBD, a venture-capital company that identifies South African technology companies that have potential for success in the global business world. The initials stand for "Here Be Dragons," the line put on ancient maps for uncharted territory.

Shuttleworth has developed Ubuntu Linux, a user-friendly version of the Linux operating system for computers. He owns 65 percent of ImpiLinux, a version that is compatible with all 11 official South African languages.

Shuttleworth has funded several foundations connected with his interests. One fosters new approaches to education. An international group he supports works at resolving the digital divide between the educated class and the poor in the Third World.

Besides his philanthropy, Shuttleworth has used his personal fortune to become one of the first space visitors. He spent seven months in training in Moscow before lifting off in the Soyuz spacecraft in 2002. He spent eight days at the international space station, taking part in experiments related to AIDS research. The trip cost him some $20 million.

References: wiki. www.markshuttleworth.com, www.bridges.com; www.tsf.org.za.

SISULU, Nontsikelelo Albertina

(South Africa, 1918–)

Nontsikelelo Albertina Sisulu is the most prominent women's leader in the African National Congress (ANC) and the antiapartheid movement generally. She has been a party stalwart, providing leadership during the difficult years when most members of the ANC high command were either in prison or in exile.

A Xhosa from a poor Transkei family, she trained as a nurse and midwife in Johannesburg. Around 1940 she met her future husband, Walter SISULU, and joined the ANC Youth League. Albertina had a calming and maturing effect on Walter, an anti-White militant with deep resentment of his mixed-blood parentage. "I am Black enough for both of us," she once said. They married in 1944 and settled into a cinderblock house in Soweto, outside of Johannesburg, where the family lived for 45 years. In this home Albertina bore and raised five children, all of whom became political activists. Her married life was one of great sacrifice. Between 1953 and 1964, Walter was imprisoned eight times and was then sentenced to Robben Island until 1989.

In 1948, Albertina joined the ANC Women's League and was a founder in the nonracial Federation of South African Women in 1954. She led demonstrations against the extension of the pass laws to women, which required Africans to carry racial identification cards at all times. In 1958 she and Winnie MADIKIZELA-MANDELA were jailed together for their opposition to women's passes. She also developed massive women's opposition to the Bantu education system, which restricted educational opportunities for Black children. The women's movement was a target of many of the attacks against the ANC and other antiapartheid groups. In 1963, after the banning of the ANC, and while her husband was in hiding underground, Sisulu was arrested and held in solitary confinement for three months and then placed under banning orders for 19 years, including 10 years of dusk-to-dawn house arrest. It is the longest record of such restrictions imposed on anyone in South Africa.

Albertina had a hard life with Walter often abroad and later imprisoned. She was harassed, jailed, two of her children fled into exile and she tried to raise three other children plus three adopted ones from her deceased sister-in-law. Several of her imprisonments were in solitary confinement, in one case for a year without charges being brought. This she somehow survived on a midwife's small stipend. All her children were jailed at one point or another.

In 1983, Sisulu was elected president of the Federation of African Women. Soon after, she was arrested for singing at an ANC funeral and covering the casket with the forbidden ANC flag. Released on appeal, she was elected co-president of the United Democratic Front (UDF), an umbrella group of hundreds of organizations opposed to apartheid. It united Black and White opposition and provided a legal front for the ANC and other banned groups. It began to campaign against a new constitutional arrangement that included Indian and Coloured houses of parliament, subservient to the White government, but excluded Black participation. The attempted reforms launched by President P. W. BOTHA failed, and a state of emergency was imposed, unleashing severe government repression. Leaderless Black youths established mob rule in the townships. The government, seeking to make an example of its authority, flattened the Crossroads township near Cape Town in 1985. Albertina Sisulu was arrested and charged with fomenting revolution. The case was dismissed, but in 1988 her movements were again restricted in a campaign of harassment against the UDF.

Matters began to change in 1989. Sisulu, "as the patroness of the principal Black opposition group," in the words of the official invitation, was

Nontsikelelo Albertina and Walter Max Ulyate Sisulu

asked to meet with U.S. President George Bush and British Prime Minister Margaret Thatcher, both of whom had resisted economic sanctions against South Africa. She was allowed to obtain a passport and to leave the country; in her interviews overseas she minced no words about conditions in South Africa and what she saw as the West's responsibility to maintain sanctions. In October 1989, her husband was released from prison, and the ANC leadership began to organize openly. In 1990, Sisulu reconstituted the ANC Women's League and was elected its president in opposition to Winnie Madikizela-Mandela.

Her celebrated rivalry with Winnie Madikizela-Mandela stems from Sisulu's commitment to solidarity and her strong feelings about individualism within the movement. The contrast between the two could not be more striking. The charismatic and attractive Madikizela-Mandela made herself a Western media personality, while the stout and matronly Sisulu, never stylishly dressed, continues to be a movement icon. Sisulu avoided the dramatic employment of bodyguards and continued to support herself by working as a clinic nurse. When Madikizela-Mandela built a lavish mansion on top of a hill in Soweto among the houses of the poor, Sisulu commented: "That's not a house; that's a whole village." After Sisulu persuaded an irate group not to attack the house, Madikizela-Mandela never spoke to her again. Sisulu has consistently

tried to dampen the revolutionary violence of the Soweto youth while Madikizela-Mandela has provoked them. Sisulu was on the committee that was chosen to negotiate during a long Soweto rent strike, while Madikizela-Mandela refused to honor the strike in order to keep the construction permits for her house. The two have clashed over leadership of the ANC Women's League, from which Madikizela-Mandela was expelled after her conviction in connection with the death of a young boy murdered by her bodyguards. In 1993, however, Madikizela-Mandela made a remarkable comeback, defeating Sisulu for the presidency of the Women's League.

Albertina Sisulu was elected to parliament under the interim South African constitution and was given the honor of nominating Nelson MANDELA for president in 1994. Elected with her were one of her sons and one daughter; two other children declined ANC nominations.

References: adb, EWB, GSAP, PLBA. Elinor Sisulu, *Walter and Albertina Sisulu: In Our Lifetime* (2003).

SISULU, Walter Max Ulyate
(South Africa, 1912–2003)

Walter Max Ulyate Sisulu, along with his close friend and comrade Nelson MANDELA, was the most important member of the generation that led the African National Congress (ANC) through the apartheid period.

Born of a poor family in the Transkei, Sisulu had a White father, about which he was always sensitive and which engendered bitter resentment of Whites. He dropped out of school after the fourth grade in 1927 and then underwent Xhosa initiation ceremonies, which in the African tradition recognized him as an adult. During the 1930s he worked at whatever jobs he could obtain—dairyman, miner and factory worker. At various times he was also a kitchen and bakery worker. He was inspired by Clements KADALIE's Industrial and Commercial Workers' Union and in 1940 was fired from his bakery job after organizing a strike. Sisulu's pugnacious stance brought him his first jail sentence when he punched a train conductor who had confiscated a Black man's rail pass. He later began to patrol the town streets armed with a knife to protect residents from assaults and gained a reputation as a street vigilante who could send petty thugs fleeing. With the advent of World War II, Sisulu opposed the campaign to recruit African troops. He also took in a boarder named Nelson Mandela and introduced him to the ANC.

Sisulu joined a Xhosa cultural society, where he discovered another outlet for his intense nationalism. At the same time, he found a confidante and friend in Albertina Totiwe, who helped him overcome his sensitivity to his mixed-race parentage; in 1944 they married. While creating a political career of her own, Albertina SISULU provided indispensable personal support for her husband during the years that he spent banned and imprisoned.

In 1940, Sisulu joined the ANC, but his aggressive attitude left him dissatisfied with the cautious, middle-class respectability of its leadership. In 1944 he, Albertina, Oliver TAMBO, and Nelson Mandela formed the ANC Youth League, taking a militant and activist position. When the Youth League was able to topple Alfred XUMA from the ANC presidency in 1949, Sisulu defeated the Communists' candidate to become ANC secretary-general. He was able to press the ANC into accepting his Programme of Action, a response to the 1948 election of Daniel MALAN as prime minister on an apartheid platform. In 1952 the Youth League elected Chief Albert LUTHULI as ANC president and established a policy of confrontation. In that year Sisulu directed the Defiance Campaign of civil disobedience against apartheid. His organizing skills placed 8,500 volunteers in Black communities to orchestrate defiance of the laws. As a result, Sisulu was put under banning orders, which forbade him to attend public meetings, and he was forced to begin working secretly.

During the early 1950s he was repeatedly banned, arrested, jailed and harassed by the police. His collaboration with the Indian Congress and antiapartheid Whites softened his Black nationalist exclusivism, however, and convinced him that the future of South Africa lay in a multiracial society. This view was reinforced by a 1953 tour of China, Israel, the Soviet Union and Romania, where Sisulu was repelled by Stalinism but impressed by the Communist commitment to development.

In 1956 the government arrested 156 people, including the leadership of the ANC, for high treason. The trials lasted until 1961, when Sisulu and the last defendants were acquitted. By this time, the ANC had been banned and Sisulu was placed under house arrest. He was arrested six times in 1962, and in 1963 he was convicted of furthering the aims of the ANC. While out on bail, Sisulu went underground to join the ANC's armed wing, announcing his decision in a broadcast from a secret radio station. The police raided the ANC's underground headquarters and arrested Sisulu and many others. Sisulu was held in solitary confinement for 88 days and then joined Mandela on trial. Sisulu denied nothing: "The African people have the right to revolt against repression," he said, rejecting nonviolence in the face of apartheid. With convincing evidence of planned sabotage was placed before the court, the ANC lawyers feared a death sentence would be imposed and were relieved when he was sentenced to life imprisonment.

Sisulu spent 25 years in prison, from 1964 to 1989, first on Robben Island and, after 1982, at another facility. On his release, despite his advanced age, Sisulu took charge of arrangements to resurrect the structure of the ANC when it became legalized again. In 1991 he was elected ANC deputy president and was a leading figure in the negotiations with F. W. DE KLERK's government for a transition to a nonracial South Africa. He retired officially in 1994 after seeing Mandela inaugurated as president and attending the official ceremonies with his wife, son and daughter, who were elected ANC members of parliament.

References: adb, DAHB, DRWW, EB, EWB, GSAP, PLBA, RWWA, *wiki*. Elinor Sisulu, *Walter and Albertina Sisulu: In Our Lifetime* (2003).

SISULU, Zwelakhe
(South Africa, 1950–)

Zwelakhe Sisulu is one of the new generation of activist leaders in the African National Congress (ANC). He follows in the footsteps of his illustrious parents, Walter SISULU and Albertina SISULU, two of the organization's stalwarts, yet he has developed his own areas of concern and competence as a journalist. His life for many years was one long struggle with apartheid.

Sisulu fled South Africa after being jailed at 17 with his mother. He was educated in Swaziland, and in 1975 studied journalism in an apprenticeship program run by the South Africa Associated Newspapers. He worked for the *Rand Daily Mail* and then as news editor of the *Sunday Post* during a brief career until he was banned in 1980. In 1977, when the government banned the Union of Black Journalists, Sisulu began the Writers' Association of South Africa, which became the Media Workers' Association in 1980 after recruiting and organizing all Black media personnel. His first imprisonment came in 1980 for refusing to answer questions about a *Post* reporter being tried under the Terrorism Act. That year he joined the staff of the *Sowetan,* which was soon banned. From 1980 to 1983 Sisulu was unemployed and constantly harassed by the government.

In 1981 he was detained for eight months under the Terrorism Act as a potential witness, although he was never called or charged. When he was released, he was sentenced to 18 months for refusing to testify in another case, but he won on appeal, and his banning order was lifted shortly thereafter. Awarded a Niemann Fellowship for journalists at Harvard University in 1984, he spent a year in the United States. In 1985, Sisulu was appointed as the first editor of *New Nation,* a newspaper founded by the South African Catholic Bishops' Conference, but when the emergency regulations went into effect in 1986 he was again detained, this time mostly in solitary confinement. He was released in 1988 under banning orders that forbade him to return to his job or to be in the company of more than 10 people. He was placed under dusk-to-dawn house arrest.

Since the dismantling of apartheid, Sisulu has returned to his profession and has now entered the heart of the official South African media by joining the staff of the South African Broadcasting Corporation (SABC). The corporation has appointed several leading Black journalists in an effort to lead the move to a multiracial South Africa, and from 1994 to 1998 Sisulu was chief executive. He instituted affirmative action programs to require that half the employees be Black within two years. He had problems within SABC over this policy when the company lost advertising and subscribers.

His interests have expanded across Africa, where he owns 51 percent of Outdoor Network, an advertising sign company which operates in west Africa, especially in the lucrative Nigerian market. In 2005 he purchased half of Stonehouse Graphics (digital printing) and 17 percent of Aquarius Platinum. He is chair of Savannah Resources and Afriminerals Holdings.

Reference: GSAP. Zwelakhe Sisulu, *Released but Not Free* (1989).

SITHOLE, Ndabaningi
(Zimbabwe, 1920–2000)

Reverend Ndabaningi Sithole was a prominent figure in the nationalist struggle in Southern Rhodesia (now Zimbabwe). His influence waned after he became entangled in the complexities of Zimbabwean resistance politics that led up to independence. Thereafter, he never recovered his power base.

Sithole was born into a traditional society and did not become literate until he was in his teens, when he entered a mission school. Through diligence he completed a school certificate and received a correspondence degree from the University of South Africa. Torn between teaching and the ministry, he chose the latter and spent from 1953 to 1956 at Newton Theological College in Massachusetts before being ordained as a Congregationalist minister.

Sithole was appointed a school principal in Chikore, and wrote *African Nationalism* (1959), which stated his credo—a moderate appeal for interracial justice based on Christian principles. Cooperation between the races and the "healing hands" of the Church were to be the means of a true solution to Black Rhodesians' grievances. The reality was something else, however, and Sithole became distressed at both the divisions within the nationalist movement and the government's increasing oppression. In 1960 he joined Joshua NKOMO's National Democratic Party (NDP) and was forced to resign his school position. The NDP was banned in 1962, and Sithole became a founder of the Zimbabwe African People's Union (ZAPU). As dissension rose over Nkomo's leadership style, Sithole and Robert MUGABE became the leaders of a rival faction, which in 1963 became the Zimbabwe African National Union (ZANU). In 1964 both ZANU and ZAPU were banned, and Sithole, along with hundreds of others, was placed in detention for five years. In 1969 he was convicted of an assassination plot against Premier Ian SMITH and was sentenced to six years' hard labor. The accusation embittered him, not because it was false, but because it slandered his principles of nonviolence.

By the time Sithole reemerged in 1974, the armed struggle had superseded efforts at conciliation, and he went into exile to Zambia with Bishop Abel MUZOREWA. He had lost most of his influence in the nationalist movement, and his attempts to regain it were ineffectual. He and Muzorewa became rivals, and after negotiating a transition government with the White leadership, Sithole had to settle for a seat in parliament when Muzorewa took the prime minister's post. Their government was a sideshow, however, to the main liberation movements of ZAPU and ZANU. After independence in 1980, Sithole was thrust permanently onto the sidelines. In 1987 he petitioned for political asylum in the United States, where he lived for a time with his daughter. In 1994 he returned to Zimbabwe to organize a factional group to contest the 1995 elections. He was elected to parliament, but denied his seat in 1997 after being tried for treason. He returned to the United States after his appeal was suspended, and died there.

References: CA, DAHB, DRWW, EB, EWB, PLBA, *wiki.*

SIYAD BARRE, Mohammed
(Somalia, 1919?–1995)

Major-General Mohammed Siyad Barre, deposed in 1991 after 25 years as military dictator of Somalia, precipitated a breakdown of Somali society. After being expelled, he went into exile in Nigeria.

Siyad Barre's career spanned a period of extensive social and political change in Somalia. Born in what was then Italian Somaliland into a family of herders and made an orphan at 10, Siyad Barre aggressively worked to improve himself. With only an elementary education he joined the police force being formed by the British in 1941 when they captured the territory from the Italians in World War II. By 1950 he had finished secondary school and was named chief inspector, which made him the highest-placed Somali in the bureaucracy. By then he spoke Italian, English, Swahili and Arabic fluently. In 1950, Italy resumed jurisdiction from the United Nations in order to prepare Somalia for independence, and Siyad Barre was well placed for a leadership role. He was sent to Italy for training, and when independence was achieved in 1960, he was transferred to the new Somali army as vice commandant with the rank of colonel. He became a general and commandant in 1965.

Siyad Barre was not involved in politics, but he was not without political convictions. In 1969, when the president of Somalia was assassinated, Siyad Barre took power in a coup in order to end the corruption and clan conflict that was then rife. Both a Marxist and a practicing Muslim, he promoted national unity over ethnic loyalties. He improved literacy and standardized the writing of Somali in Roman script. Although Somalia has a national language and is ethnically homogeneous, clan loyalty is fierce. Siyad Barre, a Marahan, belonged to one of the smaller groups.

Siyad Barre turned to the Soviet bloc for support. Some 3,000 Soviets were based in Somalia, but they angered Siyad Barre by pressuring him to federate with Ethiopia rather than supporting his traditional claims to Somali lands in Ethiopia, Kenya and Djibouti. They turned against him in 1974 to favor Ethiopia, which resulted in a three-year border war that the Ethiopians (with Cuban military support) won. More than a million refugees fled to Somalia, seriously straining the economy. Siyad Barre increasingly turned to the Arab countries and in 1974 entered the Arab League. The same year he was elected chairman of the Organization of African Unity (OAU).

War, drought and incompetence soon brought on destitution for many. Siyad Barre began to depend more and more on trusted advisors and clan members. His "Victory Pioneers," an armed youth corps, terrorized and spied on towns and villages. Matters declined and armed resistance began to organize around clan leaders. In 1986, Siyad Barre was seriously injured in an auto accident. Civil war broke out two years later. By 1990 there were several rebel groups contending for power, and a year later Siyad Barre fled the country. Rebel forces, the largest led by General Mohammed Farah AIDID, created political chaos throughout the country. The United States intervened with troops in 1992, followed by a U.N. occupation to promote order. In the end, both were a total failure.

References: afr, DAHB, DRWW, PLBA, PLCA, RWWA, *wiki.*

SLOVO, Joe (Yossel Mashel)
(South Africa, 1926–1995)

Yossel Mashel "Joe" Slovo, longtime secretary-general of the South African Communist Party (SACP), was for a generation the only prominent White leader in the African National Congress (ANC).

Slovo was born in Lithuania and came to South Africa with his parents in 1935. An admirer of the Soviet resistence to fascism, he joined the SACP at 16, and volunteered for the Spirngbok Legion, which fought for the Allies in World War II. He worked his way through the University of the Witswatersrand, receiving a BA and then a law degree in 1951, the year that he passed the bar examinations. His legal practice centered around the defense of dissidents in political trials. After the Suppression of Communism Act was passed (1950), the SACP went underground, and Slovo and his wife of a year, Ruth First, were "named by the government," placing them on a list of dangerous persons and making it illegal for them to be quoted in print. In 1954 this restriction was extended to a complete banning from attending any political gatherings. Despite this status, Slovo contributed to the Freedom Charter, the ANC's declaration of principles. Although he was continually harassed—arrested, charged, tried and released—and several times detained, he also became active in the ANC's armed wing, *Umkhonto we Sizwe* (Spear of the Nation), attending the secret meetings of its leadership.

In 1963, Slovo went abroad on an ANC mission, and shortly after his departure the ANC leadership was arrested. Ruth First finally joined her husband after serving several months of detention. Slovo continued to work for the ANC as Umkhonto chief of staff. In 1977 he established an operational center in Mozambique, where Ruth First was murdered by a parcel bomb in 1982. When the South African press reported that he had arranged his wife's death, he sued in British courts for libel and received a £25,000 settlement, about $35,000 at that time.

In 1985, Slovo became the first White to serve on the ANC national executive, and the following year he was elected secretary-general of the SACP. He resigned his Umkhonto position in 1987 in favor of Chris HANI. To this point, Slovo had been a doctrinaire Stalinist, but by 1988 he admitted the

excesses of the Stalin era. In 1990, when the SACP was legalized, he wrote *Has Socialism Failed?* This work announced the new party line: multiparty democracy based on voting rights for all, civil liberties, and full trade union rights. Recognizing the decline of world communism, he staked out a space for the SACP within a new South Africa.

Slovo took part in all the major negotiations with the government over the transition to full democracy. His involvement initially produced tense moments with officials, because Slovo was the symbol of revolution, violence and implacable opposition to the government. However, he soon disarmed his opponents with his frankness and personal warmth. In 1992 he was elected chairman of the SACP but revealed that he had cancer. Hani's murder in 1993 was a terrible blow to the SACP, because he was regarded as the organization's actual leader. The SACP reluctantly joined the ANC in the 1994 elections. Slovo was named to Nelson MANDELA's cabinet as minister of housing, which put him in charge of the massive expansion of homes promised by the new government.

References: afr, GSAP, PLBA, RWWA, wiki.

SMITH, Ian Douglas
(Zimbabwe, 1919–)

Ian Smith, separatist prime minister of Rhodesia, affronted the international community by declaring his country independent of Great Britain in order to preserve White political and economic control. Throughout his time in office, he fought an expanding war against the liberation forces that eventually overcame Rhodesia and established Zimbabwe.

Smith was born in Southern Rhodesia and, after high school, entered the Royal Air Force, where he became a Spitfire pilot. When he was shot down over North Africa during World War II, surgeons had to reconstruct his face, leaving him with a rigid expression and an inability to smile. When he returned to action, he was shot down again, this time over Italy, where he spent five months fighting alongside Italian partisans. He escaped on foot over the Alps to reach the Allied lines.

After his discharge, Smith studied commerce at Rhodes University in South Africa, where he was active in student politics. In 1948, after his return to the family farm, he was elected to the Southern

Ian Douglas Smith

Rhodesian legislative assembly as part of the right-wing opposition to Sir Godfrey HUGGINS's United Party (UP) government. In 1953, with the establishment of the Federation of Rhodesia and Nyasaland, Smith switched to the UP and was elected to the federation parliament. He was not a notable member, although from 1958 he served as chief government whip under Prime Minister Roy WELENSKY.

In 1961, Smith made a move that gave direction to the rest of his career. He resigned from both the UP and parliament over a constitutional change to provide Black Africans representation in the Southern Rhodesian legislative assembly. With several noted anti-Black politicians, Smith formed the Rhodesian Front (RF), which was initially composed of only White supremacists and extremists. Their vow of "Rhodesia for the Rhodesians" could not disguise their real intent—the establishment of a White supremacist republic with all power in the hands of settlers. Smith selected a prominent and respected farmer, Winston Field, to lead the party, and with this increased credibility, the RF scored a momentous upset over the UP in the 1962 elections. Smith was named deputy prime minister and minister of the treasury.

The federation was at that time crumbling as Great Britain laid plans for the independence of Northern Rhodesia (Zambia) and Nyasaland (Malawi). Field now called for independence for Southern Rhodesia. Britain responded with demands for increased Black participation in government, which was totally unacceptable to the Rhodesian Front. Smith joined a right-wing revolt that toppled Field

and became prime minister in 1964, pledging to lead Rhodesia to independence as a White state.

Smith moved swiftly and decisively toward his goal, correctly assuming that Great Britain would be unable or unwilling to counter him. He arrested nationalist leaders, including Joshua NKOMO, who was accused of "dragging the country from crisis to crisis." When street disturbances followed the arrests, they were crushed by a massive use of armed force. Bolstered by his control, Smith flew to London for independence talks, finally conceding that he would accept independence on the basis of the 1961 constitution, which had originally caused him to leave the UP. This constitution called for a parliament of 50 persons of high education, income and property requirements, plus 15 of lesser attainments. For all practical purposes, that meant 50 Whites and 15 Blacks, because—regardless of education—property holdings were too restricted to allow Black representation.

Smith called for a national referendum and held an *indaba,* a consultative meeting, with all the African chiefs. The chiefs from the communal reservations were bitter foes of the nationalists, and they gave Smith the African support he needed. The referendum, boycotted by many Blacks (12,664 were eligible, compared to 89,594 Whites), endorsed independence overwhelmingly. Smith continued to dangle the threat of a unilateral declaration of independence (UDI) before the British while insisting that he favored negotiations. He then called a snap election in 1965, which returned 50 RF members to parliament. No Blacks were elected, because the 15 Black seats were uncontested. With a strengthened hand, Smith once again returned to London. Prime Minister Harold Wilson demanded progress toward Black political participation, removal of racial discrimination, and a commitment not to reverse any Black gains in the 1961 constitution. He warned Smith that a UDI would be regarded as an act of rebellion.

Smith rose to the taunt and proclaimed unilateral independence on Remembrance Day, 11 November 1965. Britain denounced the act as treason and imposed economic sanctions, which were soon followed by the those of the United States and a number of other Western countries. When the British governor declined to arrest Smith and Wilson excluded military action, Smith placed Government House under siege and cut it off so thoroughly that the governor was forced to contact London by using a public telephone on the street.

This humiliation, which delighted the White extremists, continued until 1969, when Smith proclaimed a republic and formally cut all ties with the queen. He countered the embargo by obtaining supplies, especially oil, from South Africa, where the UDI had much support. Smith also established an arms industry to supply the needs of his army and located alternate outlets for the country's agricultural exports through South Africa and the Portuguese colony of Mozambique.

The White electorate continued to support Smith, giving him 81 percent in a referendum to proclaim a republic and 73 percent for a new constitution that institutionalized segregation. Again in 1970, the RF took all seats in national elections. Smith was so confident of his power that he allowed a British commission to visit in order to determine the extent of African acceptance of the new constitution. Smith was unprepared for the riots that followed, and, in a panic, he arrested his chief critic, former premier Garfield TODD. In 1973 he made an impulsive move that cost him dearly when he closed the Zambian border because Zambia was providing a safe haven for Black nationalists. The Rhodesian Railways were dependent upon Zambian copper ore shipments, and they suffered substantial losses. These reverses were added to increased international pressures. When the Portuguese withdrew from Mozambique in 1975, Rhodesia found itself trying to contain guerrilla forces on two fronts. By 1976, Smith began to soften his stand. When South African Prime Minister Balthazar VORSTER told him bluntly that he could not count on South Africa's support in a liberation war, Smith accepted negotiations for power sharing.

In 1977, Smith began to dismantle the worst of the racial restriction acts and was successful in preventing a revolt by the extreme right wing. He dissolved parliament, and the RF members who swept the following election were more amenable to change. He announced his willingness to accept universal adult suffrage and began talks with moderate nationalist leaders, including Bishop Abel MUZOREWA and Reverend Ndabaningi SITHOLE. The nationalist baton had by that time, however, passed to Robert MUGABE and Joshua NKOMO, both of whom had mounted guerrilla campaigns. As the war continued, Whites fled the border areas, adding to the economic malaise brought on by the oil crisis of the early 1970s. In 1979, Smith accepted a shared government headed

by Muzorewa, but that move placated few Black activists. After the Lancaster House conference in London that wrote a new constitution allotting 20 seats to Whites and 80 to Blacks, Mugabe emerged the clear winner in the 1980 elections. He established the first free African government in Zimbabwe.

Smith led the White opposition but could never tolerate Mugabe personally. They had a rocky relationship that Smith made more difficult by inflammatory speeches in support of South Africa's moves to preserve apartheid. Smith was imprisoned briefly in 1981, had his personal guns confiscated, and was suspended by parliamentary vote in 1987. Ironically, it was Mugabe who supported his reinstatement. Smith continued in parliament to 1990, as long as there were seats reserved for Whites. Since his departure from parliament, he has been writing his memoirs, which he characteristically entitled *The Great Betrayal* (2002). Sensing weakness in his old nemesis, he rallied the opposition to Mugabe for the 1995 elections.

References: AB, *afr*, CB, DAHB, DRWW, EWB, HWL, PLBA, PLCA, *wiki*. Smith, *Bitter Harvest* (1981); Matthew White, *Smith of Rhodesia* (1978).

SMUTS, Jan Christiaan
(South Africa, 1870–1950)

General Jan Christiaan Smuts, a major South African figure of international political and military importance, was at the center of all South African politics during the first half of the twentieth century.

Born in the Cape Colony to a Afrikaner farming family with deep roots in South Africa, Smuts went to Christ College, Cambridge University, to study law. There he acquired a respect for English ideas and values that would mark his later work and loyalties. In 1895, Smuts returned to Cape Town as an admirer of Cecil RHODES, whom he had heard speak at Cambridge. However, Smuts was disillusioned and disheartened by Leander Starr JAMESON's abortive raid into the Transvaal and by Rhodes's involvement in it. As a result, he gave up his Cape citizenship for that of the Transvaal and moved to Johannesburg.

President "Oom Paul" KRUGER made him a state attorney and assigned him the task of reform-

Jan Christiaan Smuts

ing the corrupt detective department. Smuts gained a reputation for single-mindedness and a somewhat cold tenacity. As tensions rose between the Afrikaners and the *uitlanders,* or English immigrants, Smuts found himself caught between the groups. He was loyal to his people but also had a profound respect for the British, and he sought a means for reconciliation. When the Boer War began, however, Smuts defended his country ably and proved to be a brave commando leader. As Pretoria was about to fall, he seized the national treasury, enabling the guerrilla war to continue for two more years.

In 1905 he and Louis BOTHA formed Het Volk, an Afrikaner party of reconciliation. Botha became a lifelong friend and colleague, and the two shared a common vision of a South Africa with two equal White partners, Afrikaner and British. When they obtained self-government for the Transvaal in 1907, Smuts exulted, "Has such a miracle of trust and magnanimity ever happened before?" His positive approach to the British made Smuts their South African ally and favorite but defined him as a

turncoat and traitor to the "bitter enders" (those who rejected any cooperation with the British) among most Afrikaners.

Louis Botha and Smuts had a complementary relationship and served together in office until Botha's death. Botha was not particularly intelligent, but he had wisdom, patience and kindness. Smuts was the intellectual—calculating, aloof and unemotional. The more decisive of the two, Smuts often took action that cost him any popularity he might have had. He was the one who jailed GANDHI, while Botha worked out a compromise with him. Smuts broke the miners' strike and illegally deported the labor leaders without trial. When the 1910 Union of South Africa was achieved, Smuts was respected by most but distrusted by many.

With the outbreak of World War I, Smuts and Botha's loyalties to Britain were put to the test. Several Afrikaner leaders rose in rebellion against the joint policy of support for the British war effort; Smuts helped to suppress the revolt. He and Botha then led the invasion of South-West Africa (now Namibia) that quickly led to the South African occupation of the German colony. Nevertheless, there was bitterness against Smuts that Botha somehow largely deflected. Smuts referred to it as "this hell into which I have wandered." He was dispatched as general to head the Tanganyika campaign. Subsequently, he defeated Colonel Paul Von LETTOW-VORBECK in a long and costly struggle. Called to England as a member of the Imperial War Cabinet, Smuts found himself idolized and greeted everywhere as a war hero. He turned down the presidency of the Irish convention and the Palestine command. As a war strategist, he laid the groundwork for the Royal Air Force.

Smuts became an international figure when he joined United States President Woodrow Wilson in the call for a League of Nations. At the Versailles Peace Conference, Smuts and Botha took their last stand together, arguing for conciliation with Germany, although Smuts accepted the principle of reparations. Smuts said that the Versailles Treaty breathed "a poisonous spirit of revenge," and it took some effort for Botha to persuade him to sign it. The League of Nations, however, was Smuts's dream, and he drafted many sections of its covenant. The United States' failure to join the organization was a great disappointment. The international scene never ceased to have its attraction for him, and in 1921 he assisted in establishing the Irish Free State.

To his credit, he opposed the rising European anti-Semitism in the 1920s, and in 1930 stood against the Quota Law in South Africa, which would have limited Jewish refugees.

In 1919, Smuts returned to a depressed South Africa that had little interest in his international vision. Botha died almost immediately afterward, and Smuts inherited his post as prime minister. Nationalist Party leader James HERTZOG's opposition was rancorous, especially when public disorder caused Smuts to call out troops. In 1924, Hertzog forced Smuts out of office. Smuts turned to philosophy and wrote *Holism and Evolution* (1926), a treatise on the unity of all life. In 1933 the deepening world depression forced Hertzog to accept Smuts—the champion of ending the gold standard—into his cabinet as deputy premier. He stayed on as minister of justice until 1939, when, during World War II, Smuts again became prime minister by advocating entering the war against Germany while Hertzog, miscalculating national feelings, supported neutrality.

In 1941, Smuts was made a British field marshal and served in the Libyan and Somaliland campaigns. He played a key part in founding the United Nations after the war and authored its preamble, seemingly without any sense of irony proclaiming basic human rights that were denied under his own regime. Seen as a liberal by his enemies, he was not single-minded on the race question. Smuts had cooperated in the removal of Black Africans from the Cape Province voter rolls and accepted most of the restrictions under which Blacks suffered. In his later years, however, he seemed to feel that a gradualist approach could bring eventual racial parity, which made him utterly unprepared for the extreme racist sentiments that swept him out of office in 1948. He was replaced by the Nationalist Party under Daniel MALAN. Smuts became the leader of the opposition, watched his entire social edifice dismantled, and was unable to stem the tide of apartheid.

References: DAHB, DNB, EB, EWB, HWL, MMA, *wiki* Piet Beukes, *The Holistic Smuts: A Study in Personality* (1989); Ingham, Kenneth. *Jan Christiaan Smuts: The Conscience of a South African* (1986); Ockert Geyser, *Jan Smuts and His International Contemporaries* (2002).

SOBHUZA II
(Swaziland, 1899–1982)

Sobhuza II presided as king over the development of Swaziland from an economically exploited, weak nation on the fringes of southern African affairs to a prosperous country and important player in the region's politics. At his death, he was the world's longest-reigning monarch.

Sobhuza was selected to be king in the year of his birth, after his father's death. Sobhuza's grandmother, who served as regent, built a national school to assure his education, which he completed along with two years in South Africa. In 1903, Swaziland became a British protectorate, and in 1907 the Partitions Proclamation ceded vast tracts of land to European settlers. Installed on the throne in 1921, Sobhuza immediately moved to reverse the land concessions. He led an unsuccessful delegation to London in 1922 but refused to give up on his goal. By World War II he had wrested a compromise in which the British government purchased European lands to be reassigned to the Swazi in exchange for Swazi support in the war effort.

Agricultural modernization was his first step in economic development, and Sobhuza began a "green revolution," promoting producer cooperatives and training programs for peasants. The commercial forests that he began grew into the largest manmade timberland in Africa. He also fostered the development of natural resources until iron and asbestos mining became the leading export earners by the 1970s.

Sobhuza led his country into a peaceful transition to independence in 1968, announcing that, being late in coming to sovereignty, Swaziland could observe other African nations and avoid the "crocodile drifts" into which others had fallen. He selected those aspects of modern government that he felt were appropriate and added a Swazi flavor to them. Parliaments under him were conducted almost as consultative bodies of elders, controlled completely by his royal party, the Imbododvo. In 1973 he abrogated the constitution and thereafter ruled as an absolute ruler, through a national council that he appointed.

Sobhuza practiced a blend of traditionalism and modernization. He appeared in traditional Swazi leopard-skin loincloth and feathers, and his assumption of absolute powers was undertaken because he considered democracy "un-Swazi." The Swazi regarded him with immense personal affection, which he returned by fulfilling his role. He presided over traditional festivities and rituals and encouraged such practices as traditional medicine. By his artful balance of development and respect for ancestral ways, Sobhuza maintained control of Swazi politics, keeping at bay those who resented the absolute monarchy as well as the settlers who had hoped for a privileged position in the kingdom. Throughout his reign, Sobhuza pursued a policy of racial toleration, even as he asserted Swazi economic rights. He did not disturb settler landowners and encouraged foreign investment.

Foreign affairs were a delicate balancing act for land-locked Swaziland. Sobhuza's careful foreign policy kept his country on good terms with both his neighbors, apartheid South Africa and Marxist Mozambique. Swaziland needed Mozambique's rail system and ports to export its ore, but South Africa was its major trading partner. Sobhuza maintained correct but wary relations with this powerful neighbor. He even fostered tourism by providing the casinos, discos and sex shops that South Africa did not permit. A continuing issue between the two states has been the coastal land seized from Swaziland at the end of the last century. In 1982, Sobhuza initiated talks aimed at reacquiring this territory in order to provide the country with an outlet to the sea.

Swazi customary law does not provide for an heir, although it specifies certain characteristics for a ruler. Upon Sobhuza's death he left more than 70 official wives and some 210 children. A regency was established until a choice could be made from among his sons. In 1986 the succession passed to Prince Makosetive, who became king as MSWATI III.

References: AB, *afr*, AO, DAHB, DRWW, MMA, PLBA, *wiki*. Hilda Kuper, *Sobhuza II: Ngwanyama and King of Swaziland* (1978).

SOBUKWE, Robert Mangaliso
(South Africa, 1924–1978)

Robert Mangaliso Sobukwe, a radical nationalist, was founder and first president of the Pan-Africanist Congress (PAC).

Born into a poor Xhosa family, through hard work and outstanding intellectual ability, Sobukwe received an honors degree and teaching certificate in 1949 from Fort Hare University College. During the same year he became branch chairman of the African National Congress (ANC) Youth League, which was under the charismatic leadership of Nelson MANDELA and Oliver TAMBO. In 1952, Sobukwe was dismissed from teaching due to his involvement with the ANC's Defiance Campaign against apartheid. He joined the Department of Bantu Studies at the University of the Witwatersrand as a language teaching assistant, staying there until 1960.

Sobukwe increased his commitment to the ANC, and by 1957 he was editor of its journal, *The Africanist*. At the same time, he identified with the more radical wing of the ANC, whose members called themselves the Africanists. They were uncomfortable with both the increasing influence of the Communist party within the ANC as well as with the organization's growing multiracial character. The Africanists wanted a consciously Black organization based on African nationalism. Sobukwe argued that Black Africans could be freed only by their own efforts, and, although he espoused a nonracial democratic society for South Africa, his convictions led his opponents to label him racist. His doctrine became a source of inspiration for the later Black consciousness movement of Steve BIKO. Sobukwe's militancy prompted him to leave the ANC to found the PAC on those principles in 1959.

The first test of the new PAC came with its campaign against the pass laws. Hoping to outmaneuver the ANC, the PAC organized mass demonstrations, and at Sharpeville in March 1960, 69 were killed and 178 wounded when the police panicked and fired into a peaceful crowd. Sobukwe was arrested and served three years at hard labor for incitement to riot. He was then re-arrested and held for a further six years in solitary confinement on Robben Island—ironically, under the Supression of Communism Act. During the entire period, Sobukwe studied (his movement nickname was "Prof") and received correspondence degrees in law and economics. On his release in 1969, Sobukwe was allowed to live in Kimberley and conduct legal research, but he was placed under banning orders for five years, orders that were renewed in 1974 for another five years. In 1975 he completed requirements for admission to the bar and began a small practice in Kimberley. His long detainment brought on a lung infection, however, from which he eventually died.

References: *afr*, DAHB, DRWW, EWB, MMA, PLBA, PLCA, *wiki*. Benjamin Pogrund, *Sobukwe and Apartheid* (1991).

SOGLO, Christophe
(Benin, 1909–1984)

Christophe Soglo, military president of Dahomey (now Benin), established himself in power only after placing three predecessors in office and then deposing each one for failing. He was then himself unable to deal with the country's problems.

Born into a Fon family of chiefs, Soglo joined the French army in 1931. He distinguished himself in combat during World War II, fighting in Morocco and joining the Allied landings in Corsica, Elba and southern France. He was commissioned after the war and became military advisor to the minister of French overseas territories. Promoted to captain in 1950, he was sent to Indochina, where he won the Croix de Guerre for bravery. He was then promoted to major and was posted in Sénégal, where he remained until Dahomey became independent in 1960. Returning home, Soglo was made military advisor to President Hubert MAGA and chief of staff.

As Maga's unpopularity grew, there were general strikes and student demonstrations. In 1963, Soglo staged his first coup to end the unrest, turning over power to a triumvirate of three civilian leaders: Maga, Sourou Migan APITHY, and Justin AHOMADÉGBÉ–TOMETIN. The council broke up almost immediately. Soglo again intervened in 1964, setting up elections that brought Apithy into office as president with Ahomadégbé–Tometin as prime minister. The two clashed, and each tried to depose the other. When Ahomadégbé–Tometin attempted to gather army support behind Soglo's back, Soglo removed both officials. After a month of searching for a suitable replacement, Soglo bowed to the inevitable and took over the government himself.

Soglo attempted to alter the balance of power permanently to avoid personality cults, so he enlisted technicians and military officers, but he proved an inept administrator. He began with an ambitious agricultural and infrastructure development plan in 1966, which was combined with an economic austerity program. The popular forces that had brought down Maga now began to mobilize against Soglo as economic restructuring began to create hardships. Strikes and street riots dominated 1967 until Soglo was overthrown by younger army officers at the end of the year. Soglo went into retirement at his wife's home in France, but he was allowed to return to Benin before his death in 1984.

References: DAHB, MMA, PLBA, *wiki*.

SOILIH, Ali
(Comoros, 1936–1978)

Ali Soilih, president of the Comoros from 1975 until his death, was a radical nationalist whose rule was marked by a combination of often-contradictory policies. Soilih entered politics in the Comoros Assembly and served in the semi-autonomous government that preceded independence. Soilih favored compromise with France over the contentious issue of Mayotte, the only island that rejected independence in the 1974 plebiscite that voted to end colonial status and make the Comoros an independent country. Soilih's party was soundly defeated in elections, and Ahmed ABDALLAH declared independence. Within a month, Soilih had overthrown Abdallah in a coup, using French and Belgian mercenaries led by the French mercenary Bob DENARD. Soilih's compromise proposals failing, he invaded Mayotte, only to be repulsed by the local population.

Abandoning Mayotte to French occupation, Soilih embarked on a Marxist reorganization of the Comoros. He held a public ceremony to burn all colonial records and reduced the civil service to three bureaus that reported directly to him. Local government was turned over to *mudiria*, economic collectives responsible for government, law enforcement, markets, communications and utilities. Every citizen received a plot of land. Although his programs were popular with many people, many areas were soon terrorized by youth brigades. This breakdown in law and order prompted four coup attempts in Soilih's three years in office; then crop failures in 1977 made matters intolerable. The next year Bob Denard was again hired, this time to overthrow Soilih and return control to Abdallah. Soilih was shot two weeks later, ostensibly while trying to escape.

References: *afr*, MMA, PLBA, *wiki*.

SOMÉ, Sobonfu
(Burkina Faso, 1950s-)

Sobonfu Somé is an African traditional healer and teacher who has taken up the mission of bringing African spirituality to the West. "Sobonfu," the name her devotees use almost exclusively, means "keeper of the rituals."

Sobunfu's spiritual gifts were foretold before her birth by village diviners and elders, the customary way of identifying prophets and teachers of the ancient ways. From birth, therefore, she was brought up learning the rituals of her people, the Dagara. Dagara rituals involve healing the mind and soul to receive the potential spirituality that is all around. The Dagara believe that the spirit world surrounds everyone, but all are in need of healing to recognize and accept it. From this acceptance arises community, the center of a spiritual life. Sobonfu teaches that the purpose of ritual is to "open up the gate of healing, celebration, welcoming" by calling in the ancestors.

Sobunfu has taken her message to Europe and North America to bring healing and to build community. She hopes to move the awareness of African spirituality from the perspectives of anthropology—the study of the "other"—to acceptance as one of the world's great spiritual systems. She has written two books as part of her mission: *The Spirit of Intimacy* (2000), which takes up expressions of emotion and feeling to bring healing, and *Welcoming Spirit Home* (1999), which describes rituals for family and life events, such as birth and miscarriage. In one, a pregnant woman is put into a trance and the fetus is questioned why it is coming. The name of the child should fit the purpose in life it gives from the womb.

Sobonfu moved to the United States in 1995, but says that she will return to her village when the elders tell her her mission is complete and call her home. She and her husband, a shaman, had an arranged marriage, a process she defends.

Some critics point out that Sobonfu comes dangerously close to a presentation of the mysteries of African religion as a form of New Age faith laced with pop psychology.

Reference: www.sobonfu.com.

SOUSA, Manuel Antonio de
(Mozambique, 1835–1892)

Manuel Antonio "Gouveia" de Sousa was an East Indian settler who built a private trading empire in Mozambique. As a young man in the 1850s he was sent to Mozambique from Goa, a small Portuguese enclave on the coast of India, to manage some estates of an uncle. To protect his properties he developed an armed guard of slaves and hunters, and in a short while he dominated the area. He took the nickname Gouveia—probably a corruption of *Goan*. The Portuguese, who never controlled him, acknowledged his dominion and gave it official recognition by awarding him the title of captain major in 1863.

Sousa faced two competitors, the local African tribes and other *mestiço* (mixed race) adventurers. He built a string of defensive fortified towns on his southern perimeter to protect against cattle raiders and joined the Portuguese in a series of campaigns against a rival Afro-Portuguese clan. By 1874, Sousa was recognized as the titular ruler of Manica, his region, and he married the daughter of the ruler of Barue. He placed his infant son on the throne of his father-in-law while acting as regent, which gave him effective control of a vast section of the country. Sousa always acted in concert with Portuguese interests, but because they were barely present in the interior of Mozambique, he operated largely with a free hand.

In 1890 he met a final challenger in Cecil RHODES's British South Africa Company, which laid claim to his frontier territory in what is now Zimbabwe. As he attempted to secure the area, the British captured him and sent him to Cape Town. By the time he returned a year later, tributary chiefs had begun to break away from his empire. After a few military successes, Sousa was killed in combat by a small boy in 1892. Portuguese control of the lower Zambezi collapsed with his empire, which did not outlast him.

Reference: DAHB.

SOW FALL, Aminata
(Sénégal, 1941-)

Aminata Sow Fall is a novelist who writes in French, and a prominent figure in Sénégalese cultural circles. Sometimes her name is given as Aminata Sow FALL.

Sow Fall was born in Saint-Louis, the first French settlement in Sénégal, but completed her secondary education in Dakar, the capital. She then went to France and completed a license in modern languages before returning home as a teacher. She worked for the National Reform Commission for the Teaching of French before founding a publishing house and the African Center for Animation and Cultural Exchange, both of which she still heads.

Sow Fall published eight novels between 1976 and 2005. Of those, her first three established her as a major writer, not only in Sénégal but all Africa. *Le Revenant* (*The Ghost*, 1976) tells of a postal worker who steals to cover debts incurred by his generosity toward his family and friends. In his need, they all abandon him, but he comes back for revenge, wiser for the experience. *La Grève des Bàttu* (*The Beggars' Strike*, 1979) describes the cleansing of Dakar of its street beggars, until the Muslims realize they are a necessary part of city life, because they provide a means for *zâkat*, the Muslim requirement to give to the poorest. *L'Appel des Arènes* (*The Appeal of the Wrestling Arena*, 1982) is about the clash between Western and traditional values.

All of Sow Fall's novels deal with social issues of one sort or another, but they lack the biting satire or angry rage against the failures of African society that have marked other postcolonial African writing. They end with happy resolutions. Some of that doubtless has to do with Sénégal's relatively peaceful history since independence, and its stable economy. She herself ascribes it to the universality of the human condition, that regardless of the issues that may be particular to one culture (polygamy, for example), shared humanity allows anyone to identify with the struggles of her characters.

Reference: wiki, WLTC.

SOYINKA, Wole
(Nigeria, 1934–)

Wole Soyinka, the first Black African Nobel laureate in literature, has excelled as a playwright, poet and novelist. Although he has long been recognized in literary circles, since receiving the Nobel Prize in 1986, Soyinka has become known to a wider popular audience. He has also been a vocal critic of Nigerian politics and has been scathing in his appraisal of postcolonial independent Africa's failure.

After studies in England, Soyinka worked in the London theater and then returned to Nigeria as a playwright and professor, although those activities were punctuated by house arrest (1966–1969) and exile (1969–1976) during the military regime of General Yakubu GOWON. In 1988 he began an exile in the United States, teaching at Cornell University, Emory, and the University of Nevada, Las Vegas. In 1999, he returned to Nigeria.

A formative time in Soyinka's career was a two-year period spent with the Royal Court Theatre in London between university graduation and his return to Nigeria. He served as play-reader, actor and director, and saw his first plays staged. Soon his works, especially the popular and enduring *Trials of Brother Jero* (1960), were being performed by professional and amateur groups throughout England and Nigeria. He returned in 1960 with a Rockefeller Grant to write and do research on African drama. He continued to write plays, but in 1964 he produced the first work with political overtones, *The Republicans*.

This was a period of intense activity, during which he produced a long series of his own and others' works both in English and Yoruba and successfully directed plays in London and at the Festival of Black Arts in Dakar. Soyinka's best plays, *Brother Jero* and *Kongi's Harvest* (1965) date from this period, as does his first novel, *The Interpreters* (1965), which is an account of Nigerians returning to their homeland after studies in England. The novel touches upon the interaction that is the theme of much of Soyinka's writing: the interplay among Western influences and traditional cultural roots, Christian beliefs and ancestral gods, and professionalism and commitment to African freedom. The plays illustrate these ideas more directly. Light comedies like *The Lion and the Jewel* (1959)—in which the traditional old chief wins the lovely bride over the Westernized school teacher—and *Brother Jero*—in which an African preacher turns out to be a fraud—expose the ridiculous. The darker plays reveal deeper struggles: *Death and the King's Horseman* (1975) explores loyalty to tradition as it is overcome by change, and *The Swamp Dwellers* (1958) looks at communal responsibility in the face of social change.

Soyinka has been a prolific writer in a number of genres. Although his work is in English, he is a supporter of Yoruba theater, which he believes capable of creating a new art form for Nigeria. This new form is the cinema, which Soyinka considers the vehicle that can combine all the elements of popular theater—dance, music and drama—and blend them with traditional expressions—magic, divination, costumes and ritual. His model is *cinéma verité,* in which everyday life is the scene and the props and actors are those that are available. Not only is this style inexpensive, but it represents African reality, where life is not acted but happens. Soyinka adapted *The Swamp Dwellers* for a 1967 motion picture, and in 1971 he played the lead in a film adaptation of *Kongi's Harvest* (although he later criticized it as unfaithful to his script). In 1984 he directed his first feature film, *Blues for a Prodigal.* He has written a number of plays for radio and two for television.

Soyinka's writing often follows English with expressions in pidgin or Yoruba, weaving African words as he does African motifs into his work. He believes strongly that the African nature of his work should be apparent without any fanfare or academic explanation. In 1985 he wrote a traditional Yoruba praise chant, *Muhammed Ali at Ringside,* comparing the boxing champion to a bee, a cricket which disarms the crocodile. "Black tarantula whose antics hypnotize the foe ... Astride a weathervane they sought to trap him/Slapped the wind each time."

Soyinka once dismissed the major African literary movement, *Négritude,* in a memorable phrase, by commenting that tigers do not contemplate their "tigritude" but just act naturally by pouncing. A writer's essence should be evident in his art, he believes. The positive response by anglophone writers who applauded this statement, as well as the negative response by francophone writers, reveals perhaps that even the Western interaction in modern African writing is more subtle than Soyinka appreciates.

After the outbreak of the Biafran war, the federal government arrested Soyinka for his outspoken views, despite the fact that he was not a strong supporter of Biafra. He remained under detention for three years, during which he wrote a book of poetry and a memoir of his experience, *The Man Died* (1972). After his release, Soyinka went to England, where he stayed for seven years and continued to denounce African human rights abuses. His political concerns have not been partisan or even ideological as much as humanitarian. His defense of Salman Rushdie's *Satanic Verses* earned him death threats. He has written and spoken out against tyranny regardless of its source. In recent years this has been directed especially at Robert MUGABE in Zimbabwe.

The award of the Nobel Prize in 1986 not only recognized Soyinka's genius but also was widely seen as a coming-of-age for African writing in general. Soyinka has also undertaken the resurrection of the African literary and cultural journal *Transitions,* which he once edited before it ceased publication in 1977.

References: AA, AB, *abd, afr,* AWT, CAAS, CB, DLB, EWB, MBW, NRG, *wiki,* WLTC. Soyinka, *Ake; the Years of Childhood* (1981) and *Isara* (1991); Derek Wright, *Wole Soyinka Revisited* (1993).

SPEKE, John Hanning
(Uganda, 1827–1864)

John Hanning Speke, British explorer and adventurer, found the long-sought source of the Nile River when he discovered Lake Victoria in 1862. Since ancient times, there had been speculation about the origins of the great river, and the question captured the imagination of nineteenth-century Europe.

Speke was educated to be an army officer from his youngest days. He served for 10 years (1844–1854) in India, where he explored Tibet and the Himalayas and conceived the idea of penetrating into equatorial Africa. En route, he met Sir Richard BURTON and spent a year with the latter's expedition into Somalia. When Speke was seriously wounded in a night raid on his camp, suffering 11 spear wounds, he left Burton's expedition. After recovering, Speke spent a year in the Crimean campaign and then joined Burton again in Zanzibar in 1856. Their assignment was to confirm the existence of several inland lakes that were reported by Arab traders.

The trek was arduous, and Burton was ill, deaf and blind much of the time, but in early 1858 the two first came to Lake Tanganyika, and Speke crossed it by canoe. On the return trip, Speke parted with Burton (the two were hardly on speaking terms by that time) and headed north for 25 days to verify accounts of a vast lake. He reached it, named it Victoria Nyanza for the queen, and rejoined Burton. Speke immediately asserted that he had discovered the source of the Nile, which Burton disputed hotly. The argument became acrimonious and personal when the two returned to England, but the Royal Geographical Society, the expedition's major sponsor, honored Speke for his achievement. By this time the friendship between Speke and Burton had long ended, and they dueled in books and popular magazines, with Burton ridiculing Speke's discoveries.

In 1860, Speke sailed on a government-financed expedition to verify his claims. With a party of 217, he marched overland, under attack from hostile tribes, until he reached the court of MUTESA I, king of Buganda. After securing Mutesa's approval, Speke struck out around Lake Victoria, contacting Sir Samuel BAKER, who had been sent on a relief mission to find Speke. Baker went on to locate and name Lake Albert (after Queen Victoria's consort), and Speke continued on to Khartoum in the Sudan. He had been unable to follow the Nile exactly due to local warfare, but his arrival in Khartoum caused a sensation in England. Burton still rejected the discovery, and the two were scheduled to debate the issue. On the morning of the debate day, Speke, while hunting with an uncle, accidentally slipped crossing a stone wall, shot himself, and died. Some accounts, however, suggest that Speke committed suicide before his confrontation with Burton.

Speke's contributions to the geographical knowledge of Africa were immense. His maps and descriptions were remarkably accurate, and his 1863 book, *Journey to the Source of the Nile,* was not only an important explorer's journal but also provided valuable historical background about Uganda.

References: afr, DAHB, DNB, EB, EWB, *wiki.* Alexander Maitland, *Speke* (1971).

SSEMOGERERE, Paul Kawanga

(Uganda, 1932–)

Paul Ssemogerere, a lifelong Ugandan politician, has been a defender of democratic values, often under the most hostile conditions. Until 2005, he was leader of the Democratic Party and several times its standard-bearer.

Ssemogerere was educated at Makerere University, then from 1957 to 1973, he taught in Uganda. Already in 1961 he was elected to the colonial Legislative Council (Legco), and after independence he entered the National Assembly.

In 1956, the Democratic Party (DP) was founded on a largely Baganda and Catholic base, while Milton OBOTE responded by founding the Uganda People's Congress (UPC) on an appeal to Protestants and the tribes of the north. The old divisions that had led to civil war in the early colonial period were resurrected. Ssemogerere was an early DP activist and was named publicity chair. During Obote's first regime, he was imprisoned from 1969 to 1971. Obote was then overthrown by Idi AMIN, who had the DP's president assassinated. Ssemogerere took leadership, but the DP was almost shut down by Amin's goons. Ssemogerere barely survived an "auto accident," and he fled to the United States. He graduated from Allegheny College and finally took a Ph.D. in public administration from the University of Syracuse in 1979.

Amin was swept from power by Julius NYERERE, who sent the Tanzanian army into Uganda after Amin mounted an ill-fated invasion of northern Tanzania. Nyerere reinstalled his friend Obote in the presidency, and Ssemogerere returned from exile during what became popularly known as Obote II.

In 1980 he and Yoweri MUSEVENI challenged Obote for the presidency in an election that was widely seen as fraudulent and rigged. One member of the national election commission fled to Great Britain and took asylum. Another prominent election official disappeared. Records and ballots were destroyed. Museveni's reaction was to go into the bush and organize a guerilla war against the regime. Ssemogerere chose to stay in government and take up the role of legal opposition. For five years he was parliamentary leader of the opposition.

His subsequent history has haunted Ssemogerere ever since and caused his detractors to accuse him of selling out. When Obote was finally overthrown by the army, Ssemogerere became a minister in the short-lived transitional government. After Museveni and his National Resistance Movement (NRM) took power, Ssemogerere passed from one office to another as minister of Internal Affairs, Foreign Affairs (1988–1994) and Public Service, and deputy prime minister. He resigned from government in 1996 in order to run against Museveni.

Under Museveni, the NRM maintained a monopoly on organized politics, and political parties were banned. That forced candidates to run as independents, but with government power over the media and the NRM's organization in every village and urban neighborhood, campaigning was extremely difficult at best for any opponent of Museveni. In the 1996 presidential election, Ssemogerere polled 22.3 percent. He carried the traditional Baganda Catholic areas around Entebbe and the far north. In a weird twist, the terrorist Joseph KONY, leader of the Lord's Resistance Army, ordered his people to vote for Ssemogerere or risk death.

Ssemogerere has carried the burden of being seen as a compromiser, too willing to work with other parties even when he had values conflicts with them. He was also accused of being "soft" in the face of tough decisions. Nevertheless, he has never stopped stressing his key political values: multiparty democracy, transparency and the end of corruption.

Reference: wiki.

SSERUNKUMA, Bruno
(Uganda, 1962–)

Bruno Sserunkuma is an international prize-winning ceramicist who has been at the center of the revival of the arts in Uganda after the devastation of the years of Idi AMIN, Milton OBOTE and the civil wars. During that period, Makerere University, where Sserunkuma is based, lacked the most elementary equipment, and its art studios were looted by roving gangs.

Sserunkuma studied art at Makerere during the years immediately following the removal of Obote and the first years of the National Resistance Movement (NRM) of Yoweri MUSEVENI. He received his BFA and MFA degrees. Almost immediately he began to take part in group and solo exhibitions, first at Makerere as the arts began their slow revival, and then overseas. His pieces have been shown in Belgium, Cuba, the Netherlands and France.

Sserunkuma works with a local clay, and his pots and vases (most of his work) show themes from everyday Ganda life. Social and cultural activities and scenes are surrounded by intricate ornamental designs, many of which come from batik patterns. His style shows elongated semi-abstract figures. *Ganda School Boys* is a tall cylindrical earthenware vase encircled by stylized lads in school uniforms, arms linked behind their backs. It manages to be both affecting and evocative at the same time. Some of his bowls are painted inside and out.

STANLEY, Henry Morton
(Tanzania/Uganda/Democratic Republic of the Congo, 1841–1904)

Sir Henry Morton Stanley, Anglo-American journalist, explorer and adventurer, has been fixed in the popular mind for his rescue of Dr. David LIVINGSTONE in 1872. Besides this feat, however, he was a significant explorer in his own right, crossing the continent and securing the Congo (now the Democratic Republic of the Congo) for the king of the Belgians.

Stanley was born in Wales as John Rowlands. Probably illegitimate, he was raised in a workhouse. In his *Autobiography* (1909) he relates the brutality of the place, which included his discovery of the body of a boy who had been beaten to death by the sadistic headmaster. At age 15, Rowlands ran away after assaulting the master, but when he was rejected by all his relatives, he took a ship to the United States as a cabin boy in 1859. He was taken in by a tradesman named Henry Morton Stanley, whose name he adopted. His sponsor died soon after, and young Stanley joined the Confederate army in 1861 until he was captured at the Battle of Shiloh. Prison life was so terrible that he enlisted in the Union artillery, but his health collapsed, and he transferred to the Union navy.

After the war, Stanley became a roving journalist and war correspondent. He crossed the western plains, describing the frontier to readers in the United States, and then was sent to Turkey in 1866. The following year the *New York Herald* commissioned him to report on the British military expedition against Emperor TEWODROS of Ethiopia. His reports in 1867 and 1868 of the siege and fall of Magdala fortress scooped other papers, and he was given permission to travel for the *Herald* and report whatever he chose. He went to Crete to write of a rebellion and to Spain to report on a civil war.

In 1869 the *Herald* gave Stanley his most important assignment: to find the legendary Livingstone, who had been on an expedition for three years and was presumed lost or dead. The journalistic aspect of the expedition generated anger in Great Britain, and the Royal Geographical Society mounted its own rescue mission. In 1871, Stanley set out from Zanzibar into uncharted territory, with no experience to prepare him for the rigors of the situation. Within six months he found Livingstone in Ujiji, on the shores of Lake Tanganyika. Removing his hat in a gesture of respect, Stanley greeted the old missionary and explorer—supposedly the only White man within a thousand kilometers—with the words: "Dr. Livingstone, I presume." After providing Livingstone with desperately needed provisions and medicine, Stanley traveled with him around Lake Tanganyika until the two satisfied themselves that it was not the source of the Nile. Livingstone continued on his own, and Stanley returned to London with Livingstone's journals in 1872.

Stanley's arrival in London created a storm of protest. He was denounced as a liar, his lowly origins were proclaimed in the popular press, and Livingstone's journals were denounced as fakes. Stanley was exonerated when one of Livingstone's sons authenticated the letters and Queen Victoria publicly thanked him and sent a royal gift. His *How I Found Livingstone* (1872) sold well, but Stanley returned to the more congenial atmosphere of the United States, where he had a successful lecture tour. After a brief period of reporting the Asante war in the Gold Coast (now Ghana) from 1873 to 1874, Stanley determined to complete Livingstone's work. He was influenced by John Hanning SPEKE, who had discovered Lake Victoria and suspected that it was the fabled source of the Nile.

In 1874, Stanley left Zanzibar for Lake Victoria with a well-equipped expeditionary force. The trip went from one success to another. In 1875 he visited King MUTESA I of Buganda (now Uganda), and his impassioned letter calling for Christian missionaries led to their admission two years later. He completed the work left undone by Speke's untimely death and confirmed that the Nile originated from Lake Victoria. He then discovered Lake Edward, although hostile warriors forced him to turn back. Sailing his little craft, the *Lady Alice,* along the Congo River, he went on to a lake that he named Stanley Pool. The boat finally stopped at a series of 32 cataracts, which he named Stanley Falls. He went the last distance to the Atlantic Ocean on foot and recounted the remarkable trip in *Through the Dark Continent* (1878).

Stanley's travels and discoveries opened the interior to imperialism more than any other earlier efforts. Agents of King Leopold II of the Belgians commissioned Stanley to lead a further expedition, which he did in 1879 after Great Britain expressed no interest in the Congo. He stayed until 1884, building a chain of stations along the Congo River with four steamers to link them. He also built a

Henry Morton Stanley

road past the Stanley Falls cataracts, working with such diligence that his laborers named him *Bula Mutari,* the "rock breaker." Stanley attended the Berlin Conference of 1884–1885, which divided Africa into areas of colonial expansion for the European powers and gave the Congo to Leopold as his personal fiefdom.

Stanley's last African adventure was the relief of Eduard SCHNITZER, known better as Emin Pasha, the *khedive* of Egypt's governor of the Equatoria Province in the Sudan. The Sudanese revolt of the MAHDI had stranded Emin Pasha near Lake Albert, and Stanley led the rescue mission in 1887. He proceeded along the Congo River and then through the densest tropical forest, sometimes slowed to a kilometer a day. Most of his men died, and Stanley himself almost succumbed to fever. En route he was the first Westerner to see the Ruwenzori Mountains, the "Mountains of the Moon," but his intended task went unfulfilled. Emin Pasha not only did not want to leave, but he also felt insulted that a relief column had caused him to lose face with his African soldiers. Finally, he accompanied Stanley to Bagamoyo, on the East African coast. *In Darkest Africa*

(1890), one of Stanley's most popular books, tells his story of the trek.

In 1890, Stanley settled permanently in England, where he married and adopted a son. From 1895 to 1900 he was a Unionist member of Parliament. He continued, however, to travel. He visited the United States, Australia and New Zealand, and in 1897 he was in South Africa to speak at the opening of the Cape Town-to-Bulawayo railroad. He had seen Africa emerge from an unmapped and virtually unknown region to a continent undergoing rapid Western settlement and colonial development.

References: afr, DAHB, EB, EWB, *wiki*. Martin Dugard, *Into Africa: The Epic Adventures of Staney and Livingstone* (2004); Daniel Liebowitz and Charles Pearson, *The Last Expedition: Stanley's Mad Journey Through the Congo* (2005).

STEVENS, Siaka Probyn
(Sierra Leone, 1905–1988)

Siaka Probyn Stevens, independence leader and later president, dominated the politics of Sierra Leone from 1968 until his retirement in 1985. As a proponent of African unity and nonalignment, he was active in the Organization of African Unity (OAU) and the Nonaligned Movement. Stevens was the son of a northern Christian father and a southern Muslim mother. He married a woman of mixed ethnic background and prided himself on his diversity. At the same time he profoundly distrusted political diversity and subverted it when he could.

He received his secondary education in Freetown, the capital, and entered the Court Messenger Force in 1923. This organization was the protectorate's main police constabulary, and Stevens rose to sergeant-major before leaving in 1930. He then worked for a iron mining company, which led him to begin labor union organizing. By 1943 he was a full-time trade unionist and became secretary-general of the United Mineworkers Union in 1945. He subsequently became a city councillor and a member of the colonial Protectorate Assembly, which dealt with affairs in the interior. Stevens was appointed to represent workers' interests. In 1947 the British Trades Union Council sponsored him for a year at Ruskin College, Oxford University, where he studied industrial relations.

Stevens was an advocate for the peoples of the interior, who felt themselves excluded and patronized by the Creole elite of Freetown. In 1951 he joined Albert and Milton MARGAI in founding the Sierra Leone People's Party (SLPP). Stevens was elected to the Legislative Council (Legco) when the SLPP won the 1951 elections and became minister of lands, mines, and labor. He fell out with Milton Margai and was removed from the Legco after being re-elected in 1957. As opposition leader he attended the London conferences to negotiate independence but refused to sign the conference report. Returning home, he founded the All-People's Congress (APC) but was briefly imprisoned for conspiracy for his campaigning. He was opposition leader until 1967, when the APC won the elections. The army refused to accept the results, and Stevens was forced into exile. After a year, junior officers overthrew the coup leaders, and Stevens returned in triumph to lead the country.

Stevens promptly rewarded himself with a year's back salary. It was an omen of things to come. Violence attended future elections, and in 1978 a one-party state was proclaimed. Stevens argued that multiparty systems only encouraged ethnic conflict and division. Corruption and political unrest marked the rest of his long administration. Despite this record, Stevens was also a populist and champion of justice, especially for the neglected peoples of the hinterland regions. In a divided society, he was the main symbol of national unity. He had great organizational skills, but as time passed he assumed more and more authority for himself, trusting few others to make decisions. He began to rule by patronage. One result of his rule was the gradual destruction of the flourishing business community, which became displaced by Lebanese, Indian and other foreign investors who courted (and paid for) the patronage of "Pa Shaki," as Stevens liked to be called. The resentment that grew from this development (and the accompanying inflation) led to continuous unrest that broke out into disturbances.

Stevens's greatest achievement was remaining in power and establishing a peaceful transition for his successor. His distrust of other politicians led him to choose his army commander, Major-General Joseph MOMOH, as his successor. In 1975, Stevens brought Momoh into government and spent the next 10 years preparing him for the presidency. Even as Stevens's popularity waned, he groomed his successor and passed the presidency to Momoh in 1985 after persuading all the other possible candidates to withdraw. In retirement he wrote his memoirs but, always the shrewd politician, he expressed great disappointment when Momoh staked out his own positions and did not follow his advice.

References: afr, AO, DAHB, MMA, PLBA, PLCA, *wiki*. Stevens, *What Life Has Taught Me* (1984).

STRYDOM, Amanda
(South Africa, 1956–)

Amanda Strydom is one of the most popular and enduring entertainers in South Africa. She has performed in almost every genre—acting, singing, but above all as a beloved cabaret performer.

Strydom has issued eight original music albums, plus a compilation. In 2001 she won two "best album" awards for *Op 'n Klein Blou Ghoen*. She writes most of her own material, including songs and her one-woman shows, which have been received enthusiastically throughout the country. She writes and performs in Afrikaans and English.

All this has been accomplished on talent alone, with minimal musical training. Strydom cannot read music. She studied drama at the University of Pretoria, where she graduated in 1978. She began acting immediately in Cape Town, and in 1979 made her film debut in a leading part. Offers in theater, television and cabaret followed quickly, and she was established. She also was a radio disc jockey and began script writing.

In cabaret in 1986, Strydom sang a piece about the injustice of the apartheid pass laws, and ended with the forbidden Black power salute. The reaction was one of outrage, and she was widely attacked in the press. She suffered an attack of bipolar depression that crippled her for several years and wrote a play about her experience, *In Full Flight* (1999). Her two one-woman plays have been particularly well received. *State of the Heart* (1993) still continues to be performed, and 1994's *The Incredible Journey of Tinkerbell van Tonder* is in regular demand. Songs from both have been issued as albums, and she has taken both pieces overseas. A strong supporter of the new South Africa, Strydom was a featured performer for Nelson MANDELA's eighty-fifth birthday celebration in 2003.

Reference: www.amadastrydom.com.

SUNDIATA Keita
(Mali, 1190?–1255?)

Mansa Sundiata Keita, son of a family that had ruled Kangaba for about two centuries, became king when that small state was tributary to Susu, the regional power. His name means "the lion king." He took his country on an expansionist course, creating the Mali Empire and establishing the Keita dynasty as one of the great medieval royal families of Africa. Because he was the empire's creator, many accounts about him border on legend, but throughout the stories it is clear that he was considered to be endowed with great magical powers.

It seems that he was born crippled to a mother who, in one account, was given to the king as a gift by a hunters' society. Sundiata later became a "master hunter," which placed him in a secret fraternity whose members were considered guardians of magic power. When his half-brother succeeded to the throne, Sundiata and his mother went into voluntary exile to avoid assassination, even though he was not taken seriously as a rival because of his physical handicap.

Sundiata became headman of a village, where he built up a personal army and consolidated his power when the region was overrun by the dominant state of Susu, which had rejected Islam. Sundiata's brothers were killed by the Susu king, Sumaguru, when Kangaba fell. Various legends tell of a magic cure of Sundiata's handicap, of his assembling a large army, and of a magic potion that gave him victory. Evidently, Sundiata marched on Susu, using the hunting fraternities to gather warriors as he went. The tide turned when Sundiata's sister (who had been forced to become one of Sumaguru's wives), the leading Susu general, and the clan *griot*, or court historian, deserted to Sundiata. They revealed Sumaguru's secret magic, thus destroying his warriors' confidence in his power. Sumaguru was probably poisoned after Sundiata defeated him in the battle of Kirina in 1235. Uniting the local chiefs in a war of liberation, Sundiata forced the submission of Susu's vassal states and moved against the Ghana Empire, capturing its capital in 1240. Born Mari-Djata, at this point the new emperor took the name Sundiata; both names mean "lion king."

Sundiata appointed generals from his own age group so he could count on their loyalty, and he chose governors for subject peoples who were to rule wisely, not disturbing local customs, so that their administration would not be compared with Susu's harsh rule. The original clans that joined in the liberation war, however, retained their rights and privileges as well as their titles, acknowledging the Keita as paramount and Sundiata as *mansa,* or emperor. Each clan had a representative at Sundiata's court. In this sense, Mali became a federation of clan states that also ruled various conquered territories. Sundiata reduced ethnic prejudice by linking the great families and making kin out of potentially opposed groups. Strong fraternal ties were often forged, and these great families—Conde, Keita, Camara, Diop and Traoré+n—are still important in Mali and the region around it.

As Sundiata's empire expanded, it absorbed the trade routes to the north that crossed the Sahara Desert and the gold fields to the south. He built a new capital, Niani, at a branch of the Niger River, and it soon became a center of commerce. He bound this empire together with a monarchy based on religion and magic. Sundiata was a nominal Muslim, which was important to the Islamic traders who were also grateful to him for crushing Susu. Nevertheless, he never abandoned traditional religion, which strengthened his base among the common people, who imputed magical powers to the king and held him in awe.

References: afr, DAHB, EB, HWL, *wiki.*

SUSNEYOS
(Ethiopia, 1575?–1632)

Susneyos was emperor during a turbulent period in Ethiopian history marked by religious conflict that led to civil war and his abdication.

Susneyos, a grandson of LEBNA DENGEL, came to the throne in 1607 after a 10–year struggle against relatives in the royal family. He had spent years in the south as a *shifta* or bandit, defending the borders; his achievement of power represented a victory for a new aggressive leader. Conditions in Ethiopia were grave: several border areas were under attack, there were pretenders to throne left from the bruising fight for power, and there were plots against Susneyos because of his religious policy. He responded by taking his armies into the field, securing the borders, and conquering territory to the west and north. To stabilize his position, he reached out to European powers, especially Portugal, for aid in renovating the country and moderniz-

ing the army. He abolished many court customs, such as prostrations before the emperor, forbade the sale of slaves to Arab traders, and reduced the nobility's privileges.

Jesuit missionaries had already been introduced and had achieved significant influence in the Ethiopian Church and the court. Susneyos secretly became Catholic in 1612 and planned to join the Ethiopian Coptic Church to Rome, but his Jesuit advisors thought that this action was premature. His active promotion of Catholicism widened the gulf between himself and the nobility, who considered the national Church the foundation of Ethiopian unity. In 1622 he proclaimed Catholicism the state religion, which galvanized the opposition against him. Ethiopian Church leaders, members of the royal family who governed provinces with large armies, and most of the populace opposed Susneyos. Conflicts broke out, culminating in a battle with major losses, and Susneyos's son, FASILADAS, persuaded him to abdicate after reestablishing the Ethiopian Church. He died shortly after.

References: DAB, DAHB, *wiki.*

SUZMAN, Helen Gavronsky
(South Africa, 1917–)

Dame Helen Gavronsky Suzman, the leading parliamentary opponent of apartheid in South Africa until her retirement in 1989, served as the principal voice of White liberalism.

The daughter of wealthy Lithuanian Jewish immigrants, Helen Gavronsky was educated in a convent because other private schools rarely accepted Jews. She studied at the University of the Witwatersrand and at age 19 married Moses Suzman, a physician. After the birth of their first child, she completed her studies. In 1945 she was appointed a lecturer in economic history at Witwatersrand. In 1948, after the defeat of the United Party (UP) by the Nationalists, she formed a UP chapter at the university. She was also active in the women's section of the Torch Commando, a White, English-speaking veterans' organization that opposed removing Coloured voters from the electoral rolls in Cape Province.

In 1953, when the party was unable to find another UP candidate, Suzman ran for parliament and won in an affluent, heavily Jewish constituency. She sat in parliament for 36 years. With the declining fortunes of White liberalism in South Africa, for 13 of those years she was the sole member of the Progressive Party, which was formed in 1959 when the UP split. It was the only White party to reject apartheid, and Suzman became the parliamentary voice of the antiapartheid movement and the government's conscience. In 1974, seven other Progressives were elected, and in 1977 they became the official opposition as the Progressive Federal Party.

In 1963, Suzman cast the only vote against the bill permitting detention without charges, accusing it of plunging the country into "the morass of a totalitarian state." Again and again she spoke out against apartheid, unmasking its corruption, duplicity and total disregard of democracy. Unable to stem the flow of restrictive laws, she did her best to expose them. She registered her powerful dissent against the Sabotage Law, media controls, the establishment of ethnic "homelands," and recognition of Rhodesia's White government. An able and witty debater, she parried the anti-Semitic and racist taunts of the Nationalist members, once advising President P. W. BOTHA to visit a Black township but to do so "heavily disguised as a human being."

Suzman began to take on the aura of a one-woman resistance movement, and to honor her became a way of making an antiapartheid statement. She received seven honorary doctorates, several fellowships, and nominations for the Nobel Peace Prize. In 1989 she was named Dame Commander of the British Empire.

Throughout her political career, Suzman opposed sanctions against South Africa, insisting that they would only foster a siege mentality among Whites. She endorsed a franchise limited to those with education, proposing that about 150,000 Africans (out of more than 15 million) should be allowed to vote. For those reasons, as well as her abhorrence of its Communist ties, she never supported the African National Congress (ANC). Despite her views, she remained good friends with most of the Black leaders, who admired her integrity and courage in the antiapartheid struggle. President F. W. DE KLERK appointed her to the electoral commission to prepare for the 1994 elections—the first in South Africa open to all adults.

References: *afr*, CB, DRWW, EWB, GSAP, PLBA, *wiki*. Suzman, *In No Uncertain Terms* (1993); Joanna Strangewayes-Booth, *A Cricket in the Thorn Tree* (1976).

TAITU
(Ethiopia, 1840s-1918)

Taitu, consort and fourth wife of MENELIK II, ruled Ethiopia for the eight years during his last illness before his death. Taitu was a strong-willed woman who forged a powerful alliance with her husband, promoting his career and then replacing him when he was incapacitated.

She came from a royal family and met Menelik through her brothers, who were imprisoned with him by TEWODROS II. Politically sophisticated and educated, Taitu built strong factional support based on kinship and marriage before becoming Menelik's wife in 1883. Her political connections were a factor in helping Menelik become emperor in 1889.

Taitu was a remarkable power in her own right: she had a private army and large land holdings, she held a dominant position in determining Ethiopian Orthodox Church policy, and she was the controlling figure in palace intrigues. She opposed Menelik's conciliatory attitude toward the Italians who had imperial designs on Ethiopia, once interrupting negotiations by declaring to the Italian ambassador, "You wish Ethiopia ... as your protectorate, but this shall never be!" She led her army into battle against the Italians at Meqelle and took part in their decisive defeat at Adowa in 1895. In 1902, she also led a successful campaign against Tigréan secessionists.

In domestic policy, Taitu was progressive. She founded and named the new capital, Addis Ababa ("new flower"), financed its first hotel, and promoted education for girls. In 1906, when Menelik had his first stroke, Taitu took power. Because she was childless, she attempted to have her stepdaughter ZAUDITU named successor, but Menelik chose his grandson, IYASU V, instead. By 1910, Taitu was reduced to nursing Menelik, who died in 1914. Iyasu became emperor, but when he converted to Islam in 1916, he was deposed and replaced by Zauditu. Taitu, who had retreated to a monastery after Menelik's death, briefly reappeared with the accession of Zauditu but soon retreated as Tafari Makonnen (later HAILE SELASSIE) assumed the regency. In 1918, Taitu died of heart disease.

References: afr, DAHB, WWR, *wiki*. Chris Rosenfeld, Chris. *Empress Taytu and Menilek II* (1986).

TÄKLÄ Haymanot
(Ethiopia, 1215?–1313)

Saint Täklä Haymanot, the most revered saint in Coptic Ethiopia, was a critical figure in establishing Ethiopian national identity. He was instrumental in "restoring" the Solomonic dynasty and revitalizing monasticism, which were central to both religious and cultural life.

Täklä came from a priestly family but chose to enter a monastery rather than become a parish priest. After 20 years of study and solitude, he had acquired great personal prestige. With a small band of disciples he began an extensive missionary effort that culminated in the founding of a monastery that later became Debra Libanos, the most influential center of Christianity in Ethiopia. Debra Libanos extended its influence over most other monasteries in the Ethiopian empire and, as abbot, Täklä became the most powerful religious figure in the country. Because the *abuna,* or head of the Church, was always an Egyptian, the abbot of Debra Libanos was the highest ranking native clergyman. So important was Debra Libanos that the emperor personally named its abbot from a slate elected by the monks. Täklä's missionary effort created a buffer between the Coptic Christians and the encroachments of Islam, and it is one of the major reasons why Ethiopian Christianity survived while that of neighboring Axum and Meroé faded.

Beyond these facts, Täklä's history becomes lost in the mists of religious legend. The elaborate hagiography itself, however, marks the emergence of Amhara-language literature, in which he appears as a miracle worker. Täklä is credited with defeating (and converting) Motalami, the major traditional Ethiopian ruler of the period. Moreover, he is considered the instrument of the archangel Michael in establishing the Solomonic monarchy. Whatever his direct role, Täklä was involved, playing a conciliatory role in ending the Zagwe dynasty (1137–1270) and restoring rule that styled itself as the Solomonic dynasty, claiming direct descent from the mythical liaison between Solomon and the Queen of Sheba. The Zagwe kings were deeply religious, and many were priests. The Solomonic kings favored monks over the parish clergy and were rarely devout. Täklä, and later his disciples, founded monastic society in Ethiopia; thereby, power, education and wealth accrued to them rather than to the institutional church.

References: DAB, *dacb.*

TAMBO, Oliver Reginald
(South Africa, 1917–1993)

Oliver Reginald Tambo was for a generation the leader of the African National Congress (ANC) in exile, rallying the world community against apartheid and preparing for the day of its overthrow. A courtly and gracious gentleman who preached and lived a life of tolerance and nonviolence, he guided the ANC during a time when it most needed a steady hand to unify its contending factions. Tambo was also deeply religious and during this time was leading choirs and preparing for ordination in the Anglican Church.

Tambo was born into a peasant family in the Transkei and was educated in mission schools before attending St. Peter's Secondary School in Johannesburg, a seedbed of African leadership where he came under the influence of Father Trevor HUDDLESTON. In 1941 he received a BSc from the University of Fort Hare, but he was expelled for a student demonstration during a postgraduate year. Tambo returned to St. Peter's as a science teacher until 1947, sharing his increasing political militancy with his students and helping to shape several future ANC leaders. In 1944, Tambo joined his Fort Hare comrades Nelson MANDELA, Walter SISULU, and others to found the ANC Youth League. In 1945, Tambo was national secretary. Later he became vice president, and in 1949 he was elected to the ANC national executive. Within a few years the young members had toppled the aging and conservative ANC leadership and set the organization on a new course. Tambo recalled those days wistfully: "We were never really young. There were

no dances, hardly a cinema, but meetings, discussions every night."

Throughout this period, Tambo had also been studying law by correspondence, and in 1947 he became an articled clerk to a solicitor. In 1952 he and Mandela formed the first Black law partnership in South Africa. It was in this same year that the ANC adopted the nonviolent Programme of Action against the new apartheid legislation then being imposed. Boycotts, strikes and various forms of civil disobedience brought mass demonstrations into the streets. ANC membership went from 7,000 to 100,000. In 1955, Tambo became secretary-general of the ANC, and in 1958 he was appointed deputy president, in effect running the organization, because president Chief Albert LUTHULI was under banning orders.

During the 1950s, Tambo was constantly harassed. He was banned in 1954, forbidden to attend public meetings, and restricted to Johannesburg. In 1956, just as he was made a candidate for ordination as an Anglican priest, he was arrested and charged with treason. After a year he was released, only to be banned again in 1959. The ANC had laid elaborate plans in case the government suppressed the ANC, and in the aftermath of the Sharpeville massacre, the plans went into effect in 1960. An armed wing, Umkhonto we Sizwe (Spear of the Nation) was created, and Tambo escaped the country to establish an ANC organization in exile. Mandela, Sisulu and many other ANC leaders were tried and sentenced to life imprisonment.

After establishing himself in Tanzania, Tambo undertook the task of organization. In 1967, on the death of Luthuli, he became acting president of the ANC, and in 1977, at the suggestion of the imprisoned leaders, he assumed the title of president. He developed valuable support in Scandinavia, which resulted in a regular flow of funds.

When the Black Consciousness Movement (BCM) was brutally suppressed from 1976 to 1977 after the Soweto student riots, a torrent of young people crossed the borders and entered the Umkhonto camps that Tambo had built in Tanzania. Although it was infiltrated with spies and informers, a force of 10,000 was established, trained and politically educated. Tambo was concerned that the youth see the armed struggle as an extension of a far broader political struggle for freedom. He firmly espoused the opening line of the 1955 Freedom Charter, which he had helped to write: "South Africa belongs to all who live in it, Black and

White." He did not want Black racism to replace apartheid. Umkhonto began to launch raids against power plants, police stations, post offices and other government installations until it averaged one every two days by 1981. Tambo justified the turn to armed struggle by arguing that "in the face of systematic tyranny it becomes a duty and a right to take up arms ... we decide to embrace violence to remove a violent system."

South Africa retaliated with cross-border raids and assassinations. Joe SLOVO, the leading Communist Party member of the ANC, lost his wife, the noted Marxist writer and activist Ruth First, to a parcel bomb in 1982. The South African government attempted to persuade its allies that the ANC was a terrorist organization, which was a successful policy with the United States and Great Britain. The guerrilla actions became united with internal dissension after 1985, when Tambo called for resistance to make the townships "ungovernable." Using Radio Freedom, which he had established in the ANC's new headquarters in Zambia, Tambo precipitated a massive confrontation, to which the government responded with two unprecedented states of emergency in 1985 and 1986. Twenty-two thousand were arrested and more than 2,000 died.

Tambo now seized the initiative at the first signs of domestic and international revulsion against the government's actions. In 1985 he received a delegation of South African businessmen who came to discuss the ANC's program. He reassured them—and through them the Western world—of the ANC's commitment to a mixed economy and to a nonracial South Africa. Soon delegations of all kinds were arriving in Lusaka for what were, in effect, preliminary peace talks. Tambo used his new legitimacy to undertake 1986 discussions with the British foreign secretary and Chester Crocker, the American Assistant Secretary of State for African Affairs. The U.S. Congress imposed limited economic sanctions against South Africa that year, and Tambo was received by U.S. Secretary of State George Schultz.

In 1989, Tambo suffered the first of several strokes and was admitted to a hospital in Sweden. In 1990 he returned to South Africa from exile but passed on his ANC duties to Mandela after the latter's release from prison. Tambo died in Johannesburg.

References: afr, CB, DAHB, DRWW, EWB, GSAP, PLBA, RWWA, *wiki*. E.S. Reddy, ed. *Oliver Tambo and the Struggle against Apartheid* (1987).

TAYA, Maawiya Ould Sid'Ahmed
(Mauritania, 1943–)

Colonel Maawiya Ould Sid'Ahmed Taya, head of state and military strongman, was president of Mauritania for over 20 years. He maintained firm control in a racist state where the Black majority (70 percent of the population) is ruled by an Arab minority.

Taya joined the army as a young man and became aide to President Moktar DADDAH. In 1976 he was made commander of the northern region during the Sahara war with the Polisario guerrillas, who were trying to establish an independent Sahara Arab Democratic Republic (SADR) in Western Sahara. Two years later he was promoted to deputy chief of staff and then became a member of the ruling military council and minister of defense after the coup that removed Daddah. The council's attempt to make peace with Polisario failed, and Mohammed HAIDALLAH, a relative of Taya's, took command and named Taya head of the national police and army chief of staff (1980). In 1981, Taya was named prime minister but remained a rival for Haidallah's power.

After a 1984 coup attempt, Haidallah removed Taya from the premiership, but Taya in turn toppled Haidallah and tried to deal with the Polisario crisis. He reaffirmed recognition of the SADR while restoring relations with Morocco and Libya and settling a border dispute with Algeria. Just as his policy of friendship with Arab states was succeeding, he faced an internal conflict with Black Mauritanians, who resented what they saw as Arab domination. Communal violence between Blacks and Arabs spread during 1987 and 1988. Taya handled the crisis badly, purging Blacks from the army and tolerating attacks on Black communities. In 1989, Arabs turned on Black Sénégalese guest workers in Nouakchott, the capital, forcing 15,000 to flee. In response, Mauritanian-owned shops in Dakar, Sénégal, were looted, and Mauritania began expelling all Blacks, regardless of nationality. This resulted in about 170,000 refugees.

Taya's Arab racism was exemplified in his unwillingness to confront slavery, which is still widely practiced in Mauritania. There are approximately 100,000 slaves and 300,000 semi-slaves (indentured workers) in the country. Blacks are discriminated against in education, employment and health care. Taya tolerated the dispossession of Blacks in the south, where their lands are being turned over to Arab nomads, and he supported a policy of eliminating Black cultural traditions. In reaction, there are two Black guerrilla movements operating out of Sénégal and conducting raids into Mauritania.

Despite these internal policies, Taya was a keen supporter of the American global campaign against terrorism. He fostered an alliance of eight regional states and cracked down on militant Islamicists in Mauritania. The country was also only one of three in the Arab League to recognize Israel. These moves caused his Islamic political base to erode.

Taya permitted multiparty elections in 1992 and won in what was widely seen as a fraudulent vote. In 1997 he was elected without opposition when the major parties boycotted the election. In 2003 he won again with a jiggered vote after surviving an attempted coup. There was another attempt the following year, and finally in 2005, Taya was removed by the military. He went into exile on Qatar.

References: afr, PLBA, RWWA, *wiki*.

TAYLOR, Charles Ghankay
(Liberia/Sierra Leone, 1948–)

Charles Taylor, a terrorist who destabilized several states in West Africa, took over the presidency of Liberia, and was the first African head of state to be remanded to the International Court at the Hague, Netherlands, for crimes against humanity.

Taylor was the son of an American father and his Libero-American wife. Raised in Liberia, he went to the United States after secondary school and graduated from Bentley College in 1977. After the overthrow of the Libero-American elite with the assassination of President William TOLBERT, Taylor returned to Liberia to join the staff of Samuel DOE as director of the General Services Agency. In 1983 he fled back to Boston with $1 million in looted funds. Arrested on a Liberian warrant, Taylor managed to escape from an American prison and return to Africa, where he began plotting an insurrection. He is believed to have gone first to

Former Liberian President Charles Taylor alights from the Nigerian government plane into the waiting handcuffs of United Nations Peacekeepers who effected his arrest at Monrovia's Roberts International Airport on his arrival from Nigeria. Taylor was immediately transferred to the Special Court for Sierra Leone in Freetown.

Libya and gotten support from Col. Muammar al-Qaddafi.

Taylor then took asylum in Côte d'Ivoire under the wing of President Félix HOUPHOUËT-BOIGNY. In 1989, Taylor invaded northern Liberia from his base with a ragtag force of conscripts, child soldiers and opponents of Doe. His guerillas swept through the country and surrounded Monrovia, the capital. After another insurgent captured Doe and tortured and killed him, an interim government was set up under Dr. Amos SAWYER, while Taylor consolidated his position in the hinterland. He soon controlled the countryside by a mix of terror and bonding with traditional enemies of Doe's ethnic group. He declared himself president in 1990, although he did not take total control until 1994.

In 1991, Foday SANKOH, whom Taylor had known in Libya (and who was also supported by Qaddafi), began a civil war in Sierra Leone. Soon the two terrorists were collaborating, supporting their troops with looted diamonds. After Sankoh went into exile in 1997, Taylor continued to support his guerilla forces. In 2003, Taylor was indicted by the United National Special Court for Sierra Leone (SCSL), for crimes against humanity. On a visit to Ghana he was to be served with the warrant and arrested, but President Thabo MBEKI of South Africa intervened and he returned safely to Liberia. It was one more in his litany of prominent supporters.

Taylor was accused of human rights abuses, including the mindless maiming of civilians, forced recruitment of child soldiers, mass killings and the assassination of opponents. He also began using foreign troops, which caused the gradual escalation of the Liberian crisis into a regional one. The regional organization, the Economic Union of West African States (EUWAS), sent a peacekeeping force in, but Taylor denounced them as a front for Nigerian hegemony in the area. An election was held in 1997, and Taylor won overwhelmingly in a reasonably fair election.

In 2003, Taylor was forced to flee and given sanctuary in Nigeria under a deal arranged with President Olusegun OBASANJO. Despite a $2 million bounty authorized by the United States and being placed on Interpol's Most Wanted List, he lived in Nigeria without supervision until 2006, when Liberian President Ellen JOHNSON-SHIRLEAF requested his extradition for war crimes. A reluctant Nigeria allowed him to escape, but he was captured before he crossed the border into Cameroon, and returned to Sierra Leone for trial by the SCSL. Because his presence was a security risk, the United Nations Security Council authorized his removal to the Hague for trial.

References: afr, wiki.

TEMBO, John Zenas
(Malawi, 1932–)

John Zenas Tembo was a Malawian government and party official, and a powerful figure in the regime of Dr. Hastings Kamuzu BANDA, the life president.

Educated in Lesotho and Zimbabwe, he entered parliament in 1961, in the years immediately preceding independence. Tembo joined Dr. Banda's first government as minister of finance, serving from 1964 to 1969. Consistently loyal to Banda, Tembo survived every purge of the cabinet and rose steadily. From 1969 to 1971 he was minister of trade and industry, and from 1971 to 1984 he was governor of the Reserve Bank of Malawi, a position of great power. Tembo has also been prominent on the executive council of the official Malawi Congress Party (MCP), which he now heads.

He is the uncle of Cecilia Kadzimira, Dr. Banda's longtime "official hostess," and the two were Banda's chief advisors. He served as Banda's interpreter, because Banda spoke no African language well. Tembo was widely seen as Banda's choice for successor. He is conservative, steady and reliable—qualities that endear him to international

monetary bodies and infuriate civil rights activists. His rise was not completely smooth, and a power tussle with Dick Matenje, secretary-general of the MCP in 1983, was settled only when Matenje died in a suspicious auto crash. Banda used Tembo to deal with delicate foreign affairs, and Tembo managed the tensions between Malawi and the Frontline States over Malawi's close relationship with South Africa.

As Banda aged and became less able to maintain political control, Tembo emerged as the most dominant member of the regime. When Banda had brain surgery in 1993, Tembo was part of the three-man council chosen by the MCP to govern Malawi during the president's recovery. The MCP began a cautious process of reform, eliminating Malawi's petty prohibitions against long hair, bell-bottom trousers and short skirts, and banning detention without trial. This was not enough to restore popular support, however, and Banda and the MCP were soundly defeated in free elections in 1994. Tembo remains the leader of the MCP. He hoped to contest the presidency in 2004, but was barred after he was expelled from parliament for contempt of court. He has since returned to his post as leader of the opposition.

References: DRWW, PLBA, RWWA, wiki.

TEMPELS, Placide
(Democratic Republic of the Congo/Tanzania, 1906–1977)

Father Placide Tempels, a Belgian missionary who came to be popularly known as "Baba Placide," was the theoretician of the commune-based *Jamaa* movement.

He was born Frans Tempels, taking the religious name Placide when he became a Franciscan friar in 1924. He was ordained a priest in 1930 and went to what was then the Belgian Congo three years later. He remained there 29 years, retiring back to Belgium in 1962, where he died.

Although he was neither African nor a philosopher, Tempels wrote a seminal book, *Bantu Philosophy* (1945), attempting to analyze African thought in Western philosophical categories. His central notion, and the one most taken up by others, was to attempt to define the concept of "being" in terms of the African idea of "living force." He named it the "triple force": *uzima*, a full, strong and total life, intensity in being; *uzazi*, fecundity beyond the physical; and *mapendo*, vital unity and mutual love with all beings. "Isolation kills." He argued the need for a dialogue between the African essence—what he called "the Bantu ontology"—and Western culture.

Tempels was deeply conscious that he arrived in the Congo as a White colonizer, and "the message that God entrusted me with the inspired attitudes ... of a spiritual master, doctor of authority, religious bureaucrat, pastor of a flock which was to hear, obey and be silent." After 10 years as a missionary in the bush, questions nagged him about the people among whom he lived and of whose inner lives he knew little. He set himself the goal to think and feel African, "to have a Bantu soul." From this personal desire to identify, Tempels began reflection on African thought and thought-patterns. In the process he gathered a small group of disciples around him.

One day, in their intimate sharing, Tempels asked "Who are we?" and received the spontaneous answer, "*Jamaa*, a family." He took the name *Jamaa* for the movement of small communities that followed. He thought of it as an integrally African way of being Christian, a transformation of mission into indigenization, but it soon took on social and political overtones.

Many who received *Bantu Philosophy* with enthusiasm were quite unfamiliar with his writings on *jamaa*, a Swahili word meaning variously "community," "family" or "relationship." Similarly, most of his detractors were aware primarily of the movement of Small Christian Communities (SCCs) that sprang up. The movement counted some 200,000 adherents on the lower Congo, and Tempels seems to have influenced it even after his return to Belgium. It allowed only married couples as members, studiously eschewed politics and avoided religious fervor. The weekly gatherings were conducted in Swahili as a common tongue that fended off ethnicity. After 1970, however, their loyalties were questioned, and they were seen as a threat to the mission Churches. By this time, the approach had been adopted by Protestants as well. Its ideas began to filter into Tanzania, and were incorporated into the ill-fated commune scheme of the Mwalimu Julius NYERERE, where its political implications became manifest.

References: wiki. Tempels, *Bantu Philosophy* (1959); Johannes Fabian, *Jamaa* (1971).

TERRE BLANCHE, Eugene Ney
(South Africa, 1944–)

Eugene Ney Terre Blanche, leader of the ultra-rightist terrorist group, Afrikaner Weerstandsbeweging (Afrikaner Resistance Movement, AWB), called for a White revolution against majority rule in South Africa after power in South Africa passed to the Black majority.

After high school, Terre Blanche joined the South African national police and served as a volunteer in Namibia. He resigned five years later to begin farming and to enter White politics. He studied political systems and decided that multiparty democracy was a failure and that the only salvation for Whites in South Africa would be a return to the people's states (Volksstaat) of the Afrikaner republics. In 1973 he founded the AWB, and after six years as a secret society, it began a series of political operations. Its first extremist act was to tar and feather a historian who had given a speech against observance of Day of the Vow, the anniversary of the Afrikaner covenant sworn after the Battle of Blood River in 1838.

In 1982 the police discovered a number of arms caches in raids on AWB members, and Terre Blanche and several others were charged with terrorism. Despite the evidence, Terre Blanche received a suspended sentence. He began to predict a massive, bloody confrontation between the races. In 1986 he set up Brandweg (Sentry) as the AWB's armed wing. Using neo-Nazi rhetoric, he denounced Jews, Africans, Coloureds (people of mixed racial background) and Indians, but also showed a special hatred for Muslims, because he believed that Islam was the ultimate enemy of Afrikanerdom. The AWB supported complete racial separation, and it opposed the moves taken by President Frederik DE KLERK to end apartheid. The AWB threatened and used violence in an effort to prevent majority rule.

A sex scandal involving Terre Blanche and a prominent French journalist shook the AWB in 1989, and he was accused of alcohol abuse and womanizing. He survived the uproar but was rejected that year when he wanted to run for parliament for the Conservative Party. It had become clear that he and the AWB were too extreme for even the most right-wing parties. In 1993 a group of AWB members invaded the

Bophuthatswana homeland to prevent its dissolution and to protect its head, Lucas MANGOPE. The local police killed several members, forcing AWB armed action to go underground. Nevertheless, the AWB engineered a series of bombings that killed 21 during the campaign leading to Nelson MANDELA's election as president of South Africa. The feared wave of terrorism never materialized, however, and Terre Blanche and the AWB remain under regular police surveillance. He failed in his promise to disrupt Nelson MANDELA's first year in office "by any means necessary."

From 1997 to 2004, Terre Blanche was in prison for assault and attempted murder. He claims to have become a born-again Christian who no longer endorses racist theories. The AWB has largely faded away.

References: GSAP, PLBA, *wiki.*

TEWODROS II
(Ethiopia, 1818?–1868)

Negus Tewodros II began the process of unifying Ethiopia after the century of political disintegration known as the "era of princes," during which powerful regional warlords contended for power. He was *negus* or emperor from 1855 to his death. His name is sometimes given in its Western version, Theodore.

Tewodros was born Kassa Haylu and was raised by a half-brother who was a notorious petty warlord. In 1839, Kassa Haylu succeeded him and lived for some years as a *shifta* or outlaw bandit chief. He plundered towns and caravans in the freebooting style of the time, but what distinguished Kassa Haylu was that he redistributed his booty to local peasants, which brought him a certain measure of loyalty. He shrewdly married the granddaughter of the empress and then captured the empress in battle. For her ransom, Kassa Haylu received control of much of central Ethiopia, which he dominated by 1852. He then confronted his major rivals to the north, defeating them in a series of decisive battles that left him victor over the entire country. In 1855 he had himself crowned *negus negast* (emperor), taking the name Tewodros after a legendary figure who had been prophesied as the one who would bring order, eliminate Islam, and capture Jerusalem. The same year, he subdued Shoa province in the south, taking the future Emperor MENELIK II as prisoner.

Tewodros had been educated in monasteries and hoped to reunify Ethiopia to save it from Muslim domination. He began a number of reforms that included abolishing slavery (thus weakening the Muslims, who were deeply involved in the slave trade), reducing polygamy, and centralizing the administration. To accomplish the last goal, he attempted to undermine the feudal system, centralized taxation, and created a paid professional army. Tewodros also embarked on an ambitious program of road building and shipbuilding and established a modern armaments factory. The funds for these massive expansion projects could come from only one source: the Ethiopian Orthodox Church, which owned a substantial amount of the country's land and national wealth. His policies caused friction with the clergy, who were able to rally the people around them to erode Tewodros's base of political support among the peasantry. Tewodros then introduced Protestant missionaries and technicians, hoping to gain access to European military supplies, but his move further alienated him from the Ethiopian Church. The emperor did not prove a careful politician; his strategy of using threats and force against the Church backfired. When he tried to end its tax exemption, opposition hardened. In 1864 he imprisoned the *abuna,* the head of the Church, and punished the clergy by plundering and burning 41 churches in Gondar, causing the future YOHANNES IV to rebel against him. Dissatisfied at the lack of arms provided by the foreign Christian missionaries, he also imprisoned a number of them.

The death of his wife, whom he truly loved, devastated him, and Tewodros began a descent into violence and erratic behavior. He married again, this time unhappily, and a cruel side of his nature emerged in persecutions and brutality.

Tewodros's vast army began to suffer from desertions until it was a shadow of its former strength. One after another, regional leaders rebelled until, by 1866, he had lost control of most of the country. When a British expeditionary force landed to free British prisoners, they received the support of Yohannes. Tewodros was placed in a hopeless position. Surrounded in his fortress at Magdala, he committed suicide with a pistol sent as a gift by Queen Victoria when he first came to power. Tewodros's great achievement was beginning the unification of Ethiopia, which ended the feudal period and initiated the first tentative steps toward modernization.

References: DAB, DAHB, EB, EWB, *wiki.* Sven Rubenson, *King of Kings: Tewodros of Ethiopia* (1966).

TEWOFLOS
(Ethiopia, 1910–1974?)

Abune (Patriarch) Tewoflos was a reforming patriarch of the Ethiopian Orthodox Church who was murdered by the Dergue, the Marxist military government, in the purge of the 1970s. He is also known as Theophilos.

Tewoflos was groomed from an early age by Emperor HAILE SELASSIE in his plans to modernize and reform the Ethiopian Church. He was educated in Addis Ababa and in 1930 entered the leading monastery in the country, Debra Libanos. After a dozen years as a monk, he was brought to the imperial palace with a select group of young clergy for modern religious studies. Tewoflos was subsequently appointed as head of a new theological college. In the Coptic Orthodox tradition, only celibate priests, not married ones, may be chosen bishops. As a consequence, all Ethiopian bishops are former monks. In 1948 he was in the first group of Ethiopian bishops, and in 1950 he was promoted to archbishop and deputy to BASILIOS. On Basilios's death in 1970, Tewoflos was elected the second Ethiopian patriarch. Until Basilios, all patriarchs had been chosen from Egypt.

Tewoflos established an Ethiopian youth movement and missionary program. Outside Ethiopia he established branches of the Ethiopian Church in Trinidad, Guyana and the United States. His programs expanded after he became patriarch and focused on the education of the clergy, who were woefully undertrained. He established a training center for rural clergy, a theological college at Addis Ababa University, and sent promising younger men abroad for higher study. Liturgical reform was begun, with increased use of Amharic, the vernacular language, instead of Ge'ez, an ancient language used only in church services and understood by few Ethiopians. Tewoflos represented the Ethiopian Church at international Christian assemblies, and he presided when the World Council of Churches (WCC) met in Addis Ababa in 1971. Tewoflos, an enthusiastic ecumenist, was twice president of the

All-African Council of Churches and a strong supporter of the WCC. He began an ecumenical outreach to other Eastern Churches and the Vatican.

When Haile Selassie was overthrown in 1974, the military regime, the Dergue, moved swiftly to implement a Marxist religious policy. In a broad attack against religion, the Church's privileged status was terminated, properties were confiscated, and many clergy were arrested. After the emperor's death in 1975, Tewoflos was even forbidden to conduct services for him. The confrontation came when, as head of the Church, Tewoflos appointed five new bishops without clearance from the Dergue. Deposed and under house arrest, Tewoflos was charged with unspecified crimes against the people and was executed at an unknown time and place. No successor was named until 1977, at which time a puppet priest was chosen as patriarch by the Dergue.

Reference: dacb, DRWW, *wiki.*

THEILER, Max
(South Africa, 1988–1972)

Dr. Max Theiler was a virologist who made major contributions to the prevention of yellow fever. For the vaccine he developed, he was awarded the Nobel Prize in Medicine in 1951.

Dr. Theiler, the son of a veterinarian, studied at the University of Cape Town, then completed his medical degree in London in 1922. He moved to the Department of Tropical Medicine at Harvard University in the United States shortly after, then spent 14 years at the Rockefeller Foundation, where he was head of laboratories for the Division of Medicine and Public Health. In 1964, he joined the faculty at Yale University. He lived in the United States most of his life, but never gave up his South African citizenship.

In a series of animal experiments beginning in the 1920s, Theiler demonstrated that monkeys infected with yellow fever could be replaced for research purposes by mice, thus expanding opportunities for extended research. Proving that the cause of yellow fever was a virus and not a bacterium, his team developed his first antiviral vaccine in 1934, and by 1937 he came up with a final form which could be mass produced. It was used to vaccinate 28 million people, reducing yellow fever from a major health threat in tropical areas to a manageable one.

In his later years, Theiler turned his research interests to other tropical diseases, especially dengue fever and Japanese encephalitis. Besides the Nobel Prize, he received many other awards, including the Lasker Award in 1949. Theiler called the conquest of yellow fever "one of the great epics in medical history." And of his own role, he said it was "a great adventure and a thrilling experience."

References: afr, EB, *wiki.* Theiler, *Yellow Fever* (1951).

TIPPU TIP
(Tanzania/Democratic Republic of the Congo/Zanzibar, 1830s-1905)

Tippu Tip was the best known and most powerful of the nineteenth-century slave traders in East Africa. He established a mercantile empire that at its height employed more than 4,000 agents and controlled a territory stretching from Lake Tanganyika to central Congo. Tippu Tip traded primarily in slaves and ivory, which he bought or seized in raids and exchanged for guns, cloth and manufactured goods.

The son of a prominent Zanzibari merchant, Tippu Tip began trade expeditions at the age of 12 before expanding his caravan operations into the area of present-day Zambia and the Democratic Republic of the Congo (DRC) in the 1860s. In the course of his trade he met and befriended the British explorer and missionary David LIVINGSTONE. In 1870 he returned to the Congo with 4,000 men and established a center where he remained for 10 years. By a skillful mixture of guile and force, he either persuaded or cowed local chiefs into subservience. One old chief resigned in his favor when Tippu Tip convinced him that he was his grandnephew and heir. He took sides in local dynastic feuds and supported those who promised to be loyal to him. Other communities were awed by his firearms, and some (especially those with large caches of ivory) were conquered.

Tippu Tip took over the trading routes that Swahili and Arab merchants previously had established. He dominated the trade network so that he secured recognition as the official ruler of what are now the eastern provinces of the DRC. He entered areas that had never been explored and encountered people with such little idea of the value of ivory that after eating the elephant's meat, they threw away the tusks. The movement of large numbers of tusks required slave labor, however, and because slaving was profitable despite its appalling losses, it became the second source of his wealth. Tippu Tip ruled his empire only for trade, with no notion of state building. Consequently, farming was neglected and the continual slave and ivory raids kept the area in constant turmoil. Tippu Tip's slave empire became a place of oppression and death.

Tippu Tip realized that European influence would soon dominate, and he shrewdly cultivated his contacts. He explored with Henry STANLEY, the American journalist, and negotiated with him when Stanley began working for the king of Belgium. Until the 1880s, Tippu Tip was able to maintain his authority in the interior. In 1885, however, the Berlin Conference partitioned Africa among the competing European powers, and all Zanzibari claims were ignored. Tippu Tip's power quickly declined, and he finally agreed to work as a provincial governor for the Belgians under Stanley's jurisdiction. Ironically, Tippu Tip was charged with curbing the slave trade, and he seems to have reduced the number of slave caravans. He joined Stanley in the rescue of Eduard SCHNITZER (Emin Pasha), who was stranded in the Sudan after the MAHDI expelled the Egyptian and British from the Sudan, but Stanley blamed Tippu Tip for losses during the expedition.

After having lost most of his wealth, Tippu Tip left the Congo in 1890 for the last time and retired to Zanzibar, as the Belgians moved to complete their control over his former territory. The conflict lasted from 1892 to 1894, and both Tippu Tip's son and Emin Pasha were killed.

References: AB, DAHB, EWB, MMA, WGMC, *wiki.*

TODD, Reginald Garfield
(Zimbabwe, 1908–2002)

Reverend Sir Reginald Garfield Todd, prime minister of Southern Rhodesia (which is Zimbabwe today) from 1953 to 1958, incurred the wrath of the most conservative White settlers for his opposition to harsh restrictive legislation against Black Africans.

A New Zealander by birth, Todd came to Southern Rhodesia in 1934, after studying in South Africa, to be superintendent of the Dadaya Mission, a position that he retained until 1953. He and his wife ran a clinic and a school, where Robert MUGABE was one of his teachers. Missionary work brought him into politics over concern for African education. In 1946, Todd was elected to the legislative assembly on the United Party ticket. In 1953, when Godfrey HUGGINS became the first prime minister of the Central African Federation, which united the two Rhodesias and Nyasaland (now Malawi), Todd replaced him as territorial premier.

Todd projected a public image of concern for African rights, earning himself the reputation of being a liberal. In fact, his policies were more centrist than liberal, but in the context of southern Africa they seemed extreme to many White settlers. In the postwar years, the White settler population of Southern Rhodesia expanded threefold, with increased foreign investment and development. Many of the newcomers were from South Africa and supported Southern Rhodesia's imposition of racial apartheid laws during the 1950s.

Todd promoted African education by doubling the number of elementary schools and subsidizing secondary education at mission schools. He fostered Black landownership and took steps to open the franchise to Blacks from 2 percent to 16 percent of the electorate, but this proposal was defeated. In 1956 he appointed the Tredgold Commission to develop a plan for increased Black voter participation. This strategy was in support of British policy that favored a multiracial bloc of colonies that would counter South Africa. International business also sought an alternate base for investment in case Afrikaner nationalization threatened their holdings. The settlers, in contrast, wanted African political aspirations contained and even suppressed. Todd did not hesitate to use force to restrain labor strikes, but, nevertheless, mounting dissatisfaction with Todd's leadership reached a climax when his cabinet resigned in protest of his policies in early 1958. Defying tradition by not resigning but forming another government, he was challenged at a special party congress and was ousted. For a short time he served in the cabinet of Edgar WHITEHEAD, who succeeded him.

In 1959, Todd left the United Party to found the short-lived Central African Party, which embodied his ideas of a multiracial government. It failed to win any seats in the following election. Todd's views on race became increasingly more radical with the passing years. He became a prominent critic of the Rhodesian Front govern-ment, and when Premier Ian SMITH declared Rhodesia an independent state in defiance of Great Britain and world opinion, Todd was placed under limited confinement for a year (1965–1966), which restricted him to his farm, where he secretly aided guerilla fighters. In 1972 he was briefly imprisoned so that he could not meet a visiting British commission, and his restriction was renewed until 1976. By this time Todd was an international prisoner of conscience and was awarded the papal peace and justice medal by Pope Paul VI in 1973 and several honorary doctorates. He became an advisor to Joshua NKOMO after his release, and when independence was achieved, Todd served in the Zimbabwe senate from 1980 to 1985 before retiring from public life. He gave 3,000 acres of his farm to disabled war veterans and received his knighthood from New Zealand in 1989.

As Mugabe's rule became harsher, Todd criticized the government, and finally, Mugabe stripped him of his citizenship shortly before he died.

References: DAHB, PLBA, *wiki.*

TOIVO ja Toivo, Animba Herman
(Namibia, 1924–)

Animba Herman Toivo ja Toivo, a father of Namibian nationalism and founder of the South-West African People's Organization (SWAPO), served 18 years in South African prisons before being released and becoming SWAPO's secretary-general.

Toivo's father was a mission catechist in the Finnish Lutheran Church, responsible for preparing candidates for baptism. He gave his son a Finnish name that signified "hope of hope." Toivo studied in mission schools, took a teaching certificate, and taught in an Anglican mission school. From 1942 to 1945 he served in the South African army and then settled in Cape Town, where he became involved in a multiracial national liberation group. He took a job in the South African gold mines in 1951 but was banished to Ovamboland in northern South-West Africa (now called Namibia) in 1957 after he smuggled taped testimony about conditions among mine workers to the United Nations. In 1958 he formed the Ovamboland People's Organization

(OPO). Two years later he and the OPO joined Sam NUJOMA to found SWAPO.

Nujoma went abroad to organize SWAPO resistance, but Toivo remained in Namibia, where he was arrested in 1966 for his political activities. He was held in detention under harsh conditions and constant questioning for a year before facing trial for terrorism. He defended himself well in court, but in 1968 he was sentenced to 20 years' imprisonment (he served 16) on Robben Island, which he shared with Nelson MANDELA, Walter SISULU, and other antiapartheid nationalists. Nujoma assumed the presidency of SWAPO. In 1984, Toivo was released after a petition to the South African government by the Multiparty Conference and Dirk MUDGE. At first he was unwilling to leave, because he felt he was a more potent symbol of struggle in prison than out. When he did leave prison, he went into exile with the rest of the SWAPO leadership. He was subsequently elected secretary-general of the party.

Toivo helped prepare SWAPO for assuming power in Namibia, and in 1989 he returned for the elections. In parliament he was made minister of Mines and Energy, transferring later to minister of Labour and then to minister of Prisons. He was replaced as secretary-general at the party congress of 1991. He retired from politics in 2006, a year after the end of Nujoma's presidency.

References: afr, PLBA, RWWA, *wiki*.

TOLBERT, Richard V.
(Liberia, 1950–)

Richard V. Tolbert, nephew of the slain president William Richard TOLBERT, for whom he was named, is head of the family business holdings in Liberia.

Tolbert was educated internationally: elementary school in Liberia, secondary education in England and university in the United States. He graduated from Harvard and took a law degree from Columbia University in corporate and international law.

When he returned to the family business in 1975, the Mesurado Group of companies was the most extensive business owned by Liberians in the history of the country. It employed 5,000 in 15 companies diversified throughout the economy.

Tolbert left Liberia and returned to the United States after the brutal murder of his uncle and the coup led by Samuel DOE. He became vice president of Merrill Lynch from 1980 to 1998, then was named senior vice president of UBS Payne Webber, one of America's largest investment houses.

Tolbert is a member of the African Business Roundtable of Johannesburg, South Africa, and the Washington-based Corporate Council on Africa. He has spoken and written widely on developing business in the Third World, and continues to follow developments in Liberia. He is convinced that "if Liberians can unite and get serious, we can rebuild a great country."

TOLBERT, William Richard
(Liberia, 1913–1980)

William Richard Tolbert, the last Americo-Liberian president of Liberia before the civil war, was overthrown and executed in a coup that ended the longest elected government system in Africa.

The Americo-Liberian elite originated with freed American slaves who settled the coast in 1822 and formed the Republic of Liberia in 1847. As they became a prosperous elite, numbering less than five percent of the population, the Americo-Liberians governed much like colonial masters, largely denying education and advancement to the indigenous peoples. Tolbert's father, a former South Carolina slave, fathered some 70 children and developed a successful rice and coffee farm.

Tolbert spent most of his life in national politics as a member of the True Whig Party. In 1943 he was elected to the House of Representatives, and in 1951 he became vice president under William TUBMAN. A devout Baptist minister, Tolbert preached regularly while in office and in 1965 became the first African head of the Baptist World Alliance. For 20 years Tolbert remained in Tubman's shadow, until he succeeded the latter following his death in 1971. He then embarked on a foreign policy designed to show Liberia's independence from U.S. control.

Tolbert was an aggressive leader in Africa, openly negotiating with South Africa, becoming a founder of the Economic Community of West African States (ECOWAS) and bringing together the presidents of Guinea, Côte d'Ivoire, and Sénégal in a reconciliation meeting. In 1979, Liberia hosted the Organization of African Unity (OAU), and Tolbert was elected chair.

Domestically, Tolbert proved to be a liberal reformer, replacing corrupt officials and increasing opportunities for indigenous peoples in the hinterland. For the first time in Liberian history, he permitted an opposition party to form. He also began Africanizing the economy, long controlled by foreign (mostly U.S.) interests, which had begun to falter. But although he was essentially a benevolent despot who was amazed and offended at criticism, he had a cruel side as well. In 1979, when demonstrators protested increases in the cost of rice, Tolbert ordered the militia to fire on them, which they did, killing 74. He then jailed most of the political opposition and offered US$2,000 rewards for the rest, dead or alive. Shortly after, Tolbert was murdered by soldiers led by Sergeant Samuel K. DOE. His body was mutilated, and most of the cabinet and members of Tolbert's family were rounded up and publicly executed by firing squad. It was the end of the old Americo-Liberian elite.

References: afr, AO, DAHB, DRWW, MMA, PLBA, *wiki.* Wilton Sankawulo, *Tolbert of Liberia* (1979).

TOMBALBAYE, Ngartha François
(Chad, 1918–1975)

Ngartha François Tombalbaye, first president of his country, came to power through the efforts of Muslim dissidents, and then failed to unite the country. He governed by naked power until he was overthrown and killed in a coup.

A Protestant in a Catholic and Muslim country, he was educated in Brazzaville, French Congo. He became a teacher in the 1940s while also engaged in trade union organizing and helped to found the Chadian Progressive Party (PPT), the local affiliate of the interterritorial Rassemblement Démocratique Africain (RDA) of Félix HOUPHOUËT-BOIGNY, which was established to fight for independence in French Africa. Forced out of teaching by hostile colonial administrators, he held several unskilled jobs until being elected to the territorial legislature in 1952, in opposition to the Muslims and the French. In 1957 he was appointed Chad's member on the General Council for French Equatorial Africa

(which covered five colonial territories), and in 1959 he became prime minister of Chad after having outwitted his opponents in the PPT by turning the Muslim faction against them.

In 1960, Tombalbaye became Chad's first president, but he was unable to manage the forces of disunity that he had unleashed in his moves to win power. He imposed a harsh, autocratic rule that caused more dissension instead of the unity for which he had hoped. In 1962 he banned all opposition parties, which led several groups to take up armed struggle against the government. In addition to the guerrilla conflict, there were several coup attempts and a series of urban riots that continued to destabilize the government. This political crisis soon degenerated into open civil war, and Tombalbaye called upon the French, who provided military support until 1971. Tombalbaye began receiving aid and military supplies from Libya, despite its obvious territorial designs along their shared northern border. He also negotiated a grant from Libya and an agreement to have the Libyans expel Chadian guerrillas operating within Libya. In exchange, Tombalbaye broke relations with Israel and turned a blind eye when Libya occupied the Aouzou Strip, which it had long coveted.

In 1973, to strengthen his position, Tombalbaye launched a cultural revolution, removing the French names of towns and districts and taking the title "citizen" instead of "president." Missionaries were expelled and Christianity discouraged. Ritual initiation was required of all adult males, with the penalty for refusal being execution. Despite his best efforts, Tombalbaye's situation became increasingly desperate, and when he attempted a purge of the army, he was killed by crossfire in the coup that followed. He was replaced by General Félix MALLOUM, whom he had once imprisoned on the bizarre charge of using magical animal sacrifices to undermine Tombalbaye's power.

Tombalbaye's tumultuous and brutal rule provided the basis for ongoing political turmoil in Chad, which has continued since.

References: afr, DAHB, DRWW, MMA, PLBA, *wiki.*

TOURÉ, Ahmed Sékou
(Guinea, 1922–1984)

Ahmed Sékou Touré, one of the most radical leaders in modern African history, became in later years one of its most oppressive. His determination to reject continued association with France in the 1958 referendum was the chief cause of the dissolution of the French West African federation.

Touré was expelled from primary school at age 15 for leading a student strike. He then took a job with the postal service and became an active trade unionist, affiliating the postal union with the giant Communist labor federation, Confédération Générale du Travail. By 1945, Touré was secretary-general of the postal workers. He also formed a union federation in Guinea and West Africa and was also responsible for leading a general strike. The following year he joined the treasury department and was elected secretary-general of the treasury workers' union. It was at this time that he joined these labor activities to party politics as a founder of the Democratic Party of Guinea (PDG), the local affiliate of the Rassemblement Démocratique Africain (RDA), the interterritorial party headed by Côte d'Ivoire's Félix HOUPHOUËT-BOIGNY. He was dismissed from the treasury department for his political activities.

In 1952, Touré became secretary-general of the PDG, which he had developed into a mass movement. The following year he called a two-month general strike against the government, forcing the governor to accede to his demands; he was also elected to the territorial legislature. In 1955 he assumed the position of mayor of Conakry, and in 1956 he was elected a delegate to the French national assembly. In 1957 he was elected vice president, which at that time made him the chief executive officer of Guinea. He embarked on a development program and fostered local councils at the expense of the traditional chiefs. Throughout this period Touré was heavily courted by the Communists. He was much influenced by Marxist thinking but felt that Marxism had to be adapted to African conditions. He was anticolonial but willing to cooperate with the French to gain his ends.

In 1958, General Charles de Gaulle allowed a referendum in West Africa over the future of the colonies, expecting approval of his plan for continued postcolonial association with France among the French-speaking African states. Touré showed con-

Ahmed Sékou Touré

siderable ambivalence, at times supporting de Gaulle, at times wavering. Just before the referendum, he shifted sharply toward complete independence, and Guinea was the only colony to vote "no" on continued affiliation. Touré proclaimed proudly, "Guinea prefers poverty in freedom to riches in slavery." The French reaction was swift and draconian. France set Guinea free immediately, cut off all aid, and removed its personnel and equipment within weeks. Machinery and furniture were stripped from the evacuated offices. The telephones were removed and all files and records were sent to Paris. No Western nation would provide assistance, so Touré turned to the Communist bloc for aid. The result of Guinea's action was also the breakup of the RDA and an acceleration of the decolonization process.

At the same time, Touré's national party won 57 of 60 seats in the new parliament, after which he made Guinea a one-party state by constitutional fiat.

In foreign policy, Touré was Pan-African as well as anti-Western. In 1959, Guinea and Ghana formed a compact that was to lead to union, with Mali joining the compact in 1961. Although political union never took place, there was a basis for a common foreign policy, which in the early 1960s became the radical, anti-Western Casablanca Bloc.

After the Soviets conspired with Guinean opposition movements in 1961, Touré expelled the Soviet ambassador and arrested his opponents. Friendly relations with the USSR were later restored, but Touré avoided dependence on the Communist bloc. His major focus remained West Africa.

Guinea had extensive deposits of bauxite, uranium and diamonds, but none were developed. Income was US$140 per capita, literacy stood at 10 percent, and life expectancy at age 41. Much of the Communist bloc foreign aid provided useless materials (including a shipment of Soviet snowplows). In 1960, Guinea withdrew from the franc zone, which sacrificed French support of the currency and weakened the economy further. Kwame NKRUMAH of Ghana, one of the few leaders sympathetic to Touré, provided a £10 million (then about $28 million) loan in 1958 that helped stabilize the economy. Touré began to centralize economic authority and impose controls. The 1960s were marked by inflation, poverty and lack of economic progress.

After Nkrumah's downfall in 1966, Touré provided him asylum and gave him the honorary title of co-president. When Touré threatened to restore Nkrumah by force, however, Guinea was isolated by its neighboring states, and Côte d'Ivoire sent troops to the border. By 1970, Touré took a more conciliatory approach to the West and received some limited foreign aid. In 1982, Touré suddenly reversed his Marxist economic policy with fanfare, touring the United States seeking investments and offering a free market with "fabulous economic potential," but he attracted few investors.

Touré's goal was a one-party people's democracy based on African socialism, but his human rights record belied his theory. He tolerated no dissent and punished opposition viciously. Lacking advanced education, he was suspicious of intellectuals, who he felt had sold their birthrights for Western ideas. Touré initiated a "cultural revolution" based on ideological indoctrination, and he insisted on appointing administrators without professional qualifications. After numerous coup attempts in the 1960s, he purged the army and the PDG and relied only on loyal friends and relatives. His family used the opportunity to amass huge fortunes, and the higher ranks of the PDG became a new elite of the rich and powerful.

With Touré's mounting paranoia in the 1970s, thousands were arrested and tortured or killed. Diallo Telli, former secretary-general of the Organi-zation of African Unity, was placed in a cell where he could not stand up and was deprived of all food and water until he died. At least a dozen cabinet ministers were also executed. In 1977 a peaceful demonstration by market women was crushed by the army, resulting in dozens of deaths. When some soldiers refused to fire on unarmed women, they themselves were executed. More than a million of Guinea's population became refugees. By 1984, Touré ruled by power and fear. When he died, after being flown to the United States for heart surgery, his regime was immediately overthrown by the military with widespread popular support.

References: AB, *afr*, AO, DAHB, DRWW, DT, MMA, PLBA, PLCA, *wiki*. Ladipo Adamolekun, *Sékou Touré's Guinea: An Experiment in Nation Building* (1976).

TRAORÉ, Moussa
(Mali, 1936–)

General Moussa Traoré, military strongman and Mali's former head of state, was one of the autocrats who was swept away by the democracy movement that developed in Africa in the 1990s.

As a youth, Traoré joined the French army and was sent to the Frejus Military College. Commissioned in 1960, he became an instructor at the inter-services school at Kati. In 1968, Lieutenant Traoré led a coup against the government, personally arresting President Modibo KEITA. Mali was in the midst an economic crisis, and Keita's socialist policies were widely unpopular. The new military council advocated a mixed economy and made vague promises of a return to civilian rule. In 1971, Traoré arrested his main rivals—including one who died in captivity—and strengthened his position. Throughout the 1970s, Traoré moved toward civilian rule but had to contend with opposition on the council. Nevertheless, he successfully formed a new party, announced a five-year transition to elections, and released all political prisoners. In 1978, Traoré confronted several powerful council members with evidence of their theft of drought aid and arrested them after learning that they were planning a coup. This event left him as virtual commander of the country, and after being promoted to general, he disbanded the council, having successfully negotiated the shift from a narrow military base to a broad grassroots political party.

Civilian power-sharing brought out submerged opposition from students and teachers, who recognized that behind a facade of public participation, the army was in control. In the 1980s, Traoré defeated five coup attempts. After the 1980 student uprisings were quelled, the student leader was tortured to death. Traoré seems to have been sincere in his desire to see civilian government return but was incapable of using democratic means. He ruled by decree, and his entourage—especially his wife—became increasingly corrupt, reportedly putting US$1 billion in secret overseas bank accounts. Dissent erupted in bloody clashes in 1990 in which more than 200 died. In 1991, the Traoré regime was toppled by a military group that wasted no time in setting an election date. In a three-way race in 1992, Alpha KONARÉ became Mali's first democratically elected president. In 1992, Traoré was convicted of corruption and of ordering the 1991 massacres. He was sentenced to death, but this was commuted to life imprisonment a few months later. His wife was convicted of corruption, but both were pardoned in 2002.

References: afr, DAHB, DRWW, PLBA, *wiki.*

TREURNICHT, Andries Petrus

(South Africa, 1921–1993)

Dr. Andries Petrus Treurnicht, founder of the extreme right Conservative Party, was a leading ideological exponent of apartheid.

After secondary school, Treurnicht attended Stellenbosch University, the intellectual heart of Afrikaner culture, from 1938 to 1945, receiving a BA and MA and completing seminary studies. He was ordained in the Dutch Reformed Church (DRC) and ministered to parishes until 1960, continuing his studies until he received a Ph.D. in politics from the University of Cape Town. In 1960 he became editor of *Die Kerkebode,* a leading religious journal, which he used as a vehicle for his views. The year was significant, because in the wake of the Sharpeville massacre, the Reformed Churches reassessed their commitment to apartheid. The Sharpeville massacre—in which the police fired upon a large crowd of peaceful demonstrators, killing 72 and wounding 186+n—was a turning point after which

those who had not taken positions on apartheid were forced to do so.

At the Cottlesloe Conference, convened by the World Council of Churches (WCC), Reformed Churches from around the world rejected racism and apartheid. Prime Minister Hendrik VERWOERD led the opposition with strong support from Treurnicht and *Die Kerkebode* and defended separate development of the races so effectively that the reformist view virtually disappeared from the DRC. Treurnicht became a prominent figure in the DRC and held membership in the General Synod in 1966.

In 1967, Prime Minister Balthazar VORSTER invited Treurnicht to become editor of a new conservative daily paper in Pretoria, *Hoofstad.* Although he was on the extreme right of the National Party (NP), Treurnicht supported the party in general, and in 1971 he was elected to parliament as an NP member. His political power lay not only in his journalism but also in the Broederbond, the elite Afrikaner secret society to which most important Afrikaner leaders belonged. During the early 1970s, Treurnicht was its chairman, and in 1976 his importance was recognized by his appointment to the cabinet. As deputy minister of education that year, he triggered the Soweto uprising by his insistence on the use of Afrikaans as the language of instruction in Black schools. He resisted every attempt at reform of the apartheid system until the South African media dubbed him "Dr. No." During the government of P. W. BOTHA (1978–1989), he was increasingly alarmed by what he saw as compromise. He openly clashed with Botha over non-White power sharing and led 22 NP parliamentarians in a vote of no confidence in a 1982 party caucus.

Treurnicht was suspended as head of the Transvaal provincial NP and resigned from the cabinet and the NP to form the Conservative Party, which became the official opposition in parliament in 1987. He defended White supremacy and complete separation of the races, and when Frederik DE KLERK moved to dismantle apartheid, he called the policy one of "national suicide." Nevertheless, he rejected the violence of the neo-Nazi Afrikaner Resistance Movement of Eugene TERRE BLANCHE and was troubled by extremist threats of insurrection. He died just as he was planning to join De Klerk's negotiating forum. The Conservative Party began a sharp decline shortly after.

References: GSAP, PLBA, *wiki.*

TROVOADA, Miguel Anjos da Cunha
(São Tomé e Principe, 1937–)

Miguel Anjos da Cunha Trovoada is one of the new breed of reform presidents brought into office on the wave of pluralistic democracy that arose across Africa in the early 1990s.

An island republic in the Gulf of Guinea settled by the Portuguese and their African slaves, São Tomé has a unique mulatto population. In 1953 the plantation aristocrats massacred hundreds of *foros* (landless citizens descended from slaves) while attempting to force them into farm labor. After this traumatic event, anticolonial resistance collapsed. Independence sentiment was limited to São Tomé students in Lisbon who were in contact with nationalists from Portugal's other African colonies, Angola, Mozambique, Guinea-Bissau and Cape Verde.

After secondary school in Angola, Trovoada studied law at the University of Lisbon with his friend Manuel Pinto DA COSTA. In 1960 they formed the Movement for the Liberation of São Tomé e Principe (MLSTP) as an exile organization. Trovoada set up the MLSTP office in Gabon in 1961 with support from the liberation movements of the larger Portuguese colonies. From 1961 to 1975, Trovoada was the foreign affairs representative of the party. After almost fading from existence, the MLSTP reorganized in 1972 and received the recognition of the Organization of African Unity. With the collapse of Portuguese fascism in 1974, the new Socialist government in Lisbon conceded autonomy to the colonies, and independence fever swept the islands. After a series of disturbances and a general strike, a transitional government was established.

Trovoada was named the first premier, with Da Costa as president. The MLSTP was named the only legal party, and the country embarked on a socialist program of land expropriation and government control of all retail business. This economic policy raised dissent in the MLSTP, and Da Costa grew suspicious of Trovoada, removing him from the premiership in 1979. Accused of plotting against the government, Trovoada was imprisoned until 1981, when he went into exile in France. There he supported an underground political group, the Democratic Convergence (DC), founded in 1987.

When the Da Costa government bowed to public pressure and held a national referendum, citizens voted for a multiparty system. Trovoada returned to win the 1991 elections as a DC candidate after Da Costa withdrew.

Trovoada disbanded the secret police and then addressed the problems of the economy—inflation and the falling price of cocoa, the major export. He accepted a stringent plan for overhauling the economy that was imposed by the International Monetary Fund, but it proved so unpopular that the MLSTP captured most of the seats in 1992 municipal elections after widespread demonstrations forced Trovoada to fire his prime minister. Dissent mounted, and Trovoada was ousted in a coup in 1995, but returned to office within a week. He was re-elected president in 1996 and completed his term peacefully in 2001.

Reference: RWWA, *wiki*.

TSHISEKEDI, Étienne wa Malumba
(Democratic Republic of the Congo, 1933–)

Étienne wa Malumba Tshisekedi, one of the most resilient politicians in the Democratic Republic of the Congo (DRC), went from holding a leading position under MOBUTU Sese Seko to being his most consistent opponent. He has continued to position himself in the post-Mobutu and post-Zaïre years.

A Luba from the southern province of Kasai, Tshisekedi was educated locally before going to the University of Louvain in Belgium, where he received a doctorate in law. In the early 1960s he served as justice minister in Moïse TSHOMBE's breakaway government in Katanga (now Shaba) Province. In 1965, Mobutu appointed him to his first cabinet as minister of the interior, later transferring him to justice and then to planning. In 1967 he added the position of national secretary of the Popular Movement for Renewal (MPR), Mobutu's national ruling party. Mobutu constantly rotated and switched his cabinet and prime ministers as part of his strategy for keeping himself in power, and in 1975, Tshisekedi was unceremoniously dropped from all his posts. Meanwhile, Mobutu had begun his program of "authenticity," dropping

Christian names for African ones and renaming the country "Zaïre."

Tshisekedi remained in parliament, calling for an open, multiparty system. He founded and headed the Union for Democracy and Social Progress (UDPS) in 1982, for which he was arrested 12 times, but he nevertheless formed a parliamentary opposition group known as "The Thirteen." Its members were imprisoned and banished to their home villages but still remained the only real internal opposition to Mobutu's regime during the 1980s. On one occasion, when Tshisekedi tried to speak to a group of American congressmen on a human rights investigation, he was beaten in their presence by the police. In 1987, Tshisekedi went to Belgium, returning a year later after receiving guarantees of safety from Mobutu. At the first meeting of the UDPS, Tshisekedi was shot and then confined to a mental hospital.

In 1990, Tshisekedi was released as part of an announced liberalization of politics. As conditions reached the point of national collapse in Zaïre, Mobutu consented to a national conference to design a new government. A coalition of religious, political, labor and student groups formed the Sacred Union, which dominated the national convention, and in 1992 it chose Tshisekedi as prime minister and Laurent Monsengwo, the Catholic archbishop of Kisangani, as chairman. Both were known foes of Mobutu, and he rejected their authority. While this government stalemate took place, the country faced riots, the army went on murderous rampages, and the economy utterly disintegrated. Several cities lapsed into anarchy. In 1994 there were two parallel governments, both claiming legitimacy and neither able to control the country.

Tshisekedi's third time as prime minister lasted only a week in 1997, because a month later Laurent-Desireé KABILA overthrew Mobutu in the First Congo War. Tshisekedi became an opponent of Kabila over his authoritarian rule. He boycotted the transitional government, but in 2006 he re-entered electoral politics.

Reference: PLBA, wiki. www.tshisekedi.com.

TSHOMBE, Moïse Kapenda
(Democratic Republic of the Congo, 1919–1969)

Moïse Kapenda Tshombe, who led the province of Katanga into secession during the Congo crisis of 1960, later served as prime minister of the Democratic Republic of the Congo (DRC).

Tshombe was born into a prominent Congolese commercial family related to the former Lunda royal line. He was educated as a teacher, that being the only professional avenue open to young Congolese during the Belgian colonial administration, and studied accounting in order to take over his father's business. He proved a spendthrift and dilettante, bringing his section of the company to near bankruptcy. Nevertheless, in 1951 he inherited the family enterprise and became a prominent fixture in Elizabethville (now Lubumbashi) as president of the African chamber of commerce and member of the provincial council. His business problems were not all related to his own inadequacies, however, but were in part due to restrictions on access to credit for Africans. When Tshombe decided to enter more actively in politics, he turned his business interests over to his brothers.

After establishing a Lunda cultural society and an association for middle-class Africans, the *évolués,* Tshombe founded the Confédération des Associations du Katanga (CONAKAT) in 1958 to defend the interests of the Lunda. He opposed the municipal election system that gave three out of four seats to Luba mine workers from outside the province and called for their expulsion. A subsequent recession, which caused misery for both the Lunda and Luba, the region's two major ethnic groups, convinced Tshombe that the only reasonable future for Congo lay in a federal system that would permit regional development and limit internal migration. The simultaneous rise of a Luba party led by Patrice LUMUMBA raised the specter of centralized government and outside control. Tshombe formed a coalition with several colleagues who shared his dislike of Lumumba for their own reasons. These associates included the Katanga Union, a White separatist group that wanted to maintain its colonial position, and the Belgian multinational corporation, Union Minière, which sought protection for its rich copper holdings and detested Lumumba's radical views. Union Minière also had its own private army.

In the 1960 independence discussions in Brussels, Tshombe's views were rejected, and in the following election CONAKAT won only eight seats in the new national assembly. It did, however, do well in Katanga Province, and Tshombe was chosen provincial president. Nationally, he opposed Lumumba and supported his rival, Joseph KASAVUBU, but Kasavubu divided power with Lumumba, leaving Tshombe outside the national political arena. In the meantime, the growing violence that had already begun in 1959 began to accelerate until the country was in crisis. After the army mutinied, Tshombe hired European mercenaries and declared Katanga independent in July 1960. United Nations (U.N.) peacekeeping forces intervened but refused to enter Katanga. Lumumba, infuriated, asked the Soviet Union for troops. Soon Lumumba and Kasavubu challenged each other for authority, and MOBUTU Sese Seko, a young army commander, arrested Lumumba. When he tried to escape, Lumumba was secretly shipped to Elizabethville, where Tshombe's soldiers murdered him. Despite this collusion, Tshombe was arrested by the central government a few months later and was accused of secession and treason. He was later released after signing an agreement to recognize the government.

The U.N. forces entered Elizabethville in November 1961 to establish order, and the secretary-general, Dag Hammarskjöld, was scheduled to arrive to negotiate with Tshombe in Rhodesia, but his plane crashed under mysterious circumstances, killing him. Tshombe raised a militia to attack the U.N. troops. With support from Union Minière, Katanga continued its secessionist struggle until early 1963. Tshombe went into exile, but conditions in Congo deteriorated following a peasant rebellion. In July 1964 he returned as prime minister of the country, in the hope that he could bring some measure of control. He dealt with the crisis by recalling foreign mercenaries and ruthlessly crushing the rebellion. By late 1965 he tried to wrest the presidency from Kasavubu and fought him to a stalemate until Mobutu staged a military coup. Tshombe left for exile in Spain, but in 1967 he was sentenced to death in absentia and was then kidnapped aboard a plane over the Mediterranean and flown to detention in Algeria. He died of a reported heart attack in captivity after Algeria refused to extradite him to the DRC.

References: AB, *afr*, CB, DAB, DAHB, DT, EB, EWB, HWL, MMA, PLBA, *wiki*. Ian Colvin, *The Rise and Fall of Moise Tshombe* (1968).

TSIRANANA, Philibert
(Madagascar, 1912–1978)

Philibert Tsiranana, the first Malagache president after independence, followed an independent foreign policy that included friendship with South Africa, which led to his downfall.

He came from a peasant family in Majunga Province in the northeast of the island and spent his early years tending the family's cattle. He finally was able to begin schooling at age 12, and when he finished secondary school, he became a teacher. After 12 years in the classroom, he was sent to France to obtain a certificate in technical education.

Tsiranana entered politics as a provincial councilor in Majunga in 1952. The period 1948 to 1956 was one of severe colonial repression by the French colonial authorities in Madagascar, resulting in more than 100,000 deaths. The Catholic bishops favored the nationalist movement, supporting its moderate wing out of fear of more militant and Communist anticolonialism. With Church and government support, Tsiranana founded the Social Democratic Party (SDP) in 1956 and was elected to the French national assembly as a delegate from Madagascar. At independence in 1960, the SDP was the dominant party, and Tsiranana was selected as president. Although he proclaimed himself a socialist, he followed a fairly conservative policy. He chose to keep Madagascar in the French Community and became influential among heads of state from French-speaking Africa. He also took a strongly anti-Communist stance, even opposing the admission of China to the United Nations in 1966. His most controversial and unpopular position, however, was his maintenance of friendly relations with South Africa, which became a major trading partner for Madagascar.

Tsiranana was re-elected president in 1965 and 1972 in elections that were rigged in his favor. In 1971 there was a popular rebellion, which Tsiranana suppressed brutally. His victory in 1972, with a 99.9 percent majority, caused antigovernment demonstrations and riots by students and workers and, within a few months, Tsiranana's position had deteriorated. He handed over power to the army and retired from public life. He was replaced by Gabriel RAMANANTSOA. In 1975, however, he was accused of complicity in the murder of President Richard Ratsimandrava. He subsequently was acquitted and returned to political obscurity.

References: afr, MMA, PLBA, *wiki.*

TUBMAN, William Vacanarat Shadrach
(Liberia, 1895–1971)

William V. S. Tubman was the first Liberian president to support development of the indigenous peoples in the hinterland. He was born of the Americo-Liberian elite that governed Liberia from its foundation in 1847 until 1980. (The Americo-Liberians were descendants of freed American slaves who established a colony in Liberia in the 1820s, gradually extending their authority inland.)

Tubman's father was a Liberian general, and William entered the army at 15. He rose from private soldier to become an officer after taking part in several military excursions into the bush against indigenous rebels.

Tubman studied law and was admitted to the bar. Entering politics as a senator at age 28, he served as legal advisor to President Charles KING and quit the senate in 1930 when a slave labor controversy forced King's resignation. He returned to the senate in 1934, and three years later President Edwin Barclay appointed him to the Supreme Court.

In 1943, Tubman was Barclay's handpicked choice for president. He promoted an active foreign policy, starting with Liberian entry into World War II on the side of the Allies. By the 1960s, Tubman was an anticolonial advocate of African independence and a founder of the Organization of African Unity (OAU). He courted foreign investment with an "open door policy" of tax exemptions, tariff exemptions, and repatriation of profits. A deepwater port was built at Monrovia, and iron deposits were developed, all of which contributed to a period of prosperity and high employment. For a time in the 1950s, Liberia enjoyed the status of second-highest economic growth rate in the world. It had the world's greatest mercantile fleet, was a major exporter or iron ore, and was the world leader in rubber production. Tubman abolished the constitu-

tional term limitation for presidents and was re-elected continually until his death in 1971.

Tubman actively promoted national unity, giving the vote to both women and rural peoples. He developed social services and communications in the interior and built schools. In spite of his reforms, however, Tubman was paternalistic and brooked no opposition. He believed firmly in the rule of the Americo-Liberian elite even as he tried to bridge the socioeconomic division between them and the indigenous population. Although in later years several assassination attempts were made against him, Tubman died peacefully and widely respected.

References: AB, *afr*, CB, DAHB, EWB, MMA, PLBA, PLCA, *wiki.* Tuan Weh, *The Love of Liberty: The Rule of President V.S. Tubman in Liberia* (1976).

TURABI, Hassan Abdallah al-
(Sudan, 1932–)

Sheikh Hassan Abdallah al-Turabi, head of the National Islamic Front (NIF), was the main power behind the government of General Omar BASHIR and the leading theoretician of the Muslim fundamentalist movement.

Al-Turabi's influence in the international Islamic revival makes him one of its leading apologists. To his disciples he teaches "a modern Islam, . . . an alternative model of life" to the decay of the West. To his critics he is a source of international terrorism, a "Sudanese Svengali" whose despotism has caused the deaths of scores of thousands. He is the heir of a revivalist legacy that began in the 1920s with the creation of the Sunni Muslim Brotherhood, of which he became leader in the early 1960s. The movement attacked early Arab nationalism and rejected the secularist example of Turkey, which influenced many emerging Arab states. The Muslim Brotherhood argued that many Arab leaders were in fact not true followers of Islam's tenets and deserved to be overthrown by force in a new *jihad,* or holy war. Al-Turabi's fundamentalist outlook appeals to many Sudanese intellectuals who have become frustrated at the failures of Arab nationalism to create a society that is integrally Arab but which can still provide for the needs of the economy. Al-Turabi's followers dominate banking and business as well as the government in Sudan. One of his goals, only partially realized, is the introduction of Islamic law (*sharia*) in the Sudan.

Al-Turabi's early life is obscure, but he received a superior Western education. He earned degrees in law at the University of London and a Ph.D. from the Sorbonne, and is fluent in several languages. In the mid-1980s, he founded the NIF, which was banned, along with all political parties, after Gaafar NIMEIRY's 1969 coup. Al-Turabi was held for six years and then spent three more in exile in Libya. In 1979 he returned, reconciled with Nimiery, and was appointed attorney general. He implemented Nimeiry's imposition of Islamic law so harshly that it caused an outbreak of the southern secessionist war and the fall of Nimiery in 1985.

In fact, the NIF is the ruling faction in Sudan, although it likes to refer to itself as an "Islamic current" rather than a party. Al-Turabi's only formal position is head of the Arab and Islamic Popular Congress, an umbrella group formed to forge coalitions among Arab groups across the Middle East in order to develop a modern approach to problems of the economy and Arab culture. Former prime minister Sadiq el-MAHDI, al-Turabi's brother-in-law, who has been under house arrest since his overthrow in 1989, calls the Bashir regime, under al-Turabi's guidance, "repressive, dictatorial and tyrannical." The U.S. government has denounced Sudan as the main center for international terrorism.

As attorney general, al-Turabi developed the notorious "September Laws," which introduced Islamic legal punishments, such as public floggings for alcohol use, amputations for theft, and stoning to death for adultery. This legal policy led to denunciations by Western civil rights organizations. After Nimeiry's overthrow in 1985, the NIF fared badly in the free elections that followed and entered into a coalition with Sadiq el-Mahdi. The civil war against the Christian and traditionalist south caused tremendous hardship, and when el-Mahdi began negotiations with Colonel John GARANG, the fundamentalists began to plot against him. Just as a breakthrough seemed imminent, Bashir overthrew el-Mahdi. Al-Turabi was briefly detained but soon emerged as the power behind the regime. During the 1990s he was head of the National Islamic Front and Speaker of the National Assembly. After his falling-out with Bashir in 1999, he was stripped of the latter post.

On an unofficial visit to North America in 1992, al-Turabi was attacked and injured at the Ottawa airport, but he recovered. He now uses the incident as an example to bolster his reputation for having divine protection. He continued to make Sudan a haven for terrorist organizations, including the Abu Nidal group, Hamas, and the Islamic Jihad. From 1990 to 1996, Turabi was Osama bin Laden's patron and protector in Sudan when he took up residence there and used the Sudan as a base for terrorism. In addition, both Egypt and Saudi Arabia have accused Sudan of fostering fundamentalist plots in their countries. In 1993 a cabinet shuffle brought an marked increase in NIF presence, and the United States added Sudan to its list of states sponsoring international terrorism. He has been rumored to be behind an armed Islamic group, the Justice and Equality Movement (JEM), which is responsible for much of the genocide in Darfur.

In 2004, Bashir had Turabi arrested and imprisoned for a year, alleging a coup plot.

References: EWB, MIW, *wiki*.

TUTU, Desmond Mpilo
(South Africa, 1931–)

Archbishop Desmond Mpilo Tutu, retired head of the Anglican Church in South Africa, was the leading spokesman of nonviolent resistance to apartheid during the 1980s, for which he was awarded the Nobel Peace Prize in 1984.

Tutu was born in the Transvaal and spent his teen years in Johannesburg, where his mother had taken work at a mission school for the blind. His religious faith was deeply strengthened by the staff's compassion and dedication, and shortly thereafter he met Father Trevor HUDDLESTON, whom he has termed the greatest single influence on his life. Huddleston, then just beginning his career as the leading White foe of apartheid, spent time with Tutu, including daily visits for almost two years when Tutu was in the hospital with tuberculosis. Unable to afford medical school fees after high school, Tutu received a teacher's certificate from the Bantu Normal College in 1953 and a correspondence degree from the University of South Africa the following year. He taught for several years until the government's Bantu education program, guaranteeing second-class status for Black South Africans, took effect. Along with many other teachers, Tutu resigned in 1957.

Desmond Mpilo Tutu

He decided to enter the Anglican clergy and placed himself under the direction of the Mirfield Fathers, Huddleston's religious community. From them he learned their high-church patterns of daily prayer, liturgy and meditation, but he also absorbed their strong sense of Christian social justice. He went on to theological studies at St. Peter's Seminary, taking his degree in 1960 and being ordained a deacon. A year later he was ordained an Anglican priest. He spent two years as a curate and then went to London for further study from 1962 to 1966. For the next three years he taught theology and was chaplain at Fort Hare University and then at the National University of Lesotho from 1969 to 1972. He then returned to England for three years as director of the Theological Education Fund, a World Council of Churches scholarship program. Tutu returned to South Africa in 1975 as dean of Johannesburg, and his clerical career moved swiftly: he was bishop of Lesotho from 1976 to 1978, secretary-general of the South African Council of Churches (SACC) from 1978 to 1985, Anglican bishop of Johannesburg (1985), and archbishop of Cape Town and head of the Anglican Church in South Africa from 1986 to 1996. He was the first Black South African primate in the Church. Tutu was also president of the All-Africa Council of Churches (AACC) from 1987 to 1997.

Throughout his rise in Church circles, Tutu was increasingly involved in confronting the patterns of violence in the townships and their root cause: the country's apartheid regime. Firmly committed to a policy of Christian nonviolence, Tutu nevertheless was unable to be a passive bystander, and he used his SACC position as a world pulpit. He argued that "to be impartial is to have taken sides already." He strongly endorsed economic sanctions against South Africa on a 1979 trip abroad, which led to his passport being lifted for two years. When he was again able to travel, Tutu made an international tour to promote sanctions, which he saw as the best nonviolent means of breaking apartheid's power. On his return, his passport was again taken, and thereafter he went abroad with a travel document stamped "nationality undetermined."

After the Soweto student riots of 1976, there was a great need for Black voices of authority, especially as most political leaders were silenced, exiled or imprisoned. Under the circumstances, Tutu's charismatic speaking style and uncompromising attitude thrust him to the forefront. Many other prominent religious leaders were against apartheid, but none had Tutu's position, charisma, dynamism and respect. Tutu also showed himself a competent administrator and organizer, and he was able to shape the SACC into a far more efficient body than when he took over its leadership. When the government backed down from banning the SACC after an investigation in 1984, no one doubted that Tutu's prestige had saved the organization. That fall he took a sabbatical at General Theological Seminary in New York, where he received the announcement that he had been awarded the Nobel Peace Prize.

Tutu returned home to a society that was descending into violent chaos. Thousands of government troops raided the townships, strikes paralyzed industry, and some 200,000 students boycotted classes. A new constitution provided token representation to Indians and Coloureds (people of mixed racial heritage) while excluding Blacks. Shortly after Tutu's return to Johannesburg, he was elected bishop. He continued to promote sanctions, witnessing the first restrictions placed on trade by the U.S. government. At the same time, violence escalated until President P. W. BOTHA declared a state of emergency. Hundreds of Africans died in township violence outside the major cities, and Tutu not only spoke out but acted against it. On one occasion, he broke through a crowd at the risk of his own life to save a police informer from a Black mob that was about to burn him to death. Time and again he served as a peacemaker in tense situations. When the position of archbishop of Cape Town came open in 1986, he made it known that he was interested, and in a contested election he was chosen primate of the Anglican Church in South Africa. He used the occasion of his installation to speak out again for sanctions, reiterating the statement that he had made when he first advocated them: "If we cannot consider all peaceful means, then people are in effect saying that there are no peaceful means."

After the end of apartheid, a serious question lingered about how to bring about justice for the atrocities of the past 40 years. It was felt that criminal trials would be divisive and even lead to civil conflict. The solution was the creation of the Peace and Reconciliation Commission, headed by Tutu from 1995 to 1998. Many feel is was his finest hour and his greatest legacy. Perpetrators were invited to testify in public. If they refused, they could be indicted for their criminal actions, but otherwise they named their own crimes and took responsibility for them. It was a cleansing process that has been a model for other states dealing with longtime violent oppression.

Tutu is a diminutive man, ebullient and spirited. At the inauguration of Nelson MANDELA as president in 1994, he could not contain himself and broke out with whoops of joy. He has been known to dance at solemn services, and his preaching is just as enthusiastic, but the style is more prophetic than emotional. Although he is close to Mandela and the African National Congress (ANC) leadership, Tutu has never joined the ANC, and, consistent with his nonviolent position, he opposed the ANC's guerrilla action during the liberation struggle. Through it all, he remains faithful to the disciplines of daily prayer and meditation that he learned from the Mirfield Fathers. He has always argued that apartheid morally destroyed both its advocates and its victims, and he has insistently called for a South African society based on racial equality. On the morning of Mandela's inaugura-

tion, he quietly entered his private chapel to celebrate the eucharist in Afrikaans.

References: AB, *adb*, *afr*, CA, CB, *dacb*, EWB, GSAP, HH, PLBA, PLCA, RWWA, *wiki*. Tutu, *The Rainbow People of God* (1995); Dennis Wepman, *Desmond Tutu* (1989) [young adult].

TUTUOLA, Amos
(Nigeria, 1920–1997)

Amos Tutuola, novelist and short story writer, was the first Nigerian writer to reach an international audience. Drawing on Yoruba tales, he adapted their oral technique, which allowed him to take advantage of his limited English. Tutuola completed only six years of elementary school and was never a part of Nigerian intellectual circles, which have often regarded him with embarrassment or disdain.

Tutuola was a metalworker in the Royal Air Force during World War II. After failing in his efforts to set up his own shop, he turned to writing and produced *The Palm-Wine Drinkard* (1952). It took his publisher seven years to produce the book, although it subsequently became a success, with more than 10 printings in the United States alone and an equal number of translations. A heroic tale, it is the account of a journey to the "Land of the Deads," from which the hero returns with a magic egg. When it is broken by greedy villagers, it hatches whips that scourge them. After it is restored, the egg condemns the villagers to famine, but a human sacrifice brings on the living rain.

Tutuola followed his first novel with seven others (the last in 1987), including *Feather Woman of the Jungle* (1962) and *Ajaiyi and His Inherited Poverty* (1967). One of his reasons for avoiding the Nigerian literary scene has been his conviction that the stories he tells come not from his creative imagination but emanate from the spirit world. Another reason might be his almost total rejection by embarrassed professional writers, who regard Tutuola's work as primitive, unlettered and incompetent. He has been accused of exploiting the very qualities that lead Western readers to snicker at African simple-mindedness. In contrast, Western critics have found Tutuola's writing naive and charming. The poet Dylan Thomas admiringly called it "very young English" for its freshness and eccentricity. None of his subsequent work, however, matched the success of his first novel.

Tutuola's fiction does not merely recount Yoruba tales (or his personal versions of them), it also recycles them in a new idiom, English as grasped by the African living in two worlds—the one of the village and the one of the city. Beyond the two is the bush, the unsettled (and unsettling) emptiness of desert, plains or rain forest. It is the traditional place of exile, where Tutuola's characters confront their destinies. Most of his work employs a journey motif, a search for someone or something that will unlock mysteries.

Curiously, since the 1970s, critical judgment on Tutuola has reversed. Africans accept his fractured English while appreciating his inventiveness. Western reviewers, however, have tired of his approach. This conflict raises the question of whether an African can use Western forms to express traditional materials without sacrificing them or rendering them into cartoons. Tutuola himself, uninterested in literary criticism, never entered the debate but continued to use English as he willed, in defiance of its grammar. His last work was a collection, *The Village Witch Doctor and Other Stories* (1990).

References: adb, afr, AA, CANR, DAHB, DLB, EWB, MBW, NRG, *wiki,* WLTC. Harold Collins, *Amos Tutuola* (1969); Oyekan Owomoyela, *Amos Tutuola Revisited* (1999).

TWINS Seven-Seven

(Nigeria, 1944–)

An artist, sculptor, musician, weaver, playwright and performer, Twins Seven-Seven is considered one of the foremost modern African artists.

Born a Yoruba prince, he was originally named Taiwo Olaniyi Wayewale-Toyeje Oyekali Osuntoki. The origin of the name "Twins Seven-Seven" is the tragedy of his mother, who bore seven sets of twins, of whom he is the only surviving child. One of his best known works is *Healing of the Abiku Children* (1973), based on the myth of an *abiku,* a child who dies shortly after birth and is reborn into the same family. In the painting, a mother has brought her twins to a diviner so that they might be freed of the cycle of death and rebirth.

Twins was trained in an artistic workshop, aloof from the academic art circles of the period. He came to world attention in his twenties through European exhibitions. His stylized art is immersed in the spirit world of Yoruba folk tales. Among his finest

work is a series of etchings based on the magical tales of Amos TUTUOLA, who created stories that he claimed were inspired by spirits. Twins's style of dense, figure-packed art was perfectly suited to Tutuola's fantasy world. All of Twins Seven-Seven's work is thronged with intricate decorative bits, often hard to interpret. Twins himself gives different interpretations of the figures and details in his works, depending on his moods.

Twins Seven-Seven prefers in recent years to use what he calls "sculpture painting," the use of raised relief on the base of the painting to give a dimensional effect. He is not averse to using whatever suits the work he is doing. At one point he abandoned brushes for applicators made from palm leaves. He finishes his work with varnish to give it luminosity.

Twins Seven-Seven has recorded since the 1960s, but he never assumed the prominence of most Afropop performers, nor has he become an international celebrity. His music is influenced by African-American jazz, but his last album, *Nigeria Beat* (1994), is notable for its use of traditional instruments and complex rhythms. Typically, however, when he has a painting exhibition, he sings and dances as part of the opening. As a youth, he dazzled dance halls with his creative riffs on the usual highlife dance styles and his outrageous costumes.

Healing of the Abiku Children, by Twins Seven Seven. Courtesy of the Indianapolis Museum of Art

In 2005, the United Nations Educational, Scientific, and Cultural Organization (UNESCO) named Twins Seven-Seven its Artist of Peace. He has taught in California and exhibited widely in Europe and America. He became chief of his village, but when the social and cultic obligations took up all his time, he moved to the United States in 2000.

UMAR Ibn Said Tall
(Sénégal/Mali/Guinea, 1794?–1864)

Al-Hajj Umar Ibn Said Tall, the founder of the Tukulor Empire, which covered much of today's Sénégal and southern Mali, led a major West African revolutionary movement. Umar was an important Muslim reformer and spread Islam in a series of religious wars that lasted until his death. With his pattern of Islamic expansion, he was followed by a number of others who were inspired by his example. His name is sometimes given as Umar TALL.

As a youth, Umar was initiated into the Tijaniyya brotherhood, a religious society, despite the fact that his father was a prominent member of the Qadiriyya sect in the Tukulor clerical caste. The Tijaniyya stressed salvation through action rather than study, but Umar became a Koranic scholar as well. He made his *hajj,* or pilgrimage, to Mecca in 1826, ranging widely in his travels in order to encounter a number of Islamic movements. He was especially impressed with the Wahhabi in central Arabia, an austere and puritanical sect with a strong anti-Turkish, anticolonial attitude. The head of the Tijaniyya brotherhood invested Umar as caliph of the Tijaniyya for all West Africa. On the return trip (1832), Umar stayed for seven years with Muhammad BELLO, the son and successor of UTHMAN Dan Fodio, founder of the Sokoto Empire. Here he amassed considerable wealth trading in gold dust, built a following, and married one of Bello's daughters.

Strengthened by his reputation as a seer, mystic and healer—and with a loyal following—Umar then established himself in present-day Guinea, where he established a religious community that became a prosperous and zealous Tijaniyya mission. From this base he traveled throughout the Senegambia region. He was convinced that faith without force would never overcome traditional religious beliefs, and he inscribed his doctrine in a book of teachings. He recommended blind obedience to the spiritual master, self-denial, and meditation as the Tijaniyya path to salvation.

In 1848, Umar began to expand his territory, taking over several smaller nearby Islamic states.

His success was due to the use of Western small arms and his legend of invincibility. In 1852 he declared a *jihad* (holy war) that lasted until his death in battle 12 years later. He denounced the existing Islamic states as being corrupted by traditional religion. He proclaimed a divine revelation to bring them to integral Islam. With a force of 10,000, Umar terrorized the chiefdoms into submission. He conquered a series of states, leading his own forces into battle. After each conquest, he compelled the defeated people to convert to Islam, but few proved faithful. At the same time, he came into conflict with the French, who were also expanding into Senegambia. Initially, his relations with them had been cordial because he received arms from French sources. When the arms supplies were cut, he turned against them and raided their trading forts along the Sénégal River. Umar and the French continued attacking each other's outposts from 1835 until 1859, when they signed a ceasefire. In 1858, Umar led a march to Karta of those who had fallen under French influence, and 40,000 people followed him.

Umar now turned to internal rebellions. His followers had joined him for a mixture of reasons, both religious and secular. Some hoped to bring about political reform, using Umar and the Islamic revival as a vehicle. The empire, so hastily put together, was never organized or administered properly, and after 1860 suppressing internal revolts replaced further expansion. Umar went to war against the Fulani people of Masina, who were followers of the Qadiriyya sect to which his father had belonged. The mission of *jihad* had become a war of conquest among Muslims, and Umar attempted to reconquer the Islamic state of Masina. It was in battle during a Muslim uprising led by Masina that Umar died when the town he was defending was burned down and he was killed in the explosion of the gunpowder stores. After a dynastic struggle—he left 50 sons—he was succeeded by one of them, Ahmadu ibn Umar, who maintained the empire until French conquest in 1896.

The flame of Islamic purification and resistance to Western influence did not die with Umar. It was taken up by Tijaniyya disciples such as MABA Diakhou Ba and Mamadu LAMINE, both of whom he trained and inspired. A further result of the *jihad* was a flowering of Islamic literature, particularly Arabic verse. Later Muslim assessments either glorify Umar, comparing him to the Prophet, or disparage him for shedding Muslim blood in fratricidal conflicts.

References: afr, DAHB, MIW, MMA, *wiki.*

USMAN dan Fodio
(Nigeria, 1754–1817)

Shehu Usman dan Fodio, who launched the Islamic revival in the Hausa states of Nigeria, created the Sokoto caliphate, one of the most powerful states in nineteenth-century Africa. His name is variously given as Uthman or Ousman.

Usman was born into a religious family that belonged to the Qadiriyya brotherhood, which was then dominant in the Hausa states. After a thorough training in Islamic theology and law and Arabic, he became an itinerant preacher around 1774 in Gobir, emphasizing reform and true Islamic observance. He attracted a following, largely due to his growing reputation for mysticism. Through the 1780s his number of supporters grew, and, even when the ruler of Gobir began persecuting Muslims, Usman was allowed to continue teaching. Through the 1790s he had a series of visions that called for him to purify Islam, by holy war (*jihad*) if necessary. The Islamic scholars were slow to accept Usman, but he had a strong following among the Fulani peasantry. The persecution that they endured under the Hausa made them hope for the arrival of the Mahdi, a divinely guided one who would liberate them and inaugurate a new age of Islam. Usman always rejected any attempt to identify him as the Mahdi, but he did take up the cause of the poor.

Around 1798 the sultan became alarmed that Usman's community was becoming a state within the state, and he began to limit it, forbidding all except Usman to preach and denying the right of conversion. In 1801 Usman's former pupil, Yunfa, became sultan and grew even more restrictive toward Usman. By 1804 his insistent criticisms of the Hausa rulers, especially his attacks on the tax system, caused a confrontation. Usman was forced to flee with his adherents; it was a sacred flight like the Prophet Muhammad's *hejira* from Mecca to Medina, and its anniversary is still observed in the Muslim calendar in Nigeria. After Usman was elected caliph, he proclaimed a holy war against the sultan and all the Hausa chiefs and took the title of *shehu,* Hausa for "sheikh."

Usman was neither an organizer nor a general, so he left the leadership of the army to his son, Muhammad BELLO, and the administration to his brother. He served as spiritual guide, attempting to mold his motley following, which consisted of ardent Islamic reformers as well as pastoralists, peasants and mere freeloaders. Some Fulani joined the *jihad* to free themselves from Hausa domination, and others joined because of a hatred for the Hausa slave trade. Within four years Gobir had fallen, and Usman turned to the neighboring states, rousing the Fulani to rebellion. The liberated areas were formed into emirates, with political organization at the service of the social and religious ideals taught by Usman. Bello established the capital at Sokoto, where Usman retired in 1809 to a life of study and prayer, passing his title of sultan of Sokoto to Bello. Although possessing a superior cavalry, Usman's forces were never able to conquer Bornu. As a result, when the British arrived in the interior of Nigeria, they found two large and powerful Muslim states, Bornu and Sokoto.

Usman was always a deeply religious man, faithful to his visions. The holy war brought some compromise of his ideals, as when he attacked his fellow Muslims of Bornu, but in general he kept to his religious beliefs. His personal life was simple to the point of austerity; he remained uncorrupted and unworldly. He composed religious poetry in both Fulani and Arabic.

References: AB, *afr*, CWAH, DAHB, EB, EWB, MIW, MMA, *wiki.* Mervyn Hiskett, *The Sword of Truth* (1973).

U TAM'SI, Gérald-Félix Tchicaya
(Congo, 1931–1988)

Gérald-Félix Tchicaya U Tam'si, one of the leading poets of French-speaking Africa, was both within and apart from the explosive movement that affirmed African rhythms and motifs. He never embraced the *Négritude* school, yet he was lavishly praised by its founder and father-figure, Léopold SENGHOR.

He moved to Paris at age 15 when his father, a respected Congolese politician, was elected to the French national assembly. He remained in France, working at various unskilled jobs as he began writing. He added U Tam'si to the family name to distinguish himself from his father; Tchicaya U Tam'si means "little bird singing from home." From 1957 to 1960, U Tam'si wrote and produced more than a hundred African folk tales for French radio, which were published in 1968 as *Légendes Africaines*. In 1960, as a fervent disciple of Patrice LUMUMBA, he traveled to the Belgian Congo in time for independence and edited Lumumba's party paper. Upon Lumumba's assassination, U Tam'si took a position with the United Nations Educational, Scientific, and Cultural Organization (UNESCO) in Léopoldville (now Kinshasa) and then transferred to its Department of Education in Paris, where he remained for the rest of his career.

U Tam'si's poetry is often called surrealist because it shares some elements with that genre—random images, stream of consciousness, and indifference to grammar and punctuation. "Written poetry follows a grammatical logic. My logic is my own; it is a logic of reverberation," he argues. Senghor said of U Tam'si's poems: "They are fireworks, an erupting volcano." Although his themes come from Africa, especially its landscape, U Tam'si is universal in his perspective. His nostalgia for the mythical African past is devoid of appeals to the ancestors or other notable aspects of African thought. His work evokes universal feelings in its readers. In *Feu de Brousse* (*Brush Fire*, 1957) he explores being Black in Europe, but the real theme is alienation. *A Triche Coeur* (*Cheating Heart*, 1958) reflects struggles with personal identity. Only with *Epitome* (1962), which contains his best verses, does U Tam'si become overtly political by confronting the disintegration in the Congo Republic after independence. This volume won the Dakar Festival of Black Arts poetry prize in 1966. In 1978 he was awarded the Grand Prize for Literature from the Congo Republic.

By 1980, already established as a major presence in French African poetry, U Tam'si turned to other literary fields. He published a novel and a collection of short stories that year, both of which were well received. A second novel (1982) was his last work.

References: AA, CA, MBW, NRG, *wiki*, WLTC.

VAN DER MERWE, Anna-Mart

(South Africa, 1950s-)

Anna-Mart Van der Merwe is a leading South African actress who is popular for her television appearances as well as her stage work. She performs in both English and Afrikaans.

Van der Merwe studied drama at the University of Cape Town, and worked first at the Performing Arts Council, which sponsored a theater group. She developed into a prominent lead actress in both classical and contemporary plays, rising to greatest popularity, however, for her leading roles in South African television, where she has been a regular in several series. Van der Merwe has also made several films. In all media she has performed with both Afrikaans and English scripts. In 1994 she received the Artes Award as Best Actress, and in 2000 the Avanti Award for Best Supporting Actress.

Not only is Van der Merwe talented, but her versatility is amazing. In a small drama market like South Africa, the ability to perform in several styles is highly valued. It is common for plays to open in Cape Town and then make a tour of arts festivals around the country. Van der Merwe regularly performs in dramas, television soap operas, even detective mysteries. Yet she is outstanding in the repertoire of classical English theater. Her performance of Regan in Shakespeare's *King Lear* was widely praised by reviewers. In 2006, she played in an Afrikaans-language version of Eugene O'Neill's *Desire Under the Elms*, set in rural South Africa. One reviewer called her performance "raw, emotionally tense and honest." She has appeared in a dozen television dramas, several films and over a dozen plays.

VAN DER POST, Laurens Jan

(South Africa, 1906–1996)

Sir Laurens van der Post was a noted writer, conservationist and explorer whose adventures often became the basis of his novels and non-fiction.

The son of an Afrikaner lawyer and veteran of the Boer War, van der Post was raised on a traditional Afrikaner farm, the thirteenth of 15 children. Despite a conservative upbringing, he would go on to became a sophisticated man of the world who broke out of the narrow confines of Afrikaner society. He was close to the British royal family, especially Prince Charles, and was Prince William's godfather. He was knighted by Queen Elizabeth in 1981.

It was this very global perspective that led van der Post to become one of the earliest Afrikaner critics of South African racial policy, long before apartheid was codified in 1948. *In the Province* (1934) was the first book against racial segregation written by an Afrikaner, and one of the first by any White South African. In 1925 he helped found an antiapartheid journal written in Afrikaans. As a consequence, he was forced to leave South Africa and went to Japan, where *In the Province* was later written. He returned to Cape Town as a journalist, and he and his new wife began associating with the

Lauren Jan van der Post

literary and art communities. In 1931 he moved to England where he wrote, mixed with the Bloomsbury literary society and took up farming.

When World War II broke out, he became an officer and took part in the Ethiopian campaign against the Italians. Since he spoke Dutch, he was then posted to Indonesia to organize the retreat of Allied forces as the Japanese advanced. He was captured in 1942 and spent three years in a Japanese prisoner-of-war camp on Java. From this experience came *The Seed and the Sower* (1963), which was made into the film *Merry Christmas, Mr. Lawrence* (1983) with David Bowie. Two non-fiction works were also based on his prison camp years. He helped negotiate between the Dutch and the independence movement, and ended his Java years as British military attaché. He returned to South Africa, but with the victory of the apartheid forces of David MALAN, the family moved to England, where he remained, with long trips back to Africa, until his death.

Van der Post loved the bush and spent long periods living off the land among the remaining hunter-gatherers in the Kalahari Desert of Botswana. One trip resulted in a six-part television series for the British Broadcasting Company (BBC). His books *The World of the Kalahari* (1958) and *The Heart of the Hunter* (1961) both won literary awards, and two others books followed. These are his best-known works. In later years he would even write the African volume of the TIME-LIFE cooking series, with delightful accounts of cooking wild game. His narratives of the life of the San people are idealized, presenting them as a people of mystical spirituality, living in harmony with the land.

Van der Post's fiction is less significant, although in its time it was well received. He published novels, a collection of novellas, and short stories—in total, 25 books. He was also interested in the mystical and spiritual. He met the psychologist Carl Jung and was immensely influenced by him. They remained friends for 16 years. In 1971 he wrote a television documentary on Jung, and followed that with a biography of Jung and his own experience with Jungian thought (1975). He explored Eastern religions as well and introduced Prince Charles to them.

Van der Post's great popularity generated a reaction after his death, and his books and life were the objects of negative attacks. Interest in his writing waned and has not yet revived.

References: adb, afr, CA, CANR, EB, *wiki*. Frederic Carpenter, *Laurens Van Der Post* (1969); J. D. F. Jones, *Teller of Many Tales* (2001).

VAN GRAAN, Michael "Mike"
(South Africa, 1959–)

Mike Van Graan is a major figure in the arts community in South Africa. He is a noted (and acerbic) critic who took upon himself the task of forging an arts policy for post-apartheid South Africa. He is also a successful playwright and performer.

During his university years, Van Graan became involved with Student Christian Action, a militant antiapartheid movement. He became a national organizer and was sent to the United States and Latin America for a year on a theology exchange sponsored by the Institute for Contextual Theology, which was then refining its theory of African liberation theology. Van Graan then worked for the Institute on the promotion of the Kairos Document. In 1986, the state of emergency put an end to these efforts.

Part of Van Graan's activism during his religious-based years was the use of street theater. Here he honed his skills in writing and directing. When apartheid ended, Van Graan was director of the Community Arts Project (CAP) in Cape Town, a position from which he undertook nothing less than a coordination and restructuring of the arts community throughout South Africa. He was convinced that the arts must be free of all partisan control so that it might speak the truth as it saw it. In the first flush of the new freedom, there was considerable funding available for the arts, and Van Graan took full advantage of it. He proved himself an able administrator, a good mobilizer, and an inspiring mentor. He brought a higher degree of professionalization to theater. His position for a "free" art ran counter to the engaged and politicized movements connected with the freedom movements, and when he withdrew from the CAP, it caused confusion and disintegration.

Van Graan fell victim to his own approaches as he was dropped by CAP. It proved fortuitous, however, as he soon found a place with the Congress of South African Writers (COSAW). COSAW had impeccable liberation credentials, and when Van Graan issued a call for Arts for All, a coordinating policy group independent of political organizations, including the dominant African National Congress (ANC), he created a new dynamic in the arts. In a series of moves, he drafted policies based on wide consultation through national convocations. As unity emerged and the politicized groups faded, artists and writers themselves began taking control of arts policy. Van Graan ended as general secretary of the National Arts Coalition.

Van Graan stepped away from direct leadership to found his own consulting group, Article 27. It organizes arts festivals throughout the country. Van Graan also publishes a weekly arts commentary on the Internet that gives him a public forum. He is as critical of attempts by the ANC government to manipulate the arts as he was of its predecessors. Some see him as a firm guide of South African arts policy and a brilliant arts critic, while his opponents accuse him of arrogance and hubris. A cursory glance at his Internet musings show him to be opinionated, incisive and on top of every arts development in South Africa. He can poke fun at political correctness as he did with his "Dummies Guide to Being or Becoming an African for the Four Main Population Groups." He can be sarcastic about the obtuseness of bureaucrats ("There is no money for films, but there is money for film awards"), or flay the hyper-patriots of the "new" South Africa ("Being proud, flag-waving South Africans doesn't mean we have to be happy-clappy rainbowists, blind to anything that shakes our confidence in our country"). He can tweak the Americans ("weapons of mass distraction"), prick the pompous ("Mbeki, the musical") and celebrate the demise of the National Arts Council ("Send out the clowns"). His columns are avidly read and gossiped about, but always taken seriously.

Van Graan's own plays have been successful and well received by both the public and the critics. *Dinner Talk* (1998) was performed nationally (and still is from time to time), and was taken to the Netherlands and England. He has also performed in most of his plays. In 2006 he produced *Some Mothers' Sons*, the story of a White lawyer who defends a Black man under apartheid, only to be defended by him 20 years later when conditions and roles are reversed.

Reference: adb. www.artslink.co.za.

VERWOERD, Hendrik Frensch
(South Africa, 1901–1966)

Dr. Hendrik Frensch Verwoerd was the intellectual defender of apartheid and its legislative architect. He transformed a shapeless racist doctrine into a coherent political theory.

Verwoerd's missionary family emigrated to South Africa from the Netherlands when he was a child, and he was raised in Cape Town in a deeply religious Calvinist atmosphere. After a brilliant record at Stellenbosch University, the intellectual cradle of Afrikaner nationalism, he did graduate work in Hamburg, Leipzig and Berlin, culminating in a doctorate from Stellenbosch University in South Africa. Appointed professor of applied psychology at Stellenbosch in 1928, he became professor of sociology there in 1932.

Verwoerd took an early interest in racial politics, joining a delegation of professors who opposed providing sanctuary to Jewish refugees from Nazi Germany. He became a member of the National Party (NP) and also joined the Broederbond, the secret society of Afrikaner men that included most of the elite. Verwoerd first distinguished himself by organizing a symposium on the problem of Afrikaner poverty. A popular speaker and writer, he was soon a national figure and the voice of Afrikaner nationalist thought.

In 1937, Verwoerd left his teaching post to become editor of *Die Transvaler,* an Afrikaans newspaper that gave him a platform for his views. Bitterly opposed to liberal democracy, Verwoerd flirted with Nazi racial purity doctrines, and his views supported fascism. When the *Johannesburg Star* accused him of Nazi sympathies in 1943, he sued for libel but lost the case. Verwoerd's position on race excluded any possibility of cooperation except on the basis of complete separation. He argued that only conflict would take place in "intermingled communities" and that separate development would be fairest for all. He was successful in convincing the Afrikaners that racial segregation was not mere White supremacy but a means of providing respect and dignity for Blacks as well as Whites in parallel cultural streams of advancement. He called it "grand apartheid," based on various discredited racial ideas and segregationist policies. Verwoerd admitted the assumption of White superiority, calling his Bantustan (tribal "homeland") scheme, which was the cornerstone of his program, "buying the White man his freedom and right to retain domination in his country."

Verwoerd stood for parliament in the fateful 1948 election that brought Daniel MALAN and the NP to power, but he was rejected. The NP rewarded him with an appointment to the senate in 1950, where he became party floor leader and from which, unchallenged by election, he was named minister of Bantu affairs. Under Malan, Verwoerd became the architect of apartheid and felt no compunction about the toll its implementation took on the Black population. Totally convinced of his plans' moral superiority, he set to work to complete the separation of the races. His goal was to resettle all "detribalized" Africans, except those needed for cheap labor, in homelands. The workers who remained, technically resident aliens, were forbidden to bring their spouses or families with them.

The methods were draconian. Pass laws defined everyone's race and controlled residence, education and work opportunities. Marriage and sexual relations between persons of different races were made punishable by law. African property rights were abolished for urban areas, and business permits for Blacks were severely limited. All future post-elementary education for Blacks was limited to the Bantustans. Black neighborhoods in the cities were bulldozed and their residents were moved into townships in inhospitable areas. The keystone of the plan was the Bantustan program to provide homelands for each African ethnic group and repatriate its members there. Verwoerd proposed to revive chieftaincies and reinstate traditional government as "natural" for Africans. His most destructive move was the Bantu Education Act (1953) to centralize education in his ministry and align it with apartheid. He challenged the White Churches, which had controlled much of African education, on the grounds that they taught foreign European ideals, saying: "The Bantu must be guided to serve his own community . . . it is of no avail for him to receive a training which has as its aim absorption in the European community while he cannot and will not be absorbed there." The Bantu Education Act made the schools battlegrounds against apartheid and breeding grounds for Black opposition.

In 1958, having been in both Malan's and his successor's cabinets, Verwoerd was elected prime minister in a controversial NP caucus. His eight years in office gave him the authority to see his plans put into effect. In 1960 a referendum narrowly gave him approval to withdraw from the Commonwealth and make South Africa a republic, thus depriving English-speaking citizens of their British nationality. At the same time, he began forcing Black South Africans onto the Bantustans, creating several nominally independent states (recognized by no other nation). This removed them from any claim to South African status. When challenged on this issue, Verwoerd argued that it was a progressive move, allowing Blacks freedom from White rule. African political movements such as the African National Congress (ANC) and the Pan-Africanist Congress (PAC) were banned, and Nelson MANDELA, Walter SISULU and most of the ANC and PAC leadership were imprisoned. Banning (an extreme form of house arrest), strict political censorship of publications, and the suspension of civil rights gradually turned South Africa into a police state, which maintained a thin veneer of openness and false prosperity. After 1961, Helen SUZMAN remained as the only antiapartheid member of parliament.

In the 1966 elections, for the first time, the NP polled substantial numbers of English-speaking votes. There had been a failed assassination attempt in 1960, when Verwoerd was wounded, but he was at the height of his power when a second one was successful. He was stabbed to death on the floor of parliament shortly after the elections.

References: AB, *afr*, DAHB, EB, EWB, HWL, MMA, PLBA, PLCA, *wiki*. Henry Kenney, *Architect of Apartheid: H. F. Verwoerd* (1980).

VIEIRA, João Bernardo "Nino"
(Guinea-Bissau, 1939–)

Brigadier-General João Bernardo "Nino" Vieira was military head of state from the 1980 coup that removed Luis CABRAL, the first president, to 1999. An early member of the African Party for the Independence of Guinea and Cape Verde (PAIGC), he has proved to be as able a politician as he was a soldier. He surprised many when he made a comeback in 2005 as the elected president.

Vieira was an electrician when he joined the PAIGC in 1960. He left for Conakry in neighboring Guinea. (Guinea and Guinea-Bissau are distinct countries, and Guinea-Bissau added the name of its capital to avoid confusion between them.) There he attended a party school led by Amílcar CABRAL, the leader of the revolution. Vieira spent the next four years as the political officer with the southern guerrilla force, and then in 1964 he was sent to China for military training. He returned to become commander of the southern front and vice president of the war council. After 1970 he was in charge of the entire military effort, which had taken over more than half of Guinea-Bissau. Popular among his troops, who gave him the nickname "Nino," he was an effective commander. In 1973 he was made secretary-general of the PAIGC, and when elections were conducted in the liberated zones that year, he was chosen to head the national assembly while Luis Cabral became president. The following year Guinea-Bissau became independent, and Vieira continued as commander of the armed forces until 1978, when he was named prime minister.

The major political issue of the 1970s was the merger of Guinea-Bissau and the Cape Verde islands into one nation. Most of the PAIGC leadership, including Cabral, were Cape Verdean *mestiços* (people of mixed-race), which caused resentment among Black Guineans. In 1980, Vieira took power in what amounted to a mainland coup. Cape Verde broke relations with Guinea-Bissau, which were not restored for two years. Relations with Guinea were also strained by the coup, reviving a longtime border dispute that had been ignored during the liberation war. The matter was finally decided by the International Court of Justice (ICJ) in 1985. Vieira removed Cabral's pro-Soviet ministers, replacing them with technocrats, and he moved closer to the West.

Vieira's main challenge was the economy, however, and in a shift away from the orthodox socialism of the PAIGC, he embarked on a program of liberalization. State controls were reduced and foreign investment encouraged. The currency was devalued by over 40 percent in 1987 as part of a package worked out with the International Monetary Fund. The economic changes brought increased inflation and hardship, and coup plots were discovered in 1983, 1985 and 1987. Vieira responded with authoritarian rule, but in 1991, after discussions with the other former Portuguese colonies in Africa, he announced the legalization of opposition parties. Proposed elections were held in 1994. Vieira led in the first round and won with a small majority

in the run-off. Both elections were considered free and fair.

A coup attempt led to a brief but bitter civil war, and Vieira went into exile in Portugal. When democratic elections were restored he returned to contest the presidency and won, again in a run-off.

References: afr, PLBA, RWWA, *wiki.*

VILAKAZI, Benedict Wallet Bambatha
(South Africa, 1906–1947)

Benedict Wallet Bambatha Vilakazi, the creator of modern Zulu poetry, was a teacher and scholar of the Zulu language.

After earning a teacher's certificate, Vilakazi taught and studied at various Catholic seminaries until deciding in 1933 that he did not want to pursue the priesthood. He joined the staff of the Ohlange Institute and worked with John DUBE, founder of the African National Congress, author of the first Zulu novel, and composer-collector of Zulu folk songs. Through his diligence, Vilakazi passed all levels of the state examinations to achieve a BA degree in the Zulu language from the University of South Africa.

In the 1930s, Vilakazi began publishing his poetry, and in 1935 he published the first volume of modern Zulu verse, which was followed by a second volume in 1945. Vilakazi's poetry combined elements of the Zulu oral tradition, with its chanting quality, with Western poetic techniques. Vilakazi was influenced by the English Romantics, especially Percy Bysshe Shelley. His earlier work uses rhyme and stanzas, but by the 1940s he was writing in a style closer to the Zulu oral tradition. The traditional oral praise-song, the *izibongo,* provided a tone and approach for dealing with contemporary issues, including racial segregation and abuse. He also expressed emotion and feeling, something foreign to the traditional praise poem, which dealt with exploits of warriors and the greatness of chiefs. In the 1930s, Vilakazi also published three Zulu novels, but his fiction, although prize-winning and popular, was not as outstanding as his poetry. Its main contribution was to use modern themes and settings for the first time in Zulu fiction.

In 1935, Vilakazi was appointed as the first African to teach at the University of the Witwatersrand in Johannesburg. He received MA and DLitt degrees there and was the first African to receive an earned doctorate in South Africa. His scholarly writing, on various aspects of Zulu literature, culminated in the publication of the *Zulu-English Dictionary* (1948), completed after his death by a colleague and still the standard work on the language. At the time of his death, Vilakazi was a professor at the Roma University College, Lesotho, and president of the Catholic African Teachers' Association.

References: AA, DAHB, MBW, *wiki.* D.B.Z. Ntuli, *The Poetry of B. W. Vilakazi* (1984).

VORSTER, Balthazar
(South Africa, 1915–1983)

Balthazar Vorster, one of the most ardent right-wing advocates of apartheid, served as prime minister of South Africa from 1966 to 1978, and as president from 1978 to 1979.

Born into an Afrikaner family in the Eastern Cape, he studied law at Stellenbosch University, the center of Afrikaner national and cultural consciousness. At Stellenbosch he came to know Hendrik VERWOERD, whose teaching and racial theories inspired him, and he entered campus politics with fellow student P. W. BOTHA. He began his legal practice in Port Elizabeth after graduation in 1938 but soon became embroiled in politics as World War II loomed. He joined the *Ossewabrandwag*, "Ox-Wagon Guard," a fanatical anti-British group, and became a "general" in its paramilitary wing. The *Ossewabrandwag* was pro-Nazi, believing in White supremacy, the Afrikaner destiny to rule a racially pure South Africa, and the danger of a worldwide Jewish conspiracy. When James HERTZOG lost his attempt to keep South Africa neutral in the war, he was replaced by Jan Christiaan SMUTS as prime minister. Vorster became an outspoken supporter of Hitler in this climate and, as a leader of the paramilitary wing, was deeply involved in its campaign of sabotage: cutting telegraph lines, bombing post offices and related activities. In late 1942 he was sentenced to 18 months' imprisonment.

After the war Vorster joined the Nationalist Party (NP) but was at first rebuffed in his attempts to run for office. In 1953 he was elected to parliament and was promoted to the cabinet in 1958. After Dr. Verwoerd became premier in 1958, Vorster was appointed minister of justice and police in 1961. He was now positioned to become the main agency for the suppression of Black dissent, which was growing as the result of apartheid legislation enacted earlier. He strengthened the police and had their powers extended by the 1962 Sabotage Act. Announcing in parliament that "the rights of free speech, assembly and protest are getting out of hand," Vorster moved to limit any opposition by a variety of drastic means. Detention without trial, house arrest and press censorship were common, but the most effective policy was banning, by which persons were restricted to their homes, ordered to report to the police, and kept under police supervision. Banned persons could not be quoted in the press, have their photos appear or meet socially with more than one person.

Vorster's appointment was part of Verwoerd's response to the 1960 Sharpeville massacre and its aftermath, and after Verwoerd's assassination in 1966, the NP sought a leader with a reputation for toughness. The NP's right wing, the Dutch Reformed Church, and the Broederbond (a secret society of radical Afrikaner nationalists) all supported Vorster, and he was elected prime minister. If they expected a fanatic or extremist, they were surprised. Once in office, Vorster proved more of a pragmatist than an extremist ideologue. He overcame a move by the NP's hard right wing to dislodge him in 1968, winning decisively in the 1970 elections, and even began to make overtures toward Black African nations. This effort, however, did not dampen Black resistance. Popular uprisings broke out in Johannesburg's Black suburbs in 1976 over the imposition of Afrikaans as the language of school instruction. Some 500 were killed in riots in Soweto, and street battles spread to other towns. In 1977 the political crisis was intensified when Steve BIKO, leader of the Black consciousness movement, died in detention from a police beating.

Throughout the 1970s the issue of apartheid become internationalized. South Africa was excluded from international sports, including the Olympic Games. Trade relations were reduced, and in 1977 the United Nations voted for economic sanctions against South Africa. In response, Vorster expanded the national arms industry in order to make South Africa self-sufficient in military equipment, including aircraft. He was a supporter of breakaway Rhodesia in its attempt to maintain an all-White government and used South African troops to keep his hostile neighbors (especially Angola) destabilized and fragile. In this last effort he had the tacit support of the United States, which publicly deplored apartheid but depended upon South Africa as a regional power in the Cold War.

Vorster was brought down by neither his apartheid policies nor his handling of foreign policy, but by a press investigation into media bribery.

Evidence demonstrated that his information minister had paid television and newspaper editors from a secret Swiss bank account. Vorster resigned as prime minister and was replaced by P. W. BOTHA. Vorster took the largely ceremonial state presidency for a year but was forced from that post as well.

References: afr, AO, CB, DAHB, EWB, HWL, MMA, PLBA, wiki.

WADE, Abdoulaye
(Sénégal, 1927–)

Maître Dr. Abdoulaye Wade, a lawyer and economist, the most formidable opposition leader in Sénégal, finally became president in 2001. One of the last of the Pan-Africanists who once dreamed of a United States of Africa, he is a force for multiparty democracy.

Wade was educated in Sénégal before studying in France, where he received a doctorate in law, allowing him to use the title *maître* (master). He returned home to practice and later became dean of the faculty of law and economics at Dakar University. Until 1974 he was a member of the radical wing of the governing Socialist Party of Léopold SENGHOR. In 1974, Senghor permitted the formation of opposition parties, and Wade broke away to found the Sénégalese Democratic Party (PDS). The PDS was a youth-oriented party of the left, and in 1976, Senghor named it one of the three parties officially sanctioned by the constitution. This official decree also required the party ideologies to be defined by law, and, in a strange twist, the PDS was placed to the political right of the Socialists.

Wade stood for president against Senghor in 1978 but was badly defeated. When Senghor resigned, Wade also contested presidential elections against Abdou DIOUF in 1983, 1988 and 1993. The PDS remained the major opposition party, but Wade never personally fared well in the elections, even though in 1988 there was evidence of massive voting fraud. The PDS receives its support from the cities and from Casamance, a small enclave geographically separated from the rest of Sénégal, which is important because of its oil reserves and its active separatist movement. Protests over the 1988 elections were so significant that Wade was detained for several months, after which he went into exile in Paris.

Diouf made attempts to include Wade in the government on his return in 1989, and in 1991 he was appointed minister of state. He remained in that post over a year before resigning in order to run for president again in 1993. In that short time he negotiated an end to hostilities in Casamance and also mediated a government settlement in the Democratic Republic of the Congo, then known as Zaïre. At home, Wade formed a coalition of 16 opposition groups, but again, his defeat caused disturbances, and he was arrested.

In 2000, Wade contested the elections again against Diouf, and this time he unseated him. For a year, the PDS struggled as the opposition in parliament, but in 2001 they took a majority. Wade is a strong supporter of a free market economy and individual human rights. He has had continuing tension with the Gambia, and was accused of fostering a coup attempt there. He has had a long personal friendship with Col. Muamar Gaddhafi of Libya, who made a state visit for Sénégal's 2006 anniversary of independence, and then announced a quarter-billion-dollar development along the coast.
References: PLBA, RWWA, *wiki*.

WAKIL, Idris Abdul
(Tanzania, 1925–2000)

Idris Abdul Wakil was president of the island of Zanzibar and vice president of Tanzania through the late 1980s. He struggled against secessionist moves to separate Zanzibar from the united republic.

After being locally educated, Wakil attended Makerere University (then the University of East Africa) in Kampala, Uganda, where he graduated in 1948 with a degree in education. During the 1950s he taught and was headmaster of schools in Zanzibar while also becoming active in the Afro-Shirazi Party (ASP). He was elected to the Zanzibar national assembly in 1962. Shortly after independence in 1963, however, a Black radical faction overthrew the sultan and established a "people's republic" governed by the ASP. In 1964, President Julius NYERERE of Tanganyika brought about a merger of the two states into a single political entity, Tanzania. Zanzibar continued to have its own internal rule and a president who also served as vice president of Tanzania. In all other respects, the two countries function as one nation.

At the time of the merger, Wakil was a member of the governing Revolutionary Council and minister of education. In the search for Zanzibaris for the union government, Wakil was made minister for information and tourism. In 1967 he entered the diplomatic service as ambassador to West Germany (1967–1969) with later service in the Netherlands (1969–1973) and Guinea (1973–1977). He followed this with two years as director of protocol at the foreign ministry. In 1980, Wakil returned to island politics as speaker of the Zanzibari assembly.

In 1984, Nyerere retired as president of Tanzania, and the ruling party began the replacement process. The Zanzibari vice president had earlier been forced to resign because of anti-union rioting in Zanzibar. He was replaced by Ali Hassan MWINYI, the president of Zanzibar. Wakil was invited to stand for the Tanzanian presidency but deferred to Mwinyi, leaving the presidency of Zanzibar open for him.

Wakil ran unopposed but received only 61 percent of the vote, which foreshadowed the troubles he would face. He was very unpopular on the island of Pemba, which is linked politically to Zanzibar but has always favored a capitalist economy. In 1988 the opponents of union with the mainland intensified the tensions between Arabs and Africans, and there were civil disturbances. Some Iranian-funded Islamic radicals may have been involved. Wakil accused some of his ministers of an attempted coup, and he took control of the armed forces. In 1990 he decided not to stand for reelection and withdrew from politics.

References: PLBA, RWWA.

WALLACE-JOHNSON, Isaac Theophilus Akunna

(Sierra Leone, 1894–1965)

Isaac Theophilus Akunna Wallace-Johnson, an ardent Pan-Africanist and crusading journalist, was known primarily for his work as a trade union organizer. A committed militant, Wallace-Johnson was a leading radical voice in West Africa during the colonial period.

Wallace-Johnson was born into a poor Creole family with a proud lineage of political and religious leaders. At age 18 he entered the colonial service. He immediately began organizing the workers and within a year led a strike of customs workers, for which he was dismissed. He was reinstated but continued to demand better wages and working conditions, and this time he was transferred to the army, where he served until 1920. He next worked for the Freetown City Council but left to become a merchant seaman in 1926 after his organizing efforts there showed few results. He joined the British Seamen's Union and established its journal, the *Seafarer*.

At this point, Wallace-Johnson embarked on a 12–year period of wandering, widening his experience and developing an international network of left-wing political contacts. In Lagos, Nigeria, he worked for a time on the *Daily Times* and then went to Germany to an international conference of Black workers. He returned to Nigeria to found its first labor union in 1930. This effort brought him an invitation to the Soviet Union, where he attended a labor congress and briefly studied communism. For a brief period he was associate editor of a Paris Communist paper, *Negro Worker*. During his Soviet trip and for all of his Communist writings, he used the pseudonym W. Daniels.

Wallace-Johnson became editor of the *Nigerian Daily Telegraph* on his return to Lagos in 1932, but this lasted only a year, during which time his offices were raided seven times. During this period, however, he became allied with Herbert MACAULAY, the noted Nigerian nationalist. Wallace-Johnson's next stop was the Gold Coast (now Ghana), where he wrote for two newspapers and organized the West Coast Youth League. During the Italian invasion of Ethiopia in 1936, he wrote an inflammatory article attacking Christianity as a form of colonial exploitation. As a result, he was arrested for sedition. Wallace-Johnson took his case to the Privy Council in London, where the sedition charge was dismissed but his fine was sustained because he had made "an unwarranted attack on religion." He stayed in England for two years, during which his important friendship with Jomo KENYATTA was solidified. He became involved with a circle of Pan-Africanists, who were dedicated to some sort of eventual unification of Africa after colonialism was defeated. One of these was the Trinidadian, George Padmore, who influenced his thought. Wallace-Johnson established two newspapers to publicize their convictions. From this point, Pan-Africanism supplanted his attraction to communism.

In 1938, Wallace-Johnson returned to Sierra Leone and was an instant hero when 2,000 copies of his Pan-Africanist newspapers were confiscated from his luggage. He became even more active in organizing: the West African Civil Liberties and Defense League, a new paper (the *African Standard)*, eight separate trade unions, and a Youth League. The Youth League became a mass movement, and in 1939 it played a critical role in supporting a series of strikes. These confrontations resulted in the passage of laws against sedition and supporting freedom of the press. Wallace-Johnson, who was feared by the colonial authorities, was arrested for an article accusing the district commissioner of Bonthe of flogging an African to death. British authorities used World War II as a convenient justification to keep Wallace-Johnson in detention until 1944, shifting him from place to place under appalling conditions. His last location, ironically, was internal exile in a mosquito-infested part of Bonthe, where, undaunted, he formed a union among the uneducated local population and began literacy classes.

In 1945, Wallace-Johnson, Padmore, and Kwame NKRUMAH organized the Manchester Pan-African Congress, but most of Wallace-Johnson's postwar efforts centered on Sierra Leone. He assisted in the merger of a number of political groups into the National Council of the Colony of Sierra Leone (NCCSL) and was elected to the Legislative Council (Legco) under their banner. He was re-elected in 1957 by another party and then went on to found his own organization, the Radical Democrats. When he opposed a proposal to give the majority of Legco seats to the peoples of the interior, who were always disdained by the Creoles, he lost much of his support and respect. In 1960 he was a delegate to the independence negotiations, but he played a negligible role in independent Sierra Leone. He died in an auto accident in Accra, Ghana.

References: DAB, EWB, MMA, WGMC.

WATTA, Chehem Mohamed

(Djibouti, 1962–)

Dr. Chehem Watta lives two lives as the foremost contemporary Djibouti poet and an international administrator in the fight against HIV/AIDS.

Watta was born in Djibouti (then French Somaliland), on the Horn of Africa, during the colonial period. His family were herdspeople. After studies in France, he returned in 1985 to take up posts with the United Nations Development Program in its anti-HIV/AIDS office.

Between 1997 and 2000, Watta published three volumes of poetry in French. His verse celebrates the nomadic people of Djibouti and laments the negative effects of modernization. He describes the desert in terms taken from the oral traditions of the nomads. In the second of his volumes he takes up daily life in Djibouti and begins to explore the meaning of *khat*, a mild narcotic in almost universal use in the country. He is alternatingly serious and mocking, and his writing has been compared to the French poet Arthur Rimbaud.

In 2003, Watta received his doctorate at the University of Paris VIII in psychology, with a thesis on the relationship between *khat* use and AIDS. *Khat* is an herbal stimulant widely used as a recreational drug in East Africa. In some ethnic groups it is thought to have divine qualities. Its perceived mystical qualities plus the lowering of inhibitions lead to wider sexual relationships and greater exposure to HIV/AIDS. The cultic aspect of *khat* use serves to justify the breakdown of traditional social norms, and also brings *khat* into conflict with Islam. Regardless, it is a major export crop from Djibouti and Somalia.

Watta currently lives in Paris and works with the United States Agency for International Development (USAID). He continues to write poetry, and in 2006 was part of the "Tour de France of Writers" which made a grand circle of the country, giving readings in schools.

WEAH, George Manneh "Oppong"

(Liberia, 1966–)

George "Oppong" Weah had a successful career in soccer, and then returned to his native Liberia to challenge Ellen JOHNSON-SHIRLEAF for the presidency in the first free elections in decades. He is a populist and charismatic leader with a flamboyant style that especially appeals to the young.

Weah began playing with Invincible Eleven in Liberia and Tonnerre Kalala in Cameroon before moving to Europe in 1988. His distinguished international soccer career began with Monaco, which he helped win the French Cup in 1991. He then played for Paris Saint-Germaine for three years. He was at his best with AC Milan (1995–2000), however, where he won the Golden Ball Award as best European player (1995). At the same time he was named World Player of the Year. He then played briefly for the British premiership sides Chelsea and Manchester City, and closed his career with Al-Jazira FC in the United Arab Emirates. In 2004, the soccer legend Pelé named Weah as one of the top greatest living soccer players. He played forward, and in eight of his first 10 years he scored between 10 and 18 goals per season. He was three times named African Player of the Year, and in 1998, African Player of the Century.

On his return to Liberia, Weah worked with the Liberian national team as an investor, player-manager and coach. He also founded a junior team to develop new talent.

In 1997, Weah was named a goodwill ambassador for the United Nations Educational, Scientific, and Cultural Organization (UNESCO), taking part in immunization campaigns and ant-AIDS publicity in West Africa, the United Kingdom and the Netherlands. He was required to step down from his UNESCO role when he entered Liberian politics.

Weah's 2004 announcement for the presidency of Liberia was greeted with great public acclaim. After questions about his citizenship were settled (he was said to have taken French citizenship at one point, and he was a permanent resident of the United States), he was certified to stand in the election. He won the first round of voting against Ellen Johnson-Shirleaf and several minor candidates, but he lost the run-off to her. At first, Weah protested the validity of the vote, and for a few weeks it seemed as if he might lead his supporters back into the streets, touching off a new phase of the civil war. In late 2005, however, he accepted the results and conceded.

Weah's following came largely from the youth and those who felt that with his personal wealth, he might be immune to the endemic corruption that has plagued Liberia. His lack of any political experience hampered him, and in the final result, an overwhelming vote for Johnson-Shirleaf by women put her in office as the first African woman president in history.

References: adb, EB. www.friendsofgeorgeweah.com.

WELENSKY, Roy
(Zimbabwe/Zambia, 1907–1991)

Sir Roy Welensky, the second and last prime minister of the Federation of Rhodesia and Nyasaland, was a tough and combative politician who was unable to preserve his dream of a united, White-dominated Central African federation.

Welensky was born in Southern Rhodesia (now Zimbabwe), the thirteenth child of a Lithuanian immigrant father and an Afrikaner mother. He liked to describe himself as "half Jewish, half Afrikaner and 100 percent British." He left school at age 14 and began working for the Rhodesian railways as a fireman and an engineer. For two years he was heavyweight boxing champion of the Rhodesias before he was sent off to Northern Rhodesia (now Zambia) after he took the lead in a bruising railway strike. Because of his union base, Welensky was elected to the Legislative Council (Legco) in Northern Rhodesia in 1938, thus beginning a long political career. He remained on the Legco until 1953, serving as head of its elected members' caucus after 1946. He was honored by King George VI for his work as manpower director during World War II.

In 1941, Welensky formed the Labour Party, which was committed to protecting White workers from African competition. He was a strong supporter of independent White rule for the Rhodesias, and he joined Southern Rhodesia's premier, Godfrey HUGGINS, in leading the campaign for a federation of the Rhodesias and Nyasaland under settler control. In 1953, the year he was knighted, he saw this goal achieved and took a seat in the new federal assembly. Huggins was selected as prime minister, and Welensky soon became his deputy. When Huggins retired in 1956, Welensky was the logical choice for his post.

The federation faced mounting criticism from Black leaders, which led to confrontation and agitation. Great Britain wanted the federation to evolve into a multiracial political entity, but Welensky opposed any form of power sharing. He remained to the end a believer in the superiority of White civilization. At every step, he opposed attempts to establish African majority rule. He made blustering statements about taking the federation out of the British Commonwealth and making it independent, thus laying the groundwork for Southern Rhodesia's later Unilateral Declaration of Independence (UDI) under Ian SMITH. Conditions in the federation began to unravel in 1963 under African and British pressure, and it collapsed the following year when Northern Rhodesia and Nyasaland were granted independence as Zambia and Malawi, respectively. Bitter at what he regarded as British betrayal, he wrote *Welensky, 4,000 Days* (1964), attacking British policy. Although he had advocated independence for the federation, he opposed it for Southern Rhodesia, the last remaining part. He moved to Salisbury in 1964 to challenge a Rhodesian Front candidate in a by-election on an anti-separation platform but was resoundingly defeated. In 1980 he retired to Great Britain.

Welensky was a huge man, standing over six feet and weighing some 320 pounds. He was energetic in his efforts in politics, overcoming a slum background and anti-Semitism to assume leadership. In particular, he was convinced that he understood the plight of Black Africans because of his own personal history. He opposed separatism and apartheid, but his version of "partnership" under the guidance of Whites did not appear much more progressive to Black leaders. In the end, he was caught between the march of African nationalism on one hand and the intransigence of White supremacy on the other.

References: CB, DAHB, DRWW, EB, EWB, *wiki*. Gary Allighan, *The Welensky Story* (1962).

WEMBA, "Papa"
(Democratic Republic of the Congo, 1949–)

Papa Wemba is a Congolese superstar singer who has played with some of the most popular bands in the country since the 1970s. He was named Best African Artist at the Kora Music Awards in 1996 and 1998. He tours regularly in France and Belgium. His real name is Jules Shungu Wembadio.

Wemba sings *soukous*, the popular Congolese dance music. With Papa Wemba it shades into a Latino sound, which extends his appeal from his youth base to a somewhat older crowd. He claims that all his dance music has traditional roots, but the influence of Cuban rhumba is quite apparent.

Wemba has been accused of tuning his music to others' ears. When he went to Paris in 1987, he muted his Congolese pop to adapt to European dance music. While it proved commercially successful in Europe and opened doors for him there, it did not sit well in the Congo, and he lost some of his following at home. He now plays in two styles, doing straight Congo pop for his African albums and performances, and a crossover (some would say "watered down") version for Western consumption. During MOBUTU Sese Seko's "authenticity" campaign, Wemba introduced log drums into his music, and adopted "bush wear" clothing.

Many popular entertainers have eccentricities, and Papa Wemba is no exception. He is an active *sapeur* (fashionista) in an association (The Society of Cool and Elegant People) for those who wear flamboyant designer clothing and try to be as flashy as possible. He provided the music for a film, *The Importance of Being Elegant* (2003), which is all about self-aggrandizement. The cult has raised fashion consciousness to the level of a religion, and its idols are certain Japanese fashion designers.

Wemba's behavior, too, sometime crosses the lines of propriety or even legality. In 2004 he was convicted in France for immigrant smuggling, with the sentence suspended after four months. When 200 Africans turned up at immigration with false papers (for which they each had paid $4,500), claiming to be members of Papa Wemba's band, he was arrested.

References: DMM, GEPM, *wiki*. http://papawemba.chez-alice.fr.

WHITEHEAD, Edgar Cuthbert
(Zimbabwe, 1905–1971)

Sir Edgar Cuthbert Whitehead was a settler politician and prime minister of Southern Rhodesia (Zimbabwe) whose administration saw progress in reducing racial discrimination but also severe restrictions on Black political action that resulted in violent protests.

Whitehead was the son of a British diplomat, but poor health, which dogged him throughout his life, caused him to settle in Southern Rhodesia in 1928 after his graduation from Oxford University. After two years in the civil service, he became a successful farmer and an active member of the farmowners' associations. In 1939 he entered politics as a member of the White-dominated parliament, but soon thereafter he left to become an officer in the British army in World War II, during which he served in West Africa and London. After the war, Whitehead remained briefly in London as Southern Rhodesia's high commissioner to Great Britain and then was appointed finance minister in Godfrey HUGGINS's government. His health forced him to resign after a controversial tenure (1946–1953), during which he became a staunch supporter of the federation of the Rhodesias and Nyasaland (now Malawi). The federation was formed the year he left the ministry, and Whitehead became its representative to the United States. In 1958 he was recalled to Southern Rhodesia to become premier as a compromise candidate of the ruling United Federal Party (UFP).

Whitehead's term of office (1958–1962) left an ambiguous legacy. He sincerely desired to bring Blacks and Whites together and sought to convince the latter of the eventual need for a multiracial society. This only succeeded in alienating the Whites, who were unbending on the racial question; it also angered Blacks, who sought a faster pace toward equality. Whitehead preached moderation but did not hesitate to use force. In 1959 he declared a state of emergency, using the recent riots in neighboring Nyasaland as an excuse. He arrested 500 people, banned the leading African party, and strengthened security laws. Instead of preventing disturbances as he had hoped, Whitehead's policies actually provoked them. Urban riots broke out in the capital of Salisbury in 1960 and spread to other cities. The next year Whitehead promulgated a new constitution that increased Black representation slightly, but its gradualism only further incensed African leaders. At the same time he lost the support of the White leadership, which accused him of catering to Africans. Whitehead's drift toward conservatism during his administration did not match the swift lurch to the right among the White electorate. Whitehead and his policy of moderate gradualism were defeated in the 1962 elections. His reforms were too much, too soon for the Whites and too little, too late for Black leaders. He had woefully underestimated the racist appeal of the Rhodesian Front party, and he led the parliamentary opposition until 1965, when Southern Rhodesia broke away from Britain and set itself on a path of racial exclusion.

References: DAHB, MMA, PLBA, *wiki.*

WITBOOI, Henrik
(Namibia, 1840s-1905)

Henrik Witbooi, the last and greatest of the Witbooi chiefs, led the African resistance to German imperialism. The Witbooi clan (the Nama) led a major branch of the Khoikhoi who emigrated from South Africa in the 1840s, bringing Dutch language and customs with them.

Witbooi became a Christian in 1868 and was imbued with a sense of divine mission. In 1880 he was almost killed in a surprise attack by his old enemy, the Herero chief MAHERERO, which convinced him that he was chosen by God to conquer the Herero and extend his kingdom. Shortly thereafter, he attempted to break away from his father and tried to leave with a band of Christians, but the Herero blocked his way. In 1888, Paul Visser, his brother-in-law, removed and then executed Witbooi's father, after which Witbooi killed Visser and became the undisputed leader of the clan.

In 1890 encroaching German power threatened, and Witbooi was required to submit as a number of weaker chiefs had done. Theodor LEUTWIN, the German administrator, demanded: "You still refuse to accept German supremacy.... In comparison with the German Emperor you are but a small chief. To submit yourself to him would not be a disgrace but an honor." Witbooi responded, "The Lord God has established various kingdoms in the world. Therefore I know and believe that it is no sin or crime that I should wish to remain the independent chief of my land and people."

Defeated in 1904, Witbooi accepted Leutwin's protection and made the best of a bad bargain. He supplied the German troops and joined with them in campaigns against mutual enemies. In 1903, however, Samuel MAHERERO had led the Herero people in a rebellion against the Germans, and the following year he called upon Witbooi to join him. At the same time, a prophet from Cape Colony influenced Witbooi to resist. Leutwin was removed in 1904, and Witbooi considered himself freed of his alliance with the Germans, so he joined the revolt. Unfortunately, the two forces acted independently, and when Witbooi went into battle, he was killed. The revolt continued for two more years, but finally all armed resistance was eliminated.

References: CWAH, DAHB, MMA, *wiki.*

WOBOGO, Mogho Naaba
(Burkina Faso, ?–1904)

Mogho Naaba Wobogo—the thirtieth *mogho naaba,* or ruler, of the Mossi kingdom of Ouagadougou—was known for his fierce resistance to French imperial expansion into his kingdom.

Wobogo (known before his enthronement as Boukary Koutou) received an Islamic education and was literate in Arabic. The Mossi states in this period had passed their zenith and were in the midst of a political crisis, plagued with petty wars and dynastic conflicts. When Boukary's father died in 1850, he contended for the throne but lost out to a brother. Boukary led a civil war, and after he lost, he withdrew into his own territory. When the brother died in 1889, Boukary forced the election by surrounding the electoral council with troops. He assumed the name Wobogo, which means "the elephant." Himself a former armed dissident, Wobogo faced a civil war in one of his provinces, but the royal forces were exhausted, and he recruited Zerma mercenaries from across the Volta River. This proved a disastrous move, as they laid waste the countryside and had to be subdued.

The other rivalry in the area was between the French and British, and both began to court the new ruler. Wobogo was suspicious of all Europeans and told one emissary: "I find my country good just as it is. Consider yourself fortunate that I do not order your head to be cut off. Go away now, and above all, never come back." Wobogo finally signed a friendship treaty with the British in 1894, but his suspicions were confirmed when the French invaded Ouagadougou in 1896. He resisted in vain when several of his vassal chiefs deserted him, and the French burned his capital. Wobogo retreated but continued guerrilla warfare. The French deposed him and placed his youngest brother Sighiri on the throne, but two provinces remained loyal. In a surprise attack, the French drove Wobogo's remaining troops across the border into the Gold Coast (now Ghana), where he appealed to Britain under the terms of the 1894 treaty. With the British

commander, Wobogo's forces reached almost to the capital when they learned that Britain had ceded the Mossi lands to France. Embittered, Wobogo resisted for a while but finally returned to the Gold Coast, where he lived in exile until his death.

References: DAHB, MMA.

WOODS, Donald
(South Africa, 1933–2001)

Donald Woods, longtime South African journalist and antiapartheid activist, was best known for exposing the facts behind the murder of his friend, Steve BIKO. Woods went on to write Biko's biography, but he became popular after the film based on it and his own escape from South Africa, *Cry Freedom* (1987).

Woods was a fifth-generation South African, descended from early British settlers. He studied law at the University of Cape Town, but found journalism more attractive as a career. He began as a reporter and worked his way up to editor at the *Daily Dispatch* from 1965 to 1977. He was at that point a rather complacent White South African, never a supporter of apartheid but a critic of radical Black opposition. At one point, Mamphela RAMPHELE challenged him to confront the realities of oppression and introduced him to Biko. The two became friends, which soon attracted the surveillance of the security police. After the Bantu Education Act demonstrations resulted in the shooting of unarmed students who were protesting mandatory teaching in Afrikaans, Biko's Black Consciousness Movement was banned.

Woods also was banned and confined to his home. Biko was arrested, bludgeoned mercilessly, chained and taken 750 miles to Pretoria in the back of a van, where he was pronounced dead. The story was then given out that he died from a hunger strike. Somehow, Woods was able to get into the morgue and photograph the battered body, and when the pictures appeared in the *Daily Dispatch*, the government was internationally shamed.

When Woods discovered that a T-shirt with Biko's picture on it sent to his child was permeated with acid, he feared for his family's safety. He disguised himself as a priest, hitchhiked over 300 miles and swam a swollen river to escape to Lesotho. His family joined him and together they went to Great Britain, which granted them political asylum.

Woods became an ardent campaigner for sanctions against South Africa, lobbying legislators and lecturing in 42 countries. After Woods published *Biko* (1978), he was invited to be the first private citizen to address the United Nations Security Council.

Sir Richard Attenborough adapted *Cry Freedom* from *Biko*, adding the account of Woods's escape. The film was nominated for three Academy Awards, but it was not without its critics. *The New York Times* lamented that the film, "with its potential for focusing worldwide attention on the plight of Black South Africans, should concentrate its energies on a White man."

After 13 years in exile, Woods visited South Africa in 1990, as apartheid was dying, but he never returned to live there. In 1994 he came back to vote in the first free election in South Africa, and the crowd parted before him to allow Woods to be the first to cast his vote.

Reference: CA, EB, *wiki.* Woods, *Asking for Trouble* (1981) and *Rainbow Nation Revisited: South Africa's Decade of Democracy* (2000).

WRIGHT, Ernest Jenner
(Sierra Leone, 1892–1955)

Dr. Ernest Jenner Wright was a pioneer African medical researcher and one of the leading figures in the British Colonial Medical Service. Born into an elite Sierra Leone family, the son of a lawyer, he was typical of his class. Gentle, retiring and kind, with a strong sense of *noblesse oblige,* he willingly entered into the life of public service that was expected of him.

Wright was sent to England for grammar school and completed his secondary studies in Belgium. He undertook medical studies at the University of London with great success, attaining membership in the Royal College of Surgeons with a diploma in tropical medicine. He practiced obstetrics in Liverpool and was resident medical officer in Birmingham before returning home to join the Colonial Medical Service.

Wright's contributions to tropical medicine and pediatrics are highly significant. He was the first medical researcher to identify tropical rickets, and he later became a strong proponent of prenatal care, which was virtually unknown in the colonies. His medical interests were broad, and his research included studies, for example on psychotherapy and witchcraft. His medical leadership was recognized with the award of an MBE (Member of the British Empire) in 1936. In addition, Wright was a bibliophile and numismatist who established an extensive library and amassed one of the most complete coin collections in Africa.

Reference: DAB.

XUMA, Alfred Bitini

(South Africa, 1893?–1962)

Dr. Alfred Bitini Xuma was president-general of the African National Congress (ANC) from 1940 to 1949, during one of its lowest points, and was instrumental in forming a youth wing that supported a new leadership cadre that supplanted him.

Xuma was born into an aristocratic but poor Xhosa family, and his rags-to-riches story became part of his legend. He began as a herdboy in the Transkei who, by dint of hard work, became a teacher and saved his money for higher education. He spent 14 years abroad, obtaining a degree in agriculture at Tuskegee Institute in Alabama and an M.D. at Northwestern University in Evanston, Illinois. He worked 14-hour days to pay his way at Tuskegee and yet graduated with an honors degree. After a stint at the famed Mayo Clinic, he specialized in surgery and midwifery in Hungary and continued his research in England, where he took a Ph.D. in tropical medicine. He then returned to South Africa to establish a successful practice in Sophiatown.

He was never comfortable with working-class Blacks, so the Xuma family's social set was largely White. Nonetheless, he gradually became involved in political affairs as conditions for Black South Africans worsened under the regime of James HERTZOG. Blacks were stripped of the franchise in 1936 by an unwise compromise on the part of the All-African Convention (AAC), an umbrella group uniting a number of Black organizations. Xuma was deputy president of the AAC at the time. The Great Depression and World War II brought extensive suffering to the urban settlements, including a 60 percent mortality rate among African children in Port Elizabeth, primarily due to malnutrition.

In 1940 Xuma was elected president-general of the ANC. He was a moderate who avoided political confrontation. He did, however, bring to the ANC considerable organizational skills. He expelled corrupt officers, reorganized the administration, and brought respect and competence to the group.

Xuma removed the power of the chiefs in the ANC and gave women equal rights. He also saw the need for building coalitions; most notably, he forged a bond with the Indian National Congress that laid the groundwork for later mass demonstrations. Xuma made several attempts to organize protests during his presidency, but none was effective. Throughout his presidency, however, he did attempt to attract younger members to the ANC. After a few years there were a number of young, well-educated and militant members who began to chafe under the ANC's benevolent but passive leadership. In 1944, the reformists—led by Nelson MANDELA, Oliver TAMBO and Walter SISULU—informed Xuma that they wanted to form a youth wing. Xuma resisted the program of action proposed by the radicals, but they went ahead and became a powerful force in the ANC, finally securing his reluctant blessing.

Increasingly, the moderate and radical wings of the ANC came into conflict. Xuma addressed the United Nations in 1946 on behalf of the anticolonial cause, while the youth wing members plotted demonstrations against the visit of the British royal family. Much to Xuma's chagrin, he found that the radicals often sided with the growing presence of Communists in the ANC. The ANC was shaken by the shock waves of apartheid legislation that passed after the election of Dr. Daniel MALAN in 1948. In response, the radicals ousted Xuma in the 1949 ANC elections. He reacted angrily, denouncing them as "half castes" (several were legally classified as Coloured), but he soon lost all influence in the ANC, although he did lead a protest against the declaration of Sophiatown as a White area. After he was removed forcibly from his home to make way for a White family, he died in obscurity.

References: afr, DAHB, MMA. Steven Gish, *Alfred B. Xuma: African, American, South African* (2000).

YACOB, Zara

(Ethiopia, 1592–1692)

Zara Yacob (not to be confused with the Negus ZARA Yaqob) was the most important premodern philosopher from Africa. He is also known as Zar'a Ya'eqob and Warqye. His Christian name means "Seed of Jacob."

Yacob was born in Axum, the ancient capital and religious center, and received an education in traditional Ethiopian schools, which at that time would have been largely religious. He was tutored in the Hebrew and Christian Scriptures for 10 years, especially the Psalms, which had a profound effect on him. He studied both European and Coptic scholars, but he later wrote that "often their interpretation did not agree with my reason, but I withheld my opinion and hid in my heart all the thoughts of my mind." He had begun to wrestle with the problem of the relationship between faith and reason.

During Yacob's childhood and youth, Ethiopia was in turmoil caused by religious conflict. The Muslims had almost overcome the Christian provinces, and after they were held at bay, Catholic missionaries entered the country along with Portuguese influences. The Emperor SUSNEYOS (1575?–1632) came to power after 10 years of strife, and in 1622 attempted to impose Catholicism as the state religion. In the ensuing conflicts, tens of thousands of Ethiopians died in battles with the Catholic faction. Ten years later, Susneyos was deposed and the Orthodox Church was reinstated as the national faith by FASILADAS. Although the Church was re-established as the center of national identity, Ethiopia entered a period of long decline. This confusion and national debate on religion, identity and relations with the wider world dominated public discourse throughout Yacob's life. As a consequence, he was familiar with the thought of Coptic Orthodoxy, Catholicism (with its European philosophies and theology) and Islam. There is some indication that he was also interested in Indian Hindu thought.

All this was a bit dangerous in a volatile religious atmosphere. He was denounced to Susneyos as a free-thinker and fled south with his precious book of the Psalms. In Shoa, the southernmost province, he lived in a cave for two years, meditating and forming his philosophical thought. This was published later in Ge'ez, the national language, as *Hatata* (1867). It has been compared to the thought of his French contemporary, René Descartes' *Discourse on Method* (1637). What is unique about Yacob's work is its departure from the traditional oral literature by putting his thought in written form.

Yacob was rehabilitated when Fasiladas came to power, but that did not mean he embraced all the values of Orthodoxy. He rejected the superiority of monasticism over marriage, for example, despite the fact that Coptic Orthodoxy is a highly monastic religion. Departing from a completely religious perspective, he argued for the superiority of reason over faith, although he held that all truth is in harmony. Analytical thought will reveal truth to the sincere seeker, he argued, and he rejected subjectivism. His chief interpreter, Claude Sumner, suggests that "modern philosophy, in the sense of a personal rationalistic critical investigation, began in Ethiopia with Zara Yacob at the same time as in England and France."

References: Teodros Kiras, *Zara Yacob: Rationality of the Human Heart* (2005); Claude Sumner, *Classical Ethiopian Philosophy* (1985).

YAMBIO

(Sudan, 1820s-1905)

Yambio, ruler of the Zande people in southern Sudan, successfully resisted Arab slavers and united a divided kingdom, but spent much of his life in warfare to defend his people's rights and territory.

When Yambio's father died in 1869, Zande territory was divided up among the sons, although Yambio received the title of chief. Arab traders, who found the southern Sudan an important source for slaves, wanted to keep the Zande disunited and played one faction against another. Yambio strove alone to unite his people and embarked on an antislavery crusade. In 1870 he drove out an armed slaving caravan and then rebuffed attacks by a merchant prince with a private army. By 1880 he had united the Zande and then had to contend with the Egyptians, who were establishing control over the Sudan. In 1881 he defeated an Egyptian army, but in 1882 a larger force captured him. The uprising of the MAHDI temporarily ended Egyptian intervention, and Yambio was freed in 1884. However, he refused to cooperate with the Mahdists and returned home to reassert his political authority.

After spending much of the 1890s consolidating their position in central Sudan, the Mahdists in 1897 were ready to attack Yambio. He repelled them, and the Mahdist state fell in 1899. This success brought no relief for the Zande, as Yambio now found himself in the middle of colonial rivalries. The European powers attempted to seize every advantage and section of land in their competition to create colonial empires. Pressed from the north by the British and from the south by the Belgians, Yambio found the neighboring chiefs choosing sides rather than defending their independence. In 1904 he led 10,000 Zande warriors in an attack on Belgian forces, who were well entrenched in fortifications. Traditional weapons proved no match for modern firearms, and having lost the best of his fighting forces, Yambio had to withdraw. Within a year the British overcame the demoralized Zande, and Yambio died in prison a few weeks after the final defeat. The kingdom was partitioned among his sons and came under British domination, but Zande armed guerrilla resistance continued until 1918.

Reference: DAHB.

YAMÉOGO, Maurice
(Burkina Faso, 1921–1993)

Maurice Yaméogo, the first post-independence president of his country, then called Haute Volta (Upper Volta), headed a poorly managed and corrupt administration that was overthrown in a military coup in 1966.

Yaméogo became a colonial civil servant after completing secondary studies in a seminary. Deciding not to become a priest, his first political activity was in the Christian labor movement. In 1966 he

was elected to the territorial legislature. In the pre-independence government he served as agriculture and interior minister, and he became head of the government upon the death of his predecessor. Yaméogo, a member of the Mossi minority, joined the Rassemblement Démocratique Africain (RDA), the interterritorial party dominated by Félix HOUPHOUËT-BOIGNY of Côte d'Ivoire, and in 1959 he led Upper Volta out of the West African federation, causing it to collapse. In 1960 he banned all opposition and became president of the new Republic of Upper Volta.

Yaméogo's tenure was marked by corruption and political authoritarianism. The economy declined, yet the president flaunted his personal wealth, marrying a beauty queen in an ostentatious wedding ceremony and then taking a lavish honeymoon that brought him public ridicule. He suppressed all opposition and ruled largely by decree, engineering his re-election with 99.98 percent of the vote. His extravagant lifestyle eroded government finances, while he ordered austerity for the country and cut the wages of all public employees.

In 1966 the unions called a general strike, which caused riots and the breakdown of order. The military under General Sangoulé LAMIZANA assumed control, and Yaméogo was held in detention, where he attempted suicide. In 1969 he was tried for embezzlement and sentenced to five years' hard labor and the seizure of all his property. The following year he was amnestied without civil rights when the government was returned to civilian rule, which excluded him from power even though his party won the election. When Thomas SANKARA came to power in 1983, he was again placed under a restriction order (1983–1984) due to his meddling in politics. He went into exile in Côte d'Ivoire and died there.

References: DAHB, PLBA, *wiki*.

YAR'ADUA, Shehu Musa
(Nigeria, 1943–1997)

Shehu Musa Yar'Adua was a Nigerian businessman and political figure who died in prison, where he had been sentenced for treason after he demanded that the military government of General Sani ABACHA turn over power to a democratically elected civilian authority. He had been vice president of Nigeria from 1976 to 1979.

During the First Republic, Yar'Adua's father was elected to the House of Representatives, sparking the young Shehu's interest in public service. He first embarked on a military career, and after secondary school he attended the British Royal Military Academy at Sandhurst. With the outbreak of the Biafran secession and the civil war, he rose quickly through the officer ranks. He distinguished himself when troops under his command took Onitsha in 1967 in what proved to be the deciding battle that ended the war.

The civil war devastated Nigeria and divided it along sectarian and ethnic lines. Several million Nigerians died and many starved as conditions deteriorated. Schools, clinics and agriculture were all destroyed. Yar'Adua was profoundly affected by the experience, and it was a turning point in his conviction that national unity was the only path for Nigeria. That put him in opposition to those who favored a federalist state based on religion and tribe.

Yar'Adua became federal commissioner of transport in 1976 while still in the army. He cleared the congestion of the ports, which were vital to the emerging oil industry. The following year, the president, Mohammed MURTALA, was assassinated and replaced by the transitional military rule of General Olesegun OBASANJO. Yar'Adua was promoted to major-general and chief of staff and subsequently, vice president.

In 1979, Obasanjo turned the government over to civilian authority, and Yar'Adua began a novel political experiment, the People's Front of Nigeria (PFN). Tightly organized, national in scope and avoiding all attempts to become ethnic or religious, it soon became the leading political vehicle in the country. General Ibrahim BABANGIDA, who had seized power, decided on something even more novel: two artificial national parties based on ideology. Yar'Adua emerged as the contender for the center-left Social Democratic Party (SDP). Babangida abruptly cancelled the party primaries and nullified the results.

Yar'Adua retired and set up a number of businesses in agriculture, banking, oil and publishing. He also became active in Muslim affairs and was chair of the National Mosque Committee, which oversaw fundraising and the building of the National Mosque in the new capital, Abuja. He contented himself with serving as an advisor in politics.

The increased corruption and sectionalism of Abacha's regime (1993–1998) caused several coup plots. In 1995, Yar'Adua was accused of treason and sentenced to death, later commuted to life imprisonment. His friends deserted him and Yar'Adua became a political pariah. He was intermittently ill in jail and denied proper medical care until he collapsed and died. Abacha's son was later charged with murdering Yar'Adua by lethal injection, but he was freed in 2002 by the Nigerian Supreme Court.

Reference: EB, *wiki.* Jacqueline Farris, *Shehu Musa Yar'Adua: A Life of Service* (2004). www.yaraduacente.org.

YHOMBI-OPANGO, Joachim
(Congo, 1939–)

Colonel Joachim Yhombi-Opango was head of state in the Congo Republic from 1977 to 1979 and prime minister from 1993 to 1996. He is typical of a number of military politicians who have led African countries since independence.

Yhombi-Opango entered the French army in 1957 and received officer training in France. After independence in 1960 he served in a wide variety of positions. He was military attaché in Moscow, headed the prestigious paratroop battalion, and commanded the national police. During this period Congo became a one-party state, governed after 1969 by the Congolese Labor Party (PCT). The government in the 1960s based itself on what it termed "scientific socialism," a vague sort of Marxism. In 1969, however, Congo took a sharp turn to the left and declared itself a "people's republic." Yhombi-Opango was named chief of staff by President Marien NGOUABI in 1970.

Yhombi-Opango's influence and position grew over the next few years. In 1973 he joined the party politburo, its policymaking body. In 1975 he was named director of public works, and in 1977 he became chairman of the PCT military committee. Yhombi-Opango was a military leader with a pragmatic approach to politics and no interest in political ideology. He was known to boast in private of his ignorance of Marxist theory, although in public he took the party line. In 1977, Ngouabi was assassinated, and the PCT turned control over to the military committee. Yhombi-Opango was named head of state and instituted rule by decree, first ordering the execution of former President Alphonse MASSEMBA-DÉBAT, who was accused of plotting the assassination.

Yhombi-Opango did not prove particularly competent as an administrator, and his rule was dictatorial and oppressive. He had never had a strong base in the party, whose failed economic policies he openly criticized. He was considered more favorable to the West, which rankled the left wing of the PCT. His high-handed style alienated many in the army, which was his only real source of support. In 1978 he survived a coup attempt, but during the next year pressures forced him to resign. He was replaced by his deputy, Denis SASSOU-NGUESSO, who had used his position to plot the ouster. Yhombi-Opango was expelled from the PCT, had his property confiscated, and was put in detention until 1984 in an air force camp guarded by Cuban troops. Again in 1988, after a year-long uprising in the north, Yhombi-Opango was once again imprisoned; he was confined until 1990. In 1991 the PCT agreed to permit a multiparty system as part of a move away from Marxism. More than a hundred parties registered, among them a coalition group, the Forces of Change, which included Yhombi-Opango's party, the Rally of Democracy and Development (RDD). In the 1992 elections it won 10 percent of the presidential vote and one senate seat.

President Pascal Lissouba surprised many when he named Yhombi-Opango to the position of prime minister in 1993. The appointment touched off demonstrations, and a rival government was set up in protest. In the following months a number of people died in riots. Yhombi-Opango stepped down right before the collapse of the Congo into a series of civil wars.

Reference: afr, PLBA.

YOHANNES IV
(Ethiopia, 1831–1889)

Negus Yohannes IV successfully unified Ethiopia and resisted attempts by outside powers to subdue the country. He provided for a succession that would consolidate his gains, laying the groundwork for maintaining Ethiopia's independence.

Known as Kassai, he was descended from the Tigre royal family and was therefore positioned to become a regional warlord in the decentralized

system that kept Ethiopia divided. Through his mother he also claimed decent from King Solomon. At first on good terms with Emperor TEWODROS II, he was appointed a military commander and then *ras* (governor) of Tigre in 1864. He fell out with the emperor almost immediately over religious policy. A devout Christian, Ras Kassai rebelled when Tewodros imprisoned the head of the Ethiopian Orthodox Church and plundered the churches of Gondar. In 1867, Kassai declared Tigre independent and sent a delegation to Egypt to secure its own bishop. The following year he allied himself with a British expeditionary force that was sent to free British prisoners held by Tewodros. In gratitude, Britain presented him with 12 pieces of artillery and 750 rifles after Tewodros's defeat and suicide. Kassai then plunged into the struggle for control of the country. When Tewodros's successor demanded that Kassai's bishop be turned over to him, war began. Tigre was invaded, but Kassai's superior forces defeated the emperor and captured him. There was no patriarch of the Church, and Kassai applied to the head of the Coptic Church in Egypt, as was the custom, and was sent a new patriarch so that he could be crowned in the traditional way. In 1872, Kassai became emperor as Yohannes IV.

Yohannes followed a relentless policy of unification, facing the need to subdue the regional warlords, build up the Ethiopian Church as a base of national identity, and defend the country from invading forces. By 1874 he had brought four provinces under his control, treating them in a conciliatory fashion to earn their loyalty. Those rivals whom he could not subdue directly, he allowed to be regional powers. In 1878 he reached an agreement with MENELIK II, the king of Shoa, and in 1882 he married his son to Menelik's daughter ZAUDITU to bind the alliance. Yohannes also promised Menelik the succession to the throne.

His attempts at religious unification were less successful, largely due to Islamic resistance. In 1878 he introduced a forced conversion program but soon withdrew it when he realized that it would jeopardize rather than increase national unity. From ancient times, bishops of the Ethiopian Orthodox Church had been appointed from Egypt, a policy that Yohannes did not initially challenge. He raised the number of Egyptian bishops from one to four, however, with instructions to them to oversee a purification of the Church. Christian competition was removed by the expulsion of foreign missionaries.

The major threats facing a united Ethiopia were external. Taking advantage of the confusion after Tewodros's death, the Egyptians had occupied all the entry routes to the country by the time Yohannes was crowned. When diplomacy failed, Yohannes advanced against the Egyptian forces and defeated them in battle in 1875 and 1876. Three years later, the *khedive* of Egypt sent General Charles GORDON to negotiate a treaty of friendship, but Yohannes demanded a large indemnity, return of the remaining occupied territories and several coastal areas, and the right to appoint his own bishops for Ethiopia. The talks broke down, but Egypt ceased to be a threat.

Far more serious was the revivalist Islamic movement of the MAHDI in the Sudan, which broke Egyptian power there and led to the death of Gordon in 1885. Yohannes concluded a favorable treaty with Egypt and Great Britain in 1884, receiving land and free passage from the port of Massawa in exchange for permission for Egyptian troops to retreat through Ethiopia. When the Mahdi rejected peace overtures for religious reasons, Yohannes marched against the Sudanese and defeated them in several battles, taking pressure off the beleaguered Egyptians. Yohannes was then betrayed when the Italians entrenched themselves at Massawa with British approval. He marched against the Italians and defeated them at Dogali in 1887 but was in no position to press his advantage, because the Mahdists had again crossed the frontier. Yohannes mobilized the entire country against the invaders and counterattacked, invading the Sudan. On the verge of victory at Metemmah, he was mortally wounded, and the armies fought to a standstill. The Mahdists retreated but carried Yohannes's head on a pike to be displayed in Khartoum. On his deathbed, Yohannes attempted to name his nephew as his successor, revealing that he was his natural son. But after a dynastic fight, Menelik succeeded Yohannes and, building on his accomplishments, became the most powerful Ethiopian emperor of modern times.

References: DAB, DAHB, EB, *wiki*. Zewde Gabre-Sellassie, *Yohannes IV of Ethiopia* (1975).

YOKO
(Sierra Leone, 1849?–1906)

Madam Yoko was ruler of the Mende confederacy for almost 30 years, building it into one of the largest political units in the interior of Sierra Leone. The Mende formed great warrior kingdoms, in which the women played exceptional political roles. Madam Yoko, the most famous of these leaders, rose to prominence after 1845, which marked the end of the slave trade in the region and the expansion of British interests from the coast into the interior.

Yoko was an accomplished dancer and became the trainer of girls in the initiation rites for the women's secret society. In an unusual—although not unprecedented—move, she was also initiated into the men's secret society. She divorced her first husband and was widowed by her second, after which she married his nephew, according to custom. She became involved in political affairs, at which she proved adept, and succeeded her husband on his death in 1878, as he had requested. She had a talent for diplomacy and built alliances with neighboring groups, especially the British. They supported her efforts, stationing frontier police at her disposal. When she complained of a rival who was raiding her trade convoys, they arrested and deported him. When the Hut Tax Rebellion broke out in 1898 under BAI BUREH, the Mende supported the rebels, but Yoko remained loyal to the British. She was rewarded with increased territory and, under the system of indirect rule that delegated authority to loyal rulers, she centralized control over the Mende chiefs.

Critics of Yoko have held that her importance has been greatly exaggerated. They present her as a wily schemer who undermined other Mende chiefs and was the creation of colonial authorities. Some scholars contend that after 1878 she first spent some time as headwoman of a small town and then engineered her chieftaincy with British colonial support. Her critics accuse her of subverting the customary constitutional basis of the Mende political system. She was also rumored to have died by suicide because she feared old age.

References: DAB, DAHB.

YOULOU, Fulbert
(Congo, 1917–1972)

Abbé Fulbert Youlou advocated autonomy within a French community rather than independent French-speaking African states but, nevertheless, became the first president of the Congo Republic, the former French Congo.

Youlou entered a seminary after elementary school and studied in Congo, French Cameroon, and Gabon before being ordained a priest in 1946. Having spent several years as a teacher in a mission school, he was active with youth groups while leading a parish in Brazzaville. This background led him into politics and increasing conflict with Church authorities. He stood for election to the French national assembly in 1955 but lost his bid.

In 1956, Youlou formed a political party and founded a magazine to publicize his positions, which appealed to his Balali ethnic minority. The Balali had been on the sidelines of Congolese politics nationally, but were the largest group in the capital. Youlou mobilized the Balali and was elected mayor of Brazzaville in 1956, after campaigning in his white cassock. The Church then suspended him from priestly duties; he later left the priesthood and married.

The 1957 territorial elections produced a deadlocked legislature, and Youlou maneuvered skillfully until he undermined the coalition government and emerged as prime minister a year later. At the same time, his party became the local affiliate of the Rassemblement Démocratique Africain (RDA), a regional grouping under Côte d'Ivoire's Félix HOUPHOUËT-BOIGNY. In the 1958 referendum on the future of French West Africa, Youlou supported the position that called for autonomy within the French community, rather than full independence. He carried Congo, but the desired federation failed and in 1960 the Congo Republic gained independence with Youlou as the first president. He turned to authoritarian rule to consolidate his power. He redistricted parliamentary seats to manipulate elections and confirmed his position by a 1961 unopposed presidential election in which he received 97 percent of the vote. His plans for creating a single-party system were interrupted by the coup that deposed him.

In foreign affairs, Youlou was pro-Western. He was deeply involved in the conflict in neighboring Democratic Republic of the Congo (DRC), having been an early supporter of Joseph KASAVUBU, to whom he offered help in eliminating Prime Minister Patrice LUMUMBA. When Moïse TSHOMBE attempted his secession in the DRC's Katanga Province, Youlou espoused his cause (without success) among the other French-speaking countries of Africa. Congo was dependent on French subsidies, and Youlou seems to have been influenced by conservative French advisors. The ending of most French aid influenced his downfall, forcing Youlou to impose harsh economic controls and causing serious inflation. Rioting in Brazzaville forced the military to restore order; Youlou resigned and was arrested. He managed to escape and fled to the DRC, where he plotted an invasion of the Congo Republic from across the river. When MOBUTU Sese Seko took power in the DRC, however, Youlou sought asylum in Spain, where he eventually died.

References: afr, DAHB, EWB, MMA, PLBA. Remy Boutet, *Les "Trois glorieuses," ou la Chute de Fulbert Youlou* (*The "Three Gloriouses," or the Fall of Fulbert Youlou*, 1990).

YX?, Emile
(South Africa, 1968–)

YX ?, born Emile Jansen, is a leading hip-hop entertainer and community activist who has used his celebrity to further development among youth in the urban slums of South Africa.

As Emile Jansen he was an elementary school teacher for several years before forming a rap group, Black Noise, in 1992. The following year he founded *Youth Magazine* and *Da Juice Hip Hop*, both of which he still edits. In the first dozen years of performing, Black Noise issued 10 CDs, one of which was a solo of YX?'s. Seven albums have used their own material and the others use material culled from their community projects. They have formed their own label, both to maintain artistic and commercial control of their material, but also to demonstrate their self-help theories.

Black Noise's performances are legendary, with YX? fronting the group with a dazzling combination of rap, break dancing and capoeira (a Brazilian fusion of martial arts and dance movement). His raps address the problems common to youth in South Africa—violent crime, racism, HIV/AIDS. Racism for Emile is not about the wider Black-White tensions of South African society, but that experienced by the youth of the Cape Flats. Emile, himself a Coloured (mixed race) South African, raps about racism between Black and brown, African and Indian. One of his recurring themes is identity and belonging. In his concerns, YX? prides himself on never having left the dedication to children and youth that began with his teaching career.

Black Noise has released one album abroad and took third place at the 1997 international break dancing competitions in Germany. They have performed across Europe, especially in Sweden, where their rap lyrics address the issue of racism that is directed at immigrant groups. Their latest album, *Rotational Heights* (2005), is on a Swedish label.

YX ? began a program of community-based re-education groups to talk through problems, which he dubbed TEAACH (The Educational Alternative Awakening Corrupted Heads). He calls for African role models for young people, where they can see their identity in an admired adult. A second program is Heal the Hood, a roving program that mimics a concert tour where discussions are joined to rap, music, theater and poetry slams.

As if all this is not enough, YX? has started African Battle Cry, a series of hip-hop workshops for young performers.

All this is supported by the band's touring and CDs. Black Noise performs constantly, but its high point was performing at the inauguration of President Nelson MANDELA.

References: adb. YX?, *My Hip Hop Is African and Proud* (2004). http://blacknoise.co.za; http://healthehood.org.

ZARA Yaqob
(Ethiopia, 1399?–1468)

Emperor Zara Yaqob (Jacob), one of the greatest Ethiopian kings, was a progressive reformer of both the national Coptic Orthodox Church and the state. During a 34–year reign (1434–1468) he centralized imperial power by replacing local warlords with government administrators, brought extensive neighboring lands under his authority, substantially completed the Christianization of Ethiopia, and united himself with the Orthodox Church and its monastic leadership.

Zara faced a major Islamic challenge when he took the throne, which he did only after his three brothers died. He completely reorganized the army, which enabled him to crush a Muslim invasion in 1445 and close off the Islamic threat. He completed further government reforms to bring both the central and provincial administrations under his control. A harsh man, Zara executed three of his daughters for following occult religious practices and had his wife flogged to death when she attempted a palace coup in favor of her son. Nevertheless, he appointed women as administrators and provincial governors, which in fifteenth-century Ethiopia was remarkable.

Zara was educated in monasteries and always remained interested in theology as well as religious politics. He settled a divisive controversy over the observance of the Sabbath early in his rule. He sent delegates to the papal Council of Florence (1431–1445) and forged other links with the papacy and Western Christianity. His religious writings include the "Creed of the Ethiopian Church" and five other theological treatises, but he also encouraged literature in general. His interest in theological matters backfired somewhat, however, as it encouraged speculation that led to disputes and heresies, especially over the doctrine of the nature of the Holy Trinity. Yet he brooked no disagreement when the abbot of Debra Libanos, the senior Ethiopian cleric (since the patriarch was always an Egyptian), confronted him over his brutality with political opponents. He had the abbot beaten and imprisoned, and allowed to die of his injuries.

Zara's reform of the Orthodox Church was a mix of religious zeal and administrative cunning. He converted several provinces with the first systematic program of evangelization since that of St. TÄKLÄ Haymanot. By founding churches and monasteries and maintaining control, Zara asserted his authority over the Church. He placed cooperative monks as abbots in major monasteries, suppressed superstition, and reformed the Church calendar. He was not without his own superstitions, however, and when Halley's comet appeared in 1456, he saw it as a sign from God. In response, he built the Debre Berhan Monastery and made it his new capital.

References: DAB, *dacb*, DAHB, *wiki*.

ZAUDITU
(Ethiopia, 1876–1930)

Empress Zauditu, daughter of MENELIK II, was empress from 1916 to 1930 and was the first woman to rule modern Ethiopia. Her entire life was caught up in palace intrigues and the confusion of the royal line during that period. She was a traditionalist and a deeply religious woman.

Zauditu was the stepdaughter of the Empress TAITU, who became her patron and promoted her cause as the successor of Menelik. The emperor, unwilling to name a woman, instead chose his grandson, IYASU V. Iyasu considered Zauditu a potential threat and exiled her and her husband to a distant post. In 1916, Iyasu announced his conversion to Islam, which had been long suspected, and he was deposed. Zauditu was a compromise candidate, but her accession was dependent upon conditions. She had been married four times, the last time to a member of a powerful family. Zauditu was obliged to abandon him to avoid future dynastic claims. (She herself had no living children.) The major condition, however, was the appointment of her ambitious second cousin, Ras Tafari Makonnen (who later became emperor as HAILE SELASSIE) to be regent with the title of "regent and heir apparent." Zauditu's official title was *Negiste Negest* (Queen of Kings) rather than the male title of *Negus Negest* (King of Kings). She was to be the last Ethiopian ruler in the direct Solomonic line.

Zauditu's first concern was the deposed Iyasu, who led a rebel contingent against her. His forces were defeated, but he escaped and stayed on the run for several years. He was finally captured, but Zauditu had conflicted feelings about him. Utterly devoted to her father's memory, she could not shake her belief that somehow Iyasu had a greater claim to the throne than she.

Zauditu was a profoundly religious woman and a strong traditionalist, naturally suspicious of her pro-Western cousin Ras Tafari. Her reign was divided and confused because a triumvirate governed: Zauditu as empress controlled internal administration, Habta Giorgis was commander-in-chief of the armed forces, and Ras Tafari was regent. Zauditu often found herself caught between the more liberal modernizers led by Ras Tafari and the conservative religious group headed by Habta Giorgis. Ras Tafari, however, continued in ascendancy. During Zauditu's reign, Ethiopia joined the League of Nations (1923) and abolished slavery (1924), but this was largely the work of Ras Tafari. When Habta Giorgis died in 1926, Ras Tafari took power and Zauditu retreated more and more into a private religious mysticism.

In 1928, Ras Tafari precipitated a crisis over a trifling matter of protocol and demanded to be crowned *negus,* or king. Zauditu conceded, and her estranged husband, then serving as governor of the north, rose in rebellion. He was killed in battle against Ras Tafari, and the shocked Zauditu died the following day after hearing the news.

References: DAB, DAHB, WWR, *wiki.*

ZENAWI, Meles Legesse
(Ethiopia, 1955–)

Meles Legesse Zenawi, guerrilla leader of the Tigrean People's Liberation Front (TPLF) and head of state in Ethiopia since expelling MENGISTU Haile Mariam in 1991, has proved a political pragmatist in attempting to deal with Ethiopia's massive problems.

Zenawi was a medical student when he abandoned his studies to join the guerrillas in 1974,

before the fall of Emperor HAILE SELASSIE. His committed Marxism intensified after Mengistu came to power. Zenawi became convinced, however, that Mengistu was using Marxism as a cover for his own drive for power.

Zenawi was a founder of the TPLF in 1975. It was one of several groups fighting for the independence of Tigre province, and he ruthlessly eliminated rivals until the TPLF took control of several areas, established local governments and services, and began the long campaign against the central government. It forged an alliance with the Eritrean People's Liberation Front (EPLF) of ISSAYAS Afeworki and by 1980 controlled much of Tigre.

In 1985, Zenawi took over the TPLF in a bruising leadership contest. This conflict produced some tensions with the EPLF, but by 1989 the two forces were marching on the capital, Addis Ababa. The Ethiopian army, corrupt and filled with reluctant conscripts, suffered from desertions and internal conflict. Zenawi established an umbrella group, the Ethiopian People's Revolutionary Democratic Front (EPRDF) to incorporate all anti-Mengistu factions and to create a national base. In 1991 he was elected the EPRDF's head, after which he cautiously dropped most references to Marxism in favor of an approach more acceptable to the West. An interim government was established with the EPRDF firmly in charge, but that did not guarantee national unity.

Zenawi faced a host of problems: the country was in disarray and without resources, there were several separatist movements, and agriculture had been ruined by collectivization. He began an economic liberalization program, redistributing land, devaluing the currency, and reducing the bureaucracy. He sharply cut military spending, but that only created a problem of increased unemployment as combatants went into the private sector and found no work. Civil rights were restored, and Eritrea was allowed to secede and become independent. Zenawi has not been able to deal with separatist groups, especially the Oromo Liberation Front (OLF), which has withdrawn from the EPRDF. Democratic rights are not granted evenly, and several ethnic groups feel marginalized. Oromo dissent has brought retaliation, including the detention of more than 20,000 OLF guerrillas.

Most serious has been an ongoing border war with Eritrea, which the United Nations and the African Union have attempted to mediate. It has resulted in many casualties and a drop in support for

Zenawi, as well as a loss of prestige abroad, where the war is seen as futile and meaningless.

Zenawi has consolidated his power, using the excuse of the border wars, which have drained the treasury. He has become more dictatorial and eroded the earlier grants of freedom. After the most recent elections, 4,000 political opponents were imprisoned. The press has been closed down, and labor leaders and intellectuals were charged with treason and genocide. Some ascribe the necessity of tight control to the Eritrean conflict, to which has been added an extremely serious drought in 2006 that has brought starvation and emigration to the countryside.

Reference: afr, RWWA, *wiki*.

ZERBO, Sayé
(Burkina Faso, 1932–)

Sayé Zerbo took power in 1980 in a military coup in what was then known as Upper Volta. He served as head of state for two years, until he himself was toppled and replaced by the military.

Zerbo joined the French army at age 18 and served in Algeria and Vietnam as a paratrooper. He attended the Military Preparatory School in Sénégal before being sent to France for officer training and to Côte d'Ivoire to study at the Institute for Economic and Social Development. When Upper Volta became independent in 1960, he was a captain in the army, where his talents were recognized and he rose quickly through the ranks. In 1966 he was once again sent to France in order to undertake artillery training. From 1971 to 1973 he attended the French War College. In 1974, Major Zerbo became minister of foreign affairs when General Sangoulé LAMIZANA suspended the constitution and established military rule. Zerbo returned to military life in 1976 as commander of the Combined Forces Regiment in Ouagadougou, the capital.

The Lamizana government continuously failed to deal with strikes and shortages of staple foods. In response, Zerbo used his position to mount a coup in 1980 that overthrew the Lamizana regime and established a military government. He was unable to contain the unions, however, and wildcat strikes regularly paralyzed the country, despite official efforts at repressing the union movement. Zerbo also banned political parties and attempted to rein

in the incompetent bureaucracy. His administration was a weak one, noted for its corruption, and it was overthrown in another military coup in 1982 in which Zerbo was replaced by Jean Baptiste OUÉDRAOGO. Zerbo was subsequently accused of embezzling £28 million (US$119 million in current dollar value). Zerbo has spent the subsequent years either in prison or under house arrest.

References: afr, PLBA, RWWA.

ZUMA, Jacob Gedleyihlekisa
(South Africa, 1942–)

Jacob Zuma rose to be executive vice president of South Africa and a major contender for the presidency until charges of corruption and rape brought him down.

Zuma is one of the few leaders of the dominant African National Congress (ANC) from KwaZulu Province, the stronghold of the Inkatha Freedom Party of Mangosuthu BUTHELEZI. When his father died in Zuma's childhood, he lost any opportunity for schooling, and he is self-educated. At 17 he joined the ANC, and when it was banned three years later, he joined its military wing, Umkhonto we Sizwe. His cadre was discovered and 45 members were arrested and charged with treason. Zuma served 10 years at the maximum-security prison on Robben Island, with Nelson MANDELA. He went underground as soon as he was released, but was too well known to the security police, and so he fled the country in 1975 for Swaziland and then Mozambique. His task in Mozambique was to provide for the thousands of exiles who left South Africa in the wake of the Soweto uprisings. Most were angry young men who had been radicalized by the uprising and were ripe for recruitment to Umkhonto.

Zuma was transferred to Zambia in 1987, after pressure from the South African government forced Mozambique to expel him. In Zambia he became head of intelligence for Umkhonto. By this time he had been on the National Executive of the ANC for 10 years.

When the ANC was unbanned, Zuma returned to KwaZulu to try to win support for the ANC among his fellow Zulus, whose nationalist opposition to the ANC was fanned by Buthelezi. He was involved in KwaZulu affairs, and stood aside when Thabo MBEKI was chosen to run for deputy president with Mandela in 1994. Zuma became national chair of the ANC instead and spent five years in the KwaZulu provincial government. When Mbeki succeeded to the presidency in 1999, Zuma became executive deputy president and was assumed to be next in line for the presidency. He made several forays into African affairs, especially as negotiator in the Burundi peace process.

After complaints were made that Zuma had profited from payoffs in an arms deal, he was investigated, and the prosecutor declared that there was corruption involved, but not enough evidence for conviction. The ANC stood firmly behind Zuma. A second scandal was exposed in 2005, when his financial advisor was sentenced to 15 years' imprisonment, with Zuma implicated in corruption. After two weeks of dithering, Mbeki relieved Zuma of his post. He remains a serious contender for the presidential election in 2009, although later rape charges, though he was found not guilty, may change that.

Reference: wiki.

ZWANGENDABA
(Tanzania/South Africa/Zimbabwe/Zambia, 1785?–1848)

Zwangendaba, creator of the powerful Nguni nation, led them on the longest migration in nineteenth-century Africa, lasting over 25 years. During a period of widespread political instability in southern Africa, constant warfare caused the destruction of entire tribes and nations. Refugee fragments of these groups were absorbed by raiding bands, or became new nations, such as the Zulu or Nguni, which came into being by absorbing fragmented tribes. Some of the newly formed groups were merely marauding bands, while others became large nomadic states, settling into an area for a few years before moving on, either under military pressure or in search of new opportunities. This period, known as the *difaqane,* or "crushing," was caused by Zulu expansionism, ecological disturbances, and European intervention.

Zwangendaba became chief of the Jere clan around 1815 and settled in the northern part of present-day South Africa, near modern Swaziland. The Jere were the nucleus of the Nguni nation. The Zulus destabilized their territory and caused them to move as a body. After the defeat of the larger state to which the Jere owed allegiance in 1818, Zwangendaba led his people north, seeking safety. What distinguished the Nguni from bandit groups was their absorption of defeated peoples and their assimilation of various cultures. Zwangendaba employed the Zulu regimental form of infantry, making his warriors a formidable force. His continuous integration of both captives and volunteers increased the size of his growing kingdom, in which diverse peoples soon outnumbered the original Jere nucleus.

The Nguni crossed into Mozambique in 1822 and remained until about 1830, when they were driven out by other fleeing communities. Following the Zambezi River into what is now Zimbabwe, the Nguni absorbed a number of Shona people and broke the power of the Changamire Empire, killing its chief. In 1835 Zwangendaba began moving north into the area of present-day Zambia, incorporating along the way large numbers of people after destroying their villages. The entire migration covered a thousand miles (about 1,600 kilometers). Zwangendaba subsequently reached what is now Tanzania and founded a community there. After his death, the Nguni split into five branches and moved into new territories.

References: DAHB, EB, *wiki.*

ZWELITHINI, Goodwill kaBhekuzulu
(South Africa, 1948–)

King Goodwill Zwelithini has been the traditional ruler of the Zulu nation since 1971. He was for a long time in a power struggle with the chief minister of KwaZulu, Mangosuthu BUTHELEZI.

Zwelithini was the eldest son of the previous king, and he was educated at the College of Chiefs and in the royal palace. He was named king in 1968 on his father's death, but a regent was appointed in his stead until 1971. The official South African government position is that he was away for higher studies, but it seems he went into exile, fearing for his life. The South Africans, well aware of the prestige of the Zulu king among his people, engaged in a bitter contest over the appointment of the regent. In the end, Zwelithini was crowned. The constitution makes the kingship ceremonial, and it draws its budget from that of the provincial chief minister. Buthelezi and the king clashed early on in Zwelithini's reign. Buthelezi accused the king of meddling in politics in 1975, and the two traded barbs and denunciations.

Buthelezi moved to limit the influence of the king, and progressively forbade him to grant interviews without a government minister present and limited his finances. The two leaders patched over their differences and came together after violence arose between Buthelezi's supporters and those of the United Democratic Front (UDF). When African National Congress (ANC) President Oliver TAMBO accused the KwaZulu government of fomenting the riots, Zwelithini demanded an apology. (Buthelezi did not protest that foray into politics.)

Zwelithini has never been close to the ANC. He refused to support its policy of international sanctions against apartheid South Africa, and several times he openly criticized its leadership. A bit of this was smoothed over in 1992 when President Nelson MANDELA assured Zwelithini of the continuation of his position under the new South African constitution.

Zwelithini has been criticized for his lavish lifestyle. He has six wives and 27 children.

Reference: wiki. Otty Nxumalo, *King of Goodwill* (2003).

References

AA   Donald Herdeck. *African Authors.* Vol. 1. Washington: Inscape, 1974.

AB   Viginia Knight (ed.), *African Biography.* Detroit: Dale Research, 3 volumes, 1999.

adb   www.africadatabase.org. Sponsored by the Africa Centre, London.

afr   Kwame Anthony Appiah and Henry Louis Gates. *Africana.* New York: Civitas, 2nd edition, 5 volumes, 2005.

AH   Naomi Mitchison. *African Heroes.* New York: Farrar Straus &. Giroux, 1969 [young adult].

AO   *The Annual Obituary.* Detroit: St. James Press, 1980-.

AWT   Cosmo Pieterse and Dennis Duerden (eds.) *African Writers Talking.* New York: Africana, 1972.

BPAR   Gary Stewart. *Breakout: Profiles in African Rhythm.* Chicago: University of Chicago Press, 1992.

CA   *Contemporary Authors,* 1- 164.

CAAS   *Contemporary Authors, Autobiography Series,* 1–16.

CANR   *Contemporary Authors, New Revision Series,* 1–38.

CB   *Current Biography.* New York: H. W Wilson 1940-.

CBB   *Contemporary Black Biography.* Detroit: Gale Research, 1992.

CM   Michael LaBlanc (ed.). *Contemporary Musicians.* Detroit: Gale Research, 6 volumes, 1992.

CWAH   Carter Woodson. *African Heroes and Heroines.* Washington: Associated Publishers, 1939.

DAB   *Dictionary of African Biography.* Algonac, V and New York: Reference Publications, vol. 1, 1977; vol. 2, 1979.

dacb   www.dacb.org. Dictionary of African Christian Biography, sponsored by the Overseas Ministry Study Center. Many of the articles referenced here are from the first edition of this book.

DAHB   Mark Lipschutz and R. Kent Rasmussen. *Dictionary of African Historical Biography.* Berkeley: University of California Press, 2nd edition, 1986.

DLB   *Dictionary of Literary Biography.* Detroit: Gale Research, 128 volumes, 1978–1993.

DMM   Stanley Sadie (ed.), *The New Grove Dictionary of Music and Musicians.* New York: Macmillan, 2nd edition, 29 volumes, 2001.

DNB   *Dictionary of National Biography.* London: Oxford University Press, 27 volumes, 1921–1959.

DRWW   John Dickie and Alan Rake. *Who's Who in Africa.* London: African Development, 1973.

EB   *www.britannica.com.* Complete reference to the *Encyclopedia Britannica* volumes, with full text.

EWB   *Encyclopedia of World Biography.* Palatine, IL: Heraty, 18 volumes, 1973–1992.

GEPM   Colin Larkin (ed.), *Guiness Encyclopedia of Popular Music.* Middlesex, UK: Guiness Publishers, 2nd edition, 6 volumes, 1995.

GSAP   Shelagh Gastrow (ed.). *Who's Who in South African Politics.* New York: Hans Zell, 3d edition, 1990.

HH   Ray Browne (ed.). *Contemporary Heroes and Heroines.* Detroit: Gale Research, 2 volumes, 1990,1992.

HWL   Anne Commire (ed.). *Historic World Leaders.* Detroit: Gale Research, 5 volumes, 1994.

LKW   Beverly Golemba. *Lesser-Known Women.* Boulder, CO: Lynne Rienner, 1992.

MBW   Michael Popkin (ed.). *Modern Black Writers.* New York: Frederick Ungar, 1978.

MIW   *Oxford Encyclopedia of the Modern Islamic World.* New York: Oxford University Press, 4 volumes, 1995.

MM   A Ralph Ewechue (ed.). Makers *of Modern Africa.* 2d edition. London: Africa Books, 1991.

NRG   *A New Reader's Guide to African Literature.* London: Heinemann, 2nd edition, 1983.

PAS   African Academy of Sciences. *Profiles of African Scientists.* Nairobi: Academy Science Publishers. 1st ed., 1990; 2nd ed., 1991; 3rd ed., 1996.

PLBA   John A. Wiseman. *Political Leaders in Black Africa.* Brookfield, VT: Edward Elgar Publishing, 1991.

PLCA   Harvey Glickman (ed.). *Political Leaders of Contemporary Africa South of the Sahara.* Westport, CT: Greenwood Press, 1992.

RWWA   Alan Rake. *Who's Who in Africa: Leaders for the 1990s.* Metuchen, NJ: Scarecrow Press, 1992.

WAM   Ronnie Graham. The *World of African Music.* London: Pluto Press, 2 volumes, 1988, 1992.

WGMC   J. A. Rogers. *World's Great Men of Color.* New York: Macmillan, 2 volumes, 1974.

wiki   www.wikipedia.org. A massive encyclopedia on all topics, but not juried or fact-checked by staff. Written anonymously by volunteer writers. The African articles are of good quality, but should always be checked against another source.

WLTC   *Encyclopedia of World Literature in the 20th Century*. Detroit: St. James Press, revised edition, 4 volumes, 1999.

WWR   Guida Jackson. *Women Rulers Through the Ages*. Santa Barbara: ABC-CLIO, 2nd edition, 1999. (The 1st edition, 1990, was entitled *Women Who Ruled*.)

Entries by Nation

Angola
AFONSO I
ALVERE I
Alexandre DO NASCIMENTO
José Eduardo DOS SANTOS
Lopo NASCIMENTO
Antônio Agostino NETO
NZINGA Mbande
Holden ROBERTO
Jonas SAVIMBI

Benin
AGONGLO
Justin AHOMADÉGBÉ-TOMETIN
Sourou Migan APITHY
BEHANZIN
Bernard GANTIN
GEZO
GLELE
Mathieu KÉRÉKOU
Angelique KIDJO
Hubert MAGA
Godfrey Ubeti NZAMUJO
Christophe SOGLO

Botswana
BATHOEN I
Gaositwe CHIEPE
Bessie HEAD
KHAMA III
Seretse KHAMA
David LIVINGSTONE
Quett MASIRE
Peter MMUSI

Burkina Faso
Blaise COMPAORÉ
Sangoulé LAMIZANA
Bernard Lédéa OUÉDRAOGO
Idrissa OUÉDRAOGO
Rasmane OUÉDRAOGO
Thomas SANKARA
Sobonfu SOMÉ
WOBOGO
Maurice YAMÉOGO
Sayé ZERBO

Burundi
Jean-Baptiste BAGAZA
Pierre BUYOYA
Michel MICOMBERO ;bf
MWAMBUTSA IV

Pontien NDABANEZE

Cameroon
Ahmadou AHIDJO
Rudolf BELL
Mongo BETI
Calixthe BEYALA
Paul BIYA
Jacques ECKEBIL
John Ngu FONCHA
Engelbert MVENG
Phillipe Louis OMBEDE
Ferdinand OYONO
Martin-Paul SAMBA

Cape Verde
Amílcar CABRAL
Cesaria EVORA
António Mascarenhas MONTIERO
Arsitides PEREIRA
Pedro PIRES

Central African Republic
Bartélemy BOGANDA
Jean-Bédel BOKASSA
David DACKO
Félix EBOUÉ
Abdré KOLINGBA

Chad
Idriss DÉBY
Félix EBOUÉ
Hisséne HARBRÉ
Félix MALLOUM
Goukouni OUEDDEI
Ngartha TOMBALBAYE

Comoros
Ahmed ABDALLAH Abderrahman
Said Mohammed CHEIKH
Bob DENARD
Said Mohammed DJOHAR
Ali MROIVILI
Ali SOILIH

Congo
AFONSO I
ALVERE I
Pierre Savorgnan de BRAZZA
DIOGO I
Mary KINGSLEY

Congo *(continued)*
Alphonse MASEMBA-DÉBAT
Marien NGOUABI
Denis SASSOU-NGUESSO
Félix U TAMSI
Joachim YHOMBI-OPANGO
Fulbert YOULOU

Democratic Republic of the Congo
AFONSO I
ALVERE I
Jean-Pierre BEMBA
Joseph DIANGIENDA
DIOGO I
FRANCO
Laurent-Désiré KABILA
Pepé KALLÉ
KANDA Bongo Man
Joseph KASAVUBU
Simon KIMBANGU
KIMPA Vita
Mary KINGSLEY
Tabu LEY Rochereau
Patrice LUMUMBA
Joseph MALULA
MOBUTU Sese Seko
V.Y. MUDIMBE
NICO
Henry Morton STANLEY
Placide TEMPELS
TIPPU TIP
Étienne TSHISIKEDI
Moïse TSHOMBE
"Papa" WEMBA

Côte d'Ivoire
Gabriel d'ARBOUSSIER
Louis ARCHINARD
Charles Konan BANNY
Louis BINGER
Jeanne de CAVALLY
Bernard DADIÉ
William Wadé HARRIS
Félix HOUPHOUËT-BOIGNY
Christian LATTIER
Allasane OUATTARA
Bakari OUATTARA

Djibouti
Hassan GOULED Aptidon
Chehem WATTA

Equatorial Africa
Richard Francis BURTON
Francisco MACÍAS NGUEMA
Teodoro OBIANG Nguema

Eritrea
Gebrelu GEBREMARIAM Dessu
ISSAIAS Afeworki

Ethiopia
AHMAD Ibn Ibrahim al-Ghazi
Lemma AKLILU
BASILIOS
Abebe BIKILA
Kenenisa BEKELE
Skunder BOGHOSSIAN
ELESBAAN
EZANA
FASILADAS
FRUMENTIUS
GALADÈWOS
Haile GEBRSELASSIE
Rudolfo GRAZIANI
Kidane HAILE MICHAEL
HAILE SELASSIE
IYASU V
Johann Ludwig KRAPF
LALIBELA
LEBNA DENGEL
MENELIK II
MENGISTU Haile Mariam
Richard PANKHURST
PAULOS
SUSNEYOS
TAITU
TÄKLÄ Haymanot
TWEODROS II
TEWOFLOS
YOHANNES IV
Zar'a YA'ECOB
ZARA Yakub
ZAUDITU
Meles ZENAWI

Gabon
Omar BONGO
Pierre Savorgnan de BRAZZA
Mary KINGSLEY
Léon M'BA
André RAPONDA-WALKER
Albert SCHWEITZER

The Gambia

Dawda JAWARA
Mamadu LAMINE
MABA Diakhou Ba
Mungo PARK

Ghana

Ignatius ACHEAMPONG
Kobena Eyi ACQUAH
Amishadai Larson ADU
James E.K. AGGREY
John AGGREY
Ama Ata AIDOO
Frederick AKUFFO
Francis ALLOTEY
Anton Wilhelm AMO
Nana AMPADOU
Joseph ANKRAH
Kofi ANNAN
James ANQUANDAH
Kwame Anthony APPIAH
Kofi AWOONOR
Edward AYENSU
James Hutton BREW
Jude Kofi BUCKNOR
Kofi BUSIA
Joseph CASELEY-HAYFORD
J.B. DANQUAH
Emmanuel GLOVER
William Wadé HARRIS
Sally MUGABE
Azumah NELSON
J.H. Kwabena NKETIA
Kwame NKRUMAH
Ester OCLOO
OSEI Bonsu
OSEI Tutu
PREMPEH I
PREMPEH II
Alexander QUAISON-SACKEY
Philip QUAQUE
Jerry RAWLINGS
Reggie ROCKSTONE

Guinea

Louis ARCHINARD
CAMARA Laye
Lansana CONTÉ
Joseph GALLIENI
Miriam MAKEBA
SAMORI Touré
Sékou TOURÉ

Guinea-Bissau

Amílcar CABRAL
Luis CABRAL
João Bernardo VIERA

Kenya

Abednego AJUOGA
Mohammed AMIN
Robert BADEN-POWELL
Ibn BATTUTA
Karen BLIXEN
Manilal Premchand CHANDRIA
Stephen CHERONO
Joyce CHEPCHUMBA
Lord DELAMERE
Abdullah Saleh al-FARSY
Vasco da GAMA
Ndungi GITHUKU
Mwai KIBAKI
Bildad KAGGIA
Kip KEINO
Jomo KENYATTA
Margaret KENYATTA
Dedan KIMATHI
David KIVULI
Johann Ludwig KRAPF
Louis LEAKEY
Mary LEAKEY
Richard LEAKEY
Wangari MAATHAI
Beryl MARKHAM
Ali MAZRUI
MBARUK al-Mazrui
Tom MBOYA
Daniel arap MOI
Michere Githae MUGO
MUMIA wa Shiundu
John MUTINGA
Meja MWANGI
Ngugi wa THIONG'O
John NGUGI
Thomas ODHIAMBO
Oginga ODINGA
Grace OGOT

Lesotho

Francis COILLARD
Lebua JONATHAN
Justin LEKHANYA
MASUPHA
MMANTHATISI
Thomas MOFOLO
MOSHWESHWE I
MOSHWESHWE II
Elias RAMAEMA

Liberia
Benjamin ANDERSON
Jehudi ASHMUN
Edward BLYDEN
Gyude BRYANT
Lott CAREY
Samuel DOE
William Wadé HARRIS
Ellen JOHNSON-SHIRLEAF
Henry JOHNSTON
Charles KING
Joseph ROBERTS
Edward ROYE
Amos SAWYER
Charles TAYLOR
Richard V. TOLBERT
William TOLBERT
William TUBMAN
George "Oppong" WEAH

Madagascar
Jean-Joseph RABÉARIVELO
Gabriel RAMANANTSOA
RANAVALONA I
RANAVALONA III
Marc RAVALOMANANA
Albert Rakoto RATSIMANANGA
Didier RATSIRAKA
Philibert TSIRANANA

Malawi
Hasting Kamuzu BANDA
John CHILEMBWE
Hnery Masauko CHIPEMBERE
Orton CHIRWA
Vera CHIRWA
Henry JOHNSTON
Elliott KAMWANA
Legson KAYIRA
Michael KHUMALO ARBS
David LIVINGSTONE
Jack MAPANJE
Thandika MKANAWIRE
Felix MNTHALI
Edison MPINA
Bakili MUZULI
Iqbal SACRANIE
John TEMBO
ZWAGENDABA

Mali
ABDALLAH Ibn Yasin
Sunni ALI
AMADOU Ibn Umar Tall
Louis ARCHINARD

Ibn BATTUTA
DAWUD
Félix EBOUÉ
Joseph GALLIENI
Amadou HAMALLAH Haydara
ISHAQ II
Modibo KEITA
Alpha Oumar KONARÉ
Kandia KOUYATÉ
MUHAMMAD Ture
Mansa MUSA
SAMORI Touré
SUNDIATA Keita
Moussa TRAORÉ
UMAR Ibn Said Tall

Mauritania
ABDALLAH Ibn Yasin
Moktar Ould DADDAH
Mohammed Khouna Ould HAIDALLA
Amadou HAMMALLAH Haydara
Maawiya Ould Sid'Ahmed TAYA

Mauritius
Henry BARKLY
Donald CAMERON
Anerood JUGNAUTH
Anna PATTEN
Seewoosagur RAMGOOLAM
Prega RAMSAMY

Mozambique
Joachim CHISSANO
Afonso DHLAKAMA
EUSEBIO
GUNGUNYANE
Graça MACHEL
Samora MACHEL
Mario MACHUNGO
MATAKA Nyambi
Eduardo MONDLANE
Maria de Lourdes MUTOLA
Manuel Antonio de SOUSA

Namibia
Jan Junker AFRIKANER
Frankie FREDERICKS
Hage GEINGOB
Theo Ben GURIRAB
Hosea KUTAKO
Paul von LETTOW-VORBECK
Theodor LEUTWIN
MAHERERO
Laurie MARKER
Dirk MUDGE

Namibia *(continued)*
Sam NUJOMA
Animba TOIVO ja Toivo
Henrik WITBOOI

Niger
ALI Gaji
Sunni ALI
Djibo BAKARY
DAWUD
Ibn BATTUTA
Hamani DIORI
IDRIS Aloma
ISHAQ II
Muhammad al-KANEMI
Seyni KOUNTCHÉ
MUHAMMAD Ture
Ide OUMAROU
Ali SAIBOU

Nigeria
Sani ABACHA
ABIODUN
Adigun Ade ABIODUN
Philip ABIODUN
Siddiq ABUBAKAR III
Chinua ACHEBE
King Sunny ADÉ
Adebayo ADEDEJI
Pete AKINOLA
AKITOYE
ALALI
ALI Gaji
Babajide ALO
Obuefi Nwagu ANEKE
Eleazar ANYAOKU
Clement ANYIWO
Francis ARINZE
AREOGUN of Osi-Ilorin
Michael ASOKHIA
ATTIHIRU Amadu
Obafemi AWOLOWO
Nnamdi AZIKIWE
Nafiu BABA AHMED
Joseph BABALOLA
Ibrahim BABANGIDA
William BAIKIE
Abubakar Tafewa BALEWA
"George" BANDELE
Ahmadu BELLO
Muhammad BELLO
Richard BLAIZE
Garrick BRAIDE
Muhammadu BUHARI
Donald CAMERON
Kevin CARROLL

John Pepper CLARK
Samwel CROWTHER
Olusegun DIPEOLU
Cyprian EKWENSI
Buchi EMECHETA
Benedict ENWONWU
Olaudah EQUIANO
Lamidi FAYEKE
Toyin FALOLA
Tayo FATUNLA
George GOLDIE
Yakubu GOWON
HAYATU Ibn Said
Lawrence IBUKUN
IDRIS Aloma
Julius IHONVBERE
JAJA
James JOHNSON
Henry JOHNSTON
Muhammad al-KANEMI
Fela Anikulapo-KUTI
Frederick LUGARD
Akinlawon MABOGUNJE
Herbert MACAULAY
Murtala MUHAMMED
Clement NWANKWO
Godfrey Ubeti NZAMUJO
Olusegun OBASANJO
Wale OGUNYEMI
Chukwuemeka OJUKWU
Christopher OKIGBO
Sonny OKOSUNS
Ben OKRI
'Funmi OLONISAKIN
OLOWE of Ise
Josiah OSHITELU
Mungo PARK
Fumilayo RANSOME-KUTI
Ken SARO-WIWA
Shehu SHAGARI
Yinka SHONIBARE
Wole SOYINKA
Amos TUTUOLA
TWINS Seven-Seven
UTHMAN Dan Fodio
Shehu Musa YAR'ADUA

Rwanda
Diane FOSSEY
Juvénal HABYARIMANA
Alexis KAGAME
Paul KAGAME
Grégoire KAYIBANDA
KIGERI IV Rwabugiri
MUTARA III Rutagigwa

São Tomé e Príncipe
Manuel Pinto DA COSTA
Miguel TROVOADA

Sénégal
AMADOU Ibn Umar Tall
Gabriel d'ARBOUSSIER
Mariama BÂ
Amadou BAMBA
Louis BINGER
Pierre BOILAT
Blaise DIAGNE
Alioune DIOP
Birago DIOP
Chiekh Anta DIOP
David DIOP
Djibril DIOP-MEMBETY
Abdou DIOUF
Galandou DIOUF
Alfred DODDS
Joseph GALLIENI
Lamine GUÈYE
Ann Marie JAVOUHEY
Mamadou LAMINE
MABA Diakhou Ba
Amadou M'BOW
Mansa MUSA
Youssou N'DOUR
Pierre SANÉ
Ousmane SEMBÈNE
Léopold Sédar SENGHOR
Aminata SOW FALL
UMAR Ibn Said Tall
Abdoulaye WADE

Seychelles
James MANCHAM
France-Albert RENÉ

Sierra Leone
BAI BUREH
Edward BLYDEN
Abbas BUNDU
Josepg CINQUE
Adelaide CASELY-HAYFORD
John EZZIDIO
Afrcanus HORTON
James JOHNSON
Albert MARGAI
Milton MARGAI
Joseph MOMOH
Davidson NICOL
SAMORI Touré
Foday SANKOH
Siaka STEVENS

Isaac WALLACE-JOHNSON
Ernest Jenner WRIGHT
Madam YOKO

Somalia
Starlin ABDI ARUSH
Iman ABDULMAJID
Mohammed Farah AIDID
Nuriddin FARAH
MUHAMMAD Abdullah Hassan
Aden Abdullah OSMAN
Mohammed SIYAD BARRE

South Africa
Peter ABRAHAMS
Raymond ACKERMAN
Robert BADEN-POWELL
Margaret BALLINGER
BAMBATHA
Baredn BARENDS
Henry BARKLY
Christiaan BARNARD
Barnett BARNATO
Alfred BEIT
Willie BESTER
Steve BIKO
Alan BOESAK
Louis BOTHA
P.W. BOTHA
Roelof BOTHA
Johannes BRAND
Breyten BREYTENBACH
André BRINK
Dennis BRUTUS
Zola BUDD
Sidney BUNTING
Mangosuthu BUTHELEZI
Achmad CASSIEM
CETSHWAYO
Yvonne CHAKA CHAKA
Arthur CHASKALSON
Frank CHICANE
J.M. COETZEE
Wessek "Hansie" CRONJE
Frederik Willem DE KLERK
DINGANE
DINGISWAYO
DINUZULU
Basil "Dolly" D'OLIVIERA
John DUBE
Stephanus DU TOIT
FAKU
Athol FUGARD
Mohandas GANDHI
Rider HAGGARD
Wendy de la HARPE

South Africa (continued)

Chris HANI
Bessie HEAD
James HERTZOG
HINTSA
Bantu HOLOMISA
Mike HORN
Denis HURLEY
Trevor HUDDLESTON
John Tengo JABAVU
Leander Starr JAMESON
Helen JOSEPH
Clements KADALIE
Horatio KITCHENER
Moeketsi KOENA
Stephanus Paulus KRUGER
Mandla "Bear" KUMALO
LANGALIBALELE
Alex LA GUMA
Colin LEGUM
Albert LUTHULI
Ernest MANCOBA
Winnie MADIKIZELA-MANDELA
Miriam MAKEBA
Daniel MALAN
Magnus MALAN
Nelson MANDELA
Lucas MANCOPE
Hugh MASEKELA
MAWA
Thabo MBEKI
Precious McKENZIE
Zakes MDA
MHLAKAZA
Smangaliso MKHATSHWA
MMANTHATISI
Joe MODISE
Robert MOFFATZephania MOTHOPENG
Es'kia MPHALELE
Vusamazulu Credo MUTWA
MZILIKAZI
NANDI
Beyers NAUDÉ
Bernard NCUBE
Albert NOLAN
Alfred NZO
Harry OPPENHEIMER
Alan PATON
John PHILIP
Sol PLAATJE
Gary PLAYER
Graeme POLLOCK
Andries PRETORIUS
Marthinus PRETORIUS
Lucas RADEBE
Cyril RAMAPHOSA

Memphela RAMPHELE
Cecil RHODES
Tracey ROSE
Olive SCHREINER
William SCHREINER
Pixley SEME
Mosima "Tokyo" SEXWALE
Joseph SHABALALA
SHAKA
Mark SHUTTLEWORTH
Albertina SISULU
Walter SISULU
Zwelakhe SISULU
Joe SLOVO
Jan Christiaan SMUTS
Robert SOBUKWE
Amanda STRYDOM
Helen SUZMAN
Oliver TAMBO
E.N. TERRE BLANCHE
Max THEILER
Andries TREURNICHT
Desmond TUTU
Anna-Mart VAN DER MERWE
Laurens VAN DER POST
Michael VAN GRAAN
Hendrik VERWOERD
Benedict VILAKAZI
Balthazar VORSTER
Donald WOODS
Alfred XUMA
Emile YX?
Jacob ZUMA
ZWAGENDABA
Goodwill ZWELITHINI

Sudan

Ibrahim ABBOUD
ABDULLAHI Ibn Mohammad
Samuel BAKER
Josephine BAKHITA
Omar Hassan BASHIR
John GARANG
Charles George "Chinese" GORDON
Horatio KITCHENER
The MAHDI
Sadiq al-MAHDI
Gaafar NIMIERY
Eduard SCHNITZER
Hassan al-TURABI
YAMBIO

Swaziland

BHUNU
Makhosini DALAMINI
Lydia MAKHUBU

Swaziland *(continued)*
MSWATI II
MSWATI III
SOBHUZA II

Tanzania
Muhammed Said ABDULLA
BARGHASH Ibn Said
Richard Francis BURTON
Donald CAMERON
Jane GOODALL
Henry JOHNSTON
Hugh Martin KAYAMBA
KINJIKITILE Ngwale
Johann Ludwig KRAPF
Paul von LETTOW-VORBECK
David LIVINGSTONE
Reginald Abraham MENGI
MKWAWA
Ali Hassan MWINYI
Julius NYERERE
NYUNGU ya Mawe
Remmy ONGALA
Shabaan ROBERT
SAID
Salim Ahmed SALIM
Henry Morton STANLEY
Placide TEMPELS
TIPPU TIP
Idris Abdul WAKIL
ZWAGENDABA

Togo
Gnassingbé Étienne EYADÉMA
Nicolas GRUNITSKY
Sylvanus OLYMPIO

Uganda
Idi AMIN Dada
George Henry Okello ABUNGU
Yasmin ALIBHAI-BROWN
Elizabeth BAGAAYA
Zarina BHIMJI
Godfrey BINAISA
Henry JOHNSTON
KABAREGA
Apolo KAGGWA
Joseph KIWANUKA
Joseph KONY
Alice LAKWENA
Cliff LUBWA P'CHONG
Frederick LUGARD
Janani LUWUM
Karoli LWANGA
Musajjakawa MALAKI

Mahmood MAMDANI
Yoweri MUSEVENI
MUTESA I
Edward MUTESA II
MWANGA II
Milton OBOTE
OKOT p'Bitek
John Hanning SPEKE
Paul SSEMOGERERE
Bruno SSERUNKUUMA
Henry Morton STANLEY

Zambia
Frederick CHILUBA
Francis COILLARD
Dennis DE JONG
Kenneth KAUNDA
Alice LENSHINA
David LIVINGSTONE
LEWANIKA Lubosi
Ng'andu Peter MAGANDE
Emmanuel MILINGO
Vernon MWAANGA
Harry NKUMBULA
Roy WELENSKY
ZWAGENDABA

Zimbabwe
Canaan BANANA
Mark Gova CHAVUNDUKA
Bernard CHIDZERO
Charles COUGHLAN
Tsitsi DAMGAREMBGA
GATSI Rusere
Keith GODDARD
Godfrey HUGGINS
Leander Starr JAMESON
George Payne KAHARI
LOBENGULA
LOTSHE
Colleen MADAMOMBE
Strive MASIYIWA
Bernard MATEMERA
MKWATI
Harold MOFFAT
Robert MUGABE
Sally MUGABE
Abel MUZOREWA
MZILIKAZI
Pius NCUBE
Joshua NKOMO
NYANHEHWE
Cecil RHODES
Roland ROWLAND
Ndabaningi SITHOLE
Ian SMITH

Zimbabwe *(continued)*
Garfield TODD
Roy WELENSKY

Edgar WHITEHEAD
ZWAGENDABA

Africa since Independence: Nations and Major Leaders

Date of independence and name of former colonial power appear in parentheses following the name of each independent nation.

Angola *(1975, Portugal)*
Antônio Agostinho NETO (1975–1979)
José Eduardo DOS SANTOS (1979–)

Benin *(Dahomey, 1960–1975) (1960, France)*
Hubert MAGA (1960–1963)
Christophe SOGLO (1963–1964)
Sourou Migan APITHY (1964–1965)
Christophe SOGLO (1965–1967)
Alphonse Alley (1967–1968)
Emile-Derlin Zinsou (1968–1969)
Paul Emile de Souza (1969–1970)
Hubert MAGA (1970–1972)
Justin AHOMADÉGBÉ-TOMETIN (1972)
Mathieu KÉRÉKOU (1972–1991)
Nicephore Soglo (1991–1996)
Mathieu KÉRÉKOU (1996–2006)
Yayi Boni (2006–)

Botswana *(1966, Great Britain)*
Seretse KHAMA (1966–1980)
Quett MASIRE (1980–1998)
Festus Gontebanye Mogae (1998–)

Burkina Faso *(Haute Volta/Upper Volta, 1960–1984) (1960, France)*
Maurice YAMÉOGO (1960–1966)
Sangoulé LAMIZANA (1966–1970)
Gerard Ouédraogo (1970–1974)
Sangoulé LAMIZANA (1974–1980)
Sayé ZERBO (1980–1982)
Jean-Baptiste Ouédraogo (1982–1983)
Thomas SANKARA (1983–1987)
Blaise COMPAORÉ (1987–)

Burundi *(1962, Belgium)*
Mwami MWAMBUTSA IV (1962–1966)
MwamiNtareV (1966)
Michel MICOMBERO (1966–1976)
Jean-Baptiste BAGAZA (1976–1987)
Pierre BUYOYA (1987–1993)
Melchior Ndadaye (1993)
Cyprien Ntaryamira (1993–1994)
Sylvestre Ntibantunganya (1994–1996)
Pierre BUYOYA (1996–2003)
Domitien Ndayizeye (2003–2005)

Pierre Nkurunziza (2005–)

Cabo Verde. See Cape Verde

Cape Verde *(1975, Portugal)*
Aristides PEREIRA (1975–1991)
António Mascarenhas MONTEIRO (1991–2001)
Pedro Pires (2001–)

Cameroon *(1960–1961, Republic of East Cameroon, France; 1961–1972, Federal Republic of Cameroon, including part of a British trust territory; 1972, joined to form the United Cameroon Republic)*
Ahmadou AHIDJO (1960–1982)
Paul BIYA (1982–)

Central African Republic *(Central African Empire, 1976–1979) (I960, France)*
David DACKO (1960–1965)
Jean-Bédel BOKASSA (1966–1979)
David DACKO (1979–1981)
Andre KOUNGBA (1981–1993)
Ange-Félix Patasse (1993–2002)
François Bozizé (2002–)

Chad *(I960, France)*
Ngartha Francois TOMBALBAYE (1960–1975)
Félix MALLOUM (1975–1979)
Goukouni OUEDDEI (1979–1982)
Hissène HABRE (1982–1990)
Idriss DÉBY (1990–)

Comoros *(1975, France.* See also Mayotte)
Ahmed ABDALLAH Abderrahman (1975)
Ali SOILIH (1975–1978)
Ahmed ABDALLAH Abderrahman / Muhammad Ahmed (co-presidents, 1978)
Ahmed ABDALLAH Abderrahman (1978–1989)
Said DJOHAR (1989–1996)
Mohamed Taki Abdulkarim (1996–1998)
Tajidine ben Said Massounde (interim, 1998–1999)
Azali Assoumani (1996–2006)
Ahmed Abdallah Sambi (2006–)

Congo *(1960; France)*
Fulbert YOULOU (1960–1963)
Alphonse MASSEMBA-DÉBAT (1963–1968)
Marten NGOUABI (1968–1977)
Joachim YHOMBI-OPANGO (1977–1979)
Denis SASSOU-NGUESSO (1979–1992)
Pascal Lissouba (1992–2002)
Denis SASSOU-NGUESSO (2002–)

Congo-Brazzaville. See Congo

Congo, Democratic Republic *(Republic of the Congo-Léopoldville, 1960–1966; Democratic Republic of the Congo-Kinshasa, 1966–1971; Zaïre, 1971–1997; Democratic Republic of the Congo, 1997–) (1960, Belgium)*
Joseph KASAVUBU (1960–1965)
MOBUTU Sese Seko (1965–1997)
Laurent-Désiré KABILA (1997–2001)
Joseph Kabila (2001–)

Congo-Kinshasa. See Congo, Democratic Republic

Côte d'Ivoire *(1960, France)*
Felix HOUPHOUËT-BOIGNY (1960–1993)
Henri Konan Bédié (1993–1999)
Robert Guéi (1999–2000)
Laurent Gbagbo (2000–)

Dahomey. See Benin

Djibouti *(1977, France)*
Hassan GOULED Aptidon (1977–1999)
Ismael Omar Guelleh (1999–)

Equatorial Guinea *(1968, Spain)*
Francisco MACÍAS NGUEMA (1968–1979)
Teodoro OBIANG Nguema (1979–)

Eritrea *(1993, Ethiopia)*
ISSAIAS Afeworki (provisional government, 1991–1993; president, 1993–)

Ethiopia *(not colonized)*
TEWODROS II (1855–1868)
Takla Giorgis II (1868–1872)
YOHANNES IV (1872–1889)
MENELIK II (1889–1913)
IYASU V (1914–1916)
ZAUDITU (empress, 1916–1930)
HAILE SELASSIE (regent, 1916–1928; king, 1928–1932; emperor, 1930–1974)
Aman Andom (1974)

Teferi Banti (1974–1977)
MENGISTU Haile Mariam (1974–1991)
Meles ZENAWI (1991–1995)
Negasa Gidada (1995–2001)
Girima Wolde-Giyorgis Lucha (2001–)

Gabon *(1960, France)*
Leon M'BA (1960–1967)
Omar BONGO (1967–)

The Gambia *(1965, Great Britain)*
Dawda JAWARA (1965–1994)
Yahyah Jammeh (1994–)

Ghana *(1957, Great Britain)*
Kwame NKRUMAH (1957–1966)
Joseph ANKRAH (1966–1969)
Akwasi Afrifa (1969)
Presidential Commission (1969–1970)
Edward Akufo-Addo (1970–1972)
Ignatius ACHEAMPONG (1972–1978)
Frederick AKUFFO (1978–1979)
Jerry RAWLINGS (1979)
Hilla Limann (1979–1981)
Jerry RAWLINGS (1981–2001)
John Agyekum Kufuor (2001–)

Guinea *(1958, France)*
Sékou TOURÉ (1958–1984)
Lansana CONTÉ (1984–)

Guinea-Bissau *(1974, Portugal)*
Luís de Almeida CABRAL (1974–1980)
João Bernardo VIEIRA (1980–1999)
Kuma Ialá (2000–2003)
Military Council (2003–2005)
João Bernardo VIEIRA (2005–)

Ivory Coast. See Côte d'Ivoire

Kenya *(1963, Great Britain)*
Jomo KENYATTA (1963–1978)
Daniel arap MOI (1978–2002)
Mwai KIBAKI (2002–)

Lesotho *(1966, Great Britain)*
MOSHWESHWE II (1966–1970; titular monarch, 1970–1990)
Leabua JONATHAN (PM, 1970–1986)
Justin LEKHANYA (PM, 1986–1991)
Letsie III (titular monarch, 1990–1994)
Elias RAMAEMA (PM, 1991–1993)
Ntsu Mokhehle (PM, 1993–1994)
Letsie III (governing monarch, 1994–1995)

Lesotho *(continued)*
MOSHWESHWE II (titular monarch, 1995–1996)
Letsie III (titular monarch, 1996–)

Liberia *(1847, seized from tribal chiefs)*
Joseph ROBERTS (1848–1856)
Stephen Benson (1856–1864)
Daniel Bashiel Warner (1964–1868)
James Spriggs-Payne (1868–1870)
Edward ROYE (1870–1871)
James Smith (1871–1872)
Joseph ROBERTS (1872–1876)
James Spriggs-Payne (1876–1878)
Anthony Gardiner (1878–1883)
Alfred Russell (1883–1884)
Hilary Johnson (1884–1893)
Joseph Cheeseman (1892–1896)
William Coleman (1896–1900)
Garretson Gibson (1900–1904)
Arthur Barclay (1904–1912)
Daniel Howard (1912–1920)
Charles KING (1920–1930)
Edwin Barclay (1930–1944)
William V S. TUBMAN (1944–1971)
William R. TOLBERT (1971–1980)
Samuel K. DOE (1980–1990)
Amos SAWYER (1990–1994)
Charles TAYLOR (1997–2003)
Gyude BRYANT (interim, 2003–2006)
Ellen JOHNSON-SHIRLEAF (2006–)

Madagascar *(1960; France)*
Philibert TSIRANANA (1960–1972)
Gabriel RAMANANTSOA (1972–1975)
Didier RATSIRAKA (1975–1993)
Albert Zafy (1993–1996)
Didier RATSIRAKA (1997–2001)
Marc RAVALOMANANA (2001–)

Malgache Republic. See Madagascar

Malagasy. See Madagascar

Malawi (1964, Great *Britain)*
Hastings Kamuzu BANDA (1964–1994)
Bakili Muluzi (1994–2004)
Bingu wa Mutharika (2004–)

Mali *(1959, France)*
Modibo KEITA (1960–1968)
MoussaTRAORÉ (1968–1991)
Amadou Toumani Touré (1991–1992)
Alpha Oumar Konaré (1992–2002)
Amadou Toumani Touré (2002–)

Mauritania *(1960, France)*
Moktar Ould DADDAH (1961–1978)
Mustapha Ould Muhammed Salek (1978–1979)
Mohamed Ould Ahmed Louly (1979–1980)
Mohammed Khouna Ould HAIDALLA (1980–1988)
Maawiya Ould Sid'Ahmed TAYA (1984–2005)
Ely Ould Mohamed Vall (Military Council, 2005–)

Mauritius *(1986, Great Britain)*
Seewoosagur RAMGOOLAM (PM, 1968–1982)
Aneerood JUGNAUTH (PM, 1982–)
Cassam Uteem (President, 1993–2002)
Karl Offman (2002–2003)
Anerood JUGNAUTH (2003–)

Mayotte *(French Territory since 1977, claimed by Comoros)*

Mozambique *(1975, Portugal)*
Samora MACHEL (1975–1986)
Joaquim CHISSANO (1986–2005)
Armando Guebreza (2005–)

Namibia *(1990, South Africa)*
Sam NUJOMA (1990–2005)
Hifikepunye Pohamba (2005–)

Niger *(1960, France)*
Hamani DIORI (1960–1974)
Seyni KOUNTCHÉ (1974–1987)
Ali SAIBOU (1987–1993)
Mahamane Ousmane (1993–1996)
Ibrahim Baré Maïnassara (1996–1999)
Tandja Mamadou (1999–)

Nigeria *(1960, Great Britain)*
Nnamdi AZIKIWE (president, 1963–1966)
Abubakar Tafawa BALEWA (PM, 1960–1966)
Johnson Aguiyi-Ironsi (1966)
Yakubu GOWON (1966–1975)
Murtala MUHAMMED (1975–1976)
Olusegun OBASANJO (1976–1979)
Shehu SHAGARI (1979–1983)
Muhammadu BUHARI (1983–1983)
Ibrahim BABANGIDA (1985–1993)
Sani ABACHA (1993–1998)
Abdulsalami Abubakar (1998–1999)
Olusegun OBASANJO (1999–)

Northern Rhodesia. See Zimbabwe

Republic of South Africa. See South Africa

Réunion *(French Overseas Department since 1946)*

Rwanda *(1962, Belgium)*
Grégoire KAYIBANDA (1962–1973)
Juvenal HABYARIMANA (1973–1994)
Pasteur Bizimungu (1994–2004)
Paul KAGAME (2000–)

São Tomé e Príncipe *(1975, Portugal)*
Manuel Pinto DA COSTA (1975–1991)
Miguel TROVOADA (1991–2001)
Fradique de Menezes (2001–)

Sénégal *(1960, France)*
Léopold Sédar SENGHOR (1960–1981)
Abdou DIOUF (1981–2000)
Abdoulaye WADE (2000–)

Seychelles *(1976, Great Britain)*
James MANCHAM (1976–1977)
France Albert RENÉ (1977–2004)
James Michel (2004–)

Sierra Leone *(1961, Great Britain)*
Milton MARGAI (1961–1964)
Albert MARGAI (1964–1967)
Andrew Juxon-Smith (1967–1968)
Siaka STEVENS (1968–1985)
Joseph MOMOH (1985–1992)
Valentine Strasser (1992–1996)
Ahmad Tejah Kabbah (1996–1997)
Johnny Paul Koroma (1997–1998)
Ahmad Tejah Kabbah (1998–)

Somalia *(1960, Great Britain and Italy)*
Aden Abdullah OSMAN (1960–1967)
Abdirashid Ali Shirmarke (1967–1969)
Mohammed SIYAD BARRE (1969–1991)
Ali Mahdi Mohammed (disputed, 1991–1992)
United Nations occupation (1992–1995)
no central government (1995–)

Somaliland *(Unrecognized secession from Somalia, 1991, colonial British Somaliland)*
Abdirahman Mohamed Ali (1991–1993)
Mohamed Ibrahim Egal (1993–2002)
Dahir Riyal Kahin (2002–)

South West Africa. See Namibia

South Africa *(1910, Great Britain)*
Louis BOTHA (1910–1919)
Jan SMUTS (1919–1924)
James HERTZOG (1924–1939)
Jan SMUTS (1939–1948)
Daniel E MALAN (1948–1954)
J. G. Strijdom (1954–1958)
Hendrik VERWOERD (PM, 1958–1961; president, 1961–1966)
Balthazar J. VORSTER (1966–1978)
Pieter W BOTHA (1978–1989)
Frederik Willem DE KLERK (1989–1994)
Nelson MANDELA (1994–1999)
Thabo MBEKI (1999–)

Sudan *(1956, British-Egyptian Condominium)*
Ismail al-Azhari (1956)
AbdallahKhalil (1956–1958)
Ibrahim ABBOUD (1958–1964)
Sayed al-Khatim al-Khalifa (1964–1965)
Mohammed Ahmed Mahgoub (1965–1966)
Sadiq al-MAHDI (1966–1967)
Mohammed Ahmed Mahgoub (1967–1969)
Gafaar NIMEIRY (1969–1985)
Abdel Rahman Swar Al-Dahab (1985–1986)
Ahmed Ali el-Mirghani (1986–1989)
Omar Hassan BASHIR (1989–)

Swaziland *(1968, Great Britain)*
SOBHUZA II (1921–1982)
Ntombi Thwala (queen regent, 1982–1983)
MSWATI III (1986–)

Tanganyika. See Tanzania

Tanzania *(1961, Tanganyika; 1963, Zanzibar, both fromGreat Britain; united, 1964)*
Julius K. NYERERE (1961–1985)
Ali Hassan MWINYI (1985–1995)
Benjamin Mkapa (1995–2005)
Jakaya Mrisho Kikwete (2005–)

Togo *(1960, France)*
Sylvanus OLYMPIO (1960–1963)
Nicolas GRUNITZKY (1963–1967)
Étienne Gnassingbé EYADÉMA (1967–2005)
Faure Gnassingbé (2005–)

Uganda *(1962, Great Britain)*
Milton OBOTE (1962–1971)
Idi AMIN Dada (1971–1979)
Yusuf Lule (1979)

Uganda *(continued)*
Godfrey BINAISA (1979–1980)
Paulo Muwanga (1980)
Milton OBOTE (1980–1985)
Tito Okello Lutwa (1985–1986)
Yoweri MUSEVENI (1986–)

United Cameroon Republic. See Cameroon

Upper Volta. See Burkina Faso

Zaïre. See Congo, Democratic Republic

Zambia *(1964; Great Britain)*
Kenneth KAUNDA (1964–1991)
Frederick CHILUBA (1991–2001)
Levy Mwanawasa (2001–)

Zanzibar *(1963, Great Britain; 1964 merged with Tanganyika to form Tanzania)*
Seyyid Jamshid bin Khalifa (1963–1964)

Jamshid bin Abdullah (1964, until merger)

Presidents of Zanzibar and vice presidents of Tanzania:
Abeid Amani Karume (1964–1972)
Aboud Jumbe (1972–1984)
Ali Hassan MWINYI (1984–1985)
Idris Abdul WAKIL (1985–1990)
Salmin Amour (1990–2000)
Abeid Amani Karume (2000–)

Zimbabwe *(1965, from Great Britain as Rhodesia; 1980, from Rhodesia)*
Ian SMITH (PM of Rhodesia, 1965–1978)
Executive Council (1978–1979)
Josiah Gumede (president of Zimbabwe/Rhodesia, 1979–1980)
Canaan BANANA (president of Zimbabwe, 1980–1987)
Robert MUGABE (PM, 1980–1987; executive president, 1987–)

Illustration Credits

Special thanks to Reynaldo Reyes and Veena Manchanda at the United Nations Photo Library for their generous assistance.

INDEX

T

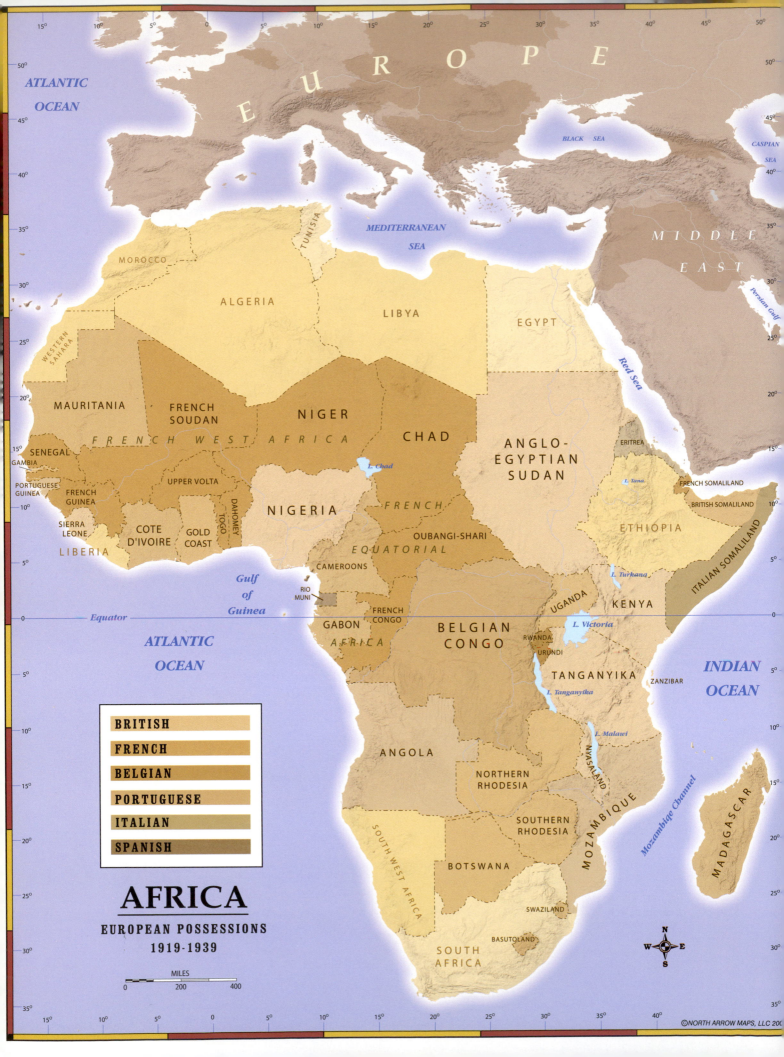

AFRICA

MAJOR NATURAL RESOURCES

OIL/NATURAL GAS	
DIAMONDS	◇
GOLD	
PLATINUM	
COAL	
COPPER	
IRON	
URANIUM	

MILES
0   200   400

©NORTH ARROW MAPS, LLC 2006

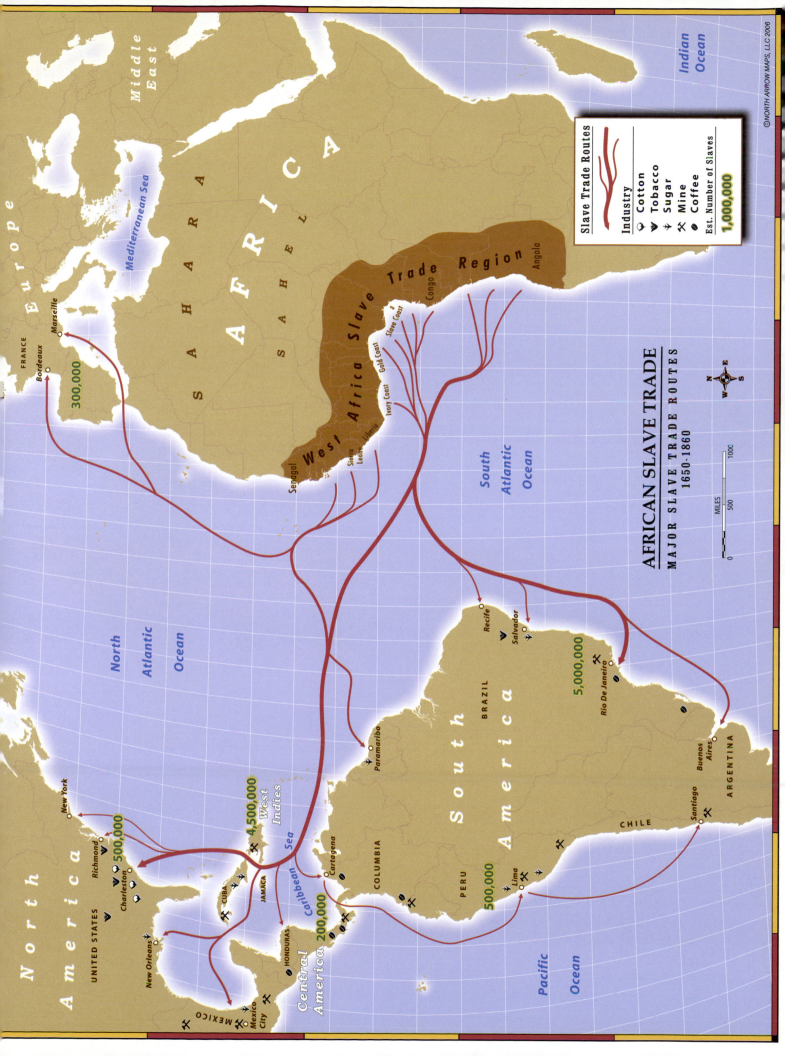

AFRICAN SLAVE TRADE

MAJOR SLAVE TRADE ROUTES 1650-1860

Slave Trade Routes

Industry
- ♌ Cotton
- ⚓ Tobacco
- ✈ Sugar
- ✗ Mine
- ◗ Coffee

Est. Number of Slaves
1,000,000

©NORTH ARROW MAPS, LLC 2006

Indian Ocean

Europe

Middle East

Mediterranean Sea

S A H A R A

A F R I C A

S A H E L

West Africa Slave Trade Region

Congo

Angola

Slave Coast

Gold Coast

Ivory Coast

Liberia

Sierra Leone

Senegal

FRANCE

Marseille

Bordeaux

300,000

North Atlantic Ocean

South Atlantic Ocean

Recife

Salvador

5,000,000

Rio De Janeiro

BRAZIL

S o u t h   A m e r i c a

Paramaribo

Buenos Aires

ARGENTINA

Santiago

CHILE

PERU

Lima

500,000

COLUMBIA

Cartagena

Caribbean Sea

West Indies

4,500,000

CUBA

JAMAICA

HONDURAS

Central America

200,000

New Orleans

Mexico City

MEXICO

UNITED STATES

New York

Richmond

Charleston

500,000

N o r t h   A m e r i c a

Pacific Ocean

MILES
0   500   1000

N
W   E
S

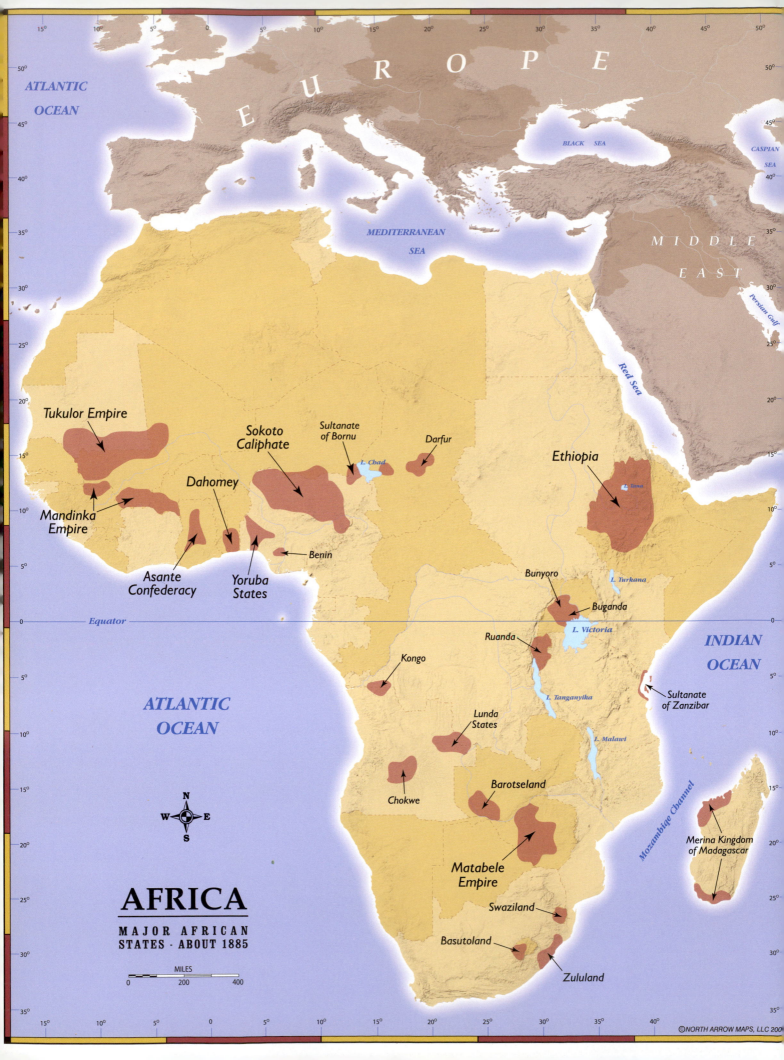

ATLANTIC
OCEAN

E U R O P E

BLACK SEA

CASPIAN
SEA

MEDITERRANEAN
SEA

M I D D L E

E A S T

Persian Gulf

Red Sea

Tukulor Empire

Sokoto
Caliphate

Sultanate
of Bornu

L. Chad

Darfur

Ethiopia

L. Tana

Dahomey

Mandinka
Empire

Benin

Asante
Confederacy

Yoruba
States

Bunyoro

L. Turkana

Buganda

Ruanda

L. Victoria

INDIAN

OCEAN

Equator

Kongo

L. Tanganyika

Sultanate
of Zanzibar

ATLANTIC

OCEAN

Lunda
States

L. Malawi

Chokwe

Barotseland

Mozambique Channel

Merina Kingdom
of Madagascar

Matabele
Empire

N
W   E
S

Swaziland

AFRICA

Basutoland

MAJOR AFRICAN
STATES - ABOUT 1885

Zululand

MILES

0   200   400

©NORTH ARROW MAPS, LLC 200